MARKETING

KU-367-613

MARKETING

CONCEPTS AND STRATEGIES

SECOND EUROPEAN EDITION

Sally Dibb
University of Warwick

Lyndon Simkin
University of Warwick

William M. Pride
Texas A & M University

O. C. Ferrell
Memphis State University

HOUGHTON MIFFLIN COMPANY   BOSTON   LONDON

This book is to be sold only in the territory to which it has been consigned. It is not for sale in the United States and its territories or in Canada.

Copyright © 1994 by Houghton Mifflin Company. All rights reserved.

No part of this work may be reproduced or transmitted in any form or by any means, electronic or mechanical, including photocopying and recording, or by any information storage or retrieval system without the prior written permission of Houghton Mifflin Company unless such copying is expressly permitted by federal copyright law. Address inquiries to College Permissions, Houghton Mifflin Company, 222 Berkeley Street, Boston, MA 02116-3764.

Printed in the U.S.A.

Library of Congress Catalog Card Number 93-78693

ISBN: 0-395-66928-6

123456789-DW 07 96 95 94 93

BRIEF CONTENTS

CONTENTS

2 The Marketing Environment

CONTENTS

3 Segmenting Markets, Targeting and Positioning

x

Managing the Product Mix

Product Positioning

Managing Products After Commercialisation

Summary

Important Terms

Discussion and Review Questions

CASES

MARKETING INSIGHTS

PART III DISTRIBUTION (PLACE) DECISIONS

10   Marketing Channels

The Structures and Types of Marketing Channels

Justifications for Intermediaries

Functions of Intermediaries

Channel Integration

Intensity of Market Coverage

CONTENTS

Strategic Issues in Physical Distribution

Summary

Important Terms

Discussion and Review Questions

PART IV **PROMOTION DECISIONS**

 14 Promotion: An Overview

The Role of Promotion

Promotion and the Communication Process

Promotion and the Product Adoption Process

The Promotional Mix

Summary

Important Terms

Discussion and Review Questions

PART IV   PROMOTION DECISIONS

14   Promotion: An Overview

PART V   PRICING DECISIONS   475

17   Pricing Concepts   476

xxii

18   Setting Prices   498

PREFACE

In the 1980s, few expected the Berlin Wall to come tumbling down, resulting eventually in the unification of Germany. Few could have predicted that 1991 would commence with a major war in the Persian Gulf involving many Western powers. Who in the late 1980s would have predicted the break-up of the Soviet Union or the horrors of civil war in the former Yugoslavia? There is no question that we live in an increasingly complex and changing world. Recent political and economic upheavals have shaken established systems to their foundations; ease of communication and commercial exchange has created a global society; and for many people, environmental concerns have become a number one priority. To provide insights into marketing in such a changing environment, *Marketing: Concepts and Strategies,* Second European Edition presents a comprehensive framework, integrating traditional marketing concepts with the realities of the 1990s.

The study of marketing has always been relevant because it is a key element in the functioning of today's society. Our economy, our lifestyles, and our physical well being are directly or indirectly influenced by marketing activities. *Marketing: Concepts and Strategies* is a leading text in Europe because it provides comprehensive coverage of the subject of marketing while stimulating student interest through its readable, accessible style and extensive use of up to date, topical examples.

For many years, *Marketing: Concepts and Strategies* has led the market in America. However, many European business schools and colleges also realised the text had significant merits, ranging from its comprehensive coverage of key marketing concepts and strategic issues; to its integrated use of product and market examples, background statistics, and explanation of current trends and practices; to its lively, colourful presentation. It seemed a natural progression, then, to further enhance the basic features of the text for the European market by publishing a version re-written specifically for that audience. Thus, with numerous suggestions from colleagues and students, we have focused on facts and issues particular to Europe in the 1990s—especially those relating to the marketing research industry, the advertising and promotions industry, and the marketing environment in general. The examples, cases, and marketing insights included in this text involve products, brands, and markets well known to European consumers, industrial markets, and marketers. Particular attention is given to this text's many users in the UK, Eire, Belgium, the Netherlands, Norway and Sweden.

CHANGES IN THIS EDITION

Marketing: Concepts and Strategies has always focused on the concepts most relevant to the development and implementation of marketing strategies. To kee~ new developments in the teaching and practice of marketing, this editi more comprehensive coverage of the key topics of market segmentation, ~

positioning (clearly explaining the link between these tasks); and the most comprehensive and up to date coverage of international marketing and of marketing ethics and social responsibility—an increasingly important area of concern to consumers and marketers alike. With the much vaunted 1992/3 deregulatory changes in the European Community (EC), a great emphasis has been placed on elements of the marketing environment which do, and increasingly will, impact upon the activities of marketing organisations within Europe. Part VI, Strategy, has been thoroughly overhauled to include more about marketing strategy *per se* and competition.

- The marketing environment, of great concern to all marketers, impacts on consumers, suppliers and marketers. With changing boundaries and political philosophies in Europe and deregulation within the European Community, the marketing environment is likely to impact even more on marketing activities within Europe. Changing consumer attitudes towards environmental issues and the increasing importance of the "Green" movement also will have major influences on the way consumers perceive products, what companies will have to provide, and the way marketing will function.
- Market segmentation has for many years been recognised as a key prerequisite to the development of successful marketing strategy. A rewritten chapter focuses on the rationale behind market segmentation, its effective use, and methods for segmenting markets. The chapter continues to look at the necessity for targeting segments and then the need and process for positioning products and brands successfully into targeted segments against competitors' products.
- A new chapter on branding and packaging examines the requirements for successful brands and the growing concerns for environmentally friendly packaging.
- The chapter relating to strategic marketing has been updated to include a greater focus on creating the differential advantage and examining strategies for competing effectively. Competitive positionings, warfare strategies, and competitor scanning are core issues introduced to this chapter.
- Marketing planning acts as a link between strategies and action. This important topic has been re-examined with the addition of many practical insights.
- The chapter entitled Marketing Ethics and Social Responsibility provides a new approach to one of the most important yet misunderstood topics in marketing, offering a framework for understanding ethical decision-making and delineating ethical issues that students will confront in the real world of marketing. Emphasis is also placed on the need for social responsibility in organisations and providing approaches for making socially responsible decisions that are effective and successful in the business community.
- The services marketing chapter now includes the latest thoughts regarding the extended marketing mix and the problems in creating a differential advantage.
- The international chapter has been completely revised to include a section on regional trade alliances and markets. Topics include the "unification" of Europe and the EC, and the impact of increasing integration of eastern Europe within continental Europe; Pacific Rim nations; and the U.S. and Canada Free Trade Agreement.

The overall design and basic features of the text were carefully reviewed and revised, following discussions with lecturers and students, to make the material as fresh and appealing as possible.

- We have created a new attractive visual presentation of the content to stimulate readers' interest. In addition, we have made the writing more lively, readable, and concise.

- We have also included many new examples of challenges facing real organisations as they market products and attempt to take advantage of unexpected opportunities in this changing world.
- Marketing Insights new for this edition integrate fundamental marketing issues and concepts with the real world practices of marketing. These inserts are generally about well known companies. They focus on issues that students will be able to relate to easily.
- Each chapter continues to include two cases, most of which are completely new for this edition.

In addition, text coverage has been completely revised and up dated to include major changes and additions such as the following:

- A greater emphasis on environmental issues and the protection of our environment, plus EC and changing regulatory influence (see especially Chapters 2 and 22).
- Coverage on lifestyles and segmentation bases, plus recent research findings in the area of segmentation (see Chapter 3).
- The latest research and new developments in our understanding of consumer buying behaviour (see Chapter 4).
- Material on recent developments, issues and the nature of the marketing research industry (see Chapter 6).
- More in-depth discussion of branding and of packaging (see Chapter 8).
- A section on retail positioning and expanded coverage on retail locations and types of retailers (see Chapter 12).
- An up dated section on recent findings related to information processing and communication in marketing, plus a discussion of the aims of promotion in modern marketing (see Chapter 14).
- A more concise and strategic approach to understanding the nature and impact of advertising, publicity and sponsorship, taking account of the recent growth of the public relations industry (see Chapter 15).
- Completely revised and up dated sections on sales promotion and direct mail (see Chapter 16).
- A completely reorganised marketing strategy part: four chapters examine marketing strategy, strategic market planning, analytical portfolio tools, competition, competitive positions and competitors' strategies; marketing planning, forecasting and the marketing audit; organisation, implementation and control; and, ethics and social responsibility in marketing (see Chapters 19–22).
- Up dated and increased depth of coverage on business-to-business and organisational marketing (sec Chapter 23).
- More in-depth coverage of services marketing incorporating the latest research in this area and increased emphasis of non-business marketing as a subset of services marketing; particular attention to the 7 Ps of the services marketing mix and the problems in creating a differential advantage in services (see Chapter 24).

Despite these changes, we believe that users of the first edition will find the second European edition to have the same strengths that have made *Marketing: Concepts and Strategies* so successful. This edition, like its predecessor, explores the depth and breadth of the field, combining detailed real examples with comprehensive coverage of marketing concepts and strategies used widely throughout the business world. Focusing on the universal concerns of marketing decision-makers, we demonstrate that marketing is a vital and challenging field of study—and a part of our world that influences almost everything we do.

FEATURES OF THE SECOND EUROPEAN EDITION

Our goal has been to provide a comprehensive and practical introduction to marketing, easy both to teach and to read. The entire book is structured to excite students about marketing and to make learning comprehensive and efficient.

- *Learning objectives* open each chapter, providing students with an overview of new concepts and each chapter's focus.
- A *vignette* introduces each chapter's marketing issues using up to date product or market examples.
- *Examples* of familiar products and organisations make concrete and specific the generalisations of marketing theory.
- Two *Marketing Insights* in each chapter focus on recognisable companies and products, extending the discussion of marketing topics and decisions.
- Numerous *figures, tables,* and *photographs* augment the text and increase comprehension. Where appropriate, current trade and industry statistics are presented to add perspective.
- A complete chapter *summary* reviews the major topics discussed.
- A *list of important terms* (highlighted in the text) provides a study aid, helping students expand their marketing vocabulary.
- *Discussion and review questions* encourage further study and exploration of chapter material (with associated material in the Tutor's Manual).
- Two concise, stimulating *cases* provoke discussion at the end of each chapter.
- A *diagram of the text's organisation* at the beginning of each part shows students how material in the upcoming part relates to the rest of the book.
- An *appendix* discusses career opportunities in marketing and its associated areas.
- A *glossary* at the end of the text defines close to 700 important marketing terms.
- A *name index* and a *subject index* enable students to find topics of interest quickly.

TEXT ORGANISATION

We have organised the seven parts of *Marketing: Concepts and Strategies* to give students a theoretical and practical understanding of marketing decision-making. Part I presents an overview of marketing, discusses general marketing concepts, and considers the marketing environment, types of markets, target market analysis, buyer behaviour, and marketing research. Part II focuses on the conceptualisation, development, and management of products, brands and packaging. Part III examines marketing channels, institutions and physical distribution. Part IV covers promotion decisions and methods, including advertising, personal selling, sales promotion, publicity, sponsorship and direct mail. Part V is devoted to pricing decisions. Part VI examines marketing management and marketing strategy, with a discussion of ethics and social responsibility in marketing. Part VII explores strategic decisions in industrial or organisational, service, non-business, and international marketing.

SUPPLEMENTS

The package for this text includes several aids to both teaching and learning:

- *Tutor's Manual.* This manual includes for each chapter: purpose and perspective, lecture outline, answers to text questions, and comments on cases. It also includes a video guide and, new to this edition, alternative syllabi.

- *Colour transparencies* of key figures and tables.
- *Videos.* The video guide for use with these video segments is found in the Tutor's Manual.

Through the years, lecturers and students have sent us many helpful suggestions for improving the text and ancillary components. We invite your comments, questions, or criticisms. We want to do our best to provide materials that enhance the teaching and learning of marketing concepts and strategies. Your suggestions will be sincerely appreciated.

Sally Dibb
Lyndon Simkin
William M. Pride
O. C. Ferrell

ACKNOWLEDGEMENTS

This text would not have happened without the support and encouragement of American authors William Pride and O. C. Ferrell, plus the comments and enthusiasm from fellow marketing lecturers at Warwick and, above all, from our students past and present. Specific thanks must go to:

- Robin Wensley, Professor of Marketing and Strategic Management and Chairman of Warwick Business School, for sustained encouragement and motivation
- Graham Cameron and all at Littlehampton
- Sue Foxon, Sheila Frost, Elizabeth Routledge and Panayiotis Panayiotou
- John Bradley and everyone at JCB
- John Wriage at Cogent and David Lake at Countrywide
- Warwick University's Business Information Service
- Susan Kahn, Margaret Kearney and Greg Tobin in Boston
- The editors and staff of *Marketing* magazine, *Marketing Week,* and *Campaign* for keeping us all abreast of current practices and trends

A number of individuals have made many helpful comments and recommendations in their reviews of this or earlier editions. We appreciate the generous help of these reviewers.

John Bradley
JCB

U. B. Bradley
City of London Polytechnic

Roger Brooks
Aston University

Debra Chelms
University of Westminster

L. de Chernatony
City University Business School

Tinus Van Drunen
Universiteit Twente (Netherlands)

Minoo Farhangmehr
Univerisdade Do Minho

Phil Flood
College of Marketing & Design, Dublin

William Fowler
University of Salford

Robert Grafton-Small
St. Andrews University

Paul James
HES(ISER) Rotterdam

Hans Kasper
University of Limburg

Patricia J. Kell
*South East Derbyshire College of
Further Education*

David W. Marshall
University of Edinburgh

Pierre B. McDonagh
University of Wales, Cardiff

Carla Millar
University of Greenwich

John Milliken
University of Ulster

Raj Singh Minhas
Sheffield University

Daniel A. Moss
University of Stirling

Paul Oakley
University of Brighton

Elaine O'Brien
University of Strathclyde

Adrian Palmer
De Montfort University

Ruth Rettie
Kingston University

Elizabeth A. Smit
Universiteit Twente (Netherlands)

Alexandra Uhlmann
Ashridge Management College

Blav Vodopivec
University of Ljubljana

Michael P. Walsh
Cork Regional Technical College

Eric Waarts
Erasmus University

Nigel Whichelo
Leeds Business School

Ken Wright
*West Australia College of Advanced
Education—Churchland Campus*

MARKETING

I AN ANALYSIS OF MARKETING OPPORTUNITIES

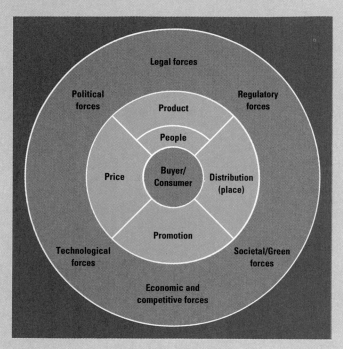

Part I introduces marketing, providing a broad perspective from which to explore and analyse various components of the marketing discipline. The first chapter defines marketing and discusses why an understanding of it is useful in many aspects of everyday life, including one's career. There is an overview of general strategic marketing issues such as market opportunity analysis, target markets, and marketing mix development. Marketers should understand how environmental forces can affect customers and their responses to marketing strategies. Chapter 2 outlines political, legal, regulatory, societal/green, technological, and economic and competitive forces in the environment. Chapter 3 focuses on one of the major steps in the development of a marketing strategy: selecting and analysing target markets. Understanding elements that affect buying decisions enables marketers to better analyse customers' needs and evaluate how specific marketing strategies can satisfy those needs. Chapter 4 examines consumer buying decision processes and factors that influence buying decisions. Organisational markets, organisational buyers, the buying centre, and the organisational buying decision process are considered in Chapter 5. Chapter 6 includes a discussion of the role of a marketing information system and the basic steps in the marketing research process. Information and marketing intelligence are essential for sound marketing decision-making. ∎

1 AN OVERVIEW OF STRATEGIC MARKETING

Objectives

To understand the definition of marketing

To understand why a person should study marketing

To gain insight into the basic elements of the marketing concept and its implementation

To understand the major components of a marketing strategy

To gain a sense of general strategic marketing issues, such as market opportunity analysis, target market selection, and marketing mix development

*F*or many years, Pepsi-Cola and Coca-Cola have been fighting for market share in the war of the soft drinks. As the battle has developed, the competition has switched from the regular to diet sectors, with a range of new product variants to satisfy the changing needs of customers. For PepsiCo and Coca-Cola, makers of the leading brands, the challenge has been to stay one step ahead of each other, in tune with these customer requirements.

PepsiCo International's plan to double sales outside its native United States is known as "Vision 2000". With a switch in energies away from its snack food division firmly towards the Pepsi soft drink brand, the company is making Japan the top priority. In a development of the "Pepsi Challenge", the Japanese campaign focuses on comparing Pepsi and Coke. The results have been encouraging—an independent survey suggests Pepsi sales have risen 50 per cent during the two month life of the campaign.

Meanwhile, in an attempt to reach the highly fragmented global market, Coca-Cola has launched a campaign costing millions, which spans almost all of its 195 markets. The company is also keeping close tabs on Europe with the recent launch of its cola based sugar free soft drink, Tab Clear. The UK launch follows just two weeks behind Tab Clear's introduction in the US. With the advertising line "Suddenly everything is clear", the drink is aimed to attract consumers who are not loyal to cola (the so called "brand switchers"). Early indications are that the product will compete mainly against the fruit carbonates, like Lilt, Sunkist, Fanta, Sprite, Gini and Tango.

As the battle continues, the giants in the soft drinks market are having to shift their focus away from the children's market towards adults. Changes in Europe's demographic make-up—there has been a 20 per cent fall in the numbers of 15 to 24 year olds in the UK alone, with a rise in numbers of 25 to 24 year olds—are leading the move. Already in the US, Belgium and Germany, 35 year olds consume more soft drinks annually than 15 year olds. According to Coca-Cola GB's external affairs manager;

> We haven't reached that stage here yet. But we do believe that as the soft drink market matures in the UK, people will retain the soft drinking habit as they grow older. ■

SOURCES: Suzanne Bidlake, "Coca-Cola keeps tab on UK market", *Marketing*, 21 January 1993; Yumiko Ono, "Pepsi challenges Japanese taboo as it ribs Coke", *Wall Street Journal*, 6 March pp. B1–B3; Fiona Plant, "Coke goes global with latest work", *Campaign*, 19 February 1993; Plant, "Coke kicks off £10m media review", *Campaign,* 22 January 1993; David Kilburn, "P challenge: double Japan share", *Advertising Age*, 10 December 1990, p. 36.

PepsiCo and Coca-Cola both have responded to a changing market-place. Demographics have altered and consumers are apparently more health-conscious. Competitive product launches have forced the introduction of new products from both these giants of the soft drinks market.

The first chapter is an overview of the concepts and decisions covered in this text. This chapter first develops a definition of marketing and explains each element of the definition. The focus is then on some of the reasons why people should study marketing. The marketing concept is introduced and several issues associated with successful implementation are examined. The major tasks associated with marketing strategy are defined and discussed: market opportunity analysis, target market selection, marketing mix development, and management of marketing activities. This chapter concludes by discussing the organisation of this text.

MARKETING DEFINED

If you ask several people what *marketing* is, they will respond with a variety of descriptions: "advertising", "selling", "conning people", "targeting", "packaging".[1] Marketing encompasses many more activities than most people realise. Since it is practised and studied for many different reasons, it has been, and continues to be, defined in many ways, for academic, research or applied business purposes. According to the UK Chartered Institute of Marketing,

> Marketing is the management process responsible for identifying, anticipating and satisfying consumers' requirements profitably.

A rather different definition has been developed by the American Marketing Association (AMA):

> Marketing is the process of planning and executing the conception, pricing, promotion, and distribution of ideas, goods, and services to create exchanges that satisfy individual and organizational goals.[2]

These definitions are widely accepted by academics and marketing managers.[3] They emphasise that marketing focuses on planning and executing activities to satisfy customers' demands. Whereas earlier definitions restricted marketing as a business activity, these definitions are broad enough to indicate that marketing can occur in non-business organisations.

Although both of the above definitions are acceptable, it is possible to define marketing still more broadly. A definition of marketing should indicate that marketing consists of activities performed by individuals and organisations. In addition, it should acknowledge that marketing activities occur in a dynamic environment. Thus we define **marketing** as follows:

> Marketing consists of individual and organisational activities that facilitate and expedite satisfying exchange relationships in a dynamic environment through the creation, distribution, promotion and pricing of goods, services and ideas.

In this definition, an **exchange** is the provision or transfer of goods, services, and ideas in return for something of value. Any product may be involved in a marketing exchange. Each component is examined more closely in the following sections.

Marketing Consists of Activities

Marketing products effectively requires many activities. Some are performed by producers; some are accomplished by intermediaries, who buy products from producers

TABLE 1.1 *Possible decisions and activities associated with marketing mix variables*

MARKETING MIX VARIABLES	POSSIBLE DECISIONS AND ACTIVITIES
PRODUCT	Develop and test market new products; modify existing products; eliminate products that do not satisfy customers' desires; formulate brand names and branding policies; create product guarantees and establish procedures for fulfilling guarantees; plan packages, including materials, sizes, shapes, colours and designs
DISTRIBUTION (PLACE)	Analyse various types of distribution channels; design appropriate distribution channels; design an effective programme for dealer relations; establish distribution centres; formulate and implement procedures for efficient product handling; set up inventory controls; analyse transportation methods; minimise total distribution costs; analyse possible locations for plants and wholesale or retail outlets
PROMOTION	Set promotional objectives; determine major types of promotion to be used; select and schedule advertising media; develop advertising messages; measure the effectiveness of advertisements; recruit and train salespersons; formulate payment programmes for sales personnel; establish sales territories; plan and implement sales promotion efforts such as free samples, coupons, displays, competitions, sales contests, and co-operative advertising programmes; prepare and disseminate publicity releases; evaluate sponsorships and provide direct mail
PRICE	Analyse competitors' prices; formulate pricing policies; determine method or methods used to set prices; set prices; determine discounts for various types of buyer; establish conditions and terms of sales
PEOPLE	Manipulate the marketing mix (marketers); make products and services available (intermediaries); provide market for products (consumers)

or from other intermediaries and resell them; and some are even performed by purchasers. Marketing does not include all human and organisational activities, but only those aimed at facilitating and expediting exchanges. Table 1.1 lists several major categories and examples of marketing activities. Note that this list is not all-inclusive. Each activity could be subdivided into more specific activities.

Marketing Is Performed by Individuals and Organisations

All organisations perform marketing activities to facilitate exchanges. Businesses as well as non-business organisations such as colleges and universities, charitable organisations, community theatres, and hospitals perform marketing activities. For example, colleges and universities and their students engage in exchanges. To receive instruction, knowledge, entertainment, a degree, the use of facilities, and sometimes room and board, students give up time, money and perhaps services in the form of labour; they may also give up opportunities to do other things. Many organisations engage in marketing activities. In the UK, various police forces have surveyed their communities in order to prioritise services and reassure the general public that people's concerns will be addressed. Even the sole owner of and worker in a small corner shop decides which products will sell, arranges deliveries to the shop, prices and displays products, advertises and serves customers.

Marketing Facilitates Satisfying Exchange Relationships

For an exchange to take place, four conditions must exist. First, two or more individuals, groups or organisations must participate. Second, each party must possess something of value that the other party desires. Third, each party must be willing to give up its "something of value" to receive the "something of value" held by the other party.

FIGURE 1.1
Exchange between buyer and seller

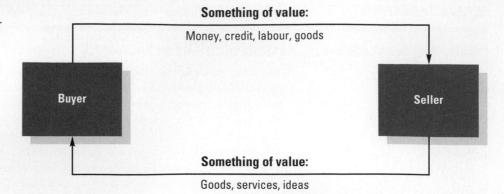

The objective of a marketing exchange is to receive something that is desired more than what is given up to get it, that is, a reward in excess of costs. Fourth, the parties to the exchange must be able to communicate with each other to make their "somethings of value" available.[4]

Figure 1.1 illustrates the process of exchange. The arrows indicate that the parties communicate and that each has something of value available to exchange. Note, though, that an exchange will not necessarily take place just because these four conditions exist. Nevertheless, even if there is no exchange, marketing activities still have occurred. The "somethings of value" held by the two parties are most often products and/or financial resources, such as money or credit. When an exchange occurs, products are traded for other products or for financial resources.

An exchange should be *satisfying* to both the buyer and the seller. In fact, in a study of marketing managers, 32 per cent indicated that creating customer satisfaction was the most important concept in a definition of marketing.[5] Marketing activities, then, should be orientated towards creating and maintaining satisfying exchange relationships. To maintain an exchange relationship, the buyer must be satisfied with the goods, service or idea obtained in the exchange; the seller must be satisfied with the financial reward or something else of value received in the exchange. For instance, to encourage satisfying exchange relationships with its customers, BBL stresses clear and concise communications (see Figure 1.2).

Maintaining a positive relationship with buyers is an important goal for a seller, regardless of whether the seller is marketing cereal, financial services or a construction plant. Through buyer-seller interaction, the buyer develops expectations about the seller's future behaviour. To fulfil these expectations, the seller must deliver on promises made. Over time, a healthy buyer-seller relationship results in interdependencies between the two parties. The buyer depends on the seller to furnish information, parts and service; to be available; and to provide satisfying products in the future. Andersen Consulting's advertising emphasises the company's skills and expertise to reassure existing and potential clients (see Figure 1.3).

Marketing Occurs in a Dynamic Environment

The marketing environment consists of many changing forces: laws, regulations, political activities, societal pressures, changing economic conditions and technological advances. Each of these dynamic forces has an impact on how effectively marketing activities can facilitate and expedite exchanges. For example, the development and acceptance of facsimile (fax) machines has given businesses another vehicle through which to promote their products. Some office suppliers and restaurants send adver-

FIGURE 1.2 *Marketing exchange*

Bank BBL tries to ensure that the exchange process is facilitated through clear communication with customers.

SOURCE: Young and Rubicam—Brussels.

tisements about their goods and services to businesses and individuals through their fax machines. Another example is the impact EC regulations have had on reducing distribution headaches within much of Europe.

Marketing Focuses on Goods, Services and Ideas

Marketing means more than simply advertising or selling a product; it involves developing and managing a product that will satisfy certain needs. It focuses on making the product available at the right place, at the right time, at a price that is acceptable to customers and with the right people. It also requires transmitting the kind of information that will help customers determine whether the product will in fact be able to satisfy their needs. Marketing Insight 1.1 discusses IKEA's successful use of marketing.

Marketing Involves Products, Distribution, Promotion, Pricing and People

The word *product* has been used a number of times in this chapter. For purposes of discussion in this text, a *product* is viewed as being a good, a service, or an idea. A *good* is a physical entity one can touch. A Ford Escort, a compact disc player, Kellogg's Frosties, a bar of soap and a kitten in a pet shop are examples of goods. A *service* is the application of human and mechanical efforts to people or objects in order to provide intangible benefits to customers. Services such as air travel, dry cleaning, hairdressing, banking, medical care and child care are just as real as goods, but an individual actually touch them. *Ideas* include concepts, philosophies, images an

FIGURE 1.3
Building satisfying customer relationships
To successfully implement the marketing concept, organisations must place a high priority on satisfying customers. By emphasising its business and technology skills, Andersen Consulting shows that it can help companies perform more effectively.

SOURCE: Reprinted with permission of Andersen Consulting.

instance, a marriage counsellor gives couples ideas and advice to help improve their relationships. Other marketers of ideas include political parties, churches, schools and marketing lecturers.

WHY STUDY MARKETING?

Marketing Activities Are Used in Many Organisations

The relevancy of marketing as a topic worth studying is apparent from the definition of marketing just presented. This section discusses several less obvious reasons why marketing should be studied.

In Europe and the United States between 25 and 33 per cent of all civilian workers perform marketing activities. The marketing field offers a variety of interesting and challenging career opportunities, such as personal selling, advertising, packaging, transport, storage, marketing research, product development, wholesaling, retailing and consultancy. In addition, many individuals who work for non-business organisations engage in marketing activities. Marketing skills are used to promote political, cultural, church, civic and charitable activities. The advertisement in Figure 1.4 encourages support of the World Wide Fund for Nature, a non-profit organisation. Whether a person earns a living through marketing activities or performs them without compensation in non-business settings, marketing knowledge and skills are valuable assets.

SWEDEN'S IKEA MARCHES ON

When Swedish home furnishings retailer IKEA opened its first store in the UK, a retail shed near the M6 at Warrington, curious shoppers found queues jamming nearby roads, parking spaces at a premium, and retailing analysts by the score. With just one store, IKEA had the UK furniture industry on its toes: large retail groups and manufacturers alike feared large market share losses. With its acquisition of the UK's Habitat, IKEA has conquered yet another territory.

IKEA has grown from one store in 1958 to close to 100 stores in 22 countries, 17,000 employees and sales of over SEK20 billion (£1.7 billion). Close to 85 per cent of sales are from within Europe, but recent expansion in North America, South East Asia, and Australasia is now increasing *rest of the world* sales—despite some initial franchising difficulties in certain territories. IKEA's distinctive catalogue is produced in-house and now printed in 12 languages. IKEA is perhaps one of the world's most successful retailers with a brand name that is known, recognised and discussed; a retail concept which stands for value, style and quality; everything for the home under one roof, with easy parking, children's play areas and cafés—"a day out"! As the company succinctly states in its advertising:

IKEA: the furnishings store from Sweden
More for your money

Low prices have been the key to IKEA's success, but price alone cannot create an internationally long term marketing success story. Products are updated consistently to match consumers' expectations and lifestyles. In-store service and staff training are integral to the IKEA shopping experience. Sites are chosen to maximise catchment areas, to make access easy for shoppers, and to bring the brand name to the attention of the whole community. Logistics give IKEA an edge, with carefully managed ordering and delivery reducing both stockholdings and stock-outs. Promotion emphasises the style without expense philosophy and the IKEA name. The result has been a country by country revolution as staid furniture markets have been rejuvenated with the entry of IKEA. Shoppers intending to buy just a sofa return home with a sofa, a chair, some lamps, and a general excitement about a new store where they can buy home furnishings at unbelievable prices.

IKEA has its ideals and operating philosophies: standards matter. IKEA has a forceful, well directed marketing strategy actioned through a tightly developed marketing mix. The result is a successful, expanding company, satisfied target customers and unhappy competitors.

SOURCES: *IKEA Facts,* 1990 and 1992; B. Solomon, "A Swedish company corners the business: worldwide", *Management Review,* 80(4), 1991, pp. 10–13; B. Saporito, "IKEA's got 'em lining up", *Fortune,* 123(5), 11 March 1991, p. 72; *Key Note,* 1989 and 1992; Peter Wingard, Warwick MBA.

CHAPTER 1   An Overview of Strategic

J.m. (6), introvert type, moet huis uit wegens sloop.
Zkt. m. spoed opvang. Bij voork. bosrijke omgeving.

FIGURE 1.4 *Promotion of a non-profit organisation*
The World Wide Fund for Nature uses marketing efforts to obtain contributions.
SOURCE: World Wide Fund for Nature.

Marketing Activities Are Important to Businesses and the Economy

A business organisation must sell products to survive and to grow. Directly or indirectly, marketing activities help sell an organisation's products. By doing so, they generate financial resources that can be used to develop innovative products. New products allow a firm to better satisfy customers' changing needs, which in turn enables the firm to generate more profits. For example, each year *Fortune* magazine publishes a list of what its staff considers the top products. Recently, among these products of the year were the Sony Video Walkman, NEC Ultralite Laptop computer, Ricoh Mirai camera, Max Factor's No Colour Mascara, and Wilson Profile tennis racket.[6] All these products produced considerable profit for the firms that introduced them.

Europe's highly complex economy depends heavily on marketing activities. They help produce the profits that are essential not only to the survival of individual businesses, but also to the health and ultimate survival of the economy as a whole. Profits are essential to economic growth because without them businesses find it difficult, if not impossible, to buy more raw materials, hire more employees, attract more capital and create the additional products which in turn make more profits.

Marketing Knowledge Enhances Consumer Awareness

Besides contributing to a country's economic well being, marketing activities permeate everyone's lives. In fact, they help to improve the quality of life. Studying marketing activities enables the costs, benefits and flaws of marketing to be evaluated. The need for improvement and ways to accomplish changes can be determined. For example, an unsatisfactory experience with a guarantee may lead consumers to demand

SWEDEN'S IKEA MARCHES ON

When Swedish home furnishings retailer IKEA opened its first store in the UK, a retail shed near the M6 at Warrington, curious shoppers found queues jamming nearby roads, parking spaces at a premium, and retailing analysts by the score. With just one store, IKEA had the UK furniture industry on its toes: large retail groups and manufacturers alike feared large market share losses. With its acquisition of the UK's Habitat, IKEA has conquered yet another territory.

IKEA has grown from one store in 1958 to close to 100 stores in 22 countries, 17,000 employees and sales of over SEK20 billion (£1.7 billion). Close to 85 per cent of sales are from within Europe, but recent expansion in North America, South East Asia, and Australasia is now increasing *rest of the world* sales—despite some initial franchising difficulties in certain territories. IKEA's distinctive catalogue is produced in-house and now printed in 12 languages. IKEA is perhaps one of the world's most successful retailers with a brand name that is known, recognised and discussed; a retail concept which stands for value, style and quality; everything for the home under one roof, with easy parking, children's play areas and cafés—"a day out"! As the company succinctly states in its advertising:

IKEA: the furnishings store from Sweden
More for your money

Low prices have been the key to IKEA's success, but price alone cannot create an internationally long term marketing success story. Products are updated consistently to match consumers' expectations and lifestyles. In-store service and staff training are integral to the IKEA shopping experience. Sites are chosen to maximise catchment areas, to make access easy for shoppers, and to bring the brand name to the attention of the whole community. Logistics give IKEA an edge, with carefully managed ordering and delivery reducing both stockholdings and stock-outs. Promotion emphasises the style without expense philosophy and the IKEA name. The result has been a country by country revolution as staid furniture markets have been rejuvenated with the entry of IKEA. Shoppers intending to buy just a sofa return home with a sofa, a chair, some lamps, and a general excitement about a new store where they can buy home furnishings at unbelievable prices.

IKEA has its ideals and operating philosophies: standards matter. IKEA has a forceful, well directed marketing strategy actioned through a tightly developed marketing mix. The result is a successful, expanding company, satisfied target customers and unhappy competitors.

SOURCES: *IKEA Facts,* 1990 and 1992; B. Solomon, "A Swedish company corners the business: worldwide", *Management Review,* 80(4), 1991, pp. 10–13; B. Saporito, "IKEA's got 'em lining up", *Fortune,* 123(5), 11 March 1991, p. 72; *Key Note,* 1989 and 1992; Peter Wingard, Warwick MBA.

FIGURE 1.4 *Promotion of a non-profit organisation*
The World Wide Fund for Nature uses marketing efforts to obtain contributions.

SOURCE: World Wide Fund for Nature.

Marketing Activities Are Important to Businesses and the Economy

A business organisation must sell products to survive and to grow. Directly or indirectly, marketing activities help sell an organisation's products. By doing so, they generate financial resources that can be used to develop innovative products. New products allow a firm to better satisfy customers' changing needs, which in turn enables the firm to generate more profits. For example, each year *Fortune* magazine publishes a list of what its staff considers the top products. Recently, among these products of the year were the Sony Video Walkman, NEC Ultralite Laptop computer, Ricoh Mirai camera, Max Factor's No Colour Mascara, and Wilson Profile tennis racket.[6] All these products produced considerable profit for the firms that introduced them.

Europe's highly complex economy depends heavily on marketing activities. They help produce the profits that are essential not only to the survival of individual businesses, but also to the health and ultimate survival of the economy as a whole. Profits are essential to economic growth because without them businesses find it difficult, if not impossible, to buy more raw materials, hire more employees, attract more capital, and create the additional products which in turn make more profits.

Marketing Knowledge Enhances Consumer Awareness

Besides contributing to a country's economic well being, marketing activities permeate everyone's lives. In fact, they help to improve the quality of life. Studying marketing activities enables the costs, benefits and flaws of marketing to be evaluated. The need for improvement and ways to accomplish changes can be determined. For example, an unsatisfactory experience with a guarantee may lead consumers to demand that

TABLE 1.2 *Popular marketing myths*

MYTHS	STRONGLY AGREE	SOMEWHAT AGREE	NEITHER AGREE NOR DISAGREE	SOMEWHAT DISAGREE	STRONGLY DISAGREE
Marketing is selling	14%	34%	26%	18%	8%
Marketers persuade	21%	25%	20%	11%	23%
Dealers' profits significantly increase prices consumers pay	21%	32%	12%	8%	27%
Marketing depends on advertising	17%	44%	12%	9%	18%
Strategic planning is nothing to do with marketing	19%	19%	21%	17%	24%

SOURCES: Student surveys.

laws be enforced more strictly to make sellers fulfil their promises. Similarly, there may be the desire for more information about a product—or more accurate information—before purchase. Understanding marketing leads to the evaluation of the corrective measures (such as laws, regulations and industry guidelines) that may be required to stop unfair, misleading or unethical marketing practices. The results of the survey presented in Table 1.2 indicate that there is a considerable lack of knowledge about marketing activities, as reflected by the sizeable proportion of respondents who agree with the myths in the table.

Marketing Costs Consume a Sizeable Portion of Buyers' Incomes

The study of marketing emphasises that many marketing activities are necessary to provide people with satisfying goods and services. Obviously, these marketing activities cost money. A family with a monthly income of £1,000, of which £300 goes on taxes and savings, spends about £700 on goods and services. Of this amount, typically £350 goes for marketing activities. Clearly, if marketing expenses consume that much income, it is necessary to know how this money is used.

THE MARKETING CONCEPT

Some organisations have tried to be successful by buying land, building a factory, equipping it with people and machines, and then making a product that they believe consumers need. However, these organisations frequently fail to attract buyers with what they have to offer because they defined their business as "making a product" rather than as "helping potential customers satisfy their needs and wants". Such organisations have failed to implement the marketing concept. It is not enough to be "product led", no matter how good the product. An organisation must be in tune with consumer requirements.

According to the **marketing concept,** an organisation should try to p̶͟ ̶͟prod-ucts that satisfy customers' needs through a co-ordinated set of activities lows the organisation to achieve its goals. Customer satisfaction is the ma̶ marketing concept. First, an organisation must find out what will satisfy customers. With this information, it then attempts to create satisfying products. But the process does not end there. The organisation must continue to alter, adapt and develop products to keep pace with customers' changing desires and preferences. The marketing concept stresses the importance of customers and emphasises that marketing activities begin and end with them.

In attempting to satisfy customers, businesses must consider not only short run, immediate needs but also broad, long term desires. Trying to satisfy customers' current needs by sacrificing their long term desires will only create future dissatisfaction. For instance, people want efficient, low cost energy to power their homes and cars, yet they react adversely to energy producers who pollute the air and water, kill wildlife or cause disease or birth defects. To meet these short and long run needs and desires, a firm must co-ordinate all its activities. Production, finance, accounting, personnel and marketing departments must work together.

The marketing concept is not a second definition of marketing. It is a way of thinking—a management philosophy guiding an organisation's overall activities. This philosophy affects all the efforts of the organisation, not just marketing activities. However, the marketing concept is by no means a philanthropic philosophy aimed at helping customers at the expense of the organisation. A firm that adopts the marketing concept must not only satisfy its customers' objectives but also achieve its own goals, or it will not stay in business long. The overall goals of a business might be directed towards increasing profits, share of the market, sales, or a combination of all three. The marketing concept stresses that an organisation can best achieve its goals by providing customer satisfaction. Thus, implementing the marketing concept should benefit the organisation as well as its customers.

Evolution of the Marketing Concept

The marketing concept may seem like an obvious and sensible approach to running a business. However, businesspeople have not always believed that the best way to make sales and profits is to satisfy customers. A famous example is the marketing philosophy for cars widely attributed to Henry Ford in the early 1900s: "The customers can have any colour car they want as long as it is black". The philosophy of the marketing concept emerged in the third major era in the history of business, preceded by the production and the sales eras. Surprisingly, nearly forty years after the marketing era began, many businesses still have not adopted the marketing concept.

The Production Era.   During the second half of the nineteenth century, the Industrial Revolution was in full swing in Europe and the United States. Electricity, railways, the division of labour, the assembly line and mass production made it possible to manufacture products more efficiently. With new technology and new ways of using labour, products poured into the market-place, where consumer demand for manufactured goods was strong. This production orientation continued into the early part of this century, encouraged by the scientific management movement that championed rigidly structured jobs and pay based on output.

The Sales Era.   In the 1920s, the strong consumer demand for products subsided. Businesses realised that products, which by this time could be made quite efficiently, would have to be "sold" to consumers. From the mid-1920s to the early 1950s, businesses viewed sales as the major means of increasing profits. As a result, this period came to have a sales orientation. Businesspeople believed that the most important marketing activities were personal selling and advertising.

The Marketing Era. By the early 1950s, some businesspeople began to recognise that efficient production and extensive promotion of products did not guarantee that customers would buy them. These businesses, and many others since then, found that they must first determine what customers want and then produce it, rather than simply make products first and then try to change customers' needs to correspond to what was being produced. As more organisations have realised the importance of knowing customers' needs, businesses have entered into the marketing era—the era of customer orientation.

Implementing the Marketing Concept

A philosophy may sound reasonable and look good on paper, but that does not mean it can be put into practice easily. The marketing concept is a case in point. To implement it, an organisation must focus on some general conditions and recognise several problems. Because of these conditions and problems, the marketing concept has yet to be fully accepted by many businesses.

Because the marketing concept affects all types of business activities, and not just marketing activities, the top management of an organisation must adopt it wholeheartedly. High level executives must incorporate the marketing concept into their philosophies of business management so completely that it becomes the basis for all the goals and decisions that they set for their firms. They must also convince other members of the organisation to accept the changes in policies and operations that flow from their acceptance of the marketing concept. Costs and budgetary controls are important, products and manufacturing essential, and personnel management necessary, but all are to no avail if the organisation's products or services are not desired by the targeted customers.

As the first step, management must establish an information system that enables it to discover customers' real needs and to use the information to create satisfying products. Because such a system is usually expensive, management must be willing to commit money and time for development and maintenance. Without an adequate information system, an organisation cannot be customer orientated.

Management's second major task is to restructure the organisation. If a company is to satisfy customers' objectives as well as its own, it must co-ordinate all its activities. To achieve this, the internal operations and the overall objectives of one or more departments may need restructuring. If the head of the marketing unit is not a member of the organisation's top level management, he or she should be. Some departments may have to be abolished and new ones created. Implementing the marketing concept demands the support not only of top management, but also of managers and staff at all levels within the organisation.

Even when the basic conditions of establishing an information system and reorganising the company are met, the firm's new marketing approach may not work perfectly. First, there is a limit to a firm's ability to satisfy customers' needs for a particular product. In a mass production economy, most business organisations cannot tailor products to fit the exact needs of each customer. Second, although a company may attempt to learn what customers want, it may be unable to do so, and when the organisation does correctly identify customers' needs, it often has a difficult time developing a product that satisfies those needs. Many companies spend considerable time and money to research customers' needs and yet still create some products that do not sell well. Third, by striving to satisfy one particular segment of society, a firm sometimes dissatisfies other segments. Certainly, government and non-business organisat~~~~~~~~~~experience this problem. Fourth, a business organisation may have diffi~~~~~~~~employee morale during any restructuring needed to co-ordinate the~~~~~~~ous departments. Management must clearly explain the reason~~~~

changes and communicate its own enthusiasm for the marketing concept. Adoption of the marketing philosophy takes time, resources, endurance and commitment.

MARKETING STRATEGY

To achieve the broad goal of expediting desirable exchanges, an organisation's marketing managers are responsible for developing and managing marketing strategies. Specifically, a **marketing strategy** encompasses selecting and analysing a target market (the group of people whom the organisation wants to reach) and creating and maintaining an appropriate **marketing mix** (product, distribution, promotion, price and people) that will satisfy those people in the target market. A marketing strategy articulates a plan for the best use of the organisation's resources and tactics to meet its objectives.

When marketing managers attempt to develop and manage marketing activities, they must deal with two broad sets of variables: those relating to the marketing mix and those that make up the marketing environment. The marketing mix decision variables—product, distribution, promotion, price and people—are factors over which an organisation has control. As Figure 1.5 shows, these variables are constructed around the buyer or consumer. The marketing environment variables are political, legal, regulatory, societal/green, technological, and economic and competitive forces. These factors are subject to less control by an organisation, but they affect buyers' needs as well as marketing managers' decisions regarding marketing mix variables.

To develop and manage marketing strategies, marketers must focus on several marketing tasks: marketing opportunity analysis, target market selection, marketing mix development, and effective marketing management. Figure 1.6 lists these tasks, along with the chapters of this book in which they are discussed.

Marketing Opportunity Analysis

A *marketing opportunity* exists when circumstances allow an organisation to take action towards reaching a particular group of customers. An opportunity provides a favourable chance or opening for the firm to generate sales from identifiable markets. For example, during a heat wave, marketers of electric fans have a marketing opportunity—an opportunity to reach customers who need electric fans.

Marketers should be capable of recognising and analysing marketing opportunities. An organisation's long term survival depends on developing products that satisfy its customers. Few organisations can assume that products popular today will interest buyers ten years from now. A marketing organisation can choose among several alternatives for continued product development through which it can achieve its objectives and satisfy buyers. It can modify existing products (for example, by removing preservatives from jams and sauces to address increasing health consciousness among customers), introduce new products (such as Kellogg's Pop-Tarts or Batchelors' Micro Chef), and delete some that customers no longer want (such as disc cameras or turntables). A company may also try to market its products to a greater number of customers, convince current customers to use more of a product, or perhaps expand marketing activities into additional countries. Diversification into new product offerings through internal efforts or through acquisitions of other organisations may be viable options for a firm. For example, BSN Groupe, a French consumer goods marketer of pasta, bakery goods and other products, bought RJR Nabisco's European consumer goods division, gaining the rights to market a number of highly successful Nabisco products in Europe, and Grand Metropolitan's purchase of Pillsbury led to the European appearance of Häagen-Dazs premium adult ice creams. An organisation's

FIGURE 1.5
*Components of the
marketing mix and
marketing environment*

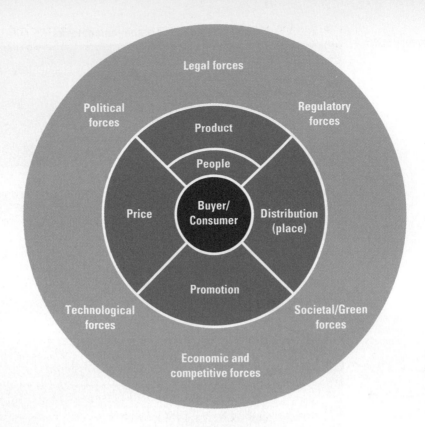

ability to pursue any of these alternatives successfully depends on its internal characteristics and the forces within the marketing environment.

Internal Organisational Factors.   The primary factors inside an organisation that should be considered when analysing marketing opportunities are organisational objectives, financial resources, managerial skills, organisational strengths and weaknesses and cost structures. Most organisations have overall organisational objectives. Some marketing opportunities may be consistent with these objectives; other are not, and to pursue them is hazardous. Frequently, the pursuit of such opportunities ends in failure or forces the company to alter its long term objectives.

Obviously, a firm's financial resources constrain the type of marketing opportunities it can pursue. Typically, an organisation does not develop projects that can bring economic catastrophe. In some situations, however, a firm must invest in a high risk opportunity, because the costs of not pursuing the project are so high. Thus, despite an economic recession and reduced house and road building, construction equipment manufacturer JCB continues to launch new ranges and enter new markets. It developed and launched its 1993 Compact Division, at a cost of millions, to respond to changing market requirements.

The skills and experience of management also limit the types of opportunities that an organisation can pursue. A company must be particularly cautious when exploring the possibility of entering unfamiliar markets with new products. If it lacks appropriate managerial skills and experience, the firm can sometimes acquire them by hiring additional managerial personnel.

Like people, most organisations have strengths and weaknesses. B
types of operation in which a company is engaged, it normally has e

CHAPTER 1   An Overview of Strategi

FIGURE 1.6
Marketing strategy tasks

Generic marketing management tasks

Marketing opportunity analysis and target market selection

- The marketing environment (Chapter 2)
- Target market evaluation (Chapter 3)
- Consumer markets and buying behaviour (Chapter 4)
- Organisational markets and buying behaviour (Chapter 5)
- Marketing research and information systems (Chapter 6)

Marketing mix development

- Product, branding and packaging decisions (Chapters 7, 8 and 9)
- Distribution (place) decisions (Chapters 10, 11, 12 and 13)
- Promotion decisions (Chapters 14, 15 and 16)
- Pricing decisions (Chapters 17 and 18)
- Supplementary decisions (Chapters 15, 21 and 22)

Marketing management

- Strategic market planning and competitive strategy (Chapters 19 and 20)
- Implementing strategies and measuring performance (Chapter 21)
- Marketing ethics and social responsibility (Chapter 22)

specialised skills and technological information. Such characteristics are a strength when launching marketing strategies that require them. However, they may be a weakness if the company tries to compete in new, unrelated product areas.

An organisation's cost structure may be an advantage if the company pursues certain marketing opportunities and a disadvantage if it pursues others. Such factors as geographic location, employee skills, access to raw materials and type of equipment and facilities all can affect the cost structure.

Marketing Environment Forces. The **marketing environment,** which consists of political, legal, regulatory, societal/green, technological, and economic and competitive forces, surrounds the buyer (consumer) and the marketing mix (see Figure 1.5). Each major environmental force is explored in considerable depth in Chapter 2. Marketers know that they cannot predict changes in the marketing environment with certainty, as illustrated in Marketing Insight 1.2. Even so, over the years, marketers have become more systematic in taking these forces into account when planning their competitive actions.[7]

Marketing environment forces affect a marketer's ability to facilitate and expedite exchanges in three general ways. First, they influence customers by affecting their lifestyles, standards of living and preferences and needs for products. Because a marketing manager tries to develop and adjust the marketing mix to satisfy consumers, the effects of environmental forces on customers also have an indirect impact on the marketing mix components. Second, marketing environment forces help determine whether and how a marketing manager can perform certain marketing activities. Third, the environmental forces may affect a marketing manager's decisions and actions by influencing buyers' reactions to the firm's marketing mix.

Although forces in the marketing environment are sometimes viewed as "uncontrollables", a marketing manager may be able to influence one or more of them. However, marketing environment forces fluctuate quickly and dramatically, which is one reason why marketing is so interesting and challenging. Because these forces are highly interrelated, a change in one may cause others to change. For example, from Freons in fridges to additives in foods, most consumers have become increasingly aware of health and environmental issues. Manufacturers have altered product specifications and production methods. Legislators and regulatory bodies have also responded to expert and consumer opinions, forcing companies to rethink their manufacturing and marketing policies, with new regulations and informal agreements.

Even though changes in the marketing environment produce uncertainty for marketers and, at times, hurt marketing efforts, they can also create opportunities. After the 1989 oil spills, for example, more companies began developing and marketing products designed to contain or dissipate spilled oil. Thus a marketer must be aware of changes in environmental forces not only to adjust to and influence them but also to capitalise on the opportunities they provide.

Marketing Strategy: Target Market Selection

A **target market** is a group of persons for whom a firm creates and maintains a marketing mix that specifically fits the needs and preferences of that group. When choosing a target market, marketing managers try to evaluate possible markets to see how entering them would affect the company's sales, costs and profits. Marketers also attempt to determine whether the organisation has the resources to produce a marketing mix that meets the needs of a particular target market and whether satisfying those needs is consistent with the firm's overall objectives. The size and number of competitors already marketing products in possible target markets are also of concern.

Marketing managers may define a target market as a vast number of people or as a relatively small group. For example, Ford produces cars suitable for the bulk of the population (although specific models are quite narrowly targeted: the family runaround Fiesta or the executive Scorpio). Porsche focuses its marketing effort on a small proportion of the population. Porsche believes that it can compete more effectively by concentrating on an affluent target market. Although a business may concentrate its efforts on one target market through a single marketing mix, businesses often focus on several target markets by developing and employing multiple marketing mixes. Reebok, for example, markets different types of shoes to meet the specific needs of joggers, walkers, aerobics enthusiasts and other groups.

Target market selection is crucial to generating productive marketing efforts. At times, products and organisations fail because marketers do not identify the appropriate customer groups at which to aim their efforts. Organisations that try to be all things to all people typically end up not satisfying the needs of any customer group very well. It is important for an organisation's management to designate which customer groups the firm is trying to serve and to have adequate information about these customers. The identification and analysis of a target market provide a foundation on which a marketing mix can be developed.

Marketing Strategy: Marketing Mix Development

As mentioned earlier, the marketing mix consists of four major components: product, distribution, promotion and price. Increasingly, people are becoming th[e] nent. These components are called marketing mix decision variables b[keting manager decides what type of each component to use and in wh[primary goal of a marketing manager is to create and maintain a mark[

LE SHUTTLE: P&O FIGHTS BACK

For decades, the majority of tourists leaving the UK for France or Benelux travelled with their cars on the cross-Channel ferries. For German, Dutch and French tourists wishing to explore Britain and Eire, the car ferries were a popular option. Flights were used more for business and longer haul visitors, were costly and required car hire or a thorough knowledge of public transport networks in a foreign land. Car ferry operators fought initially on price or availability of routes, but as the 1980s drew to a close, service levels, duty free shopping and on-board entertainment became the focus.

Now the strategies have changed. The big three ferry operators—P&O European Ferries, Sealink-Stena Line and Hoverspeed—are engaged in fierce competition both with each other and with the airlines of Europe. In addition, now there is the Channel Tunnel. Motorists will be able to load themselves and their vehicles on purpose-built rail wagons and be transported under the Channel between France and England for roughly the same price as a cross Channel ferry but with considerable time savings. Eurotunnel first advertised its service—Le Shuttle—through agency BMP DDB Needham in 1992, aiming at the freight market. During 1993, public relations activities brought Le Shuttle to the attention of consumers throughout Europe.

Expecting to be fully operational by 1996, Eurotunnel hopes to attract half of the annual 12 million car ferry passengers onto its tracks beneath the Channel, plus an additional one million passengers who previously were deterred from travelling by sea or air. Car ferry brand leader P&O with 54 per cent of the current market has responded aggressively to the forthcoming attack from the Channel Tunnel. P&O has invested £500 million in new, larger, faster, more comfortable ferries, with a further £5 million for a reservation system for travel agents. In 1993, £3.5 million was spent on advertising, re-

satisfies consumers' needs for a general product type. Notice in Figure 1.5 that the marketing mix is built around the buyer (as is stressed by the marketing concept). Bear in mind, too, that the forces of the marketing environment affect the marketing mix variables in many ways.

Marketing mix variables often are viewed as controllable variables because they can be changed. However, there are limits to how much these variables can be altered. For example, because of economic conditions or government regulations, a manager may not be free to adjust prices daily. Changes in sizes, colours, shapes and designs of most tangible goods are expensive; therefore, such product features cannot be altered very often. In addition, promotional campaigns and the methods used to distribute products ordinarily cannot be changed overnight. People, too, require training and motivating, and cannot be recruited or sacked overnight.

Marketing managers must develop a marketing mix that precisely matches the needs of the people in the target market. Before they can do so, they have to collect in-

inforcing P&O's brand name, routes and reputation. The advertising also stressed the spacious, comfortable ferries with a wide choice of bars and restaurants, duty free shopping and on-board entertainment—the implication being that a car ferry journey may take longer, but is less claustrophobic, more comfortable and less boring than Le Shuttle's expected service.

All the ferry companies are emphasising what were once secondary aspects of their service—the additional amenities and facilities on board the new generation of super ferries:

> On board you'll be eased effortlessly into the holiday spirit as you wander from the pool to a movie or from the bar to the cabaret.

The main operators have changed their advertising agencies in order to gain fresh ideas for the battle with a debt-ridden but highly professional and aggressive Eurotunnel. In addition, several operators are diversifying into other leisure or transport activities, into new markets and with new car ferry routes to Iberia and Scandinavia (not served by the new Channel Tunnel).

The marketing environment has altered dramatically with the impending launch of Le Shuttle. Ferry operators' product offerings have been redefined, branding strengthened and promotional strategy significantly re-thought over the past two years. Strategies and tactics have altered as a new mode of transport and competitor enters the market-place.

SOURCES: Penny Kiernan, "Gale warning for the ferry firms", *Marketing Week*, 16 November 1992, pp. 15–16; Clare Sambrook, "Sealink Stena drops WCRS", *Marketing*, 5 November 1992; "Kevin Morley grabs Sally Line business", *Marketing Week*, 19 February 1993, p. 19; Robert Dwek, "Computing Group joins Le Shuttle", *Marketing*, 17 December 1992, p. 10; P&O advertising, 1993.

depth, up-to-date information about those needs. The information might include data about the age, income, ethnic origin, sex and educational level of people in the target market; their preferences for product features; their attitudes towards competitors' products; and the frequency and intensity with which they use the product. Armed with these kinds of data, marketing managers are better able to develop a product, distribution system, promotion programme and price that satisfy the people in the target market.

This section looks more closely at the decisions and activities related to each marketing mix variable (product, distribution, promotion, price and people). Table 1.1 on page 5 contains a partial list of the decisions and activities associated with each marketing mix variable.

The Product Variable.   As noted earlier, a product can be a good, a service, or an idea. The **product variable** is the aspect of the marketing mix that deals with researching consumers' product wants and designing a product with the desired characteristics. It also involves the creation or alteration of packages and brand names and may include decisions about guarantees and repair services. The actual production of products is not a marketing activity.

Product variable decisions and related activities are important because they directly involve creating products and services that satisfy consumers' needs and wants. To maintain a satisfying set of products that will help an organisation achieve its goals, a marketer must be able to develop new products, modify existing ones, and eliminate those that no longer satisfy buyers or yield acceptable profits. For example, after realising that competitors were capturing large shares of the low calorie market, Heinz introduced new product items under its Weight Watchers name.

The Distribution (Place) Variable.   To satisfy consumers, products must be available at the right time and in a convenient location. In dealing with the **distribution (place) variable,** a marketing manager seeks to make products available in the quantities desired to as many customers as possible and to keep the total inventory, transport and storage costs as low as possible. A marketing manager may become involved in selecting and motivating intermediaries (wholesalers and retailers), establishing and maintaining inventory control procedures, and developing and managing transport and storage systems.

The Promotion Variable.   The **promotion variable** relates to activities used to inform one or more groups of people about an organisation and its products. Promotion can be aimed at increasing public awareness of an organisation and of new or existing products. In addition, promotion can serve to educate consumers about product features or to urge people to take a particular stance on a political or social issue. It may also be used to keep interest strong in an established product that has been available for decades. The advertisement in Figure 1.7 is an example.

The Price Variable.   The **price variable** relates to activities associated with establishing pricing policies and determining product prices. Price is a critical component of the marketing mix because consumers are concerned about the value obtained in an exchange. Price often is used as a competitive tool; in fact, extremely intense price competition sometimes leads to price wars. For example, airlines like United, British Airways and Virgin Atlantic Airways are engaged in ruthless price-cutting in the battle for transatlantic routes. Price can also help to establish a product's image. For instance, if Chanel tried to sell Chanel No. 5 in a two litre bottle for £3, consumers probably would not buy it because the low price would destroy the prestigious image of Chanel's deluxe brand.

Product, distribution, promotion and *price* are the principal elements of the marketing mix. Marketers of services include people as a core element. Writers such as Kotler include people as part of the augmented product element. Whether part of the product element or a separate element of the marketing mix, there is no doubt that people are important. As marketers they manipulate the rest of the marketing mix. As intermediaries in the marketing channel they help make products and services available to the market-place. As consumers or buyers they create the need for the field of marketing.

Developing and maintaining an effective marketing mix is a major requirement for a strong marketing strategy. Thus, as indicated in Figure 1.6, a large portion of this text (Chapters 7 through 18) focuses on the concepts, decisions and activities associated with the components of the marketing mix.

FIGURE 1.7
Promoting an established brand
Wedgwood uses advertising to remind the consumer about the craftsmanship involved in producing its porcelain.

SOURCE: Courtesy of Wedgwood.

Marketing Management

Marketing Management is a process of planning, organising, implementing and controlling marketing activities to facilitate and expedite exchanges effectively and efficiently. Effectiveness and efficiency are important dimensions of this definition. Effectiveness is the degree to which an exchange helps achieve an organisation's objectives. Efficiency is the minimisation of resources an organisation must spend to achieve a specific level of desired exchanges. Thus the overall goal of marketing management is to facilitate highly desirable exchanges and to minimise as much as possible the costs of doing so.

Planning is a systematic process of assessing opportunities and resources, determining marketing objectives, developing a marketing strategy and developing plans for implementation and control. Planning determines when and how marketing activities will be performed and who is to perform them. It forces marketing managers to think ahead, to establish objectives, and to consider future marketing activities. Effective planning also reduces or eliminates daily crises.

Organising marketing activities refers to developing the internal structure of the marketing unit. The structure is the key to directing marketing activities. The marketing unit can be organised by function, product, region, type of customer, or a combination of all four.

Proper implementation of marketing plans hinges on co-ordination of marketing activities, motivation of marketing personnel, and effective communication within the unit. Marketing managers must motivate marketing personnel, co-ordinate their activities, and integrate their activities both with those in other areas of the company and with the marketing efforts of personnel in external organisations, such as advertising agencies and marketing research firms. An organisation's communication system must allow the marketing manager to stay in contact with high level management, with managers of other functional areas within the firm, and with personnel involved in marketing activities both inside and outside the organisation.

The marketing control process consists of establishing performance standards, evaluating actual performance by comparing it with established standards, and reducing the difference between desired and actual performance. An effective control process has four requirements. It should ensure a rate of information flow that allows the marketing manager to quickly detect differences between actual and planned levels of performance. It must accurately monitor different kinds of activities and be flexible enough to accommodate changes. The control process must be economical so that its costs are low relative to the costs that would arise if there were no controls. Finally, the control process should be designed so that both managers and subordinates can understand it. To maintain effective marketing control, an organisation needs to develop a comprehensive control process that evaluates marketing operations at regular intervals. Chapters 20 and 21 examine the planning, organising, implementing and controlling of marketing activities in greater detail.

THE ORGANISATION OF THIS BOOK

Figure 1.5 is a map of the overall organisation of this book. Chapter 2 discusses the marketing environment variables listed in the outer portion of Figure 1.5 The text then moves to the centre of the figure, analysing markets, buyers and marketing research in Chapters 3, 4, 5 and 6. Chapters 7 through 18 explore the marketing mix variables, starting with the product variable and moving clockwise around Figure 1.5. Chapters 19, 20 and 21 discuss strategic marketing, marketing planning, organisation, implementation and control. Chapter 22 explores marketing ethics and social responsibility. Chapters 23, 24 and 25 scrutinise decisions and activities that are unique to business-to-business marketing, international marketing and services marketing. If, as you study, you wonder where the text is leading, look again at Figure 1.5.

SUMMARY

Marketing consists of individual and organisational activities that facilitate and expedite satisfying exchange relationships in a dynamic environment through the creation, distribution, promotion and pricing of goods, services and ideas. An exchange is the provision or transfer of goods, services and ideas in return for something of value. Four conditions must exist for an exchange to occur: (1) two or more individuals, groups or organisations must participate; (2) each party must have something of value desired by the other; (3) each party must be willing to give up what it has in order to receive the value held by the other; and (4) the parties to the exchange must be able to communicate with each other to make their "somethings of value" available. In an exchange, products are traded either for other products or for financial resources, such as cash or credit. Products can be goods, services or ideas.

It is important to study marketing because it permeates society. Marketing activities are performed in both business and non-business organisations. Moreover, marketing activities help business organisations generate profits and income, the life-blood of an economy. The study of marketing enhances consumer awareness. Finally, marketing costs absorb about half of what the consumer spends.

The marketing concept is a management philosophy which prompts a business organisation to try to satisfy customers' needs through a co-ordinated set of activities that also allows the organisation to achieve its goals. Customer satisfaction is the major objective of the marketing concept. The philosophy of the marketing concept emerged during the 1950s, after the production and the sales eras. To make the marketing concept work, top management must accept it as an overall management philosophy. Implementing the marketing concept requires an efficient information system and sometimes the restructuring of the organisation.

Marketing strategy involves selecting and analysing a target market (the group of people whom the organisation wants to reach) and creating and maintaining an appropriate marketing mix (product, distribution, promotion, price and people) to satisfy this market. Marketing strategy requires that managers focus on four tasks to achieve set objectives: (1) marketing opportunity analysis, (2) target market selection, (3) marketing mix development and (4) marketing management.

Marketers should be able to recognise and analyse marketing opportunities, which are circumstances that allow an organisation to take action towards reaching a particular group of customers. Marketing opportunity analysis involves reviewing both internal factors (organisational objectives, financial resources, managerial skills, organisational strengths, organisational weaknesses and cost structures) and external ones (the political, legal, regulatory, societal/green, technological, and economic and competitive forces of the marketing environment).

A target market is a group of persons for whom a firm creates and maintains a marketing mix that specifically fits the needs and preferences of that group. It is important for an organisation's management to designate which customer groups the firm is trying to serve and to have some information about these customers. The identification and analysis of a target market provide a foundation on which a marketing mix can be developed.

The four principal variables that make up the marketing mix are product, price, promotion and distribution. The product variable is the aspect of the marketing mix that deals with researching consumers' wants and designing a product with the desired characteristics. A marketing manager tries to make products available in the quantities desired to as many customers as possible and to keep the total inventory, transport and storage costs as low as possible—the distribution variable. The promotion variable relates to activities used to inform one or more groups of people about an organisation and its products. The price variable refers to establishing pricing policies and determining product prices. People control the marketing mix, facilitate the product's distribution and sale, and—as consumers or buyers—give marketing its rationale. Marketing exists to encourage consumer satisfaction.

Marketing management is a process of planning, organising, implementing and controlling marketing activities to facilitate and expedite exchanges effectively and efficiently. Planning is a systematic process of assessing opportunities and resources, determining marketing objectives, developing a marketing strategy, and developing plans for implementation and control. Organising marketing activities refers to developing the internal structure of the marketing unit. Properly implementing marketing plans depends on co-ordination of marketing activities, motivating marketing personnel, and effectively communicating within the unit. The marketing control process consists of establishing performance standards, evaluating actual performance by comparing it with established standards, and reducing the difference between desired and actual performance.

IMPORTANT TERMS

Marketing
Exchange
Marketing concept
Marketing strategy
Marketing mix
Marketing environment

Target market
Product variable
Distribution (place) variable
Promotion variable
Price variable
Marketing management

DISCUSSION AND REVIEW QUESTIONS

1. What is marketing? How did you define marketing before you read this chapter?
2. Why should someone study marketing?
3. Discuss the basic elements of the marketing concept. Which businesses in your area use this concept? In your opinion, have these businesses adopted the marketing concept? Explain.
4. Identify several business organisations in your area that obviously have not adopted the marketing concept. What characteristics of these organisations indicate non-acceptance of the marketing concept?
5. Describe the major components of a marketing strategy. How are the components related?
6. Identify the tasks involved in developing a marketing strategy.
7. What are the primary issues that marketing managers consider when conducting a market opportunity analysis?
8. What are the variables in the marketing environment? How much control does a marketing manager have over environmental variables?
9. Why is the selection of a target market such an important issue?
10. Why are the elements of the marketing mix known as variables? What are these variables?
11. What type of management activities are involved in the marketing management process?

■ CASES

1.1 Coffee in Europe: No Instant Success in the UK for Holland's Douwe Egberts

Douwe Egberts, one of the major players in Europe's coffee market, is expanding rapidly since the company's takeover in 1978 by US foods and consumer products group Sara Lee. The coffee market in western Europe is worth £8 billion annually, with Nestlé and Philip Morris leading and Douwe Egberts third. By the 1990s, nearly all of Sara Lee's coffee and grocery division profits came from the Dutch-based Douwe Egberts.

One product, roasted coffee, accounts for 53 per cent of Douwe Egberts' sales. Core product areas of coffee, tea and tobacco are now supported with household and personal care products in line with the parent company's portfolio, but still Douwe remains primarily a Dutch trading company with coffee its mainstay.

Active in coffee throughout Europe, Douwe has leadership in Belgium through five brands, including Douwe Egberts and Jacqmotte; in France, where Maison du Café has 15 per cent market share; in Hungary; in Spain, where Marcilla and vacuum-packed decaffeinated products take 21 per cent of the market; the Netherlands, with 73 per cent market share through brands Douwe Egberts, Van Nelle, Supra and Kanis & Gunninck; and in Denmark, with 27 per cent and Merrild as the leading brand. In the UK, only about 10 per cent of sales are of roasted and ground coffee, with 90 per cent for instant coffee brands. The trend is for consumption of more "real" coffee in the UK, to the advantage of leading producers Melitta, Lyons Tetley and Douwe Egberts.

Douwe Egberts entered the eastern European markets initially through Hungary, acquiring the largest Hungarian tea and coffee packer, Compack. "Westernised" Hungarians were selected to run this operation: Douwe recognised the need to keep Compack in the managerial hands of locals who understand not only the customers but also the complex working practices and ways for motivating Compack's workforce. In 1992, Sara Lee acquired Czechoslovakia's leading tea and coffee producer for Douwe, Balirny Praha of Prague. Douwe is currently examining further opportunities in what was once a protected and inaccessible eastern Europe, including production and sales operations in Poland and the former USSR, where there is already an export office. The next region for expansion is expected to be the Pacific Rim, including China.

For many years Douwe Egberts' overriding goal was to prevent the global ambitions of Switzerland's Nestlé and America's Philip Morris from pushing Douwe Egberts out of its strong position in Europe. This led to a whole host of separate brands and little co-ordination between territories. Now there is a central strategy depending on well-defined marketing programmes. Mainstream brands are the focus, controlled from the international marketing office in Utrecht. The cost of launching a new brand, such as the company's Eurobrand "Piazza", increasingly means new product launches must be shown to have appeal across national borders.

Away from the pan-European level, national brands are supported alongside the company's core brands. Managers are allowed a degree of flexibility in addressing the needs of their own target markets and necessary modifications to the marketing mix. Distribution networks are rarely similar country to country, but Douwe has also permitted a level of variation in pricing, branding and promotional work, as well as to the coffee's very taste and packaging. Consumer desires change quite significantly country to country, region to region.

SOURCES: Sara Lee annual report and accounts, 1991 and 1992; Argus Research Corporation; Reuters; Caroline Farquhar; Douwe Egberts, Utrecht.

Questions for Discussion

1. How have changing political issues given Douwe Egberts new market opportunities?
2. Why has Douwe Egberts decided to concentrate on its Eurobrands? Why is the company still supporting its national brands?
3. Why have consumers' tastes in the UK restricted Douwe's presence?

1.2 Hotels: Marketing Mix and Customer Targeting

With a turnover approaching £3 billion, Forte (formerly THF) is one of the world's leading hotel and catering organisations. Three hundred and thirty hotels and 30,000 bedrooms make Forte the UK's market leader from Mount Charlotte Thistle's 14,000 bedrooms and Queens Moat Houses' 11,000. Under family control, Forte for decades focused on the UK tourist industry, expanding during the 1960s and 1970s into business travel through PostHouse and larger city-based hotels. The acquisition of the 4-star Crest chain in the upbeat late 1980s firmly established Forte as a leader in business accommodation, conferences and exhibitions. The THF logo appeared at an ever-increasing rate across the world, with business and deluxe hotels in most major international locations. Market changes have seen the ubiquitous THF brand replaced. Now there is a more sophisticated edge to Forte's marketing, with brands such as Forte Travelodge, Forte Posthouse, Forte Crest, Forte Heritage and Forte Grand aimed at different sets of customers; each brand has its own marketing mix.

The 1990s, though, have brought their own problems for Forte and its rivals. The economic downturn has reduced both tourism and business travel or conferences. The competitors are more aggressive, from companies as diverse as France's Accor, the UK's Copthorne chain or American Marriott. The Gulf War and central European conflicts have hit tourism and business travel, too. Price discounting is rife in an industry where bed occupancy is on the decline. Empty rooms mean under-utilised facilities, no cash flow and no profits. For business travellers, room rates of £110 per night can be negotiated down to £45. Leisure weekend breakers can find themselves in the same rooms for as little as £40 for two nights, including breakfast!

Forte and its rivals are becoming more sophisticated in their marketing: clearer targeting of certain customer groups supported with well defined marketing programmes and sales forces. The leading operators have realised for some time that there are distinct groups of customers, including

- international business travellers
- international tourists
- domestic business users
- domestic leisure breakers
- banqueting and functions

Each customer group requires a unique marketing mix: from airport, city-centre, business park or holiday resort locations, to differing price points, hotel facilities, selling and promotion. In the right location with a wide mix of amenities, one hotel can, with *several* selling and promotional strategies, appeal to more than one of these customer groups. For other hotels, size restrictions and siting force more specific targeting.

Holiday Inn, now owned by brewer Bass, has responded to the market's changing requirements. All 5,000 hotels worldwide had a uniform product concept and branding. Now there are four brands:

- Holiday Inn. "A consistently high standard of product and service, offering good value for money across the globe." Guests—whether on business or travelling for pleasure—have large, well appointed rooms, room service, a choice of business facilities and meeting rooms, with most hotels having leisure facilities, a swimming pool, and free parking.
- Holiday Inn Crown Plaza. These are superior Holiday Inn hotels located mainly in city centres with "superb amenities and facilities".
- Holiday Inn Garden Court. Smaller 3 star hotels on the edge of cities in Europe. Holiday Inn standard bedrooms, but with bistro, fitness room, and generally few frills: "designed for today's busy traveller".
- Holiday Inn Express. "For people desiring a comfortable room but with no real need for restaurant, business or leisure facilities".

Whether Forte or Holiday Inn, the variety of customer groups and requirements had led to an increased level of marketing activity with new brands and several supporting marketing mixes. Competitor activity is fierce in a market severely affected by the external marketing environment, be it Gulf War, IRA terrorism, or economic recession.

SOURCES: "THF to rename?", *Caterer and Hotel Keeper*, 10–16 January 1991, p. 12; MEAL; English Tourist Board; Forte and Holiday Inn promotional literature; Clare Sambrook, "Marriott: a name to contend with", *Marketing*, 3 September 1992, pp. 16–18.

Questions for Discussion

1. Why is a single Holiday Inn brand and product no longer adequate to serve the whole travel market?
2. Why are leading hotel groups aiming different marketing programmes (mixes) at separate customer groups?
3. Which aspects of the marketing environment impact on the hotel and catering industry? Explain how and why.

2 THE MARKETING ENVIRONMENT

Objectives

To understand the concept of the marketing environment and the importance of environmental scanning and analysis

To identify the types of political forces in the marketing environment

To understand how laws and their interpretation influence marketing practices

To determine how government regulations and self-regulatory agencies affect marketing activities

To identify societal issues that marketers must deal with as they make decisions

To explore the effects of new technology on society and on marketing activities

To understand how economic and competitive factors affect organisations' ability to compete and customers' willingness and ability to buy products

Stabburet, a dominant force in Norway's food industry, produces meats, tinned goods, jams, pizzas and frozen foods. Stabburet's meats division distributes direct to buying groups and hundreds of retailers throughout the country. The wholesale arm distributes the company's other food lines to retailers and caterers through an extensive network of wholesalers.

Stabburet, part of the Orkla Borregaard conglomerate, owes its leading position partly to the unique nature of Norway's economy. The traditional trading hinterland has been Finland, Sweden, Denmark and Germany. To date, a semi-protectionist economy has defended Norwegian companies from leading international competitors. A string of centre line political coalitions has led to reasonably consistent economic policy, with high levels of government intervention and regulation. Norway's policy and supporting subsidies aimed at self-sufficiency in food production have been in Stabburet's favour.

Norway has watched the EC expand. Sweden's decision to join the majority of western European states has put increasing pressure on Norway to follow suit. Within government and the population there is mixed opinion, but membership would have significant implications for companies such as Stabburet. Protectionism would disappear, and the international food groups such as Unilever or General Foods would find Norway a more attractive market to enter with fewer restrictive practices. Stabburet would need to respond to these potential threats, and to the opportunities posed by easier access to EC member states' markets. Political decisions will significantly alter Stabburet's trading position, creating challenges to be addressed through the company's marketing. ∎

SOURCES: "Okt konkurransekraft det beste importvernet", *Norges Kjobmannsblad*, 73(6), 1991, pp. 16–17; *Norges Markedsdata;* Leslie Tunbridge; Stabburet reports; "Norkla", *Morges Kjobmannsblad,* 73(12), 1991, pp. 24–5; Orkla Borregaard annual reports.

As illustrated by Stabburet's experiences in Norway, various forces can have a tremendous impact on the decisions and activities of marketers. This chapter explores the political, legal, regulatory, societal, technological, economic and competitive forces that make up the marketing environment. The first section defines the marketing environment and considers why it is critical to scan and analyse it and explores the major elements of the marketing environment. The chapter then goes on to discuss the political forces that generate government actions affecting marketing activities, the effects of laws and regulatory agencies on these activities, the desires and expectations of society and the major dimensions of the technological forces in the environment. The final section considers the effects of general economic conditions—prosperity, recession, depression and recovery—and also examines several types of economic forces that influence companies' ability to compete and consumers' willingness and ability to buy.

EXAMINING AND RESPONDING TO THE MARKETING ENVIRONMENT

The **marketing environment** consists of external forces that directly or indirectly influence an organisation's acquisition of inputs and generation of outputs. Inputs might include personnel, financial resources, raw materials and information. Outputs could be information (such as advertisements), packages, goods, services or ideas. As indicated in Chapter 1 and as shown in Figure 1.5, the marketing environment consists of six categories of forces: political, legal, regulatory, societal/green, technological, economic and competitive. Although there are numerous environmental factors, most fall into one of these six categories.

Whether they fluctuate rapidly or slowly, environmental forces are always dynamic. Changes in the marketing environment create uncertainty, threats and opportunities for marketers. Although the future is not very predictable, marketers can estimate what will happen. It can be stated with certainty that marketers will continue to modify their marketing strategies in response to the dynamic environment. Marketing managers who fail to recognise changes in environmental forces leave their firms unprepared to capitalise on marketing opportunities or to cope with threats created by changes in the environment. If an organisation cannot deal with an unfavourable environment, it may go under. On Merseyside and Tyneside during the OPEC led recession of the mid-1970s many manufacturers cut back on their workforces, causing unemployment rates of over 40 per cent in many suburbs. Many local retailers and small shopkeepers, restaurants and take-aways, and garages had not anticipated the extent of the unemployment or its effect on their businesses. Dozens of small, local businesses closed down. The 1990 Gulf crisis caused huge rises in the price of petrol. The car buying public became even more concerned about fuel consumption, with a resultant decline in the sales of high horsepower sports cars and executive saloons. The Gulf crisis also hit business travel and tourism, affecting the fortunes of many airlines and hotel operators. Civil war in what was once Yugoslavia has had tragic implications for the peoples of that region and an economic impact on the tour operators who specialised in holidays to the Yugoslavian coastline. Thus monitoring the environment is crucial to an organisation's survival and to the long term achievement of its goals.

Environmental Scanning and Analysis

To monitor changes in the marketing environment effectively, marketers must engage in environmental scanning and analysis. **Environmental scanning** is the process of collecting information about the forces in the marketing environment. Scanning involves observation; perusal of secondary sources, such as business, trade, government and general interest publications; and marketing research. However, managers must be careful not to gather so much information that sheer volume makes analysis impossible.

Environmental analysis is the process of assessing and interpreting the information gathered through environmental scanning. A manager evaluates the information for accuracy, tries to resolve inconsistencies in the data, and, if warranted, assigns significance to the findings. Through analysis, a marketing manager seeks to describe current environmental changes and to predict future changes. By evaluating these changes, the manager should be able to determine possible threats and opportunities linked to environmental fluctuations. Understanding the current state of the marketing environment and recognising the threats and opportunities arising from changes within it, help marketing managers assess the performance of current marketing efforts and develop marketing strategies for the future.

JCB, the construction equipment producer, allocates individual managers the task of monitoring aspects of the marketing environment: political, legal, regulatory, societal—particularly the green movement—technological, and economical and competitive. A small committee meets to prepare short papers and presentations to interested colleagues. When the laws relating to roadworks altered, making contractors responsible for the safety of their sites and the long term quality of the inlaid road surface, JCB recognised that many of its customers would have to alter their working practices as a result. So the company produced guides to assist these contractors in responding to the new legislation. In so doing, JCB was able to enhance its image and at the same time promote its products.

Responding to Environmental Forces

In responding to environmental forces, marketing managers can take two general approaches: to accept environmental forces as uncontrollable or to confront and mould them. If environmental forces are viewed as uncontrollable, the organisation remains passive and reactive towards the environment. Instead of trying to influence forces in the environment, its marketing managers tend to adjust current marketing strategies to environmental changes. They approach market opportunities discovered through environmental scanning and analysis with caution. On the other hand, marketing managers who believe that environmental forces can be shaped adopt a proactive approach. For example, if a market is blocked by traditional environmental constraints, marketing managers may apply economic, psychological, political and promotional skills to gain access to it or operate within it. Once they identify what blocks a market opportunity, marketers can assess the power of the various parties involved and develop strategies to try to overcome environmental forces.[1]

In trying to influence environmental forces, marketing management may seek to create market opportunities or to extract greater benefits relative to costs from existing market opportunities. For instance, a firm losing sales to competitors with lower priced products may strive to develop technology that would make its production processes more efficient; greater efficiency would allow it to lower the prices of its own products.

Political action is another way of affecting environmental forces. UK retailers, for example, are lobbying government to permit full Sunday trading and legal opening of retail outlets. A proactive approach can be constructive and bring desired results. However, managers must recognise that there are limits on how much an environmental force can be shaped and that these limits vary across environmental forces. Although an organisation may be able to influence the enactment of laws through lobbying, it is unlikely that a single organisation can significantly increase the national birthrate or move the economy from recession to prosperity.

Generalisations are not possible. It cannot be stated that either of these approaches to environmental response is better than the other. For some organisations, the passive, reactive approach is more appropriate, but for other firms, the aggressive approach leads to better performance. The selection of a particular approach depends on an organisation's managerial philosophies, objectives, financial resources, customers and human skills, and on the composition of the set of environmental forces within which the organisation operates.

The rest of this chapter explores in detail each of the six environmental forces—political, legal, regulatory, societal/green, technological, and economic and competitive.

POLITICAL FORCES

The political, legal and regulatory forces of the marketing environment are closely interrelated. Legislation is enacted, legal decisions are interpreted by the courts, and regulatory agencies are created and operated, for the most part, by persons elected or appointed to political offices or by civil servants. Legislation and regulations (or the lack of them) reflect the current political outlook. Consequently, the political force of the marketing environment has the potential to influence marketing decisions and strategies.

Marketing organisations need to maintain good relations with elected political officials for several reasons. When political officials are well disposed towards particular firms or industries, they are less likely to create or enforce laws and regulations unfavourable to these companies. For example, political officials who believe that oil companies are making honest efforts to control pollution are unlikely to create and enforce highly restrictive pollution control laws. In addition, governments are big buyers, and political officials can influence how much a government agency purchases and from whom. Finally, political officials can play key roles in helping organisations secure foreign markets.

Many marketers view political forces as beyond their control; they simply try to adjust to conditions that arise from those forces. Some firms, however, seek to influence political events by helping to elect to political office individuals who regard them positively. Much of this help is in the form of contributions to political parties. A sizeable contribution to a campaign fund may carry with it an implicit understanding that the party, if elected, will perform political favours for the contributing firm. There are, though, strict laws governing donations and lobbying in most countries.

LEGAL FORCES

A number of laws influence marketing decisions and activities. This discussion focuses on procompetitive and consumer protection laws and their interpretation.

Procompetitive Legislation

Procompetitive legislation is enacted to preserve competition and to end various practices deemed unacceptable by society. Some of the most important of these are discussed next in greater detail.

Monopolies and Mergers.   In the UK the Secretary of State for Trade and Industry and the Director General of the **Office of Fair Trading** can refer monopolies for investigation by the **Monopolies and Mergers Commission,** an independent body whose members are drawn from a variety of backgrounds, including lawyers, economists, industrialists and trade unionists. The legislation defines a monopoly as a situation where at least a quarter of a particular kind of good or service is supplied by a single person or a group of connected companies, or by two or more people acting in a way which prevents, restricts or distorts competition. Local monopolies can also be referred to the commission.

If the commission finds that a monopoly operates against the public interest, the Secretary of State for Trade and Industry has power to take action to remedy or prevent the harm which the commission considers may exist. Alternatively, the Director General may be asked to negotiate undertakings to remedy the adverse effects identified by the commission. The government believes that the market is a better judge than itself of the advantages and disadvantages of mergers, so most takeovers and proposed mergers are allowed to be decided by the companies' shareholders. However, when too much power would be placed in the hands of one organisation, company or person, the government will insist on a Monopolies and Mergers Commission appraisal. If the commission believes it is against the public interest for a takeover or merger to proceed, then it will prohibit any agreement between the companies or organisations involved.

The EC has a minister responsible for competition. In recent years, he has ruled on anti-competitive practices in many industries, from airlines to financial services, forcing companies to alter their trading practices and encouraging competition from a broader base of organisations.

Financial Services Act 1986.   The Director General of the Office of Fair Trading is required to consider the implications for competition of rules, regulations, guidance and other arrangements and practices of the regulatory bodies, investment exchanges and clearing houses. The Director General must report to the Secretary of State for Trade and Industry whenever a significant or potentially significant effect on competition has been identified. This legislation is for the protection of investors, and the Secretary of State may refuse or revoke recognition of the organisation or require it to make alterations to its activities.

Anti-competitive Practices.   The Director General of the Office of Fair Trading can investigate any business practice, whether in the public or private sector, which may restrict, distort or prevent competition in the production, supply or acquisition of goods or services in Britain. The Secretary of State has power to take remedial action.

Restrictive Trade Practices Act 1976.   If two or more people who are party to the supply of goods or services in Britain accept some limitation on their freedom to make their own decisions about matters such as prices or conditions of sale, the Office of Fair Trading must be notified and such an agreement must be registered. Once an agreement has been registered, the Director General is under a general duty to refer it to the Restrictive Practices Court, and the court must declare the restrictions in it contrary to the public interest unless the parties can satisfy the court that the public interest is not an issue. The vast majority of agreements never reach the court because parties elect to give up the restrictions rather than go through such a procedure.

European Community.   The objective of the European Community's competition policy is to ensure that there is free and fair competition in trade between member states and that the government trade barriers which the **Treaty of Rome** seeks to dismantle are not replaced by private barriers which fragment the Common Market. The EC has powers to investigate and terminate alleged infringements and in The Treaty of Rome prohibits agreements or concertive practices which trade between member states and aims to prevent restriction or distortion of competition within the Common Market.[2]

Most countries have similar legislation. For example, in America the Sherman Antitrust Act prevents monopolistic situations; the Clayton Act specifically prohibits price discrimination; and the Federal Trade Commission Act broadly prohibits unfair methods of competition and empowers the Federal Trade Commission to work with the Department of Justice to enforce the provisions of the Clayton Act. The Wheeler-Lea Act essentially makes unfair and deceptive acts or practices unlawful, regardless of whether they incur competition. The Robinson-Patman Act deals with discriminatory price differentials.[3]

Consumer Protection Legislation

The second category of regulatory laws, *consumer protection legislation,* is not a recent development. However, consumer protection laws mushroomed in the mid-1960s and early 1970s. A number of them deal with consumer safety, while others relate to the sale of various hazardous products such as flammable fabrics and toys that might injure children. In the UK, the Fair Trading Act (1973) provides a machinery—headed by the Director General of the Office of Fair Trading—for continuous review of consumer affairs, for actions dealing with trading practices which unfairly affect consumers' interests, for action against persistent offenders under existing law, and for the negotiation of self-regulatory codes of practice to raise trading standards.

Consumers' interests with regard to the purity of food, the description and performance of goods and services, and pricing information are safeguarded by the Food Act (1984), the Medicines Act (1968), the Misrepresentations Act (1967), the Trade Descriptions Act (1968), the Prices Act (1974), the Unfair Contract Terms Act (1977), the Sale of Goods Act (1979), the Supply of Goods and Services Act (1982), and the Consumer Protection Act (1987). The marking and accuracy of quantities are regulated by the Weights and Measures Act (1985). The Consumer Credit Act of 1974 provides comprehensive protection for consumers who enter into credit or hire transactions. The Consumer Protection Act of 1987 implements a harmonised European Community code of civil law covering product liability, creates a general criminal offence of supplying unsafe consumer goods, makes it an offence to give any misleading price indication and consolidates the powers provided under safety related acts. The Financial Services Act (1986) offers greater protection to investors by establishing a new regulatory framework for the industry.

In addition, consumer advice and information are provided to the general public at the local level by the Citizens' Advice Bureaux and the Trading Standards or Consumer Protection departments of local authorities, and in some areas by specialist Consumer Advice Centres. The independent, non-statutory National Consumer Council, which receives government finance, ensures that consumers' views are made known to those in government and industry. Nationalised industries have consumer councils whose members investigate questions of concern to the consumer, and many trade associations in industry and commerce have established codes or practice. In addition, several private organisations work to further consumer interests, the largest of which is the **Consumers' Association,** funded by the subscriptions of its membership of over one million people. The association conducts an extensive programme of comparative testing of goods and investigation of services; its views and test reports are published in its monthly magazines and other publications.

Interpreting Laws

Laws certainly have the potential to influence marketing activities, but the actual effects of the laws are determined by how marketers and the courts interpret them. Laws seem to be quite specific because they contain many complex clauses and subclauses. In reality, however, many laws and regulations are stated in vague terms that force marketers to rely on legal advice rather than their own understanding and common sense. Because of this vagueness, some organisations attempt to gauge the limits of certain laws by operating in a legally questionable way to see how far they can go with certain practices before being prosecuted. Other marketers, however, interpret regulations and statutes very conservatively and strictly to avoid violating a vague law. Case 2.1 illustrates the impact of laws and their frequent ambiguity.

Although court rulings directly affect businesses accused of specific violations, they also have a broader, less direct impact on other businesses. When marketers try to interpret laws in relation to specific marketing practices, they often analyse recent court decisions, both to understand better what the law is intended to do and to gain a clearer sense of how the courts are likely to interpret it in the future.

REGULATORY FORCES

Interpretation alone does not determine the effectiveness of laws and regulations; the level of enforcement by regulatory agencies is also significant. Some regulatory agencies are created and administered by government units; others are sponsored by non-governmental sources.

UK Government

Ministry of Agriculture, Fisheries and Food. This ministry develops and controls policies for agriculture, horticulture, fisheries and food, and has responsibilities for environmental and rural issues and food policies.

Department of Employment. This department controls the Employment Service, employment policy and legislation; training policy and legislation; health and safety at work; industrial relations; wages councils; equal opportunities; small firms and tourism; statistics on labour and industrial matters for the UK; the Careers Service; and international representation on employment matters.

Department of the Environment. The DoE controls policies for planning and regional development, local government, new towns, housing, construction, inner city matters, environmental protection, water, the countryside, sports and recreation, conservation, historic buildings and ancient monuments.

Export Credit Guarantee Department. This department is responsible for the provision of insurance for exporters against the risk of not being paid for goods and services, access to bank finance for exports, and insurance cover for new investment overseas.

Central Statistical Office. The office prepares and interprets statistics needed for central economic and social policies and management; it co-ordinates the statistical work of other departments.

Department for Trade and Industry. The DTI controls industrial and commercial policy, promotion of enterprise and competition in the UK and abroad, investor and consumer protection. Specific responsibilities include industrial innovatio̶n̶ ̶r̶e̶-
gional industrial policy; business development, management develop̶

ness/education links; international trade policy; commercial relations and export promotions; competition policy; company law; insolvency; consumer protection and safety; radio regulations; and intellectual property.

Department of Transport.   This department is responsible for land, sea and air transport; sponsorship of the nationalised transport authorities and British Rail; domestic and international civil aviation; international transport agreements; shipping and ports industries; navigation issues, HM Coastguard and marine pollution; motorways and trunk roads; road safety; and overseeing local authority transport.

These examples of British government departments are not unusual. Similar administrative bodies exist in most countries. Increasingly in the EC, political, legal and regulatory forces are being harmonised to reflect common standards and enforcement.

Local Authorities

The functions of the UK local authorities are far-reaching; some are primary duties, whereas others are purely discretionary. Broadly speaking, functions are divided between county and district councils on the basis that the county council is responsible for matters requiring planning and administration over wide areas or requiring the support of substantial resources, and district councils on the whole administer functions of a more local significance. English county councils are generally responsible for strategic planning, transport planning, highways, traffic regulations, local education, consumer protection, refuse disposal, police, the fire service, libraries and the personal social services. District councils are responsible for environmental health, housing decisions, most planning applications and refuse collection. They may also provide some museums, art galleries, and parks. At both county and district council level, arrangements depend on local agreements.

Most countries in Europe have a similar structure: resource hungry issues with wide ranging social and political consequences are controlled centrally. Planning and service provision within the community are viewed as being better controlled at the local level by the communities which themselves will experience the advantages or problems resulting from such decision-making. The European Community aims to establish commonly accepted parameters for planning, service provision and regulation, and a framework to assist in inter- and intra-country disputes.

Non-governmental Regulatory Forces

In the absence of governmental regulatory forces and in an attempt to prevent government intervention, some businesses try to regulate themselves. For example, many newspapers have voluntarily banned advertisements for telephone chat services which were being used for undesirable activities, not technically illegal. Trade associations in a number of industries have developed self-regulatory programmes. Even though these programmes are not a direct outgrowth of laws, many were established to stop or stall the development of laws and governmental regulatory groups that would regulate the associations' marketing practices. Sometimes trade associations establish codes of ethics by which their members must abide or risk censure by other members, or even exclusion from the programme. For example, many cigarette manufacturers have agreed, through a code of ethics, not to advertise their products to children and teenagers. The ITC Code of Advertising Standards and Practice aims to keep broadcast advertising "legal, decent, honest and truthful".[4]

Self-regulatory programmes have several advantages over governmental laws and regulatory agencies. They are usually less expensive to establish and implement, and their guidelines are generally more realistic and operational. In addition, effective industry self-regulatory programmes reduce the need to expand government bureaucracy. However, these programmes also have several limitations. When a trade association creates a set of industry guidelines for its members, non-member firms do not have to abide by them. In addition, many self-regulatory programmes lack the tools or the authority to enforce guidelines. Finally, guidelines in self-regulatory programmes are often less strict than those established by government agencies.

Deregulation

Governments can drastically alter the environment for companies. In the UK the privatisation of the public utilities created new terms and conditions for their suppliers and subcontractors. The state's sales of Jaguar and Rover in the car industry and of British Airways created commercially lean companies which suddenly had new impetus to be major competitors in their industries. Deregulation in the European Community has created opportunities across borders and also new threats. Car manufacturers were previously able to restrict certain models to specific countries. They placed rigorous controls on their dealers (forbidding them to retail cars produced by rival manufacturers in the same showroom or on the same site), many of which have been swept aside. Marketing Insight 2.1 highlights some of the changes instigated by EC deregulation in 1993.

SOCIETAL/GREEN FORCES

Societal/green forces comprise the structure and dynamics of individuals and groups and the issues that engage them. Society becomes concerned about marketers' activities when those activities have questionable or negative consequences. For example, in recent times well publicised incidents of unethical behaviour by marketers and others have perturbed and even angered consumers. Chapter 22 takes a detailed look at marketing ethics and social responsibility. When marketers do a good job of satisfying society, praise or positive evaluation rarely follows. Society expects marketers to provide a high standard of living and to protect the general quality of life. This section examines some of society's expectations, the vehicles used to express those expectations, and the problems and opportunities that marketers experience as they try to deal with society's often contradictory wishes.

Living Standards and Quality of Life

In society, most people want more than just the bare necessities; they want to achieve the highest standard of living possible. For example, there is a desire for homes which offer not only protection from the elements but also comfort and a satisfactory lifestyle. People want food that is safe and readily available, in many varieties and in easily prepared forms. Clothing protects our bodies, but many consumers want a variety of clothing for adornment and to project an "image" to others. Consumers want vehicles that provide rapid, safe and efficient travel. They want communication systems that give information from around the globe—a desire apparent in the popularity of products such as facsimile machines and the 24 hour news coverage provided by the cable and satellite television networks. In addition, there is demand for sophisticated medical services that prolong life expectancy and improve physical appearance. Education is expected to help consumers acquire and enjoy a higher standard of living.

Society's high material standard of living often is not enough. Many desire a high degree of quality in their lives. People do not want to spend all their waking hours working: they seek leisure time for hobbies, voluntary work, recreation and relaxation. The quality of life is enhanced by leisure time, clean air and water, an unlittered beach, conservation of wildlife and natural resources, and security from radiation and substances. A number of companies are expressing concerns about the

MARKETING INSIGHT 2.1

REGULATORY CHANGES IMPACT ON BUSINESS

The first of January 1993 heralded significant changes throughout Europe. As news broadcasts and press headlines explained, "the Single Euro-Market is here!" For over a decade bureaucrats in the EC had been steering member countries towards an agreement which would make trade and commerce within the European Community simpler to conduct and more uniform. The UK Government's Department for Trade and Industry highlighted some of the changes in its press releases.

- *Duty.* No more quotas for duty paid goods brought back from holidays and business trips within the EC.
- *Professional permits.* Professionally qualified workers such as nurses or teachers can work in other EC countries without lengthy retraining.
- *Exports.* Businesses will be able to tender for government contracts in other member states. Less "red tape" for companies importing or exporting in the EC.
- *Inward investment.* The enlarged single market is expected to be more attractive for investment by North American and Pacific Rim countries, particularly American and Japanese corporations.
- *Competition and choice.* Opportunities and threats as companies offer products and services across national borders, competing with domestic suppliers.
- *Working practices.* Increasing pressure for member states to agree on working conditions, pay, hours and legislation.
- *Safety.* Europe wide safety standards for products produced in and imported to the EC.
- *Airline deregulation.* The end of preferential treatment for national flag carriers, with greater competition and more flexible pricing.
- *Transport.* Uniform safety levels. Less bureaucratic entry into EC states for HGVs. Two way haulage loads. Fewer restrictive working practices.
- *VAT collection.* More uniform sales and purchase taxes. Simpler collection systems for companies trading across national borders.
- *Harmonisation.* Common operating and trading standards. Products such as mobile phones to work across Europe.
- *Immigration.* Fast tracking through customs for EC nationals. More opportunities to live and work in other EC countries.

Easier access between EC member countries and the removal of duty paid goods allowances had an immediate effect, but for working practices and product harmonisation it will be several years before changes are really noticeable. In certain industries, such as airlines or car retailing, implementation of the new regulations may not occur fully until the end of the century. For consumers, companies and governments, practices from the 1980s are suddenly no longer relevant owing to these EC regulatory changes.

SOURCES: DTI press office, 1993; "Our single Euro-market is here", *Le Magazine*, January–February 1993, pp. A8–A9.

FIGURE 2.1 *Environmentally concerned consumers*
The charities have not been slow to latch onto the "greening consumer". Here, the Royal Society for the Protection of Birds is hoping to persuade businesses to enter in joint promotions.

SOURCE: Advertisement produced by International Marketing and Promotions (London) for the RSPB.

As illustrated in Figure 2.1, the charities have not been slow to latch onto the "greening concerns" and social concerns.

Because of these desires, consumers have become increasingly concerned about environmental issues such as pollution, waste disposal and the so called greenhouse effect. Society's concerns have created both threats and opportunities for marketers. For example, one of society's biggest environmental problems is lack of space for refuse disposal, especially of plastic materials such as disposable nappies and Styrofoam packaging, which are not biodegradable. In the United States, several cities have passed laws banning the use of all plastic packaging in stores and restaurants, and governments around the world are considering similar legislation. This trend has created problems for McDonald's and other fast food restaurants, which have now developed packaging alternatives. Other firms, however, see such environmental problems as opportunities. Procter & Gamble, for example, markets cleaners in bottles made of recycled plastic.[5] Environmentally responsible, or green, marketing is increasingly extensive. For example, the German companies Audi, Volkswagen and BMW are manufacturing "cleaner" cars, which do not pollute the atmosphere as much as traditional ones. Italian chemical companies are investing billions to reduce toxic wastes from their plants, and British industry is investing equally large sums emissions from power stations and to treat sewage more effectively.[6]

The **green movement** is concerned about these environmental issues.

ago few consumers were concerned about the well being of their natural environment—their planet. Resources were not seen as scarce, pollution was poorly acknowledged, and people had a short term—perhaps selfish—perspective. Now there is a growing awareness which is affecting everyone: consumers, manufacturers and legislators.

Supermarket shelves are rapidly filling with packaging which can be recycled or reused and products for which manufacturing processes have altered. Children are now taught in the classroom to "re-educate" their parents to take a more responsible view of the earth's environment. The changes are not just in the supermarkets and schools, as highlighted by BMW in Marketing Insight 2.2. The rising importance and role of the green aspect of the societal forces must not be underestimated.

As these examples illustrate, changes in the forces of the marketing environment require careful monitoring and often demand a clear and effective response. Since marketing activities are a vital part of the total business structure, marketers have a responsibility to help provide what members of society want and to minimise what they do not want.

Consumer Movement Forces

The **consumer movement** is a diverse collection of independent individuals, groups and organisations who seek to protect the rights of consumers. The main issues pursued by the consumer movement fall into three categories: environmental protection, product performance and safety, and information disclosure. The movement's major forces are individual consumer advocates, consumer organisations and other interest groups, consumer education, and consumer laws.

Consumer advocates, such as David Tench, take it upon themselves to protect the rights of consumers. They band together into consumer organisations, either voluntarily or under government sponsorship. Some organisations, such as the Consumers' Association, operate nationally, whereas others are active at local levels. They inform and organise other consumers, raise issues, help businesses develop consumer orientated programmes, and pressure legislators to enact consumer protection laws. Some consumer advocates and organisations encourage consumers to boycott products and businesses to which they have objections.

Educating consumers to make wiser purchasing decisions is perhaps one of the most far-reaching aspects of the consumer movement. Increasingly, consumer education is becoming a part of school curricula and adult education courses. These courses cover many topics—for instance, what major factors should be considered when buying specific products, such as insurance, housing, cars, appliances and furnitures, clothes, and food. The courses also cover the provision of certain consumer protection laws and provide the sources of information that can help individuals become knowledgeable consumers.

TECHNOLOGICAL FORCES

The word *technology* brings to mind creations of progress such as computers, superconductors, lasers and heart transplants. Even though such items are outgrowths of technology, none of them is technology. **Technology** has been defined as the knowledge of how to accomplish tasks and goals.[7] Often this knowledge comes from scientific research. The effects of technology are broad in scope and today exert a tremendous influence on everyone's lives.

Technology grows out of research performed by businesses, universities and non-profit organisations. Much of this research is paid for by governments, which support investigations in a variety of areas, including health, defence, agriculture, energy and

SOCIAL AWARENESS: RECYCLING THE CONSUMER

The European Recovery and Recycling Association (ERRA) is indicative of the growing concern for the environment and the awareness by the consumer of this social issue. With members including Cadbury Schweppes, Coca-Cola, Heineken, Nestlé, L'Oreal, Petrofina and Tetra Pak, Brussels based ERRA has developed a recycling scheme which could lead to the regular collection of discarded packaging; containers and bottles from housing estates, factories, schools, offices and shops; and their sorting and reuse. The scheme in many countries is far from becoming reality, requiring the significant commitment of government, local authorities and, of course, consumers. However, ERRA exists, supported by an extensive array of manufacturers and environmental pressure groups. The public's interest in the environment, in safeguarding the planet and its resources for generations to come, has led to companies paying real attention to the green lobby.

BMW, the German deluxe car maker, has been stressing the "recyclability" of its vehicles in its television and press advertising for its 3 Series range. BMW's cars are produced using more environmentally friendly production processes, with a greater proportion of components suitable for reworking. BMW's commitment to the future, however, goes further. In Landshut, Germany, it has a recycling factory. Two workers can strip all the reusable parts from a 1970s car in under 45 minutes, including the careful draining of all fluids, at a cost of about £90.

Landshut's role is as a huge scrap merchant, but one that adheres to the strictest code of ethical working practices with the latest understanding of how to dispose of "dead" vehicles with the least harm to the environment. BMW executives support the notion of a European wide initiative, requiring an authorised recycler to issue a disposal certificate for every car at the end of its life. Until such a certificate is issued, the last registered owner would continue to be liable to pay road taxes. This initiative would eventually require legislation and the support of governments. Meanwhile, several leading car manufacturers have joined forces, adopting a standardised colour coding for all reusable parts.

The investment for BMW is significant, but anticipating eventual EC legislation to enforce recycling, the German manufacturer believes it is thinking strategically and is working towards maintaining its position as a major producer of vehicles. BMW has 14 partner recycling plants worldwide, with its first UK site in Sussex. By 1995, the company hopes to have an international network, with more than 15 sites in the UK. Simultaneously, BMW is striving to make more of its cars reclaimable; 40 per cent of the current 3 Series can be stripped down and reused.

SOURCES: "The can and bottle story: environment", Coca-Cola & Schweppes Beverages Ltd, 1993; "Helping to solve the waste management puzzle", ERRA, Brussels, 1991; John Eisenhammer, "Where cars will go when they die", *The Independent on Sunday*, 21 February 1993, pp. 24–5; "Helping the earth begins at home", Central Office of In Department of the Environment, HMSO, 1992; BMW 3 Series promotional mat

CHAPTER 2   The Marketing En

pollution. Because much centrally funded research requires the use of specialised machinery, personnel and facilities, a sizeable proportion of this research is conducted by large business organisations or research institutions that already possess the necessary specialised equipment and people.

The rapid technological growth of the last several decades is expected to continue through the 1990s. Areas that hold great technological promise include digital electronics, artificial intelligence, superconductors, materials research and biotechnology. Current research is investigating new forms of memory chips and computers that are a hundred times faster and smaller than current models. Because these and other technological developments will clearly have an impact on buyers' and marketers' decisions, it is important to discuss here the effects of technology on society and marketers and to consider several factors that influence the adoption and use of technology.

The Impact of Technology

Marketers must be aware of new developments in technology and their possible effects because technology can and does affect marketing activities in many different ways. Consumers' technological knowledge influences their desires for goods and services (see Figure 2.2). To provide marketing mixes that satisfy consumers, marketers must be aware of these influences.

The various ways in which technology affects marketing activities fall into two broad categories. It affects consumers and society in general; and it influences what, how, when and where products are marketed.

Effects of Technology on Society.

Technology determines how consumers as members of society satisfy their physiological needs. In various ways and to varying degrees, eating and drinking habits, sleeping patterns, sexual activities and health care are all influenced by both existing technology and changes in technology. Technological developments have improved standards of living, thus creating more leisure time; they have also enhanced information, entertainment and education.

Nevertheless, technology can detract from the quality of life through undesirable side effects, such as unemployment, polluted air and water, and other health hazards. Some people believe that further applications of technology can soften or eliminate these undesirable side effects. Others argue, however, that the best way to improve the quality of our lives is to decrease the use of technology.

Effects of Technology on Marketing.

Technology also affects the types of products that marketers can offer. The introduction and general acceptance of cassette tapes and compact discs drove manufacturers of vinyl long-playing (LP) albums out of business or forced them to invest in new technology. Yet this technology provided new marketing opportunities for recording artists and producers, record companies, retailers and those in related industries. The following items are only a few of the many thousands of existing products that were not available to consumers 20 years ago: disposable 35mm cameras, cellular telephones, ultralight laptop computers, high resolution televisions and hand held video cameras.

Computer technology helps make warehouse storage and keeping track of stored products more efficient and, therefore, less expensive. Often these savings can be passed on to consumers in the form of lower prices. Because of technological changes in communications, marketers now can reach large masses of people through a variety of media more efficiently. The development and widespread use of facsimile machines and services, for example, allows marketers to send their advertisements or sales specifications directly to selected groups of customers who want their products.

Technological advances in transport enable consumers to travel further and more

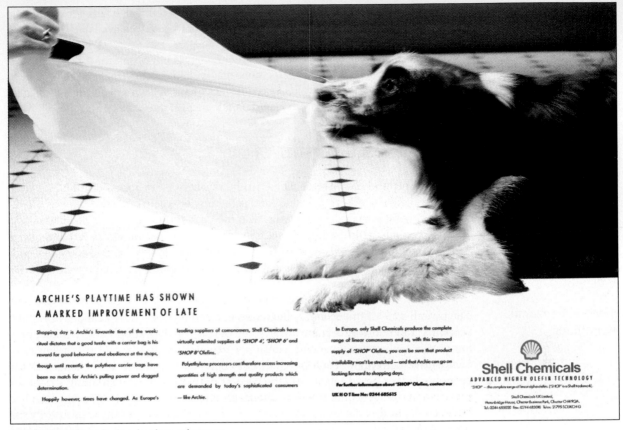

FIGURE 2.2 *Chemical technology advances*
Shell Chemicals offers consumers improved, high strength polythene carrier bags.

SOURCE: Courtesy of Shell Chemicals.

often to shop at a larger number of stores. Changes in transport also have affected producers' ability to get products to retailers and wholesalers. The ability of present day manufacturers of relatively lightweight products to reach any of their dealers within 24 hours (via overnight express delivery services, such as TNT and Federal Express) would astound their counterparts of 50 years ago.

Adoption and Use of Technology

Through a procedure known as **technology assessment,** some managers try to foresee the effects of new products and processes on their firm's operation, on other business organisations and on society in general. With the information gained through a technology assessment, management tries to estimate whether the benefits of using a specific kind of technology outweigh the costs to the firm and to society at large. The degree to which a business is technologically based will also influence how its management responds to technology. Firms whose products and product changes grow out of recent technology strive to gather and use technological information.

Although available technology could radically improve their products (or other parts of the marketing mix), some companies may put off applying this technology as long as their competitors do not try to use it. The extent to which a firm can protect inventions stemming from research also influences its use of technology. How secure a product is from imitation depends on how easily it can be copied by others without violating its patent. If new products and processes cannot be protected through patents, a company is less likely to market them and make the benefits of its research available to competitors.

How a company uses (or does not use) technology is important for its long run survival. A firm that makes the wrong decisions may well lose out to the competition. Poor decisions may also affect its profits by requiring expensive corrective actions. Poor decisions about technological forces may even drive a firm out of business.

ECONOMIC AND COMPETITIVE FORCES

The economic and competitive forces in the marketing environment influence both marketers' and customers' decisions and activities. This section first examines the effects of general economic conditions, also focusing on buying power, willingness to spend, spending patterns and competition. Then the discussion moves to competitive forces, including types of competitive structures, competitive tools and some methods for monitoring competitive behaviour. The strategic importance of competition is discussed in Chapter 19.

General Economic Conditions

The overall state of the economy fluctuates in all countries. These changes in general economic conditions affect (and are affected by) the forces of supply and demand, buying power, willingness to spend, consumer expenditure levels, and the intensity of competitive behaviour. Therefore, current economic conditions and changes in the economy have a broad impact on the success of organisations' marketing strategies. Fluctuations in the economy follow a general pattern often referred to as the business cycle. In the traditional view, the business cycle consists of four stages: prosperity, recession, depression and recovery.

During **prosperity,** unemployment is low and total income is relatively high. Assuming a low inflation rate, this combination causes buying power to be high. To the extent that the economic outlook remains prosperous, consumers generally are willing to buy. In the prosperity stage, marketers often expand their marketing mixes (product, distribution, promotion, price and people) to take advantage of the increased buying power. They sometimes capture a larger market share by intensifying distribution and promotion efforts.

Because unemployment rises during a **recession,** total buying power declines. The pessimism that accompanies a recession often stifles both consumer and business spending. As buying power decreases, many consumers become more price and value-conscious; they look for products that are basic and functional. For instance, people ordinarily reduce their consumption of more expensive convenience foods and strive to save money by growing and preparing more of their own food. Individuals buy fewer durable goods and more repair and do-it-yourself products. During a recession, some firms make the mistake of drastically reducing their marketing efforts and thus damage their ability to survive. Obviously, marketers should consider some revision of their marketing activities during a recessionary period. Because consumers are more concerned about the functional value of products, a company must focus its marketing research on determining precisely what product functions buyers want and then make sure that these functions become part of its products. Promotional efforts should emphasise value and utility.

A **depression** is a period in which unemployment is extremely high, wages are very low, total disposable income is at a minimum, and consumers lack confidence in the economy. Governments have used both monetary and fiscal policies to offset the effects of recession and depression. Monetary policies are employed to control the money supply, which in turn affects spending, saving and investment by both individuals and businesses. Through the establishment of fiscal policies, the government is able to influence the amount of savings and expenditures by adjusting the tax structure and by changing the levels of government spending. Some economic experts believe that the effective use of monetary and fiscal policies can completely eliminate depressions from the business cycle.

Recovery is the stage of the business cycle in which the economy moves from depression or recession to prosperity. During this period, the high unemployment rate begins to decline, total disposable income increases, and the economic gloom that lessened consumers' willingness to buy subsides. Both the ability and the willingness to buy rise. Marketers face some problems during recovery—for example, the difficulty of ascertaining how quickly prosperity will return and of forecasting the level of prosperity that will be attained. In this stage, marketers should maintain as much flexibility in their marketing strategies as possible to be able to make the needed adjustments as the economy moves from recession to prosperity.

Consumer Demand and Spending Behaviour

Marketers must understand the factors that determine whether, what, where and when people buy. Chapters 3 and 4 look at behavioural factors underlying these choices, but here the focus is on the economic components: buying power, willingness to purchase and spending patterns.

Buying Power.   The strength of a person's **buying power** depends on the size of the resources that enable the individual to purchase and on the state of the economy. The resources that make up buying power are goods, services and financial holdings. Fluctuations of the business cycle affect buying power because they influence price levels and interest rates. For example, during inflationary periods, when prices are rising, buying power decreases because more pounds or ECUs are required to buy products. Table 2.1 compares 1980 and 1990 prices for selected food products. Table 2.2 shows quickly increasing and declining retail prices.

The major financial sources of buying power are income, credit and wealth. From an individual's viewpoint, **income** is the amount of money received through wages, rents, investments, pensions and subsidy payments for a given period, such as a month or a year. Normally, this money is allocated among taxes, spending for goods and services, and savings. The average annual family income in the United States is approximately $25,986; in the United Kingdom it is £15,118.[8] However, because of the differences in people's educational levels, abilities, occupations and wealth, income is not equally distributed in any country.

Marketers are most interested in the amount of money that is left after payment of taxes. After-tax income is called **disposable income** and is used for spending or saving. Because disposable income is a ready source of buying power, the total amount available in a nation is important to marketers. Several factors affect the size of total disposable income. One, of course, is the total amount of income. Total national income is affected by wage levels, rate of unemployment, interest rates and dividend rates. These factors in turn affect the size of disposable income. Because disposable income is the income left after taxes are paid, the number of taxes and their amount directly affect the size of total disposable income. When taxes rise, disposable income declines; when taxes fall, disposable income increases.

Disposable income that is available for spending and saving after an individual has purchased the basic necessities of food, clothing and shelter is called **discretionary income.** People use discretionary income to purchase entertainment, holidays, cars,

TABLE 2.1 *A comparison of 1980 and 1990 prices for selected grocery products*

PRODUCT	AVERAGE[a] PRICE (PENCE)		PRODUCT	AVERAGE[a] PRICE (PENCE)	
	1990	1980		1990	1980
Beef: home-killed			**Butter**		
Rump steak[b]	376	235	Home produced, per 250 g	61	43
Stewing steak	181	113	New Zealand, per 250 g	58	42
Lamb: home-killed			Danish, per 250 g	71	46
Loin (with bone)	274	152	**Lard, per 250 g**	17	15
Shoulder (with bone)	132	98	**Cheese** – Cheddar type	150	94
Leg (with bone)	222	145	**Eggs**		
Lamb: imported (frozen)			Size 2 (65–70 g), per dozen	124	71
Loin (with bone)	192	111	Size 4 (55–60 g), per dozen	106	65
Shoulder (with bone)	92	76	**Milk**		
Leg (with bone)	177	117	Pasteurised, per pint	30	17
Pork: home-killed			**Coffee**		
Leg (foot off)	142	92	Pure, instant, per 100 g	131	102
Loin (with bone)	176	111	**Sugar**		
Bacon			Granulated, per kg	59	35
Streaky[b]	134	82	**Fresh vegetables**		
Gammon[b]	211	126	White potatoes	19	7
Back, not vacuum packed	205	117	Red potatoes	19	8
Ham (not shoulder), per 4 oz	74	163	Potatoes, new loose	30	13
Pork Sausages	101	61	Tomatoes	69	52
Pork luncheon meat, 12 oz can	53	38	Cabbage, greens	35	13
Corned beef, 12 oz can	91	84	Cauliflower, each	60	21
Chicken: roasting, oven ready			Carrots	40	13
Fresh or chilled 3 lb	98	52	Onions	34	16
Fresh and smoked fish			Mushrooms, per 4 oz	32	16
Cod fillets	249	107	**Fresh fruit**		
Haddock fillets	277	116	Apples, dessert	46	24
Bread			Pears, dessert	58	28
White loaf, sliced, 800 g	50	34	Oranges, each	20	22
Brown loaf, sliced, small	43	25	Bananas	53	27

[a] Per lb unless otherwise stated.
[b] Or Scottish equivalent.

SOURCE: *Employment Gazette,* Central Statistical Office, June 1980 and July 1990. Crown Copyright. Reprinted by permission of the Controller of Her Majesty's Stationery Office.

education, pets and pet supplies, furniture, appliances and so on. Changes in total discretionary income affect the sales of these products—especially cars, furniture, large appliances and other costly durable goods.

Credit enables people to spend future income now or in the near future. However, credit increases current buying power at the expense of future buying power. Several factors determine whether consumers use or forgo credit. First, credit must be available to them. Interest rates, too, affect consumers' decisions to use credit, especially

TABLE 2.2 *UK retail prices: Detailed figures for various groups, subgroups and sections for November 1992*

	INDEX (JAN. 1987 =100)	PERCENTAGE CHANGE OVER (MONTHS) 1	PERCENTAGE CHANGE OVER (MONTHS) 12		INDEX (JAN. 1987 =100)	PERCENTAGE CHANGE OVER (MONTHS) 1	PERCENTAGE CHANGE OVER (MONTHS) 12
ALL ITEMS	139.7	−0.1	3.0	**FOOD** (continued)			
Food and catering	132.4	0.0	1.5	Potatoes	118.7		−5
Alcohol and tobacco	149.5	0.2	6.2	of which, unprocessed			
Housing and household				potatoes	95.5		−17
expenditure	145.1	−0.5	2.7	Vegetables	108.3		−9
Personal expenditure	129.2	−0.1	1.7	of which, other fresh			
Travel and leisure	138.4	0.1	4.0	vegetables	99.1		−14
All items excluding				Fruit	114.0		−15
seasonal food	140.5	−0.1	3.4	of which, fresh fruit	110.5		−20
All items excluding food	142.1	−0.1	3.5	Other foods	135.2		2
Seasonal food	106.3	−0.2	−12.4	**CATERING**	150.7	0.3	5.2
Food excluding seasonal	130.9	−0.2		Restaurant meals	150.0		5
All items excluding			2.4	Canteen meals	154.6		7
housing	135.6	0.1	3.0	Take-aways and snacks	150.2		6
All items excluding				**ALCOHOLIC DRINK**	150.7	−0.1	5.1
mortgage interest	137.9	0.1	3.6	Beer	155.1		5
Consumer durables	116.8	0.0	−0.4	on sales	157.7		5
FOOD	127.3	−0.1	0.4	off sales	137.2		4
Bread	134.7		4	Wines and spirits	144.5		5
Cereals	134.9		0	on sales	150.9		5
Biscuits and cakes	135.9		3	off sales	139.8		5
Beef	126.8		1	**TOBACCO**	147.1	0.8	8.5
Lamb	108.0		9	Cigarettes	148.0		9
of which, home-				Tobacco	140.8		8
killed lamb	105.9		12	**HOUSING**	160.4	−1.2	3.5
Pork	122.8		2	Rent	170.7		9
Bacon	137.9		5	Mortgage interest			
Poultry	110.0		-2	payments	177.0		−5
Other meat	123.2		0	Rates and community			
Fish	129.5		2	charges	136.6		13
of which, fresh fish	145.2		2	Water and other			
Butter	127.2		2	payments	191.8		10
Oil and fats	124.7		-1	Repairs and			
Cheese	135.7		10	maintenance charges	145.1		3
Eggs	112.3		0	Do-it-yourself materials	142.3		3
Milk, fresh	139.5		4	Dwelling insurance and			
Milk products	137.1		2	ground rent	199.9		3
Tea	149.7		-2	**FUEL AND LIGHT**	127.8	0.1	−0.4
Coffee and other hot				Coal and solid fuels	118.6		2
drinks	91.1		0	Electricity	142.7		2
Soft drinks	153.3		4	Gas	114.6		−4
Sugar and preserves	136.5		-2	Oil and other fuels	116.7		−1
Sweets and chocolates	122.7		4				

TABLE 2.2 *UK retail prices: Detailed figures for various groups, subgroups and sections for November 1992 (continued)*

	INDEX (JAN. 1987 =100)	PERCENTAGE CHANGE OVER (MONTHS)			INDEX (JAN. 1987 =100)	PERCENTAGE CHANGE OVER (MONTHS)	
		1	12			1	12
HOUSEHOLD GOODS	127.9	0.5	2.0	**MOTORING**			
Furniture	128.6		1	**EXPENDITURE**	140.3	0.0	4.2
Furnishings	124.2		0	Purchase of motor			
Electrical appliances	113.3		0	vehicles	127.3		0
Other household				Maintenance of motor			
equipment	131.2		0	vehicles	156.0		6
Household consumables	145.8		5	Petrol and oil	137.1		4
Pet care	121.7		4	Vehicles tax and			
HOUSEHOLD				insurance	175.0		15
SERVICES	138.5	0.4	3.9	**FARES AND OTHER**			
Postage	138.2		0	**TRAVEL COSTS**	146.1	0.3	5.6
Telephones, tele-				Rail fares	152.2		7
messages, etc.	120.6		0	Bus and coach fares	155.9		5
Domestic services	152.7		5	Other travel costs	134.8		5
Fees and subscriptions	148.4		7	**LEISURE GOODS**	121.6	0.3	1.8
CLOTHING AND				Audio-visual equipment	82.6		–5
FOOTWEAR	121.1	–0.4	–0.6	Records and tapes	112.6		2
Men's outerwear	121.8		–1	Toys, photographic and			
Women's outerwear	111.6		–2	sports goods	121.0		1
Children's outerwear	119.5		–1	Books and newspapers	155.3		6
Other clothing	136.9		2	Gardening products	138.0		3
Footwear	124.2		0	**LEISURE SERVICES**	153.0	–0.3	5.9
PERSONAL GOODS				Television licences and			
AND SERVICES	144.6	0.3	5.5	rentals	118.4		1
Personal articles	115.1		2	Entertainment and			
Chemists' goods	149.5		5	other recreation	173.5		8
Personal services	172.6		9				

NOTES:
1. Indices are given to one decimal place to provide as much information as is available, but precision is greater at higher levels of aggregation, that is, at sub-group and group levels.
2. The structure of the published components of the index was recast in February 1987.

SOURCE: *Employment Gazette*, Central Statistical Office, January 1993. Crown Copyright. Reprinted by permission of the Controller of Her Majesty's Stationery Office.

for expensive purchases such as homes, appliances and cars. When credit charges are high, consumers are more likely to delay buying expensive items. Use of credit is also affected by credit terms, such as the size of the down payment and the amount and number of monthly payments.

A person can have a high income and very little wealth. It is also possible, but not likely, for a person to have great wealth but not much income. **Wealth** is the accumulation of past income, natural resources and financial resources. It may exist in many

TABLE 2.3 *Family spending: A report on the 1991 family expenditure survey*

	GROSS NORMAL WEEKLY INCOME OF HOUSEHOLD					
	Lowest 20%	2nd quintile group	3rd quintile group	4th quintile group	Highest 20%	All households
Total number of households	1,411	1,411	1,412	1,411	1,411	7,056
Total number of persons	2,118	2,961	3,595	4,079	4,336	17,089
Total number of adults	1,708	2,319	2,655	2,939	3,313	12,934
AVERAGE NUMBER OF PERSONS PER HOUSEHOLD						
All persons	1.501	2.099	2.546	2.891	3.073	2.422
Males	0.562	0.958	1.254	1.497	1.573	1.169
Females	0.939	1.140	1.292	1.394	1.500	1.253
Adults	1.210	1.644	1.880	2.083	2.348	1.833
Persons under 65	0.595	0.960	1.567	1.936	2.218	1.455
Persons 65 and over	0.616	0.683	0.313	0.147	0.130	0.378
Children	0.291	0.455	0.666	0.808	0.725	0.589
Children under 5	0.129	0.136	0.260	0.225	0.170	0.184
Children 5 and under 18	0.151	0.305	0.435	0.550	0.559	0.400
Persons working	0.240	0.587	1.246	1.709	2.072	1.171
Persons not working	1.262	1.512	1.300	1.181	1.001	1.251
Men 65 and over; Women 60 and over	0.661	0.738	0.347	0.163	0.132	0.408
Others	0.600	0.774	0.953	1.018	0.869	0.843
Average age of head of household	60	57	48	43	45	51

	NUMBER OF HOUSEHOLDS					
HOUSING BY TYPE OF TENURE						
Rented unfurnished	960	519	300	127	46	1,952
Rented furnished	71	51	56	22	35	235
Rent-free	30	40	37	16	16	139
Owner-occupied	350	801	1,019	1,246	1,314	4,730

[a]This information is available on a regional basis.
[b]Percentage standard error.

forms, including cash, securities, savings accounts, jewellery, antiques and property. Like income, wealth is unevenly distributed. The significance of wealth to marketers is that as people become wealthier they gain buying power in three ways: they can use their wealth to make current purchases, to generate income and to acquire large amounts of credit.

Buying power information is available from government sources, trade associations and research agencies. One of the most current and comprehensive sources of buying power data is the Central Statistical Office's *National Income and Expenditur* Table 2.3 shows this survey's findings on effective buying income data power data.

COMMODITY OR SERVICE GROUP TOTALS[a]	AVERAGE WEEKLY HOUSEHOLD EXPENDITURE (£)					
	Lowest 20%	2nd quintile group	3rd quintile group	4th quintile group	Highest 20%	All households
Housing:						
Gross	36.60	46.02	51.76	60.04	81.96	55.27
	(1.3)[b]	(1.4)[b]	(1.3)[b]	(1.5)[b]	(2.0)[b]	(0.8)[b]
Net	19.39	40.68	50.31	59.35	81.47	50.24
	(2.7)	(1.7)	(1.4)	(1.5)	(2.0)	(1.0)
Fuel, light, and power	9.47	11.39	12.10	12.70	15.61	12.25
	(1.6)	(1.7)	(1.7)	(1.5)	(1.5)	(0.7)
Food	21.07	34.30	45.84	55.81	76.63	46.13
	(1.5)	(1.4)	(1.3)	(1.1)	(1.3)	(0.8)
Alcoholic drink	2.91	5.53	10.23	13.95	21.53	10.83
	(5.9)	(4.4)	(3.4)	(3.2)	(4.2)	(2.2)
Tobacco	3.25	4.85	5.78	6.14	5.72	5.15
	(4.6)	(4.2)	(4.2)	(4.1)	(5.0)	(2.0)
Clothing and footwear	3.86	8.66	14.44	20.72	31.31	15.80
	(5.9)	(5.2)	(3.9)	(3.2)	(3.3)	(2.0)
Household goods	6.26	13.06	18.83	24.61	37.89	20.13
	(6.7)	(4.8)	(4.8)	(4.3)	(4.1)	(2.3)
Household services	4.87	8.61	11.75	14.81	24.96	13.00
	(11.7)	(7.9)	(6.7)	(3.7)	(5.5)	(3.0)
Personal goods and services	2.91	6.55	9.66	12.60	18.15	9.97
	(4.3)	(4.4)	(6.6)	(4.4)	(3.8)	(2.4)
Motoring expenditure	3.30	16.17	29.56	49.45	72.13	34.12
	(8.8)	(7.5)	(4.4)	(5.7)	(4.5)	(2.9)
Fares and other travel costs	1.75	3.11	4.96	6.50	11.57	5.58
	(6.1)	(8.0)	(6.7)	(6.8)	(6.0)	(3.4)
Leisure goods	4.02	6.31	12.11	15.11	22.73	12.06
	(10.2)	(5.1)	(5.9)	(6.4)	(7.6)	(3.7)
Leisure services	4.63	9.49	17.98	23.81	55.07	22.20
	(6.8)	(4.7)	(6.4)	(4.7)	(4.6)	(2.9)
Miscellaneous	0.26	0.79	1.47	1.96	3.47	1.59
	(29.1)	(11.7)	(15.5)	(7.6)	(7.0)	(4.9)
All expenditure groups	87.95	169.49	245.02	317.51	475.24	259.04
Percentage standard error	1.8	1.4	1.4	1.3	1.4	0.9
AVERAGE WEEKLY EXPENDITURE PER PERSON (£)						
All expenditure groups	58.59	80.75	96.24	109.83	154.65	106.95

SOURCE: "Family Expenditure Survey", Central Statistical Office, 1991. Reprinted by permission of the Controller of Her Majesty's Stationery Office.

Income, wealth and credit equip consumers to purchase goods and services. Marketing managers should be aware of current levels and expected changes in buying power in their own markets because buying power directly affects the types and quantities of goods and services that consumers purchase, as explained later in the discussion of spending patterns. Just because consumers have buying power, however, does not necessarily mean that they will buy. Consumers must also be willing to use their buying power.

Consumers' Willingness to Spend.   People's **willingness to spend** is, to some degree, related to their ability to buy. That is, people are sometimes more willing to buy if they have the buying power. However, a number of other elements also influence willingness to spend. Some elements affect specific products; others influence spending in general. A product's absolute price and its price relative to the price of substitute products influence almost everyone. The amount of satisfaction currently received or expected in the future from a product already owned may also influence consumers' desire to buy other products. Satisfaction depends not only on the quality of the functional performance of the currently owned product, but also on numerous psychological and social forces.

Factors that affect consumers' general willingness to spend are expectations about future employment, income levels, prices, family size and general economic conditions. If people are unsure whether or how long they will be employed, willingness to buy ordinarily declines. Willingness to spend may increase if people are reasonably certain of higher incomes in the future. Expectations of rising prices in the near future may also increase the willingness to spend in the present. For a given level of buying power, the larger the family, the greater the willingness to buy. One of the reasons for this relationship is that as the size of a family increases, a larger amount of money must be spent to provide the basic necessities of life to sustain the family members. Finally, perceptions of future economic conditions influence willingness to buy. For example, in the late 1980s, rising short term interest rates cooled consumers' willingness to spend.

Consumer Spending Patterns.   Marketers must be aware of the factors that influence consumers' ability and willingness to spend, but they should also analyse how consumers actually spend their disposable incomes. Marketers obtain this information by studying consumer spending patterns. **Consumer spending patterns** indicate the relative proportions of annual family expenditures or the actual amount of money spent on certain kinds of goods and services. Families are usually categorised by one of several characteristics, including family income, age of the household head, geographic area and family life-cycle. There are two types of spending patterns: comprehensive and product specific.

The percentages of family income allotted to annual expenditures for general classes of goods and services constitute **comprehensive spending patterns.** Comprehensive spending patterns or the data to develop them are available in government publications and in reports produced by the major marketing research companies and by trade associations. In Table 2.3, comprehensive spending patterns are classified by the life-cycle of the family.

Product specific spending patterns indicate the annual monetary amounts families spend for specific products within a general product class. Information sources used to construct product specific spending patterns include government publications, trade publications and consumer surveys.

A marketer uses spending patterns to analyse general trends in the ways that families spend their incomes for various kinds of products. Analyses of spending patterns yield information that a marketer can use to gain perspective and background for decision-making. However, spending patterns reflect only general trends and thus should not be used as the sole basis for making specific decisions.

Few firms, if any, operate free of competition. Broadly speaking, all firms compete with each other for consumers' money. From a more practical viewpoint, however, a business generally defines **competition** as those firms that market products that are similar to, or can be substituted for, its products in the same geographic area. For example, a local Tesco or Aldi supermarket manager views all grocery stores in a town as competitors, but almost never thinks of other types of local or out-of-town stores (DIY or electrical, for example) as competitors. This section considers the types of competitive structure and the importance of monitoring competitors.

Types of Competitive Structure.   The number of firms that control the supply of a product may affect the strength of competition. When only one or a few firms control supply, competitive factors will exert a different sort of influence on marketing activities than when there are many competitors. Table 2.4 presents four general types of competitive structure: monopoly, oligopoly, monopolistic competition and perfect competition.

A **monopoly** exists when a firm turns out a product that has no close substitutes. Because the organisation has no competitors, it completely controls the supply of the product and, as a single seller, can erect barriers to potential competitors. In reality, the monopolies that survive today are some utilities, such as telephone, electricity and cable companies, which are heavily regulated. These monopolies are tolerated because of the tremendous financial resources needed to develop and operate them; few organisations can obtain the resources to mount any competition against a local electricity producer, for example.

An **oligopoly** exists when a few sellers control the supply of a large proportion of a product. In this case, each seller must consider the reactions of other sellers to changes in marketing activities. Products facing oligopolistic competition may be homogeneous, such as aluminum, or differentiated, such as cigarettes and cars. Usually, barriers of some sort make it difficult to enter the market and compete with oligopolies. For example, because of the enormous financial outlay required, few companies or individuals could afford to enter the oil refining or steel producing industries. Moreover, some industries demand special technical or marketing skills that block the entry of many potential competitors.

Monopolistic competition exists when a firm with many potential competitors attempts to develop a differential marketing strategy to establish its own market share. For example, Levi's has established a differential advantage for its blue jeans through a well-known trade mark, design, advertising and a quality image. Although many competing brands of blue jeans are available, this firm has carved out its market share through use of a differential marketing strategy.

Perfect competition, if it existed at all, would entail a large number of sellers, not one of which could significantly influence price or supply. Products would be homogeneous, and there would be full knowledge of the market and easy entry into it. The closest thing to an example of perfect competition would be an unregulated agricultural market.

Few, if any, marketers operate in a structure of perfect competition. Perfect competition is an ideal at one end of the continuum, with monopoly at the other end. Most marketers function in a competitive environment that falls somewhere between these two extremes.

Competitive Tools.   Another set of factors that influences the level of competition is the number and types of competitive tools used by competitors. To survive, a firm uses one or several available competitive tools to deal with competitive economic forces.

TABLE 2.4 *Selected characteristics of competitive structures*

TYPE OF STRUCTURE	NUMBER OF COMPETITORS	EASE OF ENTRY INTO MARKET	PRODUCT	KNOWLEDGE OF MARKET	EXAMPLES
Monopoly	One	Many barriers	Almost no substitutes	Perfect	Railways (British Rail), many government departments
Oligopoly	Few	Some barriers	Homogeneous or differentiated (real or perceived differences) products	Imperfect	Airlines, petroleum retailers, some utility providers
Monopolistic competition	Many	Few barriers	Product differentiation with many substitutes	More knowledge than oligopoly; less than monopoly	Jeans, fast food, audio-visual
Perfect competition	Unlimited	No barriers	Homogeneous products	Perfect	The London Commodity Markets, vegetable farms

Once a company has analysed its particular competitive environment and decided which factors in that environment it can or must adapt to or influence, it can choose among the variables that it can control to strengthen its competitive position in the overall market-place.

Probably the competitive tool that most organisations grasp is price. Bic, for example, markets disposable pens and lighters that are similar to competing products but less expensive. However, there is one major problem with using price as a competitive tool: competitors will often match or beat the price. This threat is one of the primary reasons for employing non–price competitive tools that are based on the differentiation of market segments, product offering, service, promotion, distribution or enterprise.[9]

By focusing on a specific market segment, a marketer sometimes gains a competitive advantage. For instance, Saab cars and Porsche sports coupes are narrowly targeted at specific groups of consumers. Most manufacturers try to gain a competitive edge by incorporating product features that make their brands distinctive to some extent. Firms use distinguishing promotional methods to compete, such as advertising and personal selling. Competing producers sometimes use different distribution channels to prevail over one other. Retailers may compete by placing their outlets in locations that are convenient for a large number of shoppers. Dealers and distributors offer wide ranges, advice and service.

Monitoring Competition.   Marketers in an organisation need to be aware of the actions of major competitors. They should monitor what competitors are currently doing and assess the changes occurring in the competitive environment. Monitoring allows firms to determine what specific strategies competitors are following and how those strategies affect their own. It can also guide marketers as they try to develop competitive advantages and aid them in adjusting current marketing strategies, as well as in planning new ones. Information may come from direct observation or from sources such as salespeople, customers, trade publications, syndicated marketing research services, distributors and marketing studies.

An organisation needs information about competitors that will allow its marketing managers to assess the performance of its own marketing efforts. Comparing their company's performance with that of competitors helps marketing managers recognise strengths and weaknesses in their own marketing strategies. Data about market shares, product movement, sales volume and expenditure levels can be useful. However, accurate information on these matters is often difficult to obtain.

Competition exists in most markets and situations. Even charities compete with one other and with manufacturers for consumers' attention and financial commitment. Marketing places an emphasis on meeting consumers' needs and offering satisfaction. To be successful, however, competing organisations need to identify unique marketing mixes; otherwise all rival products and services will merely replicate each other. The search for a competitive edge—achieved through a differential advantage in a market over competitors—is central to effective marketing strategy. Competition is more than an aspect of the marketing environment and is explored in Chapter 19.

SUMMARY

The marketing environment consists of external forces that directly or indirectly influence an organisation's acquisition of inputs (personnel, financial resources, raw materials, information) and generation of outputs (information, packages, goods, services, ideas). The marketing environment comprises political, legal and regulatory forces; societal forces, including green concerns for the earth's natural environment; and technological forces. Along with economic forces and trends, these macro, broader aspects of the marketing environment have an impact on manufacturers and their consumers. The more narrowly focused force of competition is also of fundamental importance.

To monitor changes in these forces, marketers should practise environmental scanning and analysis. Environmental scanning is the process of collecting information about the forces in the marketing environment; environmental analysis is the process of assessing and interpreting the information obtained in scanning. This information helps marketing managers predict opportunities and threats associated with environmental fluctuation. Marketing management may assume either a passive, reactive approach or an active, aggressive approach in responding to these environmental fluctuations. The choice depends on an organisation's structure and needs and on the composition of the environmental forces which affect it.

The political, legal and regulatory forces of the marketing environment are closely interrelated. The current political outlook is reflected in legislation and regulations or the lack of them. The political environment may determine what laws and regulations affecting specific marketers are enacted and how much the government purchases and from which suppliers; it can also be important in helping organisations secure foreign markets.

Legislation affecting marketing activities can be divided into procompetitive legislation—laws designed to preserve and encourage competition—and consumer protection laws. The Restrictive Trade Practices Act and the Competition Act sought to prevent monopolies and activities that limit competition; legislation such as the Financial Services Act, the Sale of Goods Act and the Consumer Credit Act were directed towards more specific practices. Consumer protection laws generally relate to product safety and information disclosure. The actual effects of legislation are determined by how marketers and the courts interpret the laws.

Regulatory agencies influence most marketing activities. For example, the Monopolies and Mergers Commission and the Director General of fair trading usually have the power to enforce specific laws and some discretion in establishing operating rules and drawing up regulations to guide certain types of industry practices. Self-regulation by industry represents another regulatory force; marketers view this type of regulation more favourably than government action, because they have more opportunity to take part in creating the guidelines. Self-regulation may be less expensive than government regulation, and its guidelines are generally more realistic. However, such regulation generally cannot assure compliance as effectively as government agencies.

Societal forces refer to the structure and dynamics of individuals and groups and the issues that concern them. Many members of society want a high standard of living and a high quality of life, and they expect business to help them achieve these goals. Of growing concern is the well being of the earth, its resources, climate and peoples. The green movement is increasing general awareness of the natural environment and is altering product design, manufacture, packaging and use. The consumer movement is a diverse collection of independent individuals, groups and organisations that attempt to protect the rights of consumers. The major issues taken up by the consumer movement fall into three categories: environmental protection, product performance and safety, and information disclosure. Consumer rights organisations inform and organise other consumers, raise issues, help businesses develop consumer orientated programmes, and pressure legislators to enact consumer protection laws.

Technology is the knowledge of how to accomplish tasks and goals. Product development, packaging, promotion, prices and distribution systems are all influenced directly by technology. Several factors determine how much and in what way a particular business will make use of technology; these factors include the firm's ability to use technology, consumers' ability and willingness to buy technologically improved products, the firm's perception of the long run effects of applying technology, the extent to which the firm is technologically based, the degree to which technology is used as a competitive tool, and the extent to which the business can protect technological applications through patents.

The economic factors that can strongly influence marketing decisions and activities are general economic conditions, buying power, willingness to spend, spending patterns and competitive forces. The overall state of the economy fluctuates in a general pattern known as a business cycle. The stages of the business cycle are prosperity, recession, depression and recovery.

Consumers' goods, services and financial holdings make up their buying power—that is, their ability to purchase. The financial sources of buying power are income, credit and wealth. After tax income used for spending or saving is called disposable income. Disposable income left after an individual has purchased the basic necessities of food, clothing and shelter is called discretionary income. Two measures of buying power are effective buying income (which includes salaries, wages, dividends, interest, profits and rents, less taxes) and the buying power index (a weighted index consisting of population, effective buying income, and retail sales data). The factors tha consumers' willingness to spend are product price, the level of satisfaction obtained from currently used products, family size and expectations about future employment, income, prices and general economic conditions. Consumer spending patterns indicate the relative proportions of annual family expenditures or the actual amount of money spent on certain kinds of goods and services. Comprehensive spending patterns specify the percentages of family income allotted to annual expenditures for general classes of goods and services. Product specific spending patterns indicate the annual amounts families spend for specific products within a general product class.

Although all businesses compete for consumers' spending, a company's direct competitors are usually the businesses in its geographic area that market products that resemble its own or can be substituted for them. The number of firms that control the supply of a product may affect the strength of competition. There are four general types of competitive structure: monopoly, oligopoly, monopolistic competition and perfect competition. Marketers should monitor what competitors are currently doing and assess the changes occurring in the competitive environment.

IMPORTANT TERMS

Marketing environment	Depression
Environmental scanning	Recovery
Environmental analysis	Buying power
Procompetitive legislation	Income
Office of Fair Trading	Disposable income
Monopolies and Mergers	Discretionary income
Commission	Wealth
Treaty of Rome	Willingness to spend
Consumers' Association	Consumer spending patterns
Societal/green forces	Comprehensive spending patterns
Green movement	Product specific spending patterns
Consumer movement	Competition
Technology	Monopoly
Technology assessment	Oligopoly
Prosperity	Monopolistic competition
Recession	Perfect competition

DISCUSSION AND REVIEW QUESTIONS

1. Why are environmental scanning and analysis so important?
2. How are political forces related to legal and governmental regulatory forces?
3. Describe marketers' attempts to influence political forces.
4. What types of procompetitive legislation directly affect marketing practices?
5. What is the major objective of most procompetitive laws? Do the laws generally accomplish this objective? Why or why not?
6. What types of problems do marketers experience as they interpret legislation?
7. What are the goals of the Monopolies and Mergers Commission? How does it affect marketing activities?
8. Name several non-governmental regulatory forces. Do you believe that self-regulation is more or less effective than governmental regulatory agencies? Why?
9. How is the so called "green" lobby altering the shape of business?

10. Describe the consumer movement. Analyse some active consumer forces in your area.
11. What does the term *technology* mean to you?
12. How does technology affect you as a member of society? Do the benefits of technology outweigh its costs and dangers?
13. Discuss the impact of technology on marketing activities.
14. What factors determine whether a business organisation adopts and uses technology?
15. In what ways can each of the business cycle stages affect consumers' reactions to marketing strategies?
16. What business cycle stage are we experiencing currently? How is this stage affecting business firms in your area?
17. Define income, disposable income and discretionary income. How does each type of income affect consumer buying power?
18. How is consumer buying power affected by wealth and consumer credit?
19. How is buying power measured? Why should it be evaluated?
20. What factors influence a consumer's willingness to spend?

■ CASES

2.1 Buying Heinz on a Sunday

For decades Sunday was a day of rest: churches were busy, bars and restaurants operated on restricted hours, and very few shops opened their doors. Gradually this situation changed throughout the 1980s. New working practices presented more leisure time and consumers expected greater choice and variety in away from work pursuits. To many, shopping is a social activity. Increased travel and tourism enabled many Britons to experience the more relaxed shopping and licensing hours typical in many Mediterranean countries, for example.

Some businesses were noting these trends and the potential profits to be made from trading on a Sunday. A major amendment to the licensing laws in the 1980s permitted pubs to open longer and many restaurants to open all day. Continental drinking habits were coming to the UK, so why not shopping?

For retailers, though, doors remained closed. Seaside and holiday resorts allowed their shops to open seven days per week for the summer season. Throughout England and Wales, newsagents could open to distribute newspapers; forecourts could sell petrol and off-licences could open for a couple of hours at lunchtime and in the evening. For the retailers of groceries and consumer durables, shop doors remained closed. Even garden centres, allowed to open historically, could not sell garden furniture or tools on Sundays, having to chain off those display areas.

In the 1990s, the pattern has changed. DIY giants Texas and B&Q risked hefty fines to breach the Sunday trading laws and to open their doors. Despite having to pay their volunteer staff bonuses for working, Sunday trading was financially worthwhile and apparently popular with a large proportion of the general public. MPs debated the issue, with support growing for an upheaval in the Sunday trading laws. Votes for amendments were only narrowly defeated in the House of Commons. Religious leaders and shop workers' unions were appalled by the moves to bring in the seven day shopping. Campaigns were initiated to keep Sunday free from trading, with significant support from churches, unions, some of the media, and one or two retail chains which opposed the extension to opening hours and did not wish to increase staff and operating costs.

The most significant development was in 1992, when Sunday opening was introduced by the large grocery groups: Sainsbury, Tesco, Safeway and Asda. Grocery shopping is a necessity, more so than clothing or footwear; it is also a regular, frequent expedition in most households. The higher wage bills and fines imposed on retailers by some local authorities and councils did not outweigh the popularity of the move with many consumers. There were good returns for the retailers. For many households, Sunday shopping became a welcome option in a busy week's schedule. For others, it provided another leisure pursuit!

Legally, the issue went right through the English courts. There were victories on both sides, but ultimately Parliament had to abide by the existing statute books: Sunday trading for most retailers was illegal. Some of the large retailers, led by Kingfisher—owner of DIY retailer B&Q, electrical chain Comet, as well as Woolworth and Superdrug—went to the European Courts, believing the Sunday trading laws were poorly configured, ambiguous and wrongly restrictive. Initial verdicts were in these retailers' favour. More chains started to open on Sundays. Local authorities resented wasting resources to enforce legislation which seemed flawed.

The UK government admitted that the existing legislation was not clear, was difficult to enforce and was not in line with current retailing practices. Kenneth Clarke, the Home Secretary, believed he had three options to put before MPs:

- Total freedom for all shops to choose to open on Sundays
- A *Keeping Sunday Special* proposition which would allow opening only for leisure pursuits
- A reform of shops' hours which would allow some shops to open on Sundays

To many observers' surprise, in 1993 the European Court delivered its verdict on the appeals on behalf of the local authorities' right to uphold existing anti-opening laws, and against retailers' desires to open when they wished. The verdicts upheld the restricted Sunday opening laws already on the statute books and ruled against those DIY and grocery retailers which had extended their hours of operation.

The reaction was mixed. Journalists and MPs ridiculed the government's inability to act on the issue to establish working legislation which was up to date, enforceable and in line with EC regulations. Some local authorities began once more to take retailers to court for opening, while other authorities decided to take no action and to await the central government's new legislation. A few retailers closed their doors, but most continued to trade.

For consumers, regulators and retailers there was confusion; often circumstances differed from town to town. In one town, the local authority may have appeased the Keep Sunday Special lobby, by enforcing the restrictions on Sunday trading. Shoppers may, however, have been able to travel a few miles to a neighbouring town where retailers opened on a Sunday without fear of prosecution. Retailers who wanted to open thus found consistency hard to attain, different circumstances from region to region and legal development weekly. For those companies which objected to Sunday trading, there was loss of market share. John Lewis Partnership's department stores and Waitrose supermarkets, for example, saw healthy profits turn into losses as their doors remained locked on Sundays.

Changing social practices, legal, regulatory and competitive forces are all at work in the Sunday trading debate, with major implications for all those involved.

SOURCES: "Sunday trading verdict soon", *Marketing*, 12 November 1992, p. 8; John Lewis, "MP's threat to Sunday shopping", *Marketing*, 28 January 1993, p. 7; BBC TV news, November 1992–January 1993; John Lewis, "Limit to Sunday hours threatened", *Marketing*, 17 December 1992, p. 6.

Questions for Discussion

1. What changes are likely in trading practices if more lenient Sunday trading laws take effect?
2. Which aspects of the marketing environment are at work here?
3. What competitive implications from the Sunday trading debate are there for companies such as John Lewis?

2.2 Suzuki Samurai Copes with Safety Controversy

Officials of the Japanese Suzuki Motor Corp. and its American subsidiary, Suzuki of America Automotive Corp., were extremely pleased with the sales figures of the Suzuki Samurai after it was introduced in the United States in late 1985. The Samurai, a four wheel drive sport/utility vehicle, appealed to a wide range of consumers. College students, off-road enthusiasts, and urban professionals all seemed to love the sporty look and fun image of the Samurai. Its low price tag also helped sales immensely. The popularity of the Samurai might have turned it into a target, though, as more and more attention was focused on it. Today, Suzuki Samurai sales are at a low point as dealers try to cope with questions about its safety. Throughout Europe dealerships have seen a similar pattern.

Suzuki's troubles with the Samurai began when NBC in America reported on the Samurai's tendency to roll over. Soon afterwards, Consumers Union, publishers of *Consumer Reports*, gave the Samurai a "not acceptable" rating in its magazine, the first such rating the magazine had handed out in ten years. Researchers for *Consumer Reports* claim that during common evasive manoeuvres—for example, if a driver were to swerve back and forth on the road to avoid an accident—the Samurai is likely to roll over. Consumers Union was so concerned about the safety of the Samurai that it demanded that Suzuki recall the 150,000 Samurais then on the road, refund owners' purchase price, and remove the vehicle from the market. In the UK, consumer programmes and the BBC's *Top Gear* widely reported the situation in America.

One of several lawsuits has been filed against Suzuki by a Pennsylvania physician on behalf of all Samurai owners. The doctor believes that Suzuki purposely attempted to conceal knowledge of the Samurai's instability. Another lawsuit charges that Suzuki promoted the safety of the Samurai even though the company knew the vehicle was unsafe. The suit maintains that Suzuki and the firm that handles its public relations and advertising continuously committed mail and wire fraud and conspiracy to screen the Samurai's design flaws. The lawsuit refers to the National Traffic Highway Safety Administration's figures that show 44 Samurai roll-over incidents resulting in at least 25 deaths and more than 60 injuries.

Suzuki officials maintain that the Samurai is as safe as any other four wheel drive vehicle. A high ranking Suzuki executive called *Consumer Reports'* roll-over accounts "defamatory". Suzuki executives charge that *Consumer Reports'* researchers changed their roll-over test methodology when they were testing the Samurai. Furthermore, regarding the 25 deaths linked to Samurai roll-overs, Suzuki directors assert that more than 50 per cent of the accidents in which these deaths occurred can be attributed to drunk drivers.

Unlike German Audi AG officials, who initially did not respond to consumer complaints of sudden acceleration in their Audi 5000, Suzuki executives are aggressively battling the allegations against the Samurai. Suzuki officials have increased their advertising budget to publicly address safety issues. Suzuki has placed more than $1.5 million into its television media schedule to respond to the *Consumer Reports* indictment. A few months after the *Consumer Reports* article became public, Suzuki began an extensive buyer and dealer incentive programme, and sales of Samurais rocketed. Suzuki managers saw this as a sign of declining public concern over the roll-over issue. Suzuki was mistaken, however. Once it removed the generous incentives, Samurai sales began to sink again.

Suzuki officials are determined to fight their way out of this controversy, even though the fight is very expensive. Suzuki stands to lose public credibility if it cannot successfully prove the Samurai's roadworthiness. Many Suzuki officials are worried that the controversy surrounding the Samurai will spread to other Suzuki products and that sales figures of its other cars and even motorcycles will be adversely affected.

Meanwhile, Suzuki continues to sell Samurais, even though the figures are not as high as anticipated before the controversy. Suzuki managers were pleased when the Center for Auto Safety's petition to the federal government for the recall of Samurais was refused. Suzuki will have to work hard to restore the reputation of its Samurai. The Japanese car company may have a difficult time keeping the sporty little four-wheel-drive on the road.

SOURCES: Cleveland Horton and Raymond Serafin, "Wounded by Samurai?", *Advertising Age,* 20 June 1988, p. 101; " 'Samurai rollover rap is bum', Suzuki says", *Ward's AutoWorld,* July 1988, p. 34; "Samurai sales hit record", *Chicago Sun Times,* 6 September 1988; Janice Steinberg, "Suzuki acts to right slipping Samurai sales", *Advertising Age,* 25 July 1988, p. S-10; "Suit charged safety fraud by Suzuki", *Star-Ledger* (Newark, N.J.), 15 June 1988; "Suzuki calls consumer group's safety tests on Samurai 'flawed' ", *Los Angeles Times*, 10 June 1988; "Suzuki revamps ads to combat safety charges", *Detroit News*, 4 March 1988; "Ten products that made news in 1988", *Advertising Age,* 2 January 1989, p. 12; *Top Gear,* BBC, 1989.

Questions for Discussion

1. What kinds of environmental forces is Suzuki facing regarding the safety issue?
2. Evaluate Suzuki's way of dealing with the safety controversy.
3. What improvements could be made in Suzuki's approach to coping with the safety issue?

3 SEGMENTING MARKETS, TARGETING AND POSITIONING

Objectives

- To understand the definition of a market

- To recognise different types of markets

- To learn how firms segment markets

- To understand targeting decisions

- To learn about strategies for positioning

*B*aby food market leader Heinz has 53 per cent of the £108 million UK infant meals market. Supermarket shelves are full of rival baby foods bearing the labels of Milupa, Heinz, Cow & Gate and a host of retailer own label brands. Periodically, new flavours and formulations are introduced; spaghetti bolognese one week, beef and carrot broth another. In general though, the target market for these products is all families with babies or small children.

Now Heinz is trying to refine its mass market appeal by targeting the baby food needs of minority groups. As part of its £10 million marketing outlay for the year, the company is set to launch radio and press advertisements aimed specifically at the Asian community. Initially, the campaign will be confined to the Hindi press and radio in selected regions of the UK. Heinz intends to generate additional interest in the promotion with locally organised newspaper coverage and consumer competitions.

For Heinz this promotion does not represent a change of direction. The company has already developed a full range of foods geared towards vegetarian families and approved by the Vegetarian Society. Now the company will promote this same product line to Asian families. According to product manager Roger Hobbs, "Part of the radio campaign's function is to highlight the availability of our vegetarian range and its suitability for Asian babies". Market leaders and niche marketers alike tend to target specific customer segments in order to gain an edge over competition and to ensure that their products are exactly what consumers want. In this instance, Heinz has realised the opportunity to offer Asian families baby foods which take into account their cultural and religious beliefs. ■

SOURCES: Robert Dwek, "Heinz targets Asians with baby foods range", *Marketing*, 26 March 1992, p.3; *The Marketing Pocket Book 1993*, The Advertising Association in association with NTC publications Ltd; Claire Murphy, "Baby drinks firms defend position", *Marketing Week*, 6 November 1992; Mike Johnson, "Milupa rejects 'lying' claim over sugar", *Marketing*, 21 May 1992, p.4.

ompanies like Heinz realise that not all consumers want the same things. To satisfy these different needs it is necessary for companies to single out groups of customers and aim some or all of their marketing activities at these groups. The key is then to develop and maintain a marketing mix which satisfies the particular requirements of customers in these groups. In this example Heinz is trying to develop a marketing mix which appeals to a particular ethnic group.

This chapter considers the nature of markets, first defining the term and describing the different types. It then reviews the concepts of segmentation, targeting and positioning by considering the variables used to segment markets. Next, it considers the strategies often used to select target markets and approaches to product positioning. Finally, it discusses market measurement and primary sales forecasting techniques.

What Are Markets?

The word *market* has a number of meanings. It used to refer primarily to the place where goods were bought and sold. It can also refer to a large geographic area. In some cases the word refers to the relationship between the demand and supply of a specific product. For instance, "What is the state of the market for oil?" Sometimes, "market" is used to mean the act of selling something.

For the purposes of this text, a **market** is an aggregate of people who, as individuals or in organisations, have needs for products in a product class and who have the ability, willingness and authority to purchase such products. In general use, the term *market* sometimes refers to the total population—or mass market—that buys products. However, our definition is more specific; it refers to persons seeking products in a specific product category. For example, students are part of the market for textbooks, as well as being markets for calculators, pens and pencils, paper, food, music and other products. Obviously, there are many different markets in any economy. In this section, the requirements for markets are considered in conjunction with these different types.

Requirements for a Market

For a group of people to be a market, the members of the group must meet the following four requirements.

1. They must need or want a particular product or service. If they do not, then that group is not a market.
2. They must have the ability to purchase the product. Ability to purchase is related to buying power, which consists of resources such as money, goods and services that can be traded in an exchange situation.
3. They must be willing to use their buying power.
4. They must have the authority to buy the specific products.

Individuals can have the desire, the buying power and the willingness to purchase certain products but may not be authorised to do so. For example, school students may have the desire, the money and the willingness to buy alcoholic beverages; but a brewer does not consider them a market because until they are 18 years old, they are prohibited by law from buying alcohol. An aggregate of people that lacks any one of the four requirements thus does not constitute a market.

Types of Markets

Markets can be divided into two categories: consumer markets and organisational or industrial markets. These categories are based on the characteristics of the individuals and groups that make up a specific market and the purposes for which they buy products. A **consumer market** consists of purchasers and/or individuals in their households who intend to consume or benefit from the purchased products and who do not buy products for the main purpose of making a profit. Each of us belongs to numerous consumer markets for such products as housing, food, clothing, vehicles, personal services, appliances, furniture and recreational equipment. Consumer markets are discussed in more detail in Chapter 4.

An **organisational,** or **industrial, market** consists of individuals or groups that purchase a specific kind of product for one of three purposes: resale, direct use in producing other products or use in general daily operations. The four categories of organisational, or industrial, markets—producer, reseller, government and institutional—are discussed in Chapter 5.

SELECTING TARGET MARKETS

In Chapter 1 a marketing strategy is defined as having two components: (1) the selection of the organisation's target market and (2) the creation and maintenance of a marketing mix that satisfies that market's needs for a specific product. Regardless of the general types of markets on which a firm focuses, marketing management must select the firm's target markets. The next section examines two general approaches to identifying target markets: the total market approach and market segmentation.

Total Market Approach or Market Segmentation?

In some situations marketers define the total market for a particular product or service as their target market. Companies which develop a single marketing mix aimed at all potential customers in a market are said to be adopting an **undifferentiated** or **total market approach.** The assumption is that all customers in the market have similar needs and wants and can, therefore, be satisfied with a single marketing mix—a standard product or service, similar price levels, one method of distribution and a promotional mix aimed at everyone.

Increasingly, marketers in both consumer and industrial markets are facing the fact that no two customers are ever exactly the same. Different individuals and organisations have varying characteristics, needs, wants and interests. The result is that there are few markets where a single product or service is satisfactory for all. The extensive array of goods on supermarket shelves reflects basic differences in customers' requirements. The trend, it seems, is away from a mass marketing approach. Even markets which were traditionally undifferentiated are undergoing change, with an ever increasing number of products on offer. For instance, the market for food seasoning used to be dominated by salt. Now, low sodium substitutes are being offered as alternatives for the increasingly health conscious consumer (See Figure 3.1).

The mass marketing approach is appropriate only under two conditions. The first occurs when there is little variation in the needs of customers for a specific product and is increasingly rare. The market for clothing, for example, is one which does not fall into this category because of the wide variation in customer preferences. The second condition is that the organisation must develop and sustain one marketing mix which satisfies everyone. If the number of customers is large, the commitment in terms of company resources and managerial expertise can be considerable.

When an undifferentiated approach is inappropriate or impractical, marketers use market segmentation to try to improve customer satisfaction. This technique involves

FIGURE 3.1

Appealing to a particular market segment Klinge Foods offers Lo Salt to health conscious consumers.

SOURCE: All copy and Trade Mark rights belong to Klinge Foods Ltd 6750YN Scotland.

CHALLENGE

LESS FAT MORE FIBRE
LESS SALT

Trying to improve the eating habits of a modern family can be a complicated and mind-boggling task.

However there's nothing complex or mysterious about LoSalt, the reduced sodium salt alternative. It contains all the flavour of common salt but only a third of its sodium.

Substitute LoSalt for common salt, at the table and in cooking to reduce your family's salt intake.

LoSalt is supporting the Family Heart Association's Cholesterol Countdown Campaign. Are you?

ALL THE FLAVOUR
FOR ALL THE FAMILY

Good Sense with Salt

For free samples and more information on LoSalt or the Family Heart Association write your name and address on a stamped addressed envelope (approx 6½" x 9½") and send off to Klinge Foods Ltd, Family Heart Association Offer, 7 Albion Way, East Kilbride G75 0YN.
LoSalt is a trademark of Klinge Foods Ltd.

FIGURE 3.2
*Market segmentation
approach*

identifying groups of customers in markets who share similar buying needs and characteristics. By identifying and understanding such groups, marketers are better able to develop product or service benefits which are appropriate for them (See Figure 3.2). They do this by creating new product and branding concepts which are backed up with promotional campaigns to appeal to particular target segments. Decisions about pricing and distribution strategies are also made with specific segments in mind. For example, clothing sold through Victoria's Secret is manufactured for youthful female consumers. This is reflected in both the product styling and the promotional campaign.

APPLYING MARKET SEGMENTATION

Markets in which all consumers have different requirements are termed **heterogeneous markets.** For example, the market for ladies' lingerie is quite diverse. Marks & Spencer sells undergarments to customers seeking practical products of good quality, whereas Janet Reger lines are aimed at a more up market, exclusive customer.

In completely heterogeneous markets the only way to satisfy everyone is by offering tailor made or bespoke products. This unusual situation is more prevalent in organisational markets, where, for example, plant machinery is designed for a specific task and situation. However, in the vast majority of markets the aggregation of customers into groups with similar product needs and wants is perfectly feasible. **Market segmentation** is the process by which customers in markets with some heterogeneity can be grouped into smaller, more similar or homogeneous segments. In so doing, a balance is sought between obtaining reasonably substantial groups and ensuring sufficient similarity to allow individuals to be offered a standard marketing mix. For example, Alton Towers, a leading UK theme park, directed the advertisement in Figure 3.3 to the lucrative corporate market.

Having identified market segments, marketers must decide which, if any, they intend to enter. A marketing programme which covers all elements of the marketing mix can then be designed to suit the particular requirements of those segments targeted. Sears owned British Shoe Corporation dominated the UK footwear retailing sector, mainly through medium and budget priced chains such as Dolcis, Saxone and Freeman Hardy Willis. The company realised it was not catering for the upper end of the market, which had lower volumes but higher unit margins. Cable & Co. was duly launched to cater for this segment of the market.

Companies which have turned to market segmentation have done so with good reason. Amex, Burtons and TSB have all demonstrated that success can follow the effec-

FIGURE 3.3

*Supplying a heteroge-
neous market*
Alton Towers is the UK's
leading theme park. Man-
agement has identified a
growing demand for cor-
porate fun days and AGMs
staged at the theme park.
By no means Alton
Towers' core market, this
segment is sufficiently
lucrative to prompt this
advertisement.

SOURCE: Courtesy of Alton Towers

tive implementation of market segmentation strategies. In the UK market for tea (see Marketing Insight 3.1), segmentation has been essential in order to satisfy the diverse customer needs.

Careful segmentation can make it easier for firms to identify different market opportunities. By having a better understanding of different customer groups, companies can more easily exploit opportunities which arise. For example, segmentation can help minor players in the market to achieve a foothold in a particular niche, perhaps by identifying an opportunity not directly exploited by market leaders. In general, segmentation helps companies pursue four types of product and market opportunities:

1. *Market Penetration,* which increases the percentage of sales in present markets by taking sales from the competition. For example, McDonald's and Burger King engage in advertising programmes which compete for each other's market share.
2. *Product Development,* which offers new or improved products to existing markets by expanding the range of products on offer. For example, the washing powder market has undergone much change over recent years with the introduction of new micro-powders and products specifically aimed at washing coloured clothing.
3. *Market Development,* which develops existing products in new markets by finding new applications and/or customer groups. Evian, one of the major the market for mineral water, now offers its product in a mist spray.

MARKETING INSIGHT 3.1

THE CASE OF TEA

Tea, central to the British way of life, with 200 million cups drunk each day, is a market in transition. The recent proliferation of product offerings apparently relates to differences in the drink's preparation and use. Customers with varying needs are having different product types and forms targeted at them. Perhaps the most critical factor is the way the user prepares the drink.

In terms of product use, there are obvious, distinctive customer groups for manufacturers to target. Not everyone, though, is looking for the same benefits when they buy. For some, the level of convenience is important; for others, flavour and quality are the key. Improving tea bag and instant tea technology has largely satisfied the need for convenience and has made the drink a real alternative to instant coffee, particularly in the work environment. Manufacturers have responded to varying flavour and quality requirements with a host of different quality blends and types of tea, such as Earl Grey, Ceylon and China. There are also less obvious aspects which are entwined with British culture. Tradition tells us that the tea pot must be warmed, only freshly boiled water used and the drink left to brew. For many customers the act of preparing, and in some cases sharing, the drink is essential to the enjoyment. To these customers, tea bags, and especially instant tea mixes, are often regarded as unacceptable forms of the product.

	FORM OF PRODUCT	BRAND
TEA POT	Loose Leaf	Twinings
	Standard Tea Bags	Sainsbury's Kenya Blend
CUP OR MUG	One-cup Tea Bags	
	Tag Bags	Typhoo One Cup
	Round Tea Bags	Tetley
	Instant	PG Instant

Brumisateur atomiser (see Figure 3.4) is being marketed as a new concept in skin moisturisers.

4. *Diversification,* which involves moving into different markets by offering new products. For example, Bic followed its success in the ballpoint pen market by moving into disposable razors and perfumes.

THE ADVANTAGES OF MARKET SEGMENTATION

Segmentation has a number of advantages associated with it which make it easier for companies to develop and capitalise on opportunities such as those described above. These advantages can be considered at the customer level, in relation to the competition, or in terms of the effectiveness of resource allocation and strategic planning.

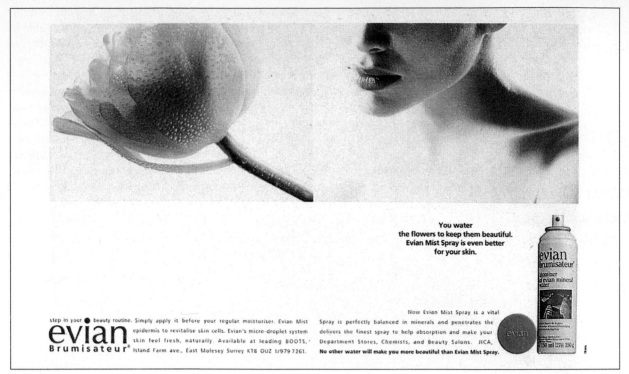

FIGURE 3.4 *Developing existing products in new markets*
Evian, one of the major players in the market for mineral water, now offers its product as a mist spray for skin care.

SOURCE: Courtesy of PBWA Advertising, Inc. for Laboratoire d'Hygiene Dermatologique d'Evian.

Customer Analysis

By segmenting markets it is possible to achieve a better understanding not only of customers' needs and wants but also of their other characteristics. The sharper focus which segmentation offers allows the personal, situational and behavioural factors which characterise customers in a particular segment to be considered. In short, questions about how, why and what customers buy can be addressed. If they are closely in touch with segments, marketers can be responsive to even slight changes in what target customers want. An appropriate response can then follow much more quickly.

Competitor Analysis

Most markets are characterised by intense competition. Within this environment, companies need to understand the nature of the competition they face. Who are the main competitors? At which segments are they targeting their products? Answering these and other similar questions allows marketers to make decisions about which are the most appropriate segments to target and what kind of competitive advantage should be sought. Companies that do not understand how the market is divided up risk competing head on against larger organisations with superior resources.

Effective Resource Allocation

All companies have limited resources. To target the whole of the market is usually unrealistic. The effectiveness of personnel and material resources can be greatly improved when they are more narrowly focused on a particular segment of customers.

The benefits which segmentation offers are illustrated in the following example. Despite recent problems, IBM is still regarded as something of a legend in the computer industry. During the 1960s, the company recognised that there was a need for certain industry standards. IBM argued that, when customers' needs changed, it would not be feasible to dispose of existing equipment and expertise and begin again. There was a need to upgrade to equipment which spoke similar languages and had similar physiology. Through this insight, IBM became that standard. The company was able to offer a complete package of service, training, consultancy, maintenance and software support. It built its corporate image to the point where the "in" industry "joke" suggested that the data processing manager who bought non-IBM equipment which failed would be rapidly moving jobs. For IBM's competitors this powerful competitive advantage presented a dilemma. How could they compete successfully against such odds? Curiously, for some companies the best solution was not to compete at all. These organisations chose to work around IBM, to specialise and focus on certain segments or niches in the market. For example, NCR concentrated on the retailing and banking markets, Apple on the education market. Some of the software companies (for example, Microsoft) adopted a similar strategy.

Strategic Marketing Planning

Companies which operate in a number of segments are unlikely to follow the same strategic plans in all of them. Dividing markets up allows marketers to develop plans that give special consideration to the particular needs and requirements of customers in different segments. The time-scale covered by the strategic plan can also be structured accordingly, because some segments change more rapidly than others. The market for recorded music is a typical example. While tastes in classical music remain fairly steady, tastes in pop change very rapidly. Companies like EMI clearly need to consider this factor when developing corporate plans.

SEGMENTING, TARGETING AND POSITIONING

Market segmentation takes place in three stages: segmentation, targeting and positioning. Figure 3.5 gives an overview of these stages.

Segmenting the Market

There are many ways in which customers can be grouped and markets segmented. In separate markets, different variables are appropriate. The key is to understand which are the most suitable for distinguishing between different product requirements. Understanding as much as possible about what the customers in segments are really like is also important. Marketers who "know" their targets are more likely to design an appropriate marketing mix for them. For example, of all sectors of retailing, only the furniture retailers experienced no real growth during the buoyant 1980s. Consumer research revealed that product design and quality were viewed as uninspiring, thus providing little incentive for customers to make replacement purchases. What was surprising for most furniture retailers was that consumers were often forced to decide between buying new living-room or dining-room furniture and going abroad for a first or second holiday each year. Companies had to gear their promotion accordingly—attempting to make their products appear more exciting while taking into account the various budgeting considerations of a typical household.

Targeting Strategy

Once segments have been identified, decisions about which and how many customer groups to target can be made. There are several options:

- Concentrate on a single segment with one product.
- Offer one product to a number of segments.
- Target a different product at each of a number of segments.

These options are explored in more detail later in this chapter. The choices companies make must take into consideration the resource implications of following a particular

FIGURE 3.5
Basic elements of segmentation

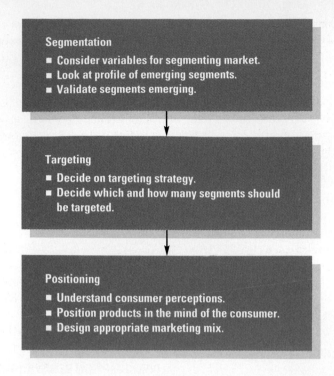

Segmentation
- Consider variables for segmenting market.
- Look at profile of emerging segments.
- Validate segments emerging.

Targeting
- Decide on targeting strategy.
- Decide which and how many segments should be targeted.

Positioning
- Understand consumer perceptions.
- Position products in the mind of the consumer.
- Design appropriate marketing mix.

strategy. The actions of NCR and Apple described above illustrate that careful focusing of resources is essential.

Positioning the Product

Companies must decide precisely how and where in targeted segments to aim a product or products, brand or brands. The needs and wants of targeted customers must be translated into a tangible mix of product/service, price, promotion and distribution. The consumers' view of the product and where it is positioned relative to the competition is particularly critical. After all, the paying public does not always perceive a product or brand in the way the manufacturer would like. The Sinclair C5, for example, was, to the dismay of those who developed it, perceived as an object of ridicule.

SELECTING SEGMENTATION VARIABLES

Segmentation variables or **bases** are the dimensions or characteristics of individuals, groups or organisations that are used for dividing a total market into segments. There is no single or best way to segment a market. Companies must choose from an array of different options.[1,2] In consumer markets, background customer characteristics like age, sex and occupation—which are relatively easy to obtain and measure through observation and questioning—are very widely used. In organisational markets, customer size, location and product use are often the focus.

Several factors are considered in selecting segmentation variables. The variables chosen should relate to customers' needs for, uses of or behaviour towards the product. Indeed, there is no "magic" associated with segmentation. Clifford and Cavanagh succinctly put the technique into perspective:

> High growth companies succeed by identifying and meeting the needs of ce~~rtain kinds of~~
> customer, not all customers, for special kinds of products and service, not all p~~roducts and~~
> services. Business academics call this market segmentation. Entrepreneurs c~~all it common~~
> sense.[3]

TABLE 3.1 *Variables for segmenting consumer markets*

BASIC CUSTOMER CHARACTERISTICS

Because of the ease with which information concerning basic customer characteristics can be obtained and measured, the use of these variables is widespread.

DEMOGRAPHICS

Age
Sex
Family
Race
Religion

The family life-cycle concept is an imaginative way of combining demographic variables.

SOCIO-ECONOMICS

Income
Occupation
Education
Social class

Different income groups have different aspirations in terms of cars, housing, education, etc.

GEOGRAPHIC LOCATION

Country
Region
Type of urban area (conurbation/village)
Type of housing (affluent suburbs/inner city)

PERSONALITY, MOTIVES AND LIFESTYLE

Holiday companies often use lifestyle to segment the market. Club Med, for example, concentrates on young singles while other tour operators cater especially for senior citizens or young families.

PRODUCT RELATED BEHAVIOURAL CHARACTERISTICS

PURCHASE BEHAVIOUR

Customers for frozen ready meals may be highly brand loyal to Heinz or Birds Eye or may shop purely on the basis of price.

PURCHASE OCCASION

A motorist making an emergency purchase of a replacement tyre, while on a trip far from home, is less likely to haggle about price than the customer who has a chance to "shop around".

BENEFITS SOUGHT

When customers buy washing powder or fabric conditioner they seek different benefits. For some, cleaning power and softness are essential while for others a product's environmental friendliness is the key. Ecover products try to cater for this latter group.

CONSUMPTION BEHAVIOUR AND USER STATUS

Examining consumption patterns can indicate where companies should be concentrating their efforts. Light or non-users are often neglected. The important question to ask is why consumption in these groups is low.

ATTITUDE TO PRODUCT

Different customers have different perceptions and preferences of products offered. Car manufacturers from Skoda to Porsche are in the business of designing cars to match customer preferences, changing perceptions as necessary.

Stereo equipment marketers might segment the stereo market on the basis of income and age—but not on the basis of religion, because one person's music equipment needs do not differ much from those of persons of other religions. Furthermore, if individuals or organisations in a total market are to be classified accurately, the segmentation variable must be measurable. For example, segmenting a market on the basis of intelligence or moral standards would be quite difficult because these attributes are hard to measure accurately.

Variables for Segmenting Consumer Markets

Companies developing their strategy for segmentation can choose one or several variables or bases from a wide range of choices. Table 3.1 comprehensively illustrates the options available for the marketer of consumer goods. These divide into variables like demographics and socio-economics that relate to basic customer characteristics and product related behavioural factors, such as purchase and usage behaviour.

TABLE 3.2 *European population statistics and projections (000's)*

	POPULATION AT LAST CENSUS				PREDICTION FOR 1995		
	Year	0–14	15–64	65+	0–14	15–64	65+
BELGIUM	1981	1,972	6,422	1,415	1,766	6,404	1,559
DENMARK	1981	968	3,151	1,005	849	3,455	804
FRANCE	1982	n/a	n/a	n/a	11,194	37,338	7,807
WEST GERMANY	1970	14,071	38,574	8,006	9,502	41,004	9,477
GREECE	1981	n/a	n/a	n/a	2,347	6,434	1,387
IRELAND	1981	1,044	2,030	369	1,161	2,533	389
ITALY	1981	12,128	36,944	7,485	9,307	39,071	9,128
LUXEMBOURG	1981	67	248	50	71	253	49
NETHERLANDS	1971	n/a	n/a	n/a	2,653	10,325	2,050
PORTUGAL	1981	n/a	n/a	n/a	2,129	7,263	1,427
SPAIN	1981	9,686	20,189	7,871	7,647	26,745	5,630
UNITED KINGDOM	1981	11,455	35,465	8,169	11,593	37,385	9,166

SOURCES: UN Population and Vital Statistics Report; National Statistical Offices; UN World Population Prospects, European Marketing Data and Statistics, 1990.

Basic Customer Characteristics

Demographic Variables.   The ease with which demographic variables can be measured has largely contributed to their widespread usage in segmenting markets. The characteristics most often used include age, sex, family, race and religion. Because these factors can be closely related to customers' product needs and purchasing behaviour, understanding them often helps target their efforts more effectively. Manufacturers of house cleaners and bleaches, such as Lever and Procter & Gamble, offer their products in a range of different sizes to satisfy the needs of consumers ranging from singles to large families.

Age is widely used for segmentation purposes. The marketing of ready to eat breakfast cereals is typical of this. For example, Kellogg's targets children with fun products designed to appeal to younger tastes—Frosties and Coco Pops. Meanwhile, the more nutrition and fitness conscious adult market is served with high fibre and low sugar products such as Nutri Grain and Fruit 'n Fibre. In the service sector too there is no longer a standard offering for all. For example, in banking, efforts are increasingly focused on age related segments. The very young customer, university undergraduates and people over 50 are all offered packages tailored to their particular needs.

Population statistics help marketers to understand and keep track of changing age profiles. The population of Europe, which is increasing at a rate of 0.6 per cent a year, expects to see a 25 per cent fall in the 15 to 25 year old age band between 1985 and 1995, with the biggest drop in Germany and Denmark (see Table 3.2). Over the same time period, however, the number of 25 to 45 year olds is expected to rise. Given the relative affluence of this particular group, a wide range of companies (for example, the leisure and service industries) might expect to reap the benefits of this increase by the turn of the century. Interestingly, though the advertisement in Figure 3.6 is promoting a newspaper for children aged 8 to 12, it is also targeted towards these children's parents, who are most likely to be in the 25 to 45 year old group.

In some markets, including clothes, cosmetics, alcoholic drinks, book

FIGURE 3.6
Combining segmentation variables
In this advertisement, *The Daily Telegraph* is promoting its newspaper for children, while targeting its message to both older and younger readers.

SOURCE: Courtesy of the Daily Telegraph.

and even cigarettes, gender has long been a key demographic variable. In other markets, its use is more recent. European Community statistics show that while women and girls represent 51.4 per cent of the population, men and boys account for 48.6 per cent. The confectionery market is one which traditionally did not segment on the basis of sex. Chocolate manufacturers, including Cadburys, tried to change this by developing assortments aimed primarily at men. In general, despite the care which was taken in each product's design, packaging and promotion, they were not successful.

Marketers have also turned to ethnicity as a means of segmenting markets for goods such as food, music and clothing, and for services such as banking and insurance. The US Hispanic population illustrates the importance of ethnicity as a segmentation variable. Comprising people of Mexican, Cuban, Puerto Rican, and Central and South American heritage, this ethnic group is growing five times faster than the general population. Consequently, more and more companies that market consumer packaged goods—including Campbell Soup Co. and Procter & Gamble—have been targeting US Hispanic consumers. They view the Hispanic segment as attractive because of its size and growth potential. However, targeting Hispanic customers is not an easy task. For example, although marketers have long believed that Hispanic consumers are exceptionally brand loyal and prefer Spanish language broadcast media, recent research has failed to support this notion. Not only do advertisers disagree about the merits of Spanish language media; they also question whether it is appropriate to advertise to Mexicans, Puerto Ricans and Cubans using a common Spanish language.[4] Each culture has its own unique language—thus, to lump Hispanic groups together does not

FIGURE 3.7
Pattern of expenditure by decile groups of gross income (1991)

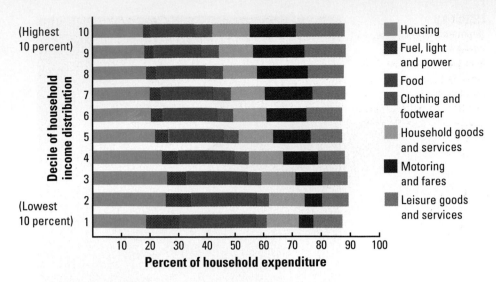

FIGURE 3.7
Pattern of expenditure by decile groups of gross income (1991)

Note: Percentages are expenditure on commodity or service group as a percentage of total household expenditure.

SOURCE: "Family Expenditure Survey", Central Statistical Office, 1991. Reprinted by permission of the Controller of Her Majesty's Stationery Office.

allow the message to effectively reach each segment. These findings suggest that marketers should carefully research the Hispanic market segment before developing marketing mixes for it.

Product needs also vary according to marital status and by number and age of children. Figure 3.7 illustrates patterns of expenditure on a full range of products for different household types. These factors are collectively taken into consideration by the *family life-cycle* concept. Some of the more obvious markets where the impact of different life-cycles is seen are tourism, housing and financial services. The family life-cycle has been broken down in several different ways. Table 3.3 illustrates a fairly comprehensive scheme which is sometimes used.

TABLE 3.3 *Wells and Gubar life-cycle stages*

Bachelor stage (young single people not living with parents)
Newly married couples without children
Full nest I (youngest child under 6)
Full nest II (youngest child 6 or over)
Full nest III (older married couple with dependent children)
Empty nest I (no children living at home, family head in work)
Empty nest II (family head retired)
Solitary survivor (in work)
Solitary survivor (retired)

SOURCE: From *Consumer Market Research Handbook*, 3rd ed., R. Worcester and J. Downham, eds. (ESOMAR) (England: McGraw-Hill Book Company (UK) Ltd, 1986), p. 394. Courtesy of the European Society for Opinion and Marketing Research, Amsterdam.

FIGURE 3.8

Segmentation according to socio-economic variables

This advertisement clearly aims at consumers who are high earners.

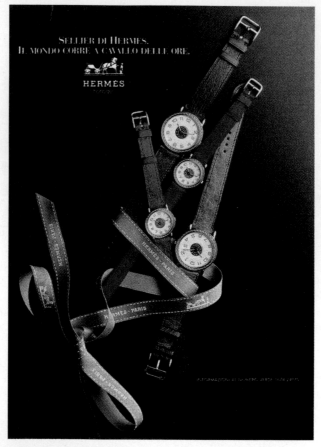

SOURCE: Courtesy of Hermes.

The scheme is based on the assumption that individuals in different life-cycle stages have varying product needs. Marketers can respond to this by targeting such groups with marketing mixes designed to capitalise on the differences. For example, parents whose children have grown up and left home tend to have more disposable income than those with young children. Relative spend on the home, holidays and new cars therefore tends to be higher. Critics of the life-cycle concept point out that it can be difficult to decide to which categories families belong. In some cases, such as single-parent families and couples without children, households do not appear to fit in at all.

Obviously, this discussion of demographic variables is not exhaustive. However, the variables described above probably represent the most widely used demographics. Other examples of the use of demographics include segmenting the cosmetic and hair-care markets on the basis of race and directing certain types of foods and clothing towards people of specific religious sects.

Socio-Economic Variables. This group of variables includes income, occupation, education and social class. Some marketing academics and practitioners include certain of these variables under the demographics label.

Income can be a very useful way of dividing markets because it strongly influences people's product needs. It affects their ability to buy (discussed in Chapter 2) and their aspirations for a certain style of living. Obvious products in this category include housing, furniture, clothing, cars, food and certain kinds of sporting goods. For example, the watches shown in Figure 3.8 are clearly aimed at very high earners.

The occupation of the household head is known to have an impact on the types of products and services which are purchased. The type of housing which individuals and families own or rent is strongly linked to this variable (see Table 3.4). It is obvious, for example, that sales of products for refurbishment and decoration, such as paints, fabrics and wallpapers, will be dominated by those professions which have owner-occupier status.

Other socio-economic variables which may be used to segment markets include education level and social class. For example, both of these variables are frequently used to aggregate readers of daily newpapers.

Geographic Variables.   The needs of consumers in different geographic locations may be affected by their local climate, terrain, natural resources and population density. Markets may be divided into regions because one or more geographic variables may cause customers' needs to differ from one region to another. A company that sells products throughout the European Community will, for example, need to reflect the different languages spoken in the labelling of its goods.

City size can be an important segmentation variable. Some marketers want to focus their efforts on cities of a certain size. For example, one franchised restaurant organisation will not locate in cities of less than 100,000 people. It has concluded that a smaller population base could make the operation unprofitable. The same company may add a second, or even a third, restaurant once the city reaches a certain size. Other firms, however, seek out opportunities in smaller towns. The major petroleum retailers, such as Esso and Shell, have traffic density thresholds, below which they perceive a local market as unviable. It is, therefore, quite common—particularly in villages and small towns in rural areas—for petroleum retailing to be dominated by independent garage owners and the smaller petroleum companies.

Market density refers to the number of potential customers within a unit of land area, such as a square kilometre (1,200 square yards). Although market density is generally related to population density, the correlation is not exact. For example, in two different geographic markets of approximately equal size and population, the market density for office supplies might be much higher in the first than in the second if the first contains a significantly greater proportion of business customers. Market density may be a useful segmentation variable because low density markets often require different sales advertising, and distribution activities from high density markets.

In Europe, climate can be used as a geographic segmentation variable. Companies entering new markets in Europe increasingly need to consider the impact of climate on their customer base. For example, washing machines sold in Italy do not require such fast spin speeds as those sold in Germany because the climate is much sunnier. Other markets affected by climate include air conditioning and heating equipment, clothing, gardening equipment, recreational products and building materials.

Locality: ACORN.   ACORN (A Classification of Residential Neighbourhoods) develops geographic location as a segmentation base one stage further. Information taken from census data allows people to be grouped according to a number of factors, including geography, socio-economics and culture. In total, 40 different variables are considered, among them household size, number of cars, type of occupation and family size and characteristics.

The underlying concept is that customers living in different residential neighbourhoods have different profiles in respect of these variables. Their product needs in terms of styling and features therefore also vary. Consumers can be cla   ACORN on the basis of the postcode of their home. They can then be all of the groups in Table 3.5.

TABLE 3.4 *Expenditure of household by occupation of head of household (000's)*

	OCCUPATION OF HEAD OF HOUSEHOLD							
	Profes-sional	Employers and managers	Inter-mediate non-manual	Junior non-manual	Skilled manual	Semi-skilled manual	Unskilled manual	All house-holds with employee heads
TOTAL NUMBER OF HOUSEHOLDS	290	770	459	423	983	537	166	3,698
TOTAL NUMBER OF PERSONS	844	2,187	1,147	987	2,980	1,458	472	10,276
TOTAL NUMBER OF ADULTS	579	1,547	858	725	2,109	1,016	321	7,287
HOUSING BY TYPE OF TENURE								
Rented unfurnished	11	39	53	69	232	197	82	712
Local authority	5	25	36	50	183	157	75	549
Housing association	2	7	5	5	29	17	4	71
Other	4	7	12	14	20	23	3	92
Rented furnished	21	22	34	27	19	21	3	165
Rent-free	13	7	11	9	7	22	2	73
Owner-occupied	245	702	361	318	725	297	79	2,748
In process of purchase	219	621	308	259	615	223	53	2,318
Owned outright	26	81	53	59	110	74	26	430

SOURCE: "Family Expenditure Survey", Central Statistical Office, 1991. Reprinted by permission of the Controller of Her Majesty's Stationery Office.

TABLE 3.5 *The* ACORN *consumer targeting classification*

CATEGORIES	% POP.	GROUPS	% POP.
A Thriving	19.8	1 Wealthy Achievers, Suburban Areas	15.1
		2 Affluent Greys, Rural Communities	2.3
		3 Prosperous Pensioners, Retirement Areas	2.3
B Expanding	11.6	4 Affluent Executives, Family Areas	3.7
		5 Well-off Workers, Family Areas	7.8
C Rising	7.5	6 Afflluent Urbanites, Town & City Areas	2.2
		7 Prosperous Professionals, Metropolitan Areas	2.1
		8 Better-Off Executives, Inner City Areas	3.2
D Settling	24.1	9 Comfortable Middle Agers, Mature Home Owning Areas	13.4
		10 Skilled Workers, Home Owning Areas	10.7
E Aspiring	13.7	11 New Home Owners, Mature Communities	9.8
		12 White Collar Workers, Better-Off Multi-Ethnic Areas	4.0
F Striving	22.8	13 Older People, Less Prosperous Areas	3.6
		14 Council Estate Residents, Better-Off Homes	11.6
		15 Council Estate Residents, High Unemployment	2.7
		16 Council Estate Residents, Greatest Hardship	2.8
		17 People in Multi-Ethnic, Low-Income Areas	2.1
Unclassified	0.5		0.5

SOURCE: © CACI Limited, 1993 (Source: OPCS and GRO(S) © Crown Copyright 1991). All rights reserved. ACORN is a registered servicemark of CACI Limited.

These categories further subdivide to give a total of 17 groups and 54 neighborhood types (see Figure 3.9). For example, the Aspiring (E) category splits into:

- new home owners, mature communities
- white collar workers, better-off multi-ethnic areas

FIGURE 3.9

ACORN Category C, Group 6, Type 17
CACI's ACORN classification, based on demographic data from the Census, is used extensively by marketers and planners in Great Britain for profiling purchasing and lifestyle behaviour. ACORN classifies people into 6 categories, which are subdivided into 17 groups and 54 neighborhood types. This illustration is for ACORN category C, Group 6, Type 17: Flats & Mortgages, Singles & Young Working Couples. This type is found in affluent areas in London, the Home Counties and central Scotland.

SOURCE: CACI and ACORN are the trademarks and/or servicemarks of CACI Limited.

Personality, Motives and Lifestyle.   Marketers sometimes use variables such as personality characteristics, motives and lifestyle to segment markets. The variables can be used by themselves to segment a market or in combination with other types.

Personality characteristics are useful when a product is similar to many competing products and consumers' needs are not significantly affected by other segmentation variables. However, attempting to segment a market according to personality characteristics has caused problems. Although marketing practitioners have long believed that consumer choice and product use should vary with personality and lifestyle, marketing research has shown only weak relationships. However, the weakness of such relationships may not be the result of lack of association between consumer choice and personality traits. Personality traits are difficult to measure accurately, because most existing personality tests were developed for clinical use, not for segmentation purposes. As the reliability of more recent measurement instruments increases, a greater association between personality and consumer behaviour has been demonstrated.[5] It has been shown that personality sometimes influences the clothes, make-up and hair styles which individuals adopt. Links with other purchase behaviour also seem likely.

When a market is segmented according to a motive, it is divided on the basis of consumers' reasons for making a purchase. Product durability, economy, convenience and status are all motives affecting the types of product purchased and the choice of stores in which they are bought. For example, one motive for the purchase of large jars of supermarket branded instant coffee is economy. At the other extreme, some customers visit specialist coffee retailers so that their coffee beans can be ground to order. Such retailers market their product in terms of its status to consumers who place particular importance on their self-image.

TABLE 3.6 *Characteristics related to activities, interests and opinions*

ACTIVITIES	INTERESTS	OPINIONS
Work	Family	Themselves
Hobbies	Home	Social issues
Social events	Job	Politics
Vacation	Community	Business
Entertainment	Recreation	Economics
Club membership	Fashion	Education
Community	Food	Products
Shopping	Media	Future
Sports	Achievements	Culture

SOURCE: Reprinted, adapted, from Joseph Plummer, "The concept and application of life style segmentation", *Journal of Marketing*, January 1974, p. 34. Reprinted by permission of the American Marketing Association.

Lifestyle segmentation groups individuals according to how they spend their time, the importance of items in their surroundings (their homes or their jobs, for example), their beliefs about themselves and broad issues, and some socio-economic characteristics such as income and education.[6] Lifestyle analysis provides a broad view of buyers because it encompasses numerous characteristics related to people's activities, interests and opinions (see Table 3.6). It can be thought of as going beyond a simple understanding of personality.

Psychographics is the main technique used to measure lifestyle. However, its use has been, and probably will continue to be, limited for several reasons. First, psychographic variables are more difficult to measure accurately than are other types of segmentation variables. Second, the relationships among psychographic variables and consumers' needs are sometimes obscure and unproven. Third, segments that result from psychographic segmentation may not be reachable.[7] For example, a marketer may determine that highly compulsive individuals want a certain type of clothing. However, no specific stores or particular media—such as television or radio programmes, newspapers or magazines—appeal precisely to this group and this group alone. Psychographic variables can sometimes offer a useful way of better understanding segments which have been defined using other base variables.

Product Related Behavioural Characteristics

Marketers can also segment markets on the basis of an aspect of consumers' behaviour towards the product. This might relate to the way the particular product is used or purchased, for example, or perhaps to the benefits which consumers require from it.

Purchase behaviour can be a useful way of distinguishing between groups of customers, giving marketers insight into the most appropriate marketing mix. For example, brand loyal customers may require a different kind of treatment from those who switch between brands. On pack sales promotions are often geared towards building loyalty in brand switchers.

It is often possible to distinguish between customers in terms of the occasion on which they buy a particular product. In different sets of circumstances the customer can be seen to apply different product selection criteria. Inevitably, this will have an impact on the choice which is made. For instance, a customer who replaces a car tyre in an emergency situation will probably be less concerned about price than one who is routinely maintaining his or her car.

Benefit segmentation is the division of a market according to the benefits consumers want from the product.[8] Although most types of market segmentation are based on the assumption that there is a relationship between the variable and customers' needs, benefit segmentation is different in that the benefits the customers seek *are* their product needs. Thus individuals are segmented directly according to their needs. By determining the benefits desired, marketers may be able to divide people into groups seeking certain sets of benefits. Marketing Insight 3.2 shows how the benefits sought by consumers from skin products are changing.

The effectiveness of benefit segmentation depends on several conditions. First, the benefits people seek must be identifiable. Second, using these benefits, marketers must be able to divide people into recognisable segments. Finally, one or more of the resulting segments must be accessible to the firms' marketing efforts.

Individuals can be divided into users and non-users of a particular product. Users can then be classified further as heavy, moderate or light. To satisfy a specific user group, marketers sometimes create a distinctive product, set special prices or initiate special promotion and distribution activities. Thus airlines such as British Airways or KLM offer frequent flier programmes to reward their regular customers with free trips and discounts for car hire and hotel accommodation. Light users or non-users of products often receive little attention from manufacturers. There is a tendency sometimes to dismiss these groups when developing a marketing programme. For example, research in the holiday industry tends to focus on feedback from current customers, often forgetting to question why non-users failed to buy.

How customers use or apply the product may also determine segmentation. To satisfy customers who use a product in a certain way, some feature—say, packaging, size, texture or colour—may have to be designed with special care to make the product easier to use, more convenient or more environmentally friendly. For instance, McDonald's increasingly packages its hamburgers in paper cartons because consumers are becoming concerned about the long term effects on the environment of using non-biodegradable packaging materials. In addition, special distribution, promotion or pricing activities may have to be created.

The varying attitude of customers towards products is another set of variables which can be used to segment markets. Clothing retailers like River Island and Zy are particularly conscious of this. While one customer seeks outfits which are practical and comfortable, another is concerned with achieving a highly fashionable image.

As this brief discussion shows, consumer markets can be divided according to numerous characteristics. However, some of these variables are not particularly helpful for segmenting industrial or organisational markets.

Variables for Segmenting Organisational Markets

Like consumer markets, industrial or organisational markets are sometimes segmented, but the marketer's aim is to satisfy the needs of organisations for products. Marketers may segment organisational markets according to geographic location, type of organisation, customer size and product use.

Geographic Location. The demand for some consumer products can vary considerably by geographic area because of differences in climate, terrain, customer preferences or similar factors. Demand for organisational products also varies according to geographic location. For example, the producers of certain types of timber divide their markets geographically because their customers' needs vary regionally. Geographic segmentation may be especially appropriate for reaching industries that are concen-

CRUELTY FREE COSMETICS: A GROWING NICHE

The skin care market is changing. In just five years, the UK market has grown to £328 million, up more than 25 per cent. The demographic profile of the market is also changing. As the proportion of older customers has increased, new opportunities have emerged for products designed with older skin in mind. The range of products aimed at the male customer is also on the increase. According to Cussons' Managing Director, "Even UK men, who were until recently unenthusiastic about personal washing, are becoming big users and purchasers of toiletries".

Retailers Sainsbury, Superdrug, Boots, Marks & Spencer, Co-Op and Tesco are responding to another market change. These retailers have joined the offensive in the market for cruelty free toiletries and cosmetics, with cruelty free retailer own label products proclaiming "Against Animal Testing", "Not Tested on Animals" and "Produced Without Cruelty to Animals". While this section has traditionally been the bastion of niche companies like Beauty Without Cruelty (BWC), changing customer concerns and values are now raising the stakes for major manufacturers to compete in this market.

The shift in consumer attitudes has occurred for a number of reasons. First, the appearance on the high street of Body Shop, with its natural, green image and cruelty free products, provided alternatives hitherto not readily available at the mass market level. Now Body Shop has been followed by a host of copy-cat, franchised organisations; and even the major retailers have followed suit. Second, there has been a steady increase in public concern for animal rights. An opinion poll in 1989 indicated that well over three quarters of the population are against animal testing in the preparation of cosmetics. In more recent research, Mintel discovered that nearly four out of ten adults make deliberate efforts to buy products which have not been tested on animals. Finally, support from the national press has helped to keep public concern about animal testing firmly on the agenda.

For pressure groups and consumers which support moves to reduce animal testing, this is good news. For manufacturers and retailers, it offers a strategic opportunity for new products. And for those companies which choose to continue testing their products on animals, the threat of reduced market share is very real. Consumer attitudes are unlikely to revert.

SOURCES: Steve McIvor, "Beauty and the Beasts", *Marketing Week,* 20 November 1992; Jo-Anne Walker, "Wash and Grow", *Marketing Week,* 20 November 1992; "Making a Clean Break", research by Nielsen, *Marketing Week,* 20 November 1992.

FIGURE 3.10
Single variable segmentation

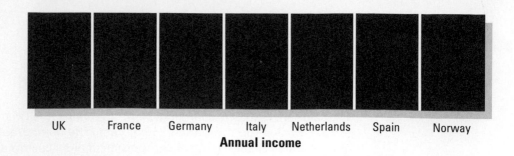

trated in certain locations, for example, textiles in West Yorkshire, cutlery in Sheffield, brewing in Burton and lace in Nottingham. Examples of such concentration in Europe include heavy industry around Lille or in the Ruhr Valley and banking in Zurich.

Type of Organisation.   A company sometimes segments a market by the types of organisations within that market. Different types of organisations often require different product features, distribution systems, price structures and selling strategies. Given these variations, a firm may either concentrate on a single segment with one marketing mix (concentration strategy) or focus on several groups with multiple mixes (multisegment strategy). A paint manufacturer could segment customers into several groups, such as paint wholesalers, do-it-yourself retail outlets, vehicle manufacturers, decorators and housing developers.

Customer Size.   An organisation's size may affect its purchasing procedures and the types and quantities of products it wants. Size can thus be an effective variable for segmenting an organisational market. To reach a segment of a particular size, marketers may have to adjust one or more marketing mix components. For example, customers who buy in extremely large quantities are sometimes offered discounts. In addition, marketers often have to expand personal selling efforts to serve larger organisational buyers properly. Because the needs of larger and smaller buyers tend to be quite distinct, marketers frequently use different marketing practices to reach various customer groups.

Use of Product.   Certain products, especially basic raw materials such as steel, petrol, plastics and timber, are used in numerous ways. How a company uses products affects the types and amounts of the products purchased, as well as the method of making the purchase. For example, computers are used for engineering purposes, basic scientific research and business operations such as word processing, bookkeeping and telephone service. A computer producer may segment the computer market by types of use because organisations' needs for computer hardware and software depend on the purpose for which the products are purchased.

Single Variable or Multivariable Segmentation

Selecting the appropriate variable for market segmentation is an important marketing management decision, because the variable is the primary factor in defining the target market. So far, segmentation by one variable has been discussed. In fact, more than one variable can be used, and marketers must decide on the number of variables to include.

Single variable segmentation is achieved by using only one variable. The segmentation shown in Figure 3.10 is based on country of origin alone. (Although the areas on the graph are the same size, the segments are not necessarily equal in size or sales potential.) Single variable segmentation, the simplest form of segmentation, is

FIGURE 3.11
*Multivariable
segmentation*

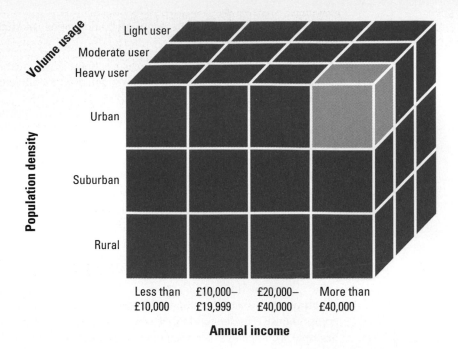

the easiest to perform. However, a single characteristic gives marketers only moderate precision in designing a marketing mix to satisfy individuals in a specific segment.

To achieve **multivariable segmentation,** more than one characteristic is used to divide a total market (see Figure 3.11). Notice in the figure that the market is segmented by three variables: annual income, population density and volume usage. The people in the highlighted segment earn more than £40,000, are urban dwellers and are heavy users. Multivariable segmentation provides more information about the individuals in each segment than does single variable segmentation. More is known about the people in each segment of Figure 3.11 than about those in the segments of Figure 3.10. This additional information may allow a company to develop a marketing mix that will satisfy customers in a given segment more precisely.

The major disadvantage of multivariable segmentation is that the larger the number of variables used, the greater the number of resulting segments. This proliferation reduces the sales potential of many of the segments. Compare, for example, the number and size of the segments in Figure 3.10 with the number and size of those in Figure 3.11.

The use of additional variables can help create and maintain a more exact and satisfying marketing mix. However, when deciding on single variable or multivariable segmentation, a marketing manager must consider whether additional variables will actually help improve the firm's marketing mix. If using a second or third variable does not provide information that ensures greater precision, there is little reason to spend more money to gain information about the extra variables.

SEGMENTATION EFFECTIVENESS

Whatever base variables are used, haphazard implementation can lead to ineffective market segmentation, missed opportunities and inappropriate investment. Satisfying the following criteria can help to avoid problems of this type. The first assumption is that there are real differences, after all, in the needs of consumers for the product or service. There is no value in segmenting a homogeneous market. In addition, segments revealed must be

- *measurable:* easy to identify and measure. Some basis must be found for effectively separating individuals into groups or segments with relatively homogeneous product or service needs.
- *substantial:* large enough to be sufficiently profitable to justify developing and maintaining a specific marketing mix.
- *accessible:* easy to reach with the marketing mix developed. For example, the promotional effort should target the relevant consumers.
- *stable:* the question of segment stability over time is not often addressed. If companies are to make strategic decisions on the basis of revealed segments, they need to be reasonably certain that those segments will be around long enough for action to be taken.

UNDERSTANDING THE PROFILE OF MARKET SEGMENTS

Whatever the variable, or combination of variables, used to group customers, a more comprehensive understanding of what those individuals are like will be needed. For example, a company which segments the market for shoes on the basis of age, focusing on customers in their late teens, would do well to understand as much as possible about its particular target group in other respects. What reference groups influence them? Where do they live? Where and when do they shop? What social background are they from? What motivates them? The more comprehensive the image developed, the better the opportunity to develop an effective marketing mix with maximum appeal.

Building up a fuller picture of target segments is sometimes called profiling; the variables used in the description are termed **descriptors.** The types of descriptors available to marketers are the same as the variables used to segment markets in the first place, that is, demographics, socio-economics and so on. This is sometimes a cause of confusion for students who struggle to remember whether they are dealing with base or descriptor variables. The simplest explanation is that while base variables should discriminate between customer needs, descriptors are simply used to enrich the picture, to help summarise what else can be gleaned about the customers in a particular segment. This gives added inspiration to the creative team developing the product and promotional material and helps to fine-tune decisions on price and distribution. Overall, the aim is to maximise the impact of the marketing mix on the customer, relative to the competition.

TARGETING STRATEGIES

Decisions about targeting centre on two major segmentation strategies: the concentration strategy and the multisegment strategy. Whether a company chooses to adopt one or the other, the decisions which are made should be based on a clear understanding of company capabilities and resources, the nature of the competition and the characteristics of the product markets in question.

Concentration Strategy

When an organisation directs its marketing efforts towards a single market segment by creating and maintaining one marketing mix, it is employing a **concentration strategy.** The fashion house Chanel, for example, targets the exclusive fashion segment, directing its marketing effort towards high income customers who want to own the most chic apparel. The chief advantage of the concentration strategy is that it allows a firm

FIGURE 3.12
Multisegment strategy

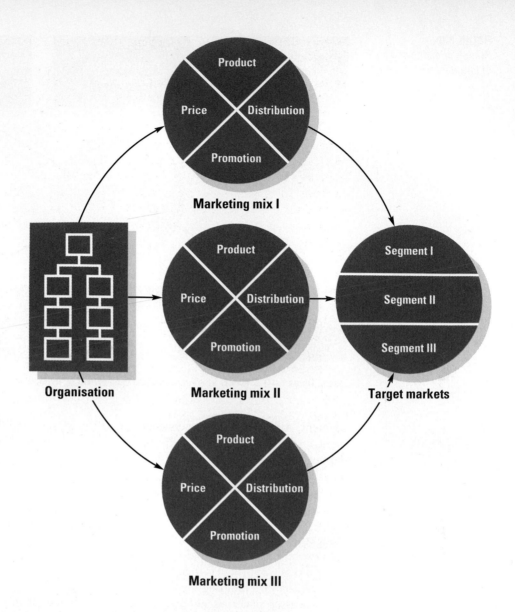

Marketing mix I

Marketing mix II

Organisation

Target markets

Marketing mix III

to specialise. The firm can analyse the characteristics and needs of a distinct customer group and then focus all its energies on satisfying that group's needs. A firm can generate a large sales volume by reaching a single segment. In addition, concentrating on a single segment permits a firm with limited resources to compete with much larger organisations, which may have overlooked some smaller segments.

Concentrating on one segment also means that a company puts all its eggs in one basket—clearly a disadvantage. If a company's sales depend on a single segment and the segment's demand for the product declines, the company's financial strength declines as well. Moreover, when a firm penetrates one segment and becomes well entrenched, its popularity may keep it from moving into other segments. For example, Ferrari would have trouble moving into the economy car segment, whereas Lada would find it difficult to enter the luxury car segment.

Multisegment Strategy

With a **multisegment strategy** (see Figure 3.12), an organisation directs its marketing efforts at two or more segments by developing a marketing mix for each selec

FIGURE 3.13
Factors affecting choice of target market strategy

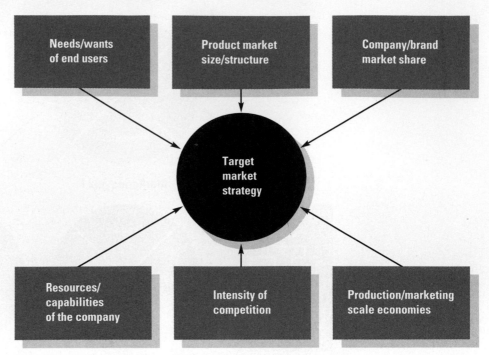

SOURCE: Data from D. Cravens, *Strategic Marketing* (Homewood, III: Irwin, 1982).

segment. After a firm uses a concentration strategy successfully in one market segment, it sometimes expands its efforts to additional segments. For example, Jockey underwear has traditionally been aimed at one segment: men. However, the company now markets underwear for women and children as well. The marketing mixes used for a multisegment strategy may vary as to product differences, distribution methods, promotion methods and prices.

A business can usually increase its sales in the aggregate market through a multisegment strategy because the firm's mixes are being aimed at more people. A company with excess production capacity may find a multisegment strategy advantageous because the sale of products to additional segments may absorb this excess capacity. On the other hand, a multisegment strategy often demands a greater number of production processes, materials and people; thus production costs may be higher than with a concentration strategy. Keep in mind also that a firm using a multisegment strategy ordinarily experiences higher marketing costs. Because this strategy usually requires more research and several different promotion plans and distribution methods, the costs of planning, organising, implementing and controlling marketing activities increase. Figure 3.13 highlights the factors which affect the choice of target market segments and which require consideration prior to entering a particular segment or segments.

POSITIONING

Figure 3.5 illustrated the link between market segmentation, targeting and positioning. Having identified the segments in a market and decided on which segment (or segments) to target, a company must position its product, service or idea. According to Wind, a product's positioning is the place a product occupies in a given market, as perceived by the relevant group of customers; that group of customers is known as the target segment of the market.[9]

Harrison states that the position of a product is

the sum of those attributes normally ascribed to it by the consumers—its standing, its quality, the type of people who use it, its strengths, its weaknesses, any other unusual or memorable characteristics it may possess, its price and the value it represents.[10]

Positioning starts with a product—a piece of merchandise, a service, a company, an institution or even a person. **Positioning** is not what is done to the product, it is what is created in the minds of the target customers; the product is positioned in the minds of these customers and is given an image.[11] There may be a few cosmetic changes to the product—to its name, price, packaging, styling or channel of distribution—but these are to facilitate the successful promotion of the image desired by the target customers. The product must be perceived by the selected target customers to have a distinct image and position vis-à-vis its competitors. Product differentiation is widely viewed as the key to successful marketing; the product must stand out and have a clearly defined position.

Determining a Position

Positions are described by variables and within parameters which are important to the customers and which essentially are selected by them. Price may be the key in grocery shopping, service level in selecting a bank, quality and reliability in buying computer hardware, value for money in choosing which theme park to visit. In-depth market research (often focus group discussions) is required if customer motivations and expectations in a particular market are to be fully understood. Management's intuition is not always sufficient. For example, research revealed that consumers often have to decide between replacement living-room or dining-room furniture and a family package holiday abroad. Managers at most leading furniture retailers perceived other furniture retailers to be their competitors, when in reality they were additionally competing for consumers' disposable income against other diverse product areas. In this budget conscious sector of the furniture buying market, retailers believed only price to be important. In-depth research proved that value for money, a concept which includes product quality and durability in addition to price, was perceived to be the main purchase consideration.

Consumers generally assign positions to a company or a product which is the market leader—and which probably has the highest profile—and the limited number of competitors they can recollect are oriented to this market leader. Occasionally the brand which consumers regard as the market leader may not be the genuine market leader in terms of market share, but simply the one most visible at that time, possibly because of heavy promotional exposure. Customers respond to the attributes of a product and to its promotional imagery, but the product's position as perceived by its target customers is affected by the reputation and image of the company, coupled with its other products, and by the activities of its competitors. For example, bad publicity, such as that recently experienced by British Airways following allegations of dirty tricks against Virgin Atlantic, can negatively affect a brand's positioning.

In-depth market research leads to an understanding of how consumers perceive products, which marketing variables they believe to be most important and by what magnitude. Such research examines consumer perceptions of various brands or companies which operate in the market under scrutiny. **Perceptual mapping** is a tool commonly adopted by marketers and marketing researchers to visually depict such

FIGURE 3.14
Positioning map of hypothetical consumer preferences

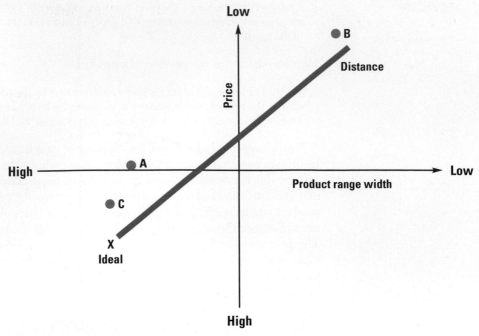

SOURCE: From D. Knee and D. Walters, *Strategy in Retailing* (Herts., England: Philip Allan, 1985), p. 27. Reproduced by permission of Philip Allan, a division of Prentice-Hall International.

consumer perceptions and prioritising of brands and their perceived attributes. Figure 3.14 illustrates a hypothetical example in which consumers thought product range width and price were the key characteristics of the market. A cross marks the ideal position, with high product range width and above average price (typical of high quality shopping goods such as cameras or hi-fi systems). Brands (or companies) *A* and *C* are perceived as being relatively close to the ideal—their pricing policy does not fully match the image required—but brand (or company) *B* is viewed as being too cheap, with inadequate product range width. Figure 3.15 illustrates how consumers of children's wear in the UK realised that the positioning of Adams (see Case 3.1) had shifted to reflect improvements in the quality of its merchandise, stores and personnel. Adams had successfully repositioned its brand to move away from being perceived as a budget orientated retailer.

Steps in Determining a Positioning Plan

There should be no mystique associated with positioning a product. Common sense and a step-by-step approach lead to a product's clear positioning:

1. Define the segments in a particular market.
2. Decide which segment (or segments) to target.
3. Understand what the target consumers expect and believe to be most important when deciding on the purchase.
4. Develop a product (or products) which caters specifically for these needs and expectations.
5. Evaluate the positioning and images, as perceived by the target customers, of competing products in the selected market segment (or segments).
6. Select an image which sets the product (or products) apart from the competing products, thus ensuring that the chosen image matches the aspirations of the target customers. (The selected positioning and imagery must be credible: consumers

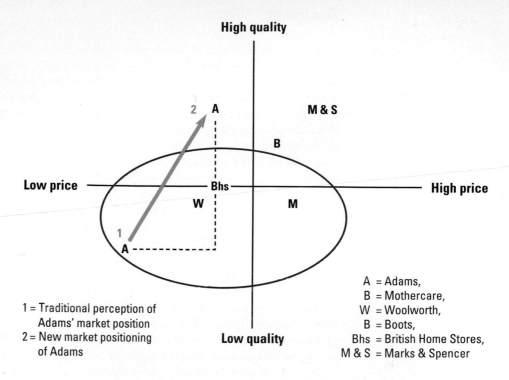

1 = Traditional perception of Adams' market position
2 = New market positioning of Adams

A = Adams,
B = Mothercare,
W = Woolworth,
B = Boots,
Bhs = British Home Stores,
M & S = Marks & Spencer

would not believe Lada or Skoda if they promoted their cars in the same manner as Porsche or Lotus.)

7. Tell target consumers about the product (promotion) as well as making it readily available at the right price: this is the development of the full marketing mix.

EVALUATING MARKETS AND FORECASTING SALES

Whether taking a total market approach or opting for segmentation, a marketer must be able to measure the sales potential of the chosen target market or markets. Moreover, a marketing manager must determine the portion or share of the selected market that the firm can capture relative to its objectives, resources and managerial skills, as well as to those of its competitors. Developing and maintaining a marketing mix consume a considerable amount of a company's resources. Thus the target market or markets selected must have enough sales potential to justify the costs of developing and maintaining one or more marketing mixes.

The potential for sales can be measured along several dimensions, including product, geographic area, time and level of competition.[12] With respect to product, potential sales can be estimated for a specific product item (for example, Diet Coke) or an entire product line (for example, Coca-Cola, Coca-Cola classic, Diet Coke, Diet caffeine-free Coke, and Cherry Coca-Cola are one product line). A manager must also determine the geographic area to be included in the estimate. In relation to time, sales potential estimates can be short range (one year or less), medium range (one to five years), or long range (longer than five years). The competitive level specifies whether sales are being estimated for a single firm or for an entire industry. Thus marketers measure sales potential both for the entire market and for their own firms and then develop a sales forecast. A detailed discussion of market potential, sales potential and sales forecasting is given in Chapter 20.

Summary

A market is an aggregate of people who, as individuals or as organisations, have needs for products in a product class and who have the ability, willingness and authority to purchase such products. A consumer market consists of purchasers and/or individuals in their households who intend to consume or benefit from the purchased products and who do not buy products for the main purpose of making a profit. An organisational or industrial market consists of persons and groups who purchase a specific kind of product for resale, direct use in producing other products or use in day-to-day operations. Profit is not always necessarily a motive. Because products are classified according to use, the same product may be classified as both a consumer product and an organisational product.

Marketers use two general approaches to identify their target markets: the total market and the market segmentation approaches. A firm using a total market approach designs a single marketing mix and directs it at an entire market for a particular product. The total market approach can be effective when a large proportion of individuals in the total market have similar needs for the product and the organisation can develop and maintain a single marketing mix to satisfy those needs.

Markets made up of individuals with diverse product needs are called heterogeneous markets. The market segmentation approach divides the total market into groups consisting of people who have similar product needs. Profiling segments using descriptor variables can help the marketer build up a fuller picture and design a marketing mix (or mixes) that more precisely matches the needs of persons in a selected segment (or segments). A market segment is a group of individuals, groups or organisations sharing one or more similar characteristics that cause them to have relatively similar product needs. There are two major types of targeting strategy. In the concentration strategy, the organisation directs its marketing efforts towards a single market segment through one marketing mix. In the multisegment strategy, the organisation develops different marketing mixes for two or more segments. The decisions which are made about the appropriate segment or segments to enter are linked to (amongst others) considerations about company resources, expertise and the nature of customers and competitors.

Certain conditions must exist for market segmentation to be effective. First, consumers' needs for the product should be heterogeneous. Second, the segments of the market should be measurable so that the segments can be compared with respect to estimated sales potential, costs and profits. Third, at least one segment must be substantial enough to have the profit potential to justify developing and maintaining a special marketing mix for that segment. Fourth, the firm must be able to access the chosen segment with a particular marketing mix. Fifth, the segment should be reasonably stable over time.

Segmentation variables are the dimensions or characteristics of individuals, groups or organisations used for dividing a total market into segments. The segmentation variable should be related to customers' needs for, uses of or behaviour towards the product. Segmentation variables for consumer markets can be grouped into two broad categories which relate either to customer characteristics—demographics (age, sex, family, race, religion), socio-economics (income, occupation, education, social class), geography (country, region, urban area, housing), personality, motives and lifestyle— or to product related behaviour—purchase behavior and occasion, benefits sought, consumption behaviour and user status, and attitude to product. Segmentation variables for organisational markets include geographic factors, type of organisation, customer size and product use. Besides selecting the appropriate segmentation variable, a marketer must also decide how many variables to use. Single variable segmentation involves only one variable, but in multivariable segmentation, more than one characteristic is used to divide a total market.

Having decided which segment or segments to target, the marketer must position the product: it must have a clearly defined image in the minds of its target consumers. The product's positioning must be perceived by its consumers to be different from the positions of competing products. Perceptual maps assist marketers in graphically depicting the relative positions of the products in a particular market. Although a product's attributes and styling, along with its pricing, service levels and channel of distribution, contribute to how consumers perceive the product, a marketer uses mainly promotion to establish a product's positioning. Whichever segments marketers target, irrespective of the positioning adopted, they must be able to measure the sales potential of the target market or markets.

IMPORTANT TERMS

Market
Consumer market
Organisational, or industrial, market
Total market (or undifferentiated)
    approach
Heterogeneous markets
Market segmentation
Segmentation variables (bases)
Market density

Benefit segmentation
Single variable segmentation
Multivariable segmentation
Descriptors
Concentration strategy
Multisegment strategy
Positioning
Perceptual mapping

DISCUSSION AND REVIEW QUESTIONS

1. What is a market? What are the requirements for a market?
2. In your local area, is there a group of people with unsatisfied product needs who represent a market? Could this market be reached by a business organisation? Why or why not?
3. Identify and describe the two major types of market. Give examples of each.
4. What is the total market approach? Under what conditions is it most useful? Describe a current situation in which a company is using a total market approach. Is the business successful? Why or why not?
5. What is the market segmentation approach? Describe the basic conditions required for effective segmentation. Identify several firms that use the segmentation approach.
6. List the differences between the concentration and the multisegment strategies. Describe the advantages and disadvantages of each strategy.
7. Identify and describe four major categories of variables that can be used to segment consumer markets. Give examples of product markets that are segmented by variables in each category.
8. What dimensions are used to segment industrial or organisational markets?
9. How do marketers decide whether to use single variable or multivariable segmentation? Give examples of product markets that are divided through multivariable segmentation.
10. Choose a product and discuss how it could be best positioned in the mark

■ CASES

3.1 Targeting in Children's Wear

Until the launch of Terence Conran's Mothercare chain, children's clothes had been marketed through large department stores and independently owned single shops, with each town generally having two or three such specialists. Mothercare, offering clothes and hardware such as cots and prams to parents of infants and toddlers, was a tremendous success. Mothercare's financial worries in the 1980s coincided with the rise of Adams Childrenswear, part of the Sears retailing group. From its humble origins as a budget driven family business in the Midlands, Adams has become one of the UK's most successful retailers, with expansion plans in South East Asia, the Middle East and mainland Europe. Adams' success is the result of sound marketing principles: a well defined retailing formula clearly targeted at a specific market segment, with customer satisfaction a priority.

"Our mission is simple . . . To become the No. 1 specialist children's wear retailers in the United Kingdom through the achievement of excellence throughout our business". From being a loss-making "me too" in a market dominated by Mothercare, Woolworth and Boots, Adams has emerged as market leader. In 1987–88 net sales were £18 million from 126 stores; now they are close to £200 million from 300 stores and nationwide. The possibility of franchising the name, merchandise and concept outside the UK offers an opportunity for continued growth. Sears was sufficiently committed to the Adams operation and its proven ability to push sales beyond £300 per square foot to allocate £50 million for new store openings and refurbishment.

What has led to the success and turnaround of Adams? Clear thinking and the development of a marketing strategy have enabled the management to take advantage both of range omissions in Marks & Spencer and BhS and financial problems in Mothercare. Adams researched its market, evaluating each competitor and determining the positioning of the major players (see Figure 3.15). This analysis was supported by extensive marketing research designed to determine the needs and expectations of targeted consumers: children up to the age of eight, their parents and grandparents.

Traditionally, Adams' trading proposition had been price driven, but as the company knew, "Price alone will not be a sufficient differential advantage to take Adams forward to market leadership". Adams opted to focus on design—of stores and merchandise—and on quality, service, value and convenience. The consumer research revealed that product quality and durability dominated buyers' decision-making. Adams has an in-house quality control and product testing department which is well resourced and increasingly sets industry standards. Young mothers often lack time and mobility, so convenience of branch locations, entrances and store layout are key determinants of store choice. First-time parents are often inexperienced shoppers for children's wear, so Adams' training emphasises customer service and advice. With clothing retailer Next, furniture manufacturers IKEA, grocers Sainsbury and skin care products chain Body Shop all helping to create fashion and design conscious consumers, Adams' colourfully co-ordinated merchandise and stores have proved popular with its target market.

Behind the scenes, the company has invested heavily in systems and computer programmes to facilitate its expansion. All branches are networked to the Nuneaton headquarters with EPOS (electronic point-of-sale data capture), giving automatic stock replenishment and sales records. Major suppliers are directly linked to Adams' headquarters, with orders arriving as required to a fully automated and robotised warehouse and distribution centre. Computer packages assist with store location, layout and shelf space allocation, merchandise planning, stock control and distribution, credit control and financial planning.

Adams' understanding of its marketplace has led to further innovations. In 1992, the first branches of its new Pride & Joy chain opened. While rivals Boots and Mothercare cater to parents of infants, toddlers and young children, Adams has split these consumers into two segments. Prams, pushchairs, cots are bulky, slow moving items which shoppers with babies and very young children need but which eat up space in a children's clothing store. These consumers have more functional requirements for clothes and baby equipment than do families with children aged three to eight. Adams has focused its Pride & Joy operation directly on mothers-to-be and parents of very young children, leaving its Adams chain to target the children's market for clothes.

SOURCES: "Adams 1987–1992", Adams Childrenswear Ltd; John Thornhill, "Why eight is a lucky number", *Financial Times,* 13 December 1990; "Sears—Adams Childrenswear", *Harvest,* 1990 and 1993.

Questions for Discussion

1. What is Adams' target market?
2. How has Adams used the steps of the positioning process?
3. How is Adams positioned relative to its competitors?

3.2 JCB: Industrial Segments

Construction and agricultural equipment manufacturers produce a diversity of machines designed to cut and dig, carry and load, tunnel and excavate, climb on tracks up severe slopes or travel on public highways at speeds of up to 45 miles per hour. Some are designed to carry many tonnes of earth or rubble, others only small loads in often confined spaces.

The product ranges of most manufacturers have expanded gradually. Some companies have diversified and added new product groups, while others concentrate on developing improved models in existing product groups. Sales and marketing activities are often geared towards the different product groups, with teams of managers handling one set of products across national borders and customer groups. Distribution can be set up in a similar way: JCB customers may have to deal with several salespeople—even dealers—when sourcing machines from different product groups.

The customers are almost as varied as the product technology. Their needs are also diverse: the contractor, who wants a few telescopic handlers and backhoe loaders; the farmer, who uses harvesters, tractors, combines and telehandlers, but who perhaps purchases only tractors and telescopic handlers; the plant hirer, whose staple products are backhoe loaders, skid-steer loaders, mini excavators and telescopic handlers, which are rented out to contractors and individual users; the large house building and quarrying companies, who have purchasing officers and large fleets. In general, the industry tends to group customers by product technology, industrial sector and country. These divisions have arisen historically for practical reasons and do not necessarily relate to different customer needs.

It is estimated that the construction equipment industry is worth close to $50 billion worldwide. The major players include US companies Caterpillar and Case—which focus on large earthmoving and construction equipment—and Japanese challengers Komatsu, Hitachi and Kubota. UK based JCB dominates the medium sized machinery market in Europe. The JCB backhoe loader—the familiar yellow digger—sets the industry standard.

Although much of the company's success is built on the backhoe, JCB has a

The Customers	The Products
agriculture	all-terrain trucks
civil engineering	articulated dump trucks
contractors	asphalt finishers
defence departments	attachments
earthmoving	backhoe loaders
house building	combines
industrial services	crawler dozers
landscaping	crawler excavators
local authorities	crawler loaders
manufacturing services	fork lifts
mining and quarrying	harvesters
plant hire	mini-excavators
public utilities	motor graders
tool hire	motor scrapers
waste disposal	rigid dump trucks
	rough-terrain lift trucks
	skid-steer loaders
	spreaders
	telescopic handlers
	tractors
	wheeled excavators
	wheeled loaders

range of other construction products and continually seeks ways to improve its relationship with its customer base. In early 1993, the company launched its new skid-steer range, positioning it as the safest and most environmentally friendly in the industry. At the same time JCB realised that the needs of buyers of skid steers and other small equipment, such as the mini-excavator and smaller backhoe loaders, could be better served by a single division. With this in mind, the company has recently launched its Compact Division, which handles the sales and service of these smaller machines.

The Compact Division cuts across traditional industry sectorisation of customers and selling, recognising that users of smaller equipment, irrespective of their business sector or country of origin, share common needs and expectations. These customers require a sales, service and distribution operation geared specifically to their needs. JCB's use of targeting and market segmentation through its Compact Division has given the company a significant advantage in its market.

SOURCES: Tony McBurnie and David Clutterbuck, *Give Your Company the Marketing Edge* (London: Penguin Books, 1988); "The JCB experience", JCB, 1992; JCB company reports; Matthew Lynn, "Digging for victory", *Business*, October 1990, pp. 112–15.

Questions for Discussion

1. How is the construction equipment and agricultural machinery market segmented?
2. Does this segmentation satisfy the usual requirement that segments contain customers with homogeneous needs? Explain why.
3. How has JCB's Compact Division developed a fresh segmentation approach in this market?
4. What other ways could be used to segment this market?

4 CONSUMER BUYING BEHAVIOUR

Objectives

To understand the different types of consumer buying behaviour

To recognise the stages of the consumer buying decision process and understand how this process relates to different types of buying decisions

To explore how personal factors may affect the consumer buying decision process

To learn about the psychological factors that may affect the consumer buying decision process

To examine the social factors that influence the consumer buying decision process

To understand why it is important for marketers to attempt to understand consumer buying behaviour and the role of this behaviour in marketing strategy

The concern of consumers about the environmental impact of products they buy and use is on the increase. Shoppers are thus giving more careful consideration to the way in which they buy a host of everyday products. Even the criteria being considered are shifting, as buyers trade bulky boxes and plastic wrappers for unbleached products which can be recycled. For green minded shoppers, however, such moves towards more environmentally considerate options can be problematic. A plethora of confusing and misleading claims about competing brands further complicates buying decisions.

A new system of "eco-labels" is designed to make life simpler for shoppers. To qualify for the new label, products will need to be shown to be the least damaging in their class according to a variety of environment related criteria: consumption of raw materials and energy, noise, pollution of land, water and air, and the generation of solid waste. Some of the first products to be considered will be detergents, white goods (fridges, freezers, washing machines and dishwashers), household paper products such as kitchen roll and facial tissues, and paints.

While pressure groups like Friends of the Earth see trends towards eco-labelling as encouraging, concerns remain about the standards a product will need to meet to be included. Some feel that what is needed is a more discerning system which will grade products and compel those not meeting minimum requirements to be withdrawn from sale. ■

SOURCES: Melanie Flinn, "Label drive aimed at green shoppers", *Coventry Evening Telegraph*, 4 June 1992; Melanie Flinn, "New labels won't wash", *Coventry Evening Telegraph*, 3 February 1993; John Lewis. "Labour demands swift eco laws", *Marketing*, 4 February 1993.

The way in which consumers choose products from their supermarket shelves reveals a great deal about their characteristics and personalities. "Green" shoppers, for example, display their concern for environmental issues by spending time and effort seeking out ecologically sensitive products. The decision processes and actions of people involved in buying and using products are known as their **buying behaviour. Consumer buying behaviour** refers to the buying behaviour of ultimate consumers, those who purchase products for personal or household use, not for business purposes.[1]

A number of factors suggest that marketers should analyse consumer buying behaviour. First, buyers' reactions to a firm's marketing strategy have a great impact on the firm's success. Second, as indicated in Chapter 1, the marketing concept stresses that a firm should create a marketing mix that satisfies customers. To find out what satisfies customers, marketers must examine the main influences on what, where, when and how consumers buy. Third, by gaining a better understanding of the factors that affect buying behaviour, marketers can better predict how consumers will respond to marketing strategies. Ultimately, this information helps companies to compete more effectively in the marketplace.

Although marketers may try to understand and influence consumer buying behaviour, they cannot control it. Some critics credit them with the ability to manipulate buyers, but marketers have neither the power nor the knowledge to do so. Their knowledge of behaviour comes from what psychologists, social psychologists and sociologists know about human behaviour in general. Even if marketers wanted to manipulate buyers, the lack of laws and principles in the behavioural sciences would prevent them from doing so.

This chapter begins by examining the types of decision-making in which consumers engage. It then analyses the major stages of the consumer buying decision process and the personal, pyschological and social factors that influence it. The chapter concludes by assessing the importance of understanding consumer buying behaviour.

TYPES OF CONSUMER BUYING BEHAVIOUR

Consumers usually want to create and maintain a collection of products that satisfy their needs and wants in both the present and future. To achieve this objective, consumers make many purchasing decisions. For example, people make many decisions daily regarding food, clothing, shelter, medical care, education, recreation or transport. As they make these decisions, they engage in different decision-making behaviour. The amount of time and effort, both mental and physical, that buyers expend in decision-making varies considerably from situation to situation—and from consumer to consumer. Consumer decisions can thus be classified into one of three broad categories: routine response behaviour, limited decision-making and extensive decision-making.[2]

A consumer practises **routine response behaviour** when buying frequently purchased, low cost items that need very little search and decision effort. When buying such items, a consumer may prefer a particular brand, but he or she is familiar with several brands in the product class and views more than one as being acceptable. The products a consumer buys through routine response behaviour are purchased almost automatically. Most buyers, for example, do not spend much time or mental effort choosing a newspaper or food for their dog. If the supermarket has no Pedigree Chum in stock, the buyers will probably select an alternative brand instead.

Buyers engage in **limited decision-making** when they buy products occasionally and when they need to obtain information about an unfamiliar brand in a familiar product category. This type of decision-making requires a moderate amount of time for information gathering and deliberation. For example, if Procter & Gamble introduces an improved Tide washing powder, buyers will seek additional information about the new product, perhaps by asking a friend who has used the product or watching a commercial, before they make a trial purchase. Similarly, if a well known brand appears in a new form—for example, the recently introduced concentrated washing powders—the consumer will take extra time.

The most complex decision-making behaviour, **extensive decision-making,** comes into play when a purchase involves unfamiliar, expensive or infrequently bought products—for instance, cars, homes, holidays or health insurance. The buyer uses many criteria to evaluate alternative brands or choices and spends much time seeking information and comparing alternative brands before deciding on the purchase.

By contrast, **impulse buying** involves no conscious planning but a powerful, persistent urge to buy something immediately. For some individuals, impulse buying may be the dominant buying behaviour. Impulse buying, however, often provokes emotional conflicts. For example, a woman may purchase a new outfit seen in a shop window, but later regret spending the money because her finances are limited that month. Marketers often capitalise on the tendency towards impulse buying—for example, by placing magazines and confectionery next to supermarket checkout counters.

The purchase of a particular product does not always elicit the same type of decision-making behaviour.[3] In some instances, buyers engage in extensive decision-making the first time they purchase a certain kind of product but find that limited decision-making suffices when they buy the product again. If a routinely purchased, formerly satisfying brand no longer pleases, a consumer may use either limited or extensive decision processes to switch to a new brand. For example, if the petrol a driver normally buys is making the car's engine knock, she may seek out a higher octane brand through limited or extensive decision-making.

THE CONSUMER BUYING DECISION PROCESS

As defined earlier, a major part of buying behaviour is the decision process used in making purchases. The **consumer buying decision process,** shown in Figure 4.1, includes five stages: (1) problem recognition, (2) information search, (3) evaluation of alternatives, (4) purchase and (5) post-purchase evaluation. Before examining each stage, consider these important points. First, the actual act of purchasing is only one stage in the process; the process is begun several stages before the actual purchase. Second, even though it is suggested that a purchase always occurs, not all decision processes lead to a purchase; the individual may end the process at any stage. It is also possible that a different sequence of stages will be followed, with buyers revisiting certain stages. Finally, consumer decisions do not always include all five stages. Persons engaged in extensive decision-making usually go through all stages of this decision process, whereas those engaged in limited decision-making and routine response behaviour may omit some stages.

Problem Recognition   Problem recognition occurs when a buyer becomes aware that there is a difference between a desired state and an actual condition. For example, consider a sales manager who needs to keep a record of appointments. When, at the end of the year, her old diary

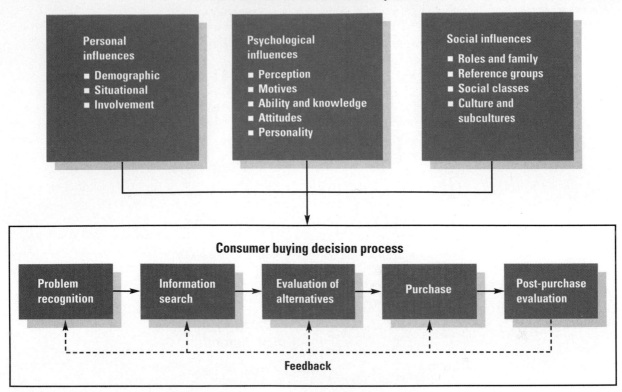

Possible influences on the decision process

Personal influences
- Demographic
- Situational
- Involvement

Psychological influences
- Perception
- Motives
- Ability and knowledge
- Attitudes
- Personality

Social influences
- Roles and family
- Reference groups
- Social classes
- Culture and subcultures

Consumer buying decision process

Problem recognition → Information search → Evaluation of alternatives → Purchase → Post-purchase evaluation

Feedback

FIGURE 4.1 *Consumer buying decision process and possible influences on the process*

is finished, she recognises that a difference exists between the desired state—a current diary—and the actual condition—an out-of-date one. She therefore makes the decision to buy a new diary.

Sometimes a person has a problem or need but is unaware of it. As shown in Figure 4.2, some consumers might not be aware that there is a range of natural, decongestant products suitable for the whole family. Marketers use sales personnel, advertising and packaging to help trigger recognition of such needs or problems. For example, a university bookshop may advertise business and scientific calculators in the university newspaper at the beginning of the term. Students who see the advertisement may recognise that they need calculators for their course work. The speed of consumer problem recognition can be either slow or rapid, depending on the individual concerned and the way in which need recognition was triggered.

Information Search

After recognising the problem or need, the buyer (if continuing the decision process) searches for information about products that will help resolve the problem or satisfy the need. For example, the above mentioned sales manager, after recognising the need for a new diary, may search for information about different types and brands. Information is acquired over time from the consumer's surroundings. However, it is important to remember that the impact of the information depends on how the consumer interprets it.

There are two aspects to an information search. In the **internal search,** buyers search their memory for information about products that might solve the problem. If

FIGURE 4.2
Problem recognition
Olbas Oil states the advantages of its product clearly to consumers.

FIGURE 4.2
Problem recognition
Olbas Oil states the advantages of its product clearly to consumers.

SOURCE: G. R. Lane Health Products.

they cannot retrieve enough information from their memory for a decision, they seek additional information in an **external search.** The external search may focus on communication with friends and colleagues, comparison of available brands and prices, marketer dominated sources and/or public sources. An individual's personal contacts—friends, relatives, associates—are often viewed as credible sources of information because the consumer trusts and respects them. Utilising marketer dominated sources of information, which include salespersons, advertising, package labelling, and in-store demonstrations and displays typically does not require much effort on the consumer's part. Buyers can also obtain information from public sources—for instance, government reports, news stories, consumer publications and reports from product testing organisations. Consumers frequently value information from public sources highly because they perceive it as factual and unbiased. Many companies try to capitalise on these sources—when favourable to them—in their public relations. The external search is also characterised by the extensiveness, manner and order in which brands, stores, attributes and sources are considered. For example, a man choosing a bottle of perfume for his mother's birthday may examine several brands at a number of different department stores before reaching a final decision.

Consumer groups are increasingly demanding access to all relevant product information. However, the greater the quantity of information available, the more the buyer may be overloaded with information. Research indicates that consumers make poorer choices when faced with large amounts of information.[4] Improving the quality of information and stressing features important to buyers in the decision process may help buyers make better purchase decisions.

How consumers use and process the information obtained in their search depends on features of the information itself, namely, availability, quantity, quality, repetition and format. If all the necessary information for a decision is available in the store, consumers may have no need to conduct an internal information search. Having all information externally available makes the consumer's decision process easier,[5] increases utilisation of the information, and may thus facilitate a purchase. It is important to recognise that adequate information may not always be available. Sometimes consumers must make do with whatever data are on hand at the time of purchase. For example, a consumer buying an airline ticket to pay an unplanned, urgent visit to a sick relative is not in a position to review all relevant sources of information.

Repetition, a technique well known to advertisers, increases consumer learning of information. When seeing or hearing an advertising message for the first time, the recipient may not grasp all its important details but learns more details as the message is repeated. Nevertheless, even when commercials are initially effective, repetition eventually causes the phenomenon of "wear-out": consumers pay less attention to the commercial and respond to it less favourably than they did at first.[6] Consumers are more likely to be receptive to repetition when making a low involvement purchase. Involvement refers to the level of interest, emotion and activity which the consumer is prepared to expend on a particular purchase.

The format in which information is transmitted to the buyer may also determine its use. Information can be presented verbally, numerically or visually. For many consumer tasks, pictures are remembered better than words, and the combination of pictures and words further enhances learning.[7] Consequently, marketers pay great attention to the visual components of their advertising materials.

A successful information search yields a group of brands that a buyer views as possible alternatives. This group of products is sometimes called the buyer's *evoked set*. For example, an evoked set of calculators might include those made by Texas Instruments, Hewlett-Packard, Tandy, Sharp and Casio.

Evaluation of Alternatives

To evaluate the products in the evoked set, a buyer establishes criteria for comparing the products. These criteria are the characteristics or features that the buyer wants (or does not want). For example, one calculator buyer may want a solar powered calculator with a large display and large buttons, whereas another may have no preference as to the size of features but dislike solar powered calculators. The buyer also assigns a certain **salience,** or level of importance, to each criterion; some features and characteristics carry more weight than others. The salience of criteria varies from buyer to buyer. For example, when choosing a newspaper one buyer may consider the political stance of the editorial to be crucial, while another might place more importance on the quality and coverage of sports. Using the criteria, a buyer rates and eventually ranks the brands in the evoked set. The evaluation stage may yield no brand that the buyer is willing to purchase; in that case, a further information search may be necessary.

Marketers can influence consumers' evaluation by *framing* the alternatives—that is, by the manner in which the alternative and its attributes are described. Framing can make a characteristic seem more important to a consumer and can facilitate its recall from memory. For example, by stressing the low calorie content of a microwave meal, a frozen food manufacturer can encourage the consumer to consider this particular aspect significant. Framing affects the decision processes of inexperienced buyers more than those of experienced ones.[8] If the evaluation of alternatives yields one or more brands that the consumer is willing to buy, the consumer is ready to move on to the next stage of the decision process—the purchase.

Purchase

The purchase stage, when the consumer chooses the product or brand to be bought, is mainly the outcome of the consumer's evaluation of alternatives, but other factors have an impact, too. The closeness of alternative stores and product availability can both influence which brand is purchased. For example, if the brand the buyer ranked highest is not available, the brand that is ranked second may be purchased instead.

During this stage, the buyer also picks the seller from whom he or she will buy the product. The choice of the seller may affect the final product selection—and so may the terms of sale, which, if negotiable, are determined during the purchase decision stage. Other issues such as price, delivery, guarantees, service agreements, installation and credit arrangements are discussed and settled. Finally, the purchase takes place, although in some cases the consumer terminates the buying decision process before reaching that point.

Post-purchase Evaluation

Once the purchase has taken place, the buyer begins evaluating the product to check whether its actual performance meets expected levels. Many of the criteria used in evaluating alternatives are applied again during the post-purchase evaluation. This stage will determine whether the consumer is satisfied or dissatisfied. Either outcome strongly influences consumers' motivation and information processing. Consumers' satisfaction or dissatisfaction determines whether they make a complaint, communicate with other possible buyers, and purchase the produce again.[9] The impact of the post-purchase evaluation is illustrated by the feedback loop in Figure 4.1.

Shortly after the purchase of an expensive product, the post-purchase evaluation may result in **cognitive dissonance**—doubts that occur because the buyer questions whether the right decision was made in purchasing the product. For example, after buying an expensive leather briefcase, a schoolteacher may feel guilty about the purchase or worry about whether it was the right brand and quality. A buyer who experiences cognitive dissonance may attempt to return the product or may seek positive information about it to justify that choice.

As shown in Figure 4.1, three major categories of influences are believed to affect the consumer buying decision process: personal, psychological and social factors. The remainder of this chapter focuses on these factors. Although each major factor is discussed separately, it is important to realise that it is a combination of their effects which influences the consumer decision process.

PERSONAL FACTORS INFLUENCING THE BUYING DECISION PROCESS

Personal factors are unique to a particular person. Many different personal factors can influence purchasing decisions. In this section three types are considered: demographic factors, situational factors and level of involvement.

Demographic Factors

Demographic factors are individual characteristics such as age, sex, race, ethnic origin, income, family life-cycle and occupation. (These and other characteristics were discussed in Chapter 3 as possible variables for segmentation purposes.) Demographic factors have a bearing on who is involved in family decision-making. For example, it is estimated that by the mid-1990s the UK will have the largest market for children's toys and clothes in the EC and the highest proportion of children in the population. Table 4.1 shows the EC official population projections by age and sex for the year 1995.

Children aged 6 to 17 are known to have more influence in the buying decision

TABLE 4.1 *Projected demographic population by age and sex, 1995 official forecasts (in thousands)*

EC MEMBERS	TOTAL	MALE	FEMALE	0–14	15–64	65 +	NOTES
Belgium	9,729	4,747	4,982	1,766	6,404	1,559	
Denmark	5,108	2,507	2,601	849	3,455	804	
France	56,338	27,756	28,582	11,194	37,338	7,807	a
Germany: East	16,998	8,231	8,767	3,447	11,362	2,189	
Germany: West	59,983	29,118	30,864	9,502	41,004	9,477	a
Greece	10,168	5,053	5,115	2,347	6,434	1,387	
Ireland	4,083	2,051	2,032	1,161	2,533	389	a
Italy	57,506	27,960	29,546	9,307	39,071	9,128	
Luxembourg	373	182	191	71	253	49	
Netherlands	15,028	7,413	7,615	2,653	10,325	2,050	
Portugal	10,819	5,273	5,547	2,129	7,263	1,427	
Spain	40,022	19,706	20,316	7,647	26,745	5,630	
United Kingdom	58,144	28,483	29,661	11,593	37,385	9,166	
EC TOTAL	**344,299**	**168,480**	**175,819**	**63,666**	**229,572**	**51,062**	

^aUN estimates (medium variant)

SOURCE: National Statistical Offices/UN World Population Prospects; "European Marketing Data & Statistics", *Euromonitor*, 1993, p. 147. Reprinted by permission.

process for breakfast cereals, ice cream, soft drinks, holidays and even the family car than ever before.[10] This influence is increasingly reflected in the way such products are designed and marketed. For example, cereal boxes frequently carry offers specifically targeted at young children. Demographic factors may also partially govern behaviour during a specific stage of the decision process. During the information stage, for example, a person's age and income may affect the number and types of information sources used and the amount of time devoted to seeking information.

Demographic factors also affect the extent and way in which a person uses products in a specific product category. While consumers aged 15 to 24 may purchase furniture, appliances and other household basics as they establish their own households, those aged 45 to 54 spend more money on luxury and leisure products after their children have left home.[11] Brand preferences, store choice and timing of purchases are other areas on which demographic factors have some impact. Consider, for example, how differences in occupation result in variations in product needs. A schoolteacher may earn roughly the same annually as a plumber. Yet the teacher and the plumber spend their incomes differently, because the product needs that arise from these two occupations vary considerably. Although both occupations require the purchase of work clothes, the teacher buys suits and the plumber buys jeans and work shirts. The vehicles they drive also vary to some extent. Where and what they eat for lunch are likely to be different. Finally, the "tools" that they purchase and use in their work are not the same. Thus occupation clearly affects consumer buying behaviour.

Situational Factors

Situational factors are the external circumstances or conditions that exist when a consumer is making a purchase decision. Sometimes a consumer changes buying behaviour as a result of an unexpected situation. For example, someone who has been temporarily immobilised by a car accident may shop by mail order in the short term, even if he or she would not usually do so. In other cases, a change in situation may arise which causes a person to lengthen or terminate the buying decision process. For instance, a consumer who is considering taking an exotic safari holiday and is laid off from work during the stage of evaluating alternatives may decide to reject the purchase entirely.

The effects of situational factors can be felt throughout the buying decision process in a variety of ways. Uncertainty about future marital status may sway a consumer against making a purchase. On the other hand, a conviction that the supply of a particular product is sharply limited may impel a person to buy it. For example, consumers have purchased and hoarded petrol, food products and even toilet tissue when these products were believed to be in short supply. Even the weather may affect buying behaviour. A hurricane warning usually sends US coastal residents rushing to stock up on bottled water, batteries and emergency food supplies in just the same way as EC citizens hurry to buy candles in times of threatened electricity power cuts. These and other situational factors can change rapidly; their influence on purchase decisions is generally as sudden as it is short lived.

The amount of time a consumer has available to make a decision is a situational factor which strongly influences buying decisions. If there is little time for selecting and purchasing a product, a person may quickly decide to buy a readily available brand. The amount of available time also affects the way consumers process the information contained in advertisements[12] and the length of the stages within the decision process. For example, if a family is planning to buy a dishwasher for a new house, its members may gather and consider a great deal of information. They may read consumer magazines, talk to friends and salespersons, look at a number of advertisements, and spend a good deal of time on comparative shopping in a number of stores. However, if the

FIGURE 4.3 *Reaching consumers who have a high level of involvement*
Choosing the perfect wedding dress is a high involvement purchase decision, as leading bridal supplier Pronuptià realises.

SOURCE: Photograph by Geoff Smith and Carol Naylor.

family's 20 year old Hotpoint dishwasher suddenly breaks down and cannot be repaired, the extent of the information search, the number of alternatives considered and the amount of comparative shopping may be much more restricted. Indeed, given the time factor, if these family members were reasonably satisfied with the performance of the old machine and service arrangements, they may buy another Hotpoint because they know the brand.

Level of Involvement

Many aspects of consumer buying decisions are affected by the individual's **level of involvement.** This term refers to the level of interest, emotional commitment and time spent searching for a product in a particular situation. A buyer's level of involvement determines why he or she is motivated to seek information about certain products and brands but virtually ignores others. The extensiveness of the buying decision process varies greatly with the consumer's level of involvement. The sequence of the steps in this process may also be altered. Low involvement buyers may form an attitude towards a product—perhaps as a result of an advertising campaign—and evaluate its features after purchasing it rather than before.[13] Conversely, high involvement buyers spend much time and effort researching their purchase beforehand. Figure 4.3 and Marketing Insight 4.1 illustrate and discuss the purchase of a wedding dress—a particularly high involvement purchase decision.

THE INVOLVEMENT OF MARRIAGE

Getting married is big business. Each year in Europe, vast amounts of money are spent on engagement rings and wedding bands, outfits for the bridal party, receptions and honeymoons, wedding cars and photographers, wedding magazines and books. Family weddings not only provide an event to remember for the couple making a lifelong commitment to each other but also offer relatives and friends the chance to meet up in happy circumstances to renew acquaintanceships.

For most brides-to-be, buying a wedding dress is a particularly important part of the event. Though traditions vary enormously depending on religion and culture, many European brides traditionally marry dressed in white or cream. Whatever the culture, religion and nationality of the bride, it is common for the process of buying the dress to begin many months before the wedding day. After some deliberation, often accompanied by a close relative or friend, the bride begins by visiting a number of bridal wear retailers. The search for a suitable dress will probably extend to several stores, perhaps in more than one town. Many styles and fabrics may be considered and several tried. Even then, it is unlikely that a decision will be made on the first outing. Time is taken to think carefully about the options, costs, accessories and schedules; and the preferred store is possibly revisited several times before a definite decision is reached.

The uniqueness of the purchase, its emotional significance, the length of time taken and the associated risk all make this a high involvement decision. The outcome of the purchase will be long lasting, recorded for posterity in the couple's wedding album and/or video recording. According to Assael, consumers are most likely to be very involved with a product when that product

is important to the consumer
is of special interest to the consumer
has high emotional appeal
involves significant risk, either financial or social
can be linked to group norms

In this sense, a wedding dress is just one part, albeit a highly visible one, of a high involvement event. It takes place amidst the planning of a host of other wedding activities: the choice of date, venue, music and readings, selection of reception venues and menus, drawing up of guest lists and design of seating plans, organisation of the honeymoon and budgeting.

SOURCES: Giles Laurent and Jean-Noel Kapferer, "Measuring consumer involvement profiles", *Journal of Marketing Research*, 22, February 1985, pp. 41–53; Henry Assael, *Consumer Behavior and Marketing Action* (Boston: PWS-Kent Publishing Co., 1992), p. 30.

A consumer's level of involvement depends on a number of factors. Consumers tend to be more involved in the purchase of high priced goods and products that are visible to others, such as clothing, furniture or cars. As levels of perceived risk increase, involvement levels are likely to rise. Furthermore, individuals may experience enduring involvement with a product class. *Enduring involvement* is an ongoing interest in a product class because of personal relevance. For example, people often have enduring involvement with products associated with their leisure activities. These individuals engage in ongoing search and information gathering processes for these products over extensive periods of time, irrespective of whether or not a purchase is imminent. Photography enthusiasts enjoy reading about and examining new types of cameras and films; horse enthusiasts visit shows even if they are not taking part.

Buyers may also experience *situational involvement* resulting from the particular circumstance or environment in which they find themselves. This type of involvement, sometimes also called pre-purchase involvement, is temporary because the conditions that triggered the high degree of involvement may change.[14] If a man is searching for an engagement ring for his prospective fiancée, for example, he will probably experience a high level of involvement in the purchase decision. His information search and evaluation of alternatives may be extensive. However, once the selection has been made, he no longer sees an engagement ring as being personally relevant.

Many purchase decisions do not generate great involvement on the consumer's part. When the involvement level is low, as with routine response purchases, then buying is almost automatic, and the information search and evaluation of alternatives are extremely limited. For example, food shopping represents low involvement purchase decisions for many consumers; products are chosen out of habit and with minimal effort.

PSYCHOLOGICAL FACTORS INFLUENCING THE BUYING DECISION PROCESS

Psychological factors operating within individuals partly determine people's general behaviour and thus influence their behaviour as consumers. The primary psychological influences on consumer behaviour are (1) perceptions, (2) motives, (3) ability and knowledge, (4) attitudes and (5) personality. Even though these psychological factors operate internally, it will become apparent later in this chaper that they are very much affected by social forces outside the individual.

Perception

Are the birds in Figure 4.4 flying to the left or right? It could be either way depending on how you perceive the birds. Different people perceive the same thing at the same time in different ways. Similarly, the same individual at different times may perceive the same item in a number of ways. **Perception** is the process of selecting, organising and interpreting information inputs to produce meaning. **Information inputs** are the sensations received through sight, taste, hearing, smell and touch. Each time we see an advertisement, listen to the radio, visit a restaurant or use a product, we receive information inputs.

As the definition indicates, perception consists of three steps. Although individuals receive numerous pieces of information at once, only a few of them reach awareness. Certain inputs are selected while others are ignored, because consumers do not have the ability to be conscious of every input at the same time. This phenomenon is sometimes called **selective exposure** because people select inputs that are to be exposed to their awareness. A child concentrating on painting a picture may not be aware of the noise of other children playing around him or her, that the light is on, or that the paint

FIGURE 4.4
Perception
Are the birds flying to the
left or to the right?

SOURCE: © 1938 Escher Foundation R-Baarn-Holland. All rights reserved.

has dripped onto the floor. Even though these inputs are being received, the child will ignore them until they are mentioned.

Why do some types of information reach awareness while others do not? An input is more likely to reach awareness if it relates to an anticipated event. For example, a family hoping to visit a travelling circus is more likely to take account of a notice about such an event which is delivered in the mail. An input is more likely to reach awareness if the information helps satisfy current needs. Thus hungry people are more likely to notice a commercial for Kentucky Fried Chicken than those who are not. Finally, an input is more likely to reach awareness if its intensity changes significantly. When a store manager reduces a price slightly, consumers may not notice because the change is not significant, but if the manager cuts the price in half, they are much more likely to recognise the reduction.

The selective nature of perception leads to two other conditions: selective distortion and selective retention. **Selective distortion** is the changing or twisting of currently received information. This condition can occur when a person receives information that is inconsistent with personal feelings or beliefs. For example, an individual who hears an advertisement promoting a brand he or she dislikes is likely to distort the information to make it more consistent with previous views. The advertisement may therefore have much less impact than on another consumer who views the same brand more favourably. In the **selective retention** phenomenon, a person remembers information inputs that support personal feelings and beliefs and forgets inputs that do not. After hearing a sales presentation and leaving the shop, a customer may forget many of the selling points if they contradict pre-existing beliefs.

The information inputs that do reach awareness are not received in an organised form. To produce meaning, an individual must enter the second step of the perceptual process—organise and integrate the new information with that already stored in memory. Although this step is usually carried out quickly, it may take longer when the individual is considering an unfamiliar product area.

Interpretation—the third step in the perceptual process—is the assignment of meaning to what has been organised. A person bases interpretation on what is familiar, on knowledge already stored in memory. For this reason, a company that changes a package design or logo faces a major problem. Since people look for the product in the old, familiar package, they may not recognise it in the new one. Unless a package or logo change is accompanied by a promotional programme that makes people aware of the change, a firm may lose sales. Even in cases where such a programme is conducted, positive reaction from the consumer cannot be guaranteed.

Although marketers cannot control people's perceptions, they often try to influence them. Several problems may arise from such attempts, however. First, a consumer's perceptual process may operate in such a way that a seller's information never reaches that person. For example, a buyer may block out a shop assistant's sales presentation. Second, a buyer may receive a seller's information but perceive it differently from the way the seller intended. For example, when a toothpaste producer advertises that "35 per cent of the people who use this toothpaste have less decay", a customer could infer that 65 per cent of the people who use the product have more tooth decay. Third, buyers who perceive information inputs to be inconsistent with their prior beliefs are likely to forget the information quickly. Thus if a salesperson tells a prospective car buyer that a particular model is highly reliable and requires few repairs but the customer has a preconceived opinion that this model is poor quality, he or she probably will not retain the information very long. The problem of interpreting information is made more complex by the large number of information inputs which consumers encounter each day.[15]

In addition to perceptions of packages, products, brands and organisations, individuals also have self-perceptions. That perception is called the person's **self-concept** or self-image. It is reasonable to believe that a person's self-concept affects purchase decisions and consumption behaviour. The results of some studies suggest that buyers purchase products that reflect and enhance their self-concepts. For instance, one person might buy designer snakeskin shoes to project an up market image, while another may buy Reebok trainers to enhance acceptability among that person's peer group.

Motives

A **motive** is an internal energy giving force that directs a person's activities towards satisfying a need or achieving a goal. Motivation is the set of mechanisms for controlling movement towards goals.[16] A buyer's actions at any time are affected by a set of motives rather than by just one. Each buyer's motives are unique and, at a single point in time, some motives in the set have priority, but the priorities of motives vary from one time to another. For example, a person's motives for having a cup of coffee are much stronger right after waking up than just before going to bed. Motivation also affects the direction and intensity of behaviour. Individuals must choose which goals to pursue at a particular time.

Motives influencing where a person purchases products on a regular basis are called **patronage motives.** A buyer may use a particular shop because of such patronage motives as price, service, location, honesty, product variety or friendliness of salespeople. To capitalise on patronage motives, a marketer should try to determine why regular customers patronise a store and then emphasise these characteristics in the store's marketing mix. Useful lessons can also be learnt by understanding people's reasons for patronising competing brands or outlets.

Motivation research can be used to analyse the major motives that influence consumers to buy or not buy their products. Measuring motive is not always straightforward. In Figure 4.5 Pretty Polly is marketing its ladies' tights and stockings to

FIGURE 4.5
Identifying consumer motives
Pretty Polly's advertising appeals to the search for glamour—a motive for purchasing its product.

SOURCE: Courtesy of Pretty Polly.

consumers seeking a glamorous but comfortable image. Motives which are subconscious are especially hard to judge, because people are by definition unaware of them and marketers thus cannot elicit them through direct questioning. Most motivation research relies on interviews or projective techniques.

When researchers study motives through interviews, they may use individual in-depth interviews, focus groups or a combination of the two. In an **in-depth interview,** the researcher tries to get the subject to talk freely about anything at all in order to create an informal atmosphere. Although there is some variation in approach, usually the researcher asks general, non-directed questions and then probes the subject's answers by asking for clarification. An in-depth interview may last for several hours. In a **focus group,** the interviewer—through leadership that is not highly structured—tries to generate discussion about one or several topics in a group of 6 to 12 people. Through what is said in the discussion, the interviewer attempts to discover people's motives relating to some issue such as the use of a product. The researcher usually cannot probe as far in a focus group as in an in-depth interview, and some products may not be suitable for such group discussion. To determine the subconscious motives reflected in the interviews, motivation researchers must be extremely well trained in clinical psychology. The use of sound and video recordings can simplify the process of analysis. Interviewers' skill in uncovering subconscious motives from what is said in an interview determines the effectiveness of their research. Both in-depth and focus group techniques can yield a variety of information. For example, they might help marketers discover why customers continue to buy high cholesterol red meats despite the fact that most say they are working towards reducing their intake of high fat foods.

Projective techniques are tests in which subjects are asked to perform specific tasks for particular reasons, while actually being evaluated for other purposes. Such tests are based on the assumption that subjects will unconsciously "project" their motives as they perform the required tasks. However, subjects should always be informed that the test is an unstructured evaluation. Researchers trained in projective techniques can analyse the materials a subject produces and make predictions about the subject's subconscious motives. Some common types of projective techniques are word association tests, sentence completion tests and bubble drawings. These are illustrated in Figure 4.6.

Motivation research techniques can be reasonably effective but are far from perfect. Marketers who want to research people's motives should obtain the services of professional psychologists skilled in the methods of motivation research.

Ability and Knowledge

Individuals vary in their **ability**—their competence and efficiency in performing tasks. One ability of interest to marketers is an individual's capacity to learn. **Learning** refers to changes in a person's behaviour caused by information and experience. The consequences of behaviour strongly influence the learning process. Behaviour that results in satisfying consequences tends to be repeated. For example, when a consumer buys a box of Kellogg's Bran Flakes and enjoys them, he or she is more likely to buy the same cereal next time. In fact, the individual will probably continue to purchase that brand until it no longer provides satisfaction. But when the effects of the behaviour are no longer satisfying, the person will switch to a different brand, perhaps, or maybe start eating croissants for breakfast instead.

When making purchasing decisions, buyers have to process information. Individuals have differing abilities in this regard. For example, when purchasing a camera, a well-educated potential buyer who has experience with cameras may be able to read, comprehend and synthesise the considerable quantities of information found in the technical brochures for various competing brands. On the other hand, another buyer with more limited abilities may be incapable of performing this task and will have to rely on information obtained from advertisements or from a sales representative of a particular brand.

Another aspect of an individual's ability is knowledge. **Knowledge** has two components: familiarity with the product and expertise, which is the individual's ability to apply the product.[17] The duration and intensity of the buying decision process depends on the buyer's familiarity with or prior experience in purchasing and using the product. For example, in Figure 4.7, Prestige, a well known manufacturer of cookware, bakeware and utensils, builds consumer awareness by informing potential purchasers of the versatility, quality, and functionality of its products. The individual's knowledge influences his or her search for, recall and use of information.[18]

When making purchase decisions, inexperienced buyers may use different types of information from more experienced shoppers who are familiar with the product and purchase situation. Inexperienced buyers use price as an indicator of quality more frequently than buyers who have some knowledge of a particular product category.[19] Thus two potential purchasers of an antique desk may use quite different types of information in making their purchase decision. The less experienced buyer is likely to judge the desk's value by the price, whereas the more experienced buyer may seek information about the craftsman, period and place of origin in order to judge the desk's quality and value.

Consumers who lack expertise are more likely to seek the advice of others when making a purchase. More experienced buyers have greater confidence; they also have more knowledge about the product or service and can tell which features are reliable indicators of product quality. For example, consider two families choosing a long haul

FIGURE 4.6
Common types of projective techniques

Word Association Tests

Subjects are asked to say what words come into their minds when a particular topic/product is mentioned.

Fresh foods are . . .	Frozen foods are . . .
Natural	Processed
Fresh	Quick
Healthy	Simple
Expensive	Convenient
Good for you	Preservatives
Real	Manufactured

Sentence Completion Tests

Subjects are asked to complete the sentences.

"People who drink additive-free soft drinks are . . ."

"People who look for the ingredients on packets before they buy them are . . ."

"People who buy decaffeinated coffee are . . ."

Bubble Drawings

Subjects are asked to say what the man is thinking.

SOURCE: Prepared with help from Peter Jackson, Adsearch, London.

holiday. Members of one family are unused to overseas travel, are unsure of the suitability of locations offered in travel brochures and do not understand how to investigate flight options or medical and insurance requirements. Members of the other family have taken holidays abroad regularly in many countries. Although on this occasion they intend to visit a country which is new to them, they are sufficiently conversant with this type of travel to make their purchase without assistance and with confidence.

Marketers sometimes help customers to learn about their products and to gain experience with them. Free samples encourage trial and reduce purchase risk. In-store

FIGURE 4.7
Building consumer awareness
Prestige increases aware-ness of its products by expanding consumers' knowledge about its range of cookware.

SOURCE: Courtesy of Prestige Group UK PLC.

demonstrations aid consumers in acquiring knowledge of product uses. Test drives give new car purchasers some experience of a car's features. Consumers also learn when they experience products indirectly, by way of information from salespeople, advertisements, friends and relatives. Through sales personnel and advertisements, marketers offer information before (and sometimes after) purchases to influence what consumers learn and to create a more favourable attitude towards the products.

Although marketers seek to influence what a consumer learns, their attempts are seldom fully successful. Marketers encounter problems in attracting and holding consumers' attention, providing consumers with the kinds of information that are important for making purchase decisions, and convincing them to try the product. These attempts are most likely to be successful when carefully designed to appeal to the target market.

Attitude

Attitude refers to knowledge and positive or negative feelings about an object or activity. The objects or acts towards which we have attitudes may be tangible or intangible, living or non-living. Some attitudes relate to things which have a major impact on our lives, while others are less important. For example, we have attitudes towards sex, religion, politics and music, just as we do towards cars, football and pizza.

An individual learns attitudes through experience and interaction with other people. Just as attitudes are learned, they can also be changed. Nevertheless, an individual's attitudes remain generally stable and do not change from moment to moment. Likewise, at any one time, a person's attitudes do not all have equal impact; some are stronger than others. For example, an individual who has recently had his or her car stolen may develop attitudes towards rising crime which are particularly clearly defined.

Consumer attitudes towards a firm and its products greatly influence the success or failure of the firm's marketing strategy. When consumers have strong negative attitudes towards one or more aspects of a firm's marketing practices, they may not only stop using the firm's product but also urge their relatives and friends to do likewise. For example, following concern about apartheid in South Africa, many consumers in Europe chose to boycott South African products. Likewise, when an oil spill from the supertanker *Exxon Valdez* fouled beaches and killed wildlife in Alaska's Prince William Sound, the public judged Exxon's response to cleaning up the spill as inadequate and cosmetic. As a result, many consumers boycotted Exxon products. Nearly 20,000 Exxon credit card holders cut up their cards and sent them back to Exxon, exhorting their friends to do the same.

Since attitudes can play such an important part in determining consumer behaviour, marketers should measure consumer attitudes towards prices, package designs, brand names, advertisements, salespeople, repair services, store locations, features of existing or proposed products, and social responsibility activities. Several methods can help marketers gauge these attitudes. One of the simplest ways is to question people directly. A marketing research agency carrying out attitude research for Heineken, for example, might ask respondents for opinions about the packaging and advertising of beer. Projective techniques used in motivation research can also be employed to measure attitudes. Sometimes marketers evaluate attitudes through attitude scales. An **attitude scale** usually consists of a series of adjectives, phrases or sentences about an object. Subjects are asked to indicate the intensity of their feelings towards the object by reacting to the adjectives, phrases or sentences in a certain way. For example, if a marketer were measuring people's attitudes towards energy efficiency, respondents might be asked to state the degree to which they agree or disagree with a number of statements, such as "Extra loft insulation can lead to substantially reduced fuel bills".

When marketers determine that a significant number of consumers have strong negative attitudes towards an aspect of a marketing mix, they may try to change consumer attitudes to make them more favourable. This task is generally long, expensive and difficult and may require extensive promotional efforts. For example, in the UK, the Milk Marketing Board has used advertising to focus consumers' attention on the nutritional and energy value of milk. This publicity contradicts some of the health concerns about cholesterol in dairy products. Similarly, manufacturers of detergents and household cleaners have been trying to respond to consumer desires for more environmentally sympathetic products.

Personality

Personality includes all the internal traits and behaviours that make a person unique. Each person's unique personality arises from both heredity and personal experiences. Personalities are typically described as having one or more characteristics, such as compulsiveness, ambitiousness, gregariousness, dogmatism, authoritarianism, introversion, extroversion, aggressiveness, competitiveness. Marketing researchers attempt to find relationships among such characteristics and buying behaviour. Even though a few links between several personality characteristics and buyer behaviour have been determined, the results of many studies have been inconclusive. Some researchers see the apparently weak association between personality and buying behaviour as due to unreliable measures rather than a lack of relationship.[20] A number of marketers are convinced that a consumer's personality does influence the types and brands of products purchased. For example, the type of clothing or cars that people buy, as well as the way their hair is styled and the leisure activities they engage in, may reflect one or more personality characteristics.

At times, marketers aim advertising campaigns at general types of personalities. In doing so, they use positively valued personality characteristics, such as gregariousness, independence or competitiveness. Products promoted this way include drinks, cars, cigarettes, clothing and computer games. For example, Nintendo advertising aims to appeal to young, trendy consumers.

SOCIAL FACTORS INFLUENCING THE BUYING DECISION PROCESS

The forces that other people exert on buying behaviour are called **social factors.** As shown in Figure 4.1, they can be grouped into four major areas: (1) roles and family, (2) reference groups, (3) social classes and (4) culture and subcultures.

Roles and Family

All of us occupy positions within groups, organisations and institutions. Associated with each position is a **role**—a set of actions and activities that a person in a particular position is supposed to perform, based on the expectations of both the individual and surrounding persons. Because people occupy numerous positions, they also have many roles. For example, a woman may perform the roles of mother, wife, grandmother, schoolteacher, part-time university student and singer at the local operatic society. Thus there are several sets of expectations placed on each person's behaviour.

An individual's roles influence both general behaviour and buying behaviour. The demands of a person's many roles may be inconsistent and confusing. To illustrate, assume that a man is thinking about buying a boat. While he wants a boat for fishing, his children want one suitable for water skiing. His wife wants him to delay the boat purchase until next year. A colleague at work insists that he should buy a particular brand, known for high performance. Thus an individual's buying behaviour is partially affected by the input and opinions of family and friends.

Family roles relate directly to purchase decisions. The male head of household is likely to be involved heavily in the purchase of products such as household insurance and alcohol. Although female roles have changed, women still make buying decisions related to many household items, including healthcare products, washing products, household cleaners and food. Husbands and wives participate jointly in the purchase of a variety of products, especially durable goods. Some students aged 16 to 24 may be rebellious; their brand loyalty can be quite changeable. Marketers frequently promote their products during school and college holidays to catch this hard-to-reach group at a time when they are more receptive to a promotional message.[21] Others in this age group may seek their parents' advice about products with which they are not personally familiar. For example, many college students bank with the same bank as their parents. Children are making many purchase decisions and influencing numerous household purchase decisions that traditionally were made only by husbands and wives. Some buying decisions are made by the whole family. For example, parents and children will usually all be involved in choosing the family holiday. When two or more family members participate in a purchase, their roles may dictate that each is responsible for performing certain tasks: initiating the idea, gathering information, deciding whether to buy the product, or selecting the specific brand. The particular tasks performed depend on the types of products being considered.

Marketers need to be aware of how roles affect buying behaviour. To develop a marketing mix that precisely meets the needs of the target market, marketers must know not only who does the actual buying but also what other roles influence the purchase. Because sex roles are changing so rapidly, marketers must ensure that their information is current and accurate.

Reference Groups

A group becomes a **reference group** when an individual identifies with it so much that he or she takes on many of the values, attitudes or behaviour of group members. The person who views a group as a reference group may or may not know the actual size of the group. Most people have several reference groups, such as families, friends and religious, civic and professional organisations.

A group can be a negative reference group for an individual. Someone may have been a part of a specific group at one time but later rejected its values and members. One can also specifically take action to avoid a particular group.[22] However, in this discussion reference groups mean those that the individual involved views positively.

A reference group may serve as a point of comparison and a source of information for an individual. A customer's behaviour may change to be more in line with the actions and beliefs of group members. For example, a person might stop buying one brand of soft drink and switch to another on the advice of members of the reference group. Generally, the more conspicuous a product, the more likely it is that the brand decision will be influenced by reference groups. An individual may also seek information from the reference group about other factors regarding a prospective purchase, such as where to buy a certain product. The degree to which a reference group will affect a purchase decision depends on an individual's susceptibility to its influence and the strength of his or her involvement with the group. Young people are often especially susceptible to this kind of influence.

A marketer sometimes tries to use reference group influence in advertisements by suggesting that people in a specific group buy a product and are highly satisfied with it. In this type of appeal, the advertiser hopes that many people will accept the suggested group as a reference group and buy (or react more favourably to) the product as a result. Whether this kind of advertising succeeds depends on three factors: how effectively the advertisement communicates the message, the type of product, and the individual's susceptibility to reference group influence.

Social Classes

Within all societies, people rank others into higher or lower positions of respect. This ranking results in social classes. A **social class** is an open group of individuals who have similar social rank. A class is referred to as "open" because people can move into and out of it. The criteria for grouping people into classes vary from one society to another. In the UK, as in other western countries, many factors are taken into account, including occupation, education, income, wealth, race, ethnic group and possessions. In the former Soviet Union, wealth and income are less important in determining social class than education and occupation: although Russian doctors and scientists do not make a great deal of money, they are highly valued in Russian society. A person who is ranking someone does not necessarily apply all of a society's criteria. The number and importance of the factors chosen depend on the characteristics of the individual being ranked and the values of the person who is doing the ranking. For example, one individual may particularly respect status within a church or religious sect, while another may regard it as having little relevance.

To some degree, persons within social classes develop and assume common patterns of behaviour. They may have similar attitudes, values, language patterns and possessions. Social class influences many aspects of people's lives. For example, it affects whom they marry, their likelihood of having children and the children's chances of surviving infancy. It influences childhood training, choice of religion, selection of occupation and how people spend their time. Because social class has a bearing on so many aspects of a person's life, it also affects buying decisions. For example, upper class Europeans seem to prefer luxury cars, such as the BMW and Mercedes-Benz, which symbolise their status, income and financial comfort.

Social class determines to some extent the type, quality and quantity of products that

TABLE 4.2 *Socio-economic classification (JICNARS)*

SOCIAL GRADE	SOCIAL STATUS	HEAD OF HOUSEHOLD'S OCCUPATION	APPROXIMATE PERCENTAGE OF FAMILIES
A	Upper middle class	Higher managerial, administrative or professional	3
B	Middle class	Intermediate managerial, administrative or professional	10
C1	Lower middle class	Supervisory or clerical and junior managerial, administrative or professional	24
C2	Skilled working class	Skilled manual workers	30
D	Working class	Semi and unskilled manual workers	25
E	Those at lowest levels of subsistence	State pensioners or widows (no other earner), casual or lowest grade workers	8

A—Upper middle class: The head of the household is a successful business or professional person, senior civil servant, or has considerable private means. A young person in some of these occupations who has not fully established himself/herself may still be found in Grade B, though he/she should eventually reach grade A. In country or suburban areas, A-grade householders usually live in large detached houses or in expensive flats. In towns, they may live in expensive flats or town houses in the better parts of town.

B—Middle class: In general, the heads of B-grade households will be quite senior people but not at the very top of their profession or business. They are quite well off, but their style of life is generally respectable rather than rich or luxurious . . . non-earners will be living on private pensions or on fairly modest private means.

C1—Lower middle class: In general it is made up of the families of small tradespeople and non-manual workers who carry out less important administrative, supervisory and clerical jobs, i.e., what are sometimes called "white-collar" workers.

C2—Skilled working class: Consists in the main of skilled manual workers and their families: the serving of an apprenticeship may be a guide to membership of this class.

D—Semi-skilled and unskilled working class: Consists entirely of manual workers, generally semi-skilled or unskilled.

E—Those at lowest levels of subsistence: Consists of old age pensioners, widows and their families, casual workers and those who, through sickness or unemployment, are dependent on social security schemes, or have very small private means.

SOURCE: From Peter M. Chisnall, *Marketing: A Behavioural Analysis* (Berkshire, England: McGraw-Hill Publishing Co. Ltd, 1976), pp. 114–15. Reprinted by permission.

a person buys and uses. Social class also affects an individual's shopping patterns and the types of stores patronised. Advertisements are sometimes based on an appeal to a specific social class. See Table 4.2 for an analysis of the categories of social class in the UK.

Culture and Sub-cultures

Culture is everything in our surroundings that is made by human beings. It consists of tangible items, such as food, furniture, buildings, clothing and tools, and intangible

FIGURE 4.8

Appealing to cultural standards
Kellogg's takes advantage of strong cultural acceptance of healthy foods by promoting key attributes of its cereal.

SOURCE: Used by permission of the Kellogg Company.

concepts, such as education, the legal system, healthcare and religion. Culture also includes the values and wide range of behaviours that are acceptable within a specific society. The concepts, values and behaviours that make up a culture are learned and passed on from one generation to the next.

Culture influences buying behaviour because it permeates daily life. Culture determines what people wear and eat, where they live and travel. Certainly, society's interest in the healthiness of food has affected companies' approaches to developing and promoting their products. It also influences how consumers buy and use products and the satisfaction gained from them. In Figure 4.8 Kellogg's promotes the health benefits of its Common Sense Bran cereal to health conscious consumers. In many western cultures, shortage of time is a growing problem because of the rise in the number of women who work and the current emphasis placed on physical and mental self-development. Many people do time saving shopping and buy convenience and labour saving products to cope with this problem.[23]

Because culture, to some degree, determines how products are purchased and used, it in turn affects the development, promotion, distribution and pricing of products. Food marketers, for example, have had to make a multitude of changes in their marketing efforts. Thirty years ago most families ate at least two meals a day together, and the mother devoted four to six hours a day to preparing those meals. Now more than 60 per cent of women aged 25 to 54 are employed outside the home, and average family incomes have risen considerably. These shifts, along with lack of time, have resulted in dramatic increases in the per capita consumption of shelf-stable foods like Pot Rice and Pot Noodles, frozen meals and take-away foods.[24] Changes in breakfast habits, for example, have been especially marked, as consumers increasingly seek quick and easy to prepare food products. Kellogg's recently launched Pop-Tarts in an attempt to capitalise on this shift in eating behaviour. Marketing Insight 4.2 shows the impact of local

KEEPING EUROPE'S WASHING CLEAN

European manufacturers of white goods—washing machines, dishwashers, fridges and freezers—need to cater to many cultural and regional variations across the markets they serve. In the UK, consumer preference for front loading washing machines results in a product quite different from the top loading French equivalent. But not all variations are caused by differing consumer preferences. The warm, sunny climate in Italy also has an effect on product features. Here, much slower spin speeds are required by the clothes washing public than in Germany, where the climate is much colder and wetter. With the increasing use of electric tumble dryers, it is not clear for how long this difference will be significant.

Meanwhile, also in Germany, the powerful environmental movement is having an impact on the products offered to the consumer. For example, Freon gas in fridges and freezers has already been outlawed, and a move towards washing machines which use less water seems inevitable.

Local and cultural differences also influence advertising and promotion strategies. Whirlpool-Philips is unusual in its attempts to implement advertising at the pan-European level. Most manufacturers communicate at a local level, because they believe this helps to overcome differences in the way advertising messages are interpreted. Some also argue that traditional, American style advertising is unpopular in certain European markets.

Although there has been much discussion about possible convergence of product offerings in European markets, it is not yet clear how much regional differences can or will be ignored. For key industry players the challenge is to establish the values, opinions, attitudes, behaviour and expectations of consumers in order to identify similarities and differences between them.

Armed with a better understanding of the needs of key customer groups across Europe, manufacturers should be better able to match consumer requirements and make comparisons across national boundaries. Although the potential of merged marketing programmes is still unknown, opportunities exist to rationalise the way customers are grouped, thus reducing marketing costs.

SOURCES: Peter Wingard, "*A study of six Swedish firms' approach to marketing*", Warwick Business School MBA Programme, 1991; S. Whelan, "Scharp vision", *Marketing*, 26 January 1989, p. 29; T. A. Stewart, "A heartland industry takes on the world", *Fortune*, 121 (6), 12 March 1990, pp. 110–12; J. Kapstein, "The fast spinning machine that blew a gasket", *Business Week*, 10 September 1990, pp. 50–2; C. Harris, "Women of Europe put Whirlpool in a spin", *Financial Times*, 30 October 1990.

and cultural differences on a different type of product—consumer white goods, such as washing machines, fridges and freezers.

When marketers sell products overseas, they often see the tremendous impact that culture has on the purchase and use of products. International marketers find that people in other regions of the world have different attitudes, values and needs, which in turn call for different methods of doing business, as well as different types of marketing mixes. For example, the Nestlé Rowntree product Smarties uses different colours in different countries to reflect local laws governing the use of artificial colourings. Some international marketers fail because they do not or cannot adjust to cultural differences. The effect of culture on international marketing programmes is discussed in greater detail in Chaper 24.

A culture can be divided into **sub-cultures** according to geographic regions or human characteristics, such as age or ethnic background. In any country, there are a number of different sub-cultures. Within these, there are even greater similarities in people's attitudes, values and actions than within the broader culture. Relative to other sub-cultures, individuals in a certain sub-culture may have stronger preferences for specific types of clothing, furniture or foods. For example, consumption of haggis tends to be confined to Scotland rather than England or Wales. Meanwhile, European teenagers seek out the latest trends in fashion from retailers like Benetton.

Marketers must recognise that even though their operations are confined to one country, state or city, sub-cultural differences may dictate considerable variations in what products people buy. There will also be differences in how people make purchases—and variations in when they make them as well. To deal effectively with these differences, marketers may have to alter their product, promotion, distribution systems, price or people to satisfy members of particular sub-cultures.

Understanding Consumer Behaviour

Marketers try to understand consumer buying behaviour so that they can offer consumers greater satisfaction. An appreciation of how and why individuals buy products and services helps marketers design more appealing marketing programmes. Yet a certain amount of customer dissatisfaction remains. Some marketers have not adopted the marketing concept, are not consumer orientated and do not regard customer satisfaction as a primary objective. Moreover, because the tools for analysing consumer behaviour are imprecise, marketers may not be able to determine accurately what is highly satisfying to buyers. Finally, even if marketers know what increases consumer satisfaction, they may not be able to provide it.

Understanding consumer behaviour is an important task for marketers. Even though research on consumer buying behaviour has not supplied all the knowledge that marketers need, progress has been made during the last 20 years and is likely to continue in the next 200. Not only will refinements in research methods yield more information about consumer behaviour, but the pressures of an increasingly competitive business environment will also make obtaining such information much more urgent for marketers.

Summary

Buying behaviour refers to the decision processes and acts of people involved in buying and using products. Consumer buying behaviour refers to the buying behaviour of ultimate consumers, those who purchase products for personal or household use, not for business purposes. Analysing consumer buying behaviour is important to marketers; if they are able to determine what satisfies customers, they can implement the marketing concept and better predict how consumers will respond to different marketing programmes.

Consumer decisions can be classified into three categories: routine response behaviour, limited decision-making and extensive decision-making. A consumer uses routine response behaviour when buying frequently purchased, low cost, low risk items that require very little search and decision effort. Limited decision-making is used for products purchased occasionally or when a buyer needs to acquire information about an unfamiliar brand in a familiar product category. Extensive decision-making is used when purchasing an unfamiliar, expensive, high risk or infrequently bought product. Impulse buying is an unplanned buying behaviour involving a powerful, persistent urge to buy something immediately. The purchase of a certain product does not always elicit the same type of decision-making behaviour. Individuals differ in their response to purchase situations. Even the same individual may make a different decision in other circumstances.

The consumer buying decision process includes five stages: problem recognition, information search, evaluation of alternatives, purchase and post-purchase evaluation. Decision processes do not always culminate in a purchase, and not all consumer decisions include all five stages. Problem recognition occurs when a buyer becomes aware that there is a difference between a desired state and an actual condition. After recognising the problem or need, the buyer searches for information about products that will help resolve the problem or satisfy the need. In the internal search, buyers search their memories for information about products that might solve the problem. If they are unable to retrieve from memory sufficient information to make a decision, they seek additional information through an external search. A successful search will yield a group of brands, called an evoked set, that a buyer views as possible alternatives. To evaluate the products in the evoked set, a buyer establishes certain criteria by which to compare, rate and rank the different products. Marketers can influence consumers' evaluation by framing the alternatives.

In the purchase stage, the consumer selects the product or brand on the basis of results from the evaluation stage and on other dimensions. The buyer also chooses the seller from whom he or she will buy the product. After the purchase, the buyer evaluates the product to determine if its actual performance meets expected levels. Shortly after the purchase of an expensive product, for example, the post-purchase evaluation may provoke cognitive dissonance, dissatisfaction brought on by the consumer's doubts as to whether he or she should have bought the product in the first place or would have been better off buying another brand that had also ranked high in the evaluation. The results of the post-purchase evaluation will affect future buying behaviour.

Three major categories of influences are believed to affect the consumer buying decision process: personal, psychological and social factors. A personal factor is one that is unique to a particular person. Personal factors include demographic factors, situational factors and level of involvement. Demographic factors are individual characteristics such as age, sex, race, ethnic origin, income, family life-cycle and occupation. Situational factors are the external circumstances or conditions that exist when a consumer is making a purchase decision. The time available to make a decision is a situational factor that strongly influences consumer buying decisions. An individual's level of involvement—the importance and intensity of interest in a product in a particular situation—also affects the buying decision process. Enduring involvement is an ongoing interest in a product class because of personal relevance. Situational involvement is a temporary interest resulting from the particular circumstance or environment in which buyers find themselves.

Psychological factors partly determine people's general behaviour and thus influence their behaviour as consumers. The primary psychological influences on consumer behaviour are perception, motives, ability and knowledge, attitudes and personality. Perception is the process of selecting, organising and interpreting information inputs (the sensations received through sight, taste, hearing, smell and touch) to produce meaning. Selective exposure is the phenomenon of people selecting the inputs that are to be exposed to their awareness; selective distortion is the changing or twisting of currently received information. When a person remembers information inputs that support personal feelings and beliefs and forgets inputs that do not, the phenomenon is called selective retention. The second step of the perceptual process requires organising and integrating the new information with that already stored in memory. Interpretation—the third step in the perceptual process—is the assignment of meaning to what has been organised. In addition to perceptions of packages, products, brands and organisations, individuals also have a self-concept, or self-image.

A motive is an internal, energy giving force directing a person's activities towards satisfying a need or achieving a goal. Patronage motives influence where a person purchases products on a regular basis. To analyse the major motives that influence consumers to buy or not buy their products, marketers conduct motivation research, using in-depth interviews, focus groups or projective techniques. Common types of projective techniques include word association tests, bubble drawings and sentence completion tests.

Individuals vary in their ability—their competence and efficiency in performing tasks. Ability includes both learning and knowledge. Learning refers to changes in a person's behaviour caused by information and experience. Knowledge has two components: familiarity with the product and expertise—the individual's ability to apply the product.

Attitude refers to knowledge and positive or negative feelings about an object or activity. Consumer attitudes towards a firm and its products greatly influence the success or failure of the firm's marketing strategy. Marketers measure consumers' attitudes with projective techniques and attitude scales.

Personality comprises all the internal traits and behaviours that make a person unique. Some marketers believe that personality does influence the types and brands of products purchased.

The forces that other people exert on buying behaviour are called social factors. Social factors include the influence of roles and family, reference groups, social classes, and culture and sub-cultures. All of us occupy positions within groups, organisations and institutions, and each position has a role—a set of actions and activities that a person in a particular position is supposed to perform, based on the expectations of both the individual and surrounding persons. A group is a reference group when an individual identifies with the group so much that he or she takes on many of the values, attitudes or behaviours of group members. A social class is an open group of individuals who have similar social rank. Culture is everything in our surroundings that is made by human beings. A culture can be divided into sub-cultures on the basis of geographic regions or human characteristics, such as age or ethnic background.

Marketers try to understand consumer buying behaviour so that they can offer consumers greater satisfaction. Refinements in research methods will yield more information about consumer behaviour, and the pressure of an increasingly competitive business environment will spur marketers to seek fuller understanding of consumer decision processes.

IMPORTANT TERMS

Buying behaviour
Consumer buying behaviour
Routine response behaviour
Limited decision-making
Extensive decision-making
Impulse buying
Consumer buying
  decision process
Internal search
External search
Salience
Cognitive dissonance
Personal factors
Demographic factors
Situational factors
Level of involvement
Psychological factors
Perception
Information inputs
Selective exposure

Selective distortion
Selective retention
Self-concept
Motive
Patronage motives
In-depth interview
Focus group
Projective techniques
Ability
Learning
Knowledge
Attitude
Attitude scale
Personality
Social factors
Role
Reference group
Social class
Culture
Sub-cultures

DISCUSSION AND REVIEW QUESTIONS

1. Name the types of buying behaviour consumers use. List some products that you have bought using each type of behaviour. Have you ever bought a product on impulse? In what circumstances?
2. What are the major stages in the consumer buying decision process? Are all these stages used in all consumer purchase decisions?
3. What are the personal factors that affect the consumer buying decision process? How do they affect the process?
4. How does a consumer's level of involvement affect his or her purchase behaviour?
5. What is the function of time in a consumer's purchasing decision process?
6. What is selective exposure? Why do humans engage in it?
7. How do marketers attempt to shape consumers' learning?
8. Why are marketers concerned about consumer attitudes?
9. How do roles affect a person's buying behaviour?
10. Describe reference groups. How do they influence buying behaviour? Name some of your own reference groups.
11. In what ways does social class affect a person's purchase decisions?
12. What is culture? How does it affect a person's buying behaviour?
13. Describe the sub-cultures to which you belong. Identify buying behaviour that is unique to your sub-culture.
14. What is the impact of post-purchase evaluation on future buying decisions?

4.1   IKEA: Stylish Home Furnishings at Affordable Prices

Swedish company IKEA is a mass market producer of cheap and stylish home furnishings which appear to transcend national boundaries. The company was founded in 1943 by Ingvar Kamprad, a small town handyman from southern Sweden, who devised the company name by combining his initials with the first initials of his farm (Elmtaryd) and the parish (Agunnaryd) where he was raised. Today, IKEA's business mission is clear. In the words of the company's founder, "We shall offer a wide range of furnishing items of good design and function, at prices so low that the majority of people can afford to buy them".

Since expanding internationally in 1973, IKEA's incremental growth approach to spreading into overseas markets has continued. Now located in more than twenty countries, the company almost tripled its turnover worldwide between 1984 and 1990 (see table). Offering affordable and varied furniture is central to IKEA's strategy. The company maintains its cost advantages by doing what it does best and concentrates on its core business and on the adoption of a long term strategy.

YEAR	OUTLETS	COUNTRIES	CO-WORKERS	TURNOVER (SEK m)
1954	1	1	15	3
1964	2	2	250	79
1974	10	5	1,500	616
1984	66	17	8,300	6,770
1990	86	21	16,850	19,400

SOURCE: From *IKEA Facts 1990*. Used with permission.

IKEA's ability to maintain its success across so many markets is impressive. Some studies suggest that one possible reason for this success is that when prices are very competitive cultural barriers become smaller and it becomes easier to reach a larger percentage of the total furniture buying population. To maintain its low cost base, the company needs to shift volume, which it does by selling broadly the same range of stylish, flat packed Swedish products in all of its stores worldwide.

Price is not the only reason for IKEA's success. In the design of its stores and products, IKEA has done much to appeal to consumers' underlying reasons for buying. The company understands that shopping is a purposeful activity: people buy in order to make their lives richer. In IKEA's case, the challenge has been to make the apparent essence of a Swedish lifestyle—beautiful homes and high quality living—available at affordable prices.

Consumer interest in IKEA has revived the flagging fortunes of furniture retailers. In areas where new IKEA stores have opened, the company's lively approach has led to an increase in the time spent shopping for home related products. Research also suggests that the proportion of the income which consumers are prepared to spend on these products is increasing. IKEA therefore believes it is competing with purchases of new cars and holidays—anything which claims the disposable income in the consumer's pocket— not just from other furniture retailers.

Although the company does not deliberately use demographic and psychographic variables to segment its customer base, IKEA products seem to appeal particularly to people in their twenties and thirties. In order to expand the product line further into other life-cycle stages, the company is trying to grow with its customers by adopting a policy of offering products which cater to families with teenage children and those whose children have left home.

While IKEA recognises that consumers shop to improve their lives, the company also acknowledges their practical needs. People are much more likely to visit retail outlets which are conveniently located and where the shopping experience is fun. IKEA meets these important needs by locating its stores close to motorways and major trunk roads and by offering extensive parking, child care, toilet and restaurant facilities. A full range of furnishings is presented in real room settings which combine expensive, high risk purchases such as living-room suites and carpets with cheaper, lower involvement items such as pictures, ornaments and lampshades.

SOURCES: Peter Wingard, "*A study of six Swedish firms' approach to marketing*", Warwick Business School MBA Programme, 1991; S. Redmond, "Home Truths", *Marketing*, 7 April 1988; J. Bamford and A. Dunlap Smith, "Why competitors shop for ideas at IKEA", *Business Week*, 9 October 1989; P. Corwin, "The Vikings are back—with furniture", *Discount Merchandiser*, 27 (4), April 1987; B. Saporito, "IKEA's got 'em lining up", *Fortune*, 123 (5), 11 March 1991; J. Reynolds, "IKEA: a competitive company with style", *Retail and Distribution Management*, 16 (3), 1988; "Report on the UK Furniture Market", *Key Note*, 1989.

Questions for Discussion

1. How do families go about purchasing a new item of furniture? Who influences and who is involved in the buying decision?
2. What factors influence the way in which a newly married couple buys furniture?
3. How important is price to IKEA because of its position as a retailer of home furnishings?

4.2 Mattessons Re-positions Its Products

During 1989 and 1990 there were numerous food scares within the European Community. In the UK, fears about salmonella and listeria reaped havoc in many key food areas. For months, egg sales plummeted as a result; and beef sales have yet to recover following the discovery of Mad Cow disease and its possible mobility through the food chain to reach human consumers. The rapidly growing sector of ready-to-eat chilled foods was also thrown into recession by the discovery of listeria in products on many supermarket shelves. Paté, too, suffered following a listeria scare.

Unilever subsidiary Mattessons Wall's has emerged from the battering of the recent food safety scares with a radical repositioning and massive cash boost for its paté to sliced meat brand Mattessons. A £3.5 million television and press campaign will bury the brand's familiar mnemonic catch lines—such as "try saying Mattessons without saying mmm"—in an attempt to move up market with more adult orientated lifestyle advertising.

The move sees the re-introduction of Mattessons' paté after the listeria scare forced them off supermarket shelves in July 1990. Unilever claims, though, that the brand repositioning is not connected with the crisis and has in fact been planned for eighteen months. Mattessons has jettisoned its former strategy and is aiming to satisfy the needs of an increasingly educated and discerning consumer.

Mattessons claims 42 per cent of the £14 million branded paté market and 65 per cent of the £130 million sliced meat sales, but admits that sales of paté fell by 30 per cent during the listeria scare. Unilever switched its Belgium supplier of paté and revamped its production process. Now paté is cooked in the tubs which are sold to the consumer, lowering the risk of infection caused by the transfer of food from factory moulds to retail packs.

Despite the scare, the re-launch, re-positioning and promotional campaigns do not stress the safety issue. Unilever believes that consumers remember the listeria scare but do not associate it with the Mattessons brand. Instead, the company is pushing the quality and taste of its re-positioned paté products.

SOURCES: Mike Johnson and Alan Mitchell, "Crisis in food", *Marketing*, 26 October 1990, pp. 24–9; Mike Johnson, "Mattessons' move up market puts paté back on shelves", *Marketing*, 5 April 1990, p. 4; Karen Hoggan, "Meat industry banks on recipe data to beef up sales", *Marketing*, 27 September 1990, p. 5.

Questions for Discussion

1. An attitude refers to knowledge and positive or negative feelings about an object or activity. How have attitudes towards fresh foods changed during the last few years?
2. How might the UK meat industry change consumer attitudes towards its products?
3. How can culture and subculture explain the consumption of beef or paté? How might an industry body or manufacturer use this information to develop a marketing strategy for the consumption of its products?

5 ORGANISATIONAL MARKETS AND BUYING BEHAVIOUR

Objectives

- To become familiar with the various types of organisational markets

- To identify the major characteristics of organisational buyers and transactions

- To understand several attributes of organisational demand

- To become familiar with the major components of a buying centre

- To understand the relationship between industrial buyers and sellers

- To understand the stages of the organisational buying decision process and the factors that affect this process

*E*mployees at 3M are continually trying to discover products to fill industrial and organisational niches. And the creative spirit at 3M gives employees the opportunity and encouragement to keep producing technological breakthroughs. The company actively encourages innovation by allowing employees to spend up to 15 per cent of their work time on their own projects. Special 3M Genesis grants are available to allow researchers funding of up to £40,000 to support new ideas. If a new product is successfully developed, those developing it are allowed to be active in its ongoing management.

One 3M chemist created a special filter to clean lubricants in metalworking shops. The market for the filter, even though it worked very well, was judged to be worth less than £1 million. Management was so impressed, though, that it allowed the employee to continue to develop the filter and eventually enter into a joint venture with a 3M customer, PPG Industries. The company, which sells paint-primer systems to car manufacturers, had been having difficulties with the filters it was using for straining impurities from the paint. The 3M filter worked much better. Since then, the filters have also proved efficient strainers for machine oil, paint, edible oils, water and beer—all in all, a £$15 million market. It is not surprising that some business experts regard 3M as the most innovative company in the world! ▪

SOURCES: Russell Mitchell, "Masters of innovation", *Business Week,* 10 April 1989, pp. 58–63; Margaret Nelson, "Top priority at 3M is communications", *Purchasing,* 10 March 1988, pp. 104–5, 109; Thomas Osborn, "How 3M manages for innovation", *Marketing Communications*, November–December 1988, pp. 17–22.

n Chapter 3 an organisational or industrial market was defined as consisting of individuals or groups that purchase a specific type of product for resale, for use in making other products, or for use in daily operations.

This chapter looks more closely at organisational markets and organisational buying decision processes. The first section discusses the various kinds of organisational markets and the types of buyers that make up these markets. The next section explores several dimensions of organisational buying, such as the characteristics of the transactions, the attributes and concerns of the buyers, the methods of buying, and the distinctive features of the demand for products sold to organisational purchasers. Finally, the chapter examines organisational buying decisions by considering how they are arrived at and who makes the purchases.

TYPES OF ORGANISATIONAL MARKETS

Chapter 3 identified four kinds of organisational, or industrial, markets: producers, resellers, governments and institutions. The following section describes the characteristics of the customers that make up these markets. Table 5.1 shows the employment patterns in these markets across Europe.

Producer Markets

Individuals and business organisations that purchase products for the purpose of making a profit by using them to produce other products or by using them in their own operations are classified as **producer markets.** Producer markets include buyers of raw materials, semi-finished and finished items used to produce other products. For example, a manufacturer buys raw materials and component parts to use directly in the production of its products. In Figure 5.1, Forros Rayon uses silk as a lining fabric. Grocers and supermarkets are producer markets for numerous support products, such as paper and plastic bags, displays, scanners and floor care products. Farmers are producer markets for farm machinery, fertiliser, seed and livestock. Producer markets cover a broad array of industries, ranging from agriculture, forestry, fisheries and mining to construction, transport, communications and public utilities. The number of business units in European producer markets is enormous.

Manufacturers tend to be geographically concentrated. This concentration occurs in Europe too, with heavy industry centred on the Ruhr Valley in Germany and on the Midlands and North West in the UK. Sometimes an industrial marketer may be able to serve customers more efficiently as a result. Within certain areas, production in just a few industries may account for a sizeable proportion of total industrial output.

Reseller Markets

Reseller markets consist of intermediaries, such as wholesalers and retailers, who buy finished goods and resell them to make a profit. (Wholesalers and retailers are discussed in Chapters 11 and 12.) Other than making minor alterations, resellers do not change the physical characteristics of the products they handle. With the exception of items that producers sell directly to consumers, all products sold to consumer markets are first sold to reseller markets.

Wholesalers purchase products for resale to retailers, to other wholesalers and to producers, governments and institutions. Although some highly technical products are sold directly to end users, many products are sold through wholesalers, who in turn sell products to other firms in the distribution system. Thus wholesalers are very important in helping to get a producer's product to customers. Wholesalers often carry many products, perhaps as many as 250,000 items. From the reseller's point of view, having access to such an array of products from a single source makes it much simpler to buy

TABLE 5.1 *Percentage of the workforce employed in different sectors across Europe, 1989*

SECTOR	BELGIUM[a]	DENMARK[a]	FRANCE[a]	GERMANY[a]	GREECE[b]	IRELAND[a]	ITALY[a]	NETHERLANDS[a]	NORWAY[c]	PORTUGAL[a]	SPAIN[d]	SWEDEN[a]	SWITZERLAND[a]
Agriculture, forestry	2.7	5.6	6.1	3.4	25.3	15.0	9.0	4.6	5.8	17.8	11.8	3.2	5.6
Mining, quarrying	0.2	0.1	0.4	0.7	0.6	0.7	1.1	0.2	1.0	0.8	0.6	0.3	0.1
Manufacturing	21.0	20.2	21.3	31.5	19.5	19.7	22.5	18.9	14.6	25.1	22.3	20.1	24.7
Electricity, gas, water	0.8	0.8	0.9	0.9	1.0	1.2	–	0.7	1.0	0.9	0.7	0.8	0.6
Construction	6.3	6.5	7.3	6.6	6.5	7.0	8.8	6.5	6.5	8.1	9.7	7.0	9.5
Wholesale retail, restaurants, hotels	17.0	14.8	17.3	16.3	17.0	17.4	21.5	17.6	17.6	15.5	20.2	14.1	20.6
Transport, storage and communications	6.9	7.2	6.4	5.8	6.6	6.1	5.4	6.1	8.1	4.5	5.8	7.2	6.1
Finance, insurance and business services	8.8	9.4	10.0	7.9	4.6	8.2	4.2	10.3	7.6	4.6	5.4	9.0	10.6
Community, social and personal services	34.9	34.5	30.2	26.7	18.9	24.6	27.5	34.2	37.5	22.8	23.4	38.2	21.9
Not defined	1.3	1.1	–	–	–	0.4	–	0.9	0.3	–	–	0.1	–

SOURCE: *European Marketing Pocket Book, 1993,* NTC Publications Ltd. Used with permission. Individual Country Contributions as below.

Notes: [a] *Labour Force Statistics,* (OECD), World Bank, 1990
[b] *Labour Force Statistics,* (OECD), World Bank, 1990 (1989 figures)
[c] *Statistisk Årbok,* 1992 (1991 figures)
[d] *Labour Force Statistics,* (OECD), Instituto Nacional de Estadistica, 1990
[e] Swedish Statistics Office, 1991.

Los Forros Rayón son la cara oculta de la moda.
Una cara noble. Suave. Confortable. Cómoda.
Una cara que, hasta hoy, ha estado tan oculta
como la otra cara de la Luna.

La cara oculta de la moda.

FORROS RAYON
PRENDAS CON CUERPO Y ALMA

FIGURE 5.1 *Focus on producer markets*
Forros Rayon emphasises the uses of silk in its producer markets.

SOURCE: Agency: SCACS, S. A.; Creative Director: Juame Anglada; Photographer: Peggegrin Arara.

a variety of items. When inventories are vast, the reordering of products is normally automated and the wholesaler's initial purchase decisions are made by professional buyers and buying committees.

Retailers purchase products and resell them to final consumers. Some retailers carry a large number of items. Chemists, for example, may stock up to 12,000 items, and some supermarkets may handle as many as 20,000 different products. In small, family owned retail stores, the owner frequently makes purchasing decisions. Large department stores have one or more employees in each department who are responsible for buying products for that department. As for chain stores, a buyer or buying committee in the central office frequently decides whether a product will be made available for selection by store managers. For most products, however, local store managers make the actual buying decisions for a particular store.

When making purchase decisions, resellers consider several factors. They evaluate the level of demand for a product to determine in what quantity and at what prices it can be resold. They assess the amount of space required to handle a product relative to its potential profit. Sometimes resellers will put a product on trial for a fixed period, allowing them to judge customers' reactions and to make better informed decisions about shelf space and positions as a result. Retailers, for example, sometimes evaluate products on the basis of sales per square meter of selling area. Since customers often depend on a reseller to have a product when they need it, a reseller typically evaluates a supplier's ability to provide adequate quantities when and where wanted. Resellers also take into account the ease of placing orders and the availability of technical assistance and training programmes from the producer. More broadly, when resellers consider buying a product not previously carried, they try to determine whether the product competes with or complements products the firm is currently handling. These types of concerns distinguish reseller markets from other markets. Sometimes resellers will start stocking a new line of products in response to specific requests from customers. Marketers dealing with reseller markets must recognise these needs and be able to serve them.

Government Markets

National and local governments make up **government markets.** They spend billions of pounds annually for a variety of goods and services to support their internal operations and to provide the public with education, water, energy, national defence, road systems and health care. Table 5.2 shows UK central government expenditure on goods and services from 1981 to 1991. In Europe, the amount spent by local governments varies from country to country depending on the level and cost of services provided. With the start of the European single market, the services provided by different governments may eventually become standardised.

The types and quantities of products bought by government markets reflect social demands on various government agencies. As the public's needs for government services change, so do the government markets' demands for products. Because government agencies spend public funds to buy the products they need to provide services, they are accountable to the public. This accountability is responsible for their relatively complex set of buying procedures. Some firms, unwilling to deal with so much red tape, do not even try to sell to government buyers. However, many marketers have learned to deal efficiently with government procedures and do not find them a stumbling block. For certain companies, such as British Aerospace, and for certain products, such as defence related items, the government may be the only customer.

Governments usually make their purchases through bids or negotiated contracts. To make a sale under the bid system, a firm must apply and receive approval to be placed on a list of qualified bidders. When a government unit wants to buy, it sends out a detailed description of the products to these qualified bidders. Businesses that wish to sell such products then submit bids. The government unit is usually required to accept the lowest bid. When buying non-standard or highly complex products, a government unit often uses a negotiated contract. Under this procedure, the government unit selects only a few firms, negotiates specifications and terms, and eventually awards the contract to one of the negotiating firms. Most large defence contracts held by such companies as GEC, Ferranti and Plessey are reached through negotiated contracts.

Although government markets have complicated requirements, they can also be very lucrative. When government departments or health care providers modernise obsolete computer systems, for example, successful bidders can make many millions of pounds during the life of a contract, which may last for five years or more. Some firms have established separate departments to facilitate marketing to government units, while others specialise entirely in this area.

Institutional Markets

Organisations that seek to achieve charitable, educational, community or other non-business goals constitute **institutional markets.** Members of institutional markets include libraries, museums, universities, charitable organisations and some churches and hospitals. Institutions purchase millions of pounds' worth of products annually to provide goods, services and ideas to club members, congregations, students and

TABLE 5.2 *UK central government: Current account (£ million)*

EXPENDITURE	1981	1982	1983	1984	1985	1986	1987	1988	1989	1990	1991
Final consumption:											
Current expenditure on goods and services:											
General public services	2,433	2,701	2,791	2,716	2,870	3,094	3,145	3,454	4,278	4,703	4,739
Defence	12,523	14,274	15,584	16,839	17,855	18,593	18,661	19,282	20,447	22,182	24,401
Public order and safety	1,127	1,259	1,406	1,581	1,598	1,954	2,140	2,413	2,689	3,060	3,958
Education	702	797	851	879	975	1,085	1,099	1,131	1,247	1,400	1,603
Health	12,631	13,199	14,994	15,741	16,763	17,956	19,765	21,771	23,577	25,853	29,076
Social security	1,273	1,461	1,505	1,560	1,670	1,607	2,050	2,285	2,380	2,532	2,927
Housing and community amenity	34	44	37	52	38	43	125	136	170	300	288
Recreational and cultural affairs	151	155	223	217	202	240	282	369	419	474	551
Fuel and energy	163	153	206	243	264	304	281	167	303	237	280
Agriculture, forestry and fishing	375	378	373	308	382	400	504	478	481	585	610
Mining and mineral resources, manufacturing and construction	319	324	299	335	388	354	358	419	358	346	579
Transport and communications	350	433	424	371	430	440	538	523	689	700	780
Other economic affairs and services	1,025	1,011	1,117	1,404	1,461	1,655	1,913	1,879	2,005	3,057	3,000
Total current expenditure on goods and services[1]	33,106	36,189	39,810	42,246	44,896	47,725	50,861	54,307	59,043	65,429	72,792
Non-trading capital consumption	773	811	844	896	983	1,076	1,179	1,303	1,484	1,623	1,650
Total final consumption	33,879	37,000	40,654	43,142	45,879	48,801	52,040	55,610	60,527	67,052	74,442

1. Net of the following income from fees and charges, etc. (£ million):

1981	1982	1983	1984	1985	1986	1987	1988	1989	1990	1991
2,290	2,616	2,901	2,741	2,287	1,970	2,026	2,255	2,489	2,484	2,466

SOURCE: United Kingdom National Accounts, Central Statistical Office, 1992. Reprinted by permission of the Controller of Her Majesty's Stationery Office.

others. Because such institutions often have different goals and fewer resources than other types of organisations, marketers may use special marketing activities to serve these markets.

DIMENSIONS OF ORGANISATIONAL BUYING

Having clarified the different types of organisational customers, the next step is to consider the dimensions of organisational buying. After first examining several characteristics of organisational transactions this section then discusses several attributes of organisational buyers and some of their primary concerns when making purchase decisions. Next it looks at methods of organisational buying and the major types of purchases organisations make. The section concludes with a discussion of how the demand for industrial products differs from the demand for consumer products.

Characteristics of Organisational Transactions

Although the marketing concept is applicable to organisational and consumer markets equally, there are several fundamental differences between the transactions which occur in each. Organisational buyers tend to order in much larger quantities than do individual consumers. Suppliers must often sell their products in large quantities to make profits; consequently, they prefer not to sell to customers who place small orders.

Generally, organisational purchases are negotiated less frequently than consumer sales. Some purchases involve expensive items, such as machinery or office equipment, that are used for a number of years (see Figure 5.2). Other products, such as raw materials and component items, are used continuously in production and may have to be supplied frequently. However, the contract regarding the terms of sale of these items is likely to be a long term agreement, requiring negotiations, for example, every third year.

Although negotiations in organisational sales are less frequent than in consumer sales, they may take much longer. Purchasing decisions are often made by a committee; orders are frequently large, expensive and complex; and products may be custom built. There is a good chance that several people or departments in the purchasing organisation will be involved. One department might express a need for a product; a second department might develop its specifications; a third might stipulate the maximum amount to be spent; and a fourth might actually place the order. This approach allows individuals with relevant expertise to be incorporated into the process when required.

One practice unique to organisational sales is **reciprocity,** an arrangement in which two organisations agree to buy from each other. In some countries, reciprocal agreements that threaten competition are illegal and action may be taken to stop anticompetitive reciprocal practices. None the less, it is reasonable to believe that a certain amount of reciprocal dealing occurs among small businesses and, to a lesser extent, among larger companies as well. Reciprocity can create a problem because coercive measures may be used to enforce it. Also, because reciprocity influences purchasing agents to deal only with certain suppliers, it can lower morale among agents and lead to less than optimal purchases.[1]

Attributes of Organisational Buyers

Organisational buyers are usually thought of as being different from consumer buyers in their purchasing behaviour because they are better informed about the products they purchase. To make purchasing decisions that fulfil an organisation's needs, organisational buyers demand detailed information about a product's functional features and technical specifications.

Organisational buyers, however, also have personal goals that may influence their buying behaviour. Most organisational buyers seek the psychological satisfaction that

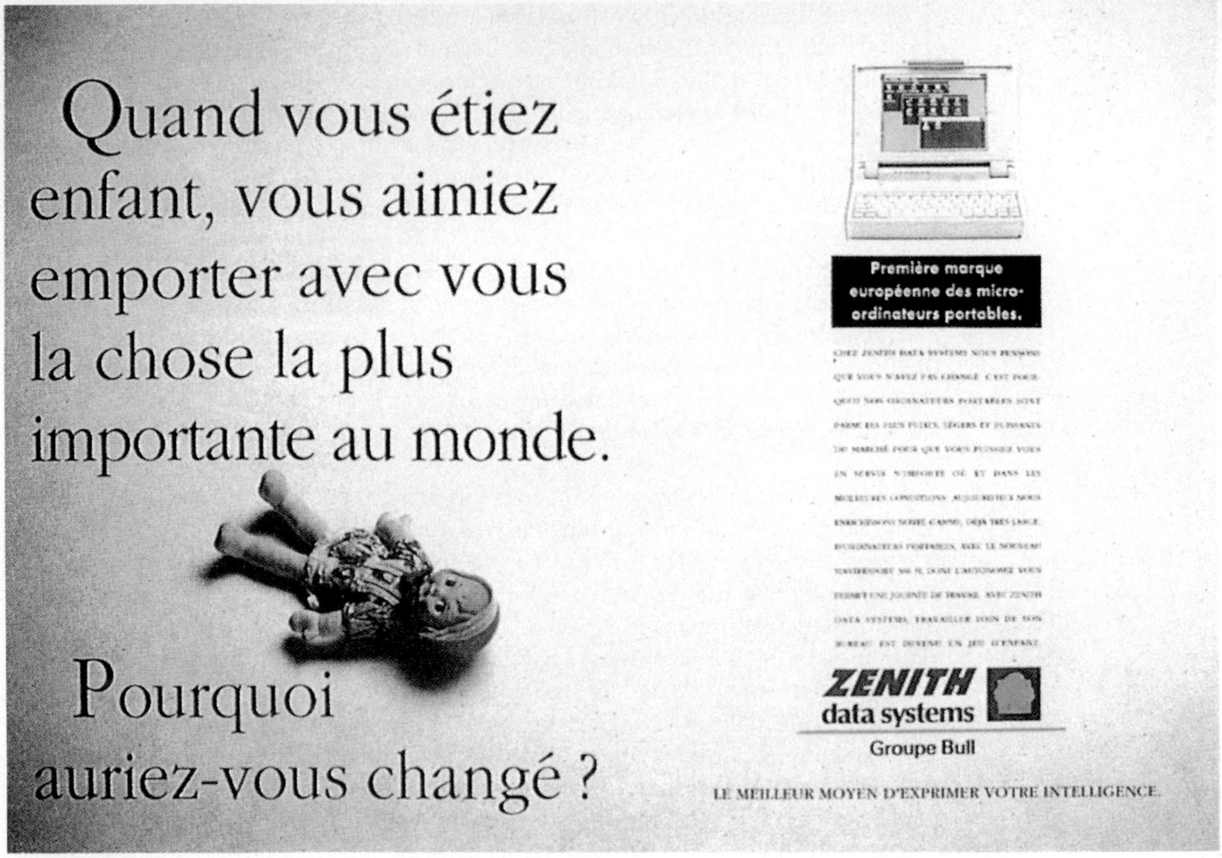

FIGURE 5.2 *One type of organisational purchase*

SOURCE: Photography courtesy of Kevin Summers.

comes with promotion and financial rewards. In general, agents are most likely to achieve these personal goals when they consistently exhibit rational organisational buying behaviour and are thus performing their jobs in ways that help their firms achieve their organisational objectives. Suppose, though, that an organisational buyer develops a close friendship with a certain supplier. If the buyer values the friendship more than organisational promotion or financial rewards, he or she may behave irrationally from the firm's point of view. Dealing exclusively with that supplier regardless of better prices, quality or service from competitors may indicate an unhealthy or unethical alliance between the buyer and seller. Some companies require more than one person to be involved in buying products in order to safeguard against the possible development of such unhealthy relationships.

Primary Concerns of Organisational Buyers

When they make purchasing decisions, organisational customers take into account a variety of factors. Among their chief considerations are quality, delivery, service and price.[2] Product range and innovation may also be significant considerations.

Most organisational customers try to achieve and maintain a specific level of quality in the products they offer to their target markets. To accomplish this goal, they often buy their products on the basis of a set of expressed characteristics, commonly called *specifications*. Thus these allow an organisational buyer to evaluate the quality of the products being considered according to a given list of features and thus to determine whether or not they meet the organisation's needs.

Meeting specifications is extremely important to organisational customers. If a product fails to meet specifications and malfunctions for the ultimate consumer, the organisational customer may drop that product's supplier and switch to a different one. On the other hand, an organisational buyer is usually cautious about buying products that exceed specifications, because such products often cost more and thus increase the organisation's production costs. Suppliers therefore need to design their products carefully to come as close as possible to their customers' specifications without incurring any unnecessary extras.

Organisational buyers also value service. The services offered by suppliers directly and indirectly influence organisational customers' costs, sales and profits. When tangible goods are the same or quite similar—as is true in the case of most raw materials—they may have the same specifications and be sold at the same price in the same kind of containers. Under such conditions, the mix of services an organisational marketer provides to its customers represents its greatest opportunity to gain a competitive advantage.

Among the most commonly expected services are market information, inventory maintenance, on-time delivery, repair services and credit. Specific services vary in importance, however, and the mix of services companies need is also affected by environmental conditions. In times of recession, for example, services are in greater demand as companies delay replacing capital equipment. Organisational buyers in general are likely to need technical product information, data regarding demand, information about general economic conditions or supply and delivery information. It is critical for suppliers to maintain an adequate inventory in order to keep products accessible when an organisational buyer needs them and to reduce the buyer's inventory requirements and costs. Since organisational buyers are usually responsible for ensuring that the organisation has products on hand and ready for use when needed, on-time delivery is crucial. Furthermore, reliable, on-time delivery by suppliers saves the organisational customers money, enabling them to carry less inventory. Organisational purchasers of machinery are especially concerned about obtaining repair services and replacement parts quickly, because equipment that cannot be used is costly. Caterpillar, a manufacturer of earthmoving, construction and materials handling machinery, has built an international reputation, as well as high profits, by providing prompt service and replacement parts for its products around the world.

Suppliers can also give extra value to organisational buyers by offering credit. Credit helps to improve an organisational customer's cash flow, reduce the peaks and troughs of capital requirements and thus lower the firm's cost of capital. Although no single supplier can provide every possible service to its organisational customers, a marketing oriented supplier will try to create a service mix that satisfies the target market.

Providing service has become even more critical for organisational marketers because customer expectations of service have broadened. Now, for instance, communication channels that allow customers to ask questions, complain, submit orders and trace shipments are indispensable. Organisational marketers also need to strive for uniformity of service, simplicity, truthfulness and accuracy; to develop customer service objectives; and to monitor or audit their customer service programmes. Firms can monitor the quality of their service by formally surveying customers or calling on them informally to ask questions about the service they have received. Marketers with a strong customer service programme reap a reward: their customers keep coming back long after the first sale.[3] For their programme to succeed, however, they must conduct research to determine customers' expectations in regard to product quality and service.[4] With customer expectations increasing, it is becoming more difficult for companies to achieve a differential advantage in these areas.[5] Marketing Insight 5.1 explains one company's efforts to stay in touch with customer expectations.

ASEA BROWN BOVERI GROUP: ACT GLOBALLY, THINK LOCALLY

Swedish based Asea Brown Boveri Group (ABB) provides electrical systems and equipment worldwide to customers in the electrical power generation, transmission, industrial, environmental control and mass transit markets. The company aims to develop its business globally while maintaining the flexibility of local market presence through centralised reporting within a decentralised structure.

ABB segments its customers into business areas based on product type and application. These areas are in turn grouped into eight business segments, each with its own demands in terms of the systems technology and sales approach to which ABB must respond. The company organises its efforts through *business area leaders,* who are responsible for strategic planning and decide which markets and customers to serve.

In order to keep its diverse customer base satisfied, ABB has implemented its own mix of Total Quality Management, Just-in-Time and Time-Based Management philosophies. The initiative aims to put the customer first and to offer higher standards of quality, delivery and customer support. Staff rotation and teamwork are encouraged, and sales and marketing, product development and production departments work together in functional units.

With interests in so many national markets, ABB is susceptible to a variety of important changes in environmental conditions. Most significantly, the European power equipment industry is becoming increasingly oligopolistic as a result of mergers and acquisitions. It also seems likely that EC prices will fall as the procurement of power plants opens up from 1993. Although ABB is optimistic about its chances in the European Community, not everyone agrees. In 1988 *The Economist* made the following observation:

> ABB may continue to suffer discrimination in public procurement after 1992 in those EC countries where it lacks a subsidiary that ranks alongside domestic competitors . . . National preference (in power systems) is such an ingrained habit that local favourites always have a definite and usually decisive advantage everywhere—GEC in the UK, and Northern Electric and Westinghouse in the United States, Hitachi in Japan and so on.

Concern for the environment is also affecting ABB's market. As it moves forward into the mid-1990s, the company seeks to capitalise on its experience in environmentally friendly technology by making products for use in green applications. Understanding and responding to changes of this type are all part of the company's relationship building philosophy, which helps it stay in touch with market needs.

SOURCES: Peter Wingard, "A study of six Swedish firms' approach to marketing", Warwick Business School MBA Programme, 1991; ABB company report, 1990; "Asea Brown Boveri: power play", *The Economist,* 28 May 1988; W. Taylor, "The logic of global business: an interview with ABB's Percy Barnevik", *Harvard Business Review,* March–April 1991.

Price matters greatly to an organisational customer because it influences operating costs and costs of goods sold, and these costs affect the customer's selling price and profit margin. When purchasing major equipment, an industrial buyer views the price as the amount of investment necessary to obtain a certain level of return or savings. Thus an organisational purchaser is likely to compare the price of a machine with the value of the benefits that the machine will yield. Caterpillar lost market share to foreign competitors because its prices were too high. An organisational buyer does not compare alternative products by price alone, though; other factors, such as product quality and supplier services, are also major elements in the purchase decision. For example, one study found that in the buying decision process for mainframe computer software operating systems, buyers indicated that intangible attributes, such as the seller's credibility and understanding of the buyer's needs, were very important in the decision process.[6]

Methods of Organisational Buying

Although no two organisational buyers go about their jobs in the same way, most use one or more of the following purchase methods: *description, inspection, sampling* or *negotiation*. When the products being purchased are commonly standardised according to certain characteristics (such as size, shape, weight and colour) and graded using such standards, an organisational buyer may be able to purchase simply by describing or specifying quantity, grade and other attributes. Agricultural produce often falls into this category. In some cases, a buyer may specify a particular brand or its equivalent when describing the desired product. Purchases on the basis of description are especially common between a buyer and seller who have established an ongoing relationship built on trust.

Certain products, such as large industrial machinery, used vehicles and buildings, have unique characteristics and are likely to vary in condition. For example, a factory unit which is for sale may need to be redecorated and have a dampproof coarse inserted. Consequently, organisational buyers of such products must base their purchase decisions on inspection.

In buying based on sampling, a sample of the product is taken from the lot and evaluated. It is assumed that the characteristics of this sample represent the entire lot. This method is appropriate when the product is homogeneous—for instance, plastic bags— and examination of the entire lot is not physically or economically feasible.

Some industrial purchasing relies on negotiated contracts. In certain instances, an organisational buyer describes exactly what is needed and then asks sellers to submit bids. The buyer may take the most attractive bids and negotiate with those suppliers. In other cases, the buyer may not be able to identify specifically what is to be purchased but can provide only a general description—as might be the case for a special piece of custom made equipment. A buyer and seller might negotiate a contract that specifies a base price and contains provisions for the payment of additional costs and fees. These contracts are most likely to be used for one off projects, such as buildings and capital equipment.

Types of Organisational Purchases

Most organisational purchases are one of three types: new task purchase, modified re-buy purchase or straight re-buy purchase. The type of purchase affects the number of individuals involved and the length of the buying process. In a **new task purchase,** an organisation makes an initial purchase of an item to be used to perform a new job or to solve a new problem. A new task purchase may require the development of product specifications, supplier specifications and procedures for future purchases of that product. To make the initial purchase, the organisational buyer usually needs a good deal of information. A new task purchase is important to a supplier, for if the organisational buyer is satisfied with the product, the supplier may be able to sell the buyer large quantities of the product over a period of years.

In a **modified re-buy purchase,** a new task purchase is changed the second or third time it is ordered, or the requirements associated with a straight re-buy purchase are modified. For example, an organisational buyer might seek faster delivery, lower prices or a different quality of product specifications. When modified re-buying occurs, regular suppliers may become more competitive to keep the account. Competing suppliers may have the opportunity to obtain the business.

A **straight re-buy purchase** occurs when a buyer purchases the same products again routinely under approximately the same terms of sale. For example, when reordering photocopying paper, a buyer requires little additional information. The buyer tends to use familiar suppliers that have provided satisfactory service and products in the past. These suppliers try to set up automatic reordering systems to make reordering easy and convenient for organisational buyers. A supplier may even monitor the organisational buyer's inventory and indicate to the buyer what needs to be ordered.

Demand for Industrial Products

Products sold to organisational customers are called industrial products and, consequently, the demand for these products is called industrial demand. Unlike consumer demand, industrial demand is (1) derived, (2) inelastic, (3) joint and (4) more fluctuating. In discussing each of these characteristics, it is important to remember that the demand for different types of industrial products varies.

Derived Demand.   Because organisational customers, especially producers, buy products to be used directly or indirectly in the production of goods and services to satisfy consumers' needs, the demand for industrial products derives from the demand for consumer products; it is therefore called **derived demand.** For example, the demand for car seat belts derives from consumer demand for cars. In the long run, no industrial demand is totally unrelated to consumer demand.

The derived nature of industrial demand usually occurs at a number of levels. Industrial sellers at different levels are affected by a change in consumer demand for a particular product. For instance, consumers today are more concerned with good health and nutrition than ever before and as a result are purchasing food products containing less cholesterol, saturated fats, sugar and salt. When consumers stopped buying high cholesterol cooking fats and margarine, the demand for equipment used in manufacturing these products also dropped. Thus factors influencing consumer buying of various food products ultimately affected food processors, equipment manufacturers, suppliers of raw materials, and even fast food restaurants, which have had to switch to using vegetable oils for frying. Changes in derived demand result from a chain reaction. When consumer demand for a product changes, a wave is set in motion that affects demand for all the items involved in the production of that consumer product.

Inelastic Demand.   The demand for many industrial products at the industry level is inelastic, that is, a price increase or decrease will not significantly alter demand for the item. (The concept of price elasticity of demand is discussed further in Chapter 18.) Because many industrial products contain a number of parts, price increases that affect only one or two parts of the product may yield only a slightly higher per unit production cost. Of course, when a sizeable price increase for a component represents a large proportion of the total product's cost, demand may become more elastic, because the component price increase will cause the price at the consumer level to rise sharply. For example, if manufacturers of aircraft engines substantially increase the price of these engines, forcing Boeing in turn to raise the prices of its aircraft, the demand for aircraft may become more elastic as airlines reconsider whether they can afford them. An increase in the price of windscreens, however, is unlikely greatly to affect the price of the aircraft or the demand for them.

The characteristic of inelasticity applies only to industry demand for the industrial product, not to the demand curve faced by an individual firm. For example, suppose that a spark plug producer increases the price of spark plugs sold to manufacturers of small engines while its competitors continue to maintain their lower prices. The spark plug manufacturer would probably experience reduced unit sales because most small engine producers would switch to the lower priced brands. A specific organisation is vulnerable to elastic demand, even though industry demand for a particular product is inelastic.

Joint Demand.   The demand for certain industrial products, especially raw materials and components, is subject to joint demand. **Joint demand** occurs when two or more items are used in combination to produce a product. For example, a firm that manufactures cork notice boards for schools and colleges needs supplies of cork and wood to produce the item; these two products are demanded jointly. A shortage of cork will cause a drop in the production of wooden surrounds for notice boards.

Understanding the effects of joint demand is particularly important for a marketer selling multiple jointly demanded items. Such a marketer must realise that when a customer begins purchasing one of the jointly demanded items, a good opportunity exists for selling related products. Similarly, when customers purchase a number of jointly demanded products, the producer must exercise extreme caution to avoid shortages of any one of them, because such shortages jeopardise the marketer's sales of all the jointly demanded products. The susceptibility of producers to the shortage of a particular item is clearly illustrated when industrial action at companies producing car components results in a halt in production at major car manufacturers.

Fluctuating Demand.   As already mentioned, the demand for industrial products may fluctuate enormously because it is derived from consumer demand. In general, when particular consumer products are in high demand, their producers buy large quantities of raw materials and components to ensure that they can meet long run production requirements. In addition, these producers may expand their production capacity, which entails the acquisition of new equipment and machinery, more workers, a greater need for industrial services, and more raw materials and component parts.

Conversely, a decline in the demand for certain consumer goods significantly reduces the demand for industrial products used to produce those goods. In fact, under such conditions, a marketer's sales of certain products may come to a temporary standstill. When consumer demand is low, industrial customers cut their purchases of raw materials and components and stop buying equipment and machinery, even for replacement purposes. This trend is especially pronounced during periods of recession.

A marketer of industrial products may notice changes in demand when its customers change their inventory policies, perhaps because of expectations about future demand. For example, if several dishwasher manufacturers who buy timers from one producer increase their inventory of timers from a two week to a one month supply, the timer producer will experience a significant immediate increase in demand.

Sometimes price changes can lead to surprising temporary changes in demand. A price increase for an industrial item may initially cause organisational customers to buy more of the item because they expect the price to rise further. Similarly, demand for an industrial product may be significantly lower following a price cut as buyers wait for further price reductions. Such behaviour is often observed in companies purchasing information technology. Fluctuations in demand can be significant in industries in which price changes occur frequently.

ORGANISATIONAL BUYING DECISIONS

Organisational (or **industrial**) **buying behaviour** refers to the purchase behaviour of producers, resellers, government units and institutions. Although several of the same factors affect consumer buying behaviour (discussed in Chapter 4) also influence organisational buying behaviour, a number of factors are unique to the latter. This section first analyses the buying centre to learn who participates in making organisational purchase decisions and then focuses on the stages of the buying decision process and the factors that affect it.

The Buying Centre

Relatively few organisational purchase decisions are made by just one person; mostly, they are made through a buying centre. The **buying centre** refers to the group of people within an organisation who are involved in making organisational purchase decisions. These individuals include users, influencers, buyers, deciders and gatekeepers, although one person may perform several of these roles.[7] Participants in the buying process share the goals and risks associated with their decisions.

Users are the organisation members who actually use the product being acquired. They frequently initiate the purchase process and/or generate the specifications for the purchase. After the purchase, they also evaluate the product's performance relative to the specifications. Although users do not ordinarily have sufficient power to make the final decision to buy, it is important that their views be considered. A user who is not happy with a piece of machinery may not work as efficiently as one who is. Influencers are often technical personnel, such as engineers, who help develop the specifications and evaluate alternative products. Technical personnel are especially important influencers when the products being considered involve new, advanced technology.

Buyers are responsible for selecting suppliers and actually negotiating the terms of purchase. They may also become involved in developing specifications. Buyers are sometimes called purchasing agents or purchasing managers. Their choices of suppliers and products, especially for new task purchases, are heavily influenced by persons occupying other roles in the buying centre. For straight re-buy purchases, the buyer plays a major role in the selection of suppliers and in negotiations with them. Deciders actually choose the products and suppliers. Although buyers may be the deciders, it is not unusual for different people to occupy these roles. For routinely purchased items, buyers are commonly the deciders. However, a buyer may not be authorised to make purchases that exceed a certain monetary value, in which case higher level management personnel are the deciders. Gatekeepers, such as secretaries and technical personnel, control the flow of information to and among the persons who occupy the other roles in the buying centre. Buyers who deal directly with suppliers may also be gatekeepers because they can control the flow of information. The flow of information from supplier sales representatives to users and influencers is often controlled by personnel in the purchasing department. Unfortunately, relations between members of the buying centre at times can become strained. Marketing Insight 5.2 considers the effects such problems can have on the buying centre's performance.

The number and structure of an organisation's buying centres are affected by its size and market position, by the volume and types of products being purchased, and by the

INTERDEPARTMENTAL CONFLICT AFFECTS PERFORMANCE OF BUYING CENTRES

Almost all organisational buying decisions are made through the buying centre—a group of people from different departments given the responsibility of purchasing products and services for the organisation. Members of the buying centre will often have different goals and objectives, depending upon the particular department for which they work. For example, when a company which manufactures agricultural pesticides and fertilisers replaces testing equipment, key influencers might include senior managers, engineers and scientists as well as the purchasing manager. As these members attempt to reach acceptable purchase choices, weighing such factors as product specifications, supplier capabilities, service and price, the potential for conflict is always present.

Conflict within the buying centre can have both good and bad outcomes on the purchase decision. Conflict in the purchasing process can ensure that the organisation's best interests as a whole are preserved. Similarly, conflict can slow down the purchase decision, ensuring that careful consideration is given to product specifications and the choice of supplier *before* the actual purchase is made. However, conflict can also cause problems. Too much conflict can slow the purchasing process to the point of being inefficient. In addition, conflict can create negative feelings among members of the buying centre—ultimately creating frustration and confusion in the purchasing process.

What causes conflict in the buying centre? Recent research indicates at least three major causes. First, organisations that reward employees for attaining departmental rather than organisational goals tend to experience

firm's overall managerial philosophy regarding exactly who should be involved in purchase decisions. A marketer attempting to sell to an organisational customer should determine who is in the buying centre, the types of decisions each individual makes, and which individuals are the most influential in the decision process. Then, if it is not possible to contact all members of the buying centre the marketer will be in a position to contact those who have the most influence.

Exchange Relationships Between Buyers and Sellers

When a company buys a product or service from another company, both organisations become involved in an exchange process. During the transaction, both buyer and seller will exchange items of value in return for something else. For example, when a truck manufacturer makes a sale to a retailer, it will provide the buyer with a package of benefits that include the vehicle, basic product information, maintenance documentation, warranty details and a variety of payment options. In exchange the buyer will agree to pay the price negotiated with the manufacturer. Figure 5.3 shows the range of factors which can be exchanged during the purchase process.

It is often in the interests of both parties to develop long term relationships. If buy-

greater conflict in their purchasing process because different departments are working for different goals. For example, the research and development department at the agricultural manufacturer may demand an expensive piece of equipment because of its unique specifications. However, if the accounting department hesitates to spend the money, conflict is bound to occur. To overcome this problem, management must change the reward system to emphasise the achievement of overall organisational goals rather than departmental ones.

The second and third reasons for conflict—unclear responsibilities and barriers to communication—are closely related. Different members of the buying centre must have clear responsibilities in the purchasing process. However, they cannot hope to understand their responsibilities without clear, open communication among all members of the buying centre, as well as between the buying centre and top management. The key to eliminating conflict in the buying centre is promoting full, open communication among departments. In this way, members of the organisation will understand their responsibilities and will work toward fulfilling organisational goals.

SOURCES: Donald W. Barclay, "Interdepartmental conflict in organizational buying: the impact of the organizational context", *Journal of Marketing Research,* May 1991, pp. 145–59; Ajay Kohli, "Determinants of influence in organizational buying: a contingency approach", *Journal of Marketing,* July 1989, pp. 50–65; Robert J. Thomas, "Bases of power in organizational buying decisions", *Industrial Marketing Management,* 13, October 1984, pp. 209–16; Robert J. Thomas, "Industrial market segmentation on buying center purchase responsibilities", Journal of the Academy of Marketing Science, Summer 1989, pp. 243–52.

ing and selling companies are used to dealing with each other, they are more likely to be able to adapt to each other's needs and to reach an agreement quickly and easily. Long term relationships are often attractive to both companies because they reduce the level of risk (financial and practical) associated with the purchase. The trend towards long term relationships has resulted in the development of what is called *relationship management.*[8] This process encourages a match between the seller's competitive advantage and the buyer's requirements over the life-cycle of the item being purchased.

Stages of the Organisational Buying Decision Process

Like consumers, organisations follow a buying decision process. This process is summarised on the right hand side of Figure 5.4. In the first stage, one or more individuals recognise that a problem or need exists. Problem recognition may arise under a variety of circumstances, either from inside or outside the company. For example, a machine might reach the end of its working life and need to be replaced, or technological advances might dictate the need for a new approach to manufacturing. Individuals in the buying centre, such as users, influencers or buyers, may be involved in problem

FIGURE 5.3

The exchange process in organisational buying

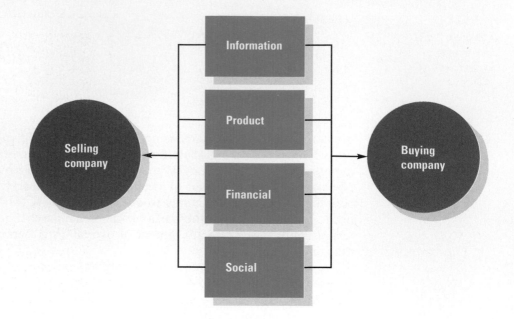

recognition, but it may be stimulated by external sources, such as sales representatives or customers.

The second stage of the process—development of product specifications—requires organisational participants to assess the problem or need and determine what will be necessary to resolve or satisfy it. During this stage, users and influencers, such as technical personnel and engineers, often provide information and advice for developing product specifications. By assessing and describing needs, the organisation should be able to establish product specifications.

Searching for possible products to solve the problem and then locating suitable suppliers is the third stage in the decision process. Search activities may involve looking in company files and trade directories, contacting suppliers for information, visiting trade shows, soliciting proposals from known suppliers, and examining catalogues and trade publications. The advertisement in Figure 5.5 is an example of information available in trade publications. Some suppliers may be viewed as unacceptable because they are not large enough to supply the quantities needed, and others may have poor records of delivery and service. In some instances the product may not be available from any existing supplier and the buyer must then find a company that can design and build the product.

If all goes well, the search stage will result in a list of several alternative products and suppliers. The fourth stage is evaluating the products on the list to determine which ones (if any) meet the product specifications developed in the second stage. The advertisement in Figure 5.6 stresses the product performance characteristics of DRG Envelopes and helps potential customers determine if the product meets their specifications. At this point, too, various suppliers are evaluated according to multiple criteria, such as price, service and ability to deliver.

The results of the deliberations and assessments in the fourth stage are used during the fifth stage to select the most appropriate product and supplier. In some cases, the buyer may decide on several suppliers. In others, only one supplier is selected—a situation which is known as sole sourcing. Sole sourcing has traditionally been discouraged except when a product is available from only one company; companies that have con-

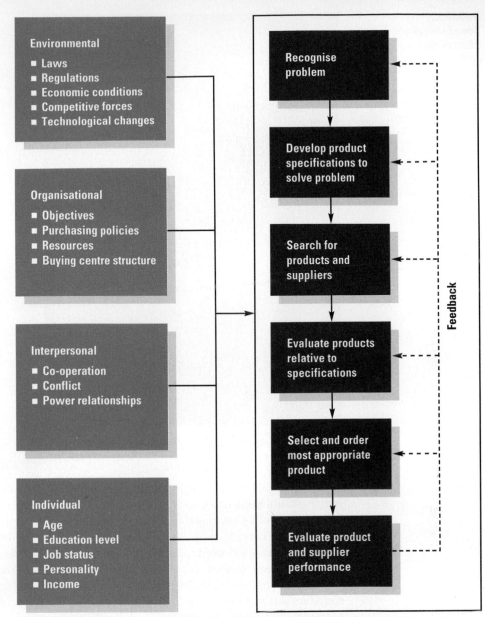

FIGURE 5.4
Organisational buying decision process and factors that may influence it

Environmental
- Laws
- Regulations
- Economic conditions
- Competitive forces
- Technological changes

Organisational
- Objectives
- Purchasing policies
- Resources
- Buying centre structure

Interpersonal
- Co-operation
- Conflict
- Power relationships

Individual
- Age
- Education level
- Job status
- Personality
- Income

Recognise problem

Develop product specifications to solve problem

Search for products and suppliers

Evaluate products relative to specifications

Select and order most appropriate product

Evaluate product and supplier performance

Feedback

SOURCE: Adapted from Frederick E. Webster, Jr, and Yoram Wind, *Organizational Buying Behavior,* © 1972, pp. 33–7. Adapted by permission of Prentice-Hall, Englewood Cliffs, N.J.

tracts with national governments are often required to have several sources for an item.

Sole sourcing is becoming more popular today, partly because such an arrangement means better communications between buyer and supplier, stability and higher profits for the supplier, and often lower prices for the buyer. However, most organisations still prefer to purchase goods and services from several suppliers to reduce the possibility of disruption caused by strikes, shortages or bankruptcy. The actual product is ordered in this fifth stage and specific details regarding terms, credit arrangements, delivery dates and methods, and technical assistance are worked out.

FIGURE 5.5
Trade publication information
Agency Hukuhodo uses advertisements in marketing trade publications to inform potential customers about its creativity.

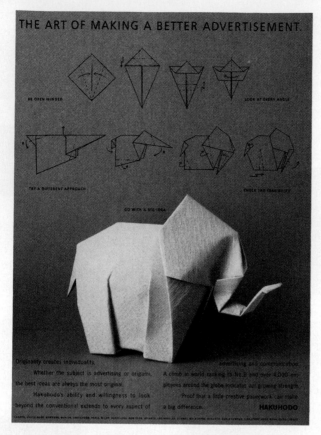

SOURCE: Produced by Hakuhodo, Tokyo for worldwide use.

During the sixth stage, the product's performance is evaluated by comparing it with specifications. Sometimes, even though the product meets the specifications, its performance does not adequately solve the problem or satisfy the need recognised in the first stage. In that case, the product specifications must be adjusted. The supplier's performance is also evaluated during this stage, and if it is found wanting, the organisational purchaser seeks corrective action from the supplier or searches for a new supplier. Buyers are increasingly concerned with obtaining high quality service from suppliers and may formally set performance targets for them. The results of such performance evaluations become feedback for the other stages and influence future organisational purchase decisions.

This organisational buying decision process is used in its entirety primarily for new task purchases. Several of the stages, but not necessarily all, are used for modified re-buying and straight re-buying, and fewer individuals are likely to be involved in these decisions.

Influences on Organisational Buying

Figure 5.4 also lists the four major categories of factors that influence organisational buying decisions: environmental, organisational, interpersonal and individual.

You may remember from Chapter 2 that environmental factors are uncontrollable forces such as politics, laws, regulations and regulatory agencies, activities of interest groups, changes in the economy, competitors' actions and technological changes. These forces generate a considerable amount of uncertainty for an organisation, which can make individuals in the buying centre apprehensive about certain types of pur-

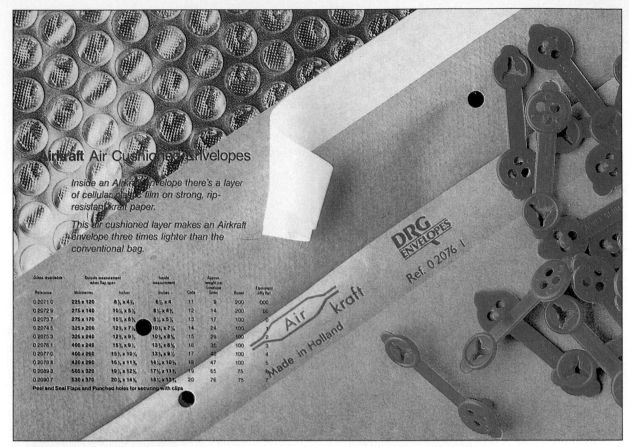

FIGURE 5.6 *Does the product meet specifications?*
The maker of DRG Envelopes emphasises product performance characteristics to assure customers that the product meets or exceeds their specifications.

SOURCE: John Dickinson Stationery.

chases. Changes in one or more environmental forces can create new purchasing opportunities and make yesterday's purchase decisions look terrible. For example, poor trading conditions can make a decision to invest in new factory premises seem ill advised, however attractive the move appeared at the time. Organisations need to approach these types of buying decisions with special caution.

Organisational factors that influence the organisational buying decision process include the buyer's objectives, purchasing policies and resources, as well as the size and composition of its buying centre. An organisation may have certain buying policies to which buying centre participants must conform. For instance, a firm's policies may mandate long term contracts, perhaps longer than most sellers desire. The nature of an organisation's financial resources may require special credit arrangements. Any of these conditions could affect purchase decision processes.

Interpersonal factors are the relationships among the people in the buying centre, where the use of power and the level of conflict significantly influence organisational buying decisions. Certain persons in the buying centre may be better communicators than others and thus more persuasive. Often these interpersonal dynamics are hidden, making them difficult for marketers to assess.

Individual factors are the personal characteristics of individuals in the buying centre, such as age, education, personality and position in the organisation. For example, a 55 year old manager who has been in the organisation for 25 years may affect the decisions of the buying centre differently than will a 30 year old person who has been employed for only two years. How influential these factors will be depends on the buying situation, the type of product being purchased and whether the purchase is new task, modified re-buy or straight re-buy. The negotiating styles of people will undoubtedly vary within an organisation and from one organisation to another. To be effective, a marketer needs to know customers well enough to be aware of these individual factors and the affects they may have on purchase decisions.

SUMMARY

Organisational markets consist of individuals and groups that purchase a specific kind of product for resale, for direct use in producing other products, or for use in day to day operations. Producer markets include those individuals and business organisations that purchase products for the purpose of making a profit by using them either to produce other products or in their own operations. Intermediaries who buy finished products and resell them for the purpose of making a profit are classified as reseller markets. Government markets consist of national and local governments, which spend billions of pounds annually for goods and services to support their internal operations and provide citizens with needed services. Organisations that seek to achieve charitable, educational, community or other non-profit goals constitute institutional markets.

Organisational transactions differ from consumer transactions in several ways. The transactions tend to be larger, and negotiations occur less frequently, though they are often lengthy. Organisational transactions sometimes involve more than one person or one department in the purchasing organisation. They may also involve reciprocity, an arrangement in which two organisations agree to buy from each other, although some countries have strict rules governing such agreements. Organisational customers are usually viewed as more rational and more likely to seek information about a product's features and technical specifications than are ultimate consumers.

When purchasing products, organisational customers must be particularly concerned about quality, delivery, service and price. Quality is important because it directly affects the quality of the organisational buyer's ultimate product. To achieve an exact standard, organisations often buy their products on the basis of a set of expressed characteristics, called specifications. Reliable and quick delivery is crucial to many organisations whose production lines must be fed with a continuous supply of component parts and raw materials. Because services can have a direct influence on a firm's costs, sales and profits, such matters as market information, on-time delivery and availability of parts can be crucial to an organisational buyer. Although an organisational customer does not decide which products to purchase solely by their price, cost is of prime concern because it directly influences a firm's profitability.

Organisational buyers use several purchasing methods, including description, inspection, sampling and negotiation. Most organisational purchases are new task, modified re-buy or straight re-buy. In a new task purchase, an organisation makes an initial purchase of an item to be used to perform a new job or to solve a problem. In modified re-buying, a new task purchase is changed the second or third time it is ordered, or the requirements associated with a straight re-buy purchase are modified. A straight re-buy purchase occurs when a buyer purchases the same products routinely under approximately the same terms of sale.

Industrial demand differs from consumer demand along several dimensions. Industrial demand derives from the demand for consumer products. At the industry level, industrial demand is inelastic. If the price of an industrial item changes, demand for the product will not change proportionally. Some industrial products are subject to joint demand, which occurs when two or more items are used in combination to make a product. Finally, because industrial demand ultimately derives from consumer demand, the demand for industrial products can fluctuate widely.

Organisational, or industrial, buying behaviour refers to the purchase behaviour of producers, resellers, government units and institutions. Organisational purchase decisions are made through a buying centre—the group of people who are involved in making organisational purchase decisions. Users are those in the organisation who actually use the product. Influencers help develop the specifications and evaluate alternative products for possible use. Buyers are responsible for selecting the suppliers and negotiating the terms of the purchases. Deciders choose the products and suppliers. Gatekeepers control the flow of information to and among persons who occupy the other roles in the buying centre.

When a company buys a product or service from another company, both organisations enter into a process during which items of value are exchanged in return for something else.

The stages of the organisational buying decision process are problem recognition, development of product specifications to solve the problem, search for products and suppliers, evaluation of products relative to specifications, selection and ordering of the most appropriate product, and evaluation of the product's and the supplier's performance. The evaluation of product and supplies will directly affect future purchasing decisions.

Four categories of factors influence organisational buying decisions: environmental, organisational, interpersonal and individual. Environmental factors include laws and regulations, economic conditions, competitive forces and technological changes. Organisational factors include the buyer's objectives, purchasing policies and resources, as well as the size and composition of its buying centre. Interpersonal factors refer to the relationships among the people in the buying centre. Individual factors refer to the personal characteristics of individuals in the buying centre, such as age, education, personality, position in the organisation and income.

IMPORTANT TERMS

Producer markets
Reseller markets
Government markets
Institutional markets
Reciprocity
New task purchase
Modified re-buy purchase

Straight re-buy purchase
Derived demand
Joint demand
Organisational (or industrial) buying
  behaviour
Buying centre

DISCUSSION AND REVIEW QUESTIONS

1. Identify, describe and give examples of four major types of organisational markets.
2. Why are organisational buyers generally considered more rational in regard to their purchasing behaviour than are ultimate consumers?

3. What are the primary concerns of organisational buyers?
4. List several characteristics that differentiate organisational transactions from consumer ones.
5. What are the commonly used methods of organisational buying?
6. Why do buyers involved in a straight re-buy purchase require less information than those making a new task purchase?
7. How does industrial demand differ from consumer demand?
8. What are the major components of a buying centre?
9. Identify the stages of the organisational buying decision process. How is this decision process used when making straight re-buys?
10. What impact does the evaluation of a particular purchase have on future buying decisions?
11. How do environmental, organisational, interpersonal and individual factors affect organisational purchases?

■ CASES

5.1 Changing the Supply of Car Parts

Companies supplying automotive parts to garages which service and repair cars and other vehicles are having to respond to sweeping market changes. In the UK and Benelux countries, the balance of outlet types is shifting away from the traditional independent garages and franchises of car manufacturers towards specialist and "fast-fit" operations. Increasingly complex vehicle specifications seem to be responsible for the growing specialisation, with all its associated computer diagnostics—too expensive and complex for most garages. Meanwhile, the rise in fortunes of fast-fit operators, such as Kwik Fit, has stemmed from the increasing demands of car owners for competitive pricing and fast service. Their popularity looks set to spread throughout many other European countries in the near future.

While the needs of the car owning public are seen to be changing, most consumers have little idea of, or interest in, the actual parts which are fitted to their cars. It is true that car owners do have an interest in the availability, quality and price of parts used in their vehicles, but the choice of brand is invariably left to the garage installing the item. For Lucas Aftermarket Operations, the division of Lucas Automotive which provides vehicle parts, the buyer to be influenced is therefore the installer (garage) rather than the vehicle owner.

In order to hit its target customers, Lucas must gear its selling efforts to the needs of the changing installer base. In the present situation, the company must respond to the differing requirements of both new and old types of installers. Although each customer will require a slightly different mix of product, price, delivery, quality and service, Lucas seeks economies of scale by looking for similarities in the needs of the different types of installer.

To serve its customers, Lucas Aftermarket Operations has at its disposal a host of Lucas branded depots and fitting centres, as well as independent distributors and dealers. Altogether, 16 major Lucas distribution centres worldwide are supported by numerous independent distributors, and the company has access to a total of around 4,000 authorised outlets in more than 100 countries. The distribution channels are as complex as they are extensive, reaching a large number of alternative customer types via numerous different routes—and sometimes through many different intermediaries.

Although Lucas' wide ranging distribution coverage gives the company access to many markets worldwide, the complexity of the channels can impose undue distance between the points of supply and consumption. When the distance (both real and psychological) is great, it can be more difficult to understand and satisfy the installer's needs. One possible solution is to forge closer links between suppliers, distributors, retailers and garages, resulting in greater co-operation between players with jointly agreed product ranges and methods of installation. Shorter distribution channels, although implemented in response to changing customer needs, will cut out stages and people in the organisational buying process.

SOURCES: Sally Dibb, "Satisfying installer needs in the UK car parts market", *International Journal of Retail and Distribution Management,* 20(3), May-June 1992, pp. 20–6; T. Drakeford, "Distribution can change your business", *Logistics and Distribution Management,* December 1987, pp. 18–20; John Wormald and Erik Arnold, "Change and opportunities in the automotive aftermarket", Booz Allen and Hamilton International (UK) Ltd, *EIU,* European Motor Business, November 1989, pp. 125–51; "Garages/Car Servicing", *Mintel,* Marketing Intelligence Report, May 1988, pp. 101–17; Lucas annual report, 1992.

Questions for Discussion

1. Who are Lucas' customers?
2. What types of organisational markets (as classified in this chapter) purchase the products Lucas makes?
3. Would most purchases of Lucas' products be new task, modified re-buy or straight re-buy? Why?
4. What advantages might shorter distribution channels have for Lucas' customers?

5.2 Institutional Buying

Institutional buying can be extremely complex or very straightforward and simple. Warwick Business School, in common with many University departments, "purchases" certain items from the University's central stores and departments, as well as dealing directly with manufacturers and service providers. Some of these activities are routine re-buys, while many are specialist one off purchases. However, even where items are bought on a fairly regular basis for similar needs and from regular suppliers, budgetary and internal political requirements often lead to a protracted decision-making process in which many influencers are involved in determining the purchasing time-scale, suppliers and product specifications.

For example, photocopying paper is a frequent, routine re-buy, and Xerox paper is bought on a regular basis. Similarly, most stationery requirements are frequent repeat purchases from an ongoing supplier base. At the other extreme, the building of the School's new teaching and conference complex and extensions to its existing office facilities involved lengthy discussions within the School regarding teaching, research and administrative needs, as well as the view of itself that the School wanted to portray to its various publics and employees. The final decision was not taken by the Business School alone. The University, as provider of land, much of the funding and support facilities, remained actively involved throughout the process. Because of the large sums of money involved, tenders were sought for the building and capital work, requiring detailed specifications to be determined.

More typical of the School's buying behaviour is the purchase of computer hardware and software for individual research groups or members of faculty. Each teaching group has its own budget requirements, while the School has overall budget constraints and needs, and the parent University has some influence on how money and resources are allocated. Each individual faculty member makes a bid for equipment (detailing requirements) to his or her teaching group, which in turn—if the bid is accepted—passes it on to a committee in the Information Systems Support Unit. In the light of the School's overall resource structure and current needs, and taking into account University guidelines, the committee will either approve, defer or reject the bid. Very often, even though the process seems complex, this decision-making can be relatively quick. However, depending on the University calendar and people's availability, there are occasions when the process seems to be extremely protracted.

For a seller attempting to gain a foothold in such a market, clearly there are many customers and influencers that the promotional material and sales representative must target, with differing messages. The user of such computer equipment needs to understand its capabilities, reliability and user-friendliness. The budget holders need to take into consideration cost versus reliability and product specification, as well as how the individual purchase fits into related purchases being made by the School for other members of staff and within the University as a whole.

This situation is typical for many corporations, organisations and service businesses. It is difficult to generalise purchasing decisions within such institutions; many different types of buying, decision-makers and influencers exist, all with varying time-scales, emotional and economic requirements, and political considerations.

SOURCES: Michael Hutt and Thomas Speh, *Business Marketing Management* (Chicago: Dryden Press, 1989); E. Jerome McCarthy and William D. Perreault, *Basic Marketing* (Homewood, Ill.: Irwin, 1990); J. Paul Peter and Gerry C. Olson, *Consumer Behaviour: Marketing Strategy Perspectives* (Homewood, Ill.: Irwin, 1987); Donald Cowell, *The Marketing of Services* (London: Heinemann, 1984).

Questions for Discussion

1. Within large corporations and institutions, is it typical for committee decision-making and buying to take place?
2. How difficult is it to centralise buying practices in organisational markets?
3. How could a supplier of computer hardware (for example, personal computers) identify customers, influencers and decision-makers in such an organisation?

6 MARKETING RESEARCH AND INFORMATION SYSTEMS

To understand the importance of and relationship between research and information systems in marketing decision-making

To distinguish between research and intuition in solving marketing problems

To learn the five basic steps for conducting a marketing research project

To understand the fundamental methods of gathering data for marketing research

*A*n international quality survey conducted by Gallup for the American Society for Quality Control interviewed 1,008 consumers in America, 1,446 in Japan and 1,000 in Germany. The survey enabled opinions of consumers in three of the world's major economies to be compared on questions of product and service quality. Observers of the US market could note changes over time, as similar research had been undertaken in 1985 and 1988.

In 1988, only 48 per cent of US consumers in the survey had given American products high marks for quality. By 1991, this proportion was up to 55 per cent. Unfortunately for US exporters, German and Japanese consumers did not agree; only 17 per cent of Japanese and 26 per cent of German consumers gave American products high marks. The rankings differed clearly by country. All consumers placed their own products first, except for televisions and video cassette recorders, for which all consumers favoured Japanese products. US consumers placed German and Japanese products after their country's products. German consumers put American products in second place and Japanese third. The Japanese preferred German products to US products, putting both well behind their own.

American and Japanese consumers surveyed both listed brand name as the core determinant of perceived product quality. Americans then considered word-of-mouth opinions, past experience and performance. The Japanese were concerned about performance and ease of use. German consumers regarded price as the most important factor, followed by brand name, appearance and durability. The survey showed that American manufacturers had a great deal of ground to make up in order to compete more effectively outside their home markets. The research results also revealed how consumer perceptions and expectations differ by country and between product groups. Manufacturers and marketers must take account of these variations in developing their products, brand positionings and marketing mixes. ∎

SOURCE: "Looking for quality in a world marketplace", ASQC/Gallup, 1991.

To implement the marketing concept, marketers require information about the characteristics, needs and wants of their target markets. Given the intense competition in today's market-place, it is unwise to develop a product and then look for a market where it can be profitably sold. (The Sinclair C5 electric car is a prime example.) Marketing research and information systems that provide practical, unbiased information help firms avoid assumptions and misunderstandings that could result in poor marketing performance.

This chapter focuses on the ways of gathering information needed to make marketing decisions, first distinguishing between managing information within an organisation (a marketing information system) and conducting marketing research. The discussion next moves on to the role of marketing research in decision-making and problem solving, compares it with intuition, and examines the individual steps of the marketing research process. The chapter also takes a close look at experimentation and various methods of collecting data. The final section considers the importance of marketing research and marketing information systems.

DEFINING MARKETING RESEARCH AND MARKETING INFORMATION SYSTEMS

Marketing research is the systematic design, collection, interpretation and reporting of information to help marketers solve specific marketing problems or take advantage of marketing opportunities. It is a process for gathering information not currently available to decision-makers. Marketing research is conducted on a special project basis, and research methods are adapted both to the problems being studied and to changes in the environment. Table 6.1 lists the main problem categories for which European marketers use marketing research. The marketing research industry is huge, highly competitive and increasingly dominated by international research agencies. Figure 6.1 reveals the scope of the marketing research industry throughout Europe. Table 6.2 identifies the major marketing research agencies worldwide.

The Market Research Society defines research as follows:

> the collection and analysis of data from a sample of individuals or organisations relating to their characteristics, behaviour, attitudes, opinions or possessions. It includes all forms of marketing and social research such as consumer and industrial surveys, psychological investigations, observational and panel studies.[1]

There are broadly two types of marketing research: **quantitative** and **qualitative.** In quantitative research, techniques and sample sizes lead to the collection of data which can be statistically analysed and whose results can be expressed numerically. These data tend to come from large surveys, sales data or market forecasts. Qualitative research deals with information too difficult or expensive to quantify: subjective opinions and value judgements not amenable to statistical analysis and quantification.[2]

A **marketing information system (MIS)** is the framework for the day to day management and structuring of information gathered regularly from sources both inside and outside an organisation. As such, an MIS provides a continuous flow of information about prices, advertising expenditure, sales, competition and distribution expenses. When information systems are strategically created and then institutionalised throughout an organisation, their value is enhanced.[3] Figure 6.2 illustrates the chief components of an MIS.

The inputs into a marketing information system include the information sources inside and outside the firm assumed to be useful for future decision-making. Processing

TABLE 6.1 *Future needs of marketing research in the European Community*

FORECAST DIRECTION OF MARKETING RESEARCH SPEND BY TYPE OVER NEXT 5 YEARS

	Top 6 Spend Currently	*More* Will Be Spent	*Less* Will Be Spent	Difference (More-Less)
Total number interviewed	184	184	184	
Percentage of users saying:	100	100	100	100
Usership & Attitude	59	37	2	35
Product Testing	56	34	6	28
Advertising Evaluation	49	28	6	22
Retail Audits	48	20	11	9
Consumer/Customer Panels	45	15	13	2
Corporate Image	41	21	8	13
Advertising Development	39	20	5	15
Campaign Tracking	38	21	5	16
Customer Satisfaction	38	21	3	18
Concept Evaluation	37	24	3	21
Distribution/Price Checks	14	9	1	8
Media (readership/viewing)	13	4	3	1
Post Launch Studies	13	8	1	7
Opinion/Social/Employee	13	8	3	5
Total Mix Testing	9	6	–	6
Sales Prediction (final mix)	9	6	2	4
Pack Testing	9	4	1	3
Price Testing/Modelling	5	2	2	–
Market Modelling	5	4	1	3
Sales Prediction (unfinished mix)	5	4	1	3
"Other Research"	9	5	1	4

SOURCE: "ESOMAR annual market study", European Society for Opinion and Marketing Research, July 1989.

information involves classifying it and developing categories for meaningful storage and retrieval. Marketing decision-makers then determine which information—the output—is useful for making decisions. Finally, feedback enables those who are responsible for gathering internal and external data to adjust the information inputs systematically.[4]

Regular reports of sales by product or market categories, data on inventory levels, and records of salespersons' activities are all examples of information that is useful in making decisions. In the MIS, the means of gathering data receive less attention than do the procedures for expediting the flow of information. The main focus of the marketing information system is on data storage and retrieval, as well as on computer capabilities and management's information requirements. RJR Nabisco, for example,

FIGURE 6.1
European marketing research markets, 1990
The total is approximately 2,474 million ECUs.

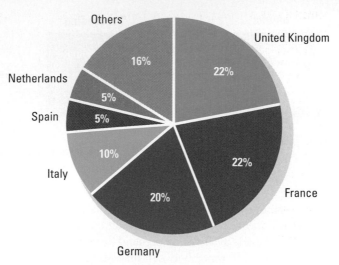

SOURCE: ESOMAR, the European Society for Opinion and Marketing Research, J. J. Viottastraat 29, 10/1 JP Amsterdam, The Netherlands. Tel: 31-20-664-2141 Fax: 31-20-664-2922.

TABLE 6.2 *World Top 10 Marketing Research Companies, 1990*

RESEARCH COMPANY	TURNOVER (MILLION ECU)[1]	COUNTRIES WITH OFFICE[2]	HEAD OFFICE	OWNERSHIP
1. A. C. Nielsen	868	32	USA	Dun & Bradstreet, USA
2. IMS International	454	62[3]	USA/UK	Dun & Bradstreet, USA
3. IRI	214	4[3]	USA	Public Company, USA
4. GfK	178	26	D	Public Company, D
5. Arbitron	138[4]	1	USA	Ceridian Corp., USA
6. Sofrès/Cecodis	131	8	F	Fimalac-led Group, F
7. Research International	113	40	UK	WPP, UK
8. Westat	88	1	USA	Private Company, USA
9. Infratest Burke	87[5]	13	D	Private Company, D
10. Video Research	82	1	J	Dentsu et al, J

[1] Excluding associates.
[2] Including associates.
[3] No 1992 information available; these data refer to the 1991 market situation.
[4] Estimate (J. Honomichl/*Marketing News*).
[5] Turnover relates to the year ending 9/92.

SOURCE: ESOMAR, the European Society for Opinion and Marketing Research, J. J. Viottastraat 29, 10/1 JP Amsterdam, The Netherlands. Tel: 31-20-664-2141 Fax: 31-20-664-2922.

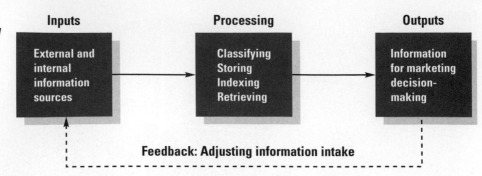

FIGURE 6.2
An organisation's marketing information system

Inputs

External and internal information sources

Processing

Classifying
Storing
Indexing
Retrieving

Outputs

Information for marketing decision-making

Feedback: Adjusting information intake

handles hundreds of thousands of consumer contacts each year, usually enquiries about product usage, nutrition and ingredients. This consumer feedback is computerised and made available on demand throughout the company's operating divisions.

The main difference between marketing research and marketing information systems is that marketing research is an information gathering process for specific situations, whereas an MIS provides continuous data input for an organisation. Nonrecurring decisions that deal with the dynamics of the marketing environment often call for a data search structured according to the problem and decision. Marketing research is usually characterised by in-depth analyses of major problems or issues. Often the information needed is available only from sources outside an organisation's formal channels of information. For instance, an organisation may want to know something about its competitors or to gain an unbiased understanding of its own customers. Such information needs may require an independent investigation by a marketing research firm.

Data brought into the organisation through marketing research become part of its **marketing databank,** a file of data collected through both the MIS and marketing research projects. The marketing databank allows researchers to retrieve information that is useful for addressing problems quite different from those that prompted the original data collection. Often a research study developed for one purpose proves valuable for developing a research method or indicating problems in researching a particular topic. For instance, data obtained from a study by Ford Motors on the buying behaviour of purchasers of its models may be used in planning future models. Consequently, marketers should classify and store in the databank all data from marketing research and the MIS to facilitate their use in future marketing decisions.

Databanks vary widely from one organisation to another. In a small organisation, the databank may simply be a large notebook, but many organisations employ a computer storage and retrieval system to handle the large volume of data. Figure 6.3 illustrates how marketing decision-makers combine research findings with data from an MIS to develop a databank. Although many organisations do not use the term *databank*, they still have some system for storing information. Smaller organisations may not use the terms *MIS* and *marketing research,* but they normally do perform these marketing activities. All organisations have some **marketing intelligence,** although often it is found to be inadequate for specific problem solving, leading to ad hoc commissioning of marketing research. Marketing intelligence is the composite of all data and ideas available within an organisation, for example, a company or a marketing department.

After a marketing information system—of whatever size and complexity—has been established, information should be related to marketing planning.[5] The following section discusses how marketers use marketing information, intuition and judgement in making decisions.

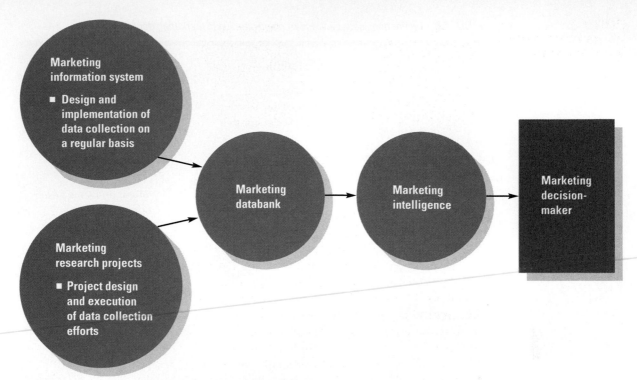

FIGURE 6.3 *Combining marketing research and the marketing information system*

INFORMATION NEEDS AND DECISION-MAKING

The real value of marketing research and marketing information systems is measured by improvements in a marketer's ability to make decisions. Marketers should treat information in the same manner as other resources utilised by the firm, and they must weigh the costs of obtaining information against the benefits derived. Information is worthwhile if it results in marketing mixes that better satisy the needs of the firm's target markets, leads to increased sales and profits, or helps the firm achieve some other goal.

Marketing research and marketing information systems provide the organisation with customer feedback, without which a marketer cannot understand the dynamics of the market-place. As managers recognise its benefits, they assign marketing research a much larger role in decision-making. For example, Japanese managers, who put much more faith in information they get directly from wholesalers and retailers, are beginning to grasp the importance of consumer surveys and scientific methods of marketing research as they seek ways to diversify their companies.[6]

The increase in marketing research activities represents a transition from intuitive to scientific problem solving. In relying on **intuition,** marketing managers base decisions on personal knowledge and past experience. However, in **scientific decision-making,** managers take an orderly and logical approach to gathering information. They seek facts on a systematic basis, and they apply methods other than trial and error or generalisation from experience.

Despite the obvious value of formal research, marketing decisions are often made without it. Certainly, minor, low risk problems that must be dealt with at once can and should be handled on the basis of personal judgement and common sense. If good de-

TABLE 6.3 *Distinctions between research and intuition in marketing decision-making*

	RESEARCH	**INTUITION**
NATURE	Formal planning, predicting based on scientific approach	Preference based on personal feelings
METHODS	Logic, systematic methods, statistical inference	Experience and demonstration
CONTRIBUTIONS	General hypotheses for making predictions, classifying relevant variables, carrying out systematic description and classification	Minor problems solved quickly through consideration of experience, practical consequences
SITUATION	High risk decision-making involving high costs, investment, strategic change or long term effects	Low risk problem solving and decision-making

cisions can be made with the help of currently available information, costly formal research may be superfluous. However, as the financial, social or ethical risks increase or the possible courses of action multiply, full scale research as a prerequisite for marketing decision-making becomes both desirable and rewarding.

The suggestion here is not that intuition has no value in marketing decision-making. Successful decisions blend both research and intuition. Statistics, mathematics and logic are powerful tools in problem solving, and the information they provide can reduce the uncertainty of predictions based on limited experience. But these tools do not necessarily bring out the right answers. Consider an extreme example. A marketing research study conducted for Xerox Corporation in the late 1950s indicated a very limited market for an automatic photocopier. Xerox management judged that the researchers had drawn the wrong conclusions from the study and decided to launch the product anyway. That product, the Xerox 914 copier, was an instant success. An immediate backlog of orders developed, and the rest is history. Though the Xerox example is an extreme one, by and large a proper blend of research and intuition offers the best formula for a correct decision. Table 6.3 distinguishes between the roles of research and intuition in decision-making.

THE MARKETING RESEARCH PROCESS

To maintain the control needed for obtaining accurate information, marketers approach marketing research in logical steps. The difference between good and bad research depends on the quality of the input, which includes effective control over the

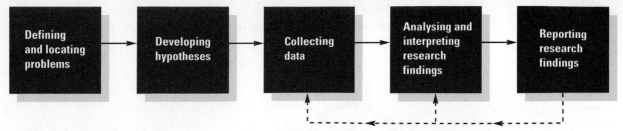

FIGURE 6.4 *The five steps of the marketing research process*

entire marketing research process. Figure 6.4 illustrates the five steps of the marketing research process: (1) defining and locating problems, (2) developing hypotheses, (3) collecting data, (4) analysing and interpreting research findings, and (5) reporting research findings. These five steps should be viewed as an overall approach to conducting research rather than a rigid set of rules to be followed in each project. In planning research projects, marketers must think about each of the steps and how they can best be adjusted for each particular problem.

DEFINING AND LOCATING PROBLEMS

Problem definition, the first step towards finding a solution or launching a research study, focuses on uncovering the nature and boundaries of a negative, or positive, situation or question. The first sign of a problem is usually a departure from some normal function, such as conflicts between or failures in attaining objectives. If a company's objective is a 12 per cent return on investment and the current return is 6 per cent, this discrepancy should be a warning flag. It is a symptom that something inside or outside the organisation has blocked the attainment of the desired goal or that the goal is unrealistic. Decreasing sales, increasing expenses or decreasing profits also signal problems. Conversely, when an organisation experiences a dramatic rise in sales, or some other positive event, it may conduct marketing research to discover the reasons and maximise the opportunities stemming from them. In Figure 6.5 CACI promotes its ability to isolate and identify problems.

To pin down the specific causes of the problem through research, marketers must define the problem and its scope in a way that requires probing beneath the superficial symptoms. The interaction between the marketing manager and the marketing researcher should yield a clear definition of the problem. Depending on their abilities, the manager and the researcher can apply various methods to shape this definition. Traditionally, problem formulation has been viewed as a subjective, creative process. Today, however, more objective and systematic approaches are utilised. For example, the Delphi method for problem definition consists of a series of interviews with a panel of experts. With repeated interviews, the range of responses converges towards a "correct" definition of the problem.[7] This method introduces structure as well as objectivity into the process of problem definition. Researchers and decision-makers should remain in the problem definition stage until they have determined precisely what they want from the research and how they will use it.

The research objective specifies what information is needed to solve the problem. Deciding how to refine a broad, indefinite problem into a clearly defined and researchable statement is a prerequisite for the next step in planning the research: developing the type of hypothesis that best fits the problem.

FIGURE 6.5
Defining and locating problems

CACI Information Services promotes its ability to target the most appropriate consumer types and their locations for profitable marketing investment.

SOURCE: CACI and ACORN are the trademarks and/or servicemarks of CACI Limited.

DEVELOPING HYPOTHESES

The objective statement of a marketing research project should include hypotheses drawn from both previous research and expected research findings. A **hypothesis** is an informed guess or assumption about a certain problem or set of circumstances. It is based on all the insight and knowledge available about the problem from previous research studies and other sources. As information is gathered, a researcher can test the hypothesis. For example, a food manufacturer such as H. J. Heinz might propose the hypothesis that children today have more influence on their families' buying decisions for ketchup and other grocery products. A marketing researcher would then gather data, perhaps through surveys of children and their parents, and draw conclusions as to whether or not the hypothesis was correct. Sometimes several hypotheses are developed during the actual study; the hypotheses that are accepted or rejected become the study's chief conclusions.

COLLECTING DATA

The kind of hypothesis being tested determines which approach will be used for gathering general data: exploratory, descriptive or causal. When marketers need more information about a problem or want to make a tentative hypothesis more specific, they may conduct **exploratory studies.** For instance, they may review the information in the firm's databank or examine publicly available data. Questioning knowledgeable people inside and outside the organisation may also yield new insights into the problem. An advantage of the exploratory approach is that it permits marketers to conduct mini-studies with a very restricted database.

If marketers need to understand the characteristics of certain phenomena to solve a particular problem, **descriptive studies** can aid them. Such studies may range from general surveys of consumers' education, occupation or age to specifics on how many consumers purchased Ice Cream Mars last month or how many adults between the ages of 18 and 30 eat some form of high fibre cereal at least three times a week. Some descriptive studies require statistical analysis and predictive tools. For example, a researcher trying to find out how many people will vote for a certain political candidate may have to survey registered voters to predict the results. Descriptive studies generally demand much prior knowledge and assume that the problem is clearly defined. The marketers' major task is to choose adequate methods of collecting and measuring data.

Hypotheses about causal relationships call for a more complex approach than a descriptive study. In **causal studies,** it is assumed that a particular variable X causes a variable Y. Marketers must plan the research so that the data collected prove or disprove that X causes Y. To do so, marketers must try to hold constant all variables except X and Y. For example, to find out whether new carpeting, curtains, and ceiling fans increase the leasing rate in a block of flats, marketers need to keep all variables constant except the new furnishings and the leasing rate. Table 6.4 compares the features of these types of research studies.

Marketing researchers have two types of data at their disposal. **Primary data** are observed and recorded or collected directly from respondents. This type of data must be gathered by observing phenomena or surveying respondents. **Secondary data** are compiled inside or outside the organisation for some purpose other than the current investigation. Secondary data include general reports supplied to an enterprise by various data services. Such reports might concern market share, retail inventory levels and consumer buying behaviour. Figure 6.6 illustrates how primary and secondary sources differ. Commonly, secondary data are already available in private or public reports or

TABLE 6.4 *Comparison of data gathering approaches*

PROJECT COMPONENT	EXPLORATORY STUDIES	DESCRIPTIVE OR CAUSAL STUDIES
PURPOSE	Provide general insights	Confirm insights Verify hypotheses
DATA SOURCES	Ill defined	Well defined
COLLECTION FORM	Open-ended	Structured
SAMPLE	Small	Large
COLLECTION PROCEDURE	Flexible	Rigid
DATA ANALYSIS	Informal	Formal
RECOMMENDATIONS	Tentative	Conclusive

SOURCE: Adapted from A. Parasuraman, *Marketing Research,* First Edition. Copyright © 1986 by Addison-Wesley Publishing Co., Inc. Used with permission.

FIGURE 6.6
Approaches to collecting data

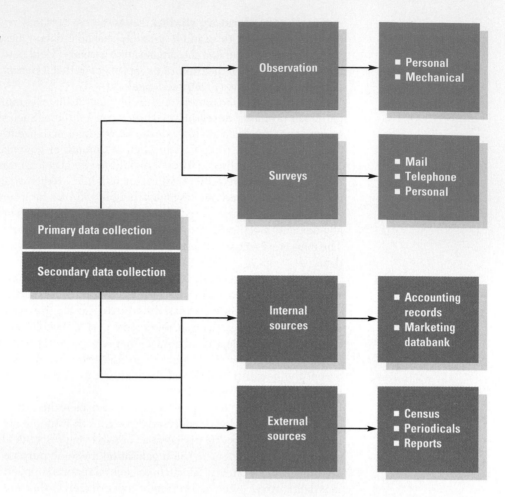

have been collected and stored by the organisation itself. Because secondary data are already available—"second-hand"—to save time and money they should be examined prior to the collection of any primary data. Clearly, primary data collection is bespoke and therefore both time consuming and costly. For relatively straightforward problems, secondary data may prove adequate. More complex or risky situations may require specific primary data collection. Figure 6.7 illustrates the Royal Mail's data collection services. The next sections discuss the methods of gathering both secondary and primary data.

Secondary Data Collection

Marketers often begin the marketing research process by gathering secondary data. They may use available reports and other information from both internal and external sources to study a marketing problem.

Internal sources of secondary data can contribute tremendously to research. An organisation's marketing databank may contain information about past marketing activities, such as sales records and research reports, which can be used to test hypotheses and pinpoint problems. An organisation's accounting records are also an excellent source of data but, strangely enough, are often overlooked. The large volume of data that an accounting department collects does not automatically flow to the marketing area. As a result, detailed information about costs, sales, customer accounts or profits by product category may not be part of the MIS. This situation occurs particularly in organisations that do not store marketing information on a systematic basis.

FIGURE 6.7
Collecting data
The Royal Mail promotes a range of services to the marketing research and direct mail industries, emphasising its comprehensive and up to date databases.

SOURCE: Advertisement reproduced by permission of The Post Office.

Secondary data can also be gleaned from periodicals, government publications and unpublished sources. Periodicals such as *Investors' Chronicle, Marketing, Campaign, Marketing Week, The Wall Street Journal* and *Fortune* print general information that is helpful for defining problems and developing hypotheses. *Business Monitor* contains sales data for major industries. Table 6.5 summarises the major external sources of secondary data, excluding syndicated services.

Syndicated data services periodically collect general information, which they sell to clients. BARB, for example, supplies television stations and media buyers with estimates of the number of viewers at specific times. SAMI furnishes monthly information that describes market shares for specific types of manufacturers. Nielsen and AGB provide data about products primarily sold through retailers. This information includes total sales in a product category, sales of clients' own brands, and sales of important competing brands. In the US, the Market Research Corporation of America (MRCA) collects data through a national panel of consumers to provide information about purchases. The data on brands maintained by the MRCA are classified by age, race, sex, education, occupation and family size. Similar samples exist in most countries.

Another type of secondary data, which is available for a fee, is demographic analysis. Companies, such as CACI or CCN, that specialise in demographic databanks have special knowledge and sophisticated computer systems to work with the very complex census databanks. As a result, they are able to respond to specialised requests. Such in-

TABLE 6.5   *Guide to external sources of secondary data*

TRADE JOURNALS	Virtually every industry or type of business has a trade journal. These journals give a feel for the industry—its size, degree of competition, range of companies involved, and problems. To find trade journals in the field of interest, check *The Source Book*, a reference book that lists periodicals by subject.
TRADE ASSOCIATIONS	Almost every industry, product category and profession has its own association. Depending on the strength of each group, they often conduct research, publish journals, conduct training sessions and hold conferences. A telephone call or a letter to the association may yield information not available in published sources.
INTERNATIONAL SOURCES	Periodical indexes, such as *Anbar*, are particularly useful for overseas product or company information. More general sources include the *United Nations Statistical Yearbook* and the *International Labour Organisation's Yearbook of Labour Statistics.*
GOVERNMENTS	Governments, through their various departments and agencies, collect, analyse and publish statistics on practically everything. Government documents also have their own set of indexes. A useful index for government generated information in the UK is the government's weekly *British Business.*
BOOKS IN PRINT (BIP)	BIP is a two volume reference book found in most libraries. All books issued by publishers and currently in print are listed by subject, title and author.
PERIODICAL INDEXES	Library reference sections contain indexes on virtually every discipline. *ABI Inform,* for example, indexes each article in all major periodicals.
COMPUTERISED LITERATURE RETRIEVAL DATABASES	Literature retrieval databases are periodical indexes stored in a computer. Books and dissertations are also included. Key words (such as the name of a subject) are used to search a database and generate references. Examples include Textline and Harvest.

formation may be valuable in tracking demographic changes that have implications for consumer behaviour and the targeting of products.[8]

Primary Data Collection

The collection of primary data is a more lengthy and complex process than the collection of secondary data. The acquisition of primary data often requires an experimental approach to determine which variable or variables caused an event to occur.

Experimentation.   **Experimentation** involves maintaining certain variables constant so that the effects of the experimental variables can be measured. For instance, when the WordPerfect Corp. tests a change in its WordPerfect word processing computer program, all variables should be held constant except the change in the program. **Marketing experimentation** is a set of rules and procedures by which data gathering is organised to expedite analysis and interpretation.

In experimentation, an **independent variable** (a variable not influenced by or dependent on other variables) is manipulated and the resulting changes measured in a **dependent variable** (a variable contingent on, or restricted to, one value or a set of values assumed by the independent variable). Figure 6.8 illustrates the relationship between these variables. For example, when Houghton Mifflin Company introduces a new edition of its *American Heritage Dictionary*, it may want to estimate the number of dictionaries that could be sold at various levels of advertising expenditure and prices. The dependent variable would be sales, the independent variables would be advertising expenditures and price. Researchers would design the experiment to control other independent variables that might influence sales, such as distribution and variations of the product.

In designing experiments, marketing researchers must ensure that their research techniques are both reliable and valid. A research technique has **reliability** if it produces almost identical results in successive repeated trials. But a reliable technique is not necessarily valid. To have **validity,** the method must measure what it is supposed to measure, not something else. A valid research method provides data that can be used to test the hypothesis being investigated. For example, recent experiments on cold fusion by scientists at various institutions have been held to lack both reliability and validity because the results of the experiments were not repeated in successive trials and the scientists are not sure whether their experiments were measuring energy produced as a result of fusion or some other process.

In America, one marketing research company, Information Resources, Inc., has brought a new dimension to experimental research by combining cable television, supermarket scanners and computers. The company has placed its BehaviorScan microcomputers on televisions in thousands of households in major cities. The company can thus track every commercial its panelists watch and every purchase they make in a supermarket or chemist's. The information provided by Information Resources helps marketers assess the effectiveness of their advertising by determining whether a viewer saw a particular advertisement and whether the advertisement led the viewer to buy the product.[9] Marketing Insight 6.1 discusses how the use of technology in marketing research assists with experimentation and marketing decision-making.

Experiments may be conducted in the laboratory or in the field; each research setting has advantages and disadvantages. In *laboratory settings*, participants or respon-

FIGURE 6.8
Relationship between independent and dependent variables

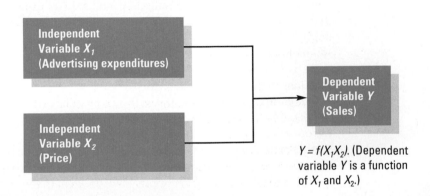

$Y = f(X_1, X_2)$. (Dependent variable Y is a function of X_1 and X_2.)

TECHNOLOGY COMES TO MARKETING RESEARCH

AGB's Superpanel, launched in 1990, took the supermarket barcode wands one step further. No longer was scanning only for the benefit of retailers' stock control. Some 8,500 households—28,000 individual consumers—were provided with barcode swipe wands in their kitchens. Weekly shopping purchases were swiped, first by the checkout assistants and a second time in the consumer's home. The collected data were automatically downloaded by telephone hook to AGB's central computer. The resulting analyses enabled AGB to relate consumer purchases by retailer and manufacturer brands to demographics and lifestyles. The sales of one brand could be examined by type of household, stockist retailers, competitive purchases and brand switching, pricing policies and promotional activity. Technology allowed this data collection to take place on a weekly—even daily—basis.

According to AGB, 12 million marketing research interviews now take place each year in the UK. Around 70 per cent are pen-and-paper or clipboard exercises—small scale, ad hoc surveys. Five hundred interviews in a survey do not warrant the use of software and laptop computers by interviewers. Close to 70 per cent of all sales in America are barcoded, and Europe is following suit. Even most cars sold now have a barcode! Anticipating significant growth in electronic point-of-sale and in-home data capture, AGB has invested over £12 million in three years to create Superpanel.

In America, the barcode technology is being developed by leading food manufacturers to target specific consumers. Companies such as Quaker Oats, Kraft General Foods and Procter & Gamble are developing in-house databases which should soon include the names and addresses of 25 per cent of their end user customers—the shoppers in the supermarkets. The

dents are invited to a central location to react or respond to experimental stimuli. In such an isolated setting it is possible to control independent variables that might influence the outcome of an experiment. The features of laboratory settings might include a taste kitchen, video equipment, slide projectors, tape recorders, one-way mirrors, central telephone banks and interview rooms. In an experiment to determine the influence of price (independent variable) on sales of a new canned soup (dependent variable), respondents would be invited to a laboratory—a room with table, chairs and sample soups—before the soup was available in stores. The soup would be placed on a table with competitors' soups. Analysts would then question respondents about their reactions to the soup at various prices.

One problem with a laboratory setting is its isolation from the real world. It is simply not possible to duplicate all the conditions that affect choices in the market-place. On the other hand, by controlling variables that cannot be controlled in the real world, laboratory experiments can focus on variables that marketers think may be significant for the success of a marketing strategy. Test market laboratories are being used more frequently today.[10]

names and data in this "relationship marketing" are collected from scanners at supermarket checkouts and from individually coded money back coupons mailed directly to millions of households. Once the personalised coupon has been redeemed, the consumer's code is instantly recorded in the scanner's database and purchases can be monitored.

Quaker Oats was a pioneer of this approach. It sent 10 coupons apiece to 18 million shoppers, each coupon inscribed with a separate family code and packaged with "involvement devices" such as competition entries and tie-ins with television programmes. Despite the high costs, double those for standard mailings, and the lengthy lead time before a database could be compiled from the feedback, other manufacturers quickly emulated Quaker Oats's initiative. Many US shoppers now carry "customer convenience cards", which reward—usually with price discounts—their compliance and brand loyalty.

Barcode scanning—in stores, at home and for manufacturers—is creating the biggest advance in data capture since the marketing research industry discovered telephone interviewing. The use of scanners, telecommunications and software has increased sample sizes and the amount and accuracy of the information collected, and it has reduced the time lags between data collection, analysis and interpretation of results.

SOURCES: Larry Black, "Homing in on the American household", *The Independent on Sunday,* 10 March 1991, p. IB21; Bill Blyth at AGB; Phil Dourado, "Clipboard makes way for barcode", *The Independent on Sunday,* 13 January 1991, p. IB21; AGB promotional video; Suzanne Bidlake, "Tesco plans smart loyalty breakthrough", *Marketing,* 14 January 1993, p. 3.

The experimental approach can also be used in *field settings.* A taste test of Stork SB margarine conducted in a supermarket is one example of an experiment in a field setting. Field settings give the marketer an opportunity to obtain a more direct test of marketing decisions than do laboratory settings.

There are, however, several limitations to field experiments. Field experiments can be influenced or biased by unexpected events, such as the weather or major economic news. Carry-over effects of field experiments are impossible to avoid. What respondents have been asked to do in one time period will influence what they do in the next. For example, evaluations of competing advertisements may influence attempts to obtain objective evaluations of a firm's proposed advertising. The fact that they have viewed previous advertising influences respondents' evaluation of future advertising. Respondents may not co-operate properly because they do not understand their role in the experiment. Finally, only a small number of variables can be controlled in field experiments. It is impossible, for example, to control competitors' advertising or their attempts to influence the outcome of the experiment. Tactics that competitors can use to thwart field efforts include couponing, reducing prices temporarily and increasing advertising frequency.

Experimentation is used in marketing research to improve hypothesis testing. However, whether experiments are conducted in the laboratory or in the field, many assumptions must be made to limit the number of factors and isolate causes. Marketing decision-makers must recognise that assumptions may diminish the reliability of the research findings. For example, viewing proposed advertisements on a video cassette recorder in a laboratory is different from watching the advertisements on television at home.

The gathering of primary data through experimentation may involve the use of sampling, survey methods, observation or some combination of these techniques.

Sampling. By systematically choosing a limited number of units, or **sample**, to represent the characteristics of a total population, marketers can project the reactions of a total market or market segment. The objective of **sampling** in marketing research, therefore, is to select representative units from a total population. Sampling procedures are used in studying the likelihood of events based on assumptions about the future.

Since the time and the resources available for research are limited, it would be almost impossible to investigate all the members of a population. A **population,** or "universe", comprises all elements, units or individuals that are of interest to researchers for a specific study. For example, if a Gallup poll is designed to predict the results of an election, all the registered voters in the country would constitute the population. A representative national sample of several thousand registered voters would be selected in the Gallup poll to project the probable voting outcome. The projection would be based on the assumption that no major political events would occur before the election. Sampling techniques allow marketers to predict buying behaviour fairly accurately on the basis of the responses from a representative portion of the population of interest. Sampling methods include random sampling, stratified sampling, area sampling and quota sampling.

When marketers employ **random sampling,** all the units in a population have an equal chance of appearing in the sample. Random sampling is basic probability sampling. The various events that can occur have an equal or known chance of taking place. For example, a specific playing card in a pack has a 1/52 probability of being drawn at any one time. Similarly, if every student at a university or college has a unique identification number and these numbers are mixed up in a large basket, each student's number would have a known probability of being selected. Sample units are ordinarily chosen by selecting from a table of random numbers statistically generated so that each digit from zero to nine will have an equal probability of occurring in each position in the sequence. The sequentially numbered elements of a population are sampled randomly by selecting the units whose numbers appear in the table of random numbers.

In **stratified sampling,** the population of interest is divided into groups according to a common characteristic or attribute, and a probability sample is then conducted within each group. Employing a stratified sample may reduce some of the error that could occur as a result of using a simple random sample. By ensuring that each major group or segment of the population receives its proportionate share of sample units, investigators avoid including too many or too few sample units from each stratum. Usually, samples are stratified when researchers believe that there may be variations among different types of respondents. For example, many political opinion surveys are stratified by sex, race and age.

Area sampling involves two stages: (1) selecting a probability sample of geographic areas, such as streets, census tracts or census enumeration districts, and (2) selecting units or individuals within the selected geographic areas for the sample. This approach is a variation of stratified sampling, with the geographic areas serving as the segments, or primary units, used in sampling. To select the units or individuals within the geographic areas, researchers may choose every nth house or unit, or they may adopt random selection procedures to pick out a given number of units or individuals from a total listing within the selected geographic areas. Area sampling may be used when a complete list of the population is not available.

Quota sampling differs from other forms of sampling in that it is judgemental; that is, the final choice of respondents is left to the interviewers. A study of consumers who wear glasses, for example, may be conducted by interviewing any person who wears glasses. In quota sampling, there are some controls—usually limited to two or three variables such as age, sex and education—over the selection of respondents. The controls attempt to ensure that representative categories of respondents are interviewed. In the marketing research industry, quota sampling is by far the most commonly employed form of sampling.

Quota samples are unique because they are not probability samples; not everyone has an equal chance of being selected. Therefore, sampling error cannot be measured statistically. Quota samples are used most often in exploratory studies, in which hypotheses are being developed. Often a small quota sample will not be projected to the total population, although the findings may provide valuable insights into a problem. Quota samples are useful when people with some unusual characteristic are found and questioned about the topic of interest. A probability sample used to study people allergic to cats would be highly inefficient.

Survey Methods.   **Survey methods** include interviews by mail or telephone and personal interviews. Selection of a survey method depends on the nature of the problem, the data needed to test the hypothesis, and the resources, such as funding and personnel, that are available to the researcher. Table 6.6 summarises and compares the advantages of the various methods. Researchers must know exactly what type of information is needed to test the hypothesis and what type of information can be obtained through interviewing. Table 6.7 lists the most frequently used consumer survey techniques for consumer goods and services. Table 6.8 summarises marketing research issues and techniques in the UK.

Gathering information through surveys is becoming more difficult because respondent rates are declining. There is also an indication that people with higher incomes and education are most likely to respond. Problems include difficulty in hiring qualified interviewers and respondents' reluctance to take part in surveys because of overlong questionnaires, dull topics and time pressures.[11] Moreover, fear of crime makes respondents unwilling to trust interviewers. The use of "sugging"—sales techniques disguised as market surveys—has also contributed to decreased respondent co-operation.

In *mail surveys*, questionnaires are sent to respondents, who are encouraged to complete and return them. Mail surveys are used most often when the individuals chosen for questioning are spread over a wide area and funds for the survey are limited. A mail survey is the least expensive survey method as long as the response rate is high enough to produce reliable results. The main disadvantages of mail surveys are the possibility of a low response rate or of misleading results, if respondents are significantly different from the population being sampled.

Researchers can boost response rates in mail surveys by offering respondents some incentive to return the questionnaire. Incentives and follow-ups have consistently been found to increase response rates. On the other hand, promises of anonymity, special appeals for co-operation, and questionnaire length have no apparent impact on the

TABLE 6.6 *Comparison of the three basic survey methods*

	MAIL SURVEYS	TELEPHONE SURVEYS	PERSONAL INTERVIEW SURVEYS
ECONOMY	Potentially the lowest cost per interview if there is an adequate return rate; increased postage rates are raising costs	Avoids interviewers' travel expenses; less expensive than in-home interviews; most common survey method	In-home interviewing is the most expensive interviewing method; shopping mall and focus group interviewing may lower costs
FLEXIBILITY	Inflexible; questionnaire must be short, easy for respondents to complete; no probing questions; may take more time to implement than other survey methods	Flexible because interviewers can ask probing questions, encourage respondents to answer questions; rapport may be gained, but observations are impossible	Most flexible method; respondents can react to visual materials, help fill out questionnaire; because observation is possible, demographic data are more accurate; in-depth probes are possible
INTERVIEWER BIAS	Interviewer bias eliminated; questionnaires can be returned anonymously (although often they are coded)	Some anonymity; may be hard to develop trust among respondents	Refusals may be decreased by interviewers' rapport-building efforts; interviewers' personal attributes may bias respondents
SAMPLING AND RESPONDENTS' CO-OPERATION	Obtaining a complete mailing list is difficult; non-response is a major disadvantage—33 per cent response rates are common in consumer surveys; 1–2 per cent rates in business-to-business surveys	Sample must be limited to respondents with telephones and listed numbers; engaged signals, no answers and non-response—including refusals—are problems; samples must cope with out at work non-responses.	Not at homes are more difficult to deal with; focus groups, shopping mall interviewing may overcome these problems.

SOURCE: Adapted from Milton M. Pressley, "Try these tips to get 50% to 70% response rate from mail surveys of commercial populations", *Marketing News,* 21 January 1983, p. 16. Reprinted by permission of American Marketing Association.

response rate. Other techniques for increasing the response rate, such as advance notification, personalisation of survey materials, type of postage, corporate or university sponsorship, or foot-in-the-door techniques, have had mixed results, varying according to the population surveyed.[12] Although such techniques may help increase the response rates, they can introduce sample composition bias, or non-response bias, which results when those responding to a survey differ in some important respect from those not responding to the survey. In other words, response enhancing techniques may

TABLE 6.7   *Changes in the frequency of use of survey research techniques*

	1978	1983	1987	1987 vs 1983
Long distance telephone	90%	91%	98%	+7
Shopping mall intercepts	89%	90%	86%	−4
Focus groups	87%	90%	98%	+8
Mail panel	53%	57%	67%	10
Custom mail	46%	33%	43%	+10
Purchase diary	46%	48%	37%	−11
Door to door	61%	47%	39%	−8
Trade surveys	33%	39%	40%	+1
Local telephone	67%	61%	°	°
Scanner panel	°	°	39%	°
Average number named	5.7	5.6	5.5	

° Not measured.

SOURCE: *Practices, Trends and Expectations for the Market Research Industry 1987,* Market Facts, Inc., 29 April 1987, p. 23. Reprinted by permission.

alienate some people in the sample and appeal to others, making the results non-representative of the population of interest. Perhaps because of these problems and the others discussed earlier, the firms surveyed in Table 6.7 spent less than 5 per cent of their research funds on mail surveys.[13]

Premiums or incentives encouraging respondents to return questionnaires have been effective in developing panels of respondents who are regularly interviewed by mail. Mail panels, selected to represent a market or market segment, are especially useful for evaluating new products, providing general information about consumers, and providing records of consumers' purchases. As Table 6.7 indicates, 67 per cent of the companies surveyed used consumer mail panels, but these panels represented a major budget share for less than 15 per cent of the companies.[14] It is interesting that 37 per cent of the sample used consumer purchase diaries. (These surveys are similar to mail panels, but consumers keep track of purchases only.) Consumer mail panels and consumer purchase diaries are much more widely used than custom mail surveys, but they do have shortcomings. Research indicates that the people who take the time to fill out a consumer diary have a higher income and are better educated than the general population. If researchers include less well educated consumers in the panel, they must risk poorer response rates.[15]

In *telephone surveys*, respondents' answers to a questionnaire are recorded by interviewers on the phone. A telephone survey has some advantages over a mail survey. The rate of response is higher because it takes less effort to answer the telephone and talk than to fill out a questionnaire and return it. If there are enough interviewers, telephone surveys can be conducted very quickly. Thus they can be used by political candidates or organisations seeking an immediate reaction to an event. In addition, this survey technique permits interviewers to gain a rapport with respondents and ask probing questions. According to a survey by the Council of American Survey Research Organizations (CASRO), telephone interviewing is the preferred survey method in more than 40 per cent of the projects conducted by commercial survey research

TABLE 6.8   *The nature of the UK marketing research industry in 1991*

AMSO 'LEAGUE TABLE' 1992 BY UK TURNOVER

Rank order	1992 turnover £000's	Change % 1991–1992
1 Taylor Nelson ACB plc	49,867	−0.9
2 Nielsen	43,732	+14.0
3 MAI Research Ltd	31,952	+2.0
4 Millward Brown	27,400	+17.4
5 Research International Ltd	26,272	+23.4
6 BMRB International Ltd	18,938	+6.2
7 RSL—Research Services Ltd	14,155	+39.6
8 The Research Business Group Ltd	12,078	+37.8
9 MORI	10,138	+12.0
10 The MBL Group plc	7,383	+18.4
11 The Harris Research Centre	6,874	+8.4
12 Infratest Burke Group Ltd	5,294	+4.1
13 Social Surveys (Gallup Poll) Ltd	5,360	+4.2
14 Martin Hamblin Research Ltd	5,027	+43.0
15 Public Attitude Surveys (PAS)	4,735	+15.9
16 Gordon Simmons Research Group	4,523	+10.2
17 FD5 Market Research Group Ltd	3,523	−8.8
18 Research and Auditing Services Ltd	3,003	+8.9
19 Pegram Walters Associates Ltd	2,640	+20.0
20 Business & Market Research plc	2,058	+12.8
21 GfK Great Britain Ltd	1,744	+51.3
22 IRB International Ltd	1,741	+6.2
23 CRAM International Ltd	1,820	+0.9
24 Scantech Ltd	1,280	+62.2
25 Marketing Sciences Ltd	1,220	+2110
26 Marketing Direction Ltd	588	−42.1
Total	203,015	+11.3

NATURE OF FIELDWORK: PERCENTAGE OF RESEARCH TURNOVER ACCOUNTED FOR BY DIFFERENT INTERVIEW METHODS

	1991 %	1992 %
Personal interview	55	54
Telephone interview	15	16
Hall test	12	11
Group discussion	10	10
Self-completion, including postal	8	9

firms.[16] The data in Table 6.7 show that virtually all the firms surveyed used telephone interviewing.

Telephone interviews do have drawbacks. They are limited to oral communication; visual aids or observation cannot be included. Interpreters of results must make adjustments for subjects who are not at home or who do not have telephones. Surveys

SOURCE OF REVENUE

Type of client company	1991 £ millions	Change %
Food and soft drinks	47.4	−9
Media	26.4	+9
Public services and utilities	25.1	+15
Health and beauty aids	22.1	+16
Alcoholic drinks	21.9	+5
Government (central and local)	17.2	+39
Pharmaceutical companies	16.0	+25
Financial services	15.8	+9
Vehicle manufacturers	14.1	+1
Business and industrial	13.2	+11
Advertising agencies	10.6	+7
Household products	10.6	+38
Retailers	9.7	+24
Travel and tourism	9.1	+31
Household durables and hardware	5.2	+80
Tobacco	3.8	+8
Oil	3.8	−17
Other direct clients	19.6	—
Within AMSO companies (mainly subcontracted fieldwork)	1.5	—

SOURCE: Association of Market Survey Organizations—the United Kingdom's leading trade body. Used with permission.

Note: The year to year change is calculated on a comparable basis. Changes in and within membership mean that the data shown are not directly comparable with the data published in 1992 for 1991.

which specify quotas of respondents hit problems of non-response: secretaries "gate-keep" calls at businesses, thereby preventing researchers from talking to their targets; adult members of households who work outside the home are difficult to contact—and calls in the evening will not be welcome as people want to relax after work.

Telephone surveys, like mail and personal interview surveys, are sometimes used to develop panels of respondents who can be interviewed repeatedly to measure changes in attitudes or behaviour. Reliance on such panels is increasing.

Computer assisted telephone interviewing integrates questionnaire, data collection and tabulations and provides data to aid decision-makers in the shortest time possible. In computer assisted telephone interviewing, the paper questionnaire is replaced by a computer monitor or video screen. Responses are entered on a terminal keyboard, or the interviewer can use a light pen (a pen shaped torch) to record a response on a light sensitive screen. On the most advanced devices, the interviewer merely points to the appropriate response on a touch sensitive screen with his or her finger. Open-ended responses can be typed on the keyboard or recorded with paper and pencil.

Computer assisted telephone interviewing saves time and facilitates monitoring the progress of interviews. Entry functions are largely eliminated; the computer determines which question to display on the screen, skipping irrelevant questions. Because data are available as soon as they are entered into the system, cumbersome hand computations are avoided and interim results can be quickly retrieved. With some systems, a laptop microcomputer may be taken to off-site locations for use in data analysis. Some researchers say that computer assisted telephone interviewing—including hardware, software and operation costs—is less expensive than conventional paper and pencil methods.[17]

Marketing researchers have traditionally favoured the *personal interview survey*, chiefly because of its flexibility. Various audio-visual aids—pictures, products, diagrams or pre-recorded advertising copy—can be incorporated into a personal interview. Rapport gained through direct interaction usually permits more in-depth interviewing, including probes, follow-up questions or psychological tests. In addition, because personal interviews can be longer, they can yield more information. Finally, respondents can be selected more carefully, and reasons for non-response can be explored.

The nature of personal interviews has changed. In the past, most personal interviews, which were based on random sampling or pre-arranged appointments, were conducted in the respondent's home. Today, most personal interviews are conducted in shopping centres or malls. *Shopping mall intercept interviews* involve interviewing a percentage of persons who pass by certain "intercept" points in a centre. Although there are many variations of this technique, Table 6.7 indicates that shopping mall intercept interviewing is the third most popular survey technique, after telephone and focus group interviewing. By 1987, not only did 86 per cent of the major consumer goods and services companies use this technique, but almost half reported that shopping mall intercept interviewing was their major expenditure on survey research.[18]

Like any face to face interviewing method, shopping centre intercept interviewing has many advantages. The interviewer is in a position to recognise and react to respondents' non-verbal indications of confusion. Respondents can be shown product prototypes, videotapes of commercials and the like, and reactions can be sought. The environment lets the researcher deal with complex situations. For example, in taste tests, researchers know that all the respondents are reacting to the same product, which can be prepared and monitored from the mall test kitchen or some other facility. In addition, lower cost, greater control and the ability to conduct tests requiring bulky equipment make shopping mall intercept interviews popular.

Research indicates that given a comparable sample of respondents, shopping mall intercept interviewing is a suitable substitute for telephone interviewing.[19] In addition, there seem to be no significant differences in the completeness of consumer responses between telephone interviewing and shopping mall intercept interviewing. In fact, for questions dealing with socially desirable behaviour, shopping mall intercept respondents appear to be more honest about their past behaviour.[20]

In *on-site computer interviewing*, a variation of the mall intercept interview, respondents complete a self-administered questionnaire displayed on a computer monitor. In America, MAX (Machine Answered eXamination), a microcomputer based software package developed by POPULUS Inc., conducts such interviews in shopping malls. After a brief lesson on how to operate MAX, respondents can proceed through the survey at their own pace. According to its developers, MAX provides not only faster and more accurate information but also consistency, for each respondent is asked questions in the same way. MAX is flexible because it can ask different sets of relevant questions depending on the respondent's previous answers. In addition, respondents' answers are entered directly into a computer and do not need to be coded and keyed in before being analysed; nor is there any chance of information being incorrectly encoded. Its developers assert that "MAX is the interviewer we would all like to be. MAX is patient, nonjudgmental, remembering all that he is taught, and he keeps track of every answer."[21]

The object of a *focus group interview* is to observe group interaction when members are exposed to an idea or concept. Often these interviews are conducted informally, without a structured questionnaire. Consumer attitudes, behaviour, lifestyles, needs and desires can be explored in a flexible and creative manner through focus group interviews. Table 6.7 indicates that 98 per cent of the firms surveyed used focus group interviewing in 1987. Questions are open-ended and stimulate consumers to answer in their own words. Researchers can ask probing questions to clarify something they do not fully understand or something unexpected and interesting that may help to explain consumer behaviour. When Cadbury used information obtained from focus groups to change its advertising and test product concepts, the new advertisements and product launches pushed up sales.[22] Case 6.2 describes the future of this marketing research technique.

Quali-depth interviews are 25 to 30 minute intercept interviews which incorporate some of the in-depth advantages of focus groups with the speed and researcher's flexibility for intercept studies. Typically, intercepted consumers are taken to a nearby hall or café and asked more probing and searching questions than is possible in a 3 to 4 minute intercept interview. They can also be shown a greater variety of stimulus material.

Another research technique is the *in-home (door to door) interview.* As Table 6.7 indicates, 39 per cent of the largest consumer companies use this technique. Because it may be desirable to eliminate group influence, the in-home interview offers a clear advantage when thoroughness of self-disclosure is important. In an in-depth interview of 45 to 90 minutes, respondents can be probed to reveal their real motivations, feelings, behaviours and aspirations. In-depth interviews permit the discovery of emotional "hot buttons" that provide psychological insights.[23]

Questionnaire Construction.   A carefully constructed questionnaire is essential to the success of any survey. Questions must be designed to elicit information that meets the study's data requirements. These questions must be clear, easy to understand and directed towards a specific objective. Researchers need to define the objective before trying to develop a questionnaire because the objective determines the substance of the questions and the amount of detail. A common mistake in constructing questionnaires is to ask questions that interest the researchers but do not yield information useful in deciding whether to accept or reject a hypothesis. Finally, the most important rule in composing questions is to maintain impartiality.

The questions are usually of three kinds: open-ended, dichotomous and multiple choice.

OPEN-ENDED QUESTION
What is your general opinion of the American Express Optima Card?

_____

_____

_____

DICHOTOMOUS QUESTION
Do you presently have an American Express Optima Card?
Yes   ____
No   ____

MULTIPLE CHOICE QUESTION

What age group are you in?

Under 20	____
20–29	____
30–39	____
40–49	____
50–59	____
60 and over	____

The design of questionnaires is extremely important because it will affect the validity and usefulness of the results. It is therefore useful to test questionnaires on a few respondents before conducting the full survey. The questions must relate to the research objectives. The layout of the questionnaire must not be off-putting to respondents or to the researchers conducting the work. These days, carefully laid out questionnaires can be read and analysed by computers. Open-ended questions can be the most revealing, but are time consuming—and therefore off-putting—for respondents, as well as difficult to analyse across respondents. Dichotomous questions are straightforward but not very revealing; and often the answer is not a full *yes* or *no.* Multiple choice questions are popular, but care must be exercised in the choice of categories. Most questionnaires include a mix of question styles.

Researchers must be very careful in wording questions that a respondent might consider too personal or that might require him or her to admit to activities that other people are likely to condemn. Questions of this type should be worded in such a way as to make them less offensive, and are often placed towards the end of the questionnaire.

For testing special markets, where individuals (for instance executives, scientists and engineers) are likely to own or have access to a personal computer, questionnaires may be programmed on a computer disk and the disk delivered through the mail. This technique may cost less than a telephone interview and eliminate bias by simplifying flow patterns in answering questions. Respondents see less clutter on the screen than on a printed questionnaire; the novelty of the approach may also spark their interest and compel their attention.

Observation Methods.　　　When using **observation methods,** researchers record respondents' overt behaviour, taking note of physical conditions and events. Direct contact with respondents is avoided; instead, their actions are examined and noted systematically. For example, researchers might use observation methods to answer the question, "How long does the average McDonald's restaurant customer have to wait in line before being served?"

Observation may also be combined with interviews. For example, during personal interviews, the condition of a respondent's home or other possessions may be observed and recorded, and demographic information such as ethnic origin, approximate age and sex can be confirmed by direct observation. As discussed in Marketing Insight 6.2, observation is not confined to consumers; shops and service establishments can be observed, too, through "mystery shopper" research.

Data gathered through observation can sometimes be biased if the respondent is aware of the observation process. An observer can be placed in a natural market environment, such as a grocery store, without biasing or influencing shoppers' actions. However, if the presence of a human observer is likely to bias the outcome or if human sensory abilities are inadequate, mechanical means may be used to record behaviour. **Mechanical observation devices** include cameras, recorders, counting machines and equipment to record physiological changes in individuals. For instance, a special camera can be used to record the eye movements of respondents looking at an advertisement and to detect the sequence of reading and the parts of the advertisement that receive greatest attention. Electric scanners in supermarkets are mechanical observation devices that offer an exciting opportunity for marketing research. Scanner technology can provide accurate data on sales and consumers' purchase patterns, and marketing researchers may buy such data from the supermarket. (See Case 6.1.)

Observation is straightforward and avoids a central problem of survey methods: motivating respondents to state their true feelings or opinions. However, observation tends to be descriptive. When it is the only method of data collection, it may not provide insights into causal relationships. Another drawback is that analyses based on observation are subject to the biases of the observer or the limitations of the mechanical device.

ANALYSING AND INTERPRETING RESEARCH FINDINGS

After collecting data to test their hypotheses, marketers analyse and interpret the research findings. Interpretation is easier if marketers carefully plan their data analysis methods early in the research process. They should also allow for continual evaluation of the data during the entire collection period. They can then gain valuable insight into areas that ought to be probed during the formal interpretation. It is important to give consideration to data analysis techniques prior to the collection of data. Many students discover after a survey has been completed, for example, how different wording or ordering of questions, as well as of categories, could have reduced the complexity of the analysis. It also helps when interpreting findings to keep in mind the target audience for the results—the report or presentation—so that the level of analysis and interpretation of the findings can be geared to their understanding.

The first step in drawing conclusions from most research is displaying the data in table format. If marketers intend to apply the results to individual categories of the things or people being studied, cross-tabulation may be quite useful, especially in tabulating joint occurrences. For example, a cross-tabulation of data using the two variables, gender and purchase rates of car tyres, would show differences in how men and women purchase car tyres. Various statistical procedures exist that facilitate the simultaneous analysis and examine the interactions of many variables.[24]

After the data are tabulated, they must be analysed. **Statistical interpretation** focuses on what is typical or what deviates from the average. It indicates how widely responses vary and how they are distributed in relation to the variable being measured. This interpretation is another facet of marketing research that relies on marketers' judgement or intuition. Moreover, when they interpret statistics, marketers must take into account estimates of expected error or deviation from the true values of the population. The analysis of data may lead reseachers to accept or reject the hypothesis being studied.

Data require careful interpretation by the marketer. If the results of a study are valid, the decision-maker should take action; however, if it is discovered that a question has been incorrectly worded, the results should be ignored. For example, if a study by an electricity company reveals that 50 per cent of its customers believe that meter-readers are "friendly", is that finding good, bad or indifferent? Two important benchmarks help interpret the result: how the 50 per cent figure compares with that for competitors and how it compares with a previous time period. The point is that man-

MARKETING INSIGHT 6.2

SERVICE AS SEEN BY THE CUSTOMER

Retailers and providers of services depend increasingly not only on the products they sell or deliver but also on the ability, attitude and quality of their personnel and the internal environment of their branch outlets. The regional directors and head office managers who check such standards all too often enter through the staff door at the rear of the branch, focusing primarily on operations and not on customer concerns. The branch's customers enter from the front, having first seen the exterior of the branch. They deal with all levels of personnel, not just the manager or manageress to whom the visiting director talks. These customers are not wrapped up in the company's products and operations; they seek help and advice. They expect courtesy and professionalism.

Sketchley, the leading UK chain of dry cleaners, realised that its management tended to assess branches in terms of operational efficiency and the maintenance of working areas. Visiting managers were not looking at their branches from the customer's point of view. Customer Concern, a research specialist in site visits, instigated a programme of branch visits, which included having items of their staff members' clothing dry cleaned. Branches were assessed according to external appearance, use of company promotional offers, cleanliness and upkeep, friendliness, attitude and knowledgeability of staff, quality and delivery of the cleaned garments. Branch by branch comparisons were drawn up using regional league tables as a way of congratulating the "good" branches and encouraging the poorer branches to improve.

Customers buy a company's products; quite often the company's management never does, instead requesting items direct from storage at staff discount rates without ever visiting shops or showrooms. Car manufacturers give their senior management vehicles and offer all employees highly attractive deals. The result is that few senior managers ever visit a showroom

agers must understand the research results and relate the results to a context that permits effective decision-making.[25]

REPORTING RESEARCH FINDINGS

The final step in the marketing research process is reporting the research findings. Before preparing the report, the marketer must take a clear, objective look at the findings to see how well the gathered facts answer the research question or support or negate the hypotheses posed in the beginning. In most cases, it is extremely doubtful that the study can provide everything needed to answer the research question. Thus in the report the researcher must point out the deficiencies and the reasons for them, perhaps suggesting areas which require further investigation.

or dealer—even their servicing is taken care of—so they never see the "sharp end", their dealers, as customers.

Rover Cars instigated a programme of "mystery shopper" surveys. This programme involved visits by bogus potential car buyers to dealers to rate the upkeep and appearance of showrooms, technical knowledge and attitude of personnel, quality of displays, negotiating criteria and adherence to company policies. Dealers did not know who the bogus buyers were, nor when they were to visit. Service reception staff were similarly targeted. A favourite ploy by the researchers was to book a car service by telephone and then phone again to cancel, judging the receptionist's response to the lost business. As a result of these frequent, always anonymous, visits, Rover was able to improve the standards of its dealers, the attitude of their personnel and ultimately the quality of its service and customer satisfaction.

This form of marketing research, "mystery shopper", is one of the fastest-growing areas in the industry. The largest company in the UK, BEM, has 2,000 mystery shoppers on its books, many working part-time; and its annual sales exceed £2 million. BEM's employees are trained to evaluate how customers are greeted, how the store looks and whether shop assistants understand the products on sale. They are expected to blend in inconspicuously while assessing branches; they are not loud customers visibly asking awkward questions. Whether it's in British Rail stations, Sears' shoe shops, B&Q DIY sheds or Allied Breweries' Ansells pubs, mystery shopper researchers are evaluating standards and service quality and supplying management with measures of performance and benchmarks against which improvements can be made.

SOURCES: Helen Slingsby, "Mystery customers stalk the shop flaws", *The Independent on Sunday*, October 1992, p. IB 23; Customer Concern and BEM promotional literature; Rover Cars; Sketchley.

The report presenting the results is usually a formal, written one. Researchers must allow time for the writing task when they plan and schedule the project. Since the report is a means of communicating with the decision-makers who will use the research findings, researchers need to determine beforehand how much detail and supporting data to include. They should keep in mind that corporate executives prefer reports that are short, clear and simply expressed. Often researchers will give their summary and recommendations first, especially if decision-makers do not have time to study how the results were obtained. A technical report allows its users to analyse data and interpret recommendations because it describes the research methods and procedures and the most important data gathered. Thus researchers must recognise the needs and expectations of the report user and adapt to them.

When marketing decision-makers have a firm grasp of research methods and procedures, they are better able to integrate reported findings and personal experience.

If marketers can spot limitations in research from reading the report, their personal experience assumes additional importance in the decision-making process. Marketers who cannot understand basic statistical assumptions and data gathering procedures may misuse research findings. Consequently, report writers should be aware of the backgrounds and research abilities of those who will rely on the report in making decisions. Clear explanations presented in plain language make it easier for decision-makers to apply the findings and less likely that a report will be misused or ignored. Talking to potential research users before writing a report can help researchers supply information that will indeed improve decision-making.

THE IMPORTANCE OF ETHICAL MARKETING RESEARCH

Marketing research and systematic information gathering increase the chances of successful marketing. Many companies, and even entire industries, have failed because of a lack of marketing research. The conventional wisdom about the evaluation and use of marketing research by marketing managers suggests that in future managers will rely on marketing research to reduce uncertainty and to make better informed decisions than they could without such information.[26]

Clearly, marketing research and information systems are vital to marketing decision-making. Because of this, it is essential that ethical standards be established and followed. Attempts to stamp out shoddy practices and establish generally acceptable procedures for conducting research are important developments in marketing research. Other issues of great concern relate to researchers' honesty, manipulation of research techniques, data manipulation, invasion of privacy and failure to disclose the purpose or sponsorship of a study in some situations. Too often respondents are unfairly manipulated and research clients are not told about flaws in data.

One common practice that hurts the image of marketing research is "sugging" ("selling under the guise of marketing research"). A leading marketing research association (ESOMAR) is encouraging research companies and marketing research firms worldwide to adopt codes and policies prohibiting this practice.[27] In the UK, the Market Research Society lays down strict guidelines.

Because so many parties are involved in the marketing research process, developing shared ethical concern is difficult. The relationships among respondents who cooperate and share information, interviewing companies, marketing research agencies that manage projects and organisations that use the data are interdependent and complex. Ethical conflict typically occurs because the parties involved in the marketing research process have different objectives. For example, the organisation that uses data tends to be results oriented, and success is often based on performance rather than a set of standards. On the other hand, a data gathering sub-contractor is evaluated on the ability to follow a specific set of standards or rules. The relationships among all participants in marketing research must be understood so that decision-making becomes ethical. Without clear understanding and agreement, including mutual adoption of standards, ethical conflict will lead to mistrust and questionable research results.[28]

Marketing research is essential in planning and developing marketing strategies. Information about target markets provides vital input in planning the marketing mix and controlling marketing activities. It is no secret that companies can use information technology as a key to gaining an advantage over the competition.[29] In short, the marketing concept—the marketing philosophy of customer orientation—can be implemented better when adequate information about customers, competition and trends is available.

SUMMARY

To implement the marketing concept, marketers need information about the characteristics, needs and wants of their target markets. Marketing research and information systems that furnish practical, unbiased information help firms avoid the assumptions and misunderstandings that could lead to poor marketing performance.

Marketing research is the systematic design, collection, interpretation and reporting of information to help marketers solve specific marketing problems or take advantage of marketing opportunities. Marketing research is conducted on a special project basis, with the research methods adapted to the problems being studied and to changes in the environment. Quantitative research leads to findings which can be quantified and statistically analysed. Qualitative research examines subjective opinions and value judgements.

The marketing information system (MIS) is a framework for the day to day managing and structuring of information regularly gathered from sources both inside and outside an organisation. The inputs into a marketing information system include the information sources inside and outside the firm considered useful for future decision-making. Processing information involves classifying it and developing categories for meaningful storage and retrieval. Marketing decision-makers then determine which information—the output—is useful for making decisions. Feedback enables those who are responsible for gathering internal and external data to adjust the information inputs systematically. Data brought into the organisation through marketing research become part of its marketing databank, a file of data collected through both the MIS and marketing research projects. Any information—an idea or piece of research—which assists in decision-making is marketing intelligence.

The increase in marketing research activities represents a transition from intuitive to scientific problem solving. Intuitive decisions are made on the basis of personal knowledge and past experience. Scientific decision-making is an orderly, logical and systematic approach. Minor, non-recurring problems can be handled successfully by intuition. As the number of risks and alternative solutions increases, the use of research becomes more desirable and rewarding.

The five basic steps of planning marketing research are (1) defining and locating problems, (2) developing hypotheses, (3) collecting data, (4) analysing and interpreting research findings, and (5) reporting the findings.

Defining and locating the problem—the first step towards finding a solution or launching a research study—means uncovering the nature and boundaries of a negative, or positive, situation or question. A problem must be clearly defined for marketers to develop a hypothesis—an informed guess or assumption about that problem or set of circumstances—which is the second step in the research process.

To test the accuracy of hypotheses, researchers collect data—the third step in the research process. Researchers may use exploratory, descriptive or causal studies. Secondary data are compiled inside or outside the organisation for some purpose other than the current investigation. Secondary data may be collected from an organisation's databank and other internal sources; from periodicals, government publications and unpublished sources; and from syndicated data services, which collect general information and sell it to clients. Secondary data should be examined prior to the collection of any primary data.

Primary data are observed and recorded or collected directly from respondents. Experimentation involves maintaining as constants those factors that are related to or may affect the variables under investigation, so that the effects of the experimental variables can be measured. Marketing experimentation is a set of rules and procedures according to which the task of data gathering is organised to expedite analysis and interpretation. In experimentation, an independent variable is manipulated and the resulting changes are measured in a dependent variable. Research techniques are reliable if they produce almost identical results in successive repeated trials; they are valid if they measure what they are supposed to measure and not something else. Experiments may take place in laboratory settings, which provide maximum control over influential factors, or in field settings, which are preferred when marketers want experimentation to take place in natural surroundings.

Other methods of collecting primary data include sampling, surveys and observation. Sampling involves selecting representative units from a total population. In random sampling, all the units in a population have an equal chance of appearing in the sample. In stratified sampling, the population of interest is divided into groups according to a common characteristic or attribute, and then a probability sample is conducted within each group. Area sampling involves selecting a probability sample of geographic areas such as streets, census tracts or census enumeration districts, and selecting units or individuals within the selected geographic areas for the sample. Quota sampling differs from other forms of sampling in that it is judgemental.

Survey methods include mail surveys, telephone surveys, computer assisted telephone interviews and personal interview surveys, such as shopping mall intercept interviews, on-site computer interviews, focus group interviews and in-home interviews. Questionnaires are instruments used to obtain information from respondents and to record observations; they should be unbiased and objective. Observation methods involve researchers recording respondents' overt behaviour and taking note of physical conditions and events. Observation may be facilitated by mechanical observation devices.

To apply research findings to decision-making, marketers must interpret and report their findings properly. Statistical interpretation is analysis that focuses on what is typical or what deviates from the average. After interpreting their research findings, researchers must prepare a report of the findings that the decision-makers can use and understand.

Marketing research and systematic information gathering increase the probability of successful marketing. Because marketing research is essential to the planning and development of marketing strategies, attempts to eliminate unethical marketing research practices and establish generally acceptable procedures for conducting research are important goals. However, because so many parties are involved in the marketing research process, shared ethical concern is difficult to achieve.

IMPORTANT TERMS

Marketing research
Quantitative research
Qualitative research
Marketing information system (MIS)
Marketing databank
Marketing intelligence
Intuition
Scientific decision-making
Problem definition
Hypothesis

Exploratory studies
Descriptive studies
Causal studies
Primary data
Secondary data
Syndicated data services
Experimentation
Marketing experimentation
Independent variable
Dependent variable

Reliability
Validity
Sample
Sampling
Population
Random sampling
Stratified sampling

Area sampling
Quota sampling
Survey methods
Observation methods
Mechanical observation devices
Statistical interpretation

DISCUSSION AND REVIEW QUESTIONS

1. What is the MIS likely to include in a small organisation? Do all organisations have a marketing databank?
2. What is the difference between marketing research and marketing information systems? In what ways do marketing research and the MIS overlap?
3. What are the differences between quantitative and qualitative marketing research?
4. How do the benefits of decisions guided by marketing research compare with those of intuitive decision-making? How do marketing decision-makers know when it will be worthwhile to conduct research?
5. Give specific examples of situations in which intuitive decision-making would probably be more appropriate than marketing research.
6. What is the difference between defining a research problem and developing a hypothesis?
7. What are the major limitations of using secondary data to solve marketing problems?
8. List some of the problems of conducting a laboratory experiment on respondents' reactions to the taste of different brands of beer. How would these problems differ from those of a field study of beer taste preferences?
9. In what situation would it be best to use random sampling? Quota sampling? Stratified or area sampling?
10. *Non-response* is the inability or refusal of some respondents to co-operate in a survey. What are some ways to decrease non-response in personal door to door surveys?
11. Suggest some ways to encourage respondents to co-operate in mail surveys.
12. If a survey of all homes with listed telephone numbers is conducted, what sampling design should be used?
13. Give some examples of marketing problems that could be solved through information gained from observation.
14. Why is questionnaire design important? Why should questionnaires be tested?
15. What is "sugging"? Why is it damaging to the marketing research industry?

■ CASES

6.1 Research Agencies Battle to Scan

A. C. Nielsen is one of the world's largest marketing research companies. In the retail tracking business, Nielsen has close to 90 per cent of the market. Manufacturers and retailers use these data to monitor the performance of individual manufacturer brands such as Persil or Kellogg's Cornflakes, retailer own label brands such as Sainsbury's

Novon, the relative success of separate food, grocery and electrical categories, the market shares of major retail groups or the impact of promotional campaigns and price variations by store, town, region or nationally.

Nielsen's hold over the market for such supermarket scanning data is about to be broken with the appearance in Europe of fellow US research house, IRI. In America, IRI's Infoscan has edged ahead of Nielsen's Scantrack. IRI plans to take the lead in Europe, too. Infoscan is jointly owned by IRI, Taylor Nelson and the German retail auditor GFK. IRI launched Infoscan in the UK, France and Germany in 1993, and during 1994 plans to enter three additional countries scanning data collection and analysis markets. IRI's Infoscan will include details on why goods are sold, not just when and where. Data will come from over 1,000 stores, including convenience outlets, the major supermarket retailers Asda, Gateway, Tesco, Safeway and Sainsbury, and Superdrug (for data on beauty aids).

IRI claims to offer more user-friendly tracking data from more stores using leading-edge software. Nielsen is retaliating by reminding the market that it offers a highly reliable and proven service as "the leading edge supplier of information systems around the world". Nielsen is stressing its overall knowledge of this market and its additional products, Scan*Pro and Homescan. Nielsen has signed up with superstore retailer Safeway to supply named account data, while IRI has opted for a similar deal with supermarket rival Asda. Nielsen's pioneering deal with Safeway, revealing specific sales data from Safeway suppliers and manufacturers, rather than general sales data not specific to a particular retailer or site, has broken new ground. It is likely that Nielsen's near monopoly of this £25 million UK market will become a buyer's market, with accounts playing off Nielsen and IRI in order to obtain the latest data at the most competitive rates.

The need for information has mushroomed, and the major research houses have invested heavily in developing these scanning research systems. Manufacturers need the information in order to plan brand strategies and identify market opportunities for new launches. These data prove invaluable in monitoring both the effects of their own marketing mixes and the impact of their rivals. For retailers, the data assist in merchandise planning: ordering the desirable brands and products, taking account of rival retailers' performances and analysing regional variations.

Away from the market for scanning data, Nielsen has responded to IRI's threat by developing its strength as the leading coupon response and sales promotions monitoring agency. PPA is the result of Nielsen's co-operation with geodemographic house CCN. Instead of reporting just the number of responses received to consumer sales promotions, CCN's geodemographic profiling system Mosaic enables full geodemographic customer profiling of respondents, leading to more accurate targeting of future campaigns. Nielsen handles around 2 million sales promotion responses each day in the UK for around 500 manufacturers. The research giant believes that the combination of its coupon response analysis and CCN's Mosaic profiling provides the opportunity for retailers and manufacturers to

- produce geodemographic profiles of customers who respond to coupon based sales promotions
- target more accurately next time those customers likely to be positive respondents
- identify the "best" retail outlets for local and national promotions
- select the most relevant media and promotions for specific brands

The marketing research industry, like any other market, is constantly evolving: new technology in particular is altering the methods of data collection and analysis in retail tracking and large scale survey research (see also Marketing Insight 6.1). Major research houses are launching new products and entering more countries to compete headon around the world. For the users of research data of this nature—manufacturers, distributors and retailers—the increased competition and investment in systems are leading to the rapid availability of more accurate data for more and more products.

SOURCES: Robert Dwek, "NDL and Pinpoint offer firms targeting plan", *Marketing*, 5 November 1992, p. 3; Robert Dwek, "Nielsen sets up analysis service", *Marketing*, 3 December 1992, p.12; "IRI to rival Nielsen with retail track", *Marketing Week*, 20 November 1992, p. 6; Alan Mitchell, "Information war sparked as US firm tackles Nielsen", *Marketing*, 19 November 1992, p. 3; "Safeway offers weekly monitor", *Marketing*, 9 July 1992, p. 4.

Questions for Discussion

1. What advantages do manufacturers gain from the rapid turnaround of Scantrack and Infoscan data?
2. How can manufacturers such as Kellogg's or Unilever use such data?
3. How can analysis of these scanning data help retailers such as Aldi, Carrefour, Safeway or Sainsbury?
4. Is the increasing competition between rival market research agencies detrimental to the services they offer or beneficial to their clients? Why?

6.2 Focus Group Interviewing: In-Depth Views from Group Discussions

Focus group interviews, which are generally informal group discussions about marketing ideas or concepts conducted by a marketer or marketing research firm, are used by most major organisations in developing marketing or business plans. In the 1980s, focus group interviewing became one of the most widely practised types of marketing research, expanding from the packaged goods industry into financial services, hard goods and industrial applications.

However, the function of focus group interviewing is expected to change in the 1990s. Traditionally, companies have relied on focus group interviews to define the input going into quantitative studies, but the new trend is to conduct focus group interviews after tabulating research results, to provide insight into why the results were achieved. The trend is also towards higher costs (the average today is £800 to £1,500 for an extended, video recorded group).

Other changes pertain to moderator guides and their reports. The moderator guides will be expected to involve clients in the development process. Their reports will concentrate on providing conclusions that interpret the findings and on making recommendations for action by the client. The reports will also contain fewer actual quotations from individual focus group participants. The post–focus group debriefing techniques are also being altered. The shift is towards disciplined debriefing that asks participants their reactions to the group session. Such debriefing can provide the link between concept development and application and serve as a rough check on validity and reliability.

Another new development in focus group interviewing is the use of electronics to offer three-way capabilities. Computerised decision-making software can supplement research findings and consolidate opinions from three different audiences. For example, in health care research in a hospital setting, the three audiences would be former patients, physicians and employees. The advantages of using electronics include easier scheduling of participating groups and more interaction among the three audiences.

A major UK service retailer was faced with declining sales and two new competitors. In order to re-establish itself as the dominant force in its market, it decided to undertake some in-depth qualitative marketing research using focus groups. The retailer's

GROUP COMPOSITION	SOCIAL CLASS*	LOCATION
1.† Male 25–39, white-collar commuters	A, B	Eastcheap
2. Male 40–55, white-collar commuters	A, B	Hitchin
3. Female 25–44, executives/PAs	A, B, C1	Bristol
4. Female 25–44, semi-skilled	C2	Working
5.† Female 35–40 "housewives"	A, B	Leamington
6. Female 25–34, "housewives"	C1, C2	Sheffield
7.† Male 18–29, young earners	C1, C2	Ealing
8. Female 18–29, young earners	C1, C2	Telford

*For social-class definitions, see Table 4.2, p. 119.
†Held in branches after hours

new competitors were opening stores at the rate of six per month, and the company realised it had to act quickly to defend its position. However, it had conducted no consumer research for many years and was uncertain why its customers preferred its stores, how competitors were perceived and what types of people constituted its customer profile. Before modifying its marketing mix and launching an advertising campaign to combat its new competitors, the company had to gain a better understanding of its target market. For approximately £10,000, using a specialist consumer qualitative agency, the company, in just three weeks, had a good "feel" for its standing in its core trading area, as perceived by customers. The table shows that the information resulted from a fairly "standard" programme of focus groups.

Each group had eight consumers, four of whom were shoppers in the retailer's stores, four of whom shopped in competitors' stores. Each group lasted three hours, and a free merchandise voucher and buffet meal were provided for delegates. The same moderator ran all eight groups to maintain consistency. Each session was tape-recorded, the tapes being transcribed later into a report and presentation to the retailer's board of directors. Two sessions were video recorded, and several were secretly viewed by the company's marketing executives.

SOURCES: Lynne Cunningham, "Electronic focus groups offer 3-way capability", *Marketing News*, 8 January 1990, pp. 22, 39; Thomas L. Greenbaum, "Focus group spurt predicted for the '90s", *Marketing News*, 8 January 1990, pp. 21, 22; and Nino DeNicola, "Debriefing sessions: the missing link in focus groups", *Marketing News*, 8 January 1990, pp. 20, 22; Peter Jackson, Adsearch, Richmond.

Questions for Discussion

1. What are the strengths and benefits of focus group marketing research?
2. This retailer chose to commission a programme of focus groups. Given the aims of the company's research, what other research tools might the company have used? Explain your selection.

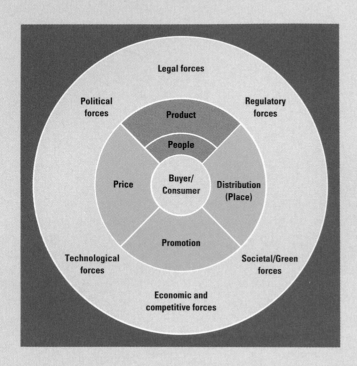

It is now appropriate to analyse the decisions and activities associated with developing and maintaining effective marketing mixes. Parts II through V focus on the major components of the marketing mix: product, distribution, promotion and price. Specifically Part II explores the product ingredient of the marketing mix. Chapter 7 introduces basic concepts and relationships that must be understood if one is to make effective product decisions. Chapter 8 looks at branding, packaging and labelling. Chapter 9 analyses a variety of dimensions regarding product management, such as the ways in which a firm can be organised to manage products, the development and positioning of products, product modification and phasing out products. ∎

7 PRODUCT CONCEPTS

Objectives

To learn how marketers define products

To understand how to classify products

To become familiar with the concepts of product item, product line and product mix and understand how they are connected

To understand the concept of product life-cycle

To understand the types of organisational structures used to manage products

*H*eineken is Europe's largest brewer. While more than half of its sales are European, worldwide, Heineken is second only to US based Anheuser-Busch. Heineken beer is recognised around the globe. With a presence in 150 countries and more than three quarters of sales originating outside the domestic Dutch market, Heineken has been described as the most international beer brand.

Despite its activities in the US, South East Asia and Asia, Heineken recognises the significance of its strength in Europe—a particularly significant market, which accounts for over 40 per cent of world beer sales. Here, despite the mass appeal of the Heineken brand, to stay a step ahead of the competition the company has to adjust its product mix to suit the needs of different countries, fitting in with local cultures and tastes. In general, Heineken achieves this goal by offering a choice of three core brands in each European country:

- A local brand, aimed at the standard and largest market segment. In Italy this is Dreher, in France '33' and in Spain Aguila Pilsener.
- A brand targeted at the upper market segment. Sometimes this is a locally produced brand, such as the Spanish Aguila Master; in other cases a newer Heineken brand, Amstel, is preferred.
- The Heineken brand itself, aimed at the premium market segment. The beer offered may be manufactured locally or exported from the Netherlands. Either way, the Dutch head office works hard to maintain product quality and brand image.

Branding policy in the UK differs slightly from that implemented in other parts of Europe. The standard Heineken brand there is a lower strength version of the beer offered in Europe. The lower strength lager first became popular in pubs across the UK in the 1960s. Now, with the increasing sophistication of the UK beer drinker, the company has introduced the Heineken Export Strength brand—more closely akin to the Heineken offered throughout Europe. ■

SOURCES: Caroline Farquhar, Warwick MBA, 1991–2; "The Netherlands trade review—the beverage market", Economic Intelligence Unit, *Marketing in Europe,* No. 347, October 1991, p. 36; Heineken annual report and accounts, 1991; Barclays de Zoute Wedd Securities, "Heineken company report", February 1992; "European brewing—industry report", SG Warburg Securities, 1991.

The product is an important variable in the marketing mix. Products such as the Heineken beer brand are among a firm's most crucial and visible contacts with buyers. If a company's products do not meet its customers' desires and needs, the company will need to adjust its offering in order to survive. Developing a successful product, as Heineken has done, requires knowledge of fundamental marketing and product concepts.

This chapter's first section introduces and defines the concepts that help clarify what a product is and looks at how buyers view products. The next section examines the concepts of product mix and product line as an introduction to product planning. The chapter then explores the stages of the product life-cycle. Each life-cycle stage generally requires a specific marketing strategy, operates within a certain competitive environment, and has its own sales and profit pattern. The final section discusses the elements which make up a product.

WHAT IS A PRODUCT?

A **product** is everything, both favourable and unfavourable, that is received in an exchange. It is a complexity of tangible and intangible attributes, including functional, social and psychological utilities or benefits.[1] A product can be an idea, a service, a good or any combination of these three. This definition also covers supporting services that go with goods, such as installation, guarantees, product information and promises of repair or maintenance. A **good** is a tangible physical entity, such as a box of Lindt chocolate or a Disney videotape. A **service,** by contrast, is intangible; it is the result of the application of human and mechanical efforts to people or objects. Examples of services include TNT overnight delivery, medical examinations and child care. (Chapter 24 provides a detailed discussion of services marketing.) **Ideas** are concepts, philosophies, images or issues. They provide the psychological stimulus to solve problems or adjust to the environment. For example, Oxfam provides famine relief and attempts to improve the long term prospects of people in hunger stricken countries.

When buyers purchase a product, they are really buying the benefits and satisfaction they think the product will provide. A Mazda MX5 sports car, for example, is purchased for excitement and fun, not just for transport. Services, in particular, are bought on the basis of promises of satisfaction. Promises, with the images and appearances of symbols, help consumers make judgements about tangible and intangible products.[2] Often, symbols and cues are used to make intangible products more tangible or real to the consumer. MasterCard, for example, uses globes to symbolise the firm's financial power and worldwide coverage.

CLASSIFYING PRODUCTS

Products fall into one of two general categories. Products purchased to satisfy personal and family needs are **consumer products.** Those bought for use in a firm's operations or to make other products are **industrial products.** Consumers buy products to satisfy their personal wants, whereas industrial buyers seek to satisfy the goals of their organisations.

The same item can be both a consumer product and an industrial product. For example, when consumers purchase light bulbs for their homes, light bulbs are classified as consumer products. However, when a large corporation purchases light bulbs to provide lighting in a factory or office, the light bulbs are considered industrial products because they are used in the daily operations of the firm. Thus the buyer's intent—or the ultimate use of the product—determines whether an item is classified as a consumer or an industrial product. It is common for more people to be involved in buying an industrial product than in a consumer purchase.

Why is it important to know about product classifications? The main reason is that classes of products are aimed at particular target markets, and classification affects distribution, promotion and pricing decisions. Furthermore, the types of marketing activities and efforts needed, in short, the entire marketing mix, differ according to how a product is classified. This section examines the characteristics of consumer and industrial products and explores the marketing activities associated with some of them.

Consumer Products

The most widely accepted approach to classifying consumer products relies on the common characteristics of consumer buying behaviour. It divides products into four categories: convenience, shopping, specialty and unsought products. However, not all buyers behave in the same way when purchasing a specific type of product. Thus a single product can fit into all four categories. To minimise this problem, marketers think in terms of how buyers *generally* behave when purchasing a specific item. In addition, they recognise that the "correct" classification can be determined only by considering a particular firm's intended target market. The four traditional categories of consumer products should be examined with these thoughts in mind.

Convenience Products. **Convenience products** are relatively inexpensive, frequently purchased and rapidly consumed items on which buyers exert only minimal purchasing effort. They range from bread, soft drinks and chewing gum to petrol and newspapers. The buyer spends little time planning the purchase or comparing available brands or sellers. Even a buyer who prefers a specific brand will readily choose a substitute if the preferred brand is not conveniently available.

Classifying a product as a convenience product has several implications for a firm's marketing strategy. A convenience product is normally marketed through many retail outlets. Because sellers experience high inventory turnover, per unit gross margins can be relatively low. Producers of convenience products such as Smiths crisps and Crest toothpaste expect little promotional effort at the retail level and thus must provide it themselves in the form of advertising and sales promotion. Packaging is also an important element of the marketing mix for convenience products. The package may have to sell the product, because many convenience items are available only on a self-service basis at the retail level. The use of on-pack sales promotion is one way to maximise the impact of the package.

Shopping Products. **Shopping products** are items which are more carefully chosen than convenience products. In fact, buyers are willing to expend considerable effort in planning and purchasing these items. They allocate time for comparing stores and brands with respect to prices, credit, product features, qualities, services and perhaps guarantees. Appliances, furniture, bicycles, stereos, jewellery and cameras (as shown in Figure 7.1) are examples of shopping products. These products are expected to last a fairly long time and are bought less often than convenience items. Even though shopping products are more expensive than convenience products, few buyers of shopping products are particularly brand loyal. If they were, they would be unwilling to shop and compare among brands.

To market a shopping product effectively, a marketer considers several key issues. Shopping products require fewer retail outlets than convenience products. Because

FIGURE 7.1 *Shopping product*
Sony cameras, as well as most other brands of camera, are shopping products.

SOURCE: Courtesy of Sony Europa.

they are purchased less frequently, inventory turnover is lower and middlemen expect to receive higher gross margins. Although large sums of money may be required to advertise shopping products, an even larger percentage of resources is likely to be used for personal selling. Indeed, the quality of the service may be a factor in the consumer's choice of outlet. Usually, the producer and the middlemen expect some co-operation from one another with respect to providing parts and repair services and performing promotional activities.

Specialty Products.   **Specialty products** possess one or more unique characteristics, and a significant group of buyers is willing to expend considerable effort to obtain them. Buyers actually plan the purchase of a specialty product; they know exactly what they want and will not accept a substitute. An example of a specialty product is a painting by L. S. Lowry or a Cartier watch. When searching for specialty products, buyers do not compare alternatives; they are concerned primarily with finding an outlet that has a pre-selected product available.

The fact that an item is a specialty product can affect a firm's marketing efforts in several ways. Specialty products are often distributed through a limited number of retail outlets. For some consumers this limited availability accentuates the exclusivity of the product. Some companies, for example, Chanel, go to considerable lengths to control this aspect of their distribution. Like shopping goods, specialty products are purchased infrequently, causing lower inventory turnover and thus requiring relatively high gross margins.

Unsought Products.   **Unsought products** are purchased when a sudden problem must be solved or when aggressive selling is used to obtain a sale that otherwise would not take place. In general, the consumer does not think of buying these products regularly. Emergency car repairs and headstones are examples of unsought products. Life insurance and encyclopaedias, in contrast, are examples of products that need aggressive personal selling. The salesperson tries to make consumers aware of the benefits that can be derived from buying such products.

Industrial Products

Industrial products are usually purchased on the basis of an organisation's goals and objectives. Generally, the functional aspects of the product are more important than the psychological rewards sometimes associated with consumer products. Industrial products can be classified into seven categories according to their characteristics and intended uses: raw materials, major equipment, accessory equipment, component parts, process materials, consumable supplies and industrial services.[3]

Raw Materials.   **Raw materials** are the basic materials that become part of physical products. They include minerals, chemicals, agricultural products and materials from forests and oceans. They are usually bought and sold in relatively large quantities according to grades and specifications.

Major Equipment.   **Major equipment** includes large tools and machines used for production purposes, such as cranes and spray-painting machinery. Normally, major equipment is expensive and intended to be used in a production process for a considerable length of time. Some major equipment is custom made to perform specific functions for a particular organisation. For example GEC Large Machines manufactures purpose built gears and turbines. Other items are standardised and perform similar tasks for many types of firms. Because major equipment is so expensive, purchase decisions are often made by high level management. In some cases the purchase process will be long and complicated. Marketers of major equipment frequently must provide a variety of services, including installation, training, repair and maintenance assistance, and even help in financing the purchase. Often manufacturers of major equipment build up long term relationships with their customers so that they can better adapt to their needs.

Accessory Equipment.   **Accessory equipment** does not become a part of the final physical product but is used in production or office activities. Marketing Insight 7.1 discusses computer software packages used by companies to expedite other activities. Examples include typewriters, fractional horsepower motors, calculators and tools. Compared with major equipment, accessory items are usually much cheaper; purchased routinely, with less negotiation; and treated as expenditure items rather than capital items because they are not expected to last as long. Accessory products are standardised items that can be used in several aspects of a firm's operations. More outlets are required for distributing accessory equipment than for major equipment, but sellers do not have to provide the multitude of services expected of major equipment marketers.

MICROSOFT WINDOWS

Once again the brilliant minds at computer software company Microsoft have developed a winner: Microsoft Windows. Described as a "pick and click" system, version 3.1 has precipitated a meteoric rise in Windows' fortunes since its launch in May 1990. In the first six weeks alone over 3 million copies were sold. Now it is estimated that more than 20 million copies are in use around the world, with an estimated one million more being shipped to customers each month. For software companies the popularity of the Windows system means that software programs can run on a number of different operating systems—including PC operating system, MS-DOS and, most recently, Windows. However, the intrinsic appeal and simplicity of the mouse driven Windows look set to ensure its long term popularity for the innovative Microsoft company.

For many industrial customers the Windows operating system offers a host of benefits: it is easy to use, attractive to look at and—perhaps most significantly—has a common user interface (CUI). The CUI means that users apply the same commands, through the same system of menus, to a wide range of different programs. The result is that once users have become familiar with commands from one software package, they can move on to another with minimum fuss.

It is perhaps not surprising that Microsoft Windows has attracted positive interest and feedback across all industry sectors. According to brewery giant Bass, the installation of Windows in its marketing department is helping to improve co-ordination of projects by making analysis, planning, data access and communications more efficient. Advertising agency Saatchi & Saatchi is also a strong convert, claiming that the installation of Windows allows personnel to switch easily from machine to machine and move quickly through a variety of packages. This maximum flexibility with minimum learning is particularly welcome in Saatchi's high pressured and fast moving environment. Although the agency does not force employees to use computer-based technology, those that do are unstinting in their praise. Of course, switching to a new operating system is not without its costs. Some organisations, such as Mars, are getting around this difficulty in the short term by offering managers a choice of systems when replacing hardware. But whatever routes companies are taking to convert to Windows, the widespread acceptance of another Microsoft masterpiece seems clear.

SOURCES: Chris Long, "Bill Gates: one man as his brand", *Marketing,* 18 February 1993, pp. 24–6; "See the stars of page and screen", Windows for Marketers, *Marketing,* 11 February 1993, p. 4; Ron Condon, "It's the sound and vision thing", Windows for Marketers, *Marketing,* 11 February 1993, pp. 12–13; Ron Condon, "Laptop lunacy licked", Windows for Marketers, *Marketing,* 11 February 1993, pp. 10–11.

Current data shows 25% of all computer print ribbon is made with ICI fibre. How's that for world trade figures?

ICI manufactures in 40 countries and sells to over 150.

ICI World Class

FIGURE 7.2   *An example of a process material*
ICI fibre is a process material used in the manufacture of computer print ribbon.

SOURCE: Courtesy of ICI, UK. Created by Saatchi & Saatchi.

Component Parts.   **Component parts** become a part of the physical product and are either finished items ready for assembly or products that need little processing before assembly. Although they become part of a larger product, component parts can often be easily identified and distinguished. Microchips, switches, screws and wires are all component parts of a personal computer. Buyers purchase such items according to their own specifications or industry standards. They expect the parts to be of specified quality and delivered on time so that production is not slowed or stopped. Producers that are primarily assemblers, such as most lawn mower or car manufacturers, depend heavily on the suppliers of component parts.

Process Materials.   **Process materials** are used directly in the production of other products. Unlike component parts, however, process materials are not readily identifiable. For example, Reichhold Chemicals markets a treated fibre product: a phenolic-resin, sheet moulding compound which is used in the production of flight deck instrument panels and aircraft cabin interiors. Although the material is not identifiable in the finished aircraft, it retards burning, smoke and formation of toxic gas if moulded components are subjected to fire or high temperatures. In Figure 7.2, ICI promotes the fact that 25 per cent of all computer print ribbon is made with ICI fibre. As with component parts, process materials are purchased according to industry standards or the purchaser's specifications.

Consumable Supplies.   **Consumable supplies** facilitate production and operations but do not become part of the finished product. Paper, pencils, oils, cleaning agents and paints are in this category. Because such supplies are standardised items used in a variety of situations, they are purchased by many different types of organisations. Consumable supplies are commonly sold through numerous outlets and are purchased routinely. To ensure that supplies are available when needed, buyers often deal with more than one seller. Because these supplies can be divided into three subcategories—maintenance, repair and operating (or overhaul) supplies—they are sometimes called **MRO items.**

Industrial Services.   **Industrial services** are the intangible products that many organisations use in their operations. They include financial, legal, marketing research, computer programming and operation, caretaking and printing services for business. Purchasers must decide whether to provide their own services internally or obtain them outside the organisation. This decision depends largely on the costs associated with each alternative and the frequency with which the services are needed.

THE THREE LEVELS OF PRODUCT

The product may appear obvious—a tin of baked beans or a JCB digger—but generally the purchaser is buying much more than some beans or an earthmover. To be motivated to make the purchase, there must be a perceived or real core benefit or service to be gained from the product. This level of product, termed the **core product,** is illustrated in Figure 7.3. The **actual product** is a composite of several factors: the features and capabilities offered, quality and durability, design and product styling, packaging, and, often of great importance, the brand name.

In order to make the purchase, the consumer will often require the assistance of sales personnel; there may be delivery and payment credit requirements and, for bulky or very technical products, advice regarding installation. The level of warranty backup and after sales support, particularly for innovative, highly technical or high value goods, will be of concern to most consumers. Increasingly, the overall level of customer service constitutes part of the purchase criteria, and in many markets it is deemed integral to the product on offer. These "support" issues form what is termed the **augmented product** (see Figure 7.3).

When a £20,000 Rover 800 executive car is purchased, the vehicle's performance specification and design may have encouraged the sale. Speed of delivery and credit payment terms may have been essential to the conclusion of the deal. The brand's image, particularly in the case of a car costing £20,000, will also have influenced the sale. Once behind the wheel of the Rover car, its new owner will expect reliability and efficient, friendly, convenient service in the course of maintenance being required. The purchase might have been lost at the outset had the salesperson mishandled the initial enquiry. Repeat servicing business and the subsequent sale of another new car would equally be ruled out if the owner encountered incompetent, unhelpful service engineers. The core benefit may have been a car to facilitate journeys to work, transport for the family or the acquisition of a recognised status symbol.

This example is not unusual. For most consumer or industrial products and services, the consumer is aware of—and influenced by—the three levels of the product: core,

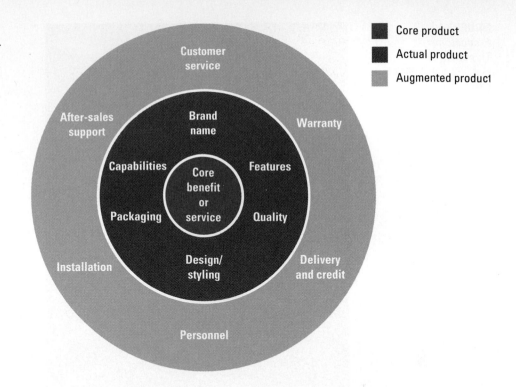

FIGURE 7.3
The three levels of product: core, actual and augmented

■ Core product
■ Actual product
■ Augmented product

Customer service

After-sales support

Warranty

Brand name

Capabilities

Features

Core benefit or service

Packaging

Quality

Installation

Design/ styling

Delivery and credit

Personnel

actual and augmented. Of growing importance to many marketers is the role of personnel, who facilitate most product exchanges. Without people, there would be no marketing. In companies they design, produce, market and sell products and services. In the distribution channel they help to make products available to the market-place. As consumers, people make decisions and ultimately adopt products for use and consumption. Companies endeavour to educate their target customers: promotional activity explains product usage, presents an image for the product and convinces customers that they have a reason to purchase. More attention is now being paid to the skills, attitudes and motivations of personnel involved in the marketing channel. Most companies are recognising the key role played by their personnel, particularly in their interaction with consumers. As explained in Chapter 24, this role is especially significant for services, but as discussed in Chapter 1, personnel also constitutes an essential ingredient of the marketing mix for consumer and industrial goods.

PRODUCT LINE AND PRODUCT MIX

Marketers must understand the relationships among all the products of their organisation if they are to co-ordinate the marketing of the total group of products. The following concepts help describe the relationships among an organisation's products. A **product item** is a specific version of a product that can be designated as a distinct offering among an organisation's products, for example, Cadbury's Dairy Milk chocolate. A **product line** includes a group of closely related product items that are considered a unit because of marketing, technical or end use considerations. All the chocolate bars manufactured by Cadbury's constitute one of its product lines. Figure 7.4 illustrates the product line for The Watch Gallery. To come up with the optimum product line,

FIGURE 7.4
Product line
This collection of
watches constitutes
part of the Watch
Gallery's product line.

SOURCE: Courtesy of The Watch Gallery.

marketers must understand buyers' goals. Specific items in a product line reflect the desires of different target markets or the different needs of consumers.

A **product mix** is the composite, or total, group of products that an organisation makes available to customers. For example, all the personal care products, laundry detergent products and other products that Procter & Gamble manufactures constitute its product mix. The **depth** of a product mix is measured by the number of different products offered in each product line. The **width** of a product mix is measured by the number of product lines a company offers. Figure 7.5 shows the width of the product mix and the depth of each product line for selected Procter & Gamble products in the US. Procter & Gamble is known for using distinctive technology, branding, packaging and consumer advertising to promote individual items in its detergent product line. Tide, Bold, and Ariel—all Procter & Gamble detergents—share similar distribution channels and manufacturing facilities. Yet due to variations in product formula and attributes, each is promoted as distinct, adding depth to the product line.

PRODUCT LIFE-CYCLES

Just as biological cycles progress through growth and decline, so do product life-cycles. A new product is introduced into the market-place; it grows; matures; and when it loses appeal and sales decline, it is terminated.[4] Recall that the earlier definition of a product focused on tangible and intangible attributes. The total product might be not just a

Laundry Detergents	Toothpastes	Bar Soaps	Deodorants	Shampoos
Ivory Snow 1930	Crest 1955	Ivory 1879	Secret 1956	Prell 1946
Dreft 1933	Gleem 1952	Kirk's 1885	Sure 1972	Head & Shoulders 1961
Tide 1946	Denquel 1980	Camay 1926	Old Spice 1990	Pantene 1965
Cheer 1950		Zest 1952		Vidal Sassoon 1974
Bold 1965		Safeguard 1963		Pert Plus 1979
Gain 1966		Coast 1974		Ivory 1983
Era 1972				
Solo 1979				
Liquid Tide 1984				
Liquid Bold-3 1985				
Liquid Cheer 1986				
Liquid Lemon Dash 1987				
Tide with bleach 1988				
Liquid Dreft 1989				
Liquid Ivory Snow 1989				

Product line depth (vertical axis)

Product mix width

SOURCE: Information provided and reprinted by permission of The Procter & Gamble Company, Public Affairs Division, 1 Procter & Gamble Plaza, Cincinnati, OH 45202-3315.

good, but also the ideas and services attached to it. Packaging, branding and labelling techniques alter or help create products, so marketers can modify product life-cycles. (Marketing strategies for different life-cycle stages are discussed in Chapter 9.)

As Figure 7.6 shows, a **product life-cycle** has four major stages: (1) introduction, (2) growth, (3) maturity and (4) decline. As a product moves through its cycle, the strategies relating to competition, promotion, distribution, pricing and market information must be periodically evaluated and possibly changed. Astute marketing managers use the life-cycle concept to make sure that the introduction, alteration and termination of a product are timed and executed properly. By understanding the typical life-cycle pattern, marketers are better able to maintain profitable products and drop unprofitable ones.

Introduction

The **introduction stage** of the life-cycle begins at a product's first appearance in the market-place, when sales are zero and profits are negative. Profits are below zero because a new product incurs development cases, initial revenues are low and at the same time a company must generally incur large expenses for promotion and distribution. As time passes, sales should move upwards from zero, and profits should also build up from the negative position due to high expenses (see Figure 7.6).

Because of cost, very few product introductions represent major inventions. Developing and introducing a new product can mean an outlay of many millions of pounds. The failure rate for new products is quite high, ranging from 60 to 90 per cent depending on the industry and how product failure is defined. For example, in the food

FIGURE 7.6
The four stages of the product life-cycle

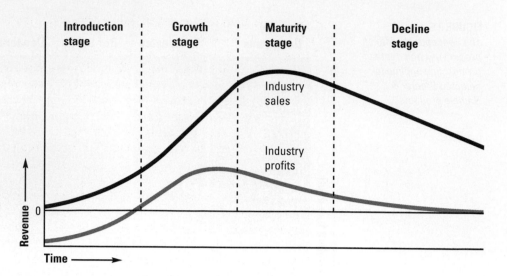

and drinks industry, 80 per cent of all new products fail.[5] More typically, product introductions involve a new magazine, a new type of portable phone or a new fashion in clothing rather than a major product innovation.

Potential buyers must be made aware of the new product's features, uses and advantages. Two difficulties may arise at this point. Only a few sellers may have the resources, technological knowledge and marketing know-how to launch the product successfully; and the initial product price may have to be high in order to recoup expensive marketing research or development costs. Given these difficulties, it is not surprising that many products never get beyond the introduction stage; indeed many are never launched commercially at all.

Growth

During the **growth stage,** sales rise rapidly and profits reach a peak and then start to decline (see Figure 7.6). The growth stage is critical to a product's survival because competitive reactions to its success during this period will affect the product's life expectancy. For example, Mars successfully launched Ice Cream Mars, the first ice cream version of an established confectioner product. Today the product competes with around a dozen other brands. Already some of the competing brands have failed—time will show how many others follow. Profits decline late in the growth stage as more competitors enter the market, driving prices down and creating the need for heavy promotional expenses. At this point a typical marketing strategy encourages strong brand loyalty, perhaps using sales promotion, and competes with aggressive emulators of the product. During the growth stage, an organisation tries to strengthen its market share and develop a competitive position by emphasising the product's benefits.

Aggressive promotional pricing, including price cuts, is typical during the growth stage. The mobile telephone industry is currently in the growth stage, and competitors are entering the market. Cellnet and Vodaphone are having to battle hard to maintain their existing positions in this competitive arena.

Maturity

During the **maturity stage,** the sales curve peaks and starts to decline, and profits continue to decline (see Figure 7.6). This stage is characterised by severe competition, with many brands in the market. Competitors emphasise improvements and differences in their versions of the product. Inevitably, during the maturity stage some weaker competitors are squeezed out or switch their attentions to other products. For example, some brands of compact disc players will perish as the product moves through the maturity stage.

During the maturity phase, the producers who remain in the market must make fresh promotional and distribution efforts. These efforts must focus on dealers as much as on consumers, to ensure that brand visibility is maintained at the point of sale. Advertising and dealer orientated promotions are typical during this stage of the product life-cycle. The promoters must also take into account the fact that, as the product reaches maturity, buyers' knowledge of it attains a high level. Consumers of the product are no longer inexperienced generalists but rather experienced specialists.

Decline

During the **decline stage,** sales fall rapidly (see Figure 7.6). New technology or a new social trend may cause product sales to take a sharp turn downwards. When this happens, the marketer considers pruning items from the product line to eliminate those not earning a profit. At this time, too, the marketer may cut promotion efforts, eliminate marginal distributors and, finally, plan to phase out the product.

Because most businesses have a product mix consisting of multiple products, a firm's destiny is rarely tied to one product. A composite of life-cycle patterns is formed when various products in the mix are at different stages in the cycle. As one product is declining, other products are in the introduction, growth or maturity stage. Marketers must deal with the dual problems of prolonging the life of existing products and introducing new products to meet organisational sales goals. For example, Kodak has prolonged the product life-cycle of its 110mm cameras by adding built-in flashes, waterproof bodies and other features. But Kodak has also continued to introduce new products, including the disposable 35mm Kodak Fling; Breeze, a new line of 35mm cameras; and Ektar, a new line of colour films designed specifically for 35mm single-lens reflex cameras. Chapter 9 further explores the development of new products and considers how they can be managed in their various life-cycle stages.

OTHER PRODUCT RELATED CHARACTERISTICS

When developing products, marketers make many decisions. Some of these decisions involve the physical characteristics of the product; others focus on less tangible support services that are very much a part of the total product.

Physical Characteristics of the Product

A crucial question that arises during product development is how much quality to build into the product. A major dimension of quality is durability. Higher quality often demands better materials and more expensive processing, increasing production costs and, ultimately, the product's price. In determining the specific level of quality required, a marketer must decide approximately what price the target market views as acceptable. In addition, a marketer usually tries to set a level for a specific product consistent with the firm's other products that carry a similar brand. Obviously, the quality of competing brands is another consideration.

A product's physical features require careful consideration by marketers and by those in research and development. Product development personnel at Gillette spent considerable resources dealing with the Sensor razor's physical features (see Marketing Insight 7.2). The prime basis for decisions about the physical features of a product should be the needs and wants of the target market. If marketers do not know what physical features people in the target market want in a product, it is highly unlikely that the product will be satisfactory. For example, Rover holds customer clinics offering people the opportunity to examine their product range and comment on desired features. Even a firm whose existing products have been designed to satisfy target market

MARKETING INSIGHT 7.2

GILLETTE SERIES LINKS IN TO GILLETTE SENSOR SUCCESS

Amidst a wave of media interest and advertising hype, Gillette has launched a range of men's toiletries simultaneously in the UK, US and Canada. Known as the Gillette Series, the range—which includes 13 personal care products, from aftershaves to antiperspirants—will be priced 25 per cent above current leading brands. The advertising copy builds on the existing Gillette theme "The best a man can get . . .". With a $125 million spend on advertising alone, and agreed shelf space alongside existing Gillette products in major supermarket and chemist outlets, the transatlantic campaign aims to ensure maximum visibility for the new Series products. The launch was backed by the distribution of 5 million samples to carefully selected homes.

Management hopes that the launch of the Gillette Series will ride on the back of the successful Gillette Sensor razor, which allowed the company to regain market share lost to Bic Corporation's disposable razors. In 1977, a Gillette design engineer came up with the concept of a shaving cartridge that would float on springs, giving a very comfortable and close shave. Many years later, Gillette assembled a nine member Sensor task force that worked on the razor seven days a week for 15 months. Like the Series, the Sensor was launched simultaneously in the UK, US and Canada. Now the Sensor is sold in over 50 countries, a position which Gillette hopes the Series products will emulate. Altogether, the activities associated with the Sensor launch were a great success, with unprecedented demand immediately following the launch advertising. Consumers, it seemed, could not get enough of the razor, and retailers quickly ran out of stock.

The Gillette Series is pitched to compete head to head with Procter & Gamble's Old Spice and Unilever's Sure and Lynx products. Management believes that innovative packaging and use of "natural" ingredients will help give the Series a competitive advantage. Gillette is also optimistic that cannibalisation of its Naturel Plus and Right Guard products will be kept to a minimum. The company hopes that its new foray into men's toiletries will be as well received as the launch of Sensor.

SOURCES: Paul Mellor, "The best a man can get?", *Marketing,* 15 October 1992, p. 2; Alison Fahey, "Gillette readies Sensor", *Advertising Age,* 18 September 1989, pp. 1, 81; Alison Fahey, "Sensor sensation", *Advertising Age,* 5 February 1990, pp. 4, 49; Keith Hammonds, "Do high-tech razors have the edge?", *Business Week,* 22 January 1990, p. 83; Keith Hammonds, "How a $4 razor ends up costing £300 million", *Business Week,* 29 January 1990, pp. 62–3.

desires should continue to assess these desires periodically to determine whether they have changed enough to require alterations in the product.

Supportive Product Related Services

All products, whether they are goods or not, possess intangible qualities. "When prospective customers can't experience the product in advance, they are asked to buy what are essentially promises—promises of satisfaction. Even tangible, testable, feelable, smellable products are, before they're bought, largely just promises."[6] There are many product related services and product intangibles but three of the most common are guarantees, repairs and replacements, and credit.

The type of guarantee a firm provides can be a critical issue for buyers, especially when expensive, technically complex goods such as appliances are involved. A **guarantee** specifies what the producer will do if the product malfunctions. In recent years, government actions have required a guarantor to state more simply and specifically the terms and conditions under which the firm will take action. Because guarantees must be more precise today, marketers are using them more vigorously as tools to give their brands a competitive advantage. Retailers, such as Dixons, which sells electrical brown goods, including compact disc players and Camcorders, are increasingly using guarantees as a competitive tool by providing longer periods of guarantee protection.

Although it is more difficult to provide guarantees for services than for goods, some service marketers do guarantee customer satisfaction. An effective service guarantee should be unconditional, easy to understand and communicate, meaningful, easy to invoke, and easy and quick to collect on. The customer can return a product and get a replacement, a refund or a credit for the returned good. Photographic processors such as SupaSnaps offer free processing on prints not ready within 24 hours. Such guarantees of satisfying the customer are beneficial because they force the service provider to focus on customers' definitions of good service. They also provide clear performance standards, generate feedback from customers on the quality of the service and help build customer loyalty and sales.[7]

A marketer must also be concerned with establishing a system to provide replacement parts and repair services. This support service is especially important for expensive, complex industrial products that buyers expect to last a long time. For example, farmers expect agricultural machinery manufacturers like Massey Ferguson to be able to provide replacement parts quickly and without fuss. Although the producer may furnish these services directly to buyers, it is more common for the producer to provide such services through regional service centres or middlemen. Regardless of how services are provided, it is important to customers that they be performed quickly and correctly.

Finally, a firm must sometimes provide credit services to customers. Even though credit services place a financial burden on an organisation, they can yield several benefits. One of them is that a firm may acquire and maintain a stable market share. Many major oil companies, for example, have competed effectively against petrol discounters by providing credit services. For marketers of relatively expensive items, offering credit services enables a larger number of people to buy the product, thus enlarging the market for the item. Another reason for offering credit services is to earn interest income from customers. The types of credit services offered depend on the characteristics of target market members, the firm's financial resources, the type of products sold and the types of credit services that competitors offer.

Summary

A product is everything, both favourable and unfavourable, that is received in an exchange. It is a complex set of tangible and intangible attributes, including functional, social and psychological utilities or benefits. A product can be an idea, a service, a good or any combination of these three. When consumers purchase a product, they are buying the benefits and satisfaction that they think the product will provide.

Products can be classified on the basis of the buyer's intentions. Thus consumer products are those purchased to satisfy personal and family needs. Industrial products, on the other hand, are purchased for use in a firm's operations or to make other products. Consumer products can be subdivided into convenience, shopping, specialty and unsought products. Industrial products can be divided into raw materials, major equipment, accessory equipment, component parts, process materials, consumable supplies and industrial services.

The purchaser buys a core benefit or service in addition to the product's brand name, features, capabilities, quality, packaging and design. Increasingly, aspects of the augmented product are important considerations for purchasers of consumer goods, services and industrial goods. Guarantees, delivery and credit, personnel, installation, often sales support and customer service are integral to the actual product's appeal and perceived benefits. The role of personnel in particular is of fundamental concern to marketers; people now form a central part of the marketing mix. It is important to remember that a product has three levels: core, actual and augmented.

A product item is a specific version of a product that can be designated as a distinct offering among an organisation's products. A product line is a group of closely related product items that are considered a unit because of marketing, technical or end use considerations. The composite, or total, group of products that an organisation makes available to customers is called the product mix. The depth of a product mix is measured by the number of different products offered in each product line. The width of the product mix is measured by the number of product lines a company offers.

The product life-cycle describes how product items in an industry move through (1) introduction, (2) growth, (3) maturity and (4) decline. The life-cycle concept is used to make sure that the introduction, alteration and termination of a product are timed and executed properly. The sales curve is at zero at introduction, rises at an increasing rate during growth, peaks at maturity and then declines. Profits peak towards the end of the growth stage of the product life-cycle. The life expectancy of a product is based on buyers' wants, the availability of competing products and other environmental conditions. Most businesses have a composite of life-cycle patterns for various products. It is important to manage existing products and develop new ones to keep the overall sales performance at a desired level.

When creating products, marketers must take into account other product related considerations, such as physical characteristics and less tangible support services. Specific physical product characteristics that require attention are the level of quality, product features, textures, colours and sizes. Support services that may be viewed as part of the total product include guarantees, repairs and replacements, and credit services.

IMPORTANT TERMS

Product	Accessory equipment
Good	Component parts
Service	Process materials
Ideas	Consumable supplies
Consumer products	MRO items
Industrial products	Industrial services
Convenience products	Core product
Shopping products	Actual product
Specialty products	Augmented product
Unsought products	Product item
Raw materials	Product line
Major equipment	Product mix

Depth (of product mix)
Width (of product mix)
Product life-cycle
Introduction stage

Growth stage
Maturity stage
Decline stage
Guarantee

Discussion and Review Questions

1. List the tangible and intangible attributes of a spiral notebook. Compare the benefits of the spiral notebook with those of an intangible product such as life insurance.
2. A product has been referred to as a "psychological bundle of satisfaction". Is this a good definition of a product? Why or why not?
3. Is a roll of carpet in a shop a consumer product or an industrial product? Defend your answer.
4. How do convenience products and shopping products differ? What are the distinguishing characteristics of each type of product?
5. Would a stereo system that sells for £400 be a convenience, shopping or specialty product?
6. In the category of industrial products, how do component parts differ from process materials?
7. How does an organisation's product mix relate to its development of a product line? When should an enterprise add depth to its product lines rather than width to its product mix?
8. How do industry profits change as a product moves through the four stages of its life-cycle?
9. What is the relationship between the concepts of product mix and product life-cycle?
10. What factors must marketers consider when deciding what quality level to build into a product? What support services can be offered to back up product quality?

■ Cases

7.1 Computers for All: Changing Trends for Personal Computers

International Business Machines (IBM) has been a leader in the computer industry since the 1960s. Several of its products, including the System/370 mainframe computers and the IBM PC line of personal computers, set the standards for many computer manufacturers. Despite IBM's reputation for providing high quality computers and strong customer service, there are those who have lost faith in the company. In a 1990 survey of more than 100 of IBM's major customers, complaints commonly cited the company's lack of applications software, poor integration of its different computer product lines and difficult to use systems. Customer dissatisfaction has translated into declining sales, profits and market share; in 1993 IBM announced the biggest losses in US corporate history.

Recognising that the company's performance has not always been adequate, senior managers are instigating a reorganisation which they hope will make the company more responsive to customers' needs and more competitive in a stagnating computer market. The aim is to boost sales, speed up new product development, slim down the corporate structure, and improve products and customer service. IBM has combined its personal computer and typewriter divisions because customers of these products have similar needs. It has also merged its mainframe division with the less profitable mid-size computer division. To help reduce the bureaucracy that slows down new product development and makes customers dissatisfied, the organisation has been somewhat decentralised, with decision-making responsibilities spread over six major product and marketing divisions. Although these efforts have improved the company's performance, IBM is still experiencing slow growth, in part because of increasing competition in its mainframe and personal computer markets.

In the personal computer market, part of the increased competition is being generated by Apple Computers, which is trying to increase the mass market appeal of its Macintosh computer. The recent launch of the Macintosh Performa series marks an attempt by the company to get a grip on the mass consumer market. There are four different models to choose from—each offering computer, mouse, software and after service support.

- Performa 200: Costs £799 including VAT. Lightweight, black and white screen, suitable for word processing and simple business applications.
- Performa 400: Costs £1,099 including VAT. The appearance and capabilities of a standard PC with colour screen. (Likely to be the most popular version.)
- Performa 600: Costs £1,899 including VAT. Colour screen, powerful business computer.
- Performa 600CD: Costs £2,199 including VAT. Fitted with a CD player. This version will play computer CDs (computer games), audio CDs and the latest Kodak PhotoCDs, which store photographs.

The Claris Works software included with the computers is an integrated package which combines word processing, database, graphics and spreadsheet facilities. The system will allow users at work and at home to produce documents, prepare graphs and illustrations, and keep accounts. User security is assured by a system of passwords, so that children can use the machine for games without jeopardising the household accounts.

SOURCES: Mat Toor, "Apple launches its consumer Performa", *Marketing*, 11 February 1993; Kim Wilson, "The kitchen computer", *Daily Mail*, 15 February 1993; Helen Slingsby, "Apple bites into families market", *Marketing Week*, 12 February 1993.

Questions for Discussion

1. In what ways can IBM benefit from the reorganisational steps its management has taken?
2. How can the market for personal computers be segmented?
3. To which segments of the PC market is Apple trying to appeal?

7.2   Disney Expands Its Product Mix

After the death of its founder, Walt Disney, in 1966, the Walt Disney Company seemed to lose its creative edge. As other studios diversified into television and video, Disney seemed content with its library of feature films and animated classics. The company was producing only three or four new films a year, most of which failed at the box office. Disney also pulled out of television after 29 years of network programming. By the mid-1980s, Disney was dependent on theme parks and property development for about 75 per cent of its revenues.

Today, however, Disney executives are intent on recapturing—and building on—the old Disney magic. Company executives say the Disney name, culture, films and library are the company's biggest resources, and Disney's plan is to rejuvenate old assets and simultaneously develop new ones. While continuing its traditional appeal to the family segment of the film market, Disney, through its Touchstone Pictures division, is turning out films for adult audiences as well. The company is releasing both old and new programmes for television syndication and testing new promotional and licensing projects. In addition, the Disney theme park has been exported. The Tokyo Disneyland is attracting millions of people a year, and a $2 billion Euro Disneyland opened near Paris in 1992. Disney's overall strategy is to channel the company's revived creativity into improved theme parks, to use the parks to generate interest in Disney films and to promote both parks and merchandise through Disney television shows.

Disney received its new lease on life a few years ago when threats of a corporate takeover prompted the company to replace its top executives. The new management moved quickly to tap the resources of the Disney television and film library. About two hundred Disney films and cartoon packages are now available on video cassette, and other classic films, such as *Snow White*, will now be released every five years instead of every seven. The studio plans to release one new animated film for children every 18 months and about a dozen adult films a year.

Disney is back on network television as well, with the return of the *Disney Sunday Movie*. The company also produces the comedy show *The Golden Girls*, along with two top rated Saturday morning cartoon shows. Following the lead of other studios, Disney has moved into television syndication by marketing packages of feature films, old cartoons and *Wonderful World of Disney* programmes. The company is syndicating *The Disney Afternoon*, a block of children's cartoons that will run from 3 p.m. to 5 p.m. New shows are also being produced for syndication. They include the popular game show *Win, Lose or Draw*, a business news programme, and film reviews by Gene Siskel and Roger Ebert. In an otherwise flat cable television market, the number of subscribers to the family orientated Disney Channel has jumped dramatically—to 4 million. The channel now offers 24 hour features and more original programming than any other pay service. Disney has even signed an agreement with the Chinese government to broadcast a weekly television series starring Mickey Mouse and Donald Duck. The company may license the Chinese to produce Disney merchandise as well.

In the United States, too, marketing of Disney characters is receiving considerable emphasis. Recently, Mickey, Donald and others visited hospital wards and marched in parades in a 120 city tour. Snow White and all seven dwarfs made a special appearance on the floor of the New York Stock Exchange to promote the celebration of Snow White's 50th birthday. Minnie Mouse now has a trendy new look and appears on clothing and watches and in a fashion doll line. Disney is also working with toy companies to develop new characters, such as Fluppy Dogs and Wuzzles, both of which will be sold in stores and featured in television shows. In addition, the company has opened non-tourist retail outlets. Located primarily in shopping malls, Disney stores carry both licensed products and exclusive theme park merchandise.

Disney's revitalised market presence has been credited with increasing attendance at the Disney theme parks to more than 50 million people. In Florida, Disney has recently completed new hotels and a movie studio/tour attraction. Moreover, Disney is constructing a 50 acre water park and adding $1.4 billion worth of new attractions to Walt Disney World. The company is also considering regional centres that would combine restaurants and shopping with evening entertainment. In a recent move, Disney announced plans to extend its expertise into the European time-share business by launching the Disney Vacation Club. The new concept offers holidaymakers accommodations in purpose built facilities at Florida's Disney World. The price is a once only payment of £7,000, which will give club members access to accommodation at Disney

World, or over 100 other destinations around the world. It is not yet clear whether the company plans to build vacation clubs at other Disney sites.

Disney intends eventually to reduce the company's financial dependence on parks and hotels. The strategy is to triple the proportion of company profits from films and television and to acquire such distribution outlets as cinemas, television stations and record companies. Recent business deals with Procter & Gamble, McDonald's, Coca-Cola, Time, M&M/Mars, and Sears, Roebuck and Co. will help increase Disney's profits and market presence still further.

SOURCES: Dudley Clendinen, "Disney's mouse of marketing", *New York Times*, 22 November 1986, p. 41–L; Pamela Ellis-Simon, "Hi Ho, Hi Ho", *Marketing & Media Decisions,* September 1986, pp. 52–4; Andrea Gabor and Steve L. Hawkins, "Of mice and money in the magic kingdom", *U.S. News & World Report,* 22 December 1986, pp. 44–6; Ronald Grover, "Disney's magic", *Business Week,* 9 March 1987, pp. 62–5; Scott Hume,"Sears gains exclusivity with Disney contract", *Advertising Age,* 23 November 1987, p. 63; Stephen Koepp, "Do you believe in magic?", *Time,* 25 April 1988, pp. 66–76; Marcy Magiera, "Disney tries retailing", *Advertising Age,* 1 June 1987, p. 80; Myron Magnet, "Putting magic back in the kingdom", *Fortune,* 5 January 1987, p. 65; Raymond Roel, "Disney's marketing touch", *Direct Marketing,* January 1987, pp. 50–3; Stephen J. Sansweet, "Disney Co. cartoons are going to China in commercial foray", *Wall Street Journal,* 23 October 1986, p. 19; Susan Spillman, "Animation draws on its storied past", *USA Today,* 15 November 1989, pp. 1B–2B; Wayne Walley, "Disney enlists Time Inc., Mars to honor Mickey", *Advertising Age,* 6 June 1988, pp. 3, 110; Wayne Walley, "P & G, Disney link videos, products", *Advertising Age,* 18 January 1988, p. 1; and Wayne Walley, "Roger Rabbit makes splash", *Advertising Age,* 27 June 1988, pp. 3, 110; "Disney hunts marketer for Euro timeshare club", *Marketing Week,* 19 February 1993, p. 5.

Questions for Discussion

1. Disney's product mix consists of many products. Does Disney have product lines? If so, what are they?
2. Disney labels many of its new films for adults as Touchstone Productions. With a famous name like Disney, why does the firm not use the Disney name?
3. Do the products in the Disney product mix have product life-cycles? Explain.

8 BRANDING AND PACKAGING

Objectives

To understand the types and benefits of brands and how to select, protect and license them

To become aware of the major packaging functions and design considerations and of the way in which packaging is used in marketing strategies

To examine the functions of labelling and the legal issues associated with labelling

*C*oca-Cola started 1993 in dynamic style by launching a 500 ml plastic version of its classic contoured Coke bottle. The new packaging helps to extend strong Coke branding even further, and Coca-Cola is highly optimistic about the new bottle's potential. Early research suggests that 30 per cent of customers will be motivated to purchase the bottle on the basis of shape alone. To help ensure the project's success, Coca-Cola's biggest marketing budget ever includes a plan to spend more than three times as much as the company's closest competitor. This aggressive marketing stance reflects managerial opinion that advertising spend is a critical factor in determining sales growth.

The launch of the new plastic bottle is also supported by a joint promotion with Sega, a video game company which is launching a new product to upgrade its Megadrive video game, the Mega CD. The promotion offers consumers instant wins and a range of exciting prizes, including 300 Mega CDs and Megadrives, 500 portable Game Gear systems and 1,000 Sonic the Hedgehog baseball jackets. Sega's links with Coca-Cola are consistent with the former's interest in being associated with world beating brands. According to Sega Europe's marketing director, Sega is positioning its products on the basis of strong and credible branding. The company believes that strong branding will make it easier in the long term to introduce and gain acceptance for new products.

Coca-Cola's joint promotion with Sega reflects the company's intention to focus more attention on teenagers and pre-teens—both groups of key importance to the soft drinks market. With a series of 26 new advertisements, to which consumers should find it easy to relate, the message has moved on from "Can't Beat the Feeling" to "Always Coca-Cola". Whatever the changes, the commitment to the Coca-Cola brand seems set for another decade. ■

SOURCES: Lindsay McMurdo, "Game, set and thrash", *Marketing Week,* 19 February 1993, pp. 28–31; Mat Toor, "Coke revives icon bottle and guns for youth", *Marketing,* 4 March 1993, p. 6; Claire Murphy, "Campaign that's always changing", *Marketing Week,* 19 February 1993, pp. 15–16; Coca-Cola in £1m link with Sega", *Marketing Week,* 5 March 1993, p. 8.

Brands and packages are part of a product's tangible features, the verbal and physical cues that help customers identify the products they want and influence their choices when they are unsure. Coca-Cola is perhaps the ultimate example of a company for whom branding and packaging play an important role in marketing strategy. A good brand is distinct and memorable; without one, firms could not differentiate their products and shoppers' choices would essentially be arbitrary. A good package design is cost effective, safe, environmentally responsible and valuable as a promotional tool.

The first part of this chapter defines branding, its benefits to customers and sellers and the various types of brands. The next section discusses how companies choose brands, how they protect them, the various branding policies that companies employ and brand licensing. The chapter then examines the critical role of packaging as part of the product and how it is marketed. The following section explores the functions of packaging, issues to consider in packaging design, how the package can be a major element in marketing strategy and packaging criticisms. The chapter concludes with a discussion of labelling and other product related features, including the product's physical characteristics and supportive product related services.

BRANDING

In addition to making decisions about actual products, marketers must make many decisions associated with branding, such as brands, brand names, brand marks, trade marks and trade names. A **brand** is a name, term, design, symbol or any other feature that identifies one seller's good or service as distinct from those of other sellers. A brand may identify one item, a family of items or all items of that seller.[1] A **brand name** is that part of a brand that can be spoken—including letters, words and numbers—such as Coca-Cola. A brand name is often a product's only distinguishing characteristic. Without the brand name, a firm could not identify its products. To consumers, brand names are as fundamental as the product itself. Brand names simplify shopping, guarantee a specific level of quality and allow self-expression.[2] Table 8.1 lists the 20 most powerful brands in the world based on surveys of over 10,000 respon-

TABLE 8.1 *Top world brands*

WORLD	WORLD
1. Coca-Cola	11. Rolls Royce
2. Sony	12. Honda
3. Mercedes-Benz	13. Panasonic
4. Kodak	14. Levi's
5. Disney	15. Kleenex
6. Nestlé	16. Ford
7. Toyota	17. Volkswagen
8. McDonald's	18. Kellogg's
9. IBM	19. Porsche
10. Pepsi Cola	20. Polaroid

SOURCE: Landor Associates' ImagePower Survey, 1990 (New York). Used by permission.

dents in the US, Japan and Europe. These ratings reflect both brand recognition (awareness) and esteem scores.

The element of a brand that is not made up of words but is often a symbol or design is called a **brand mark.** One example is the symbol of a baby on Procter & Gamble's Fairy Liquid detergent. Occasionally brand marks are modified for local markets. For example, Microsoft tops its brand name with a butterfly in France, a fish in Portugal and a sun in Spain. A **trade mark** is a legal designation indicating that the owner has exclusive use of a brand or a part of a brand and that others are prohibited by law from using it. To protect a brand name or brand mark a company must register it as a trade mark with the appropriate patenting office. Finally, a **trade name** is the full and legal name of an organisation, such as Ford Motor Company or Safeway Stores, rather than the name of a specific product.

Benefits of Branding

Branding provides benefits for both buyers and sellers.[3] Brands help buyers identify specific products that they do and do not like, a process which in turn facilitates the purchase of items that satisfy their needs and reduces the time required to purchase the product. Without brands, product selection would be quite random, because buyers could have no assurance that they were purchasing what they preferred. A brand also helps buyers evaluate the quality of a product, especially when they are unable to judge its characteristics. In other words, a purchaser for whom a brand symbolises a certain quality level will transfer that perception of quality to the unknown item. A brand thus helps to reduce a buyer's perceived risk of purchase. In addition, it may offer the psychological reward that comes from owning a brand that symbolises status. Certain brands of watches (Rolex) and of cars (Rolls Royce) fall into this category.

Sellers benefit from branding because each company's brands identify its products, which makes repeat purchasing easier for consumers. Branding helps a firm introduce a new product that carries the name of one or more of its existing products, because buyers are already familiar with the firm's existing brands. For example, Heinz regularly introduces new tinned products. Because consumers are used to buying the brand and have a high regard for its quality, they are likely to try the new offerings. Branding also facilitates promotional efforts because the promotion of each branded product indirectly promotes all other products that are similarly branded.

Branding also helps sellers by fostering brand loyalty. Brand loyalty is a strongly motivated and long standing decision to purchase a product or service. To the extent that buyers become loyal to a specific brand, the company's market share for that product achieves a certain level of stability, allowing the firm to use its resources more efficiently.[4] When a firm succeeds in fostering some degree of customer loyalty to a brand, it can charge a premium price for the product. For example, brand loyal buyers of Anadin aspirin are willing to pay two or three times more for Anadin than for a store brand of aspirin with the same amount of pain relieving agent. However, brand loyalty is declining, partly because of marketers' increased reliance on sales, coupons and other short term promotions, and partly because of the sometimes overwhelming array of similar new products from which consumers can choose. A Wall Street Journal survey found that 12 per cent of consumers are not loyal to any brand, whereas 47 per cent are brand loyal for one to five product types. Only 2 per cent of the respondents were brand loyal for more than 16 product types (see Figure 8.1). To stimulate loyalty to their brands, some marketers are stressing image advertising, mailing personalised catalogues and magazines to regular users and creating membership clubs for brand users.[5] Sometimes consumers make repeat purchases of products for reasons other than brand loyalty. Spurious loyalty is not stable and may result from non-availability of alternative brands or the way in which products are displayed in retail outlets.

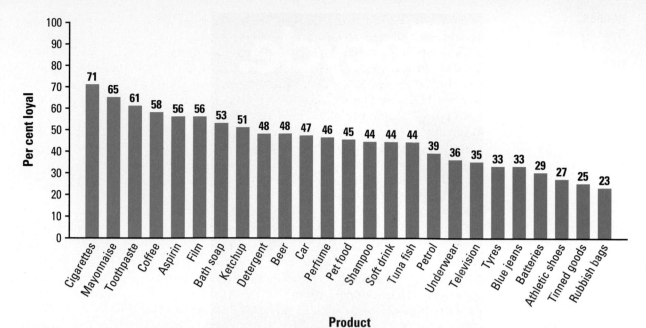

FIGURE 8.1 *Percentage of users of selected products who are loyal to one brand*

SOURCE: *Wall Street Journal,* October 19, 1989, p. B1. Reprinted by permission of Dow Jones & Company, Inc.
© 1989 Dow Jones & Company, Inc. All Rights Reserved Worldwide.

Types of Brands

There are three categories of brands: manufacturer brands, own label brands (also called private brands, store brands or dealer brands) and generic brands. **Manufacturer brands** are initiated by producers and ensure that producers are identified with their products at the point of purchase—for example, Green Giant, Apple Computer and Wall's ice cream. A manufacturer brand usually requires a producer to become involved in distribution, promotion and, to some extent, pricing decisions. Brand loyalty is encouraged by promotion, quality control and guarantees; it is a valuable asset to a manufacturer. The producer tries to stimulate demand for the product, which tends to encourage middlemen to make the product available.

Own label brands are initiated and owned by resellers—wholesalers or retailers. The major characteristic of own label brands is that the manufacturers are not identified on the products. Retailers and wholesalers use these brands to develop more efficient promotion, to generate higher gross margins and to improve store images. Own label brands give retailers or wholesalers freedom to purchase products of a specified quality at the lowest cost without disclosing the identity of the manufacturer. Wholesale brands include Roca, Family Choice, Happy Shopper and Lifestyle. Familiar retailer brands names include St. Michael (Marks & Spencer), Yessica (C & A) and George (Asda). Many successful own label brands are distributed nationally. Matsui domestic appliances (Currys) are as well known as most name brands. Sometimes retailers with successful distributor brands start manufacturing their own products to gain more control over product costs, quality and design in the hope of increasing profits. While one might think that store brands appeal most strongly to lower income shoppers or to up market shoppers who compare labels, studies indicate that buyers of own label brands have characteristics that match those of the overall population.[6] Figure 8.2 presents an example of a well known manufacturer brand, Levi's.

FIGURE 8.2
Types of brands
Levi's is a manufacturer
brand.

SOURCE: Levi Strauss and Company.

Some marketers of products that have traditionally been branded have embarked on a policy of not branding, often called generic branding. A **generic brand** indicates only the product category (such as aluminium foil) and does not include the company name or other identifying terms. Usually generic brands are sold at lower prices than are comparable branded items. Although at one time generic brands may have represented as much as 10 per cent of all retail grocery sales, today they account for less than 1 per cent.[7]

Competition between manufacturer brands and own label brands (sometimes called "the battle of the brands") is intensifying in several major product categories, particularly tinned foods, breakfast cereal, sugar and soft drinks. Own label brands now account for around 13 per cent of all supermarket sales.[8] As shown in Figure 8.3, both men and women are quite favourable towards own label brands of food products, with women (still the major grocery purchasers) even more favourable than men. For manufacturers, developing multiple manufacturer brands and distribution systems has been an effective means of combating the increased competition from own label brands. By developing a new brand name, a producer can adjust various elements of a marketing mix to appeal to a different target market. For example, Scott Paper has developed lower priced brands of paper towels; it has tailored its new products to a target market that tends to purchase own label brands.

Manufacturers find it hard to ignore the marketing opportunities that come from producing own label brands for resellers. If a manufacturer refuses to produce an own label brand for a reseller, a competing manufacturer will. Moreover, the production of own label brands allows the manufacturer to use excess capacity during periods when its own brands are at non-peak production. The ultimate decision whether to produce an own label or a manufacturer brand depends on a company's resources, production capabilities and goals.

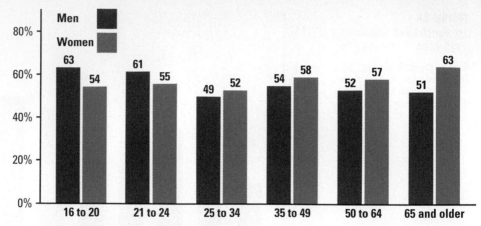

SOURCE: *Yankelovich Monitor®,* © 1991. Used with permission.

Protecting a Brand

Marketers should consider a number of factors when they choose a brand name. The name should be easy for customers—including foreign buyers, if the firm intends to market its products in other countries—to say, spell and recall. Short, one syllable names such as Mars or Tide satisfy this requirement. The brand name should indicate the product's major benefits and, if possible, should suggest in a positive way the product's uses and special characteristics; negative or offensive references should be avoided. For example, a deodorant should be branded with a name that signals freshness, dryness or long lasting protection, as do Sure, Right Guard and Arrid Extra Dry. The brand should be distinctive, to set it apart from competing brands. If a marketer intends to use a brand for a product line, it must be compatible with all products in the line. Finally, a brand should be designed so that it can be used and recognised in all of the various types of media. Finding the right brand name has become a challenging task, because many obvious product names have already been used. Figure 8.4 shows trade mark registrations in the UK between 1980 and 1989.

How are brand names derived? Brand names can be created from single or multiple words—for example, Bic or Findus Lean Cuisine. Initials, numbers or sometimes combinations are used to create brands such as IBM PC or PS 2. At times, words, numbers and initials are combined to yield brand names such as Mazda MX5 or Mitsubishi 3000GT. To avoid terms that have negative connotations, marketers sometimes use fabricated words that have absolutely no meaning at the point when they are created—for example, Kodak and Esso. Occasionally, a brand is simply brought out of storage and used as is or modified. Firms often maintain banks of registered brands, some of which may have been used in the past. Cadillac, for example, has a bank of approximately 360 registered trade marks. The LaSalle brand, used in the 1920s and 1930s, may be called up for a new Cadillac model soon to be introduced.[9] Possible brand names are sometimes tested in focus groups or in other settings to assess customers' reactions.

Who actually creates brand names? Brand names can be created internally by the organisation. Sometimes a name is suggested by individuals who are close to the development of the product. Some organisations have committees that participate in brand name creation and approval. Large companies that introduce numerous new products annually are likely to have a department that develops brand names. At times, outside consultants are used in the process of developing brand names. An organisation may also hire a company that specialises in brand name development.

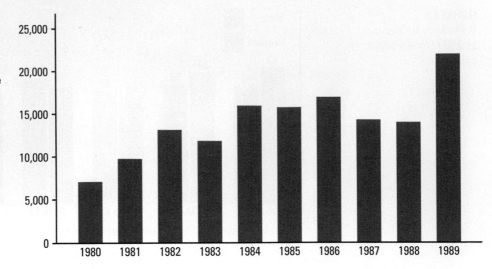

FIGURE 8.4
UK trade marks registered 1980–1989

SOURCE: Crown Copyright. Reprinted by permission of the Controller of Her Majesty's Stationery Office.

Even though most of the important branding considerations apply to both goods and services, services branding has some additional dimensions. The brand of the service is usually the same as the company name. For example, American Express, Vidal Sassoon, Pronto Print and Sheraton are names of companies and the services that they provide. Whereas companies that produce tangible goods (such as Procter & Gamble) can use separate brand names for separate products (such as Ariel, Head & Shoulders, Flash and Camay), service providers (such as British Airways) are perceived by customers as having one brand name, even though they offer multiple products (first class, business class and economy). Because the service brand name and company name are so closely interrelated, a service brand name must be flexible enough to encompass a variety of current services, as well as new ones that the company might offer in the future. Geographical references like "western" and descriptive terms like "trucking" limit the scope of associations that can be made with the brand name. "Northwest Airlines" is not a good name if the company begins flying south and east.[10] Frequently, a service marketer will employ a symbol along with its brand name to make the brand distinctive and to communicate a certain image. In Figure 8.5, Britannia Building Society includes a symbol within its logo to enhance the recognition of its brand.

Choosing a Brand Name

Marketers need to design brands that can be protected easily through registration. Amongst the most difficult to protect are generic words, such as aluminium foil, surnames and descriptive geographic or functional names.[11] Because of their designs, some brands can be legally infringed upon more easily than others. Although registration provides trade mark protection, a firm should develop a system for ensuring that its trade marks will be renewed as needed. To protect its exclusive rights to a brand, the company must make certain that the selected brand is not likely to be considered an infringement on any existing brand already registered with the relevant patent office. This task may be complex because infringement is determined by the courts, which base their decisions on whether a brand causes consumers to be confused, mistaken or deceived about the source of the product. McDonald's is one company that aggressively protects its trade marks against infringement; it has brought charges against a number of companies with "Mc" names because it fears that the use of the "Mc" will give consumers the impression that these companies are associated with or owned by McDonald's.

DON'T MAKE A MOVE UNTIL YOU'VE CHECKED WITH US.

FIGURE 8.5 *Using a symbol with a brand name*
Britannia Building Society uses a symbol to make its brand distinctive. Marketers hope this symbol will conjure images of safety and protection for consumers.

SOURCE: Courtesy of Britannia Building Society.

If possible, marketers must guard against allowing a brand name to become a generic term used to refer to a general product category. Generic terms cannot be protected as exclusive brand names. For example, names such as aspirin, escalator and shredded wheat—all brand names at one time—were eventually declared generic terms that refer to product classes; thus they no longer could be protected. To keep a brand name from becoming a generic term, the firm should spell the name with a capital letter and use it as an adjective to modify the name of the general product class, as in Kellogg's Coco Pops.[12] Including the word *brand* just after the brand name is also helpful. An organisation can deal with this problem directly by advertising that its brand is a trade mark and should not be used generically. The firm can also indicate that the brand is a registered trade mark by using the symbol ®.

Firms that try to protect a brand in a foreign country frequently encounter problems. In many countries, brand registration is not possible; the first firm to use a brand in such a country has the rights to it. In some instances, a company has actually had to buy its own brand rights from a firm in a foreign country because the foreign firm was the first user in that country.

Marketers trying to protect their brands must also contend with brand counterfeiting. In many countries, for instance, it is possible to buy fake General Motors parts, fake Rolex watches, fake Chanel perfume, fake Microsoft software, fake Walt Disney character dolls and a host of other products illegally marketed by manufacturers that do not own the brands. Many counterfeit products are manufactured overseas—in South Korea, Italy or Taiwan, for example—but some are counterfeited in the countries in which they are sold. The International Anti-Counterfeiting Coalition estimates that roughly $60 billion in annual world trade involves counterfeit merchandise. The sale of this merchandise obviously reduces the brand owners' revenues from marketing their own legitimate products.

Brand counterfeiting is particularly harmful because the usually inferior counterfeit product undermines consumers' confidence in the brand and their loyalty to it. After unknowingly purchasing a counterfeit product, the buyer may blame the legitimate manufacturer if the product is of low quality or—even worse—if its use results in damage or injury. Since counterfeiting has become such a serious problem, many firms are taking legal action against counterfeiters. Others have adopted such measures as modifying the product or the packaging to make counterfeit items easier to detect, conducting public awareness campaigns and monitoring distributors to ensure that they stock only legitimate brands.[13]

Branding Policies

Before it establishes branding policies, a firm must first decide whether to brand its products at all. If a company's product is homogeneous and similar to competitors' products, it may be difficult to brand. Raw materials—such as coal, salt, sand and milk—are hard to brand because of the homogeneity of such products and their physical characteristics. Marketers must also consider the degree to which consumers differentiate among brands of a product. For example, while brand may be an important factor in the purchase of coffee, snacks and frozen foods, it is not usually so important a consideration in buying light bulbs, cheese and cling film.

If a firm chooses to brand its products, it may opt for one or more of the following branding policies: individual, overall family, line family and brand extension branding. **Individual branding** is a policy of naming each product differently. Procter & Gamble relies on an individual branding policy for its line of fabric washing products, which includes Tide, Bold, Daz and Dreft. A major advantage of individual branding is that if an organisation introduces a poor product, the negative images associated with it will not contaminate the company's other products. An individual branding policy may also facilitate market segmentation when a firm wishes to enter many segments of the same market. Separate, unrelated names can be used, and each brand can be aimed at a specific segment.

In **overall family branding,** all of a firm's products are branded with the same name or at least part of the name, such as Kraft, Heinz, Microsoft or Ford. In some cases, a company's name is combined with other words to brand items. Heinz uses its name on its products along with a generic description of the item, such as Heinz Salad Cream, Heinz Baked Beans, Heinz Spaghetti and Heinz Tomato Soup. The quality image of its products increases consumer confidence in what they are buying. This brand consistency is stressed in Heinz advertisements (see Figure 8.6). Unlike individual branding, overall family branding means that the promotion of one item with the family brand promotes the firm's other products.

Sometimes an organisation uses family branding only for products within a single line. This policy is called **line family branding.** Colgate-Palmolive, for example, produces a line of cleaning products that include a cleanser, a powdered detergent and a liquid cleaner all with the name Ajax. Colgate also produces several brands of toothpaste, none of which carries the Ajax brand.

Brand extension branding occurs when a firm uses one of its existing brand names as part of a brand for an improved or new product that is usually in the same product category as the existing brand. The makers of Timotei Shampoo extended the name to hair conditioner and skin care products. There is one major difference between line family branding and brand extension branding. With line family branding, all products in the line carry the same name, but with brand extension branding this is not the case. The producer of Arrid deodorant, for example, also makes other brands of deodorants.

An organisation is not limited to a single branding policy. Instead, branding policy is influenced by the number of products and product lines the company produces, the

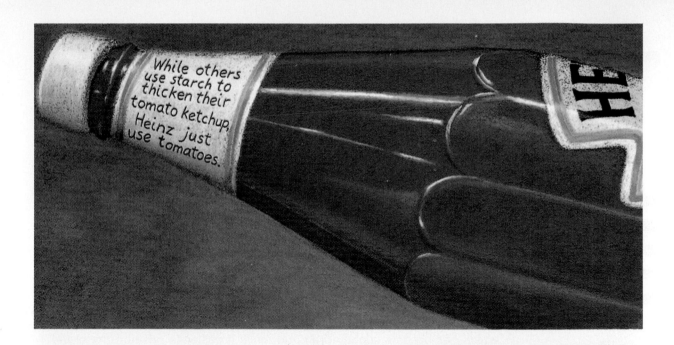

FIGURE 8.6 *Overall family branding*
Heinz uses its name on its products, along with a generic description of the item.

SOURCE: Courtesy of Heinz.

characteristics of its target markets, the number and types of competing products available and the size of its resources. Anheuser-Busch, for example, uses both individual and brand extension branding. Most of the brands are individual brands; however, the Michelob Light brand is an extension of the Michelob brand. Sometimes companies must update brands so that they remain fresh and interesting (see Marketing Insight 8.1).

NAME CHANGE FOR KENTUCKY FRIED CHICKEN

Customers of Kentucky Fried Chicken may soon see a change at their favourite fast food outlet. In response to changing market conditions, the company is looking at ways to overhaul its brand identity. As part of this move, it is testing a take away only concept, using red and blue livery in place of the famous red. While Colonel Sanders retains his role as brand mascot and prominence on the shop fascia, the name Kentucky Fried Chicken is being shortened to "KFC Express". Opinions about the ultimate extent of the branding switch are divided. Currently, around 50 of the 290 outlets are being switched to the KFC branding, but some restaurant managers believe that all outlets will eventually change over.

The reasons for the change are almost certainly linked to the increasing challenges which the fast food market presents. Updating the Kentucky Fried Chicken brand identity should help provide a welcome boost to an image which has become slightly tired and make it easier to position the brand away from the host of copycats such as Favourite Chicken and Southern Fried Chicken. Management at Kentucky Fried Chicken is also testing dishes with grilled, baked and rotisserie cooked chicken in order to respond to the increasingly health conscious consumer. Removing the word *fried* from the company's branding further emphasises this shift.

It is not just Kentucky Fried Chicken's brand identity that is changing. Location policy is also being updated: management is improving the brand's visibility by reducing the number of secondary sites that outlets occupy and moving into prime high street positions. Such changes are vital to enable the company to respond to an increasingly competitive market-place that includes McDonald's, Burger King, Pizza Hut and Pizzaland, as well as a host of independents—all offering the fast food consumer more choice than ever before. For Kentucky Fried Chicken the threat from giants McDonald's and Burger King is particularly acute as both these companies increase their range of chicken dishes.

The rewards for success are considerable in a market where the key players are set for growth. During the 1990s alone, it is anticipated that McDonald's will open a further 400 to 500 outlets outside the US, while PepsiCo (whose portfolio includes Pizza Hut and Taco Bell as well as Kentucky Fried Chicken) plans to increase its international outlets by 80 per cent.

SOURCES: Paul Meller, "KFC cooks up new look for food fight", *Marketing,* 11 March 1993; "Kentucky Fried Chicken pushes take away option", *Marketing Week,* 12 March 1993.

Brand Licensing

A recent trend in branding strategies involves the licensing of trade marks. By means of a licensing agreement, a company may permit approved manufacturers to use its trade mark on other products for a licensing fee. Royalties may be as low as 2 per cent of wholesale revenues or higher than 10 per cent. The licensee is responsible for all manufacturing, selling and advertising functions and bears the costs if the licensed product fails. Not long ago, only a few firms licensed their corporate trade marks but today the licensing business is worth billions of pounds and is growing. Harley-Davidson, for example, has authorised the use of its name on non-motorcycle products such as cologne, wine coolers, gold rings and shirts. Disney also licenses its brand for use on a range of products.

The advantages of licensing range from extra revenues and low cost to free publicity, new images and trade mark protection. For example, Coca-Cola has licensed its trade mark for use on glassware, radios, trucks and clothing in the hope of protecting its trade mark. Similarly, Jaguar has licensed a range of leisure wear. However, brand licensing is not without drawbacks. The major ones are a lack of manufacturing control, which could hurt the company's name, and the undesirability of bombarding consumers with too many unrelated products bearing the same name. Licensing arrangements can also fail because of poor timing, inappropriate distribution channels or mismatching of product and name.

PACKAGING

Packaging involves the development of a container and label, complete with graphic design for a product. A package can be a vital part of a product, making it more versatile, safer or easier to use. Like a brand name, a package can influence customers' attitudes towards a product and thus affect their purchase decisions. For example, several producers of sauces, salad dressings and ketchups have packaged their products in squeezable containers to make use and storage more convenient. Package characteristics help shape buyers' impressions of a product at the time of purchase or during use. This section examines the main functions of packaging and considers several major packaging decisions. The role of the package in marketing strategy is also analysed.

Packaging Functions

Effective packaging means more than simply putting products into containers and covering them with wrappers. First of all, packaging materials serve the basic purpose of protecting the product and maintaining its functional form. Fluids such as milk, orange juice and hair spray need packages that preserve and protect them; the packaging should prevent damage that could affect the product's usefulness and increase costs. Since product tampering has become a problem for marketers of many types of goods, several packaging techniques have been developed to counter this danger. Some packages are also designed to foil shoplifters.

Another function of packaging is to offer convenience for consumers. For example, small, sealed packages —individual sized boxes or plastic bags that contain liquids and do not require refrigeration—strongly appeal to children and young adults with active lifestyles. The size or shape of a package may relate to the product's storage, convenience of use or replacement rate. Small, single serving tins of fruit, such as Del Monte's Fruitinni, may prevent waste and make storage easier. Low, regular shaped packets may be easier to stack and use cupboard space more efficiently. A third function of packaging is to promote a product by communicating its features, uses, benefits and image. At times, a reusable package is developed to make the product more desirable. For example, ice cream containers can be used again as food storage containers.

Major Packaging Considerations

When developing packages, marketers must take many factors into account. Some of these factors relate to consumers needs; others relate to the requirements of resellers. Obviously, one major consideration is cost. Although a variety of packaging materials, processes and designs is available, some are rather expensive. In recent years, buyers have shown a willingness to pay more for improved packaging, but there are limits.

Marketers should try to determine, through research, just how much customers are willing to pay for packages.

As already mentioned, developing tamper resistant packaging is very important. Although no package is tamper proof, marketers can develop packages which are difficult to tamper with and which also make any tampering evident to resellers and consumers. Because new, safer packaging technologies are being explored, marketers should be aware of changes in packaging technology and legislation and be prepared to make modifications that will ensure consumer safety. One packaging innovation includes an inner pouch that displays the word *open* when air has entered the pouch after opening. Marketers also have an obligation to inform the public of the possibilities and risks of product tampering by educating consumers to recognise possible tampering and by placing warnings on packaging.[14] For example, the tops of many sauce and condiment bottles now have plastic seals around them, so that consumers can be confident that they have not been opened. Baby food manufacturers, such as Cow & Gate and Heinz have taken this protection method one step further by using special metal jar tops with pop-up discs which shows when a jar has been opened. This move followed cases of tampering in which foreign bodies were introduced into baby foods. Now the special tops expressly warn consumers to watch out for tampering. Although effective tamper resistant packaging may be expensive to develop, when balanced against the costs of lost sales, loss of consumer confidence and company reputation, and potentially expensive product liability lawsuits, the costs of ensuring consumer safety are minimal.[15]

Marketers should consider how much consistency is desirable in an organisation's package designs. The best policy may be not to attempt consistency, especially if a firm's products are unrelated or aimed at vastly different target markets. To promote an overall company image, a firm may decide that all packages are to be similar or include one major element of the design. This approach is called **family packaging.** Sometimes it is used only for lines of products, as with Campbell soups, Weight Watchers foods and Planters nuts.

A package's promotional role is an important consideration. Through verbal and non-verbal symbols, the package can inform potential buyers about the product's content, features, uses, advantages and hazards. A firm can create desirable images and associations by its choice of colour, design, shape and texture. Many cosmetics manufacturers, for example, design their packages to create impressions of richness, luxury and exclusiveness. A package performs a promotional function when it is designed to be safer or more convenient to use, if such characteristics help stimulate demand.

To develop a package that has a definite promotional value, a designer must consider size, shape, texture, colour and graphics. Beyond the obvious limitation that the package must be large enough to hold the product, a package can be designed to appear taller or shorter. For instance, thin vertical lines make a package look taller; wide horizontal stripes make it look shorter. A marketer may want a package to appear taller because many people perceive something that is taller as being larger.

Colours on packages are often chosen to attract attention. People associate specific colours with certain feelings and experiences. Red, for example, is linked with fire, blood, danger and anger; yellow suggests sunlight, caution, warmth and vitality; blue can imply coldness, sky, water and sadness.[16] When selecting packaging colours, marketers must decide whether a particular colour will evoke positive or negative feelings when it is linked to a specific product. Rarely, for example, do processors package meat or bread in green materials, because customers may associate green with mould. However, recent concern about the state of the environment has, in general, led to an increase in the use of green coloured packaging. Marketers must also decide whether a specific target market will respond favourably or unfavourably to a particular colour. Cosmetics for women are more likely to be sold in pastel packaging than are personal care products for men. Packages designed to appeal to children often use primary colours and bold designs.

Packaging must also meet the needs of resellers. Wholesalers and retailers consider whether a package facilitates transportation, storage and handling. Packages must allow these resellers to make maximum use of storage space, both in transit and in the shops. Products should be packed so that sales staff can transfer them to the shelves with ease. Shape and weight of packaging are also important. Resellers may refuse to carry certain products if their packages are cumbersome. Figure 8.7 shows how these factors have been taken into consideration by Cuprinol's Castlepak™ woodcare varnish container.

A final consideration is whether to develop packages that are environmentally responsible. A Cable News Network report on the growing refuse disposal problem in the US stated that nearly 50 per cent of all rubbish consists of discarded plastic packaging, such as polystyrene containers, plastic soft drink bottles, carrier bags and other packaging.[17] Plastic packaging material does not biodegrade, and paper requires the destruction of valuable forest lands. Consequently, a number of companies are recycling more materials and exploring packaging alternatives, helped by the packaging experts such as Tetra Pak. H. J. Heinz, for example, is looking for alternatives to its plastic ketchup squeeze bottles. Marketing Insight 8.2 examines some of the latest packaging innovations.

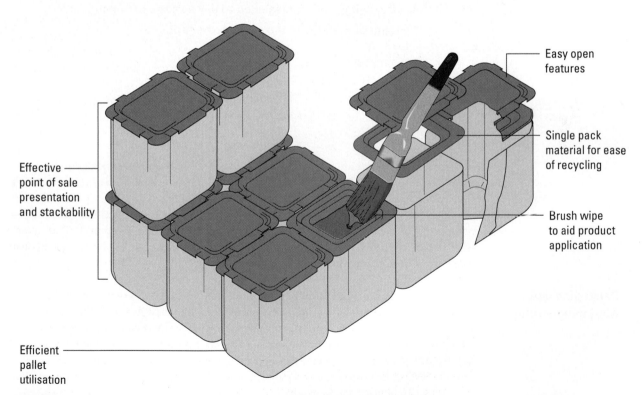

FIGURE 8.7 *Cuprinol's Castlepak™ woodcare varnish container highlights how environmental consumer usage and operation needs can be incorporated into a single packaging solution.*

SOURCE: Courtesy of *Marketing Magazine,* London.

MARKETING INSIGHT 8.2

NEW DEVELOPMENTS IN 3D PACKAGING DESIGN

Three dimensional packaging does much more than protect products and make them easy to distribute, handle and use.

For marketers, 3D packaging can help differentiate a brand, add value or simply aid consumer recognition. The distinctive shape of the Coca-Cola bottle, recognised worldwide, is synonymous with the brand. The importance of creative packaging design is well established. Maximum packaging design benefits requires an integrated approach which considers financial, manufacturing, distribution and marketing requirements. In some companies this total business approach is achieved by forming staff teams with representatives from all business areas. The teams will consider all aspects of packaging design—materials, size and shape, opening and closure features, material conversion efficiency, retail storage and display, transportability, disposability, filling speed and costs.

Growing consumer concern about the environment and government targets for recycling are putting new pressures on packaging design and development, in addition to all the other marketing and operational requirements of the process. As they look for ways to increase the environmental friendliness of their packaging, companies need to ask a series of questions:

- Can the amount of material in the package be reduced?
- Can the size of the package be reduced?
- Is recyclable material a possibility?
- Are the necessary recycling processes available?
- Are the raw materials used easy to replenish?

Companies that decide to develop environmentally responsible packaging have not always received a positive response. For example, customers' responses to Wendy's new paper plates and coffee cups have been mixed; some customers prefer the old non-biodegradable foam packages. Other companies searching for alternatives to environmentally harmful packaging have experienced similar problems.[18] Thus marketers must carefully balance society's desires to preserve the environment against consumers' desires for convenience.

Packaging and Marketing Strategy

Packaging can be a major component of a marketing strategy. A new cap or closure, a better box or wrapping, or a more convenient container may give a product a competitive advantage. The right type of package for a new product can help it gain market recognition very quickly. In the case of existing brands, marketers should periodically re-evaluate packages. Especially for consumer convenience products, marketers should view packaging as a major strategic tool. This section examines ways in which packaging can be used strategically.

Altering the Package. At times, a marketer changes a package because the existing design is no longer in style, especially when compared with competitive products. In

Environmental concerns are causing companies to reconsider the appropriateness of traditional packaging materials. For example, glass is coming back to supermarket shelves, while new developments in the use of plastics and paper/board are leading to improvements in recyclability. Even when companies are able to move towards more ecologically sympathetic packaging, there may be hidden problems. For example, the process of recycling itself may waste energy and create pollution. To ensure that the disadvantages of changing packaging design do not outweigh the benefits, a company should undertake a "cradle to grave" analysis of the proposed packaging, looking at all aspects of its manufacture, distribution, use and disposal.

In the rush to meet consumer demands and regulatory requirements, companies are in danger of introducing ineffective packaging solutions. For example, manufacturers have recently introduced flexible refill pouches as a replacement for plastic bottles. To the consumer, who sees plastic bottles as bulky and difficult to dispose of, this seems to be a positive step. In practice, the lightweight alternative may look better; but it is awkward to distribute and difficult to recycle.

SOURCES: CGM, *Marketing Guide 14: 3D Packaging Design,* Haymarket Publishing Services Ltd, 1992; John S. Blyth, "Packaging for competitive advantage", *Management Review,* May 1990, p. 64; Dagmar Mussey and Juliana Kanteng, "Packaging strict green rules", *Advertising Age,* 2 December 1991, p. S-10.

Figure 8.8, Ovaltine's packaging was up-dated to boost the brand's image. Smith and Nephew has recently redesigned its simple range of toiletries to show that the products have evolved with the times. A package also may be redesigned because new product features need to be highlighted on the package, or because new packaging materials have become available. An organisation may decide to change a product's packaging to make the product more convenient or safer to use, or to re-position the product. A major redesign of a simple package costs about £15,000, and the redesign for a line of products may cost up to £200,000.[19] Choosing the right packaging material is an important consideration when redesigning. Different materials vary in popularity at different times. For example, glass is becoming more popular as views on the environment and the need for recyclability come to the fore.[20]

Secondary Use Packaging. A secondary use package is one that can be reused for purposes other than its initial use. For example, a margarine container can be re-used to store leftovers, a jam jar can be used as a drinking glass, and shortbread tins can be re-used for storing cakes and biscuits. Secondary use packages can be viewed by customers as adding value to products. If customers value this type of packaging, then its use should stimulate unit sales.

FIGURE 8.8
Innovative packaging
The importance of packaging design cannot be underestimated. Consultant Jones Knowles Ritchie successfully up-dated the image of the well established malted drink Ovaltine without alienating traditional users.

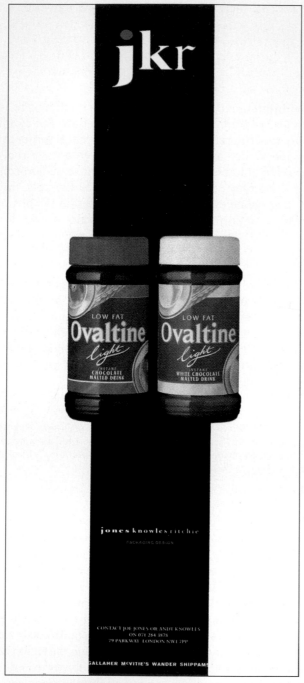

SOURCE: Courtesy of Wander Limited.

Category Consistent Packaging.   Category consistent packaging means that the product is packaged in line with the packaging practices associated with a particular product category. Some product categories—for example, mayonnaise, mustard, ketchup and jam—have traditional package shapes. Other product categories are characterised by recognisable colour combinations—red and white for soup; red and yellow for tea; red, white and blue for Ritz-like crackers. When an organisation introduces a brand in one of these product categories, marketers will often use traditional package shapes and colour combinations to ensure that customers will recognise the new product as being in that specific product category.

Innovative Packaging.   Sometimes, a marketer will employ a unique cap, design, applicator or other feature to make the product competitively distinctive. Such packaging can be effective when the innovation makes the product safer or easier to use, or when the unique package provides better protection for the product. In some instances, marketers use innovative or unique packages that are inconsistent with traditional packaging practices to make the brand stand out relative to its competitors. Procter & Gamble, for example, used an innovative, crush-proof cylinder to package its Pringles potato crisps. Innovative packaging generally requires considerable resources, not only for the package design itself but also to make customers aware of the unique package and its benefit. Sometimes, innovative packaging can change the way in which consumers use a product. The introduction of cardboard boxed, single serving soft drinks made it easier for consumers to have a drink while travelling by car, train and plane. Even cyclists can drink with ease while on the move!

Multiple Packaging.   Rather than packaging a single unit of the product, marketers sometimes use twin packs, tri-packs, six-packs or other forms of multiple packaging. For certain types of products, multiple packaging is used to increase demand because it increases the amount of the product available at the point of consumption (in consumers' houses, for example). However, multiple packaging does not work for all types of products. Consumers would not use additional table salt simply because an extra box is in the pantry. Multiple packaging can make products easier to handle and store, as in the case of six-packs for soft drinks; it can also facilitate special price offers, such as two-for-one sales. In addition, multiple packaging may increase consumer acceptance of the product by encouraging the buyer to try the product several times.

Handling Improved Packaging.   Packaging of a product may be changed to make it easier to handle in the distribution channel—for example, changing the outer carton, special bundling, shrink wrapping or palletising. In some cases the shape of the package may need to be changed. For example, an ice cream producer may change from a cylindrical package to a rectangular one to facilitate handling. In addition, at the retail level the ice cream producer may be able to get more shelf facings with a rectangular package as opposed to a round one. Outer containers for products are sometimes changed so that they will proceed more easily through automated warehousing systems.

As package designs improve, it becomes harder for any one product to dominate because of packaging. However, marketers still attempt to gain a competitive edge through packaging. Case 8.2 looks at the benefits offered by a new type of packaging. Skilled artists and package designers who have experience in marketing research test packaging to see what sells well, not just what is aesthetically appealing. Since the typical large store stocks 15,000 items or more, products that stand out are more likely to be bought.

Criticisms of Packaging

The last several decades have seen a number of improvements in packaging. However, some packaging problems still need to be resolved.

Some packages suffer from functional problems in that they simply do not work well. The packaging for flour and sugar is, at best, not better than poor. Both grocers and consumers are very much aware that these packages leak and are easily torn. Can anyone open and close a bag of flour without spilling at least a little bit? Certain packages such as biscuit tins, milk cartons with fold-out spouts and potato crisp bags are frequently difficult to open. The traditional shapes of packages for products such as ketchup and salad dressing make the products inconvenient to use. Have you ever questioned when tapping on a ketchup bottle why the producer didn't put ketchup in a mayonnaise jar?

As discussed earlier, certain types of packaging are being questioned in regard to recyclability and biodegradability. For example, throw-away bottles take considerably more resources to produce than do re-usable glass bottles.

Although many steps have been taken to make packaging safer, critics still focus on the safety issues. Containers with sharp edges and easily broken glass bottles are sometimes viewed as a threat to safety. Certain types of plastic packaging and aerosol containers represent possible health hazards.

At times, packaging is viewed as being deceptive. Package shape, graphic design and certain colours may be used to make a product appear larger than it actually is. The inconsistent use of certain size designations—such as "giant," "economy," "family," "king," and "super"—can certainly lead to customer confusion. Although customers have traditionally liked attractive, effective, convenient packaging, the cost of such packaging is high. For some products, such as cosmetics, the cost of the package is higher than the cost of the product itself.

Labelling

Labelling is very closely interrelated with packaging and can be used in a variety of promotional, informational and legal ways. The label can be used to facilitate the identification of a product by presenting the brand and a unique graphic design. For example, Heinz's ketchup is easy to identify on a supermarket shelf because the brand name is easy to read and is coupled with a distinctive, crown-like graphic design. Labels have a descriptive function. For certain types of products, the label indicates the grade of the product, especially for tinned fruit. Labels can describe the source of the product, its contents and major features, how to use the product, how to care for the product, nutritional information, type and style of the product, and size and number of servings. The label can play a promotional function through the use of graphics that attract attention. The food and drug administrations and consumer protection agencies in different countries have varying requirements in terms of warnings, instructions, certifications and manufacturer's identifications. Increasingly, however, the EC is demanding similar standards in all member countries. Despite the fact that consumers have responded favourably to the inclusion of this type of information on labels, evidence as to whether they actually use it has been mixed. Several studies indicate that consumers do not use nutritional information, whereas other studies indicate that the information is useful. Labels can also promote a manufacturer's other products or encourage proper use of products and therefore greater satisfaction with them.

The label for many products includes a **universal product code (UPC),** sometimes known as a **barcode,** which is a series of thick and thin lines that identifies the product and provides inventory and pricing information that can be read by an electronic scanner. The UPC is read electronically at the retail checkout counter. This information is used by retailers and producers for price and inventory control purposes.

Colour and eye-catching graphics on labels overcome the jumble of words—known to designers as "mouse print"—that have been added to satisfy government regulations. Because so many similar products are available, an attention getting device or silent salesperson is needed to attract interest. As one of the most visible parts of a product, the label is an important element in a marketing mix.

SUMMARY

A brand is a name, term, design, symbol or any other feature that identifies one seller's good or service and distinguishes it from those of other sellers. A brand name is that part of a brand that can be spoken; the element that cannot be spoken is called a brand mark. A trade mark is a legal designation indicating that the owner has exclusive use of a brand or part of a brand and that others are prohibited by law from using it. A trade name is the legal name of an organisation. Branding helps buyers identify and evaluate products, helps sellers facilitate repeat purchasing and product introduction, and fosters brand loyalty. A manufacturer brand, initiated by the producer, makes it possible to associate the firm more easily with its products at the point of purchase. An own label brand is initiated and owned by a reseller. A generic brand indicates only the product category and does not include the company name or other identifying terms. Manufacturers combat the growing competition from own label brands by developing multiple brands. When selecting a brand, a marketer should choose one that is easy to say, spell and recall, and that alludes to the product's uses, benefits or special characteristics. Brand names are created inside an organisation by individuals, committees or branding departments, or by outside consultants. Brand names can be devised from words, initials, numbers, nonsense words or a combination of these. Services as well as products are branded, often with the company name and an accompanying symbol that makes the brand distinctive or conveys a desired image.

Producers protect ownership of their brands through patent and trade mark offices. Marketers at a company must make certain that their selected brand name does not infringe on an already registered brand by confusing or deceiving consumers about the source of the product. In many countries, brand registration is on a first-come, first-served basis, making protection more difficult. Brand counterfeiting, increasingly common, has potential for undermining consumer confidence in and loyalty to a brand. Companies brand their products in several ways. Individual branding designates a unique name for each of a company's products; overall family branding identifies all of a firm's products with the single name; line family branding assigns all products within a single line the same name; and brand extension branding applies an existing name to a new or improved product. Trade mark licensing enables producers to earn extra revenue, receive low cost or free publicity and protect their trade marks. Through a licensing agreement, and for a licensing fee, a firm may permit approved manufacturers to use its trade mark on other products.

Packaging involves development of a container and graphic design for a product. Effective packaging offers protection, economy, safety and convenience. It can influence the customer's purchase decision by promoting features, uses, benefits and image. When developing a package, marketers must consider cost relative to how much the target market is willing to pay. Other considerations include how to make the package tamper resistant, whether to use multiple packaging and family packaging, how to design the package as an effective promotional tool, how best to accommodate resellers and whether to develop environmentally responsible packaging. Packaging can be an important part of an overall marketing strategy. Firms choose particular colours, designs, shapes and textures to create desirable images and associations. Producers alter packages to convey new features or to make them safer or more convenient. If a package has a secondary use, the product's value to the consumer may be increased. Category consistent packaging makes products more easily recognised by consumers, and innovative packaging enhances a product's distinctiveness. Consumers may criticise packaging that doesn't work well, poses health or safety problems, is deceptive in some way, or is not biodegradable or recyclable.

Labelling is an important aspect of packaging for promotional, informational and legal reasons. Because labels are attention getting devices, they are significant features in the marketing mix. Various regulatory agencies can require that products be labelled or marked with warnings, instructions, certifications, nutritional information and manufacturer's identification.

IMPORTANT TERMS

Brand	Individual branding
Brand name	Overall family branding
Brand mark	Line family branding
Trade mark	Brand extension branding
Trade name	Family packaging
Manufacturer brand	Labelling
Own label brand	Universal product code (UPC)
Generic brand	Barcode

DISCUSSION AND REVIEW QUESTIONS

1. What is the difference between a brand and a brand name? Compare and contrast the terms *brand mark* and *trade mark*.
2. How does branding benefit customers and organisations?
3. What are the advantages associated with brand loyalty?
4. What are the distinguishing characteristics of own label brands?
5. Given the competition between own label brands and manufacturer brands, should manufacturers be concerned about the popularity of own label brands? How should manufacturers fight back in the brand battle?
6. Identify and explain the major considerations consumers take into account when selecting a brand.
7. The brand name Xerox is sometimes used generically to refer to photocopying machines. How can Xerox Corporation protect this brand name?
8. Identify and explain the four major branding policies and give examples of each. Can a firm use more than one policy at a time? Explain your answer.
9. What are the major advantages and disadvantages of licensing?
10. Describe the functions that a package can perform. Which function is most important? Why?
11. When developing a package, what are the major issues that a marketer should consider?
12. In what ways can packaging be used as a strategic tool?
13. What are the major criticisms of packaging?
14. What are the major functions of labelling?

8.1 KP Heads for Market Leadership

Snack giant KP has its sights set on half of the snacks, crisps and nuts markets. The company has given itself until the year 2000 to achieve a 50 per cent share of this £1.5 billion market in the UK. Such a goal does not seem unreasonable considering that since 1982, KP has managed to increase its market share by 10 per cent to 40 per cent.

The threat to KP comes from giant PepsiCo, which the company managed to topple from market leadership for the first time in 1990. In a closely fought contest for market share, PepsiCo disputes the figures which put KP on top. While KP bases its market share on volume tonnes sold (19.2 per cent of KP's business comes from its production of own label products for supermarkets), PepsiCo says that branded sales are what matters and calculates its success using figures for branded products only—putting it at 42.6 per cent—ahead by around 14 per cent. Now PepsiCo plans to merge its Smiths and Walkers subsidiaries to strengthen its branding further, a move which KP hopes will distract PepsiCo's attention from the battle for market supremacy.

New products provide the key to KP's strategy. According to the company's marketing director, around two thirds of growth will be centered on new products. As new products are added to the range, the company will consider rationalising its existing portfolio. Those snacks and crisps which fail to reach the £20 million level are likely to be dropped. Currently, the values of KP's top four nibbles are £95 million for Hula Hoops, followed by £90 million for KP Nuts, followed by The Real McCoys and Skips, worth £48 million and £45 million respectively.

CORE SNACK BRANDS

KP

Hula Hoops	KP Nuts
The Real McCoys	Skips
Solo Lower Fat Crisps	Frisps
Roysters	Discos
Brannigans	

PEPSICO

Walkers Crisps	Smiths Quavers
Monster Munch	Smiths Crisps
Tudor Crisps	French Fries
Ruffles	Looney Tunes
Planters Nuts	Smiths Squares
Smiths Tuba Loops	Smiths Crinkles
Frazzles	Smiths Chip Sticks
Big D nuts	

The merger between Walkers and Smiths means that the PepsiCo range will soon undergo a transition. Monster Munch and Smiths Quavers are to be relaunched as Walkers Quavers and Walkers Monster Munch. This is part of a PepsiCo move, backed by £6.5 million marketing spend, to use the Walkers brand to support its key products. Other changes include the introduction of salt and vinegar flavoured Quavers (to attract children) and mixed cheese to appeal to "housewives".

KP's recent launch of Roysters Steam Nuts is indicative of the company's drive for innovative products. Representing the company's first move to extend a brand into a new sector, the product follows naturally on from the 1992 introduction of Roysters. The extra large peanuts will be available in three tempting flavours: Kentucky Smoke, Louisiana Hot Spice and New York Smoke. KP hopes that the move will provide it with a 5 per cent stake of the £136 million nuts market. According to KP's Marketing Director, the Steam Nuts brand has connotations of tradition and intrigue which should boost a flagging market.

SOURCES: Suzanne Bidlake, "Snack attack by KP demands a crisp reply", *Marketing*, 21 January 1993; Suzanne Bidlake, "KP extends Roysters to grab 5% of market", *Marketing*, 21 January 1993; Juliana Koranteng, "Quavers revamp for battle with Hula Hoops", *Marketing*, 21 January 1993.

Questions for Discussion

1. To what category of consumer products do snacks, crisps and nuts belong?
2. Is branding important in this market? Why?
3. What is meant by "brand extension". Why is KP engaging in brand extension?

8.2 Stepcan: Innovative Packaging Design

In 1988, Metal Box (MB) developed a container to rival the tin can: the Stepcan. The unique packaging, manufactured by the Stretch Tube Extrusion Process, was made of flexible, transparent plastic with a metal, ring-pull lid. Stepcan was resealable and gave consumers the opportunity of viewing the container's contents. Initial marketing research justified the company's belief that consumers would prefer the non-breakable Stepcan with its clearly viewed contents. Indeed, consumers claimed they would happily pay a price premium. From the resellers' viewpoint, the Stepcan offered a range of advantages over some other types of packaging: it was simple to fill, convenient and light to transport, and easy to display at the point of sale. Some of the more obvious benefits of the Stepcan package are as follows:

- *Clarity*
  Consumers can view the product they are buying and seemingly judge its quality for themselves.
- *High quality image*
  Consumers who are used to eating tinned fruit but fancy a change from their usual products feel that Stepcan offers a more socially acceptable alternative, especially for guests.
- *Long shelf life*
  Stepcan offers similar benefits to tinned foods for retailers and consumers not wishing to continually restock.
- *Lightweight and shatter-proof*
  In parts of Europe, bottled fruit and vegetables sold in glass packaging have been popular for many years. Stepcan offers the same visibility benefits of its glass cousin but is light to carry and is non-breakable.
- *Easy to open ends*
  The use of plastic overlids to reseal the packing allows easy storage in the refrigerator after opening.
- *Stackable*
  Many packaging innovations have come to grief because they fail to take distributors' needs into consideration. Stepcan is as easy to store as conventional tinned foods.

- *Reusable*

  Stepcan can be used as a handy storage container once its contents have been used.
- *Interchangeable on canning lines*

  From an operational viewpoint, Stepcan offers many of the same benefits as the traditional tin can, being easy to switch into the canning process. Even the need to label is minimal.

Marks & Spencer wanted exclusivity for the packaging innovation. Sainsbury, Waitrose and Tesco all expressed an interest. Marks & Spencer won the first round, and Stepcans containing fruit cocktail were test marketed in a number of locations at a variety of price levels. Eventually, the product was given a price tag of £1.29, some three times the price of a similar weight of conventional tinned fruit cocktail. When put on supermarket shelves adjacent to competing tinned brands, Stepcan consistently outsold them, sometimes by more than three times as much. As more retailers started to stock Stepcans for their own label products, more product lines were found to be suitable for this type of packaging. The simple design allows new labels to be added with the minimum of fuss. All in all, Stepcan represents a packaging design which appears to fulfill a mix of operational and marketing requirements.

SOURCES: "M and S adopts clear plastics Stepcan for premium fruit pack presentation", *Packaging News*, May 1988; "Stepcan: the choice is clear", Metal Box food promotional literature, 1988; "What's in a can?", *Inside News*, Marks & Spencer plc. April/May 1989; "Full speed ahead", *Metal Box News*, April 1988, p. 1.

Questions for Discussion

1. What benefits does Stepcan offer customers? Which do you think are the most important?
2. Why might Metal Box have difficulty maintaining its premium price in the long term?
3. How practical is Stepcan for retailers and distributors?
4. What long term threats might Stepcan face?

9 PRODUCT MANAGEMENT

Objectives

To become aware of organisational alternatives for managing products

To understand the importance and role of product development in the marketing mix

To become aware of how existing products can be modified

To learn how product deletion can be used to improve product mixes

To gain insight into how businesses develop a product idea into a commercial product

To acquire knowledge of product positioning and the management of products during the various stages of a product's life-cycle

A t a time when some branding giants are launching new lines—PepsiCo and Coca-Cola have recently extended their ranges to include Pepsi Max and Tab Clear—others are seeking to re-establish some of the old favourites. The return of 1970s fashion styles has been accompanied by comebacks from Packamac rainwear to Spam tinned meat and Brylcreem. Even Gossard's Wonderbra is enjoying a new lease of life with the introduction of a range of up-dated styles and colours, backed with a "Say Goodbye to Your Feet" advertising campaign. The Hasbro toy company's Action Man, discontinued in 1987, has also made a welcome return, spurred by consumer demand. The launch of four new Action Men—one with electronic sight and sound weapons—will be supported by television advertising and will also be available with a host of armoury and accessories.

A combination of consumer nostalgia—as seen in the return of flared trousers and platform shoes—and recession seems responsible for the spate of brand revivals. According to Coley Porter Bell group account director Jill Marshall, "In hard times you become aware of the sheer cost and the risk of new product development". Capitalising on a feeling of consumer nostalgia by re-establishing old and well loved brands offers companies alternative and less risky ways to further their business interests.

The revival which is taking place encompasses a host of both familiar and little known brands, ranging from those which had previously been withdrawn to others, like Spam and Brylcreem, which had merely fallen from consumer grace. The list of revived products even includes current market favourites, such as Lucozade, Silvikrin and TSB. For companies trying to make the most of precious resources, the opportunity to capitalise on fashion changes and consumer nostalgia is welcome. ■

SOURCES: Helen Jones, "Revival of the fittest", *Marketing Week*, 19 March 1993, pp. 32–5; Claire Murphy, "SmithKline unwraps global brand strategy", *Marketing Week*, 12 March 1993, p. 7; "TSB likes to say yes to overhaul", *Marketing Week*, 5 March 1993, p. 9; "SmithKline relaunches Silvikrin range", *Marketing Week*, 5 March 1993, p. 10.

To compete effectively and achieve their goals, organisations must be able to adjust their product mix in response to changes in buyers' preferences. A firm often has to modify existing products, introduce new products or eliminate products that were successful perhaps only a few years ago. For companies such as those described in the chapter opener, re-introducing an old favourite can be appropriate in some situations. These adjustments and the way a firm is organised to make them are facets of product management.

This chapter first examines how businesses are organised to develop and manage products. It then looks at several ways to improve a product mix. They include modifying the quality, function or style of products; deleting weak products; and developing new products. The process of developing a new product is described in detail from idea generation to commercialisation. The next section examines product positioning—how marketers decide where a product should fit into the field of competing products and which benefits to emphasise. The chapter concludes by considering issues and decisions associated with managing a product through the growth, maturity and declining stages of its life-cycle.

ORGANISING TO MANAGE PRODUCTS

A company must often manage a complex set of products, markets or both. Often, too, it finds that the traditional functional form of organisation—in which managers specialise in business functions such as advertising, sales and distribution—does not fit its needs. Consequently, management must find an organisational approach that accomplishes the tasks necessary to develop and manage products. Alternatives to functional organisation include the product manager approach, the marketing manager approach and the venture team approach.

A **product manager** is responsible for a product, a product line or several distinct products that make up an interrelated group within a multiproduct organisation. A **brand manager,** on the other hand, is responsible for a single brand, for example, Lipton's Yellow Label tea or Mars bars. A product or brand manager operates cross-functionally to co-ordinate the activities, information and strategies involved in marketing an assigned product. Product managers and brand managers plan marketing activities to achieve objectives by co-ordinating a mix of distribution, promotion (especially sales promotion and advertising) and price. They must consider packaging and branding decisions and work closely with personnel in research and development, engineering and production. Marketing research helps product managers to understand consumers and find target markets. The product manager or brand manager approach to organisation is used by many large, multiple product companies in the consumer package goods business.

A **marketing manager** is responsible for managing the marketing activities that serve a particular group or class of customers. This organisational approach is particularly effective when a firm engages in different types of marketing activities to provide products to diverse customer groups. A company might have one marketing manager for industrial markets and another for consumer markets. These broad market categories might be broken down into more limited market responsibilities.

A **venture** or **project team** is designed to create entirely new products that may be aimed at new markets. Unlike a product or marketing manager, a venture team is responsible for all aspects of a product's development: research and development, production and engineering, finance and accounting, and marketing. Venture teams work outside established divisions to create inventive approaches to new products and markets. As a result of this flexibility, new products can be developed to take advantage of opportunities in highly segmented markets.

The members of a venture team come from different functional areas of an organisation. When the commercial potential of a new product has been demonstrated, the members may return to their functional areas, or they may join a new or existing division to manage the product. The new product may be turned over to an existing division, a marketing manager or a product manager. Innovative organisational forms such as venture teams are necessary for many companies, especially well established firms operating primarily in mature markets. These companies must take a dual approach to marketing organisation. They must accommodate the management of mature products and also encourage the development of new ones.[1]

MANAGING THE PRODUCT MIX

To provide products that satisfy target markets and achieve the organisation's objectives, a marketer must develop, alter and maintain an effective product mix (although seldom can the same product mix be effective for long). An organisation's product mix may need several types of adjustments. Because customers' attitudes and product preferences change, their desire for a product may decline. People's fashion preferences obviously change quite often, but their attitudes to and preferences for most products also change over time.

In some cases a company needs to alter its product mix for competitive reasons. A marketer may have to delete a product from the mix because a competitor dominates the market for that product. Similarly, a firm may have to introduce a new product or modify an existing one to compete more effectively. A marketer may expand a firm's product mix to take advantage of excess marketing and production capacity.

Regardless of the reasons for altering a product mix, the product mix must be managed. In strategic market planning, many marketers rely on the portfolio approach for managing the product mix. The **product portfolio approach** tries to create specific marketing strategies to achieve a balanced mix of products that will bring maximum profits in the long run. The most time consuming task in a portfolio analysis is collecting data about the products and their performance along selected dimensions. Hard data must first be obtained from the company's marketing information system (MIS)— for instance, on sales, profitability, market share and industry growth. Product portfolio models are examined in detail in Chapter 19. This chapter looks at three major ways to improve a product mix: modifying an existing product, deleting a product, and developing a new product.

Modifying Existing Products

Product modification means changing one or more characteristics of a firm's product. This strategy is most likely to be used in the maturity stage of the product life-cycle to give a firm's existing brand a competitive advantage. Altering a product mix in this way entails less risk than developing a new product because the product is already established in the market.

If certain conditions are met, product modification can improve a firm's product mix. First, the product must be modifiable. Second, existing customers must be able to perceive that a modification has been made (assuming that the modified item is still aimed at them). Third, the modification should make the product more consistent with customers' desires so that it provides greater satisfaction. If these conditions are not met, it is unlikely that the product modification, however innovative, will be successful. Product modifications fall into three major categories: quality, function and style modifications.

Quality Modifications. **Quality modifications** are changes that relate to a product's dependability and durability. Usually, they are executed by altering the materials or the production process. Reducing a product's quality may allow an organisation to lower its price and direct the item at a larger target market.

By contrast, increasing the quality of a product may give a firm an advantage over competing brands. In fact, quality improvement has become a major tool for successfully competing with foreign marketers. Higher quality may enable a company to charge a higher price by creating customer loyalty and by lowering customer sensitivity to price. However, higher quality may require the use of more expensive components, less standardised production processes and other manufacturing and management techniques that force a firm to charge higher prices.[2] At the beginning of the 1990s, concern for quality increased significantly, with many firms, such as Rover, Volvo and Caterpillar, finding ways both to increase quality and reduce costs.

Functional Modifications. Changes that affect a product's versatility, effectiveness, convenience or safety are called **functional modifications;** they usually require the product to be redesigned. Typical product categories which have undergone considerable functional modifications include kitchen appliances, office and farm equipment, and cleaning products. Functional modifications can make a product useful to more people, thus enlarging its market. This type of change can place a product in a favourable competitive position by providing benefits competing items do not offer. Functional modifications can also help an organisation achieve and maintain a progressive image. For example, washing machine manufacturers such as Whirlpool have developed appliances which use less heat and water. At times, too, functional modifications are made to reduce the possibility of product liability claims.

Style Modifications. **Style modifications** change the sensory appeal of a product by altering its taste, texture, sound, smell or visual characteristics. In making a purchase decision a buyer is swayed by how a product looks, smells, tastes, feels or sounds. Thus a style modification may strongly affect purchases. For years car makers have relied on style modifications to update their products.

Through style modifications, a firm can differentiate its product from competing brands and thus gain a sizeable market share, as Bang & Olufsen demonstrates in Figure 9.1. The major drawback in using style modifications is that their value is highly subjective. Although a firm may strive to improve the product's style, customers may actually find the modified product less appealing. Some organisations try to minimise these problems by altering product style in subtle ways.

Deleting Products

Generally, a product cannot satisfy target market customers and contribute to the achievement of an organisation's overall goals indefinitely. **Product deletion** is the process of eliminating a product that no longer satisfies a sufficient number of customers. A declining product reduces an organisation's profitability and drains resources that could be used instead to modify other products or develop new ones. A marginal product may require shorter production runs, which can increase per unit production costs. Finally, when a dying product completely loses favour with customers, the negative feelings may transfer to some of the company's other products.

FIGURE 9.1
Functional modification
Up market leader Bang & Olufsen's innovative range of televisions brings versatility of location and is remote controlled.

SOURCE: Courtesy of Bang & Olufsen.

Improves breakfast television. And gives music while you work.

Put one of our beautifully styled televisions in your kitchen and you get more than you might think.

VisionClear technology for perfect pictures, even in morning sunlight. A motorised stand rotates the set to face you. One remote control lets you watch and program your Bang & Olufsen video, even though it's in the next room. Or operate and play music from our hi-fi systems, that might be in another room, through its hi-fi stereo loudspeakers.

So for breakfast TV, yesterday's drama or some music while you work take a good look at Bang & Olufsen...

MUCH MORE THAN TELEVISION

Bang & Olufsen

For our information pack or your nearest dealer call free on **0800 100 130** or write Freepost to Bang & Olufsen, Box 143, FREEPOST (BS4335), Bristol. BS1 3YX.

Most organisations find it difficult to delete a product. It was probably a hard decision for Austin Rover to drop the TR7 sports car and admit that it was a failure. A decision to drop a product may be opposed by management and other employees who feel the product is necessary in the product mix. Salespeople who still have some loyal customers are especially upset when a product is dropped. Considerable resources and effort are sometimes spent in trying to improve the product's marketing mix enough to increase sales and thus avoid having to delete it.

Some organisations delete products only after they have become heavy financial burdens. Robert Maxwell's newspaper the London *Daily News* closed after only a few weeks, having lost £25 million. A better approach is to institute some form of systematic review to evaluate each product and monitor its impact on the overall effectiveness of the firm's product mix. Such a review should analyse a product's contribution to the firm's sales for a given period and include estimates of future sales, costs and profits associated with the product. It should also gauge the value of making changes in the marketing strategy to improve the product's performance. A systematic review allows an organisation to improve product performance and to ascertain when to delete products. Although many companies do systematically review their product mixes, one research study found that few companies have formal, written policies on the process of deleting products. The study also found that most companies base their decisions to delete weak products on poor sales and profit potential, low compatibility with the firm's business strategies, unfavourable market outlook and historical declines in profitability.[3]

Basically, there are three way to delete a product: phase it out, run it out or drop it immediately (see Figure 9.2). A phase out approach lets the product decline without a change in the marketing strategy. No attempt is made to give the product new life. A run out policy exploits any strengths left in the product. Intensifying marketing efforts in core markets or eliminating some marketing expenditures, such as advertising, may

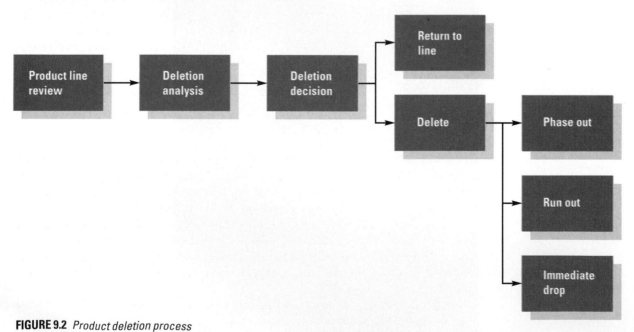

FIGURE 9.2 *Product deletion process*

SOURCE: Martin L. Bell, *Marketing: Concepts and Strategy,* 3rd ed., p. 267; copyright © 1979, Houghton Mifflin Company. Reproduced by permission of Mrs. Martin L. Bell.

cause a sudden spurt of profits. This approach is commonly taken for technologically obsolete products, such as older models of computers and calculators. Some car manufacturers use a run out approach to dispose of certain models just before a new launch. Often the price is reduced to get a sales spurt. The third alternative, dropping an unprofitable product immediately, is the best strategy when losses are too great to prolong the product's life.

Developing New Products

Developing and introducing new products is frequently expensive and risky. Thousands of new consumer products are introduced annually, and, as indicated in Chapter 7, anywhere from 60 to 90 per cent of them fail. Lack of research is the main reason new products fail. Other often cited causes of failure are technical problems in design or production and errors in timing the product's introduction. Although developing new products is risky, so is failing to introduce new products. For example, the makers of Timex watches gained a large share of the watch market through effective marketing strategies during the 1960s and early 1970s. By 1983, Timex's market share had slipped considerably, in part because the company had failed to introduce new products. In recent times, however, Timex has introduced a number of new products and regained market share.

The term *new product* can have more than one meaning. It may refer to a genuinely new product—such as the digital watch once was—offering innovative benefits. But products that are merely different and distinctly better are also often viewed as new. The following items (listed in no particular order) are product innovations of the last 30 years: Post-It note pads, disposable lighters, birth control pills, personal computers, felt tip pens, seat belts, video cassette recorders, deep fat fryers, compact disc players and soft contact lenses. Thus, a new product can be an innovative variation of an existing product, such as The Invergordon shown in Figure 9.3. It can also be a product that a given firm has not marketed previously, although similar products may be available from other companies. The first company to introduce a video cassette recorder, for example, clearly was launching a new product. However, if Boeing introduced its own brand of video cassette recorder, this would also be viewed as a new product for Boeing, because that organisation has not previously marketed such products.

Before a product is introduced, it goes through the six phases of **new product development** shown in Figure 9.4: (1) idea generation, (2) screening, (3) business analysis, (4) product development, (5) test marketing and (6) commercialisation. A product may be dropped, and many are, at any of these stages of development. This section examines the process through which products are developed from the inception of an idea to a product offered for sale.

Idea Generation. Businesses and other organisations seek product ideas that will help them achieve their objectives. This activity is **idea generation.** The fact that only a few ideas are good enough to be commercially successful underscores the difficulty of the task. Although some organisations get their ideas almost by chance, firms trying to manage their product mixes effectively usually develop systematic approaches for generating new product ideas. At the heart of innovation is a purposeful, focused effort to identify new ways to serve a market. Unexpected occurrences, incongruities, new needs, industry and market changes, and demographic changes may all indicate new opportunities.[4]

New product ideas can come from several sources. They may come from internal sources—marketing managers, researchers, sales personnel, engineers, or other organisational personnel. Brainstorming and incentives or rewards for good ideas are typical intrafirm devices for stimulating the development of ideas. The company 3M is

FIGURE 9.3
A new product
The Invergordon is an example of a new product.

SOURCE: Courtesy of the Invergordon Distillers Limited.

well known for encouraging the generation of new ideas. The idea for 3M's Post-It adhesive backed yellow notes came from an employee. As a church choir member, he used slips of paper for marking songs in his hymn book. Because the pieces of paper fell out, he suggested developing an adhesive backed note.[5] Hewlett-Packard keeps its labs open to engineers 24 hours a day to help generate ideas; it also encourages its researchers to devote 10 per cent of company time to exploring their own ideas for new products.[6]

New product ideas may also arise from sources outside the firm—customers, competitors, advertising agencies, management consultants, and private research organisations. Johnson & Johnson, for example, acquired the technology for its new, clear orthodontic braces through a joint venture with Saphikon, the developer of the technology behind the braces.[7] Sometimes, potential buyers of a product are questioned in depth to discover what attributes would appeal to them. Asking weekend fishermen

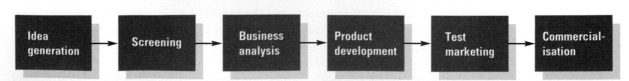

FIGURE 9.4   *Phases of new product development*

what they wanted in a sonar fish finder led Techsonic to develop its LCR (liquid crystal recorder) fish finder. In the US, annual sales of the LCR reached $31 million within one year. The practice of asking customers what they want from its products has helped Techsonic maintain its leadership in the industry.[8]

Screening Ideas.   In the process of **screening ideas,** those with the greatest potential are selected for further review. During screening, product ideas are analysed to determine whether they match the organisation's objectives and resources. The company's overall ability to produce and market the product is also analysed. Other aspects of an idea that should be weighed are the nature and wants of buyers and possible environmental changes. More new product ideas are rejected during the idea screening phase than during any other phase.

Sometimes a check-list of new product requirements is used when making screening decisions, thus encouraging evaluators to be systematic and reducing the changes of their overlooking some fact. If a critical factor on the check-list remains unclear, the type of formal marketing research described in Chapter 6 may be needed. To screen ideas properly, it may be necessary to test product concepts; a product concept and its benefits can be described or shown to consumers. Several product concepts may be tested to discover which might appeal most to a particular target market. The role of marketing research in the new product development is considered in Marketing Insight 9.1.

Business Analysis.   During the **business analysis** stage, the product idea is evaluated to determine its potential contribution to the firm's sales, costs and profits. In the course of a business analysis, evaluators ask a variety of questions: Does the product fit in with the organisation's existing product mix? Does the company have the right expertise to develop the new product? Is demand strong enough to justify entering the market and will the demand endure? What types of environmental and competitive changes can be expected, and how will these changes affect the product's future sales, costs and profits? Are the organisation's research, development, engineering and production capabilities adequate? If new facilities must be constructed, how quickly can they be built and how much will they cost? Is the necessary financing for development and commercialisation on hand or obtainable at terms consistent with a favourable return on investment? Will the new product or idea benefit the company's existing portfolio of products? Is there any danger that existing products or services will be cannibalised?

In the business analysis stage, firms seek market information. The results of consumer polls, along with secondary data, supply the specifics needed for estimating potential sales, costs and profits. At this point, a research budget should explore the financial objectives and related considerations for the new product.

Product Development.   **Product development** is the phase in which the organisation finds out if it is technically feasible to produce the product and if it can be produced at costs low enough to make the final price reasonable. To test its acceptability, the idea or concept is converted into a prototype, or working model. Case 9.1 considers the role of concept cars in the development of new vehicles. The prototype should reveal tangible and intangible attributes associated with the product in consumers' minds. The product's design, mechanical features and intangible aspects must be linked to wants in the market-place. Failure to determine how consumers feel about the product and how they would use it may lead to the product's failure. For example,

WHY PRODUCTS FAIL: A MARKETING RESEARCH GAP

The importance of marketing research and information systems is best understood by looking at product failures. Eight out of ten new products eventually fail. Strong marketing research can help companies reduce the likelihood of product failures.

Fab 1 Shot was introduced in 1987 as a single packet detergent and fabric softener. To beat competitors to the market, Colgate-Palmolive introduced the product across the US without first test marketing it. The company targeted promotion for the product at large families, when in fact the actual consumers were singles, college students and people living in flats. These consumers want convenience at any price, whereas large families are more concerned with cost and controlling the amount of detergent in each load. Without marketing efforts targeted at the appropriate segment, Fab 1 Shot was a failure. Thus accurate test data are invaluable in positioning a product in the appropriate demographic segment of the market.

When the film *Crocodile Dundee* was popular, so too was anything Australian. In jumped Australia's Foster's Lager beer in the late 1980s. Foster's promotion revolved around its Australian heritage. But when the Australian fever ended, Foster's lost more than 40 per cent of its sales. In a highly competitive market, Foster's failed to convey a clear image to consumers beyond its Australian origins, and the product never found a market niche of its own. Targeting a saturated market requires marketing research to determine niches that may have an interest in the product.

In the late 1980s, four new colognes for men and women were introduced. There was nothing too unusual about the colognes except their brand name: Bic. Upon introducing the product, Bic sank £13/£14 million into its marketing campaign, but disappointing sales contributed to a 22 per cent drop in company profits. Advertising for the colognes focused more on the novel shape of the package—similar to a lighter—and less on the fragrance. Consumers were confused by the packaging and reluctant to purchase a cologne that they could not test before purchasing. More extensive marketing research could have revealed that the Bic brand name had been overextended. What makes for a great pen, lighter or razor doesn't necessarily create a great cologne.

These examples highlight the importance of marketing research, test marketing, and establishing marketing information systems both within and outside of the company. Without critical research, products may fail, resulting in substantial losses.

SOURCES: Cara Appelbaum, "Overextending a brand", *Adweek's Marketing Week,* 5 November 1990, p. 21; Cara Appelbaum, "Targeting the wrong demographic", *Adweek's Marketing Week,* 5 November 1990, p. 20; Laura Bird, "Unnecessary 'innovations'", *Adweek's Marketing Week,* 5 November 1990, p. 24; Matthew Grimm, "Targeting a saturated market", *Adweek's Marketing Week,* 5 November 1990, p. 21; David Kiley, "Conditions that change", *Adweek's Marketing Week,* 5 November 1990, p. 25; and Dan Koeppel, "Insensitivity to a market's concern", *Adweek's Marketing Week,* 5 November 1990, p. 25.

the Sinclair C5 electric buggy was developed as a serious on-road, single seater car for city or country use. But, drivers were positioned too low to the ground to feel safe in heavy traffic. Campus students ended up using the remaining stocks as on-pavement runabouts. Testing to determine how consumers view the product idea is therefore a critical part of the product development stage. As indicated in Case 9.1, car manufacturers such as Peugeot and Citroën invest considerable energy and resources in researching and developing new products. In many cases concept cars are developed to enable them to be fully tested.

The development phase of a new product is frequently lengthy and expensive; thus a relatively small number of product ideas are put into development. If the product appears sufficiently successful during this stage to merit testing, then during the latter part of the development stage marketers begin to make decisions regarding branding, packaging, labelling, pricing and promotion for use in the test marketing stage.

Test Marketing.   A limited introduction of a product in geographic areas chosen to represent the intended market is called **test marketing.** Its aim is to determine the reactions of probable buyers. For example, after McDonald's developed fried chicken products for its fast food menu, it test marketed the idea in certain McDonald's restaurants to find out how those customers felt about eating chicken at McDonald's.[9] The company followed a similar strategy for test marketing its range of salads and pizza. Kentucky Fried Chicken is now test marketing its new KFC Express brand in selected parts of the UK. Test marketing is *not* an extension of the development stage; it is a sample launching of the entire marketing mix. Test marketing should be conducted only after the product has gone through development and after initial plans regarding the other marketing mix variables have been made.

Companies of all sizes use test marketing to lessen the risk of product failure. The dangers of introducing an untested product include undercutting already profitable products and, should the new product fail, loss of credibility with distributors and customers. When Lever Brothers launched Wisk—previously only a washing powder—in liquid form in 1986, the firm had misjudged consumer usage. Many blocked washing machines later, P&G offered liquid Ariel with Arielettes, containers to be placed inside the machines together with the clothes. Reformulations have now overcome the problems with Wisk and its competitors.

Test marketing provides several benefits. It lets marketers expose a product in a natural marketing environment to gauge its sales performance. While the product is being marketed in a limited area, the company can seek to identify weaknesses in the product or in other parts of the marketing mix. A product weakness discovered after a nationwide introduction can be expensive to correct. Moreover, if consumers' early reactions are negative, marketers may not be able to persuade consumers to try the product again. Thus making adjustments after test marketing can be crucial to the success of a new product. Test marketing also allows marketers to experiment with variations in advertising, price and packaging in different test areas and to measure the extent of brand awareness, brand switching and repeat purchases that result from alterations in the marketing mix.

The accuracy of test marketing results often hinges on where the tests are conducted. Selection of appropriate test areas is very important. The validity of test market results depends heavily on selecting test sites that provide an accurate representation of the intended target market. The criteria used for choosing test cities or television regions depend on the product's characteristics, the target market's characteristics, and the firm's objectives and resources. Even though the selection criteria will vary from one company to another, the kind of questions that Table 9.1 presents can be helpful in assessing a potential test market.

TABLE 9.1 *Questions to consider when choosing test markets*

1. Is the area typical of planned distribution outlets?
2. Is the city relatively isolated from other cities?
3. What local media are available, and are they co-operative?
4. Does the area have a dominant television station? Does it have multiple newspapers, magazines and radio stations?
5. Does the city contain a diversified cross-section of ages, religions, and cultural/societal preferences?
6. Are the purchasing habits atypical?
7. Is the city's per capita income typical?
8. Does the city have a good record as a test city?
9. Would testing efforts be easily "jammed" by competitors?
10. Does the city have stable year round sales?
11. Are retailers who will co-operate available?
12. Are research and audit services available?
13. Is the area free from unusual influences, such as one industry's dominance or heavy tourist traffic?

SOURCE: Adapted from "A checklist for selecting test markets", copyright 1982 *Sales & Marketing Management*. Reprinted by permission of Sales & Marketing Management.

Test marketing is not without risks, however. Not only is it expensive, but also a firm's competitors may try to interfere. A competitor may attempt to "jam" the test programme by increasing advertising or promotions, lowering prices or offering special incentives—all to combat the recognition and purchase of a new brand. Any such devices can invalidate test results. Sometimes, too, competitors copy the product in the testing stage and rush to introduce a similar product. It is therefore desirable to move quickly and commercialise as soon as possible after testing.

Because of these risks, many companies are using alternative methods to gauge consumer preferences. One such method is simulated test marketing. Typically, consumers at shopping centres are asked to view an advertisement for a new product and given a free sample to take home. These consumers are subsequently interviewed over the phone and asked to rate the product. The major advantages of simulated test marketing are lower costs, tighter security, and, consequently, a reduction in the flow of information to competitors and the elimination of jamming. Scanner based test marketing is another, more sophisticated version of the traditional test marketing method.[10] Some marketing research firms, such as A. C. Nielsen, offer test marketing services to help provide independent assessment of products.

Commercialisation. During the **commercialisation** phase, plans for full scale manufacturing and marketing must be refined and settled, and budgets for the project must be prepared. Early in the commercialisation phase, marketing management analyses the results of test marketing to find out what changes in the marketing mix are needed before the product is introduced. For example, the results of test marketing may tell the marketers to change one or more of the product's physical attributes, modify the distribution plans to include more retail outlets, alter promotional efforts or change the product's price. The results of test marketing helped Metal Box choose the most appropriate price for its Stepcan product. It is important that companies treat test marketing findings with care to ensure the validity of their projections.

During this phase, the organisation also has to gear up for production. Consequently, it may face sizeable capital expenditures for plant and equipment and may need to hire additional personnel.

The product enters the market during the commercialisation phase. When introducing a product, marketers often spend enormous sums of money for advertising, personal selling and other types of promotion. These expenses, together with capital outlays, can make commercialisation extremely costly; such expenditures may not be recovered for several years. For example, when Coca-Cola introduced Tab Clear, the company spent millions of pounds on advertising to communicate the new product's attributes.

Commercialisation is easier when customers accept the product rapidly, which they are more likely to do if marketers can make them aware of a product's benefits. The following stages of the **product adoption process** are generally recognised as those that buyers go through in accepting a product:

1. *Awareness.* The buyer becomes aware of the product.
2. *Interest.* The buyer seeks information and is generally receptive to learning about the product.
3. *Evaluation.* The buyer considers the product's benefits and determines whether to try it.
4. *Trial.* The buyer examines, tests, or tries the product to determine its usefulness relative to his or her needs.
5. *Adoption.* The buyer purchases the product and can be expected to use it when the need for this general types of product arises again.[11]

This adoption model has several implications for the commercialisation phase. First, the company must promote the product to create widespread awareness of its existence and its benefits. Samples or simulated trials should be arranged to help buyers make initial purchase decisions. At the same time, marketers should emphasise quality control and provide solid guarantees to reinforce buyer opinion during the evaluation stage. Finally, production and physical distribution must be linked to patterns of adoption and repeat purchases. (The product adoption process is also discussed in Chapter 14.) When launching a new product, companies should be aware that buyers differ in the speed with which they adopt a product. Identifying buyers who are most open to new products can help expedite this process.

Products are not usually launched nationwide overnight but are introduced through a process called a roll out. In a roll out, a product is introduced in stages, starting in a set of geographic areas and gradually expanding into adjacent areas. Thus, Cadbury's Wispa bar appeared initially in the North East of England. It may take several years to market the product nationally. Sometimes the test cities are used as initial marketing areas, and the introduction becomes a natural extension of test marketing.

Gradual product introduction is popular for several reasons. It reduces the risks of introducing a new product. If the product fails, the firm will experience smaller losses if the item has been introduced in only a few geographic areas than if it has been marketed nationally. Furthermore, a company cannot introduce a product nationwide overnight because the system of wholesalers and retailers required to distribute it cannot be established immediately. The development of a distribution network may take considerable time. Also, the number of units needed to satisfy the national demand for a successful product can be enormous, and a firm usually cannot produce the required quantities in a short time.

Despite the good reasons for introducing a product gradually, marketers realise that this approach creates some competitive problems. A gradual introduction allows competitors to observe what a firm is doing and to monitor results, just as the firm's own marketers are doing. If competitors see that the newly introduced product is successful, they may enter the same target market quickly with similar products. In addition, as a product is introduced region by region, competitors may expand their marketing efforts to offset promotion of the new product.

PRODUCT POSITIONING

The term **product positioning** refers to the decisions and activities intended to create and maintain a certain concept of the firm's product (relative to competitive brands) in customers' minds. In Figure 9.5, Philips claims technological breakthrough, sound reproduction improvements and recording capability, with minimum disturbance to consumers' music collections. When marketers introduce a product, they attempt to position it so that it seems to possess the characteristics the target market most desires. This projected image is crucial. The *product position* is the customer's concept of this product's attributes relative to the attributes of competitive brands. Fairy Liquid, a washing up liquid, has been positioned as being gentle to hands and long lasting, as well as providing value for money when compared with competing brands.

Product positioning is part of a natural progression when market segmentation is used. Segmentation lets the firm aim a given brand and marketing mix at a portion of the total market. Effective product positioning helps serve a specific market segment by creating an appropriate concept in the minds of customers in that market segment. For example, Lucozade traditionally had the image of a "pick me up" to be drunk during illness. When advertisements featuring sick and ailing children became less appropriate than when the brand was first introduced, Beecham Foods re-positioned the product by switching its promotion focus to healthy adults. The company substituted advertisements featuring well known athletes, so that the "pick me up" concept was not lost. This re-positioning also allowed Beecham to launch new "isotonic" variants of the Lucozade brand.

A firm can position a product to compete head on with another brand, as PepsiCo has done against Coca-Cola, or to avoid competition, as 7-Up has done relative to other soft drink producers. Head to head competition may be a marketer's positioning objective if the product's performance characteristics are at least equal to competitive brands and its prices lower. Head to head positioning may be appropriate even when the price is higher if the product's performance characteristics are superior. Conversely, positioning to avoid competition may be best when the product's performance characteristics are not significantly different from those of competing brands. Moreover, positioning a brand to avoid competition may be appropriate when that brand has unique characteristics that are important to some buyers. Ford's drive to improve vehicle security presents an opportunity to position its cars to avoid direct competition and comparison with rivals. Volvo, for example, has for years positioned itself away from competitors by focusing on the safety characteristics of its cars. Competitors sometimes mention safety issues in their advertisements only temporarily.

FIGURE 9.5

Product positioning
Philips' positioning for its technologically advanced digital compact cassette system claims CD reproduction quality with the ability to play users' existing libraries of cassettes: innovation without the need to do away with music collections.

SOURCE: Courtesy of Philips International.

Avoiding competition is critical when a firm introduces a brand into a market in which it already has one or more brands. Marketers usually want to avoid cannibalising sales of their existing brands, unless the new brand generates substantially larger profits. When Coca-Cola re-introduced Tab, it attempted to position the cola so as to minimise the adverse effects on diet Coke sales. Similarly, when KP introduces a new snack brand, it must take care to ensure that sales of other KP brands do not suffer.

If a product has been planned properly, its attributes and brand image will give it the distinctive appeal needed. Style, shape, construction, quality of work and colour help create the image and the appeal. Of course buyers are more likely to purchase the product if they can easily identify the benefits. When the new product does not offer some preferred attributes, there is room for another new product or for re-positioning an existing product.[12]

MANAGING PRODUCTS AFTER COMMERCIALISATION

Most new products start off slowly and seldom generate enough sales to produce profits immediately. As buyers learn about the new product, marketers should be alert for weaknesses and ready to make corrections quickly, in order to prevent the product's early demise. Car manufacturers expect to modify slight design flaws when launching new car models. In some cases, it may be necessary to recall models which have already been sold. Any such recalls must be executed with the minimum of difficulty to avoid damage to the brand image. Marketing strategy should be designed to attract the segment that is most interested and has the fewest objections. If any of these factors need adjustment, this action, too, must be taken quickly to sustain demand. As the sales curve moves upwards and the break even point is reached, the growth stage begins.

Marketing Strategy in the Growth Stage

As sales increase, management must support the momentum by adjusting the marketing strategy. The goal is to establish the product's position and to fortify it by encouraging brand loyalty. As profits increase, the organisation must brace itself for the entrance of aggressive competitors, who may make specialised appeals to selected market segments. Marketing Insight 9.2 discusses the competitive challenges faced by a new magazine.

During the growth stage, product offerings may have to be expanded. To achieve greater penetration of an overall market, segmentation may have to be used more intensely. That would require developing product variations to satisfy the needs of customers in several different market segments. Marketers should analyse the product position regarding competing products and correct weak or omitted attributes. Further quality, functional or style modifications may be required.

Gaps in the marketing channels should be filled during the growth period. Once a product has won acceptance, new distribution outlets may be easier to obtain. Sometimes marketers tend to move from an **exclusive** or **selective** exposure to a more **intensive** network of dealers to achieve greater market penetration. Marketers must also make sure that the physical distribution system is running efficiently and delivering supplies to distributors before their inventories are exhausted. Because competition increases during the growth period, service adjustments and prompt credit for defective products are important marketing tools.

Advertising expenditure may be lowered slightly from the high level of the introductory stage but still needs to be quite substantial. As sales increase, promotion costs should drop as a percentage of total sales. A falling ratio between promotion expenditure and sales should contribute significantly to increased profits. The advertising messages should stress brand benefits and emphasise the product's position. Coupons and samples may be used to increase market share.

After recovering development costs, a business may be able to lower prices. As sales volume increases, efficiencies in production can result in lower costs. These savings may be passed on to buyers. If demand remains strong and there are few competitive threats, prices tend to remain stable. If price cuts are feasible, they can improve price competition and discourage new competitors from entering the market. For example, when compact disc players were introduced in the early 1980s, they carried an £800 price tag. Primarily because of the price, the product was positioned as a "toy for audiophiles"—a very small market segment. To generate mass market demand, compact disc player manufacturers dropped their prices to around £150, and the cost of discs also dropped. The price is now at a point where the margin is low but the turnover is high, and more homes are now investing in compact disc players. A similar pattern is emerging in the sale of mobile phones.

Marketing Strategy for Mature Products

As many products are in the maturity stage of their life-cycles, marketers must always be ready to improve the product and marketing mix. During maturity, the competitive situation stabilises and some of the weaker competitors drop out. It has been suggested that as a product matures, its customers become more experienced and specialised

NEW TITLE HITS HEALTH AND BEAUTY MAGAZINES

A new arrival has challenged women's health and beauty magazines. The UK launch of Presse Publishing's *Top Santé Health and Beauty* was the biggest since the introduction of *Vanity Fair* in 1991. The campaign broke with a 30 second television commercial, the responsibility of advertising agency Saatchi & Saatchi, which was charged with promoting the £1 million launch. The choice of agency was clearly aimed at utilising Saatchi's considerable experience in the sector (the company had already been involved in launching both *Elle* and *Cosmopolitan* magazines).

Top Santé Health and Beauty was not an entirely new product. The French version of the monthly magazine already enjoyed considerable success. With more than 700,000 copies sold every month, the magazine is France's biggest health and beauty magazine. Now 25 to 44 year old women in the UK are being targeted with a carefully designed mix of exclusive editorial and advertising material. According to Elizabeth Rees-Jones, managing director of Presse Publishing, "We wanted all of the ads to reflect what we were doing editorially, and so we went for particularly exclusive advertisers". Among the select band of companies advertising in the first issue were Avon, Vichy, Braun and Seven Seas.

Top Santé has found itself in a highly competitive market-place. Key competition has come from the titles of The National Magazine Company (NatMags) and Condé Nast. NatMags currently has the largest slice of the UK market for women's magazines, selling one million copies of *Cosmopolitan, She* and *Company* each month. In general, NatMags has benefited from circulation rises despite the recession—management believes that magazines represent a cheap way for depressed consumers to indulge. The Condé Nast portfolio, which includes *Vogue, Tatler* and *Vanity Fair,* is aimed at the up market end of the sector, each title having a distinctive personality. *Vogue,* for example, uses top class models and photographers, earning it an ABC demographic circulation of more than 185,000 copies.

Despite the formidably competitive situation, Rees-Jones, who has more than 30 years of experience in the publishing business, looks set to establish Presse Publishing's new offering in the magazine market. As managing director, she had a strong personal involvement in the project; when surveying French magazines, it was she who noticed the success of Top Santé and who subsequently was the driving force behind its UK introduction.

SOURCES: Tina Mistry, "Advertisers put faith in new title", *Campaign,* 26 February 1993, p. 17; Tina Mistry, "Rees-Jones heads for healthy return", *Campaign,* 26 February 1993, p. 25; "National magazine religiously follows a branded philosophy", Magazine Focus, *Marketing,* 25 February 1993, p. VIII; "Condé Nast glossies are in vogue", Magazine Focus, *Marketing,* 25 February 1993, p. VIII.

(especially for industrial products), while market segmentation opportunities increase. As customers gain knowledge, the benefits they seek may change as well. Thus new marketing strategies may be called for.[13]

Marketers may need to alter the product's quality or otherwise modify it. A product may be rejuvenated through different packaging, new models or style changes. Sales and market share may be maintained or strengthened by developing new uses for the product.

During the maturity stage of the cycle, marketers actively encourage dealers to support the product. Dealers may be offered promotional assistance in lowering their inventory costs. In general, marketers go to great lengths to serve dealers and provide incentives for selling the manufacturer's brand, partly because own label or retailer brands are a threat at this time. As discussed in Chapter 8, own label brands are both an opportunity and a threat to manufacturers, who may be able to sell their products through recognised own label or retailer brand names as well as their own. However, own label or retailer brands frequently undermine manufacturers' brands. Yet if manufacturers refuse to sell to own label dealers, competitors may take advantage of this opportunity.

To maintain market share during the maturity stage requires moderate and sometimes heavy advertising expenditure. Advertising messages focus on differentiating a brand from numerous competitors, and sales promotion efforts are aimed at both consumers and resellers.

A greater mixture of pricing strategies is used during the maturity stage. In some cases, strong price competition occurs and price wars may break out. On the other hand, firms may compete in other ways than through price. Marketers develop price flexibility to differentiate offerings in product lines. Markdowns and price incentives are more common, but prices may rise if distribution and production costs increase.

Marketing Strategy for Declining Products

As a product's sales curve turns downwards, industry profits continue to fall. A business can justify maintaining a product as long as it contributes to profits or enhances the overall effectiveness of a product mix. In this stage, marketers must determine whether to eliminate the product or seek to reposition it in an attempt to extend its life. Usually, a declining product has lost its distinctiveness because similar competing products have been introduced. Competition engenders increased substitution and brand switching as buyers become insensitive to minor product differences. For these reasons, marketers do little to change a product's style, design or other attributes during its decline. New technology, product substitutes or environmental considerations may also indicate that the time has come to delete a product. For example, the ill-fated Betamax video cassette technology was quickly pushed out by the VHS format.

During a product's decline, outlets with strong sales volumes are maintained and unprofitable outlets are weeded out. An entire marketing channel may be eliminated if it does not contribute adequately to profits. Sometimes a new marketing channel, such as a factory outlet, will be used to liquidate remaining inventory of an obsolete product. As sales decline, the product becomes more obscure, but loyal buyers seek out dealers who carry it.

Advertising expenditure is at a minimum. Advertising or special offers may slow the rate of decline. Sales promotions, such as coupons and premiums, may temporarily regain buyers' attention. As the product continues to decline, the sales staff shifts its emphasis to more profitable products.

To have a product return a profit may be more important to a firm than to maintain a certain market share through repricing. To squeeze out all possible remaining profits, marketers may maintain the price despite declining sales and competitive pressures. Prices may even be increased as costs rise if a loyal core market still wants the product. In other situations, the price may be cut to reduce existing inventory so that the product can be deleted. Severe price reductions may be required if a new product is making an existing product obsolete.

SUMMARY

Developing and managing products is critical to an organisation's survival and growth. The various approaches available for organising product management share common activities, functions and decisions necessary to guide a product through its life-cycle. A product manager is responsible for a product, a product line or several distinct products that make up an interrelated group within a multiproduct organisation. A brand manager is a product manager who is responsible for a single brand. Marketing managers are responsible for managing the marketing activities that serve a particular group or class of customers. A venture or project team is sometimes used to create entirely new products that may be aimed at new markets.

The product portfolio approach attempts to create specific marketing strategies to achieve a balanced product mix that will produce maximum long run profits. To maximise the effectiveness of a product mix, an organisation usually has to alter its mix through modification of existing products, deletion of a product or new product development. Product modification involves changing one or more characteristics of a firm's product. This approach to altering a product mix can be effective when the product is modifiable, when customers can perceive the change and when customers want the modification. Quality modifications are changes that relate to a product's dependability and durability. Changes that affect a product's versatility, effectiveness, convenience or safety are called functional modifications. Style modifications change the sensory appeal of a product.

Product deletion is the process of eliminating a product that no longer satisfies a sufficient number of customers. Although a firm's personnel may oppose product deletion, weak products are unprofitable, consume too much time and effort, may require shorter production runs and can create an unfavourable impression of the firm's other products. A product mix should be systematically reviewed to determine when to delete products. Products to be deleted can be phased out, run out or dropped immediately.

A new product may be an innovation that has never been sold by any organisation, or it can be a product that a given firm has not marketed previously, although similar products have been available from other organisations. Before a product is introduced, it goes through the six phases of new product development. In the idea generation phase, new product ideas may come from internal or external sources. In the process of screening ideas, those with the greatest potential are selected for further review. During the business analysis stage, the product idea is evaluated to determine its potential contribution to the firm's sales, costs and profits. Product development is the stage in which the organisation finds out if it is technically feasible to produce the product and if it can be produced at costs low enough for the final price to be reasonable. Test marketing is a limited introduction of a product in areas chosen to represent the intended market. The decision to enter the commercialisation phase means that full scale production of the product begins and a complete marketing strategy is developed. The process that buyers go through in accepting a product includes awareness, interest, evaluation, trial and adoption.

Product positioning comprises the decisions and activities intended to create and maintain a certain concept of the firm's product (relative to competitive brands) in customers' minds. Product positioning is part of a natural progression when market segmentation is used. A firm can position a product to compete head on with another brand or to avoid competition.

As a product moves through its life-cycle, marketing strategies may require continual adaptation. In the growth stage, it is important to develop brand loyalty and a market position. In the maturity stage, a product may be modified or new market segments may be developed to rejuvenate its sales. A product that is declining may be maintained as long as it makes a contribution to profits or enhances the product mix. Marketers must determine whether to eliminate the declining product or to re-position it to extend its life.

IMPORTANT TERMS

Product manager	New product development
Brand manager	Idea generation
Marketing manager	Screening ideas
Venture or project team	Business analysis
Product portfolio approach	Product development
Product modification	Test marketing
Quality modifications	Commercialisation
Functional modifications	Product adoption process
Style modifications	Product positioning
Product deletion	

DISCUSSION AND REVIEW QUESTIONS

1. What organisational alternatives are available to a firm with two product lines, each consisting of four product items?
2. When is it more appropriate to use a product manager than a marketing manager? When might an alternative or combined approach be used?
3. What type of organisation might use a venture team to develop new products? What are the advantages and disadvantages of such a team?
4. Do small companies that manufacture one or two products need to be concerned about developing and managing products? Why or why not?
5. Why is product development a cross-functional activity within an organisation? That is, why must finance, engineering, manufacturing and other functional areas be involved?
6. Develop information sources for new product ideas for the car industry.
7. Some firms believe that they can omit test marketing. What are some of the advantages and disadvantages of test marketing?
8. Under what conditions is product modification appropriate for changing a product mix? How does a quality modification differ from a functional modification? Can an organisation make one modification without making the other?
9. How can a company prolong the life of a mature product? What actions should be taken to try to stem the product's decline?
10. Give several reasons why an organisation might be unable to eliminate an unprofitable product.

9.1   New Product Development and the Concept Car

Car manufacturers are well used to the stresses associated with new product development. The costs and difficulties of the process must be vigorously tackled by companies wishing to generate high sales and remain in the forefront of technological development. In spite of recessionary pressures and falling car sales, the industry is investing in the future with a host of new and revised model designs. The year 1993 witnessed the introduction of the Mercedes-Benz C-Series; Fiat's new three door Tipo and Cinquecento city car, the Alfa Romeo 210 bhp 164 Super and 230 bhp 164 Super Green Cloverleaf; Renault's Safrane, R21 and the new Espace; Peugeot's five door 306, Ford's Sierra replacement, the Mondeo; and Citroën's Xantia, to mention a few. Even those manufacturers not launching new models in the near future are seeking to improve and upgrade their existing portfolios. For example, Jaguar's 1993 range includes improved versions of the well loved XJ6 saloon and XJS sports car.

For many manufacturers, developing so called concept cars is an important part of the new product development process which helps new techniques, technologies, materials and production processes to be tested and evaluated. Renault's striking model, the Racoon, described by the company as a "freedom car of tomorrow", is just one example of the concept cars which appear at motor shows around the world. The four wheel drive vehicle is amphibious, has a telephone, fax machine and computer based navigation aids, and was designed using revolutionary product development techniques. Although the vehicle may look unusual to today's consumers, there are precedents which show that today's concept cars do sometimes appear in showrooms in the future.

When it was introduced at the Geneva motor show, the Aston Martin lagonda Vignale created quite a sensation. However, despite the high performance, excellent standards of accommodation and obvious good looks of the model, this too is a concept car. The company's reason for developing the Vignale was to test the future potential for producing hand built cars by investigating a range of design and production techniques and materials. According to Aston Martin's Lagonda chief executive, Walter Haynes, "There is a place for the handmade luxury car in the future but it has to be fuel efficient and innovative and capable of being a car for life". While the company does not intend to begin commercial production of the Vignale, the development of the car is considered to have been very beneficial to the company's plans for new product development.

Aston Martin is not alone in trying to predict the changes which the twenty-first century will bring. According to the UK Motor Industry Research Association (MIRA), a move towards electrically powered vehicles is likely. It is estimated that by 2010 there may be over 10 million electric cars worldwide, with annual sales running as high as 2 million. The growth seems likely, given increasing concerns about the harmful impact of petrol driven vehicles on the environment. If European companies are to maintain their stake in car production, inevitably they must direct more attention towards developing low emission, electrical vehicle technology. Such programmes will no doubt be accompanied by the development of further concept cars, vehicle trials and long run testing.

Already, the Japanese government is doing much to encourage the development of such technology. So far there has been less activity in Europe, where only the French government displays a similar degree of commitment. According to MIRA's head of automotive services, Dr. Martin White, "People believe the well publicised problems of pollution in Los Angeles are unique to that city and its suburbs sitting as they do in a geographic bowl. But even our own inner-city areas, with their tower blocks and poor air circulation, can suffer the consequences of a similar and relatively effective pollution trap".

Whatever developments the future may bring for car manufacturing, the use of product and concept testing will continue to play an important role in the changing face of car design.

SOURCES: Stewart Smith, "Peugeot keeps it in the family", Telegraph Motoring, *Coventry Evening Telegraph,* 16 March 1993, p. 23; "Citroën peps up Volcane's image", Telegraph Motoring, *Coventry Evening Telegraph*, 16 March 1993, p. 24; "Face of the future", Telegraph Motoring, *Coventry Evening Telegraph*, 16 March 1993, p. 24; "A grand cavalcade", Fast Lane 93, *Coventry Evening Telegraph,* February 1993, pp. 8–9; "Luxurious Lagonda", Fast Lane 93, *Coventry Evening Telegraph*, February 1993, p. 11; "The shape of things to come", Fast Lane 93, *Coventry Evening Telegraph,* February 1993, p. 11.

Questions for Discussion

1. Why is it important for car manufacturers to develop concept cars?
2. What other forms of research and testing are relevant to the launch of a new model?
3. How can consumers' views of concept cars displayed at motor shows feed into the new product development process for production cars?

9.2 Harley-Davidson's Product Management

Harley-Davidson Motor Co., which has its headquarters in Milwaukee, Wisconsin, has come roaring back to profitability after a decade of troubles. Strong competition from Japanese motorcycle manufacturers—Honda, Suzuki, Yamaha and Kawasaki—caused Harley's market share for superheavyweight motorcycles (motorcycles with engine displacements greater than 850 cubic centimeters) to drop from 99.7 per cent in 1972 to 23 per cent in 1983. Harley simply could not compete with Japan's high-tech machines, low prices and attractive designs. Harley executives were forced to re-evaluate their entire organisation. Today Harley is once again the US market share leader for superheavyweight motorcycles with significant sales and brand awareness throughout Europe, largely because of its commitment to new product development and improved product quality.

Realising the importance of product quality, Harley product managers understood that they had to turn to their customers for help. They began surveying customers to determine what was wanted in or on a motorcycle. Harley learned that motorcyclists are very vocal about their likes and dislikes: motorcycle enthusiasts were eager to share their views on Harley products and how they could be improved.

Because of huge growth in the early 1970s, Harley had been more interested in increasing production than in developing new products or improving product quality. The resulting motorcycles were inferior and outdated when compared with Japanese vehicles. When Harley sales figures plummeted, its executives knew that they had to undertake drastic modifications to ensure the company's survival. They increased the annual research and development budget from $2 million to $14 million.

Willie G. Davidson, Harley's Vice-President for styling and the grandson of one of the founders, began to attend motorcycle rallies to gather ideas for potential product innovations. Seeing that many motorcyclists liked to customise their machines, he noted the most promising customer "developments" and suggested that Harley mimic these in the factory. In 1980, Harley engineers created a completely redesigned chassis and a new line of engines ranging from 883 to 1340 cc displacement. Davidson first invented a new model, the Super Glide, and then introduced the Low Rider, the Wide Glide and other successful models.

A senior Vice-President at Harley-Davidson views Davidson as an artistic genius. According to this executive, Davidson performed virtual miracles by simply manipulating transfers and paint in the years before Harley-Davidson was able to bring new engines on stream. Harley's survival may be due to the new models Davidson was able to create by cosmetically changing existing models. The Japanese motorcycle makers started copying Harley designs.

Customer complaints caused the company to introduce its quality audit programme. A few days before a new model, the Café Racer, was scheduled to come off the production line, an employee shocked a Harley executive with news of severe defects in the model. Deciding to make the Café Racer a new symbol of Harley-Davidson product quality, the CEO dispatched a team of engineers, service supervisors and manufacturing managers to correct the problems. It cost the company about $100,000 to mend only 100 Café Racers, but management believed that the investment in quality was worth it.

Harley improved the quality of its products by implementing three integrated programmes: just-in-time manufacturing (called "materials-as-needed", or "MAN", at Harley), statistical operator control (SOC) and heavy reliance on employee involvement. The MAN system freed Harley from a bulky inventory and increased plant productivity. SOC gives assembly line workers responsibility for the quality of individual parts. By consulting with line workers, Harley managers and engineers have been able to improve manufacturing processes and, consequently, improve motorcycles. None of these successful programmes required large capital investment—Harley improved product quality by enhancing procedures.

Harley's product development strategies continue to evolve as the company grows stronger. The company has even called its new power train the Evolution Engine. Clearly, Harley executives are determined to keep their customers happy and the product innovations rolling. Harley's machines are in great demand. In the UK, potential dealers are lining up for approval to stock the latest machines. Media coverage for any new product development is intense and critically positive. Harley's present emphasis on quality products that meet customers' expectations is a far cry from the losing position of the late 1970s.

SOURCES: Vaughn Beals, "Harley-Davidson: an American success story", *Journal for Quality and Participation,* June 1988, pp. A19–A23; Vaughn Beals, "Operation Recovery", *Success,* February 1989, p. 16; "How Harley beat back the Japanese", *Fortune,* 25 September 1989, pp. 155, 157, 162, 164; Tani Mayer, "Harley-Davidson rides high", *Financial World,* 18 October 1988, pp. 16, 18; Gary Miller, "Harley's Teerlink thrives as rank-and-file kind of guy", *Business Journal,* Milwaukee, Wisconsin, 17 July 1989, TRN 39: E9.

Questions for Discussion

1. Why did Harley's share of the superheavyweight motorcycle market drop so drastically between 1972 and 1983?
2. What sources did Harley use to generate new product ideas?
3. What steps has Harley taken to regain its competitiveness?

PART III

DISTRIBUTION (PLACE) DECISIONS

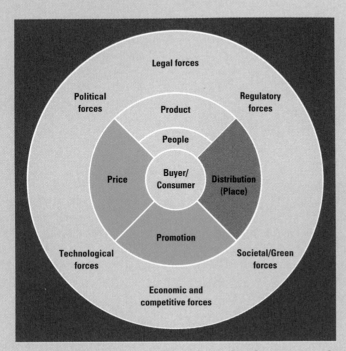

Providing customers with satisfying products is important but not enough for successful marketing strategies. These products must also be available in adequate quantities in accessible locations at the times when customers desire them. The chapters in Part III deal with the distribution of products and the marketing channels and institutions that provide the structure for making products available. Chapter 10 discusses the structure and functions of marketing channels and presents an overview of institutions that make up these channels. Chapter 11 analyses the types of wholesalers and their functions. Chapter 12 focuses on retailing and retailers, specifically, the types of retailers and their roles and functions in marketing channels. Finally, Chapter 13 analyses the decisions and activities associated with the physical distribution of products, such as order processing, materials handling, warehousing, inventory management and transport. ∎

10 MARKETING CHANNELS

Objectives

To understand the marketing channel concept and the types of marketing intermediaries in the channel

To discuss the justification of channel members

To examine the structure and function of the channel system

To explore the power dimensions of channels, especially the concepts of co-operation, conflict and leadership

*T*he face of toy retailing is changing. The small, traditional, town centre outlet is under siege from out of town retail shed and catalogue showrooms such as Argos and Children's World. Both types of outlet offer the consumer more competitive prices and greater variety than ever before. Indeed, the catalogue showrooms seem to encourage the consumer to cut out personal shopping altogether; children's noses pressed against the shop window could become a sight of the past.

Toys "Я" Us is almost certainly the best known of the retail toy sheds. To achieve this position, the company underwent considerable expansion through the 1980s, which accelerated towards the decade's end. In the company's major markets in the US, Canada, UK, Germany and France, growth has been organic, through ownership. Meanwhile, joint venture deals have aided expansion into Singapore, Hong Kong, Malaysia and Taiwan. But wherever they come from, the customers encounter few surprises. One Toys "Я" Us looks pretty much like another in size, styling and product assortment. In each of the company's markets, sourcing is relatively straightforward. The outcome is a standard customer offering with a solid 80 per cent of the different product lines sold the same in each of the company's stores.

Where the stores are sited depends on the location of local warehousing. Although store design allows for 40 per cent of usable space to be given over to warehousing, the high level of off-peak buying demands further facilities. Policy in the US has been to back up a group of between three and six stores with local warehousing, but in Europe and other overseas markets it is not always possible to provide this level of support. ∎

SOURCES: S. N. Chakravarty, "Will toys 'b' great?", *Forbes,* 22 February 1988; A. Dunkin, K. H. Hammonds and M. Maremont, "How Toys "Я" Us controls the game board", *Business Week,* 19 December 1988, pp. 58–60; Risto Laulajainen, "Two retailers go global: the geographical dimension", *The International Review of Retail, Distribution and Consumer Research,* 1 October 1991, pp. 607–26; M. J. Schoifet and H. Gralla, "The king of the category killers", *Shopping Centers Today,* May 1990, pp. 27–30; Toys "Я" Us, UK HQ.

Distribution refers to activities that make products available to customers when and where they want to purchase them. It is sometimes referred to as the *Place* element in the marketing mix of the *Ps:* Product, Place (distribution), Promotion, Price and People. Choosing which channels of distribution to use is a major decision in the development of marketing strategies.

This chapter focuses on the description and analysis of channels of distribution, or marketing channels, first discussing the main types of channels and their structures and then explaining the need for intermediaries, as well as analysing the functions they perform. Next are outlined several forms of channel integration. Consideration is given to how marketers determine the appropriate intensity of market coverage for a product and how they consider a number of factors when selecting suitable channels of distribution. After examining behavioural patterns within marketing channels, the chapter concludes by looking at several legal issues affecting channel management.

THE STRUCTURES AND TYPES OF MARKETING CHANNELS

A **channel of distribution** (sometimes called a **marketing channel**) is a group of individuals and organisations that direct the flow of products from producers to customers. Providing customer benefits should be the driving force behind all marketing channel activities. Buyers' needs and behaviour are therefore important concerns of channel members.

Making products available benefits customers. Channels of distribution make products available at the right time, in the right place, and in the right quantity by providing such product enhancing functions as transport and storage. Although consumers do not see the distribution of a product, they value the product availability that channels of distribution make possible. Consumers soon complain when a channel breaks down and their desired product or service is suddenly unavailable.

Most, but not all, channels of distribution have marketing intermediaries. A **marketing intermediary,** or middleman, links producers to other middlemen or to ultimate users of the products. Marketing intermediaries perform the activities described in Table 10.1. There are two major types of intermediaries: merchants and functional middlemen (agents and brokers). **Merchants** take title to products and resell them, whereas **functional middlemen** do not take title.

Both retailers and wholesalers are intermediaries. Retailers purchase products for the purpose of reselling them to ultimate consumers. Merchant wholesalers resell products to other wholesalers and to retailers. Functional wholesalers, such as agents and brokers, expedite exchanges among producers and resellers and are compensated by fees or commissions. For purposes of discussion in this chapter, all wholesalers are considered merchant middlemen unless otherwise specified.

Channel members share certain significant characteristics. Each member has different responsibilities within the overall structure of the distribution system, but mutual profit and success can be attained only if channel members co-operate in delivering products to the market.

Although distribution decisions need not precede other marketing decisions, they do exercise a powerful influence on the rest of the marketing mix. Channel decisions are critical because they determine a product's market presence and buyers' accessibility to the product. The strategic significance of these decisions is further heightened by the fact that they entail long term commitments. For example, it is much easier for

TABLE 10.1 *Marketing channel activities that intermediaries perform*

CATEGORY OF MARKETING ACTIVITIES	POSSIBLE ACTIVITIES REQUIRED
Marketing information	Analyse information such as sales data; perform or commission marketing research studies
Marketing management	Establish objectives; plan activities; manage and co-ordinate financing, personnel and risk taking; evaluate and control channel activities
Facilitating exchange	Choose and stock product assortments that match the needs of buyers
Promotion	Set promotional objectives, co-ordinate advertising, personal selling, sales promotion, publicity, direct mail and packaging
Price	Establish pricing policies and terms of sales
Physical distribution	Manage transport, warehousing, materials handling, inventory control and communication

an organisation to change prices or packaging than to change distribution systems already in place.

Because the marketing channel most appropriate for one product may be less suitable for another, many different distribution paths have been developed in most countries. The links in any channel, however, are the merchants (including producers) and agents who oversee the movement of products through that channel. Although there are many various marketing channels, they can be classified generally as channels for consumer products or channels for industrial products.

Channels for Consumer Products

Figure 10.1 illustrates several channels used in the distribution of consumer products. Besides the channels listed, a manufacturer may use sales branches or sales offices.

Channel A describes the direct movement of goods from producer to consumers. Customers who pick their own fruit from commercial orchards or buy double glazing from door-to-door salespeople are acquiring products through a direct channel. A producer who sells goods directly from the factory to end users and ultimate consumers is using a direct marketing channel. Although this channel is the simplest, it is not necessarily the cheapest or the most efficient method of distribution.

Channel B, which moves goods from producer to retailers and then to consumers, is the frequent choice of large retailers, for they can buy in quantity from a manufacturer. Such retailers as Marks & Spencer, Sainsbury, Aldi and Carrefour, for example, sell clothing, food and many other items they have purchased directly from the producers. Cars are also commonly sold through this type of marketing channel.

A long standing distribution channel, especially for consumer products, channel C takes goods from producer to wholesalers, then to retailers, and finally to consumers. This option is very practical for a producer who sells to hundreds of thousands of consumers through thousands of retailers. A single producer finds it hard to do business directly with thousands of retailers. For example, consider the number of retailers that market Wrigley's chewing gum. It would be extremely difficult, if not impossible, for

FIGURE 10.1
Typical marketing channels for consumer products

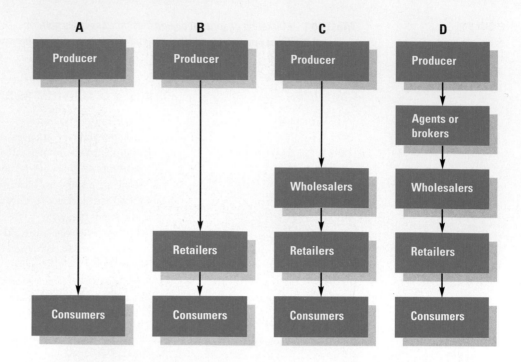

Wrigley's to deal directly with all the retailers that sell its brand of gum. Manufacturers of tobacco products, alcoholic beverages, some home appliances, hardware and many convenience goods sell their products to wholesalers, who then sell to retailers, who in turn do business with individual consumers.

Channel D—through which goods pass from producer to agents to wholesalers to retailers, and only then to consumers—is frequently used for products intended for mass distribution, such as processed food. For example, to place its biscuit line in specific retail outlets, a food processor may hire an agent (or a food broker) to sell the biscuits to wholesalers. The wholesalers then sell the biscuits to supermarkets, vending machine operators and other retail outlets.

Contrary to popular opinion, a long channel may be the most efficient distribution channel for certain consumer goods. When several channel intermediaries are available to perform specialised functions, costs may be lower than if one channel member is responsible for all the functions in all territories.

Channels for Industrial Products

Figure 10.2 shows four of the most common channels for industrial products. As with consumer products, manufacturers of industrial products sometimes work with more than one level of wholesalers.

Channel E illustrates the direct channel for industrial products. In contrast with consumer goods, many industrial products—especially expensive equipment, such as steam generators, aircraft and mainframe computers—are sold directly to the buyers. For example, GEC sells its huge power station generating turbines directly to the generating authorities and large corporate buyers. The direct channel is most feasible for many manufacturers of industrial goods because they have fewer customers, and those customers may be clustered geographically. Buyers of complex industrial products can also receive technical assistance from the manufacturer more easily in a direct channel.

If a particular line of industrial products is aimed at a larger number of customers, the manufacturer may use a marketing channel which includes industrial distributors, merchants who take title to products (channel F). Construction products made by

FIGURE 10.2
Typical marketing channels for industrial products

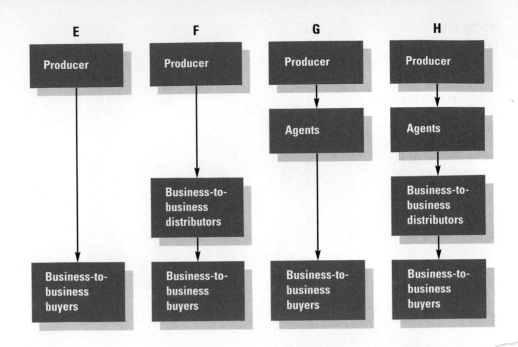

Case or JCB, for example, are sold through industrial distributors. Building materials, operating supplies and air conditioning equipment are frequently channelled through industrial distributors.

Channel G—producer to agents to industrial buyers—is often the choice when a manufacturer without a marketing department needs market information, when a company is too small to field its own sales force or when a firm wants to introduce a new product or to enter a new market without using its own salespeople. Thus a large soya bean producer might sell its product to animal food processors through an agent.

Channel H is a variation of channel G: goods move from producer to agents to industrial distributors and then to industrial buyers. A manufacturer without a sales force may rely on this channel if its industrial customers purchase products in small quantities or if they must be resupplied frequently and therefore need access to decentralised inventories. Japanese manufacturers of electronic components, for example, work through export agents who sell to industrial distributors serving small producers or dealers overseas. Chapter 23 presents more information about marketing channels for industrial products.

Multiple Marketing Channels

To reach diverse target markets, a manufacturer may use several marketing channels simultaneously, with each channel involving a different group of intermediaries. For example, a manufacturer turns to multiple channels when the same product is directed to both consumers and industrial customers. When Twinings sells tea bags for household use, the tea bags are sold to supermarkets through grocery wholesalers or, in some cases, directly to the retailers, whereas the tea bags going to restaurants or institutions follow a different distribution channel. In some instances, a producer may prefer **dual distribution**: the use of two or more marketing channels for distributing the same products to the same target market. Villeroy & Boch is a respected supplier of fine china and glassware to households across the world. The company also has ranges for the catering industry, sold and promoted through a separate marketing channel (see Figure 10.3). Dual distribution can cause dissatisfaction among wholesalers and smaller retailers.

FIGURE 10.3

Dual distribution
Villeroy & Boch produces fine china and glassware, retailed to consumers through department stores and specialist china stores. The company also produces ranges aimed at the catering industry, promoted in specialist trade magazines.

SOURCE: Courtesy of Villeroy & Boch.

JUSTIFICATIONS FOR INTERMEDIARIES

Even if producers and buyers are located in the same city, there are costs associated with exchanges. As Figure 10.4 shows, if 5 buyers purchase the products of 5 producers, 25 transactions are required. If a single intermediary serves both producers and buyers, the number of transactions can be reduced to 10. Intermediaries become specialists in facilitating exchanges. They provide valuable assistance because of their access to, and control over, important resources for the proper functioning of the marketing channel.

Nevertheless, the press, consumers, public officials and marketers freely criticise intermediaries, especially wholesalers. Table 10.2 indicates that in a recent US survey of the general public 74 per cent believed that "wholesalers frequently make high profits, significantly increasing prices the consumers pay". The critics accuse wholesalers of being inefficient and parasitic, and consumers often wish to make the distribution channel as short as possible. Consumers assume that the fewer the intermediaries, the lower the prices of goods sold to them. It is obvious that, because threats to eliminate them come from both ends of the marketing channel, wholesalers must be careful to perform only those marketing activities that are truly desired. To survive, they must be more efficient and more service orientated than alternative marketing institutions.

Critics who suggest that eliminating wholesalers would lower prices for consumers do not recognise that this would not eliminate the need for the services wholesalers

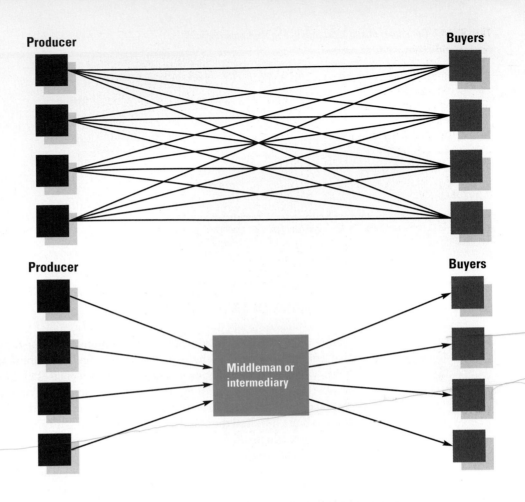

FIGURE 10.4
Efficiency in exchanges provided by an intermediary

Producer　　　　　　　　　　　　　　　　　Buyers

Producer　　　　　　　　　　　　　　　　　Buyers

Middleman or intermediary

provide. Other institutions would have to perform those services, and consumers would still have to fund them. In addition, all producers would have to deal directly with retailers or consumers, meaning that every producer would have to keep voluminous records and recruit enough personnel to deal with every customer. Even in a direct channel, consumers might end up paying a great deal more for products because prices would reflect the costs of inefficient producers' operations.

To illustrate the efficient service that wholesalers provide, assume that all wholesalers were eliminated. Because there are millions of retail stores in Europe, a widely purchased consumer product—say confectionery—would require an extraordinary number of sales contacts, possibly more than a million, to maintain the current level of product exposure. For example, Mars would have to deliver its confectionery, purchase and service thousands of vending machines, establish warehouses all over Europe and maintain fleets of delivery vans. Selling and distribution costs for confectionery would rocket. Instead of a few contacts with food brokers, large retail organisations and various merchant wholesalers, confectionery manufacturers would face hundreds of thousands of expensive contacts with and shipments to smaller retailers. Such an operation would be highly inefficient, and its costs would necessarily be passed on to consumers. Chocolate bars would cost more, and they would be much harder to find. Ultimately it is clear that wholesalers provide a far more efficient and less expensive service not only for manufacturers but for consumers as well.

TABLE 10.2 *Consumer misunderstanding about wholesalers*

Statement: *Wholesalers frequently make high profits, significantly increasing the prices consumers pay.*

	TOTAL %	MALE %	FEMALE %
Strongly agree	35.5	33	38
Somewhat agree	38	40	36
Neither agree nor disagree	16	14	18
Somewhat disagree	8	9	7
Strongly disagree	2.5	4	1

SOURCE: O. C. Ferrell and William M. Pride, National multistage area probability sample of 2,045 households, 1985. Reprinted by permission of the authors.

FUNCTIONS OF INTERMEDIARIES

Before the functions of intermediaries are examined in some detail, it should be noted that a distribution network helps overcome two major distribution problems. Consider a firm which manufactures jeans. The company specialises in the goods it can produce most efficiently: denim clothing. To make jeans the most economical way possible, the producer turns out a hundred thousand pairs of jeans each day. Few persons, however, want to buy a hundred thousand pairs of jeans. Thus the quantity of jeans that the company can produce efficiently is more than the average customer wants. The result is called a *discrepancy in quantity.*

An **assortment** is a combination of products put together to provide benefits. A consumer creates and holds an assortment. The set of products made available to customers is an organisation's assortment. Most consumers want a broad assortment of products. In addition to jeans, a consumer wants to buy shoes, food, a car, a stereo, soft drinks and many other products. Yet our jeans manufacturer has a narrow assortment because it makes only jeans (and perhaps a few other denim clothes). There is a *discrepancy in assortment* because a consumer wants a broad assortment but an individual manufacturer produces a narrow assortment.

Quantity and assortment discrepancies are resolved through the sorting activities of intermediaries in a marketing channel. **Sorting activities** are functions that allow channel members to divide roles and separate tasks. Sorting activities, as Figure 10.5 shows, may be grouped into four main tasks: sorting out, accumulation, allocation, and assorting of products.[1]

Sorting Out

Sorting out, the first step in developing an assortment, is the separating of conglomerates of heterogeneous products into relatively uniform, homogeneous groups based on product characteristics such as size, shape, weight or colour. Sorting out is especially common in the marketing of agricultural products and other raw materials, which vary widely in size, grade and quality and would be largely unusable in an undifferentiated mass. A tomato crop, for example, must be sorted into tomatoes suitable for canning, those suitable for making tomato juice and those to be sold in retail food stores.

Sorting out for specific products follows a set of predetermined standards. The sorter must know how many classifications to use and the criteria for each classification, and must usually provide for a group of miscellaneous left-overs as well. Certain

FIGURE 10.5
Sorting activities conducted by intermediaries

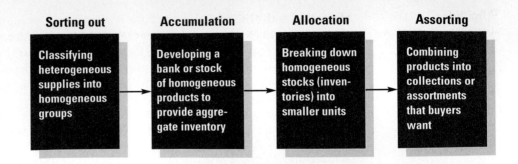

Sorting out	Accumulation	Allocation	Assorting
Classifying heterogeneous supplies into homogeneous groups	Developing a bank or stock of homogeneous products to provide aggregate inventory	Breaking down homogeneous stocks (inventories) into smaller units	Combining products into collections or assortments that buyers want

product characteristics can be categorised more easily than others; appearance and size of agricultural products are more readily apparent than flavour or nutritional content, for instance. Because the overall quality of a crop or supply of raw material is likely to vary from year to year or from region to region, classifications must be somewhat flexible.

Changing consumer needs and new manufacturing techniques influence the sorting out process. If sorting out results in manufactured goods with minor defects, these damaged or irregular products are often marketed at lower prices through factory outlet stores, which are growing in consumer popularity. Improved processing also permits the use of materials that might have been culled previously, such as the paper and aluminum now being recycled. In some industries, producers have stopped using natural materials because the manufacturing process demands the greater uniformity possible only with synthetic materials. Sorting out thus helps alleviate discrepancies in assortment by making relatively homogeneous products available for the next step, accumulation.

Accumulation

Accumulation is the development of a bank or inventory of homogeneous products which have similar production or demand requirements. Farmers who grow relatively small quantities of tomatoes, for example, transport their sorted tomatoes to central collection points, where they are accumulated in large lots for movement into the next level of the channel.

Combining many small groups of similar products into larger groups serves several purposes. Products move through subsequent marketing channels more economically in large quantities because transport rates are lower for bulk loads. In addition, accumulation gives buyers a steady supply of products in large volumes. If Del Monte had to make frequent purchases of small amounts of tomatoes from individual farmers, the company's tomato products would be produced much less efficiently. Instead, Del Monte buys bulk loads of tomatoes through brokers, thus maintaining a continuous supply of uniform quality materials for processing. Accumulation lets producers continuously use up stocks and replenish them, thus minimising losses from interruptions in the supply of materials.

For both buyer and seller, accumulation also alleviates some of the problems associated with price fluctuations and highly seasonal materials. Buyers may obtain large volume purchases at lower prices because sellers are anxious to dispose of perishable goods; purchasing agents may accumulate stocks of materials in anticipation of price rises. In other cases, sellers may receive higher prices because they enter into long-term supply contracts with producers or they agree to store accumulated materials until the producer is ready for them. Accumulation thus relieves discrepancies in quantity. It enables intermediaries to build up specialised inventories and allocate products according to customers' needs.

Allocation is the breaking down of large homogeneous inventories into smaller lots. This process, which addresses discrepancies in quantity, enables wholesalers to buy efficiently in lorry or container loads and then apportion products by cases to other channel members. A food wholesaler, for instance, serves as a depot, allocating products according to market demand. The wholesaler may divide a single lorry load of Del Monte canned tomatoes among several retail food stores.

Because supply and demand are seldom in perfect balance, allocation is influenced by several factors (and can sometimes resemble rationing). At times price is the overriding consideration. The highest bidder, or perhaps the buyer placing the largest order, is allocated most of the stock. At other times an intermediary gives preference to customers whose loyalty has been established or to those whose businesses show the most growth potential. In still other cases, products are allocated through compromise and negotiation.

Depending on the product, allocation may begin with the manufacturer and continue through several levels of intermediaries, including retailers. Allocation ends when the ultimate user selects the desired quantity of a particular product from the assortment of products available.

Assorting is the process of combining products into collections or assortments which buyers want to have available in one place. Assorting eliminates discrepancies in assortment by grouping products to satisfy buyers. The same food wholesaler that supplies supermarkets with Del Monte tomato products may also buy canned goods from competing food processors so that grocery stores can choose from a wide assortment of canned fruits and vegetables.

Buyers want an assortment of products at one location because of some task they want to perform or some problem they want solved. A buyer looking for a variety of products, all serving different purposes, requires a broad assortment from which to choose; a buyer with more precise needs or interests will seek out a narrower, and deeper, product assortment.

Assorting is especially important to retailers, and they strive to create assortments that match the demands of consumers who patronise their stores. Although no single customer is likely to buy one of everything in the store, a retailer must anticipate the probability of purchase and provide a satisfactory range of product choices. The risk involved is greater for some retailers than for others. For example, supermarkets purchase staple foods repeatedly, and these items can be stocked with little risk. But clothing retailers who misjudge consumer demand for "hot" fashion items can lose money if their assortments contain too few (or too many) of these products. Discrepancies in assortment reappear, in fact, when retailers fail to keep pace with shifts in consumer attitudes. New specialists—such as retail outlets for computer products or video games—may even enter the market to provide assortments existing retailers do not offer.

Channel Integration

Channel functions may be transferred among intermediaries and to producers and even customers. This section examines how channel members can either combine and control most activities or pass them on to another channel member. Remember, though, that the channel member cannot eliminate functions; unless buyers themselves perform the functions, they must pay for the labour and resources needed for the functions to be performed. The statement that "you can eliminate middlemen but you can't eliminate their functions" is an accepted principle of marketing.

Many marketing channels are determined by consensus. Producers and intermediaries co-ordinate their efforts for mutual benefit. Some marketing channels, however, are organised and controlled by a single leader, which can be a producer, a wholesaler, or a retailer, depending on the industry. The channel leader may establish channel policies and co-ordinate the development of the marketing mix. Marks & Spencer and IKEA, for example, are channel leaders for several of the many products they sell.

The various links or stages of the channel may be combined under the management of a channel leader either horizontally or vertically. Integration may stabilise supply, reduce costs, and increase co-ordination of channel members.

Vertical Channel Integration

Combining two or more stages of the channel under one management is **vertical channel integration.** One member of a marketing channel may purchase the operations of another member or simply perform the functions of the other member, eliminating the need for that intermediary as a separate entity. Total vertical integration encompasses all functions from production to ultimate buyer; it is exemplified by oil companies that own oil wells, pipelines, refineries, terminals and service stations.

Whereas members of conventional channel systems work independently and seldom co-operate, participants in vertical channel integration co-ordinate their efforts to reach a desired target market. This more progressive approach to distribution enables channel members to regard other members as extensions of their own operations. At one end of an integrated channel, for example, a manufacturer might provide advertising and training assistance, and the retailer at the other end would buy the manufacturer's products in quantity and actively promote them.

In the past, integration has been successfully institutionalised in marketing channels called vertical marketing systems. A **vertical marketing system** (**VMS**) is a marketing channel in which a single channel member co-ordinates or manages channel activities to achieve efficient, low cost distribution aimed at satisfying target market customers. Because the efforts of individual channel members are combined in a VMS, marketing activities can be co-ordinated for maximum effectiveness and economy, without duplication of services. Vertical marketing systems are also competitive, accounting for a growing share of retail sales in consumer goods.

Most vertical marketing systems today take one of three forms: corporate, administered or contractual. The *corporate* VMS combines all stages of the marketing channel, from producers to consumers, under a single ownership. For example, Shell (see Figure 10.6) established a corporate VMS operating corporate owned production facilities and service stations. Supermarket chains that own food processing plants and large retailers that purchase wholesaling and production facilities are other examples of corporate VMSs. Figure 10.7 contrasts a conventional marketing channel with a VMS, which consolidates marketing functions and institutions.

In an *administered* VMS, channel members are independent, but a high level of inter-organisational management is achieved by informal co-ordination. Members of an administered VMS may agree, for example, to adopt uniform accounting and ordering procedures and to co-operate in promotional activities. Although individual channel members maintain their autonomy, as in conventional marketing channels, one channel member (such as the producer or a large retailer) dominates the administered VMS, so that distribution decisions take into account the system as a whole. Because of its size and power as a retailer, Marks & Spencer exercises a strong influence over the independent manufacturers in its marketing channels, as do Kellogg's (cereals) and Volvo (cars and trucks).

Under a *contractual* VMS, the most popular type of vertical marketing system, inter-organisational relationships are formalised through contracts. Channel members are linked by legal agreements that spell out each member's rights and obligations. For in-

Where do you find vast wheat fields with perfect water-skiing?

Europe. One place more than ever, but still home to an incredible diversity of lifestyles and cultures. And, as a company that has grown from this diversity,

Shell sees it as an opportunity, not an obstacle. In the wheat fields of Northern Germany, for example, a herbicide developed by Shell helps

maintain the yield of the summer harvest. Meanwhile, in the Greek Islands, tourists' speedboats no longer foul the seawater thanks

to Shell's new biodegradable marine engine oil. Small things, perhaps, to a big corporation. But not to a local company. A company like Shell.

FIGURE 10.6 *Corporate vertical marketing system (VMS)*
With control of oil and gas fields, refineries, distribution depots and garage forecourts, Shell has created a corporate VMS.

SOURCE: Courtesy of Shell Chemicals.

stance, franchise organisations such as McDonald's and Kentucky Fried Chicken are contractual VMSs. Other contractual VMSs include wholesaler sponsored groups such as Mace or IGA (Independent Grocers' Alliance) stores, in which independent retailers band together under the contractual leadership of a wholesaler. Retailer sponsored co-operatives, which own and operate their own wholesalers, are a third type of contractual VMS.

Horizontal Channel Integration

Combining institutions at the same level of operation under one management constitutes **horizontal channel integration.** An organisation may integrate horizontally by merging with other organisations at the same level in a marketing channel level. For example, the owner of a dry cleaning firm might buy and combine several other existing dry cleaning establishments. Horizontal integration may enable a firm to generate sufficient sales revenue to integrate vertically as well.

Although horizontal integration permits efficiencies and economies of scale in purchasing, marketing research, advertising and specialised personnel, it is not always the most effective method of improving distribution. Problems of "bigness" often follow, resulting in decreased flexibility, difficulties in co-ordination, and the need for additional marketing research and large scale planning. Unless distribution functions for the various units can be performed more efficiently under unified management than under the previously separate managements, horizontal integration will not reduce costs or improve the competitive position of the integrating firm.

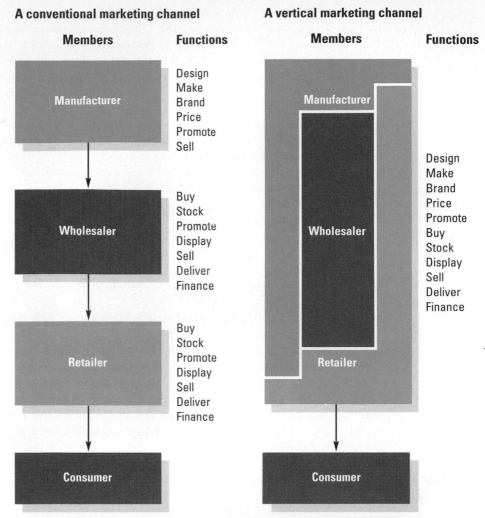

A conventional marketing channel

Members   Functions

Manufacturer — Design / Make / Brand / Price / Promote / Sell

Wholesaler — Buy / Stock / Promote / Display / Sell / Deliver / Finance

Retailer — Buy / Stock / Promote / Display / Sell / Deliver / Finance

Consumer

A vertical marketing channel

Members   Functions

Manufacturer

Wholesaler — Design / Make / Brand / Price / Promote / Buy / Stock / Display / Sell / Deliver / Finance

Retailer

Consumer

SOURCE: Adapted figure from *Strategic Marketing,* by David J. Kollat et al., copyright © 1972 by The Dryden Press, a division of Holt, Rinehart and Winston, Inc., reprinted by permission of the publisher.

INTENSITY OF MARKET COVERAGE

Characteristics of the product and the target market determine the kind of coverage a product should get, that is, the number and kinds of outlets in which it is sold. To achieve the desired intensity of market coverage, distribution must correspond to the behaviour patterns of buyers. Chapter 7 divides consumer products into three categories—convenience products, shopping products and specialty products—according to how consumers make purchases. In considering products for purchase, consumers take into account the replacement rate, product adjustment (services), duration of consumption, time required to find the product and similar factors.[2] These variables directly affect the intensity of market coverage. Three major levels of market coverage are intensive, selective and exclusive distribution.

Intensive Distribution

In **intensive distribution,** all available outlets are used for distributing a product. Intensive distribution is appropriate for convenience products such as bread, chewing-gum, beer and newspapers. To consumers, availability means a store located nearby and minimum time necessary to search for the product at the store. Sales may have a direct relationship to availability. The successful sale of bread and milk at service stations or of petrol at convenience grocery stores has shown that the availability of these products is more important than the nature of the outlet. Convenience products have a high replacement rate and require almost no service. To meet these demands, intensive distribution is necessary, and multiple channels may be used to sell through all possible outlets.

Producers of packaged consumer items rely on intensive distribution. In fact, intensive distribution is one of Procter & Gamble's key strengths. It is fairly easy for this company to formulate marketing strategies for many of its products (soaps, detergents, food and juice products, and personal care products) because consumers want availability provided quickly and intensively.

Selective Distribution

In **selective distribution,** only some available outlets in an area are chosen to distribute a product. Selective distribution is appropriate for shopping products. Durable goods such as electrical appliances and stereos usually fall into this category. Such products are more expensive than convenience goods. Consumers are willing to spend more searching time visiting several retail outlets to compare prices, designs, styles and other features.

Selective distribution is desirable when a special effort—such as customer service from a channel member—is important. Shopping products require differentiation at the point of purchase. To motivate retailers to provide adequate pre-sale service, selective distribution and company owned stores are often used. Many industrial products are sold on a selective basis to maintain a certain degree of control over the distribution process. For example, agricultural herbicides are distributed on a selective basis because dealers must offer services to buyers, such as instructions about how to apply the herbicides safely or the option of having the dealer apply the herbicide.

Exclusive Distribution

In **exclusive distribution,** only one outlet is used in a relatively large geographic area. Exclusive distribution is suitable for products that are purchased rather infrequently, consumed over a long period of time, or require service or information to fit them to buyers' needs. Exclusive distribution is not appropriate for convenience products and many shopping products. It is often used as an incentive to sellers when only a limited market is available for products. For example, cars such as the Aston Martin are sold on an exclusive basis. Royal Copenhagen's premium china is retailed through carefully selected, exclusive retail outlets (see Figure 10.8). A producer who uses exclusive distribution generally expects a dealer to be very co-operative with respect to carrying a complete inventory, sending personnel for sales and service training, participating in promotional programmes and providing excellent customer service.

SELECTION OF DISTRIBUTION CHANNELS

The process of selecting appropriate distribution channels for a product is often complex for a variety of reasons. Producers must choose specific intermediaries carefully, evaluating their sales and profit levels, performance records, other products carried, clientele, availability and so forth. But producers must also examine other factors that influence distribution channel selection, including organisational objectives and resources, market characteristics, buyer behaviour, product attributes and environmental forces.

FIGURE 10.8 *Using exclusive distribution*
Royal Copenhagen china controls its choice of retail outlets.

SOURCE: Royal Copenhagen A/S Denmark.

**Organisational
Objectives and
Resources**

A producer must consider what it is trying to accomplish in the market-place and what resources can be brought to bear on the task. A company's objectives may be broad—such as higher profits, increased market share and greater responsiveness to customers—or narrow, such as replacing an intermediary that has left the channel. The organisation may possess sufficient financial and marketing clout to control its distribution channels—for example, by engaging in direct marketing or by operating its own fleet of lorries. On the other hand, an organisation may have no interest in performing distribution services or may be forced by lack of resources and experience to depend on middlemen.

The company must also evaluate the effectiveness of past distribution relationships and methods in light of its current goals. One firm might decide to maintain its basic channel structure but add members for increased coverage in new territories. Another company might alter its distribution channel so as to provide same-day delivery on all orders. When selecting distribution channels, organisational factors and objectives are important considerations.

**Market
Characteristics**

Beyond the basic division between consumer markets and industrial markets, several market variables influence the design of distribution channels. Geography is one factor; in most cases, the greater the distance between the producer and its markets, the less expensive is distribution through intermediaries rather than through direct sales. A related consideration is market density. If customers tend to be clustered in several locations, the producer may be able to eliminate middlemen. Transport, storage, communication and negotiation are specific functions performed more efficiently in high density markets. Market size—measured by the number of potential customers in a consumer or industrial market—is yet another variable. Direct sales may be effective if a producer has relatively few buyers for a product, but for larger markets the services of middlemen may be required.[3]

Buyer Behaviour

Buyer behaviour is a crucial consideration in selecting distribution channels. To be able to match intermediaries with customers, the producer must have specific, current information about customers who are buying the product and when and where they are buying it.[4] How customers buy is important as well. A manufacturer might find direct selling economically feasible for large volume sales but inappropriate for small orders.

The producer must also understand how buyer specifications vary according to whether buyers perceive products as convenience, shopping or specialty items (see Chapter 7). Customers for chewing gum, for example, are likely to buy the product frequently (even impulsively) from a variety of outlets. Buyers of home computers, however, carefully evaluate product features, dealers, prices and after sales services. Buying patterns influence the selection of channels.

Buyers may be reached most effectively when producers are creative in opening up new distribution channels. In the UK, effective distribution, the essential tool in the highly competitive soft drinks sector, is forcing brand leader Coca-Cola and Schweppes Beverages (CCSB) to find creative ways of extending distribution. CCSB has launched a company, Vendleader, to increase penetration of sales through vending machines.

Product Attributes

Another variable in the selection of distribution channels is the product itself. Because producers of complex industrial products must often provide technical services to buyers both before and after the sale, these products are usually shipped directly to buyers. Perishable or highly fashionable consumer products with short shelf lives are also marketed through short channels. In other cases, distribution patterns are influenced by the product's value; the lower the price per unit, the longer the distribution chain. Additional factors to consider are the weight, bulkiness and relative ease of handling the products. Producers may find wholesalers and retailers reluctant to carry items that create storage or display problems.[5]

Environmental Forces

Finally, producers making decisions about distribution channels must consider forces in the total marketing environment—that is, such issues as competition, ecology, economic conditions, technology, society and law. Technology, for example, has made possible electronic scanners, computerised inventory systems such as EPOS (electronic point of sale) and electronic shopping devices, all of which are altering present distribution systems and making it harder for technologically unsophisticated firms to remain competitive. Changing family patterns and the emergence of important minority consumer groups are driving producers to seek new distribution methods for reaching market segments, and sometimes this search results in non-traditional approaches which increase competitive pressures. Interest rates, inflation and other economic variables affect members of distribution channels at every level. Environmental forces are numerous and complex and must be taken into account if distribution efforts are to be appropriate, efficient and effective. EC regulation changes in 1993 had an impact on the retailing of cars, described in Marketing Insight 10.1.

CAR DISTRIBUTION IN THE EC

For decades, most car manufacturers have maintained networks in Europe for retailing and servicing their models alone. In Germany, Portugal or the UK car showrooms are decked out in the corporate colours of BMW, Saab or Rover. A few showrooms are owned by the manufacturers themselves: French manufacturers Citroën and Renault operate a small proportion of the Citroën and Renault retail outlets in several countries. On the whole, however, car showrooms are owned by companies independent of the manufacturers on whose behalf they display, stock, sell and service vehicles.

Manufacturers design and produce vehicles with the intention of gaining market share and making profits. The showroom franchise holders also want to make profits. Despite this interdependent relationship, the power and control have tended to be in the hands of the manufacturers. Dealerships are often one off sites, with the owner's business focused on one showroom. Even where there are larger groups—companies such as Lex or Quicks, for example, operate 20 or so showrooms—power has still remained with the manufacturer.

The leverage and coercion would vary depending on the power of the brand. Marques such as BMW or Mercedes put significantly more pressure on dealers than did Skoda or Yugo to comply with uniform showroom designs, layouts, selling techniques, discounting and payment terms.

Most manufacturers in the past used their position to establish control over their dealers' stock levels, site standards, training of personnel, computing systems and financial arrangements. Consequently, most showrooms sold only one manufacturer's vehicles.

With the relaxation of trading regulations in the EC in 1993, dealers have found the power shifting towards them. The more powerful, desirable marques still exercise significant control over their dealers, who want very much to match these manufacturers' standards. Nevertheless, change has occurred at all levels.

Some dealers have introduced a second manufacturer's models alongside their existing franchise. Others have built separate showrooms adjacent to their existing operation, offering the consumer several manufacturers' cars at one location. Dealers have started to specialise: the four wheel drive, off road showroom containing vehicles from five or six manufacturers; or high performance sports coupes from several manufacturers under one roof. Even large retail groups are considering entering the market to sell family vehicles from a variety of manufacturers under one roof. The balance of power is no longer so firmly in the hands of the major car manufacturers.

SOURCES: "Car firms push ahead," Robert Dwek, *Marketing,* 14 January 1993. p. 2; Willem Molle, "The economics of European integration", Aldershot: Dartmouth, 1990; Guy de Jonquieres and David Buchan, "Japanese car import agreement threatened by EC disarray", *Financial Times*, 25 September 1990, p. 1c; Paolo Cecchini, "The European challenge 1992", Wildwood House, 1988; and Tony Cutler, Colin Haslam, John Williams, Karel Williams, *1992—The Struggle for Europe* (New York: BERG, 1989).

BEHAVIOUR OF CHANNEL MEMBERS

The marketing channel is a social system with its own conventions and behaviour patterns. Each channel member performs a different role in the system and agrees (implicitly or explicitly) to accept certain rights, responsibilities, rewards and sanctions for non-conformity. Moreover, each channel member expects certain things of every other channel member. Retailers, for instance, expect wholesalers to maintain adequate inventories and to deliver goods on time. For their part, wholesalers expect retailers to honour payment agreements and to keep them informed of inventory needs. It must be remembered that often channel members are companies in their own right, with profit goals, cash flow needs, shareholders and their own marketing strategies and programmes. This section discusses several issues related to channel member behaviour, including co-operation, conflict and leadership. Marketers need to understand these behavioural issues to make effective channel decisions.

Channel Co-operative

Channel co-operation is vital if each member is to gain something from other members.[6] Without co-operation, neither overall channel goals nor member goals can be realised. Policies must be developed that support all essential channel members; otherwise, failure of one link in the chain could destroy the channel.

There are several ways to improve channel co-operation. A marketing channel should consider itself a unified system, competing with other systems. This way, individual members will be less likely to take actions that would create disadvantages for other members. Similarly, channel members should agree to direct their efforts towards a common target market so that channel roles can be structured for maximum marketing effectiveness, which in turn can help members achieve their individual objectives. It is crucial to define precisely the tasks that each member of the channel is to perform. This definition provides a basis for reviewing the intermediaries' performance and helps reduce conflicts because each channel member knows exactly what is expected of it.

Channel Conflict

Although all channel members work toward the same general goal—distributing products profitably and efficiently—members may sometimes disagree about the best methods for attaining this goal. Each channel member wants to maximise its own profits while maintaining as much autonomy as possible. However, if this self-interest creates misunderstanding about role expectations, the end result is frustration and conflict for the whole channel. For individual organisations to function together in a single social system, each channel member must clearly communicate and understand role expectations.

Because channel integration and co-ordination are achieved through role behaviour, channel conflict often stems from perceived or real un-met role expectations. That is, members of the channel expect a given channel member to conduct itself in a certain way and to make a particular contribution to the total system. Wholesalers expect producers to monitor quality control and production scheduling, and they expect retailers to market products effectively. Producers and retailers expect wholesalers to provide co-ordination, functional services and communication. But if members do not fulfil their roles—for example, if wholesalers or producers fail to deliver products on time or the producers' pricing policies cut into the margins of downstream channel members—conflict may ensue.

Channel conflicts also arise when dealers over emphasise competing products or diversify into product lines traditionally handled by other, more specialised intermediaries. In some cases, conflict develops because producers strive to increase efficiency by circumventing intermediaries, as is happening in marketing channels for microcomputer software and video games. Many software-only stores are establishing direct relationships with software producers, by-passing wholesale distributors altogether. Some dishonest retailers are also pirating software or making unauthorised copies, thus cheating other channel members out of their due compensation. Consequently, suspicion and mistrust are heightening tensions in software marketing channels.[7]

A manufacturer embroiled in channel conflict may ship late (or not at all), withdraw financing, use promotion to build consumer brand loyalty, and operate or franchise its own retail outlet. To retaliate, a retailer may develop store brands, refuse to stock certain items, focus its buying power on one supplier or group of suppliers and seek to strengthen its position in the marketing channel. Although there is no single method for resolving conflict, an atmosphere of co-operation can be re-established if two conditions are met. First, the role of each channel member must be specified. To minimise misunderstanding, all members must be able to expect unambiguous, agreed on levels of performance from one another. Second, channel members must institute certain measures of channel co-ordination, a task which requires leadership and the benevolent exercise of control.[8] To prevent channel conflict, producers or other channel members may provide competing resellers with different brands, allocate markets among resellers, define direct sales policies to clarify potential conflict over large accounts, negotiate territorial issues between regional distributors and provide recognition to certain resellers for the importance of their role in distributing to others. Hallmark, for example, distributes its Ambassador greetings card line in discount stores and its name brand Hallmark line in up market department and specialist card stores, thus limiting the amount of competition among retailers carrying its products.[9]

Channel Leadership

The effectiveness of marketing channels hinges on channel leadership. Producers, retailers or wholesalers may assume this leadership. To become a leader, a channel member must want to influence and direct overall channel performance. Furthermore, to attain desired objectives, the leader must possess **channel power,** which is the ability to influence another channel member's goal achievement. As Figure 10.9 shows, the channel leader derives power from seven sources, two of them economic and five non-economic.

The five non-economic sources of power—reward, expert, referent, legitimate and coercive—are crucial for establishing leadership. A channel leader gains reward power by providing financial benefits. Expert power exists when other channel members believe that the leader provides special expertise required for the channel to function properly. Referent power emerges when other members strongly identify with and emulate the leader. Legitimate power is based on a superior-subordinate relationship. Coercive power is a function of the leader's ability to punish other channel members.[10]

In many countries, producers assume the leadership role in marketing channels. A manufacturer—whose large scale production efficiency demands increasing sales volume—may exercise power by giving channel members financing, business advice, ordering assistance, advertising and support materials. For example, BMW and Mercedes-Benz control their dealers totally, specifying showroom design and layout, discount levels and quotas of models. Coercion causes dealer dissatisfaction that is stronger than any impact from rewards, so the use of coercive power can be a major cause of channel conflict.[11]

Retailers can also function as channel leaders, and with the domination of national chains and own label merchandise they are increasingly doing so. Marketing Insight 10.2 describes Sainsbury's battle with Unilever and Procter & Gamble. Small retailers,

FIGURE 10.9
Determinants of channel leadership

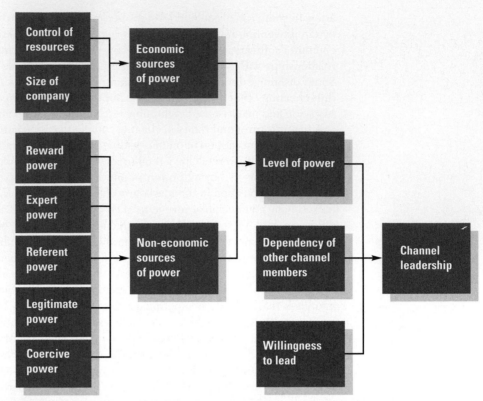

SOURCE: R. D. Michman and S. D. Sibley, *Marketing Channels and Strategies,* 2nd ed. (Worthington, Ohio: Publishing Horizons, Inc., 1980), p. 413. Reproduced by permission.

too, may share in the leadership role when they command particular consumer respect and patronage in local or regional markets. Among large retailers, Carrefour, IKEA, Marks & Spencer and Sainsbury base their channel leadership on wide public exposure to their products. These retailers control many brands and sometimes replace un-co-operative producers. Marks & Spencer exercises power by dictating manufacturing techniques, lead times, quality levels and product specifications.

Wholesalers assume channel leadership roles as well, although they were more powerful decades ago, when most manufacturers and retailers were small, underfinanced and widely scattered. Today wholesaler leaders may form voluntary chains with several retailers, which they supply with bulk buying or management services or which market their own brands. In return, the retailers shift most of their purchasing to the wholesaler leader. In Scandinavia, buying groups act as wholesalers, with bulk ordering price advantages, expert advertising and purchasing. Other wholesaler leaders such as Intersport or Mace might also help retailers with store layouts, accounting and inventory control.

LEGAL ISSUES IN CHANNEL MANAGEMENT

The multitude of laws governing channel management are based on the general principle that the public is best served when competition and free trade are protected. Under the authority of such national legislation as the UK's Monopolies and Mergers Commission, Fair Trading Act, Prices Act, Trade Description Act and

Consumer Protection Act, or EC Competition Laws and dictats, the courts and regulatory agencies determine under what circumstances channel management practices violate this underlying principle and must be restricted and when these practices may be permitted. Although channel managers are not expected to be legal experts, they should be aware that attempts to control distribution functions may have legal repercussions. The following practices are among those frequently subject to legal restraint.

Restricted Sales Territories

To tighten its control over the distribution of its products, a manufacturer may try to prohibit intermediaries from selling its products outside designated sales territories. The intermediaries themselves often favour this practice because it lets them avoid competition for the producer's brands within their own territories. Many companies have long followed the policy of restricting sales in this fashion. In recent years, the courts have adopted conflicting positions in regard to restricted sales territories. Although they have deemed restricted sales territories a restraint of trade among intermediaries handling the same brands (except for small or newly established companies), the courts have also held that exclusive territories can actually promote competition among dealers handling different brands. At present, the producer's intent in establishing restricted territories and the overall effect of doing so on the market must be evaluated for each case individually.

Tying Contracts

When a supplier (usually a manufacturer or franchiser) furnishes a product to a channel member with the stipulation that the channel member must purchase other products as well, a *tying contract* exists.[12] Suppliers, for instance, may institute tying arrangements to move weaker products along with more popular items. To use another example, a franchiser may tie the purchase of equipment and supplies to the sale of franchises, justifying the policy as necessary for quality control and protection of the franchiser's reputation.

A related practice is full line forcing. In this situation, a supplier requires that channel members purchase the supplier's entire line to obtain any of the products. Manufacturers sometimes use full line forcing to ensure that intermediaries accept new products and that a suitable range of products is available to customers.

The courts accept tying contracts when the supplier alone can provide products of a certain quality, when the intermediary is free to carry competing products as well and when a company has just entered the market. Most other tying contracts are considered illegal.

Exclusive Dealing

When a manufacturer forbids an intermediary to carry products of competing manufacturers, the arrangement is called *exclusive dealing*. A manufacturer receives considerable market protection in an exclusive dealing arrangement and may cut off shipments to an intermediary who violates such an agreement.

An exclusive dealing contract is generally legally permitted if dealers and customers in a given market have access to similar products or if the exclusive dealing contract strengthens an otherwise weak competitor.

Refusal to Deal

Producers have the right to choose the channel members with whom they will do business (and the right not to choose others). Within existing distribution channels, however, suppliers may not refuse to deal with wholesalers or dealers just because these wholesalers or dealers have resisted policies that are anticompetitive or in restraint of trade. Suppliers are further prohibited from organising some channel members in refusal to deal actions against other members who choose not to comply with illegal policies.[13]

NOVON DETERGENT ATTACKS ALL KNOWN BRANDS

Once a small London grocer's, Sainsbury has expanded during the past 10 years to reach Scotland and the bulk of the British Isles. Its Sainsbury chain is the most successful retailer in the UK and leads the highly profitable grocery sector where, despite the economic recession in the early 1990s, profits continued to rise. With hypermarket chain Savacentre and DIY chain Homebase, the Sainsbury family—one of the richest in Europe—has established its company alongside Marks & Spencer as a high quality, service orientated retailer known to consumers as trustworthy, safe and reliable.

Sainsbury has never been afraid to introduce new practices in retailing. From in-store baking, cafeterias and baby care facilities to trend setting alcohol and food products, the company endeavours to keep abreast of consumer needs. A few years ago, the company temporarily destocked Kellogg's cereals in a much publicised battle with the US food manufacturer. Now Sainsbury is taking on the detergent giants Unilever and Procter & Gamble (P&G).

In the autumn of 1992 Sainsbury launched its own detergent brand, Novon. Sainsbury's shoppers are used to being offered Sainsbury labelled products, including detergents. But Novon is different. It is packaged and sold as if it were a manufacturer's proprietary brand, similar to Procter & Gamble's Fairy or Unilever's Persil. The intention is to run Novon alongside Sainsbury's own label products, and those from manufacturers such as Procter & Gamble or Unilever, "to create a brand", according to advertising agency Abbott Mead Vickers BBDO, "which is a legitimate option for the housewife without forgetting it has Sainsbury's endorsement". Within six

SUMMARY

Distribution refers to activities that make products available to customers when and where they want to purchase them. A channel of distribution, or marketing channel, is a group of individuals and organisations that direct the flow of products from producers to customers. In most channels of distribution, producers and customers are linked by marketing intermediaries or middlemen, called merchants if they take title to products and functional middlemen if they do not take title. Channel structure reflects the division of responsibilities among members.

Channels of distribution are broadly classified as channels for consumer products or channels for industrial products. Within these two broad categories, different marketing channels are used for different products. Although some consumer goods move directly from producer to consumers, consumer product channels that include wholesalers and retailers are usually more economical and efficient. Industrial goods move directly from producer to end users more frequently than do consumer goods. Channels for industrial products may also include agents, industrial distributors or both. Most producers have dual or multiple channels so that the distribution system can be adjusted for various target markets.

weeks of Novon's launch, Sainsbury had doubled its share of the detergent market, largely through a campaign of in-store posters, vouchers, sampling and promotions. Against P & G/Unilever's combined £140 million advertising spend in the UK, Sainsbury's Novon enjoyed a successful debut.

As Sainsbury is the UK's largest grocery retailer, manufacturers of detergents with long standing, high profile brands now have a dilemma. Novon gives them a reason for confrontation, but Sainsbury is also a major outlet for Unilever and P & G. While disappointed by Sainsbury's move into branding, these manufacturers need the co-operation of the UK's premier grocery chain in order to maintain their presence in the supermarkets and, ultimately, in most consumers' homes.

Sainsbury, for its part, risks alienating some of its major suppliers. It is possible that Sainsbury's preferential buying and delivery terms may be affected. For the manufacturers there is a threat, but one not particularly open to retaliation. It is unusual for both suppliers and retailers to share such powerful positions in a market-place. For other suppliers too, this innovation represents a warning sign. Sainsbury admits that the success of its Novon brand is encouraging the retailer to consider introducing other "brands", including food lines.

SOURCES: "Sainsbury takes on Persil brands", *Marketing*, 12 November 1992, p. 3; "Sainsbury guns for top grocery brands", Alan Mitchell, *Marketing*, 10 December 1992, p. 3; "Unilever signals bold food drive", Alan Mitchell, *Marketing*, 21 January 1993, p. 3; Abbott Mead Vickers BBDO, London.

Although intermediaries can be eliminated, their functions are vital and cannot be dropped; these activities must be performed by someone in the marketing channel or passed on to customers. Because intermediaries serve both producers and buyers, they reduce the total number of transactions that would otherwise be needed to move products from producer to ultimate users. Intermediaries' specialised functions also help keep down costs.

An assortment is a combination of products assembled to provide benefits. Intermediaries perform sorting activities essential to the development of product assortments. Sorting activities allow channel members to divide roles and separate tasks. Through the basic tasks of sorting out, accumulating, allocating and assorting products for buyers, intermediaries resolve discrepancies in quantity and assortment. The number and characteristics of intermediaries are determined by the assortments and by the expertise needed to perform distribution activities.

Integration of marketing channels brings various activities under the management of one channel member. Vertical integration combines two or more stages of the channel under one management. The vertical marketing system is managed centrally for the mutual benefit of all channel members. Vertical marketing systems may be corporate, administered or contractual. Horizontal integration combines institutions at the same level of channel operation under a single management.

A marketing channel is managed so that products receive appropriate market coverage. In choosing intensive distribution, producers strive to make a product available to all possible dealers. In selective distribution, dealers are screened to choose those most qualified for exposing a product properly. Exclusive distribution usually gives one dealer exclusive rights to sell a product in a large geographic area.

When selecting distribution channels for products, manufacturers evaluate potential channel members carefully. Producers also consider the organisation's objectives and available resources; the location, density and size of a market; buyers' behaviour in the target market; characteristics of the product; and outside forces in the marketing environment.

A marketing channel is a social system in which individuals and organisations are linked by a common goal: the profitable and efficient distribution of goods and services. The positions or roles of channel members are associated with rights, responsibilities and rewards, as well as sanctions for non-conformity. Channels function most efficiently when members co-operate, but when they deviate from their roles, channel conflict can arise. Effective marketing channels are usually a result of channel leadership.

Channel leaders can facilitate or hinder the attainment of other members' goals, and they derive this power from authority, coercion, rewards, referents or expertise. Producers are in an excellent position to structure channel policy and to use technical expertise and consumer acceptance to influence other channel members. Retailers gain channel control through consumer confidence, wide product mixes and intimate knowledge of consumers. Wholesalers and buying groups become channel leaders when they have expertise that other channel members value and when they can co-ordinate functions to match supply with demand.

Important Terms

Channel of distribution (marketing channel)
Marketing intermediary
Merchants
Functional middlemen
Dual distribution
Assortment
Sorting activities
Sorting out
Accumulation

Allocation
Assorting
Vertical channel integration
Vertical marketing system (VMS)
Horizontal channel integration
Intensive distribution
Selective distribution
Exclusive distribution
Channel power

Discussion and Review Questions

1. Compare and contrast the four major types of marketing channels for consumer products. Through which type of channel is each of the following products most likely to be distributed: (a) new cars, (b) cheese biscuits, (c) cut-your-own Christmas trees, (d) new textbooks, (e) sofas, (f) soft drinks?
2. "Shorter channels are usually a more direct means of distribution and therefore are more efficient". Comment on this statement.

3. Describe an industrial distributor. What types of products are marketed through industrial distributors?
4. Under what conditions is a producer most likely to use more than one marketing channel?
5. Why do consumers often blame intermediaries for distribution inefficiencies? List several reasons.
6. How do the major functions that intermediaries perform help resolve the discrepancies in assortment and quantity?
7. How does the number of intermediaries in the channel relate to the assortments retailers need?
8. Can one channel member perform all channel functions?
9. Identify and explain the major factors that influence decision-makers' selection of marketing channels.
10. Name and describe firms that use (a) vertical integration and (b) horizontal integration in their marketing channels.
11. Explain the major characteristics of each of the three types of vertical marketing systems (VMSs).
12. Explain the differences among intensive, selective and exclusive methods of distribution.
13. "Channel co-operation requires that members support the overall channel goals to achieve individual goals". Comment on this statement.
14. How do power bases within the channel influence the selection of the channel leader?

■ CASES

10.1 Firstdirect: Midland's Advantage Through Innovative Channels

> With *Firstdirect* you can do your banking when it suits you, not when it suits us. We're open every hour, of every day, 365 days a year. So, if you want to transfer cash on a Sunday or set up a standing order late at night, you just ring up. And yes, you always talk to a real person. Because everything's done by phone, you can also bank from wherever you are . . . at home or in the office. And all calls are charged at local rate.

Most consumers have a bank cheque account from which cash is drawn, bills are paid and cheques written, and into which salaries, pensions or grant cheques are paid. For many consumers, the bank is a high street or shopping mall office—imposing, formal and often intimidating. Whether it's National Westminster, Barclays or TSB in the UK; ABN AMRO or Rabobank in the Netherlands, each high street bank is fairly alike, with similar products and services, personnel, branch layouts, locations and opening hours. Differentiation has been difficult to achieve and generally impossible to maintain over any length of time as competitors have copied rivals' moves. Promotional strategy and brand image have been the focus for most banking organisations, supported with more minor tactical changes in, for example, opening hours or service charges. For the majority of bank account holders, however, the branch—with its restricted openings, formal ambience and town centre location—is the only point of contact for the bulk of transactions.

Firstdirect, owned by Midland Bank, but managed separately, broke the mould in 1989. Launched with a massive £6 million promotional campaign, *Firstdirect* bypassed the traditional marketing channel. *Firstdirect* has no branches, no branch overhead and operating costs. It provides free banking, unlike its high street competitors with their system of bank charges combined with interest paid on positive balances.

Firstdirect is a telephone banking service which offers full current and deposit account facilities, cheque books, automatic bill payment and ATM "hole in the wall" cash cards through Midland's international service-till network.

Midland has established a purpose built administrative centre for *Firstdirect* in Leeds, guaranteeing immediate, personal response to calls 24 hours a day. All normal banking transactions can be completed over the telephone. Initial reactions have been positive, with many non-Midland account holders switching to the innovative new style of banking. The more traditional consumer—who equates the marbled halls of the Victorian branches with heritage, security and traditional values—has been less easily converted. For the targeted, more financially aware and independent income earner, *Firstdirect* is proving very popular.

Firstdirect's services and products are not new, but the chosen marketing channel—no branches, only the telephone—is totally innovative. Customers no longer have to reach inaccessible, parked-up, town centre branches with queues and restricted opening hours. *Firstdirect* has introduced a service, alien to some more traditional tastes perhaps, which is more readily available and with fewer costs. Many thousands of consumers have welcomed the launch of this new option, but millions have preferred to bank the traditional way. The start for *Firstdirect* has been highly encouraging, but it remains to be seen how successful the concept becomes and whether rivals choose to emulate *Firstdirect*'s methods.

SOURCES: "Midland fails to bank on a third successive win", *Marketing*, 19 July 1990, p. 7; "Taxis fare well with Firstdirect", Mat Toor, *Marketing*, 19 April 1990, p. 1; "Banking industry report", Salomon Brothers, 1992; *Firstdirect* advertising, 1993; *Firstdirect* factfile, 1993.

Questions for Discussion

1. Why is innovation in marketing channels generally difficult to achieve?
2. Why is *Firstdirect* different from its rivals? What gives it differentiation?
3. Why might some potential customers of *Firstdirect* have reservations about the innovative nature of the service?

10.2   Bols: Revitalised for the 1990s

Bols liqueurs are well known throughout the world, but there is much more to the Dutch distiller than creamy yellow advocaat. Just in the world's top 10 spirits manufacturers and distributors, Bols employs 2,000 people and produces spirits, aperitifs, non-alcoholic wines, mineral water, fruit juices and soft drinks. Bols produces its own branded drinks but also own label brands for various buying groups and retailers. Founded by Lucas Bols in 1575, the company's heritage is based upon distilling high quality liqueurs. During the 1980s, Bols had to make some difficult decisions, the most significant of which was to diversify from its main spirits business and enter the low and non-alcoholic beverage market in line with growing consumer demand for these products. Bols also divested third party agency business, brand franchises held to produce and distribute other manufacturers' brands.

The shift away from the traditional liqueur business was quite fundamental. The Netherlands' trading position and ties with the Spice Islands in the Far East had allowed Bols' products to take on a very distinctive character: highly coloured, with a consistent, premium quality taste. The non-alcoholic drinks share few of these traits. Bols' distribution had traded the company's liqueur spirits throughout Europe for centuries. The 1980s distribution focused on establishing Bols' spirit liqueur brands in bars and restaurants, as well as off licences and retail outlets. In most countries the distribution for soft drinks and low alcohol wines was quite different.

In Benelux, Bols and leading rival Heineken were both suffering from severe price competition and eroding margins. As a result the two companies formed the joint venture Bols Benelux, with Heineken under Bols' management. The combined muscle saw margins improve by 8 per cent and sales of spirits rise by 30 per cent. Today, Bols Benelux has 40 per cent of the Dutch market. In Italy, Bols took advantage of the rise in sparkling wine and non-alcoholic drink consumption, purchasing Ottavio Riccadonna (now Bols Italy) to become the fourth largest producer of sparkling wines in Italy. Bols' lemonade, Lemonsoda, is the brand leader, and in mineral water the company has a toe-hold of 2 per cent and is seeking further acquisitions.

In France a number of strategically prudent acquisitions has led to Bols becoming a major force in the high quality wine market, exporting to the USA, UK and the Netherlands. Bols Strothmann, created in the 1980s with the acquisition of the Strothmann distillery, has given Bols a presence in Germany at a time when German unification has opened up significant new markets to the east. There are successes in Spain, where sherries are exported to the UK, and in Switzerland; and agreements have been entered into in Hungary, Czechoslovakia and other eastern European countries. Only 14 per cent of business comes from outside Europe, but recently this proportion has expanded rapidly, particularly through new offices in Singapore, New York, Brazil and Argentina.

Bols had to make hard decisions as its historical core product, spirits, declined worldwide and beers, wines and non-alcoholic beverages gained market share. The company diversified, but only within the drinks industry with which it was familiar. New lines, particularly soft drinks and low alcohol sparkling wines, have heralded an upturn in the company's fortunes, coupled with wider geographic activity away from the European heartland. Sales in 1989 had dropped 10 per cent, but in 1990 they rose 8 per cent and 11.3 per cent in 1991, by which time profits were Dfl 144,300,000 at a margin of 10.8 per cent.

Distribution in the drinks industry is complicated and highly competitive. Several countries, including the UK, are dominated by third party specialist distributors who have access to retail chains and independent shops through wholesalers, bars, restaurants and entertainment facilities. Bols has adopted a variety of methods to expand its activities, including organic growth—mainly in its Benelux base—acquisition and contractual arrangements with leading distributors such as JR Phillips. Bols' experience in spirits gave it access to several markets, but the most direct approach to expanding and achieving distribution penetration came through the acquisition of leading players that already had distribution networks and outlets.

SOURCES: "Bols–company report", Barclays De Zoete Wedd Securities, January 1992; Bols: Review of operations, 1990; "Bols", UBS Phillips & Drew, April 1992; "Bols" FT Analysis, May 1992; "Spirits and liqueurs in the Netherlands", Economist Intelligence Unit, Issue 338, 1991; "The Beverages Industry", Economist Intelligence Unit, Issue 347, 1991; Caroline Farquhar (with thanks).

Questions for Discussion

1. What forced Bols to consider diversification?
2. What possible options were available to Bols to help the company reverse its declining fortunes?
3. What implications did Bols' new strategy in the 1980s have for its distribution and channel management?

11 WHOLESALING

Objectives

- To understand the nature of wholesaling in the marketing channel

- To learn about wholesalers' activities

- To understand how wholesalers are classified

- To examine organisations that facilitate wholesaling

- To explore changing patterns in wholesaling

McKesson Corporation is the leading wholesale distributor of health care products in the United States. Though it also distributes beauty aids, general merchandise, specialty foods, bottled water and office supplies, its primary line of business is drug/pharmaceutical wholesaling. Throughout its existence, McKesson has revolutionised the health care industry by providing retailers with distribution innovations, new avenues of customer support and electronic information systems.

Decades ago, Mckesson executives realised that because their firm offered the same physical products as its competitors, it needed to differentiate itself from other drug wholesalers by offering retailers more services and benefits. McKesson's Economost electronic order entry system assisted retailers in cutting costs. Giving retailers the capability to automatically order products using hand-held order entry devices, McKesson reduced retailers' labour costs, product costs and inventory holdings.

McKesson set out to assist in particular smaller retail chemists that were competing with the larger health care chains. It organised these stores into purchasing co-operatives, which could then receive volume discounts comparable to the ones given to giant chain operations. Using research gathered by its sales force, McKesson learned that the smaller stores wanted help with marketing research, shelf management planning, centralised warehousing and storage, and co-operative advertising and joint marketing. McKesson assisted them in all these areas, thus establishing a loyal base of customers. Because of McKesson's efforts, the smaller chemists were able to offer consumers reduced prices and better services—making them more profitable and stable enterprises. ■

Based on information in Eric Clemons and Michael Row, "A strategic information system: McKesson Drug Company's Economost", *Planning Review*, September-October 1988, pp. 14–19; Meghan O'Leary, "Getting the most out of buying at cost", *CIO*, August 1989, pp. 86–8; and William L. Trombetta, "Channel systems: an idea whose time has come in health care marketing", *Journal of Health Care Marketing*, September 1989, pp. 26–35.

This chapter focuses on wholesaling activities (such as those provided by McKesson) within a marketing channel. Wholesaling is viewed here as all exchanges among organisations and individuals in marketing channels, except transactions with ultimate consumers. This chapter examines the importance of wholesalers and their functions, noting the services they render to producers and retailers alike, then classifies various types of wholesalers and facilitating organisations. Finally, changing patterns in wholesaling are explored.

The Nature and Importance of Wholesaling

Wholesaling comprises all transactions in which the purchaser intends to use the product for resale, for making other products or for general business operations. It does not include exchanges with ultimate consumers. Wholesaling establishments are engaged primarily in selling products directly to industrial, reseller, government and institutional users.

A **wholesaler** is an individual or organisation engaged in facilitating and expediting exchanges that are primarily wholesale transactions. Only occasionally does a wholesaler engage in retail transactions, which are sales to ultimate consumers.

The Activities of Wholesalers

In America and in Europe more than 50 per cent of all products are exchanged, or their exchange is negotiated, through wholesaling institutions. Owing to the strength of large, national retailers, in the UK wholesaling is not as important in consumer markets. There are also far fewer wholesalers. For example, just 27 wholesale companies and buying groups account for 85 per cent of the grocery wholesale market. In Scandinavia, Iberia and much of eastern Europe, wholesaling companies (or buying groups) account for the bulk of exchanges. Of course, it is important to remember that the distribution of all goods requires wholesaling activities, whether or not a wholesaling institution is involved. Table 11.1 lists the major activities wholesalers perform. The activities are not mutually exclusive; individual wholesalers may perform more or fewer activities than Table 11.1 shows. Wholesalers provide marketing activities for organisations above and below them in the marketing channel.

Services for Producers

Producers, above wholesalers in the marketing channel, have a distinct advantage when they use wholesalers. Wholesalers perform specialised accumulation and allocation functions for a number of products, thus allowing producers to concentrate on developing and manufacturing products that match consumers' wants.

Wholesalers provide other services to producers as well. By selling a manufacturer's products to retailers and other customers and by initiating sales contacts with the manufacturer, wholesalers serve as an extension of the producer's sales force. Wholesalers also provide four forms of financial assistance. They often pay the costs of transporting goods; they reduce a producer's warehousing expenses and inventory investment by holding goods in inventory; they extend credit and assume the losses from buyers who turn out to be poor credit risks; and when they buy a producer's entire output and pay promptly or in cash, they are a source of working capital. In addition, wholesalers are conduits for information within the marketing channel, keeping manufacturers up to date on market developments and passing along the manufacturers' promotional plans to other middlemen in the channel.

TABLE 11.1 *Major wholesaling activities*

ACTIVITY	DESCRIPTION
Wholesale management	Planning, organising, staffing and controlling wholesaling operations
Negotiating with suppliers	Serving as the purchasing agent for customers by negotiating supplies
Promotion	Providing a sales force, advertising, sales promotion and publicity
Warehousing and product handling	Receiving, storing and stock keeping, order processing, packaging, shipping outgoing orders and materials handling
Transport	Arranging and making local and long distance shipments
Inventory control and data-processing	Controlling physical inventory, book keeping, recording transactions, keeping records for financial analysis
Security	Safeguarding merchandise
Pricing	Developing prices and providing price quotations
Financing and budgeting	Extending credit, borrowing, making capital investments and forecasting cash flow
Management and marketing assistance to clients	Supplying information about markets and products and providing advisory services to assist customers in their sales efforts

Ideally, many producers would like more direct interaction with retailers. Wholesalers, however, usually have closer contact with retailers because of their strategic position in the marketing channel. Besides, even though a producer's own sales force is probably more effective in its selling efforts, the costs of maintaining a sales force and performing the activities normally done by wholesalers are usually higher than the benefits received from better selling. Wholesalers can also spread their costs over many more products than most producers, resulting in lower costs per product unit. For these reasons, many producers have chosen to control promotion and influence the pricing of products and have shifted transport, warehousing and financing functions to wholesalers.

Services for Retailers Wholesalers help their retailer customers select inventory. In industries where obtaining supplies is important, skilled buying is essential. A wholesaler who buys is a specialist in understanding market conditions and an expert at negotiating final purchases. For example, based on its understanding of local customer needs and market conditions, a building supply wholesaler purchases inventory ahead of season so that it can provide its retail customers with the building supplies they want when they want them.[1] A retailer's buyer can thus avoid the responsibility of looking for and coordinating supply sources. Moreover, if the wholesaler makes purchases for several different buyers, expenses can be shared by all customers. Another advantage is that a manufacturer's salespersons can offer retailers only a few products at a time, but independent wholesalers have a wide range of products available.

By buying in large quantities and delivering to customers in smaller lots, a wholesaler can perform physical distribution activities—such as transport, materials handling, inventory planning, communication and warehousing—more efficiently and can provide more service than a producer or retailer would be able to do with its own physical distribution system. Furthermore, wholesalers can provide quick and frequent delivery even when demand fluctuates. They are experienced in providing fast delivery at low cost, thus allowing the producer and the wholesalers' customers to avoid risks associated with holding large product inventories.

Because they carry products for many customers, wholesalers can maintain a wide product line at a relatively low cost. Often wholesalers can perform storage and warehousing activities more efficiently, permitting retailers to concentrate on other marketing activities. When wholesalers provide storage and warehousing, they generally take on the ownership function as well, an arrangement that frees retailers' and producers' capital for other purposes.

Wholesalers are very important in reaching global markets. Approximately 85 per cent of all prescription drugs sold in Europe go through wholesalers that are within national borders. In the future, it is anticipated that more wholesalers will operate across borders, particularly as changing EC regulations reduce EC restrictions.[2]

CLASSIFYING WHOLESALERS

Many types of wholesalers meet the different needs of producers and retailers. In addition, new institutions and establishments develop in response to producers and retail organisations that want to take over wholesaling functions. Wholesalers adjust their activities as the contours of the marketing environment change.

Wholesalers are classified along several dimensions. Whether a wholesaler is owned by the producer influences how it is classified. Wholesalers are also grouped according to whether they take title to (actually own) the products they handle. The range of services provided is another criterion used for classification. Finally, wholesalers are classified according to the breadth and depth of their product lines. Using these dimensions, this section discusses three general categories, or types, of wholesaling establishments: (1) merchant wholesalers, (2) agents and brokers, and (3) manufacturers' sales branches and offices.

Merchant Wholesalers

Merchant wholesalers are wholesalers that take title to goods and assume the risks associated with ownership. These independently owned businesses, which make up about two thirds of all wholesale establishments, generally buy and resell products to industrial or retail customers. A producer is likely to use merchant wholesalers when selling directly to customers would not be economically feasible. From the producer's point of view, merchant wholesalers are also valuable for providing market coverage, making sales contacts, storing inventory, handling orders, collecting market information and furnishing customer support.[3] Some merchant wholesalers are even involved in packaging and developing own label brands to help their retailer customers be competitive.

During the past 30 years, merchant wholesalers have expanded their share of the wholesale market despite competition from other types of intermediaries. Now, they often account for more than half of all wholesale revenues.[4] As a rule, merchant wholesalers for industrial products are better established and earn higher profits than consumer goods merchant wholesalers; the latter normally deal in products of lower unit value and face more competition from other middlemen. Industrial product wholesalers are also more likely to have selective distribution arrangements with manufacturers because of the technical nature of many industrial products.

Merchant wholesalers go by various names, including wholesaler, jobber, distributor, assembler, exporter and importer.[5] They fall into one of two broad categories: full service and limited service. Figure 11.1 illustrates the different types of merchant wholesalers.

Full Service Merchant Wholesalers.   **Full service wholesalers** are middlemen who offer the widest possible range of wholesaling functions. Their customers rely on them for product availability, suitable assortments, bulk breaking (breaking large quantities into smaller ones), financial assistance, and technical advice and service.[6] Full service wholesalers provide numerous marketing services to interested customers. Many large grocery wholesalers, for example, help retailers with store design, site selection, personnel training, financing, merchandising, advertising, coupon redemption and scanning. Although full service wholesalers often earn higher gross margins than other wholesalers, their operating expenses are also higher because they perform a wider range of functions. Full service merchant wholesalers may handle either consumer products or industrial products and are categorised as general merchandise, limited line or specialty line wholesalers.

General Merchandise Wholesalers.   **General merchandise wholesalers** are middlemen who carry a wide product mix but offer limited depth within the product lines. They deal in such products as medicines, hardware, non-perishable foods, cosmetics, detergents and tobacco. General merchandise wholesalers develop strong, mutually beneficial relationships with local grocery stores, hardware and appliance shops, and local department stores, which are their typical customers. The small retailers often obtain everything they need from these wholesalers. General merchandise wholesalers for industrial customers provide supplies and accessories and are sometimes called *industrial distributors* or *mill supply houses*.

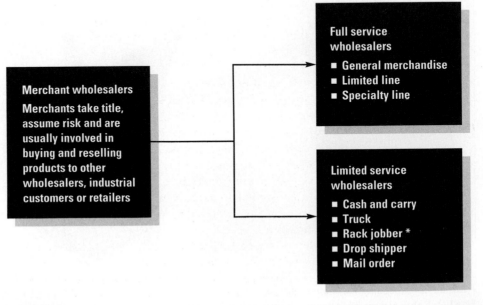

FIGURE 11.1
Types of merchant wholesalers

* Rack jobbers, in many cases, provide such a large number of services that they can be classified as full service, specialty line wholesalers.

Limited Line Wholesalers.   **Limited line wholesalers** are wholesalers who carry only a few product lines, such as groceries, lighting fixtures or oil well drilling equipment, but offer an extensive assortment of products within those lines. They provide a range of services similar to those of full service merchandise wholesalers. Limited line wholesalers for industrial goods serve relatively large geographic areas and provide technical expertise; in consumer goods, they supply single or limited line retailers. Computerworld, for example, is a limited line wholesaler of single and multi-user computer systems, dealing in six manufacturers' hardware but a limited number of product lines.

Specialty Line Wholesalers.   Of all the wholesalers, **specialty line wholesalers** are the middlemen who carry the narrowest range of products, usually a single product line or a few items within a product line. For example, wholesalers who carry shellfish, fruit or other food delicacies such as cheeses (see Figure 11.2) are specialty line wholesalers. Marketing Update 11.1 discusses a successful specialty coffee wholesaler. Specialty line wholesalers understand the particular requirements of the ultimate buyers and offer customers detailed product knowledge and depth of choice. To provide sales assistance to retailers, specialty wholesalers may set up displays and arrange merchandise. In industrial markets, specialty whole-

FIGURE 11.2   *Specialty line wholesaling*

Fine Dutch cheeses are often handled by specialty line wholesalers.

SOURCE: Raymond Meier.

MARKETING UPDATE 11.1

SPECIALIST GROCERY WHOLESALING—CARWARDINES

Established in 1903, Carwardines retails quality coffees via high street shops and cafés. It is a small business, with a turnover of only a few hundred thousand pounds. Since 1988, the company has concentrated on the wholesale of quality coffees with a delivery and machinery service to the retail trade. Carwardines aims to provide absolutely fresh, quality coffee blends—roasted, ground and packed to clients' specifications; filter machinery for those who need it; and speedy, reliable delivery service to its customers. For a wholesaler, Carwardines is a particularly customer orientated business.

Concentrating on companies in London, Carwardines has three key target groups of customers:

- Predominantly up market food and drink retailers such as cafés, sandwich shops and hotels, which themselves attract a discerning clientele
- Businesses such as firms of solicitors and estate agents within London wishing to provide their guests and employees with premium quality coffee
- A discerning set of customers who are willing to pay a premium price for top quality taste and branded coffee

For such a specialist wholesaler/supplier dealing only in one product area, Carwardines has limited resources but must maintain high levels of customer service and product quality. There is little advertising undertaken, but much effort is put into personal selling and sales promotion (price discounts with bulk buying, machinery on loan, gifts to major customers). The company very much depends on reputation in a very competitive market, with a relatively small customer base.

From being a product orientated company, Carwardines has increasingly realised the need to develop a proactive marketing strategy and, in particular, to place more emphasis on promotional activity, in order to maintain existing business and to grow both geographically and in terms of volume of customers.

SOURCES: Carwardines promotional literature; "Carwardines of London: Promotional Strategy", Dirk Sickmuller, University of Warwick, 1991; and J. Nicholson, Director, Carwardines.

salers are often better able than manufacturers to give customers technical advice and service.

Rack jobbers are specialty line wholesalers who own and maintain their own display racks in supermarkets and drugstores. They specialise in non-food items—particularly branded, widely advertised products sold on a self-service basis—which the retailers themselves prefer not to order and stock because of risk or inconvenience. Health and beauty aids, toys, books, magazines, hardware, housewares and stationery are typical products rack jobbers handle. The rack jobbers send out delivery persons to set up displays, mark merchandise, stock shelves and keep billing and inventory records; retailers need only furnish the space. Most rack jobbers operate on consignment and take back unsold products.

Limited Service Merchant Wholesalers. **Limited service wholesalers** provide only some marketing services and specialise in a few functions. Producers perform the remaining functions, or the functions are passed on to customers or other middlemen. Limited service wholesalers take title to merchandise, but in many cases, they do not deliver merchandise, grant credit, provide marketing information, store inventory, or plan ahead for customers' future needs. Because they offer only restricted services, limited service wholesalers are compensated with lower rates and thus earn smaller profit margins than full service wholesalers.

Although certain types of limited service wholesalers are few in number, they are important in the distribution of such products as specialty foods, perishable items, construction materials and coal. This section discusses the specific functions of three typical limited service wholesalers: cash and carry wholesalers, drop shippers, and mail order wholesalers. (Table 11.2 summarises the services these wholesalers provide.)

Cash and Carry Wholesalers. **Cash and carry wholesalers** are middlemen whose customers—usually small retailers and small industrial firms—will pay cash and furnish transport. In some cases, full service wholesalers set up cash and carry departments because they cannot otherwise supply small retailers profitably. Cash and carry middlemen usually handle a limited line of products with a high turnover rate—for instance, groceries, building materials, electrical supplies or office supplies. Marketing Insight 11.2 highlights the growth of Dutch cash and carry giant, Makro.

Booker Cash and Carry has a national network in the UK of retail warehouses stocking fresh and frozen foods, cigarettes, wines and spirits, and meat and provisions. Selling to the trade only, Booker offers bulk discounts to hotels, restaurants, the catering industry and small, local shops.

Cash and carry wholesaling developed after 1920, when independent retailers began experiencing competitive pressure from large chain stores. Today cash and carry wholesaling offers advantages to wholesalers and customers alike.[7] The wholesaler has

TABLE 11.2   *Various services provided by limited service merchant wholesalers*

	CASH AND CARRY	DROP SHIPPER[a]	MAIL ORDER
Physical possession of merchandise	Yes	No	Yes
Personal sales calls on customers	No	No	No
Information about market conditions	No	Yes	Yes
Advice to customers	No	Yes	No
Stocking and maintenance of merchandise in customers' stores	No	No	No
Credit to customers	No	Yes	Some
Delivery of merchandise to customers	No	No	No

[a] Also called desk jobber.

THE MARCH OF MAKRO

The cash and carry sector was shaken up with the entry of Holland's Makro, a self-service wholesaler. Makro is part of SHV Holdings, a large international distribution and energy company and the sixth largest company in the Netherlands after Shell, Unilever, Philips, AKZO and Ahold. With sales of £700 million, 7,000 employees and 21 UK sites, Makro has quickly moved into fifth place, with around 8 per cent of the market. The UK operation is only a small part of Makro's European business.

Makro's latest two openings in Aberdeen and Croydon are, at over 3,000 square metres (about 100,000 square feet), more than twice the average size for a cash and carry warehouse. These depots have the latest computer systems, customer service points and in-store displays. Makro serves the trade as a cash and carry wholesaler of groceries, fresh foods, wines, spirits, beer and cigarettes, household goods, clothing, toys and sports equipment. The company retails a clutch of own label brands in these categories, including Aro, Louis Chevalier and Roca.

In a relatively traditional sector dominated by four long standing companies, Dutch Makro has had a major impact in a short time. Its mix of merchandise is more comprehensive than its competitors, forcing several, such as Booker and Landmark, to rethink their merchandising strategies. Because depth and breadth of stock within individual product categories are not as extensive as those of UK rivals, the industry has been prompted to re-think, and most companies have reduced the number of lines stocked. Although not the first wholesaler with own label products, Makro's promotion of its own ranges has encouraged its competitors to divert more attention to this area, which now accounts for 20 per cent of all sales in the cash and carry sector.

Makro's biggest impact has perhaps been in the sales and marketing techniques it has brought to the UK. Cash and carry warehouses used to be dowdy depots which paid little attention to layout, upkeep, design or ambience and demonstrated even less regard for customer service and satisfaction. Price was the name of the game: customers could buy in bulk at a discount but were offered few additional benefits. Makro's philosophy brings to the cash and carry sector the retailing techniques of the hypermarket: carefully controlled branch designs and layouts, high levels of staff training and a significant emphasis on building ongoing relationships with customers. Customers are wooed with more enticing warehouse stores and better customer service. In addition, sales teams monitor customers' orders and offer incentives to regular purchasers. As customer needs and buying habits change, so do Makro's depots, merchandising and marketing. The secretive Dutch company has earned a glowing reputation in its UK market.

SOURCES: Makro Leicester; *Marketing Pocket Book* (Henley: NTC Publications, 1993); "Cash and carry outlets", Keynote Publications, 1992; Harvest; Business Information Service, University of Warwick.

no expenditures for outside salespersons, marketing, research, promotion, credit or delivery, and the customer benefits from lower prices and immediate access to products. Many small retailers whose accounts were refused by other wholesalers have survived because of cash and carry wholesalers.

Drop Shippers.　**Drop shippers,** also known as desk jobbers, are intermediaries who take title to goods and negotiate sales but never take actual possession of products. They forward orders from retailers, industrial buyers, or other wholesalers to manufacturers and then arrange for large shipments of items to be delivered directly from producers to customers. The drop shipper assumes responsibility for the products during the entire transaction, including the costs of any unsold goods.

Drop shippers are most commonly used in large volume purchases of bulky goods, such as coal, coke, oil, chemicals, lumber and building materials. Normally sold in wagon loads, these products are expensive to handle and ship relative to their unit value; extra loading and unloading is an added (and unnecessary) expense. One trend in this form of wholesaling is the use of more drop shipping from manufacturers to supermarkets.[8] A drop shipment eliminates warehousing and deferred deliveries to the stores, and large supermarkets can sell entire lorry loads of products rapidly enough to make drop shipping profitable.[9]

Because drop shippers incur no inventory costs and provide only minimal promotional assistance, they have low operating costs and can pass along some of the savings to their customers. In some cases, drop shippers do offer planning services, credit and personal selling.

Mail Order Wholesalers.　**Mail order wholesalers** use catalogues instead of sales forces to sell products to retail, industrial and institutional buyers. This is a convenient and effective method of selling small items to customers in remote areas. Mail order enables buyers to choose particular catalogue items and then send in their orders and receive shipments through the postal service or other carriers. Wholesalers can thus generate sales in locations that otherwise would be unprofitable to service.

Wholesale mail order houses generally feature cosmetics, specialty foods, hardware, sporting goods, business and office supplies, and car parts. They usually require payment in cash or by credit card, and they give discounts for large orders. Mail order wholesalers hold goods in inventory and offer some planning services but seldom provide assistance with promotional efforts.

Agents and Brokers　Agents and brokers (see Figure 11.3) negotiate purchases and expedite sales but do not take title to products. They are **functional middlemen,** intermediaries who perform a limited number of marketing activities in exchange for a commission, which is generally based on the product's selling price. **Agents** are middlemen who represent buyers or sellers on a permanent basis. **Brokers** are usually middlemen whom either buyers or sellers employ temporarily. Together, agents and brokers account for 11.6 per cent of the total sales volume of all US wholesalers, for example.[10]

Although agents and brokers perform even fewer functions than limited service wholesalers, they are usually specialists in particular products or types of customer and can provide valuable sales expertise. They know their markets well and often form long lasting associations with customers. Agents and brokers enable manufacturers to expand sales when resources are limited, to benefit from the services of a trained sales force and to hold personal selling costs down. However, despite the advantages they offer, agents and brokers face increased competition from merchant wholesalers, manufacturers' sales branches and offices, and direct sales efforts.

FIGURE 11.3

Types of agents and brokers

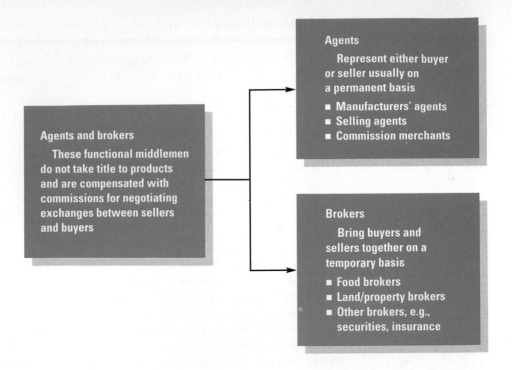

This section concentrates on three types of agents: manufacturers' agents, selling agents and commission merchants, as well as examining the brokers' role in bringing about exchanges between buyers and sellers. Table 11.3 summarises these services.

Manufacturers' Agents.   **Manufacturers' agents**—who account for over half of all agent wholesalers—are independent middlemen who represent two or more sellers and usually offer customers complete product lines. They sell and take orders year-round, much as a manufacturer's sales office does. Restricted to a particular territory, a manufacturers' agent handles non-competing and complementary products. The relationship between the agent and each manufacturer is governed by written agreements explicitly outlining territories, selling price, order handling, and terms of sale relating to delivery, service and warranties. Manufacturers' agents are commonly used in the sale of clothing and accessories, machinery and equipment, iron, steel, furniture, automotive products, electrical goods and certain food items.

Although most manufacturers' agents run small enterprises, their employees are professional, highly skilled salespeople. The agents' major advantages, in fact, are their wide range of contacts and strong customer relationships. These intermediaries help large producers minimise the costs of developing new sales territories and adjust sales strategies for different products in different locations. Agents are also useful to small producers who cannot afford outside sales forces of their own, because they incur no costs until the agents have actually sold something. By concentrating on a limited number of products, agents can mount an aggressive sales effort that would be impossible with any other distribution method except producer owned sales branches and offices. In addition, agents are able to spread operating expenses among non-competing products and thus offer each manufacturer lower prices for services rendered.

The chief disadvantage of using agents is the higher commission rate (usually 10 to 15 per cent) they charge for new product sales. When sales of a new product begin to build, total selling costs go up, and producers sometimes transfer the selling function

TABLE 11.3 *Various services agents and brokers provide*

	BROKERS	MANUFACTURERS' AGENTS	SELLING AGENTS	COMMISSION MERCHANTS
Physical possession of merchandise	No	Some	No	Yes
Long term relationship with buyers or sellers	No	Yes	Yes	Yes
Representation of competing product lines	Yes	No	No	Yes
Limited geographic territory	No	Yes	No	No
Credit to customers	No	No	Yes	Some
Delivery of merchandise to customers	No	Some	Yes	Yes

to in-house sales representatives. For this reason, agents try to avoid depending on a single product line; most work for more than one manufacturer.

Manufacturers' agents have little or no control over producers' pricing and marketing policies. They do not extend credit, and they may not be able to provide technical advice. They do occasionally store and transport products, assist with planning, and provide promotional support. Some agents help retailers advertise and maintain a service organisation. The more services offered, the higher the agent's commission.

Selling Agents.   **Selling agents** market either all of a specified product line or a manufacturer's entire output. They perform every wholesaling activity except taking title to products. Selling agents usually assume the sales function for several producers at a time and are often used in place of a marketing department. In contrast to other agent wholesalers, selling agents generally have no territorial limits and have complete authority over prices, promotion and distribution. They play a key role in the advertising, marketing research and credit policies of the sellers they represent, at times even advising on product development and packaging.

Selling agents, who account for about 1 per cent of the wholesale trade, are used most often by small producers or by manufacturers who find it difficult to maintain a marketing department because of seasonal production or other factors. A producer having financial problems may also engage a selling agent. By so doing, the producer relinquishes some control of the business but may gain working capital by avoiding immediate marketing costs.

To avoid conflicts of interest, selling agents represent non-competing product lines. The agents play an important part in the distribution of coal and textiles, and they also sometimes handle canned foods, household furnishings, clothing, lumber and metal products. In these industries, competitive pressures increase the importance of marketing relative to production, and the selling agent is a source of essential marketing and financial expertise.

Commission Merchants.   **Commission merchants** are agents who receive goods on consignment from local sellers and negotiate sales in large central markets. Most often found in agricultural marketing, commission merchants take possession of commodities in lorry loads, arrange for any necessary grading or storage and transport the commodities to auction or markets where they are sold. When sales have been completed, an agent deducts a commission plus the expense of making the sale and then turns over the profits to the producer.

Sometimes called factor merchants, these agents may have broad powers regarding prices and terms of sale, and they specialise in obtaining the best price possible under market conditions. Commission merchants offer planning assistance and sometimes extend credit, but they do not usually provide promotional support. Because commission merchants deal in large volumes, their per unit costs are usually low. Their services are most useful to small producers who must get products to buyers but choose not to field a sales force or accompany the goods to market themselves. In addition to farm products, commission merchants may handle textiles, art, furniture or seafood products.

Businesses—including farms—that use commission merchants have little control over pricing, although the seller can specify a minimum price. Generally, the seller is able to supervise the agent's actions through a check of the commodity prices published regularly in newspapers. Large producers, however, need to maintain closer contact with the market and so have limited need for commission merchants.

Brokers.   Brokers seek out buyers or sellers and help negotiate exchanges. In other words, brokers' primary purpose is to bring buyers and sellers together. Thus brokers perform fewer functions than other intermediaries. They are not involved in financing or physical possession, have no authority to set prices and assume almost no risks. Instead, they offer their customers specialised knowledge of a particular commodity and a network of established contacts.

Brokers are especially useful to sellers of certain types of products who market those products only occasionally. Sellers of used machinery, seasonal food products, financial securities and land/property may not know of potential buyers. A broker can furnish this information. The party who engages the broker's services—usually the seller—pays the broker's commission when the transaction is completed.

Food brokers—the most common type of broker—are intermediaries who sell food and general merchandise items to retailer owned and merchant wholesalers, grocery chains, industrial buyers and food processors. Food brokers enable buyers and sellers to adjust to fluctuating market conditions; they also aid in grading, negotiating and inspecting foods (in some cases they store and deliver products). Because of the seasonal nature of food production, the association between broker and producer is temporary—though many mutually beneficial broker-producer relationships are resumed year after year. Because food brokers provide a range of services on a somewhat permanent basis and operate in specific geographic territories, they can more accurately be described as manufacturers' agents.

Manufacturers' Sales Branches and Offices   Sometimes called manufacturers' wholesalers, manufacturers' sales branches and offices resemble merchant wholesalers' operations. These producer owned middlemen account for about 9 per cent of wholesale establishments and generate approximately one third (31 per cent) of all wholesale sales.[11]

Sales branches are manufacturer owned middlemen selling products and providing support services to the manufacturer's sales force, especially in locations where large customers are concentrated and demand is high. They offer credit, deliver goods, give promotional assistance and furnish other services. In many cases, they carry inventory (although this practice often duplicates the functions of other channel members and is now declining). Customers include retailers, industrial buyers and other wholesalers. Branch operations are common in the electrical supplies, plumbing, lumber and car parts industries.

Sales offices are manufacturer owned operations that provide services normally associated with agents. Like sales branches, they are located away from manufacturing plants, but unlike branches, they carry no inventory. A manufacturer's sales offices or branches may sell products which enhance the manufacturer's own product line. For example, Hiram Walker, a distiller, imports wine from Spain to increase the number of products that its sales offices can offer wholesalers.

Manufacturers may set up sales branches or sales offices so that they can reach customers more effectively by performing wholesaling functions themselves. A manufacturer may also set up these branches or offices when required specialised wholesaling services are not available through existing middlemen. In some situations, however, a manufacturer may bypass its wholesaling organisation entirely—for example, if the producer decides to serve large retailer customers directly. One major distiller bottles own label spirits for a UK grocery chain and separates this operation completely from the company's sales office, which serves other retailers.

FACILITATING AGENCIES

The total marketing channel is more than a chain linking the producer, intermediary and buyer. **Facilitating agencies**—transport companies, insurance companies, advertising agencies, marketing research agencies and financial institutions—may perform activities that enhance channel functions. Note, however, that any of the functions these facilitating agencies perform may be taken over by the regular marketing intermediaries in the marketing channel.

The basic difference between channel members and facilitating agencies is that channel members perform the negotiating functions (buying, selling and transferring title), whereas facilitating agencies do not.[12] In other words, facilitating agencies assist in the operation of the channel but do not sell products. The channel manager may view the facilitating agency as a subcontractor to which various distribution tasks can be farmed out according to the principle of specialisation and division of labour.[13] Channel members (producers, wholesalers, distributors or retailers) may rely on facilitating agencies because they believe that these independent businesses will perform various activities more efficiently and more effectively than they themselves could. Facilitating agencies are functional specialists who perform special tasks for channel members without getting involved in directing or controlling channel decisions. The following sections describe the ways in which facilitating agencies provide assistance in expediting the flow of products through marketing channels.

Public Warehouses

Public warehouses are storage facilities available for a fee. Producers, wholesalers and retailers may rent space in a warehouse instead of constructing their own facilities or using a merchant wholesaler's storage services. Many warehouses also order, deliver, collect accounts and maintain display rooms where potential buyers can inspect products.

To use goods as collateral for a loan, a channel member may place products in a bonded warehouse. If it is too impractical or expensive physically to transfer goods, the channel member may arrange for a public warehouser to verify that goods are in the member's own facilities and then issue receipts for lenders.[14] Under this arrangement, the channel member retains possession of the products but the warehouser has control. Many field public warehousers know where their clients can borrow working capital and are sometimes able to arrange low cost loans.

Finance Companies

Wholesalers and retailers may be able to obtain financing by transferring ownership of products to a sales finance company or bank while retaining physical possession of the goods. Often called "floor planning", this form of financing enables wholesalers and retailers—especially car and appliance dealers—to offer a greater selection of products for customers and thus increase sales. Loans may be due immediately upon sale; so products financed this way are usually well known, sell relatively easily and present little risk.

Other financing functions are performed by factors—organisations that provide clients with working capital by buying their accounts receivable or by lending money, using the accounts receivable as collateral. Most factors minimise their own risks by specialising in particular industries, in order to better evaluate individual channel members within those industries. Factors usually lend money for a longer time than banks. They may help clients improve their credit and collection policies and may also provide management expertise.

Transport Companies

Rail, road, air and other carriers are facilitating organisations that help manufacturers and retailers transport products. Each form of transport has its own advantages. Railways ship large volumes of bulky goods at low cost; in fact, outside the UK, a "unit train" is the cheapest form of overland transport for ore, grain or other commodities. Air transport is relatively expensive but is often preferred for shipping high value or perishable goods. Trucks, which usually carry short haul, high value goods, now carry more and more products because factories are moving closer to their markets. As a result of technological advances, pipelines now transport powdered solids and fluidised solid materials, as well as petroleum and natural gas.

Transport companies sometimes take over the functions of other middlemen. Because of the ease and speed of using air transport for certain types of products, parcel express companies, such as DHL (see Figure 11.4), can eliminate the need to maintain large inventories and branch warehouses. In other cases, freight forwarders perform accumulation functions by combining less than full shipments into full loads and passing on the savings to customers—perhaps charging a wagon rate rather than a less than wagon rate.

Trade Shows and Trade Markets

Trade shows and trade markets enable manufacturers or wholesalers to exhibit products to potential buyers and thus help the selling and buying functions. **Trade shows** are industry exhibitions that offer both selling and non-selling benefits.[15] On the selling side, trade shows let vendors identify prospects; gain access to key decision-makers; disseminate facts about their products, services and personnel; and actually sell products and service current accounts through contacts at the show.[16] Trade shows also allow a firm to reach potential buyers who have not been approached through regular selling efforts. In fact, research indicates that most trade show visitors have not been contacted by a sales representative of any company within the past year, and many are therefore willing to travel several hundred miles to attend trade shows to learn about new goods and services.[17] The non-selling benefits include opportunities to maintain the company image with competitors, customers and the industry; gather information about competitors' products and prices; and identify potential channel members.[18] Trade shows have a positive influence on other important marketing variables, such as maintaining or enhancing company morale, product testing, and product evaluation.

Trade shows can permit direct buyer-seller interaction and may eliminate the need for agents. Companies exhibit at trade shows because of the high concentration of prospective buyers for their products. Studies show that it takes, on average, 5.1 sales calls to close an industrial sale but less than 1 sales call (0.8) to close a trade show lead. The explanation for the latter figure is that more than half of the customers who purchase a product based on information gained at a trade show order the product by mail or by phone after the show. When customers use these more impersonal methods to

FIGURE 11.4

Facilitating agencies

Parcel express companies such as DHL, Federal Express, and UPS facilitate and sometimes perform functions of marketing channel members.

"I know production will be affected without them. Yes, of course their systems will track each dispatch. I checked. They left today and will be there before 10:00 am as usual. Yes, I promise."

WE KEEP YOUR PROMISES

SOURCE: Courtesy of DHL.

gather information, the need for major sales calls to provide such information is eliminated.[19]

Trade markets are relatively permanent facilities that firms can rent to exhibit products year-round. At these markets, such products as furniture, home decorating supplies, toys, clothing and gift items are sold to wholesalers and retailers. In the United States, trade markets are located in several major cities, including New York, Chicago, Dallas, High Point (North Carolina), Atlanta and Los Angeles. The Dallas Market Center, which includes the Dallas Trade Mart, the Home Furnishing Mart, the World Trade Center, the Decorative Center, Market Hall, InfoMart, and the Apparel Mart, is housed in six buildings designed specifically for the convenience of professional buyers. Paris, Rotterdam and London all have centres, similar in scale to Birmingham's National Exhibition Centre, which offers a 240 hectare (600 acre) site, with open display areas, plus 125,000 square metres (156,000 square yards) of covered exhibition space, hotels, parking for thousands of cars, and rail and air links.

CHANGING PATTERNS IN WHOLESALING

The nature of the wholesaling industry is changing. The distinction between wholesaling activities that any business can perform and the traditional wholesaling establishment is becoming blurred. Changes in the nature of the marketing environment itself have transformed various aspects of the industry. For instance, they have brought about an increasing reliance on computer technology to expedite the ordering, delivery and handling of goods. The trend towards globalisation of world markets has resulted in other changes, and astute wholesalers are responding to them. The two predominant shifts in wholesaling today are the consolidation of the wholesaling industry and the development of new types of retailers.

Wholesalers Consolidate Power

Like most major industries, the wholesale industry is experiencing a great number of mergers. Wholesaling firms are acquiring or merging with other firms primarily to achieve more efficiency in the face of declining profit margins. Consolidation also gives larger wholesalers more pricing power over producers. Some analysts have expressed concern that wholesalers' increased price clout will increase the number of single-source supply deals, which may reduce competition among wholesalers, as well as retailers and producers. Nevertheless, the trend towards consolidation of wholesaling firms appears to be continuing.[20] It is also crossing national borders, as many European companies take advantage of the EC's cross-border trade and regulatory improvements.

One of the results of the current wave of consolidation in the wholesale industry is that more wholesalers are specialising. For example, McKesson Corporation once distributed chemicals, wines and spirits but now focuses only on medicines. The new larger wholesalers can also afford to purchase and use more modern technology to manage inventories physically, provide computerised ordering services and even help manage their retail customers' operations.[21]

New Types of Wholesalers

The trend towards larger retailers—superstores and the like (discussed in Chapter 12)—will offer opportunities as well as dangers for wholesaling establishments. Opportunities will develop from the expanded product lines of these mass merchandisers. A merchant wholesaler of groceries, for instance, may want to add other low cost, high volume products sold in superstores. On the other hand, some limited function merchant wholesalers may no longer have a role to play. For example, the volume of sales may eliminate the need for rack jobbers, who usually handle slowly moving products that are purchased in limited quantities. The future of independent wholesalers, agents and brokers depends on their ability to delineate markets and furnish desired services.

SUMMARY

Wholesaling includes all transactions in which the purchaser intends to use the product for resale, for making other products or for general business operations. It does *not* include exchanges with the ultimate consumers. Wholesalers are individuals or organisations that facilitate and expedite primarily wholesale transactions.

Except in the UK consumer markets, where the large multiple retailers dominate, more than half of all goods are exchanged through wholesalers, although the distribution of any product requires that someone must perform wholesaling activities, whether or not a wholesaling institution is involved. For producers, wholesalers perform specialised accumulation and allocation functions for a number of products, letting the producers concentrate on manufacturing the products. For retailers, wholesalers provide buying expertise, wide product lines, efficient distribution, and warehousing and storage service.

Various types of wholesalers serve different market segments. How a wholesaler is classified depends on whether the wholesaler is owned by a producer, whether it takes title to products, the range of services it provides, and the breadth and depth of its product lines. The three general categories of wholesalers are merchant wholesalers, agents and brokers, and manufacturers' sales branches and offices.

Merchant wholesalers are independently owned businesses that take title to goods and assume risk; they make up about two thirds of all wholesale firms. They are either full service wholesalers, offering the widest possible range of wholesaling functions, or limited service wholesalers, providing only some marketing services and specialising in a few functions. Full service merchant wholesalers include general merchandise wholesalers, which offer a wide but relatively shallow product mix; limited line wholesalers, which offer extensive assortments in a few product lines; and specialty line wholesalers, which offer great depth in a single product line or in a few items within a line. Rack jobbers are specialty line wholesalers that own and service display racks in supermarkets and chemists. There are three types of limited service merchant wholesalers. Cash and carry wholesalers sell to small businesses, require payment in cash and do not deliver. Drop shippers own goods and negotiate sales but never take possession of products. Mail order wholesalers sell to retail, industrial and institutional buyers through direct mail catalogues.

Agents and brokers, sometimes called functional middlemen, negotiate purchases and expedite sales but do not take title to products. They are usually specialists and provide valuable sales expertise. Agents represent buyers or sellers on a permanent basis. Manufacturers' agents offer customers the complete product lines of two or more sellers; selling agents market a complete product line or a producer's entire output and perform every wholesaling function except taking title to products; commission merchants receive goods on consignment from local sellers and negotiate sales in large central markets. Brokers, such as food brokers, negotiate exchanges between buyers and sellers on a temporary basis.

Manufacturers' sales branches and offices are vertically integrated units owned by manufacturers. Branches sell products and provide support services for the manufacturer's sales force in a given location. Sales offices carry no inventory and function much as agents do.

Facilitating agencies do not buy, sell or take title but perform certain wholesaling functions. They include public warehouses, finance companies, transport companies, and trade shows and trade markets. In some instances, these organisations eliminate the need for a wholesaling establishment.

The nature of the wholesaling industry is changing in response to changes in the marketing environment. The predominant changes are the increasing consolidation of the wholesaling industry and the growth of new types of wholesalers.

IMPORTANT TERMS

Wholesaling	Agents
Wholesaler	Brokers
Merchant wholesalers	Manufacturers' agents
Full service wholesalers	Selling agents
General merchandise wholesalers	Commission merchants
Limited line wholesalers	Food brokers
Specialty line wholesalers	Sales branches
Rack jobbers	Sales offices
Limited service wholesalers	Facilitating agencies
Cash and carry wholesalers	Public warehouses
Drop shippers	Trade shows
Mail order wholesalers	Trade markets
Functional middlemen	

DISCUSSION AND REVIEW QUESTIONS

1. Is there a distinction between wholesalers and wholesaling? If so, what is it?
2. Would it be appropriate for a wholesaler to stock both interior wall paint and office supplies? In what circumstances would this product mix be logical?
3. What services do wholesalers provide to producers and retailers?
4. Drop shippers take title to products but do not accept physical possession. Commission merchants take physical possession of products but do not accept title. Defend the logic of classifying drop shippers as wholesale merchants and commission merchants as agents.
5. What are the advantages of using agents to replace merchant wholesalers? What are the disadvantages?
6. What, if any, are the differences in the marketing functions that manufacturers' agents and selling agents perform?
7. Why are manufacturers' sales offices and branches classified as wholesalers? Which independent wholesalers are replaced by manufacturers' sales branches? Which independent wholesalers are replaced by manufacturers' sales offices?
8. "Public warehouses are really wholesale establishments". Please comment.
9. Discuss the role of facilitating organisations. Identify three facilitating organisations and explain how each type performs this role.

■ CASES

11.1 Anheuser-Busch and Its Wholesalers

St Louis-based Anheuser-Busch, Inc., is the world's largest brewing company, with a market share that is increasing steadily. It currently produces one out of every three beers sold in the US. Anheuser-Busch's brewery sales have recently neared $6.5 billion. Its products include Budweiser, Michelob, Michelob Light, Bud Light, Bud Dry and Michelob Classic Dark.

In the US and in Caribbean countries, Anheuser-Busch distributes beer through a network of about 1,000 independently owned wholesalers and 10 company owned wholesale operations—a distribution system considered the strongest in the brewing industry. Anheuser-Busch's independent wholesalers employ about 30,000 people, more than 18,000 of whom work in direct beer marketing positions. (One Anheuser-Busch distributor is Frank Sinatra, who owns Somerset Distributing in California.) Company owned distributorships employ about 1,600 people. Wholesalers handle volumes ranging from 870 barrels to 1.1 million barrels annually.

Anheuser-Busch's effective distribution system is bolstered by a variety of cooperative arrangements with wholesalers. For example, the company tries to ensure that its beers are sold to wholesalers FOB (free on board) from the "least cost" brewery. That is, the wholesaler must supply or pay for transport from the brewery that can provide the product at the lowest shipping cost. But if a product must be shipped at a higher cost—perhaps because the nearest brewery does not produce a specific package—Anheuser-Busch compensates the wholesaler for the difference in cost. The company's traffic department also helps wholesalers arrange transport. Some 20 years ago, Anheuser-Busch introduced its wholesaler equity programme, and recently expanded it to give distributors exclusive territories where permitted by law. A wholesaler advisory panel, a cross-section of wholesalers and top company managers, meets regularly to discuss and act on industry issues.

In addition, the 10 distributorships in the company's wholesale operations division serve as a testing ground for programmes which are made available to independent wholesalers. In one case, the company developed computer software to help wholesalers maximise retail shelf space. Anheuser-Busch wholesalers receive group discounts on computers, trucks and insurance and can take company courses ranging from draught beer basics to dynamics of business readings. To build morale among wholesalers, Anheuser-Busch puts top executives in charge of its biggest volume states (the company's president, August Busch III, handles California himself). Furthermore, every three years, the company throws a Las Vegas-style wholesalers' convention, with appearances by such celebrities as Bob Hope and Paul Newman.

Anheuser-Busch's most evident support for its distributors is its backing of special promotions: sporting events, college parties, rodeos and festivals. The company may pay as much as half the cost of these events, in co-operation with local wholesalers. To improve sales of Michelob Light, for example, a local New York distributor decided to hold a Michelob Light Concentration Day. On that day, only Michelob Light was delivered to retailers. Tuxedo clad representatives from the St Louis headquarters rode on delivery vans, accompanied by two Playboy Playmates. The distributorship sold 21,000 cases of Michelob Light in one day (it normally takes 20 days to sell that amount), and Anheuser-Busch is now staging Concentration Days in other cities.

The company has helped support everything from Chicago's Lithuanian festival to the Iron Man Triathlon in Hawaii. Just before Coors moved into the New York—New Jersey market, Anheuser-Busch supplied its wholesalers with a 300 page "Coors Defence Plan", along with funding for promotional events that might have attracted Coors sponsorship. Coors was unable to reach an agreement with any major beer wholesalers and had to distribute through a soft drink bottler instead.

For distributors, however, the price of such generous corporate support is unquestioned loyalty. Anheuser-Busch asks more of its wholesalers than any other brewer. Each year all distributors are requested to contribute ideas for local promotions—one for every brand. Furthermore, although the distributors are independent business owners, technically free to sell whatever they choose, Anheuser-Busch takes a dim view of wholesalers who decide to carry a competing product. When a Florida distributorship added Heineken and Amstel Light to its line, 22 Anheuser-Busch field managers swarmed in and rode on the company's vans for a week, and the distributor and his general manager were summoned to St Louis for a meeting with top management.

Anheuser-Busch defends its policies, maintaining that the company will not allow "greedy" wholesalers to jeopardise market share. Although Anheuser-Busch has a lead over all other brewers, the company is taking no chances. It has enthusiastically entered and is actively pursuing its foreign markets, especially in the UK, where it is trying to establish an equally effective distribution system. Anheuser-Busch has launched several non-beer beverages in recent years, including L.A. (a low alcohol beer), Dewey Stevens (a low calorie wine cooler aimed at women), and Zeltzer Seltzer (a flavoured sparkling water). So far these products have not been marketed aggressively, and they may never be highly profitable. But with rival brewers entering these new markets, Anheuser-Busch wants to be able to supply its distributors with competing products. Along with its share of the market, say Anheuser-Busch executives, the company intends to maintain its share of wholesalers.

SOURCES: Anheuser-Busch Cos., Inc., *Annual Report*, 1986; Paul Hemp, " 'King of beers' in a bitter battle in Britain", *Wall Street Journal*, 9 June 1988, p. 26; Michael Oneal, "Anheuser-Busch: the scandal may be small beer after all", *Business Week*, 11 May 1987, pp. 72–3; and Patricia Sellers, "How Busch wins in a doggy market", *Fortune*, 22 June 1987, pp. 99–100.

Questions for Discussion

1. Are Anheuser-Busch's wholesalers merchant wholesalers? Explain your answer. Are they full service or limited service wholesalers? Why?
2. Why does Anheuser-Busch give its wholesale distributors so much support?
3. Why has Anheuser-Busch introduced non-beer products? Evaluate this practice.

11.2 Cash and Carry No Longer Just Discounts

Heinz boss Tony O'Reilly heads Fitzwilton group, a major Irish motor, cash and carry and industrial group, trading as M6 Cash and Carry in Britain. Despite the sector's worth of close to £8.5 billion in 1992, O'Reilly described UK cash and carry trading conditions as the "toughest in recent years, with volumes and sales just keeping pace with inflation". The boom years of the mid-1980s encouraged numerous new entrants, but now there is over capacity, with declining numbers of depots and increasing liquidations. This squeeze has hit the smaller operators most; the largest companies are consolidating their grip on the sector: Booker, Landmark, Nurdin & Peacock, and NISA-Today's have over 70 per cent of the market. This concentration replicates the grocery retailing scene of the late 1960s, when supermarket groups merged to produce a handful of dominant players.

COMPANY	MARKET	NUMBER OF DEPOTS	
	Share (per cent)	1989	1992
Booker	22	171	166
Today's	15.5	86	90
Landmark	17	75	90
Nurdin & Peacock	15	38	50
Sterling	4.7	31	39
Mojo	1.4	25	24
Makro	7.6	15	21
Watson & Philip	2	14	12
Batleys	5	11	11

SOURCE: Key Note, 1992.

Although price remains a core trading proposition, service and brand image are increasingly important. Customers are being offered better service, together with assistance in building their own company image through local press and television advertising. The leading cash and carry companies are offering marketing support to their key accounts not just to stimulate sales but also to build up those customers' loyalty to their nearby warehouse. These changes have been accompanied by a rise in average sales per depot from £9.2 million in 1986 to £14.9 million in 1991.

Depots have been up-rated by the leading groups, with new equipment, better stocking systems and improved physical distribution. They have also initiated sales promotions campaigns and incentive programmes. Computerisation has helped lower costs and improve efficiency. With Germany's Siemens Nixdorf, Booker has created MIDAS (management information depot application system), giving each of its depots a comprehensive invoicing, mailing, sales data, customer information and stock control system. This system has improved Booker's ability to target customers and monitor stock needs. Systems such as MIDAS have enabled the leading companies to reduce their product lines. For example, Nurdin & Peacock used to carry 60,000 lines but has now reduced its coverage to 40,000 and is aiming to reach 30,000 without alienating customers.

Branches are being rationalised, both to respond to the recession and to benefit from cost economies and enhanced computer systems. For example, companies are either consolidating three outdated neighbouring depots, into one central, spacious, service orientated depot, or they are closing a branch while extending and refurbishing a neighbouring one. Own label lines are taking up to 20 per cent of cash and carry sales, among the most popular being Booker's grocery Family Choice label and its catering Chef's Larder range; Landmark's Lifestyle; and Nurdin & Peacock's Happy Shopper. There are own label brands in most of the key product areas: grocery, catering (for the catering trade), confectionery, wines, spirits, lager and beer, and cigarettes. Own label brands are even available for some fresh foods, shirts and sports equipment (Makro), and garden products (Nurdin & Peacock). Companies have also established specialist sales teams to provide expert advice and service. For example, Nurdin & Peacock has separate teams handling independent grocers, garage forecourts and newsagents, and the catering trade.

Significant investment has gone into staff training, new stores, computer systems, sales teams and the development of own label products. The overriding aim has been to provide customers with a better service which is closely in tune with their needs, even down to offering marketing advice and support for customers' promotional campaigns. As the sector has evolved, customer service and modernised operations have taken a prime position. The cash and carry sector now involves much more than pure discounting.

SOURCES: "Cash & Carry Outlets", Key Note, 1992; IGD Research Services; Harvest; Booker promotional material.

Questions for Discussion

1. How are the major cash and carry companies responding to changing customer needs?
2. How are computerised retailing systems contributing to improved customer service?
3. Why are cash and carry companies offering marketing and promotional advice to their customers?

12 RETAILING

Objectives

To understand the purpose and function of retailers in the marketing channel

To describe and distinguish major types of retailers and locations

To understand non-store retailing and franchising

To learn about strategic issues in retailing

*B*AA owns and operates seven airports in the UK, including Heathrow, Gatwick and rapidly expanding Stanstead. BAA's 72 million passengers account for 70 per cent of the UK's air passenger traffic. The company, privatised in 1987, builds and manages terminals and runways and handles security. Chief executive Sir John Egan, former champion of Jaguar Cars, intends to keep London as the "hub of Europe", ahead of challengers Paris, Frankfurt, Amsterdam and Vienna.

A couple of years ago Egan instigated a policy review which emphasised a commitment to quality service, on-site competition, and the introduction of branded operations and concessions. All proposals followed extensive marketing research. Three tax-free operators currently compete for the available business: Allders, Forte and Harrods. SAS, Häagen-Dazs and Garfunkels compete for catering business, along with big names such as Upper Crust, Granary, Casey Jones and Burger King. The BAA Skyshop brand disappeared and was replaced with Forte bookshops and market leaders W. H. Smith and John Menzies.

With the EC planning to phase out intra-community duty free trade by 1996, Egan sees retail operations as the way to continue BAA's impressive profits record. Already 10 per cent of terminal space—46,000 square metres (500,000 square feet)—is devoted to retailing. Egan intends to double this, with the help of retailing director Barry Gibson, whose record of senior positions at Littlewoods, Burton Group and Jean Machine have well equipped him for the task.

BAA has taken bored and restless passengers waiting for flights and put them into shops, selling well known brands and a variety of merchandise. Research from 120,000 interviews each year has shown that retail outlets are a high priority for passengers. The following are now offered: Bally, Benetton, Body Shop, Sock Shop, Aquascutum, Burberry, Harrods, Thomas Pink. The captive audience is appreciative of the changes, as are the retailers. Tie Rack's sales at Heathrow are £27,000 per square metre (£3,000 per square foot) annually, 10 times the ratio the company's high street stores achieve. Heathrow's Terminal 4 is to house BAA's first "serious" shopping mall, with 20 retailers, natural daylight, shopping trolleys and big brands. Experiments with technology selling include an interactive video screen offering merchandise, the opportunity to view merchandise on screen or listen to music recordings, and a credit card swipe facility to make the purchase. ∎

SOURCES: BAA press office; Bunhill, *The Independent on Sunday,* 21 February 1993, p. IB40; "BAA talks shop on airport retailing", Clare Sambrook, Marketing, 29 October 1992, pp. 25–30.

Marketing research has enabled BAA to develop facilities in line with passengers' wishes and a marketing strategy which has enhanced its profits. Marketing methods which satisfy consumers serve well as the guiding philosophy of retailing. Retailers are an important link in the marketing channel because they are both marketers and customers for producers and wholesalers. They perform many marketing activities, such as buying, selling, grading, risk taking and developing information about consumers' wants. Of all marketers, retailers are the most visible to ultimate consumers. They are in a strategic position to gain feedback from consumers and to relay ideas to producers and intermediaries in the marketing channel. Retailing is an extraordinarily dynamic area of marketing.

This chapter examines the nature of retailing and its importance in supplying consumers with goods and services. It discusses the major retail locations and types of retail stores and describes several forms of non-store retailing, such as in-home retailing, telemarketing, automatic vending and mail order retailing. This chapter also looks at franchising, a retailing form which continues to grow in popularity. Finally, it presents several strategic issues in retailing: location, product assortment, retail positioning, atmospherics, store image, scrambled merchandising, the wheel of retailing, the balance of retailing, retail technology and the impact of the deregulation of the European Community.

THE NATURE OF RETAILING

Retailing includes all transactions in which the buyer intends to consume the product through personal, family or household use. The buyers in retail transactions are ultimate consumers. A **retailer**, then, is an organisation which purchases products for the purpose of reselling them to ultimate consumers. Although most retailers' sales are to consumers, non-retail transactions occasionally occur when retailers sell products to other businesses. Retailing activities usually take place in a store or in a service establishment, but exchanges through telephone selling, vending machines and mail order retailing occur outside stores.

It is common knowledge that retailing is important to the economy, being a large employer and major service sector component. Table 12.1, for example, shows the vol-

TABLE 12.1 *Volume/value of UK retail sales, 1985–1991*

VOLUME SALES BY ALL RETAILERS, 1985–91
(index: 1985 = 100; %)

	1985	1986	1987	1988	1989	1990	1991
Index	100.0	105.3	110.7	117.7	119.9	120.4	119.5
% change	4.7	5.3	5.1	6.3	1.9	0.4	–0.7

VALUE OF SALES BY ALL RETAILERS, 1986–90
(£ mn; index: 1985 = 100; %)

Sales value	—	95,660	103,220	113,240	120,800	128,710	134,960
Index		108.8	117.4	128.8	137.4	146.4	153.5
% change		8.8	7.9	9.7	6.7	6.6	4.8

SOURCE: From *Retail Trade Review.* Published by The Economist Intelligence Unit, London.

ume and value of retail sales in the UK between 1985 and 1991. As the table shows, sales volume has increased more than fourfold over this time period. Also, most personal income is spent in retail stores.

By providing assortments of products to match consumers' wants, retailers create place, time and possession utilities. *Place utility* means moving products from wholesalers or producers to a location where consumers want to buy them. *Time utility* involves maintaining specific business hours to make products available when consumers want them. *Possession utility* means facilitating the transfer of ownership or use of a product to consumers.

In the case of services such as hairdressing, dry cleaning, restaurants and car repairs, retailers themselves develop most of the product utilities. The services of such retailers provide aspects of *form utility* associated with the production process. Retailers of services usually have more direct contact with consumers and more opportunity to alter the product in the marketing mix.

RETAIL LOCATIONS

Central Business District

The traditional hub of most cities and towns is the **central business district (CBD),** the focus for shopping, banking and commerce and hence the busiest part of the whole area for traffic, public transport and pedestrians. Examples are London's Oxford and Regent streets, the Champs Elysées in Paris and Berlin's Kurfürstendamm.[1] The CBD is subdivided into zones: generally retailers are clustered together in a zone; banking and insurance companies locate together; legal offices occupy neighbouring premises; municipal offices and amenities are built on adjoining plots (town hall, library, law courts, art galleries).

Within the shopping zone certain streets at the centre of the zone will have the main shops and the highest levels of pedestrian foot-fall. In this area, known as the prime pitch, the key traders or magnets (Marks & Spencer, Boots or major department stores) will occupy prominent sites, so generating much of the footfall. Other retailers vie to be located close to these key traders so as to benefit from the customer traffic they generate. The highest rents are therefore paid for such sites. The CBD shopping centre—the city or town centre—generally offers shopping goods and some convenience items. Clothing, footwear, jewellery, cosmetics and financial services dominate the CBD. For the most part, grocers have moved out of town.

Property developers build shopping malls or centres in and around the CBD. Each development has one or more magnets (big name variety or department stores) both to attract shoppers and to encourage other retailers to locate within the development. Most city centres now have one covered shopping centre development (e.g., Eldon Square in Newcastle, Arndale Centre in Manchester).[2] On streets adjacent to this area of prime pitch, rents are lower but so is foot-fall. These secondary sites are suitable for specialty retailers or discounters, which have either lower margins or lower customer thresholds (the number of customers required to make a profit). Figure 12.1 shows the composition of a typical central business district (CBD).

Suburban Centres

Historically, as urban areas expanded during the early part of the twentieth century, they joined and subsequently swallowed up neighbouring towns and villages. The shopping centres of these settlements survived to become **suburban centres** of the now larger city or town. Where the expansion of the town was planned, suburban centres were created at major road junctions to cater for local shopping needs and reduce

FIGURE 12.1

The composition of a typical central business district (CBD)

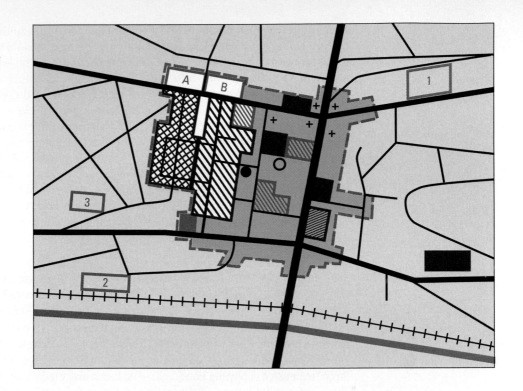

⌐⌐	CBD	▨ Banks, building societies, insurance companies	B	Town hall, art gallery, library
1	Bus station	▨ Solicitors/legal	▨	Covered shopping centres/malls
2	Railway station	Central shopping area	○	Peak land value intersection (retail)
3	Coach station	Head Post Office		Zone in transition*
▬	Main road	Department stores	●	Peak overall land value (CBD)
—	Minor road	▨ Market hall		
++	Railway	A Law courts	▬	Sports stadium
▬	Canal		+	Cinema/theatre

*The zone in transition is the land use between the CBD and suburban housing areas: light manufacturing, transport termini, wholesaling, garages, medical, mult-family residences.

SOURCE: Lyndon Simkin and Sally Dibb

demands and congestion in the CBD.[3] Suburban centres tend to offer convenience goods (frequently demanded, cheaper items such as groceries and drugs) and some shopping goods (clothing and footwear). Apart from a supermarket or limited range variety store (such as Woolworth), the shops tend to be small store outlets from 150 to 250 square metres (1,650 to 2,750 square feet); many are privately owned—unlike those in the CBD—and not part of national chains.

Edge of Town

During the 1970s, as rents in the CBD rose and sites sufficient for large, open-plan stores became harder to obtain, retailers looked to the green fields adjacent to outer ring roads for expansion. The superstore era had dawned as the major grocery, carpets and furniture, electrical and DIY* retailers opened free-standing "sheds". Needing more space to display stock and sell their goods than they could afford or obtain in the CBD or even suburban centre, but still requiring high traffic levels, they sought sites adjacent to major arteries into the CBD. Initially, planning authorities protected greenbelt and undeveloped land, so the retailers occupied disused warehouses and factory units in once thriving industrial and commercial areas.

The planners then began to realise that stylish retail outlets could brighten up areas, create employment, attract traffic and rejuvenate decaying zones. Major retail chains such as the grocery retailers with their frequently purchased convenience goods attracted large volumes of traffic. Relocating these stores to non-retail areas of the city, and particularly to **edge of town** sites, helped redistribute traffic volumes and make use of the latest infrastructure. Retailers no longer had to occupy run down warehouses; they could acquire undeveloped land and provide purpose built stores, parking facilities and amenities for their customers.[4]

Retail Parks

The progression of the out of town concept and relaxation of planning regulations by local authorities led to the mid-1980s initiation of the **retail park,** in which free-standing superstores, each over 2,500 square metres (27,500 square feet) are grouped together to form retail villages or parks. Located close to major roads, they offer extensive free parking. Most of the stores offer one floor shopping with wide ranges. Grocery superstores locate so as to be easily accessible to their consumers, as do the retailers of large, expensive shopping goods: carpets, furniture, electrical goods, toys. The extensive ranges and displays of DIY retailers make such locations viable.

Increasingly, planners are for the first time allowing clothing and footwear retailers to locate out of town. They initially feared the demise of the CBD, but forecasts now show that both CBD and out of town centres can survive serving the same town or city. Most retail parks, for example, West Thurrock on the M25 London orbital motorway, provide only superstores, but some have shopping malls of specialty and chain stores, such as Birmingham's Merry Hill or Gateshead's Metro Centre. Leisure facilities are frequently incorporated to cater for a family day out: ice skating rinks, cinemas, children's play areas, restaurants, fast food outlets and food courts (see Figure 12.2).

MAJOR STORE TYPES

Department and Variety Stores

Department stores are physically large—around 25,000 square metres (275,000 square feet)—and occupy prominent positions in the traditional heart of the town or city, the central shopping centre. Most towns have at least one such store; larger towns and cities have the population size to support several. The smaller town's department store is generally independently owned, whereas the larger store groups such as Debenhams, House of Fraser, John Lewis, or Allders in the UK, AuHPrintemps in France, El Corte Ingles in Spain, or Karlstadt in Germany, have stores in many cities. Within a department store, related product lines are organised into separate departments such as cosmetics, men's and women's fashions and accessories, housewares, home furnishings, haberdashery and toys. Each department functions as a self-contained business unit and the buyers for individual departments are fairly autonomous. Financial services, hairdressing, and restaurants or coffee shops act as additional pulls to attract customers into the store.

Quite often concessionaires operate shops within shops. Brides is the largest retailer

*DIY (do-it-yourself) merchandise includes building materials, hardware, plumbing and electrical goods, kitchen units and gardening requirements.)

FIGURE 12.2
The out of town shopping mall has reached Europe Gateshead's Metro Centre offers the major retail chains plus extensive leisure amenities and catering facilities.

SOURCE: Courtesy of The Metro Centre.

of wedding apparel in the UK. The company has its own bridal shops and agencies in secondary locations but also operates the bridal departments in most Debenhams and House of Fraser department stores (see Figure 12.3). Brides either pays a fixed rental per square metre of space occupied in the host department store or pays a percentage commission on its volume of business. In department stores, concessions or shops within shops are typical for fashion clothing, cosmetics and housewares.

Throughout the 1970s and 1980s, with the growth of shopping malls and covered centres, the explosion in the number of specialty shops and the move to out of town shopping, the demise of department stores was predicted. Yet they are still at the heart of many CBD shopping centres. With new management teams and investment, most departmental store groups are once again thriving and expanding, building new stores in towns where they were not previously represented and in out of town retail parks, as well as refurbishing existing outlets.

Variety stores tend to be slightly smaller and often are more specialised, offering a reduced range of merchandise. Their appeal tends to be middle market, price points are more critical and the selection of additional services is limited, usually just coffee shops. C&A focuses on men's, women's and children's clothing; Marks & Spencer on clothing and food; BhS and Littlewoods on clothing and housewares; Woolworth on housewares, records and tapes, children's clothes and confectionery. Variety stores are

FIGURE 12.3
A shop within a shop
Brides occupies a prominent position in this Debenhams store.

SOURCE: Courtesy of Bridal Fashions Ltd.

characterised by low cost facilities, self-service shopping, central payment points and multiple purchases; they appeal to large, heterogeneous target markets, especially price conscious customers.

Grocery Supermarkets, Superstores and Hypermarkets

In the 1960s, led by Sainsbury, Tesco and Fine Fare, grocery retailers expanded into 1,000 square metre (11,000 square foot) supermarkets, either in the city centre or within suburban centres. As product ranges grew, self-service requirements called for more space; and as city centre rents rose, the age of the superstore arrived. Size requirements grew further still, and there was an exodus from the city centre. In the 1980s the average grocery superstore grew from 2,500 square metres to 5,500 square metres (27,500 to 61,000 square feet) and moved away from the suburban centre to either free-standing superstore sites or edge of town retail parks.

Supermarkets and grocery **superstores** are large, self-service stores which carry a complete line of food products as well as other convenience items—cosmetics, nonprescription drugs and kitchenwares. Some, such as Asda or Tesco, sell clothing and small electrical appliances. Grocery superstores are laid out in departments for maximum efficiency in stocking and handling products but have central checkout facilities by the exits to the ample, free parking. Prices are considerably lower than in the independently owned supermarkets based in suburban shopping centres or in neighbourhood grocery shops. Price conscious consumers demanding greater choice, improved packaging and refrigeration, as well as widespread car ownership, spurred the huge growth of the major grocery superstore retailers: Sainsbury, Tesco, Asda, Gateway and Safeway.

Of the top retailers in Europe (see Table 12.2, Table 12.3 and Table 12.4), many are superstore trading grocery companies. They are at the forefront of retail technology—

TABLE 12.2   *Sales of top ten retailers in the UK*

MAJOR DISTRIBUTION CHAINS

Rank	Company	Category	Financial year ending	Group sales[1] £ million
1	J. Sainsbury	Food, DIY, hypermarkets	1991	7,813
2	Tesco	Food	1991	6,346
3	Marks & Spencer	Food/non-food	1991	5,775
4	Argyll Group	Food	1991	4,496
5	Asda Group	Food/non-food	1991	4,468
6	Isosceles	Food/non-food	1991	3,483
7	Kingfisher	Non-food	1991	3,117
8	Boots	Non-food	1991	3,042
9	Sears	Non-food/mail order	1991	2,163
10	John Lewis	Food/non-food	1991	1,978

Note: [1]Retailing (including overseas) only, excluding, VAT.

SOURCE: Marketing Pocket Book. Copyright © 1992 by NTC Publications. Used with permission.

TABLE 12.3   *The UK's major retailers (Top 100 retailers in the UK by sub-sector)*

SUB-SECTOR	NUMBER OF RETAILERS IN THE TOP 100	SALES (£bn)	PERCENTAGE OF TOTAL SALES OF TOP 100
Grocers	12	20,740.9	35
Other food specialists	10	2,029.7	3.4
CTNs (news agents)	4	525	0.9
Off licences	5	1,056	1.8
Clothing	7	2,523	4.3
Footwear	3	385	0.6
Furniture/carpets/household goods	6	1,451.9	2.5
Electrical and music goods	2	1,933	3.3
DIY and hardware	3	594	1.0
TV rental	2	1,470.5	2.5

SOURCE: Reprinted by permission of Corporate Intelligence Research Publications Limited/*Marketing,* 30 March 1990.

TABLE 12.4 *Europe's main retail groups, 1990–1991*

SPAIN	Pta. million		WEST GERMANY*	DM million
El Corte Ingles	662,621		Tengelmann	37,230
Ifa Española	401,059		Rewe, Zentral	29,415
Pryca	313,000		Edeka	22,000
Sogero	281,906		Aldi	12,200
Seleoctherica	255,00		Otto Versand	14,358
Maesa	251,215		Karstadt	12,961
ITALY	Lr. billion		Metrol Kaufhof	11,278
Rinascente	2,715		Quelle	10,652
Standa	2,623		**NORWAY**	NOK million
Despar	2,300		NKL (Co-op)	6,929
Benetton	1,275		Hagen	5,750
Coin	745		Joh Johannson	5,642
Unico-op Firenze	710		Narvesen	2,272
FRANCE	Fr. million		Staff	2,244
Leclerc	100,000		**EIRE**	£1R million
Intermeaché	96,000		Dunnes	840
Carrefour	75,841		Power-Supermarkets	550
Auchan	64,000		Musgrave	400
Promodès	58,477		Supergwinn	155
Casino	44,900		Allced	125
Système U	32,500		**DENMARK**	DKr. million
NETHERLANDS	Fl. million		Co-ops	29,128
Ahold	8,785		Dansk Supermarked	13,000
Albert Heijh	2,231		Dagrofa	7,000
Vendex	6,848		Edeka (Hoki)	3,400
KBB	5,054		Oceka/NH	3,000
Schuitema	3,020		Sam Koclo/Prima	2,600
Aldi	1,750			

*Figures for the unified Germany are not yet available.

SOURCES: Authors; Warwick University Business Information Service; *Euromonitor;* DTI.

bar scanning **EPOS** (electronic point of sale) tills, shelf allocation modelling, robotised warehouse stacking—and of monitoring changes in customer attitudes and expectations. Increasingly, to gain an edge over the competition, they are launching more own label products with attributes equal to, if not better than, the manufacturers' brands which are also on sale. Marketing Insight 12.1 describes how the grocery retailers have led the transition in Europe, crossing national borders to trade in many countries. This move has been led by the discounters, such as Aldi, Netto and Carrefour.

Hypermarkets take the benefits of the superstore even further, using their greater size—over 9,000 square metres (100,000 square feet)—to give the customer a wider range and depth of products. They are common in the US, France and Germany, but there are few genuine hypermarkets in the UK, except perhaps for Sainsbury's Savacentre.

SUPERMARKETERS EXPAND ACROSS EUROPE

The German company Aldi, one of Europe's largest retailers, led the assault into the UK grocery sector. In just three years close to 70 discount stores opened in the Midlands and North of England. In late 1992, the French giant Carrefour announced its intention to launch its Ed discount operation in the South of England, becoming the first non-UK discounter to challenge Kwik Save in the South of the country. Twelve Ed The Discount Grocery stores are planned initially, each around 1,000 square metres (11,000 square feet) in area, plus parking. Unlike Aldi, or Danish Netto, which operates in the North East, Ed will sell more manufacturers' brands than the retailer's own label. German discounter Norma, which has 700 stores outside the UK, is also entering the South East of England with an operation similar to Aldi's.

While retailers have dabbled outside their country of origin, hardly any retailers outside the grocery sector have spread their marque away from their original heartland. The few exceptions are IKEA and previously Habitat in home furnishings, Marks & Spencer in clothing and foods, and, most notably, Body Shop in skin and body care. There are signs in many sectors, from electricals to footwear, that this situation is changing. The grocery sector, however, has long led the way, and not just through the quickly growing Aldi or Carrefour.

The UK based voluntary group SPAR has a significant presence throughout Europe. Most SPAR stores are owned by individual entrepreneurs or companies trading from small regional chains of 20 to 30 shops. In 1992 SPAR decided to run its first pan-European promotion—pushing well known manufacturers' brands at low prices across 14 countries. Simultaneously, SPAR developed a new image for its own label products, an image which could be used throughout its network of convenience stores in Europe. The company has encountered various problems. For its pan-European promotions, supplying manufacturers were concerned about maintaining uniform brand positioning and pricing from country to country. Most brands, including SPAR's own label, occupy different positionings from one country to the next. This problem was to prove more fundamental to the roll-out and strategic use of the SPAR own label brand, particularly between Spain, Germany, Holland and the UK. The brand occupies a discount position, except in the UK, where it enjoys a slightly more up market image.

SOURCES: "Cut price Carrefour targets UK", Suzanne Bidlake, *Marketing,* 19 November 1992, p. 3; "Norma and Carrefour invade UK", *Marketing Week,* 22 January 1993, p. 6; Aldi Appointments, *The Independent on Sunday,* 7 March 1993, p. IB39; "Spar slashes brand prices over Europe", Kate Trollope, *Marketing,* 11 June 1992, p. 8.

Asda, based in Leeds, began as a discount retailer of grocery products in the northern industrial regions of the UK. Needing large premises but unable to gain planning permission to build on green field sites, the company operated initially from redundant cinemas and converted industrial warehouses. As the superstore era blossomed,

Asda was a guiding force. Today the company is the market leader in superstore grocery retailing, with over one hundred purpose built free-standing superstores offering manufacturer and Asda branded goods. The stores have over 4,500 square metres (50,000 square feet) of one floor retail space, pleasing ambience and additional amenities such as cafés, crèche facilities and ample free parking. The company has a new distribution network, fully computerised and centralised, with on-line EPOS systems monitoring the exact stock requirements of each store.

Discount Sheds and Superstores

The move away from the city or town centre was not confined to multiple grocery retailers. Furniture, carpets and electrical appliances require large display areas, ranges with strength in depth and, if possible, one floor shopping. The concentration of retailers in the city centre led to limited store opening opportunities (large enough sites were hard to find) and to high rents. When the electrical retailer Comet and furniture retailers Queensway and MFI sought out of town sites, they too were initially forced by the planning authorities to occupy disused warehouses and industrial units along arteries into the city centre. As the planners reviewed their regulations, these firms, along with the major DIY and toy retailers, developed purpose built discount "sheds" or retail warehouses. Originally free-standing, these 2,000 to 3,500 square metre (22,000 to 39,000 square foot) stores are increasingly found in edge of town retail parks.

The **discount sheds** are cheaply constructed, one storey retail stores with no window displays and few add-on amenities. Orientated towards car-borne shoppers, they have large, free car parks and spacious stock facilities to enable shoppers to take delivery of their purchases immediately. Checkout points and customer services are kept to a minimum. As major retail groups have seen the cost benefits of location out of town, more companies have opened out of town, free-standing or retail park superstores. Many customers would not tolerate the minimalist approach to ambience and service levels. Construction is still basic, but more resources are devoted to shop fitting expertise and customer service. US Toys "Я" Us and Sweden's IKEA typify the new generation of superstores. Most retail groups selling electrical goods, carpets, furniture, toys, groceries or DIY goods, not just the discounters, now operate superstores. Increasingly, major variety store companies, departmental store groups, and clothing and footwear retailers are developing superstores: Marks & Spencer, Debenhams and Sears are among them.

Specialty Shops

Most shopping centres and towns have a major department store. At the other end of the spectrum is the traditional corner shop. Few small shops these days retail a variety of product groups. In suburban areas such shops tend to specialise in retailing one convenience product category—newsagents with cigarettes and newspapers, greengrocers, chemists, hair salons, etc. In the town centre (CBD) few retailers of convenience goods, with their low margins, can afford the rents and business tax. Instead, the small store retailers—250 square metres (2,750 square feet) and under—in the town centre specialise in shopping or comparison items: clothing, footwear, records and tapes, cosmetics, jewellery. Ownership of such retail outlets is increasingly concentrated in the hands of a few major retail groups (see Table 12.5), some of which also have retail brands which operate as department stores or out of town superstores. **Specialty shops** offer self-service but a greater level of assistance from store personnel. A typical 300 square metre (3,300 square feet) footwear or clothing retail store will have window displays to entice passing pedestrians, one or two checkout points and three or four assistants. Such stores depend on the town centre's general parking facilities and on proximity to a key trader, such as Boots or Marks & Spencer, which will generate pedestrian traffic.

TABLE 12.5 *Large retail groups*

Boots (chemists, car accessories, DIY)	Boots, Halfords, Do-It-All (with W. H. Smith), A.G. Stanley, FADS
Burton Group (fashion clothing shops and department stores)	Burton, Top Man, Principles/Principles for Men, Top Shop, Evans, Dorothy Perkins, Champion Sport, Secrets, Radius, Alias, Harvey Nichols and Debenhams
Dixons (electricals, computers)	Dixons, Currys, PC World
John Menzies (books, newsagency, toys)	Hammicks; John Menzies; Early Learning Centres
Kingfisher (variety stores, chemists, electricals, DIY)	Woolworth, Superdrug, Comet, B&Q
Pentos (greetings cards, books, office supplies)	Athena; Dillons; Ryman
Signet (jewellery, leather goods))	Ratners, H. Samuel, James Walker, Watches of Switzerland, Zales, Ernest Jones, Dqua, Salisbury's
J. Sainsbury (grocery, DIY)	Sainsbury, Savacentre; Homebase
Sears (footwear, fashion clothing, jewellery, sportswear, children's wear, mail order, department stores)	British Shoe Corporation (Freeman Hardy Willis, Trueform, Dolcis, Bertie, Cable & Co., Lilley & Skinner, Saxone, Manfield, Roland Cartier, Curtess, Shoe City); Fosters, Hornes, Zy, Bradleys, Your Price; Miss Selfridge, Wallis, Warehouse; Milletts Leisure, Olympus Sports Pro-Performance; Adams Childrenswear, Pride & Joy; Selfridges; Freemans
W. H. Smith (newsagency, books, records/tapes, DIY)	W. H. Smith, Waterstone, Paperchase, Our Price, Wee Three Records (USA), Do-It-All (with Boots)
Storehouse (fashion clothing, children's wear, variety stores)	Richard Shops, Blazer, Mothercare, BhS

Convenience Stores

As the number of neighbourhood grocery stores declined in the 1960s and 1970s with the expansion of the superstore based national grocery chains, a niche emerged in the market to be filled by **convenience stores.** These shops sell essential groceries, alcoholic drinks, drugs and newspapers outside the traditional 9.00 a.m. to 6.00 p.m. shopping hours. The major superstores extended their opening hours to 8.00 p.m. to facilitate after work shopping, but no major retailers catered for "emergency" or top up shopping. There was a resurgence of the traditional corner shop located in suburban housing estates, offering limited ranges but extended opening hours. Consumers pay a slight price premium but receive convenience in terms of location and opening hours.

In the 1970s and 1980s, the voluntary groups (Spar, Mace, VG) and national retail groups such as Circle K and 7/Eleven repositioned their brands into the "open all hours" top-up or emergency shopping niche.

Markets and Cash and Carry Warehouses

In most towns there are wholesale **markets** selling meat, greengrocery, fruit, flowers and fish from which specialty retailers make their inventory purchases. Traditional, too, is the general retail market either in recently refurbished Victorian market halls or in council provided modern halls adjacent to the town centre shopping malls. Such market halls sell fresh foods, clothing and housewares, and they cater for budget conscious shoppers who typically have a middle and down market social profile.

Cash and carry warehouses, such as Booker or Makro, retail extensive ranges of groceries, tobacco, alcohol, beverages and confectionery to newsagents, small supermarkets and convenience stores, and the catering trade (hotels, guest houses, restaurants and cafés). By purchasing from manufacturers in bulk, cash and carry companies can offer substantial price savings to their customers, who in turn can add a retail margin without alienating their customers. Many countries, particularly Scandinavia, have hybrid outlets that combine the speciality shop, convenience store and cash and carry warehouse. Buying groups link small, often privately owned local retailers with similar shops; collectively their purchasing power is enhanced, and they increasingly operate their own wholesale warehouses and offer own label brands.

Catalogue Showrooms

In a **catalogue showroom** one item of each product class is on display and the remaining inventory is stored out of the buyer's reach. Using catalogues which have been mailed to their homes or are on counters in the store, customers order the goods at their leisure. Shop assistants usually complete the order form and then collect the merchandise from the adjoining warehouse. Catalogue showrooms, such as Argos or Index, regularly sell goods below list prices and often provide goods immediately. Higher product turnover, fewer losses through damage or shoplifting and lower labour costs lead to their reduced retail prices. Jewellery, luggage, photographic equipment, toys, small appliances, housewares, sporting goods, garden furniture and power tools are the most commonly available items, listed by category and brand in the company's catalogue.

Categories

Table 12.6 summarises the major categories of retailing as defined in official DTI statistics. It is worth noting that the categories with the most stores do not necessarily top the league for highest turnover or profitability. The superstore and department store retailers have relatively fewer outlets but they account for large floor areas and include many of the UK's main retail groups. European, and UK in particular, retail statistics are notoriously poor, being based on infrequent estimates rather than regular censuses. Agencies such as AGB, Euromonitor, Jordans, Mintel and Verdict produce regular reports on retail sectors and consumer expectations based on commissioned marketing research surveys. These are available by subscription or occasionally, for the newest versions, through business libraries. These agencies tend to use categories similar to those discussed by the retail trade itself rather than the stilted, amalgamated official classification:

Food/grocery • CTN (confectionery, tobacco, news) • Off-licence beverages
Men's/women's wear • Children's wear • Footwear/leather goods
Furniture/carpets/soft furnishings
Electrical (small appliances, brown and white goods)
Hardware • DIY

TABLE 12.6 *UK retail trade by sectors (standardised sectors)*

	FOOD RETAILERS		DRINK, CONFECTIONERY, AND TOBACCO RETAILERS		CLOTHING, FOOTWEAR AND LEATHER GOODS RETAILERS		HOUSEHOLD GOODS SHOPS		OTHER NON-FOOD RETAILERS		MIXED RETAIL BUSINESSES		HIRE AND REPAIR BUSINESS	
	1987	1988	1987	1988	1987	1988	1987	1988	1987	1988	1987	1988	1987	1988
BUSINESS (NUMBER)	73,681	67,755	47,296	48,893	31,162	30,170	42,760	45,678	38,973	39,604	4,937	3,528	2,045	2,204
OUTLETS (NUMBERS)	98,016	87,758	59,810	60,877	58,380	57,768	60,406	63,795	52,473	52,944	11,363	9,402	5,020	5,703
TURNOVER (£ MN)	35,880	38,311	10,363	11,180	10,077	11,068	17,001	18,827	8,812	10,051	18,354	19,835	1,288	1,292
AVERAGE TURNOVER PER OUTLET (£'000)	366	437	173	184	173	192	281	295	168	190	2,084	2,110	257	227
SHARE OF SALES (%)	35.2	34.7	10.2	10.1	9.9	10.0	16.7	17.0	8.7	9.1	18.0	17.9	1.3	1.2
GROSS MARGIN (%)	21.9	22.8	17.8	18.2	41.4	43.4	32.0	34.1	33.2	33.0	34.7	33.2	72.5	69.8

SOURCE: From *Retail Trade Review*. Published by The Economist Intelligence Unit, London.

Chemist/druggist
Books/greetings cards
Jewellers
Toys
Mixed retail businesses
Mail order
Restaurants/cafés/catering • Hotels
Banking/financial services

NON-STORE RETAILING AND HOME RETAILING

Non-store retailing is the selling of goods or services outside the confines of a retail facility. This form of retailing accounts for an increasing percentage of sales and includes personal sales methods, such as in-home retailing and telemarketing, and non-personal sales methods, such as automatic vending and mail order retailing (which includes catalogue retailing).

Certain non-store retailing methods are in the category of **direct marketing:** the use of non-personal media or telesales to introduce products to consumers, who then purchase the products by mail or telephone. In the case of telephone orders, salespeople may be required to complete the sales. Telemarketing, mail order and catalogue retailing are all examples of direct marketing, as are sales generated by coupons, direct mail and Freephone bell gratis 0800 numbers.

In-Home Retailing

In-home retailing is selling via personal contacts with consumers in their own homes. Organisations such as Avon, Amway and Betterware send representatives to the homes of pre-selected prospects. Traditionally, in-home retailing relied on a random, door-to-door approach. Some companies now use a more efficient approach. They first identify prospects by reaching them by phone or mail or intercepting them in shopping malls or at consumer trade fairs. These initial contacts are limited to a brief introduction and the setting of appointments.

Some in-home selling, however, is still undertaken without information about sales prospects. Door-to-door selling without a pre-arranged appointment represents a tiny proportion of total retail sales, less than 1 per cent. Because it has so often been associated with unscrupulous and fraudulent techniques, it is illegal in some communities. Generally, this method is regarded unfavourably because so many door-to-door salespeople are under trained and poorly supervised. A big disadvantage of door-to-door selling is the large expenditure, effort and time it demands. Sales commissions are usually 25 to 50 per cent (or more) of the retail price; as a result, consumers often pay more than a product is worth. Door-to-door selling is used most often when a product is unsought—for instance, encyclopaedias, which most consumers would not be likely to purchase in a store.

A variation of in-home retailing is the home demonstration or party plan, which such companies as Tupperware, Ann Summers and Mary Kay Cosmetics use successfully. One consumer acts as host and invites a number of friends to view merchandise at his or her home, where a salesperson is on hand to demonstrate the products. The home demonstration is more efficient for the sales representative than contacting each prospect door-to-door, and the congenial atmosphere partly overcomes consumers' suspicions and encourages them to buy. Home demonstrations also meet the buyers' needs for convenience and personal service. Commissions and selling costs make this form of retailing expensive, however. Additionally, successful party plan selling requires both a network of friends and neighbours who have the time to attend such social gatherings and a large number of effective salespersons. With so many household members now holding full time jobs, both prospects and sales representatives are harder to recruit. The growth of interactive telephone-computer home shopping may also cut into party plan sales.

Telemarketing

More and more organisations—IBM, Merrill Lynch, Avis, Ford, Quaker Oats, Time and American Express, to name a few—are using the telephone to strengthen the effectiveness of traditional marketing methods. **Telemarketing** is direct selling of goods and services by telephone based on either a cold canvass of the telephone directory or a pre-screened list of prospective clients. (In some areas, certain telephone numbers are listed with an asterisk to indicate the people who consider sales solicitations a nuisance and do not want to be bothered.) Telemarketing can generate sales leads, improve customer service, speed up collection of over due accounts, raise funds for non-profit groups and gather market data.[5]

In some cases, telemarketing uses advertising encouraging consumers to initiate a call or to request information about placing an order. This type of retailing is only a small part of total retail sales, but its use is growing. According to AT&T, US companies spent $13.6 billion in one year on telemarketing phone calls and equipment (phones, lines and computers). Telephone Marketing Resources, a US telemarketing firm, estimates telephone sales of goods and services at $75 billion annually (the figure includes business to consumer sales and business to business sales).[6] Experts believe that similar growth will be seen in Europe in the next few years. Research indicates that telemarketing is most successful when combined with other marketing strategies, such as direct mail or advertising in newspapers, radio and television.

Automatic Vending

Automatic vending makes use of machines and accounts for less than 1 per cent of all retail sales. In the UK there are approximately 650,000 vending machines. Locations and the percentage of sales each generates are as follows:[7]

Plants and factories	38%
Public locations (e.g. stores)	26
Offices	16
Colleges and universities	6
Government facilities	3
Hospitals and nursing homes	3
Primary and secondary schools	2
Others	6

Video game machines provide an entertainment service, and many banks now offer machines that dispense cash or offer other services, but these uses of vending machines are not reported in total vending sales volume.

Automatic vending is one of the most impersonal forms of retailing. Small, standardised, routinely purchased products (chewing gum, sweets, newspapers, cigarettes, soft drinks, coffee) can be sold in machines because consumers usually buy them at the nearest available location. Machines in areas of heavy traffic provide efficient and continuous services to consumers. The elimination of sales personnel and the small amount of space necessary for vending machines give this retailing method some advantages over stores. The advantages are partly offset by the expense of the frequent servicing and repair needed.

**Mail Order
Retailing**

Mail order retailing involves selling by description because buyers usually do not see the actual product until it arrives in the mail. Sellers contact buyers through direct mail, catalogues, television, radio, magazines and newspapers. A wide assortment of products such as compact discs, books and clothing is sold to consumers through the mail. Placing mail orders by telephone is increasingly common. The advantages of mail order selling include efficiency and convenience. Mail order houses, such as Freemans or Grattan, can be located in remote, low cost areas and avoid the expenses of store fixtures. Eliminating personal selling efforts and store operations may result in tremendous savings that can be passed along to consumers in the form of lower prices. On the other hand, mail order retailing is inflexible, provides limited service and is more appropriate for specialty products than for convenience products.

When **catalogue retailing** (a specific type of mail order retailing) is used, customers receive their orders by mail (see Figure 12.4), or they may pick them up if the catalogue retailer has stores, as does Littlewoods. Although in-store visits result in some catalogue orders, most are placed by mail or telephone. In the US, General Foods created Thomas Garroway Ltd., a mail order service supplying gourmet pasta, cheese, coffee and similar items. Other packaged goods manufacturers involved in catalogue retailing include Hanes, Nestlé, Thomas J. Lipton, Sunkist and Whitman Chocolates.[8] These catalogue retailers are able to reach many two income families who have more money and less time for special shopping. In the UK manufacturers and store focused retail groups tend not to be involved with catalogue or home shopping.

FIGURE 12.4 *Catalogue retailing*
The 3 Suisses mail order house promotes an extensive product mix to its customers.

SOURCE: Courtesy of Julian Meijer Associates.

The specialist mail order companies such as GUS and Freemans dominate this sector. The UK mail order market is worth over £5.4 billion, having grown by 113 per cent since 1982.[9] As described in Case 12.2 it is a sector likely to be assisted by new technology and the changing leisure habits of consumers.

FRANCHISING

Franchising is an arrangement whereby a supplier, or franchisor, grants a dealer, or franchisee, the right to sell products in exchange for some type of consideration. For example, the franchisor may receive some percentage of total sales in exchange for furnishing equipment, buildings, management know-how, marketing assistance and branding to the franchisee. The franchisee supplies labour and capital, operates the franchised business and agrees to abide by the provisions of the franchise agreement. This next section looks at the major types of retail franchises, the advantages and disadvantages of franchising, and trends in franchising.

Major Types of Retail Franchises

Retail franchise arrangements can generally be classified as one of three general types. In the first arrangement, a manufacturer authorises a number of retail stores to sell a certain brand name item. This franchise arrangement, one of the oldest, is common in the sales of cars and trucks, farm equipment, earthmoving equipment and petroleum. The majority of all petrol is sold through franchised independent retail service stations, and franchised dealers handle virtually all sales of new cars and trucks. In the second type of retail franchise, a producer licenses distributors to sell a given product to retailers. This franchising arrangement is common in the soft drinks industry. Most international manufacturers of soft drink syrups—Coca-Cola, Pepsi-Cola—franchise independent bottlers, which then serve retailers. In the third type of retail franchise, a franchisor supplies brand names, techniques, or other services, instead of a complete product. The franchisor may provide certain production and distribution services, but its primary role in the arrangement is the careful development and control of marketing strategies. This approach to franchising, which is the most typical today, is used by many organisations, including Holiday Inn, McDonald's, Avis, Hertz, Kentucky Fried Chicken, Body Shop, Holland & Barrett, Pronuptia and Benetton, as described in Marketing Insight 12.2.

Advantages and Disadvantages of Franchising

Franchising offers several advantages to both the franchisee and the franchisor. It enables a franchisee to start a business with limited capital and to make use of the business experience of others. Moreover, an outlet with a nationally advertised name, such as Body Shop or Burger King, is often assured of customers as soon as it opens. If business problems arise, the franchisee can obtain guidance and advice from the franchisor at little or no cost. Franchised outlets are generally more successful than independently owned businesses: only 5 to 8 per cent of franchised retail businesses fail during the first two years of operation, whereas approximately 54 per cent of independent retail businesses fail during that period.[10] The franchisee also receives materials to use in local advertising and can take part in national promotional campaigns sponsored by the franchisor.

The franchisor gains fast and selective distribution of its products through franchise arrangements without incurring the high cost of constructing and operating its own outlets. The franchisor therefore has more capital available to expand production and to use for advertising. At the same time, it can ensure, through the franchise agreement, that outlets are maintained and operated to its own standards. The franchisor

FRANCHISING ALL OVER

A press campaign in 1993 by McDonald's was not targeted at its customers. Instead, it sought franchisees, as the advertisement's header explained:

> "Here's something for hungry entrepreneurs to get their teeth into".

In the UK McDonald's owns the bulk of its 470 restaurants, but in many other territories most are owned and operated by franchise holders. The fast food giant, eager to speed up its expansion and reduce its capital outlay, is offering budding entrepreneurs the chance to own and run their own McDonald's restaurant. The requirements include entrepreneurial spirit, the ability to lead and motivate staff, sound financial skills, the successful completion of a vigorous training programme and £50,000 to lease an existing restaurant or £150,000 to £240,000 to purchase a new or existing restaurant.

McDonald's offers one of the best known brands in the world, a proven trading concept, training, advice and promotional support. For the franchisee, however, individual success depends on his or her own abilities, commitment and business skills.

McDonald's has a successful track record of viable franchises all around the world. Not all franchises have been so fortunate. From dry cleaning operations to mobile car maintenance, baked potato outlets to security systems, the bankruptcy courts are littered with the records of failed franchises. Nevertheless, the annual Franchise Exhibition sees thousands of visitors seeking information and business opportunities offered by franchising. For well known brands such as Pizza Hut, McDonald's, Body Shop and the print shop Kall-Kwik, franchising has brought considerable rewards for both brand owner and franchise holder.

For the franchisee, it is essential that there be a clearly defined brand proposition, and one which is in demand. The franchise holder must be paying for a marketing asset which is well perceived by the target market. It must be a well thought out business proposition. Identified customer needs, competitive forces and environmental trends all need to support a viable financial analysis and cash flow forecast. The British Franchise Association stresses that a franchise is not something for nothing; taking on a franchise is not a cut-price way to establish a high profile, well branded operation and make the franchisee's fortune overnight. A franchise agreement is a business deal. The brand and concept must be in sufficient demand by the target public to warrant the purchase of the franchise and the setting up of the business. Like any other type of business, stresses the Association, a franchise opportunity requires thorough marketing and financial analyses. With annual sales approaching £5 billion, franchising in the UK is quickly emulating patterns in Europe and North America.

SOURCES: "A low risk guide to franchising", Roger Trapp, *The Independent on Sunday*, 11 October 1992, p. IB23; McDonald's advertisements, February 1993; "Buy yourself a brand name", Roger Trapp, *The Independent on Sunday*, 21 February 1993, p. IB26; British Franchise Association literature.

also benefits from the fact that the franchisee, being a sole proprietor in most cases, is likely to be very highly motivated to succeed. The success of the franchise means more sales, which translate into higher royalties for the franchisor.

Despite their numerous advantages, franchise arrangements also have several drawbacks. The franchisor can dictate many aspects of the business: decor, the design of employees' uniforms, types of signs and numerous details of business operations. In addition, franchisees must pay to use the franchisor's name, products and assistance. Usually, there is a one-time franchise fee and continuing royalty and advertising fees, collected as a percentage of sales. In addition, franchisees often must work very hard, putting in 10 and 12 hour days, six days a week. In some cases, franchise agreements are not uniform: one franchisee may pay more than another for the same services. The franchisor also gives up a certain amount of control when entering into a franchise agreement. Consequently, individual establishments may not be operated exactly as the franchisor would operate them.

Trends in Franchising

Franchising has been used since the early 1990s, primarily for service stations and car dealerships. However, it has grown enormously since the mid-1960s. This growth has generally paralleled the expansion of the fast food industry—the industry in which franchising is widely used. Of course, franchising is not limited to fast foods. Franchise arrangements for health clubs, pest control, hair salons and travel agencies are widespread. The estate agency industry has also experienced a rapid increase in franchising. The largest franchising sectors, ranked by sales, are car and truck dealers (52 per cent), service stations (14 per cent), restaurants (10 per cent), and non-food retailing (5 per cent).[11]

STRATEGIC ISSUES IN RETAILING

Consumers often have vague reasons for making a retail purchase. Whereas most industrial purchases are based on economic planning and necessity, consumer purchases often result from social influences and psychological factors. Because consumers shop for a variety of reasons—to search for specific items, to escape boredom or to learn about something new—retailers must do more than simply fill space with merchandise; they must make desired products available, create stimulating environments for shopping and develop marketing strategies that increase store patronage. This section discusses how store location, property ownership, product assortment, retail positioning, atmospherics/design, store image, scrambled merchandising, central/regional management, technology, distribution, the wheel of retailing and EC deregulation affect these retailing objectives.

Location

Location, the least flexible of the strategic retailing issues, is one of the most important, because location dictates the limited geographic trading area from which a store must draw its customers.[12] Thus retailers consider a variety of factors when evaluating potential locations, including the location of the firm's target customers within the trading area, the economic climate in the region, the kinds of products being sold, the availability of public transport, customer characteristics and competitors' locations.[13] The relative ease of movement to and from the site is important, so that pedestrian and vehicular traffic, parking and transport must all be taken into account. Most retailers prefer sites with high pedestrian traffic; preliminary site investigations often include a pedestrian count to determine how many of the passers by are truly prospective customers. Similarly, the nature of the area's vehicular traffic is analysed. Certain retailers, such as service stations and convenience stores, depend on large numbers of car-borne customers but try to avoid overly congested locations. In addition, parking space must be adequate for projected demand, and transport networks (major thoroughfares and public transport) must be able to accommodate customers and delivery vehicles.

Retailers also evaluate the characteristics of the site itself: the other stores in the area, particularly the proximity of key traders or magnets; the size, shape and visibility of the plot or building under consideration; and the rental, leasing or ownership terms under which the building may be occupied. Retailers also look for compatibility with nearby retailers because stores that complement one another draw more customers for everyone. This is particularly true for clothing, footwear and jewellery retailers.[14] When making site location decisions, retailers must select from among several general types of location: free-standing structures, traditional business districts, neighbourhood/suburban shopping centres, out of town superstores and retail parks. In recent years retailers have been moving away from the traditional store assessment procedure of pedestrian counts and "eye-balling" the immediate site's location. Various agencies—notably CACI and SAMI—have detailed databases examining each shopping centre. Computer modelling, such as SLAM (Store Location Assessment Model), has become more widespread, bringing a basis of objectivity to what was previously an intuitive decision-making process, based on few hard facts.[15]

Property Ownership

Property ownership is perpetually an issue in retailing. Some companies, such as Marks & Spencer, own the majority of their property portfolio. This gives security of tenure, saves on rents and lease negotiations, and adds to the book value of the company. To release operating funds, companies often engage in "sale and leaseback" deals. Property companies buy the freehold to add to their assets but give a favourable lease immediately to the retailer. In recent years companies which once held the freehold for most of their stores have sold off property to make available operating funds for new computer systems, store refurbishment or new store openings. Companies such as the Burton Group or Next argue that they are primarily retailers and funds should not be tied up in property ownership. Retailers that locate mainly in covered shopping centres and in retail parks generally have to accept lease agreements as the centre's developer maintains ownership of the property.

Product Assortment

The **product assortments** which retailers develop vary considerably in breadth and depth. As discussed earlier, retail stores are often classified according to their product assortments. Conversely, a store's type affects the breadth and depth of its product offerings, as shown in Figure 12.5. Thus a specialty store has a single product line but considerable depth in that line. Tie Rack stores and Fannie May Candy Shops, for example, carry only one line of products but many items within that line. In contrast, discount stores may have a wide product mix (such as housewares, automotive services, clothing and food). Department stores may have a wide product mix with different product line depths. Nevertheless, it is usually difficult to maintain both a wide and a deep product mix because of the inventories required. In addition, some producers prefer to distribute through retailers that offer less variety so that their products get more exposure and are less affected by the presence of competing brands.

Issues of product assortment are often a matter of what and how much to carry. When retailers decide what should be included in their product assortments, they consider the assortment's purpose, status and completeness.[16] *Purpose* relates to how well an assortment satisfies consumers and at the same time furthers the retailer's goals. *Status* identifies by rank the relative importance of each product in an assortment: for example, motor oil might have low status in a store that sells convenience foods. *Completeness* means that an assortment includes the products necessary to satisfy a

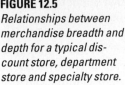

FIGURE 12.5

Relationships between merchandise breadth and depth for a typical discount store, department store and specialty store.

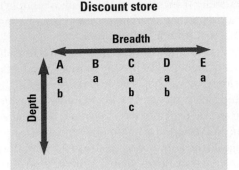

Discount store

Breadth

Depth

A B C D E
a a a a a
b b b
c

Department store

Breadth

Depth

A B C D E
a a a a a
b b b b b
c c c c c
d d
e

Specialty store

Breadth

Depth

A
a
b
c
d
e
f

The capital letters represent the number of product lines, and the small letters depict the choices in any one product line. Thus it can be seen that discount stores are wide and shallow in merchandise assortment. Specialty stores, at the other extreme, have few product lines, but much more depth in the few they carry. The typical department store falls in between, having a broad assortment with many merchandise lines and medium depth in each line.

SOURCE: Robert F. Hartley, *Retailing: Challenge and Opportunity,* 3rd ed., p. 118. Copyright © 1984 by Houghton Mifflin Company. Used by permission.

store's customers; the assortment is incomplete when some products are missing. An assortment of convenience foods must include milk to be complete because most consumers expect to be able to buy milk when purchasing other food products. New products are added to (and declining products are deleted from) an assortment when they meet (or fail to meet) the retailer's standards of purpose, status and completeness.

The retailer also considers the quality of the products to be offered. The store may limit its assortments to expensive, high quality goods for upper income market segments; it may stock cheap, low quality products for low income buyers; or it may try to attract several market segments by offering a range of quality within its total product assortment.

How much to include in an assortment depends on the needs of the retailer's target market. A discount store's customers expect a wide and shallow product mix, whereas specialty store shoppers prefer narrow and deep assortments. If a retailer can increase sales by increasing product variety, the assortment may be enlarged. If a broader product mix ties up too much floor space or creates storage problems, however, the retailer may stock only the products that generate the greatest sales. Other factors that affect product assortment decisions are the personnel, store image, inventory control methods and the financial risks involved.[17]

Retail Positioning

Because of the emergence of new types of store (discount warehouses, superstores, hypermarkets) and the expansion of product offerings by traditional stores, competition among retailers is intense. Thus it is important for management to consider the retail organisation's market positioning.[18] **Retail positioning** involves identifying an unserved or under served market niche, or segment, and serving it through a strategy that distinguishes the retailer from others in the minds of people in that segment.[19] The retailer must have a proposition, trading concept, brand image or merchandise policy which is visibly different from its competitors.

There are several ways in which retailers position themselves.[20] A retailer may position itself as a seller of high quality, premium priced products providing many services. A store such as Selfridges, which specialises in expensive high fashion clothing and jewellery, sophisticated electronics and exclusive home furnishings, might be expected to provide wrapping and delivery services, personal shopping consultants and restaurant facilities. Fortnum & Mason, for example, emphasises superlative service and even hires pianists to play in the entrance of its store.[21] Dixons, the electrical retailer, is often referred to as "the grown man's toy shop". Another type of retail organisation, such as IKEA, may be positioned as a marketer of reasonable quality products at everyday low prices.

| Atmospherics | Atmospherics are often used to help position a retailer. **Atmospherics** are the physical elements in a store's design which appeal to consumers' emotions and encourage them to buy. Exterior and interior characteristics, layout and displays all contribute to a store's atmosphere. Department stores, restaurants, hotels, service stations and shops combine these elements in different ways to create specific atmospheres that may be perceived as warm, fresh, functional or exciting. |

Exterior atmospheric elements include the appearance of the store front, the window displays, store entrances and degree of traffic congestion. Exterior atmospherics are particularly important to new customers, who tend to judge an unfamiliar store by its outside appearance and may not enter the store if they feel intimidated by the building or inconvenienced by the car park. Because consumers form general impressions of shopping centres and business districts, the businesses and neighbourhoods surrounding a store will affect how buyers perceive the atmosphere of a store.

Interior atmospheric elements include aesthetic considerations such as lighting, wall and floor coverings, changing rooms and store fixtures. Interior sensory elements also contribute to atmosphere. Colour, for example, can attract shoppers to a retail display. Many fast food restaurants use bright colours such as red and yellow because these have been shown to make customers feel hungrier and eat faster, thus increasing turnover. Sound is another important sensory component of atmosphere and may consist of silence, soft music or even noisiness. Scent may be relevant as well; within a store, the odour of perfume suggests an image different from that suggested by the smell of prepared food. A store's layout—arrangement of departments, width of aisles, grouping of products and location of cashiers—is yet another determinant of atmosphere. Closely related to store layout is the element of crowding. A crowded store may restrict exploratory shopping, impede mobility and decrease shopping efficiency. An apparently empty store, however, may imply unpopularity and deter shoppers from entering.

Once the exterior and interior characteristics and store layout have been determined, displays are added. Displays enhance the store's atmosphere and give customers information about products. When displays carry out a store-wide theme, during the Christmas season, for instance, they attract customers' attention and generate sales. So do displays that present several related products in a group, or ensemble. Interior displays of products stacked or hanging neatly on racks create one kind of atmosphere; marked down items grouped together on a bargain table produce a different kind.

Retailers must determine the atmosphere the target market seeks and then adjust atmospheric variables to encourage the desired awareness and action in consumers. High fashion boutiques generally strive for an atmosphere of luxury and novelty; discount department stores must not seem too exclusive and expensive. To appeal to multiple market segments, a retailer may create different atmospheres for different operations within the store; for example, the discount basement, the sports department and the women's shoe department may each have a distinctive atmosphere.

Store Image

To attract customers, a retail store must project an image—a functional and psychological picture in the consumer's mind—that is acceptable to its target market. Although heavily dependent on atmospherics and design, a store's image is also shaped by its reputation for integrity, the number of services offered, location, merchandise assortments, pricing policies, promotional activities, community involvement and the retail brand's positioning.[22]

Characteristics of the target market—social class, lifestyle, income level and past buying behaviour—help form store image as well. How consumers perceive the store can be a major determinant of store patronage. Consumers from lower socio-economic groups tend to patronise small, high margin, high service food stores and prefer small, friendly building societies/loan companies over large, impersonal banks, even though these companies charge high interest. Affluent consumers look for exclusive, high quality establishments that offer prestige products and labels.

Retailers should be aware of the multiple factors that contribute to store image and recognise that perceptions of image vary. For example, one study found that in America consumers perceived Wal-Mart and K mart differently although the two sold almost the same products in stores that looked quite similar, offered the same prices, and even had similar names. Researchers discovered that Wal-Mart shoppers spent more money at Wal-Mart and were more satisfied with the store than K mart shoppers were with K mart, in part because of differences in the retailers' images. For example, Wal-Mart employees wore waistcoats; K mart employees did not. Wal-Mart purchases were packed in paper bags while K mart used plastic bags. Wal-Mart had wider aisles, recessed lighting and carpeting in some departments. Even the retailers' logos affected consumers' perceptions: Wal-Mart's simple white and brown logo appeared friendly and "less blatantly commercial", while K mart's red and turquoise blue logo conveyed the impression that the stores had not changed much since the 1960s. These atmospheric elements gave consumers the impression that Wal-Mart was more "upmarket", warmer, and friendlier than K mart.[23]

Scrambled Merchandising

When retailers add unrelated products and product lines, particularly fast moving items that can be sold in volume, to an existing product mix, they are practising **scrambled merchandising.** For example, a convenience store might start selling lawn fertiliser. Retailers adopting this strategy hope to accomplish one or more of the following: (1) to convert their stores into one stop shopping centres, (2) to generate more traffic, (3) to realise higher profit margins, (4) to increase impulse purchases.

In scrambling merchandise, retailers must deal with diverse marketing channels and thus may reduce their own buying, selling and servicing expertise. The practice can also blur a store's image in consumers' minds, making it more difficult for a retailer to succeed in today's highly competitive, saturated markets. Finally, scrambled merchandising intensifies competition among traditionally distinct types of stores and forces suppliers to adjust distribution systems so that new channel members can be accommodated. Asda is predominantly a grocery retailer; however, most stores carry the "George" clothing ranges. The company retails small electrical appliances, DIY goods and car accessories in some stores but not in others. During the summer months, gardening supplies and equipment are sold. In the months leading up to Christmas, such floor space is given over to children's toys and gifts.

The Wheel of Retailing

As new types of retail businesses come into being, they strive to fill niches in the dynamic environment of retailing. One hypothesis regarding the evolution and development of new types of retail stores is the **wheel of retailing**. According to this theory, new retailers often enter the market-place with low prices, margins and status. The new competitors' low prices are usually the result of innovative cost cutting procedures, and they soon attract imitators. Gradually, as these businesses attempt to broaden their customer base and increase sales, their operations and facilities become more elaborate and more expensive. They may move to more desirable locations, begin to carry higher quality merchandise or add customer services. Eventually, they emerge at the high end of the price/cost/service scales, competing with newer discount retailers who are following the same evolutionary process.[24]

For example, supermarkets have undergone many changes since their introduction in the 1920s. Initially, they provided limited services in exchange for lower food prices. However, over time they developed a variety of new services, including free coffee, gourmet food sections and children's play areas. Now supermarkets are being challenged by superstores and hypermarkets, which offer more product choices than the original supermarkets and have undercut supermarket prices.

Figure 12.6 illustrates the wheel of retailing for department stores and discounters. Department stores such as Debenhams started out as high volume, low cost merchants competing with general stores and other small retailers; discount houses developed later, in response to the rising expenses of services in department stores. Many discounters now appear to be following the wheel of retailing by offering more services, better locations, high quality inventories and, therefore, higher prices. Some discount houses are almost indistinguishable from department stores.

Like most hypotheses, the wheel of retailing may not fit every case. For example, it

FIGURE 12.6
The wheel of retailing, which explains the origin and evolution of new types of retail stores.

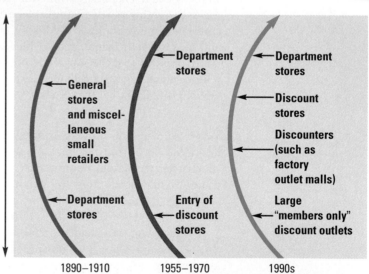

If the "wheel" is considered to be turning slowly in the direction of the arrows, then the department stores around 1900 and the discounters later can be viewed as coming on the scene at the low end of the wheel. As it turns slowly, they move with it, becoming higher price operations, and at the same time leaving room for lower price firms to gain entry at the low end of the wheel.

SOURCE: Adapted from Robert F. Hartley, *Retailing: Challenge and Opportunity,* 3rd ed., p. 42. Copyright © 1984 by Houghton Mifflin Company. Used by permission.

does not adequately explain the development of convenience stores, specialty stores, department store branches and vending machine operations. Another major weakness of the theory is that it does not predict what retailing innovations will develop, or when. Still, the hypothesis works reasonably well in industrialised, expanding economies.

Current Trends

In addition to the strategic issues highlighted above, mention must also be made of some current trends with strategic implications. The **balance of retailing** is a well-documented subject: the balance of negotiating and buying power between retailers and their suppliers.[25] As more retailers devote shelf space to their own label branded goods, the major manufacturers find themselves squeezed out. In the clothing market nearly all retailers now give precedence to their own label goods. Marks & Spencer takes the situation to the extreme: only St Michael (Marks & Spencer's own label) goods are on sale. The company dictates quality levels, lead times, packaging and delivery conditions, and often the price it will pay to its suppliers![26] A few years ago retailer Sainsbury threatened to de-stock Kellogg's cereals totally and Kellogg's refused to supply Sainsbury. Two giant brands were locked in a power struggle. Increasingly compromise and negotiation are leading to deals beneficial to both sides of the equation: retailers receive preferential treatment and buying terms while manufacturers receive contracts to supply major retail chains exclusively with their own label needs, often alongside their own manufacturer brands.[27]

Technology. Retailers are turning to **retail technology** for improved productivity and often to create a competitive edge. Table 12.7 shows the current levels of electronic systems penetration in UK retailing. Bar scanning and electronic point of sale (EPOS) systems enable companies to monitor exact consumer spending patterns on a store by store basis, to prevent stock-outs and to have detailed sales data to add weight to negotiations with suppliers. EFTPOS (electronic funds transfer at point of sale) equipment facilitates speedy payment for goods, thereby reducing checkout queues; the rapid debiting of customer accounts is to the benefit of the retailer's bank account and cash flow. Video screens and video walls bring a new medium for the promotion of goods and services, as well as for the transfer of information. The spread of computer systems has enabled consultants to develop computer graphic tools for the modelling of store location choice, customer demographics and shelf space allocation.[28]

Retail technology is not cheap—£60,000 to bring a typical shoe shop on-line with an EPOS system—but it often allows decision-makers to be fully aware of sales trends and customer needs. When linked to the warehouse network, the EPOS process brings increased speed and efficiency to the physical distribution process. Most national retail groups are centralising their distribution.[29] The grocery companies, for instance, have one or two huge, centrally located warehouses close to the heart of the motorway network. Through EPOS data, each store's exact requirements are dispatched from the central warehouse to match actual daily or weekly sales patterns. Often the warehouse is automated, with robotised handling. This reduces stock holdings in the store itself and centrally, and minimises safety stocks (the "extra" stock held to cater for surges in demand or supplier delays).[30]

Dixons and Currys have two major warehouses which receive most of their deliveries from manufacturers. Small appliances are dispatched to individual stores—to match each store's sales patterns—but white goods (too large to occupy branch space productively) are held at regional warehouses, each of which serves 30 or 40 branches and delivers direct to customers rather than to the shops. Prior to the introduction of EPOS and the move to warehouse centralisation, such fine-tuning would not have been possible.

	STORES ON-LINE (%)	SALES ON-LINE (%)	DPP SYSTEMS	AUTOMATIC STOCK RE-ORDERING	REGIONAL/ EXPERIMENTAL/ PRICING	EDI
Boots (BTC)	29	65	X	X	X	X
Burton	20	17				
Dixons—Currys	100	100		°		X
—Dixons	100	100		°		X
Empire	N/A	100	X			°
Etam	0	0				
GUS	N/A	100	X	°		°
Kingfisher						
—F. W. Woolworth	Part	10		°		°
—Comet	100	100		°		°
—B&Q	75	85	X	X		X
—Superdrug	0	0				
Marks & Spencer	90	95		°		X
Next	85	90		X		X
Ratners	95	98		X		
Sears	35	45	°	°		°
W. H. Smith						
—Do-It-All	100	100	X	X	X	X
—Our Price	0	0		X		X
—UK/Retail/ Books	70	85	X	X	°	°
Storehouse						
—Mothercare	100	100		X		X
—BhS	100	100		X		X
Wickes—Wickes	100	100	X	X		X
—Malden	100	100	°			

° used to some extent.
DPP = Direct Product Profitability; EDI = Electronic Data Interface

SOURCE: *International Journal of Retail & Distribution Management*, Vol. 18, No. 2, p. 44. Copyright © 1989 by MCB University Press, West Yorkshire, England. Used with permission of Morgan Stanley International.

Europe 1992/93.   Deregulation of the European Community in 1992/93 had various implications for European retailers. Market leaders in the UK, for example, once perceived as unassailable, are on a European scale relatively small. A grocery retailer with 8 per cent of the UK market may have 0.5 per cent of the European market. Large UK groups which previously bought out smaller regional UK retailers now find themselves being targeted for takeover by French and German retail groups. More non-UK–based companies are establishing footholds in the UK market, which was previously relatively free from Continental European competition (see Marketing Insight 12.1). For many years, particularly in the more affluent South East of England, retailers have found it difficult to attract high calibre sales assistants and managers in competition for employment with other industrial sectors. Current research is anticipating an exaggeration of the problem as many UK residents move across the Channel to find employment in France and beyond.

Summary

Retailing includes all transactions in which the buyer intends to consume the product through personal, family or household use. Retailers, organisations which sell products primarily to ultimate consumers, are important links in the marketing channel because they are customers for wholesalers and producers. Most retailing takes place inside stores or service establishments, but retail exchanges may also occur outside stores through telemarketing, vending machines, and mail order catalogues. Retail institutions provide place, time and possession utilities. In the case of services, retailers develop most of the product's form utility as well.

Retail stores are often classified according to width of product mix and depth of product lines. The major types of retail stores are department stores, variety stores, hypermarkets, superstores and supermarkets, discount sheds, specialty shops, convenience stores, markets, cash and carry outlets and catalogue showrooms. Department stores are large retail employers and characterised by wide product mixes in considerable depth for most product lines. Their product lines are organised into separate departments that function much as self-contained businesses do.

Specialty retailers offer substantial assortments in a few product lines. They include traditional specialty retailers, which carry narrow product mixes with deep product lines. Retail stores locate in the central business district—the traditional centre of the town—in suburban centres, in edge of town, free-standing superstores, or in retail parks. The national chains occupy the prime pitch sites in the CBD and the edge of town sheds. Locally based independent retailers tend to dominate in the suburbs and focus on convenience and some comparison goods.

Non-store retailing is the selling of goods or services outside the confines of a retail facility. Direct marketing is the use of non-personal media or telesales to introduce products to consumers, who then purchase the products by mail or telephone. Forms of non-store retailing include in-home retailing (selling via personal contacts with consumers in their own homes), telemarketing (direct selling of goods and services by telephone based either on a cold canvass of the telephone directory or on a pre-screened list of prospective clients), automatic vending (selling through machines), and mail order retailing (selling by description because buyers usually do not see the actual product until it arrives in the mail).

Franchising is an arrangement whereby a supplier grants a dealer the right to sell products in exchange for some type of consideration. Retail franchises are of three general types: a manufacturer may authorise a number of retail stores to sell a certain brand name item; a producer may license distributors to sell a given product to retailers; or a franchisor may supply brand names, techniques or other services instead of a complete product. Franchise arrangements have a number of advantages and disadvantages over traditional business forms, and their use is increasing.

To increase sales and store patronage, retailers must consider several strategic issues. Location determines the trading area from which a store must draw its customers and should be evaluated carefully. When evaluating potential sites, retailers take into account a variety of factors, including the location of the firm's target market within the trading area, the kinds of products being sold, the availability of public transport, customer characteristics and competitors' locations. The retailer must decide whether to invest heavily in owning freeholds or to negotiate leases. Retailers can choose among several types of locations: free-standing structures, traditional business districts, neighbourhood/suburban shopping centres, regional shopping centres or retail parks. The width, depth and quality of the product assortment should be of the kind that can satisfy the retailer's target market customers.

Retail positioning involves identifying an unserved or under served market niche, or segment, and serving the segment through a strategy that distinguishes the retailer from others in people's minds. Atmospherics and design comprise the physical elements of a store's design that can be adjusted to appeal to consumers' emotions and thus induce them to buy. Store image, which various consumers perceive differently, derives not only from atmosphere, but also from location, products offered, customer services, prices, promotion and the store's overall reputation. Scrambled merchandising adds unrelated product lines to an existing product mix and is being used by a growing number of stores to generate sales.

The "wheel of retailing" hypothesis holds that new retail institutions start as low status, low margin and low price operators. As they develop, they increase service and prices and eventually become vulnerable to newer institutions, which enter the market and repeat the cycle. However, the hypothesis may not apply in every case. There is an ever-changing balance of power between retailers and their suppliers, emphasised by the growth of retailers' own label brands, which compete with manufacturers' brands. EPOS and other systems have revolutionised retailing and—when coupled with new, often centralised, warehouse networks—have reduced stock holdings, improved productivity, and minimised the risk of stock-outs. The reduction of European Community border controls and regulations is making the retailing environment much more fluid and dynamic: it holds new opportunities for expansion or strategic alliances in other countries, but it also carries the risk of takeover and increased competition in domestic markets.

IMPORTANT TERMS

Retailing	Catalogue showroom
Retailer	Non-store retailing
Central business	Direct marketing
district (CBD)	In-home retailing
Suburban centres	Telemarketing
Edge of town	Automatic vending
Retail park	Mail order retailing
Department stores	Catalogue retailing
Variety stores	Franchising
Supermarkets	Location
Superstores	Product assortment
EPOS	Retail positioning
Hypermarkets	Atmospherics
Discount sheds	Scrambled merchandising
Specialty shops	Wheel of retailing
Convenience stores	Balance of retailing
Markets	Retail technology
Cash and	
carry warehouses	

DISCUSSION AND REVIEW QUESTIONS

1. What are the major differences between specialty shops and department stores?
2. How does a superstore differ from a supermarket?
3. Evaluate the following statement: "Direct marketing and non-store retailing are roughly the same thing".
4. Why is door-to-door selling a form of retailing? Some consumers feel that direct mail orders skip the retailer. Is this true?
5. If you were to open a retail business, would you prefer to open an independent store or to own a store under a franchise arrangement? Explain your preference.
6. What major issues should be considered when determining a retail site location?
7. Describe the major types of shopping centre. Give examples of each type in your area.
8. How does atmosphere add value to products sold in a store? How important are atmospherics for convenience stores?
9. How should one determine the best retail store atmosphere?
10. Discuss the major factors that help determine a retail store's image.
11. Is it possible for a single retail store to have an overall image that appeals to sophisticated shoppers, extravagant ones and bargain hunters? Why or why not?
12. In what ways does the use of scrambled merchandising affect a store's image?
13. How has technology improved retail productivity?
14. What are the likely effects of EC deregulation on retailing in the EC?

■ CASES

12.1   Aldi Expands

While the major UK grocery retailers recently positioned themselves as middle to up market, providing extensive ranges, own label goods, improved customer service and large stores with carefully conceived facilities and atmospherics, the budget conscious sector of the market was left in the hands of Kwik Save.

With only 2,500 lines and concentrating on manufacturer brands, no-frills service and small supermarkets in town centres or in the suburbs, Kwik Save has become one of the UK's most successful companies.

Now, however, the market is changing. Aldi, the German discounter, has opened its first branches in the Midlands. Already one of Europe's largest grocery retailers, Aldi offers no luxuries, no customer services and secondary sites with no expense devoted to store design and fitting out. Aldi concentrates on many of its own label products but they—along with manufacturer brands—are displayed in their shipping containers (in boxes). A limited range of essentials for C2/DE shoppers, for whom price is the key, is the Aldi approach.

Discount grocery retailing has not been successful in the UK. Tesco is still shaking off its former discount image; Supasave went into liquidation in 1982; Pricerite was carved up by Shoppers Paradise and Argyll; Shoppers Paradise itself was devoured and rebranded by Gateway in 1986. The only success story has been Kwik Save. For Aldi, however, UK grocery margins of 5 to 7 per cent are perceived as high, enticing the company into the UK. It remains to be seen whether Aldi can create a network of branches large enough to give it the necessary scale economies to trade on price. UK consumers have yet to accept its discount, limited range positioning in a market led by

DIFFERENT VIEWS OF SUCCESSFUL UK FOOD RETAILERS, SELECTED RATIOS AND RANKING

Company	Turnover (£m)	Operating profit (£m)	Market value (£m)	% return on net assets	% return on equity	Sales growth	PE ratio	Added value[1]
Sainsbury	5,659(1)[2]	369(1)	3,365(1)	21(4)	21(3)	11(2)	13.5(2)	12.3(3)
Tesco	4,717(2)	274(2)	2,350(2)	23(3)	18(4)	7(3)	12.6(4)	12.5(2)
Gateway	4,516(3)	205(3)	1,703(4)	21(5)	17(6)	−19(6)	10.8(6)	6.6(5)
Argyll	3,500(4)	156(4)	1,661(5)	25(2)	24(2)	1(4)	13.3(3)	10.1(4)
Asda	2,708(5)	156(5)	1,913(3)	18(6)	18(5)	1(5)	11.5(5)	1.2(6)
Kwik Save	1,181(6)	58(6)	848(6)	41(1)	27(1)	18(1)	17.6(1)	26.8(1)

[1] As percentage of input costs.
[2] All rankings in brackets.

SOURCE: John Kay, "Different Views of Successful UK Food Retailers, Selected Ratios and Ranking," *Accountancy*. Reprinted by permission.

such high profile retailers as Sainsbury, Tesco, Gateway, Argyll (Safeway), Asda and Marks & Spencer.

Aldi describes its UK operation as "new", "dynamic", and "fast moving". In just three years, it opened 65 stores, predominantly in the Midlands and North of England, centred on two state of the art regional distribution centres in Leicestershire and Manchester. With 3,500 stores in Europe and the US, the German discount supermarket chain has succeeded in each country it has entered. Compared with UK discount rival Kwik Save and more up market leaders Sainsbury, Tesco or Safeway, Aldi is still a niche player in a highly competitive market. The success of Kwik Save, one of the UK's most profitable retailers, shows that there is the opportunity for price driven supermarkets to compete with their superstore rivals. Danish, French and German discount rivals have also targeted the UK, and Kwik Save has speeded up its store opening programme.

SOURCES: "King of the discounts invades the south", *Marketing*, 13 September 1990, pp. 38–9; "Aldi arrives", *Marketing*, 9 May 1990, p. 3; and Nigel Cope, "Aldi cuts the cackle", *Business,* June 1990, pp. 78–80; "Cut price Carrefour targets UK", Suzanne Bidlake, *Marketing*, 19 November 1992, p. 3; "Norma and Carrefour invade UK", *Marketing Week,* 22 January 1993, p. 6; Aldi appointments, *The Independent on Sunday,* 7 March 1993, p. IB39.

Questions for Discussion

1. Why are retailers targeting other countries for store expansion?
2. What market opportunities has Aldi exploited in the UK?
3. What problems now oppose the continued rapid expansion of Aldi's no-frills discount chain?

12.2 Technology to Increase Home Shopping: Catalogue Retailer Littlewoods Stays Ahead

Throughout the 1970s and 1980s, pundits were predicting the demise of the traditional home catalogue shopping companies, such as Littlewoods, Freemans, Great Universal Stores and Otto Versand's Grattan. Instead, Next's Directory and a whole host of specialist operators such as Innovations entered a market which is far from obsolete. One in three consumers now buys goods at home, through catalogue retailing, a market set for important technological changes.

John Moores started his mail order business from one office, a little warehouse, with one secretary. Already a millionaire from his football pools operation, Moores wanted to see if he could "make another million from nothing". Pools customers were recruited as customers for mail order, and they in turn persuaded relatives, friends and neighbours to buy from Moores' catalogues. In its first year, the Littlewoods catalogue division had sales of £100,000. In 1936, sales hit £4 million. Today Littlewoods accounts for 28 per cent of a market worth £3.5 billion, dealing with £2 million worth of orders each working day and despatching 40 million parcels annually to UK homes.

Sixty years of Littlewoods' catalogue sales have echoed consumer changes. When it all began in the 1930s, most people had never travelled more than 50 miles from their birthplace, there was an economic slump, women "slaved" as housewives, few houses had electricity, even large towns had only a few shops, and there was no such entity as a supermarket. In the 1940s Littlewoods joined the war effort, supplying 13,000 food packs daily for troops in Burma, 12 million shells, 750 Wellington bomber bodies, 50,000 rubber dinghies and 5 million parachutes. A fireside chair cost £2, a three piece suite £8, a double bed or vacuum cleaner £3, a diamond ring £1.50 and gas irons 50p. By the present Queen's coronation in 1953, half the population crammed into bars and lucky neighbours' houses to watch the ceremony on television. Tea, sugar, butter and cheese were still rationed, an electric iron cost £2.40 and a ballpoint pen £1.74 in the still austere 1950s.

The swinging 1960s brought a credit driven society seeking consumer durables and more stylish merchandise: transistor radios for £12.60, cine cameras at £55, a sewing machine for £38. In the 1970s inflation soared to 15.9 per cent and Britain joined the European Common Market. A radio cost £6.65 or 20 weeks at 33p; a superior three-piece suite £75.75 or £1.51 a week for 50 weeks. A Hotpoint washing machine cost £131.29 and a Hoovermatic £103.85. The 1980s, the decade of Margaret Thatcher, heralded increased consumer spending and prosperity, rising unemployment and crime, and inner city riots. The microchip arrived in nearly every household, and the yuppies wheeled and dealed their way to inherit the land! Health foods and non-smoking grew in popularity, home ownership rocketed, and nearly all households had a television set, a fridge and central heating. AIDS imposed its tragic effects on society and people worried more about the world's starving millions and under privileged.

Throughout all of these evolving, and at times dramatic, consumer changes, Littlewoods led the catalogue sector. In retailing, the burgeoning of retail chains nationwide and even internationally created a shopping conscious consumer happy to see increased choice and rapid development of new shopping centres, malls and retail parks. With the adoption of the US superstore concept and out of town retailing, many analysts predicted the demise of high street retailers and home catalogue shopping. Sears, Freemans, Grattan, GUS and Littlewoods did all suffer during the early 1980s, but the adoption of sound marketing principles led to rekindled fortunes.

These companies monitored changing consumer tastes and trends more closely, altering their merchandise ranges and prices accordingly. They created new identities for separate catalogues, each targeted at slightly different groups of customers. For example, German acquired Grattan trades through several catalogues: Grattan—a household name—Kaleidoscope, Scotcade, You & Yours, Look Again and Agency One. Freemans operates as Freemans, Complete Essentials, Clothkits, We Are, Direct Collection and the Jan Harvey Collection. Each catalogue has a different mix of styles and merchandise, price points and sourcing, giving each its own positioning in a highly competitive market-place. In addition to the clothing and household goods dominated catalogues of the major companies, there are niche specialists offering narrowly focused ranges, including perfumes and cosmetics, toys and novelty goods, home/office stationery and equipment, photographic products, car accessories and specialty foods.

The sector is far from in decline. Littlewoods believes that leisure trends and the increasing use of in-home technology favour the continued success of catalogue retailing. The company expects technology to make it possible to buy almost anything while sitting in an armchair at home. Already, personal financial business from insurance to current account banking can be conducted over the telephone or through home computers. Catalogues can be made available on home computers or displayed through videodiscs on television screens. Investments in such technologies are high, but the competitive advantage is potentially great so long as consumers accept the innovations. In the interim, Littlewoods has kept its options open; in addition to its catalogue business, the company operates a chain of high street variety stores, Littlewoods and close to 200 Index catalogue stores in town centres and retail parks. In mail order, though, Littlewoods and its rivals anticipate the dawning of a whole new era of catalogue retailing and home shopping.

SOURCES: Littlewoods; Freemans; Grattan; *The Marketing Pocket Book 1993* (Henley-on-Thames: NTC), p. 60; "Rise and rise of mail order shopping", Barbara Argument, *Coventry Evening Telegraph*, 1 September 1992, pp. L2–3. With grateful thanks to the *Coventry Evening Telegraph* and Littlewoods.

Questions for Discussion

1. What threats have faced the catalogue retailers?
2. How have these been addressed?
3. What are the current trends in the home shopping sector?

13 PHYSICAL DISTRIBUTION

Objectives

To understand how physical distribution activities are integrated into marketing channels and overall marketing strategies

To examine three important physical distribution objectives: customer service, total distribution costs and cost trade-offs

To learn how efficient order processing facilitates product flow

To illustrate how materials handling is a part of physical distribution activities

To learn how warehousing facilitates the storage and movement functions in physical distribution

To understand how inventory management is conducted to develop and maintain adequate assortments of products for target markets

To gain insight into how transport modes, which bridge the producer-customer gap, are selected and co-ordinated

M.S. Carriers is a relatively new trucking company with a low key approach to managing quality physical distribution service to marketing channel members. Whereas many companies spend a great deal to promote their quality improvement efforts to potential customers and the general public, M.S. Carriers chooses not to flaunt its customer orientation. In a short time M.S. Carriers has become a leader in its industry and was recently rated in the top five in its division by *Distribution* magazine. Instead of promoting its efforts externally, the company focuses on constant internal improvement in the way it services its customers—marketing channel members. One of M.S. Carriers' divisions provides service to private companies, in some cases taking over a manufacturer's private trucking operations. Manufacturers, retailers or wholesalers often run their trucks empty on a return trip after delivering cargo, but M.S. Carriers uses its service and marketing network to contract cargo to haul back on the return (an activity until recently often prohibited in Europe, but not under new EC regulations). The channel member benefits by reducing costs and distribution problems, while M.S. Carriers makes a profit.

In an effort to place even more emphasis on continuous process improvement through quality management, M.S. Carriers hired Darryl Jackson, the company's external quality consultant, as Executive Vice President and Chief Operating Officer to oversee the day to day operations of the company. This move allows the company's CEO, Mike Starnes, to focus on developing and expanding "niche" markets while providing missing links in customer service. M.S. Carriers' basic quality service principles are customer focus, total employee involvement, proper performance measurement and improvement of the systems and processes within the company. Over 75 per cent of the company's 1,800 employees are lorry drivers, and a great deal of effort has been directed at helping them do a better job. In an industry in which turnover is rampant, M.S. Carriers improved its driver turnover rate 35 per cent from 1990 to 1991 by allocating more money for training and boosting drivers' wages 24 per cent. M.S. Carriers is succeeding in an industry in which many transportation firms have failed in recent years. ∎

SOURCES: Based on information from David Yawn, "M.S. Carriers looks into satellite-tracking system", *Memphis Business Journal,* 18–22 November 1991, p. 8; David Flaum, "Adviser gets role at M.S. Carriers" *(Memphis) Commercial Appeal,* 11 November 1991, p. B3; and Mike Eigo, "Partnership pays for TL Carrier", *Fleet Owner,* November 1988, pp. 103–8.

M.S. Carriers provides quality customer service to marketing channel members. The company's service orientation helps manufacturers, wholesalers and retailers in the physical distribution of their products. Physical distribution deals with the movement and handling of goods and the processing of orders, activities necessary to provide a level of service that will satisfy customers. Even though physical distribution is costly, it creates time and place utility, which maximises the value of products by delivering them when and where they are wanted.

This chapter describes how marketing decisions are related to physical distribution. After considering basic physical distribution concepts, it outlines the major objectives of physical distribution. Next it examines each major distribution function: order processing, materials handling, warehousing, inventory management and transport. The chapter closes with a discussion of marketing strategy considerations in physical distribution. In reading this chapter, it is important to keep in mind how significant customer service is to physical distribution and how physical distribution is related to marketing channels.

The Importance of Physical Distribution

Physical distribution is a set of activities—consisting of order processing, materials handling, warehousing, inventory management and transport—used in the movement of products from producers to consumers and end users. Planning an effective physical distribution system can be a significant decision in developing a marketing strategy. A company that has the right goods in the right place at the right time in the right quantity and with the right support services is able to sell more than competitors who fail to accomplish these goals. Physical distribution is an important variable in a marketing strategy because it can decrease costs and increase customer satisfaction. In fact, speed of delivery, along with service and dependability, is often as important to buyers as cost. In some situations, for example, the emergency provision of a spare part for vital production line machinery, it may even be the single most important factor.

Physical distribution deals with physical movement and inventory holding (storing and tracking inventory until it is needed) both within and among marketing channel members. Often one channel member will arrange the movement of goods for all channel members involved in exchanges. For example, a packing company ships fresh salmon and champagne (often by air) to remote markets on a routine basis. Frequently, buyers are found while the goods are in transit.

The physical distribution system is often adjusted to meet the needs of a channel member. For example, an agricultural equipment dealer who keeps a low inventory of replacement parts requires the fastest and most dependable service when parts not in stock are needed. In this case, the distribution cost may be a minor consideration when compared with service, dependability and promptness.

Physical Distribution Objectives

For most companies, the main objective of physical distribution is to decrease costs while increasing service. In the real world, however, few distribution systems manage to achieve these goals in equal measure. The large inventories and rapid transport essential to high levels of customer service drive up costs. On the other hand, reduced inventories and slower, cheaper shipping methods cause customer dissatisfaction. Physical distribution managers strive for a reasonable balance of service, costs and resources. They determine what level of customer service is acceptable yet realistic, develop a "system" outlook of calculating total distribution costs and trade higher costs at one stage of distribution for savings in another. In this section these three performance objectives are examined more closely.

Customer Service

In varying degrees, all organisations attempt to satisfy customer needs and wants through a set of activities known collectively as customer service. Many companies claim that service to the customer is their top priority. These companies see service as being as important in attracting customers and building sales as the cost or quality of the organisation's products.

Customers require a variety of services. At the most basic level, they need fair prices, acceptable product quality and dependable deliveries.[1] In the physical distribution area, availability, promptness and quality are the most important dimensions of customer service. These are the main factors that determine how satisfied customers are likely to be with a supplier's physical distribution activities.[2] Customers seeking a higher level of customer service may also want sizeable inventories, efficient order processing, availability of emergency shipments, progress reports, post sale services, prompt replacement of defective items and warranties. Customers' inventory requirements influence the level of physical distribution service they expect. For example, customers who want to minimise inventory storage and shipping costs may require that suppliers assume the cost of maintaining inventory in the marketing channel, or the cost of premium transport.[3] Because service needs vary from customer to customer, companies must analyse—and adapt to—customer preferences. Attention to customer needs and preferences is crucial to increasing sales and obtaining repeat sales. A company's failure to provide the desired level of service may mean the loss of customers. Without customers there can be no profit.

Companies must also examine the service levels competitors offer and match those standards, at least when the costs of providing the services can be balanced by the sales generated. For example, companies may step up their efforts to identify the causes of customer complaints or institute corrective measures for billing and shipping errors. In extremely competitive businesses, such as the market for vehicle parts, firms may concentrate on product availability. To compete effectively, manufacturers may strive for inventory levels and order processing speeds that are deemed unnecessary and too costly in other industries.[4]

Services are provided most effectively when service standards are developed and stated in terms that are specific, measurable and appropriate for the product: for example, "Guaranteed delivery within 48 hours". Standards should be communicated clearly to both customers and employees and rigorously enforced. In many cases, it is necessary to maintain a policy of minimum order size to ensure that transactions are profitable; that is, special service charges are added to orders smaller than a specified quantity. Many carrier companies operate on this basis. Many service policies also spell out delivery times and provisions for back-ordering, returning goods and obtaining emergency shipments. The overall objective of any service policy should be to improve customer service just to the point beyond which increased sales would be negated by increased distribution costs.

Total Distribution Costs

Although physical distribution managers try to minimise the costs of each element in the system—order processing, materials handling, inventory, warehousing and transport—decreasing costs in one area often raises them in another. By using a total cost approach to physical distribution, managers can view the distribution system as a whole, not as a collection of unrelated activities. The emphasis shifts from lowering the separate costs of individual functions to minimising the total cost of the entire distribution system.

The total cost approach calls for analysing the costs of all possible distribution alternatives, even those considered too impractical or expensive. Total cost analyses weigh inventory levels against warehousing expenses, materials handling costs against various modes of transport and all distribution costs against customer service standards. The costs of potential sales losses from lower performance levels are also considered. In many cases, accounting procedures and statistical methods can be used to figure total costs. Where hundreds of combinations of distribution variables are possible, computer simulations may be helpful. In no case is a distribution system's lowest total cost the result of using a combination of the cheapest functions; instead, it is the lowest overall cost compatible with the company's stated service objectives.

Cost Trade-offs

A distribution system that attempts to provide a specific level of customer service for the lowest possible total cost must use cost trade-offs to resolve conflicts about resource allocations. That is, higher costs in one area of the distribution system must be offset by lower costs in another area if the total system is to remain cost effective.

Trade-offs are strategic decisions to combine (and re-combine) resources for greatest cost effectiveness. When distribution managers regard the system as a network of interlocking functions, trade-offs become useful tools in a unified distribution strategy. The furniture retailer IKEA uses a system of trade-offs. To ensure that each store carries enough inventory to satisfy customers in the area, IKEA groups its retail outlets into regions, each served by a separate distribution centre. In addition, each IKEA store carries a five week back stock of inventory. Thus IKEA has chosen to trade higher inventory warehousing costs for improved customer service.[5]

Now that several of the physical distribution objectives that marketers may pursue have been considered, it is time to take a closer look at specific physical distribution activities. For the remainder of the chapter, the focus is on order processing, materials handling, warehousing, inventory management and transport.

ORDER PROCESSING

Order processing—the first stage in a physical distribution system—is the receipt and transmission of sales order information. Although management sometimes overlooks the importance of these activities, efficient order processing facilitates product flow. Computerised order processing, used by many firms, speeds the flow of information from customer to seller.[6] When carried out quickly and accurately, order processing contributes to customer satisfaction, repeat orders and increased profits.

Generally, there are three main tasks in order processing: order entry, order handling and order delivery.[7] Order entry begins when customers or salespeople place purchase orders by mail, telephone or computer. In some companies, sales service representatives receive and enter orders personally and also handle complaints, prepare progress reports and forward sales order information.[8]

The next task, order handling, involves several activities. Once an order has been entered, it is transmitted to the warehouse, where the availability of the product is verified, and to the credit department, where prices, terms and the customer's credit rating are checked. If the credit department approves the purchase, the warehouse begins to fill the order. If the requested product is not in stock, a production order is sent to the factory or the customer is offered a substitute item.

When the order has been filled and packed for shipment, the warehouse schedules pick up with an appropriate carrier. If the customer is willing to pay for rush service, priority transport is used. The customer is sent an invoice, inventory records are adjusted and the order is delivered.

Order processing can be manual or electronic, depending on which method provides the greatest speed and accuracy within cost limits. Manual processing suffices for a small volume of orders and is more flexible in special situations; electronic processing is more practical for a large volume of orders and lets a company integrate order processing, production planning, inventory, accounting and transport planning into a total information system.[9] Many leading retail groups, with products from groceries to electrical goods, have their stores networked to the head office. Suppliers are also electronically linked to the retailers' head offices, so that stock can be ordered electronically.

MATERIALS HANDLING

Materials handling, or physical handling of products, is important for efficient warehouse operations, as well as in transport from points of production to points of consumption. The characteristics of the product itself often determine how it will be handled. For example, fresh dairy produce has unique characteristics that determine how it can be moved and stored.

Materials handling procedures and techniques should increase the usable capacity of a warehouse, reduce the number of times a good is handled, and improve service to customers and increase their satisfaction with the product. Packaging, loading, movement and labelling systems must be co-ordinated to maximise cost reduction and customer satisfaction.

In Chapter 8 it was noted that the protective functions of packaging are important considerations in product development. Appropriate decisions about packaging materials and methods allow for the most efficient physical handling; most companies employ packaging consultants or specialists to accomplish this important task. Materials handling equipment is used in the design of handling systems. **Unit loading** is grouping one or more boxes on a pallet or skid; it permits movement of efficient loads by mechanical means, such as fork-lifts, trucks or conveyor systems. **Containerisation** is the practice of consolidating many items into a single large container that is sealed at its point of origin and opened at its destination (see Figure 13.1). The container are usually 2.5 metres (8 feet) wide, 2.5 metres (8 feet) high, and 3, 6, 7.5 or 12 metres (10, 20, 25, or 40 feet) long. They can be conveniently stacked and sorted as units at the point of loading; because individual items are not handled in transit, containerisation greatly increases efficiency and security in shipping.

WAREHOUSING

Warehousing, the design and operation of facilities for storing and moving goods, is an important physical distribution function. Warehousing provides time utility by enabling firms to compensate for dissimilar production and consumption rates. That is, when mass production creates a greater stock of goods than can be sold immediately, companies may warehouse the surplus goods until customers are ready to buy. Warehousing also helps stabilise the prices and availability of seasonal items. Following is a description of the basic functions of warehouses and the different types of ware-

FIGURE 13.1

Containerisation
Cast is a container shipping firm that ships products worldwide.

SOURCE: Courtesy of Cast North America (1983) Inc.

houses available. The distribution centres, special warehouse operations designed so that goods can be moved rapidly, are also examined.

Warehousing Functions

Warehousing is not limited simply to storage of goods. When warehouses receive goods by wagon loads or lorry loads, they break the shipments down into smaller quantities for individual customers; when goods arrive in small lots, the warehouses assemble the lots into bulk loads that can be shipped out more economically.[10] Warehouses perform these basic distribution functions:

1. *Receiving goods.* The merchandise is accepted, and the warehouse assumes responsibility for it.
2. *Identifying goods.* The appropriate stock keeping units are recorded, along with the quantity of each item received. The item may be marked with a physical code, tag or other label; or it may be identified by an item code (a code on the carrier or container) or by physical properties.
3. *Sorting goods.* The merchandise is sorted for storage in appropriate areas.
4. *Dispatching goods to storage.* The merchandise is put away so that it can be retrieved when necessary.
5. *Holding goods.* The merchandise is kept in storage and properly protected until needed.

6. *Recalling and picking goods.* Items customers have ordered are efficiently retrieved from storage and prepared for the next step.
7. *Marshalling the shipment.* The items making up a single shipment are brought together and checked for completeness or explainable omissions. Order records are prepared or modified as necessary.
8. *Dispatching the shipment.* The consolidated order is packaged suitably and directed to the right transport vehicle. Necessary shipping and accounting documents are prepared.[11]

Types of Warehouses

A company's choice of warehouse facilities is an important strategic consideration. By using the right warehouse, a company may be able to reduce transport and inventory costs or improve its service to customers; the wrong warehouse may drain company resources. For example, a company which produces processed foods must locate its warehousing close to main transport routes to facilitate delivery to supermarkets in different parts of the country. Besides deciding how many facilities to operate and where to locate them, a company must determine which type of warehouse will be most appropriate. Warehouses fall into two general categories: private and public. In many cases, a combination of private and public facilities provides the most flexible approach to warehousing.

Private Warehouses. A **private warehouse** is operated by a company for shipping and storing its own products. Private warehouses are usually leased or purchased when a firm believes that its warehouse needs in given geographic markets are so substantial and so stable that it can make a long term commitment to fixed facilities. They are also appropriate for firms that require special handling and storage features and want to control the design and operation of the warehouse. Marketing Insight 13.1 describes British Tubes Stockholding's warehousing and distribution functions.

Some of the largest users of private warehouses are retail chain stores.[12] Retailers such as Aldi, Marks & Spencer, Texas or Carrefour find it economical to integrate the warehousing function with purchasing for and distribution to their retail outlets. When sales volumes are fairly stable, ownership and control of a private warehouse may provide benefits, such as property appreciation. Private warehouses, however, face fixed costs, such as insurance, taxes, maintenance and debt expense. They also allow little flexibility when firms wish to move inventories to more strategic locations. Before tying up capital in a private warehouse or entering into a long term lease, a company should consider its resources, the level of its expertise in warehouse management and the role of the warehouse in its overall marketing strategy.

Public Warehouses. **Public warehouses** rent storage space and related physical distribution facilities to other companies and sometimes provide distribution services such as receiving and unloading products, inspecting, reshipping, filling orders, financing, displaying products and co-ordinating shipments. They are especially useful to firms with seasonal production or low volume storage needs, companies with inventories that must be maintained in many locations, firms that are testing or entering new markets and business operations that own private warehouses but occasionally require additional storage space. Public warehouses can also serve as collection points during product recall programmes. Whereas private warehouses have fixed costs, public warehouses' costs are variable (and often lower) because users rent space and purchase warehousing services only as needed.

In addition, many public warehouses furnish security for products that are being used as collateral for loans, a service that can be provided at either the warehouse or

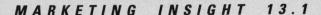

BRITISH TUBES STOCKHOLDING—AD HOC DISTRIBUTION

Steel stockholding in Europe is dominated by the nationalised industries' stockholding subsidiaries; in the UK the recently privatised British Steel subsidiaries have nearly half of the market. British Tubes Stockholding (BTS), for example, accounts for a quarter of the market and has seven warehouses throughout the UK as well as two central distribution centres. BTS customers range from small general engineers to major oil companies. Market sectors include general engineering, shipbuilding, pipework fabricators, power generation contractors, management contractors, off-shore fabricators, oil companies, petrochemical and gas industries. BTS provides an international service for direct shipment to worldwide destinations.

BTS, like the other major stockholders, Brown and Tawse and Walkers, has grown by acquiring smaller, often locally orientated independents. Its distribution network is, therefore, rather ad hoc: two new, purpose built warehouses that can handle the whole product range; some warehouses capable of stocking only a limited range; some outdated premises built many years ago with limited vehicle access and poor handling facilities; non-uniform coverage areas—some deal nationally, others locally, many intrude on neighbouring sales or delivery territories. In one case, the area sales force is capable of generating 40 per cent more business volume than its warehouse can supply.

A new network of warehouses is now being developed. Large, infrequently demanded, bulky items are to be stocked centrally, still providing delivery in under 24 hours—better than the market requires—and all regional warehouses will have a product range in line with their customer requirements. New locations close to motorways will enable easy delivery from factories and importers while allowing easy collection from or delivery to customers in each region. Warehousing in the South East will be able to cater for exports into Europe and act as a deterrent to Dutch and French competitors. A computer monitors all stockholding, orders, and deliveries, minimizing stock outs and excess holdings.

SOURCES: BTS management, 1988–1990; BTS promotional material, "Buying from your local winning team", 1988; "British Steel's solid strength", *Investors Chronicle,* 16–22 February 1990, p. 50; "British Steel: manufacturer and distributor", *Investors Chronicle,* 15–21 June 1990, p. 52.

the site of the owner's inventory. A **field public warehouse** is a warehouse established by a public warehouse at the owner's inventory location. The warehouser becomes the custodian of the products and issues a receipt that can be used as collateral for a loan. Public warehouses can also provide **bonded storage**, a warehousing arrangement under which imported or taxable products are not released until the owners of the products have paid customs duties, taxes or other fees. Bonded warehouses enable firms to defer tax payments on such items until the products are delivered to customers.

The Distribution Centre. A **distribution centre** is a large, centralised warehouse that receives goods from factories and suppliers, regroups them into orders and ships them to customers quickly; its focus is on active movement of goods rather than passive storage.[13] Distribution centres are specially designed for the rapid flow of products. They are usually one storey buildings (to eliminate lifts) and have access to transport networks, such as motorways or railway lines. Many distribution centres are highly automated operations in which computer directed robots, fork-lifts and hoists collect and move products to loading docks. Although some public warehouses offer such specialised services, most distribution centres are privately owned. They serve customers in regional markets and in some cases function as consolidation points for a company's branch warehouses.

Distribution centres offer several benefits, the most important of which is improved customer service. Distribution centres ensure product availability by maintaining full product lines. The speed of their operations cuts delivery time to a minimum. In addition, they reduce costs. Instead of having to make many smaller shipments to scattered warehouses and customers, factories can ship large quantities of goods directly to distribution centres at bulk load rates, thus lowering transport costs; furthermore, rapid turnover of inventory lessens that need for warehouses and cuts storage costs. Some distribution centres also facilitate production by receiving and consolidating raw materials and providing final assembly for some products.

INVENTORY MANAGEMENT

Inventory management involves developing and maintaining adequate assortments of products to meet customers' needs. Because a firm's investment in inventory usually represents 30 to 50 per cent of its total assets, inventory decisions have a significant impact on physical distribution costs and the level of customer service provided. When too few products are carried in inventory, the result is **stock outs,** or shortages of products, which cause brand switching, lower sales and loss of customers. But when too many products (or too many slow moving products) are carried, costs increase, as do the risks of product obsolescence, pilferage and damage. The objective of inventory management, therefore, is to minimise inventory costs while maintaining an adequate supply of goods. Marketing Insight 13.2 shows how staff at Benetton use high technology equipment to ensure that the company's inventory is managed efficiently.

There are three types of inventory costs. *Carrying costs* are holding costs; they include expenditures for storage space and materials handling, financing, insurance, taxes and losses from spoilage of goods. *Replenishment costs* are related to the purchase of merchandise. The price of goods, handling charges and expenses for order processing contribute to replenishment costs. *Stock out costs* include sales lost when demand for goods exceeds supply on hand and the clerical and processing expenses of back-ordering. A company must control all the costs of obtaining and maintaining inventory in order to achieve its profit goals. Management must therefore have a clear idea of the level of each type of cost incurred.

Inventory managers deal with two issues of particular importance. They must know when to reorder and how much merchandise to order. For example, many high street banks no longer require current account customers to order new cheque books. Once a certain cheque number is reached, a new book is automatically sent to the customer. The **reorder point** is the inventory level which signals that more inventory should be ordered. Three factors determine the reorder point: the expected time between the date an order is placed and the date the goods are received and made ready for resale to customers; the rate at which a product is sold or used up; and the quantity of **safety**

MARKETING INSIGHT 13.2

BENETTON'S INTERNATIONAL ELECTRONIC DATA INTERCHANGE SYSTEM

How important can eight people be to a multinational clothing manufacturer and retailer? To Benetton, the Italian casual wear company, the eight people who run the warehouse that handles the distribution of 50 million pieces of clothing a year are extremely important. These eight people are responsible for processing 230,000 articles of clothing a day to serve 4,500 stores, of which 1,500 are located in Italy, 700 in the United States and 350 in the UK. Though sales in the garment industry have sagged recently, Benetton is still moving tremendous amounts of knit and cotton clothing. After their small clothing business expanded into an international fashion sensation, executives at Benetton realised that highly efficient physical distribution methods were a must.

Benetton has linked its sales agents, factory and warehouse together using an international electronic data interchange (EDI) system. Suppose a student in London wants to buy a Benetton sweater identical to his older brother's. He goes to a Benetton store and searches for it, only to be disappointed when he finds that the sweater is not there. The salesperson assures him that the sweater will arrive in a month. The salesperson then calls a Benetton sales agent, who places the sweater order on a personal computer. Three times a day, this information is collected and sent to the company's mainframe system in Italy, where the computer searches inventory data to find out if the requested item is in stock. If not, an order automatically travels to a machine that cuts the materials and immediately starts to knit the sweater. Workers put the finished sweater in a box with a barcoded label and send it to the warehouse. In the warehouse, a computer commands a robot to retrieve the sweater and any other merchandise that needs to be transported to the same store.

Through efficient management of physical distribution activities and the use of the latest technologically advanced equipment, Benetton ensures that its products are available to consumers when and where they want them. Close attention to physical distribution activities has helped the company achieve its objectives and become a major competitor in the fashion industry.

SOURCES: Barbara DePompa, "More power at your fingertips", *Information Week,* 23 December 1991, p. 22; Lory Zottola, "The united systems of Benetton", *Computerworld,* 2 April 1990, p. 70; Brian Dumaine, "How managers can succeed through speed", *Fortune,* 13 February 1989, p. 59; and Martha Groves, "Retailer Benetton hopes to crack Soviet market", *Los Angeles Times,* 7 January 1989, sec. IV, pp. 2, 4.

stock on hand, or inventory needed to prevent stock outs. The optimum level of safety stock depends on the general demand and the standard of customer service to be provided. If a firm is to avoid shortages without tying up too much capital in inventory, some systematic method for determining reorder points is essential.

The inventory manager faces several trade-offs when reordering merchandise. Large safety stocks ensure product availability and thus improve the level of customer service; they also lower order processing costs because orders are placed less frequently. Small safety stocks, on the other hand, cause frequent reorders and high order processing costs but reduce the overall cost of carrying inventory. (Figure 13.2 illustrates two order systems involving different order quantities but the same level of safety stocks. Figure 13.2(a) shows inventory levels for a given demand of infrequent orders; Figure 13.2(b) illustrates the levels needed to fill frequent orders at the same demand.)

To quantify this trade-off between carrying costs and order processing costs, a model for an **economic order quantity (EOQ)** has been developed (see Figure 13.3); it specifies the order size that minimises the total cost of ordering and carrying inventory.[14] The fundamental relationships underlying the widely accepted EOQ model are the basis of many inventory control systems. Keep in mind, however, that the objective of minimum total inventory cost must be balanced against the customer service level necessary for maximum profits. Therefore, because increased costs of carrying inventory are usually associated with a higher level of customer service, the order quantity will often lie to the right of the optimal point in the figure, leading to a higher total cost for ordering and larger carrying inventory.

Fluctuations in demand, for example, in times of economic recession, mean that it is not always easy to predict changing inventory levels. When management miscalculates reorder points or order quantities, inventory problems develop. Warning signs include an inventory that grows at a faster rate than sales, surplus or obsolete inventory, customer deliveries that are consistently late or lead times that are too long, inventory that represents a growing percentage of assets, and large inventory adjustments or write-offs.[15] However, there are several tools for improving inventory control. From a technical standpoint, an inventory system can be planned so that the number of products sold and the number of products in stock are determined at certain checkpoints. The control may be as simple as tearing off a code number from each product sold so that the correct sizes, colours and models can be tabulated and reordered. Many bookshops insert reorder slips of paper into each item of stock, which can be removed at the checkout. A sizeable amount of technologically advanced electronic equipment is available to assist with inventory management. In many larger stores, such as Tesco and Toys "Я" Us stores, checkout terminals connected to central computer systems instantaneously update inventory and sales records. For continuous, automatic updating of inventory records, some firms use pressure sensitive circuits installed under ordinary industrial shelving to weigh inventory, convert the weight to units, and display any inventory changes on a video screen or computer printout.

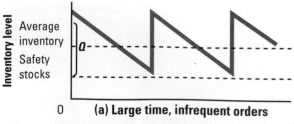
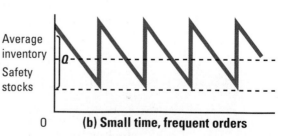

Q = quantity.

FIGURE 13.2 *Effects of order size on an inventory system*

FIGURE 13.3
*Economic order quantity
(EOQ) model*

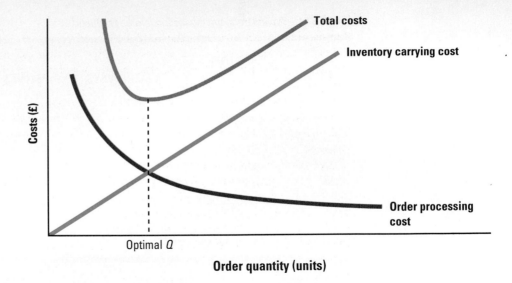

Various techniques have also been used successfully to improve inventory management. The just-in-time concept, widely used in Japan, calls for companies to maintain low inventory levels and purchase products and materials in small quantities, just at the moment they are needed for production. Ford Motor Company, for example, sometimes receives supply deliveries as often as every two hours.[16] Just-in-time inventory management depends on a high level of co-ordination between producers and suppliers, but the technique enables companies to eliminate waste and reduce inventory costs significantly. When Polaroid implemented just-in-time techniques as part of its zero-base pricing programme to reduce the overall cost of purchased materials, equipment and services, it saved an average of £15 million per year.[17]

Another inventory management technique, the 80/20 rule, holds that fast moving products should generate a higher level of customer service than slow moving products, on the theory that 20 per cent of the items account for 80 per cent of the sales. Thus an inventory manager attempts to keep an adequate supply of fast selling items and a minimal supply of the slower moving products.

TRANSPORTATION

Transportation adds time and place utility to a product by moving it from where it is made to where it is purchased and used.[18] Because product availability and timely deliveries are so dependent on transport functions, a firm's choice of transport directly affects customer service. A firm may even build its distribution and marketing strategy around a unique transport system if the system ensures on-time deliveries that will give the firm a competitive edge. This section considers the principal modes of transport, the criteria companies use to select one mode over another and several methods of co-ordinating transport service. Table 13.1 illustrates typical transport modes for various products.

Transport Modes

There are five major **transport modes,** or methods of moving goods: railways, motor vehicles, inland waterways, airways and pipelines. Each mode offers unique advantages; many companies have adopted physical handling procedures that facilitate the use of two or more modes in combination (see Table 13.2).

TABLE 13.1 *Typical transport modes for various products*

RAILWAYS	MOTOR VEHICLES	WATERWAYS	PIPELINES	AIRWAYS
Coal	Clothing	Petroleum	Oil	Flowers
Grain	Paper goods	Chemicals	Processed coal	Perishable food
Chemicals	Computers	Iron ore	Natural gas	Instruments
Timber	Books	Bauxite	Water	Emergency parts
Cars	Fresh fruit	Grain		Overnight mail
Iron	Livestock			

TABLE 13.2 *UK trade by transport modes*

MODE	IMPORTS (000 TONNES)	EXPORTS (000 TONNES)
Railways	540	481
Road	6,281	4,513
Ship	53,344	82,920

Motor Vehicles.   Motor vehicles provide the most flexible schedules and routes of all major transport modes because they can go almost anywhere. Lorries have a unique ability to move goods directly from factory or warehouse to customer, so they are often used in conjunction with other forms of transport that cannot provide door-to-door deliveries.

Although motor vehicles usually travel much faster than trains, they are more vulnerable to bad weather, and their services are more expensive. Lorries are also subject to the size and weight restrictions of the products they carry. In addition, carriers are sometimes criticised for high levels of loss and damage to freight and for delays due to rehandling of small shipments. In response, the road haulage industry is turning to computerised tracking of shipments and developing new equipment to speed loading and unloading.[19] Companies are paying more attention to route planning to ensure that goods are delivered as efficiently as possible. Figure 13.4 illustrates three types of routes which can be used. The choice of route will depend on vehicle capacity, order size, geographical characteristics of the territory and existence of suitable major routes.[20] In Europe, particularly the UK, road haulage dominates in the distribution of most consumer and industrial products. Quick, flexible and relatively cost efficient, it has overtaken rail, and motorway improvements will further strengthen its position.

Railways.   Railways carry heavy, bulky freight that must be shipped over land for long distances. Railways commonly carry minerals, sand, timber, pulp, chemicals and farm products, as well as low value manufactured goods and an increasing number of cars. They are especially efficient for transporting full car loads, which require less handling—and can therefore be shipped at lower rates—than smaller quantities. Some

Area routes connect customers in concentratred areas.

Arc (circumferential) routes link customers in arcs at different distances from the distribution centre.

Radial routes link customers in radial groups to and from the distribution centre.

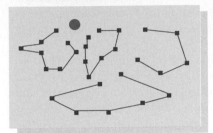 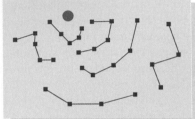 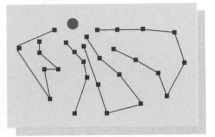

FIGURE 13.4 *Planning distribution routes*

companies locate their factories or warehouses near major rail lines or on spur lines for convenient loading and unloading.

Although railways haul intercity freight, their share of the transport market has declined in recent years. High fixed costs, shortages of rail wagons during peak periods, poor maintenance of tracks and equipment, and increased competition from other carriers, mainly road hauliers, have plagued European rail operators. The Channel Tunnel will be rail orientated. Already British Rail and its French counterpart are building freight depots at numerous strategic locations in anticipation of increased rail freight. The partial privatisation of British Rail will further complicate the situation in the UK.

Inland Waterways.   Water transport is the cheapest method of shipping heavy, low value, non-perishable goods such as coal, grain, sand and petroleum products. Water carriers offer considerable capacity. Barges that travel along inland rivers, canals and navigation systems can haul many times the weight of one railway wagon.

However, many markets are accessible to water only with supplementary rail or road transport. Furthermore, water transport is extremely slow and sometimes comes to a standstill during freezing weather. Companies that depend on water may ship their entire inventory during the summer and then store it for winter use. Droughts and floods also create difficulties for users of inland waterway transport. Because water transport is extremely fuel efficient, its volume is expected to double by the year 2000 but it will still represent only a very small percentage of total shipping.[21]

Airways.   Air transport is the fastest and most expensive form of shipping. It is used most often for perishable goods; for high value, low bulk items; and for products that must be delivered quickly over long distances, such as emergency shipments. The capacity of air transport is limited only by the capacity of individual aircraft. Medium-range jets can carry about 18,000 kilos (40,000 pounds) of freight, and some new jet cargo planes equipped to carry containers can accommodate more than 90,000 kilos (200,000 pounds). Most air carriers transport a combination of passengers, freight and mail.[22]

Although air transport accounts for less than 1 per cent of total tonne-miles carried, its importance as a mode of transport is growing. Despite its expense, air transit can reduce warehousing and packaging costs and also losses from theft and damage, thus helping to offset total costs. However, the ground transport needed for pick up and final delivery adds to cost and transit time.

Pipelines.   Pipelines, the most automated transport mode, usually belong to the shipper and carry the shipper's products. Most pipelines carry petroleum products or chemicals. For example, the Trans-Alaska Pipeline, owned and operated by a consortium of oil companies that includes Exxon, Mobil and British Petroleum, transports crude oil for its owners from remote oil drilling sites in central Alaska to shipping terminals on the coast. Slurry pipelines have been developed to carry pulverised coal, grain or wood chips suspended in water.

Pipelines move products slowly but continuously and at relatively low cost. They are a reliable mode of transport and ensure low product damage and theft. However, their contents are subject to as much as 1 per cent shrinkage, usually from evaporation, and products must be shipped in minimum quantities of 25,000 barrels for efficient pipeline operation.[23] British and Scandinavian North Sea oil and natural gas depend on pipelines for transport and distribution. They have also been a source of concern to environmentalists, who fear that installation and leaks could harm plants and animals. Time will tell whether the safety record of pipelines is better or worse than traditional methods, for example, the use of oil tankers, for moving oil.

Criteria for Selecting Transport

Marketers select a transport mode on the basis of costs, transit time (speed), reliability, capability, accessibility, security and traceability.[24] Table 13.3 summarises various cost and performance considerations that help determine the selection of transport modes. It is important to remember that these relationships are approximations and that the choice of a transport mode involves many trade-offs.

Costs.   Marketers compare alternative means of transport to determine whether the benefits from a more expensive mode are worth the higher costs. Air freight carriers provide many benefits, such as high speed, reliability, security and traceability, but at higher costs relative to other transport modes. When speed is less important, marketers prefer lower costs.

Recently, marketers have been able to cut expenses and increase efficiency. Railways, airlines, road hauliers, barges and pipeline companies have all become more competitive and more responsive to customers' needs. Surveys reveal that in recent years transport costs per tonne and as a percentage of sales have declined, now averaging 7.5 per cent of sales. This figure varies by industry, of course: electrical machinery, textiles and instruments have transport costs of only 3 or 4 per cent of sales, whereas timber products, chemicals and food have transport costs close to 15 per cent of sales.

Transit Time.   Transit time is the total time a carrier has possession of goods, including the time required for pick up and delivery, handling and movement between the points of origin and destination. Closely related to transit time is frequency, or number of shipments per day. Transit time obviously affects a marketer's ability to provide service, but there are some less obvious implications as well. A shipper can take advantage of transit time to process orders for goods en route, a capability especially important for agricultural and raw materials shippers. Some railways also let shipments already in transit be redirected, for maximum flexibility in selecting markets. For example, a consignment of seafood may be shipped to a closer destination if the seafood is in danger of going bad.

Reliability.   The total reliability of a transport mode is determined by the consistency of service provided. Marketers must be able to count on their carriers to deliver goods on time and in an acceptable condition. Along with transit time, reliability affects a marketer's inventory costs, which include sales lost when merchandise is not avail-

TABLE 13.3 *Ranking of transport modes by selection criteria, highest to lowest*

	COST	TRANSIT TIME	RELIABILITY	CAPABILITY	ACCES- SIBILITY	SECURITY	TRACE- ABILITY
MOST	Air	Water	Pipeline	Water	Road	Pipeline	Air
	Pipeline	Rail	Rail	Road	Rail	Water	Road
	Rail	Pipeline	Road	Rail	Air	Rail	Rail
	Road	Road	Air	Air	Water	Air	Water
LEAST	Water	Air	Water	Pipeline	Pipeline	Road	Pipeline

SOURCE: Selected information adapted from J.L. Heskett, Robert Ivie and J. Nicholas Glaskowsky, *Business Logistics* (New York: Ronald Press, 1973). Reprinted by permission of John Wiley & Sons, Inc.

able. Unreliable transport necessitates maintaining higher inventory levels to avoid stock-outs. Reliable delivery service, on the other hand, enables customers to save money by reducing inventories, for example, if a pharmacist knows that suppliers can deliver drugs within hours of ordering, he or she can carry a smaller inventory.

Capability.   Capability is the ability of a transport mode to provide the appropriate equipment and conditions for moving specific kinds of goods. For example, many products must be shipped under controlled temperature and humidity. Other products, such as liquids or gases, require special equipment or facilities for their shipment.

Accessibility.   A carrier's accessibility refers to its ability to move goods over a specific route or network (rail lines, waterways or roads).

Security.   A transport mode's security is measured by the physical condition of goods upon delivery. A business organisation does not incur costs directly when goods are lost or damaged, because the carrier is usually held liable in these cases. Nevertheless, poor service and lack of security will indirectly lead to increased costs and lower profits for the firm, since damaged or lost goods are not available for immediate sale or use. In some cases companies find it necessary to transport products using courier companies such as Securicor.

Traceability.   Traceability is the relative ease with which a shipment can be located and transferred (or found if it is lost). Quick traceability is a convenience that some firms value highly. Shippers have learned that the ability to trace shipments, along with prompt invoicing and processing of claims, increases customer loyalty and improves a firm's image in the market-place.[25]

Co-ordinating Transport Services

To take advantage of the benefits various types of carriers offer, and to compensate for their deficiencies, marketers often must combine and co-ordinate two or more modes of transport. In recent years, **intermodal transport**, as this integrated approach is sometimes called, has become easier because of new developments within the transport industry.

Several kinds of intermodal shipping are available, all combining the flexibility of road haulage with the low cost or speed of other forms of transport. Containerisation, discussed earlier, facilitates intermodal transport by consolidating shipments into sealed containers for transport by piggyback (shipping that combines truck trailers and railway flatcars), fishyback (truck trailers and water carriers), and birdy-back (truck trailers and air carriers). As transport costs increase, intermodal services gain popularity. Intermodal services have been estimated to cost 25 to 40 per cent less than all-road transport in the US, where they account for about 12 to 16 per cent of total transport business.[26]

Specialised agencies, **freight forwarders,** provide other forms of transport co-ordination. These firms combine shipments from several organisations into efficient lot sizes. Small loads—less than 225 kilos (500 pounds)—are much more expensive to ship than full lorry loads and frequently must be consolidated. The freight forwarder takes small loads from various shippers, buys transport space from carriers and arranges for the goods to be delivered to their respective buyers. The freight forwarder's profits come from the margin between the higher, less than car load rates charged to each shipper and the lower car load rates the agency pays. Because large shipments require less handling, the use of a freight forwarder can speed transit time. Freight forwarders can also determine the most efficient carriers and routes and are useful for shipping goods to foreign markets.

One other transport innovation is the development of **megacarriers,** freight companies that provide several methods of shipment, such as rail, road and air service. Air carriers have increased their ground transport services. As they have expanded the range of transport alternatives, carriers have also put greater stress on customer service.

Strategic Issues in Physical Distribution

The physical distribution functions discussed in this chapter—order processing, materials handling, warehousing, inventory management and transport—account for about one third of all marketing costs. Moreover, these functions have a significant impact on customer service and satisfaction, which are of prime importance to marketers. Effective marketers accept considerable responsibility for the design and control of the physical distribution system. They work to ensure that the organisation's overall marketing strategy is enhanced by physical distribution, with its dual objectives of decreasing costs while increasing customer service.

The strategic importance of physical distribution is evident in all elements of the marketing mix. Product design and packaging must allow for efficient stacking, storage and transport; decisions to differentiate products by size, colour and style must take into account the additional demands that will be placed on warehousing and shipping facilities. Competitive pricing may depend on a firm's ability to provide reliable delivery or emergency shipments of replacement parts; a firm trying to lower its inventory costs may offer quantity discounts to encourage large purchases. Promotional campaigns must be co-ordinated with distribution functions so that advertised products are available to buyers; order processing departments must be able to handle additional sales order information efficiently. Distribution planners must consider warehousing and transport costs, which may influence—for example—the firm's policy on stock outs or its choice to centralise (or decentralise) its inventory.

No single distribution system is ideal for all situations, and any system must be evaluated continually and adapted as necessary. For instance, pressures to adjust service levels or reduce costs may lead to a total restructuring of the marketing channel relationships; changes in transport, warehousing, materials handling and inventory may affect speed of delivery, reliability and economy of service. Marketing strategists must consider customers' changing needs and preferences and recognise that changes in any one of the major distribution functions will necessarily affect all other functions.

Consumer orientated marketers will analyse the various characteristics of their target markets and then design distribution systems to provide products at acceptable costs.

SUMMARY

Physical distribution is a set of activities that moves products from producers to consumers, or end users. These activities include order processing, materials handling, warehousing, inventory management and transport. An effective physical distribution system can be an important component of an overall marketing strategy, because it can decrease costs and lead to higher levels of customer satisfaction. Physical distribution activities should be integrated with marketing channel decisions and should be adjusted to meet the unique needs of a channel member. For most firms, physical distribution accounts for about one fifth of a product's retail price.

The main objective of physical distribution is to decrease costs while increasing customer service. Physical distribution managers therefore try to balance service, distribution costs and resources. Companies must adapt to customers' needs and preferences, offer service comparable to—or better than—that of their competitors, and develop and communicate desirable customer service policies. The costs of providing service are minimised most effectively through the total cost approach, which evaluates the costs of the system as a whole rather than as a collection of separate activities. Cost trade-offs must often be used to offset higher costs in one area of distribution against lower costs in another area.

Order processing, the first stage in a physical distribution system, is the receipt and transmission of sales order information. Order processing consists of three main tasks. Order entry is the placement of purchase orders from customers or salespeople by mail, telephone or computer. Order handling involves checking customer credit, verifying product availability and preparing products for shipping. Order delivery is provided by the carrier most suitable for a desired level of customer service. Order processing may be done manually or electronically, depending on which method gives the greatest speed and accuracy within cost limits.

Materials handling, or the physical handling of products, is an important element of physical distribution. Packaging, loading and movement systems must be co-ordinated to take into account both cost reduction and customer requirements. Basic handling systems include unit loading on pallets or skids, movement by mechanical devices and containerisation.

Warehousing involves the design and operation of facilities for storing and moving goods. It is important for companies to select suitable warehousing conveniently located close to main transport routes. Private warehouses are owned and operated by a company for the purpose of distributing its own products. Public warehouses are business organisations that rent storage space and related physical distribution facilities to other firms. Public warehouses may furnish security for products that are being used as collateral for loans by establishing field warehouses. They may also provide bonded storage for companies wishing to defer tax payments on imported or taxable products. Distribution centres are large, centralised warehouses specially designed to facilitate the rapid movement of goods to customers. In many cases, a combination of private and public facilities provides the most flexible approach to warehousing.

The objective of inventory management is to minimise inventory costs while maintaining a supply of goods adequate for customers' needs. All inventory costs—carrying, replenishment and stock out costs—must be controlled if profit goals are to be met. To avoid stock outs without tying up too much capital in inventory, a firm must have a systematic method of determining a reorder point, the inventory level at which more inventory is ordered. The trade-offs between the costs of carrying larger average safety stocks and the costs of frequent orders can be quantified using the economic order quantity (EOQ) model. Inventory problems may take the form of surplus inventory, late deliveries, write offs and inventory that is too large in proportion to sales or assets. Methods for improving inventory management include systems that continuously monitor stock levels and techniques such as just-in-time management and the 80/20 rule.

Transport adds time and place utility to a product by moving it from where it is made to where it is purchased and used. The five major modes of transporting goods are motor vehicles, railways, inland waterways, airways and pipelines. Marketers evaluate transport modes with respect to costs, transit time (speed), reliability, capability, accessibility, security and traceability; final selection of a transport mode involves many trade-offs. Intermodal transport allows marketers to combine the advantages of two or more modes of transport; this method is facilitated by containerisation, freight forwarders—who co-ordinate transport by combining small shipments from several organisations into efficient lot sizes—and megacarriers—freight companies that offer several methods of shipment.

Physical distribution affects every element of the marketing mix: product, price, promotion and distribution. To give customers products at acceptable prices, marketers consider consumers' changing needs and any shifts within the major distribution functions. They then adapt existing physical distribution systems for greater effectiveness. Physical distribution functions account for about one third of all marketing costs and have a significant impact on customer satisfaction. Therefore, effective marketers are actively involved in the design and control of physical distribution systems.

IMPORTANT TERMS

Physical distribution	Distribution centre
Order processing	Stock outs
Materials handling	Reorder point
Unit loading	Safety stock
Containerisation	Economic order quantity (EOQ)
Warehousing	Transport modes
Private warehouse	Intermodal transport
Public warehouses	Freight forwarders
Field public warehouse	Megacarriers
Bonded storage	

DISCUSSION AND REVIEW QUESTIONS

1. Discuss the cost and service trade-offs involved in developing a physical distribution system.
2. What factors must physical distribution managers consider when developing a customer service mix?
3. Why should physical distribution managers develop service standards?
4. What is the advantage of using a total cost approach to distribution?
5. What are the main tasks involved in order processing?
6. Discuss the advantages of using an electronic order processing system. Which types of organisation are most likely to use such a system?

7. How does a product's package affect materials handling procedures and techniques?
8. What is containerisation? Discuss the major benefits of containerisation.
9. Explain the major differences between private and public warehouses. What is a field public warehouse?
10. What characteristics should a suitable warehouse possess?
11. In what circumstances should a firm use a private warehouse instead of a public one?
12. The focus of distribution centres is on active movement of goods. Discuss how distribution centres are designed for the rapid flow of products.
13. Describe the costs associated with inventory management.
14. Explain the trade-offs inventory managers face when reordering merchandise.
15. How can managers improve inventory control? Give specific examples of techniques.
16. Compare the five major transport modes in terms of costs, transit time, reliability, capability, accessibility, security and traceability.
17. What is transit time, and how does it affect physical distribution decisions?
18. Discuss how marketers can combine or co-ordinate two or more modes of transport. What advantage do they gain by doing this?
19. Identify the type of containerised shipping available to physical distribution managers.
20. Discuss how the elements of the marketing mix affect physical distribution strategy.

■ CASES

13.1 Transportation Industry Faces a Packaging Dilemma

Many companies are facing a dilemma in their choice of cushioning materials to protect their products during distribution. The use of polystyrene peanuts, the most common cushioning material, is provoking increasing criticism from both consumers and environmentalists for several reasons. First, polystyrene peanuts are made from petroleum, a non-renewable resource. Second, the peanuts are not biodegradable; they remain in the environment anywhere from 400 to 1,000 years. Third, some peanuts contain chlorofluorocarbons (CFCs) that are released during incineration. CFCs are widely known for their damaging effects to the earth's ozone layer. Finally, the peanuts produce static electricity, making them useless for cushioning sensitive electronic equipment.

The purpose of any cushioning material is to protect a package's contents from harm during the distribution process. Internal packaging is important because if it fails to do its job, the quality of the package's contents becomes a secondary concern. However, in the face of increased environmental awareness, many companies are discovering that their choice of packaging materials is fast becoming an important issue with their customers.

There are several alternatives to polystyrene peanuts, each having advantages and disadvantages. One of the cleverest alternatives is popcorn, which many industry experts say could be the answer to the dilemma. Popcorn is attractive because it is biodegradable and costs one quarter as much as polystyrene peanuts. Likewise, unpopped popcorn is less expensive to ship and store before it is needed. However, in some countries popcorn is not an option at present because it is considered a food, not a packaging material. Many countries forbid the use of popcorn as a cushioning material until a method can be found to prevent people from eating it after it has been used for shipping purposes.

Billed as a direct alternative to polystyrene peanuts, Eco-Foam is made from a special hybrid corn and is composed of 95 per cent cornstarch, making it fully biodegradable and less prone to static electricity. Eco-Foam, which looks a lot like polystyrene peanuts, is attractive because it can be used with the same dispensing equipment as peanuts. Thus a company that currently uses peanuts can switch to Eco-Foam with very little inconvenience. However, Eco-Foam is more expensive and has one major drawback: it fully disintegrates when it gets wet. This makes Eco-foam impractical for use in shipping liquid-filled containers or in situations in which the threat of water damage is high. In addition, Eco-foam has a tendency to shrink when exposed to high heat and humidity, which is always a possibility in a vehicle trailer or on a train.

Quadra-Pak, a third alternative, is fully biodegradable and recyclable, contains no CFCs and is produced totally from refuse materials. Quadra-Pak is made by stacking heavyweight paper in layers that are then cut into strips 10 centimetres (4 inches) long and 0.3 centimetres (0.125 inches) wide. The cut lengths are then compacted into an accordion shape that makes them act as if spring loaded. The finished product measures about 2.5 centimetres (1 inch) long but expands when it is jostled. The result is a packing material that protects from all sides while preventing a carton's contents from moving about. Although Quadra-Pak possesses superior cushioning properties to peanuts, it is more expensive to manufacture and cannot be used with current dispensing equipment.

Other alternatives include Bio-Puffs—a loose-fill foam packaging peanut that biodegrades within weeks or months—and vermiculite, a naturally occurring mineral used by the military to ship munitions in Operation Desert Storm. With so many alternatives and the relentless pressure of environmentalists to use more environmentally friendly packing materials, the Polystyrene Packaging Council (PPC) is crying foul. PPC admits that CFCs were once a problem, but even then, it argues, only 2 per cent of all polystyrene contained CFCs, and their use was phased out of polystyrene production in 1989. To curb negative publicity, the PPC—along with four producers of polystyrene peanuts—is creating a peanut recycling programme.

While many packaging options exist, there is no perfect answer to the current dilemma. All of the options have good and bad characteristics. For the most part, companies currently choose a packing material on the basis of cost and performance. Ultimately, however, the choice of material will depend more and more upon the needs of the customer and the material's impact on the environment.

SOURCES: Jerry Drisaldi, "Protective packaging: it's your responsibility", *Inbound Logistics*, November 1991, p. 39; Walter L. Weart, "Packaging dilemmas: the sequel", *Inbound Logistics,* June 1991, pp. 27–9; Bob Freiday, "Popcorn, peanuts, and Quadra-Paks", *Inbound Logistics*, February 1991, pp. 25–8; and "Environmental concerns influence packaging", *Inbound Logistics,* June 1990, p. 4.

Questions for Discussion

1. What are the advantages and disadvantages of each of the packaging alternatives discussed above?
2. How does a company's choice of packaging materials affect its ability to serve customer needs?
3. Overall, which packing material would you choose? Why? How would your decision change if you were shipping electronic equipment? Glass? Liquid filled containers?

13.2 EC Transport Deregulation

In 1982, the UK government privatised the National Freight Company (NFC). Forty per cent of the shareholding is owned by the 25,000 employees. The company now has a turnover of close of £1,500 million, up from £461 million in 1982, covering transport, distribution, parcels and property development under the BRS, Lynx Express, SPD and Hoults brands.

Excel Logistics, as NFC's distribution division was renamed in 1989, is operating in an increasingly competitive market. There has been significant fall out, with the larger operators gaining dominance over the smaller, independent companies.

Excel, like all European hauliers, is trading in a dynamic environment. The harmonisation of Europe in 1992—when the European Community removed much inter-country legislation and bureaucracy—has significant implications for all physical distribution in the EC, particularly for road hauliers.

When the national borders and transport regulations are removed, it is predicted that cross-Europe routes will improve, there will be standardisation across countries of technical, legal and taxation requirements, and fewer delays at customs posts (which currently can equal a day for a journey from the UK to Italy). Transport costs will be reduced with the end of "cabotage", whereby UK operators, for example, often have to return with empty vehicles because they are not allowed to pick up loads in other EC countries. With minimal borders and few regulations, interstate trade is set to increase, but so is the ability of hauliers to operate and seek business in more countries, leading to more competition and further shake out.

Hauliers are increasing their share of road transport. Only the major retailers, which are investing heavily in creating company owned distribution networks and infrastructure, are seeing an increase in own account haulage.

UK FREIGHT TRANSPORT BY ROAD (BILLION TONNE-KILOMETRES)

	1984	1985	1986	1987
Public haulage	62.3	66.6	68.7	77.1
Own account haulage	34.2	32.5	32.4	31.5

Throughout the EC, companies that are relatively strong but already facing stiff competition, such as Excel/NFC in the UK, will face new competitors, a dramatically altered trading environment and new marketing challenges.

SOURCES: Office for Official Publications of the European Community (Brussels), *The European Community Transport Policy*, 1984; London: Keynote, *The Road Haulage Industry*, 1989; London: Jordans, *Britain's Top 300 Road Haulage Companies*, 1988; and M. Labrou, "Ten marketing cases", University of Warwick, MBA dissertation, 1989.

Questions for Discussion

1. Can NFC continue to focus on being a UK operator?
2. How dependent are transport and distribution on external factors for growth or decline?
3. How real are the benefits to transport of EC deregulation?

PART IV PROMOTION DECISIONS

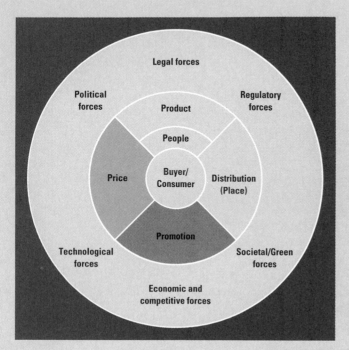

Part IV focuses on communications with target market members. A specific marketing mix cannot satisfy people in a particular target market unless they are aware of the product and where to find it. Some promotion decisions and activities relate to a specific marketing mix, whereas others, broader in scope, are geared to promoting the whole organisation. Chapter 14 presents an overview of promotion, describing the communication process and the major promotion methods that can be included in promotional mixes. Chapter 15 analyses the major steps required to develop an advertising campaign, explains what public relations and publicity are and how they can be used, and discusses the growing role of sponsorship. Chapter 16 deals with the management of personal selling and the role it can play in a firm's promotional mix. This chapter also explores the general characteristics of sales promotion and sales promotion techniques and the nature of direct mail. ■

14

PROMOTION: AN OVERVIEW

Objectives

To understand the role of promotion in the marketing mix

To examine the process of communication

To understand the product adoption process and its implications for promotional efforts

To understand the aims of promotion

To explore the elements of the promotional mix

To acquire an overview of the major methods of promotion

To explore factors that affect the choice of promotional methods

*T*he music industry depends not only on the ability of artists to record and perform but also on the skills of marketing managers and publicity officers in the large recording companies such as EMI, Sony or Virgin. In 1980 the Postcard label released "Falling and Laughing" by Orange Juice in a plain brown paper sleeve, arguing that the record would sell on merit alone. The recording is reported to have notched up 41 sales. In 1983 the ZTT label released the debut single by Frankie Goes to Hollywood, "Relax", supported by personal selling, advertising, sales promotion and significant publicity. The result was 2.4 million sales.

Although the ability and quality of artists are critical factors, promotional support is clearly essential for commercial success. The death of Queen lead singer Freddie Mercury did not end sales of either Queen recordings or Mercury's solo singles. Instead, through shrewd marketing that capitalised on the loyalty of Queen fans, both Queen and Mercury topped the charts world-wide.

In the case of a newly signed band, the record company uses PR to "hype" the signing, the band and any newsworthy characteristics of its music, gigs or individual members. Contacts are used to gain gig bookings, and "promo" recordings are made for distribution to clubs and radio stations. With luck, the recording is picked up and given air time, which—supported with more publicity—leads to media coverage and the possible playlisting of the recording for regular broadcasting. Flyers, posters and other printed items will add to the increasing promotional coverage. "Pluggers" work on behalf of the record companies to gain air time on radio and in clubs, visiting DJs and station managers to peddle their wares. Sales activity may warrant promotional videos aimed at television coverage and further, more polished recordings. These then form the foundation for additional publicity, interviews and media coverage. If the record (CD) sells, a television appearance may encourage the record company to bring out new format special editions and remixes. Low sales will lead to discounting and a new strategy: different promotional activity or the end of the recording contract. ∎

SOURCES: Neal Martin; Fives Records; HMV; Mute Records; *Q* magazine, December 1987, March 1988, May 1988, June 1988, June 1989, April 1990.

O
rganisations use various promotional approaches to communicate with target markets, as the preceding example illustrates. This chapter looks at the general dimensions of promotion, defining promotion in the context of marketing and examining its roles. Next, to understand how promotion works, the chapter analyses the meaning and process of communication, as well as the product adoption process. The remainder of the chapter discusses the major types of promotional methods and the factors that influence an organisation's decision to use specific methods of promotion.

THE ROLE OF PROMOTION

People's attitudes towards promotion vary. Some hold that promotional activities, particularly advertising and personal selling, paint a distorted picture of reality because they provide the customer with only selected information. According to this view, the repetition of similar themes in promotion has brought about changes in social values, such as increased materialism.[1] Proponents of this view hold that promotional activities are unnecessary and wasteful and that promotion costs (especially advertising) are high—sometimes excessively so—resulting in higher prices. Others take a positive view. They believe that advertising messages often project wholesome values—such as affection, generosity or patriotism[2]—or that advertising, as a powerful economic force, can free countries from poverty by communicating information.[3] It has also been argued that advertising of consumer products was a factor in the decline of communism and the move towards a free enterprise system in eastern Europe. However, none of these impressions is completely accurate.

The role of **promotion** in a company is to communicate with individuals, groups or organisations with the aim of directly or indirectly facilitating exchanges by informing and persuading one or more of the audiences to accept the firm's products.[4] PepsiCo, for example, recruited pop star Michael Jackson to communicate the benefits of its cola drink. Rock Against Drugs (RAD), a non-profit organisation, employs popular rock musicians, such as Lou Reed, to communicate its anti-drug messages to teenagers and young adults. Like PepsiCo and RAD, marketers try to communicate with selected audiences about their company and its goods, services and ideas in order to facilitate exchanges. Marketing Insight 14.1 describes how Häagen-Dazs used and continues to use promotion to gain a new position for its superpremium "adult" ice cream.

Marketers indirectly facilitate exchanges by focusing information about company activities and products on interest groups (such as environmental and consumer groups), current and potential investors, regulatory agencies, and society in general. Some marketers use *cause related marketing,* which links the purchase of their products to philanthropic efforts for a particular cause. Cause related marketing often helps a marketer boost sales and generate goodwill through contributions to causes that members of its target markets want to support. For example, American Express used cause related marketing to encourage its credit card holders to use their cards more often and thus help to rebuild the Statue of Liberty. American Express pledged to donate a percentage of the value of all purchases charged on its cards to rebuilding the statue.[5] Similarly, Procter & Gamble has tied promotional efforts for some of its products with contributions to the Special Olympics. Oxfam promotes use of the Visa card.

Viewed from this wider perspective, promotion can play a comprehensive communication role. Some promotional activities, such as publicity and public relations, can be directed towards helping a company justify its existence and maintain positive, healthy relationships between itself and various groups in the marketing environment.

HÄAGEN-DAZS: PROMOTING AN ADULT ICE CREAM

Häagen-Dazs makes the best selling superpremium ice cream in North America. Its luscious ingredients include chocolate from Benelux, vanilla from Madagascar, Brazilian coffee, Oregon strawberries, nuts from Hawaii and Switzerland—and the text on the packaging serenely asserts that it is the world's best ice cream. Since Grand Metropolitan's takeover of Pillsbury, Häagen-Dazs has come to Europe in a big way. In just two years, sales in Britain, France and Germany have climbed from £3 million to £45 million, with consumers happily paying two or three times the cost of rival, traditional brands for this premium product.

London's Leicester Square shop served close to one million ice cream lovers in its first year. The success of the Victor Hugo Plaza shop in Paris, now the company's second busiest, led to the establishment of its first European factory in France. Häagen-Dazs shops are planned for Italy, Spain, Benelux and Scandinavia by the end of the decade. The appealing flavours can now be found not only in the company's shops but also at airports, in cafés and in carefully selected delicatessens, with rapidly growing popularity.

The product's high quality has been essential in maintaining a loyal customer following, but it was promotional work that led to the successful take-off of what was, until recently, an unheard of brand in Europe. Free tasting was a major prong of attack; over 5 million free cupfuls of ice cream were given away during the company's European launch. Thousands of retailers, cafés and delis were supplied with branded freezers both to display and carefully look after the new premium ice cream. Häagen-Dazs spent £30 million on advertising, stressing the de luxe ingredients, unusual flavours and novelty of the product. Europeans currently eat 22 per cent of the 3 billion gallons of ice cream consumed worldwide. Häagen-Dazs plans to increase consumption by appealing to more than traditional ice cream lovers.

The summer afternoon stroll with an ice cream cornet, the family trip to a fun park or beach, a snack during a film or concert, the sticky climax of a birthday party feast had long been the core market for Wall's and Lyons Maid. Ice Cream Mars changed all that by creating an ice cream bar suitable for any occasion and particularly attractive to adults. Häagen-Dazs goes further! Press adverts, artistically shot, often in black and white, feature lithe, semi-nude couples entwined in exotic poses while feeding each other Häagen-Dazs ice cream. The appeal of vanilla ice cream bars hand-dipped in Belgian chocolate and rolled in roasted almonds now seems hard to resist for adults everywhere. The advertising imagery promotes an adult, up market, glamorous positioning for this superpremium ice cream.

SOURCES: G. Mead, "Sex, ice and videod beer", *Financial Times,* 26 September 1992, p. 5; "Saucy way to sell a Knickerbocker Glory—Häagen-Dazs' new ice cream campaign", *Financial Times,* 8 August 1991, p. 8; "Häagen-Dazs is using sex to secure an up market niche in Britain's £400 m ice cream market", *Observer,* 4 August 1991, p. 25; M. Carter, "The luxury ice cream market", *Marketing Week,* 22 May 1992, p. 30; "European push by Häagen-Dazs", *The New York Times,* 12 November 1991; "They're all screaming for Häagen-Dazs", *Business Week,* 14 October 1991, p. 121.

FIGURE 14.1
Information flows into and out of an organisation.

Record companies, television stations, media and personalities gave their services free to facilitate the global Live Aid fund raising activities.

Although a company can direct a single type of communication—such as an advertisement—towards numerous audiences, marketers often design a communication precisely for a specific target market. A company frequently communicates several different messages concurrently, each to a different group. For example, McDonald's may direct one communication towards customers for its Big Mac, a second message towards investors about the firm's stable growth and a third communication towards society in general regarding the company's Ronald McDonald Houses, which provide support to families of children suffering from cancer.

To gain maximum benefit from promotional efforts, marketers must make every effort to properly plan, implement, co-ordinate and control communications. Effective promotional activities are based on information from the marketing environment, often obtained from an organisation's marketing information system (see Figure 14.1). How effectively marketers can use promotion to maintain positive relationships depends largely on the quantity and quality of information an organisation takes in. For example, scares in the UK about the contamination of baby food led manufacturers to inform customers about specially developed safety tops. The problem was that the customers could see when a tinned food had been tampered with, but found it more difficult to detect tampering when it came to food sold in glass jars. The manufacturers therefore stressed the safety "button" on jar lids, which popped up when the seal had been broken. Because the basic role of promotion is to communicate, it is important to analyse what communication is and how the communication process works.

PROMOTION AND THE COMMUNICATION PROCESS

Communication can be viewed as the transmission of information.[6] For communication to take place, however, both the sender and the receiver of the information must share some common ground. They must share an understanding of the symbols used to transmit information, usually pictures or words. For instance, an individual transmitting the following message may believe he or she is communicating with you:

在工廠吾人製造化粧品, 在商店吾人銷售希望。

However, communication has not taken place because few of you understand the intended message.[7] Thus **communication** is defined here as a sharing of meaning.[8] Implicit in this definition is the notion of transmission of information, because sharing necessitates transmission.

As Figure 14.2 shows, communication begins with a source. A **source** is a person, group or organisation that has a meaning it intends and attempts to share with an audience. For example, a source could be a salesperson who wishes to communicate a sales

FIGURE 14.2
The communication process

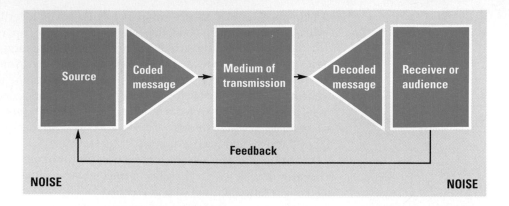

message or an organisation that wants to send a message to thousands of consumers through an advertisement. A **receiver** is the individual, group or organisation that decodes a coded message. A receiving audience is two or more receivers who decode a message. The intended receivers, or audience, of an advertisement for Cellnet cellular telephones, for example, might be businesspeople who must frequently travel by car. The source may be Cellnet or companies, such as Securicor Communications, which installs and supplies Cellnet phones.

To transmit meaning, a source must convert the meaning into a series of signs that represent ideas or concepts. This is called the **coding process,** or *encoding*. When coding meaning into a message, a source must take into account certain characteristics of the receiver or audience. First, to share meaning, the source should use signs that are familiar to the receiver or audience. Marketers who understand this fact realise how important it is to know their target market and to make sure that an advertisement, for example, is written in language that the target market can understand. Thus when Du Pont advertised its Stainmaster carpeting, it did not mention the name of the chemical used to make the carpet resistant to stains, because it would have had little meaning to consumers seeing the advertisement. There have been some notable problems in the translation of advertisements. For example, a beer advertisement translated from English to Spanish using the tag line "Sueltate" was supposed to mean "Let go!" but actually invited readers to "Get diarrhoea!". An airline advertisement translated to entice Spanish speakers to fly first class on leather seats invited them instead to fly naked.[9] Thus it is important that people fully understand the language used in promotion.

Second, when coding a meaning, a source should try to use signs that the receiver or audience uses for referring to the concepts the source intends. Marketers should generally avoid signs that can have several meanings for an audience. For example, an international advertiser of soft drinks should avoid using the word *soda* as a general term for soft drinks. Although in some places soda is taken to mean "soft drink," in others it may connote bicarbonate of soda, an ice cream drink, or something that one mixes with Scotch whisky.

To share a coded meaning with the receiver or audience, a source must select and use a medium of transmission. A **medium of transmission** carries the coded message from the source to the receiver or audience. Transmission media include ink on paper, vibrations of air waves produced by vocal cords, chalk marks on a chalkboard and electronically produced vibrations of air waves, as in radio and television signals.

When a source chooses an inappropriate medium of transmission, several problems may arise. A coded message may reach some receivers, but not the right ones. For example, suppose a local theatre group spends most of its advertising budget on radio advertisements. If theatre-goers depend mainly on newspapers for information about local drama, then the theatre will not reach its intended target audience. Coded messages may also reach intended receivers in an incomplete form because the intensity of the transmission is weak. For example, radio signals can be received effectively only over a limited range that may vary depending on climatic conditions. Members of the target audience who live on the fringe of the broadcasting area may receive a weak signal; others well within the broadcasting area may also receive an incomplete message if they listen to their radios while driving or studying.

In the **decoding process,** signs are converted into concepts and ideas. Seldom does a receiver decode exactly the same meaning that a source coded. When the result of decoding is different from what was coded, **noise** exists. Noise has many sources and may affect any or all parts of the communication process. When a source selects a medium of transmission through which an audience does not expect to receive a message, noise is likely to occur. Noise sometimes arises within the medium of transmission itself. Radio static, faulty printing processes and laryngitis are sources of noise. Interference on viewers' television sets during an advertisement is noise and lessens the impact of the message. Noise also occurs when a source uses a sign that is unfamiliar to the receiver or that has a different meaning from the one the source intended. Noise may also originate in the receiver. As Chapter 4 discusses, a receiver may be unaware of a coded message because his or her perceptual processes block it out or because the coded message is too obscure.

The receiver's response to a message is **feedback** to the source. The source usually expects and normally receives feedback, although it may not be immediate. During feedback, the receiver or audience is the source of a message that is directed towards the original source, which then becomes a receiver. Feedback is coded, sent through a medium of transmission, and is decoded by the receiver, the source of the original communication. It is logical, then, to think of communication as a circular process.

During face to face communication, such as in personal selling or product sampling, both verbal and non-verbal feedback can be immediate. Instant feedback lets communicators adjust their messages quickly to improve the effectiveness of their communication. For example, when a salesperson realises through feedback that a customer does not understand a sales presentation, he or she adapts the presentation to make it more meaningful to the customer. In interpersonal communication, feedback occurs through talking, touching, smiling, nodding, eye movements and other body movements and postures.

When mass communication such as advertising is used, feedback is often slow and difficult to recognise. If EuroDisney increased its advertising in order to increase the number of visitors, it might be 6 to 18 months before the theme park could recognise the effects of the expanded advertising. Although it is harder to recognise, feedback does exist for mass communication. Figure 14.3 illustrates a unique programme developed by Minolta to obtain feedback on whether its message was received by its target market. Advertisers, for example, obtain feedback in the form of changes in sales volume or in consumers' attitudes and awareness levels, monitored through tracking research.

Each communication channel has a limit on the volume of information it can handle effectively. This limit, called **channel capacity,** is determined by the least efficient component of the communication process. To illustrate this, think about communications that depend on vocal speech. An individual source can talk only so fast, and there is a limit to how much an individual receiver can take in aurally. Beyond that point, additional messages cannot be decoded; thus meaning cannot be shared. Although a radio announcer can read several hundred words a minute, a one minute advertising

FIGURE 14.3

Getting feedback
With this direct response press advertisement, Minolta in France can judge the impact of its campaign.

SOURCE: Minolta France S.A.

message should not exceed 150 words because most announcers cannot articulate the words into understandable messages at a rate beyond 150 words per minute. This figure is the limit for both source and receiver, and marketers should keep this in mind when developing radio commercials. At times, a firm creates a television advertisement that contains several types of visual material and several forms of audio messages, all transmitted to viewers at the same time. Such communication may not be totally effective, because receivers cannot decode all the messages simultaneously.

Now that the basic communication process has been explored, it is worth considering more specifically how promotion is used to influence individuals, groups or organisations to accept or adopt a firm's products. Although the product adoption process was briefly touched upon in Chapter 9, it is discussed more fully in the following section in order to provide a better understanding of the conditions under which promotion occurs.

PROMOTION AND THE PRODUCT ADOPTION PROCESS

Marketers do not promote simply to inform, educate and entertain; they communicate to facilitate satisfying exchanges. One long run purpose of promotion is to influence and encourage buyers to accept or adopt goods, services and ideas. At times, an advertisement may be informative or entertaining, yet it may fail to get the audience to purchase the product. For example, some ads for business computers seem to be weak in communicating benefits—they focus instead on getting customers to feel good about

FIGURE 14.4 *Building awareness*

JCB launched its skid steer initially with this teaser advertisement (left) before running the second advertisement which revealed the actual product (right).

SOURCE: Client: John Bradley, JCB Sales Ltd. Agency: CB Brookes Advertising Ltd.

the product. The ultimate effectiveness of promotion is determined by the degree to which it affects product adoption among potential buyers or increases the frequency of current buyers' purchases.

To establish realistic expectations about what promotion can do, product adoption should not be viewed as a one step process. Rarely can a single promotional activity cause an individual to buy a previously unfamiliar product. The acceptance of a product involves many steps. Although there are several ways to look at the **product adoption process,** it is commonly divided into five stages: awareness, interest, evaluation, trial and adoption.[10]

In the awareness stage, individuals become aware that the product exists, but they have little information about it and are not concerned about obtaining more. When Peugeot launched its 405 model, for example, it used provocative teaser advertisements, which showed burning fields but no car. Later adverts did show the 405. In Figure 14.4 JCB's teaser advertisement (left) did not reveal its innovative single arm skid steer; later adverts did (right). Consumers enter the interest stage when they are motivated to obtain information about the product's features, uses, advantages, disadvantages, price or location. During the evaluation stage, individuals consider whether the product will satisfy certain criteria that are crucial for meeting their specific needs. In the trial stage, they use or experience the product for the first time, possibly by pur-

SOURCE: Client: John Bradley, JCB Sales Ltd. Agency: CB Brookes Advertising Ltd.

chasing a small quantity, by taking advantage of a free sample or demonstration or by borrowing the product from someone. Supermarkets, for example, frequently offer special promotions to encourage consumers to taste products such as cheese, cooked meats, snacks or pizza. During this stage, potential adopters determine the usefulness of the product under the specific conditions for which they need it.

Individuals move into the adoption stage by choosing the specific product when they need a product of that general type. It cannot be assumed, however, that because a person enters the adoption process she or he will eventually adopt the new product. Rejection may occur at any stage, including adoption. Both product adoption and product rejection can be temporary or permanent.

For the most part, people respond to different information sources at different stages of the adoption process. Figure 14.5 illustrates the most effective sources for each stage. Mass communication sources, such as television advertising, are often effective for moving large numbers of people into the awareness stage. Producers of consumer goods commonly use massive advertising campaigns when introducing new products. They do so to create product awareness as quickly as possible within a large portion of the target market.

Mass communications may also be effective for people in the interest stage who want to learn more about a product. During the evaluation stage, individuals often seek information, opinions and reinforcement from personal sources—relatives, friends and associates. In the trial stage, individuals depend on salespeople for information about how to use the product properly to get the most out of it. Marketers must use ad-

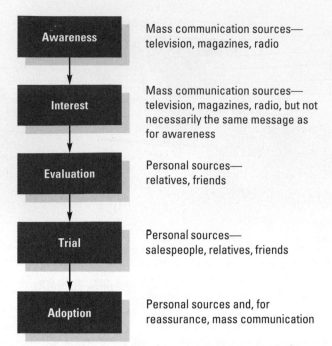

Awareness — Mass communication sources—television, magazines, radio

Interest — Mass communication sources—television, magazines, radio, but not necessarily the same message as for awareness

Evaluation — Personal sources—relatives, friends

Trial — Personal sources—salespeople, relatives, friends

Adoption — Personal sources and, for reassurance, mass communication

vertising carefully when consumers are in the trial stage. If advertisements greatly exaggerate the benefits of a product, the consumer may be disappointed when the product does not meet expectations.[11] It is best to avoid creating expectations that cannot be satisfied, because rejection at this stage will prevent adoption. Friends and peers may also be important sources during the trial stage. By the time the adoption stage has been reached, both personal communication from sales personnel and mass communication through advertisements may be required. Even though the particular stage of the adoption process may influence the types of information sources consumers use, marketers must remember that other factors, such as the product's characteristics, price and uses, as well as the characteristics of customers, also affect the types of information sources that buyers desire and believe.

Because people in different stages of the adoption process often require different types of information, marketers designing a promotional campaign must determine what stage of the adoption process a particular target audience is in before they can develop the message. Potential adopters in the interest stage will need different information from people who have already reached the trial stage.

When an organisation introduces a new product, people do not all begin the adoption process at the same time, and they do not move through the process at the same speed. Of those people who eventually adopt the product, some enter the adoption process rather quickly, whereas others start considerably later. For most products, too, there is a group of non-adopters who never begin the process.

Product Adopter Categories

Depending on the length of time it takes them to adopt a new product, people can be divided into five major adopter categories: innovators, early adopters, early majority, late majority and laggards.[12] Figure 14.6 shows each adopter category and indicates the percentage of total adopters that it typically represents. **Innovators** are the first to adopt a new product. They enjoy trying new products and tend to be venturesome. **Early adopters** choose new products carefully and are viewed as "the people to check

FIGURE 14.6
Distribution of product adopter categories

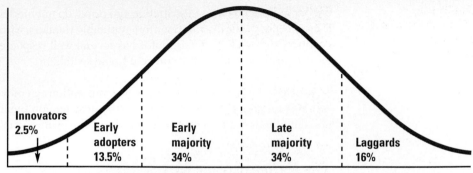

Innovators
2.5%

Early
adopters
13.5%

Early
majority
34%

Late
majority
34%

Laggards
16%

SOURCE: Reprinted with permission of the Free Press, a division of Macmillan Inc., from *Diffusion of Innovations,* 3rd. ed., by Everett H. Rogers. Copyright © 1962, 1971, 1983 by The Free Press.

with" by those in the remaining adopter categories. People in the **early majority** adopt just prior to the average person; they are deliberate and cautious in trying new products. **Late majority** people, who are quite sceptical about new products, eventually adopt them because of economic necessity or social pressure. **Laggards,** the last to adopt a new product, are orientated towards the past. They are suspicious of new products, and when they finally adopt the innovation, it may already have been replaced by a newer product. When developing promotional efforts, a marketer should bear in mind that people in different adopter categories often need different forms of communication and different types of information.

Aims of Promotion Communication

Product adoption is a major focus for any promotional activity. There are, though, five basic communications aims, which are defined as follows.[13]

Category Need.   The consumer must realise he or she wants a particular product—particularly for innovative new category product launches—and must perceive a **category need** in order to be motivated even to consider a product. When compact disc players were launched, many consumers had perfectly adequate album and/or cassette based hi-fi systems and did not see any need to purchase a compact disc player.

Brand Awareness.   The consumer must be able to identify (recognise or recall) a manufacturer's brand within the category in sufficient detail to make a purchase. **Brand awareness** means that the manufacturer must make its brand stand out, initially through product attributes supported by distinctive promotional activity. Sony wants consumers to be aware of *its* compact disc players rather than Aiwa or Amstrad players.

Brand Attitude.   Emotions and logic or cognitive beliefs combine to give the consumer a particular impression of a product. This **brand attitude** directs consumer choice towards a particular brand. Companies need customers to have a positive view of their brands.

Brand Purchase Intention.   Once a category need and brand awareness are established, if the consumer's brand attitude is favourable, he or she will decide to purchase the particular product and take steps to do so, showing **brand purchase intention.**

Purchase Facilitation.   Having decided to buy, the consumer requires the product to be readily available at a convenient location, at a suitable price and from a familiar dealer **(purchase facilitation).** The manufacturer must ensure that other marketing factors (product, people, distribution and price) do not hinder the purchase. Sony customers expect wide distribution from reputable retailers, with no budget pricing. Sony produces high quality goods, but it has several well respected competitors and must ensure product availability to prevent brand switching.

To provide a better understanding of how promotion can move people closer to the acceptance of goods, services and ideas, the next section focuses on the major promotional methods available to an organisation—the promotional mix.

THE PROMOTIONAL MIX

Several types of promotional methods can be used to communicate with individuals, groups and organisations. When an organisation combines specific ingredients to promote a particular product, that combination constitutes the promotional mix for that product. The four traditional ingredients of a **promotional mix** are advertising, personal selling, public relations and sales promotion. Increasingly, sponsorship and direct mail are elements of the promotional mix in their own right (see Figure 14.7). For some products, firms use all these ingredients; for other products, two or three will suffice. This section analyses the major ingredients of a promotional mix and the chief factors that influence an organisation to include specific ingredients in the promotional mix for a specific product. Chapters 15 and 16 examine the promotional mix in greater detail.

Promotional Mix Ingredients

At this point consideration is given to some general characteristics of advertising, personal selling, public relations, sales promotion, sponsorship and direct mail.

Advertising.   **Advertising** is a paid form of non-personal communication about an organisation and its products that is transmitted to a target audience through a mass medium such as television, radio, newspapers, magazines, direct mail, public transport, outdoor displays or catalogues. Individuals and organisations use advertising to promote goods, services, ideas, issues and people. Because it is highly flexible, advertising offers the options of reaching an extremely large target audience or focusing on a small, precisely defined segment of the population. For instance, McDonald's advertising focuses on a large audience of potential fast food consumers, ranging from children to adults, whereas advertising for DeBeers' diamonds focuses on a much smaller and specialised target market.

Advertising offers several benefits. It can be an extremely cost efficient promotional method because it reaches a vast number of people at a low cost per person. For example, the cost of a four colour, one page advertisement in the *Sunday Telegraph* magazine is £7,000. Because the magazine reaches 700,000 readers, the cost of reaching 1,000 subscribers is only £10. Advertising also lets the user repeat the message a number of times. Unilever advertises many of its products (cleaning products, foods, cosmetics) on television, in magazines and through outdoor advertising. In addition, advertising a product in a certain way can add to its value. For example, BMW cars are advertised as having more sophistication, style and technical innovation than Honda, Toyota and other Japanese companies' vehicles. The visibility that an organisation gains from advertising enhances the firm's public image.

Advertising also has several disadvantages. Even though the cost per person reached may be low, the absolute monetary outlay can be extremely high, especially for advertisements shown during popular television programmes. These high costs can limit,

FIGURE 14.7
Possible ingredients of an organisation's promotional mix

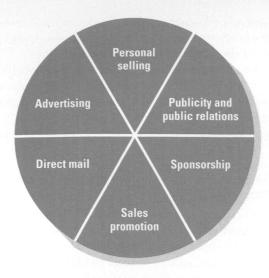

and sometimes prevent, the use of advertising in a promotional mix. Moreover, advertising rarely provides rapid feedback. Measuring its effect on sales is difficult, and it ordinarily has a less persuasive impact on customers than personal selling.[14]

Personal Selling.   **Personal selling** involves informing customers and persuading them to purchase products through personal communication in an exchange situation. The phrase *to purchase products* should be interpreted broadly to encompass the acceptance of ideas and issues. Telemarketing, which Chapter 12 describes as direct selling over the telephone, relies heavily on personal selling.

Personal selling has both advantages and limitations when compared with advertising. Advertising is general communication aimed at a relatively large target audience, whereas personal selling involves more specific communication aimed at one or several persons. Reaching one person through personal selling costs considerably more than doing so through advertising, but personal selling efforts often have a greater impact on customers. Personal selling also provides immediate feedback, which allows marketers to adjust their message to improve communication. It helps them determine and respond to customers' needs for information.

When a salesperson and customer meet face to face, they use several types of interpersonal communication. Obviously, the predominating communication form is language—both speech and writing. In addition, a salesperson and customer frequently use **kinesic communication,** or body language, by moving their heads, eyes, arms, hands, legs or torsos. Winking, head nodding, hand gestures and arm motions are forms of kinesic communication. A good salesperson can often evaluate a prospect's interest in a product or presentation by watching for eye contact and head nodding. **Proxemic communication,** a less obvious form of communication used in personal selling, occurs when either person varies the physical distance that separates the two people. When a customer backs away from a salesperson, for example, that individual may be indicating that he or she is not interested in the product or may be expressing dislike for the salesperson. Touching, or **tactile communication,** can also be used; shaking hands is a common form of tactile communication in many countries.

Publicity and Public Relations.   **Publicity** refers to non-personal communication in news story form about an organisation or its products, or both, that is transmitted through a mass medium at no charge. Examples of publicity include magazine, newspaper, radio and television news stories about new retail stores, new products or personnel changes in an organisation. Although both advertising and publicity are transmitted through mass communication, the sponsor does not pay the media costs for publicity and is not identified. Nevertheless, publicity should never be viewed as free communication. There are clear costs associated with preparing news releases and encouraging media personnel to broadcast or print them. A firm that uses publicity regularly must have employees to perform these activities or obtain the services of a public relations firm or an advertising agency. Either way, the firm bears the costs of the activities.

Publicity must be planned and implemented so that it is compatible with, and supportive of, other elements in the promotional mix. However, publicity cannot always be controlled to the extent that other elements of the promotional mix can be. For example, just as Perrier's contamination problems appeared to be easing, a BBC television programme showed that the "bottled at source" packaging was misleading because the bubbles were added during the bottling process. Sainsbury, the UK's major grocery retailer, refused for many months to re-stock Perrier until the wording on the packaging was altered, creating further adverse publicity for the French company. Marketing Insight 14.2 explains how Benetton's advertising caused the Italian company to rethink its promotion and provided extra work for its publicity department. The **public relations** mechanism manages and controls the use of effective publicity (see Chapter 15).

Sales Promotion.   **Sales promotion** is an activity or material that acts as a direct inducement by offering added value to or incentive for the product to resellers, sales people or consumers.[15] Examples of sales promotion include coupons and tokens (see Figure 14.8), bonuses and contests used to enhance the sales of a product. The term *sales promotion* should not be confused with *promotion;* sales promotion is but a part of the more comprehensive area of promotion, encompassing personal selling, advertising, publicity, sponsorship and direct mail. Some sales promotions, however, are closely associated with additional elements of the promotional mix (see Chapter 15). Currently, marketers spend about half as much on sales promotion as they do on advertising. Sales promotion appears to be growing in use more than advertising.

Marketers frequently rely on sales promotion to improve the effectiveness of other promotional mix ingredients, especially advertising and personal selling. For example, some firms allocate 25 per cent of their annual promotional budget to trade shows in order to introduce new products, meet key industrial personnel, and identify likely prospects.[16]

Marketers design sales promotion to produce immediate, short run sales increases. For example, the major brewers such as Heineken and Whitbread use a continuous programme of sales promotion techniques to boost sales in the highly competitive beer and lager market: free drinks and prize competitions, scratch cards and trade incentives.

Generally, if a company employs advertising or personal selling, it either depends on them continuously or turns to them cyclically. However, a marketer's use of sales promotion tends to be irregular. Many products are seasonal. For example, Thomas Cook and Lunn Poly promote summer package holidays predominantly in the winter and spring months. Qualcast pushes its lawn mowers and other gardening equipment from Easter onwards.

Sponsorship.   **Sponsorship** is the financial or material support of an event, activity, person, organisation or product by an unrelated organisation or donor. Funds are made available to the recipient of the sponsorship in return for the prominent expo-

BENETTON BARES ALL

Italian clothing giant Benetton, known for its vibrant colours and fashionable knitwear, has never been shy of seeking media attention in order to gain consumer awareness. In the early 1990s two campaigns not only created headlines but also provoked shock around the world. First, huge billboards brought a blood covered newborn baby still attached to the umbilical cord to the streets of many towns and cities. With not an item of Benetton clothing in sight, complaints broke all records; watchdog bodies forced Benetton to remove the offending advertisements. In the UK the Advertising Standards Authority received over 800 complaints, while members of the public also contacted Trading Standards officials and even the police. On previous occasions Benetton's awareness generating, colourful campaigns had tackled such weighty issues as racial equality, civil rights, birth control and world peace.

A year later, the world's media covered Benetton's new campaign, which broke in America and featured an AIDS victim lying dead in hospital in the arms of his grieving father, surrounded by distraught family members. Public opinion was again outraged, and the campaign never reached most European markets. The adverts were branded sensational, insensitive and irrelevant to the promotion of Benetton's merchandise and shops.

In 1993, the company's $25 million global campaign replaced the images of a dying AIDS victim and oil drenched gulls with that of a naked Luciano Benetton, the company's chairman. The strap line read, "I want my clothes back". Still as bizarre as previous Benetton campaigns, this one avoided adverse media coverage and aimed to present a more sympathetic, caring image for the company. The new adverts "combined the advertising of a brand with concrete social concerns", being run in association with the International Red Cross and clothing charity Coritas. The adverts appealed to consumers to take their old, unwanted clothes to any Benetton shop where collection bins were located. The clothes were sent to the world's numerous trouble spots.

According to Benetton, the campaign was not just an attempt to patch up its battle-scarred brand image. ("There will always be the cynical point of view, but we never expected everyone to be with us.") The company remains unrepentant about past campaigns. ("All we ever wanted was for people to understand our point of view.") Either way, the new charity orientated campaign caught the positive attention of the world's media while continuing to attract the attention of consumers worldwide and reinforce the Benetton brand.

SOURCES: Reuters; ASA; "Benetton bares all for charity", Mat Toor, *Marketing,* 28 January 1993, p. 4; *Marketing,* 8 September 1991; *Marketing,* 19 September 1991; *Campaign,* 27 September 1991; Lindsay Fowler.

FIGURE 14.8

*Example of a sales
promotion*
Tokens or coupons are
common sales promotions.

FREE FROM **SPECIAL K**
PURE AND SIMPLE.

Special K has always helped to look after your body. And now it can
do the same for your complexion. Collect eight tokens from **Special K**
packs (here are two to get you started). Send them to us, and in return,
we'll send you a 160 ml bottle from the Pure and Simple skin care range,
absolutely free. Kellogg's **Special K**. Now with added cleanser, toner
and moisturiser from Pure and Simple.

SOURCE: Printed by permission of the Kellogg Company of Great Britain
Limited.

sure of the benefactor's generosity, products and brands. Sponsorship is no longer confined to the arts or the sporting world, although many galleries, theatrical companies,
sports events and teams could not survive without sponsorship. Research and development, buildings, degree courses, charitable events—all often benefit from sponsorship. The donor or sponsor gains the benefits of enhanced company, brand or
individual reputation and awareness, as well as possibly improved morale and employee relations.

Direct Mail.   The direct mail industry takes a significant slice of the promotional
budgets for many companies and organisations. Few households and companies fail to
receive direct mail solicitations. **Direct mail** is used to entice prospective customers
or charitable donors directly to invest in products, services or worthy causes.
Throughout Europe, direct mail is used as a pre-sell technique prior to a sales call, to
generate orders, qualify prospects for a sales call, follow up a sale, announce special or
localised sales, and raise funds for charities and non-profit organisations. Good database management is essential, and the material must be carefully targeted to overcome
the growing public aversion to "junk mail".

   Now that the basic components of an organisation's promotional mix have been discussed, it is important to consider how that mix is created. The factors and conditions
which affect the selection of the promotional methods a specific organisation uses in its
promotional mix for a particular product need to be examined.

Marketers vary the composition of promotional mixes for many reasons. Although all six ingredients can be included in a promotional mix, frequently a marketer selects fewer than six. In addition, many firms that market multiple product lines use several promotional mixes simultaneously.

An organisation's promotional mix (or mixes) is not an unchanging part of the marketing mix. Marketers can and do change the composition of their promotional mixes. The specific promotional mix ingredients employed and the intensity with which they are used depend on a variety of factors, including the organisation's promotional resources, objectives and policies; characteristics of the target market; characteristics of the product; and cost and availability of promotional methods.

Promotional Resources, Objectives and Policies. The quality of an organisation's promotional resources affects the number and relative intensity of promotional methods that can be included in a promotional mix. If a company's promotional budget is extremely limited, the firm is likely to rely on personal selling because it is easier to measure a salesperson's contribution to sales than to measure the effect of advertising. A business must have a sizeable promotional budget if it is to use regional or national advertising and sales promotion activities. Organisations with extensive promotional resources usually can include more ingredients in their promotional mixes. However, having larger promotional budgets does not imply that they necessarily will use a greater number of promotional methods.

An organisation's promotional objectives and policies also influence the types of promotion used. If a company's objective is to create mass awareness of a new convenience good, its promotional mix is likely to lean heavily towards advertising, sales promotion and possibly publicity. If a company hopes to educate consumers about the features of durable goods, such as home appliances, its promotional mix may combine a moderate amount of advertising, possibly some sales promotion efforts designed to attract customers to retail stores and a great deal of personal selling, this being an excellent way to inform customers about these types of products. If a firm's objective is to produce immediate sales of consumer non-durables, such as paper products and many grocery goods, the promotional mix will probably stress advertising and sales promotion efforts.

Characteristics of the Target Market. The size, geographic distribution and socio-economic characteristics of an organisation's target market also help dictate the ingredients to be included in a product's promotional mix. To some degree, market size determines the composition of the mix. If the size is quite limited, the promotional mix will probably emphasise personal selling, which can be quite effective for reaching small numbers of people. Organisations that sell to industrial markets and firms that market their products through only a few wholesalers frequently make personal selling the major component of their promotional mixes. When markets for a product consist of millions of customers, organisations use advertising and sales promotion because these methods can reach masses of people at a low cost per person. The Coca-Cola Company attempted to reach consumers through a non-traditional vehicle when it placed a commercial for diet Coke in the introduction to the home video version of the 1989 blockbuster *Batman.* Warner Home Video, the distributor of *Batman,* believed that it would sell more than 10 million copies of the video cassette, exposing millions of consumers to the diet Coke message at a low cost per person.[17]

The geographic distribution of a firm's customers can affect the combination of promotional methods used. Personal selling is more feasible if a company's customers are concentrated in a small area than if they are dispersed across a vast region. When the company's customers are numerous and dispersed, advertising may be more practical.

The distribution of a target market's socio-economic characteristics, such as age, income or education, may dictate the types of promotional techniques that a marketer selects. For example, personal selling may be much more successful than print advertisements for communicating with poorly educated people, because it allows meaning or product attributes to be explained face to face.

Characteristics of the Product. Generally, promotional mixes for industrial products concentrate on personal selling. In promoting consumer goods, on the other hand, advertising plays a major role. This generalisation should be treated cautiously, however. Industrial goods producers do use some advertising to promote their goods, particularly in the trade press. Advertisements for computers, road building equipment and aircraft are not altogether uncommon, and some sales promotion is used to promote industrial goods. Personal selling is used extensively for services and consumer durables, such as home appliances, cars and houses, and consumer convenience items are promoted mainly through advertising and sales promotion. Publicity appears in promotional mixes for industrial goods, consumer goods and for services. Many organisations use direct mail, and more are now examining the growing use of corporate sponsorship.

Marketers of highly seasonal products are often forced to emphasise advertising, and possibly sales promotion, because off-season sales will not support an extensive year round sales force. Although many toy producers have sales forces to sell to re-sellers, a number of these companies depend to a large extent on advertising to promote their products.

The price of a product also influences the composition of the promotional mix. High priced products call for more personal selling because consumers associate greater risk with the purchase of such products and usually want the advice of a salesperson. Few consumers, for example, would be willing to purchase a refrigerator or personal computer from a self-service establishment. For low priced convenience items, marketers use advertising rather than personal selling at the retail level. The profit margins on many of these items are too low to justify the use of salespeople, and most customers do not need advice from sales personnel when buying such products.

A further consideration in creating an effective promotional mix is the stage of the product life-cycle. During the introduction stage, a good deal of advertising may be necessary for both industrial and consumer products to make potential users aware of a new product. For many products, personal selling and sales promotion are helpful as well at this stage. In the case of consumer non-durables, the growth and maturity stages call for a heavy emphasis on advertising. Industrial products, on the other hand, often require a concentration of personal selling and some sales promotion efforts during these stages. In the decline stage, marketers usually decrease their promotional activities, especially advertising. Promotional efforts in the decline stage often centre on personal selling and sales promotion efforts.

The intensity of market coverage is still another factor affecting the composition of the promotional mix. When a product is marketed through intensive distribution, the firm depends strongly on advertising and sales promotion. A number of convenience products, such as lotions, cereals and coffee, are promoted through samples, coupons and cash refunds. Where marketers have opted for selective distribution, marketing mixes vary considerably as to type and amount of promotional methods. Items handled through exclusive distribution frequently demand more personal selling and less advertising. Expensive watches, furs and high quality furniture are typical products promoted heavily through personal selling.

A product's use also affects the combination of promotional methods. Manufacturers of highly personal products, such as non-prescription contraceptives, feminine hygiene products and haemorrhoid treatments, count on advertising for promotion because many users do not like to talk to sales personnel about such products.

Cost and Availability of Promotional Methods.   The cost of promotional methods is a major factor to analyse when developing a promotional mix. National advertising and sales promotion efforts require large expenditures. For example, in the UK, television transmission charges for advertising in 1989 were £1,990 million and production costs were £296 million.[18] However, if the efforts are effective in reaching extremely large numbers of people, the cost per individual reached may be quite small, possibly a few pennies per person. Moreover, not all forms of advertising are expensive. Many small, local businesses advertise their products through local newspapers, magazines, radio stations, outdoor signs and public transport.

Another consideration that marketers must explore when formulating a promotional mix is the availability of promotional techniques. Despite the tremendous number of media vehicles, a firm may find that no available advertising medium effectively reaches a certain market. For example, a product may be banned from being advertised on television, as are cigarettes in many countries. A stockbroker may find no suitable advertising medium for investors in Tottenham Hotspur Football Club: should the stockbroker use financial publications, sports magazines or general media? The problem of media availability becomes even more pronounced when marketers try to advertise in other countries. Some media, such as television, simply may not be available to advertisers. Television advertising in Scandinavia is minimal. In the UK only seven minutes of advertising are permitted per hour of television. The media that are available may not be open to certain types of advertisements. For example, in West Germany, advertisers were forbidden to make brand comparisons in television advertisements. Other promotional methods have limitations as well. An organisation may wish to increase the size of its sales force but be unable to find qualified personnel. In America, some state laws prohibit the use of certain types of sales promotion activities, such as contests. Such prohibited techniques are thus "unavailable" in those locales.

Push Policy Versus Pull Policy

Another element that marketers should consider when they plan a promotional mix is whether to use a push policy or a pull policy. With a **push policy,** the producer promotes the product only to the next institution down the marketing channel. For instance, in a marketing channel with wholesalers and retailers, the producer promotes to the wholesaler, in this case the channel member just below the producer (see Figure 14.9). Each channel member in turn promotes to the next channel member. A push policy normally stresses personal selling. Sometimes sales promotion, direct mail and advertising are used in conjunction with personal selling to push the products down through the channel.

As Figure 14.9 shows, a firm using a **pull policy** promotes directly to consumers with the intention of developing a strong consumer demand for the products. It does so through advertising, sales promotion, direct mail, sponsorship and packaging that helps manufacturers build and maintain market share.[19] Because consumers are persuaded to seek the products in retail stores, retailers will in turn go to wholesalers or the producer to buy the products. The policy is thus intended to "pull" the goods down through the channel by creating demand at the consumer level.

FIGURE 14.9
Comparison of push and pull promotional strategies

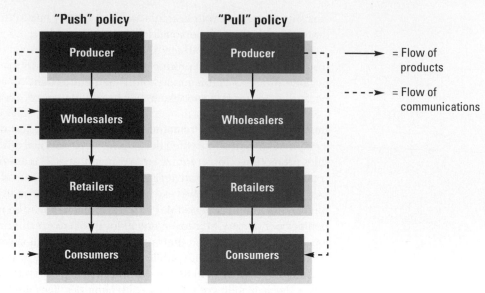

A push policy can be combined with a pull policy. Mars, for example, has a pull policy aimed at the consumer: sponsorship of events and advertising create awareness; packaging, sales promotions—such as competitions or discounts—and direct mail prompt product trial and adoption. Simultaneously, the company's push policy of trade advertising, sales promotions and personal selling persuades channel members to stock and retail its products.

SUMMARY

The primary role of promotion is to communicate with individuals, groups or organisations in the environment with the aim of directly or indirectly facilitating exchanges.

Communication is a sharing of meaning. The communication process involves several steps. First, the source translates the meaning into code, a process known as coding or encoding. The source should employ signs familiar to the receiver or audience and choose signs that the receiver or audience uses for referring to the concepts or ideas being promoted. The coded message is sent through a medium of transmission to the receiver or audience. The receiver or audience then decodes the message and usually supplies feedback to the source. When the decoded message differs from the encoded one, a condition called noise exists.

The long run purpose of promotion is to influence and encourage customers to accept or adopt goods, services and ideas. The product adoption process consists of five stages. In the awareness stage, individuals become aware of the product. People move into the interest stage when they seek more information about the product. In the evaluation stage, individuals decide whether the product will meet certain criteria that are crucial for satisfying their needs. During the trial stage, the consumer actually tries the product. In the adoption stage, the consumer decides to use the product on a regular basis. Rejection of the product may occur at any stage. The adopters can be divided into five major categories—innovators, early adopters, early majority, late majority and laggards—according to the length of time it takes them to start using a new product.

A manufacturer or retailer must establish a category need for a product. Consumers must be aware of a company's brands and have a favourable brand attitude towards the products. If the consumer decides to make a purchase, the company's overall marketing policy must guarantee distribution, suitable product quality and attributes, and set the relevant price points. These are all areas of successful promotional activity.

The promotional mix for a product may include the four major promotional methods: advertising, personal selling, publicity and sales promotion, as well as the growing areas of direct mail and sponsorship. Advertising is a paid form of non-personal communication about an organisation and its products that is transmitted to a target audience through a mass medium. Personal selling is a process of informing customers and persuading them to purchase products through personal communication in an exchange situation. Publicity is non-personal communication in news story form, about an organisation, its products, or both, that is transmitted through a mass medium at no charge, controlled by the public relations mechanism. Sales promotion is an activity or material that acts as a direct inducement by offering added value to or incentive for the product to resellers, salespeople or consumers. Sponsorship involves financial or material support for an organisation, product or event in return for prominent public recognition and display of the sponsor's name, products or services. Direct mail involves mailing information, selling or donation packages to consumers and businesses to solicit interest in products or services, purchases or charitable donations.

There are several major determinants of what promotional methods to include in a promotional mix for a product: the organisation's promotional resources, objectives and policies; the characteristics of the target market; the characteristics of the product; and the cost and availability of promotional methods. Marketers must also consider whether to use a push policy or a pull policy, or a combination of the two. With a push policy, the producer promotes the product only to the next institution down the marketing channel. Normally, a push policy stresses personal selling. A firm that uses a pull policy promotes directly to consumers with the intention of developing a strong consumer demand for the products. Once consumers are persuaded to seek the products in retail stores, retailers in turn go to wholesalers or the producer to buy the products.

IMPORTANT TERMS

Promotion
Communication
Source
Receiver
Coding process
Medium of transmission
Decoding process
Noise
Feedback
Channel capacity
Product adoption process
Innovators
Early adopters
Early majority
Late majority
Laggards
Category need

Brand awareness
Brand attitude
Brand purchase intention
Purchase facilitation
Promotional mix
Advertising
Personal selling
Kinesic communication
Proxemic communication
Tactile communication
Publicity
Public relations
Sales promotion
Sponsorship
Direct mail
Push Policy
Pull policy

DISCUSSION AND REVIEW QUESTIONS

1. What is the major task of promotion? Do firms ever use promotion to accomplish this task and fail? If so, give several examples.
2. What is communication? Describe the communication process. Is it possible to communicate without using all the elements in the communication process? If so, which ones can be omitted?
3. Identify several causes of noise. How can a source reduce noise?
4. Describe the product adoption process. In certain circumstances, is it possible for a person to omit one or more of the stages in adopting a new product? Explain your answer.
5. Describe a product that many people are in the process of adopting. Have you begun the adoption process for this product? If so, what stage have you reached?
6. What is category need? Illustrate your answer with examples.
7. Identify and briefly describe the major promotional methods that can be included in an organisation's promotional mix. How does publicity differ from advertising?
8. What forms of interpersonal communication besides language can be used in personal selling?
9. How do market characteristics determine which promotional methods to include in a promotional mix? Assume that a company is planning to promote a cereal to both adults and children. Along what major dimensions would these two promotional efforts have to be different?
10. How can a product's characteristics affect the composition of its promotional mix?
11. Evaluate the following statement: "Appropriate advertising media are always available if a company can afford them".
12. Explain the difference between a pull policy and a push policy. Under what conditions should each policy be used?

■ CASES

14.1 The Energizer Bunny Marches On and On . . . Straight into Duracell's Pink Bunny

"Nothing outlasts the Energizer. They keep going and going. . . ." To effectively communicate the message that its Energizer batteries last a long, long time, the Ever Ready Battery Co. introduced in America what has been called one of the cleverest advertising campaigns in television history. With the Energizer brand's introduction into Europe, the Energizer Bunny has encountered an aggressive pink rival.

In a series of television advertisements, the Energizer Bunny's batteries last so long that he escapes from a real advertisement for the batteries and marches through parodied advertisements for fictional products such as instant coffee, air freshener, late-night albums by obscure artists, soft drinks and Château Marmoset wine. After several seconds of a seemingly real advertisement for "Chug-a-Cherry Cola," for example, E.B. encounters a young man dancing upside down on the ceiling. In an advertisement for a fictitious phone company, the bunny knocks down the partition dividing two callers, poking fun at telephone trunk call advertising. After following the real 60 second battery advertisement for several weeks, the 15 second parody spots now air alone, enhancing the surprise effect.

Chiat/Day/Mojo, the campaign's creators, pay attention to the tiniest details in the parodied advertisements, even down to a "use only as directed" disclaimer for the fake nasal spray. The ads emphasise that "nothing outlasts the Energizer. They keep going and going and going . . . ," just as E.B. keeps going and going, even into other commercials. The campaign works because of the elements of surprise and humour. The long lasting message is clearly evident, and the phone spots amuse consumers while standing out from the barrage of television advertising. Company executives say they have received hundreds of positive letters about the campaign, and one Energizer Bunny ad recently won a Clio award for the year's best video spot.

Emboldened by the success of the campaign, E.B. is turning up in surprisingly new places. He marches through advertisements for real products like Purina Cat Chow in America. (Ralston Purina Co. is the corporate parent for both Ever Ready and Cat Chow.) In this advertisement, E.B. dances along with a woman and her cat to the well known "chow-chow-chow" step of the Purina Cat chow campaign. He breaks through a page of full type in print ads running in issues of *Newsweek, People, Sports Illustrated, Time* and *U.S. News & World Report.* In his cinema debut, he interrupts a preview parody for a fictitious French film, *Dance with Your Feet.* Right in the middle of a dancer's romantic interlude, in barges E.B. He is even appearing soon on packages of Ever Ready batteries and in in-store promotions.

One nagging concern for both Ever Ready and its advertising agency is continuing customer confusion over which brand of battery the bunny advertisements promote. In a recent American survey by Video Storyboard Tests, 40 per cent of the respondents who remember the bunny think he advertises Duracell batteries, Ever Ready's number one competitor. This is a throwback to an earlier Duracell advertisement which featured toy bunnies. Although some experts are advising Ever Ready to spend more time advertising the Energizer name and less on the bunny, the company is confident that this is a normal "lag time" before people consistently link the bunny to the battery.

Despite its overwhelming popularity, the campaign's effect on sales is ambiguous. Recent Nielsen figures place Duracell in the number one spot in America with 42.1 per cent of all alkaline battery sales, and Ever Ready in second place with 36.7 per cent, down slightly from the previous year. Ever Ready's own figures, however, indicate that it is the undisputed market share leader. In addition, Ever Ready consumer research shows unaided brand awareness up 33 per cent, television commercial awareness up 43 per cent and recall of the product's "long lasting" message up 49 per cent.

Increasing consumer demand from the campaign has forced retailers to respond by moving Energizer battery displays to more prominent spaces in their stores. In fact, E.B. is so popular that an offer for a stuffed E.B. doll in the US drew 20,000 requests in two weeks—a response 20 times larger than a typical mail offer generates. The bunny gained some extra publicity when an impostor E.B. appeared on the *Late Night with David Letterman* television programme. In a recent Coors Brewing Company advertisement, actor Leslie Nielsen—dressed in bunny ears, cottontail and pink bunny feet—marched through an advertisement for light beer while a voice-over announced that Coors Light sales keep on "growing and growing". Although Ever Ready initiated talks with Coors to try to stop the advertisement from airing, some analysts assert that battery sales will actually benefit from the humour and extra exposure. So far, Ralston Purina has turned down hundreds of offers to license E.B. for sale in retail stores, but the success of California Raisins toys and Domino's Pizza Noid doll may encourage company executives to change their minds.

In time for Christmas sales, however, Duracell rekindled its "enormously popular" pink bunny property with a £4 million national television campaign in the UK through agency BSB Dorland. Observers thought this was a clever way of spiking Ever Ready's guns just as the company imported the US brand Energizer and its drum beating bunny to replace the flagging Ever Ready Gold Seal alkaline battery line. Research in the UK shows the pink bunny to be clearly associated with Duracell, which has 30 per cent of the market compared with Ever Ready's 25.5 per cent. The Energizer Bunny has hit Europe, though, with Duracell spreading its pink bunny rival to stem Ever Ready's energizer introduction.

SOURCES: Ira Teinowitz, "Coors in a (rabbit) stew over parody", *Advertising Age,* 29 April 1991, pp. 1, 50; Julie Liesse, "Bunny back to battle Duracell", *Advertising Age,* 17 September 1990, pp. 4, 78; "Ever Ready's Bunny to be in the movies", *Los Angeles Times,* 11 September 1990, p. D6; Joann S. Lublin, "Bunny at the movies", *Wall Street Journal,* 11 September 1990, p. B6; Joanne Lipman, "Too many think the Bunny is Duracell's, not Ever Ready's", *Wall Street Journal,* 31 July 1990, pp. B1, B7; Dan Cook, "The rabbit's feat", *California Business,* 1 June 1990; Stuart Elliott and Sal Ruibal, "E.B. and Bo led '89 dream team", *USA Today,* 28 December 1989, p. 6B; Stuart Elliott, "He's back: Energizer Bunny's beat goes on", *USA Today,* 6 December 1989, p. 2B; Julie Liesse Erickson, "Energizer Bunny will plug Purina", *Advertising Age,* 4 December 1989, pp. 1, 54; Stuart Elliott, "Energizer ads march to different drummer", *USA Today,* 24 October 1989, p. 1B; Julie Liesse Erickson, "Energizer Bunny gets the jump", *Advertising Age,* 23 October 1989, p. 4; and Bob Garfield, "Energizer's parody campaign is one bunny of a concept", *Advertising Age,* 23 October 1989, p. 120; "Bunny leaps back into Duracell's defence", Mattoor, *Marketing,* 8 October 1992, p. 7; "Energizer: the birth of a brand", Mattoor, *Marketing,* 4 March 1993, pp. 20–1.

Questions for Discussion

1. In America, why are the Energizer battery advertisements so successful?
2. What is the advertising platform for the Energizer Bunny campaign?
3. What is the nature of the publicity that Ever Ready gained with the Energizer Bunny campaign? Distinguish between the publicity and the advertising in this campaign.
4. How can Ever Ready's Energizer Bunny work to Duracell's advantage?

14.2 Boosting the Doorstep Pinta

In 1991 the National Dairy Council (NDC) worked with advertising agency BMP DDB Needham to produce an advertising campaign which successfully halted the decline in UK doorstep deliveries of milk. Sales had declined significantly throughout the 1980s as milk became more widely distributed in more convenience stores, garage forecourts, newsagents and supermarkets, with keen pricing to combat the convenience of daily home deliveries. The advertising hoped to persuade customers that this personal, convenient and regular service provided by the traditional "milkman" justified a higher price than for milk in the shops. The Dancing Milk Bottle campaign was a tremendous success, leading to increased sales and the award of the prestigious 1992 IPA Advertising Effectiveness Gold Award.

The NDC is the co-ordinating body for the dairy industry in England and Wales, focusing on information and promotional activities. The organisation represents the interests of most of the leading dairies, promoting not only milk as a product but also the service milkmen provide. Milk sales had declined overall by 2 per cent since 1985. Fewer children in the population, health worries about the fat content in milk and the increasing consumption of milk substitutes and soft drinks were the primary reasons for this decline. The NDC was worried about the sharp decline in purchases from the doorstep milkman. In a market worth £3.2 billion, the NDC's milkmen had lost one million customers a year, so that by 1991 only 62 per cent of households bought from a milkman, compared with 90 per cent in 1980.

The first attempt to stem this decline began with a television campaign in 1988, which promoted the milkman service using famous personalities such as athlete Daley Thompson. Although awareness of milk improved following this campaign, the decline was not completely reversed. The 1991 Dancing Milk Bottles, still in use, did successfully address the declining sales. This campaign aimed to present a rational and emotional argument to consumers in favour of milkmen, while simultaneously boosting the self-esteem of the milkmen themselves. The core target audience was deemed to be the brand switchers those consumers who bought from both milkmen and retail outlets. They needed to be "tied in" to their milkman service and discouraged from purchasing from stores. "Busy mums" were identified as those being most in need of the convenience and flexibility offered by doorstep deliveries to the home.

The advertisements stressed several features of the service:

- Full range of milks, including skimmed
- Flexibility of quickly changed orders
- Recycling of collected bottles
- No need to carry heavy, spillable milk
- Friendly, charming, caring milkmen

These were compiled into a "wake up to milk" campaign which emphasised the delivery to the consumer's doorstep.

There were six advertisements in the sequence. "Daybreak" was a 60 second spot which familiarised everyone with the milkman, showing him to be a cheerful person working for the consumer's convenience while he/she sleeps and an integral part of the community. The advert illustrated the flexibility of the service and ease of modifying an order. To avoid stereotyping consumers, no customers were depicted in the advert. Instead, the advert focused on the milkman, and to give a sense of vitality, his dancing milk bottles.

"Garden Path", a 10 second advertisement, emphasised the recycling and environmentally friendly nature of the service. Two other 10 second spots highlighted specific features of the service; "Threesome" featured the variety of milk types offered, and "Carrier Bag" explained the benefit of not needing to carry heavy milk from the supermarket in already cumbersome shopping bags. "Yellow Pages" flagged up the directory as a source for contacting local milkmen to arrange deliveries, but was rarely screened. "Bad Weather" showed snowbound houses still receiving their doorstep pints and was screened during the inclement winter months. The longer "Daybreak" advert was generally featured at the start of a commercial break in a television programme; a 10 second advert concluded the same break to emphasise one of the milkman service's functional benefits, while other companies' advertisements were shown in between.

The campaign identified clear objectives and sought to target a specific audience with a carefully concocted message. The results? According to agency BMP DDB Needham, the campaign in 1991 generated £22.5 million extra profit for NDC, with an adspend of only £5.1 million—a fourfold return. More consumers switched to purchasing only from milkmen, rather than from both milkmen and stores; milkmen's individual orders increased; and cancellations declined. Spontaneous recall tracking research indicated a very successful 67 per cent awareness of the advertisements, with 91 per cent recall in prompted tests.

SOURCES: "Liquid milk report. An era of achievement", National Dairy Council, 1992; "IPA advertising effectiveness awards 1992 report", *Marketing*, 1992; IB 365 students; "The roundsman's chronicle—special edition", National Dairy Council, 1992; BMP DDB Needham video cassette.

Questions for Discussion

1. What was the message of the Dancing Milk Bottles campaign?
2. Who were the targets of the advertising campaign?
3. How did the campaign's success form the basis for PR activity?

15 ADVERTISING, PUBLICITY AND SPONSORSHIP

Objectives

- To explore the uses of advertising

- To become aware of the major steps involved in developing an advertising campaign

- To find out who is responsible for developing advertising campaigns

- To gain an understanding of publicity and public relations

- To analyse how publicity can be used

- To understand the nature of corporate sponsorship

*I*n the furious competition for market share in the huge but maturing £17 billion global athletic shoe industry, some companies are willing to take high risks. One such company is Reebok International. For several years, Reebok and its rival Nike have engaged in an intense strategic marketing war. In early 1990 Reebok's ad agency struggled to come up with a brilliant ad campaign for the Reebok Pump shoe that would challenge the successful Nike Air campaign. The result was a television advertisement featuring bungee jumpers—people who leap from high places tethered at the ankles by giant elastic ropes. The advertisement opens with two men standing on a bridge, 50 meters (180 feet) above whitewater rapids and rocks. Both are wearing basketball shoes—one man in Nike Air hightops and the other in Reebok's Pump. Then the two men free-fall to the sound of clothes flapping in the wind. At the end, the Reebok wearer is shown safely hanging upside down above the water; the other cord holds only a pair of empty Nike Airs. The announcer says, "The Pump from Reebok—it fits a little better than your ordinary athletic shoe".

The advertisement certainly caught people's attention and generated publicity, but it was the wrong kind. Many people viewed the sly joke about violent death as extraordinarily cruel, and consumers complained that children might try the dangerous stunt. Although the advertisement was originally planned as a £20 million, three week campaign, in several territories, including North America, Europe and South East Asia, Reebok took it off the air after six days. The company later attempted to re-run the commercial with disclaimers, but many major television companies refused to air it.

Amongst the clutter of television advertising, how does a company get attention, make a statement? What is certain is that associating a competitor's product with death raises an ethical issue. The Reebok campaign generated a great deal of adverse publicity: Reebok's public relations team had to work overtime to calm critics in the media and to reassure consumers. Stockists of Reebok footwear also were unhappy and did not want their reputations damaged by Reebok's apparent insensitivity. Existing advertisements filled gaps in the schedule, but Reebok's agency had to think up a whole new campaign in a hurry. Meanwhile, Nike could benefit from Reebok's promotional error. ■

SOURCES: Based on information from Laura Jereski, "Can Paul Fireman put the bounce back in Reebok?", *Business Week,* 18 June 1990, pp. 181–2; Bob Garfield, "Good taste takes deep dive in bungee ad for Reebok Pump", *Advertising Age,* 26 March 1990, p. 52; Marcy Mageira, "Nike edges Reebok, L.A. Gear Sprinting", *Advertising Age,* 25 September 1989, p. 93; "Reebok Pacific man takes UK job", *Marketing Week,* 14 January 1993, p. 5; "Reebok hires word chief", *Marketing Week,* 15 January 1993, p. 7; Lindsay McMurdo, "Above the plimsoll line", *Marketing Week,* 8 November 1992, pp. 32–5.

This chapter explores the many dimensions of advertising, publicity and sponsorship. The chapter initially focuses on how advertising is used and then goes on to examine the major steps by which an advertising campaign is developed, describing who is responsible for developing such campaigns. After analysing publicity and comparing its characteristics with those of advertising, the chapter explores the different forms publicity may take. The following section considers how publicity is used and what is required for an effective public relations programme. After discussing negative publicity and some problems associated with the use of publicity, the chapter concludes with a look at the increasing use of corporate sponsorship in the promotional mix.

THE NATURE OF ADVERTISING

Advertising permeates everyone's daily lives. At times people view it positively; at other times they avoid it by taping television programmes and then zapping over the advertisements as they watch later by pressing the video cassette recorder's fast-forward button.[1] Some advertising informs, persuades or entertains; some of it bores, even insults. For example, consumer groups have been whitewashing billboards advertising tobacco products because they believe such advertisements encourage children to smoke.[2]

As mentioned in Chapter 14, **advertising** is a paid form of non-personal communication that is transmitted through mass media such as television, radio, newspapers, magazines, direct mail, pubic transport vehicles and outdoor displays. An organisation can use advertising to reach a variety of audiences, ranging from small, precise groups, such as the stamp collectors of the Highlands, to extremely large audiences, such as all the buyers of fax machines in Sweden.

When people are asked to name major advertisers, most immediately mention business organisations. (See Table 15.1 for a listing of the top 10 advertisers by country in Europe for 1992–1993.) However, many types of organisations—including governments, churches, universities, civic groups and charitable organisations—take advantage of advertising. For example, the UK government is one of the largest advertisers: "Heroin Screws You Up", Employment Training, the DTI Enterprise Initiative are just a few examples. So even though advertising is analysed here in the context of business organisations, it should be borne in mind that much of the discussion applies to all types of organisations.

Marketers sometimes give advertising more credit than it deserves. This attitude causes them to use advertising when they should not. For example, manufacturers of basic products such as sugar, flour and salt often try to differentiate their products, with minimal success. Over the years, Saxa has nevertheless tried to position its salt as different from the competition with the advertising slogan "Saxa Table Salt—lets the flavour flow".

Under certain conditions, advertising can work effectively for an organisation. The questions in Table 15.2 raise some general points that a marketer should consider when assessing the potential value of advertising as an ingredient in a product's promotional mix. The list is not all-inclusive. Numerous factors have a bearing on whether advertising should be used at all, and if so, to what extent.

THE USES OF ADVERTISING

Advertising can serve a variety of purposes. Individuals and organisations use it to promote products and organisations, to stimulate demand, to offset competitors' advertis-

TABLE 15.1 *Top 10 advertisers by country in Europe, 1992–1993*

FRANCE
Renault
PSA-Peugeot
Procter & Gamble
PSA-Citroën
Sopad Nestlé
Henkel France
Ford France
La Francaise des Jeux
Fiat
Lever

GERMANY
C&A
Procter & Gamble
Springer-Verlag
Union Dt. Lebensm. Werke
Ferrero
SA-Sonstige Anzeigen
Mercedes-Benz
Opel
Jacobs Suchard
Ford

DENMARK
FDB
Dansk Supermarked
Magasin
Colgate-Palmolive
Lever
Procter & Gamble
Nordisk Kellog's
Carlsberg Bryggerierne
Kraft General Foods
MD Foods

BELGIUM
Procter & Gamble
GIB Group
BSN-Gervais Danone
Etat Belge
L'Oreal
Interbrew Belgium
D'Ieteren
Henkel
Master Foods
Nestlé Belgilux

NETHERLANDS
Procter & Gamble
Albert Heyn
Rijksvoorlichtingsdienst
Lever
Van den Bergh Foods
PTT Telecom
C&A
Heineken
Postbank
Mars

PORTUGAL
Industrias Lever Portuguesa
Fiat Auto Portuguesa
Renault Portuguesa
Mocar (Alfa Romeo & Peugeot)
Nestlé Portugal
Grupo Refrigor
Banco Comercio Industria
Fima Industria Alimentar
Iglo-Industrias Gelados
Citroën

SPAIN
Grupo SEAT-Audi-Volkswagen
Fasa Renault
Citroën Hispania
Grupo Nestlé
El Corte Ingles
Unilever
Fiat
Grupo BSN
Peugeot-Talbot
Leche Pascual

FINLAND
Aro-Yhtymä (car sales)
Valio (food)
Kesko (conglomerate)
Op-Ryhmä (bank)
Korpivaara (cars)
Sp-Ryhmä (bank)
Procter & Gamble (detergents)
Lever (detergents)
Veho (car sales)
Postipankki (bank)

SWEDEN
ICA
Kooperativa Förbundet
Televerket
Vivo-Favör Förbundet
Sparbankemas Bank
Onoff
Ahlens
Volvo
MIO
Saab/General Motors

NORWAY
Denofa/Lilleborg
Norske Meierier
Norsk Tipping
Televerket/Direktoratet
General Motors Norge
Toyota
Statens Informasjonstjeneste
Freia
Norske Shell
Statoil

ITALY
Ferrero
Barilla
Procter & Gamble
Fiat Auto
Sagit
Saipo
Fiat Lancia
Lever
Vick International
Henkel

SWITZERLAND
Migros
Co-op
FTR (Tobacco)
Toyota
General Motors/Opel
Denner
Amag/VW
SBG/UBS
Effems
Procter & Gamble

Notes: 1. For the UK, see Table 15.3, page 411.

SOURCE: From *The European Marketing Pocketbook, 1993.* Copyright © 1993 by NTC Publications. Used with permission.

TABLE 15.2 *Some issues to consider when deciding whether to use advertising*

1. Does the product possess unique, important features?

Although homogeneous products such as cigarettes, petrol and beer have been advertised successfully, they usually require considerably more effort and expense than other products. On the other hand, products that are differentiated on physical rather than psychological dimensions are much easier to advertise. Even so, "being different" is rarely enough. The advertisability of product features is enhanced when buyers believe that those unique features are important and useful.

2. Are "hidden qualities" important to buyers?

If by viewing, feeling, tasting or smelling the product buyers can learn all there is to know about the product and its benefits, advertising will have less chance of increasing demand. Conversely, if not all product benefits are apparent to consumers on inspection and use of the product, advertising has more of a story to tell, and the probability that it can be profitably used increases. The "hidden quality" of vitamin C in oranges once helped explain why Sunkist oranges could be advertised effectively, whereas the advertising of lettuce has been a failure.

3. Is the general demand trend for the product favourable?

If the generic product category is experiencing a long-term decline, it is less likely that advertising can be used successfully for a particular brand within the category.

4. Is the market potential for the product adequate?

Advertising can be effective only when there are sufficient actual or prospective users of the brand in the target market.

5. Is the competitive environment favourable?

The size and marketing strength of competitors and their brand shares and loyalty will greatly affect the possible success of an advertising campaign. For example, a marketing effort to compete successfully against Kodak film, Heinz baked beans, or Campbell soups would demand much more than simply advertising.

6. Are general economic conditions favourable for marketing the product?

The effects of an advertising programme and the sale of all products are influenced by the overall state of the economy and by specific business conditions. For example, it is much easier to advertise and sell luxury leisure products (stereos, sailing boats, video cameras) when disposable income is high.

7. Is the organisation able and willing to spend the money required to launch an advertising campaign?

As a general rule, if the organisation is unable or unwilling to undertake an advertising expenditure that as a percentage of the total amount spent in the product category is at least equal to the market share it desires, advertising is not likely to be effective.

8. Does the firm possess sufficient marketing expertise to market the product?

The successful marketing of any product involves a complex mixture of product and consumer research, product development, packaging, pricing, financial management, promotion and distribution. Weakness in any area of marketing is an obstacle to the successful use of advertising.

SOURCE: Adapted from Charles H. Patti, "Evaluating the role of advertising", *Journal of Advertising*, Fall 1977, pp. 32–3. Reprinted by permission of the *Journal of Advertising*.

ing, to make sales personnel more effective, to increase the uses of a product, to remind and reinforce customers, and to reduce sales fluctuations (see Figure 15.1).

Promoting Products and Organisations

Advertising is used to promote goods, services, ideas, images, issues, people and indeed anything that the advertiser wants to publicise or foster. Depending on what is being promoted, advertising can be classified as institutional or product advertising. **Institutional advertising** promotes organisational images, ideas or political issues. For example, some of Seagram's advertising promotes the idea that drinking and driv-

FIGURE 15.1
Major uses of advertising

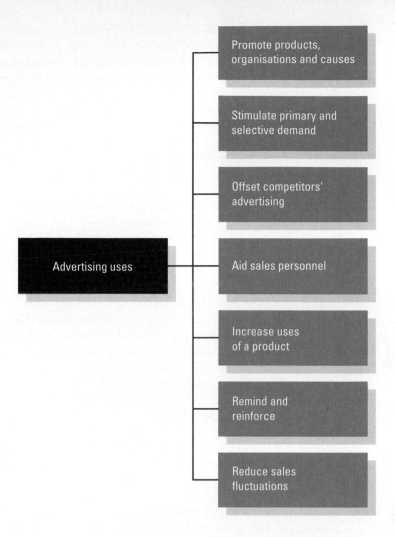

ing do not mix, in order to create and develop a socially responsible image. Hanson Trust and BOC have successfully used advertising to explain and promote their different subsidiaries and products: their corporate composition.

   Product advertising promotes goods and services. Business, government and private non-business organisations turn to it to promote the uses, features, images and benefits of their products. When Monsanto introduced a new pesticide to help farmers clean up weeds in the post harvest stubble, it used press advertising to tout the benefits of Sting CT, including a competition (a trip to Italy) and a coupon to send off for further technical details of the product.

Stimulating Primary and Selective Demand

When a specific firm is the first to introduce an innovation, it tries to stimulate *primary demand*—demand for a product category rather than a specific brand of the product—through pioneer advertising. **Pioneer advertising** informs people about a product: what it is, what it does, how it can be used and where it can be purchased. Because pioneer advertising is used in the introductory stage of the product life-cycle when there are no competitive brands, it neither emphasises the brand name nor compares brands. The first company to introduce the compact disc player, for instance, initially tried to stimulate primary demand (create category need) by emphasising the benefits of compact disc players in general rather than the benefits of its brand. Product advertising is also used sometimes to stimulate primary demand for an established product. Occasionally, an industry trade group, rather than a single firm, sponsors advertisements to stimulate primary demand. For example, to stimulate demand for milk, the Milk Marketing Board sponsors advertisements that demonstrate how healthy and pleasant milk is to drink. In Figure 15.2, advertising promotes the use of Swedish bottled water.

To build *selective demand,* or demand for a specific brand, an advertiser turns to competitive advertising. **Competitive advertising** points out a brand's uses, features and advantages that benefit consumers but may not be available in competing brands. For example, Volvo heavily promotes the safety and crash-worthiness of Volvo cars in its advertising.

Another form of competitive advertising is **comparative advertising,** in which two or more brands are compared on the basis of one or more product attributes. Companies must not, however, misrepresent the qualities or characteristics of the comparison product.

Offsetting Competitors' Advertising

When marketers advertise to offset or lessen the effects of a competitor's promotional programme, they are using **defensive advertising.** Although defensive advertising does not necessarily increase a company's sales or market share, it may prevent a loss in these areas. For example, when McDonald's first test marketed pizza, Pizza Hut countered with defensive advertising to protect its market share and sales. Pizza Hut advertised both on television and in newspapers in the two test cities, emphasising that its product is made from scratch, whereas McDonald's uses frozen dough.[3] Defensive advertising is used most often by firms in extremely competitive consumer product markets, such as the fast food industry.

Making Sales Personnel More Effective

Business organisations that stress personal selling often use advertising to improve the effectiveness of sales personnel. Advertising created specifically to support personal selling activities tries to pre-sell a product to buyers by informing them about its uses, features and benefits and by encouraging them to contact local dealers or sales representatives. This form of advertising helps salespeople find good sales prospects. Advertising is often designed to support personal selling efforts for industrial products, insurance and consumer durables, such as cars and major household appliances. For example, advertising may bring a prospective buyer to a showroom, but usually a salesperson plays a key role in closing the sale.

Increasing the Uses of a Product

The absolute demand for any product is limited because people in a market will consume only so much of it. Given both this limit on demand and competitive conditions, marketers can increase sales of a specific product in a defined geographic market only to a certain point. To improve sales beyond this point, they must either enlarge the geographic market and sell to more people or develop and promote a larger number of uses for the product. If a firm's advertising convinces buyers to use its products in more ways, the sales of the products go up. For example, Nabisco used advertising to inform consumers that its Shredded Wheat cereal contains no added sugar and is high in natural fibre, which is essential to a healthy, balanced diet. The company is thus attempting to position Shredded Wheat as part of a wholesome diet, as well as a popular children's cereal. When promoting new uses, an advertiser attempts to increase the demand for its own brand without driving up the demand for competing brands.

Reminding and Reinforcing Customers

Marketers sometimes employ **reminder advertising** to let consumers know that an established brand is still around and that it has certain uses, characteristics and benefits. Procter & Gamble, for example, reminds consumers that its Crest toothpaste is

FIGURE 15.2
*Using advertising for
product promotion*
Advertising promotes the
use of Swedish bottled
water.

SWEDISH WATER COLOUR.

RAMLÖSA THE LIGHTLY SPARKLING NATURAL MINERAL WATER FROM SWEDEN.

SOURCE: Royal Swedish Ramlosa.

still the best one for preventing cavities. **Reinforcement advertising,** on the other hand, tries to assure current users that they have made the right choice and tells them how to get the most satisfaction from the product. The aim of both reminder and reinforcement advertising is to prevent a loss in sales or market share.

**Reducing Sales
Fluctuations**

The demand for many products varies from month to month because of such factors as climate, holidays, seasons and customs. A business, however, cannot operate at peak efficiency when sales fluctuate rapidly. Changes in sales volume translate into changes in the production or inventory, personnel and financial resources it requires. To the extent that marketers can generate sales during slow periods, they can smooth out the fluctuations. When advertising reduces fluctuations, a manager can use the firm's resources more efficiently.

Advertising is often designed to stimulate business during sales slumps. For example, advertisements promoting price reductions of lawncare equipment or package holidays can increase sales during the winter months. On occasion, a business advertises that customers will get better service by coming in on certain days rather than others. During peak sales periods, a marketer may refrain from advertising to prevent over stimulating sales to the point where the firm cannot handle all the demand. For example, coupons for the delivery of pizza are often valid only from Monday to Thursday, not Friday to Sunday, which are the peak delivery days.

A firm's use of advertising depends on the firm's objectives, resources and environmental forces. The degree to which advertising accomplishes the marketer's goals depends in large part on the advertising campaign.

DEVELOPING AN ADVERTISING CAMPAIGN

An **advertising campaign** involves designing a series of advertisements and placing them in various advertising media to reach a particular target market. As Figure 15.3 indicates, the major steps in creating an advertising campaign are (1) identifying and analysing the advertising target, (2) defining the advertising objectives, (3) creating the advertising platform or property, (4) determining the advertising budget, (5) developing the media plan, (6) creating the advertising message, (7) executing the campaign and (8) evaluating the effectiveness of the advertising. The number of steps and the exact order in which they are carried out may vary according to an organisation's resources, the nature of its product, the types of target markets or audiences to be reached and the advertising agency selected.[4] These general guidelines for developing an advertising campaign are appropriate for all types of organisations.

Identifying and Analysing the Advertising Target

The **advertising target** is the group of people at which advertisements are aimed. For example, the target audience for Special K and All-Bran cereals is health-conscious adults. Identifying and analysing the advertising target are critical processes; the information they yield helps determine the other steps in developing the campaign. The advertising target often includes everyone in a firm's target market. Marketers may, however, seize some opportunities to slant a campaign at only a portion of the target market.

Advertisers analyse advertising targets to establish an information base for a campaign. Information commonly needed includes the location and geographic distribution of the target group; the distribution of age, income, ethnic origin, sex and education; and consumer attitudes regarding the purchase and use of both the advertiser's products and competing products. The exact kinds of information that an organisation will find useful depend on the type of product being advertised, the characteristics of the advertising target and the type and amount of competition. Generally, the more advertisers know about the advertising target, the more likely they are to develop an effective advertising campaign. When the advertising target is not precisely identified and properly analysed, the campaign may not succeed.

Defining the Advertising Objectives

The advertiser's next step is to consider what the firm hopes to accomplish with the campaign. Because advertising objectives guide campaign development, advertisers should define their objectives carefully to ensure that the campaign will achieve what they want. Advertising campaigns based on poorly defined objectives seldom succeed.

Advertising objectives should be stated clearly, precisely and in measurable terms. Precision and measurability allow advertisers to evaluate advertising success: to judge, at the campaign's end, whether the objectives have been met, and if so, how well. To provide precision and measurability, advertising objectives should contain benchmarks—the current condition or position of the firm—and indicate how far and in what direction the advertiser wishes to move from these benchmarks. For example, the advertiser should state the current sales level (the benchmark) and the amount of sales increase that is sought through advertising. An advertising objective also should specify a time frame, so that advertisers know exactly how long they have to accomplish the objective. Thus an advertiser with average monthly sales of £450,000 (the benchmark) might set the following objective: "Our primary advertising objective is to increase av-

FIGURE 15.3
General steps for developing and implementing an advertising campaign

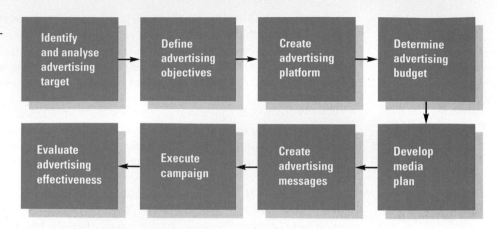

erage monthly sales from £450,000 to £540,000 within 12 months." This also tells the advertiser when evaluation of the campaign should begin.

If an advertiser defines objectives by sales, the objectives focus on raising absolute monetary sales, increasing sales by a certain percentage, or increasing the firm's market share. Alberto Culver decided to pump £12.5 million into advertising its hair care brands in 1990, mainly to revitalise Alberto VO5 shampoo and conditioners. Spend on VO5 alone was to double to £5 million to relaunch the brand, which the company believed had lost its way.[5] However, even though an advertiser's long run goal is to increase sales, not all campaigns are designed to produce immediate sales. Some campaigns are designed to increase product or brand awareness, make consumers' attitudes more favourable or increase consumers' knowledge of a product's features. These objectives are stated in terms of communication. For example, when Apple Computers introduced home computers, its initial campaign did not focus on sales but on creating brand awareness and educating consumers about the features and uses of home computers. A specific communication objective might be to increase product feature awareness from 0 to 40 per cent in the target market at the end of six months.

Creating the Advertising Platform

Before launching a political campaign, party leaders develop a political platform, which states the major issues that will be the basis of the campaign. Like a political platform, an **advertising platform** consists of the basic issues or selling points that an advertiser wishes to include in the advertising campaign. A single advertisement in an advertising campaign may contain one or several issues in the platform. Although the platform sets forth the basic issues, it does not indicate how they should be presented.

A marketer's advertising platform should consist of issues that are important to consumers. One of the best ways to determine what those issues are is to survey consumers about what they consider most important in the selection and use of the product involved. For example, Procter & Gamble has developed refill packages for some of its cleaning products. The refill packages provide a unique benefit by not adding to solid waste disposal problems.[6] Environmentally conscious consumers consider this a positive selling feature. The selling features of a product must not only be important to consumers; if possible, they should also be features that competitive products do not have.

Although research is the most effective method for determining the issues of an advertising platform, it is expensive. As a result, the advertising platform is most commonly based on the opinions of personnel within the firm and of individuals in the advertising agency, if an agency is used. This trial and error approach generally leads to some successes and some failures.

Because the advertising platform is a base on which to build the message, marketers should analyse this stage carefully. A campaign can be perfect in the selection and analysis of its advertising target, the statement of its objectives, its media strategy and the form of its message. But the campaign will still fail if the advertisements communicate information that consumers do not consider important when they select and use the product.

Determining the Advertising Budget

The **advertising budget** is the total amount of money that a marketer allocates for advertising over a period of time. It is difficult to determine this amount, because there is no way to measure the precise effects of spending a certain amount of money on advertising.

Many factors affect a firm's decision about how much to spend for advertising. The geographic size of the market and the distribution of buyers within the market have a great bearing on this decision. Both the type of product being advertised and a firm's sales volume relative to competitors' sales volumes also play a part in determining what proportion of a firm's revenue is spent on advertising. Advertising budgets for industrial products are usually quite small relative to the sales of the products, whereas consumer convenience items, such as soft drinks, soaps and cosmetics, generally have large budgets. The UK launch of Ragu pasta sauce, for example, had a budget of £2 million for two weeks' advertising and below-the-line support.

Of the many techniques used to determine the advertising budget, one of the most logical is the **objective and task approach.** Using this approach, marketers initially determine the objectives that a campaign is to achieve and then attempt to list the tasks required to accomplish them. The costs of the tasks are then calculated and added to arrive at the amount of the total budget. This approach has one main problem: marketers usually find it hard to estimate the level of effort needed to achieve certain objectives. A coffee marketer, for example, might find it extremely difficult to determine by what amount it should increase national television advertising in order to raise a brand's market share from 8 to 12 per cent. As a result of this problem, advertisers do not often use the objective and task approach.

In the more widely used **percentage of sales approach,** marketers simply multiply a firm's past sales, plus a factor for planned sales growth or declines, by a standard percentage, based on both what the firm traditionally spends on advertising and what the industry averages. This approach has one major flaw: it is based on the incorrect assumption that sales create advertising, rather than the reverse. Consequently, a marketer using the approach at a time of declining sales will reduce the amount spent on advertising. But such a reduction may further diminish sales. Though illogical, this technique has gained wide acceptance because it is easy to use and less disruptive competitively; it stabilises a firm's market share within an industry. However, in times of declining sales, many firms do increase their contribution to advertising in the hope of reversing the decline.

Another way to determine the advertising budget is the **competition matching approach.** Marketers who follow this approach try either to match their major competitors' budgets or to allocate the same percentage of sales for advertising as their competitors do. Although a wise marketer should be aware of what competitors spend on advertising, this technique should not be used by itself, because a firm's competitors probably have different advertising objectives and different resources available for advertising. Many companies and advertising agencies engage in quarterly competitive spending reviews, comparing competitors' expenditures in print, radio and television with their own spending levels. Competitive tracking of this nature occurs at both the national and regional levels.

At times, marketers use the **arbitrary approach:** a high level executive in the firm states how much can be spent on advertising for a certain time period. The arbitrary approach often leads to under spending or over spending. Although hardly a scientific budgeting technique, it is expedient.

Establishing the advertising budget is critically important. If it is set too low, the campaign cannot achieve its full potential for stimulating demand. When too much money is appropriated for advertising, the over spending that results wastes financial resources.

Developing the Media Plan

As Table 15.3 shows, advertisers spend tremendous amounts of money on advertising media. These amounts have grown rapidly during the past two decades. To derive the maximum results from media expenditures, a marketer must develop an effective media plan. A **media plan** sets forth the exact media vehicles to be used (specific magazines, television channels, newspapers and so forth) and the dates and times when the advertisements will appear. The effectiveness of the plan determines how many people in the advertising target will be exposed to the message. It also determines, to some degree, the effects of the message on those individuals. Media planning is a complex task

TABLE 15.3 *Advertising in the UK*

TOP TEN ADVERTISERS, 1991

Rank	Advertiser	Total Adspend £'000	TV %	Press %	Radio %
1	Lever Brothers (Unilever)	63,045	81.1	18.4	0.5
2	Procter & Gamble	62,494	98.2	1.3	0.5
3	Kellogg	52,506	96.0	3.2	0.8
4	Ford	47,130	54.2	43.4	2.4
5	British Telecom	46,653	69.1	28.2	2.7
6	P & G (Health & Beauty Care)	41,207	96.5	2.5	1.0
7	Nestlé	39,830	87.5	11.6	0.9
8	Vauxhall	34,339	39.5	59.3	1.3
9	Mars Confectionery	32,801	94.0	5.7	0.4
10	Kraft General Foods (Philip Morris)	32,188	91.3	8.6	0.1

TOP 10 BRANDS, 1992

Rank 92	91	Brand (Ad agency)	Spend 92 (£000s)	Spend 91 (£000s)	% change 91/92
1	1	Tesco (Lowe)	25,733	23,782	8%
2	3	Texas Homecare (Hilton Grey)	22,152	16,876	31%
3	12	MFI/Hygena (Publicis)	21,227	13,905	53%
4	7	Comet (AMV BBDO)	19,526	14,805	32%
5	2	B&Q (BSB)	17,911	19,765	-9%
6	5	Woolworth's (BSB)	17,662	15,466	14%
7	4	McDonald's (Burnetts)	16,741	16,833	-1%
8	10	Currys (Saatchis)	16,522	14,147	17%
9	8	Sainsbury's (AMV BBDO)	16,288	14,581	12%
10	11	Boots (CDP/Publicis)	16,161	13,997	15%

TABLE 15.3 *Advertising in the UK (continued)*

ADVERTISING SPEND BY MEDIA 1991

Television Category	% of total adspend	National Press Category	% of total adspend
Food	24.1	Retail & Mail Order	23.3
Household Stores	9.6	Financial	14.9
Drink	8.1	Motors	14.1
Motors	7.2	Holidays, Travel & Trans.	8.2
Financial	7.1	Institutional, Industrial	4.9
Toiletries & Cosmetics	6.8	Office Equipment	4.2
Retail & Mail Order	5.8	Leisure Equipment	4.1
Leisure Equipment	4.9	Household Equipment	3.0
Publishing	4.3	Government & Service	2.9
Pharmaceutical	3.4	Entertainment	2.8
Others	18.7	Others	17.6

Radio Category	% of total adspend	Regional Press Category	% of total adspend
Local Advertisers	28.3	Retail & Mail Order	33.2
Publishing	9.7	Motors	14.4
Entertainment	8.4	Financial	8.5
Retail & Mail Order	8.2	Holidays, Travel & Transport	7.1
Motors	6.6	Institutional, Industrial	6.5
Holidays, Travel & Transport	5.1	Household Appliances	5.6
Financial	4.7	Entertainment	4.9
Drink	4.0	Government & Service	3.5
Food	4.0	Household Equipment	3.5
Leisure Equipment	3.5	Drink	1.9
Others	17.5	Others	10.9

SOURCE: *MEAL; Campaign; The Marketing Pocketbook 1993* and *The Media Pocketbook 1992.* Copyright by NTC Publications. Used with permission.

that requires thorough analysis of the advertising target, as well as of any legal restrictions that might apply (see Marketing Insight 15.1).

To formulate a media plan, the planner selects the media for a campaign and draws up a time schedule for each medium. The media planner's primary goal is to reach the largest possible number of people in the advertising target for the amount of money spent on media. In addition, a secondary goal is to achieve the appropriate message reach and frequency for the target audience while staying within the budget. *Reach* refers to the percentage of consumers in the advertising target actually exposed to a particular advertisement in a stated time period. *Frequency* is the number of times these targeted consumers were exposed to the advertisement.

Media planners begin with rather broad decisions; eventually, however, they must make very specific choices. A planner must first decide which kinds of media to use: radio, television, newspapers, magazines, direct mail, outdoor displays, public transport or a combination of two or more of these. After making the general media decision, the planner selects specific sub-classes within each medium. Estee Lauder, for example, might advertise its Clinique cosmetic line in women's magazines, as well as during daytime, prime time and late night television.

Media planners take many factors into account as they devise a media plan. They analyse the location and demographic characteristics of people in the advertising target because the various media appeal to particular demographic groups in particular locations. For example, there are radio stations directed mainly at teenagers, magazines for men in the 18 to 34 age group and television programmes aimed at adults of both sexes. Media planners should also consider the size and type of audiences that specific media reach. Several data services collect and periodically publish information about the circulations and audiences of various media.

The cost of media is an important but troublesome consideration. Planners try to obtain the best coverage possible for the amount of money spent, yet there is no accurate way of comparing the cost and impact of a television advertisement with the cost and impact of a newspaper advertisement.

The content of the message sometimes affects the choice of media. Print media can be used more effectively than broadcast media to present many issues or numerous details. The makers of Tartare Light Fromage Frais produce wordy magazine advertisements, including recipes as well as product details, to boost demand and educate consumers about the product's uses. The advertisements appear in most women's and food magazines. If an advertiser wants to promote beautiful colours, patterns or textures, media that offer high quality colour reproduction—magazines or television—should be used instead of newspapers. For example, cosmetics can be far more effectively promoted in a full colour magazine advertisement than in a black and white newspaper advertisement. Compare the black and white and colour versions of the advertisement in Figure 15.4.

Table 15.4 provides data on the relative amounts of advertising expenditure in Europe by media. The data indicate that different countries give greater priority to certain types of advertising media. The medium selected is determined by the characteristics, advantages and disadvantages of the major media available (see Table 15.5).

Given the variety of vehicles within each medium, media planners must deal with a vast number of choices. The multitude of factors that affect media rates obviously adds to the complexity of media planning. A **cost comparison indicator** lets an advertiser compare the costs of several vehicles within a specific medium (such as two newspapers) in relation to the number of persons reached by each vehicle. For example, the "milline rate" is the cost comparison indicator for newspapers; it shows the cost of exposing a million persons to a space equal to one agate line.[*]

Creating the Advertising Message

The basic content and form of an advertising message are a function of several factors. The product's features, uses and benefits affect the content of the message. Characteristics of the people in the advertising target—their sex, age, education, ethnic origin, income, occupation and other attributes—influence both the content and form. When Procter & Gamble promotes its Crest toothpaste to children, the company emphasises the importance of daily brushing and decay control. When it markets Crest to adults, it discusses tartar and plaque. To communicate effectively, an advertiser must use words, symbols and illustrations that are meaningful, familiar and attractive to the people who constitute the advertising target.

The objectives and platform of an advertising campaign also affect the content and form of its messages. For example, if a firm's advertising objectives involve large sales

[*]An agate line is one column wide and the height of the smallest type normally used in classified newspaper advertisements. There are fourteen agate lines in one column inch.

EC ADVERTISING LEGISLATION

Already Here—*Existing European legislation*

Cross-frontier broadcasting directive The broadcasting directive which was agreed in October 1988 is designed to liberalise the transmission of television channels across national frontiers. Television also sets minimum controls on advertising. Originally, Germany and other member states pressed for highly restrictive rules on advertising "minutage" around programmes. But the directive enshrines a relatively liberal ITV style system. The directive, which was originally to have been implemented by 1990, bans tobacco advertising on television. It also includes IBA style controls on alcohol advertising and guidelines for advertising to children and sponsorship.

Misleading advertising directive Adopted in 1984, this directive provides procedures for the control of misleading advertising. It prohibits the use of misleading information about products or advertisers. It requires member states to have a supervisory body with legal powers to regulate misleading advertising; but it allows for self-regulation.

On the Way—*Proposed European legislation*

Tobacco advertising directive Proposed in March 1990, the directive puts forward a ban on "creative" ad campaigns. Press and poster ads would be restricted to pack shots on blank backgrounds, plus health warnings taking up to 20 per cent of space. The European Parliament has taken a tougher stance by backing a total ban.

Food claims The commission is pushing for a formal directive on food claims in advertising, banning the use of nutritional claims which cannot be substantiated.

Pharmaceutical directive Details on the active ingredients and recommended use of branded over-the-counter drugs must be carried in ads.

Comparative advertising The commission is circulating a preliminary text to amend the existing directive on misleading advertising to encourage direct comparisons between competing products and services. Ads will be allowed to mention competitors and their products, as long as they are fair and stick to verifiable facts.

In the Future

Alcohol The Council of Europe, which operates separately from the EC, is considering proposals that would ban all alcohol advertising carried by television channels operating in its 23 member states. But there is little chance that these will come into effect.

Financial services There have been numerous calls from Euro-MP's to restrict advertising of financial services across all media. Loans and mortgages which are offered in non-domestic currencies are current targets of Euro-MP's attention.

Car advertising   Discussions on road safety within the EC include car advertising. Failed proposals to ban references to maximum speeds and acceleration in car ads may be resurrected.

Environmental labelling   The commission is considering a system of labelling products which are considered environmentally benign.

Portrayal of women   Controversy over the portrayal of women in several member states could spill over into the EC as the European Parliament's women's rights committee presses for a review of sexism in the media.

Country by Country...

UK   Advertising restrictions agreed by media owners and advertisers face stricter Euro laws on tobacco and alcohol.

Germany   Advertising to children has become an issue. But strict limits on television ad breaks will crumble under EC legislation.

France   A total ban on tobacco advertising is expected to become law. Alcohol advertisements on television are already banned.

Italy   A ban on tobacco advertising already exists. Proposed new drink laws restrict alcohol advertising, mainly for spirits.

Spain   Already bans tobacco advertising. Television alcohol advertisement controls are also being tightened.

Greece   A ban on toy advertising on television is already in place. Advertisements for tobacco and ads for medicines are banned.

Belgium   Bans television tobacco advertising. But restrictions on ads for certain types of alcoholic drinks have been liberalised.

Portugal   Tight controls on tobacco advertising, with time restrictions on alcohol advertisements.

The Netherlands   Advertisements for tobacco on television are out; those for alcohol and sweet ads face time restrictions.

Denmark   Bans television advertising of tobacco, medicines and all but the weakest alcohol products.

Ireland   Television advertising controls largely mirror those of the UK. But a ban on press advertisements for abortion advice clinics still causes some problems.

Luxembourg   Advertisements for hard liquor are allowed on television, but sole state broadcaster RTL imposes its own ban on advertising tobacco products.

NOTE: The EC is still deliberating on its proposals, but most of them are expected to come into force by 1995.

SOURCE: *Marketing*, 2 August 1990. Reprinted by permission of *Marketing*.

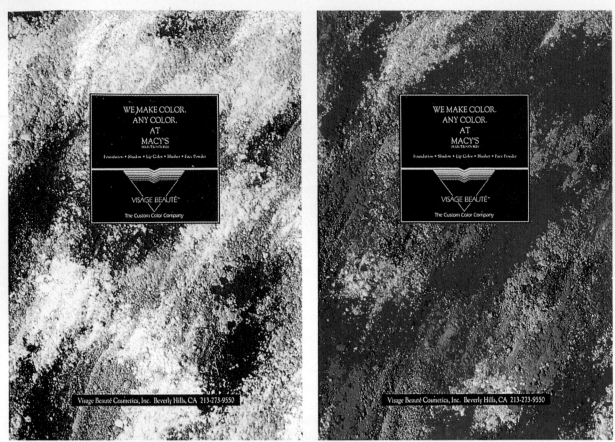

FIGURE 15.4 *Comparison of black and white and colour advertisements*
This example highlights the importance of selecting the right media for a message. This advertisement ran in *Vogue* in full colour.

SOURCE: Visage Beauté Cosmetics, Inc.

increases, the message demands hard hitting, high impact language and symbols. When campaign objectives aim at increasing brand awareness, the message may use much repetition of the brand name and words and illustrations associated with it. Thus the advertising platform is the foundation on which campaign messages are built.

The choice of media obviously influences the content and form of the message. Effective outdoor displays and short broadcast spot announcements require concise,

TABLE 15.4 *Relative percentages of advertising expenditure in Europe, by media, 1990*

	France	Germany	Italy	Spain	UK	Belgium	Netherlands	Denmark	Norway	Finland	Sweden
TV	25	13	47	32.8	31	26	13.6	7.7	1.5	11	–
Press	51	78	44.2	57.4	62.8	57	73.6	87.1	94.3	85	95.7
Radio	11	5	3.6	8.4	2	1	1.8	1.7	0.8	2	–
Posters	12	3	4.8	3	3.8	14	10.7	2.8	2.3	2	3.7
Cinema	1	1	0.4	0.4	0.4	2	0.3	0.7	1.1	–	0.6

SOURCE: "The Campaign report", *Campaign*, 30 November 1990, pp. 1–24.

TABLE 15.5 *Characteristics, advantages and disadvantages of major advertising media*

MEDIUM	TYPES	UNIT OF SALE	FACTORS AFFECTING RATES	COST COMPARISON INDICATOR	ADVANTAGES	DIS-ADVANTAGES
Newspaper	National Local Morning Evening Sunday Sunday supplement Weekly Special	Column cms/inches Counted words Printed lines Agate lines	AVolume and frequency discounts Number of colours Position charges for preferred and guaranteed positions Circulation level	Milline rate = cost per agate line × 1,000,000 divided by circulation Cost per column cm/inch	Almost everyone reads a newspaper; purchased to be read; selective for socio-economic groups: national geographic flexibility; short lead time; frequent publication; favourable for co-operative advertising; merchandising services	Short life; limited reproduction capabilities; large advertising volume limits exposure to any one advertisement
Magazine	Consumer Farm Business etc.	Pages Partial pages Column cms/inches	Circulation level Cost of publishing Type of audience Volume discounts Frequency discounts Size of advertisement Position of advertisement (covers) Number of colours Regional issues	Cost per thousand (CPM) = cost per page × 1,000 divided by circulation	Socio-economic selectivity; good reproduction; long life; prestige; geographic selectivity when regional issues are available; read in leisurely manner	High absolute monetary cost; long lead time

TABLE 15.5 *Characteristics, advantages and disadvantages of major advertising media (continued)*

MEDIUM	TYPES	UNIT OF SALE	FACTORS AFFECTING RATES	COST COMPARISON INDICATOR	ADVANTAGES	DIS-ADVANTAGES
Direct mail	Letters Catalogues Price lists Calendars Brochures Coupons Circulars Newsletters Postcards Booklets Samples	Not applicable	Cost of mailing lists Postage Production costs	Cost per contact	Little wasted circulation; highly selective; circulation controlled by advertiser; few distractions; personal; stimulates action; use of novelty; easy to measure performance; hidden from competitors	Expensive; no editorial matter to attract readers; considered junk mail by many; criticised as invasion of privacy
Radio	AM FM	Programme types Spots: 5, 10, 20, 30, 60 seconds	Time of day Audience size Length of spot or programme Volume and frequency discounts	Cost per thousand (CPM) = cost per minute × 1,000 divided by audience size	Highly mobile; low cost broadcast medium; message can be quickly changed; geographic selectivity; socio-economic selectivity	Little national radio advertising; provides only audio message; has lost prestige; short life of message; listeners' attention limited because of other activities while listening
Television	ITV Satellite Cable	Programme type Spots: 15, 20, 30, 60 seconds	Time of day Length of spot Volume and frequency discounts Audience size	Cost per thousand (CPM) = cost per minute × 1,000 divided by audience size	Reaches large audience; low cost per exposure; uses both audio and video; highly visible; high prestige; geographic and socioeconomic selectivity	High monetary costs; highly perishable message; size of audience not guaranteed; prime time limited.

Category	Types	Basis of sale	Factors	Evaluation	Advantages	Disadvantages
Inside public transport	Buses Underground	Full, half and quarter showings are sold on a monthly basis	Number of passengers Multiple-month discounts Production costs Position	Cost per thousand passengers	Low cost; "captive" audience; geographic selectivity	Does not secure quick results
Outside public transport	Buses Taxis	Full, half and quarter showings; space also rented on per unit basis	Number of advertisements Position Size	Cost per 100 exposures	Low cost; geographic selectivity; reaches broad, diverse audience	Lacks socio-economic selectivity; does not have high impact on readers
Outdoor	Papered posters/billboards Painted displays Spectaculars Poster vans	Papered posters: sold on monthly basis in multiples Painted displays and spectaculars; sold on per unit basis	Length of time purchased Land rental Cost of production Intensity of traffic Frequency and continuity discounts Location	No standard indicator	Allows for repetition; low cost; message can be placed close to the point of sale; geographic selectivity; works 24 hours a day	Message must be short and simple; no socio-economic selectivity; seldom attracts readers' full attention; criticised for being traffic hazard and blight on countryside

SOURCE: Some of the information in this table is from S. Watson Dunn and Arnold M. Barban, *Advertising: Its Role in Modern Marketing*, 6th ed. (Hinsdale, Ill.: Dryden Press, 1986); and Anthony F. McGann and J. Thomas Russell, *Advertising Media* (Homewood, Ill.: Irwin, 1981).

FIGURE 15.5
*Copy and artwork
elements of printed
advertisements*
This advertisement clearly
differentiates the basic
elements of print
advertising.

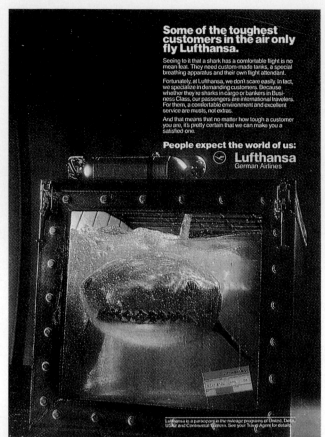

Headline

Body Copy

**Sub-headline
Signature**

Illustration

SOURCE: Lufthansa German Airlines.

simple messages. Magazine and newspaper advertisements can include more detail and long explanations. Because several different kinds of media offer geographic selectivity, a precise message can be tailored to a particular geographic section of the advertising target. Some magazine and national newspaper publishers produce **regional issues:** for a particular issue, the advertisements and editorial content of copies appearing in one geographic area differ from those appearing in other areas. A clothing manufacturer might decide to use one message in London and another in the rest of the UK. A company may also choose to advertise in only a few regions. Such geographic selectivity lets a firm use the same message in different regions at different times.

The basic components of a print advertising message are shown in Figure 15.5. The messages for most advertisements depend on the use of copy and artwork. These two elements are now examined in more detail.

Copy.   **Copy** is the verbal portion of an advertisement. It includes headlines, sub-headlines, body copy and the signature (see Figure 15.5). When preparing advertising copy, marketers attempt to move readers through a persuasive sequence called **AIDA:** attention, interest, desire and action. Not all copy need be this extensive, however.

The headline is critical because often it is the only part of the copy that people read. It should attract readers' attention and create enough interest to make them want to read the body copy. The sub-headline, if there is one, links the headline to the body copy. Sometimes it helps explain the headline.

COGENT

CUPRINOL	945	12.3.91.
30 SEC TV	SF	SECOND

"GINGER"

VISION	SOUND
Open on a large old country kitchen with some beautifully varnished pieces of furniture. Amongst these, a lovely old carver in which sits the Cuprinol man and a long refectory table, possibly oak.	(Music: At first a faithful sound effect of drumsticks on table, this rapidly becomes more musical. Instruments are chosen for their ability to mimic the sound of objects being hit.)
The wooden man (also beautifully varnished) sits at the table with a can of new Cuprinol Ultra Varnish.	
He taps the can as he speaks... (close-up on can) then puts it on to the table.	WOODEN MAN: Just how much tougher is this Ultra Varnish from Cuprinol?
Wooden man gives us an impish look then picks up a pair of drum sticks.	
His expression changes to one of deadly seriousness.	
He closes his eyes, throws his head back and launches into a frenzied battering of the table - treating it like the snare on a drum kit.	SFX: Short burst of drumming on the table top.
After perhaps three seconds of this machine-gun drumming, he stops. He looks closely at the table top.	

We look closely. It's completely unscathed.	Wooden Man: (Appreciatively) Hmm...
Satisfied with this he now goes for everything within range. The chairs become cymbals. The chair backs are great for running the drum sticks over. His foot stamps out a mean, driving rhythm on the floor. The joint is jumpin' and the varnish is getting a thumpin'. Dressers, doors, windowsills - anything within reach and even some things he has to stretch for are getting the Keith Moon treatment.	
At some stage he may drum his own legs, he may drum the floor, he may twirl the sticks.	
Everything he hits has its own peculiar, woody sound. Some things, like cupboards, give off a nice boomy sound. Others, like chair backs, are higher pitched.	
Occasionally, he may hit something like a teapot.	
He reaches a crescendo with a sustained high speed drumming, arms and sticks almost blur with the effort. The can of Ultra is bouncing across the table as the finishes, head bowed low.	
Distinctly knackered by all the effort he collapses back into the carver. Weakly surveying the unscathed varnished surfaces he says ...	Wooden Man: It's tough ...
Super: No one does wood more good.	MVO: Cuprinol.No one does wood more good.

FIGURE 15.6 *Example of a parallel script*
Agency Cogent advertises the wood preserver Cuprinol.

SOURCE: Reproduced by permission of Cuprinol Ltd. U.K.

Body copy for most advertisements consists of an introductory statement or paragraph, several explanatory paragraphs and a closing paragraph. Some copywriters have adopted a pattern or set of guidelines to develop body copy systematically: (1) identify a specific desire or problem of consumers, (2) suggest the good or service as the best way to satisfy that desire or solve that problem, (3) state the advantages and benefits of the product, (4) indicate why the advertised product is the best for the buyer's particular situation, (5) substantiate the claims and advantages, and (6) ask the buyer for action.[7]

The signature identifies the sponsor of the advertisement. It may contain several elements, including the firm's trade mark, logo, name and address. The signature should be designed to be attractive, legible, distinctive and easy to identify in a variety of sizes.

Because radio listeners often are not fully "tuned in" mentally, radio copy should be informal and conversational to attract their attention and achieve greater impact. The radio message is highly perishable. Thus radio copy should consist of short, familiar terms. Its length should not require a delivery rate exceeding approximately two and a half words per second.

In television copy, the audio material must not overpower the visual material and vice versa. However, a television message should make optimal use of its visual portion. As Figure 15.6 illustrates, copy for a television advertisement is initially written in parallel script form. The video is described in the left column and the audio in the right

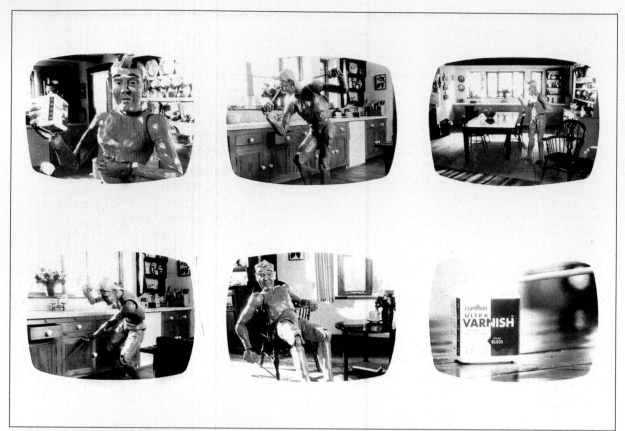

FIGURE 15.7 *Final storyboard for Cuprinol advertisement*

SOURCE: Reproduced by permission of Cuprinol Ltd. U.K.

column. When the parallel script is approved, the copywriter and the artist combine the copy with the visual material through use of a **storyboard** (see Figure 15.7), which depicts a series of miniature television screens to show the sequence of major scenes in the commercial. Technical personnel use the storyboard as a blueprint when they produce the commercial.

Artwork.   **Artwork** consists of the illustration and layout of the advertisement (see Figure 15.5). Although **illustrations** are often photographs, they can also be drawings, graphs, charts or tables. Illustrations are used to attract attention, to encourage the audience to read or listen to the copy, to communicate an idea quickly or to communicate an idea that is difficult to put into words.[8] They are especially important because consumers tend to recall the visual portion of advertisements better than the verbal portions. Advertisers use a variety of illustration techniques, which are identified and described in Table 15.6.

The **layout** of an advertisement is the physical arrangement of the illustration, headline, sub-headline, body copy and signature. The arrangement of these parts in Figure 15.5 is only one possible layout. These same elements could be arranged in many ways. The final layout is the result of several stages of preparation. As it moves through these stages, the layout helps people involved in developing the advertising campaign exchange ideas. It also provides instructions for production personnel.

TABLE 15.6 *Illustration techniques for advertisements*

ILLUSTRATION TECHNIQUE	DESCRIPTION
Product alone	Simplest method; advantageous when appearance is important, when identification is important, when trying to keep a brand name or package in the public eye, or when selling through mail order
Emphasis on special features	Shows and emphasises special details or features as well as advantages; used when product is unique because of special features
Product in setting	Shows what can be done with product; people, surroundings or environment hint at what product can do; often used in food advertisements
Product in use	Puts action into the advertisement; can remind readers of benefits gained from using product; must be careful not to make visual cliché; should not include anything that will divert attention from product; used to direct readers' eyes towards product
Product being tested	Uses test to dramatise product's uses and benefits versus competing products
Results of product's use	Emphasises satisfaction from using product; can liven up dull product; useful when nothing new can be said
Dramatising headline	Appeal of illustration dramatises headline; can emphasise appeal but dangerous to use illustrations that do not correlate with headlines
Dramatising situation	Presents problem situation or shows situation in which problem has been resolved
Comparison	Compares product with "something" established; the something must be positive and familiar to audience
Contrast	Shows difference between two products or two ideas or differences in effects between use and non-use; before and after format is a commonly used contrast technique
Diagrams, charts and graphs	Used to communicate complex information quickly; may make presentations more interesting
Phantom effects	X-ray or internal view; can see inside product; helpful to explain concealed or internal mechanism
Symbolic	Symbols used to represent abstract ideas that are difficult to illustrate; effective if readers understand symbol; must be positive correlation between symbol and idea
Testimonials	Actually shows the testifier; should use famous person or someone to whom audience can relate

SOURCE: Dorothy Cohen, *Advertising* (New York: Wiley, 1972), pp. 458–64; and S. Watson Dunn and Arnold M. Barban, *Advertising: Its Role in Modern Marketing*, 6th ed. (Hinsdale, Ill.: Dryden Press, 1986), pp. 497–98.

Executing the Campaign

The execution of an advertising campaign requires an extensive amount of planning and co-ordination. Regardless of whether or not an organisation uses an advertising agency, many people and organisations are involved in the execution of a campaign.[9] Production companies, research organisations, media firms, printers, photo engravers and commercial artists are just a few of the people and organisations that contribute to a campaign.

Implementation requires detailed schedules to ensure that various phases of the work are done on time. Advertising management personnel must evaluate the quality of the work and take corrective action when necessary. In some instances, changes have to be made during the campaign so that it meets campaign objectives more effectively.

Evaluating the Effectiveness of the Advertising

There are various ways to test the effectiveness of advertising. They include measuring achievement of advertising objectives; assessing the effectiveness of copy, illustrations or layouts; and evaluating certain media.

Advertising can be evaluated before, during and after the campaign. Evaluations performed before the campaign begins are called **pre-tests** and usually attempt to evaluate the effectiveness of one or more elements of the message. To pre-test advertisements, marketers sometimes use a **consumer focus group,** a number of people who are actual or potential buyers of the advertised product. Members are asked to judge one or several dimensions of two or more advertisements. Such tests are based on the belief that consumers are more likely than advertising experts to know what will influence them.

To measure advertising effectiveness during a campaign, marketers usually take advantage of "enquiries". In the initial stages of a campaign, an advertiser may use several direct response advertisements simultaneously, each containing a coupon or a form requesting information. The advertiser records the number of coupons that are returned from each type of advertisement. If an advertiser receives 78,528 coupons from advertisement A, 37,072 coupons from advertisement B and 47,932 coupons from advertisement C, advertisement A is judged superior to advertisements B and C. For advertisements which do not demand action—coupon filling or dialling an 0800 freephone number—enquiries are difficult to monitor.

Evaluation of advertising effectiveness after the campaign is called a **post campaign test** (or **post test**). Advertising objectives often indicate what kind of post test will be appropriate. If an advertiser sets objectives in terms of communication—product awareness, brand awareness or attitude change—then the post test should measure changes in one or more of these dimensions. Advertisers sometimes use consumer surveys or experiments to evaluate a campaign based on communication objectives. These methods are costly, however.

For campaign objectives that are stated in terms of sales, advertisers should determine the change in sales or market share that can be attributed to the campaign. Unfortunately, such changes brought about by advertising cannot be measured precisely;[10] many factors independent of advertisements affect a firm's sales and market share. Competitive actions, government actions, and changes in economic conditions, consumer preferences and weather are only a few factors that might enhance or diminish a company's sales or market share. However, by using data about past and current sales and advertising expenditures, an advertiser can make gross estimates of the effects of a campaign on sales or market share.

Because consumer surveys and experiments are so expensive, and because it is so difficult to determine the direct effects of advertising on sales, many advertisers evaluate print advertisements according to the degree to which consumers can remember them. The post test methods based on memory include recognition and recall tests. Such tests are usually performed by research organisations through consumer surveys. If a **recognition test** is used, individual respondents are shown the actual advertisement and asked whether they recognise it. If they do, the interviewer asks additional questions to determine how much of the advertisement each respondent read. When recall is evaluated, the respondents are not shown the actual advertisement but instead are asked about what they have seen or heard recently.

Recall can be measured through either unaided or aided recall methods. In an **unaided** (or **spontaneous**) **recall test,** subjects are asked to identify advertisements that they have seen recently but are given no clues to help them remember. A similar

TABLE 15.7 *Results of tested recall of advertisements*

PROMPTED RECALL				SPONTANEOUS RECALL	

PROMPTED RECALL

Q. Which of the following advertisements do you remember seeing or hearing recently?

SPONTANEOUS RECALL

Q. Thinking back over the past week, which commercials can you remember seeing or hearing?

		Account	Agency/Media buyer	%		Account	Agency/Media buyer
1	(1)	BT Share Offer	*WCRS*	86			
2	(3)	Coca-Cola	*HK McCann*	71	1	Ford	*Ogilvy & Mather*
3	(2)	McDonald's	*Leo Burnett*	71			
4	(−)	Mars ice-creams range	*Saatchi & Saatchi/Zenith*	68	2	BT	*WCRS, Simons Palmer, Saatchis*
5	(5)	Kellogg's Corn Flakes	*JWT*	65			
6	(4)	Bradford & Bingley	*Leo Burnett*	64			
7	(−)	Swinton Insurance	*Bartle Boggle Hegarty*	63	3	Coke/Coca-Cola	*HK McCann*
8	(−)	Pepsi	*Abbott Mead Vickers BBDO*	60	4	Ariel/Ariel Automatic	*Saatchi & Saatchi*
9	(−)	Ariel Colour Powder	*Saatchi & Saatchi*	59			
10	(−)	Sainsbury's Recipe	*Abbott Mead Vickers BBDO*	55	5	Persil	*JWT/Initiative*
11	(−)	Heinz Baked Beans	*BMPDDB Needham*	54	6	Renault (unspecified)	*Publicis/ Optimedia*
12	(−)	Cadbury's Caramel	*EURO RSCG/M Star*	49			
13	(−)	Kellogg's Coco Pops	*Leo Burnett/JWT*	45	7	Rover	*Kevin Morley Group/ Zenith*
14	(−)	Fiat Cinquecento	*DMD&B/M Cent*	45			
15	(−)	Comfort (New Island Fresh)	*Ogilvy & Mather*	44			
16	(−)	Persil Micro	*JWT/Initiative*	43	8	Andrex	*JWT*
17	(−)	Sega	*WCRS*	40	9	Peugeot	*EURO RSCG/ M Star*
18	(−)	Opal Fruits	*Saatchi & Saatchi/Zenith*	39			
19	(−)	Always Ultra (Super)	*DMB&B/M Cent*	36			
20	(−)	Clairol Nice 'n' Easy	*BMP DDB Needham/M Cent*	34	10	Daz (unspecified)	*Leo Burnett*

Research for the Adwatch survey is conducted exclusively for *Marketing* by Audience Selection using Phonebus, a weekly telephone omnibus survey among a sample of more than 1,000 adults aged 15 and over. The commercials in the research are chosen by the *CTC-Telepictorials* and *CIA media*. Analytical assistance from *The Planning Partnership*.

SOURCE: "Audience selection", *Marketing*, 22 July 1993, p. 12. Reprinted by permission.

procedure is used with an **aided** (or **prompted**) **recall test,** except that subjects are shown a list of products, brands, company names or trade marks to jog their memories. Several research organisations, such as Nielsen, Audience Selection and Gallup, provide research services that test recognition and recall of advertisements (see Table 15.7).

The major justification for using recognition and recall methods is that people are more likely to buy a product if they can remember an advertisement about it than if they cannot. However, recalling an advertisement does not necessarily lead to buying the product or brand advertised. Research shows that the more "likeable" an advertisement is, the more persuasive it will be with consumers. People who enjoy an advertisement are twice as likely to be convinced that the advertised brand is best. Of about 16 per cent of those who liked an advertisement, a significant number increased their preference for the brand. Only a small percentage of those who were neutral about the advertisement felt more favourable towards the brand as a result of the advertisement.[11] The type of programme in which the product is advertised can also affect consumers' feelings about the advertisement and the product it promotes. Viewers judge advertisements placed in happy programmes as more effective and recall them somewhat better.[12]

Researchers are also using a sophisticated technique called single source data to help evaluate advertisements. With this technique, individuals' behaviour is tracked from television sets to the checkout counter. Monitors are placed in pre-selected homes, and microcomputers record when the television set is on and which channel is being viewed. At the supermarket checkout, the individual in the sample household presents an identification card. The cashier records the purchases by scanner, and the data are sent to the research facility. This technique is bringing more insight into people's buying patterns than ever before (see Chapter 8).

WHO DEVELOPS THE ADVERTISING CAMPAIGN?

An advertising campaign may be handled by (1) an individual or a few people within the firm, (2) an advertising department within the organisation or (3) an advertising agency.

In very small firms, one or two individuals are responsible for advertising (and many other activities as well). Usually these individuals depend heavily on personnel at local newspapers and broadcasting stations for copywriting, artwork and advice about scheduling media.

In certain types of large businesses—especially in larger retail organisations—advertising departments create and implement advertising campaigns. Depending on the size of the advertising programme, an advertising department may consist of a few multi-skilled people or a sizeable number of specialists, such as copywriters, artists, media buyers and technical production co-ordinators. An advertising department sometimes obtains the services of independent research organisations and also hires freelance specialists when they are needed for a particular project.

When an organisation uses an advertising agency, such as Ogilvy & Mather or JWT, the firm and the agency usually develop the advertising campaign jointly. How much each party participates in the campaign's total development depends on the working relationship between the firm and the agency. Ordinarily, a firm relies on the agency for copywriting, artwork, technical production and formulation of the media plan.

An advertising agency can assist a business in several ways. An agency, especially a larger one, supplies the firm with the services of highly skilled specialists—not only copywriters, artists and production co-ordinators but also media experts, researchers and legal advisers. Agency personnel have often had broad experience in advertising and are usually more objective than a firm's employees about the organisation's products. Figure 15.8 outlines the composition of a typical advertising agency.

Because an agency traditionally receives most of its income from a 15 per cent commission on media purchases, a firm can obtain some agency services at a low or moderate cost. For example, if an agency contracts for £400,000 of television time for a firm, it receives a commission of £60,000 from the television company. Although the traditional compensation method for agencies is changing and now includes other factors, the media commission still offsets some costs of using an agency. BMP DDB Needham is considering breaking the mould; the agency would be paid by results. Clients would pay a bonus to the agency for meeting targets or receive a payback (refund) if the advertising failed to deliver.[13]

Now that advertising has been explored as a potential promotional mix ingredient, it is time to consider a related ingredient, publicity.

FIGURE 15.8
A typical advertising agency structure

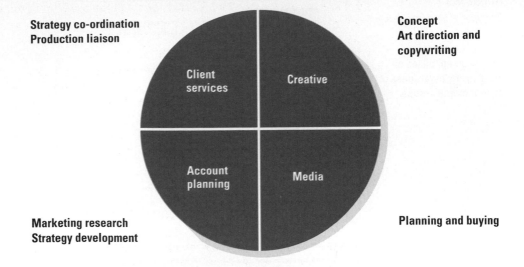

Strategy co-ordination
Production liaison

Concept
Art direction and
copywriting

Marketing research
Strategy development

Planning and buying

PUBLICITY AND PUBLIC RELATIONS

As indicated in Chapter 14, **publicity** is communication in news story form about an organisation, its products or both that is transmitted through a mass medium at no charge (although the publicity activity will incur production and personnel costs). Publicity can be presented through a variety of vehicles, several of which are examined here.

Within an organisation, publicity is sometimes viewed as part of public relations—a larger, more comprehensive communications function. **Public relations** is the planned and sustained effort to establish and maintain goodwill and mutual understanding between an organisation and its **publics:** customers, employees, shareholders, trade bodies, suppliers, government officials and society in general.[14] Publicity is the result of various public relations efforts. For example, when Tesco decided to make a special effort to stock environmentally safe products and packaging, its public relations department sent out press releases to various newspapers, magazines and television contacts, as well as to its suppliers. The result was publicity in the form of magazine articles, newspaper acknowledgements and television coverage. Towards the end of the 1980s, public reactions was the fastest growing element in the promotional mix.[15]

Publicity and Advertising Compared

Although publicity and advertising both depend on mass media, they differ in several respects. Advertising messages tend to be informative or persuasive, whereas publicity is primarily informative. Advertisements are sometimes designed to have an immediate impact on sales; publicity messages are more subdued. Publicity releases do not identify sponsors; advertisements do. The sponsor pays for media time or space for advertising, but not for publicity, and there is therefore no guarantee of inclusion. Communications through publicity are usually included as part of a programme or a print story, but advertisements are normally separated from the broadcast programmes or editorial portions of print media so that the audience or readers can easily recognise (or ignore) them. Publicity may have greater credibility than advertising among consumers because as a news story it may appear more objective. Finally, a firm can use advertising to repeat the same messages as many times as desired; publicity is generally not subject to repetition.

FIGURE 15.9

Example of a press release
Countrywide's press release for client Exel Logistics capitalises on the growing awareness of environmental issues.

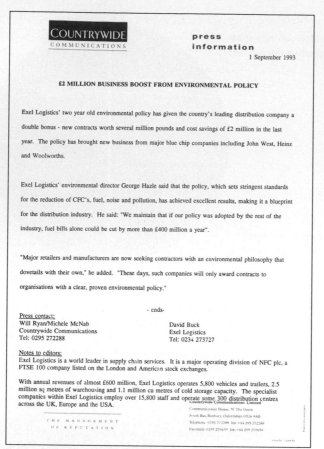

SOURCE: Reproduced by kind permission of the Countrywide Communications Group, England.

Kinds of Publicity

There are several types of publicity mechanism.[16] The most common is the **press (news) release** which is usually a single page of typewritten copy containing fewer than 300 words. A press release, sometimes called a news release, also gives the firm's or agency's name, its address and phone number, and the contact person. Car makers often use press releases to introduce new products. Figure 15.9 is an example of a press release. A **feature article** is a longer manuscript (up to 3,000 words) that is usually prepared for a specific publication. A **captioned photograph** is a photograph with a brief description explaining the picture's content. Captioned photographs are especially effective for illustrating a new or improved product with highly visible features.

There are several other kinds of publicity. A **press conference** is a meeting called to announce major news events. Media personnel are invited and are usually supplied with written materials and photographs. In addition, letters to the editor and editorials are sometimes prepared and sent to newspapers and magazines. However, newspaper editors frequently allocate space on their editorial pages to local writers and national columnists. Finally, films and tapes may be distributed to broadcasting companies in the hope that they will be aired. The broader remit of public relations also includes training personnel to meet and handle the media (journalists); arranging interviews; establishing links with VIPs and influential bodies; managing visits, seminars and meetings; and maintaining information flows within the organisation.

A marketer's choice of specific types of publicity depends on considerations that include the type of information being transmitted, the characteristics of the target audience, the receptivity of media personnel, the importance of the item to the public, and the amount of information that needs to be presented. Sometimes a marketer uses a single type of publicity in a promotional mix. In other cases, a marketer may use a variety of publicity mechanisms, with publicity being the primary ingredient in the promotional mix. **Third party endorsement** increases the credibility of publicity and public relations; this is a recommendation (written, verbal or visual) from an opinion leader or respected personality.

Uses of Publicity

Publicity has a number of uses. It can make people aware of a firm's products, brands or activities; help a company maintain a certain level of positive public visibility; and enhance a particular image, such as innovativeness or progressiveness. Companies also try to overcome negative images through publicity. Some firms seek publicity for a single purpose and others for several purposes. As Table 15.8 shows, publicity releases can tackle a multitude of specific issues. It must be remembered that an organisation has a number of audiences—customers, suppliers, distributors, shareholders, journalists—as well as its internal market: its employees and management. Publicity needs to target all of these publics.

Requirements of a Publicity Programme

For maximum benefit, a firm should create and maintain a systematic, continuous publicity programme.[17] A single individual or department—within the organisation or from its advertising agency or public relations firm—should be responsible for managing the programme. Relationships must be maintained with the media, particularly to facilitate crisis management public relations.

It is important to establish and maintain good working relationships with media personnel. Often personal contact with editors, reporters and other news personnel is essential; without their input a company may find it hard to design its publicity programme so as to facilitate the work of newspeople.

Media personnel reject a great deal of publicity material because it is poorly written or not newsworthy. To maintain an effective publicity programme, a firm must strive to avoid these flaws. Guidelines and checklists can aid it in this task. Material submitted must match the particular newspaper's style, for example, for length, punctuation and layout.

Finally, an organisation has to evaluate its publicity efforts. Usually, the effectiveness of publicity is measured by the number of releases actually published or broadcast. To monitor print media and determine which releases are published and how often, an organisation can hire a cuttings service—a firm that cuts out and sends published news releases to client companies. To measure the effectiveness of television publicity, a company can enclose a card with its publicity releases and request that the television company record its name and the dates when the news item is broadcast, but companies do not always comply. Though some television and radio tracking services do exist, they are extremely costly.

Dealing with Unfavourable Publicity

Up to this point publicity has been discussed as a planned promotional mix ingredient. However, companies may have to deal with unfavourable publicity regarding an unsafe product, an accident, the actions of a dishonest employee or some other negative event. For example, when British Airways' Lord King had to apologise publicly to a rival airline, Virgin Atlantic Airways, and its boss, Richard Branson, for a "dirty tricks campaign", BA's credibility was severely damaged and seat reservations reportedly declined significantly.[18]

Such unfavourable publicity can arise quickly and dramatically. A single negative event that produces unfavourable publicity can wipe out a company's favourable image and destroy consumer attitudes that took years to build through promotional efforts.

TABLE 15.8 *Possible topics for publicity releases*

Marketing developments
New products
New uses for old products
Research developments
Changes of marketing personnel
Large orders received
Successful bids
Awards of contracts
Special events

Company Policies
New guarantees
Changes in credit terms
Changes in distribution policies
Changes in service policies
Changes in prices

News of general interest
Annual election of directors
Meetings of the board of directors
Anniversaries of the organisation
Anniversaries of an invention
Anniversaries of the senior directors
Holidays that can be tied to the organ-
    isation's activities
Annual banquets
Conferences and special meetings
Open house to the community
Athletic events
Awards of merit to employees
Laying of cornerstone
Opening of an exhibition

Reports on current developments
Reports of experiments
Reports on industry conditions
Company progress reports
Employment, production, and sales statistics
Reports on new discoveries
Tax reports
Speeches by principals
Analyses of economic conditions
Employment gains
Financial statements
Organisation appointments
Opening of new markets
Government trade awards

Personalities—names are news
Visits by famous persons
Accomplishments of individuals
Winners of company contests
Employees' and directors' advancements
Interviews with company officials
Company employees serving as judges for
    contests
Interviews with employees

Slogans, symbols, endorsements
Company's slogan—its history and develop-
    ment
A tie-in of company activities with slogan
Creation of a slogan
The company's trade mark
The company's name plate
Product endorsements

SOURCE: Albert Wesley Frey, ed., *Marketing Handbook*, 2nd ed. (New York: Ronald Press, 1965), pp. 19–35. Copyright © 1965. Reprinted by permission of John Wiley & Sons, Inc.

Moreoever, the mass media today can disseminate information faster and to larger audiences than ever before, and bad news generally receives much attention in the media. Thus the negative publicity surrounding an unfavourable event now reaches more people.[19] By dealing effectively with a negative situation, an organisation can minimise the damage from unfavourable publicity. Marketing Insight 15.2 discusses problems of adverse publicity facing Hoover.

To protect an organisation's image, it is important to avoid unfavourable publicity or at least to lessen its effects. First and foremost, the organisation can directly reduce negative incidents and events through safety programmes, inspections and effective quality control procedures. However, because organisations obviously cannot eliminate all negative occurrences, they need to establish policies and procedures for the news coverage of such events. These policies and procedures should aim at reducing negative impact.

In most cases, organisations should expedite news coverage of negative events rather than try to discourage or block it. The expediting approach not only tends to diminish the fall out from negative events but also fosters a positive relationship with media personnel. Such a relationship is essential if news personnel are to co-operate with a company and broadcast favourable news stories about it. Facts are likely to be reported accurately, but if news coverage is discouraged, rumours and misinformation may be passed along. An unfavourable event can easily be blown up into a scandal or a tragedy. It can even cause public panic.

Crisis management involves the identification of key targets (publics) for which to provide material or publicity; the need for a well rehearsed contingency plan and public relations exercise; the ability and skills of the organisation quickly and accurately to report details of the crisis itself; and the provision of immediate access by journalists to information and personnel. Above all, the organisation must remain in control of the situation and the material being published or broadcast.

Limitations in Using Publicity

Free media publicity is a double-edged sword: the financial advantage comes with several drawbacks. If company messages are to be published or broadcast, media personnel must judge them newsworthy. Consequently, messages must be timely, interesting and accurate. Many communications simply do not qualify. It may take time and effort to convince media personnel of the news value of publicity releases. Even a top public relations consultancy achieves a hit rate of only one out of every four press releases being published in the press.

Although marketers usually encourage media personnel to air a publicity release at a certain time, they control neither the content nor the timing of the communication. Media personnel alter the length and content of publicity releases to fit publishers' or broadcasters' requirements and may even delete the parts of the message that the firm deems most important. Furthermore, media personnel use publicity releases in time slots or positions that are most convenient for them; thus the messages often appear at times or in locations that may not reach the firm's target audiences. These limitations can be frustrating. Nevertheless, properly managed publicity offers an organisation substantial benefits at relatively low cost.

This chapter concludes with an overview of corporate sponsorship: an element of the promotional mix which is increasingly apparent to many consumers and a promotional tool now used by many organisations.

SPONSORSHIP

Sponsorship is the financial or material support of an event, activity, person, organisation or product by an unrelated organisation or donor. Generally, funds will be made available to the recipient of the sponsorship deal in return for the prominent exposure of the sponsor's name or brands.

Increasing Popularity of Sponsorship

A decade or so ago sponsorship in the arts became an established form of funding for individual performances, tours, whole seasons or exhibitions; indeed some theatrical companies and galleries came to depend on it. Many orchestras, ballet, opera or theatre companies, museums and art galleries would not have survived in the face of declining government subsidies of the arts had it not been for corporate sponsorship. Sport was soon to follow, as numerous football teams found that gate receipts and pitch advertising revenues were no longer adequate to cover wage bills and operating costs.

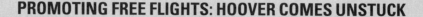

PROMOTING FREE FLIGHTS: HOOVER COMES UNSTUCK

Whether it's Sainsbury and BA, Boots and British Rail, Sony and Thomas Cook, or Bird's Eye Menumaster and National Express Coaches, retailers and manufacturers have negotiated with carriers to offer free travel or holidays to boost sales. The depressed holiday industry has welcomed the opportunity to use excess capacity and increase demand. It was not too surprising when consumer electronics giant Hoover joined the ranks of manufacturers offering free trips in order to stimulate demand for its white goods, first by offering free tickets to Europe with purchases of more than £100, then by extending the promotion to include free tickets to the USA. What was not predictable was the adverse publicity the scheme brought for Hoover.

The second promotion was supported by a high profile £1 million television campaign. The offer included two free flights to either Orlando or New York for every purchase over £100, with an additional £60 towards car hire and accommodation for purchases over £300. Hoover claimed that the tickets into Europe had constituted its most successful promotion ever, putting its £130 vacuum cleaner ahead of its £100 model and making its £380 washing machine more popular than its £330 model.

In November 1992 a *Daily Record* story, "Hoover's flight shocker", started the trouble. This story alleged that none of the airlines Hoover claimed were involved in the deal had any knowledge of the scheme and that Hoover had yet to reserve a single airline seat. The article also stated that the sales promotion company behind the offer was £500,000 in debt. In response, Hoover launched a major damage limitation exercise, including full page adverts assuring people that there was no mystery, that the offer was genuine and

While the larger clubs earn seven figure revenues from shirt sponsorship by companies such as Sony, JVC or Heineken, deals for as little as £20,000 are not uncommon in the lower leagues; either way this form of financial support is becoming essential to guarantee the survival of many clubs.

The popularity of corporate sponsorship has grown dramatically: few leading sports or arts events are without corporate sponsorship. Sponsors believe there are two key benefits to the company and its products. First and foremost, media coverage is unbridled. Volvo estimates that its £2 million investment in tennis sponsorship has been worth the equivalent of £15 million spent on advertising. Its banners are displayed at its tournaments, as are examples of its model range. Volvo advertisements and publicity appear in the programmes. The Volvo brand appears in advertising for the event, and usually the company's cars transport the celebrity players during the tournaments. Not only does the public see the company's advertisements, they cannot fail to see its brand name displayed extensively. In addition, the product is on hand for demonstration, while television coverage of the events takes the Volvo name into every tennis fan's home; radio and press coverage prominently features Volvo's name.

Few spectators at the Barcelona Olympics could have failed to notice the identities of the leading sponsors. To many sports enthusiasts, the leading competitions become generically known as the Gillette Cup, Nat West Trophy, Prudential Series or Coca-

that free flights were available. Hoover's problems did not end there, however. Media attention increased, as did stories of disgruntled consumers.

From BBC consumer affairs programme *Watchdog* to the House of Commons, questions were asked about the ethics of the deal and the apparently unfair treatment of hundreds of annoyed consumers who, having purchased a Hoover product and received their vouchers, had actually attempted to claim their prizes. Many potential holidaymakers could not get first or even second choices of dates or destination. Many were refused their choices so often that Hoover's promotions company refused to permit any travel! Over 70 MPs demanded a parliamentary investigation. Eventually, the Office of Fair Trading was brought in to investigate.

Hoover had intended neither to mislead nor to disappoint its customers, but the promotion nevertheless severely affected the firm's reputation. Circumstances combined in several well publicised cases to make a deteriorating situation even worse for the company. What began as a sales boosting, attention grabbing promotion rapidly turned into a damaging public relations nightmare for Hoover. Key directors were dismissed and the US parent had to provide millions of pounds in order to meet travellers' demands for their prizes. Twelve months later, disputes had still to be settled.

SOURCES: "Do free flights really build brands?", Clare Sambrook, *Marketing*, 15 October 1992, p. 11; "Hoover retaliates over flights offer", Mat Toor, *Marketing*, 3 December 1992, p. 3; "Hoover extends its free flights deal", Robert Dwek, *Marketing*, 29 October 1992, p. 16; BBC and ITN television news broadcasts, March and April 1993.

Cola Cup. In equestrian events, the horses' names often include the name of the sponsoring company. Visitors to Royal Shakespeare Company's performances are clearly informed of the support given by leading sponsors. Montserrat Caballe's performance at Birmingham's prestigious new Symphony Hall was made possible largely by the sponsorship of Forward Trust Group, a fact made clear in all promotional material—leaflets, advertising and publicity—and in the concert's programme.

The second benefit of corporate sponsorship is internal. Many organisations believe that their sponsorship of events helps improve the morale of their workforce. On one level, high profile, brand building sponsorship, such as Prudential Insurance's involvement with cricket, reassures the workforce and reaffirms the company's leading position in its market-place. On a more human level, sponsorship for altruistic projects, such as worthy community causes, helps give employees a "warm", positive feeling towards their employer. McDonald's support of Ronald Homes close to children's hospitals and its sponsorship of local school events not only help the communit also make its employees feel more positive towards the company.

Applications for Sponsorship

Sponsorship used to be a tool of public relations and the domain of public sultancies. Increasingly, it is a specialist area and a separate componen tional mix. Public relations consultancies still handle many sponsor growing number of specialist sponsorship advisers now introduce sponsors to appropriate recipients. It should not be thought that sponsorship is prominent only in the sports and arts worlds. It is an activity of growing importance in many fields. Universities and colleges seek sponsorship for students, technical equipment, buildings and even degree programmes. Hospitals receive and welcome the sponsorship of buildings, operating theatres, and fund raising events. Engineering and scientific research, particularly in universities and "research clubs", benefit from the sponsorship of research and development, often from organisations in completely unrelated fields of business.

No matter what the area, if a company believes its brand reputation will be enhanced and its brand awareness improved by its involvement with an organisation or an event, sponsorship becomes an important element in its promotional mix. Sponsorship can be for events or competitions, equipment or buildings, ideas or research, learning or development, animals or people, commercial or charitable causes, products or services, single activities or ongoing programmes.

Reputable Partnerships

There are ground rules to be considered by the prospective sponsor. As with any promotional activity, the sponsor must ensure that the recipient organisation, event or product is recognised by the sponsor's target audience, that it is welcome and acceptable to its target audience and that it is reputable and ethical in its dealings. The sponsor does not want to invest its promotional budget in activities not recognised by its own target market. The sponsor cannot risk becoming involved with an event or organisation which has a risqué reputation and unprofessional management; such a situation threatens the sponsor's reputation and brands. The recipient, too, needs to be wary of the donor's image and reputation.

SUMMARY

Advertising is a paid form of non-personal communication that is transmitted to consumers through mass media, such as television, radio, newspapers, magazines, direct mail, public transport and outdoor displays. Both non-business and business organisations use advertising.

Marketers use advertising in many ways. Institutional advertising promotes organisations' images and ideas, as well as political issues and candidates. Product advertising focuses on the uses, features, images and benefits of goods and services. To make people aware of a new or innovative product's existence, uses and benefits, marketers rely on pioneer advertising in the introductory stage to stimulate primary demand for a general product category. Then they switch to competitive advertising to boost selective demand by promoting a particular brand's uses, features and advantages.

Through advertising, a company can sometimes lessen the impact of a competitor's promotional programme or make its own sales force more effective. To increase market penetration, an advertiser sometimes focuses a campaign on promoting a greater number of uses for the product. Some advertisements for an established product remind consumers that the product is still around and that it has certain characteristics and uses. Marketers may try to assure users of a particular brand that they are selecting the best brand. Marketers also use advertising to smooth out fluctuations in sales.

Although marketers may vary in how they develop advertising campaigns, they should follow a general pattern. First, they must identify and analyse the advertising target. Second, they should establish what they want the campaign to accomplish by defining the advertising objectives. The third step is creating the advertising platform, which contains the basic issues to be presented in the campaign. Fourth, advertisers must decide how much money to spend on the campaign; they arrive at this decision through the objective and task approach, the percentage of sales approach, the competition matching approach, or the arbitrary approach. Fifth, they must develop the media plan by selecting and scheduling the media to be used in the campaign. In the sixth stage, advertisers use copy and artwork to create the message. In the seventh stage, they execute their advertising campaign, after extensive planning and co-ordination. Finally, advertisers must devise one or more methods for evaluating the effectiveness of the advertisements.

Advertising campaigns can be developed by personnel within the firm or in conjunction with advertising agencies. When a campaign is created by the firm's personnel, it may be developed by only a few people, or it may be the product of an advertising department within the firm. The use of an advertising agency may be advantageous to a firm because an agency can provide highly skilled, objective specialists with broad experience in the advertising field at low to moderate costs to the firm.

Publicity is communication in news story form about an organisation, its products or both, transmitted through a mass medium at no charge. Generally, publicity is part of the larger, more comprehensive communications function of public relations. Publicity is mainly informative and usually more subdued than advertising. There are many types of publicity, including news releases, feature articles, captioned photographs, press conferences, editorials, films and tapes. In addition, public relations includes training managers to handle journalists and publicity, establishing links with influential bodies and VIPs, managing visits and seminars, and providing information to employees. Marketers can use one or more of these forms to achieve a variety of objectives. Targets include consumers, suppliers, distributors, journalists and shareholders, as well as employees and managers inside the firm. Effective public relations depends on thorough identification of target publics. To have an effective publicity programme, someone—either in the organisation or in the firm's agency—must be responsible for creating and maintaining systematic and continuous publicity efforts.

An organisation should avoid negative publicity by reducing the number of negative events that result in unfavourable publicity. To diminish the impact of unfavourable publicity, an organisation should institute policies and procedures for dealing with news personnel when negative events do occur. Problems that organisations confront when seeking publicity include the reluctance of media personnel to print or broadcast releases and a lack of control over the timing and content of messages.

Sponsorship is the financial or material support of an event, activity, person, organisation or product by an unrelated organisation or donor, in return for the prominent exposure of the sponsor's name and brands. Once the domain of arts and sports, sponsorship applications are broadening. An organisation's target audiences can be communicated with through sponsorship. An additional benefit can be to raise the morale of employees within the donor organisation. Sponsor recipients must be certain of each other's ethics and behaviour.

IMPORTANT TERMS

Advertising	Reinforcement advertising
Institutional advertising	Advertising campaign
Product advertising	Advertising target
Pioneer advertising	Advertising platform
Competitive advertising	Advertising budget
Comparative advertising	Objective and task approach
Defensive advertising	Percentage of sales approach
Reminder advertising	Competition matching appro

Arbitrary approach	Recognition test
Media plan	Unaided (spontaneous) recall test
Cost comparision indicator	Aided (prompted) recall test
Regional issues	Publicity
Copy	Public relations
AIDA	Publics
Storyboard	Press (news) release
Artwork	Feature article
Illustrations	Captioned photograph
Layout	Press conference
Pre-tests	Third party endorsement
Consumer focus group	Crisis management
Post campaign test or post test	Sponsorship

DISCUSSION AND REVIEW QUESTIONS

1. What is the difference between institutional and product advertising?
2. When should advertising be used to stimulate primary demand? When should advertising be used to stimulate selective demand?
3. What are the major steps in creating an advertising campaign?
4. What is an advertising target? How does a marketer analyse the target audience after it has been identified?
5. Why is it necessary to define advertising objectives?
6. What is an advertising platform, and how is it used?
7. What factors affect the size of an advertising budget? What techniques are used to determine this budget?
8. Describe the steps required in developing a media plan.
9. What is the role of copy in an advertising message?
10. What role does an advertising agency play in developing an advertising campaign?
11. Discuss several ways to post test the effectiveness of an advertisement.
12. What is publicity? How does it differ from advertising?
13. How do organisations use publicity? Give several examples of publicity releases that you have observed recently in local media.
14. What are target publics? Why must they be carefully identified and handled by a public relations department?
15. How should an organisation handle negative publicity? Identify a recent example of a firm that received negative publicity. Did the firm deal with it effectively?
16. Explain the problems and limitations associated with using publicity. How can some of these limitations be minimised?
17. How can corporate sponsorship enhance brand awareness for a sponsoring organisation?
18. What factors must an organisation consider before selecting a sponsor or recipient organisation?

■ CASES

15.1 British Airways' Evolving Promotion

In the late 1970s British Airways (BA) had lost its way as the UK's national airline. The merger of BOAC and BEA had not gone smoothly, financial performance was poor and travel surveys showed customer satisfaction to be low. The 1979 election of a

Conservative government gave new impetus to improve, as the government wished to privatise the state owned airline. Lord King was appointed chairman in 1983, and under him the airline quickly became operationally sound, although customers had not perceived the change.

The subsequent promotional strategy can be divided into three distinct phases. From 1983 to 1985 the global campaigns of Saatchi & Saatchi aimed "to make the airline feel proud again". Employees were to feel valued and part of a successful organisation, customers were to believe BA was superior to competitors and financial institutions were to see the turnaround in BA as a prelude to privatisation. The now famous "Manhattan Landing" commercial made no attempt to demonstrate product benefits, create category need or purchase intention. The message was that BA was large and "the world's favourite airline". The campaign was hugely successful in the UK and US—BA's main markets. Sales increased by 28 per cent in the US and 13 per cent elsewhere; America voted the commercial the best of all airlines' promotion in 1984. Perceptions of BA changed.

By 1985, awareness of BA had grown. The objective then was to alter customer attitudes, particularly in the lucrative business class sector. Stressing service and comfort, advertisements were targeted at business travellers, particularly in America; "Superclub Seats", "Supercare", and "Putting People First" are examples of such advertisements. The campaign was influenced by Colin Marshall, who had recently joined BA from Avis and believed in service as a means of differentiation. Training programmes improved service levels so that the reality of the product offer matched the message of BA's promotion.

Since 1987, BA's advertising has concentrated on its "pillar" brands. BA had previously promoted a recognisable corporate image but had only haphazardly promoted its various services, such as Club Class and the Shuttles. Mike Batt joined the airline from Mars and brought marketing techniques which focused on the product rather than on the company or corporate image. He introduced the concept of pillar brands, the key products that supported the global and corporate branding already in place. The corporate identity remained part of the promotion, but the focus turned to selling specific products to particular market segments using distinctive brands—for example, Club World, Saver Shuttle, Executive Shuttle. The "Boardroom" advertisement sold Club World—a long haul service which provided comfort and convenience and enables passengers to arrive fit for work—to businesspeople. Following these branding and promotion exercises, the number of business class passengers increased by 31 per cent worldwide and 12 per cent in Europe.

SOURCES: Saatchi & Saatchi directors; *Sunday Times*, 27 May 1990; John Francis, "BA promotions in the 1980s", University of Warwick, 1990.

Questions for Discussion

1. How important is a strong corporate identity in the successful advertising of services?
2. Creating a successful platform is difficult. Keeping it fresh is more so. Discuss the problems of building on BA's powerful and innovative "Manhattan Landing" advertisement.

15.2   Public Relations and Perrier's Crisis

On 10 February 1990, in North Carolina, bottles of Perrier were found to be contaminated with benzene. For the best selling brand of mineral water in the world this meant a huge crisis. "Once a critical situation arises the most vital task is to do everything you can to reduce damage to the absolute minimum. We were fortunate that we had agreed procedures in advance and these procedures were followed absolutely", stated Perrier spokesperson Wenche Marshall Foster. "From the very beginning we were determined to keep everyone fully informed".

Perrier's crisis team in the UK moved quickly; senior executives of Perrier, its PR agency Infoplan and advertising agency Leo Burnett had been briefed before the contamination scare on the needs of crisis management. Within hours of the contamination announcement Perrier had set up tests with independent consultant Hydrotechnica so as to have accurate information to give out. The crisis team knew it had to be truthful throughout. Infoplan immediately set up a telephone information service, which dealt with 1,700 calls each day from distributors, retailers and consumers. Within three days of the crisis breaking, shelves worldwide had been cleared and all stocks returned to Perrier. The company achieved goodwill by moving so decisively. No press conferences were given. Instead, the five members of the crisis team individually met journalists for in-depth, head to head interviews to give precise and clear information and to minimise poor publicity.

Perrier risked competitors moving to take advantage of the crisis, since retailers would not leave shelves empty. Perrier, though, was the clear brand leader with the only established image worldwide. Competitors would take time to develop such strength, and their stocks were not high. Evian and others had nothing to gain from drawing further attention to Perrier's crisis, which was damaging the industry as a whole.

Perrier handled the crisis in PR textbook fashion. With 85 per cent of the American and 60 per cent of the UK market it had a great deal to lose. The company informed its publics of its problems, tackled the contamination problems and relaunched the product with new packaging and bottle sizes—clearly to be seen as new stock—with a "Welcome Back" promotional campaign. Within months, Perrier's market share was climbing back and shelf space had been regained. The company did not hide anything, it identified the various audiences to brief and it tackled its production to ensure that there were no repeat problems. Consumers, distributors, public health bodies and the media were made to feel part of Perrier's solution through the effective use of PR.

SOURCES: *Marketing Week*, 2 March 1990; *Personally Speaking*, 27 March 1990; *Fortune*, 23 April 1990.

Questions for Discussion

1. How important is it to have an ongoing commitment to public relations in the event of a crisis?
2. Could Perrier's competitors have taken more advantage of the crisis?
3. Did the same publicity message go out to all of Perrier's publics or target audiences?

16 PERSONAL SELLING, SALES PROMOTION AND DIRECT MAIL

Objectives

To understand the major purposes of personal selling

To learn the basic steps in the personal selling process

To identify the types of sales force personnel

To gain insight into sales management decisions and activities

To become aware of what sales promotion activities are and how they can be used

To become familiar with specific sales promotion methods used

To understand the role of direct mail

*T*he food industry is quite used to sales promotion. Manufacturers regularly offer on-pack promotions, free or discounted merchandise, point-of-sale displays, competitions and coupon redemptions. Retailers support manufacturers' promotions with in-store displays and demonstrations but in addition run their own competitions, discounts, on-pack offers and coupon redemption or discount schemes. In 1992, supermarket giant Tesco broke the mould with a "Computers for School" promotion which resulted in the donation of 13,000 computing systems, printers, hard disk drives and software packages worth over £3 million to 8,000 schools. So successful was this ground-breaking scheme that Tesco repeated the promotion in spring 1993.

Set to run for 12 weeks, a month longer than in 1992, "Computers for Schools '93" operated on the basis of one voucher for every £25 spent in a Tesco store. The vouchers were redeemable against a variety of Acorn computer hardware and software. The intention was for school communities to enter into the programme collectively, with 200 vouchers earning a piece of software, 4,000 a computer and 7,000 for 11 pocket books.

The sales promotion's benefits were far reaching. For Tesco, there were sales volume increases as a result of increased customer spend and higher traffic flow; 91 per cent of head teachers surveyed wanted the promotion to be repeated, and 71 per cent believed the scheme enhanced Tesco's reputation. Emulating US grocery retailer Giant Foods' link with Apple, this promotion "stressed Tesco's firm commitment to be proactive and meet community needs", according to marketing director Terry Leahy. Following the successful initial promotion, the 1993 promotion was supported with high profile public relations and an advertising campaign in the press and on television positioning Tesco as the store to "feed" children's minds. ■

SOURCES: Tesco promotional literature; "Tesco repeats schools promo", Robert Dwek, *Marketing,* March 4, 1993, p. 12; "Drop till you shop", Matt Phillips, *Marketing Week,* 19 March 1993, pp. 41–7.

A s indicated in Chapter 14, personal selling, sales promotion and direct mail are
possible ingredients in a promotional mix. Personal selling is the more widely
used. Sometimes it is a company's sole promotional tool, although it is generally used in conjunction with other promotional mix ingredients. Personal selling is becoming more professional and sophisticated, with sales personnel acting more as
consultants and advisers. The use of lap-top computers has better equipped the salesperson to satisfy customers. Lap-top computers allow the salesperson to have easier access to inventory listings and prices, to spend more time interacting with customers
and to gain more credibility with clients. Sales promotion and direct mail are also playing an increasingly important role in marketing strategies.[1]

This chapter focuses on personal selling, sales promotion and direct mail, examining
the purposes of personal selling, its basic steps, the types of salespeople and how they
are selected. It also discusses the major sales management decisions and activities,
which include setting objectives for the sales force and determining its size; recruiting,
selecting, training, compensating and motivating salespeople; managing sales territories; and controlling sales personnel. The discussion then goes on to explore several
characteristics of sales promotion, the reasons for using sales promotion and the sales
promotion methods available for use in a promotional mix. The chapter concludes with
a look at the role of direct mail.

The Nature of Personal Selling

Personal selling is the process of informing customers and persuading them to purchase products through personal communication in an exchange situation. For example, a salesperson describing the benefits of a Braun shaver to a customer in a Boots
store is using personal selling. Personal selling gives marketers the greatest freedom to
adjust a message to satisfy customers' information needs. In comparison with all other
promotional methods, personal selling is the most precise, enabling marketers to focus
on the most promising sales prospects. Other promotional mix ingredients are aimed
at groups of people, some of whom may not be prospective customers. A major disadvantage of personal selling is its cost. Generally, it is the most expensive ingredient in
the promotional mix (salaries, cars, expenses). Personal selling costs are increasing
faster than advertising costs.

Businesses spend more money on personal selling than on any other promotional
mix ingredient. Millions of people, including increasing numbers of women, earn their
living through personal selling. In the UK it is estimated that 600,000 people are directly employed as salespeople.[2] A selling career can offer high income, a great deal of
freedom, a high level of training and a high level of job satisfaction.[3] Unfortunately,
consumers often view personal selling negatively. A study of marketing students' perceptions of personal selling showed that approximately 25 per cent of the survey group
thought directly of door-to-door selling. In addition, 59 per cent of all students surveyed had a negative impression of personal selling. Major corporations, professional
sales associations (such as the Sales Lead Body) and academic institutions are making
an effort to change the negative stereotypes of salespeople.[4]

Personal selling goals vary from one firm to another. However, they usually involve
finding prospects, convincing prospects to buy and keeping customers satisfied.
Identifying potential buyers who are interested in an organisation's products is critical.
Because most potential buyers seek information before they make a purchase, salespeople must ascertain prospects' information needs and then provide the relevant
information. To do so, sales personnel must be well trained, both in regard to their
products and in regard to the selling process in general.

Salespeople need to be aware of their competitors. They need to monitor new products being developed, and they should be aware of all competitors' sales activities in their sales territories. Salespeople must emphasise the advantages their products provide when their competitors' products do not offer that specific advantage.[5] Later in this chapter this issue is discussed in greater detail.

Few businesses survive solely on profits from one sale customers. For long run survival, most marketers depend on repeat sales. A company has to keep its customers satisfied to obtain repeat purchases. Besides, satisfied customers help attract new ones by telling potential customers about the organisation and its products. Even though the whole organisation is responsible for providing customer satisfaction, much of the burden falls on salespeople. The salesperson is almost always closer to customers than anyone else in the company and often provides buyers with information and service after the sale. Such contact not only gives salespeople an opportunity to generate additional sales but also offers them a good vantage point from which to evaluate the strengths and weaknesses of the company's products and other marketing mix ingredients. Their observations are helpful in developing and maintaining a marketing mix that better satisfies both customers and the firm.

A salesperson may be involved in achieving one or more of the three general goals. In some organisations, there are people whose sole job is to find prospects. This information is relayed to salespeople, who then contact the prospects. After the sale, these same salespeople may do the follow up work, or a third group of employees may have the job of maintaining customer satisfaction. In many smaller organisations, a single person handles all these functions. No matter how many groups are involved, several major sales tasks must be performed to achieve these general goals.

ELEMENTS OF THE PERSONAL SELLING PROCESS

The exact activities involved in the selling process vary from one salesperson to another and differ for particular selling situations. No two salespeople use exactly the same selling methods. None the less, many salespeople—either consciously or unconsciously—move through a general selling process as they sell products. This process consists of seven elements, or steps: prospecting and evaluating, preparing, approaching the customer, making the presentation, overcoming objections, closing and following up.

Prospecting and Evaluating

Developing a list of potential customers is called **prospecting.** A salesperson seeks the names of prospects from the company's sales records, referrals, trade shows, newspaper announcements (of marriages, births, deaths and so on), public records, telephone directories, trade association directories, telemarketing lists[6] and many other sources. Sales personnel also use responses from advertisements that encourage interested people to send in an information request form. Seminars and meetings may produce good leads. Seminars may be targeted at particular types of clients, such as solicitors, accountants, the over-55s or specific businesspeople.

After developing the prospect list, a salesperson evaluates whether each prospect is able, willing and authorised to buy the product. On the basis of this evaluation, some prospects may be deleted, while others are deemed acceptable and ranked according to their desirability or potential.

Preparing

Before contacting acceptable prospects, a salesperson should find and analyse information about each prospect's specific product needs, current use of brands, feelings about available brands and personal characteristics. The most successful salespeople are thorough in their preparation. They prepare by identifying key decision-makers, reviewing account histories and reports, contacting other clients for information, assessing credit histories and problems, preparing sales presentations, identifying product needs and obtaining all relevant literature.[7] Being well informed about a prospect makes a salesperson better equipped to develop a presentation that precisely communicates with the prospect.

For example, Xerox developed an automated sales process to help sales personnel prepare for complex sales situations after discovering that its salespeople spent half their time on sales inhibiting activities, such as looking for forms and gathering information. Preparing an order required 5 to 13 forms, and one third of all orders were rejected because of mistakes on the forms. To overcome the problem, Xerox developed computer work stations to assist its sales force in shaping proposals, prospecting and preparing, and to link salespeople throughout the company without a piece of paper having to be touched.[8]

Approaching the Customer

The **approach,** the manner in which a salesperson contacts a potential customer, is a critical step in the sales process. In more than 80 per cent of initial sales calls, the purpose is to gather information about the buyer's needs and objectives. Creating a favourable impression and building rapport with the prospective client are also important tasks in the approach, because the prospect's first impression of the salesperson is usually a lasting one, with long run consequences. During the initial visit, the salesperson strives to develop a relationship rather than just push a product. The salesperson may have to call on a prospect several times before the product is considered.[9]

One type of approach is based on referrals. The salesperson approaches the prospect and explains that an acquaintance, an associate or a relative suggested the call. The salesperson who uses the cold canvass method calls on potential customers without their prior consent. Repeat contact is another common approach; when making the contact, the salesperson mentions a prior meeting. The exact type of approach depends on the salesperson's preferences, the product being sold, the firm's resources and the characteristics of the prospect.

Making the Presentation

During the sales presentation, the salesperson must attract and hold the prospect's attention to stimulate interest and stir up a desire for the product. The salesperson should have the prospect touch, hold or actually use the product (see Figure 16.1). If possible, the salesperson should demonstrate the product and get the prospect more involved with it to stimulate greater interest. Audio-visual materials may be used to enhance the presentation.

During the presentation, the salesperson must not only talk but also listen. The sales presentation gives the salesperson the greatest opportunity to determine the prospect's specific needs by listening to questions and comments and observing responses. Even though the salesperson has planned the presentation in advance, she or he must be able to adjust the message to meet the prospect's information needs.

Overcoming Objections

An effective salesperson usually seeks out a prospect's objections in order to address them. If they are not apparent, the salesperson cannot deal with them, and they may keep the prospect from buying. One of the best ways to overcome a prospect's objections is to anticipate and counter them before the prospect has an opportunity to raise them. However, this approach can be risky because the salesperson may mention some objections that the prospect would not have raised. If possible, the salesperson should handle objections when they arise. They can also be dealt with at the end of the presentation.

FIGURE 16.1

Enhancing the sales presentation
To stimulate interest and stir up desire for a product, the salesperson should have the prospect touch, hold, or actually use the product.

SOURCE: Printed courtesy of Sony United Kingdom Limited.

Closing

Closing is the stage in the selling process in which the salesperson asks the prospect to buy the product or products. During the presentation, the salesperson may use a "trial close" by asking questions that assume the prospect will buy the product. For example, the salesperson might ask the potential customer about financial terms, desired colours or sizes, delivery arrangements or the quantity to be purchased. The reactions to such questions usually indicate how close the prospect is to buying. A trial close allows prospects to indicate indirectly that they will buy the product without having to say those sometimes difficult words, "I'll take it".

A salesperson should try to close at several points during the presentation, because the prospect may be ready to buy. One closing strategy involves asking the potential customer to take a trial order. The sales representative should either guarantee a refund if the customer is not satisfied or make the order a free offer.[10] Often an attempt to close the sale will result in objections. Thus closing can be an important stimulus that uncovers hidden objections, which can then be addressed.

Following Up

After a successful closing, the salesperson must follow up the sale. In the follow up stage, the salesperson should determine whether the order was delivered on time and installed properly, if installation was required. He or she should contact the customer to learn what problems or questions have arisen regarding the product. The follow up stage can also be used to determine customers' future product needs.

TYPES OF SALESPEOPLE

To develop a sales force, a marketing manager must decide what kind of salesperson will sell the firm's products most effectively. Most business organisations use several different categories of sales personnel. Based on the functions they perform, salespeople can be classified into three groups: order getters, order takers and support personnel. One salesperson can, and often does, perform all three functions.

Order Getters

To obtain orders, a salesperson must inform prospects and persuade them to buy the product. The **order getter's** job is to increase the firm's sales by selling to new customers and by increasing sales to present customers. This task is sometimes called creative selling. It requires salespeople to recognise potential buyers' needs and then give them the necessary information. Order getting activities are sometimes divided into two categories: current customer sales and new business sales.

Current Customer Sales. Sales personnel who concentrate on current customers call on people and organisations that have purchased products from the firm at least once. These salespeople seek more sales from existing customers by following up previous sales. Current customers can also act as leads for new prospects.

New Business Sales. Business organisations depend on sales to new customers, at least to some degree. New business sales personnel locate prospects and convert them to buyers. Salespeople in many industries help to generate new business, but industries that depend in large part on new customer sales are insurance, heavy industrial machinery, fleet cars and office stationery.

The time-share industry uses various sales promotion techniques (direct mail, competitions, free offers) to attract potential buyers to attend seminars or open days at the time-share site. Once they are there, however, the sales force has to explain the concept of time-sharing, show the site's facilities and close the deal. It is unlikely that other promotional techniques alone would be sufficient to sign up new customers.

Order Takers

Taking orders is a repetitive task that sales staff perform to perpetuate long lasting, satisfying relationships with customers. **Order takers** seek repeat sales. One of their major objectives is to be absolutely certain that customers have sufficient product quantities where and when they are needed. Most order takers handle orders for standardised products that are purchased routinely and therefore do not require extensive sales efforts.[11] There are two groups of order takers: inside order takers and field order takers.

Inside Order Takers. In many businesses, inside order takers work in sales offices and receive orders by mail and telephone (telesales). Certain producers, wholesalers and even retailers have sales personnel who sell from within the firm rather than in the field. That does not mean that inside order takers never communicate with customers face to face. For example, salespersons in retail stores are classified as inside order takers.

Field Order Takers. Salespeople who travel to customers are referred to as "outside", or "field", order takers: the field force. Often a customer and a field order taker develop an interdependent relationship. The buyer relies on the salesperson to take orders periodically (and sometimes to deliver them), and the salesperson counts on the buyer to purchase a certain quantity of product periodically. Use of lap-top computers can improve the field order taker's tracking of inventory and orders.

Field and inside order takers should not be thought of as passive functionaries who simply record orders in a machine-like manner. Order takers generate the bulk of many organisations' total sales.

Support Personnel

Support personnel facilitate the selling function but are not usually involved solely in making sales. They are engaged primarily in marketing industrial products. They locate prospects, educate customers, build goodwill and provide service after the sale. Although there are many kinds of sales support personnel, the three most common are missionary, trade and technical.

Missionary Salespeople. **Missionary salespeople,** who are usually employed by manufacturers, assist the producer's customers in selling to their own customers. A missionary salesperson may call on retailers to inform and persuade them to buy the manufacturer's products. If the call is successful, the retailers purchase the products from wholesalers, who are the producer's customers. Manufacturers of medical supplies and pharmaceutical products often use missionary sales staff to promote their products to doctors, hospitals and retail chemists.

Trade Salespeople. **Trade salespeople** are not strictly support personnel, because they usually perform the order taking function as well. However, they direct much of their efforts towards helping customers, especially retail stores, promote the product. They are likely to restock shelves, obtain more shelf space, set up displays, provide in-store demonstrations and distribute samples to store customers. Food producers and cosmetics companies commonly employ trade salespeople.

Technical Salespeople. **Technical salespeople** give technical assistance to the organisation's current customers. They advise customers on product characteristics and applications, system designs and installation procedures. Because this job is often highly technical, the salesperson usually needs to have formal training in one of the physical sciences or in engineering. Technical sales personnel often sell technical industrial products, such as computers, heavy equipment and steel.

When hiring sales personnel, marketers seldom restrict themselves to a single category, because most firms require different types. Several factors dictate how many of each type of salesperson a particular company should have. A product's uses, characteristics, complexity, price and margin influence the kind of sales personnel used, as do the number of customers and their characteristics. The kinds of marketing channels and the intensity and type of advertising also have an impact on the selection of sales personnel.

MANAGEMENT OF THE SALES FORCE

The sales force is directly responsible for generating an organisation's primary input: sales revenue. Without adequate sales revenue, a business cannot survive long. A firm's reputation is often determined by the ethical conduct of its sales force. On the other hand, the morale and, ultimately, the success of a firm's sales force is determined in large part by adequate compensation, room for advancement, sufficient training and management support—all key areas of sales management. When these elements are not satisfactory, sales staff may leave for more satisfying jobs elsewhere. This problem of sales force turnover is the subject of Marketing Insight 16.1. It is important to eval-

MANAGING SALES FORCE TURNOVER

Sales force turnover—the replacement of employees who leave a company—is an area of increasing concern for companies that rely on personal selling. Turnover across all sales positions more than tripled from 1983 to 1988, from an average of 7.6 per cent to 27 per cent. Turnover costs the average company nearly $250,000 a year in the US and £150,000 in the UK in time spent recruiting and training replacements and in the loss of potential business.

A survey of 500 sales representatives and managers in the United States and Canada found that the top three reasons salespeople cite for leaving their jobs are inadequate compensation, lack of advancement opportunities and personality conflicts. A natural conflict often exists between salespeople, who are generally motivated by self-achievement, and managers, who are motivated by power and who often make less money than those they manage. About one third of the survey respondents indicated that better management support would improve their jobs. Although a majority of the respondents were highly satisfied with both the quality of the goods or services they sold and their companies' reputations, they were least satisfied with the things that management used to help salespeople prepare for and perform their jobs: sales tools, sales incentives and sales training programmes.

Sales force managers can reduce turnover by promoting greater job satisfaction and stronger company loyalty. Conducting surveys to determine how salespeople feel about their jobs may indicate that different reward systems are needed. High performers tend to respond to pay satisfaction; low performers generally leave when they are no longer satisfied with their jobs.

Another suggestion for reducing turnover is using an open door style of management, including weekly sessions with salespeople to spot potential problems. Other suggestions include keeping issues in perspective (for example, compensation versus other work related issues), conducting periodic audits to determine causes of job dissatisfaction, establishing recruiting standards for prospective employees and re-evaluating training programmes so that salespeople have essential product knowledge and sales skills.

SOURCES: Lynn G. Coleman, "Sales force turnover has managers wondering why", *Marketing News*, 4 December 1989, pp. 6, 21; George H. Lucas, Jr., A. Parasuraman, Robert A. Davis and Ben M. Enis, "An empirical study of salesforce turnover", *Journal of Marketing*, July 1987, pp. 34–59; Lester L. Tobias, "Is salesperson turnover bashing your bottom line?" *Business Marketing*, June 1986, pp. 78–82; George H. Lucas, Jr., Emin Babakus and Thomas N. Ingram, "An empirical test of the job satisfaction-turnover relationship: assessing the role of job performance for retail managers", *Journal of the Academy of Marketing Science*, 1990.

uate the input of salespeople because effective sales force management determines a firm's success.

This section explores eight general areas of sales management: (1) establishing sales force objectives, (2) determining sales force size, (3) recruiting and selecting sales personnel, (4) training sales personnel, (5) compensating sales personnel (6) motivating salespeople, (7) managing sales territories and (8) controlling and evaluating sales force performance.

Establishing Sales Force Objectives

To manage a sales force effectively, a sales manager must develop sales objectives. Sales objectives tell salespeople what they are expected to accomplish during a specified time period. These objectives give the sales force direction and purpose and serve as performance standards for the evaluation and control of sales personnel. For example, in Figure 16.2, Zanussi promotes high performance to help salespeople meet their sales goals. As with all types of objectives, sales objectives should be stated in precise, measurable terms and should specify the time period and the geographic areas involved.

Sales objectives are usually developed for both the total sales force and each salesperson. Objectives for the entire force are normally stated in terms of sales volume, market share or profit. Volume objectives refer to a quantity of money or sales units. For example, the objective for an electric drill manufacturer's sales force might be to sell £6 million worth of drills annually or 600,000 drills annually. When sales goals are stated in terms of market share, they usually call for an increase in the proportion of the company's sales relative to the total number of products sold by all businesses in that particular industry. When sales objectives are based on profit, they are generally stated in terms of monetary amounts or in terms of return on investment.

Sales objectives, or quotas, for an individual salesperson are commonly stated in terms of monetary or unit sales volume. Other bases used for individual sales objectives include average order size, average number of calls per time period and the ratio of orders to calls.

Determining Sales Force Size

Deciding how many salespeople to use is important because it influences the company's ability to generate sales and profits. Moreover, the size of the sales force affects the compensation methods used, salespeople's morale and overall sales force management. Sales force size must be adjusted from time to time because a firm's marketing plans change, as do markets and forces in the marketing environment. One danger is to cut back the size of the sales force to increase profits by cutting costs. The sales organisation could lose its strength and resilience, preventing it from rebounding when growth returns or better market conditions prevail. The organisation that loses capacity through cutbacks may not have the energy to accelerate.[12]

There are several analytical methods for determining the optimal size of the sales force; however, a detailed discussion of these methods is beyond the scope of this text. Although marketing managers may use one or several analytical methods, they normally temper their decisions with a good deal of subjective judgement.[13]

Recruiting and Selecting Salespeople

To create and maintain an effective sales force, a sales manager must recruit the right type of salespeople. **Recruiting** is a process by which the sales manager develops a list of applicants for sales positions. The cost of hiring, training and retaining a salesperson is soaring; currently, costs in the UK can reach £60,000 or more.[14]

To ensure that the recruiting process results in a pool of qualified salespeople from which to choose, a sales manager should establish a set of required qualifications be-

FIGURE 16.2

Establishing objectives
Zanussi promotes the high performance of its products to assist salespeople in meeting their sales goals.

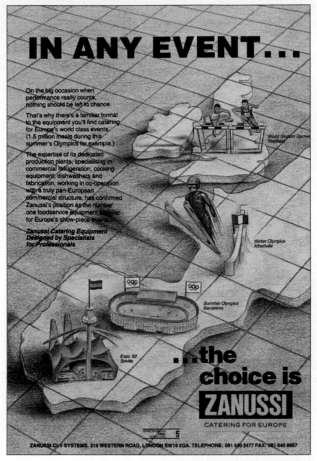

SOURCE: Advertisement reproduced by kind permission of Zanussi CLV Systems—Produced by Brand Development & Marketing.

fore beginning to recruit. Although for years marketers have attempted to identify a set of traits that characterise effective salespeople, there is currently no such set of generally accepted characteristics. Therefore, a sales manager must develop a set tailored to the sales tasks in a particular company. Two activities can help establish this set of requirements. The sales manager should prepare a job description that lists the specific tasks salespeople are to perform. The manager should also analyse the characteristics of the firm's successful salespeople, as well as those of its ineffective sales personnel. From the job description and the analysis of traits, the sales manager should be able to develop a set of specific requirements and be aware of potential weaknesses that could lead to failure.

A sales manager generally recruits applicants from several sources: departments within the firm, other firms, employment agencies, educational institutions, respondents to advertisements and individuals recommended by current employees. The specific sources a sales manager uses depend on the type of salesperson required and the manager's experiences with particular sources.

The process of hiring a sales force varies tremendously from one company to another. One technique used to determine whether potential candidates will be good salespeople is an assessment centre. Assessment centres are intense training environments that place candidates in realistic problem settings in which they must assign priorities to their activities, make decisions and act on their decisions. Candidates are judged by experienced managers or trained observers. Assessment centres have proved to be valuable in selecting good salespeople.[15]

Sales management should design a selection procedure that satisfies the company's specific needs. The process should include enough steps to yield the information needed to make accurate selection decisions. However, because each step incurs a certain expense, there should be no more steps than necessary. The stages of the selection process should be sequenced so that the more expensive steps, such as physical examination, are near the end. Fewer people will then move through the higher cost stages.

Recruitment should not be sporadic; it should be a continuous activity aimed at reaching the best applicants. The selection process should systematically and effectively match applicants' characteristics and needs with the requirements of specific selling tasks. Finally, the selection process should ensure that new sales personnel are available where and when they are needed.

Recruitment and selection of salespeople are not one-off decisions. The market and marketing environment change, as do an organisation's objectives, resources and marketing strategies. Maintaining the proper mix of salespeople thus requires the firm's sales management's continued attention.

Training Sales Personnel

Many organisations have formal training programmes; others depend on informal, on-the-job training. Some systematic training programmes are quite extensive; others are rather short and rudimentary. Regardless of whether the training programme is complex or simple, its developers must consider what to teach, whom to train, and how to train them.

A sales training programme can concentrate on the company, on products or on selling methods. Training programmes often cover all three areas. For experienced company sales staff, training usually emphasises product information, although it also describes new selling techniques and any changes in company plans, policies and procedures.

Training programmes can be aimed at newly hired salespeople, experienced sales staff, or both. Ordinarily, new sales personnel require comprehensive training, whereas experienced personnel need both refresher courses about established products and training in new product information. Training programmes can be directed at the entire sales force or at one segment of it.

Sales training may be done in the field, at educational institutions, in company facilities or in several of these locations. Some firms train new employees before assigning them to a specific sales position. Other businesses, however, put them into the field immediately and provide formal training only after they have gained a little experience. Training programmes for new personnel can be as short as several days or as long as three years, or even longer. Sales training for experienced personnel is often scheduled during a period when sales activities are not too demanding. Because training experienced salespeople is usually an ongoing effort, a firm's sales management must determine the frequency, sequencing and duration of these activities.

Sales managers, as well as other salespeople, often engage in sales training—whether daily on the job or periodically in sales meetings. Salespeople sometimes receive training from technical specialists within their own organisations. In addition, a number of individuals and organisations sell special sales training programmes. Appropriate materials for sales training programmes range from films, texts, manuals and cases to programmed learning devices and audio and video cassettes. As for teaching methods, lectures, demonstrations, simulation exercises and on-the-job training can all be effective. The choice of methods and materials for a particular sales training programme depends on the type and number of trainees, the programme's content and complexity, its length and location, the size of the training budget, the number of teachers and the teachers' preferences.

Compensating Salespeople

To develop and maintain a highly productive sales force, a business must formulate and administer a compensation plan that attracts, motivates and retains the most effective individuals. The plan should give sales management the desired level of control and provide sales personnel with an acceptable level of freedom, income and incentive. It should also be flexible, equitable, easy to administer and easy to understand. Good compensation programmes facilitate and encourage proper treatment of customers.

Even though these requirements appear to be logical and easily satisfied, it is actually quite difficult to incorporate them all into a simple programme. Some of them will be satisfied, and others will not. Studies evaluating the impact of financial incentives on sales performance indicate five general responses. For price sensitive individuals, an increase in incentives will usually increase their sales efforts, and a decrease in financial rewards will diminish their efforts. Unresponsive salespeople will sell at the same level regardless of the incentive. Leisure sensitive salespeople tend to work less when the incentive system is implemented. Income satisfiers normally adjust their performance to match their income goal. Understanding potential reactions and analysing the personalities of the sales force can help management evaluate whether an incentive programme might work.[16] Therefore, in formulating a compensation plan, sales management must strive for a proper balance of freedom, income and incentives.

The developer of a compensation programme must determine the general level of compensation required and the most desirable method of calculating it. In analysing the required compensation level, sales management must ascertain a salesperson's value to the company on the basis of the tasks and responsibilities associated with the sales position. The sales manager may consider a number of factors, including salaries of other types of personnel in the firm, competitors' compensation plans, costs of sales force turnover and the size of non-salary selling expenses and perks.

Sales compensation programmes usually reimburse salespeople for their selling expenses, provide a certain number of fringe benefits and deliver the required compensation level. To do that, a firm may use one or more of three basic compensation methods: straight salary, straight commission or a combination of salary and commission. In a **straight salary compensation plan,** salespeople are paid a specified amount per time period. This sum remains the same until they receive a pay increase or decrease. In a **straight commission compensation plan,** salespeople's compensation is determined solely by the amount of their sales for a given time period. A commission may be based on a single percentage of sales or on a sliding scale involving several sales levels and percentage rates. In a **combination compensation plan,** salespeople are paid a fixed salary plus a commission based on sales volume. Some combination programmes require a salesperson to exceed a certain sales level before earning a commission; others offer commissions for any level of sales.

Traditionally, department stores have paid salespeople straight salaries, but combination compensation plans are becoming popular. Concessionaires in Debenhams, for example, are offering commissions (averaging 6 to 8 per cent) to a large segment of their sales force. The practice has made the salespeople more attentive to a customer's presence and needs; it has also attracted older, more experienced salespeople, who tend to be in short supply.[17] Car salespeople traditionally receive low basic salaries (£5,000 to £9,500 p.a.), with the remainder coming from commission.

Table 16.1 lists the major characteristics of each sales force compensation method. Notice that the combination method is most popular. When selecting a compensation

TABLE 16.1 *Characteristics of sales force compensation methods*

COMPENSATION METHOD	FREQUENCY OF USE (%)[a]	WHEN ESPECIALLY USEFUL	ADVANTAGES	DISADVANTAGES
Straight salary	17.4	Compensating new salespeople; firm moves into new sales territories that require developmental work; salespeople need to perform many non-selling activities	Gives salesperson maximum amount of security; gives sales manager large amount of control over sales force; easy to administer; yields more predictable selling expenses	Provides no incentive; necessitates closer supervision of salespeople's activities; during sales declines, selling expenses remain at same level
Straight commission	6.5	Highly aggressive selling is required; non-selling tasks are minimised; company cannot closely control sales force activities	Provides maximum amount of incentive; by increasing commission rate, sales managers can encourage salespeople to sell certain items; selling expenses relate directly to sales resources	Salespeople have little financial security; sales manager has minimum control over sales force; may cause salespeople to give inadequate service to smaller accounts; selling costs less predictable
Combination	76.1	Sales territories have relatively similar sales potentials; firm wishes to provide incentive but still control sales force activities	Provides certain level of financial security; provides some incentive; selling expenses fluctuate with sales revenue	Selling expenses less predictable; may be difficult to administer

[a]The figures are computed from "Alternative sales compensation and incentive plans", *Sales & Marketing Management*, 17 February 1986, p. 57. *Note:* The percentage for Combination includes compensation methods that involved any combination of salary, commission or bonus.

SOURCE: Based on John P. Steinbrink, "How to pay your sales force", *Harvard Business Review,* July/August 1978.

method, sales management weighs the advantages and disadvantages shown in Table 16.1.

Proper administration of the sales force compensation programme is crucial for developing high morale and productivity among sales personnel. A good salesperson is highly marketable in today's workplace, and successful sales managers switch industries on a regular basis. Basic knowledge and skills related to sales management are in demand, and sometimes new insights can be gained from different work experiences. For example, one of British Steel's best sales managers was recruited from the grocery sector. To maintain an effective compensation programme and retain productive employees, sales management should periodically review and evaluate the plan and make necessary adjustments.

Motivating Salespeople

A sales manager should develop a systematic approach for motivating the salesforce to be productive. Motivating should not be viewed as a sporadic activity reserved for periods of sales decline. Effective sales force motivation is achieved through an organised set of activities performed continuously by the company's sales management. For example, scheduled sales meetings can motivate salespeople. Periodic sales meetings have four main functions: recognising and reinforcing the performance of salespeople, sharing sales techniques that are working, focusing employees' efforts on matching the corporate goals and evaluating their progress towards achieving these goals, and teaching the sales staff about new products and services.[18]

Although financial compensation is important, a motivational programme must also satisfy non-financial needs. Sales personnel, like other people, join organisations to satisfy personal needs and achieve personal goals. Sales managers must become aware of their sales personnel's motives and goals and then attempt to create an organisational climate that lets their salespeople satisfy their personal needs.

A sales manager can use a variety of positive motivational incentives as well as financial compensation (see Figure 16.3). For example, enjoyable working conditions, power and authority, job security and an opportunity to excel can be effective motivators. Salespeople can also be motivated by their company's efforts to make their job more productive and efficient. For example, Honeywell Information Systems developed a computerised sales support system that has increased sales productivity by 31 per cent and reduced sales force turnover by 40 per cent within a year. This system can track leads and provide customer profiles and competitor data.[19]

Sales contests and other incentive programmes can also be effective motivators. Sales contests can motivate salespeople to focus on increasing sales or new accounts, promote special items, achieve greater volume per sales call, cover territories better and increase activity in new geographic areas.[20] Some companies have found such incentive programmes to be powerful motivating tools that marketing managers can use to achieve corporate goals. Properly designed, an incentive programme can pay for itself many times over. However, for an incentive system to succeed, the marketing objectives must be accepted by the participants and prove effective in the market-place. Some organisations also use negative motivational measures: financial penalties, demotions, even terminations of employment.

Managing Sales Territories

The effectiveness of a sales force that must travel to its customers is influenced to some degree by sales management's decisions regarding sales territories. Sales managers deciding on territories must consider size, shape, routing and scheduling.

Creating Sales Territories. Several factors enter into the design of the size and shape of sales territories. First, sales managers must construct the territories so that sales potentials can be measured. Thus sales territories often consist of several geographic units for which market data are obtainable, such as census tracts, cities, counties or regions. Sales managers usually try to create territories that have similar sales potentials or require about the same amount of work. If territories have equal sales potentials, they will almost always be unequal in geographic size. The salespeople who are assigned the larger territories will have to work longer and harder to generate a certain sales volume. Conversely, if sales territories that require equal amounts of work are created, sales potentials for those territories will often vary. If sales personnel are

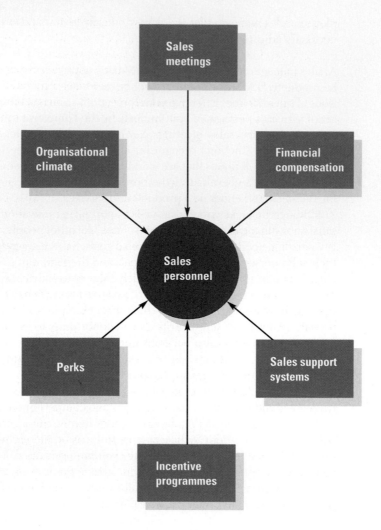

partially or fully compensated through commissions, they will have unequal income potentials. Many sales managers try to balance territorial workload and earnings potential by using differential commission rates. Although a sales manager seeks equity when developing and maintaining sales territories, some inequities will always prevail.

A territory's size and shape should also be designed to help the sales force provide the best possible customer coverage and to minimise selling costs. Territory size and shape should take into account the density and distribution of customers.

Routing and Scheduling Salespeople. The geographic size and shape of a sales territory are the most important factors affecting routing and scheduling of sales calls. Next are the number and distribution of customers within the territory, followed by the frequency and duration of sales calls. The person in charge of routing and scheduling must consider the sequence in which customers are called on, the specific roads or transport schedules to be used, the number of calls to be made in a given period and what time of day the calls will occur. In some firms, salespeople plan their own routes and schedules with little or no assistance from the sales manager; in other organisations, the sales manager draws up the routes and schedules. No matter who plans the routing and scheduling, the major goals should be to minimise salespeople's non-selling time (the time spent travelling and waiting) and maximise their selling time. The planners should try to achieve these goals in a way that holds a salesperson's travel and accommodation costs to a minimum. Many companies use agencies, such as SPA Ltd, to construct databases of actual and potential customers and associated sales territories. SPA has a database of car and lorry drive-times, even taking account of road works, which allows sales territories to be delineated. These territories can share out actual and potential customers and allocate the sales force in relation to the time taken to service them.

Controlling and Evaluating Sales Force Performance

To control and evaluate sales force activities properly, sales management needs information. A sales manager cannot observe the field sales force daily and so relies on call reports, customer feedback and invoices. Call reports identify the customers called on and present detailed information about interaction with those clients. Travelling sales personnel must often file work schedules indicating where they plan to be during specific future time periods.

The dimensions used to measure a salesperson's performance are determined largely by sales objectives. These objectives are normally set by the sales manager. If an individual's sales objective is stated in terms of sales volume, then that person should be evaluated on the basis of sales volume generated. Even though a salesperson may be assigned a major objective, he or she is ordinarily expected to achieve several related objectives as well. Thus salespeople are often judged along several dimensions. Sales managers evaluate many performance indicators, including average number of calls per day, average sales per customer, actual sales relative to sales potential, number of new customer orders, average cost per call and average gross profit per customer.

To evaluate a salesperson, a sales manager may compare one or more of these dimensions with a predetermined performance standard. However, sales management commonly compares one salesperson's current performance either with the performance of other employees operating under similar selling conditions or with his or her past performance. Sometimes management judges factors that have less direct bearing on sales performance, such as personal appearance, knowledge of the product and competitors.

After evaluating their sales force, sales managers must take any corrective action needed, because it is their job to improve the performance of the sales force. They may have to adjust performance standards, provide additional sales training or try other motivational methods. Corrective action may demand comprehensive changes in the sales force.

Many industries, especially technical ones, are monitoring their sales forces and increasing productivity through the use of lap-top (portable) computers. In part, the increasing use of computers in technical sales is a response to customers' greater technical sophistication. Product information—especially information on price, specifications and availability—helps salespeople to be more valuable. Some companies that have provided their sales forces with laptops expect a 15 to 20 per cent increase in their sales.[21]

SALES PROMOTION

The Nature of Sales Promotion

As defined earlier, **sales promotion** is an activity or material (or both) that acts as a direct inducement and offers added value to or incentive to buy the product to resellers, salespersons or consumers.[22] The sale probably would have taken place without the sales promotion activity, but not for a while; the promotion has brought the sale forward. For example, a consumer loyal to Persil washing powder may purchase a packet every four weeks. If, however, on the third week, Sainsbury or Tesco has Persil on offer or with an on-pack promotion, the consumer will probably buy a week early to take advantage of the deal. Sales promotion encompasses all promotional activities and materials other than personal selling, advertising and publicity. In competitive markets, where products are very similar, sales promotion provides additional inducements to encourage purchases. Sales promotions are designed to generate short term sales and goodwill towards the promoter. Marketing Insight 16.2 highlights Zanussi's use of trade show sales promotion to stimulate retailers' interest in its new ranges.

Sales promotion has grown dramatically in the last 10 years, largely because of the focus of business on short term profits and value and the perceived need for promotional strategies to produce short term sales boosts.[23] Current estimates in the UK suggest that consumer sales promotion is worth £2 billion annually. Include price discounting and the figure could be £4 billion higher; include trade sales promotion and the total reaches £8 billion.[24] The most significant change in promotion expenditures in recent years has been the transfer of funds usually earmarked for advertising to sales promotion. Companies now spend 54 per cent of their combined marketing services budgets on advertising and 21 per cent on sales promotion (see Figure 16.4).[25] Fundamental changes in marketing, which have led to a greater emphasis on sales promotion, mean that specialist sales promotion agencies have increased and many major advertising agencies have developed sales promotion departments.

An organisation often uses sales promotion activities in concert with other promotional efforts to facilitate personal selling, advertising or both. Figure 16.5 depicts what is known as the **ratchet effect**—the impact of using sales promotion (short term sales brought forward) and advertising (longer term build up to generate sales) together. Sales promotion efforts are not always secondary to other promotional mix ingredients. Companies sometimes use advertising and personal selling to support sales promotion activities. For example, marketers frequently use advertising to promote contests, free samples and premiums. Manufacturers' sales personnel occasionally administer sales contests for wholesale or retail salespeople. The most effective sales promotion efforts are closely interrelated with other promotional activities. Decisions regarding sales promotion therefore often affect advertising and personal selling decisions, and vice versa.

Sales Promotion Opportunities and Limitations

Sales promotion can increase sales by providing an extra incentive to purchase. There are many opportunities to motivate consumers, resellers and salespeople to take a desired action. Some kinds of sales promotion are designed specifically to stimulate resellers' demand and effectiveness; some are directed at increasing consumer demand; and still others focus on both resellers and consumers. Regardless of the purpose, marketers need to ensure that the sales promotion objectives are consistent with the organisation's overall objectives, as well as with its marketing and promotion objectives.

Although sales promotion can support a brand image, excessive price reduction sales promotion, such as coupons, can affect it adversely. Firms therefore must decide between short term sales increases and the long run need for a desired reputation and brand image.[26] As already noted, sales promotion has been catching up with advertising in total expenditure; but in the future, brand advertising may become more important relative to sales promotion. Some firms that shifted from brand advertising to sales promotion have lost market share, particularly in consumer markets where advertising is essential to maintain awareness and brand recognition. Advertising does not necessarily work better than sales promotion. There are trade-offs between these two forms

TRADE SHOWS LAUNCH NEW ZANUSSI RANGE

Italian white goods giant, Zanussi, part of the leading electrical appliances Electrolux group, chose a massive trade show as the central element in its new product launch. The 1993 new generation of cookers, fridges, dishwashers and washing machines premiered to the trade at a "no expense spared" extravaganza at Birmingham's National Exhibition Centre (NEC) organised by corporate events specialist Park Avenue. During the three day spring trade show, close to 3,000 retailers of white goods were "educated" into the new Zanussi range and brand positioning. Although in Italy Zanussi has a fairly utilitarian image, in many countries it is perceived to stand for design and innovation. Parent company Electrolux, locked in a global battle with Philips-Whirlpool, has injected substantial resources into Zanussi's new range in an attempt to maintain Zanussi's dominant position alongside the Electrolux brand, enabling a double-pronged attack on Whirlpool.

Hoover, too, launched New Wave and Classica washing machines and driers, stressing environmental benefits in terms of their production, reduced use of water and less reliance on harmful detergents. Zanussi's range had not been fully revamped for close to a decade and needed to match both competitors' developments and changing consumer concerns.

Zanussi's well remembered "appliance of science" television campaigns from the early 1980s firmly established the trade mark as a brand in consumers' minds. Television advertising has now dropped to 10 per cent of such levels and focuses on maintaining awareness of the brand in short bursts. Seventy per cent of the company's promotional budget now goes on below-the-line activities such as sales promotions. The NEC "mega" trade show is the latest in a regular series of road shows which began in 1986 to develop links with retailers.

Zanussi recognises the importance of the white goods retailer in the buying process. Retailers' in-store displays are influential, as is the advice of sales personnel. Stock levels and product availability also influence the consumer's choice. As Zanussi's Marketing Director explains, "the need to support and work closely with retailers is more crucial than ever".

The move away from above-the-line advertising to various sales promotions activities which include road shows, trade shows, point-of-sale displays, retailer incentives and training has coincided with Zanussi's gain of 1.5 per cent of the white goods market. With the recession hit electrical appliance market still led by Hotpoint with 16 per cent and Philips-Whirlpool's attack on Europe making significant inroads, Zanussi is steadily building its share. With 12 per cent of the market, the Electrolux subsidiary hopes to become the market leader in the UK before the end of the 1990s.

SOURCES: Peter Wingard; "Low exhibition spend levels out", Ken Gofton, *Marketing*, 5 November 1992, p. 12; "Zanussi trade show to boost new image", Robert Dwek, *Marketing*, 28 January 1993, p. 13; "Philips picks Vente for Euro ad post", *Marketing Week*, 15 January 1993, p. 6.

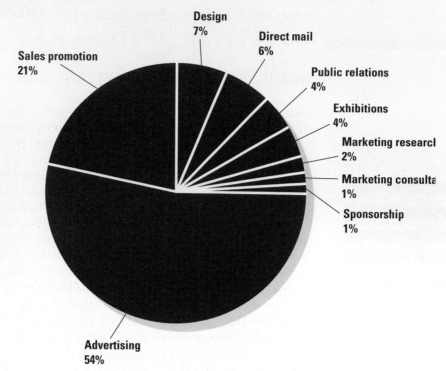

FIGURE 16.4
Breakdown of spend on marketing services (1989)

Design 7%

Direct mail 6%

Public relations 4%

Exhibitions 4%

Marketing research 2%

Marketing consulta 1%

Sponsorship 1%

Sales promotion 21%

Advertising 54%

SOURCE: Data from Mintel, Marketing Research Special Report, 1990, *Marketing,* 1990. Reprinted by permission.

FIGURE 16.5
The "ratchet effect"
Sales promotion (SP) brings forward sales but has an immediate effect. An advertising campaign (A) takes time to take off and to generate sales, but can switch other brand users and non-users. The ratchet effect has been identified in most consumer and service markets.

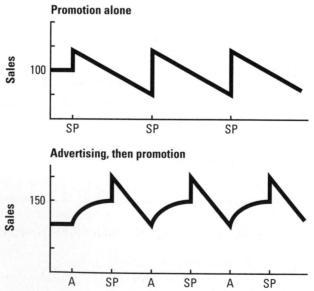

SOURCE: W. T. Moran, "Insights from pricing research", in E. B. Bailey, ed., *Pricing Practices and Strategies* (New York: The Conference Board, 1978), pp. 7 & 13. Used by permission.

of promotion, and the marketing manager must determine the right balance to achieve maximum promotional effectiveness.

SALES PROMOTION METHODS

Most sales promotion methods can be grouped into the categories of consumer sales promotion and trade sales promotion. **Consumer sales promotion techniques** encourage or stimulate consumers to patronise a specific retail store or to try a particular product. **Trade sales promotion methods** stimulate wholesalers, retailers or dealers to carry a producer's products and to market these products aggressively.

Marketers consider a number of factors before deciding which sales promotion methods to use. They must take into account both product characteristics (size, weight, costs, durability, uses, features and hazards) and target market characteristics (age, sex, income, location, density, usage rate and shopping patterns). How the product is distributed and the number and types of resellers may determine the type of method used. The competitive and legal environment may also influence the choice.

This section looks closely at several consumer and trade sales promotion methods to show what they entail and what goals they can help marketers achieve. Figure 16.6 shows how all members of a marketing channel can be engaged in sales promotion activities with different target audiences and techniques.

Consumer Sales Promotion Methods

The principal consumer sales promotion methods include coupons, demonstrations, frequent-user incentives, point-of-sale displays, free samples, money refunds, premiums, price-off offers, and consumer contests and sweepstakes.

Coupons.   **Coupons** are used to stimulate consumers to try a new or established product, to increase sales volume quickly, to attract repeat purchasers or to introduce new package sizes or features. Coupons usually reduce the purchase price of an item.

FIGURE 16.6
Uses of sales promotion in the marketing channel

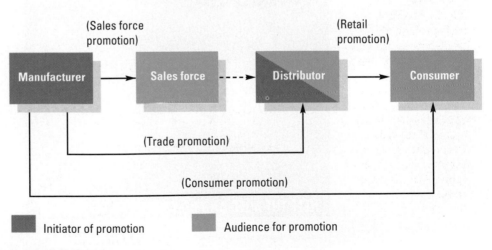

Consumer: Coupons, free samples, demonstrations, competitions
Trade (at wholesalers, retailers, salespeople): Sales competitions, free merchandise,
P.O.S. displays, plus trade shows and conferences

SOURCE: Rossiter, John and Larry Percy. *Advertising and Promotion Management.* Copyright © 1987 by McGraw-Hill, Inc. Used with permission.

For example, Figure 16.7 illustrates how Colgate-Palmolive hoped to increase sales of its Ajax product with a 10p off coupon. The savings may be deducted from the purchase price or offered as cash. For best results, coupons should be easy to recognise and state the offer clearly. The nature of the product (seasonality, maturity, frequency of purchase and so on) is the prime consideration in setting up a coupon promotion.

Several thousand manufacturers distribute coupons, which are used by approximately 80 per cent of all households. One study found that pride and satisfaction from obtaining savings through the use of coupons and price consciousness were the most important determinants of coupon use.[27] Coupons are distributed through free-standing inserts (FSIs), print advertising, direct mail/leaflet drops and in stores. Historically, FSIs have been the dominant vehicle for coupons.[28] When deciding on the proper vehicle for their coupons, marketers should consider strategies and objectives, redemption rates, availability, circulation and exclusivity. The whole coupon distribution and redemption business has become very competitive. To draw customers to their stores, grocers may double and sometimes even triple the value of the coupons they bring in. But because the practice of doubling and tripling coupons is expensive, many of these retailers have asked manufacturers to reduce the face value of the coupons they offer.[29]

There are several advantages to using coupons (see Figure 16.8). Print advertisements with coupons are often more effective than non-promotional advertising in generating brand awareness. Generally, the larger the coupon's cash offer, the better the recognition generated. Another advantage is that coupons are a good way to reward

FIGURE 16.7
Example of a coupon
Colgate-Palmolive used a 10p off coupon to increase sales of Ajax Liquid.

SOURCE: Courtesy of Colgate-Palmolive Company.

FIGURE 16.8

Sales promotion
Direct response advertisements with discount coupons are popular sales promotion approaches. Here, dandruff shampoo is on offer if the coupon is redeemed.

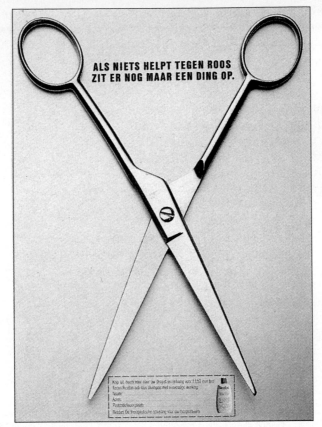

ALS NIETS HELPT TEGEN ROOS
ZIT ER NOG MAAR EEN DING OP.

SOURCE: PMS vW/Y & R.

present users of the product, win back former users and encourage purchases in larger quantities. Coupons also let manufacturers determine whether the coupons reached the intended target market because they get the coupons back.

Coupons also have drawbacks. Fraud and misredemption are possible, and the redemption period can be quite lengthy. Table 16.2 illustrates coupon distribution and redemption rates in the UK. In addition, some experts believe that coupons are losing their value because so many manufacturers are offering them, and consumers have therefore learned not to buy without some incentive, whether it be a coupon, a rebate or a refund. There has been a general decline in brand loyalty among heavy coupon users. On the other hand, many consumers redeem coupons only for products they normally buy. Studies have shown that about 75 per cent of coupons are redeemed by people who already use the brand on the coupon. So, as an incentive to try to continue to use a new brand or product, coupons have questionable success. Another problem with coupons is that stores often do not have enough of the coupon item in stock. This situation can generate ill will towards both the store and the product.[30]

Although the use of coupons as a sales promotion technique is expected to grow in the next few years, marketers' concerns about their effectiveness could well diminish their appeal. However, coupons will probably remain a major sales promotion component for stimulating trial of new products. Coupons will also be used to increase the frequency of purchase for established products that show sluggish sales. On the other hand, successful, established products may be reducing their profits if 75 per cent of the coupons are redeemed by brand loyal customers.[31]

TABLE 16.2 *Coupon redemption rates in the UK*

COUPONS—VOLUME AND EXPENDITURE

	1987	1989	1991
Number of coupons distributed (millions)	4,695	4,865	8,109
Number of coupons redeemed (millions)	411	311	451
Total value of coupons redeemed (£m)	60.4	70.0	113.0
Coupons' average face value (pence)	14.7	22.5	25.0
Manufacturers' average handling allowance° to retailers (pence per 100 coupons)	148.0	178.0	260.0
Distribution medium of coupons redeemed° (%)			
Newspaper	6	4	6
Magazine	6	4	4
Door-to-door	38	31	22
In/on pack	34	28	35
In store	5	18	23
Others	11	15	10
Average redemption rates by media (%)			
Newspaper	2.3	1.3	1.1
Magazine	2.2	1.2	1.5
Door-to-door	9.5	7.6	6.8
In/on pack	24.8	11.9	13.9

Note: °(excl. retailer tailor-made promotions)

SOURCE: From *The Marketing Pocketbook.* Copyright © 1993 by NTC Publications. Used with permission.

Demonstrations.   **Demonstrations** are excellent attention-getters. Manufacturers often use them temporarily either to encourage trial use and purchase of the product or to show how the product actually works. Because labour costs can be extremely high, demonstrations are not widely used. They can, however, be highly effective for promoting certain types of products, such as appliances, cosmetics and cars. Cosmetics marketers, such as Clinique (owned by Estee Lauder), sometime offer potential customers "makeovers" to demonstrate their products' benefits and proper application.

Frequent-User Incentives.   Many firms develop incentive programmes to reward individual consumers who engage in repeat (frequent) purchases. For example, most major international airlines offer a frequent-flyer programme through which customers who have flown a specified number of miles are rewarded with free tickets for additional travel. Thus frequent-user incentives help foster customer loyalty to a specific company or group of co-operating companies that provides extra incentives for patronage. Frequent-user incentives have also been used by service businesses, such as car hire companies, hotels, and credit card companies, as well as by marketers of consumer goods.

An older frequent-user incentive is trading stamps. **Trading stamps** are dispensed in proportion to the amount of a consumer's purchase and can be accumulated and redeemed for goods. Retailers use trading stamps to attract consumers to specific stores. Stamps are attractive to consumers as long as they do not drive up the price of goods.

They are effective for many types of retailers. Trading stamps were very popular in the 1960s, but their use as a sales promotion method declined dramatically in the 1970s. However, Green Shield stamps made a comeback and petrol retailers are offering in-house stamps redeemable for limited collections of goods.

Point-of-Sale Displays. **Point-of-sale (P-O-S) materials** include such items as outside signs, window displays, counter pieces, display racks and self-service cartons. Innovations in P-O-S displays include sniff teasers, which give off a product's aroma in the store as consumers walk within a radius of four feet, and computerised interactive displays, which ask a series of multiple choice questions and then display information on a screen to help consumers make a product decision.[32] These items, which are often supplied by producers, attract attention, inform customers and encourage retailers to carry particular products. A retailer is likely to use point-of-sale materials if they are attractive, informative, well constructed, and in harmony with the store. With two-thirds of all purchases resulting from in-store decisions, P-O-S materials can help sustain incremental sales if a brand's essential components—brand name, positioning and visual image—are the basis of the P-O-S display.[33]

A survey of retail store managers indicated that almost 90 per cent believed that P-O-S materials sell products. The retailers surveyed also said that P-O-S is essential for product introductions. Different forms of display material are carried by different types of retailers. Convenience stores, for example, favour window banners and "shelf talkers" (on-the-shelf displays or signs), whereas chain chemists prefer floor stands and devices that provide samples.[34]

Free Samples. Marketers use **free samples** for several reasons: to stimulate trial of a product, to increase sales volume in the early stages of a product's life-cycle or to obtain desirable distribution. The sampling programme should be planned as a total event, not merely a give-away.[35] Sampling is the most expensive of all sales promotion methods; production and distribution through such channels as mail delivery, door-to-door delivery, in-store distribution and on-package distribution entail very high costs. In designing a free sample, marketers should consider factors such as the seasonality of the product, the characteristics of the market and prior advertising. Free samples are not appropriate for mature products and products with a slow turnover.

Money Refunds. With **money refunds,** consumers submit proof of purchase and are mailed a specific amount of money. Usually, manufacturers demand multiple purchases of the product before a consumer can qualify for a refund. For example, Panasonic marketed a line of VHS tapes that featured a £1 rebate per tape for up to 12 purchases. A customer had to send in the sales receipt and a proof of purchase from inside each tape package. This method, used primarily to promote trial use of a product, is relatively inexpensive. Nevertheless, because money refunds sometimes generate a low response rate, they have limited impact on sales.

One of the problems with money refunds or rebates is that many people perceive the redemption process as too complicated. Consumers also have negative perceptions of manufacturers' reasons for offering rebates. They may believe that these are new, untested products or products that have not sold well. If these perceptions are not changed, rebate offers may degrade the image and desirability of the product being promoted. If the promotion objective in the rebate offer is to increase sales, an effort should be made to simplify the redemption process and proof of purchase requirements.[36]

Premiums.   **Premiums** are items offered free or at minimum cost as a bonus for purchasing a product. Vidal Sassoon offered a free, on-pack 50 ml "travel size" container of shampoo with its 200 ml size of Salon Formula shampoo. Kellogg's offered easy art books with its Variety Packs. Premiums can attract competitors' customers, introduce different sizes of established products, add variety to other promotional efforts and stimulate loyalty. Inventiveness is necessary, however; if an offer is to stand out and achieve a significant number of redemptions, the premium must be matched to both the target audience and the brand's image.[37] To be effective, premiums must be easily recognisable and desirable. Premiums are usually distributed through retail outlets or the mail, but they may also be placed on or in packages.

Price-off Offers.   A **price-off offer** gives buyers a certain amount off the regular price shown on the label or package. Similar to coupons, this method can be a strong incentive for trying the product; it can stimulate product sales, yield short lived sales increases and promote products in off-seasons. It is an easy method to control and is used frequently for specific purposes. However, if used on an ongoing basis, it reduces the price to customers who would buy at the regular price, and frequent use of price-off offers may cheapen a product's image. In addition, the method often requires special handling by retailers.

Consumer Contests and Sweepstakes.   In **consumer contests,** individuals compete for prizes based on their analytical or creative skill. This method generates traffic at the retail level. Marriott and Hertz co-sponsored a scratch-card contest with a golf theme to boost sales during the slow winter travel season. Contestants received game cards when they checked in at a Marriott hotel or hired a Hertz car and scratched off spots to see if they had won prizes such as cars, holidays or golf clubs.[38] However, marketers should exercise care in setting up a contest. Problems or errors may anger consumers or result in lawsuits. Contestants are usually more involved in consumer contests than they are in sweepstakes, which are discussed next, even though the total participation may be lower. Contests may be used in conjunction with other sales promotion methods, such as coupons.

The entrants in a **consumer sweepstake** submit their names for inclusion in a drawing for prizes. Sweepstakes are used to stimulate sales and, as with contests, are sometimes teamed with other sales promotion methods. Sweepstakes are used more often than consumer contests, and they tend to attract a greater number of participants. The cost of a sweepstake is considerably less than the cost of a contest.[39] Successful sweepstakes or competitions can generate widespread interest and short-term increases in sales or market share.

Trade Sales Promotion Methods

Producers use sales promotion methods to encourage resellers, especially retailers, to carry their products and promote them effectively. The methods include buy-back allowances, buying allowances, counts and recounts, free merchandise, merchandise allowances, co-operative advertising, dealer listings, premium or push money, sales contests and dealer loaders.

Buy-Back Allowances.   A **buy-back allowance** is a certain sum of money given to a purchaser for each unit bought after an initial deal is over. This method is a secondary incentive in which the total amount of money that resellers can receive is proportional to their purchases during an initial trade deal, such as a coupon offer. Buy-back allowances foster co-operation during an initial sales promotion effort and stimulate repurchase afterwards. The main drawback of this method is its expense.

Buying Allowances.   A **buying allowance** is a temporary price reduction to resellers for purchasing specified quantities of a product. A soap producer, for example, might give retailers £1 for each case of soap purchased. Such offers may be an incentive to handle a new product, achieve a temporary price reduction or stimulate the purchase of an item in larger than normal quantities. The buying allowance, which takes the form of money, yields profits to resellers and is simple and straightforward to use. There are no restrictions on how resellers use the money, which increases the method's effectiveness.

Counts and Recounts.   The **count and recount** promotion method is based on the payment of a specific amount of money for each product unit moved from a reseller's warehouse in a given time period. Units of a product are counted at the start of the promotion and again at the end to determine how many have moved from the warehouse. This method can reduce retail stock-outs by moving inventory out of warehouses and can also clear distribution channels of obsolete products or packages and reduce warehouse inventories. The count and recount method might benefit a producer by decreasing resellers' inventories, making resellers more likely to place new orders. However, this method is often difficult to administer and may not appeal to resellers who have small warehouses.

Free Merchandise.   **Free merchandise** is sometimes offered to resellers who purchase a stated quantity of the same or different products. Occasionally, free merchandise is used as payment for allowances provided through other sales promotion methods. To avoid handling and bookkeeping problems, the giving away of merchandise free is usually accomplished by reducing the invoice.

Merchandise Allowances.   A **merchandise allowance** is a manufacturer's agreement to pay resellers certain amounts of money for providing special promotional efforts, such as advertising or displays. This method is best suited to high volume, high profit, easily handled products. One major problem with using merchandise allowances is that some retailers perform their activities at a minimally acceptable level simply to obtain the allowances. Before paying retailers, manufacturers usually verify their performance. Manufacturers hope that the retailers' additional promotional efforts will yield substantial sales increases.

Co-operative Advertising.   **Co-operative advertising** is an arrangement whereby a manufacturer agrees to pay a certain amount of a retailer's media costs for advertising the manufacturer's products. The amount allowed is usually based on the quantities purchased. Before payment is made, a retailer must show proof that advertisements did appear. These payments give retailers additional funds for advertising. They can, however, put a severe burden on the producer's advertising budget. Some retailers exploit co-operative advertising programmes by crowding too many products into one advertisement. Some retailers cannot afford to advertise; others can afford it but do not want to advertise. Still others actually put out advertising that qualifies for an allowance but are not willing to undertake the paperwork required for reimbursement from producers.[40]

Dealer Listings.   A **dealer listing** is an advertisement that promotes a product and identifies the names of participating retailers who sell the product. Dealer listings can influence retailers to carry the product, build traffic at the retail level and encourage consumers to buy the product at participating dealers.

Premium or Push Money. **Premium** or **push money** is used to push a line of goods by providing additional compensation to salespeople. This promotion method is appropriate when personal selling is an important part of the marketing effort; it is not effective for promoting products that are sold through self-service. Although this method often helps a manufacturer obtain commitment from the sales force, it can also be very expensive.

Sales Contests. A **sales contest** is designed to motivate distributors, retailers and sales personnel by recognising outstanding achievements. The Colt Car Company, importer of Japanese made Mitsubishi cars into the UK, designed a sales contest that offered dealers an incentive trip for two to Barbados if they improved their sales figures by 10 to 12 per cent. Approximately 50 per cent of the dealers met this sales goal and won the trip.[41] To be effective, this method must be equitable for all sales personnel involved. One advantage of the method is that it can achieve participation at all levels of distribution. However, the results are temporary, and prizes are usually expensive.

Dealer Loaders. A **dealer loader** is a gift to a retailer who purchases a specified quantity of merchandise. Often dealer loaders are used to obtain special display efforts from retailers by offering essential display parts as premiums. For example, a manufacturer might design a display that includes a sterling silver tray as a major component and give the tray to the retailer. Marketers use dealer loaders to obtain new distributors and push larger quantities of goods.

This chapter concludes with an examination of direct mail, an important ingredient in the promotional mix.

DIRECT MAIL

Direct mail and telephone selling are part of the *direct selling* category described in Chapter 12. The use of direct mail to contact prospective customers and to solicit interest in products or services is not new. Advertising agencies, public relations consultancies and in particular sales promotions houses have been using mail shots for several decades. With approximately 6 per cent of all promotional budgets in consumer goods and services, its own professional bodies and trade associations, and the growing sophistication of consumer databases, the direct mail industry believes it warrants recognition as a separate element of the promotional mix alongside advertising, sales promotion, personal selling, public relations and sponsorship.

Uses for Direct Mail

Direct mail is not confined to consumers; it is an important promotional activity in many business-to-business markets. Direct mail delivers the promotional message— and sometimes the product—through the postal service, private delivery organisations and the expanding network of in-home fax machines. Direct mail is used to create brand awareness and stimulate product adoption. Throughout Europe, direct mail is widely used to generate orders, pre-sell prior to a sales call, qualify prospects for a sales call, screen out non-prospects, follow up a sale, announce special sales and localised selling initiatives, and raise funds for charities and non-profit organisations. In the UK, the average household receives six items of direct mail each month (see Table 16.3).

Attention Seeking Flashes

Direct mail packages must prompt the recipient to open them, rather than bin them as *junk mail*. "Prize inside", "Your opportunity to win", "Not a circular", "Important documentation enclosed" are just some of the popular headers or **flashes** printed promi-

TABLE 16.3   *The UK Consumer Direct Mail Industry*

A. PERCENTAGES OF MAIL ITEMS RECEIVED BY TYPE OF HOUSEHOLD

Type* of Household	Free Newspapers	Leaflets/ Coupons	Personal Mail	Direct Mail	Total
AB	11.6	14.3	51.0	23.0	100
C1	14.5	18.8	47.2	19.5	100
C2	16.9	15.7	48.3	19.0	100
DE	20.8	20.3	45.4	13.5	100
All	16.3	17.5	47.8	18.4	100

B. SENDERS OF CONSUMER DIRECT MAIL

Industry	1991 Per Cent	1989 Per Cent
Mail Order	16.9	24.3
Insurance	9.9	8.3
Charity	8.6	4.1
Banks	8.3	8.4
Retailers	7.7	7.0
Manufacturers	5.2	4.6
Credit Card	4.4	6.1
Book Club	4.4	3.9
Building Society	3.8	2.9
Gas/Electricity Board	3.5	2.9
Magazines	2.1	5.7
Estate Agents	1.4	2.6
Film Processing	0.6	0.8
Others	23.2	18.14

*For definition of social groups, see Table 4.2, p. 119.

SOURCE: Adapted from *The Media Pocket Book*, 1992, NTC Publications, Ltd. Used with permission.

nently on the address labels. In some markets, these are sufficient at least to persuade the recipient to open the package. With the boom in direct mail and the growing adverse reaction to junk mail, however, persuasive phrases are often not enough. Packaging design is becoming more important in enticing recipients, through attractive or unusual shapes and designs, to examine the detail of the direct mail shot.

The Package

The **direct mail package** is more than just the envelope. Often it is a mix of mailing envelope, covering or explanatory letter, circular, response device and return device. The mailing envelope has to overcome the recipient's inertia, often through catchy flashes and design flair. The letter needs to be personalised and clear, appeal to the beliefs and lifestyle of the recipient and elicit interest in the product or service in question. The circular contains the service or product details and specifications: colour, sizes, capabilities, prices, photographs or illustrations, and guarantees and endorsements from satisfied customers or personalities. The circular is the primary selling tool in the pack and often takes the form of a booklet, broadsheet, jumbo folder, brochure or flyer. The response device is typically an order form which must be legally correct, repeat the selling message and product benefits, simple to read and fill out, and comprehensive in the information requested. Alternatively, the response device can be an 0800 freephone telephone number or credit card hotline. The return device is any mechanism which enables the recipient to respond with an order or donation. It can be an information request form, order form or payment slip and is usually accompanied by a pre-printed—and often pre-paid—return envelope.

Mailing Lists

Eighty per cent of direct mail is opened: only 63 per cent is partially read; less still leads to an order or donation. Depending on the scale of the targeted audience, however, the costs are relatively low: design, printing, postage and the purchase or compilation of **mailing lists.** To be effective, appropriate targeting of direct mail is essential. Mailing lists must be as up-to-date as possible. There is a rule of thumb in the industry that one third of addresses on a list change each year owing to deaths and relocations. Within a year or two a list can be obsolete. Internal lists are those compiled in-house from customer addresses, account details and records of enquiries. External lists are produced by list brokers or mailing houses and bought—or rented—at commercial rates.

The suppliers of these external lists often undertake the complete direct mail operation for clients, from identification of recipients and compilation of lists to production of printed material, postage and even receipt of response devices. External lists can be either addresses of product category customers, including those of competing businesses if available, or general lists of targets with apparently suitable demographic profiles and lifestyles. Many of the leading geodemographic *databases,* such as ACORN or MOSAIC, were originally developed to assist in the targeting of direct mail.

Copy Writing

The targeting does not stop with the acquisition of a mailing list. The printed and product material included in the direct mail package must be written, designed and produced to appeal to the targets. The material must be prepared by people who understand the emotions and attitudes of the prospective customers. **Copy writing** is an important skill in the promotional mix, especially in the production of direct mail. The text must appeal to the target audience; sell the product; reassure the reader; be informative, clear and concise; and lead to a positive response.

Strengths and Weaknesses of Direct Mail

There are many advantages associated with direct mail. The medium offers a wide variety of styles and formats—more than offered by a radio or press advertisement, for example. The package can be personalised and customised. Often it will be received and read alone, not in competition with other promotions from other products and services. Marketing research and database management can lead to accurate targeting of direct mail. Sending material direct to people's homes and workplaces can hit targets otherwise inaccessible to promotional activity.

The primary disadvantage is the growing consumer view that direct mail is **junk mail** which should be consigned to the dustbin without even being opened. If used on a large scale, direct mail can prove costly—perhaps less than a sales force or television advertising, but more expensive than many public relations activities and some local or trade advertising. The direct mail packages and campaigns need to be updated to remain fresh in the fight against the junk mail image. In many countries, the paucity of up-to-date mailing lists increases the cost of direct mail, reduces the response rates and adds to consumer dislike of the concept of unsolicited direct selling through the post.

For organisations as diverse as retailer Marks & Spencer, financial services group American Express, catalogue retailer GUS, charity Oxfam, consumer goods manufacturer Unilever or British Airways, direct mail is an important, everyday component of the promotional mix. Whether it is on behalf of the starving in the Third World, double glazing for windows, fast food or book clubs, direct mail is familiar to consumers in most countries. For office supplies, maintenance services, security, computing products, and raw materials and components, in organisational markets direct mail is another important promotional tool, often supporting trade advertising and personal selling campaigns.

SUMMARY

Personal selling is the process of informing customers and persuading them to purchase products through personal communication in an exchange situation. The three general purposes of personal selling are finding prospects, convincing them to buy and keeping customers satisfied.

Many salespeople—either consciously or unconsciously—move through a general selling process as they sell products. In prospecting, the salesperson develops a list of potential customers. Before contacting acceptable prospects, the salesperson prepares by finding and analysing information about the prospects and their needs. The approach is the manner in which a salesperson contacts a potential customer. During the sales presentation, the salesperson must attract and hold the prospect's attention to stimulate interest and desire for the product. If possible, the salesperson should handle objections when they arise. Closing is the stage in the selling process when the salesperson asks the prospect to buy the product or products. After a successful closing, the salesperson must follow up the sale.

In developing a sales force, marketing managers must consider which types of salespeople will sell the firm's products most effectively. The three classifications of salespeople are order getters, order takers and support personnel. Order getters inform both current customers and new prospects and persuade them to buy. Order takers seek repeat sales and fall into two categories: inside order takers and field order takers. Sales support personnel facilitate the selling function, but their duties usually extend beyond making sales. The three types of support personnel are missionary, trade and technical salespeople.

The effectiveness of sales force management is an important determinant of a firm's success because the sales force is directly responsible for generating an organisation's sales revenue. The major decision areas and activities on which sales managers must focus are establishing sales force objectives, determining sales force size, recruiting and selecting salespeople, training sales personnel, compensating salespeople, motivating salespeople, managing sales territories, and controlling and evaluating the sales force.

Sales objectives should be stated in precise, measurable terms and specify the time period and the geographic areas involved. The size of the sales force must be adjusted from time to time because a firm's marketing plans change, as do markets and forces in the marketing environment.

Recruiting and selecting salespeople involves attracting and choosing the right type of salesperson to maintain an effective sales force. When developing a training programme, managers must consider a variety of dimensions, such as who should be trained, what should be taught and how the training should occur. Compensation of salespeople involves formulating and administrating a compensation plan that attracts, motivates and holds the right types of salespeople for the firm. Motivation of salespeople should allow the firm to attain high productivity. Managing sales territories, another aspect of sales force management, focuses on such factors as size, shape, routing and scheduling. To control and evaluate sales force performance, the sales manager must use information obtained through sales personnel's call reports, customer feedback and invoices.

Sales promotion is an activity or material (or both) that acts as a direct inducement, offering added value or incentive for the product, to resellers, salespersons or consumers. Marketers use sales promotion to identify and attract new customers, to introduce a new product and to increase reseller inventories. Sales promotion techniques fall into two general categories: consumer and trade. Consumer sales promotion methods encourage consumers to trade at specific stores or to try a specific product. These methods include coupons, demonstrations, frequent-user incentives, free samples, money refunds, premiums, price-off offers, and consumer sweepstakes and contests. Trade sales promotion techniques stimulate resellers to handle a manufacturer's products and market these products aggressively. These techniques include buy-back allowances, buying allowances, counts and recounts, free merchandise, merchandise allowances, co-operative advertising, dealer listings, premium or push money, sales contests and dealer loaders.

Direct mail uses the postal service to contact prospective customers and to solicit interest in products or services. Direct mail is widely used for consumer goods and services and also in business-to-business marketing. Increasingly, it is also important to non-profit organisations and charitable fund raising. Direct mail must be carefully designed with an attention seeking flash, good copy and a well constructed package. Mailing lists quickly become obsolete, and good database management is essential for the effective targeting of mail shots. The main problem facing the direct mail industry is the growing adverse reaction to it as "junk mail".

IMPORTANT TERMS

Personal selling
Prospecting
Approach
Closing
Order getters
Order takers
Support personnel
Missionary salespeople
Trade salespeople
Technical salespeople
Recruiting
Straight salary compensation plan
Straight commission
   compensation plan
Combination compensation plan
Sales promotion
Ratchet effect
Consumer sales promotion
   techniques
Trade sales promotion
   methods
Coupons
Demonstrations
Trading stamps

Point-of-sale (P-O-S)
   materials
Free samples
Money refunds
Premiums
Price-off offers
Consumer contests
Consumer sweepstake
Buy-back allowance
Buying allowance
Count and recount
Free merchandise
Merchandise allowance
Co-operative advertising
Dealer listing
Premium or push money
Sales contest
Dealer loader
Direct mail
Flashes
Direct mail package
Mailing lists
Copy writing
Junk mail

DISCUSSION AND REVIEW QUESTIONS

1. What is personal selling? How does personal selling differ from other types of promotional activities?
2. What are the primary purposes of personal selling?
3. Identify the elements of the personal selling process. Must a salesperson include all these elements when selling a product to a customer? Why or why not?
4. How does a salesperson find and evaluate prospects? Do you find any of these methods ethically questionable?
5. Are order getters more aggressive or creative than order takers? Why or why not?
6. Identify several characteristics of effective sales objectives.
7. How should a sales manager establish criteria for selecting sales personnel? What are the general characteristics of a good salesperson?
8. What major issues or questions should be considered when developing a sales force training programme?
9. Explain the major advantages and disadvantages of the three basic methods of compensating salespeople. In general, which method do you prefer? Why?
10. What major factors should be taken into account when designing the size and shape of a sales territory?
11. How does a sales manager—who cannot be with each salesperson in the field on a daily basis—control the performance of sales personnel?
12. What is sales promotion? Why is it used?
13. Does sales promotion work well in isolation from the other promotional mix elements?
14. For each of the following, identify and describe three techniques and give several examples: (a) consumer sales promotion methods, (b) trade sales promotion methods, (c) retail sales promotion methods.
15. What types of sales promotion methods have you observed recently?
16. How does direct mail gain the interest of its recipients?
17. What are the problems facing users of direct mail?

■ CASES

16.1 Varta's "Green" Battery

In 1988 the UK market for batteries was worth £250 million and was dominated by Ever Ready and Duracell.

	Value (%)	Volume (%)
Ever Ready	49	50
Duracell	32	22
Vidor	5	7
Varta	2	3
Own label	8	10
Others	5	8

The own label sector (Tesco, Asda, Boots) was growing quickly, with batteries produced by Ever Ready, Duracell and Vidor.

Environmentalists are concerned about disposed-of batteries which contain heavy, hazardous metals: zinc and mercury in zinc carbon batteries and cadmium in ni-cad rechargeable batteries. The Swiss government requires warning labels on batteries and restricts their mercury content; in 1989 the Swedish government banned all alkaline batteries; the European Community has reduced the permitted levels of heavy metal content and is to require all batteries to be sold with instructions on their safe disposal.

Varta AG is the largest battery producer in Europe, with a DM1.962 billion turnover in 1988. Varta produces all types of batteries but sales of consumer batteries outside Germany were DM726 million in 1988. German environmental groups have been powerful for many years, and Varta responded by developing technology which reduced the heavy metal content of its batteries. When these were launched in Europe in 1988, the UK was excluded as a market not ready to support a "green" battery.

The rapid "greening" of the UK government and consumers forced Varta executives to reconsider in 1989. Advertising began in the *Today* newspaper—"Like Today We Care about Tomorrow". A direct mail campaign sent a green box containing a copy of the paperback *Green Consumers' Guide* and a packet of Varta "green mercury free batteries that don't cost the Earth" to 500 political, business and entertainment personalities, and key retailers.

On St David's Day a cadmium free battery was launched. Packages containing the new product, together with two fresh leeks (the Welsh emblem), were distributed by courier. The direct mail was expanded, with packets of seeds and recycled card. Subsequent advertising targeted women, who buy the majority of household batteries. These advertisements featured a wistful baby and suggested the mother had a responsibility for making the world safe for her children. Varta's share of battery sales through grocery outlets rose to 14 per cent from 9 per cent as the major retailers pushed Varta's "green" batteries ahead of their own label products. The Varta PR mechanism was quick to publicise each product improvement and promotional tactic.

SOURCES: Keynote, "Dry batteries", 1988; *Management Today,* February 1989, pp. 56–60; *Marketing Week,* 12 May 1989, p. 55; and *Marketing,* 27 March 1989, p. 26.

Questions for Discussion

1. What were the reasons for Varta's success?
2. Why did large grocery retailers stock Varta batteries?
3. How important was promotion to Varta's success?

16.2 DEC's Sales Force Goes On-Line

Since 1957, when Digital Equipment Corporation was established, it has risen to the spot of number two computer maker in the world, just below its chief competitor, IBM. Faced with more hardware and software challengers in the market, as well as an industry wide slowdown, DEC is now struggling to remain at the top. Only a few years ago company profits rose 38 per cent, but more recently DEC has experienced a drop in its market share and has cut its workforce by 10,000. Declining sales have served as a catalyst for change. By linking personal computers to information networking technology, DEC is automating its sales force—to establish a more efficient sales force capable of maintaining a competitive edge.

With buzzwords like "Microserver," "Microvax II," and "ethernet" in its vocabulary, networking conjures images of science fiction full of robots and other futuristic technology usurping humanity's place in the world. However, it is really only a tool designed to serve, and in large and small companies alike, it is doing just that. Hewlett-Packard, Fina Oil and Chemical equip all their salespeople with lap-top computers, and several small businesses have saved themselves from going under by automating their sales forces. House-to-house interviewers in marketing research surveys use keyboards instead of clipboards. Meter readers for the utilities and delivery vehicles for Federal Express use barcode readers and data capture equipment during their calls. All that is needed is a computer, a modem and the communications software, which is becoming increasingly available. The most recent *Directory of Marketing Software,* a comprehensive list of sales marketing and sales software, catalogues almost 700 packages available for microcomputers, minicomputers and mainframes, compared with only 250 entries just a few years earlier. Turn on the switch and there is an electronic sales assistant, a desktop library with 24 hour access to current information and a worldwide communication system.

DEC's software, called Easynet Network, links sales, marketing and service personnel in 500 offices and 33 countries, allowing communication anytime and anyplace. Every DEC salesperson has an Easynet account accessible at the office, the customer site or at home via a personal computer. Sales personnel can use three different electronic ordering systems. Electronic Store provides customers with descriptions and pricing for every DEC product and service; over 100,000 customers have used this option to place orders. DECdirect, with a "mailing list" of 500,000 customers, is an electronic catalogue for lower priced items, with salespeople available for on-line customer assistance. One of DEC's goals over the next few years is to use DECdirect to place at least 80 per cent of its orders. EDI (electronic data interchange) provides computer-to-computer exchange of documents, such as purchase orders, enabling the sales force to respond to orders and ship products sooner. Sales representatives receive credit toward bonuses and membership in "top sales" clubs for all orders they place electronically.

Asked what they like most about being "on-line," DEC salespeople place access to information, as well as to others in the company, at the top of the list. Seventeen informational databases satisfy the sales representative's "need to know," offering information on topics such as account management, customer service, and telemarketing. One DEC sales manager reports that Easynet saves sales representatives more than one hour of research time for every sale, as well as about 60 phone calls a month, translating into a savings of over £15 million. Easynet provides communication between sales, marketing, finance and engineering personnel through electronic mail (person-to-person messages), conferencing (group discussions) and electronic bulletin boards (company wide information). As communication becomes easier, geography becomes less relevant to the sales process. On a large project, the sales manager in Frankfurt can communicate with the project manager in London, who can talk to the support personnel in Maryland—without playing telephone tag or waiting for conventional mail. Thanks to Easynet, DEC is now restructuring its sales organisation from territory based to industry based. A person formerly responsible for a geographic area—Benelux, for example—may become the sales manager for a specific industry, such as insurance or banking.

Why automate a sales force? Critics warn that computer technology may be difficult for new people to learn and that the amount of available information may overwhelm the sales force. DEC believes that computerised selling frees people from paperwork and streamlines the ordering process, giving sales personnel more time to create demands for their products and to propose solutions to meet those demands. DEC saves money and gets a better prepared, more knowledgeable sales force. After more than 20 years in business, the president of DEC remains committed to his vision of a technology driven operation. His goal is to use electronics in a continuous effort to satisfy any customer's needs for any of DEC's 100,000 products or services in less and less time at lower and lower cost.

DEC is not alone in its new philosophy. Marketing research, door-to-door selling, retailing and business-to-business selling situations are increasingly supported by IT (information technology) hardware and software. Prospect screening, order taking, delivery and after sales service can all be assisted with IT solutions, to the benefit of customers, suppliers and employees alike.

SOURCES: Thayer C. Taylor, "DEC gets its house in order", *Sales & Marketing Management,* July 1990, pp. 59–66; "Our 1990 marketing software directory", *Business Marketing,* June 1990, pp. 54, 56–8, 60–1, 70, 72; "DEC fires up an enterprise wide networking strategy", *Electronics,* September 1988; Leslie Helm, "What's next for Digital?" *Business Week,* 16 May 1988, pp. 88–92; Russ Lockwood, "What's new in on-line services", *Personal Computing,* June 1987, pp. 151–61; "Digital's high tech coup", *Dun's Business Month,* December 1986, pp. 28–9; and Nick Sullivan, "Making on-line information work for you", *Working Woman,* April 1986, pp. 111–13.

Questions for Discussion

1. In what ways does the automation of DEC's sales force help the company's sales managers do their jobs more effectively?
2. What competitive advantages are gained by equipping DEC's sales force with advanced information technology?
3. What problems may be encountered during the implementation of such automation?

PART V

PRICING DECISIONS

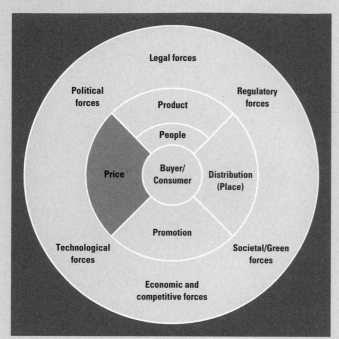

If an organisation is to provide a satisfying marketing mix, the price of its product must be acceptable to the target market. Pricing decisions can have numerous effects on other parts of the marketing mix. For example, a product's price can influence how customers perceive it, what types of marketing institutions are used in distributing it and how the product is promoted. Chapter 17, discusses the importance of price and looks at some of the characteristics of price and non-price competition. The major factors that affect marketers' pricing decisions are also discussed. Eight major stages used by marketers in establishing prices—from setting pricing objectives to establishing actual price points—are examined in Chapter 18. ∎

17 PRICING CONCEPTS

Objectives

To understand the nature and importance of price

To be aware of the characteristics of price and non-price competition

To examine various pricing objectives

To explore key factors that may influence marketers' pricing decisions

To consider issues affecting the pricing of products for industrial markets

S tatus symbols are expensive by nature—sleek European sports cars, 18-carat gold watches, and ostrichskin briefcases are all very costly. Though smaller and less expensive, fancy fountain pens have become a common sight in the hands of influential businesspeople. Such pens have high price tags and are much more difficult to maintain than ballpoints, felt tip pens or roller ball pens. However, recent sales figures indicate that the semi-obsolete fountain pen is making a comeback as the writing instrument of choice for status minded individuals.

Of the premium priced fountain pens, Montblanc pens are probably the most prestigious. Named after the highest mountain in Europe, these German made fountain pens cost from about £100 to £5,000 (for a solid gold one). The most popular model costs about £300. Prestige pricing has worked well for Montblanc, placing the pen in the same category as Rolex watches, Porsche sunglasses, BMW cars and Gucci luggage. Former US president Ronald Reagan, ex-prime minister Margaret Thatcher, and fictional super-spy James Bond all use Montblanc pens.

Parker also makes high priced "power" pens, including its revived Duofold model, which was popular during the 1920s. The Duofold comes in a blue and maroon marbled finish and sells for about £175. Waterman and S.T. Dupont also sell fine fountain pens. The Waterman Le Man series, which comes in seven sizes, is priced at around £160. Dupont pens have a distinctive Chinese lacquer finish and are priced from £200 to £300 (for the gold flecked models). ■

Based on information in Michelle Hill, "Writing in rarefied air", *Bridgewater Courier-News* (Bridgewater, N.J.), 25 June 1989, pp. G1, G2; Allen Norwood, "Pen offers status—at only $295", *Charlotte Observer*, (Charlotte, N.C.), 20 November 1988, pp. 1C, 3C; and Sharon Schlegel, "Fountain pens ink new success as status symbols", *Chicago Sun-Times*, 26 March 1989.

hese companies are using price, along with other elements, to distinguish their pens from competitive brands and to give them an exclusive, up market image. For these firms, as for most organisations, pricing is a crucial element in the marketing mix. After focusing first on the nature of price and its importance to marketers, this chapter then considers some of the characteristics of price and non-price competition. The next section explores the various types of pricing objectives that marketers may establish and examines in some detail the numerous factors that can influence pricing decisions. The chapter concludes by discussing selected issues related to the pricing of products for industrial markets.

THE NATURE OF PRICE

To a buyer, **price** is the *value* placed on what is exchanged. Something of value—usually buying power—is exchanged for satisfaction or utility. As described in Chapter 2, buying power depends on a buyer's income, credit and wealth. It is a mistake to believe that price is always money paid or some other financial consideration. In fact, trading of products—**barter**—is the oldest form of exchange. Money may or may not be involved.

Buyers' interest in price stems from their expectations about the usefulness of a product or the satisfaction they may derive from it. Because buyers have limited resources, they must allocate their buying power so that they can obtain the most desired products. Buyers must decide whether the utility gained in an exchange is worth the buying power sacrificed. Almost anything of value—ideas, services, rights and goods—can be assessed at a price, because in many societies the financial price is the measurement of value commonly used in exchanges. Thus a painting by Picasso may be valued, or priced, at £1 million. Financial price, then, quantifies value. It is the basis of most market exchanges.

Terms Used to Describe Price

Price is expressed in different terms for different exchanges. For instance, motor insurance companies charge a *premium* for protection from the cost of injuries or repairs stemming from a car accident. A police officer who stops a motorist for speeding writes a ticket that requires a *fine* to be paid. A lawyer charges a *fee,* and a *fare* is charged for a railway or taxi. A *toll* is sometimes charged for the use of bridges. *Rent* is paid for the use of equipment or for a flat. An estate agent receives a *commission* on the sale of a property. A *deposit* is made to reserve merchandise. A *tip* helps pay waitresses or waiters for their services. *Interest* is charged for loans, and *taxes* are paid for government services. The value of many products is called *price.*

Although price may be expressed in a variety of ways, it is important to remember that the purpose of this concept is to quantify and express the value of the items in a market exchange.

The Importance of Price to Marketers

As pointed out in Chapter 9, developing a product may be a lengthy process. It takes time to plan promotion and to communicate benefits. Distribution usually requires a long term commitment to dealers who will handle the product. Often price is the only aspect a marketer can change quickly to respond to changes in demand or to the actions of competitors. It must be borne in mind, however, that under certain circumstances the price variable may be relatively inflexible.

Price is also a key element in the marketing mix because it relates directly to the generation of total revenue. The following equation is an important one for the entire organisation:

$$\text{Profits} = \text{Total Revenues} - \text{Total Costs}$$

or

$$\text{Profits} = (\text{Prices} \times \text{Quantities Sold}) - \text{Total Costs}$$

Prices affect an organisation's profits, which are its lifeblood for long term survival. Price affects the profit equation in several ways. It directly influences the equation because it is a major component. It has an indirect impact because it can be a major determinant of the quantities sold. Even more indirectly, price influences total costs through its impact on quantities sold.

Because price has a psychological impact on customers, marketers can use it symbolically. By raising a price, they can emphasise the quality of a product and try to increase the status associated with its ownership. By lowering a price, they can emphasise a bargain and attract customers who go out of their way—spending extra time and effort—to save a small amount. In Figure 17.1, Granada targets students with a low price deal for TV and video rentals.

PRICE AND NON-PRICE COMPETITION

A product offering can compete on a price or non-price basis. The choice will affect not only pricing decisions and activities but also those associated with other marketing mix decision variables.

FIGURE 17.1

Price competition
Granada emphasises low price in its drive to encourage students to rent TVs and videos.

SOURCE: Granada UK Rental Ltd.

MUMM CHAMPAGNE: NEW PRICING AND RE-POSITIONING

As the Christmas 1992 festivities died down and revellers looked to New Year's Eve celebrations, few realised the significant changes occurring throughout the European Community. Britain's Prime Minister John Major lit one of hundreds of beacons to mark the dawning of a new era in intra-European trade and co-operation. The customs posts had a new, more limited focus: travellers entering the EC from other parts of the world. For businesspeople and tourists alike, the formalities of passport checks and duty free allowances when passing from country to country in the EC had changed beyond recognition. Passport checks were few, and car-borne travellers could load more goods in their cars than—according to leading motoring organisations and the police—their vehicles could safely transport.

Many EC consumers noticed no changes until their annual holidays took them into Europe. For some more alert consumers, the changes in EC regulations had an immediate impact. Car ferry operators reported brisk business and above average passenger levels as UK consumers headed for the French coastal hypermarkets to load up with cut price wines and spirits. Coach operators from the South of England were joined by operators from the Midlands and the North running "away days" to the French hypermarkets. For the hypermarkets, extra stocks were brought in and English language signage became more prominent.

There had been much talk about 1992's EC deregulation. Governments had been preparing companies and trade organisations for several years, but the low cost wines of France were the first concrete manifestation of the changes for many UK consumers. Not only the French hypermarkets were facing new and changing opportunities. The new regulations were to cause upheaval for many companies, including Seagram's, makers of Mumm champagne.

Price Competition

When **price competition** is used, a marketer emphasises price as an issue and matches or beats the prices of competitors. Bic engages in price competition by pricing its perfume or pens low and emphasising price in its advertisements. To compete effectively on a price basis, a firm should be the low cost producer of the product. If all firms producing goods in an industry charge the same price, the firm with the lowest costs is the most profitable. Firms that stress low price as a key element in the marketing mix tend to produce standardised products. A seller using price competition may change prices frequently or at least must be willing and able to do so. Whenever competitors change their prices, the seller must respond quickly and aggressively. In many countries, the postal service and United Parcel Service or DHL engage in direct price competition in their pricing of overnight air express services. In the UK, fast printing services adopt a similar approach.

Price competition gives a marketer flexibility. Prices can be altered to account for changes in the firm's costs or in demand for the product (see Marketing Insight 17.1). If competitors try to gain market share by cutting prices, an organisation competing on

Seagram's decided to sell its Mumm brand in the UK at prices similar to Mumm's French prices. Why? "We had to align our prices with those charged in France, to prevent the French coming over and buying it cheaper from here [the UK]," explained Seagram's. The price per case to the trade was set to increase £23, pushing the wholesale price per bottle up from £14.33 to £16.25. The retail price to the consumer was £17.99 but rose to over £20, pushing Mumm ahead of arch rivals Moet Chandon, Mercier and Piper Heidsieck. "We are trying to re-position Mumm with a more premium image because the current positioning is not enough to support the new bottle price."

Seagram's had to rethink its pricing differential between France and the UK for its Mumm brand as trade barriers altered and consumers had an incentive to travel further to purchase, even potentially crossing the English Channel. The existing press advertising for Mumm, through Ogilvy & Mather, had to be shelved as Mumm was re-positioned. Seagram's second champagne marque, Perrier Jouet, also received additional marketing attention to reduce any loss to the re-positioned Mumm brand.

The French hypermarkets, UK coach operators, car ferry companies and alcoholic beverages giant Seagram's were not the only companies to notice changes caused by the macro marketing environment: EC deregulation. In Seagram's case, the pricing policies of major brands had to be altered and brand positionings reassessed.

SOURCES: Paul Meller, "Mumm price follows in French fashion", *Marketing,* 28 January 1993, p. 6; the Automobile Association; BBC and ITN television news broadcasts, 1 and 2 January 1993; Paul Meller, "Champagne: missing the marque?" *Marketing,* 17 December 1992, pp. 16–19.

a price basis can react quickly to such efforts. However, a major drawback of price competition is that competitors, too, have the flexibility to adjust their prices. Thus they can quickly match or beat an organisation's price cuts. A price war may result. In the UK in the 1970s, both grocery and petrol retailers engaged in highly visible price wars. Many grocery retailers—led by Fine Fare and Tesco—traded purely on price; and their promotional material (newspaper advertisements and window posters) pushed the latest price reductions on major brands. The petrol companies and independent forecourt operators were locked in a price war in which neighbouring competing garages might reduce pump prices several times in one day in tit-for-tat reactions. Furthermore, if a user of price competition is forced to raise prices, competing firms that are not under the same pressures may decide not to raise their prices.

Non-price Competition

In **non-price competition,** a seller elects not to focus on price but instead emphasises distinctive product features, service, product quality, promotion, packaging or other factors to distinguish its product from competing brands. Since non-price competition is based on factors other than price, this approach gives an organisation the opportunity to increase its brand's unit sales through means other than changing the brand's price. For example, Galway Irish Crystal stresses heritage and product quality rather than compete on the basis of price. One major advantage of non-price competition is that a firm can build customer loyalty towards its brand. If customers prefer a brand because of non-price issues, they may not be easily lured away by competing firms and brands. Customers whose primary attraction to a store is based on non-price factors are less likely to leave their regular store for a lower competitive price. Price is not the most durable factor from the standpoint of maintaining customer loyalty.[1] But when price is the primary reason that customers buy a particular brand, the competition can attract such customers through price cuts.

Non-price competition is workable under the right conditions. A company must be able to distinguish its brand through unique product features, higher quality, customer service, promotion, packaging and the like (see Figure 17.2). Buyers must not only be able to perceive these distinguishing characteristics but must also view them as desirable. The distinguishing features that set a particular brand apart from its competitors should be difficult, if not impossible, for competitors to imitate. Finally, the organisation must extensively promote the distinguishing characteristics of the brand to establish its superiority and to set it apart from competitors in the minds of buyers.

Many European and non-US firms put less emphasis on price than do their American counterparts. They look for a competitive edge by concentrating on promotion, research and development, marketing research and marketing channel considerations. In a study of pricing strategy, five such firms stated specifically that they

FIGURE 17.2
Non-price competition
In this advertisement, the Port of Calais stresses its easy accessibility rather than the price of channel crossings.

CALAIS – shortest sea route to France and traditional landfall for generations of British travellers bound for the Continent. Modern car ferries plus seacats and hovercraft provide a choice of 100 crossings daily during the summer and never less than 50 off peak. A new motorway link direct to Calais port provides rapid access to the A26 and the entire Continental motorway network.

VIA **Calais**
– just a short cruise away.

FROM 75 MINUTES BY CAR FERRY, 45 BY SEACAT, 30 BY HOVERCRAFT.

SOURCE: Chambre de Commerce et d'industrie de Calais France.

emphasise research and development and technological superiority; competition based on price was seldom a major marketing consideration.[2]

A marketer attempting to compete on a non-price basis is still not able simply to ignore competitors' prices, however. The organisation must be aware of competitors' prices and will probably price its brand near or slightly above competing brands. As an example, Sony sells television sets in a highly competitive market and charges higher prices for its sets; but it is successful none the less. Sony's emphasis on high product quality both distinguishes it from its competitors and allows it to set higher prices. Therefore, price remains a crucial marketing mix component in situations that call for non-price competition.

PRICING OBJECTIVES

Pricing objectives are overall goals that describe what the firm wants to achieve through its pricing efforts. Because pricing objectives influence decisions in most functional areas—including finance, accounting and production—the objectives must be consistent with the organisation's overall mission and purpose. Banking is an area where pricing is a major concern. As competition has intensified, bank executives have realised that their products must be priced to meet not only short term profit goals but also long term strategic objectives.[3] Because of the many areas involved, a marketer often uses multiple pricing objectives. This section looks at a few of the typical pricing objectives that companies might set for themselves.

Survival

A fundamental pricing objective is survival. Most organisations will tolerate difficulties such as short run losses and internal upheaval if they are necessary for survival. Because price is a flexible and convenient variable to adjust, it is sometimes used to increase sales volume to levels that match the organisation's expenses.

Profit

Although businesses may claim that their objective is to maximise profits for their owners, the objective of profit maximisation is rarely operational, because its achievement is difficult to measure. Because of this difficulty, profit objectives tend to be set at levels that the owners and top level decision-makers view as satisfactory. Specific profit objectives may be stated in terms of actual monetary amounts or in terms of percentage change relative to the profits of a previous period.

Return on Investment

Pricing to attain a specified rate of return on the company's investment is a profit-related pricing objective. Most pricing objectives based on return on investment (ROI) are achieved by trial and error, because not all cost and revenue data needed to project the return on investment are available when prices are set. General Motors, for example, uses ROI pricing objectives.

The objective of return on investment may be used less as managers and marketers in diversified companies stress the creation of shareholder value. When shareholder value is used as a performance objective, strategies—including those involving price—are evaluated on the basis of the impact they will have on the value investors perceive in the firm.[4]

Market Share

Many firms establish pricing objectives to maintain or increase market share, that is, a product's sales in relation to total industry sales. For example, Volkswagen AG cut prices on its 1990 model Jettas, Golfs, Cabriolets and Carats by 5 to 14 per cent and introduced two new models—the Corrado and Passat—at unexpectedly lower prices to boost its share of the car market.[5]

Maintaining or increasing market share need not depend on growth in industry sales. Remember that an organisation can increase its market share even though sales for the total industry are decreasing. On the other hand, assuming that the overall market is growing, an organisation's sales volume may actually increase as its market share within the industry decreases.

Cash Flow

Some organisations set prices to recover cash as fast as possible. Financial managers are understandably interested in quickly recovering capital spent to develop products. This objective may have the support of the marketing manager who anticipates a short product life-cycle.

Although it may be acceptable in some situations, the use of cash flow and recovery as an objective over simplifies the value of price in contributing to profits. A disadvantage of this pricing objective could be high prices, which might allow competitors with lower prices to gain a large share of the market.

Status Quo

In some cases, an organisation may be in a favourable position and, desiring nothing more, may set an objective of status quo. Status quo objectives can focus on several dimensions—maintaining a certain market share, meeting (but not beating) competitors' prices, achieving price stability or maintaining a favourable public image. A status quo pricing objective can reduce a firm's risks by helping to stabilise demand for its products. The use of status quo pricing objectives sometimes minimises pricing as a competitive tool, leading to a climate of non-price competition in an industry.

Product Quality

A company might have the objective of product quality leadership in the industry. For example, the construction equipment manufacturer JCB aims to be ranked as one of the leading companies in its industry in terms of product quality and customer satisfaction.[6] This goal normally dictates a high price to cover the high product quality and, in some instances, the high cost of research and development. Mont Blanc pens, shown in Figure 17.3, are premium priced to cover high production costs and to help maintain their high quality image.

FACTORS AFFECTING PRICING DECISIONS

Pricing decisions can be complex because of the number of details that must be considered. Frequently there is considerable uncertainty about the reactions to price on the part of buyers, channel members, competitors and others. Price is also an important consideration in marketing planning, market analysis and sales forecasting. It is a major issue when assessing a brand's position relative to competing brands. Most factors that affect pricing decisions can be grouped into one of the eight categories shown in Figure 17.4. This section explores how each of these eight groups of factors enters into price decision-making.

Organisational and Marketing Objectives

Marketers should set prices that are consistent with the organisation's goals and mission. For example, a retailer trying to position itself as offering value for money may wish to set prices that are quite reasonable relative to product quality. In this case, a marketer would not want to set premium prices on products but would strive to price products in line with this overall organisational goal.

The firm's marketing objectives must also be considered. Decision-makers should make pricing decisions that are compatible with the organisation's marketing objectives. Say, for instance, that one of a producer's marketing objectives is a 12 per cent increase in unit sales by the end of the next year. Assuming that buyers are price sensitive,

FIGURE 17.3
Product quality pricing objective
Mont Blanc pens carry a high price to cover high production costs and to help maintain a high quality image.

SOURCE: Courtesy of Montblanc/Simplo Gmbtt. © Montblanc® Meisterstück®.

FIGURE 17.4
Factors that affect pricing decisions

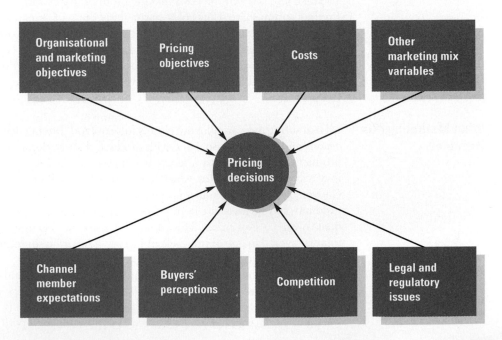

increasing the price or setting a price above the average market price would not be in line with the firm's sales objective. For example, Ford has introduced high performance, well specified model variants to the top of each of its model ranges, for example, the £23,000 Escort RS Cosworth and the £28,000 Granada Scorpio 24v. Such prices ensure that these particular models have only limited appeal. Ford's stated objective, however, is to be market leader in terms of sales volume. The company, therefore, is careful to price the great majority of its cars in line with the price expectations of the bulk of the car buying public and fleet operators—far below these £23,000 and £28,000 levels.[7]

Types of Pricing Objectives

The type of pricing objectives a marketer uses will obviously have considerable bearing on the determination of prices.[8] An objective of a certain target return on investment requires prices to be set at a level that will generate a sales volume high enough to yield the specified target. A market share pricing objective usually causes a firm to price a product below competing brands of similar quality to attract competitors' customers to the company's brand. This type of pricing can lead to lower profits. A marketer sometimes uses temporary price reductions in the hope of gaining market share. A cash flow pricing objective may cause an organisation to set a relatively high price, which can place the product at a competitive disadvantage. On the other hand, a cash flow pricing objective sometimes results in a low price sustained in the long term. However, this type of objective is more likely to be addressed by using temporary price reductions, such as sales, refunds and special discounts.

Costs

Obviously, costs must be an issue when establishing price. A firm may temporarily sell products below cost to match the competition, to generate cash flow or even to increase market share; but in the long run it cannot survive by selling its products below cost. Even when a firm has a high volume business, it cannot survive if each item is sold slightly below what it costs to produce and market. A marketer should be careful to analyse all costs so that they can be included in the total costing associated with a product.

Besides considering the costs associated with a particular product, marketers must also take into account the costs that the product shares with others in the product line. Products often share some costs, particularly those of research and development, production and distribution. Services are especially subject to cost sharing. For example, the costs of a bank building are spread over the costs of all services the bank offers.[9] Most marketers view a product's cost as a minimum, or floor, below which the product cannot be priced. Cost analysis is discussed in more detail in the next chapter and in Chapter 23.

Other Marketing Mix Variables

All marketing mix variables are closely interrelated. Pricing decisions can influence decisions and activities associated with product, distribution and promotion variables. A product's price frequently affects the demand for the item. A high price, for instance, may result in low unit sales, which in turn may lead to higher production costs per unit. Conversely, lower per unit production costs may result from a low price. For many products, buyers associate better product quality with a high price and poorer product quality with a low price. This perceived price-quality relationship influences customers' overall image of products or brands. The price sometimes determines the degree of status associated with ownership of the product.

Pricing decisions influence the number of competing brands in a product category. When a firm introduces a product, sets a relatively high price and achieves high unit sales, competitors may be attracted to this product category. If a firm uses a low price, the low profit margin may be unattractive to potential competition.

The price of a product is linked to several dimensions of its distribution. Premium-priced products are often marketed through selective or exclusive distribution; lower-priced products in the same product category may be sold through intensive distribution. For example, Cross pens are distributed through selective distribution and Bic pens through intensive distribution. The manner in which a product is stored and transported may also be associated with its price. When a producer is developing the price of a product, the profit margins of marketing channel members such as wholesalers and retailers must be considered. Channel members must be adequately compensated for the functions they perform. Inadequately compensated channel members will withdraw from a marketing channel or be poorly motivated.

The way a product is promoted can be affected by its price. Bargain prices are often included in advertisements, whereas premium prices are less likely to appear in advertising messages. The issue of a premium price is sometimes included in advertisements for up market items, such as luxury cars or fine jewellery. Higher priced products are more likely to require personal selling efforts than lower priced ones. A customer may purchase an inexpensive watch in a self-service environment but hesitate to buy an expensive watch in the same store, even if it is available there.

The price structure can affect a salesperson's relationship with customers. A complex pricing structure takes longer to explain to customers, is more likely to confuse the buyer and may cause misunderstandings that result in long term customer dissatisfaction. For example, the pricing structures of many airlines are complex and frequently confuse ticket sales agents and travellers alike.

Channel Member Expectations

When making price decisions, a producer must consider what distribution channel members (such as wholesalers and retailers) expect. A channel member certainly expects to receive a profit for the functions performed. The amount of profit expected depends on the amount that would be gained by handling a competing product instead. The amount of time and the resources required to carry the product also influence intermediaries' expectations.

Channel members often expect producers to provide discounts for large orders and quick payment. (Discounts are discussed later in this chapter.) At times, resellers expect producers to provide several support activities, such as sales training, service training, repair advisory service, co-operative advertising, sales promotions and perhaps a programme for returning unsold merchandise to the producer. These support activities clearly incur associated costs, and a producer must consider these costs when determining prices. Failure to price the product so that the producer can provide some of these support activities may cause resellers to view the product less favourably.

Buyers' Perceptions

One important question that marketers should assess when making price decisions is, "How important is the price to people in the target market?" The importance of price is not absolute; it can vary from market segment to market segment and from person to person. Members of one market segment may be more sensitive to price than members of a different target market. Moreover, the importance of price will vary across different product categories. Price may be a more important factor in the purchase of petrol than in the purchase of a pair of jeans, because buyers may be more sensitive to the price of a frequently purchased item such as petrol than to the price of jeans. Marketing Insight 17.2 examines the role of price in haute couture—up market fashion.

For numerous products, buyers have a range of acceptable prices. This range can be fairly narrow in some product categories but wider in others. A marketer should become aware of the acceptable range of prices in the relevant product category. (This issue and related ones are discussed in more detail in Chapter 18.)

HAUTE COUTURE MOVES DOWN MARKET

Names like Yves Saint Laurent, Givenchy, Christian Dior and Giorgio Armani are synonymous with haute couture: one of a kind, hand-crafted fashions priced beyond the means of all but an elite few. In the best French fashion houses, women like Princess Caroline of Monaco and Jackie Kennedy Onassis pay £20,000 for one dress, flying to Paris for fittings and waiting three months for delivery. Even "luxury ready to wear" commands extravagant prices. Most women can only admire a £1,000 dress, let alone spend £7,500 for a Saint Laurent Rive Gauche suit. To attract a larger market, many European couturiers are offering more moderately priced collections, known in the fashion industry as bridge lines.

Certainly, global recession has had an impact on the world of high fashion. The chairman of the Fédération Française reports that orders for French haute couture and up market ready to wear are declining steadily, and the chief executive of Yves Saint Laurent says orders for his custom made line are down by 50 per cent. In style conscious Italy, sales of the chic apparel dropped 12 per cent in one year. As the glamorous 1980s crashed headlong into the price conscious 1990s, consumers became less willing to spend their money on clothes just to make a fashion statement.

Many European couturiers, however, are counting on consumer willingness to spend £80–£600 for bridge collection labels. Among the down-to-earth lines are Givenchy's Life, Ungaro's Emanuel, Yves Saint Laurent's Variation, and Christian Dior's Coordonnes. In France, a Variation sports jacket sells for about £150. Although an Ungaro white sequin dress costs about £2,000, European shoppers can pick up a similar dress from the less expensive Emanuel line for £500. In the United States, almost everything in Ungaro's Emanuel collection is priced under $500. Instead of luxurious fabrics and delicate craftsmanship, Armani Jeans offers casual apparel like cotton T-shirts and denim jackets. For about £80, shoppers can walk out of a shop wearing a pair of Armani Jeans white stretch trousers and an Armani Jeans T-shirt. While these figures still look pricey, fashion marketers are confident that the prosperous middle class can afford them.

Since European haute couture houses were born in the days of Napoleon III, some women have always spent a fortune on fashion. Industry experts believe that, for the most part, those days are over. They predict that less expensive bridge lines will flourish into a £1/2 billion worldwide market, with the United States as the most enthusiastic customer. Boutiques featuring second collections are already flourishing in Rodeo Drive in Beverly Hills and in New York, Washington, D.C., London, Paris and Milan. Some designers, however, refuse to jump on the bandwagon for fear that cheaper collections will pollute the glamorous image of haute couture.

SOURCES: Barbara Rudolph, "Why chic is now cheaper", *Time,* 11 November 1991, pp. 68–70; Zina Sawaya, "Alter egos", *Forbes,* 24 June 1991, pp. 58, 61; and Blanca Riemer, Laura Zinn and Fred Kapner, "Haute couture that's not so haute", *Business Week,* 22 April 1991, p. 108; Suzanne Bidlake," Discounting UK fashion", *Marketing,* 12 November 1992, p. 2.

Consumers' perceptions of price may also be influenced by all the products in a firm's product line. The perception of price depends on a product's actual price plus the consumer's reference price, that is, the consumer's expectation of price. Exposure to a range of prices in a product line affects the consumer's expectations and perceptions of acceptable prices.[10]

Buyers' perceptions of a product relative to competing products may allow or encourage a firm to set a price that differs significantly from the prices of competing products. If the product is deemed superior to most of the competition, a premium price may be feasible. Strong brand loyalty sometimes makes it possible for the firm to charge a premium price for its product. On the other hand, if buyers view the product relatively unfavourably (without being extremely negative), a lower price may be required to generate sales. There is a considerable body of research on the relationship between price and consumers' perceptions of quality. Consumers use price as an indicator of quality when brands are unfamiliar and when the perceived risk of making unsatisfactory choices is high. They also rely on price as an indicator if there is little information available and judging a product's attributes is difficult.[11]

Competition

A marketer needs to know competitors' prices so that the firm can adjust its own prices accordingly. This does not mean that a company will necessarily match competitors' prices; it may set its price above or below theirs. However, matching competitors' fares is an important strategy for survival in the airline industry.[12]

When adjusting prices, a marketer must assess how competitors will respond. Will they change their prices (some, in fact, may not) and, if so, will they raise or lower them? For example, is it likely that as Hertz stresses its keen pricing, competitors will adjust their pricing? Chapter 2 describes several types of competitive market structures. The structure that characterises the industry to which a firm belongs affects the flexibility of price setting.

When an organisation operates as a monopoly and is unregulated, it can set whatever prices the market will bear. However, the company may avoid pricing the product at the highest possible level for fear of inviting government regulation or because it wants to penetrate a market by using a lower price. If the monopoly is regulated, it normally has less pricing flexibility; the regulatory body lets it set prices that generate a reasonable, but not excessive, return. A government owned monopoly may price products below cost to make them accessible to people who otherwise could not afford them. However, government owned monopolies sometimes charge higher prices to control demand.

In an oligopoly, only a few sellers operate, and there are high barriers to competitive entry. The motor, mainframe computer, telecommunications and steel industries exemplify oligopolies. A firm in such an industry can raise its price, hoping that its competitors will do the same. When an organisation cuts its price to gain a competitive edge, other firms are likely to follow suit. Thus very little is gained through price cuts in an oligopolistic market structure.

A market structure characterised by monopolistic competition means numerous sellers with differentiated product offerings. The products are differentiated by physical characteristics, features, quality and brand images. The distinguishing characteristics of its product may allow a company to set a different price from its competitors. However, firms engaged in a monopolistic competitive market structure are likely to practice non-price competition, discussed earlier in this chapter.

Under conditions of perfect competition, there are many sellers. Buyers view all sellers' products as the same. All firms sell their products at the going market price, and buyers will not pay more than that. This type of market structure, then, gives a marketer no flexibility in setting prices.

Legal and Regulatory Issues

At times government action sways marketers' pricing decisions. To curb inflation, the government may invoke price controls, "freeze" prices at certain levels or determine the rates at which prices can be increased. With the privatisation of once public utilities, the UK government has set up regulatory bodies which stress minimum and maximum charges (for example, OFTEL for telecommunications).

Many regulations and laws affect pricing decisions and activities. Not only must marketers refrain from fixing prices, they must also develop independent pricing policies and set prices in ways that do not even suggest collusion. Over the years, legislation has been established to safeguard the consumer and organisations from the sharp practices of other companies. In the UK, the Monopolies and Mergers Commission prevents the creation of monopolistic situations. The consumer is protected by the Trade Descriptions Act, the Fair Trading Act, the Consumer Protection Act and many more. All countries have similar legislation, and the European Community legislates to protect consumers within the community.

PRICING FOR INDUSTRIAL MARKETS OR ORGANISATIONAL MARKETS

As previously mentioned, industrial markets consist of individuals and organisations that purchase products for resale, for use in their own operations or for producing other products. Establishing prices for this category of buyers is sometimes different from setting prices for consumers. Industrial marketers have experienced much change because of economic uncertainty, sporadic supply shortages and an increasing interest in service. Differences in the size of purchases, geographic factors and transport considerations require sellers to adjust prices. This section discusses several issues unique to the pricing of industrial products, including discounts, geographic pricing, transfer pricing and price discrimination.

Price Discounting

Producers commonly provide intermediaries with discounts off list prices. Although there are many types of discounts, they usually fall into one of five categories: trade, quantity, cash and seasonal discounts, and allowances.

Trade Discounts. A reduction off the list price given by a producer to an intermediary for performing certain functions is called a **trade,** or **functional, discount.** A trade discount is usually stated in terms of a percentage or series of percentages off the list price. Intermediaries are given trade discounts as compensation for performing various functions, such as selling, transporting, storing, final processing and perhaps providing credit services. Although certain trade discounts are often a standard practice within an industry, discounts do vary considerably from one industry to another.

Quantity Discounts. Deductions from list price that reflect the economies of purchasing in large quantities are called **quantity discounts.** Price quantity discounts are used to pass on cost savings, gained through economies of scale, to the buyer. Cost savings usually occur in four areas. First, fewer but larger orders reduce per unit selling costs. Second, fixed costs, such as invoicing and sales contracts, remain the same or may even go down. Third, costs for raw materials are lower, because quantity discounts are often available to the seller. Fourth, longer production runs mean no increases in holding costs.[13] In addition, a large purchase may shift some of the storage, finance and risk taking functions to the buyer. Thus quantity discounts usually reflect legitimate reductions in costs.

Quantity discounts can be either cumulative or non-cumulative. **Cumulative discounts** are aggregated over a stated period of time. Purchases of £10,000 in a three month period, for example, might entitle the buyer to a 5 per cent, or £500, rebate. Such discounts are supposed to reflect economies in selling and encourage the buyer to purchase from one seller. **Non-cumulative discounts** are one off reductions in prices based on the number of units purchased, the monetary value of the order or the product mix purchased. Like cumulative discounts, these discounts should reflect some economies in selling or trade functions.

Cash Discounts. A **cash discount,** or simple price reduction, is given to a buyer for prompt payment or payment in cash. Accounts receivable are an expense and a collection problem for many organisations. A policy to encourage prompt payment is a popular practice and sometimes a major concern in setting prices.

Discounts are based on cash payments or cash paid within a stated time. For example, "2/10 net 30" means that a 2 per cent discount will be allowed if the account is paid within 10 days. However, if the buyer does not pay within the 10 day period, the entire balance is due within 30 days without a discount. If the account is not paid within 30 days, interest may be charged.

Seasonal Discounts. A price reduction to buyers who purchase goods or services out of season is a **seasonal discount.** These discounts let the seller maintain steadier production during the year. For example, car hire companies offer seasonal discounts in winter and early spring to encourage firms to use cars during the industry's slow months.

Allowances. Another type of reduction from the list price is an **allowance**—a concession in price to achieve a desired goal. Trade-in allowances, for example, are price reductions granted for turning in a used item when purchasing a new one. Allowances help give the buyer the ability to make the new purchase. This type of discount is popular in the aircraft industry. Another example is promotional allowances, which are price reductions granted to dealers for participating in advertising and sales support programmes intended to increase sales of a particular item.

Geographic Pricing

Geographic pricing involves reductions for transport costs or other costs associated with the physical distance between the buyer and the seller. Prices may be quoted as being F.O.B. (free-on-board) factory or destination. An **F.O.B. factory** price indicates the price of the merchandise at the factory, before it is loaded onto the carrier vehicle; it thus excludes transport costs. The buyer must pay for shipping. An **F.O.B. destination** price means that the producer absorbs the costs of shipping the merchandise to the customer. This policy may be used to attract distant customers. Although F.O.B. pricing is an easy way to price products, it is sometimes difficult for marketers to administer, especially when a firm has a wide product mix or when customers are dispersed widely. Because customers will want to know about the most economical method of shipping, the seller must keep abreast of shipping rates.

To avoid the problems involved in charging different prices to each customer, **uniform geographic pricing,** sometimes called postage stamp pricing, may be used. The same price is charged to all customers regardless of geographic location, and the price is based on average shipping costs for all customers. Petrol, paper products and office equipment are often priced on a uniform basis.

Zone prices are regional prices that take advantage of a uniform pricing system; prices are adjusted for major geographic zones as the transport costs increase. For example, a Lille manufacturer's prices may be higher for buyers in the south of France than for buyers in Paris.

Base point pricing is a geographic pricing policy that includes the price at the factory, plus freight charges from the base point nearest the buyer. This approach to pricing has virtually been abandoned because its legal status has been questioned. This policy can result in all buyers paying freight charges from one location regardless of where the product was manufactured!

When the seller absorbs all or part of the actual freight costs, **freight absorption pricing** is being used. The seller might choose this method because it wishes to do business with a particular customer or to get more business; more business will cause the average cost to fall and counter-balance the extra freight cost. This strategy is used to improve market penetration and to retain a hold in an increasingly competitive market.

Transfer Pricing

When one unit in a company sells a product to another unit, **transfer pricing** occurs. The price is determined by one of the following methods:

Actual full cost: calculated by dividing all fixed and variable expenses for a period into the number of units produced.

Standard full cost: calculated on what it would cost to produce the goods at full plant capacity.

Cost plus investment: calculated as full cost, plus the cost of a portion of the selling unit's assets used for internal needs.

Market based cost: calculated at the market price less a small discount to reflect the lack of sales effort and other expenses.

The choice of a method of transfer pricing depends on the company's management strategy and the nature of the units' interaction. The company might initially choose to determine price by the actual full cost method. But later price changes could result in a market based method or another method that the management of the company decides is best for its changed business situation.[14] An organisation must also ensure that transfer pricing is fair to all units that must purchase its goods or services.

Price Discrimination

A policy of **price discrimination** results in different prices being charged to give a group of buyers a competitive advantage. In some countries price discrimination is regarded as illegal in certain circumstances. For example, in the US price differentials are legal only when they can be justified on the basis of cost savings, when they are used to meet competition in good faith or when they do not damage competition. Thus, if customers are not in competition with one another, different prices may be charged legally. The EC is keen to stamp out price discrimination.

Price differentiation is a form of market segmentation that companies use to provide a marketing mix that satisfies different segments. Because different market segments perceive the value of a particular product differently, depending on the product's importance and value to the industrial buyer, marketers may charge different prices to different market segments. Price discrimination can also be used to modify demand patterns, support sales of other products, help move obsolete goods or excessive inventories, fill excess production capacity and respond to competitors' activities in particular markets.[15] Table 17.1 shows the principal forms of price discrimination. For price discrimination to work, several conditions are necessary:

1. The market must be segmentable.
2. The cost of segmenting should not exceed the extra revenue from price discrimination.

TABLE 17.1 *Principal forms of price discrimination*

BASES OF DISCRIMINATION	EXAMPLES
Buyers' incomes	Low priced admission to leisure and recreation facilities for the unemployed
Buyers' age	Children's haircuts, lower admission charges for students and senior citizens
Buyers' location	Zone prices and season ticket reductions for bus and train travel
Buyers' status	Lower prices to new customers, quantity discounts to big buyers
Use of product	Eat in and take away prices for fast foods
Qualities of products	Relatively higher prices for de luxe models
Labels on products	Lower prices for unbranded products
Sizes of products	Relatively lower prices for larger sizes (the "giant economy" size)
Peak and off-peak services	Lower prices for off-peak services, (excursion rates on public transport, off-season rates at resorts, holiday and evening telephone rates)

3. The practice should not breed customer discontent.
4. Competition should not be able to steal the segment that is charged the higher price.
5. The practice should not violate any applicable laws.

SUMMARY

Price is the value placed on what is exchanged. The buyer exchanges buying power—which depends on the buyer's income, credit and wealth—for satisfaction or utility. Price is not always money paid; barter, the trading of products, is the oldest form of exchange. Price is a key element in the marketing mix because it relates directly to the generation of total revenue. The profit factor can be determined mathematically by first multiplying price by quantity sold to calculate total revenues and then subtracting total costs. Price is the only variable in the marketing mix that can be adjusted quickly and easily to respond to changes in the external environment.

A product offering can compete on either a price or a non-price basis. Price competition emphasises price as the product differential. Prices fluctuate frequently, and price competition among sellers is aggressive. Non-price competition emphasises product differentiation through distinctive features, services, product quality or other factors. Establishing brand loyalty by using non-price competition works best when the product can be physically differentiated and the customer can recognise these distinguishing characteristics.

Pricing objectives are overall goals that describe the role of price in a firm's long-range plans. The most fundamental pricing objective is the organisation's survival. Price can be easily adjusted to increase sales volume or to combat competition so that the organisation can stay alive. Profit objectives, which are usually stated in terms of monetary sales volume or percentage change, are normally set at a satisfactory level rather than at a level designed for profit maximisation. A sales growth objective focuses on increasing the profit base by increasing sales volume. Pricing for return on investment (ROI) sets a specified profit as its objective. A pricing objective to maintain or increase market share implies that market position is linked to success. Other types of pricing objectives include cash flow and recovery, status quo and product quality.

A group of eight factors enters into pricing decisions: organisational and marketing objectives, pricing objectives, costs, other marketing mix variables, channel member expectations, buyers' perceptions, competition, and legal and regulatory issues. When setting prices, marketers should make decisions consistent with the organisation's goals and mission. Pricing objectives heavily influence price setting decisions. Most marketers view a product's cost as the floor below which a product cannot be priced. Due to the interrelation of the marketing mix variables, price can affect product, promotion, distribution and service level decisions. The revenue that channel members expect for the functions they perform must also be considered when making price decisions.

Buyers' perceptions of price vary. Some consumer segments are sensitive to price, but others may not be; thus before determining price, a marketer needs to be aware of its importance to the target market. Knowledge of the prices charged for competing brands is essential so that the firm can adjust its prices relative to those of competitors. Government regulations and legislation can also influence pricing decisions through laws to enhance competition and by invoking price controls—for example, to curb inflation.

Unlike consumers, industrial buyers purchase products to use in their own operations or for producing other products. When adjusting prices, industrial sellers take into consideration the size of the purchase, geographical factors and transport requirements. Producers commonly provide discounts off list prices to intermediaries. The categories of discounts include trade, quantity, cash and seasonal discounts, and allowances. A trade discount is a price reduction for performing such functions as storing, transporting, final processing or providing credit services. If an intermediary purchases in large enough quantities, the producer gives a quantity discount, which can be either cumulative or non-cumulative. A cash discount is a price reduction for prompt payment or payment in cash. Buyers who purchase goods or services out of season may be granted a seasonal discount. A final type of reduction from the list price is an allowance, such as a trade-in allowance.

Geographic pricing involves reductions for transport costs or other costs associated with the physical distance between the buyer and the seller. A price quoted as F.O.B. factory means that the buyer pays for shipping from the factory; an F.O.B. destination price means that the producer pays for shipping. This is the easiest way to price products, but it can be difficult for marketers to administer. When the seller charges a fixed average cost for transport, the practice is known as uniform geographic pricing. Zone prices take advantage of a uniform pricing system adjusted for major geographical zones as the transport costs increase. Base point pricing resembles zone pricing; prices are adjusted for shipping expenses incurred by the seller from the base point nearest the buyer. A seller who absorbs all or part of the freight costs is using freight absorption pricing.

When a price discrimination policy is adopted, different prices are charged to give a group of buyers a competitive advantage. In some countries, price differentials are legal only when they can be justified on the basis of cost savings, when they meet competition in good faith or when they do not attempt to damage competition.

IMPORTANT TERMS

Price
Barter
Price competition
Non-price competition
Pricing objectives
Trade, or functional, discount
Quantity discounts
Cumulative discounts
Non-cumulative discounts
Cash discount
Seasonal discount

Allowance
Geographic pricing
F.O.B. factory
F.O.B. destination
Uniform geographic pricing
Zone prices
Base point pricing
Freight absorption pricing
Transfer pricing
Price discrimination

DISCUSSION AND REVIEW QUESTIONS

1. Why are pricing decisions so important to an organisation?
2. Compare and contrast price and non-price competition. Describe the conditions under which each form works best.
3. How does a pricing objective of sales growth and expansion differ from a pricing objective to increase market share?
4. Why is it crucial that marketing objectives and pricing objectives be considered when making pricing decisions?
5. In what ways do other marketing mix variables affect pricing decisions?
6. What types of expectations may channel members have about producers' prices, and how do these expectations affect pricing decisions?
7. How do legal and regulatory forces influence pricing decisions?
8. Compare and contrast a trade discount and a quantity discount.
9. What is the reason for using the term F.O.B.?
10. What is the difference between a price discount and price discrimination?

■ CASES

17.1   The BMW Z1

In September 1988 at the Paris Motor Show, BMW unveiled its new sports car, the Z1. Described by critics as BMW's jaunty, expensive, two seater 170 bhp roadster with slide-down electric doors and bounce-back bodywork, the Z1 was priced at DM83,000 in West Germany. The car had been intended as a limited edition pilot project, but its entire production was immediately sold out until the end of 1990. The Z1 was priced well above the BMW 325i (whose engine and transmission it used and which had similar performance) but was priced at considerably less than, for example, the Porsche 911 Carrera Cabrie.

The planned production quota for the UK was 25 units in 1989, rising to only 50 units in 1990. Demand was significantly higher than supply, and BMW (GB) received orders—with a £5,000 deposit—many months prior to the official UK launch date. The official UK price for the Z1 in August 1989 was £36,925. However, in the summer of 1989, 16 Z1s were advertised in the press by owners or dealers, with an average price of £46,822. Gradually, these private "black market" prices dropped from a peak of £50,000 to close to the official retail price.

SOURCES: M. Labrou, "Ten marketing cases", MBA dissertation, University of Warwick, 1989; Douglas Hamilton, Reuters, 30 September 1988 and 17 October 1988; and *Autocar and Motor*, 19 July 1989.

Questions for Discussion

1. Could BMW have priced the car significantly higher (or lower) than it did? What would have been the consequences?
2. Setting production levels in such a market is not straightforward. Could BMW have predicted demand for the Z1 more accurately?
3. BMW positions itself as a prestige car manufacturer. If it were producing cars for the mass market—as Ford and Volkswagen do—would the company adopt a different pricing policy?

17.2 Perfume Discounting—Pricing Policies to Rattle the Leading Brands

For decades the leading perfume houses of Paris, London and New York have sought exclusive, premium brand positioning: Joy, Chanel No. 5 and Givenchy have been marketed as high priced, de luxe lines available only from carefully selected retailers: leading department stores, fragrance houses and only those chemists with a genuine perfumery. Even a company as reputable as Boots has failed to gain Chanel's permission to retail Chanel fragrances throughout its chain of stores. Chanel permits only the larger, more exclusive branches of Boots to stock its brands, sometimes giving preference to an independent specialist fragrance house in a town to retail its products.

While these up market brands have controlled distribution, they have also prevented price discounting. The more mass market brands, such as Revlon, Max Factor or Boots' own No. 7, have been left to take the bulk of the market on volume, pricing way below Joy, Chanel No. 5 or Givenchy. In this way, these more expensive, selectively distributed brands have nurtured an exclusive, premium image to support their higher prices.

Kingfisher, owners of Woolworths and B&Q DIY, has created the UK's leading chain of discount drugstores. Towards the end of 1992, Kingfisher's Superdrug chain caught the market-place by surprise. It brought in full in-store pharmacies to rival Boots but kept its discounting focus by reducing prices of proprietary medicines by around 10 per cent. Superdrug also looked to the perfume market, reducing the prices of the more mass market brands it stocked. Why, though, shouldn't Superdrug create full perfumery sections in its larger branches and stock the more up market, exclusive brands? More significantly, why should Superdrug not discount the prices of these leading exclusive brands of perfume, in line with the chain's general trading philosophy as a discounter?

Shock waves were felt throughout the industry. The perfume producers had spent decades creating premium priced, exclusive brands. Discounting by a retail chain was the antithesis of this strategy. Independent perfume retailers had been able to occupy prime pitch sites with high staffing levels and glamorous shop fittings on the basis of the higher margins offered by the slower selling exclusive brands. The pricing and images of these brands had for decades protected them from the national retail chains and buying groups. The large department stores were less dependent on maintaining the premium pricing, but they similarly saw their sales decline as Superdrug followed through with its plans. EC and UK trading laws and anti-price fixing legislation seemed to be on Superdrug's side, too.

It was not easy going for Superdrug. Along with the other discounters, Superdrug was refused supplies from the perfume manufacturers; the company had to source from "the grey market", mainly overseas wholesalers. The producers' PR mechanisms mobilised many industry players against the moves. Superdrug's first press advertising campaign for its discounting of fine fragrances was rejected by a string of up market colour supplements and publishing houses. According to the marketing press, colour supplements for *The Independent on Sunday*, *The Sunday Times* and *The Observer* all refused to carry the Superdrug advertisements for fear of provoking repercussions from the up market, perfume houses, all leading advertisers in these newspapers' supplements.

Prior to Christmas, the peak selling season for all perfumes—including brands such as Joy, Chanel and Givenchy—leading department store operator House of Fraser, which owns Harrods and stores in most large cities in the UK, reduced prices of many leading perfumes. Boots, too, retaliated against Superdrug's move. For example, in branches of Boots permitted to sell Chanel, a smaller Chanel No. 5 perfume dropped from around £28 to £21, a price still well ahead of the more mass market brands, but the largest discount for such a brand seen in one of its core retail outlets. Boots and House of Fraser admitted they were "reviewing daily" their pricing policies.

Years of brand building and image cultivation were in jeopardy. More to the point, the retailers were to risk reducing sales of these still lucrative brands. Superdrug wanted to enter the upper echelons of the fragrance market, but not to let discounting devalue the worth of stocking some of these brands. There were no intentions to replicate the price discounting and tit-for-tat retaliations in the DIY or grocery sectors of retailing, or in the holiday industry. The fragrance market, though, witnessed quite dramatic upheavals in a very conservative market. The entry of Superdrug, with its aggressive pricing policy and discounting, caused changes in strategies throughout the industry, by perfume producers, retailers and the media.

SOURCES: "Superdrug finds refuge in women's magazines", *Marketing Week*, 13 November 1992, p. 6; Helen Slingsby, "House of Fraser reviews scent pricing", *Marketing Week*, 18 December 1992 p. 5; Stop Press, *Marketing*, 19 November 1992, p. 7; "Eau Zone expands with new name", *Marketing Week*, 6 November 1992, p. 8; Suzanne Bidlake, "Givenchy TV ads 'plug' discounters", *Marketing*, 17 December 1992, p. 6, Suzanne Bidlake, "Perfume firms fear wrath of retailers", *Marketing*, 29 October 1992, p. 5; Suzanne Bidlake, "Asda apes Superdrug with discount scent", *Marketing*, 22 October 1992, p. 5.

Questions for Discussion

1. What were the pricing objectives of perfume manufacturers such as Chanel and Givenchy? Explain.
2. What impact could a price war have on brand loyalty in this market? Why?
3. On what criteria has competition in this market previously been based? Was the new focus on price a sensible development?

18 SETTING PRICES

Objectives

To understand the eight major stages of the process used to establish prices

To explore issues connected with selecting pricing objectives

To grasp the importance of identifying the target market's evaluation of price

To gain insight into demand curves and the price elasticity of demand

To examine the relationships between demand, costs and profits

To learn about how to analyse competitive prices

To understand the different types of pricing policies

To scrutinise the major kinds of pricing methods

Wedgwood china tableware and giftware is known throughout the world for its quality and premium branding. Similarly, Irish crystal producer Waterford is mentioned in the same breath as Gucci, Rolex and Rolls-Royce in North America and much of South East Asia. In 1986 Waterford acquired Wedgwood, creating a dominant force in the tableware and premium giftware market. The combined distribution and brand awareness helped strengthen both brands, particularly in much of Europe, Japan and Australia. Unfortunately, the economic climate did not favour sales of such fine but expensive ranges. Most of the group's divisions were losing money well into the 1990s, with operating profits predominantly coming from UK china tableware, Wedgwood's stronghold.

To expand their markets, major manufacturers introduced new products and designer pieces, such as crystal candlesticks and animal figurines. According to the most fashionable magazines, crystal glassware was the most desired giftware in the USA. Demand for Waterford's handcrafted crystal outstripped supply in stores such as Bloomingdale's. Nevertheless, Waterford's crystal operation was making heavy losses; thousands of workers in its Irish plants were made redundent.

With its new Marquis line, the venerable Irish crystal manufacturer has departed from its traditional practices by moving production into Europe—to Germany, Portugal and what once was Yugoslavia. Launched into the USA, Marquis by Waterford retails at around 30 per cent below traditional Waterford crystal lines, with smaller items starting at $30. Seen by some US observers as a range for "the less well heeled", Marquis—produced away from its Irish heartland and with price points significantly beneath historical levels—is a gamble for Waterford. The pricing is risky, but it aims to make Waterford crystal available to a new group of consumers; people with relatively high incomes who shop at the more exclusive china and glass emporiums or department stores. The pricing for Marquis is central to its positioning and to the fortunes of Waterford. ■

SOURCES: Waterford annual reports and accounts, 1991, 1992, 1993; Warwick University's business information service.

I n the crystal market, the economic recession has brought price points into prominence. Leader Waterford has responded with the launch of *Marquis*—a range that still carries the Waterford name but is significantly more accessible and affordable. Setting prices of products such as crystal giftware requires careful analysis of numerous issues. This chapter examines the eight stages of a process that marketers can use when setting prices.

Figure 18.1 illustrates these eight stages. Stage 1 is the development of a pricing objective that is congruent with the organisation's overall objectives and its marketing objectives. In stage 2, both the target market's evaluation of price and the ability of these consumers to buy must be assessed. Stage 3 requires marketers to determine the nature and price elasticity of demand. Stage 4, which consists of analysing demand, cost and profit relationships, is necessary for estimating the economic feasibility of alternative prices. Evaluation of competitors' prices, which constitutes stage 5, helps determine the role of price in the marketing strategy. Stage 6 is the selection of a pricing policy, or the guidelines for using price in the marketing mix. Stage 7 involves choosing a method for calculating the price charged to customers. Stage 8, the determining of the final price, depends on environmental forces and marketers' understanding and use of a systematic approach to establishing prices. These stages are not rigid steps that all marketers must follow but rather guidelines that provide a logical sequence for establishing prices. In some situations, additional stages may need to be included in the price setting process; in others, certain stages may not be necessary.

SELECTION OF PRICING OBJECTIVES (1)

Chapter 17 considered the various types of pricing objectives. Selecting pricing objectives is an important task because they form the basis for decisions about other stages of pricing. Thus pricing objectives must be explicitly stated. The statement of pricing objectives should include the time period during which the objectives are to be accomplished.

Marketers must be certain that the pricing objectives they set are consistent with the organisation's overall objectives and marketing objectives. Inconsistent objectives cause internal conflicts and confusion and can prevent the organisation from achieving its overall goals. Furthermore, pricing objectives inconsistent with organisational and

FIGURE 18.1
Stages for establishing prices

marketing objectives may cause marketers to make poor decisions during the other stages in the price setting process.

Organisations normally have multiple pricing objectives, some short term and others long term. For example, the pricing objective of gaining market share is normally short term in that it often requires the firm to price its product quite low relative to competitors' prices. An organisation should have one or more pricing objectives for each product. For the same product aimed at different market segments, marketers sometimes choose different pricing objectives. A marketer typically alters pricing objectives over time.

ASSESSING THE TARGET MARKET'S EVALUATION OF PRICE AND ITS ABILITY TO BUY (2)

Although it is generally assumed that price is a significant issue for buyers, the importance of price depends on the type of product, the type of target market and the purchase situation. For example, in general, buyers are probably more sensitive to petrol prices than to luggage prices. With respect to the type of target market, the price of an airline ticket is much more important to a tourist than to a business traveller. The purchase situation also affects the buyer's view of price. Most film goers would never pay, in other situations, the prices asked for soft drinks, popcorn, and confectionery in cinema foyers. By assessing the target market's evaluation of price, a marketer is in a better position to know how much emphasis to place on price. Information about the target market's price evaluation may also help a marketer determine how far above the competition a firm can set its prices.

As discussed in Chapter 3, the people who make up a market must have the ability to buy a product. Buyers must need a product, be willing to use their buying power and have the authority (by law or social custom) to buy. Their ability to buy, like their evaluation of price, has direct consequences for marketers. The ability to purchase involves such resources as money, credit, wealth and other products that could be traded in an exchange. Understanding customers' buying power and knowing how important a product is to them in comparison with other products helps marketers correctly assess the target market's evaluation of price.

DETERMINING DEMAND (3)

Determining the demand for a product is the responsibility of marketing managers, who are aided in this task by marketing researchers and forecasters. Marketing research and forecasting techniques yield estimates of sales potential or the quantity of a product that could be sold during a specific period. (Chapter 20 describes such techniques as surveys, time series analyses, correlation methods and market tests.) These estimates are helpful in establishing the relationship between a product's price and the quantity demanded.

The Demand Curve For most products, the quantity demanded goes up as the price goes down and goes down as the price goes up. Thus there is an inverse relationship between price and quantity demanded. As long as the marketing environment and buyers' needs, ability (purchasing power), willingness and authority to buy remain stable, this fundamental inverse relationship will continue.

Figure 18.2 illustrates the effect of one variable—price—on the quantity demanded. The classic **demand curve** (D1) is a graph of the quantity of products expected to be sold at various prices, if other factors remain constant.[1] It illustrates that as price falls, the quantity demanded usually rises. Demand depends on other factors in the marketing mix, including product quality, promotion and distribution. An improvement in any of these factors may cause a shift to, say, demand curve D2. In such a case, an increased quantity (Q2) will be sold at the same price (P).

There are many types of demand, and not all conform to the classic demand curve shown in Figure 18.2. Prestige products, such as selected perfumes and jewellery, seem to sell better at high prices than at low ones. These products are desirable partly because their cost makes buyers feel superior. If the price fell drastically and many people owned them, they would lose some of their appeal.

The demand curve in Figure 18.3 shows the relationship between price and quantity for prestige products. Demand is greater, not less, at higher prices. For a certain price range—from P1 to P2—the quantity demanded (Q1) goes up to Q2. After a point, however, raising the price backfires. If the price of a product goes too high, the quantity demanded goes down. The figure shows that if the price is raised from P2 to P3, quantity demanded goes back down from Q2 to Q1.

Demand Fluctuations

Changes in buyers' needs, variations in the effectiveness of other marketing mix variables, the presence of substitutes and dynamic environmental factors can influence demand. Restaurants and utility companies experience large fluctuations in demand daily. Toy manufacturers, fireworks suppliers, and air conditioning and heating contractors also face demand fluctuations because of the seasonal nature of these items. The demand for fax machines, single serving low calorie meals and fur coats has changed significantly over the last few years. In some cases, demand fluctuations are predictable. It is no surprise to restaurants and public utilities that demand fluctuates. However, changes in demand for other products may be less predictable, leading to problems for some companies. Marketing Insight 18.1 discusses the impact of price wars in the holiday industry. Although demand can fluctuate unpredictably, some firms have been able to anticipate changes in demand by correlating demand for a specific

FIGURE 18.2

Demand curve illustrating the price-quantity relationship and an increase in demand

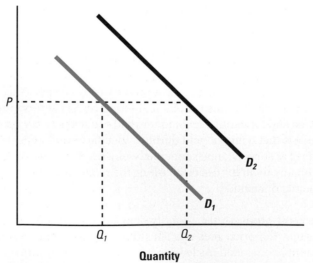

SOURCE: Reprinted from *Dictionary of Marketing Terms,* Peter D. Bennett, Ed., 1988, p. 54, published by the American Marketing Association. Used by permission.

FIGURE 18.3
*Demand curve illustrating
the relationship between
price and quantity for
prestige products*

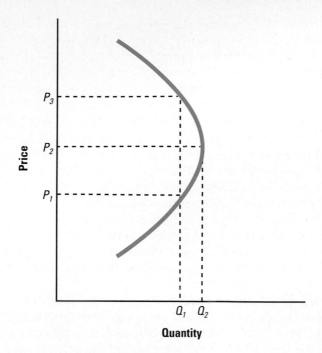

**Gauging Price
Elasticity of Demand**

product with demand for the total industry or with some other economic variable. If a brand maintains a fairly constant market share, its sales can be estimated as a percentage of industry sales.

Up to this point, the discussion has considered how marketers identify the target market's evaluation of price and its ability to purchase and how they examine demand to learn whether price is related inversely or directly to quantity. The next stage in the process is to gauge price elasticity of demand. **Price elasticity of demand** provides a measure of the sensitivity of demand to changes in price. It is formally defined as the percentage change in quantity demanded relative to a given percentage change in price[2] (see Figure 18.4). The percentage change in quantity demanded caused by a percentage change in price is much greater for elastic demand than for inelastic demand. For a product such as electricity, demand is relatively inelastic. When its price is increased, say from P1 to P2, quantity demanded goes down only a little, from Q1 to Q2. For products such as recreational vehicles, demand is relatively elastic. When price rises sharply, from P1 to P2, quantity demanded goes down a great deal, from Q1 to Q2.

If marketers can determine price elasticity of demand, it is much easier for them to set a price. By analysing total revenues as prices change, marketers can determine whether a product is "price elastic". Total revenue is price times quantity: thus 10,000 rolls of wallpaper sold in one year at a price of £10 per roll equals £100,000 of total revenue. If demand is *elastic,* a change in price causes an opposite change in total revenue—an increase in price will decrease total revenue, and a decrease in price will increase total revenue. An *inelastic* demand results in a change in the same direction in total revenue—an increase in price will increase total revenue, and a decrease in price will decrease total revenue. The following formula determines the price elasticity of demand:

$$\text{Price Elasticity of Demand} = \frac{\text{\% Change in Quantity Demanded}}{\text{\% Change in Price}}$$

HOLIDAY PRICE WARS

For television viewers throughout Europe, the winter months after Christmas throughout the 1970s and 1980s were brightened by holiday programmes and television advertisements promoting resorts, destinations, tour operators and travel agencies. As the 1980s came to a close, the market witnessed two changes. First, the promotional season began to start well before Christmas. Travel companies saw the need to compete more aggressively not only with one another but also for Christmas shoppers' disposable income. In addition, the retailers' post Christmas January sales were a significant draw on consumers' available cash. Second, the core message was no longer brochure choice or exotic destinations but price: value for money, low-cost holidays.

In the 1960s and 1970s supermarket chains and petrol forecourts had competed largely on the basis of price; they attempted little or no product or service differentiation, and their promotional campaigns emphasised only low prices. The resulting price wars sometimes led to several price reductions for the same merchandise within a working day. Motorists would travel the extra half mile to save 1 or 2 per cent on the price of a tank of petrol. Neighbouring garage forecourts would alter the advertised price of their petrol in tit-for-tat retaliations. Shoppers would visit neighbouring supermarkets to compare prices on major lines such as branded soups or breakfast cereals.

Although not as frenetic, the price wars in the holiday industry were equally fierce. Poor weather in 1992, coupled with the economic recession throughout much of Europe, made 1993 a crucial season for many travel firms. In the UK in 1992 several major operators had been forced out of business. Even Intersun, once the market leader, had ceased trading.

FIGURE 18.4
Elasticity of demand

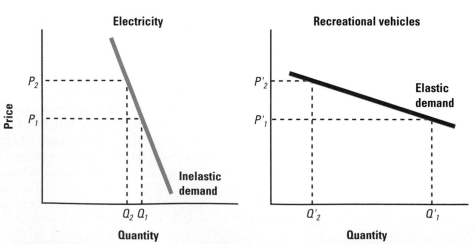

SOURCE: Reprinted from *Dictionary of Marketing Terms,* Peter D. Bennett, Ed., 1988, p. 54, published by the American Marketing Association. Used by permission.

The first shots were fired by Thomas Cook, which not only guaranteed no surcharges for its new season's holidays but reduced list prices in its brochures by 10 per cent. Leading travel agent rivals Lunn Poly and Pickford's followed suit, reducing prices. Not only the travel agencies offered reductions. Leading rival tour operators such as Thomsons and Airtours slashed their 1993 brochure prices. Europe's latest resort, EuroDisney, found itself having to offer hefty price discounts.

Industry observers were concerned that the latest price wars would harm everyone and force more companies into liquidation, as well as causing service standards for the consumer to fall as companies pared their operating costs to the bone. The independent travel agents were squeezed even more by their chain rivals, many of which were part of larger holding companies with significant funds and resources. Noel Josehides of the Association of Independent Tour Operators warned that multiples such as Lunn Poly and Pickford's were conditioning the consumer to expect constant give-aways by offering a wider range of cut price deals than ever before. Industry observers believed that several operators were selling holidays at well below cost price and that travel agents were waiving their commissions. The emphasis was on reduced prices, cash flow generation and, for many companies, short term survival.

SOURCES: Thomas Cook, Airtours, Thomson, Lunn Poly, Pickford's promotional literature, 1992–93; "Holiday discounts are 'unfair trading' ", *Marketing Week,* 22 January 1992, p. 8; Juliana Koranteng, "Travel agents unite for ad campaign", *Marketing*, 29 October 1992, p. 10.

For example, if demand falls by 8 per cent when a seller raises the price by 2 per cent, the price elasticity of demand is -4 (the negative sign indicating the inverse relationship between price and demand). If demand falls by 2 per cent when price is increased by 4 per cent, then elasticity is $-\frac{1}{2}$. The less elastic the demand, the more beneficial it is for the seller to raise the price. Products for which substitutes are not readily available and for which consumers have strong needs (for example, electricity or petrol) usually have inelastic demand.

Marketers cannot base prices solely on elasticity considerations. They must also examine the costs associated with different volumes and see what happens to profits.

ANALYSIS OF DEMAND, COST AND PROFIT RELATIONSHIPS (4)

The last section examined the role of demand in setting prices and the various costs and their relationships; this section explores the relationships between demand, cost and profit. There are two approaches to understanding demand, cost and profit relationships: marginal analysis and break even analysis.

Marginal Analysis

Marginal analysis is the examination of what happens to a firm's costs and revenues when production (or sales volume) is changed by one unit. Both production costs and revenues must be evaluated. To determine the costs of production, it is necessary to distinguish between several types of costs. **Fixed costs** do not vary with changes in the number of units produced or sold. The cost of renting a factory does not change because production increases from one shift to two shifts a day, or because twice as much wallpaper is sold. Rent may go up, but not because the factory has doubled production or revenue. **Average fixed cost,** the fixed cost per unit produced, is calculated by dividing fixed costs by the number of units produced.

Variable costs vary directly with changes in the number of units produced or sold. The wages for a second shift and the cost of twice as much paper are extra costs that occur when production is doubled. Variable costs are usually constant per unit; that is, twice as many workers and twice as much material produce twice as many rolls of wallpaper. **Average variable cost,** the variable cost per unit produced, is calculated by dividing the variable costs by the number of units produced.

Total cost is the sum of average fixed costs and average variable costs multiplied by the quantity produced. The **average total cost** is the sum of the average fixed cost and the average variable cost. **Marginal cost (MC)** is the extra cost a firm incurs when it produces one more unit of a product. Table 18.1 illustrates various costs and their relationships. Notice that the average fixed cost declines as the output increases. The average variable cost follows a U shape, as does the average total cost. Because the average total cost continues to fall after the average variable cost begins to rise, its lowest point is at a higher level of output than that of the average variable cost. The average total cost is lowest at 5 units at a cost of £22, whereas the average variable cost is lowest at 3 units at a cost of £11.67. As shown in Figure 18.5, marginal cost equals average total cost at the latter's lowest level, between 5 and 6 units of production. In Table 18.1 this occurs between 5 and 6 units of production. Average total cost decreases as long as the marginal cost is less than the average total cost, and it increases when marginal cost rises above average total cost.

Marginal revenue (MR) is the change in total revenue that occurs when a firm sells an additional unit of a product. Figure 18.6 depicts marginal revenue and a demand curve. Most firms in Europe face downward sloping demand curves for their products. In other words, they must lower their prices to sell additional units. This sit-

TABLE 18.1 *Costs and their relationships*

1	2	3	4	5	6	7
		AVERAGE	AVERAGE	AVERAGE	TOTAL	
	FIXED	FIXED COST	VARIABLE	TOTAL COST	COST	
QUANTITY	COST	(2) ÷ (1)	COST	(3) + (4)	(5) × (1)	MARGINAL COST
1	£40	£40.00	£20.00	£60.00	£60	£10
2	40	20.00	15.00	35.00	70	5
3	40	13.33	11.67	25.00	75	15
4	40	10.00	12.50	22.50	90	20
5	40	8.00	14.00	22.00	110	30
6	40	6.67	16.67	23.33	140	40
7	40	5.71	20.00	25.71	180	

FIGURE 18.5
Typical marginal cost and average cost relationships

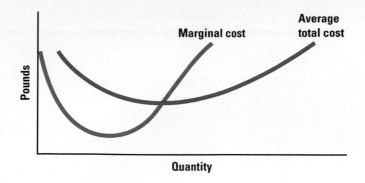

FIGURE 18.6
Typical marginal revenue and average revenue relationships

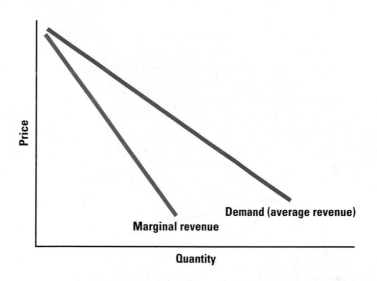

uation means that each additional product sold provides the firm with less revenue than the previous unit sold. MR then becomes less than average revenue, as Figure 18.6 shows. Eventually, MR reaches zero, and the sale of additional units merely hurts the firm.

However, before the firm can determine whether a unit makes a profit, it must know its cost, as well as its revenue, because profit equals revenue minus cost. If MR is a unit's addition to revenue and MC is a unit's addition to cost, then MR minus MC tells whether the unit is profitable or not. Table 18.2 illustrates the relationships between price, quantity sold, total revenue, marginal revenue, marginal cost and total cost. It indicates where maximum profits are possible at various combinations of price and cost.

Profit is maximised where MC = MR (see Table 18.2). In this table MC = MR at 4 units. The best price is £33.75 and the profit is £45. Up to this point, the additional revenue generated from an extra unit of sale exceeds the additional total cost. Beyond this point, the additional cost of another unit sold exceeds the additional revenue generated, and profits decrease. If the price was based on minimum average total cost—£22 (Table 18.1)—it would result in less profit: only £40 (Table 18.2) or 5 units at a price of £30 versus £45 for 4 units at a price of £33.75.

Graphically combining Figures 18.5 and 18.6 into Figure 18.7 shows that any unit for which MR exceeds MC adds to a firm's profits, and any unit for which MC exceeds MR subtracts from a firm's profits. The firm should produce at the point where MR equals MC, because this is the most profitable level of production.

TABLE 18.2 *Marginal analysis: method of obtaining maximum profit-producing price*

1 PRICE	2 QUANTITY SOLD	3 TOTAL REVENUE (1) X (2)	4 MARGINAL REVENUE	5 MARGINAL COST	6 TOTAL COST	7 PROFIT (3) – (6)
£57.00	1	£ 57	£57	£—	£ 60	£– 3
55.00	2	110	53	10	70	40
40.00	3	120	10	5	75	45
33.75ᵃ	**4**	**135**	**15**	**15**	**90**	**45**
30.00	5	150	15	20	110	40
27.00	6	162	12	30	140	22
25.00	7	175	13	40	180	–5

ᵃBoldface indicates best price-profit combination.

FIGURE 18.7
Combining the marginal cost and marginal revenue concepts for optimal profit

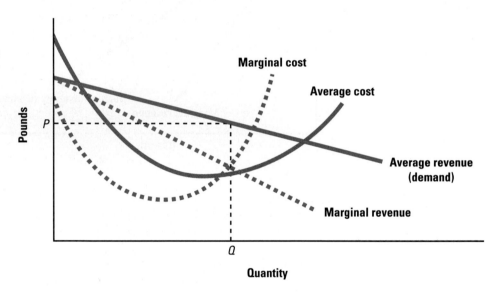

This discussion of marginal analysis may give the false impression that pricing can be highly precise. If revenue (demand) and cost (supply) remained constant, then prices could be set for maximum profits. In practice, however, cost and revenue change frequently. The competitive tactics of other firms or government action can quickly undermine a company's expectations of revenue. Thus marginal analysis is only a model from which to work. It offers little help in pricing new products before costs and revenues are established. On the other hand, in setting prices of existing products, especially in competitive situations, most marketers can benefit by understanding the relationship between marginal cost and marginal revenue.

Break Even Analysis

The point at which the costs of producing a product equal the revenue made from selling the product is the **break even point.** If a wallpaper manufacturer has total annual

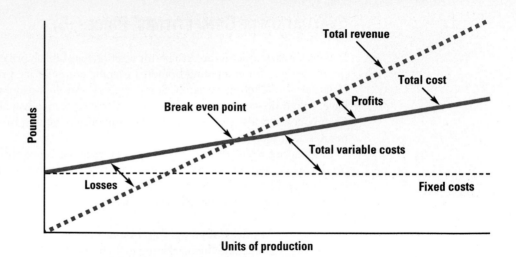

FIGURE 18.8
Determining the break even point

costs of £100,000 and in the same year it sells £100,000 worth of wallpaper, then the company has broken even: no profits, no losses.

Figure 18.8 illustrates the relationships of costs, revenue, profits and losses involved in determining the break even point. Knowing the number of units necessary to break even is important in setting the price. If a product priced at £100 per unit has an average variable cost of £60 per unit, then the contribution to fixed costs is £40. If total fixed costs are £120,000, here is the way to determine the break even point in units:

$$\text{Break even Point} = \frac{\text{Fixed Costs}}{\text{Per Unit Contribution to Fixed Costs}}$$

$$= \frac{\text{Fixed Costs}}{\text{Price-Variable Costs}}$$

$$= \frac{£120,000}{£40}$$

$$= 3,000 \text{ Units}$$

To calculate the break even point in terms of cash sales volume, multiply the break even point in units by the price per unit. In the preceding example, the break even point in terms of cash sales volume is 3,000 (units) times £100, or £300,000.

To use break even analysis effectively, a marketer should determine the break even point for each of several alternative prices. This determination allows the marketer to compare the effects on total revenue, total costs and the break even point for each price under consideration. Although this comparative analysis may not tell the marketer exactly what price to charge, it will identify highly undesirable price alternatives that should definitely be avoided.

Break even analysis is simple and straightforward. It does assume, however, that the quantity demanded is basically fixed (inelastic) and that the major task in setting prices is to recover costs. It focuses more on how to break even than on how to achieve a pricing objective, such as percentage of market share or return on investment. None the less, marketing managers can use this concept to determine whether a product will achieve at least a break even volume. In other words, it is easier to answer the question "Will we sell at least the minimum volume necessary to break even?" than the question "What volume of sales will we expect to sell?"

EVALUATION OF COMPETITORS' PRICES (5)

In most cases, marketers are in a better position to establish prices when they know the prices charged for competing brands. Learning competitors' prices may be a regular function of marketing research. Some grocery and department stores, for example, have full time comparative shoppers who systematically collect data on prices. Companies may also purchase price lists, sometimes weekly, from syndicated marketing research agencies.

Finding out what prices competitors are charging is not always easy, especially in producer and reseller markets. Competitors' price lists are often closely guarded. Even if a marketer has access to price lists, they may not reflect the actual prices at which competitive products are sold because those prices may be established through negotiation.

Knowing the prices of competing brands can be very important for a marketer. Competitors' prices and the marketing mix variables that they emphasise partly determine how important price will be to customers. Marketers in an industry in which nonprice competition prevails need competitive price information to ensure that their organisation's prices are the same as its competitors' prices. In some instances, an organisation's prices are designed to be slightly above competitors' prices to give its products an exclusive image. Alternatively, another company may use price as a competitive tool and attempt to price its product below those of competitors. Toys "Я" Us and Superdrug, for example, have each acquired a large market share through aggressive competitive prices.

SELECTION OF A PRICING POLICY (6)

A **pricing policy** is a guiding philosophy or course of action designed to influence and determine pricing decisions. Pricing policies set guidelines for achieving pricing objectives. They are an important component of an overall marketing strategy. Generally, pricing policies should answer this recurring question: "How will price be used as a variable in the marketing mix?" This question may relate to (1) introduction of new products, (2) competitive situations, (3) government pricing regulations, (4) economic conditions or (5) implementation of pricing objectives. Pricing policies help marketers solve the practical problems of establishing prices. This section examines the most common pricing policies.

Pioneer Pricing Policies

Pioneer pricing—setting the base price for a new product—is a necessary part of formulating a marketing strategy. The base price is easily adjusted (in the absence of government price controls), and its establishment is one of the most fundamental decisions in the marketing mix. The base price can be set high to recover development costs quickly or to provide a reference point for developing discount prices to different market segments.

When marketers set base prices, they also consider how quickly competitors will enter the market, whether they will mount a strong campaign on entry, and what effect their entry will have on the development of primary demand. If competitors will enter quickly with considerable marketing force and with limited effect on the primary demand, a firm may adopt a base price that will discourage their entry.

Price Skimming. **Price skimming** is charging the highest possible price that buyers who most desire the product will pay. This pioneer approach provides the most flexible introductory base price. Demand tends to be inelastic in the introductory stage of the product life-cycle (for example, the compact disc player and the pocket calculator).

Price skimming can provide several benefits, especially when a product is in the introductory stage of its life-cycle. A skimming policy can generate much needed initial cash flows to help offset sizeable developmental costs. When introducing a new model of camera, Polaroid initially uses a skimming price to defray large research and development costs. Price skimming protects the marketer from problems that arise when the price is set too low to cover costs. When a firm introduces a product, its production capacity may be limited. A skimming price can help keep demand consistent with a firm's production capabilities. The use of a skimming price may attract competition into an industry because the high price makes that type of business appear to be quite lucrative.

Penetration Price.   A **penetration price** is a price set below the prices of competing brands in order to penetrate a market and produce a larger unit sales volume. When introducing a product, a marketer sometimes uses a penetration price to gain a large market share quickly. As shown in Figure 18.9, Lufthansa's campaign stresses its "best price guarantee" low cost flights. This approach places the marketer in a less flexible position than price skimming because it is more difficult to raise a penetration price than to lower or discount a skimming price. It is not unusual for a firm to use a penetration price after having skimmed the market with a higher price.

FIGURE 18.9
Psychological pricing
Lufthansa's "best price guarantee" hopes to persuade potential flyers that the German airline offers highly competitive rates and value for money.

SOURCE: Photo courtesy of Lufthansa German Airlines.

Penetration pricing can be especially beneficial when marketers suspect that competitors could enter the market easily. First, if the penetration price lets one marketer gain a large market share quickly, competitors might be discouraged from entering the market. Second, entering the market may be less attractive to competitors when a penetration price is used, because the lower per unit price results in lower per unit profit; this may cause competitors to view the market as not being especially lucrative.

A penetration price is particularly appropriate when demand is highly elastic. Highly elastic demand means that target market members would purchase the product if it was priced at the penetration level but that few would buy the item if it was priced higher. A marketer should consider using a penetration price when a lower price would result in longer production runs, increasing production significantly and reducing the firm's per unit production costs.

Psychological Pricing

Psychological pricing encourages purchases based on emotional rather than rational responses. It is used most often at the retail level. Psychological pricing has limited use for industrial products.

Odd-Even Pricing. Through **odd-even pricing**—that is, ending the price with certain numbers—marketers try to influence buyers' perceptions of the price or the product. Odd pricing assumes that more of a product will be sold at £99.95 than at £100. Supposedly, customers will think, or at least tell friends, that the product is a bargain—not £100, mind you, but £99, plus a few insignificant pence. Also, customers are supposed to think that the store could have charged £100 but instead cut the price to the last penny or so, to £99.95. Some claim, too, that certain types of customers are more attracted by odd prices than by even ones. However, no substantial research findings support the notion that odd prices produce greater sales. None the less, even prices are far more unusual today than odd prices.

Even prices are used to give a product an exclusive or up market image. An even price supposedly will influence a customer to view the product as being a high quality, premium brand. A tie manufacturer, for example, may print on a premium silk tie packet a suggested retail price of £32 instead of £31.95; the even price of the shirt is used to enhance its up market image.

Customary Pricing. In **customary pricing,** certain goods are priced primarily on the basis of tradition. Recent economic uncertainties have made most prices fluctuate fairly widely, but the classic example of the customary, or traditional, price is the telephone call. Until the mid-1980s, UK public telephones were geared to the use of particular coins. For years the 2 pence and, later, the 10 pence slots were widely recognised. BT's initial response to rising prices was to alter the cost of units so that less call time was allowed for the same money. Since then, demands for greater flexibility of use have seen public call-boxes altered to accept most British coins.

Prestige Pricing. In **prestige pricing,** prices are set at an artificially high level to provide prestige or a quality image. In the United States, pharmacists report that some consumers complain if a prescription does not cost enough. Apparently, some consumers associate a drug's price with its potency. Consumers in Europe often associate the quality of service provided by a hairdresser with price. In some cases, this is demonstrated by a willingness to pay more than twice as much for a perm at an establishment like Vidal Sassoon than at the local hairdresser, even though the treatment given may be comparable.

Prestige pricing is used especially when buyers associate a higher price with higher quality. Typical product categories in which selected products are given prestige prices include perfumes, cars, alcoholic beverages, jewellery and electrical appliances. Dramatically lowering the prices of products with prestige prices would be inconsistent with the perceived images of such products.

Price Lining. When an organisation sets a limited number of prices for selected groups or lines of merchandise, it is using **price lining.** A retailer may have various styles and brands of men's shirts of similar quality that sell for £10. Another line of higher quality shirts may sell for £20. Price lining simplifies consumers' decision-making by holding constant one key variable in the final selection of style and brand within a line. In product line pricing, the company should look at the prices of the overall product line to ensure that the price of the new model lies within the range of existing prices for that line. Failure to consider the impact of the new model's price relative to the existing product line may change buyers' perceptions of all the models in the line.[3]

The basic assumption in price lining is that the demand is inelastic for various groups or sets of products. If the prices are attractive, customers will concentrate their purchases without responding to slight changes in price. Thus a women's dress shop that carries dresses priced at £85, £55 and £35 might not attract many more sales with a drop to, say, £83, £53 and £33. The "space" between the prices of £55 and £35, however, can stir changes in consumer response. With price lining, the demand curve looks like a series of steps, as shown in Figure 18.10.

Professional Pricing

Professional pricing is used by people who have great skill or experience in a particular field or activity. Some professionals who provide such products as medical services feel that their fees (prices) should not relate directly to their time and involvement in specific cases; rather, they charge a standard fee regardless of the problems involved in performing the job. Some estate agents' and solicitors' fees are prime examples: 2 per cent of a house sale price, plus VAT, and £300 for house conveyancing. Other professionals set prices in other ways.

The concept of professional pricing carries with it the idea that professionals have an ethical responsibility not to over charge unknowing customers. In some situations, a seller can charge customers a high price and continue to sell many units of the product. Medicine offers several examples. If a patient with high blood pressure requires four tablets a day to survive, the individual will pay for the prescription whether it costs £3 or £30 per month. In fact, the patient would purchase the pills even if the price went higher. In these situations sellers could charge exorbitant fees. Drug companies claim that despite their positions of strength in this regard, they charge "ethical" prices rather than what the market will bear. In 1989 Burroughs-Wellcome reduced the price of its AIDS drug AZT by 20 per cent, partly in response to pressure from AIDS patients and activists. However, some feel that the annual price tag for AZT treatments is still far too high.[4]

Promotional Pricing

Price is an ingredient in the marketing mix, and it is often co-ordinated with promotion. The two variables sometimes are so interrelated that the pricing policy is promotion orientated. Examples of promotional pricing include price leaders, special event pricing and experience curve pricing.

Price Leaders. Sometimes a firm prices a few products below the usual mark-up, near cost, or below cost, which results in prices known as **price leaders.** This type of pricing is used most often in supermarkets and department stores to attract consumers by giving them special low prices on a few items. Management hopes that sales of regularly priced merchandise will more than offset the reduced revenue from the price leaders.

FIGURE 18.10
Price lining

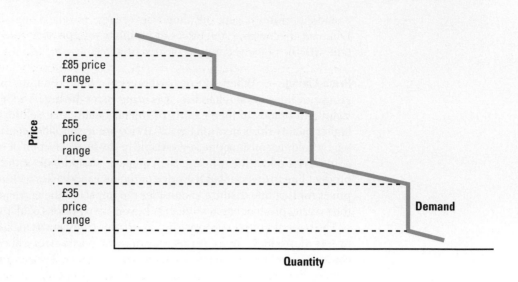

Special Event Pricing. To increase sales volume, many organisations co-ordinate price with advertising or sales promotion for seasonal or special situations. **Special event pricing** involves advertised sales or price cutting that is linked to a holiday, season or event. As shown in Figure 18.11, many companies, such as Cadbury's, organise sales which are linked to bank holidays, for example. If the pricing objective is survival, special sales events may be designed to generate the necessary operating capital. Special event pricing also entails co-ordination of production, scheduling, storage and physical distribution. Whenever there is a sales lag, special event pricing is an alternative that marketers should consider.

FIGURE 18.11
Special event pricing
Cadbury's tied in with doorstep milk deliveries with this special pricing campaign for Easter eggs.

SOURCE: Cadbury Limited.

| **Misleading Prices** | The UK Consumer Protection Act (1987) contains a code of practice intended to give advice on **misleading prices.** The act makes it illegal to mislead customers about the price at which products or services are offered for sale. However, the code—which is not legally binding—encourages companies to offer explanations whenever price comparisons or reductions are made. According to the *Which?* handbook of consumer law, "Unexplained reductions from a store's own prices should be used only if the goods have been on sale at the same store for 28 days in the preceding six months, and if the price quoted was the last price at which the goods were on sale.[5] |

| **Experience Curve Pricing** | In **experience curve pricing,** a company fixes a low price that high cost competitors cannot match and thus expands its market share. This practice is possible when a firm gains cumulative production experience and is able to reduce its manufacturing costs at a predictable rate through improved methods, materials, skills and machinery. Texas Instruments used this strategy in marketing its calculators. As described in Marketing Insight 18.2, many suppliers—and buyers—of faxes are now benefiting from tumbling prices. The experience curve depicts the inverse relationship between production costs per unit and cumulative production quantity. To take advantage of the experience curve, a company must gain a dominant market share early in a product's life-cycle. An early market share lead, with the greater cumulative production experience that it implies, will place a company further down the experience curve than its competitors. |

DEVELOPMENT OF A PRICING METHOD (7)

After selecting a pricing policy, a marketer must choose a **pricing method,** a mechanical procedure for setting prices on a regular basis. The pricing method structures the calculation of the actual price. The nature of a product, its sales volume or the amount of product the organisation carries will determine how prices are calculated. For example, a procedure for pricing the thousands of products in a supermarket must be simpler and more direct than that for calculating the price of a new earthmoving machine manufactured by Caterpillar. This section examines three market orientated pricing methods: cost orientated, demand orientated and competition orientated pricing.

| **Cost Orientated Pricing** | In **cost orientated pricing,** a monetary amount or percentage is added to the cost of a product. The method thus involves calculations of desired margins or profit margins. Cost orientated pricing methods do not necessarily take into account the economic aspects of supply and demand, nor do they necessarily relate to a specific pricing policy or ensure the attainment of pricing objectives. They are, however, simple and easy to implement. Two common cost orientated pricing methods are cost plus and mark up pricing. |

Cost Plus Pricing.   In **cost plus pricing,** the seller's costs are determined (usually during a project or after a project is completed), and the price is then set by adding a specified amount or percentage of the cost to the seller's cost. Cost plus pricing is appropriate when production costs are difficult to predict or production takes a long time. Custom made equipment and commercial construction projects are often priced by this method. The government frequently uses cost orientated pricing in granting defence contracts. One pitfall for the buyer is that the seller may increase costs to establish a larger profit base. Furthermore, some costs, such as overheads, may be difficult to determine.

MARKETING INSIGHT 18.2

FAXES IN THE HOME AS PRICES TUMBLE

Businesses are experiencing a general fax frenzy. Customers are faxing orders to restaurants, architects are faxing tentative plans to their offices and freelance artists are faxing designs everywhere. Fax machines were initially available from office supplies and telecommunications dealers; today, however, many high street retailers, for example, Dixons, sell a range of fax machines, starting at below £300. In 1992, £92 million worth of fax machines were sold in the UK and G160=-million worth in the Netherlands; over one million machines are now in use in both countries. Even BT is screening television advertisements pitched to domestic users, with the aim of increasing fax ownership and use. Canon and NEC lead the market, each with a 25 per cent share by volume. Worldwide industry leaders Sharp, Canon, Xerox and Murata achieve strength by producing relatively inexpensive machines that appeal to small and medium sized businesses.

The purchase of fax machines actually saves money for smaller companies by reducing the need for express mail service and messengers. Business analysts expect sales of fax machines to increase dramatically in the future as more and more individuals start working from home. These workers are most likely to be attracted to basic, "low end" machines costing less than £400.

Xerox created the first commercial fax machine in 1970, but it was Sharp and Murata that produced the earliest no frills models. With a continually growing list of competitors in the low priced part of the market, including price driven Amstrad, both Sharp and Murata are investing heavily in research and development to solidify their positions as industry leaders. South Korean fax machine manufacturers such as Samsung and Daewoo might pose a challenge to established companies. Analysts expect these Korean firms to drive the price of fax machines down to about £200.

Based on information in Jeffrey H. Epstein, "The future in fax", *Direct Marketing,* March 1989, pp. 28, 30; Sherli Evans, "Fax: looking fine in '89", *Industry Week,* 15 May 1989, pp. BC3-BC4, BC6-BC7; Frederick H. Katayama, "Who's fueling the fax frenzy", *Fortune,* 23 October 1989, pp. 151–2, 156; and HARVEST, *Trade Estimates/Market Assessment,* 1990, 42221438.

In periods of rapid inflation, cost plus pricing is popular, especially when the producer must use raw materials that are fluctuating in price. For industries in which cost plus pricing is common and sellers have similar costs, price competition may not be especially intense.

Mark up Pricing.   A common pricing method among retailers is **mark up pricing.** In mark up pricing, a product's price is derived by adding a predetermined percentage of the cost, called *mark up,* to the cost of the product. Although the percentage mark up in a retail store varies from one category of goods to another (35 per cent of cost for hardware items and 100 per cent of cost for greeting cards, for example), the same percentage is often used to determine the price of items within a single product category, and the same or similar percentage mark up may be standardised across an industry at the retail level. Using a rigid percentage mark up for a specific product category reduces pricing to a routine task that can be performed quickly.

Mark up can be stated as a percentage of the cost or as a percentage of the selling price. The following example illustrates how percentage mark ups are determined and points out the differences between the two methods. Assume that a retailer purchases a tin of tuna at 45 pence, adds 15 pence to the cost, and then prices the tuna at 60 pence. Here are the figures:

$$\text{Mark up as a Percentage of Cost} = \frac{\text{Mark up}}{\text{Cost}}$$

$$\text{Mark up as a Percentage of Selling Price} = \frac{\text{Mark up}}{\text{Selling Price}}$$

$$= \frac{15}{60}$$

$$= 25.0\%$$

Obviously, when discussing a percentage mark up, it is important to know whether the mark up is based on cost or selling price.

Mark ups normally reflect expectations about operating costs, risks and stock turnovers. Wholesalers and manufacturers often suggest standard retail mark ups that are considered profitable. An average percentage mark up on cost may be as high as 100 per cent or more for jewellery or as low as 20 per cent for this textbook. To the extent that retailers use similar mark ups for the same product category, price competition is reduced. In addition, using rigid mark ups is a convenient method for retailers who face numerous pricing decisions.

Demand Orientated Pricing

Rather than basing the price of a product on its cost, marketers sometimes use a pricing method based on the level of demand for the product: **demand orientated pricing.** This method results in a high price when demand for the product is strong and a low price when demand is weak. Admission to night clubs often operates on this basis, with higher prices when demand is highest, on Friday nights and at weekends. To use this method, a marketer must be able to estimate the amounts of a product that consumers will demand at different prices. The marketer then chooses the price that generates the highest total revenue. Obviously, the effectiveness of this method depends on the marketer's ability to estimate demand accurately.

A marketer may favour a demand orientated pricing method called **price differentiation** when the firm wants to use more than one price in the marketing of a specific product. Price differentiation can be based on such considerations as type of customer, type of distribution channel used or the time of the purchase. Here are several examples. A 12 ounce can of soft drink costs less from a supermarket than from a vending machine. London hotel accommodation is more expensive in the summer than in the winter. Christmas tree ornaments and cards are usually cheaper on 27 December than on 16 December. Some hotels offer special "weekender" prices (see Figure 18.12).

For price differentiation to work properly, the marketer must be able to segment a market on the basis of different strengths of demand and then keep the segments separate enough so that segment members who buy at lower prices cannot then sell to buyers in segments that are charged a higher price. This isolation could be accomplished, for example, by selling to geographically separated segments.

FIGURE 18.12
Price differentiation
Many hotels offer special reduced "weekender" prices to stimulate demand.

SOURCE: © Inter-Continental Hotels Group Ltd.

Price differentiation is often facilitated in international marketing by the geographic distance between markets. For example, the price Matsushita Electric Co. charges for cordless Panasonic telephones in Japan is eight times the price charged for cordless telephones of slightly lower quality in the United States. When a Japanese trading company reimported the US cordless phones and sold them for $80 instead of the Japanese model, which cost $657, consumers lined up to buy the cheaper telephone. To combat the reimportation, Matsushita bought up all the unsold, made for export Panasonic telephones it could find to eliminate the wide price differential. (The major difference between the telephones was that the US telephone had a range of 40 metres (130 feet) and the Japanese telephone had a range of 50 metres (165 feet), which is surprising, because the average Japanese home is much smaller than the average US home.[6]

Price differentiation can also be based on employment in a public service position. For example, many bookshops offer a 15 per cent discount to teachers.

Compared with cost orientated pricing, demand orientated pricing places a firm in a better position to reach higher profit levels, assuming that buyers value the product at levels sufficiently above its actual cost. To use demand orientated pricing, however, a marketer must be able to estimate demand at different price levels, which is often difficult to do accurately.

Competition Orientated Pricing

In using **competition orientated pricing,** an organisation considers costs and revenue to be secondary to competitors' prices. The importance of this method increases if competing products are almost homogeneous and the organisation is serving markets in which price is the key variable of the marketing strategy. A firm that uses competition orientated pricing may choose to be below competitors' prices, above competitors' prices or at the same level. The price of this textbook paid by the bookshop to the publishing company was determined using competition orientated pricing. Competition orientated pricing should help attain a pricing objective to increase sales or market share. Competition orientated pricing methods may be combined with cost approaches to arrive at price levels necessary for a profit.

DETERMINING A SPECIFIC PRICE (8)

Pricing policies and methods should direct and structure the selection of a final price. If they are to do so, it is important for marketers to establish pricing objectives, to know something about the target market and to determine demand, price elasticity, costs and competitive factors. In addition to those economic factors, the manner in which pricing is used in the marketing mix will affect the final price.

Although a systematic approach to pricing is suggested here, in practice prices are often finalised after only limited planning; or they may be set without planning, just by trial and error. Marketers then determine whether the revenue minus costs yields a profit. This approach to pricing is not recommended, because it makes it difficult to discover pricing errors. If prices are based on both unrealistic pricing methods and unrealistic sales forecasts, a firm may resort to price gimmickry to sell its products. This approach should be avoided because it can become permanent. The car industry is a current example of how pricing incentives, such as discounts, cheap credit facilities and trade-in deals, can become an essential and permanent part of pricing.

In the absence of government price controls, pricing remains a flexible and convenient way to adjust the marketing mix. In most situations, prices can be adjusted quickly—in a matter of minutes or over a few days. This flexibility and freedom do not characterise the other components of the marketing mix. Because so many complex issues are involved in establishing the right price, pricing is indeed as much an art as a science.

SUMMARY

The eight stages in the process of establishing prices are as follows: (1) selecting pricing objectives; (2) assessing the target market's evaluation of price and its ability to purchase; (3) determining demand; (4) analysing demand, cost and profit relationships; (5) analysing competitors' prices; (6) selecting a pricing policy; (7) developing a pricing method; and (8) determining a specific price.

The first stage, setting pricing objectives, is critical because pricing objectives form a foundation on which the decisions of subsequent stages are based. Organisations may use numerous pricing objectives: short term and long term ones, and different ones for different products and market segments.

The second stage in establishing prices is an assessment of the target market's evaluation of price and its ability to purchase. This stage tells a marketer how much emphasis to place on price and may help the marketer determine how far above the competition the firm can set its prices. Understanding customers' buying power and knowing how important a product is to the customers in comparison with other products helps marketers correctly assess the target market's evaluation of price.

In the third stage, the organisation must determine the demand for its product. The classic demand curve is a graph of the quantity of products expected to be sold at various prices, if other factors are held constant. It illustrates that, as price falls, the quantity demanded usually increases. However, for prestige products, there is a direct positive relationship between price and quantity demanded: demand increases as price increases. Next, price elasticity of demand—the percentage change in quantity demanded relative to a given percentage change in price—must be determined. If demand is elastic, a change in price causes an opposite change in total revenue. Inelastic demand results in parallel change in total revenue when a product's price is changed.

Analysis of demand, cost and profit relationships—the fourth stage of the process—can be accomplished through marginal analysis or break-even analysis. Marginal analysis is the examination of what happens to a firm's costs and revenues when production (or sales volume) is changed by one unit. Marginal analysis combines the demand curve with a firm's costs to develop an optimum price for maximum profit. Fixed costs do not vary with changes in the number of units produced or sold; average fixed cost is the fixed cost per unit produced. Variable costs vary directly with changes in the number of units produced or sold. Average variable cost is the variable cost per unit produced. Average total cost is the sum of the average fixed cost and average variable cost times the quantity produced. The optimum price is the point at which marginal cost (the cost associated with producing one more unit of the product) equals marginal revenue (the change in total revenue that occurs when one additional unit of the product is sold). Marginal analysis is only a model; it offers little help in pricing new products before costs and revenues are established.

Break even analysis—determining the number of units necessary to break even— is important in setting the price. The point at which the costs of production equal the revenue made from selling the product is the break even point. To use break even analysis effectively, a marketer should determine the break even point for each of several alternative prices. This determination makes it possible to compare the effects on total revenue, total costs and the break even point for each price under consideration. However, this approach assumes that the quantity demanded is basically fixed and that the major task is to set prices to recover costs.

A marketer needs to be aware of the prices charged for competing brands. This awareness allows a firm to keep its prices the same as competitors' prices when non-price competition is used. If a company uses price as a competitive tool, it can price its brand below competing brands.

A pricing policy is a guiding philosophy or course of action designed to influence and determine pricing decisions. Pricing policies help marketers solve the practical problems of establishing prices. Two types of pioneer pricing policies are price skimming and penetration pricing. With price skimming, an organisation charges the highest price that buyers who most desire the product will pay. A penetration price is a lower price designed to penetrate the market and produce a larger unit sales volume. Another pricing policy, psychological pricing, encourages purchases that are based on emotional rather than rational responses. It includes odd-even pricing, customary pricing, prestige pricing and price lining. A third pricing policy, professional pricing, is used by people who have great skill or experience in a particular field. Promotional pricing, in which price is co-ordinated with promotion, is another type of pricing policy. Price leaders and special event pricing are examples of promotional pricing. Experience curve pricing fixes a low price that high cost competitors cannot match.

Experience curve pricing is possible when experience reduces manufacturing costs at a predictable rate.

A pricing method is a mechanical procedure for assigning prices to specific products on a regular basis. Three types of pricing methods are cost orientated, demand orientated and competition orientated pricing. In using cost orientated pricing, a firm determines price by adding a monetary amount or percentage to the cost of the product. Two common cost orientated pricing methods are cost plus and mark up pricing. Demand orientated pricing is based on the level of demand for the product. To use this method, a marketer must be able to estimate the amounts of a product that buyers will demand at different prices. Demand orientated pricing results in a high price when demand for a product is strong and a low price when demand is weak. In the case of competition orientated pricing, costs and revenues are secondary to competitors' prices. Competition orientated pricing and cost approaches may be combined to arrive at price levels necessary to generate a profit.

IMPORTANT TERMS

Demand curve	Customary pricing
Price elasticity of demand	Prestige pricing
Fixed costs	Price lining
Average fixed cost	Professional pricing
Variable costs	Price leaders
Average variable cost	Special event pricing
Total cost	Misleading prices
Average total cost	Experience curve pricing
Marginal Cost (MC)	Pricing method
Marginal revenue (MR)	Cost orientated pricing
Break even point	Cost plus pricing
Pricing policy	Mark up pricing
Price skimming	Demand orientated pricing
Penetration price	Price differentiation
Psychological pricing	Competition orientated pricing
Odd-even pricing	

DISCUSSION AND REVIEW QUESTIONS

1. Identify the eight stages that make up the process of establishing prices.
2. Why do most demand curves demonstrate an inverse relationship between price and quantity?
3. List the characteristics of products that have inelastic demand. Give several examples of such products.
4. Explain why optimum profits should occur when marginal cost equals marginal revenue.
5. The Chambers Company has just gathered estimates in preparation for a break even analysis for a new product. Variable costs are £7 a unit. The additional plant will cost £48,000. The new product will be charged £18,000 a year for its share of general overheads. Advertising expenditure will be £80,000, and £55,000 will be spent on distribution. If the product sells for £12, what is the break even point in units? What is the break even point in sales volume?

6. Why should a marketer be aware of competitors' prices?
7. For what type of products would a pioneer price skimming policy be most appropriate? For what type of products would penetration pricing be more effective?
8. Why do consumers associate price with quality? When should prestige pricing be used?

■ CASES

18.1 Budget Hotels — a Burgeoning Sector

In common with most of Europe, until recently the hotel industry in the UK had been dominated by two extremes: small, privately owned, no-frills hotels aimed at sales representatives travelling on tight budgets and families seeking low cost accommodation for their summer holidays; and larger hotel groups operating chains of mid and up market hotels. In the last few years, however, there have been several fundamental changes. Many operators are truly international and own properties in many countries. Hotel groups geared to the business market have invested heavily in conference and meeting facilities. France, the UK and Germany have seen the growth of deluxe, small, rural country house hotels. Perhaps one of the most significant developments, however, has been the expansion of chains of low cost, well appointed motorway lodges. Typically of AA two star standard, with en suite bedrooms but limited catering facilities and no leisure amenities, these hotels have sprung up close to most major settlements and motorway intersections.

The small, privately owned hotels offer basic accommodation at around £20 per night with few extra facilities or amenities. The larger hotels in most town and city centres, such as the three and four star hotels owned by Forte, Queens Moat Houses, Mount Charlotte, Hilton or Holiday Inn, offer more in-room amenities plus leisure and conference facilities, but at prices from £70 to £120 per night. In the 1980s several operators identified a niche in the market between the cheaper private hotels and the more expensive branded chains: a budget conscious segment which, though price driven, requires convenient, safe locations, clean, comfortable bedrooms with television and bathroom, and somewhere close at hand for a bite to eat.

Most of the major hotel groups have entered this market, led by Forte's Travelodge chain, which now has close to 140 locations in the UK and properties in key business locations in Europe. Travelodge provides comfortable bedrooms, easy access and the reassurance of a major brand, but without any extras such as a fitness centre or business services. Indeed, the chain has no restaurants, instead, each site is shared by one of Forte's diner chains, Happy Eater or Little Chef. A room at the Travelodge—"little luxuries, little prices"—costs just over £30 per night, irrespective of whether it is occupied by one person or a family of four. Granada Lodges and Sleep Inns are similarly targeted.

Marriott (Courtyard by Marriott) and Holiday Inn (Garden Court) have also entered this budget conscious arena, but with slightly higher pricing and more facilities. Still pitched beneath Holiday Inns or Hiltons, the Garden Courts are "competitively priced three star hotels featuring all the benefits of luxury accommodation but without the extras like swimming pools and a choice of restaurants". Each does have a bistro style dining area, open plan bar and fitness centre, as well as providing in-room movies in its four star standard bedrooms. Prices per night, though, are £64.50 Sunday to Thursday and £49.50 at weekends. Locations tend to be close to major motorways— ideal for business travellers, who represent the core weekday market. Courtyard by Marriott is £62 during the week and £38 at weekends (£24 room only without breakfast). The variable pricing positions the hotels more towards bargain breaker tourists at weekends in order to use slack capacity.

The market has been further shaken up with the entry of France's Formule group. Visitors to the Formule 1 hotel on the Boongate Industrial Estate in Peterborough are greeted by a cash point machine which checks how many nights they want to stay, debits their credit cards and gives out a six-figure code allowing them to pass through the locked lobby doors and into a room. Once by their beds, red and green lights tell them when it is safe to have a bath without risk of being sluiced with detergents in the self-cleaning bathrooms. The hotel consists of prefabricated, factory built, inter-locking cabins and is maintained without staff, except for a husband and wife management team. There are no catering facilities, but fast food chains and pubs are nearby. The price is under £20 per night for up to three people sharing a room. Formule is talking about opening close to 200 such hotels in the UK. "A lot of people like the idea of staying in a quiet, cheap place without meeting anybody".

Price is a key differentiating aspect of the marketing mix for these hotel operators, but it is not always the only issue of importance to these target consumers. The hotel business, after all, is increasingly strongly branded, and as a service industry depends on additional elements of the marketing mix. Nevertheless, as France's Formule and the UK's Forte have demonstrated, there is room in this industry to trade on the basis of price, augmented with balanced supporting marketing programmes and clear positioning strategies.

SOURCES: Nick Cohen, "Anonymity for any number at automatic hotel", *The Independent*, November 1992; Holiday Inn and Travelodge promotional literature; *Marketing*, 16 August 1992, p. 4; *Leamington Spa Business Times*, August 1990, p. 5; Clare Sambrook, "Marriott: a name to contend with", *Marketing*, 3 September 1992, pp. 16–18.

Questions for Discussion

1. What opportunities is Travelodge aiming to exploit? Do its aims differ from those of Courtyard by Marriott or Holiday Inn's Garden Court?
2. Why do many hotel companies alter their price points at weekends? Is such a pricing policy seen in other industries? Why or why not?
3. Is price alone a basis for competing in this budget sector of the hotel market? Why or why not?

18.2 Toys "Я" Us—Internationally Competing Through Price

Toys "Я" Us, which leads the US toy market with its chain of over 400 warehouse style toy supermarkets spread across the country, is expanding rapidly in Europe and the Pacific Rim. In Europe its growth is fast bringing a new style and scale of toy retailing to the UK (43 branches), Germany (32), France (17), Spain (12) and Austria (5). The company has long been an innovator in both its pricing policies and its toy supermarket design. Toys "Я" Us brings customers into the store by discounting such baby care products as buggies and disposable nappies below cost. The strategy is that once parents are in the store, they will spend on toys the money they saved on the discounted baby goods.

Toys "Я" Us stores are usually located along road arteries, well away from CBD shopping malls, to keep down costs and prevent customers from being distracted by other toy merchants. Isolation from shopping malls also means that customers will load up their shopping trolleys because they do not have to lug their purchases through crowded malls.

The first Toys "Я" Us store was opened in 1957 as the Children's Supermarket (the "Rs" were printed backwards to encourage name recognition), offering brand name toys and baby goods below normal retail prices. Today, it still offers brand name toys at 20 to 50 per cent below retail price. Each store has a full stock of thousands of different toys and baby goods tracked by a computer system that almost eliminates stock outs. Managers don't place orders for toys, the toys just arrive on time, thus averting the Toys "Я" Us definition of a major disaster—not having a certain toy on display and ready to sell.

Toys "Я" Us sets its price for a particular item based on how much it projects customers will pay for it. The company then determines the price at which it is willing to purchase the toy from the manufacturer and negotiates fiercely with the manufacturer to get the toy at that price. The company has a definite advantage in negotiations because it buys in such large volume. Toy manufacturers also treat Toys "Я" Us well because the company is often a testing ground for new toys. Price is so important to the Toys "Я" Us strategy that even when demand for a toy is high and supplies are short, the company will not raise its price on the toy to make a quick profit.

Market share is the Toys "Я" Us main pricing objective; and at present it is the number one toy store in the United States. In the UK, local independent toy shops still account for the bulk of the toy market share, but in only a few years Toys "Я" Us has become the leading national chain. The company says it is willing to cut prices to retain its leading position. Other toy stores are scrambling to meet the competition from Toys "Я" Us; those that do not change their strategies wind up out of the toy market altogether. Many stores, such as K mart, or Asda in the UK, expand their toy lines only for the six week Christmas season and bring customers in with sales. Although Toys "Я" Us never holds sales, it maintains its huge selection and discount prices year round. Customers who found good buys at Toys "Я" Us at Christmas will also shop there for children's birthdays and other special days, when other retail stores have a limited selection. Even new parents who drop in to Toys "Я" Us for discounted baby products tend to return to buy toys. The company also sells sporting goods "toys", such as footballs and bicycles, suitable for teens, young adults and family members of almost any age.

Some competitors (in the UK Boots owned Children's World) have adopted the Toys "Я" Us supermarket approach and have tried to meet Toys "Я" Us prices throughout the year. Other stores are trying non-price competition by offering educational and babysitting services. However, Toys "Я" Us intends to rely on its non-price attributes of convenience, selection and inventory, as well as price competition, to hold its position.

Toys "Я" Us has expanded internationally, into Europe, Canada, Japan and other parts of Asia with close to 200 stores outside the US. The company has plans for many more stores overseas to take advantage of the world toy market, which is nearly double that of the United States. Additionally, it opened Kids "Я" Us in the United States, a chain of children's clothing stores similar to the toy stores.

Toys "Я" Us has customer loyalty behind it. Customers know that they can find *the* toy that a child wants, at the best price, at Toys "Я" Us. And if the child does not like the toy, the purchaser may return it for a full refund with no questions asked.

SOURCES: Robert J. Cole, "Toys "Я" Us to open stores in Japan within two years", *The New York Times*, 27 September 1989, pp. D1, D6; Dan Dorfman, "Toys "Я" Us : Mattel play?" *USA Today*, 28 June 1987, p. 2B; Trish Hall, "Finding gold in overalls and bibs", *The New York Times,* 25 December 1988, pp. F1, F10; Mark Maremont, Dori Jones Yang and Amy Dunkin, "Toys "Я" Us goes overseas—and finds that toys 'Я' them, too", *Business Week,* 26 January 1987, pp. 71–72; David Owen, "Where toys come from", *Atlantic Monthly,* October 1986, pp. 64–78; Jesus Sanchez, "Toymakers make a play for market", *USA Today,* 10 February 1987, pp. 1B–2B; Toys "Я" Us UK HQ, 1993.

Questions for Discussion

1. What are the major pricing objectives of Toys "Я" Us?
2. Assess the Toys "Я" Us practice of not raising the prices of products that are scarce and in high demand.
3. A major disadvantage of using price competition is that competitors can match prices. Or can they? Evaluate this potential threat for Toys "Я" Us.

PART VI

STRATEGIC MARKETING MANAGEMENT

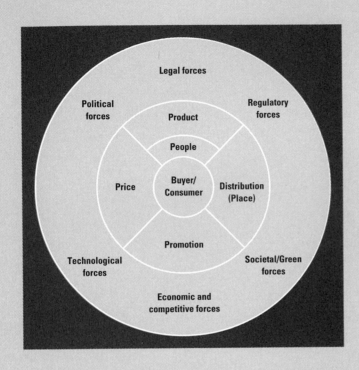

Legal forces

Political forces

Regulatory forces

Product

People

Price

Buyer/ Consumer

Distribution (Place)

Promotion

Technological forces

Societal/Green forces

Economic and competitive forces

So far this text has divided marketing into several sets of variables and has discussed the decisions and activities associated with each variable. By now, it should have made clear (1) how to analyse marketing opportunities and (2) the components of the marketing mix. It is time to put all these components together in a discussion of strategic marketing management issues. In the reality of day-to-day marketing management, marketing opportunities are identified in conjunction with marketing strategy decisions, planning and controls. The marketing mix is manipulated in order to support and implement marketing strategies and plans.

Chapter 19 presents an overview of marketing strategy, strategic market planning, key analytical tools and the nature of competition and competitors' strategies. Chapter 20 examines marketing planning—a process many successful marketing-led companies adopt in order to translate carefully thought out strategies into required marketing programmes and action. This chapter also discusses two associated topics: market potential forecasting and the marketing audit. Chapter 21 focuses on the prerequisites for implementing strategies and plans, as well as the need to measure performance. Part VI of this text concludes with Chapter 22's examination of an area of increasing importance and concern: ethical issues and considerations of social responsibility within strategic marketing. ■

19 MARKETING STRATEGY AND COMPETITIVE FORCES

Objectives

- To understand the basis of marketing strategy and the strategic market planning process

- To explore and examine three major tools to assist in strategic marketing decision-making, the analysis of market opportunities, use of resources and effective market targeting: product portfolio analysis, the market attractiveness-business position model and Profit Impact on Marketing Strategy (PIMS)

- To evaluate the role of competition and competitors' strategies in relation to the development of functional marketing strategies and activities

For years, Pepsi-Cola and Coca-Cola have been slugging it out for market share in a soft drink war, and Pepsi keeps coming in second. However, PepsiCo is more than just soft drinks. Since its 1965 merger with Frito-Lay, Inc., the company has continued to expand and now flourishes in soft drinks, snack foods and restaurants. Since 1980, sales have quadrupled. According to industry analysts, PepsiCo's ability to implement and change its marketing strategies accounts for the firm's enormous profitability.

To satisfy changing tastes in the market-place, Pepsi-Cola (the soft drink arm of PepsiCo) strives to please its target markets. Because Pepsi is popular with teens, the company cultivates the product's youthful and exciting image. It constantly updates television advertising, using music and stars with youth appeal. The company introduced Diet Pepsi to attract diet conscious consumers. In the 1990s Pepsi is concentrating on international markets in the former Soviet republics, Europe and India.

PepsiCo's snack food division, Frito-Lay, is the number one snack food company in the world. Identifying two distinct target markets—high volume youthful snackers and older, nutrition conscious snackers—Frito-Lay developed separate product mixes, different packaging and different styles of advertising and promotion for each. Adding spicier new flavours, modernising packaging and updating music in adverts are all ways Frito-Lay targets younger snackers. For consumers worried about fat and calories, the company introduced reduced fat versions of popular snacks.

PepsiCo's three restaurant chains—Pizza Hut, Taco Bell and KFC—are closing in on their number one competitor, McDonald's. Pizza Hut attracts fast food customers with the guaranteed five minute lunch. Taco Bell attracts frugal customers with value pricing. KFC attracts health conscious customers with skinless fried chicken. ∎

Sources: Based on information from PepsiCo, Inc., 1991 annual report; Patricia Sellers, "Pepsi keeps on going after no. 1", *Fortune*, 11 March 1991, pp. 62–4, 70; Laura Bird, "Pepsi's new order: snack food, global growth and profit", *Adweek's Marketing Week*, 17 December 1990, pp. 4–5; Amy Dunkin, "PepsiCo: why a top consumer marketer moved up in rank", *Business Week*, 13 April 1990, pp. 26–30; John Oldland, "Plotting strategy over a Pepsi", *Marketing*, 9 April 1990, p. 10; Frederick H. Lowe, "New 'rapping' for Pepsi can", *Chicago Sun Times*, 5 April 1990; and PepsiCo, Inc., *Products and Service*.

P art I of this text explored the analysis of market opportunities, in particular the need to understand the moves and trends in a market-place, customer behaviour and needs, and the importance of targeting the right market segments. Parts II to V focused on the marketing mix ingredients which ultimately take a product or service into a market-place to reach the targeted consumers. This chapter aims to highlight the strategic marketing considerations which help to ensure that the product or service is marketed for the benefit of the organisation as well as its targeted customers, and differently enough from its competitors' marketing programmes to give the organisation's product or service a perceived advantage over these competitors that will lead to success in the market-place. These core components of marketing strategy are illustrated in Figure 19.1.

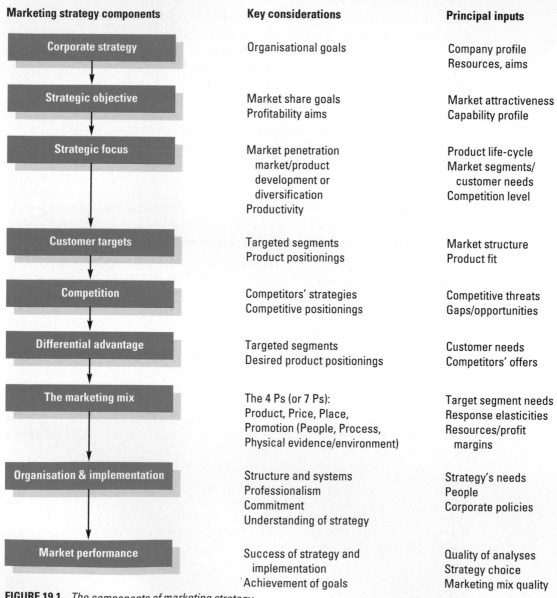

Marketing strategy components	Key considerations	Principal inputs
Corporate strategy	Organisational goals	Company profile Resources, aims
Strategic objective	Market share goals Profitability aims	Market attractiveness Capability profile
Strategic focus	Market penetration market/product development or diversification Productivity	Product life-cycle Market segments/ customer needs Competition level
Customer targets	Targeted segments Product positionings	Market structure Product fit
Competition	Competitors' strategies Competitive positionings	Competitive threats Gaps/opportunities
Differential advantage	Targeted segments Desired product positionings	Customer needs Competitors' offers
The marketing mix	The 4 Ps (or 7 Ps): Product, Price, Place, Promotion (People, Process, Physical evidence/environment)	Target segment needs Response elasticities Resources/profit margins
Organisation & implementation	Structure and systems Professionalism Commitment Understanding of strategy	Strategy's needs People Corporate policies
Market performance	Success of strategy and implementation Achievement of goals	Quality of analyses Strategy choice Marketing mix quality

FIGURE 19.1 *The components of marketing strategy*

SOURCE: Adapted from John Saunders and Veronica Wong, "In search of excellence in the UK", *Journal of Marketing Management,* 1 (2), 1985, fig. 2, p. 130.

The chapter first explores how to develop marketing strategies and then discusses strategic market planning, stressing the importance of organisational goals and corporate strategy. The next section presents some of the related analytical tools associated with the planning of a marketing strategy: the product portfolio analysis, the market attractiveness–business position model and Profit Impact on Marketing Strategy (PIMS). The chapter then focuses on competitive strategies for marketing: the role of competition, its ramifications for strategy, competitive positions and warfare strategies. Other aspects of the strategic marketing management process—marketing forecasting and marketing planning; organising, implementing and controlling—are covered in Chapters 20 and 21, respectively.

MARKETING STRATEGY DEFINED

Marketing strategy indicates the specific markets towards which activities are to be targeted and the types of competitive advantages that are to be developed and exploited.[1] Implicitly, as described in Figure 19.1, the strategy requires clear objectives and a focus in line with an organisation's corporate goals; the "right" customers must be targeted more effectively than they are by its competitors, and associated marketing mixes must be developed into marketing programmes which successfully implement the marketing strategy.

A **strategic market plan** is an outline of the methods and resources required to achieve an organisation's goals within a specific target market. It takes into account not only marketing but also all functional aspects of a business unit that must be co-ordinated. These functional aspects include production, finance and personnel. Environmental issues are an important consideration as well. The concept of the strategic business unit is used to define areas for consideration in a specific strategic market plan. Each **strategic business unit (SBU)** is a division, product line or other profit centre within the parent company. Each sells a distinct set of products to an identifiable group of customers, and each competes with a well defined set of competitors. Each SBU's revenues, costs, investments and strategic plans can be separated and evaluated apart from those of the parent company. SBUs operate in a variety of markets, which have differing growth rates, opportunities, degrees of competition and profit-making potential. The Coca-Cola Company, for example, includes the Coca-Cola European Community Group, a strategic business unit (see Figure 19.2). Strategic planners therefore must recognise the different performance capabilities of each SBU and carefully allocate resources.

The process of **strategic market planning** yields a marketing strategy that is the framework for a marketing plan. A **marketing plan** (see Chapter 20) includes the framework and entire set of activities to be performed; it is the written document or blueprint for implementing and controlling an organisation's marketing activities. Thus a strategic market plan is *not* the same as a marketing plan; it is a plan of *all* aspects of an organisation's strategy in the market-place. A marketing plan, in contrast, deals primarily with implementing the market strategy as it relates to target markets and the marketing mix.[2]

Figure 19.3 shows the components of strategic market planning. The process is based on the establishment of an organisation's overall goals, and it must stay within the bounds of the organisation's opportunities and resources. When the firm has determined its overall goals and identified its resources, it can then assess its opportunities and develop a corporate strategy. Marketing objectives must be designed so that their achievement will contribute to the corporate strategy and so that they can be accomplished through efficient use of the firm's resources.

FIGURE 19.2
An SBU in operation
The Coca-Cola European
Community Group is
charged with addressing
Europe's 12 country market,
and Norway—Europe's
largest per capita consumer
of Coca-Cola.

SOURCE: © 1993 Arthur Meyerson Photography.

To achieve its marketing objectives, an organisation must develop a marketing strategy, or a set of marketing strategies, as shown in Figure 19.3. The set of marketing strategies that are implemented and used at the same time is referred to as the organisation's **marketing programme.** Through the process of strategic market planning, an organisation can develop marketing strategies that, when properly implemented and controlled, will contribute to the achievement of its marketing objectives and its overall goals. Marketing Insight 19.1 discusses InterCity's strategy appraisal and resulting marketing programme. As mentioned before, to formulate a marketing strategy, the marketer identifies and analyses the target market and develops a marketing mix to satisfy individuals in that market. Marketing strategy is best formulated when it reflects the overall direction of the organisation and is co-ordinated with all the firm's functional areas.

As indicated in Figure 19.3, the strategic market planning process is based on an analysis of the environment, by which it is very much affected. Environmental forces can place constraints on an organisation and possibly influence its overall goals; they also affect the amount and type of resources that a firm can acquire. However, these forces can create favourable opportunities as well—opportunities that can be translated into overall organisational goals and marketing objectives. For example, when oil prices declined during the second half of the 1980s, consumers viewed cars with high petrol consumption more favourably. This situation created an opportunity for manufacturers of large vehicles, such as BMW and Volvo.

Marketers differ in their viewpoints concerning the effect of environmental variables on marketing planning and strategy. Some take a deterministic perspective, believing that firms must react to external conditions and tailor their strategies and organisational structures to deal with these conditions. According to others, however, companies can influence their environments by choosing in which markets to com-

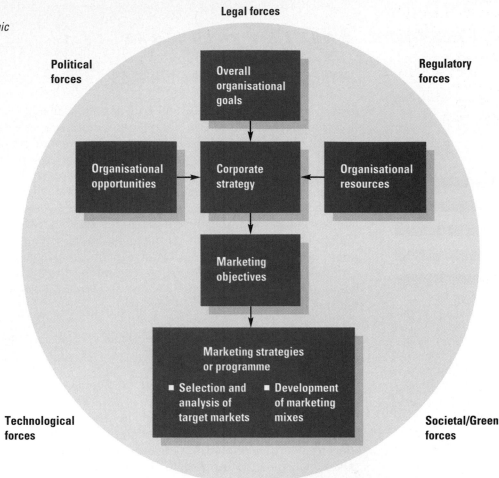

FIGURE 19.3
Components of strategic market planning

Legal forces

Political forces

Regulatory forces

Overall organisational goals

Organisational opportunities

Corporate strategy

Organisational resources

Marketing objectives

Marketing strategies or programme

- Selection and analysis of target markets
- Development of marketing mixes

Technological forces

Societal/Green forces

pete. They can also change the structures of their industries, engaging in activities such as mergers and acquisitions, demand creation or technological innovation.[3]

Regardless of which viewpoint is adopted, environmental variables play a part in the creation of a marketing strategy. When environmental variables affect an organisation's overall goals, resources, opportunities or marketing objectives, they also affect its marketing strategies, which are based on these factors. Environmental forces more directly influence the development of a marketing strategy through their impact on consumers' needs and desires. In addition, these forces have a bearing on marketing mix decisions. For instance, competition strongly influences marketing mix decisions. The organisation must diagnose the marketing mix activities it performs, taking into account competitors' marketing mix decisions, and develop some competitive advantage to support a strategy. Thus as Honda and Toyota entered the luxury car market with the Acura and Lexus models, European car makers BMW, Mercedes and Jaguar had to change their marketing strategies to maintain their market shares. They did so by lowering prices to compete with the new Japanese models.

The next sections discuss the major components of the strategic market planning process: organisational goals, organisational opportunities and resources, and corporate strategy, as well as the tools that aid in strategic market planning and some competitive marketing strategies.

INTERCITY CATERS FOR BUSINESS

British Rail employs over 100,000 staff, has a turnover close to £3 billion and a passenger volume of over 20 billion passenger miles. Divided into five business units, InterCity is the UK national passenger rail network competing for long distance passenger journeys. There are three clearly identifiable segments: business travel, leisure travel and obligatory travel (commuting).

Every business regularly needs to re-appraise its activities, and InterCity is no exception. Recognising the importance of the business market, InterCity consults customers to ascertain what they seek and whether their requirements are being met. Products may need re-launching, improving or promoting to make customers aware of them. InterCity conducted a major programme of consumer research, comparing the advantages and disadvantages for customers of rail, car and air travel. Consumers most often indicated these advantages:

Car   Privacy/Flexibility/Accessibility/Control/Speed

Plane   Standard of service/Thrill of flying/Arrive fresh

InterCity Space to move around/Work while travelling/Centre to centre

The major finding from the research, however, was that business travellers cared greatly about the status accompanying their choice of transport. Because InterCity offered less privacy and appeared less exclusive, it did not adequately meet status needs.

Knowing the problems, InterCity decided to alter its perceived position and to take steps to be viewed as a more up market product. To carry out this re-positioning, InterCity designed a marketing package aimed at increasing the status of business travel by rail, coupled with the existing advantages of lack of strain, space to move and ability to work while travelling. Executive tickets, for example, include seat reservations, 24 hours' car parking, refreshment voucher and London Underground travel. Pullman luxury carriages have been added on more services, and Pullman executive lounges have been built at various major stations.

Saatchi & Saatchi's advertising campaigns emphasised this re-positioning and the benefits of InterCity. British Rail identified what its business travellers wanted, provided the required service and communicated with existing and potential customers about the improvements and changes.

SOURCES: "How InterCity caters for its business customers", Wetherby: Target, 1990; R. Mason, InterCity marketing director 1990, British Railways Board, London; "A selection of case studies from organisations that have demonstrated excellence in marketing and recruitment", Target, Wetherby: Michael Benn and Associates, 1990; Fiona Plant, "Agencies vie for BR's £4m", *Campaign*, 19 October 1990, p. 4; Nicholas Faith, "British Rail's market express", *Business,* July 1989, pp. 52–62; Roland Rudd, "Full steam ahead for the big state sell off", *The Independent on Sunday,* 13 January 1991, pp. 4–5.

ORGANISATIONAL GOALS

A firm's organisational goals should be derived from its *mission,* the broad tasks that the organisation wants to accomplish. IBM, for example, has stated that its mission is helping businesspeople make decisions. A company's mission and overall organisational goals should guide all its planning efforts. Its goals should specify the ends, or results, that are sought. For example, a firm in serious financial trouble may be concerned solely with short run results needed for staying in business. There usually is an airline or major retailer being forced by cash shortages to take drastic action to stay in business. Lowndes Queensway, once the UK's largest retailer of carpets and furniture, several times had to renegotiate its financing with City institutions, alter payment and credit times and terms with its suppliers and ultimately identify which of its 500 superstores should be closed to save costs. The company went into receivership despite all its efforts. On the other hand, some companies have more optimistic goals. Often manufacturers such as General Motors have goals that relate to return on investment. A successful company, however, may want to sacrifice the current year's profits for the long run and at the same time pursue other goals, such as increasing market share.

ORGANISATIONAL OPPORTUNITIES AND RESOURCES

There are three major considerations in assessing opportunities and resources: evaluating market opportunities, environmental scanning (discussed in Chapter 2) and understanding the firm's capabilities. An appreciation of these elements is essential if an organisation is to build up a sustainable differential or competitive advantage.

Differential Advantage

If a marketing mix is developed which matches target market needs and expectations, and is superior to those offered by competitors, there is a real—or perceived—**differential advantage.** A differential advantage is inherent in an organisation's marketing mix if it is desired by consumers and not matched by competitors. Achieving a differential advantage, or competitive edge, requires an organisation to make the most of its opportunities and resources while offering customers a satisfactory mix of tangible and intangible benefits[4] (see Figure 19.4). When striking a balance between customer requirements on the one hand and company resources on the other, competitor activity must also be monitored. For example, there is little sense in promoting speedy distribution to customers if several large competing organisations offer a faster service. There are many different sources of differential advantage which firms can pursue. Marketing Insight 19.2 reveals how the export of American football to Europe has left the sport struggling to find a genuine differential advantage.

For some firms, such as 3M, innovativeness is the focus, while for others, like Vidal Sassoon hair salons, image plays an important part. The Body Shop concentrates on environmentally friendly cosmetics, while for multiplex cinemas the differential advantage is the choice of multiple screens at one location. Some of these ways of gaining an edge are easier to sustain than others. For example, many UK companies which have traditionally focused on low price have found this advantage difficult to maintain in the long term.[5] The airline industry is just one to be plagued by periodic price wars.

Market Opportunities

A **market opportunity** arises when the right combination of circumstances occurs at the right time to allow an organisation to take action towards reaching a target market. An opportunity provides a favourable chance or opening for the firm to generate sales from identifiable markets. For example, in reaction to the overwhelming growth in ce-

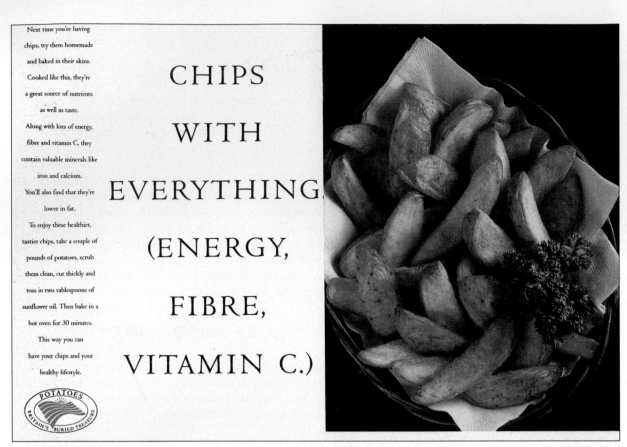

Next time you're having chips, try them homemade and baked in their skins. Cooked like this, they're a great source of nutrients as well as taste. Along with lots of energy, fibre and vitamin C, they contain valuable minerals like iron and calcium. You'll also find that they're lower in fat. To enjoy these healthier, tastier chips, take a couple of pounds of potatoes, scrub them clean, cut thickly and toss in two tablespoons of sunflower oil. Then bake in a hot oven for 30 minutes. This way you can have your chips and your healthy lifestyle.

CHIPS WITH EVERYTHING. (ENERGY, FIBRE, VITAMIN C.)

FIGURE 19.4 *Differential advantage*
Even for the mundane potato, marketers strive to create a differential advantage and respond to consumer attitudes.

SOURCE: With permission from The Potato Marketing Board of Great Britain.

reals and other foods containing oat bran (which some researchers believe helps lower cholesterol levels), the Quaker Oats Company developed an advertising campaign to remind consumers that Quaker porridge oats have always contained oat bran. The advertisements told consumers that eating porridge is "the right thing to do", and helped boost sales of Quaker Oats dramatically.[6] Increasing concerns about cancer and heart disease gave Quaker a market opportunity to reach consumers who are especially health conscious by touting the health benefits of its oats. Kellogg's also took advantage of the popularity of oat bran by creating its Common Sense™ Oat Bran cereal. Interestingly, in 1990, a study published in a leading medical journal questioned the effectivness of oat bran in lowering cholesterol, concluding that it was the elimination of high cholesterol animal products that really lowered cholesterol. Therefore, some of the oat bran mystique vanished overnight. The term *strategic window* has been used to describe what are often temporary periods of optimum fit between the key requirements of a market and the particular capabilities of a firm competing in that market.[7]

The attractiveness of market opportunities is determined by market factors, such as size and growth rate, as well as competitive, financial, economic, technological, social, ecological, legal and political factors.[8] Because each industry and product are somewhat different, the factors that determine attractiveness tend to vary.

EXPORTING AMERICAN FOOTBALL: A COMPETITIVE EDGE?

When the London Monarchs kicked off against the Frankfurt Galaxy in the opening game of the World League of American Football, a crowd of more than 23,000 cheered them on. Flag waving, song singing fans sat in the rain and cold in Barcelona to watch the New York–New Jersey Knights battle the home team Dragons, even though many didn't seem to know the difference between a first down and a touchdown. From the enthusiasm the 10 team WLAF generated overseas, it looked as if Europeans would embrace football just as they have cheeseburgers and MTV.

Over 750 million fans in more than 50 countries watched the last US Superbowl on television; and National Football League exhibition games in Europe, Canada and Japan have drawn huge crowds. Pointing to that popularity as an indicator of football's universal appeal, promoters created a new spring league made up of seven American and Canadian teams and two European ones. Cynics say that the WLAF is professional ball with mostly unknowns who are too light or too slow for the NFL, modest salaries and playing fields that often don't meet regulations, but it exudes a spontaneity and vitality that European fans are enjoying. European franchises consistently beat US WLAF franchises in game attendance, and British newspapers regularly featured more items on the WLAF than do newspapers in the United States. While the American network ABC draws dismal ratings for its Sunday telecasts of WLAF games, the World Bowl at London's Wembley Stadium attracted a near capacity crowd.

To survive, the WLAF needs to increase its number of fans. The league's best chance for success seems to rest with European fans, who are not inundated with the National Football League, basketball, hockey and baseball. Potential locations for expansion include Paris, Helsinki and even Tokyo, where promoters hope the sport won't be just another "Spring League", but "American Football". There are teething problems, though, particularly in Europe, where clubs are struggling financially. The export of American football has surprised many onlookers, but early success needs to be reinforced. An opportunity existed, but it is not clear whether American football has established a differential advantage sustainable in the face of retaliation by rival sports and leisure pursuits. Tennis, show jumping, football, cricket and rugby are revitalising their marketing in order to retain television coverage and attract the paying public. In 1992 European-American football games were cancelled. Now, the show is once more on the road.

SOURCES: Rick Reilly, "One to remember", *Sports Illustrated,* 17 June 1991, p. 46; Charles Leerhsen, Daniel Pedersen and Howard Manly, "Hold that helmet cam!" *Newsweek*, 20 May 1991, p. 60; and Rick Reilly, "World premiere", *Sports Illustrated*, 1 April 1991, pp. 40–3.

Market requirements relate to customers' needs or desired benefits. Market requirements are satisfied by components of the marketing mix that provide buyers with these benefits. Of course, buyers' perceptions of what requirements fulfil their needs and provide the desired benefits determine the success of any marketing effort. Marketers must devise strategies to outperform competitors by finding out what product attributes buyers use to select products. An attribute must be important and differentiating if it is to be useful in strategy development. When marketers fail to understand buyers' perceptions and market requirements, the result may be failure. Freemans, prior to its takeover by Sears, launched its by mail "Specialogue", aimed at yuppie men. The company failed to realise that such target customers wanted branded goods from prestigious specialty retail outlets; they did not perceive mail order shopping to be suitable for them.

Environmental Scanning

In Chapter 2 **environmental scanning** was defined as the process of collecting information about the marketing environment to help marketers identify opportunities and assist in planning. Some companies have derived substantial benefits from establishing an "environmental scanning (or monitoring) unit" within the strategic planning group or from including line management in teams or committees to conduct environmental analysis. This approach engages management in the process of environmental forecasting and enhances the likelihood of successfully integrating forecasting efforts into strategic market planning.[9] Results of forecasting research show that even simple quantitative forecasting techniques outperform the unstructured intuitive assessments of experts.[10] Many builders and developers in the UK believe that the house buying public is unwilling to pay the increased cost of energy efficient new housing. However, research suggests that consumers *are* happy to pay extra, within reason, for the increased comfort levels and reduced fuel bills associated with such property.[11]

Environmental scanning to detect changes in the environment is extremely important if a firm is to avoid crisis management. An environmental change can suddenly alter a firm's opportunities or resources. Reformulated, more effective strategies may then be needed to guide marketing efforts. For example, after the UK government legislated against heavy emissions from cars, and gave unleaded fuel tax advantages, petrol suppliers and vehicle manufacturers had to reformulate their strategies and marketing programmes.[12] Because car manufacturers had engaged in environmental scanning and were aware that such legislation might indeed be enacted because of social and political concerns, most had already begun developing plans for cars powered by clean fuel. Ford Motor Company, for example, is already testing a car that can run on methanol, ethanol, petrol or any combination of those fuels.[13] Similarly, increased concern about the cleanliness of the environment has left manufacturers looking for ways to pass on the costs of catalytic converters, which are necessary if some cars are to run on lead free fuels, to the consumer. Environmental scanning should identify new developments and determine the nature and rate of change.

Capabilities and Resources

A firm's **capabilities** relate to distinctive competencies that it has developed to do something well and efficiently. A company is likely to enjoy a differential advantage in an area where its competencies out do those of its potential competitors.[14] Often a company may possess manufacturing or technical skills that are valuable in areas outside its traditional industry. For example, BASF, known for its manufacture and development of audio and video tapes, produced a new type of lightweight plastic that has uses in other industries. **Marketing assets** highlight capabilities that managers and the market-place view as beneficially strong. These capabilities can then be stressed to the company's advantage. Customer based assets include brand image and reputation;

distribution based assets may involve density of dealers and geographic coverage; internal marketing assets include skills, experience, economies of scale, technology and resources.[15]

Today marketing planners are especially concerned with external resource constraints. Shortages in energy and other scarce economic resources often limit strategic planning options. On the other hand, planning to avoid shortages can backfire. In many countries electricity suppliers decided to build nuclear power plants in the 1970s to compensate for an expected shortfall of fossil fuels—only to find the political, social and technological problems of nuclear power almost impossible to overcome. Moreover, an adequate supply of fossil fuels still exists to power traditional plants that generate electricity. But as the public grows more concerned about pollution and the so called greenhouse effect—the increased warming of the earth caused by pollution—nuclear power plants may once again become a plausible alternative.

CORPORATE STRATEGY

Corporate strategy determines the means for utilising resources in the areas of production, finance, research and development, personnel and marketing to reach the organisation's goals. A corporate strategy determines not only the scope of the business but also its resource deployment, competitive advantages and overall co-ordination of production, finance, marketing and other functional areas. The term *corporate* in this context does not apply only to corporations; corporate strategy is used by all organisations, from the smallest sole proprietorship to the largest multinational corporation.

Corporate strategy planners are concerned with issues such as diversification, competition, differentiation, interrelationships among business units and environmental issues. Strategy planners attempt to match the resources of the organisation with the various opportunities and risks in the environment. Corporate strategy planners are also concerned with defining the scope and role of the strategic business units of the organisation so that they are co-ordinated to reach the ultimate goals desired.

TOOLS FOR STRATEGIC MARKET PLANNING

A number of tools have been proposed to aid marketing managers in their planning efforts. Based on ideas used in the management of financial portfolios, several models that classify an organisation's product portfolio have been proposed. These models allow strategic business units or products to be classified and visually displayed according to the attractiveness of various markets and the business's relative market share within those markets. Three of these tools—the Boston Consulting Group (BCG) product portfolio analysis, the market attractiveness–business position model and the Profit Impact on Marketing Strategy (PIMS)—are discussed next.

The Boston Consulting Group (BCG) Product Portfolio Analysis

Just as financial investors have different investments with varying risks and rates of return, firms have a portfolio of products characterised by different market growth rates and relative market shares. **Product portfolio analysis,** the Boston Consulting Group approach, is based on the philosophy that a product's market growth rate and its relative market share are important considerations in determining its marketing strategy. All the firm's products should be integrated into a single, overall matrix and evaluated to determine appropriate strategies for individual SBUs and the overall portfolio strategies. However, a balanced product portfolio matrix is the end result of a number of actions—not just the analysis alone. Portfolio models can be created on the basis of present and projected market growth rates and proposed market share strategies (build share, maintain share, harvest share or divest business). Managers can use these models to determine and classify each product's expected future cash contributions and future cash requirements.

Generally, managers who use a portfolio model must examine the competitive position of a product (or product line) and the opportunities for improving that product's contribution to profitability and cash flow.[16] The BCG analytical approach is more of a diagnostic tool than a guide for making strategy prescriptions.

Figure 19.5, which is based on work by the BCG, enables the marketing manager to classify a firm's products into four basic types: stars, cash cows, dogs and problem children.[17] **Stars** are products with a dominant share of the market and good prospects for growth. However, they use more cash than they generate to finance growth, add capacity and increase market share. **Cash cows** have a dominant share of the market but low prospects for growth; typically, they generate more cash than is required to maintain market share. **Dogs** have a subordinate share of the market and low prospects for growth; these products are often found in mature markets. **Problem children,** sometimes called "question marks", have a small share of a growing market and generally require a large amount of cash to build share.

The growth-share matrix in Figure 19.5 can be expanded to show a firm's whole portfolio by providing for each product (1) its cash sales volume, illustrated by the size of a circle on the matrix; (2) its market share relative to competition, represented by the horizontal position of the product on the matrix; and (3) the growth rate of the market, indicated by the position of the product in the vertical direction. It should be noted that relative market share is a company's own market share relative to the biggest competitor's. Figure 19.6 suggests marketing strategies appropriate for cash cows, stars, dogs and problem children.

FIGURE 19.5
Illustrative growth-share matrix developed by the Boston Consulting Group

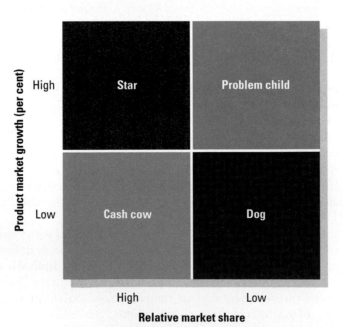

SOURCE: *Perspectives,* No. 66, "The product portfolio". Reprinted by permission from The Boston Consulting Group, Inc., Boston, MA. © copyright 1970.

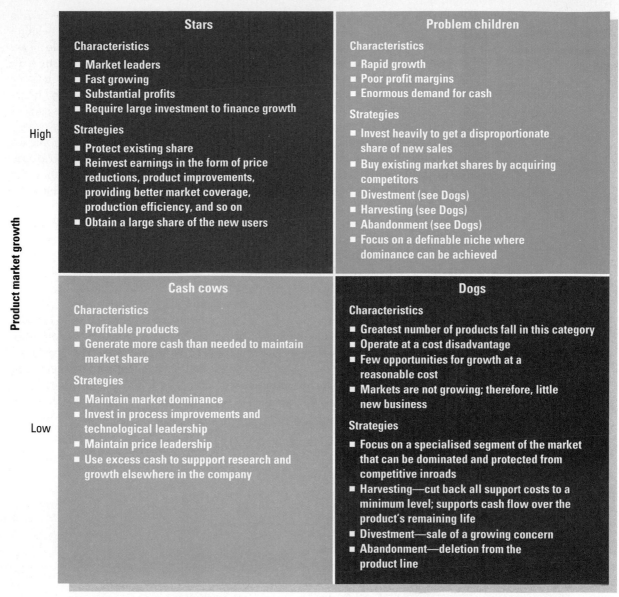

High

Low

Product market growth

Stars

Characteristics

- Market leaders
- Fast growing
- Substantial profits
- Require large investment to finance growth

Strategies

- Protect existing share
- Reinvest earnings in the form of price reductions, product improvements, providing better market coverage, production efficiency, and so on
- Obtain a large share of the new users

Problem children

Characteristics

- Rapid growth
- Poor profit margins
- Enormous demand for cash

Strategies

- Invest heavily to get a disproportionate share of new sales
- Buy existing market shares by acquiring competitors
- Divestment (see Dogs)
- Harvesting (see Dogs)
- Abandonment (see Dogs)
- Focus on a definable niche where dominance can be achieved

Cash cows

Characteristics

- Profitable products
- Generate more cash than needed to maintain market share

Strategies

- Maintain market dominance
- Invest in process improvements and technological leadership
- Maintain price leadership
- Use excess cash to support research and growth elsewhere in the company

Dogs

Characteristics

- Greatest number of products fall in this category
- Operate at a cost disadvantage
- Few opportunities for growth at a reasonable cost
- Markets are not growing; therefore, little new business

Strategies

- Focus on a specialised segment of the market that can be dominated and protected from competitive inroads
- Harvesting—cut back all support costs to a minimum level; supports cash flow over the product's remaining life
- Divestment—sale of a growing concern
- Abandonment—deletion from the product line

High   **Low**

Relative market share

FIGURE 19.6   *Characteristics and strategies for the four basic product types in the growth–share matrix*

SOURCE: Concepts in this figure adapted from George S. Day, "Diagnosing the product portfolio", *Journal of Marketing,* April 1977, pp. 30–31. Reprinted by permission of the American Marketing Association.

The long term health of an organisation depends on having some products that generate cash (and provide acceptable profits) and others that use cash to support growth. Among the indicators of overall health are the size and vulnerability of the cash cows, the prospects for the stars, if any, and the number of problem children and dogs. Particular attention must be paid to those products with large cash appetites. Unless the company has an abundant cash flow, it cannot afford to sponsor many such products at one time. If resources, including debt capacity, are spread too thinly, the company will end up with too many marginal products and will be unable to finance promising new product entries or acquisitions in the future.

Market Attractiveness– Business Position Model

The **market attractiveness–business position model,** illustrated in Figure 19.7, is another two dimensional matrix. However, rather than using single measures to define the vertical and horizontal dimensions of the matrix, the model employs multiple measurements and observations. The vertical dimension, *market attractiveness,* includes all strengths and resources that relate to the market, such as seasonality, economies of scale, competitive intensity, industry sales, and the overall cost and feasibility of entering the market. The horizontal axis, *business position,* is a composite of factors such as sales, relative market share, research and development, price competitiveness, product quality and market knowledge as they relate to the product in building market share. A slight variation of this matrix is called **General Electric's Strategic Business Planning Grid** because General Electric is credited with extending the product portfolio planning tool to examine market attractiveness and business strength.

The best situation for a firm is to have a strong business position in an attractive market. The upper left area in Figure 19.7 represents the opportunity for an invest/grow strategy, but the matrix does not indicate how to implement this strategy. The purpose of the model is to serve as a diagnostic tool to highlight SBUs that have an opportunity to grow or that should be divested or approached selectively. SBUs that occupy the invest/grow position can lose their position through faulty marketing strategies.

Decisions on allocating resources to SBUs of medium overall attractiveness should be arrived at on a basis relative to other SBUs that are either more or less attractive. The lower right area of the matrix is a low growth harvest/divest area. Harvesting is a gradual withdrawal of marketing resources on the assumption that sales will decline at a slow rate but profits will still be significant at a lower sales volume. Harvesting and divesting may be appropriate strategies for SBUs characterised by low overall attractiveness.

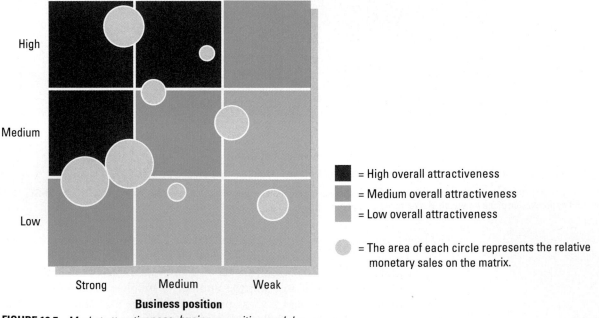

FIGURE 19.7 *Market attractiveness–business position model*

SOURCE: Adapted from Derek F. Abell and John S. Hammond, *Strategic Market Planning: Problems and Analytical Approaches,* © 1979, p. 213. Reprinted by permission of Prentice-Hall, Inc., Englewood Cliffs, N.J.

Profit Impact on Marketing Strategy (PIMS)

The US Strategic Planning Institute (SPI) developed a databank of information on 3,000 strategic business units of 200 different firms during the period 1970–1983 for the **Profit Impact on Marketing Strategy (PIMS)** research programme.[18] The sample is somewhat biased because it is composed primarily of large, profitable manufacturing firms marketing mature products; service firms and distribution companies are under-represented. However, 19 per cent of the sample is composed of international businesses.[19] The member organisations of the Institute provide confidential information on successes, failures, and marginal products. Figure 19.8 shows a PIMS data form. The data are analysed to provide members with information about how similar organisations have performed under a given set of circumstances and about the factors that contribute to success or failure in given market conditions.

The unit of observation in PIMS is the SBU. Table 19.1 shows the types of information provided on each business in the PIMS database. The PIMS database includes both diagnostic and prescriptive information to assist in analysing marketing perform-

FIGURE 19.8
Sample page from PIMS data forms

103: "LIFE CYCLE" STAGE OF PRODUCT CATEGORY

How would you describe the stage of development of the types of products or services sold by this business during the last three years? *(Check one)*

. . . Introductory Stage: Primary demand for product just starting to grow; products or services still unfamiliar to many potential users ☐ 1

. . . Growth Stage: Demand growing at 10% or more annually in real terms: technology or competitive structure still changing ☐ 2

. . . Maturity Stage: Products or services familiar to vast majority of prospective users; technology and competitve structure reasonably stable ☐ 3

. . . Decline Stage: Products viewed as commodities: weaker competitors beginning to exit ☐ 4

104: What was this business's first year of commercial sales? *(Check one)*

Prior to 1930	1930–1949	1950–1954	1955–1959	1960–1964	1965–1969	1970–1974	1975–
☐ 0	☐ 1	☐ 2	☐ 3	☐ 4	☐ 5	☐ 6	☐ 7

105: At the time this business first entered the market, was it . . . *(Check one)*

. . . One of the pioneers in first developing such products or services? ☐ 1

. . . An early follower of the pioneer(s) in a still growing, dynamic market? ☐ 2

. . . A later entrant into a more established market situation? ☐ 3

106–07: PATENTS AND TRADE SECRETS

Does this business benefit *to a significant degree* from patents, trade secrets, or other proprietary methods of production or operation . . .

106: Pertaing to products or services? NO ☐ 0 YES ☐ 1

107: Pertaining to processes? NO ☐ 0 YES ☐ 1

108: STANDARDIZATION OF PRODUCTS OR SERVICES

Are the products or services of this business . . *(Check one)*.

. . . More or less standardized for all customers? ☐ 0

. . . Designed or produced to order for individual customers? ☐ 1

109: FREQUENCY OF PRODUCT CHANGES

Is it typical practice for the business and its major competitors to change all or part of the line of products or services offered . . . *(Check one)*

. . . Annually (for example, annual model changes)? ☐ 1

. . . Seasonally? ☐ 2

. . . Peridically, but at intervals longer than one year? ☐ 3

. . . No regular, periodic pattern of change? ☐ 4

110: TECHNOLOGICAL CHANGE

Have there been major technological changes in the products offered by the business or its major competitors, or in methods of production, during the last 8 years? *(If in doubt about whether a change was "major," answer NO.)* NO ☐ 0 YES ☐ 1

SOURCE: PIMS Data Form reproduced by permission of the Strategic Planning Institute (PIMS programme), Cambridge, Mass., 1979.

TABLE 19.1   *Types of information provided on each business in the PIMS database*

Characteristics of the business environment	Structure of the production process
Long run growth rate of the market	Capital intensity (degree of automation, etc.)
Short run growth rate of the market	Degree of vertical integration
Rate of inflation of selling price levels	Capacity utilisation
Number and size of customers	Productivity of capital equipment
Purchase frequency and magnitude	Productivity of people
	Inventory levels
Competitive position of the business	
Share of the served market	**Discretionary budget allocations**
Share relative to largest competitors	Research and development budgets
Product quality relative to competitors	Advertising and promotion budgets
Prices relative to competitors	Sales force expenditures
Pay scales relative to competitors	
Marketing efforts relative to competitors	**Strategic moves**
Pattern of market segmentation	Patterns of change in the controllable
Rate of new product introductions	elements above
	Operating results
	Profitability results
	Cash flow results
	Growth results

SOURCE: Reproduced by permission of the Strategic Planning Institute [PIMS programme], Cambridge, Mass.

ance and formulating marketing strategies. The analysis focuses on options, problems, resources and opportunities.

The PIMS project has identified more than 30 factors that affect the performance of firms. These factors can be grouped into three sets of variables: (1) those relating to the structure of the market-place in which the firm competes; (2) those that describe the firm's competitive position within that market; and (3) those that relate to the strategy chosen by the firm.[20] These factors may interact, as well as directly affect performance and profitability. Some of the main findings of the PIMS project are discussed briefly below.

Strong Market Position.   Market position refers to the relative market share that a firm holds in relation to its competition. Firms that have a large share of a market tend to be the most profitable. However, it should be noted that market share does not necessarily create profitability. It is the result of business strategies such as the marketing of high quality products, or the provision of good service.

High Quality Products.   Organisations that offer products of higher quality tend to be more profitable than their competitors. They are able to demand higher prices for those products. Moreover, high quality offerings instil customer loyalty, foster repeat purchases, insulate firms from price wars and help build market share. In Figure 19.9, Coca-Cola promotes its ongoing commitment to quality. It appears impossible for firms to overcome inferior offerings with high levels of marketing expenditures. Advertising is no substitute for product quality.

FIGURE 19.9
A commitment to quality
Coca-Cola offers a high
quality product and re-
mains the number one
selling soft drink.

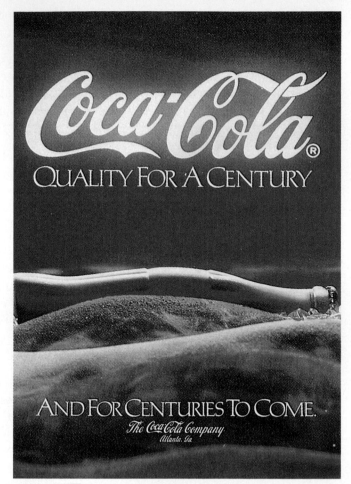

SOURCE: "Coca-Cola" and the Dynamic Ribbon device are registered trademarks of The Coca-Cola Company.

Lower Costs.   Firms achieve lower costs through economies of scale, ability to bargain with suppliers or backward integration. Low costs heighten profitability levels.

Investment and Capital Intensity.   The higher the required investment to compete
in an industry, the more pressure there is on a firm fully to use its production capacity.
Moreover, these factors tend to have a negative impact on profitability.

**Significance of
Strategic Market
Planning Approaches**

The approaches presented here provide an overview of the most popular analytical
methods used in strategic market planning. However, the Boston Consulting Group's
portfolio analysis, the market attractiveness–business position model and the Profit
Impact on Marketing Strategy research programme are used not only to diagnose
problem areas or to recognise opportunities but also to facilitate the allocation of resources among business units. They are not intended to serve as formulae for success
or prescriptive guides, which lay out cut-and-dried strategic action plans.[21] These approaches are supplements to, not substitutes for, the marketing manager's own judgement. The real test of each approach, or any integrated approach, is how well it helps
management diagnose the firm's strengths and weaknesses and prescribe strategic ac-

tions for maintaining or improving performance. The emphasis should be on making sound decisions with the aid of these analytical tools.[22]

Another word of caution regarding the use of portfolio approaches is necessary. The classification of SBUs into a specific portfolio position hinges on four factors: (1) the operational definition of the matrix dimensions; (2) the rules used to divide a dimension into high and low categories; (3) the weighting of the variables used in composite dimensions, if composite dimensions are used; and (4) the specific model used.[23] In other words, changes in any of these four factors may well result in a different classification for a single SBU.

The key to understanding the tools for strategic market planning described in this chapter is recognition that strategic market planning takes into account all aspects of a firm's strategy in the market-place. Most of this book is about functional decisions and strategies of marketing as a part of business. This chapter focuses on the recognition that all functional strategies, including marketing, production and finance, must be co-ordinated to reach organisational goals. Results of a survey of top industrial firms sponsored by the *Harvard Business Review* indicate that portfolio planning and other general planning techniques help managers strengthen their planning process and solve the problems of managing diversified industrial companies. However, the results also indicate that analytical techniques alone do not result in success. Management must blend these analyses with managerial judgement to deal with the reality of the existing situation.

There are other tools that aid strategic market planning besides those examined here. For example, for many years marketing planners have used the product life-cycle concept discussed in Chapters 7 and 9. Many firms have their own approaches to planning that incorporate, to varying degrees, some of the approaches discussed here. All strategic planning approaches have some similarity in that several of the components of strategic market planning outlined in Figure 19.3 (especially market/product relationships) are related to a plan of action for reaching objectives.

DEVELOPING COMPETITIVE STRATEGIES FOR MARKETING

After analysing business operations and business performance, the next step in strategic market planning is to determine future business directions and develop marketing strategies. A business may choose one or more competitive strategies, including intense growth, diversified growth and integrated growth. Figure 19.10 shows these competitive strategies on a product-market matrix. This matrix can help in determining growth that can be implemented through marketing strategies.

Intense Growth

Intense growth can take place when current products and current markets have the potential for increasing sales. There are three main strategies for intense growth: market penetration, market development and product development.

Market penetration is a strategy of increasing sales in current markets with current products. For example, Coca-Cola and PepsiCo try to achieve increased market share through aggressive advertising.

Market development is a strategy of increasing sales of current products in new markets. For example, a European aircraft manufacturer was able to enter the US market by offering Eastern Airlines financing that Boeing could not match. Evian devised a new use for its mineral water by developing its "Brumisateur", an atomiser spray for the skin.

Product development is a strategy of increasing sales by improving present products

FIGURE 19.10
*Ansoff's competitve
strategies*

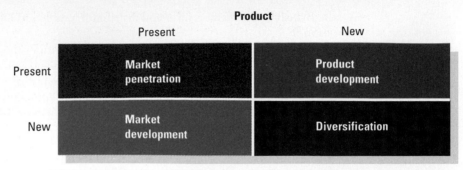

SOURCE: H. I. Ansoff, *The New Corporate Strategy* (New York, N.Y.: John Wiley & Sons, 1988), p. 83, Figure 6.1. Reproduced by permission of the author.

or developing new products for current markets. Tandem Computers, for example, has marketed specialty computers for commercial use for several years but has only recently developed its first mainframe computer—the NonStop Cyclone—to compete head on with IBM in Tandem's market.[24]

Diversified Growth

Diversified growth occurs when new products are developed to be sold in new markets. Firms have become increasingly diversified since the 1960s. Diversification offers some advantages over single business firms, because it allows firms to spread their risk across a number of markets. More important, it allows firms to make better and wider use of their management, technical and financial resources. For example, marketing expertise can be used across businesses, which may also share advertising themes, distribution channels, warehouse facilities or even sales forces.[25] The three forms of diversification are horizontal, concentric and conglomerate.

Horizontal diversification results when new products that are not technologically related to current products are introduced to current markets. Sony, for example, has diversified from electronics to film production through its purchase of Columbia Pictures. The purchase gave Sony a library of 2,700 films, including *Ghostbusters 2* and *When Harry Met Sally,* as well as 23,000 television episodes, which it may use to help establish its new line of 8mm videos.[26]

In *concentric diversification,* the marketing and technology of new products are related to current products, but the new ones are introduced into new markets. For instance, Dow Chemical is diversifying into agricultural chemicals and pharmaceuticals through joint ventures with corporations in those industries.[27]

Conglomerate diversification occurs when new products are unrelated to current technology, products or markets and are introduced to markets new to the firm. For example, Bass, the British brewer, acquired the American Holiday Inn hotel chain, and Laura Ashley, the UK clothing and furnishings company, has moved into the fragrance market with Laura Ashley No. 1.

Integrated Growth

Integrated growth can occur in the same industry that the firm is in and in three possible directions: forwards, backwards and horizontally. A company growing through forward integration takes ownership or increased control of its distribution system. For example, a shoe manufacturer might start selling its products through wholly owned retail outlets. In backward integration, a firm takes ownership or increased control of its supply systems. A newspaper company that buys a paper mill is integrating back wards. Horizontal integration occurs when a firm takes ownership or control of some of its competitors. For example, prior to its financial collapse, Polly Peck International, the British/Cypriot fruit grower and distributor, purchased Del Monte's fresh fruit division.[28]

In developing strategies, an organisation must consider the competitive positions in the market-place and formulate marketing strategies and tactics accordingly. Some authors have adopted warfare analogies to describe the strategic options for competing in a market. This chapter now examines the concept of competitive positions—as distinct from product or brand positionings, discussed in Chapter 3—and concludes with an overview of the principal warfare strategies.[29]

COMPETITIVE POSITIONS AND WARFARE

In the world of market shares, there has to be one—and only one—**market leader:** the player enjoying individually the largest slice of the market. In some industrial markets, a market leader can have a majority of industry sales, particularly when patent protection or technical innovation gives it an advantage over competitors. In most markets, however, the market leader may have only 10 to 20 per cent of the market's sales. The market leader has the highest market share and retains its competitive position by expanding the total market or expanding market share at the expense of rivals, while protecting or defending current market share by retaining its customer base.

Behind the market leader are competing companies, which are market challengers, market followers or market nichers. **Market challengers** are non-market leaders which aggressively attack rivals, including the market leader, to take more market share. In most instances, these players are number two, three and perhaps four in a market. It is important to remember, though, that to qualify as challengers these companies must be proactive and aggressive in their sales and marketing rather than passively reinforcing the existing hierarchy. It is also possible for a relative "minnow" to be a challenger; a company with 1 per cent of the market two years ago and 4.5 per cent this year is certainly one to monitor.

Market followers are low share competitors without resources, market position, research and development, or commitment to challenge for extra sales and market share. These companies tend to be the "plodders" or "me-toos" in a market, whose raison-d'être is to do as before and survive. In boom times these players can latch onto the success of their larger rivals, but in recession—or when faced with rivals' product innovation—they often struggle for business. Most markets also contain **market nichers**: companies which specialise by focusing on only a very narrow range of products (Sock Shop or Saab), or on a select band of consumers (Body Shop or Porsche). Nichers survive by finding a safe, small, profitable market segment—often apparently too small to attract the market leaders and challengers. Nichers specialise and can genuinely gear up a marketing mix that exactly matches their target customers' needs. They are vulnerable to market down turns, the entry of rival nichers and the sudden attention of the major players in the market-place.

A market leader must defend its position, while simultaneously seeking more market share. Only a market leader should consider **defensive warfare.** Strong defence involves striking a balance between waiting for market developments or competitor activity and proactively parrying competitors' thrusts. As market leader, the company must remember that a false sense of security and passive inactivity lead to disaster; the best defensive strategy is the courage to attack; and strong moves by competitors should always be blocked, never ignored. To defend its market share, a market leader must treat existing customers well and attentively and never take them for granted. The marketing mix must be continuously updated and target customer needs regularly considered. New markets, products and opportunities should always be sought and evaluated. Occasionally, if faced by a strong challenger in a small or declining market, a market leader should consider divesting and concentrating resources in its other markets.

A challenger has to attack for market share, but on what basis? The leader, and perhaps other challengers, will be strong and rich in resources. A challenger's attack must be well thought out and not suicidal in terms of the company's medium term future. In **offensive warfare,** the main consideration is the market leader's strength: where are there any chinks in the leader's armour? A challenger must identify a weakness in the leader's marketing mix and develop a genuine corresponding strength. With such a differential advantage or competitive edge, the challenger's resources may well be sufficient to steal ground successfully from the leader. Any attack, however, should be on a narrow front, where the challenger is percieved by the target customers to have an advantage and where resources can be focused. If no real weakness in the market leader exists, a challenger may attack head on. Such an attack can be successful only if there are numerous, very weak market followers, if the leader is slow to react and if a price cutting war does not result; in the latter situation, the leader's resource base may kill off the challenger's attack.

Followers are vulnerable, but careful monitoring of market, environmental and competitive trends can help ensure their survival. They must serve exactly only a few market segments, specialising rather than diversifying in terms of products and markets and making prudent use of what research and development resources are available. Nichers must watch for signs of competitor threats and possible changes in target segment customer needs; and they may need to consider product development and, ultimately, diversification. Their marketing mixes must be tailored exactly to meet the expectations of their target segment.

All organisations should know, for all their markets and target segments, which companies occupy these competitive positions. And they must alter their strategies and marketing programmes accordingly. Organisations should also review their rivals' marketing strategies and marketing programmes; many companies are surprisingly predictable. Response to rivals' pricing policies, frequency of new product launches, entry into new markets and timing of promotional campaigns, for example, can often be accurately anticipated. In this way thorough **competitor scanning** helps to establish more realistic marketing goals, develop successful strategies and programmes, and pre-empt nasty shocks caused by competitors' actions.

SUMMARY

Marketing strategy is a plan of action based on thorough analyses of market opportunities, trends in the marketing environment, customers, competitors, organisational goals, capabilities and resources. A marketing strategy aims to target customer segments of most benefit to an organisation in a manner which provides a differential advantage over competitors and matches the organisation's corporate goals.

A strategic market plan is an outline of the methods and resources required to achieve the organisation's goals within a specific target market; it takes into account all the functional areas of a business unit that must be co-ordinated. A strategic business unit (SBU) is a division, product line, or other profit centre within the parent company and is used to define areas for consideration in a specific strategic market plan. The process of strategic market planning yields a marketing strategy that is the framework for a marketing plan. A marketing plan (see Chapter 20) includes the framework and entire set of activities to be performed; it is the written document or blueprint for implementing and controlling an organisation's marketing activities.

Through the process of strategic market planning, an organisation can develop marketing strategies that, when properly implemented and controlled, will contribute to achieving the organisation's overall goals. The set of marketing strategies that are implemented and used at the same time is referred to as the organisation's marketing-programme. Environmental forces are important in—and profoundly affect—the strategic market planning process. These forces imply opportunities and threats that influence an organisation's overall goals.

A firm's organisational goals should be derived from its mission, that is, the broad tasks the organisation wants to achieve. These goals should guide planning efforts.

An organisation should strive for a differential advantage (competitive edge) in its markets. Marketing programmes and the marketing mix should emphasise desirable attributes of a company's marketing mix that its target customers consider unmatched by competitors.

There are three major considerations in assessing opportunities and resources: evaluating market opportunities, monitoring environmental forces and understanding the firm's capabilities. A market opportunity, or strategic window, opens when the right combination of circumstances occurs at the right time, allowing an organisation to take action towards a target market. An opportunity offers a favourable chance for the company to generate sales from markets. Market requirements relate to the customers' needs or desired benefits. The market requirements are satisfied by components of the marketing mix that provide buyers with these benefits. Environmental scanning is a search for information about events and relationships in a company's outside environment; such information aids marketers in planning. A firm's capabilities relate to distinctive competencies that it has developed to do something well and efficiently. A firm is likely to enjoy a differential advantage in an area in which its competencies out do those of its potential competition.

Corporate strategy determines the means for utilising resources in the areas of production, finance, research and development, personnel and marketing to reach the organisation's goals.

A number of tools have been developed to aid marketing managers in their planning efforts, including the Boston Consulting Group (BCG) product portfolio analysis, the market attractiveness–business position model and Profit Impact on Marketing Strategy (PIMS). The BCG approach is based on the philosophy that a product's market growth rate and its market share are key factors influencing marketing strategy. All the firm's products are integrated into a single, overall matrix and evaluated to determine appropriate strategies for individual SBUs and the overall portfolio strategies.

The market attractiveness–business position model is a two dimensional matrix. The market attractiveness dimension includes all the sources of strength and resources that relate to the market; competition, industry sales and the cost of competing are among the sources. The business position axis measures sales, relative market share, research and development, and other factors that relate to building a market share for a product.

The Profit Impact on Marketing Strategy (PIMS) research programme has developed a databank of confidential information on the successes, failures and marginal products of more than 3,000 strategic business units of the 200 members of the Strategic Planning Institute. The unit of observation in PIMS is an SBU. The results of PIMS include diagnostic and prescriptive information to assist in analysing marketing performance and formulating marketing strategies. The analysis focuses on options, problems, resources and opportunities.

These tools for strategic market planning are used only to diagnose problem areas or recognise opportunities. They are supplements to, not substitutes for, the marketing manager's own judgement. The real test of each approach, or any integrated approach, is how well it helps management diagnose the firm's strengths and weaknesses and prescribe strategic actions for maintaining or improving performance.

Competitive strategies that can be implemented through marketing include intense growth, diversified growth and integrated growth. Intense growth includes market penetration, market development or product development. Diversified growth include horizontal, concentric and conglomerate diversification. Integrated growth includes forwards, backwards and horizontal integration.

In developing strategies, an organisation must consider the competitive positions in the market-place. The market leader must defend its position and seek new sales opportunities. Attack may prove the best form of defence. Market challengers must aggressively seek market share gains but carefully select the basis on which to attack: a chink in the leader's armour or a quick response to changing consumer needs. Market followers are the "also-rans", prone to be squeezed in recession or in response to challengers' aggression. Market nichers specialise in terms of product and customer segment. They can very successfully tailor their marketing to their customers' needs but are vulnerable to competitors' entry into their target segments. To compete successfully, any organisation needs to consider the principles of offensive and defensive warfare.

IMPORTANT TERMS

Marketing strategy
Strategic market plan
Strategic business unit (SBU)
Strategic market planning
Marketing plan
Marketing programme
Differential advantage
Market opportunity
Market requirements
Environmental scanning
Capabilities
Marketing assets
Corporate strategy
Product portfolio analysis
Stars
Cash cows
Dogs
Problem children

Market attractiveness–business
   position model
General Electric's Strategic Business
   Planning Grid
Profit Impact on Marketing
   Strategy (PIMS)
Intense growth
Diversified growth
Integrated growth
Market leader
Market challenger
Market follower
Market nicher
Defensive warfare
Offensive warfare
Competitor scanning

DISCUSSION AND REVIEW QUESTIONS

1. Why should an organisation develop a marketing strategy? What is the difference between strategic market planning and the strategy itself?
2. Identify the major components of strategic market planning and explain how they are interrelated.

3. In what ways do environmental forces affect strategic market planning? Give specific examples.
4. What are some of the issues that must be considered in analysing a firm's opportunities and resources? How do these issues affect marketing objectives and marketing strategy?
5. Why is market opportunity analysis necessary? What are the determinants of market opportunity?
6. In relation to resource constraints, how can environmental scanning affect a firm's long term strategic market planning? Consider product costs and benefits affected by the environment.
7. What are the major considerations in developing the product portfolio grid? Define and explain the four basic types of products suggested by the Boston Consulting Group.
8. When should marketers consider using PIMS for strategic market planning?
9. Why do you think more firms are diversifying? Give some examples of diversified firms.
10. How can a market leader best defend its competitive position?
11. What are the strengths of a market nicher? In what way is a nicher vulnerable?

◼ CASES

19.1 Ireland: Marketing a Country

During the 1960s and 1970s, Ireland's economy lagged behind those of its European neighbours. The Irish government realised it needed to create more employment opportunities in industries of the future in order to establish a more affluent, outward-looking basis to the country's economy. Today Ireland has a trade surplus in excess of 11 per cent of GNP, a balance of payments surplus equivalent to 3 per cent of GNP and one of the lowest inflation rates in Europe. Membership in the EC has brought significant benefits to the country, including grants for infrastructure enhancements and improved international links. Over 1,000 international companies have been encouraged to invest in factories, distribution centres or office complexes.

From its previous dependence on agriculture, the economy has become far more balanced, with industry accounting for 35 per cent of GDP, distribution, transport and communication 18 per cent, services 31 per cent and agriculture just 10 per cent. Although not solely responsible for this change, the Industrial Development Authority (IDA) has figured prominently in Ireland's economic transformation. Established to promote industrial development, the IDA has encouraged overseas companies to locate in Ireland, creating close to 90,000 jobs; 350 US companies alone have settled on an Irish base as a gateway into the huge EC market of over 340 million consumers. Household names including IBM, Microsoft, Lotus, Norwich Union, Siemens, CIGNA, McGraw-Hill, Massachusetts Mutual, Ericsson, Philips, Fujitsu, Northern Telecom, Pratt & Whitney, Merck Sharp & Dohme, Braun, Coca-Cola and Nestlé are important investors and employers.

The IDA has succeeded not by good luck but through the development of an evolving strategy. First, it identified specific sectors of economic activity for international growth. Ireland wanted to attract the growth companies of the future, not yesteryear. Financial services, electronics, high-tech engineering, consumer products, branded food and drinks, and healthcare were earmarked to lead the economy into the Twenty-First Century. The USA, Pacific, Asia, Britain, Germany, Benelux and Scandinavia were home to these growth industries, so the IDA set up a network of 20 offices in these territories to push the Irish message.

Having targeted the growth industries, the IDA knew it had to offer benefits in order to attract any interest in locating and investing in Ireland. Research revealed several negative perceptions of the country and its people as impoverished, rural, agricultural and poorly educated. The facts paint a far different picture, and through glossy printed publicity, seminars, press involvement and various road shows, IDA personnel, politicians and leading Irish industrialists sought to convey the real story.

The message was carefully honed to reflect the target companies' concerns and to offer tangible rewards for investing in Ireland:

- A young, English speaking, highly educated workforce superior to most in Europe.
- A 10 per cent corporate tax rate up to the year 2010 and freedom to repatriate profits.
- A state of the art digital telecommunications system.
- Generous capital, employment, research and development, and training grants.
- A stable currency and low inflation rate.
- Duty free access to the EC market.
- Return on investment (29.9 per cent) more than three times the EC (9.4 per cent) and world (8.6 per cent) averages.
- Most European cities within two hours' flying time.
- A vigorous subcontracting and component supply industry.
- A unique, historic culture and quality of life with superb recreational and leisure facilities.

The pliable, capable, young workforce has been a significant attraction, as has the cultural and recreational base. The stable economy and hefty financial incentives for many companies simply helped close the deal for relocation. With extensions to Shannon International airport, the creation of the associated duty free zone trading estate—the first in the world—significant investment from both the private and public sectors and the recent development of the superb waterfront financial services centre in Dublin, the Irish strategy has worked.

An opportunity existed to create a rationale for overseas companies to put Ireland at the top of their location and investment lists. Advantages were created and existing benefits reinforced to establish a clear basis for companies to choose Ireland. Careful targeting of industries and companies, supported by comprehensive promotion, led to the establishment of operations in Ireland by over 1,000 companies.

SOURCES: Irish Embassy, London; Industrial Development Authority (IDA); IDA promotional material: "Dublin: the international financial services centre", "Ireland: put yourself in our hands in the 90s"; Shannon Development promotional literature.

Questions for Discussion

1. Why was targeting central to the IDA strategy?
2. What problems had to be overcome to attract overseas investors to locate in Ireland?
3. What benefits were offered by the IDA? How did this varied package communicate the Irish message?

19.2   Marks & Spencer: Maintaining Competitive Position

The Marks & Spencer story began in 1884 when Russian refugee Michael Marks set up a haberdashery market stall in the northern English city of Leeds. Ten years later, the empire had expanded to 10 stalls and Marks was joined by Tom Spencer. Today, with close to 700 stores in Europe, the US, Canada and the Far East and a turnover of more than £5.8 billion, Marks & Spencer has become truly international.

The company's aim of providing quality, value and service, established early on by Michael Marks and Tom Spencer, is still its goal today. The aim has been expanded to form a set of key company principles (see table) which management believes will help to ensure the company's continued success. Through its range of clothing, foods and homeware, Marks & Spencer has a powerful hold on the retailing sector. With 17 per cent of the UK clothing market and 5 per cent of food sales, the company works hard to maintain its competitive position.

Management at Marks & Spencer is acutely aware of the importance of a satisfied and brand loyal customer base. Keeping customers happy means staying in touch with, and adapting quickly to, new trends. The clothing side of the company's business accounts for approaching half of total turnover. To retain its share of this highly competitive market, Marks & Spencer has developed close links with key manufacturers, working together with them to ensure that seasonal sales patterns are reflected in the products in the stores. The company splits its clothing products into "classic" goods—which are not highly susceptible to sudden fashion fluctuations—and fashion goods—which enjoy a short life-cycle and become quickly out-moded. This categorisation helps the company match customer desires with appropriate merchandise.

Marks & Spencer does not rely just on its clothing to maintain its strong market position. The company's range of quality food is an increasingly important aspect of the business. With the 40 per cent share of turnover taken by this range looking set to increase, the company is continually seeking innovative recipes—both convenience and cordon bleu— to appeal to customers' taste buds.

Here too, ensuring quality products and customer satisfaction remains the focus. The handling of chilled foods needs to be undertaken with particular care; and Marks & Spencer has installed systems to ensure that it is. For example, the transport of produce from the point of manufacture to stores—and ultimately to the customer—is especially critical. Fleets of refrigerated lorries ensure the early arrival of produce at stores, where staff move quickly to transfer the food to cold rooms and into shop floor fridges. The Marks & Spencer commitment to quality does not end there. Comprehensive customer instructions are printed on the packs to ensure that produce is correctly stored and used in the home.

MARKS & SPENCER UK: COMPANY PRINCIPLES

Selling clothing for the family, homeware and a range of fine foods—all representing high standards of quality and value.

Creating an attractive, efficient shopping environment for customers.

Providing friendly, helpful service from well trained staff.

Sharing mutually beneficial, long term partnerships with suppliers who use modern and efficient production techniques.

Supporting British industry and buying abroad only when new ideas, technology, quality and value are not available in the UK.

Ensuring that staff and shareholders share in the success of the company.

Fostering good human relations with customers, staff, suppliers and the community.

Acting with responsibility towards the environment in all operations and, with all suppliers, in the manufacture of the goods sold.

SOURCE: *Marks & Spencer Company Facts, 1992.* Used with permission.

Marks & Spencer, currently enjoying a strong competitive position in the UK retailing sector as market leader in terms of market share, profitability and customer loyalty, considers its customers the key to continued success. Monitoring customer needs, responding quickly to them and maintaining standards of quality, service and value for money—while keeping a careful eye on the competition—are all central to keeping the customers happy.

SOURCES: *Marks & Spencer Company Facts,* 1992, Marks & Spencer plc, Baker Street, London; *Marks & Spencer Annual Report,* 1993; *A Company of Values,* Marks & Spencer plc, 1991, Baker Street, London; *Bricks and Mortar,* Marks & Spencer plc, 1991, Baker Street, London; *Food for Thought,* Marks & Spencer plc, 1991, Baker Street, London; *Spinning a Yarn,* Marks & Spencer plc, 1991, Baker Street, London.

Questions for Discussion

1. With what types of stores does Marks & Spencer compete?
2. Does Marks & Spencer have a differential advantage? If so, what is it?
3. If you were a new clothing retailer selling a full range of family clothes, how would you position your products against Marks & Spencer? What competitive position would your company be likely to occupy in the market?

20 MARKETING PLANNING AND SALES POTENTIAL

Objectives

- To gain an understanding of sales potential

- To become familiar with sales forecasting methods

- To understand the marketing planning process

- To examine the role of the SWOT analysis in marketing planning

- To gain an overview of the marketing plan

- To become aware of the major components of a marketing audit

NutraSweet Company's brand of sugar substitute has become a household name, but its exclusive patent and worldwide monopoly expired in 1992. Pressure is on the organisation to produce an equally popular and profitable product. NutraSweet believes it can present an encore performance with its fat substitute, Simplesse, a blend of proteins from milk and egg whites. Simplesse's recent approval by the US Food and Drug Administration (FDA) as the first low calorie fat substitute opens the door to a huge potential market.

To separate its brand of fat substitute from its brand of sugar substitute, NutraSweet markets Simplesse through a newly formed subsidary, Simplesse Company, and employs a marketing strategy aimed at establishing Simplesse as a "branded ingredient". The firm is working to ensure that customers will look for Simplesse, not "microparticulated protein", on product labels. NutraSweet's strategy for establishing brand identity includes persuading its customers to display the Simplesse logo—a spoon dipping into a dish—on their packaging, and introducing its own frozen dessert, Simple Pleasures.

Although Simplesse benefits from being the first fat substitute on the market, its success is far from assured. Longer than expected FDA approval time hurt, because the product is now entering a market in which everything from cereal to potato crisps is advertised as being low in fat and cholesterol. When its patent runs out in 2005, Simplesse will come up against packaged food giants Procter & Gamble, Frito-Lay, Unilever and many more, all of which are working on fat substitutes. NutraSweet's long awaited second act depends on establishing brand identity before the curtain rises on the competition. It is a well thought-out strategy, but one still to be proven.

As for NutraSweet's first core product, its same named sugar substitute, marketers have slaved long hours to maintain market leadership. Marketing planning has helped to ensure that core target markets have been carefully singled out with marketing programmes designed to maintain sales, raise brand awareness and create brand loyalty. ■

SOURCES: Robert Steyer, "Analysts trim hopes on fake fat," *St. Louis Post Dispatch*, 1 August 1991; "Fake fat of the land", *Time*, 24 June 1991, p. 41; Robert McMath, "Footloose and sugar free", *Adweek's Marketing Week*, 3 June 1991, p. 41; Julie Liesse, "Fat-free: Fad or food of the future?" *Advertising Age*, 10 September 1990, p. 6; and Molly O'Neill, "First low calorie substitute for fats is approved by US", *New York Times*, 23 February 1990.

Manipulation of the marketing mix to match target market needs and expectations constitutes a daily activity for most marketing personnel. However, as explained in the previous chapter, fundamental strategic decisions need to be addressed before the marketing mix(es) are formulated. To expedite this process and link the strategic decision-making to the development of actionable marketing programmes, many organisations turn to formal marketing planning. Some companies conduct a marketing audit as a preliminary analysis to gain a realistic understanding of the organisation, its personnel and its market. Like all business activities, marketing needs to have goals; often these are sales targets and market share objectives. To set the right goals, marketers must be able to forecast future sales and market size trends. This chapter begins with a discussion of forecasting and techniques for predicting sales. It then examines in detail the marketing planning process, including the SWOT analysis. The chapter concludes with a summary of the marketing audit.

A sales forecast is an estimation of the amount of a service or product that an organisation expects to sell during a specific period at a specified level of marketing activities. Market potential is a prediction of industry wide market size, everything else being equal, over a specified time period. Marketing planning is a systematic process involving the assessment of marketing opportunities and resources, the determination of marketing objectives and the development of a plan for implementation and control. The marketing audit, where applied, is a systematic examination of the objectives, strategies, organisation and performance of a company's marketing unit.

Forecasting in Marketing

Unfortunately, many organisations' sales and marketing activities are reactions to changes in the market-place, particularly the actions of competitors, rather than planned and carefully orchestrated activities which anticipate consumer needs and expectations. In such reactive organisations, predictions of future changes in market size and potential tend to be rudimentary or non-existent. Estimations of their own likely sales are often based only on the hunches of managers or on the status quo. The forecasting of market potential and expected sales is problematic but must be undertaken thoroughly and with as much objectivity as marketing intelligence and information permit. This section focuses on market and sales potential, and forecasting techniques.

Market and Sales Potentials

Market potential is the total amount of a product that customers will purchase within a specified period at a specific level of industry wide marketing activity. Market potential can be stated in terms of monetary value or units and can refer to a total market or to a market segment. As shown in Figure 20.1, market potential depends on economic, social and other marketing environment factors. Marketing Insight 20.1 discusses the expansion of theme park Alton Towers into new markets: forecasts were required first to help determine market potential. When analysing market potential, it is important to specify a time frame and to indicate the relevant level of industry marketing activities. One airline determined that in one year 3,300,000 customers travelled to Europe on its aircraft—more customers than any other airline had. Based on this finding, its marketers were able to estimate the market potential for European travel in the following year, taking into account other environmental factors.

Note that marketers have to assume a certain general level of marketing effort in the industry when they estimate market potential. The specific level of marketing effort certainly varies from one firm to another, but the sum of all firms' marketing activities equals industry marketing efforts. A marketing manager must also consider whether

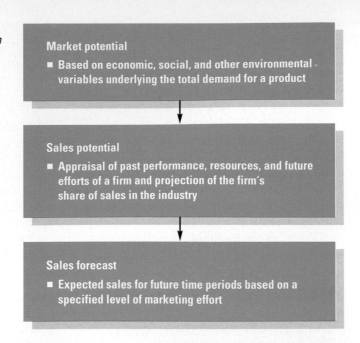

and to what extent industry marketing efforts will change. For instance, in estimating the market potential for the spreadsheet software industry, Microsoft must consider changes in marketing efforts by Lotus and other software producers. If marketing managers at Microsoft know that Lotus is planning to introduce a new version of the Lotus 1-2-3 Spreadsheet product with a new advertising campaign, this fact will contribute to Microsoft's estimate of the market potential for computer software.

Sales potential is the maximum percentage of market potential that an individual company within an industry can expect to obtain for a specific product or service. Several general factors influence a company's sales potential. First, the market potential places absolute limits on the size of the company's sales potential. Second, the magnitude of industry wide marketing activities has an indirect but definite impact on the company's sales potential. Those activities have a direct bearing on the size of the market potential. When Pizza Hut advertises home delivered pizza, for example, it indirectly promotes pizza in general; its advertisements may, in fact, help sell competitors' home delivered pizza. Third, the intensity and effectiveness of a company's marketing activities relative to those of its competitors affect the size of the company's sales potential. If a company is spending twice as much as any of its competitors on marketing efforts and if every unit of currency spent is more effective in generating sales, the firm's sales potential will be quite high compared with that of its competitors.

There are two general approaches to measuring sales potential: break down and build up. In the **break down approach**, the marketing manager first develops a general economic forecast for a specific time period. Next, market potential is estimated on the basis of this economic forecast. The company's sales potential is then derived from the general economic forecast and the estimate of market potential.

In the **build up approach,** an analyst begins by estimating how much of a product a potential buyer in a specific geographic area, such as a sales territory, will purchase in a given period. Then the analyst multiplies that amount by the total number of potential buyers in that area. The analyst performs the same calculation for each geographic area in which the firm sells products and then adds the totals for each area to calculate the market potential. To determine the sales potential, the analyst must estimate, by

PLANNING A DAY OUT—ALTON TOWERS

The theme park is a leisure park consisting of rides and attractions built around a central theme or themes. Walt Disney created the concept in America, and the Disney Corporation has since taken the concept to Japan and now to France. The UK theme park industry really took off in the early 1980s. By 1985 there were 4.5 million visitors; and by 1989, 9.5 million visitors who spent £105 million. Current figures estimate that by 1996, 12.5 million visitors will spend £182 million, although the opening of the Paris Disney World and of the Channel Tunnel may have some bearing on these. The top five theme parks in the UK are listed below:

Alton Towers	2.4 million visitors
Chessington World of Adventure	1.3
Thorpe Park	1.3
Frontierland	1.3
The American Adventure	0.7

Not only do theme parks compete with one another, though geographically many cater for purely local markets, they also compete with a whole range of day trip activities:

Museums and galleries	33.0% of day trippers
Historic properties	22.5
Wildlife attractions	10.0
Theme parks	5.5
Gardens	4.0
Other (Seaside resorts, holiday centres, etc.)	25.0

Despite the 1990–1993 economic downturn in the UK, and the crises in the Middle East and eastern Europe, all economic indicators point to an increase in leisure time and in discretionary income. Alton Towers aims to maintain its market leadership. It continually invests in new rides and facilities and is planning a £20 million holiday village next to the park (for the leisure and business conference markets). The strategy is to attract new visitors in the UK and from continental Europe, while encouraging repeat visits from current users. Key targets are young adults aged 15 to 24, families with children, school parties and, increasingly, the corporate sector for sales incentive schemes and corporate events (AGMs, product launches, sales force parties and so on). Each segment has its own marketing mix and strategy: separate price policies, promotional tactics and even product offerings. From being a day tripper park orientated towards the family, Alton Towers has monitored demographic changes and competitor activity and is planning to cater for its key segments' differing needs well into the 1990s.

SOURCES: British Tourist Authority, 1988; "Visits to tourist attractions", British Tourist, Authority, 1987–1989; *Leisure Management*, Volume 9, April 1989, and Volume 10, July 1990; Alton Towers' promotional material, 1990; K. M. Bon, "The UK leisure industry", Warwick MBA dissertation, University of Warwick, 1990.

specific levels of marketing activities, the proportion of the total market potential that the company can obtain.

For example, the marketing manager of a regional paper company with three competitors might estimate the company's sales potential for bulk gift wrapping paper using the buildup approach. The manager might determine that each of the 66 paper buyers in a single sales territory purchases an average of 10 rolls annually. For that sales territory, then, the market potential is 660 rolls annually. The analyst follows the same procedure for each of the firm's other nine sales territories and then totals the sales potential for each sales territory (see Table 20.1). Assuming that this total market potential is 18,255 rolls of paper (the quantity expected to be sold by all four paper companies), the marketing manager would estimate the company's sales potential by ascertaining that it could sell about 33 per cent of the estimated 18,255 rolls at a certain level of marketing effort. The marketing manager might develop several sales potentials, based on several levels of marketing effort.

Whether marketers use the break down or the build up approach, they depend heavily on sales estimates. To get a clearer idea of how these estimates are derived, it is essential to understand sales forecasting.

Developing Sales Forecasts

A **sales forecast** is the amount of a product that the company actually expects to sell during a specific period at a specified level of marketing activities. The sales forecast differs from the sales potential: it concentrates on what the actual sales will be at a certain level of marketing effort, whereas the sales potential assesses what sales are possible at various levels of marketing activities, based on certain environmental conditions. Businesses use the sales forecast for planning, organising, implementing and controlling their activities. The success of numerous activities depends on the accuracy of this forecast. Forecasts help to estimate market attractiveness, monitor performances, allocate resources effectively and efficiently, and gear up production to meet demand. Excess stocks are wasteful and cost money; but production set too low leads to missed sales, and perhaps customer or distributor unease.[1]

A sales forecast must be time specific. Sales projections can be short (one year or

TABLE 20.1 *The sales potential calculations for bulk wrapping paper*
(Market potential: 18,255 rolls)

TERRITORY	NUMBER OF POTENTIAL CUSTOMERS	ESTIMATED PURCHASES	TOTAL
1	66	10 rolls	660 rolls
2	62	10	620
3	55	5	275
4	28	25	700
5	119	5	595
6	50	20	1,000
7	46	10	460
8	34	15	510
9	63	10	630
10	55	10	550
		Total company sales potential	6,000 rolls

less), medium (one to five years) or long (longer than five years). The length of time chosen for the sales forecast depends on the purpose and uses of the forecast, the stability of the market, and the firm's objectives and resources.

To forecast sales, a marketer can choose from a number of forecasting methods. Some of them are arbitrary; others are more scientific, complex and time consuming. A firm's choice of method or methods depends on the costs involved, the type of product, the characteristics of the market, the time span of the forecast, the purposes of the forecast, the stability of the historical sales data, the availability of required information, and the forecasters' expertise and experience.[2] The common forecasting techniques fall into five categories: executive judgement, surveys, time series analysis, correlation methods and market tests.[3]

Executive Judgement.   At times, a company forecasts sales chiefly on the basis of **executive judgement,** which is the intuition of one or more executives. This approach is highly unscientific but expedient and inexpensive. Executive judgement may work reasonably well when product demand is relatively stable and the forecaster has years of market related experience. However, because intuition is swayed most heavily by recent experience, the forecast may be overly optimistic or overly pessimistic. Another drawback to intuition is that the forecaster has only past experience as a guide for deciding where to go in the future.

Surveys.   A second way to forecast sales is to question customers, sales personnel or experts regarding their expectations about future purchases.

Through a **customer forecasting survey,** marketers can ask customers what types and quantities of products they intend to buy during a specific period. This approach may be useful to a business that has relatively few customers. For example, a computer chip producer that markets to less than a hundred computer manufacturers could conduct a customer survey. PepsiCo, though, has millions of customers and cannot feasibly use a customer survey to forecast future sales, unless its sampling is known to reflect the entire market, which is hard to verify.

Customer surveys have several drawbacks. Customers must be able and willing to make accurate estimates of future product requirements. Although industrial buyers can sometimes estimate their anticipated purchases accurately from historical buying data and their own sales forecasts, many cannot make such estimates. In addition, for a variety of reasons, customers may not want to take part in a survey. Occasionally, a few respondents give answers that they know are incorrect, making survey results inaccurate. Moreover, customer surveys reflect buying intentions, not actual purchases. Customers' intentions may not be well formulated, and even when potential purchasers have definite buying intentions, they do not necessarily follow through with them. Finally, customer surveys consume much time and money.

In a **sales force forecasting survey,** members of the firm's sales force are asked to estimate the anticipated sales in their territories for a specified period of time. The forecaster combines these territorial estimates to arrive at a tentative forecast.

A marketer may survey the sales staff for several reasons. The most important one is that the sales staff are closer to customers on a daily basis than other company personnel; therefore they should know more about customers' future product needs. Moreover, when sales representatives assist in developing the forecast, they are more likely to work towards its achievement. Another advantage of this method is that forecasts can be prepared for single territories, for divisions consisting of several territories, for regions made up of multiple divisions and then for the total geographic market. Thus the method readily provides sales forecasts from the smallest geographic sales unit to the largest.

Despite these benefits, a sales force survey has certain limitations. Salespeople can be too optimistic or pessimistic because of recent experiences. In addition, salespeople tend to underestimate the sales potential in their territories when they believe that their sales goals will be determined by their forecasts. They also dislike paperwork because it takes up the time that could be spent selling. If the preparation of a territorial sales forecast is time consuming, the sales staff may not do the job adequately.

None the less, sales force surveys can be effective under certain conditions. If, for instance, the salespeople as a group are accurate—or at least consistent—estimators, the over estimates and under estimates should balance each other out. If the aggregate forecast is consistently over or under actual sales, then the marketer who develops the final forecast can make the necessary adjustments. Assuming that the survey is well administered, the sales force can have the satisfaction of helping to establish reasonable sales goals. It can also be assured that its forecasts are not being used to set sales quotas.

The **Delphi approach** is very popular: managers' and sales personnel's views are validated centrally, and the resulting forecasts are returned to those involved for further comment. Participants—such as field managers—make separate, individual forecasts. A central analyst independently aggregates and modifies their forecasts. This revised forecast is returned to the separate participants, who can then amend their forecasts in the context of the consolidated picture. The central analyst then collates the updated forecasts to produce the company's overall final forecast. The Delphi technique avoids many weighting and judgemental problems; the median of the group's overall response will tend to be more accurate; and the approach is useful for short, medium and long term forecasts, as well as for new product development, for which there is no historical information on which to base a forecast.

When a company wants an **expert forecasting survey,** it hires experts to help prepare the sales forecast. These experts are usually economists, management consultants, advertising executives, academics or other persons outside the firm who have solid experience in a specific market. Drawing on this experience and their analyses of available information about the company and the market, the experts prepare and present their forecasts or answer questions regarding a forecast. Using experts is expedient and relatively inexpensive. However, because they work outside the firm, experts may not be as motivated as company personnel to do an effective job.

Time Series Analysis. The technique by which the forecaster, using the firm's historical sales data, tries to discover a pattern or patterns in the firm's sales over time is called **time series analysis.** If a pattern is found, it can be used to forecast sales. This forecasting method assumes that the past sales pattern will continue in the future. The accuracy, and thus the usefulness, of time series analysis hinges on the validity of this assumption.

In a time series analysis, a forecaster usually performs four types of analysis: trend, cycle, seasonal and random factor.[4] **Trend analysis** focuses on aggregate sales data, such as a company's annual sales figure, over a period of many years to determine whether annual sales are generally rising, falling or staying about the same. Through **cycle analysis,** a forecaster analyses sales figures (often monthly sales data) over a period of three to five years to ascertain whether sales fluctuate in a consistent, periodic manner. When performing **seasonal analysis,** the analyst studies daily, weekly or monthly sales figures to evaluate the degree to which seasonal factors, such as climate and holiday activities, influence the firm's sales. **Random factor analysis** is an attempt to attribute erratic sales variations to random, non-recurrent events, such as a regional power failure, a natural disaster or political unrest in a foreign market. After performing each of these analyses, the forecaster combines the results to develop the sales forecast.

Time series analysis is an effective forecasting method for products with reasonably stable demand, but it is not useful for products with highly erratic demand. Seagram, the importer and producer of spirits and wines, uses several types of time series analysis for forecasting and has found them quite accurate. For example, Seagram's forecasts of industry sales volume has proved correct within ±1.5 per cent, and the firm's sales forecasts have been accurate within ±2 per cent.[5] Time series analysis is not always so dependable.

Correlation Methods. Like time series analysis, correlation methods are based on historical sales data. When using **correlation methods,**[6] the forecaster attempts to find a relationship between past sales and one or more variables such as population, per capita income or gross national product. To determine whether a correlation exists, the forecaster analyses the statistical relationship between changes in past sales and changes in one or more variables—a technique known as regression analysis.[7] The object of regression analysis is a mathematical formula that accurately describes a relationship between the firm's sales and one or more variables; however, the formula indicates only an association, not a causal relationship. Once an accurate formula has been established, the analyst plugs the necessary information into the formula to derive the sales forecast.

Correlation methods are useful when a precise relationship can be established. However, a forecaster seldom finds a perfect correlation. Furthermore, this method can be used only when the available historical sales data are extensive. Ordinarily, then, correlation techniques are futile for forecasting the sales of new products, or in markets where changes are frequent and extensive.

Market Tests. Conducting a **market test** involves making a product available to buyers in one or more test areas and measuring purchases and consumer responses to distribution, promotion and price. Even though test areas are often cities with populations of 200,000 to 500,000, test sites can be larger metropolitan areas or towns with populations of 50,000 to 200,000, or ITV regions. A market test provides information about consumers' actual purchases rather than about their intended purchases. In addition, purchase volume can be evaluated in relation to the intensity of other marketing activities—advertising, in-store promotions, pricing, packaging, distribution and the like. On the basis of customer response in test areas, forecasters can estimate product sales for larger geographic units. For example, Cadbury's Wispa first appeared in the Tyne Tees area of North East England. Sales showed management that the company had to build more production capacity to cope with a national roll out of the brand and full launch.

Because it does not require historical sales data, a market test is an effective tool for forecasting the sales of new products or the sales of existing products in new geographic areas. The test gives the forecaster information about customers' real actions rather than intended or estimated behaviour. A market test also gives a marketer an opportunity to test various elements of the marketing mix. But these tests are often time consuming and expensive. In addition, a marketer cannot be certain that the consumer response during a market test represents the total market response or that such a response will continue in the future.

Using Multiple Forecasting Methods

Although some businesses depend on a single sales forecasting method, most firms use several techniques. A company is sometimes forced to use several methods when it markets diverse product lines, but even for a single product line several forecasts may be needed, especially when the product is sold in different market segments. Thus a producer of car tyres may rely on one technique to forecast tyre sales for new cars and on another to forecast the sales of replacement tyres. Variation in the length of the needed forecasts may call for several forecast methods. A firm that employs one method for a short range forecast may find it inappropriate for long range forecasting. Sometimes a marketer verifies the results of one method by using one or several other methods and comparing results.[8]

MARKETING PLANNING

As noted at the start, this chapter deals with the planning aspect of marketing management. This section describes how the strategic plan is implemented. **Marketing planning** is a systematic process that involves assessing marketing opportunities and resources, determining marketing objectives and developing a plan for implementation and control. An objective of marketing planning is the creation of a marketing plan document. The marketing planning process combines the organisation's overall marketing strategy with fundamental analyses of trends in the marketing environment; company strengths, weaknesses, opportunities and threats; competitive strategies; and identification of target market segments. Ultimately, the process leads to the formulation of marketing programmes or marketing mixes which facilitate the implementation of the organisation's strategies and plans.

Figure 20.2 illustrates the **marketing planning cycle.** Note that marketing plan-

FIGURE 20.2
The marketing planning cycle

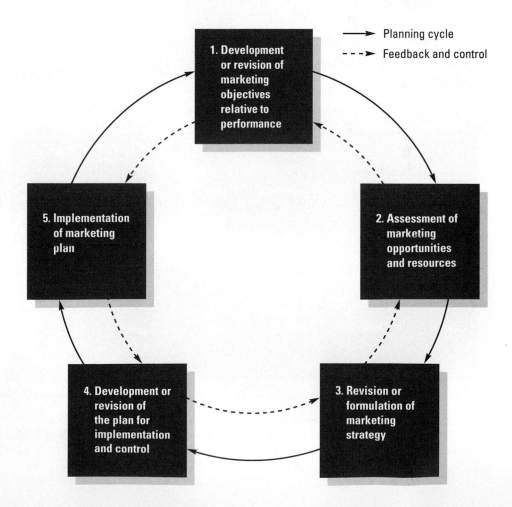

Planning cycle
----- Feedback and control

1. Development or revision of marketing objectives relative to performance

2. Assessment of marketing opportunities and resources

3. Revision or formulation of marketing strategy

4. Development or revision of the plan for implementation and control

5. Implementation of marketing plan

ning is a circular process. As the dotted feedback lines in the figure indicate, planning is not one way. Feedback is used to co-ordinate and synchronise all the stages of the planning cycle.

The duration of marketing plans varies. Plans that cover a period of one year or less are called **short range plans. Medium range plans** are usually for two to five years. Marketing plans that extend beyond five years are generally viewed as **long range plans.** These plans can sometimes cover a period as long as 20 years. Marketing managers may have short, medium, and long range plans all at the same time. Long range plans are relatively rare. However, as the marketing environment continues to change and business decisions become more complex, profitability and survival will depend more and more on the development of long range plans.[9] Many organisations choose to update fully and revise their marketing plans annually, modifying their marketing programmes and changing the detail of their marketing mix(es) as a result. Overall strategic planning is unlikely to face annual changes of such magnitude, although strategy modifications will always be needed to respond to changes in customer needs, the marketing environment and competitors' activities.

The extent to which marketing managers develop and use plans also varies. Although planning provides numerous benefits, some managers do not use formal marketing plans because they spend almost all their time dealing with daily problems, many of which would be eliminated by adequate planning. However, planning is becoming more important to marketing managers, who realise that planning is necessary

FIGURE 20.3 *The importance of marketing planning*
The Rover Mini is still in production decades since launch. Shrewd planning has enabled Rover to target changing segments and modify its smallest model to maintain consumer interest.

SOURCE: By kind permission of Rover Group Ltd.

to develop, co-ordinate and control marketing activities effectively and efficiently. (Figure 20.3 shows the value of marketing planning to Rover.) When formulating a marketing plan, a new enterprise or a firm with a new product does not have current performance to evaluate or an existing plan to revise. Therefore, its marketing planning centres on analysing available resources and options to assess opportunities. Managers can then develop marketing objectives and a strategy. In addition, many firms recognise the need to include information systems in their plans so that they can have continuous feedback and keep their marketing activities orientated towards objectives. One research study, which examined 207 different companies, found that those that have maintained or increased their planning departments during the past five years and increased their allocation of resources to planning activities out performed those whose planning departments have become smaller.[10]

To illustrate the marketing planning process, consider the decisions that went into the planning in America of the national newspaper *USA Today*. Table 20.2 lists several of the more important marketing decisions. Of course, to reach the objective, a detailed course of action was communicated throughout the organisation. In short, specific marketing plans should do the following:

1. Specify expected results so that the organisation can anticipate what its situation will be at the end of the current planning period.
2. Identify the resources needed to carry out the planned activities so that a budget can be developed.
3. Describe in sufficient detail the activities that are to take place so that responsibilities for implementation can be assigned.

TABLE 20.2   *Planning for the introduction of a national newspaper: USA Today*

Objective: Achieve 1 million in circulation by reaching an upmarket segment, primarily of males who hold professional and managerial positions and who made at least one trip of 200 miles or more within the last year.

Opportunity: Paper tends to be a second newspaper purchase for readers. *USA Today* is not in competition directly with local papers, and it is not positioned against other national newspapers/magazines.

Market: Circulation within a 200 mile radius of 15 major markets, representing 54 per cent of the US population, including such cities as Chicago, Houston, New York, Los Angeles and Denver.

Product: Superior graphic quality; appeal to the television generation through short news items, a colour weather map and other contemporary features.

Price: Competitive.

Promotion: Pedestal like vending machines with attention grabbing design and a higher position than competitors to differentiate the paper and bring it closer to eye level. Out door advertising and some print advertising promotes the paper.

Distribution: Newsstands, vending machines in busy locations and direct mail.

Implementation and control: Personnel with experience in the newspaper business who can assist in developing a systematic approach for implementing the marketing strategy and design, as well as an information system to monitor and control the results.

SOURCE: Kevin Higgins, *"USA Today* nears million reader mark", *Marketing News,* 15 April 1983, pp. 1, 5. Reprinted by permission of the American Marketing Association.

TABLE 20.3 *The core steps of the marketing planning process*

ANALYSIS

Analysis of customers' needs and perceptions: market segmentation and brand positioning

Analysis of the marketing environment and trends

Analysis of competition and competitors' strategies

Analysis of market opportunities/trends

Analysis of company's Strengths, Weaknesses, Opportunities and Threats (SWOT)

STRATEGY

Determination of core target markets; basis for competing/differential advantage;
  desired product positioning

IMPLEMENTATION

Specification of sales targets and expected results

Specification of plans for marketing mix programmes:

- products
- promotion
- distribution
- service levels
- pricing

Specification of tasks/responsibilities; timing; costs; budgets

SOURCE: Sally Dibb and Lyndon Simkin, *The Marketing Casebook.* Copyright © 1993 by Routledge. Used with permission.

4. Provide for the monitoring of activities and results so control can be exerted.[11]
5. Lead to the implementation of the organisation's marketing strategy.

There is a logical and relatively straightforward approach to marketing planning:

1. Analysis of markets and the trading environment.
2. Determination of core target markets.
3. Identification of a differential advantage (competitive edge).
4. Statement of specific goals and desired product or service positioning.
5. Development of marketing mixes to implement plans.
6. Determination of required budgets and allocation of marketing tasks.

Table 20.3 illustrates these aspects of the marketing planning process in more detail.

Obviously, the marketing plan needs to be carefully written to attain these objectives. The next section of this chapter takes a closer look at the marketing plan itself.

THE MARKETING PLAN

The marketing plan is the written document or blueprint governing all of a firm's marketing activities, including the implementation and control of those activities.[12] A marketing plan serves a number of purposes:

1. It offers a "road map" for implementing the firm's strategies and achieving its objectives.
2. It assists in management control and monitoring of implementation of strategy.

3. It informs new participants in the plan of their role and function.
4. It specifies how resources are to be allocated.
5. It stimulates thinking and makes better use of resources.
6. It assigns responsibilities, tasks and timing.
7. It makes participants aware of problems, opportunities and threats.

A company should have a plan for each marketing strategy it develops. Because such plans must be changed as forces in the company and in the environment change, marketing planning is a continuous process.

Organisations use many different formats when devising marketing plans. Plans may be written for strategic business units, product lines, individual products or brands, or specific markets. Most plans share some common ground, however, by including an executive summary; a statement of objectives; background to the market; a situation analysis and examination of realistic market opportunities; a description of environmental forces, customers' needs and market segments, and competitor activity; an outline of marketing strategy; a statement of expected sales patterns; the detail of marketing mixes required to implement the marketing plan; controls; financial requirements and budgets; and any operational considerations that arise from the marketing plan (see Table 20.4). The following sections consider the major parts of a typical marketing plan, as well as the purpose that each part serves.

| **Management or Executive Summary** | The *management summary*, or *executive summary* (often only one or two pages) should be a concise overview of the entire report, including key aims, overall strategies, fundamental conclusions and salient points regarding the suggested marketing programmes (mixes). Not many people read an entire report, tending to dip in here and there, so the management summary should be comprehensive and clear. |

| **Marketing Objectives** | *Objectives* are for the benefit of the reader, to give perspective to the report. Aims and objectives should be stated briefly, but include reference to the organisation's mission statement (corporate goals), objectives and any fundamental desires for core product groups or brands. This section describes the objectives underlying the plan. A **marketing objective** is a statement of what is to be accomplished through marketing activities. It specifies the results expected from marketing efforts. A marketing objective should be expressed in clear, simple terms so that all marketing personnel understand exactly what they are trying to achieve. It should be written in such a way that its accomplishment can be measured accurately. If a company has an objective of increasing its market share by 12 per cent, the firm should be able to measure changes in its market share accurately. A marketing objective should also indicate the time frame for accomplishing the objective. For example, a company that sets an objective of introducing three new products should state the time period in which this is to be done. |

Objectives may be stated in terms of degree of product introduction or innovation, sales volume, profitability per unit or gains in market share. They must also be consistent with the company's overall organisational goals.

| **Product/Market Background** | *Product/market background* is a necessary section. Not everyone will be fully familiar with the products and their markets. This section "scene sets," helping the readers—for example, a chief executive or advertising manager—to understand the marketing plan. |

| **Situation or SWOT Analyses** | The *SWOT* or a *situational* analysis is an important foundation for any marketing plan, helping to produce realistic and meaningful recommendations. The section in the main body of the report should be kept to a concise overview, with detailed market |

TABLE 20.4   *Parts of a marketing plan*

1. **Executive or Management Summary**
2. **Objectives**
   a. Company mission statement
   b. Detailed company objectives
   c. Product group goals
3. **Product/Market Background**
   a. Product range and explanation
   b. Market overview and sales summary
4. **Situation or SWOT Analysis**
   a. Performance of current marketing strategies
   b. Greatest challenges or threats
   c. Opportunity analysis
5. **Marketing Analyses**
   a. Marketing environment and trends
   b. Customers' needs and segments
   c. Competition and competitors' strategies
6. **Marketing Strategies**
   a. Core target markets (segments)
   b. Basis for competing/differential advantage
   c. Desired product/brand positioning
7. **Statement of Expected Sales Forecasts and Results**
8. **Marketing Programmes for Implementation**
   a. Marketing mixes
   b. Tasks and responsibilities
9. **Controls and Evaluation: Monitoring of Performance**
10. **Financial Implications/Required Budgets**
    a. Delineation of costs
    b. Expected returns on investment for implementing the marketing plan
11. **Operational Considerations**
    a. Personnel and internal communications
    b. Research and development/production needs
    c. Marketing information system
12. **Appendices**
    a. SWOT analysis details
    b. Background data and information
    c. Marketing research findings

SOURCE: Adapted from Sally Dibb and Lyndon Simkin, *The Marketing Casebook* (London: Routledge, 1993).

by market or country by country SWOTS—and their full explanations—kept to the appendices.

The **situation analysis** provides an appraisal of the difference between the company's current performance and past stated objectives. It includes a summary of data that relate to the creation of the current marketing situation. This information is obtained from both the company's external and internal environment, usually through its marketing information system. Depending on the situation, details on the composition of target market segments, marketing objectives, current marketing strategies, market trends, sales history and profitability may be included. Many marketers conduct a **SWOT analysis:** Strengths, Weaknesses, Opportunities, Threats. The first half of this analysis—strengths and weaknesses—examines the company's position, or that of its product, vis-à-vis customers, competitor activity, environmental trends and company resources. The second half of the SWOT takes this review further to examine the opportunities and threats identified and make recommendations which feed into marketing strategy and the marketing mix. The result of the situation analysis or a SWOT analysis should be a thorough understanding of the organisation's status and its standing in its markets.

Marketing Analysis

The *analysis* section is the heart of the marketing planning exercise: if incomplete or highly subjective, the recommendations are likely to be based on an inaccurate view of the market and the company's potential. This section gives a sound foundation to the recommendations and marketing programmes. It includes analyses of the marketing environment, market trends, customers, competitors, competitor positions and competitors' strategies. In Figure 20.4, such analyses helped Tilda determine a successful positioning strategy.

The marketing environment section of the marketing plan describes the current state of the marketing environment, including the legal, political, regulatory, technological, competitive, social and economic forces, as well as ethical considerations. It also makes predictions about future directions of those forces.

For example, the retailer Safeway was among the first to respond to consumer concern about the use of artificial fertilisers and pesticides. It offered its customers a choice of either regular fruit and vegetables or organically grown produce at a higher price.

As mentioned earlier, environmental forces can hamper an organisation in achieving its objectives. This section of the plan also describes the possible impact of these forces on the implementation of the marketing plan. Most marketing plans include extensive analyses of competitive, legal and regulatory forces, perhaps even creating separate sections for these influential forces of the marketing environment. It is important to note here that, because the forces of the marketing environment are dynamic, marketing plans should be reviewed and possibly modified periodically to adjust to change.

Marketing exists to enable an organisation to meet customers' needs properly. This is particularly true in the marketing planning process. The views, needs and expectations of current and potential customers are important as a basis for formal marketing planning. Without such an understanding and analysis of likely changes in customer requirements, it is impossible to safely target those markets of most benefit to the organisation's fortunes. It is also impossible to specify a correct marketing mix (or mixes).

The analysis of the marketing environment includes competitive forces and trends. As explained in the previous chapter, however, a meaningful marketing plan and associated programmes for implementation necessitate a prior comprehensive analysis of an organisation's competitive position in its markets and territories, together with an understanding of rival organisations' marketing strategies.

Marketing Strategies

Strategies should be self-evident if the analyses have been objective and thorough: which target markets are most beneficial to the company, what is to be the differential advantage or competitive edge in these markets and what is the desired product positioning. This strategy statement must be realistic and detailed enough to act upon.

This section of the marketing plan provides a broad overview of the plan for achieving the marketing objectives and, ultimately, the organisational goals. Marketing strategy focuses on defining a target market and developing a marketing mix to gain long

FIGURE 20.4
Marketing analyses
In a once commodity
market, Tilda's marketing
analysis identified a strong
positioning for its brands.
With careful planning,
Tilda has established a
worthy position in all of its
markets.

*Tilda American Long Grain Rice
goes with chil▢▢ ▢▢spare ribs,
ice cream, c▢▢ ▢▢n, steak,
bananas, du▢▢ ▢▢ burgers,
sweet corn, ▢▢ ▢▢ hot dogs,
tomatoes ▢▢ ▢▢ cucumber,
anchovies, n▢▢ ▢▢nkfurter,
egg, bacon, c▢▢ ▢▢shrooms,
onions, pineapp▢▢ ▢▢asparagus,
currants, sala▢▢ ▢▢spinach,
sweet & so▢▢ ▢▢champagne,
soy sau▢▢ ▢▢ ▢▢crayfish,
tuna, ora▢▢ ▢▢ke, salmon.*

Tilda
RICE

SOURCE: Reproduced with permission of Tilda Rice Ltd. © 1993.

run competitive and consumer advantages. There is a degree of overlap between corporate strategy and marketing strategy. Marketing strategy is unique in that it has the responsibility to assess buyer needs and the firm's potential for gaining competitive advantage, both of which ultimately must guide the corporate mission.[13] In other words, marketing strategy guides the firm's direction in relationships between customers and competitors. The bottom line is that a marketing strategy must be consistent with consumer needs, perceptions and beliefs. American Express shows highly successful individuals as card members, fulfilling consumers' perception that to be a member is a privilege (see Figure 20.5). Thus this section should describe the firm's intended target market and how product, promotion, distribution and price will be used to develop a product or brand positioning which will satisfy the needs of members of the target market.

Michael Porter[14] describes three **generic strategies** which he maintains help firms to achieve industry success (see Figure 20.6). The first is *cost leadership,* in which low cost producers exploit experience curve effects to achieve market penetration. The key is the development of a low cost structure which allows high returns even when competition is intense. Amstrad and Texas Instruments have both successfully operated as cost leaders. *Differentiation,* the second generic strategy, involves firms developing a product or service which is unique or superior in some way. Products which have this quality, whether in terms of features, image or design, often have higher than average prices. Sony stereos and Raleigh bicycles are both examples of products for which a high price can be demanded. Indeed, the price of items like these is part of the prod-

FIGURE 20.5 *Developing strategies that meet consumers' perceptions*
Celebrity endorsers enhance the American Express card's image as a privilege and an achievement of success.

SOURCE: Courtesy of American Express Europe Ltd.

FIGURE 20.6
Generic routes to competitive advantage

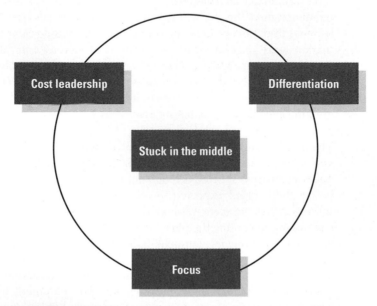

SOURCE: Based on M. E. Porter, *Competitive Strategy: Techniques for Analysing Industries and Competitors* (New York: Free Press, 1980). From *Distance Learning MBA Notes,* Warwick Business School, 1987.

ucts' character and ethos. The final generic strategy is *focus*. Here companies concentrate their efforts on particular segments of the market. In some instances this is because there are insufficient resources to compete on a larger scale. Focus allows companies like Rolex watches and Porsche in the car market to service particular subgroups of customers. Although focusing has attractions in terms of gearing the marketing mix to a quite specific and narrow customer target, the associated risks are high. The danger is that, if attacked head on, such highly specialised companies may find it difficult to develop alternative competencies. Porter warns against firms becoming "stuck in the middle" of the three strategies. If this happens, he argues, customers may not have a good reason for purchasing a company's products or services.

Expected Results

Having highlighted the strategic thrust and intention, it is important to explain the *expected results* and sales volumes to show why the strategies should be followed. These forecasts should be quantified—typically as expected units of sales and possible market shares.

Marketing Programmes for Implementation

Marketing programme recommendations are the culmination of the various analyses and statement of strategies: exactly what needs to be done, how and why. This is the detailed presentation of the proposed marketing mixes designed to achieve the goals and implement the strategies.

Each market segment to be targeted may require its own, tailor made marketing mix (as for Kraft's cheese slices in Marketing Insight 20.2). This section of the marketing plan is of paramount importance, as it gives the specific details of the marketing activity required to implement the marketing plan and to achieve the organisation's strategic goals. Each element of the marketing mix should be discussed in turn, with specific recommendations explained in sufficient detail to enable managers to put them into action. Product, people, pricing, place (distribution) and promotion must all be addressed. Associated tasks should be allocated to personnel and responsibilities for action clearly identified.

Controls and Evaluation

It is essential that *controls* be established along with measures to assess the ongoing implementation of the marketing plan. This section details how the results of the plan will be measured. For example, the results of an advertising campaign designed to increase market share may be measured in terms of increases in sales volume or improved brand recognition and acceptance by consumers. Next, a schedule for comparing the results achieved with the objectives set forth in the marketing plan is developed. Finally, guidelines may be offered outlining who is responsible for monitoring the programme and taking remedial action.

Financial Implications/ Required Budgets

The full picture may not be known, but an indication of required resources and the *financial implications* must be given. The financial projections and budgets section outlines the returns expected through implementation of the plan. The costs incurred will be weighed against expected revenues. A budget must be prepared to allocate resources in order to accomplish marketing objectives. It should contain estimates of the costs of implementing the plan, including the costs of advertising, sales force training and compensation, development of distribution channels and marketing research.

Operational Considerations

These strategies and marketing programmes may have ramifications for other product groups, sectors or territories, for research and development, for engineering and so on. The *operational implications* must be flagged up, but too much detail may be inappropriate and politically sensitive within the organisation.

KRAFT GENERAL FOODS ADJUSTS TO GLOBAL MARKETS

Kraft General Foods are marketed in over 100 countries around the world, and about 25 per cent of the firm's sales and earnings come from outside the United States. It is therefore extremely important for Kraft to be able to adapt its products and marketing strategies to international markets. Although packaged food today is increasingly a global industry, what a French family may choose to eat is probably different from what an American or Swedish family would choose to eat. Similarly, product characteristics that appeal to various cultures are likely to be different. Kraft's successful worldwide promotion of its packaged cheese slices is a good example of how the concept of adaptive marketing can be applied and of how a company needs to incorporate flexibility into its marketing strategy.

Kraft discovered several years ago that many consumers were not aware that Kraft's packaged cheese slices were dairy products—that is, made from milk—whereas some of the competitors' cheese slices were not. Advertisements emphasising that Kraft cheese was made from "5 ounces of milk" proved very successful in the American market, and it was therefore decided to use this same "dairy" emphasis in foreign markets where the product had proved successful. However, because of differences in these overseas markets, the promotion of Kraft slices had to be altered. The result was specific advertising campaigns for each nation, tailored to unique differences, yet retaining the same basic theme. For example, in Canada a different formula was used in the slices—one with 7 ounces of milk instead of 5—and there were no direct competitors, so the advertisements made no direct comparisons with other products. In Australia a more dramatic visual presentation illustrated how much milk is contained in each slice, using an implied health message directed at mothers. Finally, in the UK and Spain the differing number of slices contained in each package meant that the amount of milk shown to be included in Kraft slices had to be altered, as well as converted to volume measures such as pints and litres.

Kraft's adaptive strategy of marketing the company's cheese slices is an excellent example of how a firm often must find a blend between standardised and customised marketing. The company was able to retain the same basic message for all markets but made changes in the message so that it was relevant to each different foreign market. Kraft's overall strategy held firm for this product, but the marketing programmes which implemented its strategies needed to be modified.

SOURCE: James M. Kilts, "Company study: adaptive marketing", *Journal of Consumer Marketing,* Summer 1990, pp. 39–45.

The report should be as concise as possible. The document must, though, tell the full story and include evidence and statistics which support the strategies and marketing programmes being recommended. The use of *appendices*—so long as they are fully cross referenced in the main body of the report—helps to keep the report concise and well focused.

THE MARKETING AUDIT

A **marketing audit** is a systematic examination of the marketing group's objectives, strategies, organisation and performance. Its primary purpose is to identify weaknesses in ongoing marketing operations and plan the necessary improvements to correct these weaknesses. The marketing audit does not concern itself with the firm's marketing position; that is the purpose of the firm's marketing plan. Rather, the marketing audit evaluates how effectively the marketing organisation performed its assigned functions.[15]

Like an accounting or financial audit, a marketing audit should be conducted regularly instead of just when performance control mechanisms show that the system is out of control. The marketing audit is not a control process to be used only during a crisis, although a business in trouble may use it to isolate problems and generate solutions.

A marketing audit may be specific and focus on one or a few marketing activities, or it may be comprehensive and encompass all of a company's marketing activities. Table 20.5 lists many possible dimensions of a marketing audit. An audit might deal with only a few of these areas, or it might include them all. Its scope depends on the costs involved, the target markets served, the structure of the marketing mix and environmental conditions. The results of the audit can be used to reallocate marketing effort and to re-examine marketing opportunities. For example, after the rise in consumer interest in buying unleaded petrol during the 1980s, the oil companies realised that many customers were still using leaded fuel, because the engine performance of their cars was better. Launching the new "super" unleaded brands late in the 1980s helped to counter these problems.

The marketing audit should aid evaluation by doing the following:

1. Describing current activities and results to sales, costs, prices, profits and other performance feedback.
2. Gathering information about customers, competition and environmental developments that may affect the marketing strategy.
3. Exploring opportunities and alternatives for improving the marketing strategy.
4. Providing an overall database to be used in evaluating the attainment of organisational goals and marketing objectives.

Marketing audits can be performed internally or externally. An internal auditor may be a top level marketing executive, a company wide auditing committee or a manager from another office or of another function. Although it is more expensive, an audit by outside consultants is usually more effective; external auditors have more objectivity, more time for the audit and greater experience.

There is no single set of procedures for all marketing audits. However, firms should adhere to several general guidelines. Audits are often based on a series of questionnaires administered to the firm's personnel. These questionnaires should be developed carefully to ensure that the audit focuses on the right issues. Auditors should develop and follow a step by step plan to guarantee that the audit is systematic. When interviewing company personnel, the auditors should strive to talk to a diverse group of people from many parts of the company. The auditor should become familiar with the

TABLE 20.5 *Dimensions of a marketing audit*

Part I. The Marketing Environment Audit

Macroenvironment

A. Economic-demographic

1. What does the company expect in the way of inflation, material shortages, unemployment and credit availability in the short run, intermediate run and long run?
2. What effect will forecast trends in the size, age distribution and regional distribution of population have on the business?

B. Technological

1. What major changes are occurring in product technology? In process technology?
2. What are the major generic substitutes that might replace this product?

C. Political-legal

1. What laws are being proposed that may affect marketing strategy and tactics?
2. What national and local government actions should be watched? What is happening with pollution control, equal opportunity employment, product safety, advertising, price controls and so on that is relevant to marketing planning?

D. Cultural

1. What attitude is the public taking towards business and the types of product produced by the company?
2. What changes in consumer lifestyles and values have a bearing on the company's target markets and marketing methods?

E. Ecological

1. Will the cost and availability of natural resources directly affect the company?
2. Are there public concerns about the company's role in pollution and conservation? If so, what is the company's reaction?

Task Environment

A. Markets

1. What is happening to market size, growth, geographical distribution and profits?
2. What are the major market segments and their expected rates of growth? Which are high opportunity and low opportunity segments?

B. Customers

1. How do current customers and prospects judge the company and its competitors on reputation, product quality, service, sales force and price?
2. How do different classes of customers make their buying decisions?
3. What evolving needs and satisfactions are the buyers in this market seeking?

C. Competitors

1. Who are the major competitors? What are the objectives and strategy of each major competitor? What are their strengths and weaknesses? What are the sizes and trends in market shares?
2. What trends can be foreseen in future competition and substitutes for this product?

D. Distribution and dealers

1. What are the main trade channels bringing products to customers?
2. What are the efficiency levels and growth potentials of the different trade channels?

E. Suppliers

1. What is the outlook for the availability of key resources used in production?
2. What trends are occurring among suppliers in their patterns of selling?

F. Facilitators and marketing firms

1. What is the outlook for the cost and availability of transport services?
2. What is the outlook for the cost and availability of warehousing facilities?
3. What is the outlook for the cost and availability of financial resources?
4. How effectively is the advertising agency performing? What trends are occurring in advertising agency services?

G. Publics

1. Where are the opportunity areas or problems for the company?
2. How effectively is the company dealing with publics?

Part II. Marketing Strategy Audit

A. Business mission

1. Is the business mission clearly focused with marketing terms and is it attainable?

TABLE 20.5 *Dimensions of a marketing audit (continued)*

B. Marketing objectives and goals

1. Are the corporate objectives clearly stated? Do they lead logically to the marketing objectives?
2. Are the marketing objectives stated clearly enough to guide marketing planning and subsequent performance measurement?
3. Are the marketing objectives appropriate, given the company's competitive position, resources and opportunities? Is the appropriate strategic objective to build, hold, harvest or terminate this business?

C. Strategy

1. What is the core marketing strategy for achieving the objectives? Is it sound?
2. Are the resources budgeted to accomplish the marketing objectives inadequate, adequate or excessive?
3. Are the marketing resources allocated optimally to prime market segment, territories and products?
4. Are the marketing resources allocated optimally to the major elements of the marketing mix, i.e., product quality, service, sales force, advertising, promotion and distribution?

Part III. Marketing Organisation Audit

A. Formal structure

1. Is there a high level marketing manager with adequate authority and responsibility over those company activities that affect customer satisfaction?
2. Are the marketing responsibilities optimally structured along functional, product, end use and territorial lines?

B. Functional efficiency

1. Are there good communications and working relations between marketing and sales?
2. Is the product management system working effectively? Are the product managers able to plan profits or only sales volume?
3. Are there any groups in marketing that need more training, motivation, supervision or evaluation?

C. Interface efficiency

1. Are there any problems between marketing and manufacturing, research and development, purchasing, finance, accounting and legal departments that need attention?

Part IV: Marketing Systems Audit

A. Marketing information system

1. Is the marketing intelligence system producing accurate, sufficient and timely information about developments in the market-place?
2. Is marketing research being adequately used by company decision-makers?

B. Marketing planning system

1. Is the marketing planning system well conceived and effective?
2. Is sales forecasting and measurement of market potential soundly carried out?
3. Are sales quotas set on a proper basis?

C. Marketing control system

1. Are the control procedures (monthly, quarterly, etc.) adequate to ensure that the annual plan's objectives are being achieved?
2. Is provision made to analyse periodically the profitability of different products, markets, territories and channels of distribution?
3. Is provision made to examine and validate periodically various marketing costs?

D. New product development system

1. Is the company well organised to gather, generate and screen new product ideas?
2. Does the company do adequate concept research and business analysis before investing heavily in a new idea?
3. Does the company carry out adequate product and market testing before launching a new product?

Part V. Marketing-Productivity Audit

A. Profitability analysis

1. What is the profitability of the company's different products, served markets, territories and channels of distribution?
2. Should the company enter, expand, contract or withdraw from any business segments, and what would be the short and long run profit consequences?

B. Cost effective analysis

1. Do any marketing activities seem to have excessive costs? Are these costs valid? Can cost reducing steps be taken?

TABLE 20.5 *Dimensions of a marketing audit (continued)*

Part VI. Marketing Function Audits

A. Products

1. What are the product line objectives? Are these objectives sound? Is the current product line meeting these objectives?
2. Are there particular products that should be phased out?
3. Are there new products that are worth adding?
4. Are any products able to benefit from quality, feature or style improvements?

B. Price

1. What are the pricing objectives, policies, strategies and procedures? Are prices set on sound cost, demand and competitive criteria?
2. Do the customers see the company's prices as being in or out of line with the perceived value of its products?
3. Does the company use price promotions effectively?

C. Distribution

1. What are the distribution objectives and strategies?
2. Is there adequate market coverage and service?
3. How effective are the following channel members: distributors, manufacturers' reps, brokers, agents and so on?
4. Should the company consider changing its distribution channels?

D. Advertising, sales promotion, and publicity

1. What are the organisation's advertising objectives? Are they sound?
2. Is the right amount being spent on advertising? How is the budget determined?
3. Are the ad themes and copy effective? What do customers and the public think about the advertising?
4. Are the advertising media well chosen?
5. Is the internal advertising staff adequate?
6. Is the sales promotion budget adequate? Is there effective and sufficient use of sales promotion tools, such as samples, coupons, displays and sales contests?
7. Is the publicity budget adequate? Is the public relations staff competent and creative?

E. Sales force

1. What are the organisation's sales force objectives?
2. Is the sales force large enough to accomplish the company's objectives?
3. Is the sales force organised along the proper principle(s) of specialisation (territory, market, product)? Are there enough (or too many) sales managers to guide the field sales reps?
4. Does the sales compensation level and structure provide adequate incentive and reward?
5. Does the sales force show high morale, ability and effort?
6. Are the procedures for setting quotas and evaluating performance adequate?
7. How does the company's sales force compare with the sales forces of competitors?

SOURCE: Philip Kotler, *Marketing Management: Analysis, Planning, and Control,* 6th ed. © 1988, pp. 748–51. Adapted by permission of Prentice-Hall, Inc., Englewood Cliffs, N.J.

product line, meet headquarters staff, visit field organisations, interview customers, interview competitors and analyse information for a report on the marketing environment.[16] The audit framework and associated questionnaires should remain consistent over time, so that improvements and problems can be noted between audits.

To achieve adequate support, the auditors normally focus first on the firm's top management and then move down through the organisational hierarchy. The auditor looks for different points of view within various departments of the organisation or a mismatch between the customers' and the company's perception of the product as signs of trouble in an organisation.[17] The results of the audit should be reported in a comprehensive written document, which should include recommendations that will increase marketing productivity and determine the company's general direction.

The marketing audit lets an organisation change tactics or alter day to day activities as problems arise. For example, marketing auditors often wonder whether a change in budgeted sales activity is caused by general market conditions or is due to a change in the firm's market share.

Although the concept of auditing implies an official examination of marketing activities, many organisations audit their marketing activities informally. Any attempt to verify operating results and to compare them with standards can be considered an auditing activity. Many smaller firms probably would not use the word *audit*, but they do perform auditing activities.

Several problems may arise in an audit of marketing activities. Marketing audits can be expensive in time and money. Selecting the auditors may be difficult because objective, qualified personnel may not be available. Marketing audits can also be extremely disruptive because employees sometimes fear comprehensive evaluations, especially by outsiders. The benefits, though, are significant. The audit reveals successes and also problem areas which need to be addressed.

SUMMARY

Whether using a total market or a market segmentation approach, a marketer must be able to measure the sales potential of the target market or markets. Market potential is the total amount of a product that customers will purchase within a specified period at a specific level of industry wide marketing activity. Sales potential is the maximum percentage of market potential that an individual firm within an industry can expect to obtain for a specific product. There are two general approaches to measuring sales potential: break down and build up. A sales forecast is the amount of a product that the company actually expects to sell during a specific period of time and at a specified level of marketing activities. Several methods are used to forecast sales: executive judgement, surveys (customer, sales force and executive surveys, including the Delphi approach), time series analysis (trend analysis, cycle analysis, seasonal analysis, random factor analysis), correlation methods and market tests. Although some businesses may rely on a single sales forecasting method, most organisations employ several different techniques.

A strategic market plan is an outline of the methods and resources required to achieve the organisation's goals within a specific target market; it takes into account all the functional areas of a business unit that must be co-ordinated. A strategic business unit (SBU) is a division, product line or other profit centre within the parent company and is used to define areas for consideration in a specific strategic market plan. The process of strategic market planning yields a marketing strategy that is the framework for a marketing plan. A marketing plan includes the framework and entire set of activities to be performed; it is the written document or blueprint for implementing and controlling an organisation's marketing activities.

Through the process of strategic market planning, an organisation can develop marketing strategies that, when properly implemented and controlled, will contribute to achieving the organisation's overall goals. The set of marketing strategies that are implemented and used at the same time is referred to as the organisation's marketing programme. Environmental forces are important in the marketing planning process and profoundly affect it. These forces imply opportunities and threats that influence an organisation's overall goals.

A firm's organisational goals should be derived from its mission, the broad tasks the organisation wants to achieve. These goals should guide planning efforts.

To control marketing strategies, it is sometimes necessary to audit marketing activities. A marketing audit is a systematic examination of the marketing group's objectives, strategies, organisation and performance. A marketing audit attempts to identify what a marketing unit is doing, to evaluate the effectiveness of these activities, and to recommend future marketing activities.

IMPORTANT TERMS

Market potential

Sales potential

Break down approach

Build up approach

Sales forecast

Executive judgement

Customer forecasting survey

Sales force forecasting survey

Delphi approach

Expert forecasting survey

Time series analysis

Trend analysis

Cycle analysis

Seasonal analysis

Random factor analysis

Correlation methods

Market test

Marketing planning

Marketing planning cycle

Short range plans

Medium range plans

Long range plans

Marketing objective

Situational analysis

SWOT analysis

Generic strategies

Marketing audit

DISCUSSION AND REVIEW QUESTIONS

1. Why is a marketer concerned about sales potential when trying to find a target market?
2. What is a sales forecast, and why is it important?
3. What is the Delphi approach to forecasting? Why is it a popular tool?
4. What is marketing planning? How does it help companies to better target their market-places?
5. In what ways do marketing environmental forces affect marketing planning? Give examples.
6. What is a SWOT analysis? How does it lead to an understanding of realistic market opportunities?
7. What issues *must* be thoroughly analysed during marketing planning prior to the formulation of a marketing programme?
8. Why is it important to determine a differential advantage?
9. Porter's generic strategies warn against being "stuck in the middle". Why?
10. Why would a company uses a marketing audit?

■ CASES

20.1 Planning for International Markets

As the world shrinks and global business expands, companies often vary advertising, promotions, logos or prices to attract customers in diverse markets around the world. Advertising and particularly pricing for specific international markets are complicated by the need to understand relevant local laws, as well as local attitudes and economies.

Differences in price from one country to another often relate directly to indigenous governmental regulations, such as taxes or subsidies, or even to the prevailing political climate. An example of government's influence on pricing is the cost of petrol at pumps worldwide. While Americans complain about paying 85 pence per gallon, Germans pay £2 and the Japanese, £2.70 ; yet drivers in Mexico pay only 60 pence per gallon and those in the former Soviet Union 16 pence. What accounts in part for the disparity is whether a government saves consumers money by subsidising the price, or taxes them, thus adding to the price. The Japanese pay £1.05 in tax on every gallon they buy, whereas Russian drivers have benefited from government subsidies that keep prices low. Prices often fall prey to politics, as is the case in Korea. Government officials there decided that Korea was importing too many cars and dramatically raised the number of mandatory subway bonds consumers must buy when purchasing a foreign car. Someone choosing a Mercedes-Benz, for example, must include in the purchase price £13,000 worth of bonds.

A product's image in various world markets often affects its price. International wine pricing, for example, is particularly sensitive to image. To Europeans, California wines typically suggest lower, jug-type quality, especially in comparison with the best French and Italian wines. After adding importers' fees, duties, and shipping, Gallo charges £4.75 in the UK for a bottle of wine that retails for about £2.30 in the United States. At that price, Gallo's low quality image can't compete with choice European wines. Industry experts believe that California can perform better overseas by exporting higher priced, high quality wines.

Adding to the complexity of pricing for the global community is the wide diversity in income and standard of living. An affluent Japanese driver may find it easy to pay £2.50 a gallon for petrol, whereas a Russian citizen may be unable to pay 70 pence. To buy the least expensive GM car available in Poland, a Polish customer has to spend 125 times the average monthly salary. In Moscow, an average Russian worker will pay at least two days' wages to buy a McDonald's meal for the family. Clearly, sensitivity to the ability of customers around the world to pay the price is essential.

This example has concentrated on pricing variations country by country, but all elements of the marketing mix must be adjusted to take account of local markets, customer practices and aspects of the marketing environment. Owing to such variations, even target markets and brand positioning strategy may require modification. A strategy and associated marketing programme designed to be effective in one country or market will likely as not fail to achieve success in different territories or markets without some alteration. Companies' marketing planning processes must be both flexible and thorough so as to take account of these probable changing requirements; otherwise the resulting marketing programmes will have limited applicability.

SOURCES: Damon Darlin, "U.S. auto firms push their efforts to sell cars in Asian market", *Wall Street Journal,* 21 March 1991, p. A1; Allen R. Myerson, "Setting up an island in the Soviet storm", *New York Times,* 30 December 1990, pp. F1, F6; Lawrence M. Fisher, "California wineries look overseas", *The New York Times,* 26 December 1990, pp. D1, D5; "G.M. is selling cars in Poland", *The New York Times,* 28 August 1990, p. D4; Linda Feldmann, "Muscovites have fallen in love with a pair of golden arches", *Christian Science Monitor* 20 August 1990, p. 11; Damon Darlin, "South Korea regresses on opening markets, trade partners say", *Wall Street Journal,* 12 June 1990, pp. A1, A15; Masha Hamilton, "1st 'Beeg Mak' attack leaves Moscow agog", *Los Angeles Times,* 1 February 1990, pp. A1, A12; and Richard Homan, "Gas peddled at wide range of prices", *Washington Post* 12 January 1991.

Questions for Discussion

1. The role of marketing planning is important in any organisation, but why particularly so in companies that trade globally?
2. With such dramatic price variations between territories, why is the estimation of sales potential important?

20.2 Binney & Smith Brightens Marketing Strategy for Crayola Crayons

While Nintendo games and MTV music videos have captured children's attention, Crayola Crayons have languished on store shelves. Now Binney & Smith, a division of Hallmark Cards, is fighting back with a new marketing strategy for the venerable crayon. The company launched a huge MTV style campaign, which targets children rather than parents.

Traditionally Binney & Smith targeted Crayola Crayons at parents, using educational themes. But after recognising that children's purchasing power and influence on family purchases have increased in recent years, the company decided to change the crayon's image as an old fashioned toy to an exciting way for kids and teens to express themselves. To this end, the company developed new advertisements featuring rock music, "hip" kids and soaring colours for showing during television programmes seen by children. In-store videos provided to toy stores and retailers of children's clothing followed up the theme.

After marketing research indicated that children prefer brighter colours, the company decided to retire blue grey, green blue, lemon yellow, maize, orange red, orange yellow, raw umber and violet blue to the Crayola Hall of Fame, and replace them with the more vivid cerulean, dandelion, fuchsia, jungle green, royal purple, teal blue, vivid tangerine and wild strawberry. This decision was controversial, however. The company was inundated with phone calls, letters and petitions from people who missed the old colours. Protesters marched on the company, carrying placards with slogans like "We hate the new 8!" and "They call it a retirement, I call it a burial." RUMPS, the Raw Umber and Maize Preservation Society, finally got its way. In late 1991 the company issued a commemorative tin containing the 64 crayon box and a special pack of the eight colours dropped one year earlier. Even though kids liked the new colours, parents liked the old eight colours. The company issued a statement saying that the old colours were revived partly because the company is in the business of providing what the consumer wants.

Along with new advertisements and colours, the company introduced ColourWorks, a line of erasable crayon sticks and retractable coloured pencils and pens. In 1991 the company brought out Silver Swirls, crayons that have twirls of silver mixed in with the wax colours. Pictures coloured with Silver Swirls can be buffed to a high sheen with tissue. The new line was not only tested by children but also named by them.

Despite its new focus on children, Binney & Smith did not forget who actually holds the purse strings; the company continues to target parents with advertisements in women's and parents' magazines. The company hopes that its new strategy will lead more children to reach for Crayola Crayons instead of the Nintendo joystick.

So far, the revised strategy for Crayola seems to be working. Sales are up; shelf space in toy stores could not be better, despite stiff competition from a host of rival products and toys; and deals with airlines, fast food outlets and restaurant chains to provide "time filler" packs for children have boosted brand awareness.

SOURCES: Ellen Neuborne, "Crayola crayons have old colors back", *USA Today,* 2 October 1991, p. 2B; Ken Riddle, "Crayola draws brighter lines in the market", *Marketing (Maclean Hunter),* 21 January 1991, p. 4; Virginia Daut, "Roses were reds, violets blues till they redid Crayola's hues", *Wall Street Journal,* 11 September 1990, p. B1; and Cara Appelbaum, "Crayola launches hip bright ads for kids", *Adweek's Marketing Week,* 3 September 1990, p. 8; Beefeater Restaurants, 1993; Toys "Я" Us, Leicester, 1993.

Questions for Discussion

1. Why did Binney & Smith have to update its marketing of Crayola and change its strategy?
2. What are Crayola's target audiences? Why did the company need to approach them differently?
3. Why has the company negotiated with airlines and restaurants to offer give-aways?

21 IMPLEMENTING STRATEGIES AND MEASURING PERFORMANCE

Objectives

To understand how the marketing unit fits into a company's organisational structure

To become familiar with the ways of organising a marketing unit

To examine several issues relating to the implementation of marketing strategies

To understand the control processes used in managing marketing strategies

To learn how cost and sales analyses can be used to evaluate the performance of marketing strategies

*I*n the mid-1980s, Parker Pen Company, at the time a Wisconsin firm, sold products in 154 countries, and its marketing executives were eager to design and implement a global strategy. James Peterson, then chief executive, believed that global marketing would be crucial to the survival of the company. Profits were down, and most of the profits were generated by Manpower Temporary Services, a subsidiary. Peterson and his marketing team began production of cheap pens that could compete in the under £5 market, and they standardised everything associated with Parker products. Worldwide advertising was handled by one agency using a single theme—"Make your mark with a Parker." In addition, advertising spotlighted Parker's new, inexpensive products instead of the quality pens that were the company's trade mark.

Difficulties were encountered almost immediately. The manufacturing facilities which produced the new product line repeatedly shut down, and the number of defective products soared. In addition, the standardised advertising strategy was so general that it appealed to no one in particular. Profits plummeted, Peterson resigned and in 1986 Parker Pen was purchased by a group of British investors. Parker's strategy was flawed and its implementation poorly executed.

Now based in Newhaven, England, Parker Pen Ltd is again a profitable company, with a new marketing strategy. Parker's inexpensive pens receive less emphasis, and plans to produce disposable pens have been shelved. Except for the company's Duofold Centennial 1 carat gold nib fountain pen, which costs £250 and is targeted to a tiny market segment, global advertising has been dropped. The company has worked hard to restore its reputation for quality and reliability. Perceived value, rather than volume, is the focus. Parker, now in second position in the very competitive Japanese high end pen market with a 17 per cent market share, is again seen worldwide as a maker of high quality writing instruments. This success has led to takeover attempts, including interest from its leading rivals, but at least the company is successful and its products valued by customers. ∎

SOURCES: Geoffrey E. Duin, "Parker Pen: an old Japan hand", *Tokyo Business Today,* July 1989, pp. 50–51; and Mike Stevens, "Premiums and incentives: designs on your desk", *Marketing,* 14 April 1988, pp. 45, 47.

This chapter focuses first on the marketing unit's position in the organisation and the ways the unit itself can be organised. It goes on to examine several issues regarding the implementation of marketing strategies. The next section considers the basic components of the process of control. Finally, the chapter discusses the use of cost and sales analyses to evaluate the effectiveness of marketing strategies and measure the firm's performance.

ORGANISING MARKETING ACTIVITIES

The structure and relationships of a marketing unit, including lines of authority and responsibility that connect and co-ordinate individuals, strongly affect marketing activities. This section first looks at the place of marketing within an organisation and examines the major alternatives available for organising a marketing unit. Then it shows how marketing activities can be structured to fit into an organisation so as to contribute to the accomplishment of overall objectives.

Centralisation Versus Decentralisation

The organisational structure that a company uses to connect and co-ordinate various activities affects its success. Basic decisions relate to how various participants in the company will work together to make important decisions, as well as to co-ordinate, implement and control activities. Top managers create corporate strategies and co-ordinate lower levels. A **centralised organisation** is one in which the top level managers delegate very little authority to lower levels of the organisation. In a **decentralised organisation,** decision-making authority is delegated as far down the chain of command as possible. The decision to centralise or decentralise directly affects marketing in the organisation.

In a centralised organisation, major marketing decisions originate with top management and are transmitted to lower levels of management. A decentralised structure gives marketing managers more opportunity for making key strategic decisions. IBM has adopted a decentralised management structure so that its marketing managers have a chance to customise strategies for customers. On the other hand, Hewlett-Packard and 3M have become more centralised by consolidating functions or eliminating divisional managers.[1] Although decentralising may foster innovation and a greater responsiveness to customers, a decentralised company may be inefficient or appear to have a blurred marketing strategy when dealing with larger customers. A centralised organisation avoids confusion among the marketing staff, vagueness in marketing strategy and autonomous decision-makers who are out of control. Of course, over centralised companies often become dependent on top management and respond too slowly to be able to solve problems or seize new opportunities. Obviously, finding the right degree of centralisation for a particular company is a difficult balancing act.

The Place of Marketing in an Organisation

Because the marketing environment is so dynamic, the position of the marketing unit within the organisation has risen during the past 25 years. Companies that truly adopt the marketing concept develop a distinct organisational culture—a culture based on a shared set of beliefs that make the customer's needs the pivotal point of a company's decisions about strategy and operations.[2] Instead of developing products in a vacuum and then trying to convince consumers to buy them, companies using the marketing concept begin with an orientation towards their customers' needs and desires. If the marketing concept serves as a guiding philosophy, the marketing unit will be closely co-ordinated with other functional areas, such as production, finance, and personnel. Figure 21.1 shows the organisation of a marketing unit by types of customers. This

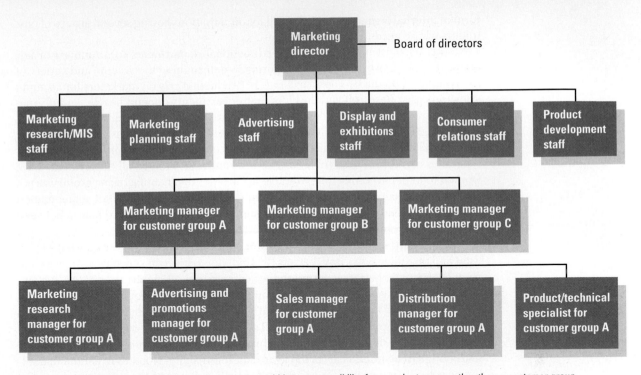

Note: In some organisations, each marketing manager would have responsibility for a product group rather than a customer group, and would be termed a product manager.

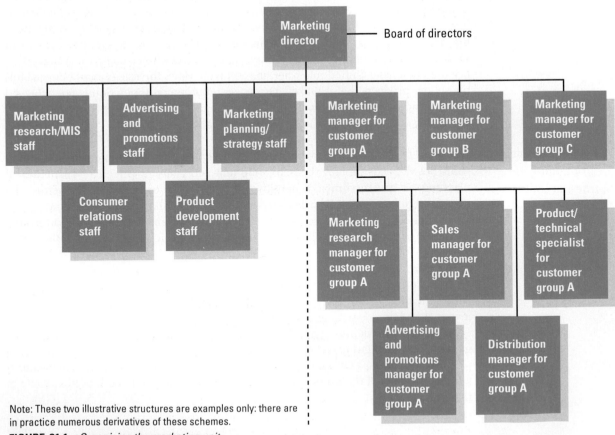

Note: These two illustrative structures are examples only: there are in practice numerous derivatives of these schemes.

FIGURE 21.1 *Organising the marketing unit*

form of internal organisation works well for organisations having several groups of customers whose needs differ significantly.

Marketing must interact with other functional departments in a number of key areas. It needs to work with manufacturing in determining the volume and variety of the company's products. Those in charge of production rely on marketers for accurate sales forecasts. Research and development departments depend heavily on information gathered by marketers about product features and benefits desired by consumers, as well as details of complaints concerning current products. Decisions made by the physical distribution department hinge on information about the urgency of delivery schedules and cost/service trade-offs.[3] For example, at Honda, all departments have worked together for a long time, whereas at Chrysler the manufacturing group was not even on the product design committee until 1981. With rapid market segmentation forcing companies to design cars even faster than in the past, co-ordination between engineering, production, marketing and finance is essential.[4]

A **marketing orientated organisation** concentrates on discovering what buyers want and providing it in a way that lets the company achieve its objectives. Such a company has an organisational culture that effectively and efficiently produces a sustainable competitive advantage. It focuses on customer analysis, competitor analysis and the integration of the firm's resources to provide customer value and satisfaction, as well as long term profits.[5] As Figure 21.2 shows, the marketing director's position is at the same level as those of the financial, production and personnel directors. Thus the marketing director takes part in top level decision-making. Note, too, that the marketing director is responsible for a variety of activities. Some of them—sales forecasting and supervision and product planning—would be under the jurisdiction of other functional managers in production or sales orientated firms.

Both the links between marketing and other functional areas (such as production, finance and personnel) and the importance of marketing to management evolve from the organisation's basic orientation. Marketing encompasses the greatest number of business functions and occupies an important position when a company is marketing orientated; it has a limited role when the company views the role of marketing as simply selling products that it makes. However, a marketing orientation is not achieved simply by redrawing the organisational chart; management must also adopt and use the marketing orientation as a management philosophy.

Major Alternatives for Organising the Marketing Unit

How effectively a firm's marketing management can plan and implement marketing strategies depends on how the marketing unit is organised. Effective organisational planning can give the firm a competitive advantage. The organisational structure of a marketing department establishes the authority relationships between marketing personnel and specifies who is responsible for making certain decisions and performing particular activities. This internal structure is the vehicle for directing marketing activities.

In organising a marketing unit, managers divide the work into specific activities and delegate responsibility and authority for those activities to people in various positions within the unit. These positions include, for example, the sales manager, the research manager and the advertising manager.

No single approach to organising a marketing unit works equally well in all businesses. A marketing unit can be organised according to (1) functions, (2) products, (3) regions or (4) types of customer. The best approach or approaches depend on the number and diversity of the firm's products, the characteristics and needs of the people in the target market and many other factors.

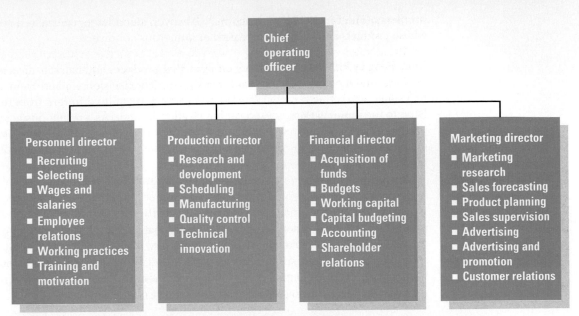

FIGURE 21.2 *Organisational chart of a marketing orientated company*

Firms often use some combination of organisation by functions, products, regions or customer types. Product features may dictate that the marketing unit be structured by products, whereas customers' characteristics require that it be organised by geographical region or by type of customer. Construction equipment leader JCB has organised by product types (crawler excavators, backhoe diggers, compact equipment and so on), but many financial institutions organise by customers, because personal banking needs differ from commercial ones. By using more than one type of organisation, a flexible marketing unit can develop and implement marketing plans to match customers' needs precisely. To develop organisational plans that give a firm a competitive advantage, four issues should be considered:

1. Which jobs or levels of jobs need to be added, deleted or modified? For example, if new products are important to the success of the firm, marketers with strong product development skills should be added to the organisation.
2. How should reporting relationships be structured to create a competitive advantage? This question is discussed further in the following descriptions of organisational structure.
3. To whom should the primary responsibility for accomplishing work be assigned? Identifying primary responsibility explicitly is critical for effective performance appraisal and reward systems.
4. Should any committees or task forces be organised?[6]

Organising by Functions.   Some marketing departments are organised by general marketing functions, such as marketing research, product development, distribution, sales, advertising and customer relations. The personnel who direct these functions report directly to the top level marketing executive. This structure is fairly common because it works well for some businesses with centralised marketing operations, such as Ford and General Motors. In more decentralised firms, such as some retailers or giants Procter & Gamble and Unilever, functional organisation can raise severe co-ordination problems. The functional approach may, however, suit a large, centralised company whose products and customers are neither numerous nor diverse.

Organising by Products.   An organisation that produces and markets diverse products may find the functional approach inadequate. The decisions and problems related to a single marketing function for one product may be quite different from those related to the same marketing function for another product. As a result, businesses that produce diverse products sometimes organise their marketing units according to product groups. Organising by product groups gives a firm the flexibility to develop special marketing mixes for different products.

The product management system, which was introduced by Procter & Gamble, operates in about 85 per cent of firms in the consumer packaged goods industry. In this structure, the product manager oversees all activities related to his or her assigned product. He or she develops product plans, sees that they are implemented, monitors the results and takes corrective action as necessary. The product manager is also responsible for acting as a liaison between the firm and its marketing environment, transmitting essential information about the environment to the company.[7] The product manager may also draw on the resources of specialised staff in the company.

Organising by Regions.   A large company that markets products nationally (or internationally) may organise its marketing activities by geographic regions. Managers of marketing functions for each region report to their regional marketing manager; all the regional marketing managers report directly to the executive marketing manager. Companies often adopt this regional structure to put more senior management personnel into the field, to get closer to customers and to enable the company to respond more quickly and efficiently to the regional competitors. This form of organisation is especially effective for a firm whose customers' characteristics and needs vary greatly from one region to another.

A firm with marketing managers for each separate region has a complete marketing staff at its headquarters to provide assistance and guidance to regional marketing managers. The major UK brewers have national headquarters and marketing centres, often in London, but regional brands, each with a marketing department, in major provincial conurbations. The regional office controls the marketing and promotion of its brand within guidelines specified by head office. However, not all firms organised by regions maintain a full marketing staff at their head offices. Firms that try to penetrate the national market intensively sometimes divide regions into sub-regions.

Organising by Type of Customer.   Sometimes the marketing unit is organised according to type of customer. This form of internal organisation works well for a firm that has several groups of customers whose needs and problems differ significantly. For example, Bic may sell pens to large retail stores, wholesalers and institutions. Retailers may want more rapid delivery of small shipments and more personal selling by the producer than do either wholesalers or institutional buyers. Because the marketing decisions and activities required for these two groups of customers differ considerably, the company may find it efficient to organise its marketing unit by type of customer.

In an organisation with a marketing department broken down by customer group, the marketing manager for each group reports to the top level marketing executive and directs most marketing activities for that group. A marketing manager controls all activities needed to market products to a specific customer group.

IMPLEMENTING MARKETING ACTIVITIES

The planning and organising functions provide purpose, direction and structure for marketing activities. However, until marketing managers implement the marketing plan, exchanges cannot occur. In fact, organisers of marketing activities can become excessively concerned with planning strategy while neglecting implementation. Before John Harvey-Jones joined ICI, some analysts believed that its management's preoccupation with procedures and plans caused the company's business to suffer. Obviously, implementation of plans is important to the success of any organisation.[8] Proper implementation of a marketing plan depends on internal marketing to employees, the motivation of personnel who perform marketing activities, effective communication within the marketing organisation, and the co-ordination of marketing activities. In Figure 21.3, Aerospatiale promotes its teamwork philosophy in business with other countries and internally.

Internal Marketing

Marketing activities cannot be effectively implemented without the co-operation of employees. Employees are the essential ingredient in increasing productivity, providing customer service, and beating the competition. Thus, in addition to marketing activities targeted at external customers, firms use internal marketing to attract, motivate and retain qualified internal customers (employees) by designing internal products (jobs) that satisfy employees' wants and needs.[9] **Internal marketing** refers to the managerial actions necessary to make all members of the marketing organisation understand and accept their respective roles in implementing the marketing strategy. This means that all personnel, from the chairman of the company down to the manual workers on the shop floor, must understand the role they play in carrying out their jobs and implementing the marketing strategy. Everyone must do his or her part to ensure that customers are satisfied. All personnel within the firm, both marketers and those who perform other functions, must recognise the tenet of customer orientation and service that underlies the marketing concept. Customer orientation is fostered by training and education and by keeping the lines of communication open throughout the firm. In recent years, public relations consultancies have worked hard with management in many companies to develop effective, friendly and informative internal channels of communication and interaction between employees and departments.

Like external marketing activities, internal marketing may involve market segmentation, product development, research, distribution and possibly public relations and sales promotion.[10] For example, an organisation may sponsor sales contests to encourage sales personnel to boost their selling efforts. Some companies, such as IBM, encourage employees to work for their companies' industrial customers for a period of time, often while continuing to receive their regular salaries. This helps the employees (and ultimately the company) to understand better the customer's needs and problems, allows them to learn valuable new skills and heightens their enthusiasm for their normal jobs. The ultimate result is more satisfied employees and improved customer relations.

Motivating Marketing Personnel

An important element in implementing the marketing plan, and in internal marketing, is motivating marketing personnel to perform effectively. People work to satisfy physical, psychological and social needs. To motivate marketing personnel, managers must discover their employees' needs and then develop motivational methods that help them satisfy those needs. It is crucial that the plan for motivating employees be fair, ethical and well understood by them. Additionally, rewards to employees must be tied

FIGURE 21.3

Implementing plans involves co-operation
Aerospatiale's teamwork message supports the idea that co-operation is needed to implement marketing strategies.

SOURCE: Courtesy of Aerospatiale.

to organisational goals. In general, to improve employee motivation, companies need to find out what workers think, how they feel and what they want. Some of this information can be obtained from an employee attitude survey. A business organisation can motivate its workers by directly linking pay with performance, informing workers how their performance affects department and corporate results, following through with appropriate compensation, promoting or implementing a flexible benefits programme and adopting a participative management approach.[11]

Consider the following example. Suppose a salesperson can sell product A or B to a particular customer, but not both products. Product A sells for £200,000 and contributes £20,000 to the company's profit margin. Product B sells for £60,000 and has a contribution margin of £40,000. If the salesperson receives a commission of 3 per cent of sales, he or she would obviously prefer to sell product A, even though the sale of product B contributes more to the company's profits. If the salesperson's commission was based on contribution margin instead of sales and the firm's goal was to maximise profits, both the firm and the salesperson would benefit more from the sale of product B.[12] By tying rewards to organisational goals, the company encourages behaviour that meets organisational goals.

Besides tying rewards to organisational goals, managers must motivate individuals by using different motivational tools, based on each individual's value system. For example, some employees value recognition more than a slight pay increase. Managers can reward employees with money, plus additional fringe benefits, prestige or recognition, or even non-financial rewards such as job autonomy, skill variety, task significance and increased feedback. A survey of Fortune 1000 companies found that "the majority of organisations feel that they get more for their money through non-cash awards, if given in addition to a basic compensation plan".[13]

Communicating Within the Marketing Unit

With good communication, marketing managers can motivate personnel and co-ordinate their efforts. Marketing managers must be able to communicate with the firm's high level management to ensure that marketing activities are consistent with the company's overall goals. Communication with top level executives keeps marketing managers aware of the company's overall plans and achievements. It also guides what the marketing unit is to do and how its activities are to be integrated with those of other departments—such as finance, production or personnel—with whose management the marketing manager must also communicate to co-ordinate marketing efforts. For example, marketing personnel must work with the production staff to help design products that customers want. To direct marketing activities, marketing managers must communicate with marketing personnel at the operations level, such as sales and advertising personnel, researchers, wholesalers, retailers and package designers.

To facilitate communication, marketing managers should establish an information system within the marketing unit. The marketing information system (discussed in Chapter 6) should allow for easy communication among marketing managers, sales managers and sales personnel. Marketers need an information system to support a variety of activities, such as planning, budgeting, sales analyses, performance evaluations and the preparation of reports. An information system should also expedite communications with other departments in the organisation and minimise destructive competition between departments for organisational resources.

Co-ordinating Marketing Activities

Because of job specialisation and differences related to marketing activities, marketing managers must synchronise individuals' actions to achieve marketing objectives. In addition, they must work closely with managers in research and development, production, finance, accounting and personnel to see that marketing activities mesh with other functions of the firm. In Figure 21.4, Sony's advertisement is the outward indication of a highly coordinated and carefully planned strategy. Marketing managers must co-ordinate the activities of marketing staff within the firm and integrate those activities with the marketing efforts of external organisations—advertising agencies, resellers (wholesalers, retailers and dealers), researchers and shippers, among others. Marketing managers can improve co-ordination by using internal marketing activities to make each employee aware of how his or her job relates to others and how his or her actions contribute to the achievement of marketing plans.

CONTROLLING MARKETING ACTIVITIES

To achieve marketing objectives as well as general organisational objectives, marketing managers must effectively control marketing efforts. The **marketing control process** consists of establishing performance standards, evaluating actual performance by comparing it with established standards and reducing the differences between desired and actual performance. This process helped Xerox to recover ground lost to competitors (see Marketing Insight 21.1). Dunkin' Donuts has developed a programme to ensure consistency throughout its franchises. Dunkin' Donuts controls the quality of operations in its franchised units by having franchisees attend Dunkin'

FIGURE 21.4
Co-ordinating marketing activities
Sony's worldwide success hinges on thorough marketing planning and comprehensive implementation of strategies across national borders.

DE SONY TR75, IDEAAL VOOR MENSEN ZONDER BAGAGERUIMTE.

SOURCE: PMSvW/Y&R.

Donuts University. Owners and managers of Dunkin' Donuts are required to take a six week training course, covering everything from customer relations and marketing to production, including a test of making 140 dozen doughnuts in 8 hours. As part of the test, an instructor randomly selects 6 of the 1,680 doughnuts made, to ascertain that they weigh around 350 grammes (12 ounces) and measure just under 20 centimetres (8 inches) when stacked. The Dunkin' Donuts University was opened to guarantee uniformity in all aspects of the business operations throughout the 1,700 franchise units.[14] The Coca-Cola Company's efforts to implement and control its marketing strategy are discussed in Marketing Insight 21.2.

Although the control function is a fundamental management activity, it has received little attention in marketing. There are both formal and informal control systems in organisations. The formal marketing control process, as mentioned before, involves performance standards, evaluation of actual performance and corrective action to remedy shortfalls (see Figure 21.5). The informal control process, however, involves self-control, social or group control, and cultural control through acceptance of a firm's value system. Which type of control system dominates depends on the environmental context of the firm.[15] These steps in the control process and the major problems they involve are discussed in the next sections.

Establishing Performance Standards

Planning and controlling are closely linked because plans include statements about what is to be accomplished. For purposes of control, these statements function as performance standards. A **performance standard** is an expected level of performance against which actual performance can be compared. Examples of performance standards might be the reduction of customers' complaints by 20 per cent, a monthly sales

CONTROLLING PERFORMANCE: XEROX'S RETURN TO LEADERSHIP

For its first 15 years, Xerox was without equal, best in an industry whose products were synonymous with its name. But in the mid-1970s challenges came from new competitors such as Canon and IBM. Japanese and US competition surpassed Xerox reprographic products in both cost and quality. Not even second best in some product categories, Xerox launched an ambitious quality improvement programme in 1984 to arrest its decline in the world market it had created. As a result, Xerox has not only halted loss of world market share but actually reversed it.

The phrase "Team Xerox" is not an empty slogan. It accurately reflects the firm's approach to tackling quality issues. Planning new products and services is based on detailed analyses of data specific to planning, managing and evaluating quality improvement. Much of this wealth of data has been amassed through an extensive network of market surveillance and customer feedback, all designed to support systematic evaluation of customer requirements.

Customer analyses include exhaustive surveys of 55,000 Xerox equipment owners. The company uses this information to develop concrete business plans with measurable targets for achieving quality improvements necessary to meet customers' needs.

Xerox measures its performance in about 240 key areas of product, service and business performance. The ultimate target for each attribute is the level of performance achieved by the world leader, regardless of industry. Gains in quality include a 78 per cent decrease in the number of defects per 100 machines; greatly increased product reliability, as measured by a 40 per cent decrease in unscheduled maintenance; increased copy quality, which has strengthened the company's position as world leader; a 27 per cent drop (nearly two hours) in service response time; and significant reductions in labour and materials overhead. Today the company has re-established itself as a world leader in copier markets.

SOURCES: Extracted from US Department of Commerce brochure, "Malcolm Baldrige National Quality Award, 1989 award winner"; Xerox Sales Force, UK.

quota of £150,000 or a 10 per cent increase per month in new customer accounts. Performance standards are also given in the form of budget accounts; that is, marketers are expected to achieve a certain objective without spending more than a given amount of resources. As stated earlier, performance standards should be tied to organisational goals. Performance standards can relate to product quality.

Evaluating Actual Performance

To compare actual performance with performance standards, marketing managers must know what marketers within the company are doing and have information about the activities of external organisations that provide the firm with marketing assistance. (Specific methods for assessing actual performance are discussed later in this chapter.)

COCA-COLA MANAGES INTERNATIONAL BOTTLERS

Coca-Cola may seem as American as apple pie, but the Coca-Cola name is one of the most recognised brands in the world. The company sells roughly 47 per cent of all the soft drinks consumed globally, more than twice as much as PepsiCo, its nearest rival. In 1989, 80 per cent of Coke's operating earnings came from foreign markets, up from 50 per cent in 1985. Amazing as it may seem, more Coca-Cola is sold in Japan each year than in the United States.

Coke's international success did not happen overnight. When most American companies were only thinking about global marketing strategies, Coke was implementing them. First, Coke carefully guided and set standards for its overseas bottling partners. To maintain control of its overseas bottlers, Coke generally invested in them, spending more than £1.5 billion in joint bottling ventures worldwide in the 1980s. If bottlers fail to perform as expected, Coke reviews their contracts and takes corrective action, sometimes resulting in ownership of its own bottling plants. When French bottler Pernod Richard S.A. disagreed with Coke over how to revive slow soft drink sales in France, the company took control to solve the problem.

The second part of Coke's international strategy consists of aggressive advertising, packaging and marketing to foreign consumers. Sometimes being "The Real Thing" isn't enough to ensure success. In many countries, such as Indonesia, Coke attempted to change consumer tastes by incorporating local tastes into the Coca-Cola formula. Thus, by buying strawberry, pineapple and banana flavoured soft drinks, Indonesians became accustomed to carbonated beverages.

By aggressively marketing to foreign consumers, Coke created markets with a high probability of success. It is this high probability of success that allows Coke to be firm but fair with its bottlers. At times, Coke's international bottlers may feel pressure to achieve the company's high standards. However, the dominance of the Coca-Cola brand in most foreign markets all but guarantees success for Coke and its bottlers. Until its competitors move to adopt global marketing strategies, Coca-Cola will remain not just "The Real Thing" but "The Only Thing" in many foreign markets. For Coca-Cola, control is fundamental to any successes.

SOURCES: "How Coke markets to the world", *Journal of Business Strategy,* September–October 1988, pp. 4–7; Michael J. McCarthy, "The real thing: as a global marketer, Coke excels by being tough and consistent", *Wall Street Journal,* 19 December 1989, pp. A1, A6; Robert McGough, "No more Mr. Nice Guy", *Financial World,* 25 July 1989, pp. 30–4.

FIGURE 21.5
The marketing control process

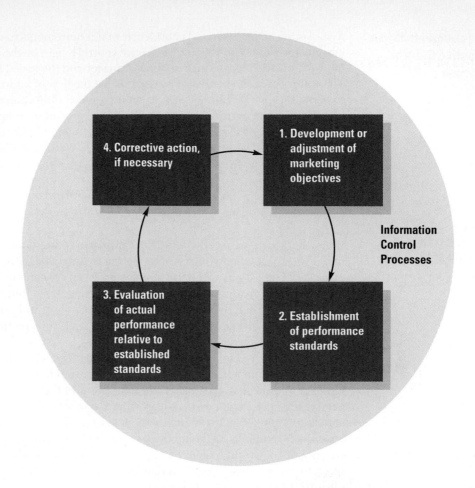

Information is required about the activities of marketing personnel at the operations level and at various marketing management levels. Most businesses obtain marketing assistance from one or more external individuals or organisations, such as advertising agencies, middlemen, marketing research firms and consultants. To maximise benefits from external sources, a firm's marketing control process must monitor their activities. Although it may be difficult to obtain the necessary information, it is impossible to measure actual performance without it.

Records of actual performance are compared with performance standards to determine whether and how much of a discrepancy exists. For example, a salesperson's actual sales are compared with his or her sales quota. If there is a significant negative discrepancy, the marketing manager takes corrective action.

Taking Corrective Action

Marketing managers have several options for reducing a discrepancy between established performance standards and actual performance. They can take steps to improve actual performance, can reduce or totally change the performance standard, or do both. Changes in actual performance may require the marketing manager to use better methods of motivating marketing personnel or find more effective techniques for co-ordinating marketing efforts.

Sometimes performance standards are unrealistic when they are written. In other cases, changes in the marketing environment make them unrealistic. For example, a company's annual sales goal may become unrealistic if several aggressive competitors enter the firm's market. In fact, changes in the marketing environment may force managers to change their marketing strategy completely.

Requirements for an Effective Control Process

A marketing manager should consider several requirements in creating and maintaining effective control processes.[16] Effective control hinges on the quantity and quality of information available to the marketing manager and the speed at which it is received. The control process should be designed so that the flow of information is rapid enough to allow the marketing manager to detect quickly differences between actual and planned levels of performance. A single control procedure is not suitable for all types of marketing activities, and internal and environmental changes affect an organisation's activities. Therefore, control procedures should be flexible enough to adjust to both varied activities and changes in the organisation's situation. For the control process to be usable, its costs must be low relative to the costs that would arise if controls were lacking. Finally, the control process should be designed so that both managers and subordinates can understand it and its requirements.

Problems in Controlling Marketing Activities

When marketing managers attempt to control marketing activities, they frequently run into several problems. Often the information required to control marketing activities is unavailable or is available only at a high cost. Even though marketing controls should be flexible enough to allow for environmental changes, the frequency, intensity and unpredictability of such changes may hamper effective control. In addition, the time lag between marketing activities and their effects limits a marketing manager's ability to measure the effectiveness of marketing activities.

Consider the problems of demand fluctuation in the video games industry. By failing to control the number of video game products offered, Nintendo (which controls 80 per cent of the US market and is at the forefront of the market in Europe), Atari and Sega glutted the market with so many video game titles that consumers were confused and disappointed with the numerous look-alike products. Companies are avoiding past mistakes by carefully analysing the success of video games and deleting older games that are no longer profitable. For example, Nintendo withdrew 18 of its 36 games to make room for new product introductions. This careful analysis and control of product offerings has helped home video games make a comeback from being a spectacular but short lived fad of the early 1980s.[17] It is estimated that soon one out of two homes will have either a Nintendo or Sega system.

Because marketing and other business activities overlap, marketing managers cannot determine the precise cost of marketing activities. Without an accurate measure of marketing costs, it is difficult to know if the effects of marketing activities are worth their expense. Finally, marketing control may be difficult because it is very hard to develop exact performance standards for marketing personnel.

METHODS OF EVALUATING PERFORMANCE

There are specific methods for assessing and improving the effectiveness of a marketing strategy. A marketer should state in the marketing plan what a marketing strategy is supposed to accomplish. These statements should set forth performance standards, which are usually stated in terms of profits, sales or costs. Actual performance must be measured in similar terms so that comparisons are possible. This section describes sales analysis and cost analysis, two general ways of evaluating the actual performance of marketing strategies.

Sales Analysis

Sales analysis uses sales figures to evaluate a firm's current performance. It is probably the most common method of evaluation, because sales data partially reflect the target market's reactions to a marketing mix and are often readily available, at least in aggregate form (see Figure 21.6).

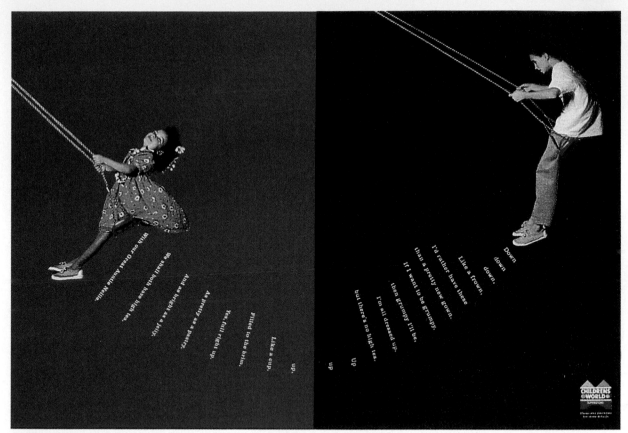

FIGURE 21.6 *Evaluating performance through sales data*
Boots' Children's World will use sales data from this summer to help predict sales of summer clothes for future years.

SOURCE: Advertising agency: GGT, London. Title of ad: Swing.

Marketers use current sales data to monitor the impact of current marketing efforts. However, that information alone is not enough. To provide useful analyses, current sales data must be compared with forecast sales, industry sales, specific competitors' sales or the costs incurred to achieve the sales volume. For example, knowing that a store attained a £600,000 sales volume this year does not tell management whether its marketing strategy has been successful. However, if managers know that expected sales were £550,000, they are then in a better position to determine the effectiveness of the firm's marketing efforts. In addition, if they know that the marketing costs needed to achieve the £600,000 volume were 12 per cent less than budgeted, they are in an even better position to analyse their marketing strategy precisely.

Types of Sales Measurements. Although sales may be measured in several ways, the basic unit of measurement is the sales transaction. A sales transaction results in a customer order for a specified quantity of an organisation's product sold under specified terms by a particular salesperson or sales group on a certain date. Many organisations record these bits of information about their transactions. With such a record, a company can analyse sales in terms of cash volume or market share.

Firms frequently use cash volume sales analysis because currency is a common denominator of sales, costs and profits (see Table 21.1). However, price increases and decreases affect total sales figures. For example, if a company increased its prices by 10

TABLE 21.1 *Top 10 UK beauty care brands, 1989[a]*

POSITION	BRAND	OWNER	SALES (£m)
1	Estée Lauder	Estée Lauder	over 100
2	Yves St Laurent	Cerus	over 100
3	L'Oréal	L'Oréal	over 100
4	Elizabeth Arden	Eli Lilly	70–100
5	Chanel	Chanel	70–100
6	Clinique	Estée Lauder	70–100
7	Christian Dior	LVMH	70–100
8	Lancôme	L'Oréal	40–70
9	Aramis	Estée Lauder	40–70
10	Helena Rubinstein	L'Oréal	40–70

[a]Sector defined as: make-up, female and male fragrance, consultant skin care

SOURCE: NCH Promotional Services. Reprinted by permission of Nielsen Marketing Services, Oxford, UK.

per cent this year and its sales volume is 10 per cent greater than last year, it has not experienced any increase in unit sales. A marketing manager who uses cash volume analysis should factor out the effects of price changes.

A firm's market share is the firm's sales of a product stated as a percentage of industry sales of that product. For example, KP, Golden Wonder, Smiths and Walkers account for around 70 per cent of the UK savoury snacks market. In the carbonated-drinks sector, Coca-Cola has a leading 16 per cent share by volume.[18] Market share analysis lets a company compare its marketing strategy with competitors' strategies. The primary reason for using market share analysis is to estimate whether sales changes have resulted from the firm's marketing strategy or from uncontrollable environmental forces. When a company's sales volume declines but its share of the market stays the same, the marketer can assume that industry sales declined (because of some uncontrollable factors) and that this decline was reflected in the firm's sales. However, if a company experiences a decline in both sales and market share, it should consider the possibility that its marketing strategy is not effective.

Even though market share analysis can be helpful in evaluating the performance of a marketing strategy, the user must interpret results cautiously. When attributing a sales decline to uncontrollable factors, a marketer must keep in mind that such factors do not affect all firms in the industry equally. Not all firms in an industry have the same objectives, and some change their objectives from one year to the next. Changes in the objectives of one company can affect the market shares of one or all companies in that industry. For example, if a competitor significantly increases promotional efforts or drastically reduces prices to increase market share, a company could lose market share despite a well designed marketing strategy. Within an industry, the entrance of new firms or the demise of established ones also affects a specific firm's market share, and market share analysts should attempt to account for these effects. Kentucky Fried Chicken (KFC), for example, probably re-evaluated its marketing strategies when McDonald's introduced its own fried chicken product.

Bases for Sales Analysis.   Whether it is based on sales volume or market share, sales analysis can be performed on aggregate sales figures or on disaggregated data. Aggregate sales analysis provides an overview of current sales. Although helpful, aggregate sales analysis is often insufficient, because it does not bring to light sales variations within the aggregate. It is not uncommon for a marketer to find that a large proportion of aggregate sales comes from a small number of products, geographic areas or customers. (This is sometimes called the "iceberg principle" because only a small part of an iceberg is visible above the water.) To find such disparities, total sales figures are usually broken down by geographic unit, salesperson, product, customer type or a combination of these categories.

In sales analysis by geographic unit, sales data can be classified by city, county, region, country or any other geographic designation for which a marketer collects sales information. Actual sales in a geographic unit can be compared with sales in a similar geographic unit, with last year's sales or with an estimated market potential for the area. For example, if a firm finds that 18 per cent of its sales are coming from an area that represents only 8 per cent of the potential sales for the product, then it can be assumed that the marketing strategy is successful in that geographic unit.

Because of the cost associated with hiring and maintaining a sales force, businesses commonly analyse sales by salesperson to determine the contribution each member of the sales force makes. Performance standards for each salesperson are often set in terms of sales quotas for a given time period. Evaluation of actual performance is accomplished by comparing a salesperson's current sales with a pre-established quota or some other standard, such as the previous period's sales. If actual sales meet or exceed the standard and the sales representative has not incurred costs above those budgeted, that person's efforts are acceptable.

Sales analysis is often performed according to product group or specific product item. Marketers break down their aggregate sales figures by product to determine the proportion that each contributed to total sales. Columbia Pictures, for example, might break down its total sales figures by box office figures for each film produced. A firm usually sets a sales volume objective—and sometimes a market share objective—for each product item or product group, and sales analysis by product is the only way to measure such objectives. A marketer can compare the breakdown of current sales by product with those of previous years. In addition, within industries for which sales data by product are available, a firm's sales by product type can be compared with industry averages. To gain an accurate picture of where sales of specific products are occurring, marketers sometimes combine sales analysis by product with sales analysis by geographic area or salesperson.

Analyses based on customers are usually broken down by type of customer. Customers can be classified by the way they use a firm's products, their distribution level (producer, wholesaler, retailer), their size, the size of orders or other characteristics. Sales analysis by customer type lets a firm ascertain whether its marketing resources are allocated in a way that achieves the greatest productivity. For example, sales analysis by type of customer may reveal that 60 per cent of the sales force is serving a group that makes only 15 per cent of total sales.

A considerable amount of information is needed for sales analyses, especially if disaggregated analyses are desired. The marketer must develop an operational system for collecting sales information; obviously, the effectiveness of the system for collecting sales information largely determines the ability of a company to develop useful sales analyses.

Marketing Cost Analysis

Although sales analysis is critical for evaluating the effectiveness of a marketing strategy, it gives only part of the picture. A marketing strategy that successfully generates sales may also be extremely costly. To obtain a complete picture, a firm must know the marketing costs associated with using a given strategy to achieve a certain sales level. **Marketing cost analysis** breaks down and classifies costs to determine which are associated with specific marketing activities. By comparing costs of previous marketing activities with results generated, a marketer can better allocate the firm's marketing resources in the future. Marketing cost analysis lets a company evaluate the effectiveness of an ongoing or recent marketing strategy by comparing sales achieved and costs incurred. By pin-pointing exactly where a company is experiencing high costs, this form of analysis can help isolate profitable or unprofitable customer segments, products or geographic areas.

For example, the market share of Komatsu, a Japanese construction equipment manufacturer, began to decline in the United States when prices increased because of the high yen value. Komatsu responded by developing an equal joint venture with Dresser Industries, making it the second largest company in this industry. The joint venture with Dresser allowed Komatsu to shift a large amount of its final assembly to the United States, to Dresser plants that had been running at 50 per cent capacity. By using Dresser's unused capacity and existing US plants, Komatsu avoided the start up costs of new construction and gained an immediate manufacturing presence in the United States.[19] This cost control tactic should enable Komatsu to use price more effectively as a marketing variable to compete with industry leader Caterpillar Tractor Co.

In some organisations, personnel in other functional areas—such as production or accounting—see marketers as primarily concerned with generating sales, regardless of the costs incurred. By conducting cost analyses, marketers can counter this criticism and put themselves in a better position to demonstrate how marketing activities contribute to generating profits. Even though hiring a sports figure such as Monica Seles is costly, in many sectors sales goals cannot be reached without large expenditures for promotion. Many advertisers believe that using celebrities helps to increase sales. Research shows that the public are good at identifying which personalities are linked to advertised brands (see Table 21.2). Ultimately, cost analysis should show if promotion costs are effective in increasing sales.

Determining Marketing Costs. The task of determining marketing costs is often complex and difficult. Simply ascertaining the costs associated with marketing a product is rarely adequate. Marketers must usually determine the marketing costs of serving specific geographical areas, market segments or even specific customers.

A first step in determining the costs is to examine accounting records. Most accounting systems classify costs into **natural accounts**—such as rent, salaries, office supplies and utilities—which are based on how the money was actually spent. Unfortunately, many natural accounts do not help explain what marketing functions were performed through the expenditure of those funds. It does little good, for example, to know that £80,000 is spent for rent each year. The analyst has no way of knowing whether the money is spent for the rental of production, storage or sales facilities. Therefore, marketing cost analysis usually requires some of the costs in natural accounts to be reclassified into **marketing function accounts,** which indicate the function performed through the expenditure of funds. Common marketing function accounts are transport, storage, order processing, selling, advertising, sales promotion, marketing research and customer credit.

Natural accounts can be reclassified into marketing function accounts as shown in the simplified example in Table 21.3. Note that a few natural accounts, such as advertising, can be reclassified easily into functional accounts because they do not have to be split across several accounts. For most of the natural accounts, however, marketers must develop criteria for assigning them to the various functional accounts. For example, the number of square metres of floor space used was the criterion for dividing the rental costs in Table 21.3 into functional accounts. In some instances, a specific mar-

TABLE 21.2 *Results of a survey testing correct association of personalities with brands*

PERSONALITY/ACCOUNT	AGENCY	PERCENTAGE CORRECT
1 Maureen Lipman—British Telecom	JWT	76
2 Daley Thompson—Lucozade	O&M	67
3 Paul Hogan—Foster's	BMPDDB Needham	63
4 Nannette Newman—Fairy Liquid	Grey	50
5 Dudley Moore—Tesco	LH-S	47
6 Billy Connolly—Kaliber	FCO	36
7 Nigel Havers/Jan Francis—Lloyds	LH-S	35
8 Richard Briers/Penelope Wilton—Nescafé	McCanns	32
9 Burt Lancaster—Foster's	BMPDDB Needham	31
10 John Barnes—Lucozade Sport	O&M	30
11 John Cleese—Schweppes	Saatchis	25
12 Warren Mitchell—British Gas	Y&R	22
13 Mel Smith/Griff Rhys Jones— Nationwide Anglio	Leagas Delaney	21
14 Twiggy—Silvikrin	O&M	20
15 Stephen Fry/Hugh Laurie— Alliance & Leicester	BMPDDB Needham	19

SOURCE: "Personalities prove there is life after death", *Marketing,* 8 February 1990, p. 7.

keting cost is incurred to perform several functions. A packaging cost, for example, could be considered a production function, a distribution function, a promotional function or all three. The marketing cost analyst must reclassify such costs across multiple functions.

Three broad categories are used in marketing cost analysis: direct costs, traceable common costs and non-traceable common costs. **Direct costs** are directly attributable to the performance of marketing functions. For example, sales force salaries might be allocated to the cost of selling a specific product item, selling in a specific geographic area or selling to a particular customer. **Traceable common costs** can be allocated indirectly, using one or several criteria, to the functions that they support. For example, if the firm spends £80,000 annually to rent space for production, storage and selling, the rental costs of storage could be determined on the basis of cost per square metre used for storage. **Non-traceable common costs** cannot be assigned according to any logical criteria and thus are assignable only on an arbitrary basis. Interest, taxes and the salaries of top management are non-traceable common costs.

The manner of dealing with these three categories of costs depends on whether the analyst uses a full cost or a direct cost approach. When a **full cost approach** is used, cost analysis includes direct costs, traceable common costs and non-traceable common costs. Proponents of this approach claim that if an accurate profit picture is desired, all costs must be included in the analysis. However, opponents point out that full costing does not yield actual costs, because non-traceable common costs are determined by arbitrary criteria. With different criteria, the full costing approach yields different results. A cost conscious operating unit can be discouraged if numerous costs are assigned to it arbitrarily. To eliminate such problems, the **direct cost approach,** which includes direct costs and traceable common costs but not non-traceable com-

TABLE 21.3 *Reclassification of natural accounts into functional accounts*

PROFIT AND LOSS STATEMENT		FUNCTIONAL ACCOUNTS					
		ADVERTISING	PERSONAL SELLING	TRANSPORT	STORAGE	MARKETING RESEARCH	NON-MARKETING
Sales	£250,000						
Cost of goods sold	45,000						
Gross profit	205,000						
Expenses (natural accounts)							
Rent	£ 14,000		£ 7,000		£6,000		£ 1,000
Salaries	72,000	£12,000	32,000	£7,000		£1,000	20,000
Supplies	4,000	1,500	1,000			1,000	500
Advertising	16,000	16,000					
Freight	4,000			2,000			2,000
Taxes	2,000				200		1,800
Insurance	1,000				600		400
Interest	3,000						3,000
Bad debts	6,000						6,000
Total	£122,000	£29,500	£40,000	£9,000	£6,800	£2,000	£34,700
Net profit	£ 83,000						

mon costs, is used. Opponents say that this approach is not accurate, because it omits one cost category.

Methods of Marketing Cost Analysis.   Marketers can use several methods to analyse costs. The methods vary in their precision. This section examines three cost analysis methods—analysis of natural accounts; analysis of functional accounts; and cost analysis by product, geographic area or customer.

Marketers can sometimes determine marketing costs by performing an analysis of natural accounts. The precision of this method depends on how detailed the firm's accounts are. For example, if accounting records contain separate accounts for production wages, sales force wages and executive salaries, the analysis can be more precise than if all wages and salaries are lumped into a single account. An analysis of natural accounts is more meaningful, and thus more useful, when current cost data can be compared with those of previous periods or with average cost figures for the entire industry. Cost analysis of natural accounts frequently treats costs as percentages of sales. The periodic use of cost to sales ratios lets a marketer ascertain cost fluctuations quickly.

As indicated earlier, the analysis of natural accounts may not shed much light on the cost of marketing activities. In such cases, natural accounts must be reclassified into marketing function accounts for analysis. Whether certain natural accounts are reclassified into functional accounts and what criteria are used to reclassify them will depend to some degree on whether the analyst is using direct costing or full costing. After natural accounts have been reclassified into functional accounts, the cost of each function is determined by adding together the costs in each functional account. Once the costs of these marketing functions have been determined, the analyst is ready to compare the resulting figures with budgeted costs, sales analysis data, cost data from earlier operating periods or perhaps average industry cost figures, if these are available.

Although marketers usually obtain a more detailed picture of marketing costs by analysing functional accounts than by analysing natural accounts, some firms need an even more precise cost analysis. The need is especially great if the firms sell several types of products, sell in multiple geographic areas or sell to a wide variety of customers. Activities vary in marketing different products in specific geographic locations to certain customer groups. Therefore, the costs of these activities also vary. By analysing the functional costs of specific product groups, geographic areas or customer groups, a marketer can find out which of these marketing entities are the most cost-effective to serve. In Table 21.4, the functional costs derived in Table 21.3 are allocated to specific product categories.

TABLE 21.4 *Functional accounts divided into product group costs*

FUNCTIONAL ACCOUNTS		PRODUCT GROUPS		
		A	B	C
Advertising	£29,500	£14,000	£ 8,000	£ 7,500
Personal selling	40,000	18,000	10,000	12,000
Transport	9,000	5,000	2,000	2,000
Storage	6,800	1,800	2,000	3,000
Marketing research	2,000		1,000	1,000
Total	£87,300	£38,800	£23,000	£25,500

A similar type of analysis could be performed for geographic areas or for specific customer groups. The criteria used to allocate the functional accounts must be developed so as to yield results that are as accurate as possible. Use of faulty criteria is likely to yield inaccurate cost estimates, which in turn lead to less effective control of marketing strategies. Marketers determine the marketing costs for various product categories, geographic areas or customer groups and then compare them with sales. This analysis lets them evaluate the effectiveness of the firm's marketing strategy or strategies.

SUMMARY

The organisation of marketing activities involves the development of an internal structure for the marketing unit. The internal structure is the key to directing marketing activities. A centralised organisation is one in which the top level managers delegate very little authority to lower levels of the firm. In a decentralised organisation, decision-making authority is delegated as far down the chain of command as possible. In a marketing orientated organisation, the focus is on finding out what buyers want and providing it in a way that lets the organisation achieve its objectives. The marketing unit can be organised by (1) functions, (2) products, (3) regions or (4) types of customer. An organisation may use only one approach or a combination.

Implementation is an important part of the marketing management process. Proper implementation of a marketing plan depends on internal marketing to employees, the motivation of personnel who perform marketing activities, effective communication within the marketing organisation and the co-ordination of marketing activities. Internal marketing refers to the managerial actions necessary to make all members of the marketing organisation understand and accept their respective roles in implementing the marketing strategy. To attract, motivate and retain qualified internal customers (employees), firms employ internal marketing by designing internal products (jobs) that satisfy employees' wants and needs. Marketing managers must also motivate marketing personnel. A company's communication system must allow the marketing manager to communicate with high level management, with managers of other functional areas in the firm and with personnel involved in marketing activities both inside and outside the organisation. Finally, marketing managers must co-ordinate the activities of marketing personnel and integrate these activities with those in other areas of the company and with the marketing efforts of personnel in external organisations.

The marketing control process consists of establishing performance standards, evaluating actual performance by comparing it with established standards and reducing the difference between desired and actual performance. Performance standards, which are established in the planning process, are expected levels of performance with which actual performance can be compared. In evaluating actual performance, marketing managers must know what marketers within the firm are doing and must have information about the activities of external organisations that provide the firm with marketing assistance. Then actual performance is compared with performance standards. Marketers must determine whether a discrepancy exists and, if so, whether it requires corrective action, such as changing the performance standards or improving actual performance.

To maintain effective marketing control, an organisation needs to develop a comprehensive control process that evaluates its marketing operations at a given time. The control of marketing activities is not a simple task. Problems encountered include environmental changes, time lags between marketing activities and their effects, and difficulty in determining the costs of marketing activities. In addition to these, it may be hard to develop performance standards.

Control of marketing strategy can be achieved through sales and cost analyses. For the purpose of analysis, sales are usually measured in terms of either cash volume or market share. For a sales analysis to be effective, it must compare current sales performance with forecast company sales, industry sales, specific competitors' sales or the costs incurred to generate the current sales volume. A sales analysis can be performed on the firm's total sales, or the total sales can be disaggregated and analysed by product, geographic area or customer group.

Marketing cost analysis involves an examination of accounts records and, frequently, a reclassification of natural accounts into marketing function accounts. Such an analysis is often difficult, because there may be no logical, clear cut way to allocate natural accounts into functional accounts. The analyst may choose either direct costing or full costing. Cost analysis can focus on (1) an aggregate cost analysis of natural accounts or functional accounts or (2) an analysis of functional accounts for products, geographic areas or customer groups.

IMPORTANT TERMS

Centralised organisation
Decentralised organisation
Marketing orientated organisation
Internal marketing
Marketing control process
Performance standard
Sales analysis
Marketing cost analysis

Natural accounts
Marketing function accounts
Direct costs
Traceable common costs
Non-traceable common costs
Full cost approach
Direct cost approach

DISCUSSION AND REVIEW QUESTIONS

1. What determines the place of marketing within an organisation? Which type of organisation is best suited to the marketing concept? Why?
2. What factors can be used to organise the internal aspects of a marketing unit? Discuss the benefits of each type of organisation.
3. Why might an organisation use multiple bases for organising its marketing unit?
4. What is internal marketing? Why is it important in implementing marketing strategies?
5. Why is motivation of marketing personnel important in implementing marketing plans?
6. How does communication help in implementing marketing plans?
7. What are the major steps of the marketing control process?
8. List and discuss the five requirements for an effective control process.
9. Discuss the major problems in controlling marketing activities.
10. What is a sales analysis? What makes it an effective control tool?
11. Identify and describe three cost analysis methods. Compare and contrast direct costing and full costing.

21.1 Paramount Pictures: Strategic Struggle

Although Hollywood studios market products which are different from those of other companies, they are, like any other business, vulnerable to threats and open to opportunities. They must develop marketing strategies and implement them if they are to produce the blockbuster films and hit television programmes that consumers want to see. Paramount Pictures Corporation is one studio that has developed successful marketing strategies.

Business is good for Paramount today; it is making blockbuster films and hit television programmes such as *Cheers, The Arsenio Hall Show* and *Star Trek: The Next Generation*. But things were not always so glamorous for the studio division of Paramount Communications Inc. (formerly Gulf & Western). In early 1986, Paramount had a dismal 1.5 per cent share of the market, down from a 1984 high of 19.1 per cent. In addition, the management team that had led the studio to glory with the films *Flashdance, An Officer and a Gentleman* and *Raiders of the Lost Ark* left for positions with 20th Century-Fox and the Walt Disney Company. Paramount became the owner of a large collection of movie flops, with the exception of one huge hit, *Beverly Hills Cop*.

Then, Frank Mancuso, a 27 year Paramount veteran, assumed the post of chairman of the company. Mancuso hired the industry's best production and marketing executives and began a strategy of establishing long term relationships between the studio and major film producers and stars. This strategy proved to be the answer to Paramount's film production woes.

Shortly after Mancuso assumed the chairmanship of Paramount, the company began turning out one hit after another—often from ideas turned down by other film studios. One such idea was a script about young naval air cadets, which Paramount produced at a cost of more than $175 million under the name *Top Gun*. *Top Gun* went on to become the top grossing hit of 1986 with revenues of $270 million. *Crocodile Dundee* in 1986 and *Beverly Hills Cop II, Fatal Attraction* and *The Untouchables* in 1987 were other Paramount success stories. By the end of 1987, Paramount had captured the number one position in the market two years in a row and a 20 per cent share of the US market. This position reflected the company's worldwide rating. Despite the 1990 box office success of *The Hunt for Red October* and *Ghost*, a 7 per cent decline in cinema attendance and several disappointing films lowered the studio's US market share to 16.4 per cent and left its international position once more vulnerable.

The secret of Paramount's fluctuating success lies partly in the whimsical entertainment tastes of consumers. However, a great deal of it can be attributed to its strategy of nurturing successful long term relationships and projects. Paramount has carefully milked one of its oldest television cash cows, *Star Trek*, with video releases of the original episodes, six feature films and the hit programme *Star Trek: The Next Generation*. Long term relationships with other cash cows and stars, such as actor/comedians Eddie Murphy and Arsenio Hall and major directors Steven Spielberg and George Lucas, have also contributed to the studio's string of winners.

Nurturing such long term relationships is the only means of securing successful sequel and television spin off development. The enormous popularity of groups of films such as the *Indiana Jones* trilogy, the series of *Star Trek* movies and more than half a dozen Eddie Murphy pictures bear out the importance of securing these long term contracts. Within the industry, Paramount's exclusive contract with Eddie Murphy has been considered to be the best of them all. Murphy's films with Paramount have a combined income of more than $1,000 million, not counting the additional revenue generated through television, video cassettes and cable television.

The success of these long term relationships has allowed Paramount to be aggressive in marketing and media usage. A prime example is the deal struck by Paramount and Time Warner to promote the opening day of *Godfather III*. Paramount agreed to advertise heavily in Time Warner publications, especially *People, Life* and *Entertainment Weekly.* In return, Time Warner supported the film's opening by showing *The Godfather,* and *The Godfather II* on the HBO television channel shortly before the premiere. It also broadcast a 30 minute special programme, *Making of the Godfather,* and a television behind the scenes look at *Godfather* stars that gave out a telephone number offering viewers a gift package. Paramount's advertisements promoted the HBO showings as well as the movie. As the result of this and other promotions, Paramount is known as the master of publicity and word of mouth promotions.

A film producing strategy based on a product line can be a gamble. Paramount risks staking its future on past successes and even on a single superstar. Some of the company's products, such as the *Star Trek* series, are already mature because of the aging of the principal actors. Others have finished: *Indiana Jones and the Last Crusade* was the last of the highly successful trilogy featuring Harrison Ford. The danger of relying on a single star is becoming more evident to Paramount studios. There was some doubt as to whether or not Eddie Murphy would make *Beverly Hills Cop III,* considered to be an automatic $100 million production.

Thus, despite its successful long term relationships and successful products, Paramount must constantly look for new product ideas and hot new stars. To shore up a 4 per cent drop in entertainment operating revenues, Paramount sold a package of 24 of its premium films to the USA television network for about $2 million per title. The studio also trimmed its staff and halved the number of films in development to 125. Paramount is currently exploring the possibility of doing a string of films based on its *Star Trek: The Next Generation* television series. It recently signed Arsenio Hall to an exclusive, long term contract and announced its own talk show, *The Maury Povich Show,* already sold to stations in 40 per cent of the United States. The firm's European operation will produce two to four films annually.

The studio continues to believe in its strategy of milking its cash cows. With a box office share just below leader Disney Studios, a $420 million production budget, and more plans for big budget, big star films, its faith seems justified. But the studio is constantly looking for and developing new stars. One company executive insists that Paramount won't just sit back, make *Star Trek VII, VIII* and *IX,* and call it a day.

The declining fortunes in the early 1980s emphasised that even in the movies, companies require strategies and marketing programmes capable of responding to consumer tastes, competitors' products and corporate expectations. In order to avoid the traumas associated with low sales and financial crises, Paramount—in common with the industry in general—has prioritised the ongoing assessment of performances on three levels: financial, human and critical acclaim.

SOURCES: Richard Behar, "Small wonders", *Time,* 11 February 1991, pp. 63–4; Charles Fleming, "Time Warner, Par in "God swap' ", *Film,* 8 October 1990, pp. 5, 85; "Paramount hoping Povich " 'Current Affair' success translates to new talk show", *Broadcasting,* October 1990, p. 32; "Tribune, Paramount part company", *Broadcasting,* 1 October 1990, p. 36; Michael Fleming, "Majors' heavyweight films to slug it out for holiday biz", *Film,* October 1990, pp. 5, 8; Paul Noglows and Judy Brennan, "Par's net hike by the book", *Finance,* September 1990, pp. 73–4; Charles Fleming, "Sequel sinks as Murphy trawls for new megadeals", *Variety,* 28 March 1990, pp. 1, 4; Dennis McDougal, "Paramount's net profit central to Buchwald suit", *Los Angeles Times,* 23 March 1990; Elizabeth Guider, "Writers flex their muscles thanks to Buchwald win", *Variety,* 17 January 1990, pp. 1, 4; Marcy Magiera, "Paramount axes DMB&B as studios watch costs", *Advertising Age,* 15 January 1990, p. 4; Laura Landro, "Paramount plans movie unit in London to tap growing international market", *Wall Street Journal*, 12 January 1990, p. B4; Laura Landro, "It's a record race for movie makers", *Wall Street Journal*, 3 November 1989, p. B2; Ronald Grover, "Fat times for studios, fatter times for stars", *Business Week*, 24 July 1989, p. 48; and Laura Landro, "Sequels and stars help top movie studios avoid major risks", *Wall Street Journal*, 6 June 1989, pp. A1, A18.

Questions for Discussion

1. What is the likely role of strategic market planning at Paramount Pictures?
2. Which environmental forces are most likely to affect the planning and the outcomes of Paramount's marketing strategies?
3. Why must Paramount have a continuous understanding of its performance and industry standing?

21.2   Timex Stands the Test Of Time

During the 1970s, watches took a technological leap forward from wind up spring mechanisms to quartz crystals, batteries and digital displays. The Timex Corporation, however, lagged behind other manufacturers in making the changes. When the Swiss-made Swatch invaded department stores and convinced customers that their watches were not just time telling devices but fashion statements, Timex was not ready to offer any competition. At Timex, reliability had always been the number one priority, certainly not style and fashion. For years, Timex's sales suffered because of a drab image, especially in contrast with the colourful Swatch.

Then came the 1990s, the decade of value. As value takes precedence over status, more price conscious consumers are attracted by quality at moderate prices than by designer labels. Timex is taking advantage of this trend to revive its 41 year old brand, the old reliable Timex watch. By blending its "value pricing" message with some trendy new designs and diversifying its product for specific niche markets, Timex is making a comeback.

Consumers can still buy an unadorned Timex watch for about £5, and analysts say that these simple styles with easy to read faces are the company's best sellers. To compete in a crowded market, however, Timex is developing stylish special collections for two separate adult divisions, dress watches and sports watches, as well as expanding its children's unit. The company has even set up studios in France and the United States to design Timex renditions of colourful creative watches. In the adult fashion arena, Timex offers women its Images line with neon accented hands, floral patterned watch bands, and over sized faces, and men the Carriage III collection. For those with poor vision, Timex created the Easy Reader with large clear numbers. Sports watch buyers can choose from models with names like Surf, Brave Wave and Magnum that are shock-resistant, water-resistant and offer features like compasses, pedometers, chronographs and thermometers. After soliciting educators' advice, the company came up with its Gizmoz watches to help children five to nine years old tell time. Colourful designs are on the band instead of the face, which displays all of the numbers and colour codes hour and minute hands. For example, black faced watches have whitehours and hour hands but green minutes and green minute hands. There is even a Lefty Gizmoz available. To appeal to parents, whose money really buys the Gizmoz watches, Timex offers a kids' loss protection plan that replaces a watch for only half the purchase price.

Timex's advertising strategy is to appeal to niche markets by reviving its traditional "durable yet inexpensive" positioning and revitalising its powerful brand identity. The famous Timex theme, "It Takes a Licking and Keeps On Ticking", takes a humorous bent in television spots where Sumo wrestlers wear Timex watches strapped to their middles as they grapple on the mat and rock musicians use Timex watches to strum their guitars. In a recent print advertising campaign, the firm featured real people who, like the Timex watches they wear, have been through rough experiences but survived to tell the tale. On television talk shows, company executives introduced the Timex *Why Pay More* magazine, featuring Timex watches as part of fashion outfits selling for under £50.

With watch sales in most countries declining, most watchmakers are concerned. At Timex, however, executives are celebrating sales and market share increases. The company now controls a larger segment of the market than its four biggest competitors combined. Timex is happy to be shedding its dowdy and boring image. Rising young professional people don't have to put their wrists behind their backs to hide a Timex any more, or announce loudly to co-workers that they are only wearing a Timex while their Rolex is being repaired. Marketing executives have carefully monitored the introduction of this strategy to (1) ensure that early signs of success or failure could be acted upon and (2) modify marketing programmes continuously in order to enhance the impact of Timex's new approach. Sales and financial performance are evaluated regularly: so far they reveal a success story. Changing fashions and aggressive competitors such as Swatch caught Timex out once before. The company does not intend to be left behind again, despite industrial relations problems in Europe. These issues have forced Timex to modify its strategies, and to rejuvenate its promotional campaigns to overcome adverse publicity from trades unions.

SOURCES: Cara Appelbaum, "High time for Timex", *Adweek's Marketing Week,* 29 July 1991, p. 24; Melissa Campanelli, "Motivating, MOTI style", *Sales & Marketing Management,* June 1991, pp. 125–6; and Jennifer Pellet, "Watching watch trends", *DM,* November 1990, pp. 56–7; BBC/ITN News Broadcasts, Spring 1993.

Questions for Discussion

1. Which environmental forces are likely to be of greatest interest to marketing managers at Timex?
2. Identify the target markets towards which Timex is aiming its products.
3. Why must Timex continuously assess its performance and the impact of its marketing?

22 MARKETING ETHICS AND SOCIAL RESPONSIBILITY

Objectives

To define and understand the importance of marketing ethics

To recognise factors that influence ethical or unethical decisions

To discuss some important ethical issues in marketing

To identify ways to improve ethical decisions in marketing

To understand the concept of social responsibility

To explore several important issues of social responsibility

To describe strategies for dealing with social dilemmas

*I*n the summer of 1990 Japanese film and camera company Fuji ran into a storm when its UK marketing team launched a revolutionary advertising campaign. As *Marketing* magazine's editorial read, opinions were mixed:

> Fuji has used the issues of racism and hostility towards handicapped people to promote its film. Does this herald a new wave of social concern in advertising, and if so, what are the pitfalls? Is it exploitation or is it a step forward?

Some media watchers thought the advertisements—which depicted everyday scenes from the lives of handicapped workers and Asian families—to be callous or exploitative, while others described them as enlightened and brilliant. For Fuji and agency Henry Howell Chaldecott Lury, the aim was to provide educational value as well as achieve brand and product awareness. Fuji was pinning its social conscience on its sleeve. Negative reaction to its campaign was not, therefore, expected. "Fuji produces the best film" was the key message; Fuji as a caring company—an opinion supported by consumer research—was the secondary message.

Fuji's advertisements were checked by the Independent Broadcasting Authority and measured against the guidelines set by the Race Relations Act and the Equal Opportunities Act. Both Mencap, the charity for the mentally handicapped, and the Commission for Racial Equality have praised the sensitivity of the advertisements. While many companies' advertisements include disabled people and those representing ethnic minorities, none previously had so prominently featured situations which for many people are an everyday aspect of life. ■

SOURCES: Suzanne Bidlake, "Shooting the victims", *Marketing*, 19 July 1990, pp. 20–1; Phil Dourado, "Parity not charity", *Marketing* 16 August 1990, pp. 26-7; Liz Levy, "Bitter-sweet charity", *Marketing*, 15 March 1990, pp. 34–5; "The old year's honours list", *Campaign*, 11 January 1991, pp. 25–31.

Most marketers avoid sensitive issues; a few abuse them. Fuji took a bold step and most consumers believe the company cared rather than exploited. The ethics of such a campaign were discussed at great length, by the companies concerned in developing the campaign, regulatory bodies, organisations representing the groups featured and the media. The issue of ethics in marketing is evolving and set to increase in prominence.

Issues such as the Fuji advertising controversy illustrate that all marketing activities can be judged as morally right or wrong by society, consumers, interest groups, competitors and others. Although most marketers operate within the limits of the law, some do engage in activities that are not considered acceptable by other marketers, consumers and society in general. A number of recently publicised incidents in marketing, such as deceptive or objectionable advertising, misleading packaging, questionable selling practices, manipulation, corruption and pollution, have raised questions as to whether specific marketing practices are acceptable and beneficial to society. The limits of acceptable marketing practices and the obligations marketers have to society are issues of marketing ethics and social responsibility.

This chapter gives an overview of the role of ethics and social responsibility in marketing decision-making. The chapter first defines marketing ethics and discusses the factors that influence ethical decision making in marketing. Next it outlines some specific ethical issues in marketing and explores ways to improve ethics in marketing decisions. The chapter then focuses on the issue of social responsibility as its core theme, looking at the impact of marketing decisions on society and developing some strategies for dealing with social responsibility dilemmas. The chapter closes by comparing and contrasting the concepts of marketing ethics and social responsibility.

THE NATURE OF MARKETING ETHICS

Although a very important concern in marketing decisions, ethics may be one of the most misunderstood and controversial concepts in marketing. No one has yet developed a universally accepted approach to dealing with marketing ethics. However, marketing personnel need to examine the concept and its application to help them make marketing decisions that are acceptable and beneficial to society. This section considers the meaning of marketing ethics.

Marketing Ethics Defined

Ethics relate to moral evaluations of decisions and actions as right or wrong on the basis of commonly accepted principles of behaviour. **Marketing ethics** are moral principles that define right and wrong behaviour in marketing. The most basic ethical issues have been formalised through laws and regulations to conform to the standards of society. At the very least, marketers are expected to obey these laws and regulations. However, it is important to realise that marketing ethics go beyond legal issues; ethical marketing decisions foster mutual trust among individuals and in marketing relationships.

Ethics are individually defined and may vary from one person to another. Although individual marketers often act in their own self-interest, there must be standards of acceptable behaviour to guide all marketing decisions. Marketers need to operate in accordance with sound moral principles based on ideals such as fairness, justice and trust.[1] Consumers generally regard unethical marketing activities—for instance, deceptive advertising, misleading selling tactics, price fixing and the deliberate marketing of harmful products—as unacceptable and often refuse to do business with marketers that engage in such practices. Thus when marketers deviate from accepted moral principles to further their own interests at the expense of others, continued marketing exchanges become difficult, if not impossible.[2]

Marketing Ethics Are Controversial

Few topics in marketing are more controversial than ethics. Most marketing decisions can be judged as right or wrong, ethical or unethical. But people have different ideas as to what is ethical or unethical depending on the nature of the organisation, their experiences in life, and their personal values. Many marketers have such strong convictions about what is morally right or wrong that they deeply resent discussions of alternative ways to make ethical decisions.

Regardless of how a person or an organisation views the acceptability of a particular activity, if society judges that activity to be wrong or unethical, then this view directly affects the organisation's ability to achieve its goals. Although not all activities deemed unethical by society may be illegal, consumer protests against a particular activity may result in legislation that restricts or bans it. When an organisation engages in unethical marketing activities, it may not only lose sales as dissatisfied consumers refuse to deal with it, it may also face lawsuits, fines and even prison for its executives. Manufacturer Hoover ran a now infamous sales promotion in late 1992 offering free flights to anyone purchasing a Hoover product valued over £100. Thousands of consumers purchased Hoover vacuum cleaners and washing machines expressly to take advantage of this offer, but many hundreds were disappointed. The offer was flawed: some of Hoover's agents acted unscrupulously; few people were offered their choice of holiday destination; BBC's Watchdog programme showed agents deliberately obstructing consumers attempting to take up the offer. Hoover had not broken any laws but was deemed by the media and consumers to have behaved unethically.[3] Such an example illustrates the importance of understanding marketing ethics and recognising ethical issues.

Because marketing ethics are so controversial, it is important to state that it is not the purpose of this chapter to question anyone's personal ethical beliefs and convictions. Nor is it the purpose of this chapter to examine the behaviour of consumers, although consumers, too, may be unethical (engaging, for instance, in coupon fraud, shoplifting and other abuses). Instead, its goal is to underscore the importance of ethical issues and ethical decision-making in marketing. Understanding the impact of ethical decisions in marketing can help people to recognise and resolve ethical issues within an organisation.

UNDERSTANDING THE ETHICAL DECISION-MAKING PROCESS

To grasp the significance of ethics in marketing decision-making, it is first necessary to examine the factors that influence the ethical decision-making process. Personal moral philosophies, organisational relationships and opportunity are three factors that interact to determine ethical decisions in marketing (see Figure 22.1).

Moral Philosophies

Moral philosophies are principles or rules that individuals use to determine the right way to behave. They provide guidelines for resolving conflicts and ensuring mutual benefit for all members of society.[4] People learn these principles and rules through socialisation by family members, social groups, religion and formal education. Each moral philosophy has its own concept of rightness or "ethicalness" and rules for behaviour. Here two distinct moral philosophies are discussed: utilitarianism and ethical formalism.

FIGURE 22.1
Factors that influence the ethical decision-making process

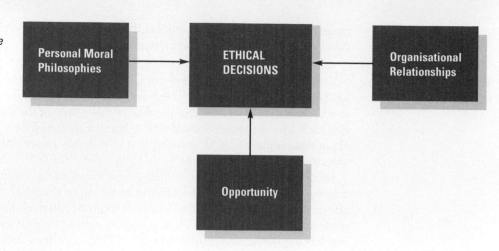

Utilitarianism.   **Utilitarianism** is a moral philosophy concerned with maximising the greatest good for the greatest number of people. Utilitarians judge an action on the basis of the consequences for all the people affected by the action. In other words, in a situation with an ethical component, utilitarians compare all possible options and select the one that promises the best results. Under utilitarianism, then, it would be unethical to act in a way that leads to personal gain at the expense of society in general. Consider the following example of an organisation adopting a utilitarian philosophy. In 1990, the offices of Delta Air Lines in Ireland received a telephone threat from terrorists that one of its transatlantic flights would be bombed. Delta decided to publicise the threat and announced that it would allow customers holding tickets on its transatlantic flights to transfer them to other airlines without penalty.[5] When Pan Am received a bomb threat in 1988, it did not notify the public; the loss of more than 200 lives in the terrorist bombing of Pan Am Flight 103 over Lockerbie and the negative publicity directed at Pan Am damaged the firm. Thus, after weighing the possible loss of life and the negative publicity surrounding a terrorist bombing or crash against the loss of revenue and profits, Delta executives probably concluded that publicising the bomb threat and letting passengers decide whether to fly on Delta would be best for consumers and for the company.

Ethical Formalism.   Other moral philosophies focus on the intentions associated with a particular behaviour and on the rights of the individual. **Ethical formalism** develops specific rules for behaviour by determining whether an action can be taken consistently as a general rule without concern for alternative results.[6] Behaviour is judged on the basis of whether it infringes individual rights or universal rules. The Golden Rule—do unto others as you would have them do unto you—exemplifies ethical formalism. So does Immanuel Kant's categorical imperative: that every action should be based on reasons that everyone could act on, at least in principle, and that action must be based on reasons that the decision-maker would be willing to have others use.[7] In marketing, ethical formalism is consistent with the idea of consumer choice. For example, consumers have a right to know about possible defects in a car or other products that involve safety.[8]

Applying Moral Philosophies to Marketing Decision-Making.   Traditionally, it has been assumed that personal moral philosophies remain constant in both work and non-work situations. However, research has shown that most business people use one moral philosophy at work and a completely different one outside work.[9]

Another study found that although personal moral philosophies and values enter into ethical decisions in business, they are not the central component that guides the decisions, actions and policies of an organisation.[10] This finding may explain why individuals switch moral philosophies between home and work and why personal values make up only one part of an organisation's total value system.

Some marketers use the logic that anything is fair which defeats the competition and increases profits. They have used warfare concepts such as "guerrilla warfare", "pre-emptive first strikes" and "counter attacks" to justify questionable and possibly unethical actions. A distinction should be made between competitors and enemies. Competitors are rivals that compete for customers and markets according to socially accepted rules, whereas central to the science of warfare is total conquest and, in some cases, elimination of the enemy. Therefore the "marketing as warfare" comparison raises ethical concerns, given the destructive nature of warfare.[11]

Others view marketing as a game, like football or boxing, in which ordinary rules and morality do not apply. For example, what if a boxer decided it was wrong to try to injure another person or a rugby player was afraid of hurting another player when he made contact? Sports have rules and referees to regulate the game to ensure safety and equality. However, because customers in marketing exchanges are not economically self-sufficient, they cannot choose to withdraw from the marketing "game". Given this condition, marketing ethics must make clear what rules do and should apply in the marketing "game". Even more important, the rules developed must be appropriate to the non-voluntary character of participation in the game. Most members of society hold that moral principles and standards of acceptable behaviour should guide decisions related to the welfare of customers.[12]

Ethical behaviour may be a function of two different dimensions of an organisation's value structure: the organisation's values and traditions, or corporate culture, and the personal moral philosophies of the organisation's individual members. An employee assumes some measure of moral responsibility by agreeing to abide by an organisation's rules and standard operating procedures. When a marketer decides to behave unethically or even illegally, it may be that competitive pressures and organisational rewards provided the incentive.

Organisational Relationships

People learn personal moral philosophies, and therefore ethical behaviour, not only from society in general but also from members of their social groups and their organisational environment. Relationships with employees, co-workers, or superiors create ethical problems, such as maintaining confidentiality in personal relations; meeting obligations, responsibilities and mutual agreements; and avoiding undue pressure that may force others to behave unethically. Employees may have to deal with assignments that they perceive as creating ethical dilemmas. For example, a salesperson may be asked to lie to a customer over the phone. Likewise, an employee who sees another employee cheating a customer must decide whether to report the incident.

Marketing managers must carefully balance their duties to the owners or shareholders who hired them to carry out the organisation's objectives and to the employees who look to them for guidance and direction. In addition, managers must also comply with society's wishes and ethical evaluations. Striking an ethical balance between these areas, then, is a difficult task for today's marketing decision-makers.

The role of top management is extremely important in developing the culture of an organisation. Most experts agree that the chief executive officer or the director in charge of marketing sets the ethical tone for the entire marketing organisation. Lower level managers take their cues from top management, yet they, too, impose some of their personal values on the company. This interaction between corporate culture and executive leadership helps determine the ethical value system of the firm.

Powerful superiors can affect employees' activities and directly influence behaviour by putting into practice the company's standards of ethics. Young marketers in particular indicate that they often go along with their superiors to demonstrate loyalty in matters related to judgements of morality. The status and power of significant others is directly related to the amount of pressure they can exert to get others to conform to their expectations. A manager in a position of authority can exert strong pressure to ensure compliance on ethically related issues. In organisations where ethical standards are vague and supervision by superiors is limited, peers may provide guidance in an ethical decision.

The role of peers (significant others) in the decision-making process depends on the person's ratio of exposure to unethical behaviour to exposure to ethical behaviour. The more a person is exposed to unethical activity in the organisational environment, the more likely it is that he or she will behave unethically.[13] Employees experience conflict between what is expected of them as workers and managers and what they expect of themselves based on their own personal ethical standards.

Opportunity

Opportunity provides another pressure that may determine whether a person will behave ethically. Opportunity is a favourable set of conditions that limit barriers or provide rewards. Rewards may be internal or external. Internal rewards are the feelings of goodness and worth a person experiences after carrying out an altruistic action. External rewards are what a person expects to receive from others in terms of values generated and provided on an exchange basis. External rewards are often received from peers and top management in the form of praise, promotions and pay raises.

If a marketer takes advantage of an opportunity to act unethically and is rewarded or suffers no penalty, he or she may repeat such acts as other opportunities arise. For example, a salesperson who receives a pay rise after using a deceptive sales presentation to increase sales is being rewarded for this behaviour and so will probably continue it. Indeed, opportunity to engage in unethical conduct is often a better predictor of unethical activities than personal values.[14]

Besides rewards and the absence of punishment, other elements in the business environment help to create opportunities. Professional codes of ethics and ethics related corporate policy also influence opportunity by prescribing what behaviours are acceptable. The larger the rewards and the lesser the punishment for unethical behaviour, the greater is the probability that unethical behaviour will be practised.

ETHICAL ISSUES IN MARKETING

A person will not make an ethical decision unless he or she recognises that a particular issue or situation has an ethical or moral component. Thus developing awareness of ethical issues is important in understanding marketing ethics. An **ethical issue** is an identifiable problem, situation or opportunity requiring an individual or organisation to choose from among several actions that must be evaluated as right or wrong, ethical or unethical. Any time an activity causes consumers to feel deceived, manipulated or cheated, a marketing ethical issue exists, regardless of the legality of that activity.

Ethical issues typically arise because of conflicts between individuals' personal moral philosophies and the marketing strategies, policies and organisational environment in which they work. Ethical issues may stem from conflicts between a marketer's attempts to achieve organisational objectives and customers' desires for safe and reliable products. For example, the Reliant Robin became highly controversial in the 1970s after consumer advocates (*That's Life* on BBC television) claimed that because

Reliant had saved money in the design of the car's steering system Reliants ran a greater risk of being involved in accidents. Similarly, organisational objectives that call for increased profits or market share may pressure marketers to steal competitors' secrets, knowingly put an unsafe product on the market or engage in some other questionable activity. For example, in South Korea, Lucky Goldstar Group markets a detergent packaged in an orange box with a whirlpool design just like Procter & Gamble's Tide brand. The product is called Tie, and Procter & Gamble does not make it or license it to Goldstar.[15] Obviously, the attempt to develop a Tide look-alike without Procter & Gamble's permission creates an ethical issue.

Regardless of the reasons behind specific ethical issues, once the issues are identified, marketers and organisations must decide how to deal with them. Thus it is essential to become familiar with many of the ethical issues that may arise in marketing so that they can be identified and resolved when they occur. Of course, it is not possible to discuss here every possible issue that could develop in the different marketing mix elements. However, this examination of a few issues can provide some direction and lead to an understanding of the ethical problems that marketers must confront.

Product Issues

In general, product related ethical issues arise when marketers fail to disclose risks associated with the product or information about its function, value or use. Competitive pressures can also create product related ethical issues. As competition intensifies and profit margins diminish, pressures can build to substitute inferior materials or product components so as to reduce costs. An ethical issue arises when marketers fail to inform customers about changes in product quality; this failure is a form of dishonesty about the nature of the product. Consider the following example. Shell launched a new petrol—the first attempt to differentiate the petrol product—Formula Shell. Despite much publicity for Formula Shell, the additives (which improved performance) were not specified. Many engines suffered from the use of the new variant; consumers were caught unawares. At great cost, the product was withdrawn. Many companies, of course, genuinely stress product features in their advertising, including aspects of product safety of concern to all consumers.

A similar ethical problem arose when the chairman of Chrysler Corporation, Lee Iacocca, learned that several Chrysler executives had driven new Chryslers with the odometers disconnected and then sold the cars as new, without disclosing that the cars had been driven. Some of the cars had been involved in accidents and repaired. In this case, however, Iacocca apologised for the company's unethical behaviour at a national press conference and developed a programme to compensate customers who had bought the pre-driven cars. Iacocca took out two page advertisements in *USA Today*, *The Wall Street Journal*, and *The New York Times* to apologise for the unethical mistake and added that "the only thing we're recalling here is our integrity". Such messages send a signal to all employees in the organisation, as well as to customers, concerning a firm's ethical standards.[16]

Promotion Issues

The communication process provides a variety of situations that can create ethical issues: for instance, false and misleading advertising and manipulative or deceptive sales promotions, tactics or publicity efforts. This section considers some ethical issues linked to advertising and personal selling. It also examines the use of bribery in personal selling situations.

Advertising. Unethical actions in advertising can destroy the trust customers have in an organisation. Sometimes adverts are questioned because they are unfair to a competitor. For example, after McDonald's introduced a chicken product in some regions of the USA, Kentucky Fried Chicken used television advertisements featuring a clown named Mr. R. McDonald being questioned by a congressional committee. In one advert, when asked what McDonald's has that Kentucky Fried Chicken does not, Mr. McDonald replies, "Toys . . . lots of toys". The CBS television network refused to broadcast the advert, saying, "We felt the commercial was unfairly denigrating to the corporate image of McDonald's". Although both the NBC and ABC networks showed the advertisements, CBS considered them ethically questionable.[17]

Abuses in advertising can range from exaggerated claims and concealed facts to outright lying. Exaggerated claims cannot be substantiated; for example, claims that a certain pain reliever or cough syrup is superior to any other on the market often cannot be verified by consumers or experts. Concealed facts are material facts deliberately omitted from a message. Perrier's packaging implies that the bubbles in its mineral water are natural and are bottled at the source. Sainsbury refused to stock this brand leader because the labelling was misleading: the bubbles are added during the bottling process and the mineral water therefore does not contain them naturally. When consumers learn that promotion messages are untrue, they may feel cheated and refuse to buy the product again; they may also complain to government or other regulatory agencies. Consequently, marketers should take care to provide all the important facts and avoid making claims that cannot be supported. Otherwise they risk alienating their customers.

Another form of advertising abuse involves ambiguous statements—statements using words so weak that the viewer, reader or listener must infer advertisers' intended messages. These "weasel" words are inherently vague and enable the advertiser to deny any intent to deceive. For example, one common "weasel" word is *help*, as in "helps prevent", "helps fight", or "helps make you feel".[18] Such advertising practices are questionable if they deceive the consumer outright. Although some marketers view such statements as acceptable, others do not. Thus vague messages remain an ethical issue in advertising.

Personal Selling.   A common problem in selling is judging what types of sales activities are acceptable. Consumers may perceive salespeople as unethical because of the common belief that sales personnel often pressure customers to purchase products they neither need nor want. Nevertheless, the sales forces of most firms, such as IBM and Procter & Gamble, are well educated, well trained and professional; and they know that they must act ethically or risk losing valuable customers and sales. Although most salespeople are ethical, some do engage in questionable actions. For example, some use very aggressive and manipulative tactics to sell almost worthless securities, gemstones, holidays, or other products over the phone. Marketing Insight 22.1 details the questionable methods employed by some time-share operators. Even though these salespeople may be fined for their activities, their unethical and often illegal actions contribute to consumers' mistrust of telephone selling and personal selling in general.

At one time or another, most salespeople face an ethical conflict in their jobs. For example, a salesperson may have to decide whether to tell a customer the truth and risk losing the customer's business, or somehow mislead the customer to appease him or her and ensure a sale. Failure to train salespeople adequately in how to deal with such situations leaves them unprepared to cope with ethical issues when they arise. Furthermore, sales personnel who are untrained and confused about what action to take when facing an ethical dilemma often experience high levels of job frustration, anxiety and stress.

Frequently, the problem of ethics has a snowball effect. Once a salesperson has deceived a customer, it becomes increasingly difficult to tell the truth later. If the customer learns of the deception, the sales representative will lose all credibility in the

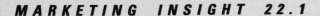

MARKETING INSIGHT 22.1

TIME-SHARE—QUESTIONABLE TACTICS

The European time-share business grew during the 1980s. Hotel apartments, villas, boats and country club accommodation are now all available: customers buy a flat or a boat for use during only a few weeks of the year. The same boat or flat is "owned" by other customers for the remainder of the year.

Various selling and promotional techniques have been used. Typically, direct mail informs people of open days near to their town and invites prospective buyers to a free champagne reception where there will be a seminar discussing a particular time-share property.

Unfortunately, this technique has been taken a step further by some unscrupulous operators. The direct mail does not overtly mention time-share or selling. Instead it implies the recipient has "definitely" won a Ford Fiesta or cash prize. The smaller print points out that collection of the prize can only be at a weekend residential time-share seminar, for example. In many cases the even smaller print states that a prize has not definitely been awarded; it is only possible to win it. Clearly, many people are taken in and do not read the small print. No illegal actions have taken place—just misleading and not completely ethical marketing tactics. The UK government has announced that it intends tightening up on time-share companies and their sales techniques.

During the early 1990s, more and more complaints against (1) "hard sell" techniques disguised as prizes or promotional offers and (2) misleading information and disappointing products were received by trading standards bodies, consumer affairs journalists and governments throughout Europe. The EC has threatened to impose strict guidelines. Those ethical and aboveboard time-share operators have drawn up a code of standards. In general the situation has improved, largely through industry self-regulation and the close attention of campaigning consumer affairs television programmes. Unfortunately, some operators persist in using misleading and underhand tactics, leaving many consumers alienated and disappointed.

SOURCES: "Borrie blasts time-share", *Marketing,* 5 July 1990; *Marketing,* 22 March 1990; Robert Dwek, "Time-share body out to foil OFT", *Marketing,* 14 June 1990, p. 13; "Curbs on holiday share gift schemes", *Coventry Evening Telegraph*", 11 December 1990, p. 14.

eyes of the customer, as well as that customer's associates and friends. Thus the manner in which a salesperson deals with an ethical issue can have far reaching consequences for both the individual and the firm.

Bribery in Selling Situations.   When payments, gifts or special favours are granted to obtain a sale or for some other reason, there is always some question of bribery. A bribe is anything given to influence improperly the outcome of a decision. Even when a bribe is offered to benefit the organisation, it is usually considered unethical, and it hurts the organisation in the long run by jeopardising trust and fairness. Table 22.1 lists

TABLE 22.1. *Which of these gifts could be considered a bribe?*

Pen and pencil set (with company logo)
Five year supply of notepads (with company logo)
Dinner at a four star French restaurant
Box of grapefruit shipped to your house each Christmas
Season tickets to sport of your choice
Weekend break
Three day, all expenses paid golfing holiday
Trip to a ski resort
Lavish trip to an exotic foreign resort
£1,000 in cash
Free PC and software

SOURCE: Adapted from E. J. Muller, "Traffigraft: is accepting a gift from a vendor a breach of ethics? To some people, it's just a perk. To others, it's poison", *Distribution*, January 1990, p. 38. © 1990 Distribution Magazine. Reprinted with permission.

some possible gifts that could be offered by a salesperson in an attempt to gain sales. Clearly, defining a bribe is often a matter of personal values and judgement. Bribery is pernicious, for it stifles fair competition among businesses and limits consumer choice.

Pricing Issues

Price fixing, predatory pricing and failure to disclose the full price associated with a purchase are typical ethical issues. The emotional and subjective nature of price creates many situations in which misunderstandings between the seller and buyer cause ethical problems. Marketers have the right to price their products so that they earn a reasonable profit, but ethical issues may crop up when a company seeks to earn high profits at the expense of its customers.

Distribution Issues

Ethical issues in distribution involve relationships among producers and marketing middlemen. Marketing middlemen, or intermediaries (wholesalers and retailers), facilitate the flow of products from the producer to the ultimate consumer. Each intermediary performs a different role and accepts certain rights, responsibilities and rewards associated with that role. For example, producers can expect retailers to honour payment agreements and keep them informed of inventory needs. Failure to make payments in a timely manner may be considered an ethical issue.

The numerous relationships between marketing intermediaries present many opportunities for conflicts and disputes, including judgements about right or wrong, ethical or unethical behaviour. Manipulating a product's availability for purposes of exploitation and using coercion to force intermediaries to behave in a specific manner are particularly serious ethical issues in the distribution sphere. For example, a powerful manufacturer can exert undue influence over an intermediary's choice of whether to handle a product or how to handle it.

Other ethical issues in distribution relate to some stores' refusal to deal with some types of middlemen. A number of conflicts are developing in the distribution of microcomputer software. Many software only stores are bypassing wholesalers and establishing direct relationships with software producers. Some dishonest stores are "hacking", or making unauthorised copies of software, preventing the producers from getting their due compensation. These occurrences have spawned suspicion and general ethical conflict in the distribution of software.[19]

Much controversy also surrounds retailers such as Tesco or Marks & Spencer, which often insist on doing business directly with a producer rather than going through an intermediary. Marks & Spencer has been accused of threatening to buy from other producers if firms refuse to sell directly to it. Similar buy direct policies are in effect at B&Q, the largest UK retailer of do-it-yourself building supplies, and at Do-It-All, the home improvement chain. These retailers, which emphasise low prices, maintain that bypassing intermediaries cuts costs and does not involve any ethical issues. However, some small companies cannot afford to maintain their own sales forces and must rely on intermediaries to sell their products to retailers. The refusal of Tesco or B&Q and others to deal with intermediaries effectively shuts these smaller companies out of the market because they cannot compete with companies that have their own sales forces.

IMPROVING ETHICAL DECISIONS IN MARKETING

Conflicts between personal moral philosophies and corporate values, organisational pressures and opportunity interact to create situations that may cause unethical behaviour. It is possible to improve ethical behaviour in an organisation by eliminating unethical personnel and improving the organisation's ethical standards.

One way to approach improvement of an organisation's ethical standards is by considering a "bad apple—bad barrel" analogy. Some people always act in their own self-interest regardless of organisational goals or accepted moral standards; they are sometimes called "bad apples". To eliminate unethical behaviour, an organisation must rid itself of these bad apples, or unethical people. It can attain this goal through screening techniques and through enforcement of ethics codes.[20] However, organisations also sometimes become "bad barrels"—not because the individuals within them are bad, but because the pressures to survive and succeed create conditions that reward unethical behaviour. A way of resolving the problem of the bad barrel is to redesign the organisation's image and culture so that it conforms to industry and societal norms of ethical behaviour.[21]

By making marketers aware of ethical issues and potential areas of conflict, it is possible to eliminate or defuse some of the ethical pressures that occur in daily marketing activities. Awareness of and sensitivity towards ethical issues can eliminate the risk of making unethical decisions. Ethical values must be built into the organisational culture and marketing strategy by establishing codes of ethics and by controlling unethical behaviour when it occurs.[22]

Codes of Ethics

It is difficult for employees to determine what is acceptable behaviour within an organisation if the organisation does not have uniform policies and standards. Without standards of behaviour, employees will generally make decisions based on their observations of how their peers and managers behave. **Codes of ethics** are formalised rules and standards that describe what the company expects of its employees. Codes of ethics encourage ethical behaviour by minimising opportunities for unethical behaviour: the company's employees know both what is expected of them and what the punishment is for violating the rules. Codes of ethics also help marketers deal with ethical issues or dilemmas that develop in daily operations by prescribing or limiting certain activities. The codes of ethics do not have to be so detailed that they take into account every situation, but they should provide general guidelines for achieving organisational goals and objectives in a morally acceptable manner. Top management should also provide leadership and guidelines in implementing the codes.

Table 22.2 presents the American Marketing Association's Code of Ethics. The code does not cover every ethical issue, but it is a useful overview of what marketers believe

TABLE 22.2 *The American Marketing Association's Code of Ethics***

Members of the American Marketing Association (AMA) are committed to ethical professional conduct. They have joined together in subscribing to this Code of Ethics embracing the following topics:

Responsibilities of the Marketer

Marketers must accept responsibility for the consequences of their activities and make every effort to ensure that their decisions, recommendations and actions function to identify, serve and satisfy all relevant publics: consumers, organisations and society. Marketers' professional conduct must be guided by:

1. The basic rule of professional ethics: not knowingly to do harm;
2. The adherence to all applicable laws and regulations;
3. The accurate representation of their education, training and experience; and
4. The active support, practice and promotion of this Code of Ethics.

Honesty and Fairness

Marketers shall uphold and advance the integrity, honour and dignity of the marketing profession by:

1. Being honest in serving consumers, clients, employees, suppliers, distributors and the public;
2. Not knowingly participating in conflict of interest without prior notice to all parties involved; and

3. Establishing equitable fee schedules including the payment or receipt of usual, customary and/or legal compensation for marketing exchanges.

Rights and Duties of Parties

Participants in the marketing exchange process should be able to expect that:

1. Products and services offered are safe and fit for their intended uses:
2. Communications about offered products and services are not deceptive;
3. All parties intend to discharge their obligations, financial and otherwise, in good faith; and
4. Appropriate internal methods exist for equitable adjustment and/or redress of grievances concerning purchases.

It is understood that the above would include, *but is not limited to*, the following responsibilities of the marketer:

In the area of product development management:

Disclosure of all substantial risks associated with product or service usage

Identification of any product component substitution that might materially change the product or impact on the buyer's purchase decision

Identification of extra cost added features

* A similar code has yet to be produced in the EC.

---

are sound moral principles for guiding marketing activities. This code could be used to help structure an organisation's code of ethics.

Controlling Unethical Behaviour

Ethical behaviour in marketing must be based on a strong moral foundation, including personal moral development and an organisational structure that encourages and rewards desired ethical action. The pressures of competition must be understood and coped with to improve ethical behaviour. The idea that marketing ethics is learned at home, at school and in family relationships does not recognise the impact of opportunity and the organisation on ethical decision-makers.

If a company is to maintain ethical behaviour, its policies, rules and standards must be worked into its control system. If the number of employees making ethical decisions on a regular basis is not satisfactory, then the company needs to determine why and take corrective action through enforcement. Enforcement of standards is what makes codes of ethics effective. If codes are mere window dressing and do not relate to what is expected or what is rewarded in the corporate culture, then they serve no purpose except to give an illusion of concern about ethical behaviour.

In the area of promotions:

Avoidance of false and misleading advertising

Rejection of high pressure manipulations, or misleading sales tactics

Avoidance of sales promotions that use deception or manipulation

In the area of distribution:

Not manipulating the availability of a product for purpose of exploitation

Not using coercion in the marketing channel

Not exerting undue influence over the resellers' choice to handle a product

In the area of pricing:

Not engaging in price fixing

Not practicing predatory pricing

Disclosing the full price associated with any purchase

In the area of marketing research:

Prohibiting selling or fund raising under the guise of conducting research

Maintaining research integrity by avoiding misrepresentation and omission of pertinent research data

Treating outside clients and suppliers fairly

Organisational Relationships

Marketers should be aware of how their behaviour may influence or impact on the behaviour of others in organisational relationships. They should not encourage or apply coercion to obtain unethical behavior in their relationships with others, such as employees, suppliers or customers.

1. Apply confidentiality and anonymity in professional relationships with regard to privileged information.

2. Meet their obligations and responsibilities in contracts and mutual agreements in a timely manner.

3. Avoid taking the work of others, in whole, or in part, and represent this work as their own or directly benefit from it without compensation or consent of the originator or owner.

4. Avoid manipulation to take advantage of situations to maximise personal welfare in a way that unfairly deprives or damages the organisation or others.

Any AMA members found to be in violation of any provision of this Code of Ethics may have his or her Association membership suspended or revoked.

SOURCE: Reprinted by permission of the American Marketing Association.

THE NATURE OF SOCIAL RESPONSIBILITY

The concepts of ethics and social responsibility are often used interchangeably, although each has a distinct meaning. **Social responsibility** in marketing refers to an organisation's obligation to maximise its positive impact and minimise its negative impact on society. Whereas ethics relate to individual decisions, social responsibility concerns the impact of an organisation's decisions on society.

For example, years ago the US brewer Anheuser-Busch test marketed a new adult beverage called Chelsea. Because it contained less than one half per cent alcohol, Chelsea was not subject to alcohol retail controls and was thus available in many shops that sell sweets and drinks to children. Consumer groups labelled the beverage "kiddie beer" and protested that the company was being socially irresponsible by making an alcoholic drink available to minors. Anheuser-Busch's first reaction was defensive; it tried to claim that the beverage was not dangerous and would not lead children to stronger drink. However, the company later decided to withdraw the beverage from the market-place and reformulate it so that it would be viewed as more acceptable by society.[23] Social responsibility, then, can be viewed as a contract with society, whereas ethics relate to carefully thought out rules of moral values that guide individual and group decision-making.

Marketing managers try to determine what accepted relationships, obligations and duties exist between the marketing organisation and society. Recognition is growing that for a firm's survival and competitive advantage, the long term value of conducting business in a socially responsible manner far outweighs short term costs.[24] To preserve socially responsible behaviour while achieving organisational goals, organisations must monitor changes and trends in society's values. For example, food companies around the world are developing and marketing healthier products in response to increasing public concern about cancer and heart disease. Furthermore, marketers must develop control procedures to ensure that daily decisions do not damage their company's relations with the public. An organisation's top management must assume some responsibility for its employees' conduct by establishing and enforcing policies.

Being socially responsible may be a noble and necessary endeavour, but it is not a simple one. To be socially responsible, marketers must confront certain major issues. Robertson's had, for four decades, used its black Golliwog brand mark on its market leading jams. Racial tension and increasingly vocal ethnic groups persuaded the company to minimise this potentially offensive symbol. Marketers therefore must determine what society wants and then predict the long term effects of their decisions, often by turning to experts such as lawyers, doctors and scientists. However, experts do not necessarily agree with one another, and the fields in which they work can yield findings that undermine previously acceptable marketing decisions.

Forty years ago, for example, tobacco marketers promoted cigarettes as being good for one's health. Now, years after the discovery that cigarette smoking is linked to cancer and other medical problems, society's attitude towards smoking is changing, and marketers are confronted with new social responsibilities, such as providing a smoke free atmosphere for customers. Most major hotel chains reserve at least some of their rooms for non-smokers, and most other businesses within the food, travel and entertainment industries provide smoke free environment or sections.

Because society is made up of many diverse groups, finding out what society as a whole wants is difficult, if not impossible. In trying to satisfy the desires of one group, marketers may dissatisfy others. For example, in the smoking debate, marketers must balance the desire of smokers to continue to smoke cigarettes against the desire of non-smokers for a smoke free environment.

Moreover, there are costs associated with many of society's demands. For example, society wants a cleaner environment and the preservation of wildlife and habitats, but it also wants low priced petrol and heating oil. Figure 22.2 illustrates how Esso acknowledges the need to care for the environment. Thus, companies that market petrol and oil must carefully balance the costs of providing low priced products against the costs of manufacturing and packaging their products in an environmentally responsible manner. Such a balance is difficult to achieve to the satisfaction of all members of society. Marketers must also evaluate the extent to which members of society are willing to pay for what they want. For instance, consumers may want more information about a product yet be unwilling to pay the costs the firm incurs in providing the data. Thus marketers who want to make socially responsible decisions may find the task difficult.

**Social Responsibility
Issues**

Although social responsibility may seem to be an abstract ideal, managers make decisions related to social responsibility on a daily basis. To be successful, a business must determine what customers, government inspectors, competitors and society in general want or expect in terms of social responsibility. The success of international retailer Body Shop has been attributed to the company's awareness of the green movement

FIGURE 22.2
Caring for the environment
Esso promotes its support of UK 2000 by its efforts to help make the environment cleaner and safer.

SOURCE: Reproduced with kind permission of Esso Petroleum UK Ltd.

and demonstration of social responsibility (see Marketing Insight 22.2). Table 22.3 summarises several major categories of social responsibility issues, which include the consumer movement, community relations, and "green" marketing.

Consumer Issues.   One of the most significant social responsibility issues in marketing is the consumer movement, which Chapter 2 defines as the efforts of independent individuals, groups and organisations to protect the rights of consumers. A number of interest groups and individuals have taken actions such as lobbying government officials and agencies, letter writing campaigns, placing advertisements and boycotting companies they consider are irresponsible.

David Tench, one of the best known consumer activists in the UK, continues to crusade for consumer rights. Consumer activism on the part of Tench and others has resulted in legislation requiring various safety features in cars: seat belts, padded dashboards, stronger door catches, headrests, shatterproof windscreens and collapsible steering columns. Activists' efforts have furthered the passage of several consumer protection laws, such as the Trade Descriptions Act 1968, the Consumer Protection Act 1987, the Fair Trading Act 1973, the Food Act 1984 and the Weights and Measures Act 1985.

THE BODY SHOP PRACTICES
GLOBAL SOCIAL RESPONSIBILITY

In 1976, Anita Roddick, then a 33 year old housewife, opened a store in Brighton to sell natural body lotions. Since then, sales and profits of The Body Shop's retail chain have grown an average of 50 per cent a year. By 1992, the company had 730 Body Shop stores (94 per cent franchised) in 41 countries, with pre-tax profits of £28 million on sales of £147.5 million. A new shop opens every two to three days. There are now over 520 outside the UK. Annual return to investors has averaged 97 per cent over the past five years. Much of The Body Shop's success can be attributed to a combination of smart retailing practices and a strong sense of social responsibility.

The Body Shop stores sell wholly natural cosmetics made from high-quality, biodegradable ingredients packaged in recyclable containers. Its products are not developed in laboratories or tested on animals like those of many other cosmetic companies. Each store is designed to be self-service, and the sales staff, while very knowledgeable about Body Shop products, provide information and do not force sales. To educate consumers about how its products are made and where their ingredients come from, the company uses bright graphics, videos and a sense of style and humour.

Anita Roddick has tried to bring a global focus and unusual values to The Body Shop. She believes that companies must be concerned with more than profits, that they must be accountable for their actions and how they affect the environment, just as people are responsible for themselves and their neighbours. This is further emphasised by The Body Shop's support of such causes as saving endangered whales and vanishing rain forests. All of these issues surround customers in the form of banners, pamphlets, T-shirts and posters emphasising the importance of social issues.

The Body Shop's unusual philosophy has helped create a passion in its employees and customers. The company maintains a school in London to teach employees about its products and the value of being socially conscious. Additionally, employees are required to put in one hour of paid company time each week towards a community project. By instigating a philosophy of social responsibility, Roddick believes that her employees will be motivated by feeling good about what they are doing.

SOURCES: Rahul Jacob,"Body Shop International: what selling will be like in the '90's", *Fortune*, 13 January 1992, pp. 63–4; Bo Burlingham, "This woman has changed business forever", Inc., June 1990, pp. 34–48; The Body Shop 1990 annual report; 1989 annual report; Bernice Huxtable, "Body care firm joins rainforest campaign, *Calgary Herald*, 11 July 1989, p. E5; and Dan Parle,"Back to nature", *Business journal*, January-February 1989, pp. 24–9; Annual report, 1992.

TABLE 22.3 *Social responsibility issues*

ISSUE	DESCRIPTION	MAJOR SOCIETAL CONCERNS
Consumer Movement	Activities undertaken by independent individuals, groups and organisations to protect their rights as consumers	The right to safety The right to be informed The right to choose The right to be heard
Community Relations	Society anxious to have marketers contribute to its wellbeing, wishing to know what businesses do to help solve social problems Communities demanding that firms listen to their grievances and ideas	Equality issues Disadvantaged members of society Safety and health Education and general welfare
Green Products and Production	Consumers insisting not only on the quality of life but also on a healthy environment so that they can maintain a high standard of living during their lifetimes	Conservation Water pollution Air pollution Land pollution

Community Relations. Social responsibility also extends to marketers' roles as community members. Individual communities expect marketers to contribute to the satisfaction and growth of their communities. Thus many marketers view social responsibility as including contributions of resources (money, products, time) to community causes such as education, the arts, recreation, disadvantaged members of the community and others. McDonald's, Tesco, Shell, Ogilvy & Mather and Hewlett Packard all have programmes that contribute funds, equipment and personnel to educational reform. Similarly, IBM donates or reduces the price of computer equipment to educational institutions. All these efforts, of course, have a positive impact on local communities, but they also indirectly help the organisations in the form of goodwill, publicity and exposure to potential future customers. Thus, although social responsibility is certainly a positive concept, most organisations do not embrace it without the expectation of some indirect long term benefit.

Green Marketing. **Green marketing** refers to the specific development, pricing, promotion and distribution of products that do not harm the environment. An independent coalition of environmentalists, scientists and marketers is one group involved in evaluating products to determine their environmental impact and marketers' commitment to the environment and producing *The Green Guide*. In Germany, several environmental groups have joined together to create a seal of approval, the Blue Angel, to distinguish products that are environmentally safe. Companies receiving this seal will be able to use it in advertising and public information campaigns and on packaging.

As discussed in Chapter 2, perhaps one of the most fundamental changes in the 1990s facing marketers and consumers alike is the tremendous growth of the green movement. Increased environmental awareness has led to changes in production methods—from product design, materials and packaging to promotion and selling messages, and even product disposal. Figure 22.3 illustrates a Dutch campaign for ecologically safe paints, recruiting support from consumers and industry.

Strategies for Dealing With Social Responsibility Issues

There are four basic strategies for systematically dealing with social responsibility issues: reaction, defence, accommodation and proaction.

Reaction Strategy. A business adopting a **reaction strategy** allows a condition or potential problem to go unresolved until the public learns about it. The situation may be known to management (as were one car maker's problems with fuel tank combustibility) or it may be unknown (as was the sudden acceleration of the Audi without direct action from the driver). In either case, the business denies responsibility but tries to resolve the problem, deal with its consequences and continue doing business as usual to minimise the negative impact.

Defence Strategy. A business using a **defence strategy** tries to minimise or avoid additional obligations linked to a problem or problems. Commonly used defence tactics include legal manoeuvring and seeking the support of trade unions that embrace

FIGURE 22.3
Social responsibility
In the Netherlands, the campaign for ecologically safe paints is recruiting support from consumers and from industry.

SOURCE: Company: Sigma Coatings; Brand: Histor; Agency: KKBR, Amsterdam; Art: Rob Sluijs; Copy: Ton Drupper.

the company's way of doing business and support the industry. Businesses often lobby to avoid government action or regulation. For example, the direct mail industry lobbied against an increase in bulk postal rate because it knew it would have to pass on these increases to its clients, advertisers and advertising agencies. Sizeable increases in postal rates could put it at a competitive disadvantage in relation to print media, such as newspaper inserts, which are not carried by mail. Thus the industry took a defensive position to protect its own and its clients' interests.

Accommodation Strategy. A business using an **accommodation strategy** assumes responsibility for its actions. A business might adopt the accommodation strategy when special interest groups are encouraging a particular action or when the business perceives that if it fails to react the government will pass a law to ensure compliance. Figure 22.4 illustrates how Persil's evolution aims to address an ecological problem.

For example, McDonald's developed a nutrition orientated advertising campaign to appease dietitians and nutritionists who had urged that accurate nutritional information should be provided on all fast food products. However, McDonald's campaign, instead of soothing the interest groups, antagonised them. The groups claimed that McDonald's portrayal of its food as healthy was inaccurate. A McDLT, chips and milkshake contain 1,283 calories, approximately 60 per cent of the entire recommended daily calorie intake for an adult woman. In addition, that meal contains 15 teaspoons of fat, 10 teaspoons of sugar, no fibre, and approximately 70 per cent of the daily al-

FIGURE 22.4
Developing products that solve ecological problems Persil is adopting an accommodation strategy.

SOURCE: Reproduced by permission of Lever Brothers (UK) Ltd.

lowance of sodium. In the USA, dietitians and nutritionists petitioned the Food and Drug Administration in the hope that it would require nutritional labelling on products to alert consumers to high levels of fat, sodium, and sugar and low levels of starch and fibre.[25] McDonald's chose to take an accommodation strategy to curtail lobbying against nutritional information disclosure when it probably should have adopted a proactive strategy.

Proactive Strategy. A business that uses a **proactive strategy** assumes responsibility for its actions and responds to accusations made against it without outside pressure or the threat of government intervention. A proactive strategy requires management, of its own free will, to support an action or cause. For example, Toyota decided to recall its popular 1990 model Lexus car to repair several defects. Although none of the defects had caused any accidents or injuries, Toyota has a reputation for quality and excellence, which it promotes heavily in advertising. Consequently, its executives probably concluded that the most responsible action to take was to deal with the defects before any injuries or deaths occurred.[26] Even if the recall should temporarily harm the Lexus image, Toyota's prompt and responsible action will probably draw a positive response from consumers in the long run.

SOCIAL RESPONSIBILITY AND MARKETING ETHICS

Although the concepts of marketing ethics and social responsibility are often used interchangeably, it is important to remember that ethics relate to individual moral evaluations—judgements about what is right or wrong in a particular decision-making situation. Social responsibility is the obligation of an organisation to maximise its positive impact and minimise its negative impact on society. Thus social responsibility deals with the total effect of marketing decisions on society. These two concepts work together; a company that supports both socially acceptable moral philosophies and individuals who act ethically is likely to make decisions that have a positive impact on society.

One way to evaluate whether a specific behaviour is ethical and socially responsible is to ask other people in an organisation if they approve of it. For social responsibility issues, contact with concerned consumer groups and industry or government regulatory groups may be helpful. Checking to see if there is a specific company policy about the activity may also resolve the issue. If other people in the organisation approve of the activity and it is legal and customary within the industry, the chances are that the activity is acceptable from both an ethical and social responsibility perspective.

A rule of thumb for ethical and social responsibility issues is that if they can withstand open discussion and result in agreements or limited debate, an acceptable solution may exist. Still, even after a final decision is reached, different viewpoints on the issue may remain. Openness is not the complete solution to the ethics problem; but it does create trust and facilitate learning relationships.[27]

SUMMARY

Marketing ethics are moral principles that define right and wrong behaviour in marketing. Most marketing decisions can be judged as ethical or unethical. Ethics are a very important concern in marketing decisions, yet they may be one of the most misunderstood and controversial concepts in marketing.

Personal moral philosophies, organisational factors and opportunity are three important components of ethical decision-making. Moral philosophies are principles or rules that individuals use to determine the right way to behave. They provide guidelines for resolving conflicts and ensuring mutual benefit for all members of society. Utilitarian moral philosophies are concerned with maximising the greatest good for the greatest number of people. Ethical formalism philosophies, on the other hand, focus on general rules for guiding behaviour and on the rights of the individual. Organisational relationships with employees or superiors create ethical problems such as maintaining confidentiality in personal relations; meeting obligations, responsibilities and mutual agreements; and avoiding undue pressure that may force others to behave unethically. Opportunity—a favourable set of conditions that limit barriers or provide internal or external rewards—to engage in unethical behaviour provides another pressure that may determine whether a person behaves ethically. If an individual uses an opportunity afforded him or her to act unethically and escapes punishment or even gains a reward, that person is more likely to repeat such acts when circumstances favour them.

An ethical issue is an identifiable problem, situation or opportunity requiring an individual or organisation to choose from between alternatives that must be evaluated as right or wrong. Ethical issues typically arise because of conflicts between individuals' personal moral philosophies and the marketing strategies, policies and organisational environment in which they work. Product-related ethical issues may develop when marketers fail to disclose risks associated with the product or information that relates to understanding the function, value or use of the product. Competitive pressures can also create product related ethical issues. The promotion process provides situations that can result in ethical issues, such as false and misleading advertising and deceptive sales tactics. Sales promotions and publicity that use deception or manipulation also create significant ethical issues. Bribery may be an ethical issue in some selling situations. The emotional and subjective nature of price creates conditions in which misunderstandings between the seller and buyer lead to ethical problems. Ethical issues in distribution relate to relationships and conflicts among producers and marketing middlemen.

Codes of ethics, which formalise what an organisation expects of its employees, minimise the opportunity for unethical behaviour because they provide rules to guide conduct and punishments for violating the rules. If the number of employees making ethical decisions on a regular basis is not satisfactory, the company needs to determine why and take corrective action through enforcement. Enforcement of standards is what makes codes of ethics effective.

Social responsibility in marketing refers to an organisation's obligation to maximise its positive impact and minimise its negative impact on society. Marketing managers try to determine what accepted relationship, obligations and duties exist between the business organisation and society.

To be successful, a business must determine what customers, government officials, competitors, and society in general want or expect in terms of social responsibility. Major categories of social responsibility issues include the consumer movement, community relations and green marketing. The consumer movement refers to the activities of independent individuals, groups and organisations in trying to protect the rights of consumers. Communities expect marketers to contribute to the satisfaction and growth of their communities. Green marketing refers to the specific development, pricing, promotion and distribution of products that do not harm the environment. The green movement is leading to tremendous changes in the 1990s for consumers, manufacturers and workers alike.

Four basic strategies for dealing with social responsibility issues are reaction, defence, accommodation and proaction. A business adopting a reaction strategy allows a condition or potential problem to go unresolved until the public learns about it. A business using the defence strategy tries to minimise or avoid additional obligations associated with a problem or problems. By using the accommodation strategy, a business assumes responsibility for its actions. A business that uses the proactive strategy assumes responsibility for its actions and responds to accusations made against it without outside pressure or the threat of government intervention.

The concepts of marketing ethics and social responsibility work together because a company that has a corporate culture built on socially acceptable moral philosophies will generally make decisions that have a positive impact on society. If other persons in the company approve of an activity and it is legal and customary within the industry, chances are the activity is ethical and socially responsible.

IMPORTANT TERMS

Marketing ethics	Social responsibility
Moral philosophies	Green marketing
Utilitarianism	Reaction strategy
Ethical formalism	Defence strategy
Ethical issue	Accommodation strategy
Codes of ethics	Proactive strategy

DISCUSSION AND REVIEW QUESTIONS

1. Why are ethics an important consideration in marketing decisions?
2. How do the factors that influence ethical or unethical decisions interact?
3. Is the view of marketing as warfare, based on seeing competitors as the enemy, a matter for ethical concern?
4. What are some of the areas that result in major ethical issues in marketing?
5. How can ethical decisions in marketing be improved?
6. How can people with different personal values join together to make ethical decisions in an organisation?
7. What is the difference between ethics and social responsibility?
8. What are major social responsibility issues?
9. Describe strategies for dealing with social responsibility issues.
10. How do you determine when a gift or payment is a bribe in marketing?

■ CASES

22.1 BMG/Arista Makes Good for Milli Vanilli Lip-Synch Hijinx

The recording industry was stunned by the disclosure that singers Rob Pilatus and Fabrice Morvan of the group Milli Vanilli did not perform the vocals for their Arista Records albums and lip-synched those recordings during their concert appearances. The group had produced only two albums—*Girl You Know It's True* and *The Remix Album*—and one video cassette recording when the announcement was made. The actions of the singers and Arista Records not only sent shock waves through the industry but angered many fans and album purchasers as well.

On 27 November 1990, a US state court judge in the Circuit Court of Cook County, Illinois, determined that the main lawsuit filed at the time—*Siegel* v. *Pilatus et al.*—could proceed as a class action suit on behalf of all recording/merchandise purchasers in the United States. In the class action suit against Milli Vanilli, Arista and the Bertelsmann Music Group (BMG), the plaintiffs claimed fraud, misrepresentation, negligence, breach of contract and breach of warranty and sought monetary relief in the form of the return of amounts paid for Milli Vanilli's recordings, merchandise and concert tickets. The plaintiffs also sought statutory and punitive damages as well as legal fees. In addition to the main class action suit, 22 other cases were also filed against the group and BMG/Arista, alleging violations of the federal Racketeer Influenced and Corrupt Organizations Act (RICO). Later that year, US federal judges in Pennsylvania and California denied motions that would have allowed these 22 cases and others to become class action suits as well.

On September 5, 1991, Judge Thomas J. O'Brien of the Circuit Court of Cook County, Illinois, preliminarily approved a proposed settlement agreed to by the plaintiffs in the *Siegel* case and BMG/Arista. Those included in the settlement were divided into three classes: recording, concert and merchandise. Members of each class were allowed to obtain certain rebates provided that they met certain eligibility conditions. Those who had purchased a Milli Vanilli recording prior to 27 November 1990 were allowed to obtain a rebate of $1.00 for a single (cassette or record), $2.00 for an album (cassette or record), and $3.00 for a compact disc purchase. Class members who had purchased Milli Vanilli concert tickets prior to 27 November 1990 were allowed to obtain a rebate of 5 per cent of the face value of a concert ticket. In the merchandise class, qualifying members were allowed to have their names included as partial donors of $250,000 to one of three charities: the T. J. Martell Foundation for leukaemia research, the American Foundation for AIDS Research, and the Rainforest Action Network and Cultural Survival. The maximum donation per class member was set at $5.00. Members of the recordings and concert classes were also allowed to donate their rebates to one of the three charities. In each case, class members were allowed to keep their recordings and merchandise. To be eligible for the rebates, class members had to send in proofs of purchase, such as liner notes from compact discs and cassettes and barcodes from records. Purchasers who did not want to accept these decisions were allowed to be excluded from the settlement.

SOURCE: *Notice of Pendency of Class Action*, US Circuit Court of Cook County, Illinois.

Questions for Discussion

1. How would you or one of your friends feel if you purchased a recording and found out that the artists were not the real performers?
2. How might the settlement and its accompanying publicity affect Arista's marketing strategy?
3. What are the implications of this case for other industries and businesses?

22.2   McDonald's Social Responsibility

The McDonald's Corporation is the largest food service organisation in the world. McDonald's competes on the basis of price and value by offering quality food products with speed and convenience in reliable, clean restaurants. Its brand is one of the most advertised in the world, and the company spends millions of pounds a year on marketing.

Customer satisfaction is the cornerstone of the McDonald's marketing strategy. The company wants to make every customer contact an enjoyable experience by serving quality food at affordable prices and providing fast, accurate, friendly service. Most people reading this case have had the McDonald's experience many times.

The philosophy of Ray Kroc, McDonald's founder, was that McDonald's and its franchises should put something back into the communities in which they do business. In addition, McDonald's believes that being a good corporate citizen means treating people with fairness and integrity and sharing success in the communities where the company operates. This philosophy is implemented in many different ways throughout the McDonald's corporation.

Quality education is a priority for most countries, and McDonald's is committed to making a contribution, whether it's in the USA, the UK, France, Switzerland or South-East Asia. Many young people who work in McDonald's stores are taught the importance of responsibility, self-discipline and good work habits. McDonald's works with parents, educators and students and believes in supporting education through various programmes that encourage and recognise scholastic achievement. The company allows school fund raising and charitable activities such as car washing days on its sites; it sponsors computer equipment; and it encourages school children to continue into higher education.

McDonald's is concerned about affirmative action and equal opportunity. The company attempts to attract minorities, women, disabled and older people and develop their potential without regard to race, sex, religion, ethnicity, educational or cultural background. McJobs is an employment programme established to assist mentally and physically challenged individuals to develop their skills and confidence to succeed. The McMasters programme attempts to recruit, train and retain some of McDonald's most valued employees—people aged 55 and over.

As a responsible corporate citizen, McDonald's is committed to protecting the environment. The company has many ongoing efforts to manage solid waste, conserve and protect natural resources, and promote sound environmental practices. Although many studies indicated that foam packaging is environmentally sound, McDonald's phased out this packaging in 1990 because of customer feedback. There are programmes within the McDonald's organisation to reduce the weight and volume of packaging, to recycle, to implement reusable materials whenever feasible and to purchase a minimum of £65 million worth a year of recycled materials for use in the construction, equipping and operations of restaurants. In addition, McDonald's refuses to purchase beef from companies that destroy tropical rain forests to create cattle grazing lands. This policy is strictly enforced and closely monitored.

Part of the philosophy of giving something back to the communities is dedicated to helping children achieve their fullest potential. Since its founding in 1984 in memory of Ray Kroc, Ronald McDonald Children's Charities (RMCC) has funded nearly 1,000 grants totalling £25 million to help support programmes in the areas of health care and medical research, specially designed rehabilitation facilities and special youth education programmes.

The Ronald McDonald House programme is the cornerstone of RMCC, providing a "home away from home" for families of seriously ill children being treated at nearby hospitals. The first Ronald McDonald House was developed 17 years ago in Philadelphia, Pennsylvania, when the NFL's Philadelphia Eagles, a children's hospital and owner/operators of McDonald's restaurants decided to establish a place where parents of sick children could be with others who understood their situation and could provide emotional support.

In 1991, the 150th Ronald McDonald House was opened. Houses are now appearing outside America: London's first has won praise from all quarters. In total, more than 2,500 bedrooms serve some 4,000 family members each night. Each house is located close to a major medical facility.

Each Ronald McDonald House is run by a local non-profit organisation composed of members of the medical community, McDonald's owner/operators, businesses and civic organisations, and parent volunteers. More than 12,000 volunteers provide the backbone of the programme, helping with all aspects of House operations, including fund raising, renovation, programme development and services to families. Families staying at Ronald McDonald Houses are asked to make a small donation per day. If that is not possible, their stay is free.

McDonald's attempts to contribute to all aspects of community life by supporting education, pursuing equal opportunity and affirmative action in employment practices, operating Ronald McDonald Children's Charities and promoting sound environmental practices. All of these activities combined demonstrate a commitment to putting something back into the communities that spend so much of their disposable income at McDonald's restaurants. Few companies can compete with the high level of commitment McDonald's has made to communities.

SOURCES: McDonald's 1990 annual report; *Ronald McDonald House Fact Sheet*, Ronald McDonald Children's Charities, Kroc Drive, Oakbrook, Ill.; *Ronald McDonald House Backgrounder*, Ronald McDonald Children's Charities, Kroc Drive, Oakbrook, Ill.; *Ronald McDonald House World*, a newsletter published for the Ronald McDonald House family, Winter 1991; and "Ronald McDonald's Children's Charities" videocassette; McDonald's in-store leaflets; McDonald's, London.

Questions for Discussion

1. Why, in your opinion, has McDonald's selected Ronald McDonald Children's Charities as one of its most visible attempts to implement social responsibility?
2. Why are environmental, educational and equal opportunity/affirmative action issues so important to the long term success of McDonald's?
3. Currently 65 per cent of all future owner/operators in training are minorities and women. What impact will this have on McDonald's operations in the future?

VII SELECTED APPLICATIONS

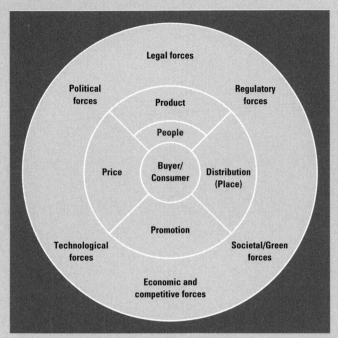

The remaining chapters in this book discuss and highlight strategic applications in organisational, business-to-business, services and international marketing. The emphasis is on the features and issues that are unique to each of these selected areas of marketing but the chapters also focus on aspects that influence formulating and implementing marketing strategies. Chapter 23 analyses the development of business-to-business, industrial marketing strategy and discusses the decisions and activities that characterise industrial or organisational marketing. Chapter 24 explores selected aspects of services and non- business marketing strategies. Chapter 25 focuses on international marketing and on the development and implementation of marketing strategies for markets across national boundaries. ■

23 BUSINESS-TO-BUSINESS MARKETING

Objectives

To understand some unique characteristics of business-to-business marketing

To learn how to select and analyse business-to-business target markets

To find out how business-to-business marketing mix components differ from the components in consumer product marketing mixes

To realise the importance of determining a differential advantage

Volvo Trucks is a wholly owned subsidiary of Volvo. In the UK it is the division which handles the importing, manufacturing, sales and marketing, and after sales support for all Volvo heavy goods vehicles. Currently, Volvo has an approximately 18 per cent market share of UK trucks over 15 tonnes.

Sales of all makes of trucks heavier than 3.5 tonnes were the highest of the decade in 1989, at 69,234. However, in the summer and autumn of 1990, sales fell by nearly 40 per cent. As the UK economic recession worsened, most hauliers cancelled or delayed orders for replacement vehicles. The UK situation was repeated throughout Europe. As a result, many suppliers, who had scheduled high levels of production based on 1989 sales, found themselves seriously overstocked.

For most of the major players in the European truck market, two major trends are dictating current marketing strategies. The decline in new vehicle sales is leading to an increased focus on the after market. The market for replacement parts is more stable and offers some degree of cushioning against the more extreme fluctuations in demand for new vehicles. Similarly, tyres, fuels and lubricants continue to sell steadily even when there is a downturn in truck sales. Most truck manufacturers are devoting more of their marketing effort to servicing, maintenance and provision of parts.

The second trend has been a move by hauliers and large companies with their own transport fleets away from purchasing new vehicles outright. There has been a switch to leasing and contract hire, whereby the truck manufacturer ultimately retains ownership of the vehicle and has to off load the vehicles when they are returned by the haulier. This development has forced marketers to learn a variety of new financial skills. They have to set leasing and contract hire rates sufficiently high to make an operating profit, bearing in mind the increased competition in the market. They must also be prepared to take back and resell large numbers of used vehicles. For the business-to-business marketer working in the truck business, the task is no longer simply one of marketing and selling new vehicles—the provision of after sales services and parts and the negotiating of complex leasing and contract hire agreements are becoming increasingly important. ■

SOURCES: "Heavy going", Automotive Management, 13 September 1990; John Griffiths, "Truck sales suffer fall in September of nearly 40%", *Financial Times*, 17 October 1990; Richard Longworth, "Glitter shadows and lights at the ends of tunnels", *Transport Week*, 22 September 1990, pp. 40–1.

Some of the problems that business-to-business marketers like those in Volvo Trucks experience resemble those of consumer product marketers, and business-to-business marketers, too, rely on basic marketing concepts and decisions. However, they apply those concepts and decisions in different ways, which take into account the nature of business-to-business markets and products.

Business-to-business marketing, also called business marketing or industrial marketing, is a set of activities directed towards facilitating and expediting exchanges involving industrial products and customers in business-to-business markets. As mentioned in Chapter 5, an industrial product differs from a consumer product in that it is purchased to be used directly or indirectly to produce other products or to be used in the operations of an organisation. Chapter 5 also classifies industrial products into seven categories: raw materials, major equipment, accessory equipment, component parts, process materials, consumable supplies and industrial services. As explained there, an organisational or business-to-business market consists of individuals or groups who purchase a specific kind of product for one of three purposes: resale, direct use in producing other products or use in general daily operations. Business-to-business markets consist of numerous types of customers, including commercial producers, resellers, governments and institutions.

Aside from product and market differences, business marketing is unique for these reasons: (1) the buyer's decision-making process, (2) characteristics of the product market and (3) the nature of environmental influences.[1] These differences influence the development and implementation of business-to-business marketing strategies.

This chapter focuses on dimensions unique to developing marketing strategies for industrial products. First, it examines the selection and analysis of business-to-business target markets. Then it discusses the distinctive features of business marketing mixes.

SELECTION AND ANALYSIS OF BUSINESS-TO-BUSINESS TARGET MARKETS

Marketing research is becoming more important in industrial marketing, especially in selecting and analysing target markets. Most of the marketing research techniques discussed in Chapter 6 can be applied to business-to-business marketing. This section focuses on important and unique approaches to selecting and analysing business-to-business target markets.

Business marketers have easy access to a considerable amount of information about potential customers, for much of this information appears in government and industry publications. However, comparable data about ultimate consumers are not available. Even though marketers may use different procedures to isolate and analyse target markets, most follow a similar pattern: (1) determining who potential customers are and how many there are, (2) locating where they are and (3) estimating their purchase potential.[2]

Determining Who Potential Customers Are and How Many There Are

Much information about industrial customers is based on the **Standard Industrial Classification (SIC) system,** which was developed to classify selected economic characteristics of industrial, commercial, financial and service organisations. In the UK this system is administered by the Central Statistical Office. Table 23.1 shows how the SIC system can be used to categorise products. The most recent SIC Manual contains 10 broad divisions, each denoted by a single digit from 0 to 9. These are subdivided into

TABLE 23.1 *The Standard Industrial Classification (SIC) System for categorising industrial customers*

0	Agriculture, forestry and fishing
1	Energy and water supply industries
2	Extraction of minerals and ores other than fuels; manufacture of metals, mineral products and chemicals
3	Metal goods, engineering and vehicles
4	Other manufacturing industries
5	Construction
6	Distribution, hotels and catering; repairs
7	Transport and communication
8	Banking, finance, insurance, business services and leasing
9	Other services

classes (each denoted by the addition of a second digit), the classes are divided into groups (three digits) and the groups into activity headings (four more digits). There are 10 divisions, 60 classes, 222 groups and 334 activity headings. For example, Division 4 (see Table 23.1), "Other manufacturing industries", has 8 classes, 50 groups and 91 activity headings. The numbering system follows that of NACE (Nomenclature Générale des Activités Économiques dans les Communautés Européennes) as far as possible.[3] To categorise manufacturers in more detail, the *Census of Distribution* further sub-divides manufacturers.

Data are available for each SIC category through various government publications and departments. Table 23.2 shows the types of information that can be obtained from government sources. Some data are available by town, county and metropolitan area. Business-to-business market data also appear in such non-government sources as Dun & Bradstreet's *Market Identifiers.*

The SIC system is a ready made tool that allows business-to-business marketers to divide industrial organisations into market segments based mainly on the type of product manufactured or handled. Although the SIC system is a vehicle for segmentation, it must be used in conjunction with other types of data to enable a specific business-to-business marketer to determine exactly which customers it can reach and how many of them can be targeted.

Input-output analysis works well in conjunction with the SIC system. This type of analysis is based on the assumption that the output or sales of one industry are the input or purchases of other industries. For example, component manufacturers provide products which form an input for manufacturers of white goods such as washing machines and fridges. **Input-output data** tell what types of industries purchase the products of a particular industry.

After discovering which industries purchase the major portion of an industry's output, the next step is to find the SIC numbers for those industries. Because firms are grouped differently in the input-output tables and the SIC system, ascertaining SIC numbers can be difficult. However, the Central Statistical Office does provide some limited conversion tables with the input-output data. These tables can assist business marketers in assigning SIC numbers to the industry categories used in the input-output analysis. Having determined the SIC numbers of the industries that buy the firm's output, a business-to-business marketer is in a position to ascertain the number of

TABLE 23.2 *Types of government information available about business-to-business markets (based on SIC categories)*

Value of industry shipments
Number of establishments
Number of employees
Exports as a percentage of shipments
Imports as a percentage of apparent consumption
Compound annual average rate of growth
Major producing areas

firms that are potential buyers nationally, by town and by county. Government publications report the number of establishments within SIC classifications, along with other types of data, such as those shown in Table 23.2.

Locating Business-to-Business Customers

At this point, business-to-business marketers know what industries purchase the kind of products their firm produces, as well as the number of establishments in those industries and certain other information. However, the marketers still have to find out the names and addresses of potential customers.

One approach to identifying and locating potential customers is to use business-to-business directories, such as *Kompass* and *Kelly's*. These sources contain such information about a firm as its name, SIC number, address, phone number and annual sales. By referring to one or more of these sources, an organisational marketer can isolate customers with certain SIC numbers, determine their locations and thus develop lists of potential customers by area.

A second approach, which is more expedient but also more expensive, is to use one of the many marketing research agencies. For example, Market Locations is able to provide lists of organisations which fall into particular SIC groups. Information can include name, location, sales volume, number of employees, type of products handled and names of chief executives. Figure 23.1 illustrates the Dutch Automobile Association's attempts to target travel agencies.

Either approach can effectively identify and locate a group of potential organisational customers. However, a business-to-business marketer probably cannot pursue all firms on the list. Because some companies have a greater purchase potential than others, the marketer must weigh up the attractiveness of each and determine which segment or segments to pursue.

In business-to-business marketing, situation specific variables may be more relevant in segmenting markets than general customer characteristics. Industrial customers concentrate on benefits sought; therefore, understanding the end use of the product is more important than the psychology of decisions or socio-economic characteristics. Segmenting by benefits rather than customer characteristics can provide insight into the structure of the market and opportunities for new customers.[4]

Estimating Purchase Potential

To estimate the purchase potential of business-to-business customers or groups of customers, a business-to-business marketer must find a relationship between the size of potential customers' purchases and a variable available in SIC data, such as the number of employees. For example, a paint manufacturer might attempt to determine the

FIGURE 23.1 *Locating business customers*
This advertisement for the Dutch Automobile Association targeted travel agencies.

SOURCE: Courtesy ANWB Royal Dutch Touring Club.

average number of gallons purchased by a specific type of potential business-to-business customer relative to the number of persons employed. If the business-to-business marketer has no previous experience in this market segment, it will probably be necessary to survey a random sample of potential customers to establish a relationship between purchase sizes and numbers of persons employed. Once this relationship has been established, it can be applied to potential customer segments to estimate their purchases. After deriving these estimates, the business-to-business marketer selects the customers to be included in the target market.

CHARACTERISTICS OF BUSINESS-TO-BUSINESS MARKETING MIXES

After selecting and analysing a target market, a business-to-business marketer must create a marketing mix that will satisfy the customers in that target market. Marketing Insight 23.1 reviews the marketing mix of a Swedish manufacturer of industrial bearings. In many respects, the general concepts and methods involved in developing a

FIGURE 23.2 *Business-to-business services*
Beton offers its services to the building industries.

SOURCE: InformationZentrum Beton Gmbtt.

business-to-business marketing mix are similar to those used in consumer product marketing. Here the focus is on the features of business-to-business marketing mixes that differ from the marketing mixes for consumer products. Each of the main components in a business-to-business marketing mix is examined: product, distribution, promotion and price. Personnel are not particularly part of the product, but they are integral to the selling and promotional activity in all markets.

Product

After selecting a target market, the business-to-business marketer has to decide how to compete. Production orientated managers fail to understand the need to develop a distinct appeal for their product to give it a competitive, or differential, advantage. Positioning the product (discussed in Chapters 3 and 9) is necessary to serve a market successfully, whether it is consumer or business-to-business.[5]

Compared with consumer marketing mixes, the product ingredients of business-to-business marketing mixes often include a greater emphasis on services, both before and after sales. Services, including on-time delivery, quality control, custom design (see Figure 23.2) and a comprehensive parts distribution system, may be important components of the product. Marketing Insight 23.2 reveals the importance of a service "package" in the shipping and forwarding industry.

SVENSKA KULLAGERFABRIKEN

Swedish company Svenska Kullagerfabriken (SKF) is world leader in the manufacture of roller bearings. SKF was founded in 1907 following the invention by its founder, Sven Wingquist, of a single groove ball-bearing. This product went on to form the basis of the organisation's success. Today, SKF's massive 20 per cent share of the world market comes from the efforts of 45,000 employees in 130 different countries. Altogether, SKF has more than 100 factories and 8,000 distributors. The company has extended its product base, through acquisitions, to include, among others, machine tools, cutting tools, seals, aircraft components and textile machinery parts. The company's customer driven objectives aim to identify customer problems, devise solutions, provide the right product and offer appropriate service support.

SKF adopts a multi-level segmentation of the market, dividing customers first according to industry type and then by product application. In meeting the needs of a diverse customer base, the company is keen to maintain superior standards of quality and customer service across all areas of its business. These aspects form the central thrust of SKF's differential advantage and, therefore, the focus of the company's marketing activity.

Product quality standards are maintained through a programme of continual product checks, both in the research and development laboratories and manufacturing facilities. Although bearings may appear to be quite simple products, they are a critical component in many types of machine. Often the bearings must operate under extreme temperature conditions or cope with severe vibration. The dangers of bearing fatigue have led SKF to investigate alternative materials and develop new types of bearings. The company is proud of its investment in research and development, which is close to 2 per cent of sales. According to company literature, "If one were to magnify a ball from a standard bearing up to the size of Mount Everest, the largest irregularity would measure no more than 50 millimetres [2 inches]."

SKF has no intention of competing on the basis of price. The emphasis on product quality and suitability, coupled with efficient delivery and after sales service, means that price is not usually the customer's primary concern. SKF has invested considerable resources in its distribution network. Having its own subsidiaries in each country allows the organisation to keep control of the sales operation and maintain its high standards. It caters for the needs of the different national markets with promotional material in 17 languages and a carefully planned global promotion that takes into account the full range of customer cultures. In designing its marketing programmes, SKF has put the needs and wants of its diverse customer base at the forefront.

SOURCES: Peter Wingard, Warwick Business School MBA Programme, 1990–91; *SKF Company Reports*, 1990, 1991; *The World of SKF*, SKF company literature, publication 3909 E, 1988; N. Webb, "The bearing industry: adding it all up", *Purchasing World*, Vol. 34, Issue 6, 1990, pp. 48–50; J. Arbrose, "SKF's strategy to counter the Japanese", *International Management* (UK), Vol. 41, Issue 6, pp. 40–7.

Before making a sale, business-to-business marketers provide potential customers with technical advice regarding product specifications, installation and applications. Many business-to-business marketers depend heavily on long term customer relationships that perpetuate sizeable repeat purchases. Therefore, business-to-business marketers also make a considerable effort to provide services after the sale. Because business-to-business customers must have products available when needed, on-time delivery is another service included in the product component of many business-to-business marketing mixes. A business-to-business marketer unable to provide on-time delivery cannot expect the marketing mix to satisfy business-to-business customers. Availability of parts must also be included in the product mixes of many business-to-business marketers in order to prevent costly production delays. The business-to-business marketer who includes availability of parts within the product component has a competitive advantage over a marketer who fails to offer this service. Furthermore, customers whose average purchases are large often desire credit; thus some business-to-business marketers include credit services in their product mixes. When planning and developing a business-to-business product mix, a business-to-business marketer of component parts and semi-finished products must realise that a customer may decide to make the items instead of buying them. In some cases, then, business-to-business marketers compete not only with one another, but with their own potential customers as well.

Frequently, industrial products must conform to standard technical specifications that business-to-business customers want. Thus business-to-business marketers often concentrate on functional product features rather than on marketing considerations. This fact has important implications for business-to-business salespeople. Rather than concentrating just on selling activities, they must assume the role of consultants, seeking to solve their customers' problems and influencing the writing of specifications.[6] For example, salespeople for computer hardware often act as consultants for software as well as the basic computer kit. Most customers now expect this level of service. In the UK many suppliers went out of business because of their inability to offer such a service.

Because industrial products are rarely sold through self-service, the major consideration in package design is protection. There is less emphasis on the package as a promotional device.

Research on business-to-business customer complaints indicates that such buyers usually complain when they encounter problems with product quality or delivery time. On the other hand, consumers' complaints refer to other problems, such as customer service and pricing. This type of buyer feedback allows business-to-business marketers to gauge marketing performance. It is important that business-to-business marketers respond to valid complaints, because the success of most industrial products depends on repeat purchases. Because buyer complaints serve a useful purpose, many industrial firms facilitate this feedback by providing customer service departments.[7]

If a business-to-business marketer is in a mature market, growth can come from attracting market share from another business marketer; alternatively, a company can look at new applications or uses for its products. JCB dominates the backhoe digger market in Europe, but the economic recession, which resulted in reduced construction of buildings and infrastructures, hit its key customers hard. The company used its existing skills and facilities to design an innovative range of very safe, single arm skid steer machines. These nimble, compact "mini diggers" are now appearing on most building sites and are entering the hire market, proving very successful for JCB. Putting user safety and environmental concerns to the fore, they lend themselves particularly well to the buyer needs in Germany and Scandinavia.

MARKETING INSIGHT 23.2

ADD ON SERVICES COST P&O DEARLY

P&O Containers, a subsidiary of P&O plc, is a major container shipping line serving most of the world's trade routes. The UK agency, part of P&O Containers, provides a full range of commercial and logistical services for UK importers and exporters shipping with P&O Containers. The agency has recently branched out by providing forwarding services for non-P&O Containers' customers.

The agency, which employs 900 people in 15 locations throughout the UK arranges bespoke packages which include combined sea-air freight services, cargo insurance, cargo consolidation, cargo management, full European distribution, EDI (Electronic Data Interchange) links, export finance, cross trade and relay links, and regulations/customs advisory service. No other container shipping company offers such a range of add on services, which for P&O supplements the company's rail services and trailer park facilities.

Expensive to provide and resource hungry to arrange, many of these services are rarely used. Few customers want all; most take advantage of only a small selection. However, as competitors offer many of these services, but not all, customers have come to expect a major player to be able to offer the full range. It may actually cost the agency to provide some; others may barely break even. Nevertheless, it is necessary for P&O Containers not only to be seen as a key shipping force but also as having the facilities and products to be able to provide customers—large or small—with the required range of services and assistance. Customer needs—real and perceived—must be catered for, and even in business-to-business marketing, service provision is a key determinant of success.

Although some of these add-on services do not contribute to P&O's profits, they do enable the company to offer a complete service. This is particularly reassuring for many of P&O's customers, given the changing trade and shipping regulations within the EC and the growth of trade with the formerly communist countries of eastern Europe. The service element of P&O's business is integral to the company's product offer and its intention to serve its industrial customers.

SOURCES: "P&O containers—the UK agency", *P&O Containers*, 1989; P&O Containers' promotional leaflets, 1988–90; "Freight forwarding in the 1990s", *Freight News Express*, 16 April 1990; "Freight forwarding", London: Keynote, 1990; "Sea-air", *British Shipper and Forwarder*, March 1988.

Distribution

The distribution ingredient in organisational marketing mixes differs from that for consumer products with respect to the types of channels used; the kinds of intermediaries available; and the transport, storage and inventory policies. None the less, the primary objective of the physical distribution of industrial products is to ensure that the right products are available when and where needed.

FIGURE 23.3
Typical marketing channels for industrial products

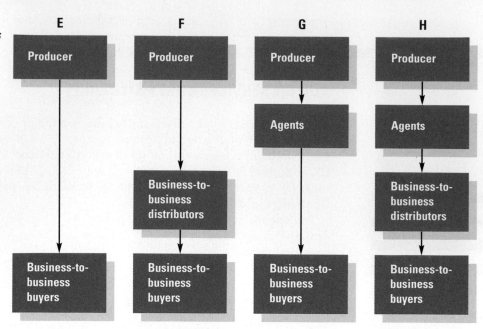

Distribution channels tend to be shorter for industrial products than for consumer products. (Figure 23.3 shows the four commonly used industrial distribution channels that were described in Chapter 10). Although **direct distribution channels,** in which products are sold directly from producers to users, are not used frequently in the distribution of consumer products, they are the most widely used for industrial products. More than half of all industrial products are sold through direct channels (channel E in Figure 23.3). Industrial buyers like to communicate directly with producers, especially when expensive or technically complex products are involved. For this reason organisational buyers prefer to purchase expensive and highly complex main frame and mini computers directly from the producers. In these circumstances, an industrial customer wants the technical assistance and personal assurances that only a producer can provide.

A second industrial distribution channel involves an industrial distributor to facilitate exchanges between the producer and customer (channel F in Figure 23.3). A **business-to-business distributor** is an independent business organisation that takes title to products and carries inventories. Such distributors are merchant wholesalers; they assume possession and ownership of goods, as well as the risks associated with ownership. Business-to-business distributors usually sell standardised items, such as maintenance supplies, production tools and small operating equipment. Some carry a wide variety of product lines; others specialise in one or a small number of lines. Industrial distributors can be most effectively used when a product has broad market appeal, is easily stocked and serviced, is sold in small quantities and is needed rapidly to avoid high losses (as is a part for an assembly-line machine).[8]

Business-to-business distributors offer sellers several advantages. They can perform the needed selling activities in local markets at relatively low cost to a manufacturer. They can reduce a producer's financial burden by providing their customers with credit services. And because industrial distributors usually maintain close relationships with their customers, they are aware of local needs and can pass on market information to producers. By holding adequate inventories in their local markets, these distributors reduce the producers' capital requirements.

There are, though, several disadvantages to using business-to-business distributors. They may be difficult to control because they are independent firms. Because they often stock competing brands, an industrial seller cannot depend on them to sell a specific brand aggressively. Furthermore, industrial distributors maintain inventories, for which they incur numerous expenses; consequently, they are less likely to handle bulky items or items that are slow sellers relative to profit margin, need specialised facilities or require extraordinary selling efforts. In some cases, business-to-business distributors lack the technical knowledge necessary to sell and service certain industrial items.

In the third business-to-business distribution channel (Channel G in Figure 23.3), a manufacturers' agent is employed. As described in Chapter 10, a manufacturers' agent or representative is an independent businessperson who sells complementary products of several producers in assigned territories and is compensated through commissions. Unlike an industrial distributor, a manufacturers' agent does not acquire title to the products and usually does not take possession. Acting as a salesperson on behalf of the producers, a manufacturers' agent has no latitude, or very little, in negotiating prices or sales terms.

Using manufacturers' agents can benefit a business marketer. These agents usually possess considerable technical and market information and have an established set of customers. For an industrial seller with highly seasonal demand, a manufacturers' agent can be an asset because the seller does not have to support a year round sales force. The fact that manufacturers' agents are paid on a commission basis may also make them an economical alternative for a firm that has extremely limited resources and cannot afford a full time sales force.

Certainly, the use of manufacturers' agents is not problem free. Even though straight commissions may be cheaper for an organisational seller, the seller may have little control over manufacturers' agents. Because of the compensation method, manufacturers' agents generally want to concentrate on their larger accounts. They are often reluctant to spend adequate time following up sales, put forward special selling efforts or provide sellers with market information when such activities reduce the amount of productive selling time. Because they rarely maintain inventories, manufacturers' agents have a limited ability to provide customers quickly with parts or repair services.

The fourth business-to-business distribution channel (Channel H in Figure 23.3) has both a manufacturers' agent and an industrial distributor between the producer and the organisational customer. This channel may be appropriate when the business marketer wishes to cover a large geographical area but maintains no sales force because demand is highly seasonal or because the firm cannot afford one. This type of channel can also be useful for a business-to-business marketer that wants to enter a new geographic market without expanding the firm's existing sales force.

So far, this discussion has implied that all channels are equally available and that an industrial producer can select the most desirable option. However, in a number of cases, only one or perhaps two channels are available for the distribution of certain types of products. An important issue in channel selection is the manner in which particular products are normally purchased. If customers ordinarily buy certain types of products directly from producers, it is unlikely that channels with intermediaries will be effective. Other dimensions that should be considered are the product's cost and physical characteristics, the costs of using various channels, the amount of technical assistance customers need and the size of product and parts inventory needed in local markets.

Physical distribution decisions regarding transport, storage and inventory control are especially important for business-to-business marketers. Some raw materials and other industrial products may require special handling; for example, toxic chemicals used in the manufacture of some products must be shipped, stored and disposed of properly to ensure that they do not harm people or the environment. In addition, the continuity of most organisational buyer-seller relationships depends on the seller having the right products available when and where the customer needs them. This requirement is so important that business-to-business marketers must sometimes make a considerable investment in order processing systems, materials handling equipment, warehousing facilities and inventory control systems. In the UK, British Tubes Stockholding, a subsidiary of British Steel, holds extensive stocks of steel tubes, pipes and girders for distribution to a variety of business markets—ranging from North Sea oil to general construction to lawnmower production.

Many industrial purchasers are moving away from traditional marketing exchange relationships, where the buyer purchases primarily on price from multiple suppliers, to more tightly knit, relational exchanges, which are long lasting, less price driven agreements between manufacturers and suppliers.[9] Just-in-time inventory management systems are providing the rationale underlying these new types of relationships. In order to reduce inventory costs and to eliminate waste, buyers purchase new stock just before it is needed in the manufacturing process. To make this system effective, they must share a great deal of information with their suppliers, since these relationships are collaborative.

Promotion

The combination of promotional efforts used in business-to-business marketing mixes generally differs from those for consumer products, especially convenience goods. The differences are evident in the emphasis on various promotional mix ingredients and the activities performed in connection with each promotional mix ingredient.

For several reasons, most organisational marketers rely on **personal selling** to a much greater extent than do consumer product marketers (except, perhaps, marketers of consumer durables). Because an industrial seller often has fewer customers, personal contact with each customer is more feasible. Some industrial products have technical features that are too numerous or too complex to explain through non-personal forms of promotion. Moreover, business-to-business purchases are frequently high in value and must be suited to the job and available where and when needed; thus business buyers want reinforcement and personal assurances from industrial sales personnel. Because business marketers depend on repeat purchases, sales personnel must follow up sales to make certain that customers know how to use the purchased items effectively, as well as to ensure that the products work properly. Personal selling is often supported with advertising activity (see Figure 23.4).

Salespeople need to perform the role of educators, showing buyers clearly how the product fits their needs. When the purchase of a product is critical to the future profitability of the business-to-business buyer, buying decision-makers gather extensive amounts of information about all alternative products. To deal with such buyers successfully, the seller must have a highly trained sales force that is knowledgeable not only about its own company's products, but also about competitors' offerings. Besides, if sales representatives offer thorough and reliable information, they can reduce the organisational buyer's uncertainty, as well as differentiate their firm's product from the competition. Finally, the gathering of information lengthens the decision-making process. Thus it is important for salespeople to be patient; not to pressure their clients as they make important, new and complex decisions; and to continue providing information to their prospects throughout the entire process.[10]

FIGURE 23.4

A typical business-to-business advertisement In industrial selling, advertising often supplements personal selling efforts.

SOURCE: Courtesy: Electricity Association. Agency: First City/BBDO, London.

As Table 23.3 illustrates, the average cost of an industrial sales call varies from industry to industry. Selling costs comprise salaries, commissions, bonuses and travel and entertainment expenses. In America, the average cost of an industrial call is $229.70.[11] It should also be noted, however, that some business-to-business sales are very large. A Boeing salesperson, for instance, closed a sale with Delta Air Lines for commercial aircraft worth $3 billion.[12] But on the average, only 350 aircraft are sold each year, resulting in sales of $105 billion. Generally, aircraft salespeople work hardest in the three to five years before a sale is made.[13]

Because of the escalating costs of advertising and personal selling, telemarketing, the creative use of the telephone to enhance the salesperson's function, is on the increase. Some of the activities in telemarketing include Freephone 0800 phone lines and personal sales workstations—assisted by data terminals—that take orders, check stock and order status, and provide shipping and invoicing information.

Although not all business-to-business sales personnel perform the same sales activities, they can generally be grouped into the following categories, as described in Chapter 16: technical, missionary, and trade or inside order takers. An inside order taker could effectively use telemarketing. Regardless of how sales personnel are classified, industrial selling activities differ from consumer sales efforts. Because organisational sellers are frequently asked for technical advice about product specifications and uses, they often need technical backgrounds and are more likely to have them than consumer sales personnel. Compared with typical buyer-seller relationships in consumer product sales, the interdependence that develops between industrial buyers and sellers is likely to be stronger, sellers count on buyers to purchase their particular products; and buyers rely on sellers to provide information, products and related services when and where needed. Although business-to-business salespeople do market their products aggressively, they almost never use "hard sell" tactics because of their role as technical consultants and the interdependence between buyers and sellers.

Advertising is emphasised less in business sales than in consumer transactions. Some of the reasons given earlier for the importance of personal selling in business-to-busi-

TABLE 23.3 *The average cost of a business-to-business sales call between selected industries in America*[a]

SIC NUMBER	INDUSTRY	NUMBER OF BUSINESS-TO-BUSINESS COMPANIES REPORTING	AVERAGE DAILY NUMBER OF SALES CALLS PER SALESPERSON	AVERAGE COST OF BUSINESS-TO-BUSINESS SALES CALL	AVERAGE DAILY SALES CALL COSTS[b] PER SALESPERSON
27	Printing and publishing	18	3.2	$148.60	$ 475.52
28	Chemicals and allied products	41	4.0	$155.20	$ 620.80
29	Petroleum and coal products	12	5.3	$ 99.10	$ 525.23
33	Primary metal industries	15	3.9	$363.90	$1,419.21
34	Fabricated metal products	113	3.9	$186.10	$ 725.79
35	Machinery, except electrical	275	3.5	$257.30	$ 900.55
3573	Electronic computing equipment (computer hardware)	17	4.2	$452.60	$1,900.92
36	Electrical and electronic equipment	137	3.5	$238.40	$ 834.40
37	Transport equipment	41	2.9	$255.90	$ 742.11
38	Instruments and related products	73	3.9	$209.50	$ 817.05
50	Wholesale trade-durable goods	29	5.1	$139.80	$ 712.98
73	Business services	30	2.8	$227.20	$ 636.16

[a]No comparable UK/EC statistics available.

[b]This cost is determined by multiplying the average daily number of calls per salesperson by the average cost per sales call for each industry.

SOURCE: Laboratory of Advertising Performance (LAP), report no. 8052.3 (date unavailable), McGraw-Hill Research. Reprinted by permission of McGraw-Hill, Inc.

ness promotional mixes explain why. However, advertising often supplements personal selling efforts. Because the cost of a business-to-business sales call is high and continues to rise, advertisements that allow sales personnel to perform more efficiently and effectively are worthwhile for industrial marketers. Advertising can make organisational customers aware of new products and brands; inform buyers about general product features, representatives and organisations; and isolate promising prospects by providing enquiry forms or the addresses and phone numbers of company representatives. To ensure that appropriate information is sent to a respondent, it is crucial that the enquiry specify the type of information desired, the name of the company and respondent, the company's SIC number and the size of the organisation.

Because the demand for most business-to-business products is derived demand, marketers can sometimes stimulate demand for their products by stimulating consumer demand. Thus an organisational marketer occasionally sponsors an advertisement promoting the products sold by the marketer's customers.

When selecting advertising media, organisational marketers primarily choose such print media as trade publications and direct mail; they seldom use broadcast media. Trade publications and direct mail reach precise groups of industrial customers and avoid wasted circulation. In addition, they are best suited for advertising messages that present numerous details and complex product information (which are frequently the types of messages that business-to-business advertisers wish to get across).

Compared with consumer product advertisements, industrial advertisements are usually less persuasive and more likely to contain a large amount of copy and numerous details. In contrast, marketers that advertise to reach ultimate consumers sometimes avoid extensive advertising copy because consumers are reluctant to read it. Business-to-business advertisers, however, believe that industrial purchasers with any interest in their products will search for information and read long messages.

Sales promotion activities, too, can play a significant role in business-to-business promotional mixes. They encompass such efforts as catalogues, trade shows and trade sales promotion methods, including merchandise allowances, buy back allowances, displays, sales contests and other methods discussed in Chapter 16. Business-to-business marketers go to great lengths and considerable expense to provide catalogues that describe their products to customers. Customers refer to various sellers' catalogues to determine specifications, terms of sale, delivery times and other information about products. Catalogues thus help buyers decide which suppliers to contact.

Trade shows can be effective vehicles for making many customer contracts in a short time. One study found that firms allocate 25 per cent of their annual promotional budgets to trade shows in order to communicate with their current and potential customers, promote their corporate image, introduce new products, meet key account executives, develop mailing lists, identify sales prospects and find out what their competitors are doing. Although trade shows take second place to personal selling, they rank above print advertising in influencing business-to-business purchases, particularly as the organisational buyers reach the stages in the buying process of need recognition and supplier evaluation.

Many firms that participate in trade shows lack specific objectives regarding what they hope to accomplish by such participation. Firms with the most successful trade show programmes have written objectives for the tasks they wish to achieve, and they carefully select the type of show in which to take part so that those attending match the firm's target market.[14]

The way in which business marketers use publicity in their promotional mixes may not be much different from the way in which marketers of consumer products use it. More companies are incorporating public relations automatically into their promotional mixes.

Price

Compared with consumer product marketers, organisational marketers face many more price constraints from legal and economic forces. With respect to economic forces, an individual industrial firm's demand is often highly elastic, requiring the firm to approximate competitors' prices. This condition often results in non-price competition and a considerable amount of price stability.

Today's route to sustainable *competitive advantage* lies in offering customers something that the competition does not offer—something that helps them increase their productivity and profitability. Firms achieve high market share not by offering low prices but by offering their customers superior value and product quality.[15] Customers are willing to pay higher prices for quality products.[16] Companies such as Caterpillar Tractor, Hewlett-Packard and 3M have shown that a value based strategy can win a commanding lead over competition. Such firms emphasise the highest quality products at slightly higher prices.

Many industrial companies are devoting increased resources to training, so that their personnel are better qualified and more willing to provide full customer service. Corporate image, reliability and flexibility in production and delivery, technical innovation, and well executed promotional activity also present opportunities to create a differential advantage (competitive edge). Price used to be the basis for differentiation in industrial markets, but price can be reduced only so far if companies are to remain viable. Although cost is still important, in most markets, companies have attempted to move away from a selling proposition based purely on low price. They have realised that "value" is not necessarily equal to a low price. Service, reliability, image and design are just a few factors in addition to price that influence many sales.

Although there are various ways to determine prices of industrial products, the three most common are administered pricing, bid pricing and negotiated pricing. With **administered pricing,** the seller determines the price (or series of prices) for a product, and the customer pays that specified price. Marketers who use this approach may employ a one price policy in which all buyers pay the same price, or they may set a series of prices that are determined by one or more discounts. In some cases, list prices are posted on a price sheet or in a catalogue. The list price is a beginning point from which trade, quantity and cash discounts are deducted. Thus the actual (net) price a business-to-business customer pays is the list price less the discount(s). When a list price is used, an industrial marketer sometimes specifies the price in terms of list price times a multiplier. For example, the price of an item might be quoted as "list price x .78", which means the buyer can purchase the product at 78 per cent of the list price. Simply changing the multiplier lets the seller revise prices without having to issue new catalogues or price sheets.

With **bid pricing,** prices are determined through sealed or open bids. When a buyer uses sealed bids, selected sellers are notified that they are to submit their bids by a certain date. Normally, the lowest bidder is awarded the contract, as long as the buyer believes that the firm is able to supply the specified products when and where needed. In an open bidding approach, several, but not all, sellers are asked to submit bids. In contrast to sealed bidding, the amounts of the bids are made public. Finally, an organisational purchaser sometimes uses negotiated bids. Under this arrangement, the customer seeks bids from a number of sellers and screens the bids. Then the customer negotiates the price and terms of sale with the most favourable bidders, until either a final transaction is consummated or negotiations are terminated with all sellers.

Sometimes a buyer will be seeking either component parts to be used in production for several years or custom built equipment to be purchased currently and through future contracts. In such instances, an industrial seller may submit an initial, less profitable bid to win "follow on" (subsequent) contracts. The seller that wins the initial contract is often substantially favoured in the competition for follow on contracts. In such a bidding situation, an industrial marketer must determine how low the initial bid should be, the probability of winning a follow on contract and the combination of bid prices on both the initial and the follow on contract that will yield an acceptable profit.[17]

For certain types of business markets, a seller's pricing component may have to allow for **negotiated pricing.** That is, even when there are stated list prices and discount structures, negotiations may determine the actual price an organisational customer pays. Negotiated pricing can benefit seller and buyer because price negotiations frequently lead to discussions of product specifications, applications and perhaps product substitutions. Such negotiations may give the seller an opportunity to provide the customer with technical assistance and perhaps sell a product that better fits the customer's requirements; the final product choice might also be more profitable for the seller. The buyer benefits by gaining more information about the array of products and terms of sale available and may acquire a more suitable product at a lower price.

Some business-to-business marketers sell in markets in which only one of these general pricing approaches prevails. Such marketers can simplify the price components of their marketing mixes. However, a number of business marketers sell to a wide variety of organisational customers and must maintain considerable flexibility in pricing.

SUMMARY

Business-to-business marketing is a set of activities directed at facilitating and expediting exchanges involving industrial products and customers in industrial markets.

Business-to-business marketers have a considerable amount of information available to them for use in planning their marketing strategies. Much of this information is based on the Standard Industrial Classification (SIC) system, which classifies businesses into major industry divisions, classes, groups and activities. The SIC system provides business marketers with information needed to identify market segments. It can best be used for this purpose in conjunction with other information, such as input-output data. After identifying target industries, the marketer can locate potential customers by using business-to-business directories or by employing a marketing research agency. The marketer must then estimate the potential purchases of organisational customers by finding a relationship between a potential customer's purchases and a variable available in published sources.

Like marketers of consumer products, an industrial marketer must develop a marketing mix that satisfies the needs of customers in the industrial target market. Personnel are not generally seen as integral to the product itself, but perhaps more than in consumer marketing they are central to the selling process and are a key part of promotional activity. The product component frequently emphasises services, which are often of primary interest to business customers. The marketer must also consider that the customer may elect to make the product rather than buy it. Industrial products must meet certain standard specifications that organisational users want.

The distribution of industrial products differs from that of consumer products in the types of channels used; the kinds of intermediaries available; and transport storage and inventory policies. A direct distribution channel is common in business marketing. Also used are channels containing manufacturers' agents, industrial distributors, or both agents and distributors. Channels are chosen on the basis of availability, the typical mode of purchase for a product and several other variables.

Personal selling is a primary ingredient of the promotional component in business-to-business marketing mixes. Sales personnel often act as technical advisers both before and after a sale. Advertising is sometimes used to supplement personal selling efforts. Industrial marketers generally use print advertisements containing more information but less persuasive content than consumer advertisements. Other promotional activities include catalogues and trade shows.

The price component for business marketing mixes is influenced by legal and economic forces to a greater extent than it is for consumer marketing mixes. Pricing may be affected by competitors' prices, as well as by the type of customer who buys the product. Increasingly, though price is still important, many companies are seeking new ways of creating a differential advantage. Value for money is important in most markets, but low price is not an effective differential advantage except in the very short term. Flexibility and reliability in production and delivery can be differentiating factors, as can technical innovation, personnel and customer service, promotional activity and even payment terms.

IMPORTANT TERMS

Business-to-business marketing	Business-to-business distributor
Standard Industrial Classification (SIC) system	Personal selling
	Administered pricing
Input-output data	Bid pricing
Direct distribution channels	Negotiated pricing

DISCUSSION AND REVIEW QUESTIONS

1. How do industrial products differ from consumer products?
2. What function does the SIC system help industrial marketers perform?
3. List some sources that a business-to-business marketer can use to determine the names and addresses of potential customers.
4. How do business marketing mixes differ from those of consumer products?
5. What are the major advantages and disadvantages of using industrial distributors?
6. Why do organisational marketers rely on personal selling more than consumer products marketers?
7. Why would a business-to-business marketer spend resources on advertising aimed at stimulating consumer demand?
8. Compare three methods of determining the price of industrial products.
9. Why must a differential advantage be based on more than just low prices?

■ CASES

23.1 Hoskyns Group plc—Success in Computer Services

Computer services companies engage in activities which are basically divided into professional services and tasks related to processing and operating. Hoskyns, operating in a highly competitive market, is one of the largest and oldest computer services companies. In 1965 the organisation was acquired by Martin Marietta, a large US aerospace company. During 1986 Hoskyns went public, when Martin Marietta sold a 25 per cent stake in the business. Further changes occurred in July 1988, when Plessey acquired Martin Marietta's remaining 68 per cent share of Hoskyns.

Throughout this period, Hoskyns continued to operate autonomously. With around 3,000 employees and more than 2,000 customers during 1988, the company maintained its reputation for consistent growth beyond that of the computer services industry as a whole (see tables).

Hoskyns's low level of exports, at only 12 per cent of turnover, is potentially a disad-

Hoskyns's turnover and profit 1983–1988

YEAR	TOTAL SALES (£m)	GROWTH OVER PREVIOUS YEAR (%)	PROFIT BEFORE TAX (£m)
1983	28.7	–	2.5
1984	40	41.3	2.8
1985	56	40	3.5
1986	67.7	20.8	4.4
1987	79	16.7	6.5
1988	110	39	9.5

Top seven computer services companies by 1988 revenue

RANK	COMPANY	UK REVENUE (£m)	TOTAL REVENUE (£m)
1	SD-Scion	100	260
2	Hoskyns	97	110
3	SEMA	95	280
4	Istel	83	85
5	EDS	75	2,823
6	Logica	70	132
7	Anderson Consultancy	67	597

vantage with the likely changes in environment associated with 1992 EC deregulation. Companies in other countries, like SEMA, have already made strong inroads into Europe. If Hoskyns is to be a successful European competitor, it must therefore capitalise on its particular strengths, which include the following:

■ Expertise on IBM, ICL, DEC and Packard hardware.
■ Modular Application Systems (MAS) software, which allows customers to use software matching their own requirements without having to order "bespoke" software.
■ Considerable breadth of services, markets and customer base and ability to offer practical, computer based solutions.
■ Creative and innovative services. For example, the launching of "Re-engineering" in 1988—a novel approach to systems developments where the underlying structure of software is retained when hardware is replaced.
■ "People" culture in its working environment, resulting in a happy and satisfied workforce.

In addition, Hoskyns has undertaken a number of useful acquisitions. During October 1987, the company acquired Thomas and Co. Ltd (TCL), a financial services specialist. This was quickly followed by the acquisition of Computer Based Training (CBT), which specialised in both distance learning and classroom based courses. In

May 1988, a further three companies were acquired. Insight Database Systems, Insight Software (Export) and Vector Software were expert in IBM mid-range computers and were bought in anticipation of the new IBM AS/400 mainframe launch. During 1988, Hoskyns moved one step closer to Europe by winning a facilities management contract with BP. This led to the opening of a new facilities management centre in Holland.

SOURCES: Michael Labrou, "Ten marketing case studies", MBA dissertation, University of Warwick, 1989; Excel Cards for Hoskyns; Dataline, 22 February 1989, p. 36; Hoskyns annual reports, 1987, 1988; *Computing*, 29 October 1987, p. 19; *Computer Weekly*, 17 July 1988, p. 124; *Electronic Times*, 28 July 1988, p. 2.

Questions for Discussion

1. Why is Hoskyns successful?
2. How might Hoskyns capitalise on its qualities to improve its chances of success in Europe after 1992?

23.2   Compaq Computer Targets Business Customers to Take Over in Europe

In businesses, banks, doctors' surgeries, department stores and homes, computers in general make work and life easier. But no single class of computer is a perfect fit for every job, and computer companies continually develop and market a variety of models to fill a variety of niches. Compaq Computer, the world's fourth largest manufacturer of desktop personal computers, primarily produces high quality, high priced versions for businesses and professional organisations that require fast, rugged and reliable machines and are willing to pay premium prices to get them. Compaq targets *Times* 1,000 type companies, including in its impressive clientele such organisations as ALCOA, the Louvre Museum in Paris, Dole Foods of Thailand, Lego Toys and the *Chicago Tribune*.

In 1982, Rod Canion, Bill Murto and Jim Harris left their executive positions with Texas Instruments, formed their own company and introduced the Compaq Portable Computer. Just four years later, Compaq made *Fortune* magazine's list of the top 500 companies in the world, faster than any other business in the history of the list. By the end of 1987, sales topped the £666 million mark. In 1989, boasting a net income of £222 million and about £1,933 million in sales, Compaq became the second largest supplier of business PCs in Europe, surpassing Apple. Although IBM still maintains better brand recognition, European consumers now view Compaq as having joined its chief competitor at the top of the PC ladder.

Until recently, Compaq has succeeded in attracting the high end of the computer market by maintaining premium prices, low key advertising and a dealership distribution strategy. Although Compaq is still highly successful in the 1990s, slowing US sales and intense competitions from lower priced catalogue companies are forcing the company to re-evaluate its methods and initiate some changes. Compaq recently discounted prices up to 40 per cent on several of its most advanced PCs. Calling it "creative pricing", one company executive said that his organisation is responding to the growing view that its products are becoming too costly, especially for smaller companies that were previously loyal Compaq customers. Responding to the reality that few retailers are equipped to sell machines as complicated as the new £15,000–£25,000 SystemPro 486, Compaq recently signed agreements with several computer consulting firms to sell the SystemPro line and opened up demonstration centres in major conurbations in its core territories to help sell the network systems. Expanding its marketing techniques beyond simple and straightforward advertising, Compaq introduced a joint worldwide promotion with Microsoft to introduce the Microsoft BallPoint Mouse, the first such pointing device designed specifically for use with laptop PCs. Compaq offered free BallPoints to buyers of any of its laptop or notebook computers. Advertisements for the promotion appeared in leading business magazines and newspapers, reinforced with direct mail packs to business users and telemarketing support.

SOURCES: "Compaq, Microsoft team for joint promotion", *Adweek,* 11 March 1991, p. 61; Mark Ivey, Barbara Buell, Jonathan B. Levine and Neil Gross, "What's in a clone: price, technology, service . . .", *Business Week,* 19 November 1990, p. 137; Thomas C. Hayes, "Compaq cuts prices on some computers", *The New York Times,* 12 September 1990; Kevin Burke, Brett Graham, Dale Miller, Steve Rikli and Chris Tiesman, *Compaq Computer Corporation Desktop Personal Computers: Marketing Plan*, working paper, Texas A&M University, fall 1990; Todd Mason, "Compaq to unveil 3 personal computers, posing big sales challenge for dealers", *Wall Street Journal,* 23 July 1990, p. B2; Jim Bartimo and Deidre A. Depke, "Compaq's muscular mini isn't knocking them out", *Business Week,* 2 July 1990, pp. 34–5; Gregory Seay, "Overseas sales boost Compaq to new heights", *Houston Post,* 27 April 1990; Deidre A. Depke, "Bloody, bowed, back together", *Business Week,* 19 March 1990, pp. 42–3; and Carla Lazzareschi, "Compaq and Businessland heal their year-long rift", *Los Angeles Times,* 8 March 1990, p. D6.

Questions for Discussion

1. Compare Compaq's new marketing strategy with its previous one.
2. Will the new strategy that Compaq is using to remain competitive diminish its premium image and thus adversely affect its efforts to market its products in the premium business segment of the personal computer market?
3. For the SystemPro line, who and what factors will influence the buying process?

24

SERVICES MARKETING

Objectives

- To understand the nature and characteristics of services

- To classify services

- To understand the development of strategies for services

- To examine the extended marketing mix for services

- To understand the problems involved in developing a competitive advantage in services

- To explore the concept of marketing services in non-business situations

- To understand the development of service strategies in non-business organisations

- To describe methods for controlling non-business service activities

*T*he 1991 merger between Algemene Bank Nederland and Amsterdam-Rotterdam Bank to create Dutch based ABN AMRO Bank produced the dominant financial institution in the Netherlands, the seventh largest bank in Europe and one of the world's top 20. With branches throughout Benelux, and over 400 in 51 other countries, ABN AMRO daily deals with thousands of customers face to face or through telecommunications.

Many consumers find banks' history and formal procedures intimidating and view them as powerful institutions with which they can enjoy little personal interaction. ABN AMRO has tackled this perception head on, recognising that fundamentally it is a service provider dealing with people, whose success depends on the attitude and ability of the bank's own personnel. In this respect, ABN AMRO realises it must behave as a service provider and adopt the practices of services marketing.

ABN AMRO places significant emphasis on its employees, who are integral to its products, marketing and the services it provides. The bank's internal marketing focuses on training and motivating its staff worldwide to deliver a consistent, friendly, proficient and superior service to ABN AMRO's many customers. ABN AMRO acknowledges it is only as good as its personnel—those people who to many customers epitomise the bank's products and services. Its human resource and marketing executives highlight these employees' skills in handling customer contact and delivering the bank's services. ■

SOURCES: Caroline Farquhar; ABN AMRO annual report & accounts; Barclays de Zoete Wedd Securities; Credit Suisse first Boston; Financial Times Analysis; "Banking industry report", Salomon Brothers, April 1992; ABN AMRO Utrecht.

This chapter presents concepts that apply specifically to the marketing of services. Services marketing involves marketing in non-profit organisations such as education, health care, charities and government, as well as for profit areas such as entertainment, tourism, finance, personal services and professional services.

The chapter first focuses on the growing importance of service industries in the economy. Second, it addresses the unique characteristics of services and the problems they present to marketers. Third, it presents various classification schemes that can help service marketers develop marketing strategies. In addition, it discusses a variety of marketing mix considerations, along with the associated problems of creating and sustaining a differential advantage (competitive edge). Finally, the chapter defines non-business marketing and examines the development of non-business marketing strategies and the control of non-business marketing activities.

THE NATURE AND CHARACTERISTICS OF SERVICES

As mentioned in Chapter 7, all products—goods, services, or ideas—possess a certain amount of intangibility. A service is an intangible product involving a deed, a performance or an effort that cannot be physically possessed.[1] It should be noted that few products can be classified as a pure good or a pure service. Consider, for example, a car. When consumers purchase a car, they take ownership of a physical item that provides transport, but the warranty associated with the purchase is a service. When the car is returned to the dealer for routine maintenance, the dealer is providing a service. When consumers hire a car, they purchase a transport service that is provided through temporary use of a car. Most products, such as cars and car hire, contain both tangible and intangible components. One component, however, will dominate, and it is this dominant component that leads to the classification of goods, services and ideas.

Figure 24.1 illustrates the tangibility concept by placing a variety of products on a continuum of tangibility and intangibility. Tangible dominant products are typically classified as goods, and intangible dominant products are typically considered services. An airline seat or hotel bed may be tangible and physical, but the airline or hotel operator is in fact providing a service: transportation or temporary accommodation. Thus, as defined in Chapter 7, services are intangible dominant products that involve the application of human and mechanical efforts to people or objects.

Growth and Importance of Services

In the United States, the increasing importance of services in the economy has led many people to call the country the world's first service economy. Service industries—encompassing trade, communications, transport, food and lodging, financial and medical services, education, government and technical services—account for about 60 per cent of the US national income and three quarters of the non-farm jobs in the United States. In the UK and in Europe, the service sector is now just as important (see Figures 24.2 and 24.3), employing 67 per cent of the workforce in the UK and 59 per cent in Europe.

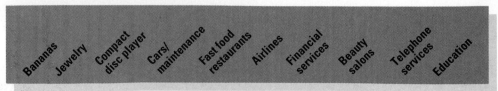

Goods (tangible) — Bananas · Jewelry · Compact disc player · Cars/maintenance · Fast food restaurants · Airlines · Financial services · Beauty salons · Telephone services · Education — Services (intangible)

FIGURE 24.1 *A continuum of product tangibility and intangibility*

FIGURE 24.2

European Community total employment by economic activity

SOURCE: *Eurostat,* 1988. Reproduced by permission of the Commission of the European Communities.

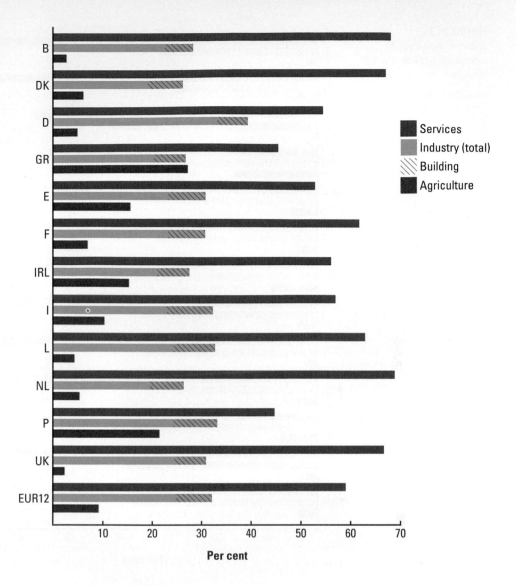

One major catalyst of the growth in **consumer services** has been general economic prosperity, which has led to an increase in financial services, travel, entertainment and personal care, with more mundane activities contracted out. Lifestyle changes have similarly encouraged expansion of the service sector. Smaller families result in more free time and relatively higher disposable income. A widespread desire for self-fulfill-ment—experience rather than ownership—leads consumers to "buy in" outside serv-ices. In the past 40 years, the number of women in the workforce has more than doubled. Consumers want to avoid tasks such as meal preparation, house cleaning, home maintenance and preparation of tax returns. Furthermore, Europeans have be-come more fitness and recreation orientated, and with greater leisure time, the de-mand for fitness and recreational facilities has escalated. In terms of demographics, the population is growing older, and this change has promoted tremendous expansion of health care services. Finally, the number and complexity of goods needing servicing have spurred demand for repair services.

Not only have consumer services grown in the economy, **business services** have prospered as well. Business or industrial services include repairs and maintenance,

FIGURE 24.3
Gross value added by economic activity (market prices)

SOURCE: *Eurostat,* 1988. Reproduced by permission of the Commission of the European Communities.

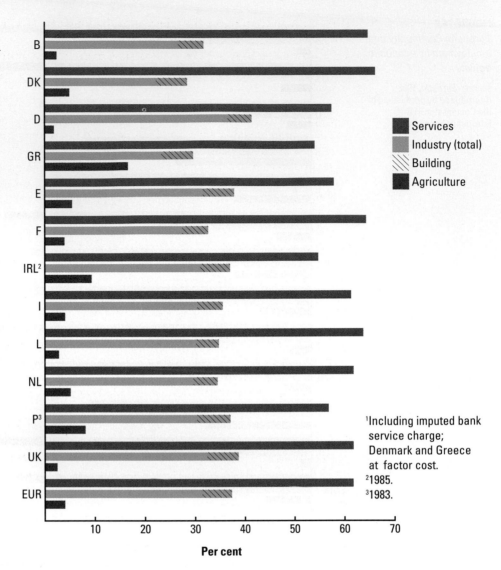

¹Including imputed bank service charge; Denmark and Greece at factor cost.
²1985.
³1983.

Per cent

consulting and professional advice, installation, equipment leasing, marketing research, advertising, temporary office personnel and caretaking services. Expenditures for business and industrial services have risen even faster than expenditures for consumer services. This growth has been attributed to the increasingly complex, specialised and competitive business environment. Large retailers such as IKEA or Marks & Spencer are successfully incorporating additional services into their retail stores. Providing additional services at one location is an excellent way to satisfy and keep customers who need and want more and more services. Burton Group operates its traditional department stores (Debenhams) but in addition offers optical services, financial services and so on. If customers enter a store for one service, they are more likely to shop at the store again or try another service that the retailer provides.[2]

For non-consumer services there are three key reasons behind the growth of business-to-business services:

■ Specialisation; the delegation of non-care tasks such as advertising, executive recruitment and car fleet management.

- Technology; the increase in sophistication leading to the "buying in" of expert knowledge and skills such as IT computing consultants.
- Flexibility; the need in many organisations to avoid fixed overhead costs. Marketing research, maintenance and cleaning are frequently only brought in on an ad hoc basis.

Characteristics of Services

The problems of service marketing are distinct from those of goods marketing.[3] To understand them, it is first necessary to understand the distinguishing characteristics of services. Services have four basic characteristics: (1) intangibility, (2) inseparability of production and consumption, (3) perishability and (4) heterogeneity.[4] Table 24.1 summarises these characteristics and the marketing problems they entail.

Intangibility stems from the fact that services are performances. They cannot be seen, touched, tasted or smelled; nor can they be possessed. Intangibility also relates to the difficulty that consumers may have in understanding service offerings.[5] Services have a few tangible attributes, called **search qualities,** that can be viewed prior to purchase. When consumers cannot view a product in advance and examine its properties, they may not understand exactly what is being offered. Even when consumers do gain sufficient knowledge about service offerings, they may not be able to evaluate the possible choices. On the other hand, services are rich in experience and credence qualities. **Experience qualities** are those qualities that can be assessed only after purchase and consumption (satisfaction, courtesy and the like). **Credence qualities** are those qualities that cannot be assessed even after purchase and consumption.[6] An appendix operation is an example of a service high in credence qualities. How many consumers are knowledgeable enough to assess the quality of an appendectomy, even after it has been performed?

A Volvo car can be test driven before being purchased. It can be viewed in the dealer's showroom and on the streets. It can—to an extent—be consumed prior to the risk taking purchase. The same is not true of a meal in a top restaurant or a theatre seat. The meal may be disappointing, as may the play, but by the time the disappointment is recognised it is too late; the service has been—at least partially—consumed and paid for.

TABLE 24.1   *Service characteristics and marketing problems*

UNIQUE SERVICE FEATURES	RESULTING MARKETING PROBLEMS
Intangibility	Cannot be stored
	Cannot be protected through patents
	Cannot be readily displayed or communicated
	Prices difficult to set
Inseparability	Consumer involved in production
	Other consumers involved in production
	Centralised mass production difficult
Perishability	Services unable to be inventories
Heterogeneity	Standardisation and quality difficult to control

SOURCE: Valarie A. Zeithaml, A. Parasuraman and Leonard L. Berry, "Problems and strategies in services marketing", *Journal of Marketing,* Spring 1985, pp. 33–46. Used by permission of the American Marketing Association.

Related to intangibility, therefore, is **inseparability** of production and consumption. Services are normally produced at the same time they are consumed. A medical examination is an example of simultaneous production and consumption. In fact, the doctor cannot possibly perform the service without the patient's presence, and the consumer is actually involved in the production process. Dining out in a restaurant is a similar example. With other services, such as air travel, many consumers are simultaneously involved in production. Because of high consumer involvement in most services, standardisation and control are difficult to maintain.

Because production and consumption are simultaneous, services are also characterised by **perishability.** The consumer of a service generally has to be present and directly involved in the consumption of the service at the time of its production. In other words, unused capacity in one time period cannot be stockpiled or inventoried for future time periods. Consider the airlines' seating capacity dilemma. Each carrier maintains a sophisticated reservations system to juggle ticket prices and ensure maximum revenues for every flight. This attempt to maximise profit on each flight has led to over booking, which means that airlines may sell tickets for more seats than are available so as to compensate for "no shows"—people who have made reservations but do not actually take that particular flight. The airlines' dilemma illustrates how service perishability presents problems very different from the supply and demand problems encountered in the marketing of goods.[7] Unoccupied seats on an airline flight cannot be stored for use on another flight that is booked to capacity. Hotel operators offer bargain breaks—discount deals—to fill under utilised capacity in slack periods; an empty room one night is a sale lost for ever.

Finally, because most services are labour intensive, they are susceptible to **heterogeneity.** For the service to be provided and consumed, the client generally meets and deals directly with the service provider's personnel. People typically perform services, and people do not always perform consistently. There may be variation from one service to another within the same organisation or variation in the service that a single individual provides from day to day and from customer to customer. A good branch manager is crucial for a company such as Pizza Hut. Poor customer reaction and branch performance can often be traced back to a poor branch manager.[8] Queuing times in McDonald's can vary greatly, often due to teamwork, speed and efficiency variations between branches. A hotel general manager has a significant impact on the attitude of the hotel's staff and thus on the running of the hotel. There may be a considerable variation in guest satisfaction, therefore, between one Hilton and another. Thus standardisation and quality are extremely difficult to control. But this fact may also lead to customising services to meet consumers' specific needs. Because of these factors, service marketers often face a dilemma: how to provide efficient, standardised service at some acceptable level of quality while simultaneously treating each customer as a unique person. Giving "good service" is a major concern of all service organisations, and it is often translated into more personalised service.

CLASSIFICATION OF SERVICES

Services are a very diverse group of products, and an organisation may provide more than one kind. Examples of services include car hire, repairs, health care, hair dressers, health centres, child care, domestic services, legal advice, banking, insurance, air travel, education, entertainment, catering, business consulting, dry cleaning and accounting. Nevertheless, services can be meaningfully analysed by using a five category classification scheme: (1) type of market, (2) degree of labour intensiveness, (3) degree of customer contact, (4) skill of service provider, and (5) goal of the service provider. Table 24.2 summarises this scheme.

Services can be viewed in terms of the market or type of customer they serve—consumer or industrial. The implications of this distinction are very similar to those for all products and therefore are not discussed here. In Figure 24.4, the International Convention Centre in Birmingham aims to attract conferences to Britain's "second city".

A second way to classify services is by degree of labour intensiveness. Many services, such as repairs, education and hair care, rely heavily on human labour. Other services, such as telecommunications, health farms/fitness centres and public transport, are more equipment intensive (although people are still integral).

Labour (people) based services are more susceptible to heterogeneity than are most equipment based services. Marketers of people based services must recognise that the service providers are often viewed as the service itself. Therefore, strategies relating to selecting, training, motivating and controlling employees are very important to the success of most service businesses.

The third way in which services can be classified is by customer contact. High contact services include health care, hotels, estate agencies and restaurants; low contact services include repairs, theatres, dry cleaning and spectator sports.[9] Note that high contact services generally involve actions that are directed towards individuals. Because these services are directed at people, the consumer must be present during production. Although it is sometimes possible for the service provider to go to the con-

TABLE 24.2 *Classification of services*

CATEGORY	EXAMPLES
TYPE OF MARKET	
Consumer	Repairs, child care, legal advice
Industrial	Consulting, caretaking services, installation
DEGREE OF LABOUR INTENSIVENESS	
Labour based	Repairs, education, haircuts
Equipment based	Telecommunications, health farms, public transport
DEGREE OF CUSTOMER CONTACT	
High	Health care, hotels, air travel
Low	Repairs, home deliveries, postal service
SKILL OF THE SERVICE PROVIDER	
Professional	Legal advice, health care, accountancy
Non-professional	Domestic services, dry cleaning, public transport
GOAL OF THE SERVICE PROVIDER	
Profit	Financial services, insurance, health care
Non-profit	Health care, education, government

FIGURE 24.4

Marketing of services to business users

The International Convention Centre in Birmingham aims to attract conferences to Britain's "second city" and to the UK's first purpose built convention centre.

SOURCE: The International Convention Centre in Birmingham.

sumer, high contact services typically require that the consumer goes to the production facility. Thus the physical appearance and ambience of the facility may be a major component of the consumer's overall evaluation of the service. The enjoyment of an evening out in a restaurant stems not just from the taste of the food but also from the decor and furnishings, general ambience, and the ability and attitude of the staff. Because the consumer must be present during production of a high contact service, the process of production may be just as important as its final outcome. For example, open plan banks and quick queue systems aim to improve the transaction process and make the service more enjoyable for the consumer.

Low contact service, in contrast, commonly involves actions directed at things. Consequently, the consumer is usually not required to be present during service delivery. The consumer's presence, however, may be required to initiate or terminate the service. The Post Office maintains a network of branches, sorting offices and vehicles. The process of sending a parcel from Cardiff to London or Lille is lengthy. Although they must be present to initiate the provision of the service, consumers need not be present during the process. The appearance of the production facilities and the interpersonal skills of actual service providers are thus not as critical in low contact services as they are in high contact services.[10]

Skill of the service provider is a fourth way to classify services. Professional services tend to be more complex and more highly regulated than non-professional services. In the case of legal advice, for example, consumers often do not know what the actual service will involve or how much it will cost until the service is completed, because the final product is very situation specific. Additionally, solicitors are regulated both by law and by professional associations.

Finally, services can be classified according to the goal of the service provider—profit or non-profit. The second half of this chapter examines non-business marketing. Most non-business organisations provide services rather than goods.

DEVELOPING MARKETING STRATEGIES FOR SERVICES

The Extended Marketing Mix for Services

The standard marketing mix comprises the "4 Ps":

- Product
- Promotion
- Price
- Distribution (Place)

The discussion about the classification of services has emphasised the importance of these additional elements:

- Process
- Physical evidence (ambience)
- People

Collectively, these seven elements—the "7 Ps"—form what is termed the **extended marketing mix for services** (see Figure 24.5).

Before examining strategic considerations for the marketing of services, creating a differential advantage and the importance of customer satisfaction, this section considers in more detail the extended marketing mix in services marketing.

Product

Goods can be defined in terms of their physical attributes, but services, because they are intangible, cannot. As pointed out earlier in the chapter, it is often difficult for consumers to understand service offerings and to evaluate possible service alternatives. British Gas, for example, has schemes to spread bill payments and to assist those financially disadvantaged, plus several methods of making payments. These services are

FIGURE 24.5
The extended marketing mix for services

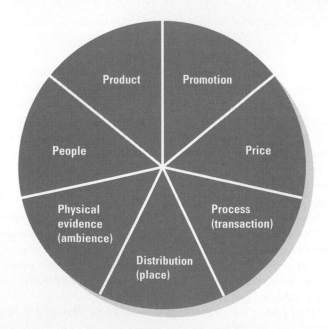

MARKETING INSIGHT 24.1

EXPANSION OF HEALTH CARE MARKETING

Private health care is far removed from the marketing of Sony Walkmans or Caterpillar earthmovers. What is the product? The consultation with a specialist? The treatment? Perhaps the speed from diagnosis to operation? The en suite, comfortable facilities? Or the improved condition and lifestyle of the patient? In the UK, BUPA is a leader in the provision of private (non-government provided) health care and has just recruited car hire company Avis's marketing director in order to rekindle its marketing.

Although there are dozens of health care companies—and more from Europe entering the UK market each year—only a handful offer the complexity of products available from BUPA. The insurance division sells health cover policies, which to many consumers represent the most visible side of BUPA. There is much more, however. BUPA owns its own hospitals, operating theatre units and health clinics. The company is thus far more than an insurance broker; and as a result, it has many publics. These include companies which subscribe for insurance cover on behalf of their employees as a "perk"; suppliers of medical equipment and drugs; the medical profession, which recommends its hospitals and facilities; insurance brokers, who recommend policies to their clients; the general and specialist media; and consumers as private purchasers of policies and as patients.

The insurance division's principal market is the corporate sector; it therefore targets sales activity at companies taking out policies for their employees. In addition, BUPA is now devoting more attention to promoting its services directly to consumers in order to increase its membership and enlarge its customer base. Television advertisements during 1992 and 1993 emphasised the relatively low cost of private health cover "from as little as £17 per month". With *fund holding* GPs taking a fresh look at private medi-

explained in advertisements. Marketing Insight 24.1 examines the nature of the service product and the growing role of marketing in the private health care sector.

There may also be tangibles (such as facilities, employees or communications) associated with a service. These tangible elements help form a part of the product and are often the only aspects of a service that can be viewed prior to purchase. Consequently, marketers must pay close attention to associated tangibles and make sure that they are consistent with the selected image of the service product.[11] For example, consumers perceive public transport at night as plagued by crime and therefore hesitate to use it. Improving the physical appearance of tube stations and reducing the time between trains are tangible cues that consumers can use to judge public transport services.

The service product is often equated with the **service provider,** for example, the bank clerk or the stylist becomes the service a bank or a beauty salon provides. Because consumers tend to view services in terms of the service personnel and because personnel are inconsistent in their behaviour, it is imperative that marketers effectively select, train, motivate and control contact people.

After testing many variables, the Strategic Planning Institute (SPI) in America decine, BUPA is also publicising its facilities and locations to the general medical profession.

In a recent rapid expansion of the private health care sector, Nuffield Hospitals and international based AMI have taken market share from BUPA. Currently BUPA's marketing has been handled regionally, but with 29 hospitals, 30 health screening clinics, 10 homes for the elderly and an occupational health service, BUPA feels the need for a formal marketing strategy and centralised control. Already the enhanced marketing activity has turned a £63-million loss into a pre-tax profit to be reinvested in BUPA's facilities.

BUPA's actions coincide with the launch of a new rival, Firstchoice, led by ex-BUPA executives. Claiming to be the UK's first health insurance broker, Firstchoice develops tailor made insurance packages and sells services from over 20 health care companies. It has established agreements with all of the market's major players, except with BUPA. Whereas most competitors target the corporate sector primarily, Firstchoice believes there is growing consumer interest in private health care cover and services.

Along with BUPA, AMI and Nuffield, Firstchoice is segmenting the marketplace and developing marketing programmes aimed at specific target audiences, employing many tools created by the marketers of the consumer goods giants. For the rapidly developing private health care industry, marketing is increasingly important.

SOURCES: "Firstchoice claims new line in health insurance", *Marketing Week*, 26 February 1993, p. 9; Penny Kiernan, "BUPA drafts in marketing chief", *Marketing Week*, 5 February 1993, p. 8; BUPA promotional literature; Firstchoice promotional literature; David Bryant, "Updating BUPA's figures", *Marketing*, 22 October 1992, p. 16.

veloped an extensive database on the impact of various business strategies on profits. The institute found that "relative perceived product *quality*" is the single most important factor in determining long term profitability. In fact, because there are generally no objective measures to evaluate the quality of professional services (medical care, legal services and so forth), the customer is actually purchasing confidence in the service provider.[12] The strength or weakness of the service provided often affects consumers' perceptions of **service product quality**. Of the companies in the SPI database, businesses that rate low on service lose market share at the rate of 2 per cent a year and average a 1 per cent return on sales. Companies that score high on service gain market share at the rate of 6 per cent a year, average a 12 per cent return on sales and charge a significantly higher price.[13] These data indicate that firms having service dominant products must score high on service quality.

Because services are performances rather than tangible goods, the concept of service quality is difficult to grasp. However, price, quality and value are important considerations of consumer choice and buying behaviour for both goods and services.[14] It should be noted that it is not objective quality that matters, but the consumer's subjective perceptions. Instead of quality meaning conformity to a set of specifications—which frequently determine levels of product quality—service quality is defined by customers.[15] Moreover, quality is frequently determined in a comparison context. In the case of services quality is determined by contrasting what the consumer expected a service to be with her or his actual service experience.[16]

Service providers and service consumers may have quite different views of what constitutes service quality. Consumers frequently enter service exchanges with a set of predetermined expectations. Whether a consumer's actual experiences exceed, match or fall below these expectations will have a great effect on future relationships between the consumer and the service provider. To improve service quality, a service provider must adjust its own behaviour to be consistent with consumers' expectations or re-educate consumers so that their expectations will parallel the service levels that can be achieved.[17] In Figure 24.6 KLM promotes its speed of service and reliability.

A study of doctor-patient relationships proposed that when professional service exceeds client expectations, a true person to person bonding relationship develops. However, the research also revealed that what doctors viewed as being quality service was not necessarily what patients perceived as quality service. Although interaction with the doctor was the primary determinant of the overall service evaluation, patients made judgements about the entire service experience, including factors such as the appearance and behaviour of receptionists, nurses and technicians; the decor; and even the appearance of the building.[18]

Other product concepts discussed in Chapters 7 and 9 are also relevant here. Management must make decisions regarding the product mix, positioning, branding

FIGURE 24.6
Providing speed of service
KLM emphasises, and explains, its speed of service and reliability.

SOURCE: Copyright KLM Royal Dutch Airlines and American Express.

and new product development of services. It can make better decisions if it analyses the organisation's service products as to **complexity** and **variability.** Complexity is determined by the number of steps required to perform the service. Variability reflects the amount of diversity allowed in each step of service provision. In a highly variable service, every step in performing the service may be unique, whereas in cases of low variability, every performance of the service is standardised.[19] For example, services provided by doctors are both complex and variable. Patient treatment may involve many steps, and the doctor has considerable discretion in shaping the treatment for each individual patient.

An examination of the complete service delivery process, including the number of steps and decisions, enables marketers to plot their service products on a complexity/variability grid, such as the one in Figure 24.7. The position of a service on the grid has implications for its positioning in the market. Furthermore, any alterations in the service delivery process that shift the position of the service on the complexity/variability grid have an impact on the positioning of the service in the market-place. Table 24.3 details the effects of such changes. When structuring the service delivery system, marketers should consider the firm's marketing goals and target market.

Promotion

As intangible dominant products, services are not easily promoted. The intangible is difficult to depict in advertising, whether the medium is print, television or radio. Service advertising should thus emphasise tangible cues that will help consumers understand and evaluate the service. The cues may be the physical facilities in which the service is performed or some relevant tangible object that symbolises the service itself.[20] For example, restaurants may stress their physical facilities—clean, elegant, casual and so on—to provide clues as to the quality or nature of the service. Insurance firms, such as Legal and General, use objects as symbols to help consumers understand their services. Legal and General's umbrella symbol reflects an image of paternalistic protection. Midland Bank's slogan "The Listening Bank" gives the impression of understanding, helpfulness and service. Service providers may also focus their advertising on the characteristics they believe customers want from their services. National Westminster Bank's promotion stresses its ability to offer unbiased, independent advice about pensions. Commercial Union Assurance—"We won't make a drama out of a crisis"—emphasises speed of service in dealing with insurance claims and the provision of assistance in sorting out the problem.

The symbols, catch-lines and imagery common to most financial organisations reflect the increasing importance of branding in services.[21] Differentiation between rival services is difficult, as is effective promotion. Branding is helping to distinguish competing services and to provide a platform for promotional activity.

FIGURE 24.7
Complexity/variability grid for medical services

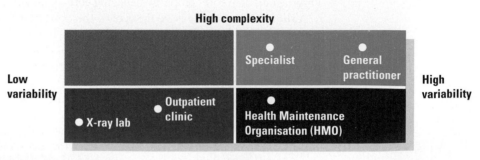

SOURCE: Adapted from Lynn Shostack, 1985 American Marketing Association Faculty Consortium on Services Marketing, Texas A&M University, 7–11 July. Reprinted by permission of the American Marketing Association.

TABLE 24.3 *Effects of shifting positions on the complexity/variability grid*

DOWNSHIFTING COMPLEXITY/VARIABILITY	UPSHIFTING COMPLEXITY/VARIABILITY
Standardises the service	Increases costs
Requires strict operating controls	Indicates higher margin/lower volume strategy
Generally widens potential market	Personalises the service
Lowers costs	Generally narrows potential market
Indicates lower margin/higher volume strategy	Makes quality more difficult to control
Can alienate existing markets	

SOURCE: Adapted from G. Lynn Shostack, 1985 American Marketing Association Faculty Consortium on Services Marketing, Texas A&M University, 7–11 July. Reprinted by permission of American Marketing Association.

In order to be successful, firms must not only maximise the difference between the value of the service to the customer and the cost of providing it; they must also design the service with employees in mind. Contact personnel are critical to the perception of quality service. They must be provided with sufficient tools and knowledge to furnish the type of service that the customer desires. Because service industries are information driven, they can substitute knowledgeable, highly trained personnel for the capital assets used in more product orientated businesses.[22]

Thus employees in a service organisation are an important secondary audience for service advertising. Variability in service quality, which arises from the labour-intensive nature of many services, is a problem for service marketers, because consumers often associate the service with the service provider. Advertising can have a positive effect on customer contact personnel. It can shape employees' perceptions of the company, their jobs and how management expects them to perform. It can be a tool for motivating, educating and communicating with employees.[23]

Personal selling is potentially powerful in services because this form of promotion lets consumers and salespeople interact. When consumers enter into a service transaction, they must, as a general rule, interact with service firm employees. Customer contact personnel can be trained to use this opportunity to reduce customer uncertainty, give reassurance, reduce dissonance and promote the reputation of the organisation.[24] Once again, therefore, properly managing contact personnel is important.

Although consumer service firms have the opportunity to interact with actual customers and those potential customers who contact them, they have little opportunity to go out into the field and solicit business from all potential consumers. The very large number of potential customers and the high cost per sales call rule out such efforts. On the other hand, marketers of industrial services, like the marketers of industrial goods, are dealing with a much more limited target market and may find personal selling the most effective way of reaching customers.

Sales promotions, such as contests, are feasible for service firms, but other types of promotions are more difficult to implement. How does a firm display a service? How does it provide a free sample without giving away the whole service? A complementary visit to a health club or a free skiing lesson could possibly be considered a free sample to entice a consumer into purchasing a membership or taking lessons. Although the role of publicity and the implementation of a publicity campaign do not differ significantly in the goods and service sectors, service marketers appear to rely on publicity much more than goods marketers do.[25]

Consumers tend to value word of mouth communications more than company sponsored communications. This preference is probably true for all products, but especially for services, because they are experiential in nature. For this reason, service firms should attempt to stimulate word of mouth communications.[26] They can do so by encouraging consumers to tell their friends about satisfactory performance. Many firms, for instance, prominently display signs urging customers to tell their friends if they like the service and to tell the firm if they do not. Some service providers, such as hairdressers, give their regular customers discounts or free services for encouraging friends to come in for a haircut. Word of mouth can be simulated through communications messages that feature a testimonial—for example, television advertisements showing consumers who vouch for the benefits of a service a particular firm offers.

One final note should be made in regard to service promotion. The promotional activities of most professional service providers, such as doctors, lawyers and accountants, are severely limited. Until recently, all these professionals were prohibited by law from advertising. Although these restrictions have now been lifted in many countries, there are still many obstacles to be overcome. Not being used to seeing professionals advertise, consumers may reject the advertisements of those who do. Furthermore, professionals are not familiar with advertising and consequently do not always develop advertisements appropriate for their services. In many countries, lawyers are being forced to consider advertising, both because many potential clients do not know that they need legal services and because there is an over supply of lawyers. Consumers want more information about legal services, and lawyers have a very poor public image.[27] On the other hand, doctors and dentists are more skeptical about the impact of advertising on their image and business. Despite the trend towards professional services advertising, the professions themselves exert pressure on their members to advertise or promote only in a limited way because such activities are still viewed as somewhat risqué.

Price

Price plays both an economic and a psychological role in the service sector, just as it does with physical goods. However, the psychological role of price in respect to services is magnified; after all, consumers must rely on price as the sole indicator of service quality when other quality indicators are absent. In its economic role, price determines revenue and influences profits. Knowing the real costs of each service provided is vital to sound pricing decisions.[28]

Services may also be bundled together and then sold for a single price. Service bundling is a practical strategy, because in many types of service there is a high ratio of fixed to variable costs and high cost sharing amongst service offerings. Moreover, the demand for certain services is often interdependent. For example, banks offer packages of banking services—current and savings accounts and credit lines that become active when customers overdraw their other accounts. Price bundling may help service marketers cross sell to their current customers or acquire new customers. The policy of price leaders also may be used by discounting the price of one service product when the customer purchases another service at full price.[29]

As noted in Table 24.1, service intangibility may complicate the setting of prices. When pricing physical goods, management can look to the cost of production (direct and indirect materials, direct and indirect labour, and overheads) as an indicator of price. It is often difficult, however, to determine the cost of service provision and thus identify a minimum price. Price competition is severe in many service areas characterised by standardisation. Usually, price is not a key variable when marketing is first implemented in an organisation. Once market segmentation and specialised services are directed to specific markets, specialised prices are set. Next comes comparative pricing as the service becomes fairly standardised. Price competition is quite common in the hotel and leisure sectors, banking and insurance.

Many services, especially professional services, are situation specific. Thus neither the service firm nor the consumer knows the extent of the service prior to production and consumption. Once again, because cost is not known beforehand, price is difficult to set. Despite the difficulties in determining cost, many service firms use cost plus pricing. Others set prices according to the competition or market demand.

Pricing of services can also help smooth out fluctuations in demand. Given the perishability of service products, this is an important function. A higher price may be used to deter or off set demand during peak periods, and a lower price may be used to stimulate demand during slack periods. British Rail's cheap day returns and Savers minimise sales declines in slack periods. Airlines rely heavily on price to help smooth out their demand, as do many other operations, such as pubs and entertainment clubs, cinemas, resorts and hotels.

Distribution (Place)

In the service context, distribution is making services available to prospective users. Marketing intermediaries are the entities between the actual service provider and the consumer that make the service more available and more convenient to use.[30] The distribution of services is very closely related to product development. Indirect distribution of services may be made possible by a tangible representation or a facilitating good, for example, a bank credit card.[31]

Almost by definition, service industries are limited to direct channels of distribution. Many services are produced and consumed simultaneously; in high contact services in particular, service providers and consumers cannot be separated. In low contact services, however, service providers may be separated from customers by intermediaries. Dry cleaners, for example, generally maintain strategically located retail stores as drop off centres, and these stores may be independent or company-owned. Consumers go to the branch to initiate and terminate service, but the actual service may be performed at a different location. The separation is possible because the service is directed towards the consumer's physical possessions, and the consumer is not required to be present during delivery.

Other service industries are developing unique ways to distribute their services. To make it more convenient for consumers to obtain their services, airlines, car hire companies and hotels have long been using intermediaries: travel agencies. In financial services marketing, the two most important strategic concerns are the application of technology and the use of electronic product delivery channels—such as automatic cash dispensers and electronic funds transfer systems—to provide customers with financial services in a more widespread and convenient manner.[32] Consumers no longer have to go to their bank for routine transactions; they can now receive service from the nearest cash dispenser or conduct transactions via telephone or fax. Bank credit cards have enabled banks to extend their credit services to consumers over widely dispersed geographic areas through an international network of intermediaries, namely, the retailers who assist consumers in applying for and using the cards.

Process

The acts of purchasing and consumption are important in all markets—consumer, industrial or service. The direct involvement of consumers in the production of most services and the perishability of these services place greater emphasis on the process of the transaction for services. Friendliness of staff and flows of information affect the customer's perception of the service product offer. Appointment or queuing systems become part of the service. Ease of payment can enhance or spoil the consumption of a service. Diners in a TGI Friday's or Old Orleans expect prompt service, informative menus, no waiting and no delays in paying their bills at the conclusion of their meals. These are operational issues which *directly* affect customer perceptions and satisfaction: they are important aspects of the marketing of services.[33]

Physical Evidence/Ambience

The environment in which a service is offered, and consumed, is central to the consumer's understanding of the service and to her or his enjoyment or satisfaction. The "feel" is very much part of the service offer. Whether in a restaurant, hospital, sports club or bank, the appearance and ambience matter. Layout, decor, up-keep; noise and aroma; general ease of access and use all become part of the service product.

People

The nature of most services requires direct interaction between the consumer and personnel representing the service provider's organisation. In many services, customers interact with one another; the organisation's staff also interact with one another. This level of human involvement must be given maximum attention if customers are to maximise their use of the service and, ultimately, their satisfaction. Employee selection, training and motivation are central considerations. A restaurant may have a superb operation, but if the chef or waiters become demoralised and unmotivated, they will begin to deliver low quality meals and inefficient service, resulting in a poor product from the consumer's point of view. Operational staff often help "produce" the service product, sell it and assist in its consumption. Many service businesses are totally dependent on their personnel, as Leo Burnett, founder of the international advertising agency which bears his names, summed up: "All our assets go down the elevator every evening"—people!

Strategic Considerations

In developing marketing strategies, the marketer must first understand what benefits the customer wants, how the marketer is perceived relative to the competition and what services consumers buy.[34] In other words, the marketer must develop the right service for the right people at the right price and at the right place. The marketer must remember to communicate with consumers so that they are aware of the need satisfying services available to them.

One of the unique challenges service marketers face is matching supply and demand. Price can be used to help smooth out demand for a service. There are other ways, too, that marketers can alter the marketing mix to deal with the problem of fluctuating demand. Through price incentives, advertising, and other promotional efforts, marketers can remind consumers of busy times and encourage them to come for service during slack periods. Additionally, the product itself can be altered to cope with fluctuating demand. Restaurants, for example, may change their menus, vary their lighting and decor, open or close the bar, and add or delete entertainment. A ski resort may install an alpine slide to attract customers during the summer. Finally, distribution can be modified to reflect changes in demand. Theatres have traditionally offered matinées during the weekend, when demand is greater, and some libraries have mobile units that travel to different locations during slack periods.[35]

Before understanding such strategies, service marketers must first grasp the pattern and determinants of demand. Does the level of demand follow a cycle? What are the causes of this cycle? Are the changes random?[36] The need to answer such questions is best illustrated through an example. An attempt to use price decreases to shift demand for public transport to off peak periods would most likely fail because of the cause of the cyclical demand for public transport: employment hours. Employees have little

TABLE 24.4 *Strategies for coping with fluctuations in demand for services*

MARKETING STRATEGIES	NON-MARKETING STRATEGIES
Use different pricing	Hire extra staff/lay off employees
Alter product	Work employees overtime/part-time
Change distribution	Crosstrain employees
Use promotional efforts	Use employees to perform non-vital tasks during slack times
	Sub-contract work/seek sub-contract work
	Slow the pace of work
	Turn away business

control over working hours and are therefore unable to take advantage of pricing incentives.

Table 24.4 summarises ways in which service firms may deal with the problem of fluctuating demand. Note that the strategies fall into two categories: marketing and non-marketing strategies. Non-marketing strategies essentially involve internal, employee related actions.[37] They may be the only available choices when fluctuations in demand are random. For example, a strike or natural disaster may cause fluctuations in consumer demand for public transport.

<table>
<tr><td>

Creating a Differential Advantage in Services

</td><td>

The aim of marketing is to satisfy customers, achieving product or brand differentiation with an advantage over competitors' products. This **differential advantage,** sometimes termed a *competitive edge,* is determined by customers' perceptions. If the targeted customers do not perceive an advantage, in marketing terms the product offers no benefit over rival products. For any product, achieving—and sustaining—a differential advantage is difficult, but for services the challenge is even greater. The intangibility of the service product and the central role of people are the prime causes of this difficulty, but there are also others:

</td></tr>
</table>

- Intangibility minimises product differentiation.
- No—or little—patent protection exists.
- Few barriers to entry enable competitors to set up and copy successful initiatives.
- The interface with customers is difficult to control.
- Growth is hard to achieve, particularly as key personnel can only be spread so far.
- Service quality is irregular.
- It is difficult to improve productivity and lower the cost to the consumer.
- Innovation leads to imitation.
- Restrictive regulations abound, particularly in the professions.

The difficulty encountered in creating a differential advantage in services underscores the importance of many of the fundamental steps in marketing. In services it is increasingly important for businesses to identify well defined target market segments in order to bring service products and the marketing mix into line with consumers' exact requirements, to evaluate competitors' service offerings and marketing programmes, and to research customers' satisfaction levels. Branding, supported with well constructed promotional campaigns, is even more central to the reinforcement and communication of any differential advantage.

Customer Satisfaction

It is essential to reiterate a major point: the marketing concept is equally applicable to goods, services and ideas. The marketing of services, like the marketing of goods, requires the identification of a viable target market segment; the development of a service concept that addresses the consumer's needs within that segment; the creation and implementation of an operating strategy that will adequately support the service concept; and the design of a service delivery system that will support the chosen operating strategy.[38]

Table 24.5 illustrates the approaches that marketers of services can take to achieve consumer satisfaction. A basic requirement of any marketing strategy, however, is a development phase, which includes defining target markets and finalising a marketing mix. The following seven preconditions need to be considered when developing a service marketing strategy.

1. Make sure that marketing occurs at all levels, from the marketing department to the point where the service is provided.
2. Allow flexibility in providing the service—when there is direct interaction with the customers, customise the service to their wants and needs.
3. Hire and maintain high quality personnel and market the organisation or service to them; often it is the people in a service organisation who differentiate the organisation from competitors.
4. Consider marketing to existing customers to increase their use of the service or create loyalty to the service provider.
5. Quickly resolve any problems in providing the service, to avoid damaging the firm's reputation for quality.
6. Use high technology to provide improved services at a lower cost. Continually evaluate how to customise the service to each consumer's unique needs.

TABLE 24.5 *Examples of approaches to consumer satisfaction for marketers of services*

SERVICE INDUSTRY	OUTCOME SOUGHT BY BUYER	TECHNICAL POSSIBILITIES	STRATEGIC POSSIBILITIES
Higher education	Educational attainment	Help lecturers to be effective teachers; offer tutoring	Admit better prepared students (or, for a fee, give them better preparation before entry)
Hospitals	Health	Instruct patients in how to manage their current problems and prevent others	Market preventive medicine services (weight loss, stress reduction and so on)
Banks	Prosperity	Offer money management courses; provide management assistance to small businesses	Market financial expertise, probably by industry specialisation
Plumbing repairs	Free flowing pipes	Provide consumers with instructions and supplies to prevent further blockages	Diversity (for example, point of use water purification systems)

SOURCE: Adapted from Betsy D. Gelb, "How marketers of intangibles can raise the odds for consumer satisfaction", *Journal of Services Marketing,* Summer 1987, p. 15. Reprinted by permission of the publisher.

MARKETING INSIGHT 24.2

MARKETING CHARITIES

Many people see marketing as a selling or advertising activity undertaken by companies such as Ford, McDonald's or Kodak. While such commercial organisations seek high returns and profits, charities seek to increase their revenues to fund their laudable causes. During the past five or six years, many leading charities and fund raising bodies have appointed marketing managers, strategists and professional public relations executives. While there is a cost to bear for recruiting such marketers, the extra revenue attracted through their efforts is expected to more than justify the additional expense.

At the NEC Marketing Show, one of the most prominent stands promotes the animal welfare charity, the RSPCA. The aim is not to persuade visitors to this exhibition to make donations. Instead the display and supporting brochure illustrate the charity's numerous joint promotional campaigns with leading household brands. The manufacturers have promoted the RSPCA on their brands' packaging and in their advertising, gaining a more "caring" image in return. In addition to exposure, the RSPCA receives a donation from these manufacturers for each item purchased during the promotion.

The RSPCA is not alone in discovering marketing. A hard hitting Christmas appeal for the leading children's charity, the NSPCC—which included one of the most successful TV charity adverts, "Ellie"—was awarded the gold award in the Direct Marketing Association's Streamline awards. Television was also selected by The Royal National Lifeboat Institution (RNLI), the UK's third largest charity, for a direct response campaign during 1993. The advertising was scheduled to coincide with a six week documentary series about

7. Brand the service to distinguish it from that of the competition. For example, instead of simply seeking a pest controller, a customer would seek assistance from Rentokil because of Rentokil's name recognition.[39]

NON-BUSINESS MARKETING

Marketing was broadly defined earlier as a set of individual and organisational activities aimed at facilitating and expediting satisfying exchanges in a dynamic environment through the creation, distribution, promotion and pricing of goods, services and ideas. Most of the previously discussed concepts and approaches to managing marketing activities also apply to non-business situations. Of special relevance is the material offered in the first half of this chapter, because many non-business organisations provide services. As a discipline, marketing is becoming increasingly important in the non-business sector, as illustrated in Marketing Insight 24.2, which looks at marketing in charities (see Figure 24.8).

Non-business marketing includes marketing activities conducted by individuals and organisations to achieve some goal other than ordinary business goals of profit, market share or return on investment. Non-business marketing can be divided into two categories: non-profit organisation marketing and social marketing. Non-profit or-the RNLI and was supported with a direct mail drop to half a million homes. The promotional activity was part of a carefully orchestrated strategy to broaden the charity's donor base. As the recession bites, charities have had to compete more aggressively for consumers' disposable income. St. John's Ambulance increased its use of direct mail campaigns in an attempt to enlarge its 15,000 strong database of regular donors. The accuracy of the mail shots was improved through the profiling of existing donors' lifestyles and geodemographic characteristics by research specialists CACI and NDL.

The World Wide Fund for Nature (WWF) is going further. In the aftermath of the Earth Summit in Rio de Janeiro, the WWF recruited a UK marketing campaigns director. The intention was to develop a more coherent marketing planning and strategy function using innovative and high profile fund raising activities instead of relying on the direct mail method traditionally used by charities. With operations in 28 countries, the WWF has achieved a significant increase in income through enhanced marketing and better image building—from £5 million per annum in the mid-1980s to £22 million.

SOURCES: Oxfam; RSPCA; Daz Valladares, "Charities find relief in targeted advertising", *Marketing Week*, 27 November 1992, p. 16; Ken Gofton, "NSPCC wins DMA prize", *Marketing*, 17 December 1992, p. 4; Paul Meller, "Amherst picks up St. John's account", *Marketing*, 26 November 1992, p. 8; "RNLI takes plunge with TV ad move", *Marketing*, 19 November 1992, p. 14; "Charities face shortage of marketers", *Marketing Week*, 29 January 1993, p. 8; "RSPCA Christmas ads help recession hit pets", *Marketing Week*, 27 November 1992, p. 8.

ganisation marketing is the application of marketing concepts and techniques to organisations such as hospitals and colleges. Social marketing is the development of programmes designed to influence the acceptability of social ideas, such as contributing to a foundation for AIDS research or getting people to recycle more newspapers, plastics and aluminium.[40]

As discussed in Chapter 1, an exchange situation exists when individuals, groups or organisations possess something that they are willing to give up in an exchange. In non-business marketing, the objects of the exchange may not be specified in financial terms. Usually, such exchanges are facilitated through **negotiation** (mutual discussion or communication of terms and methods) and **persuasion** (convincing and prevailing upon by argument). Often negotiation and persuasion are conducted without reference to or awareness of the role that marketing plays in transactions. The discussion here concerns non-business performance of marketing activities, whether the exchange is consummated or not.

The rest of this chapter first examines the concept of non-business marketing to determine how it differs from marketing activities in business organisations. Next it explores the overall objectives of non-business organisations, their marketing objectives and the development of their marketing strategies. The discussion closes by illustrating how an audit of marketing activities can promote marketing awareness in a non-business organisation.

FIGURE 24.8
Non-business marketing
The marketing of charities is expanding rapidly. Here, NCH is appealing to the business community for joint promotions.

Giving big business a human face.

Working with a charity can be a good business decision as well as a good deed.

NCH is one of Britain's leading children's charities. When you work with us the children benefit, but so does your company.

Corporate image, product awareness, employee motivation, virtually every aspect of your public image can be improved by working with us. In fact, in recent research 78% of shareholders sampled stated they would prefer to buy shares in a company that works with a charity.

For a free marketing pack, containing real case studies and information about corporate promotions and sponsorships with NCH, simply complete and return the coupon.

Please send me (Tick Box):

☐ "Partners for Success." *How to make the most of charity promotions.* ☐ "In Business with Charities." *NCH's latest market research report.*

Name _____ Title _____

Company _____

Address _____ Postcode _____

Complete and send the coupon to:
Jamus Swindells, Corporate Fundraising Manager, NCH, 85 Highbury Park, London N5 1UD. Tel. 071 226 2033 Reg. Charity no: 215301

SOURCE: Ad produced by the Johnson Agency for NCH.

Why Is Non-business Marketing Different?

Traditionally and mistakenly, people have not thought of non-business exchange activities as marketing. But consider the following example. Warwick Business School used to promote its degree courses solely through the University of Warwick's prospectuses. In the early 1980s, its main programmes received small advertising budgets. As courses were improved, the wider use of advertising increased awareness of the school and its programmes. A new corporate identity was developed by Coley Porter Bell of London and each programme, led by the MBA, developed its own full marketing mix and more extensive promotional strategy, all in line with the school's new mission statement. Many university departments and state maintained schools are now engaging in marketing strategy.

Many non-business organisations strive for effective marketing activities. Charitable organisations and supporters of social causes are major non-business marketers. Political parties, unions, religious groups and student organisations also perform marketing activities, yet they are not considered businesses. Whereas the chief beneficiary of a business enterprise is whoever owns or holds shares in it, in theory the only beneficiaries of a non-business organisation are its clients, its members or the public at large.

Non-businesses have a greater opportunity for creativity than most business organisations, but trustees or board members of non-businesses are likely to have trouble judging performance when services can be provided only by trained professionals. It is harder for administrators to evaluate the performance of doctors, lecturers or social workers than it is for sales managers to evaluate the performance of salespeople in a for profit organisation.

Another way in which non-business marketing differs from for profit marketing is that non-business is sometimes quite controversial. Non-business organisations such as Greenpeace, CND and Shelter spend lavishly on lobbying efforts to persuade government and even the courts to support their interests, in part because acceptance of their aims is not always guaranteed. However, marketing as a field of study does not attempt to define an organisation's goals or debate the issue of non-business versus business goals. Marketing attempts only to provide a body of knowledge to further an organisation's goals. Individuals must decide whether they approve of an organisation's goal orientation. Most marketers would agree that profit and consumer satisfaction are appropriate goals for business enterprises, but there probably would be considerable disagreement about the goals of a controversial non-business organisation.

Non-business Marketing Objectives

The basic aim of non-business organisations is to obtain a desired response from a target market. The response could be a change in values, a financial contribution, the donation of services or some other type of exchange. Non-business marketing objectives are shaped by the nature of the exchange and the goals of the organisation. BBC sponsored Children in Need and Comic Relief telethons have raised millions of pounds. Telethons have three specific marketing objectives: (1) to raise funds to support programmes, (2) to plead a case on behalf of disadvantaged groups and (3) to inform the public about the organisation's programmes and services. Tactically, telethons have received support by choosing good causes; generating extensive grass-roots support; portraying disadvantaged people in a positive and dignified way; developing national, regional and local support; and providing quality entertainment.[41] Figure 24.9 illustrates how the exchanges and the purpose of the organisation can influence marketing

FIGURE 24.9
Examples of marketing objectives for different types of exchanges

SOURCE: Philip Kotler, *Marketing for Nonprofit Organisations,* 2nd Ed., © 1982, p. 38. Adapted by permission of Prentice-Hall, Inc., Englewood Cliffs, N.J.

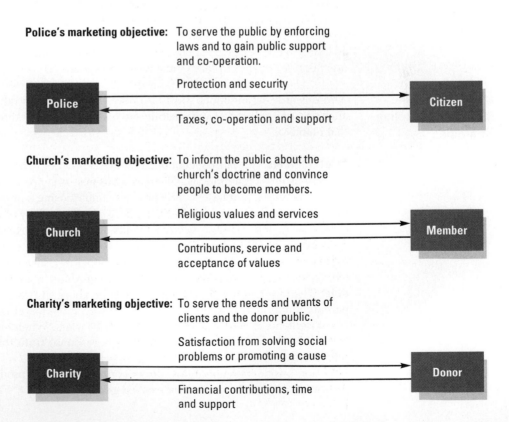

Police's marketing objective: To serve the public by enforcing laws and to gain public support and co-operation.

Police → Protection and security → Citizen
Police ← Taxes, co-operation and support ← Citizen

Church's marketing objective: To inform the public about the church's doctrine and convince people to become members.

Church → Religious values and services → Member
Church ← Contributions, service and acceptance of values ← Member

Charity's marketing objective: To serve the needs and wants of clients and the donor public.

Charity → Satisfaction from solving social problems or promoting a cause → Donor
Charity ← Financial contributions, time and support ← Donor

FIGURE 24.10

Non-business markets
The University of Warwick
serves many groups:
students, the community
at large through employ-
ment and student develop-
ment, and philanthropists
who may be looking for
worthwhile organisations
to support.

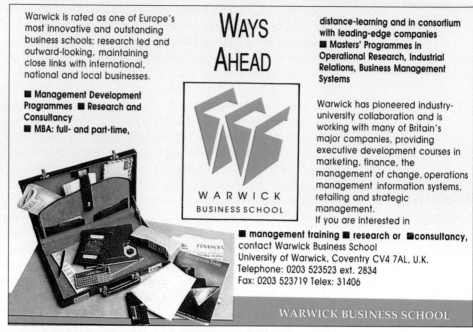

Warwick is rated as one of Europe's most innovative and outstanding business schools; research led and outward-looking, maintaining close links with international, national and local businesses.

■ **Management Development Programmes** ■ **Research and Consultancy**
■ **MBA: full- and part-time,**

WAYS AHEAD

distance-learning and in consortium with leading-edge companies
■ **Masters' Programmes in Operational Research, Industrial Relations, Business Management Systems**

Warwick has pioneered industry-university collaboration and is working with many of Britain's major companies, providing executive development courses in marketing, finance, the management of change, operations management information systems, retailing and strategic management.
If you are interested in

WARWICK BUSINESS SCHOOL

■ **management training** ■ **research or** ■ **consultancy,** contact Warwick Business School
University of Warwick, Coventry CV4 7AL, U.K.
Telephone: 0203 523523 ext. 2834
Fax: 0203 523719 Telex: 31406

WARWICK BUSINESS SCHOOL

SOURCE: Courtesy Warwick Business School, University of Warwick.

objectives. (These objectives are used as examples and may or may not apply to specific organisations.)

Non-business marketing objectives should state the rationale for an organisation's existence. An organisation that defines its marketing objective as providing a product can be left without a purpose if the product becomes obsolete. However, serving and adapting to the perceived needs and wants of a target public, or market, enhances an organisation's chance to survive and achieve its goals.

Developing Non-business Marketing Strategies

Non-business organisations must also develop marketing strategies by defining and analysing a target market and creating and maintaining a marketing mix that appeals to that market.

Target Markets. The concept of target markets needs to be revised slightly to apply to non-business organisations. Whereas a business is supposed to have target groups that are potential purchasers of its product, a non-business organisation may attempt to serve many diverse groups. In Figure 24.10, the University of Warwick is promoting excellence to potential and current students, financial supporters and the general public. A **target public** is broadly defined as a collective of individuals who have an interest in or concern about an organisation, a product or a social cause. The terms *target market* and *target public* are difficult to distinguish for many non-business organisations. The target public for campaigns warning about the dangers of solvent abuse is parents, adults and concerned teenagers. However, the target market for many of the advertisements is potential and current solvent users. When an organisation is concerned about changing values or obtaining a response from the public, it views the public as a market.[42]

In non-business organisations, direct consumers of the product are called **client publics** and indirect consumers are called **general publics**.[43] For example, the client public for a university is its student body, and its general public includes parents, graduates and the University Senate. The client public usually receives most of the attention when an organisation develops a marketing strategy. The techniques and approaches to segmenting and defining target markets discussed in Chapter 3 apply also to non-business target markets.

Developing a Marketing Mix.   A marketing mix strategy limits choices and directs marketing activities towards achieving organisation goals. The strategy should outline or develop a blueprint for making decisions about product, distribution, promotion, price and personnel. These decision variables should be blended to serve the target market.

In tackling the product variable, non-business organisations deal more often with ideas and services than with goods. Problems may evolve when an organisation fails to define what is being provided. What products do the Women's Institute, the Scout movement or the Chamber of Commerce provide? They offer a forum for social gatherings, courses, outings and a sense of co-operation. Their products are more difficult to define than the average business product. As indicated in the first part of this chapter, services are intangible and therefore need special marketing efforts. The marketing of ideas and concepts is likewise more abstract than the marketing of tangibles, and it requires considerable effort to present benefits.

Because most non-business products are ideas and services, distribution decisions relate to how these ideas and services will be made available to clients. If the product is an idea, selecting the right media (the promotional strategy) to communicate the idea will facilitate distribution. The availability of services is closely related to product decisions. By nature, services consist of assistance, convenience and availability. Availability is part of the total service. For example, making a product such as health services available calls for knowledge of such retailing concepts as site location analysis and logistics management.

Developing a channel of distribution to co-ordinate and facilitate the flow of non-business products to clients is a necessary task, but in a non-business setting the traditional concept of the marketing channel may need to be reviewed. The independent wholesalers available to a business enterprise do not exist in most non-business situations. Instead, a very short channel—non-business organisation to client—is prevalent, because production and consumption of ideas and services are often simultaneous.

Making promotional decisions may be the first sign that non-business organisations are performing marketing activities. Non-business organisations use advertising and publicity to communicate with clients and the public. Direct mail remains the primary means of fund raising for social services such as those provided by the Red Cross or Oxfam. In addition to direct mail, Oxfam uses press advertising, public relations and sponsorship. Personal selling is also used by many non-business organisations, although it may be called something else. Churches and charities rely on personal selling when they send volunteers to recruit new members or request donations. The armed forces use personal selling when recruiting officers attempt to convince men and women to enlist. Special events to obtain funds, communicate ideas or provide services are sales promotion activities. Contests, entertainment and prizes offered to attract donations resemble the sales promotion activities of business enterprises. Amnesty International, for example, has held worldwide concert tours, featuring artists such as Sting and Phil Collins, to raise funds and increase public awareness of political prisoners around the world.

The number of advertising agencies that are donating their time for public service announcements (PSAs) or public information films is increasing, and the quality of print PSAs is improving noticeably. Non-profit groups are becoming more interested in the impact of advertising on their organisations, and they realise that second rate PSAs can cause a credibility loss.[44]

Although product and promotion techniques might require only slight modification when applied to non-business organisations, pricing is generally quite different and the decision-making more complex. The different pricing concepts that the non-business organisation faces include pricing in user and donor markets. There are two types of monetary pricing: *fixed* and *variable*. Membership fees, such as the amount paid to become a friend of a zoo, represent a fixed approach to pricing, whereas zoo fund raising activities that lead to donations represent a variable pricing structure.[45]

The broadest definition of price (valuation) must be used to develop non-business marketing strategies. Financial price, an exact monetary value, may or may not be charged for a non-business product. Economists recognise the giving up of alternatives as a cost. **Opportunity cost** is the value of the benefit that is given up by selecting one alternative rather than another. This traditional economic view of price means that if a non-business organisation can persuade someone to donate time to a cause or to change his or her behaviour, the alternatives given up are a cost to (or a price paid by) the individual. Volunteers who answer phones for a university counselling service or suicide hotline, for example, give up the time they could have spent studying or doing other things, as well as the income they might have earned from working in a business organisation.

For other non-business organisations, financial price is an important part of the marketing mix. Non-business organisations today are raising money by increasing the prices of their services or starting to charge for services if they have not done so before. They are using marketing research to determine for what kinds of products people will pay.[46] Pricing strategies of non-business organisations often stress public and client welfare over equalisation of costs and revenues. If additional funds are needed to cover costs, then donations, contributions or grants may be solicited.

The additional elements of the marketing mix for services are also important in non-business marketing. Physical environment quite often poses problems: subscribers and donors want an organisation that looks "professional" but not head administrative offices that look as if precious funds have been wasted on office equipment, fittings and furniture. There needs to be a compromise: an appearance of businesslike efficiency without any extravagance. Process for transactions is increasingly important: regular donors are offered direct debits, automatic payment methods and regular information packs or leaflets detailing the recipient organisation's activities, expenditures and plans. People, too, are of importance: capable administrators, sympathetic helpers, trustworthy fund raisers—they too, must project a caring yet efficient image to the client and general publics.

Controlling Non-business Marketing Activities	To control marketing activities in non-business organisations, managers use information obtained in the marketing audit to make sure that goals are achieved. Table 24.6 lists several helpful summary statistics. It should be obvious that the data in Table 24.6 are useful for both planning and control. Control is designed to identify what activities have occurred in conformity with the marketing strategy and to take corrective action where any deviations are found. The purpose of control is not only to point out errors and mistakes but to revise organisational goals and marketing objectives as necessary. One way to measure the impact of an advertisement is to audit the number of requests for information or applications, such as those received by Oxfam, the Royal Navy (see Figure 24.11), or the WWF.

Many potential contributors decide which charities to support based on the amount of money actually used for charitable purposes. Charities are more aggressively exam-

TABLE 24.6 *Examples of data useful in controlling non-business marketing activities*

1. Product mix offerings
  A. Types of product or services
  B. Number of organisations offering the product or service

2. Financial resources
  A. Types of funding used
    1. Local government grants
    2. Government grants
    3. Foundations
    4. Public appeals
    5. Fees charges
  B. Number using each type of funding
  C. Number using combinations of funding sources

3. Size
  A. Budget (cash flows)

  B. Number of employees
    1. By organisation
    2. Total industry wide
  C. Number of volunteers
    1. By organisation
    2. Total industry wide
  D. Number of customers serviced
    1. By type of service
    2. By organisation
    3. Total industry wide

4. Facilities
  A. Number and type
    1. By organisation
    2. Total industry wide
  B. Location
    1. By address
    2. By postal code

SOURCE: Adapted from Philip D. Cooper and George E. McIlvain, "Factors Influencing marketing's ability to assist non-profit organizations", John H. Summey and Ronald D. Taylor, eds., *Evolving Marketing Thought for 1980, Proceedings of the Southern Marketing Association* (19–22 November 1980), p. 315. Used by permission.

ining their own performance and effectiveness. For example, compared with other charities, the Salvation Army contributes the most of every pound it receives to the needy; its employees are basically volunteers who work for almost nothing. Charities are making internal changes to increase their effectiveness, and many are hiring professional managers and fund raisers to help with strategic planning in developing short term and long range goals, marketing strategies and promotional plans.

To control non-business marketing activities, managers must make a proper inventory of activities performed and prepare to adjust or correct deviations from standards. Knowing where and how to look for deviations and knowing what types of deviations to expect are especially important in non-business situations. Because non-business marketing activities may not be perceived as marketing, managers must clearly define what activity is being examined and how it should function.

It may be difficult to control non-business marketing activities, because it is often hard to determine whether goals are being achieved. A homeless support group that wants to inform community members of its services may not be able to find out whether it is communicating with persons who need assistance. Surveying to discover the percentage of the population that is aware of a programme to help the homeless can show whether the awareness objective has been achieved, but it fails to indicate what percentage of people without housing has been assisted. The detection and correction of deviations from standards are certainly major purposes of control, but standards must support the organisation's overall goals. Managers can refine goals by examining the results that are being achieved and analysing the ramifications of those results.

Techniques for controlling overall marketing performance must be compatible with the nature of an organisation's operations. Obviously, it is necessary to control the mar-

FIGURE 24.11 *Measuring the impact of advertising*
The Royal Navy can measure the impact of its advertising by keeping a count of the number of requests for information.

SOURCE: © British Crown. Copyright 1993. Reproduced with the permission of the Controller of Her Britannic Majesty's Stationery office.

keting budget in most non-business organisations, but budgetary control is not tied to standards of profit and loss; responsible management of funds is the objective. Central control responsibility can facilitate orderly, efficient administration and planning. For example, most universities evaluate graduating students' progress to control and improve the quality of the educational product. The audit phase typically relies on questionnaires sent to students and eventual employers. The employer completes a questionnaire to indicate the former student's progress; the graduate completes a questionnaire to indicate what additional concepts or skills were needed to perform duties. In addition, a number of faculty members may interview certain employers and former students to obtain information for control purposes. Results of the audit are used to develop corrective action if university standards have not been met. Corrective action might include an evaluation of the deficiency and a revision of the curriculum.

SUMMARY

Services are intangible dominant products that cannot be physically possessed—the result of applying human or mechanical efforts to people or objects. They are a growing part of the economy. Services have four distinguishing characteristics: intangibility, inseparability of production and consumption, perishability and heterogeneity. Because services include a diverse group of industries, classification schemes are used to help marketers analyse their products and develop the most appropriate marketing mix. Services can be viewed in terms of type of market, degree of labour intensiveness, degree of customer contact, skill of the service provider and goal of the service provider.

When developing a marketing mix for services, several aspects deserve special consideration. Regarding product, service offerings are often difficult for consumers to understand and evaluate. The tangibles associated with a service may be the only visible aspect of the service, and marketers must manage these scarce tangibles with care. Because services are often viewed in terms of the providers, service firms must carefully select, train, motivate and control employees. Service marketers are selling long term relationships as well as performance.

Promoting services is problematic because of their intangibility. Advertising should stress the tangibles associated with the service or use some relevant tangible object. Personnel in direct contact with customers should be considered an important secondary audience for advertising. Personal selling is very powerful in service firms because customers must interact with personnel; some forms of sales promotion, however, such as displays and free samples, are difficult to implement. The final principal component of the promotion mix, publicity, is vital to many service firms. Because customers value word of mouth communications, messages should attempt to stimulate or simulate word of mouth. Many professional service providers, however, are severely restricted in their use of promotional activities.

Price plays three major roles in service firms. It plays a psychological role by indicating quality and an economic role by determining revenues. Price is also a way to help smooth out fluctuations in demand.

Service distribution channels are typically direct because of simultaneous production and consumption. However, innovative approaches such as drop off points, intermediaries and electronic distribution are being developed.

The basic marketing mix is augmented for services through the addition of people, physical evidence (ambience) and the process of transaction in order to produce the "7 Ps" or the extended marketing mix.

The intangibility of the service product, together with the importance of the people component of the extended marketing mix for services, leads to significant difficulties in creating—and sustaining—a differential advantage or a competitive edge. Increasingly, strong branding and associated promotional strategy are playing more of a role in the marketing strategy for services.

Fluctuating demand is a major problem for most service firms. Marketing strategies (the marketing mix), as well as non-marketing strategies (primarily internal, employee-based actions), can be used to deal with the problem. Before attempting to undertake any such strategies, however, service marketers must understand the patterns and determinants of demand.

Non-business marketing includes marketing activities conducted by individuals and organisations to achieve goals other than normal business goals. Non-business marketing uses most of the concepts and approaches applied to business situations.

The chief beneficiary of a business enterprise is who ever owns or holds shares in the business, but the beneficiary of a non-business enterprise should be its clients, its members or its public at large. The goals of a non-business organisation reflect its unique philosophy or mission. Some non-business organisations have very controversial goals, but many organisations exist to further generally accepted social causes.

The marketing objective of non-business organisations is to obtain a desired response from a target market. Developing a non-business marketing strategy consists of defining and analysing a target market and creating and maintaining a marketing mix. In non-business marketing, the product is usually an idea or service. Distribution is involved not so much with the movement of goods as with the communication of ideas and the delivery of services, which results in a very short marketing channel. Promotion is very important in non-business marketing; personal selling, sales promotion, advertising and publicity are all used to communicate ideas and inform people about services. Price is more difficult to define in non-business marketing because of opportunity costs and the difficulty of quantifying the values exchanged.

It is important to control non-business marketing strategies. Control is designed to identify what activities have occurred in conformity with marketing strategy and to take corrective action where deviations are found. The standards against which performance is measured must support the non-business organisation's overall goals.

IMPORTANT TERMS

Consumer services	Service product quality
Business services	Complexity
Intangibility	Variability
Search qualities	Differential advantage
Experience qualities	Non-business marketing
Credence qualities	Negotiation
Inseparability	Persuasion
Perishability	Target public
Heterogeneity	Client publics
Extended marketing mix for services	General publics
Service provider	Opportunity cost

DISCUSSION AND REVIEW QUESTIONS

1. Identify and discuss the distinguishing characteristics of services. What problems do these characteristics present to marketers?
2. What is the significance of "tangibles" in service industries?
3. Analyse a house cleaning service in terms of the five classification schemes, and discuss the implications for marketing mix development.
4. How do search, experience, and credence qualities affect the way consumers view and evaluate services?
5. Discuss the role of promotion in services marketing.
6. What additional elements must be included in the marketing mix for services? Why?
7. Why is it difficult to create and maintain a differential advantage in many service businesses?
8. Analyse the demand for dry cleaning, and discuss ways to cope with fluctuating demand.
9. Compare and contrast the controversial aspects of non-business versus business marketing.
10. Relate the concepts of product, distribution, promotion and price to a marketing strategy aimed at preventing drug abuse.
11. What are the differences between clients, publics and consumers? What is the difference between a target public and a target market?
12. What is the function of control in a non-business marketing strategy?
13. Discuss the development of a marketing strategy for a university. What marketing decisions should be made in developing this strategy?

24.1 Multiplex Cinemas: The Promise of UCI

In 1991 over 107 million cinema seats were sold in Germany. In the UK the number was 91 million, a significant rise from 72 million in 1985. Now around 11 per cent of the population claim to be "regular" film goers. Despite additional television channels and transmitting hours, relaxed regulations in terms of television censorship, the introduction of more cable and satellite television services and the increasing range of competing activities for leisure time, the cinema industry is booming. In the UK, this boom can be attributed mainly to two factors: better, more attractive cinemas in more accessible locations and a regular stream of US made "blockbuster" movies.

United Cinemas International (UCI), a joint venture between MCA and Paramount, leads the development of the new generation of cinemas: the multiplex. Each multiplex has 8 to 10 screens offering a wide choice of movies for all social groups and ages. In addition to the mainstream releases there are children's clubs, late night adult clubs and showings of critically acclaimed "art" films. The luxuriously appointed auditoria have air conditioning, extra leg room, comfortable seating, wide screens and Dolby stereo Surroundsound. All multiplexes offer extensive refreshment facilities and some, such as the Milton Keynes complex "The Point", house restaurants, a nightclub and an amusement area.

These large, often out of town developments are quite different from the traditional Victorian Regal or Roxy with one screen and limited amenities. The consumer of the 1980s came to expect more comfortable, glitzy surroundings, with easy car parking and access. The boom in cinema attendances, though, has also benefited the older, traditional town centre cinemas. The Odeon and Cannon chains are reporting increased ticket sales, as are the remaining independent cinemas.

Showcase and UCI have brought a new generation of cinemas to Europe with plans for expansion throughout the EC and Scandinavia. The UCI ethos is well defined:

> It is the philosophy of United Cinemas International to offer a complete cinematic entertainment package to every member of the family, and, in so doing, become an important part of the community. Through the concept of the multiplex cinema this philosophy will be "screened" worldwide, with UCI acting as the catalyst which will bring people back to the cinema—truly recreating the magic of the movies.

From the first UK UCI in 1985, the company now operates over 30 sites. Each, whether it has 6 or 18 screens, aims to present a wide choice of films, with top picture and sound quality based on the latest technology in luxurious, clean and well maintained surroundings. High management and staff service levels, the convenience of easily accessible sites in or near shopping and leisure complexes that have easy public transport links and ample parking, and value for money complete the UCI offer.

The goal of becoming part of the community is central to UCI's marketing. Months before a new opening, UCI liaises with community leaders to discuss ways in which the cinema and the company can help with special events or activities. Links with local arts festivals, charity fund raising, sponsorship of events, special interest films for the community, exhibitions and publicity are just a few of the activities in which UCI becomes involved. Opening galas are always staged in aid of a prominent local charity and involve people from all sectors of the local community. Celebrities turn out and often a spectacular event is staged free for everyone—perhaps a fireworks display or one off Drive-In movie, an event pioneered in Europe by UCI.

UCI believes that staff training "provides the essential foundation upon which all successful organisations base their business". A smart appearance and friendly personality are essential qualities, but "attitude" is of central importance. New recruits are taught basic skills in each main area—Box Office, Refreshment, Usher, Health & Hygiene, Fire Safety and First Aid. They take written and oral exams, gaining in status and pay as they pass each stage. The very best employees reach the coveted "Top Gun" status and receive the opportunity to enter management posts. For managers training is equally rigorous and includes orientation programmes for the UCI and multiplex philosophies and courses at UCI's Manchester training department in employment law, cinema administration, discipline and grievance procedures, communication and training skills, leadership and teamwork. Ultimately, the individual cinema can be run efficiently and for the consumer's benefit only if the manager is caring and well versed in UCI's philosophy, which is reiterated in UCI's "promise":

Thank you for choosing a UCI cinema

We promise that when you visit one of our cinemas,
Our staff will be friendly, courteous and helpful.
The foyers, corridors and auditoriums will be clean and tidy.
The toilets will be clean and fully stocked.
Refreshment areas will be clean, and refreshments
    will be served hot or cold as intended.
The film presentation will be of the highest quality,
    with crystal clear pictures and top quality sound.
If for any reason your visit is not up to our promise
    or your expectations, please see one of our duty
    managers, and let us know your views.
We value your impressions as much as we do your custom.

SOURCES: *Screen Digest*, August 1990; "The cinema industry", *Key Note*, 1990; Kok Bon; "General household survey", HMSO; UCI, "Projecting a philosophy"; "Bright lights, big picture show", *Marketing Week*, 6 February 1993, p. S6; UCI information pack.

Questions for Discussion

1. What has led to the "re-birth" of the cinema industry?
2. Compared with its numerous competitors, what advantages are offered by the multiplex concept?
3. How do the core lessons of services marketing reveal themselves in UCI's trading formula?

24.2 Beefeater Soldiers On

Until the recent introduction of American bistros such as TGI Friday's and Old Orleans, the brewery owned steak house chains dominated the mass market restaurant sector. With over 270 restaurants, Whitbread's Beefeater chain is still the market leader in this sector, followed by Toby, Porterhouse and Harvester. Beefeaters, introduced in 1974, numbered 50 by 1981. Now there are Beefeater restaurants throughout the UK and also in Germany.

The familiar red, yellow and black Tower of London Beefeater style uniforms, red decor and steak menus immediately identify the chain. Whitbread has placed great emphasis on maintaining a similar, guaranteed level of product, service and satisfaction in all Beefeater restaurants. Its goal is to offer tasty, reliable food together with efficient service, a friendly atmosphere, and value for money prices. As the table shows, the traditional restaurant chains face increasing competition from rival restaurants and the growing rate of competing catering establishments. To remain successful, the company cannot rely on its heritage alone.

MILLIONS OF MEALS SERVED UK, 1992

Hotels	500
Restaurants	340
Pubs	1,250
Fast food chains	470
Travel	400
Cafés/Take aways	1,590
Clubs/Entertainment facilities	980

Beefeater's success was attributed in the industry to its ability to target specific customer groups, its staff training and its regular modification and updating of its branding and trading concept. The Beefeater Care Programme stresses the importance of having helpful, friendly staff who are both competent and trustworthy. The Care Programme intends to maintain a "caring" culture throughout the Beefeater chain. In recent years, Beefeater restaurants have been refurbished in softer, informal, friendly colours to make the diner's experience more relaxing and enjoyable. The menus have moved away from beef steaks and now offer a greater variety of value for money meat, fish, pasta and vegetarian dishes to keep abreast of changing eating habits.

With this so called software for success, Beefeater and Whitbread expect to set—and maintain—operating and service standards, so that direct competitors are continually striving to catch up with Beefeater. Whitbread recognises the importance of pleasing its customers, whether in its pubs, in its Beefeater or TGI Friday's restaurants, or in its hotels and country clubs. The company uses its marketing mix to great effect but is conscious of the importance of its people (customers and employees), the atmosphere and appearance of its facilities, and the ease and enjoyment of the consumption of its products. By clearly defining an extended marketing mix for its service businesses and rigorously controlling standards, Whitbread hopes to gain an advantage over its competitors in its markets.

SOURCES: Marketpower Estimates, 1992; Kok Bon; Beefeater promotional literature; "Eating out", Harvest, 1992; "Leisure intelligence", Mintel, 1993; "European consumer catering", *Euromonitor*, 1992; Suzanne Bidlake, "Beefeater serves up Christmas drinks", *Marketing*, 10 December 1992, p. 8.

Questions for Discussion

1. Why does Whitbread emphasise its staff training?
2. How do the additional elements of the extended marketing mix help Beefeater gain an advantage over its competitors?

25 INTERNATIONAL MARKETING

Objectives

To define the nature of international marketing

To understand the importance of international marketing intelligence

To recognise the impact of environmental forces on international marketing efforts

To become aware of regional trade alliances and markets

To examine the potential of marketing mix standardisation among nations

To describe adaptation of the international marketing mix when standardisation is impossible

To look at ways of becoming involved in international marketing activities

*T*he chocolate confectionery business of Swiss based Jacob Suchard represents 58 per cent of its Sw. fr. 6 billion turnover. The company has been gearing up for global markets since the late 1960s, by developing global brands, such as Milka and Toblerone, and undertaking a number of strategically important acquisitions. In taking over other European confectionery companies, such as Du Lac (Italian) and Pavlides (Greek), Suchard has sought established distribution and retail channels in areas where it was not traditionally strong. This has helped the company to develop its own global brands alongside smaller, local products. The acquisition of the West German cocoa trader Van Houten in 1987 has given Suchard closer control over its raw materials.

It seems likely that, at the European level, global brands will be assisted by the single market allowing unrestricted flow of goods between EC countries. Companies with pan-European brands, including Suchard, will benefit from the advertising opportunities offered by European satellites, which are less likely to be exploited by national brands. It is probable that over several years preferences and eating habits within Europe will gradually converge as communication of this type increases. Companies such as Suchard have evolved from operating with a domestic market to being global leaders. In so doing, these international operators must seek additional marketing intelligence and data, re-think strategies and modify their marketing mixes. ∎

SOURCES: *Le Journal de Genève,* 29 April 1989, p. 9; *24 Ore* (Italian), 15 April 1987, p. 15; *Marketing Week,* 8 July 1988, p. 19; Michael Labrou, "Ten marketing cases", MBA dissertation, University of Warwick, 1989.

International marketing refers to marketing activities performed across national boundaries.[1] In many cases, serving a foreign target market requires more than minor adjustments of marketing strategies.

This chapter looks closely at the unique features of international marketing and at the marketing mix adjustments businesses make when they cross national boundaries. Beginning by examining companies' level of commitment to and degree of involvement in international marketing, the chapter then considers the importance of international marketing intelligence when a firm is moving beyond its domestic market. Next it focuses on the need to understand various environmental forces in international markets and discusses several regional alliances and markets. The chapter also analyses marketing mix standardisation and adaptation and concludes by describing a number of ways to become involved in international marketing.

Involvement in International Marketing

Before international marketing could achieve its current level of importance, enterprises with the necessary resources had to develop an interest in expanding their businesses beyond national boundaries. Once interested, marketers engage in international marketing activities at several levels of involvement. Regardless of the level of involvement, however, they must choose either to customise their marketing strategies for different regions of the world or to standardise their marketing strategies for the entire world.

Multinational Involvement

The level of involvement in international marketing covers a wide spectrum, as shown in Figure 25.1. Casual or accidental exporting is the lowest level of commitment. For example, the products of a small medical supplies manufacturer might occasionally be purchased by hospitals or clinics in nearby countries; its products might also be purchased by other countries through an export agent. Active exporting concentrates on selling activities to gain foreign market acceptance of existing products. Full scale international marketing involvement means that top management recognises the impor-

Casual or accidental exporting	Active exporting	Full scale international marketing involvement	Globalisation of markets
Occasional, unsolicited foreign orders are received. There is no real commitment to international marketing.	This is an attempt to create sales without significant changes in the firm's products and overall operations. An active effort to find foreign markets for existing products is most typical.	Markets across national boundaries are a consideration in the marketing strategy. International marketing activities are seen as a part of overall planning.	Companies try to operate as if the world were one large market, ignoring regional and national differences.

National or domestic orientation ⟵——————————————⟶ Global orientation

FIGURE 25.1 *Levels of involvement in international marketing*

SOURCE: Excerpts from *International Marketing,* Third Edition by Vern Terpstra, copyright © 1983 by The Dryden Press, reprinted by permission of the publisher.

tance of developing international marketing strategies to achieve the firm's goals. Globalisation of markets requires total commitment to international marketing; it embodies the view that the world is a single market.

Globalisation Versus Customisation of Marketing Strategies

Only full scale international marketing involvement and globalisation of markets represent a full integration of international marketing into strategic market planning. Traditional full scale international marketing involvement is based on products customised according to cultural, regional and national differences. In full scale international marketing, marketing strategies are developed to serve specific target markets. From a practical standpoint, this means that to standardise the marketing mix, the strategy needs to group countries by social, cultural, technological, political and economic similarities.

In contrast, **globalisation** involves developing marketing strategies as though the entire world (or regions of it) were a single entity; a globalised firm markets standardised products in the same way everywhere.[2] For many years, organisations have attempted to globalise the marketing mix as much as possible by employing standardised products, promotion campaigns, prices and distribution channels for all markets. The economic and competitive pay offs for globalised marketing strategies are certainly great. Brand name, product characteristics, packaging and labelling are among the easiest marketing mix variables to standardise; media allocation, retail outlets and price may be more difficult. In the end, the degree of similarity among the various environmental and market conditions determines the feasibility of globalisation.

Some companies have moved from customising or standardising products for a particular region of the world to offering globally standardised products that are advanced, functional, reliable and low in price.[3] Nike, for example, provides a standardised product worldwide. As stated earlier, a firm committed to globalisation develops marketing strategies as if the entire world (or major regions of it) were a single entity. Examples of globalised products are electrical equipment, videos, films, soft drinks, rock music, cosmetics and toothpaste. Sony televisions, Levi jeans and UK confectionery brands seem to make annual gains in the world market. Even McDonald's, Pizza Hut and Kentucky Fried Chicken restaurants seem to be widely accepted in markets throughout the world. Attempts are now being made to globalise industrial products—such as computers, robots and carbon filters—and professional engineering products—such as earthmoving equipment and communications equipment. But it remains questionable whether the promotion, pricing and distribution of these products can also be standardised.

Debate about the feasibility of globalised marketing strategies has continued since the birth of the idea in the 1960s. Surprisingly, questions about standardised advertising policies are the leading concern. However, it should be remembered that there are degrees of both customisation and globalisation. Neither strategy is implemented in its pure form.[4] The debate will doubtless continue over which products, if any, can be fully globalised. Some firms, such as Black & Decker and Coca-Cola (see Figure 25.2) have adopted globalised marketing strategies. For some products—such as soft drinks—a global marketing strategy, including advertising, seems to work well while for other products—such as beer—strategies must accommodate local, regional and national differences.[5]

INTERNATIONAL MARKETING INTELLIGENCE

Despite the debate over globalisation of markets, most firms perceive international markets as differing in some ways from domestic markets. Analyses of international

FIGURE 25.2
Example of globalisation
Coca-Cola offers globally
standardised products.

SOURCE: "Coca-Cola" and the
Dynamic Ribbon device are
registered trademarks of the
Coca-Cola Company.

markets and possible marketing efforts can be based on many dimensions. Table 25.1 lists the types of information that international marketers need.

Gathering secondary data (see Table 25.2) should be the first step in analysing a foreign market. Sources of information include government publications, financial services firms, international organisations such as the United Nations, foreign governments, and international trade organisations. UK firms seeking to market their products in Russia, for example, can obtain information about Russian markets and regulations from the Department of Trade and Industry (DTI), the Russian Chamber of Commerce and Industry, the Russian trade organisation Amtorg and numerous other organisations. Depending on the source, however, secondary data can be misleading. The reliability, validity and comparability of data from some countries are often problematic.

To overcome these shortcomings, marketers may need primary data to understand consumers' buying behaviour in the country under investigation. Marketers may have to adjust their techniques of collecting primary data for foreign markets. Attitudes towards privacy, unwillingness to be interviewed, language differences and low literacy rates can be serious research obstacles. In a bi-cultural country such as Canada, a national questionnaire that uses identical questions cannot be used because of the cultural and language differences. In many areas of Africa, where the literacy rate is low, self-administered questionnaires would never work.

Primary research should uncover significant cultural characteristics before a product is launched so that the marketing strategy is appropriate for the target market. It

TABLE 25.1 *Information needed for international marketing analyses*

PRELIMINARY SCREENING	ANALYSIS OF INDUSTRY MARKET POTENTIAL	ANALYSIS OF COMPANY SALES POTENTIAL
Demographic/Physical Environment Population size, growth, density Urban and rural distribution Climate and weather variations Shipping distance Product significant demographics Physical distribution and communications network Natural resources **Political Environment** System of government Political stability and continuity Ideological orientation Government in business Government in communications Attitudes towards foreign business (trade restrictions, tariffs, non-tariff barriers, bilateral trade agreements) National economic and developmental priorities **Economic Environment** Overall level of development Economic growth: GNP, industrial sector Role of foreign trade in economy Currency, inflation rate, availability, controls, stability of exchange rate Balance of payments Per capita income and distribution Disposable income and expenditure patterns **Social/Cultural Environment** Literacy rate, educational level Existence of middle class Similarities and differences in relation to home market Language and other cultural considerations	**Market Access** Limitations on trade: tariff levels, quotas Documentation and import regulations Local standards, practices, and other non-tariff barriers Patents and trade marks Preferential treaties Legal considerations: investment, taxation, repatriation, employment, code of laws **Product Potential** Customer needs and desires Local production, imports, consumption Exposure to and acceptance of product Availability of linking products Industry specific key indicators of demand Attitudes towards products of foreign origin Competitive offerings Availability of intermediaries Regional and local transport facilities Availability of manpower Conditions for local manufacture	**Sales Volume Forecasting** Size and concentration of customer segments Projected consumption statistics Competitive pressures Expectations of local distributors/agents **Landed Cost** Costing method for exports Domestic distribution costs International freight insurance Cost of product modification **Cost of Internal distribution** Tariffs and duties Value Added Tax Local packaging and assembly Margins/commission allowed for the trade Local distribution and inventory costs Promotional expenditures **Other Determinants of Profitability** Going price levels Competitive strengths and weaknesses Credit practices Current and projected exchange rates

SOURCE: Adapted from S. Tamer Cavusgil, "Guidelines for export market research", *Business Horizons,* November-December 1985, pp.30–1. Used by permission.

TABLE 25.2 *Sources of secondary information for international marketing*

TYPE OF INFORMATION	SOURCES	OTHER SOURCES
Foreign market information	Foreign economic trends Overseas business reports International economic indicators Foreign governments (e.g. US Department of Commerce) DTI EC (Eurostat, etc.)	*Financial Times* surveys Business International Dun & Bradstreet International Chase World Information Corp. International Trade Reporter Accounting and stock market firms Foreign trade organisations Economist Intelligence Unit
Export marketing research	Country market sectoral surveys Global market surveys International marketing research	Marketing research firms Advertising agencies Publishing companies Trade associations
International statistics	Export statistics profile Customer service statistics	Predicasts Foreign brokerage houses United Nations International Monetary Fund OECD, EC, GATT
Overseas representatives	Customised export mailing list World trader data reports Agent/distributor service	Banks International Chambers of Commerce Consulting firms Direct telephone contact
Sales leads	Trade opportunities programme Strategic and industrial product sales group Major export projects programme Export information reference room	Banks International Chambers of Commerce Consulting firms Development agencies
Reference data on foreign markets	World trader data reports	Banks International Chambers of Commerce Consulting firms Development agencies Corporate information databases

SOURCES: S. Tamer Cavusgil, "Guidelines for export market research", *Business Horizons,* November-December 1985, p. 32; and Leonard M. Fuld, "How to gather foreign intelligence without leaving home", *Market News,* 4 January 1988, pp. 24, 47. Data used by permission.

may be necessary to investigate basic patterns of social behaviour, values and attitudes to plan a final marketing strategy. Overall, the cost of obtaining such information may be higher than the cost of domestic research; the reasons include the large number of foreign markets to be investigated, the distance between the marketer and the foreign market, unfamiliar cultural and marketing practices, language differences and the scarcity or unreliability of published statistics.[6]

After analysing secondary and primary data, marketers should plan a marketing strategy. Finally, after market entry, review and control will result in decisions to withdraw from the foreign market, to continue to expand operations or to consider additional foreign markets.

ENVIRONMENTAL FORCES IN INTERNATIONAL MARKETS

A detailed analysis of the environment is essential before a company enters a foreign market. If a marketing strategy is to be effective across national borders, the complexities of all the environments involved must be understood. This section examines how the cultural, social and green, economic, political and legal, and technological forces of the marketing environment in different countries vary.

Cultural Forces

Chapter 3 defined culture as the concepts, values and tangible items, such as tools, buildings and foods, that make up a particular society. Culture is passed on from one generation to another; in a way, it is the blueprint for acceptable behaviour in a given society. When products are introduced into one nation from another, acceptance is far more likely if there are similarities between the two cultures.

The connotations associated with body motions, greetings, colours, numbers, and shapes, sizes and symbols vary considerably across cultures (Table 25.3 gives a few examples). For multinational marketers, these cultural differences have implications for product development, personal selling, advertising, packaging and pricing. For example, the illustration of feet is regarded as despicable in Thailand. An international marketer must also know a country's customs regarding male-female social interaction. In Italy it is unacceptable for a salesman to call on a woman if her husband is not at home. In Thailand certain Listerine television commericals that portrayed boy-girl romantic relationships were unacceptable.

Product adoption and use are also influenced by consumers' perceptions of other countries. When consumers are generally unfamiliar with products from another country, their perceptions of the country itself affect their attitude towards and adoption of the products. If a country has a reputation for producing quality products, and therefore has a positive image in consumers' minds, marketers from that country will want to make the country of origin well known. Conversely, marketers may want to disassociate themselves from a particular country. Because American cars have not been viewed by the world as being quality products, Chrysler, for example, may want to advertise in Japan that Colt is "not another American compact".[7]

Culture may also affect marketing negotiations and decision-making behaviour on the part of marketers, industrial buyers and other executives. Research has shown that when marketers use a problem solving approach—that is, gain information about a particular client's needs and tailor products or services to meet those needs—it leads to increased customer satisfaction in marketing negotiations in France, Germany, the United Kingdom and the United States. However, the attractiveness of the salesperson and his or her similarity to the customer increase the levels of satisfaction only for Americans. Furthermore, marketing negotiations proceed differently in the various cultures, and the role and status of the seller are more important in both the UK and France.[8]

Social Forces

Marketing activities are primarily social in purpose; therefore they are structured by the institutions of family, religion, education, health and recreation (see Figure 25.3). For example, in the UK, where listening to music on hi-fi systems is a common form of relaxation, Japanese products have a large target market. In every nation, these social

TABLE 25.3 *Sampling of cultural variations*

COUNTRY/ REGION	BODY MOTIONS	GREETINGS	COLOURS	NUMBERS	SHAPES, SIZES, SYMBOLS
Japan	Pointing to one's own chest with a forefinger indicates one wants a bath. A forefinger to the nose indicates "me".	Bowing is the traditional form of greeting.	Positive colours are in muted shades. Combinations of black, dark grey, and white have negative overtones.	Positive numbers are 1, 3, 5, 8. Negative numbers are 4, 9.	Pine, bamboo or plum patterns are positive. Cultural shapes such as Buddha shaped jars should be avoided.
India	Kissing is considered offensive and is not usually seen on television, in films or in public places.	The palms of the hands touch and the head is nodded for greeting. It is considered rude to touch or shake hands with a woman.	Positive colours are bold such as green, red, yellow or orange. Negative colours are black and white if they appear in relation to weddings.	To create brand awareness, numbers are often used as a brand name.	Animals such as parrots, elephants, tigers or cheetahs are often used as brand names or on packaging. Sexually explicit symbols are avoided.
Europe	When counting on one's fingers, "one" is often indicated by thumb, "two" by thumb and forefinger.	It is acceptable to send flowers in thanks for a dinner invitation, but not roses (for sweethearts) or chrysanthemums (for funerals).	Generally, white and blue are considered positive. Black often has negative overtones.	The numbers 3 or 7 are usually positive. 13 is a negative number.	Circles are symbols of perfection. Hearts are considered favourably at Christmas time.
Latin America	General arm gestures are used for emphasis.	The traditional greeting is a hearty embrace and slap on the back.	Popular colours are generally bright or bold yellow, red, blue or green.	Generally, 7 is a positive number. Negative numbers are 13, 14.	Respect religious symbols. Avoid national symbols such as flag colours.
Middle East	The raised eyebrow facial expression indicates "yes".	The word "no" must be mentioned three times before it is accepted.	Positive colours are brown, black, dark blues and reds. Pink, violets and yellows are not favoured.	Positive numbers are 3, 5, 7, 9; 13, 15 are negative.	Round or square shapes are acceptable. Symbols of six pointed star, raised thumb or Koranic sayings are avoided.

SOURCE: James C. Simmons, "A matter of interpretation", *American Way,* April 1983, pp. 106–111; and "Adapting export packaging to cultural differences", *Business America,* 3 December 1979, pp. 3–7.

FIGURE 25.3

The societal aspects of international marketing
Widespread acceptance of relaxing to music enables Philips to produce a range of advertisements with relevance in many markets.

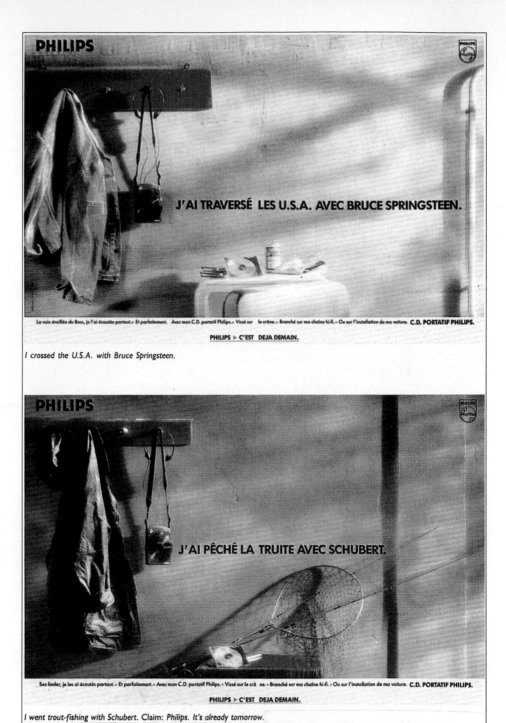

I crossed the U.S.A. with Bruce Springsteen.

I went trout-fishing with Schubert. Claim: Philips. It's already tomorrow.

SOURCE: © Philips Electronics N.V.

institutions can be identified. By finding major deviations in institutions among countries, marketers can gain insights into the adaptation of a marketing strategy. Although American football is a popular sport in the United States and a major opportunity for many television advertisers, soccer is the most popular television sport in Europe. Yet football hooliganism caused major advertisers in the United Kingdom to have second thoughts about supporting such events with vast sums spent on advertising.[9] The role of children in the family and a society's overall view of children also influence marketing activities. For example, the use of cute, cereal loving children in advertising for Kellogg's is illegal in France. In the Netherlands, children are banned from appearing in advertisements for sweets, and confectionery manufacturers are required to place a little toothbrush symbol at the end of each confectionery spot.[10]

Economic Forces

Economic differences dictate many of the adjustments that must be made in marketing abroad. The most prominent adjustments are caused by differences in standards of living, availability of credit, discretionary buying power, income distribution, national resources and conditions that affect transport.

Gross domestic product (GDP) is the total value of all goods and services produced by a country's income. A comparison of GDP for Europe, America and Japan (see Table 25.4) shows that the United States has the largest gross domestic product in the world. However, in order to attain a measure of standard of living, it is necessary to

TABLE 25.4 *Growth of real GDP in some OECD countries*

	1988	1989	1990	1991	FORECAST 1992	FORECAST 1993
United States	4.5	2.5	1.0	−0.7	2.1	3.6
Canada	4.4	2.5	0.5	−1.5	2.3	4.3
Japan	6.2	4.8	5.2	4.5	1.8	3.1
Australia	3.5	4.4	1.7	−1.9	2.6	3.7
Germany, FR	3.7	3.8	4.5	3.1	1.3	2.3
France	4.2	4.1	2.2	1.3	2.0	2.6
Italy	4.1	2.9	2.2	1.4	1.5	2.1
UK	4.2	2.3	1.0	−2.2	0.4	2.6
Spain	5.1	4.7	3.7	2.4	2.6	3.2
Netherlands	2.7	4.2	3.9	2.0	1.2	2.1
Sweden	2.3	2.4	0.5	−1.2	0.3	0.9
Switzerland	2.9	3.9	2.2	−0.5	0.9	2.0
Belgium	4.6	3.8	3.7	1.5	1.6	2.3
Austria	3.9	3.7	4.6	3.0	2.1	2.5
Denmark	0.9	0.8	1.7	1.0	2.1	2.9
Finland	5.4	5.4	0.4	−6.1	−1.3	3.3
Norway	−0.5	0.4	1.8	1.9	2.0	1.9
Greece	4.1	3.5	−0.1	1.5	1.4	2.1
Portugal	4.0	5.2	4.2	2.2	2.8	3.3
Ireland	1.4	5.6	8.3	2.3	2.4	3.1
OECD Total	**6.1**	**3.3**	**2.5**	**1.0**	**1.8**	**3.0**

SOURCE: *OECD Economic Outlook*, July 1992. Used with permission.
Note: Percentage changes from previous year.

FIGURE 25.4

Impact of trade barriers on international marketing As barriers to trade come down, opportunities are presented for some surprising enterprises.

You haven't seen Ireland until you've seen Killarney.

the world's No. 1...

AerRianta **Duty Free** at Shannon

SOURCE: Courtesy of Shannon Duty Free Shop.

divide this figure by the size of the population. In this way it is possible to gain insight into the level of discretionary income or "buying power" of individual consumers. This kind of knowledge about aggregate GDP, credit and the distribution of income provides general insights into market potential.

Opportunities for international marketers are certainly not limited to countries with the highest incomes. Some nations are progressing at a markedly faster rate than they were even a few years ago; and these countries—especially in Latin America, Africa, eastern Europe and the Middle East—have great market potential for specific products. However, marketers must first understand the political and legal environment before they can convert buying power into actual demand for specific products.

Political and Legal Forces

A country's political system, national laws, regulatory bodies, national pressure groups and courts all have great impact on international marketing. A government's policies towards public and private enterprise, consumers and foreign firms influence marketing across national boundaries. For example, the Japanese have established many barriers to imports into their country. Even though they are reducing the tariffs on thousands of items, many non-tariff barriers still make it difficult for other companies to export their products to Japan.[11] Just a few years ago, companies exporting electronic equipment to Japan had to wait for the Japanese government to inspect each item. A government's attitude towards co-operation with importers has a direct impact on the economic feasibility of exporting to that country. As barriers to trade come down, opportunities are presented (see Figure 25.4).

Differences in political and government ethical standards are enormous. The use of pay offs and bribes is deeply entrenched in many governments, while in others direct involvement in pay offs and bribes is prohibited. European companies that do not engage in such practices may have a hard time competing with foreign firms that do. Some businesses that refuse to make pay offs are forced to hire local consultants, public relations firms or advertising agencies—resulting in indirect pay offs. The ultimate decision about whether to give small tips or gifts where they are customary must be based on a company's code of ethics.

Technological Forces   Much of the marketing technology used in Europe and other industrialised regions of the world may be ill suited for developing countries. For example, advertising on television or through direct mail campaigns may be difficult in countries that lack up to date broadcasting and postal services. None the less, many countries—particularly China, South Korea, Mexico and the countries of the former Soviet Union—want to engage in international trade, often through partnerships with American, European and Japanese firms, so that they can gain valuable industrial and agricultural technology. However, in certain cases companies need permission to export goods. For example, in the UK and other EC countries, government approval is needed before defence equipment can be exported.

REGIONAL TRADE ALLIANCES AND MARKETS

Although some firms are beginning to view the world as one huge market-place, various regional trade alliances and specific markets may create difficulties or opportunities for companies engaging in international marketing. This section examines several regional trade alliances and changing markets, including the 1992 unification of Europe, the Pacific Rim markets, changing conditions in eastern Europe and the former Soviet Union, and the United States and Canada trade pact.

Europe 1992 Unification and the "European" Consumer   The unification of Europe in 1992 permits virtually free trade among the 12 member nations of the European Community (EC). Although Germany, France, Italy, the United Kingdom, Spain, the Netherlands, Belgium, Denmark, Greece, Portugal, Ireland and Luxembourg currently exist as separate markets, in 1992 they technically merged into the largest single market in the world, with more than 320 million consumers. The unification will ultimately allow marketers to develop one standardised product for all 12 nations instead of customising products to satisfy the regulations and restrictions of each country.[12] Before completely free trade can be established, a large number of barriers still need to be overcome. Some businesspeople and economists believe that because of inconsistencies between the administrations of member states—for example, VAT levels, tax systems and laws—1992 was only a symbolic date. In reality, there is likely to be continued discussion between member states over outstanding issues of this type, and it will be many years before the EC is really one deregulated market.[13]

Although the 12 nations of the EC will essentially function as one large market and consumers in the EC are likely to become more homogeneous in their needs and wants, marketers must be aware that cultural and social differences among the 12 member nations may require modifications in the marketing mix for consumers in each nation. Some researchers believe that eventually, following the 1992 unification, it will be possible to segment the European Community into six markets on the basis of cultural, geographic, demographic and economic variables. The six markets would be (1) the United Kingdom and Ireland; (2) Central and Northern France, Southern

Belgium, Central Germany and Luxembourg; (3) Spain and Portugal; (4) Southern Germany, Northern Italy and South Eastern France; (5) Greece and Southern Italy; and (6) Denmark, Northern Germany, the Netherlands and Northern Belgium.[14] Differences in taste and preferences among these markets are significant for international marketers. For example, the British prefer front loading washing machines; the French prefer top loading ones. Consumers in Spain eat far more poultry products than Germans do.[15] Preference differences may exist even within the same country, depending on the geographic region. Thus international marketing intelligence efforts are likely to remain very important in determining European consumer's needs and in developing marketing mixes that will satisfy those needs. It is also clear that EC organisations will have to face up to considerable changes in the way they operate. In sectors where there is little within-EC trade and many manufacturers, restructuring will be the most radical. For pharmaceutical companies, the prospects include harmonisation of prices and formulations and likely job losses. In this, as in other sectors, much collaborative activity through mergers and acquisitions is likely to occur.

Pacific Rim Nations

Companies of the Pacific Rim nations—Japan, China, South Korea, Taiwan, Singapore, Hong Kong, the Philippines, Malaysia, Indonesia, Australia and Indochina—have become increasingly competitive and sophisticated in their marketing efforts in the last three decades. The Japanese in particular have made tremendous inroads into world consumer markets for cars, motorcycles, watches, cameras and audio and video equipment. Products from Sony, Sanyo, Toyota, Mitsubishi, Canon, Suzuki and others are sold all over the world and have set standards of quality by which other products are often judged. Managers from other nations study and imitate Japan's highly efficient management and manufacturing techniques. However, Japan's marketing muscle has not escaped criticism. Europe and the United States rely on Japan's informal trade restraints on its exports of cars, textiles, steel, audio and video consumer products. There has also been considerable international criticism of Japan's reluctance to accept imports from other nations.

South Korea has become very successful in world markets with familiar brands such as Samsung, Daewoo and Hyundai. But even before those companies became household names, their products achieved strong success under company labels such as RCA and JC Penney, for example, in America. Korean companies are now taking market share away from Japanese companies in the world markets for video cassette recorders, colour televisions and computers, despite the fact that the Korean market for these products is limited. In Canada, the Hyundai Excel overtook Japan's Honda in just 18 months.[16] Faced with EC quotas, Hyundai is taking on Japanese and American manufacturers for a piece of the US market.

Because of its drive towards modernisation, the People's Republic of China was thought to have great market potential and opportunities for joint venture projects. However, limited consumer demand and political instability dimmed those prospects. In particular, a 1989 student pro-democracy uprising in Beijing reversed several years of business progress in China. Given the political instability, many foreign companies reduced their presence in China or left altogether; other firms became more cautious in their relations with China.[17]

Less visible Pacific Rim regions, such as Singapore, Taiwan and Hong Kong, are major manufacturing and financial centres. Singapore also has large world markets for pharmaceutical and rubber goods. Hong Kong, however, faces an uncertain future after it moves from British control to control by the People's Republic of China in 1997. Taiwan may have the most promising future of all the Pacific Rim nations. It has a strong local economy and has lowered many import barriers, sending imports up by 42 per cent, to nearly £35 billion in 1988. Taiwan is beginning to privatise state run banks and is also opening its markets to foreign firms. Some analysts believe that it may replace Hong Kong as a regional financial power centre when Hong Kong reverts to Chinese control.[18] Firms from Thailand and Malaysia are also blossoming, carving out niches in the world markets for a variety of products, from toys to car parts.[19]

Changing Relations with Eastern Europe and the CIS

Part of the former Soviet Union—the Commonwealth of Independent States (CIS)—and other eastern European nations (Poland, Hungary, the former East Germany, the former Yugoslavia, Czechoslovakia, Romania and Bulgaria), following a policy of *perestroika,* are experiencing great political and economic changes. The Communist Party's centrally planned economies are being replaced by democratic institutions in most of these countries. In fact, changes in the eastern bloc countries have been the fastest breaking developments in international marketing. As a result, they are becoming increasingly market orientated. These countries are very different in terms of technology, infrastructure, foreign investment laws and speed of change.[20]

The former Soviet leader Mikhail Gorbachev implemented widespread measures to improve the economic environment of the Soviet Union, measures aimed primarily at making his nation more responsive to the forces of supply and demand. For instance, government owned businesses were granted more autonomy to make marketing decisions.[21] Other economic reform plans included replacing the Soviet Union's system of state owned enterprises and farms with independent businesses leased or owned by workers, shareholders, co-operatives and joint ventures; overhauling the system of centrally determined prices; and setting free market prices for many products. For the first time, businesses from the West began to advertise and sell their products. *The Economist* was the first English billboard advertisement in May 1989. Although Boris Yeltsin and Mikhail Gorbachev's other successors have faced severe political, civil and economic difficulties, the move towards a market economy, with greater imports and exports, continues.

The reformers of the Soviet, Polish and Hungarian economies want to reduce trade restrictions on imports and offer incentives to encourage exports to and investment in their countries.[22] One such move involved seven UK companies, which formed a consortium to look at opportunities in the personal care and food and drink areas of the Russian market. So far, the initiative has led to a number of developments, including joint venture agreements between Tambrands and the Ukrainian ministry of public health to sell tampons to a market of 70 million women in and between Allied Lyons and the Russian ministry of trade to market 8 million gallons of ice cream a year under the Baskin-Robbins label.[23] Because of these economic and political reforms, productivity in eastern Europe and the former Soviet Union is expected to increase as workers are given more incentives and control, raising the possibility that eastern Europe will eventually become an economic powerhouse rivalling the United States and Japan. There is also speculation that some of the eastern European nations will ultimately join the European Community, allowing freer trade across all European borders.[24] In free elections, East Germany voted to re-unify with West Germany. Although there have been initial teething problems and some social unrest, the unification of Germany is likely to have a great impact on the European Community and world economy.

Because of the changing economic conditions in the eastern bloc and the former Soviet Union, there are many marketing opportunities in these countries for western European, American and Asian firms. Siemens, Federal Express, Procter & Gamble and Occidental Petroleum are among the many companies doing business in eastern Europe. The countries of eastern Europe are building new hotels and improving telephone, airline and land transport services to facilitate international trade, as well as for the benefit of their citizens.[25] Marketing Insight 25.1 highlights the actions taken by

AS THE BERLIN WALL CRUMBLED, MARKETING OPPORTUNITIES EMERGED

For nearly 30 years, the concrete Berlin Wall loomed as both a physical barrier and a symbol of the political, social and economic differences between democratic West Germany and communist East Germany. It had been erected in August 1961 to stop a massive westward flow of refugees. With the overthrow of communist regimes throughout Eastern Europe in 1989, the wall became just a physical barrier between East and West Germans. While residents and souvenir seekers chiselled away at the wall itself, the symbolic implications of the fall of the wall resulted in new marketing opportunities.

Less than a month after the dramatic decision was made to open the wall, PepsiCo, AT&T and Quintessence, which makes Jovan fragrances, filmed advertisements at the site, designed first to make an emotional appeal and second to stimulate product sales. The Quintessence advertisement depicted the reunion of a family split by the wall. An East German grandfather, laden with gifts, dropped a teddy bear while crossing through a newly opened gate in the wall. It was returned by a guard, and a "peace on earth" message flashed on the screen, followed by a list of Quintessence products. Pepsi's advertisement showed a child giving a border guard a rose with Handel's "Hallelujah Chorus" playing in the background. The AT&T advertisements focused on communication between family and friends previously separated by the wall.

The rapidly changing political climate in Europe has opened more than just the Berlin Wall for entrepreneurs willing to invest in ventures. Although such investments can be risky and the obstacles to trade are many, some companies are overcoming the obstacles and reaching trade agreements. For example, UK newspapers bought shares in German newspaper and publishing businesses, and some set up satellite printing operations for foreign editions. The late Robert Maxwell targeted Berliner Verlag GmbH. The company—which publishes two daily newspapers and a number of magazines—is owned by the political party PDS, the new name for the SED party which formerly held power in East Germany. A trade newsletter publisher is producing a newsletter about trade with eastern Europeans. One entrepreneur compared the opportunities in eastern Europe to the Gold Rush days of America. Although there is a chance to strike it rich, many companies may find only fool's gold.

SOURCES: "A batch of really off-the-wall acts", *US News & World Report,* 18 December 1989, pp. 11–12; "Colas toast crumbling of Berlin Wall", *Adweek,* 11 December 1989, p. 61; Marc Fisher, "East Germany to tear down Berlin Wall", *Commercial Appeal,* 3 January 1990, pp. A1, A10; Thomas R. King, "Berlin Wall lands role in 3 US spots", *Wall Street Journal,* 5 December 1989, p. B6; and "World news", *Marketing,* 24 May 1990, p. 4.

some firms in response to the fall of the Berlin Wall in 1989. However, because of the swift and uncontrolled nature of the changes taking place in eastern Europe and the former Soviet Union, firms considering marketing their products in these countries must carefully monitor events and proceed cautiously.

United States and Canada Trade Pact

In 1989 the United States and Canada signed the Free Trade Agreement (FTA), which essentially merged the American and Canadian markets and formed the largest free trade zone in the world. The agreement calls for the elimination of most tariffs and other trade restrictions over a 10-year period so that goods and services can flow more easily each way across the US—Canadian border. Trade between the United States and Canada already totals more than £100 billion annually, and the FTA will make trade and investment across the border even "more profitable, less cumbersome, and more secure".[26]

Although passage of the trade pact was controversial and required lengthy negotiations, most experts believe that it will enable firms in both countries to compete more successfully against Asian and European rivals. When all the provisions are in effect in the year 2000, the treaty will enlarge Canada's markets tenfold, and the United States will have unrestricted access to a market the size of California. Canadians are expected to ship more minerals, livestock and forest products to the United States; American investments in Canada and sales of paper goods are likely to increase. Some experts estimate that the gross national products of the two countries could rise by 1 to 5 per cent, as keener competition spurs companies on both sides to greater efficiency and productivity.[27] The tariff reductions mandated by the FTA will especially benefit smaller American and Canadian firms because they will allow them to create more efficient economies of scale for the unified market and to earn higher profit margins.[28]

STRATEGIC ADAPTATION OF MARKETING MIXES

Once a company determines overseas market potential and understands the foreign environment, it develops and adapts its marketing mix(es). Creating and maintaining the marketing mix is the final step in developing the international marketing strategy. Only if foreign marketing opportunities justify the risk will a company go to the expense of adapting the marketing mix. Of course, in some situations new products are developed for a specific country. In these cases, there is no existing marketing mix and no extra expense to consider in serving the foreign target market.

Product and Promotion

As Figure 25.5 shows, there are five possible strategies for adapting product and promotion across national boundaries: (1) keep product and promotion the same worldwide, (2) adapt promotion only, (3) adapt product only, (4) adapt both product and promotion and (5) invent new products.[29]

Keep Product and Promotion the Same Worldwide. This strategy attempts to use in the foreign country the product and promotion developed for the home market, an approach that seems desirable wherever possible because it eliminates the expenses of marketing research and product redevelopment. American companies PepsiCo and Coca-Cola use this approach in marketing their soft drinks. Although both translate promotional messages into the language of a particular country, they market the same product and promotion messages around the world. Despite certain inherent risks that stem from cultural differences in interpretation, exporting advertising copy does provide the efficiency of international standardisation, or globalisation. Global advertising

FIGURE 25.5
International product and promotion strategies

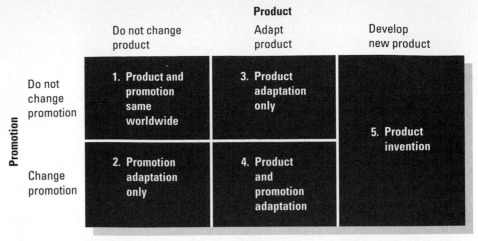

SOURCE: Adapted from Warren J. Keegan, *Global Marketing Management,* 4th ed., Englewood Cliffs, N.J.: Prentice-Hall, 1989, pp. 378–382. Used by permission.

embraces the same concept as global marketing, discussed earlier in this chapter. An advertiser can save hundreds of thousands of pounds by running the same advertisement worldwide.

Adapt Promotion Only.   This strategy leaves the product basically unchanged but modifies its promotion. For example, Coca-Cola provides similar products throughout the world but may modify the media for its advertising messages. This approach may be necessary because of language, legal or cultural differences associated with the advertising copy. When Polaroid introduced its SX-70 camera in Europe, for example, it used the same television and print advertisements featuring the same "celebrities" that it had used in the United States. However, because those featured were in fact not well known in Europe, the advertisements were not effective, and sales of the SX-70 were initially low. Only when Polaroid adapted its promotion to appeal to regional needs and tastes did the SX-70 begin to achieve success.[30] Promotional adaptation is a low cost modification compared with the costs of redeveloping engineering and production and physically changing products.

Generally, the strategy of adapting only promotion infuses advertising with the culture of people who will be exposed to it (see Figure 25.6). Often promotion combines thinking globally and acting locally. At company headquarters, a basic global marketing strategy is developed, but promotion is modified to fit each market's needs.

Adapt Product Only.   The basic assumption in modifying a product without changing its promotion is that the product will serve the same function under different conditions of use. Soap and washing powder manufacturers have adapted their products to local water conditions and washing equipment without changing their promotions. Household appliances also have been altered to use different types of electricity.

A product may have to be adjusted for legal reasons. Japan, for example, has some of the most stringent car emission requirements in the world. European cars that fail emission standards cannot be marketed in Japan. Sometimes, products must be adjusted to overcome social and cultural obstacles. American Jell-O introduced a powdered jelly mix that failed in Britain because Britons were used to buying jelly in cube form. Resistance to a product is frequently based on attitudes and ignorance about the

TR*EAU*PHÄE

Treauphy.

EIGENL*EAU*B

Bleau your own trumpet.

PR*EAU*PAGANDE

Preaupaganda.

F*EAU*REVER

FIGURE 25.6 *Adapting promotion across national boundaries*

SOURCE: Courtesy Perrier Export.

nature of new technology. It is often easier to change the product than to overcome technological biases.

Adapt Both Product and Promotion.   When a product serves a new function or is used differently in a foreign market, then both the product and its promotion need to be altered. For example, when Procter & Gamble marketed its Cheer washing powder in Japan, it promoted the product as being effective in all temperatures. Most Japanese, however, wash clothes in cold water and therefore do not care about all temperature washing. Moreover, the Japanese often add a lot of fabric softener to the wash, and Cheer did not produce many suds under those conditions. Procter & Gamble thus reformulated Cheer so that it would not be affected by the addition of fabric softeners and changed the promotion to emphasise "superior" cleaning in cold water. Cheer then became one of Procter & Gamble's most successful products in Japan.[31] Adaptation of both product and promotion is the most expensive strategy discussed so far, but it should be considered if the foreign market appears large enough.

Invent New Products.   This strategy is selected when existing products cannot meet the needs of a foreign market. General Motors developed an all purpose, jeep-like motor vehicle that can be assembled in developing nations by mechanics with no special training. The vehicle is designed to operate under varied conditions; it has standardised parts and is inexpensive. Colgate-Palmolive developed an inexpensive, all-plastic, hand powered washing machine that has the tumbling action of a modern automatic machine. The product, marketed in less developed countries, was invented for households that have no electricity. Strategies that involve the invention of products are often the most costly, but the pay off can be great.

Distribution and Pricing

Decisions about the distribution system and pricing policies are important in developing an international marketing mix. Figure 25.7 illustrates different approaches to these decisions.

Distribution.   A company can sell its product to an intermediary that is willing to buy from existing marketing channels, or it can develop new international marketing channels. Obviously, some service companies, such as Citicorp or ABN AMRO, need to develop their own distribution systems to market their products. However, many products, such as toothpaste, are distributed through intermediaries and brokers. The firm must consider distribution both between countries and within the foreign country.

In determining distribution alternatives, the existence of retailers and wholesalers that can perform marketing functions between and within countries is one major factor. If a country has a segmented retail structure consisting primarily of one person shops or street sellers, it may be difficult to develop new marketing channels for products such as packaged goods and prepared foods. Quite often in Third World countries, certain channels of distribution are characterised by ethnodomination. *Ethnodomination* occurs when an ethnic group occupies a majority position within a marketing channel. Indians, for example, own approximately 90 per cent of the cotton gins in Uganda; the Hausa tribe in Nigeria dominates the trade in kola nuts, cattle and housing; and Chinese merchants dominate the rice economy in Thailand. Marketers must be sensitive to ethnodomination and recognise that the ethnic groups operate in subcultures with a unique social and economic organisation.[32]

If the product being sold across national boundaries requires service and information, then control of the distribution process is desirable. Caterpillar, for example, sells

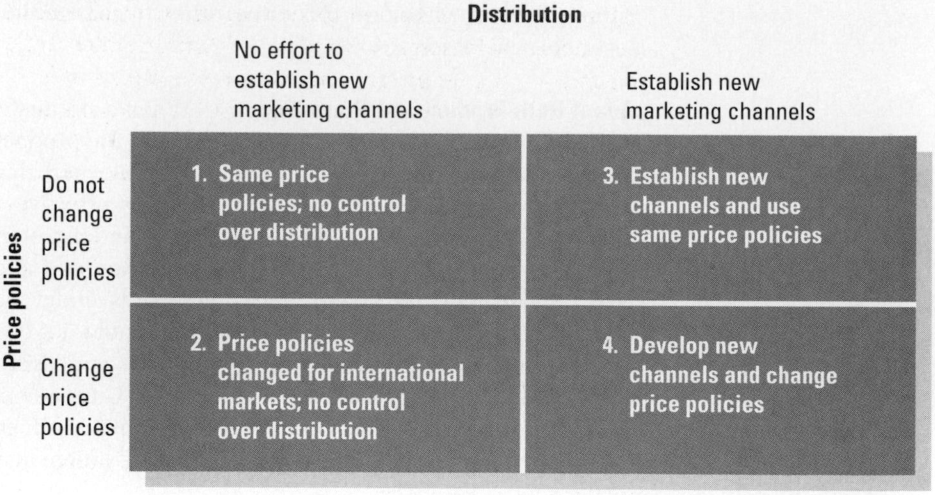

FIGURE 25.7
*Strategies for international
distribution and pricing*

Distribution

	No effort to establish new marketing channels	Establish new marketing channels
Do not change price policies	1. Same price policies; no control over distribution	3. Establish new channels and use same price policies
Change price policies	2. Price policies changed for international markets; no control over distribution	4. Develop new channels and change price policies

Price policies (vertical axis label)

more than half its construction and earthmoving equipment out of its native USA. Because it must provide services and replacement parts, Caterpillar has established its own dealers in foreign markets. Regional sales offices and technical experts are also available to support local dealers. A manufacturer of paintbrushes, on the other hand, would be more concerned about agents, wholesalers or other manufacturers that would facilitate the product's exposure in a foreign market. Control over the distribution process would not be so important for that product because services and replacement parts are not needed.

Research suggests that international firms use independently owned marketing channels when they market in countries perceived to be highly dissimilar to their home markets. However, when they market complex products, they develop vertically integrated marketing channels to gain control of distribution. To manage the distribution process from manufacturer to customer contact requires an expert sales force that must be trained specifically to sell the firm's products. Moreover, when products are unique or highly differentiated from those of current competitors, international firms also tend to design and establish vertically integrated channels.[33]

It is crucial to realise that a country's political instability can jeopardise the distribution of goods. For example, when the United States invaded Panama in late 1989, the Panama Canal was closed for several days, delaying shipments of goods through the canal. Similarly, during the political unrest in China, military activity and fighting made it difficult to move goods into and out of certain areas. Instability centring on Iraq and the Persian Gulf was having a similar effect. Thus it must be stressed again how important it is to monitor the environment when engaging in international marketing. Companies that market products in unstable nations may need to develop alternative plans to allow for sudden unrest or hostility and ensure that the distribution of their products is not jeopardised.

Pricing. The domestic and non-domestic prices of products are usually different. For example, the prices charged for Walt Disney videos in the UK, Germany and Spain will all vary, as well as being different from US prices. The increased costs of transport, supplies, taxes, tariffs and other expenses necessary to adjust a firm's operations to international marketing can raise prices. A key decision is whether the basic pricing policy will change (as discussed in Chapter 18). If it is a firm's policy not to allocate fixed costs to non-domestic sales, then lower foreign prices could result.

It is common practice for EC countries to sell off foodstuffs and pharmaceuticals at knock down prices to eastern bloc and African states respectively. This kind of sale of products in non-domestic markets—or vice versa—at lower prices (when all the costs have not been allocated or when surplus products are sold) is called **dumping.** Dumping is illegal in some countries if it damages domestic firms and workers.

A cost plus approach to international pricing is probably the most common method used because of the compounding number of costs necessary to move products from their country of origin. Of course, as the discussion of pricing policies in Chapter 18 points out, understanding consumer demand and the competitive environment is a necessary step in selecting a price.

The price charged in other countries is also a function of foreign currency exchange rates. Fluctuations in the international monetary market can change the prices charged across national boundaries on a daily basis. There has been a trend towards greater fluctuation (or float) in world money markets. For example, a sudden variation in the exchange rate, which occurs when a nation devalues its currency, can have wide ranging effects on consumer prices.

DEVELOPING ORGANISATIONAL STRUCTURES FOR INTERNATIONAL MARKETING

The level of commitment to international marketing is a major variable in deciding what kind of involvement is appropriate. A firm's options range from occasional exporting to expanding overall operations (production and marketing) into other countries. This section examines exporting, licensing, joint ventures, trading companies, direct ownership and other approaches to international involvement.

Exporting

Exporting is the lowest level of commitment to international marketing and the most flexible approach. A firm may find an exporting intermediary that can perform most marketing functions associated with selling to other countries. This approach entails minimum effort and cost. Modifications in packaging, labelling, style or colour may be the major expenses in adapting a product. There is limited risk in using export agents and merchants because there is no direct investment in the foreign country.

Export agents bring together buyers and sellers from different countries; they collect a commission for arranging sales. Export houses and export merchants purchase products from different companies and then sell them to foreign countries. They are specialists at understanding customers' needs in foreign countries.

Foreign buyers from companies and governments provide a direct method of exporting and eliminate the need for an intermediary. Foreign buyers encourage international exchange by contacting domestic firms about their needs and the opportunities available in exporting. Domestic firms that want to export with a minimum of effort and investment seek out foreign importers and buyers.

Licensing

When potential markets are found across national boundaries—and when production, technical assistance or marketing know how is required—**licensing** is an alternative to direct investment. The licensee (the owner of the foreign operation) pays commissions or royalties on sales or supplies used in manufacturing. An initial down payment or fee may be charged when the licensing agreement is signed. Exchanges of management techniques or technical assistance are primary reasons for licensing agreements. Yoplait yogurt is a French yogurt that is licensed for production in the United States; the Yoplait brand tries to maintain a French image.

Licensing is an attractive alternative to direct investment when the political stability of a foreign country is in doubt or when resources are unavailable for direct investment. Licensing is especially advantageous for small manufacturers wanting to launch a well known brand internationally. For example, all Spalding sporting products are licensed worldwide. The Questor Corporation owns the Spalding name but produces no goods itself. Pierre Cardin has issued 500 licences and Yves St Laurent 200 to make their products.[34] Löwenbrau has used licensing agreements to increase sales worldwide without committing capital to build breweries.

Joint Ventures

In international marketing, a **joint venture** is a partnership between a domestic firm and a foreign firm or government. Joint ventures are especially popular in industries that call for large investments, such as natural resources extraction or car manufacturing. Control of the joint venture can be split equally, or one party may control decision-making. Joint ventures are often a political necessity because of nationalism and governmental restrictions on foreign ownership. They also provide legitimacy in the eyes of the host country's people. Local partners have first hand knowledge of the economic and socio-political environment, access to distribution networks, or privileged access to local resources (raw material, labour management, contacts and so on). Moreover, entrepreneurs in many less developed countries actively seek associations with an overseas partner as a ready means of implementing their own corporate strategy.[35]

Joint ventures are assuming greater global importance because of cost advantages and the number of inexperienced firms entering foreign markets. They may be the result of a trade-off between a firm's desire for completely unambiguous control of an enterprise and its quest for additional resources. They may occur when internal development or acquisition is not feasible or unavailable or when the risks and constraints leave no other alternative. As project sizes increase in the face of global competition and firms attempt to spread the huge costs of technological innovation, there is increased impetus to form joint ventures.[36] Several European truck makers are considering mergers and joint ventures with other European firms to consolidate their power after the unification of EC in 1992 and the deregulation of the European haulage industry in 1993. Volvo and Renault have developed a partnership, and Britain's Leyland and the Netherlands' DAF joined forces until DAF's financial problems caused Leyland to seek new partners.[37]

Increasingly, once a joint venture succeeds, nationalism spurs a trend towards expropriating or purchasing foreign shares of the enterprise. On the other hand, a joint venture may be the only available means for entering a foreign market. For example, European construction firms bidding for business in Saudi Arabia have found that joint ventures with Arab construction companies gain local support among the handful of people who make the contracting decisions.

Strategic alliances, the newest form of international business structure, are partnerships formed to create a competitive advantage on a worldwide basis. They are very similar to joint ventures. Strategic alliances have been defined as "co-operation between two or more industrial corporations, belonging to different countries, whereby each partner seeks to add to its competencies by combining its resources with those of its partner."[38] The number of strategic alliances is growing at an estimated rate of about 20 per cent per year.[39] In fact, in some industries, such as cars and high technology, strategic alliances are becoming the predominant means of competing. International competition is so fierce and the costs of competing on a global basis so high that few firms have the individual resources to go it alone. Thus individual firms that lack all the internal resources essential for international success may seek to collaborate with other companies.[40]

The partners forming international strategic alliances often retain their distinct identities, and each brings a distinctive competence to the union. However, the firms share common long term goals. What distinguishes international strategic alliances from other business structures is that member firms in the alliance may have been traditional rivals competing for market share in the same product class.[41] Table 25.5 shows some examples of strategic alliances.[42] Marketing Insight 25.2 describes some typical marketing alliances.

Trading Companies

A **trading company** provides a link between buyers and sellers in different countries. A trading company, as its name implies, is not involved in manufacturing or owning assets related to manufacturing. It buys in one country at the lowest price consistent with quality and sells to buyers in another country. An important function of trading companies is taking title to products and undertaking all the activities necessary to move the products from the domestic country to a foreign country. For example, large grain trading companies control a major portion of the world's trade in basic food commodities. These trading companies sell agricultural commodities that are homogeneous and can be stored and moved rapidly in response to market conditions.

Trading companies reduce risk for companies interested in getting involved in international marketing. A trading company will assist producers with information about products that meet quality and price expectations in domestic or international markets. Additional services a trading company may provide include consulting, marketing research, advertising, insurance, research and development, legal assistance, warehousing and foreign exchange.

TABLE 25.5 *Examples of international strategic alliances*

PARTNERS	PRODUCTS
General Motors; Toyota	Cars
Rover; Honda	Cars
American Motors; Renault	Cars
Chrysler; Mitsubishi	Cars
Ford; Toyo Kogyo	Cars
Alfa Romeo; Nissan; Fiat	Cars
ATT; Olivetti	Office equipment; computers
Amdahl; Fujitsu	Computers
ICL; Fujitsu	Computers
ATT; Philips	Telecommunications equipment
Honeywell; L.M. Ericsson	PBX system
General Motors; Fanuc	Robotics
AEG Telefunken; JVC; Thorn-EMI; Thomson	Video recorders
General Electric; Matsushita	Electrical appliances
Corning Glass; Siemens	Optical cables
Hercules; Montedison	Polypropylene resin
United Technologies; Rolls Royce	Aircraft engines

SOURCE: S. Young, J. Hamill, C. Wheeler and R. Davies, *International Market Entry and Development,* 1st ed., London: Harvester Wheatsheaf, 1989, p. 273. Reprinted by permission of the publisher.

STRATEGIC ALLIANCES

Cathay Pacific Airways and Japan Airlines (JAL) will begin operating a direct service between Hong Kong and Sapporo on Japan's northern island of Hokkaido in their first joint venture. Cathay Pacific's manager in Sapporo, Mark Nakayasu, said the two airlines had been negotiating a joint service since May 1990 in a bid to attract more Hong Kong tourists to Hokkaido's wealthy ski resorts.

Hokkaido, considered Japan's last frontier, has a population of 5.7 million people, but accounts for one fifth of Japan's land mass. Most famous for its winter skiing and the Snow Festival in February, the island has become especially attractive to Japanese tourists and students all year round, as favourable summer temperatures range between 20° and 28°C. The two airlines hope that direct flights will promote Hokkaido not only as a winter getaway resort, but also as a year-round destination for golf, boating, sightseeing and the Japanese *onsen,* or hot bath.

It is the first joint venture operation between Cathay Pacific and Japan's national carrier. Cathay will operate a Lockheed TriStar, which can carry 281 passengers, with one JAL crew member.

Mr Nakayasu said 16 Cathay staff and more than 100 JAL staff will be involved with ground operations in Sapporo. "We need JAL to help us at Chitose Airport, but we will use Cathay's style for passenger handling and catering," he said. "No one from Cathay has been in Sapporo for 10 years, so we had to get help from JAL to avoid the risks. We decided on a joint venture at the beginning to test the waters. If we feel confident then later on we may separate".

It is not only in the airline industry that joint ventures are popular. Strategic alliances enable companies to expand, often into new territories, with reduced capital outlay and risk. Citroën is entering the car market in China through a joint venture with Second Automobile Works. The jointly controlled company Aeolus Citroën Automobile Company will produce 150,000 Citroën ZXs per year. A £50 million joint venture between Coca-Cola and Nestlé will manufacture and market a fresh range of ready made beverages under the Nescafé and Nestea brand names. Nescafé will gain a distribution system of unparalleled reach and Coca-Cola will benefit by linking with internationally recognised brand names.

SOURCES: Sondra Dunn, "Cathay and JAL link up", *South China Morning Post,* 10 September 1990; "Citroën gears up for China", *Marketing,* 24 January 1991; Karen Hoggan, "Coca-Cola/Nestlé venture revives iced tea and coffee", *Marketing,* 6 December 1990, p. 7.

Direct Ownership

Once a company makes a long term commitment to marketing in a foreign nation that has a promising political and economic environment, **direct ownership** of a foreign subsidiary or division is a possibility. Although most discussions of foreign investment concern only manufacturing equipment or personnel, the expenses of developing a

TABLE 25.6 *Top 30 European companies ranked by sales in ecu (millions)*

RANK 1993	RANK 1992	COMPANY	COUNTRY	SALES	EMPLOYEES
1	1	N.V. Kon. Nederlandse Petroleum Maatschappij	NL	82.934	57000
2		Iriistituto per la Ricostruzione Industriale	IT	51.247	407169
3	2	The British Petroleum Co. plc	UK	46.470	115250
4	4	Daimler-Benz ag	DE	46.307	381511
5		Volkswagen Aktiengesellschaft	DE	37.195	267009
6	3	Fiat Spa	IT	36.434	288500
7	8	Unilever N.V.	NL	33.070	9800
8	7	Unilever plc	UK	33.004	298000
9	5	Eni Ente Nazionale Idrocarburi	IT	32.819	131248
10	9	Siemens Aktiengesellschaft (Konzern)	DE	30.796	406000
11	11	Mercedes-Benz Aktiengesellschaft (Konzern)	DE	29.153	229957
12	16	Veba Aktiengesellschaft	DE	29.002	114537
13	14	Elf Aquitaine (Ste Natl)	FR	28.800	87000
14	10	Deutsche Bundespost	DE	27.509	580000
15	12	Nestle, SA	CH	27.272	7000
16	15	N.V. Philips' Gloeilampenfabrieken	NL	24.654	46763
17	24	Electricite De France	FR	24.595	119300
18	28	RWE Aktiengesellschaft	DE	24.316	102190
19	17	Renault SA	FR	23.817	153776
20		Mercedes-Benz Aktiengesellschaft	DE	23.671	177127
21	13	B A T Industries plc	UK	23.482	212316
22	18	PSA Peugeot Citroën	FR	22.984	157000
23	22	Alcatel Alsthom	FR	22.971	200500
24	19	BASF Aktiengesellschaft (Konzern)	DE	22.724	138533
25	26	AGIP Petroli spa	IT	22.127	20361
26	20	Hoechst Aktiengesellschaft (Konzern)	DE	21.865	179332
27	33	Metro International AG	CH	21.856	250
28		Bayer Aktiengesellschaft	DE	20.666	166325
29	31	Total	FR	20.523	40000
30	2219	Fomento de Construcciones Y Contratas, SA	ES	20.341	9000

SOURCE: *D & B Europa*, Vol. 4, 1993, p. 43. Used with permission.

separate foreign distribution system can be tremendous. The opening of retail stores in neighbouring countries can require a large financial investment in facilities, research and management. Disney's development of EuroDisney near Paris has been a huge drain on resources.

The term **multinational enterprise** refers to firms that have operations or subsidiaries located in many countries. Often the parent firm is based in one country and cultivates production, management and marketing activities in other countries. The firm's subsidiaries may be quite autonomous in order to respond to the needs of individual international markets. Firms such as ICI, Unilever and General Motors are multinational companies with worldwide operations. Table 25.6 lists the top 30

European companies, ranked by sales (turnover) in ECUs, the EC monetary unit. Most of these companies are active in many countries and several continents.

A wholly owned foreign subsidiary may be allowed to operate independently of the parent company so that its management can have more freedom to adjust to the local environment. Co-operative arrangements are developed to assist in marketing efforts, production and management. A wholly owned foreign subsidiary may export products to the home country. Some car manufacturers, such as Ford and General Motors, for example, import cars built by their foreign subsidiaries. A foreign subsidiary offers important tax, tariff and other operating advantages. One of the greatest advantages is the cross cultural approach. A subsidiary usually operates under foreign management, so that it can develop a local identity. The greatest danger in such an arrangement comes from political uncertainty: a firm may lose its foreign investment.

SUMMARY

Marketing activities performed across national boundaries are usually significantly different from domestic marketing activities. International marketers must have a profound awareness of the foreign environment. The marketing strategy is ordinarily adjusted to meet the needs and desires of markets across national boundaries.

The level of involvement in international marketing can range from casual exporting to globalisation of markets. Although most firms adjust their marketing mixes for differences in target markets, some firms are able to standardise their marketing efforts worldwide. Traditional full scale international marketing involvement is based on products customised according to cultural, regional and national differences. Globalisation, however, involves developing marketing strategies as if the entire world (or regions of it) were a single entity; a globalised firm markets standardised products in the same way everywhere.

Marketers must rely on international marketing intelligence to understand the complexities of the international marketing environment before they can formulate a marketing mix. Therefore, they collect and analyse secondary data and primary data about international markets.

Environmental aspects of special importance include cultural, social, economic, political and legal forces. Cultural aspects of the environment that are most important to international marketers include customs, concepts, values, attitudes, morals and knowledge. Marketing activities are primarily social in purpose; therefore they are structured by the institutions of family, religion, education, health and recreation. The most prominent economic forces that affect international marketing are those that can be measured by income and resources. Credit, buying power and income distribution are aggregate measures of market potential. Political and legal forces include the political system, national laws, regulatory bodies, national pressure groups and courts. The foreign policies of all nations involved in trade determine how marketing can be conducted. The level of technology helps define economic development within a nation and indicates the existence of methods to facilitate marketing.

Various regional trade alliances and specific markets are creating difficulties and opportunities for firms, including the unification of the EC with deregulation in 1993 and harmonised trade agreements, the Pacific Rim markets, changing conditions in eastern Europe and the former Soviet Union, and the United States and Canada trade pact.

After a country's environment has been analysed, marketers must develop a marketing mix and decide whether to adapt product or promotion. There are five possible strategies for adapting product and promotion across national boundaries: (1) keep product and promotion the same worldwide, (2) adapt promotion only, (3) adapt product only, (4) adapt both product and promotion and (5) invent new products. Foreign distribution channels are nearly always different from domestic ones. The allocation of costs, transport considerations or the costs of doing business in foreign nations will affect pricing.

There are several ways of getting involved in international marketing. Exporting is the easiest and most flexible method. Licensing is an alternative to direct investment; it may be necessitated by political and economic conditions. Joint ventures and strategic alliances are often appropriate when outside resources are needed, when there are governmental restrictions on foreign ownership or when changes in global markets encourage competitive consolidation. Trading companies are experts at buying products in the domestic market and selling to foreign markets, thereby taking most of the risk in international involvement. Direct ownership of foreign divisions or subsidiaries is the strongest commitment to international marketing and involves the greatest risk. When a company has operations or subsidiaries located in many countries, it is termed a multinational enterprise.

IMPORTANT TERMS

International marketing	Joint venture
Globalisation	Strategic alliances
Gross domestic product (GDP)	Trading company
Dumping	Direct ownership
Licensing	Multinational enterprise

DISCUSSION AND REVIEW QUESTIONS

1. How does international marketing differ from domestic marketing?
2. What must marketers consider before deciding whether to become involved in international marketing?
3. Are the largest industrial companies in Europe committed to international marketing? Why or why not?
4. Why is so much of this chapter devoted to an analysis of the international marketing environment?
5. A manufacturer recently exported peanut butter with a green label to a nation in the Far East. The product failed because it was associated with jungle sickness. How could this mistake have been avoided?
6. Relate the concept of reference groups (Chapter 4) to international marketing.
7. How do religious systems influence marketing activities in foreign countries?
8. Which is more important to international marketers, a country's aggregate GDP or its GDP per capita? Why?
9. If you were asked to provide a small tip (or bribe) to have a document approved in a foreign nation where this practice was customary, what would you do?
10. What should marketers consider as they decide whether to license or to enter into a joint venture in a foreign nation?
11. Discuss the impact of strategic alliances on marketing strategies.

■ CASES

25.1 Porsche AG

Founded in 1930 by Dr Ferdinand Porsche, the company known today as Porsche AG began as a research and development firm. The original company accepted contracts from individuals and firms to design new cars, aeroplanes and ships. The company built prototypes of each design and thoroughly tested them. If the firm that commissioned the work approved the design, the product was then produced by one of the large manufacturing companies in Germany. After World War II, the Porsche family experienced a period of hardship, disappointment and personal tragedy. Porsche's son, Dr Ferry Porsche, began a company to manufacture family designed sports cars in 1948. Despite depressed economic conditions, the company persevered and prospered. By 1973, Porsche AG had built and sold some 200,000 Porsches, gaining world recognition for its cars and their promise of "driving in its purest form".

Porsche today is organised into three divisions located in three suburbs of Stuttgart: the factory, in Zuffenhausen; testing, engineering and design, in Weissach; and marketing, in Ludwigsburg. The Porsche Research and Development Centre has produced the 959 race car, an aircraft engine, the TAG motor and designs for ambulances, mobile surgery units, gliders, fire engines and fork lift trucks. The company holds more than 2,000 patents, and innovations developed by Porsche are in several manufacturers' car models.

The popularity of Porsche cars stems from their reputation for outstanding performance. Not only are the cars produced in a painstaking fashion, but Porsche AG also takes maintenance and repair very seriously. Porsche mechanics receive five days of instruction each year at the Porsche marketing centre in Ludwigsburg, more training than any other car company provides. In its advertising, the company encourages customers to rely only on Porsche experts for repair and maintenance of their cars to prevent the customers from having unsatisfactory experiences with unqualified mechanics. This action further differentiates Porsche cars from the competition.

Despite Porsche's reputation for excellence, the company has fallen on hard times. It was forced to raise prices on cars sold in the US because of changes in the dollar exchange rate. Because of the price increases, a weakening US dollar, and lower priced Japanese imitations, sales in the United States dropped significantly in the late 1980s. Roughly 60 per cent of all Porsches were sold in the United States. Production in 1988 dropped from the record levels in 1986–1987 (more than 50,000 cars). This over dependence on the US market caused the firm to implement an austerity programme. The programme included lowering production output, reducing costs (lower dividends and fewer employees), revamping all three model lines and pulling out of the lower end of the luxury car market. The company is now trying to enter new markets, including Spain and Japan, to boost sales and increase profits.

Porsche is successful in markets where the social climate favours people who want to demonstrate their success and where the economic climate is conducive to the entrepreneur. Porsche management believes that its customers have high personal goals and a drive to achieve, do not like to compromise and give their best efforts every time. Although not averse to risk, they prepare thoroughly for new ventures. Porsche customers are apparently goers and doers, but not show offs. To succeed, Porsche AG must exhibit some of its customers' traits. Customers must be able to identify with the firm, to see in the company the same characteristics they see in themselves.

SOURCES: Joseph M. Callahan and Lance A. Ealey, "Porsche's Schutz reveals US marketing plans", *Industries,* March 1985, p. 50; Gred V. Guterl, John Dornberg and Kevin Sullivan, "Three to get ready",

Business Month, March 1988, pp. 42–50; "It shortens the path", Christophorous, August 1984; Maria Kielmas, "Stalled Porsche: but is there a U-turn in its future?", Barron's, 27 June 1988, pp. 14–15, 37; Ron Lewald, "Porsche's US backfire", International Management, April 1988, pp. 42–5; Richard Morais, "What price excellence?", Forbes, 17 November 1986, p. 234; Plan Your Success, 2nd ed. (Stuttgart: Dr. Ing. h.c. Ferry Porsche, 1985), pp. 1, 3; Dr. Ing. h.c. Ferry Porsche and John Bentley, We at Porsche (Garden City, N.Y.: Doubleday, 1976), p. 263; "Porsche", Ward's Auto World, January 1985, pp. 52–3; Porsche Brochure for Distribution, Stuttgart: Dr. Ing. h.c. F. Porsche AG 1984; John A. Russell, "Porsche puts high value on its people, Schutz says", Automotive News, 4 August 1986, p. 64; Gail Schares and Mark Maremont, "Jaguar and Porsche try to pull out of the slow lane", Business Week, 12 December 1988, pp. 84–5; Peter Schutz and Jack Cook, "Porsche and nichemanship", Harvard Business Review, March-April 1986, pp. 98–106; and Jesse Snyder, "Porsche looks for new brand to sell in US", Automotive News, 15 December 1986, p.1.

Questions for Discussion

1. Evaluate international marketing opportunities for Porsche AG. What are the company's strengths and weaknesses?
2. What obstacles must Porsche overcome to succeed in selling its cars in the United States?
3. What is the role of diversification in the Porsche AG corporate strategy?

25.2   MTV's Strategies in Global Markets

In 53 million American homes, pop music fans, mostly aged 16 to 34, tune in to enjoy superstars like Paula Abdul, Michael Jackson and Madonna. Working like a Top 40 radio station, MTV rotates through about 60 different music videos, selling and airing advertising to make its money. Viacom International, owner of MTV, reports that about 20 per cent of its £940 million in revenue comes from its video network. In the last few years, the number of American MTV viewers has levelled off, and MTV's US market seems to be reaching saturation. Hoping to attract new audiences and still retain its established market, MTV is concentrating on international expansion. MTV's goal, says the network's CEO, is to be in every home in the world.

When MTV made its first foreign licensing deal in Japan, company executives were just beginning to think about overseas expansion. They gave their Japanese affiliate little supervision regarding style and content. However, after one MTV executive reviewed some of the Japanese videos, she decided that they didn't convey the trendy and sophisticated image MTV tries to impart. Renegotiating the deal, the network took tighter control over quality. Subsequent expansion into Europe, South America and Australia means that today, about 200 million fans in about 38 countries can enjoy the latest pop videos from around the world.

Other cable enterprises, including Cable News Network (CNN), broadcast internationally. Unlike executives at MTV, CNN's owner, cable giant Ted Turner, elects to broadcast solely in English, primarily targeting Americans travelling in all parts of the world. MTV attempts to be sensitive to other countries' cultures by responding to their musical styles and tastes. Although every broadcast must fit into MTV guidelines, television networks outside the US employ native video jockeys who highlight locally popular stars. In Japan, MTV VJs speak almost entirely in Japanese and focus on Japanese and other international artists. English is the language of choice on 24 hour European MTV, but European and other international musicians are the stars of the videos. MTV depends on music instead of language to link its 25 country European market.

Recognised as the leading pop music expert in the United States, MTV is rapidly becoming the authority on youth culture worldwide. The network is increasingly successful in convincing record companies that it can launch artists on a worldwide scale. Adding to its list of international advertisers like Nike, Levi's and Fruit of the Loom is going a long way towards keeping MTV one step ahead of its fast growing competitor, Video Jukebox Network.

SOURCES: Andy Fry, "The year of European media revolution", *Marketing*, 28 March 1991, pp. 25–6; Peter Newcomb, "Music video wars", *Forbes*, 4 March 1991, pp. 68, 70; and Sara Nelson, "What's the big idea", *Working Woman*, July 1990, pp. 96, 98, 108.

Questions for Discussion

1. Does MTV have a uniform product globally?
2. Have local or national needs altered MTV's marketing and its product format? 3.
3. MTV's European network hinges on the English language. What problems may this cause? Are MTV's US bosses likely to be aware of these?

CAREERS IN MARKETING

SOME GENERAL ISSUES

As noted in Chapter 1, between one fourth and one third of the civilian workforces in the United States and Europe are employed in marketing related jobs. Although obviously a multitude of diverse career opportunities in marketing exists, the number of positions in different areas of the field varies. For example, millions of workers are employed in many facets of sales, but relatively few people work in public relations and marketing research.

Many non-business organisations now recognise that they do, in fact, perform marketing activities. For that reason, the number of marketing positions in government agencies, hospitals, charitable and religious groups, educational institutions and similar organisations is increasing (see Chapter 24).

Even though financial reward is not the sole criterion for selecting a career, it is only practical to consider potential earnings from a marketing job. Generally, entry level marketing personnel earn more than their counterparts in economics and social studies but not as much as people who enter accounting, chemistry or engineering positions. Starting salaries for marketing graduates average £14,000. Marketers who advance to higher level positions often earn high salaries, and a significant proportion of corporate executives held marketing jobs before attaining their top level positions.

As *Marketing* magazine's annual UK salary review indicates, there is a great range of marketing job positions and associated remuneration and perks. A marketing assistant earns on average £12,400 with no perks; a marketing manager, £26,700, with a car, pension and health cover; a marketing director, £42,600 with a full package of perks (see Table A.1). Figure A.1 shows current statistics for the proportion of men and women in each job category.

	SEX	AGE	EDUCATION	WORK EXPERIENCE	PERKS
MARKETING ASSISTANT (£12,400)	F	25.7	degree	less than 2 years	none
MARKETING EXECUTIVE (£15,600)	F	28	degree	3–5 years	contributory pension
PRODUCT BRAND MANAGER (£18,650)	F	28.6	degree	3–5 years	company car, medical insurance, contributory pension scheme
GROUP PRODUCT MANAGER (£24,800)	M	32.8	degree	6–10 years	company car, car running costs, medical insurance, contributory pension
MARKETING MANAGER (£26,700)	M	35	degree	6–15 years	company car, car running costs, medical insurance, contributory pension
MARKETING DIRECTOR (£42,600)	M	30	degree	11 + years	company car, car running costs, medical insurance, contributory pension
PROPRIETOR (£36,300)	M	44.7	degree	21 + years	company car, car running costs
MANAGING DIRECTOR/ DEPUTY MANAGING DIRECTOR (£47,550)	M	43	degree	21 + years	company car, car running costs, car telephone, medical insurance, contributory pension
CHAIRMAN/CHIEF EXECUTIVE (£49,300)	M	43.5	degree	21 + years	company car, car running costs, medical insurance, contributory pension

SOURCE: "The *Marketing* Salary Survey", *Marketing,* 17 January, 1991, pp. 19–22.

Another important issue is whether the work associated with a particular career is enjoyable and stimulating. Because you will spend almost 40 percent of your waking hours on the job, you should not allow such factors as economic conditions or status to over ride your personal goals as you select a life long career. Too often, people do not weigh these factors realistically. You should give considerable thought to your choice of career, and you should adopt a well planned, systematic approach to finding a position that meets your personal and career objectives.

After determining your objectives, you should identify the organisations that are likely to offer desirable opportunities. Learn as much as possible about these organisations before setting up employment interviews; job recruiters are impressed with applicants who have done their homework.

When making initial contact with potential employers by mail, enclose a brief, clearly written letter of introduction. After an initial interview, you should send a brief

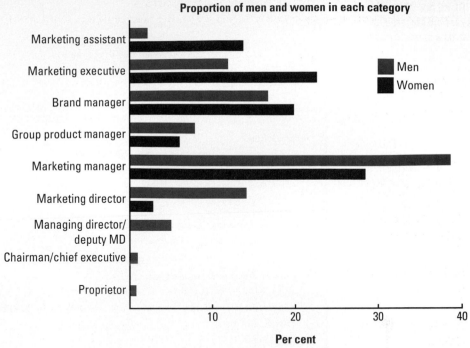

Proportion of men and women in each category

SOURCE: "The marketing salary survey", *Marketing*, 17 January 1991, p. 20

letter of thanks to the interviewer. The job of getting the right job is important, and you owe it to yourself to take this process seriously.

THE RÉSUMÉ OR CURRICULUM VITAE

The résumé or curriculum vitae (CV) is one of the keys to being considered for a good job. Because it states your qualifications, experiences, education and career goals, the résumé is a chance for a potential employer to assess your compatibility with the job requirements. For the employer's and individual's benefit, the résumé should be accurate and current.

To be effective, the résumé can be targeted towards a specific position, as Figure A.2 shows. This document is only one example of an acceptable résumé. The job target section is specific and leads directly to the applicant's qualifications for the job. Capabilities show what the applicant can do and that the person has an understanding of the job's requirements. Skills and strengths as they relate to the specific job should be highlighted. The achievement section indicates success at accomplishing tasks or goals within the job market and at school/college. The work experience section includes educational background, which adds credibility to the résumé but is not the major area of focus; the applicant's ability to function successfully in a specific job is the major emphasis.

Common suggestions for improving résumés include deleting useless information, improving organisation, using professional printing and typing, listing duties (not accomplishments), maintaining grammatical perfection and avoiding an excessively elaborate or fancy format.[1] One of the biggest problems in résumés, according to a survey of personnel experts, is distortions and lies; 36 per cent of the experts thought that this was a major problem.[2] People lie most often about previous salaries and tasks per-

FIGURE A.2

A résumé targeted towards a specific position

LORRAINE WHEELER
35 EAST PARK ROAD
REEDLEY
LEEDS, L517 9NP
(0532) 482111

EDUCATION: B.Sc. Honours, The Best University, 1984, Marketing

DATE OF BIRTH: 2/8/59

POSITION DESIRED: PRODUCT MANAGER WITH AN INTERNATIONAL FIRM PROVIDING
FUTURE CAREER DEVELOPMENT AT THE EXECUTIVE LEVEL.

QUALIFICATIONS:

* communicates well with individuals to achieve a common goal

* handles tasks efficiently and in a timely manner

* knowledge of advertising, sales, management, marketing research, packaging, pricing,
distribution, and warehousing

* co-ordinates many activities at one time

* receives and carries out assigned tasks or directives

* writes complete status or research reports

EXPERIENCE:

* Assistant Editor on student newspaper

* Treasurer of the hockey club

* Student Researcher with Dr. Steven Who, Lecturer of Marketing, The Best University

* Achieved 2.1 degree

WORK RECORD:

1984 – Present	Wiggins & Co.
	* Junior Advertising Account Executive
1981 – 1983	The Place
	* Retail sales and consumer relations
1979 – 1981	Do All Builders
	* Labourer (part time/holidays)

EDUCATION:

1981 – 1984	B. Sc. Management Science,
	The Best University, London. 2.1 Honours awarded.
	Dissertation topic: the marketing of charities.
1978 – 1980	Middlethorn Sixth Form College, Dullsville.
	A levels: English (A); Economics (B); General Studies (A).

formed in former jobs. Present career/education details in reverse order; your most recent exploits first as those are of most interest to potential employers.

TYPES OF MARKETING CAREERS

In considering marketing as a career, the first step is to evaluate broad categories of career opportunities in the areas of marketing research, sales, public relations, industrial buying, distribution management, product management, advertising, retail management and direct marketing. Keep in mind that the categories described here are not all inclusive and that each encompasses hundreds of marketing jobs.

Marketing Research

Clearly, marketing research and information systems are vital aspects of marketing decision-making. The information about buyers and environmental forces that research and information systems provide improves a marketer's ability to understand the dynamics of the market-place and make effective decisions.

Marketing researchers gather and analyse data relating to specific problems.

Marketing research firms are usually employed by a client organisation, which could be a provider of goods or services, a non-business organisation, the government, a research consulting firm or an advertising agency. The activities performed include concept testing, product testing, package testing, advertising testing, test market research and new product research.

A researcher may be involved in one or several stages of research, depending on the size of the project, the organisation of the research unit and the researcher's experience. Marketing research trainees in large organisations usually perform a considerable amount of clerical work, such as compiling secondary data from a firm's accounting and sales records and periodicals, government publications, syndicated data services and unpublished sources. A junior analyst may edit and code questionnaires or tabulate survey results. Trainees also may participate in primary data gathering by learning to conduct mail and telephone surveys, conducting personal interviews and using observational methods of primary data collection. As a marketing researcher gains experience, the researcher may become involved in defining problems and developing hypotheses; designing research procedures; and analysing, interpreting and reporting findings. Exceptional personnel may assume responsibility for entire research projects.

Although most employers consider an honours degree sufficient qualification for a marketing research trainee, many specialised positions require a graduate degree in business administration, statistics or other related fields. Today, trainees are more likely to have a marketing or statistics degree than a social science degree. Also, trainees who are capable of immediate productivity and more complex tasks are more desirable.[3] Courses in statistics, data processing, psychology, sociology, communications, economics and English composition are valuable preparations for a career in marketing research.

Marketing research provides abundant employment opportunity (see Chapter 6), especially for applicants with graduate training in marketing research, statistics, economics and the social sciences. Generally, the value of information gathered by marketing information and research systems will become more important as competition increases, thus expanding the opportunities for prospective marketing research personnel.

The three major career paths in marketing research are with independent marketing research agencies/data suppliers, advertising agency marketing research departments and marketing research departments in businesses. In a company in which marketing research plays a key role, the researcher is often a member of the marketing strategy team. Surveying or interviewing consumers is the heart of the marketing research firm's activities. A statistician selects the sample to be surveyed, analysts design the questionnaire and synthesise the gathered data into a final report, data processors tabulate the data, and the research director controls and co-ordinates all these activities so that each project is computed to the satisfaction of the client (consumer and industrial product manufacturers).[4] In marketing research agencies, a researcher deals with many clients, products and problems. Advertising agencies use research as an ingredient in developing and refining campaigns for existing or potentially new clients.[5]

Salaries in marketing research depend on the type, size and location of the firm as well as the nature of the positions. Generally, starting salaries are somewhat higher and promotions somewhat slower than in other occupations requiring similar training. In addition, the role of marketing in overall corporate planning is becoming more important as companies seek marketing information for strategic planning purposes. Marketing research directors are reporting to higher levels of management than ever before, and the number of corporate directors who receive marketing research as regular input in decision-making has doubled in recent years. The Association of Market Survey Organisations in Leamington Spa (Millward Brown) and the Market Research

Society in London produce useful guides to the marketing research business and the leading agencies.

Personal Selling. Millions of people earn a living through personal selling. Chapter 16 defines personal selling as a process of informing customers and persuading them to purchase products through personal communication in an exchange situation. Although this definition describes the general nature of many sales positions, individual selling jobs vary enormously with respect to the type of businesses and products involved, the educational background and skills required, and the specific activities sales personnel perform. Because the work is so varied, sales occupations offer numerous career opportunities for people with a wide range of qualifications, interests and goals. A sales career offers the greatest potential compensation or remuneration. The following two sections describe what is involved in wholesale and manufacturer sales.

Wholesale Sales. Wholesalers perform activities to expedite transactions in which purchases are intended for resale or to be used to make other products. Wholesalers thus provide services to both retailers and producers. They can help match producers' products to retailers' needs and can provide accumulation and allocation services that save producers time, money and resources. Some activities associated with wholesaling include planning and negotiating transactions; assisting customers with sales, advertising, sales promotion and publicity; handling transport and storage activities; providing customers with inventory control and data processing assistance; establishing prices; and giving customers technical, management and merchandising assistance.

The background wholesale personnel need depends on the nature of the product handled. A pharmaceuticals wholesaler, for example, needs extensive technical training and product knowledge and may have a degree in chemistry, biology or pharmacy. A wholesaler of standard office supplies, on the other hand, may find it more important to be familiar with various brands, suppliers and prices than to have technical knowledge about the products. A new wholesale representative may begin a career as a sales trainee or hold a non-selling job that provides experience with inventory, prices, discounts and the firm's customers.

The number of wholesale sales positions is expected to grow about as fast as the average for all occupations. Earnings for wholesale personnel vary widely because commissions often make up a large proportion of their incomes.

Manufacturer Sales. Manufacturer sales personnel sell a firm's products to wholesalers, retailers and industrial buyers; they thus perform many of the same activities wholesale salespeople handle. As is the case with wholesaling, the educational requirements for manufacturer sales depend largely on the type and complexity of the products and markets. Manufacturers of non-technical products usually hire graduates who have a social studies or business degree and give them training and information about the firm's products, prices and customers. Manufacturers of highly technical products generally prefer applicants who have degrees in fields associated with the particular industry and market involved.

More and more sophisticated marketing skills are being used in industrial sales. Business-to-business marketing originally followed the commodity approach to complete a sale, whereby the right product is in the right place at the right time and for the right price. Today industrial sales use the same marketing concepts and strategies as do marketers selling to consumers (see Chapter 23).

Employment opportunities in manufacturer sales are expected to experience average growth. Manufacturer sales personnel are well compensated and earn above average salaries. Most are paid a combination of salaries and commissions. Commissions vary according to the salesperson's efforts, abilities, and sales territory and the type of products sold.

Public Relations

Public relations encompasses a broad set of communication activities designed to create and maintain favourable relations between the organisation and its publics—customers, employees, shareholders, government officials and society in general. Public relations specialists help clients both create the image, issue or message they wish to present and communicate it to the appropriate audience. In the UK, the concentration is in London, although the agency of the year, Countrywide, is in a market town—Banbury. Starting salaries range from £8,500 to £10,500. Of all persons working in this field, 55 per cent earn over £20,000 per year, with a package of perks.[6] Communication is basic to all public relations programmes. To communicate effectively, public relations practitioners first must gather information about the firm's client publics to assess their needs, identify problems, formulate recommendations, implement new plans and evaluate current activities.

Public relations personnel disseminate large amounts of information to the organisation's client publics. Written communication is the most versatile tool of public relations, and good writing ability is essential. Public relations practitioners must be adept at writing for a variety of media and audiences. It is not unusual for a person in public relations to prepare reports, news releases, speeches, broadcast scripts, technical manuals, employee publications, shareholder reports and other communications aimed at both organisational personnel and external groups. In addition, a public relations practitioner needs a thorough knowledge of the production techniques used in preparing various communications.

Public relations personnel also establish distribution channels for the organisation's publicity. They must have a thorough understanding of the various media, their areas of specialisation, the characteristics of their target audiences and their policies regarding publicity. Anyone who hopes to succeed in public relations must develop close working relationships with numerous media personnel to enlist their interest in disseminating an organisation's communications.

Further education combined with writing or media related experience is the best preparation for a career in public relations. Some beginners have a degree in journalism, communications or public relations, but some employers prefer a business background. Courses in journalism, business administration, marketing, creative writing, psychology, sociology, political science, economics, advertising, English and public speaking are recommended. Some employers require applicants to present a portfolio of published articles, television or radio programmes, slide presentations and other work samples. Other agencies are requiring written tests that include activities such as writing sample press releases. Manufacturing firms, public utilities, transport and insurance companies, and trade and professional associations are the largest employers of public relations personnel. In addition, sizeable numbers of public relations personnel work for health-related organisations, government agencies, educational institutions, museums, and religious and service groups.

Although some larger companies provide extensive formal training for new personnel, most new public relations employees learn on the job. Beginners usually perform routine tasks such as maintaining files about company activities and searching secondary data sources for information that can be used in publicity materials. More experienced employees write press releases, speeches and articles and help plan public relations campaigns.

Employment opportunities in public relations are expected to increase faster than the average for all occupations through the 1990s. One caveat is in order, however:

competition for first jobs is keen. The prospects are best for applicants who have solid academic preparation and some media experience. Areas that are projected to offer the most opportunity are in public relations agencies in the areas of product publicity, mergers and acquistions, and financial and investor relations.[7] Abilities that differentiate candidates, such as a basic understanding of computers, are becoming increasingly important.

Industrial Buying

Industrial buyers, or purchasing agents, are responsible for maintaining an adequate supply of the goods and services that an organisation needs for operations. In general, industrial buyers purchase all items needed for direct use in producing other products and for use in the day to day operations. Industrial buyers in large firms often specialise in purchasing a single, specific class of products, for example, all petroleum based lubricants. In smaller organisations, buyers may be responsible for purchasing many different categories of items, including such goods as raw materials, component parts, office supplies and operating services.

An industrial buyer's main job is selecting suppliers who offer the best quality, service and price. When the products to be purchased are standardised, buyers may compare suppliers by examining catalogues and trade journals, making purchases by description. Buyers who purchase highly homogeneous products often meet with salespeople to examine samples and observe demonstrations. Sometimes, buyers must inspect the actual product before purchasing; in other cases, they invite suppliers to bid on large orders. Buyers who purchase specialised equipment often deal directly with manufacturers to obtain specially designed items made to specifications. After choosing a supplier and placing an order, an industrial buyer usually must trace the shipment to ensure on-time delivery. Finally, the buyer sometimes is responsible for receiving and inspecting an order and authorising payment to the shipper.

Training requirements for a career in industrial buying relate to the needs of the firm and the types of products purchased. A manufacturer of heavy machinery may prefer an applicant who has a background in engineering; a service company, on the other hand, may recruit social studies graduates. Although it is not generally required, a college degree is becoming increasingly important for buyers who wish to advance to management positions.

Employment prospects for industrial buyers are expected to increase faster than average through the 1990s. Opportunities will be excellent for individuals with a master's degree in business administration (MBA) or an honours degree in engineering, science or business administration. In addition, companies that manufacture heavy equipment, computer equipment and communications equipment will need buyers with technical backgrounds.

Distribution Management

A distribution (or traffic) manager arranges for the transport of goods within firms and through marketing channels. Transport is an essential distribution activity that permits a firm to create time and place utility for its products. It is the distribution manager's job to analyse various transport modes and select the combination that minimises cost and transit time while providing acceptable levels of reliability, capability, accessibility and security.

To accomplish this task, a distribution manager performs many activities. First, the individual must choose one or a combination of transport modes from the five major modes available: railways, motor vehicles, inland waterways, pipelines and airways. Then the distribution manager must select the specific routes the goods will travel and the particular carriers to be used, weighing such factors as freight classifications and regulations, freight charges, time schedules, shipment sizes, and loss and damage ratios. In addition, this person may be responsible for preparing shipping documents, tracing shipments, handling loss and damage claims, keeping records of freight rates and monitoring changes in government regulations and transport technology.

Distribution management employs relatively few people and is expected to grow about as fast as the average for all occupations in the near future. Manufacturing firms are the largest employers of distribution managers, although some traffic managers work for wholesalers, retail stores and consulting firms. Salaries of experienced distribution managers vary but generally are much higher than the average for all non-supervisory personnel.

Starting jobs are diverse, varying from inventory/stock control, traffic scheduling, operations management or distribution management. Inventory management is an area of great opportunity because many firms see inventory costs as high relative to foreign competition, especially that from the Japanese. Just-in-time inventory systems are designed by inventory control specialists to work with the bare minimum of inventory.[8]

Most employers prefer graduates of technical programmes or seek people who have completed courses in transport, logistics, distribution management, economics, statistics, computer science, management, marketing and commercial law. A successful distribution manager must be adept at handling technical data and be able to interpret and communicate highly technical information.

Product Management

The product manager occupies a staff position and is responsible for the success or failure of a product line. Product managers co-ordinate most of the marketing activities required to market a product; however, because they hold staff positions, they have relatively little actual authority over marketing personnel. Even so, they take on a large amount of responsibility and typically are quite well paid relative to other marketing employees. Being a product manager can be rewarding both financially and psychologically, but it can also be frustrating because of the disparity between responsibility and authority.

A product manager should have a general knowledge of advertising, transport modes, inventory control, selling and sales management, sales promotion, marketing research, design and packaging, pricing, and warehousing. The individual must be knowledgeable enough to communicate effectively with personnel in these functional areas and to make suggestions and help assess alternatives when major decisions are being made.

Product managers usually need university training in an area of business administration. A master's degree is helpful, although a person usually does not become a product manager directly out of university or polytechnic. Frequently, several years of selling and sales management are prerequisites for a product management position, which often is a major step in the career path of top level marketing executives.

Advertising

Advertising pervades daily life. As detailed in Chapter 15, business and non-business organisations use advertising in many ways and for many reasons. Advertising clearly needs individuals with diverse skills to fill a variety of jobs. Creative imagination, artistic talent and expertise in expression and persuasion are important for copywriters, artists and account executives. Sales ability and managerial skills are vital to the success of advertising managers, media buyers and production managers. Research directors must have a solid understanding of research techniques and human behaviour. As a profession, advertising is very difficult to enter; jobs are scarce. Generally, students of business studies work on the planning and strategy issues; the creative side is dominated by art school graduates.

Advertising professionals disagree on the most beneficial educational background for a career in advertising. Most employers prefer university graduates. Some employers seek individuals with degrees in advertising, journalism or business; most prefer graduates with broad classics and social studies backgrounds. Still other employers rank relevant work experience above educational background. Starting salaries are often quite low; but to gain experience in the advertising industry, employees must work their way up in the system. The entry level salaries of media assistants and account co-ordinators are often £12,000 or less.

A variety of organisations employ advertising personnel. Although advertising agencies are perhaps the most visible and glamorous of employers, many manufacturing firms, retail stores, banks, utility companies, and professional and trade associations maintain advertising departments. Advertising jobs also can be found with television and radio stations, newspapers and magazines. Other businesses that employ advertising personnel include printers, art studios, letter shops and package design firms. Specific advertising jobs include advertising manager, account executive, research director, copywriter, media specialist and production manager.[9]

Employment opportunities for advertising personnel are expected to decrease in the 1990s as agency acquisitions and mergers continue. General economic conditions, however, strongly influence the size of advertising budgets and, hence, employment opportunities. Currently there are few vacancies.

Retail Management

Several million people in the UK and in each EC country work in the retail industry. Although a career in retailing may begin in sales, there is more to retailing than simply selling. Many retail personnel occupy management positions. Besides managing the sales force, they focus on selecting and ordering merchandise, promotional activities, inventory control, customer credit operations, accounting, personnel and store security.

How retail stores are organised varies. In many large department stores, retail management personnel rarely become involved in actually selling to customers; these duties are performed by retail sales assistants. However, other types of retail organisations may require management personnel to perform selling activities from time to time.

Large retail groups offer a variety of management positions besides those at the very top, including assistant buyers, buyers, department managers, section managers, store managers, division managers, regional managers and directors of merchandising. The following list describes the general duties of four of these positions; the precise nature of these duties varies from one retail organisation to another.

A section or department manager co-ordinates inventory and promotions and interacts with buyers, salespeople and ultimately consumers. The manager performs merchandising, labour relations and managerial activities and can rarely expect to get away with as little as a 40 hour work week.

The buyer's task is more focused. In this fast-paced occupation, there is much travel, pressure and need to be open minded with respect to new and potentially successful items.

The regional manager co-ordinates the activities of several stores within a given area. Sales, promotions and procedures in general are monitored and supported.

The director of merchandising has a broad scope of managerial responsibility and reports to the managing director at the top of the organisation.

Traditionally, retail managers began their careers as sales assistants. Today, many large retailers hire university or polytechnic educated people, put them through management training programmes and then place them directly into management positions.

They frequently hire people with backgrounds in social studies or business administration. Sales and retailing are the greatest employment opportunities for marketing students.

Retail management positions can be exciting and challenging. Competent, ambitious individuals often assume a great deal of responsibility very quickly and advance rapidly. However, pay for entry level positions (management trainees) has historically been below average. This situation is changing with major specialty, department and discount stores offering entry salaries in the £13,000 to £17,000 range. In addition, a retail manager's job is physically demanding and sometimes entails long working hours. None the less, positions in retail management often provide numerous opportunities to excel and advance.

Direct Marketing

One of the most dynamic areas in marketing is direct marketing and teleselling, in which the seller uses one or more direct media (telephone, mail, print or television) to solicit a response. The telephone is a major vehicle for selling many consumer products and services. Telemarketing is direct selling to customers using a variety of technological improvements in telephone services. Much of the industry's sales come from business-to-business marketing, not from selling to consumers at home. In addition, the telemarketing industry has been growing an average of 30 per cent per year.

Direct mail catalogues appeal to market segments such as working women or people who find going to retail stores difficult or inconvenient. Newspapers and magazines offer great opportunity, especially in special market segments. *Golf Digest,* for example, is obviously a good medium for selling golfing equipment. Cable television provides many new opportunities for selling directly to consumers. Interactive cable will offer a new method to expand direct marketing by developing timely exchange opportunities for consumers.

The most important asset in direct marketing is experience. Employers often look to other industries to locate experienced professionals. In a choice between an MBA or an individual with a direct marketing background, the experienced individual would be hired.[10] This preference means that if you can obtain an entry level position in direct marketing, you will have a real advantage in developing a career.

Jobs in direct marketing include buyers, such as department store buyers, who select goods for catalogue, telephone or direct mail sales. Catalogue managers develop marketing strategies for each new catalogue that goes into the mail. Research/mailing list management involves developing lists of products that will sell in direct marketing and lists of names that will respond to a direct mail effort. Order fulfillment managers direct the shipment of products once they are sold. Nearly all not for profit organisations have fund-raising managers who use direct marketing to obtain financial support.[11]

The executive vice president of the advertising agency Young & Rubicam, Inc. in New York stated that direct marketing will have to be used "not as a tactic, but as a strategic tool".[12] Direct marketing's effectiveness is enhanced by periodic analysis of advertising and communications at all phases of contact with the consumer. Direct marketing involves all aspects of the marketing decision. It is becoming a more professional career area that provides great opportunity.

Notes

Chapter 1

1. M. Baker, "One more time—what is marketing?" in *The Marketing Book,* M. Baker, ed. (London: Heinemann/Chartered Institute of Marketing, 1991).
2. Peter D. Bennett, ed., *The Dictionary of Marketing Terms* (Chicago, Ill.: American Marketing Association, 1988), p. 115. Reprinted by permission.
3. O. C. Ferrell and George Lucas, "An evaluation of progress in the development of a definition of marketing", *Journal of the Academy of Marketing Science,* Fall 1987, p. 17.
4. Philip Kotler, *Marketing Management: Analysis, Planning, Implementation, and Control,* 6th ed. (Englewood Cliffs, N.J.: Prenticc-Hall, 1988), p. 6.
5. Ferrell and Lucas, p. 20.
6. Edward C. Baig, "Products of the year", *Fortune,* 5 December 1988, pp. 89–98.
7. Gene R. Laczniak and Robert F. Lusch, "Environment and strategy in 1995: a survey of high-level executives", *Journal of Consumer Marketing,* Spring 1986, p. 28.

Chapter 2

1. Philip Kotler, "Megamarketing", *Harvard Business Review,* March-April 1986, pp. 117–24.
2. *Britain 1990: An Official Handbook* (London: Central Office of Information, 1990).
3. Joseph Plummer, "The concept of application of life style segmentation", *Journal of Marketing,* January 1974, p. 34.
4. *The IBA Code of Advertising Standards and Practice* (London: Independent Broadcasting Authority, December 1977), p. 3. The IBA is now the ITC.
5. Brian Bremner, "A New Sales Pitch: The Environment", *Business Week,* 24 July 1989, p. 50.
6. Robin Knight, with Eleni Dimmler, "The Greening of Europe's Industries", *U.S. News & World Report,* 5 June 1989, pp. 45–6.
7. Reprinted by permission from Herbert Simon, "Technology and Environment", *Management Science,* 19 (10), June 1973. Copyright 1973, The Institute of Management Sciences.
8. Judith Waldrop, "Inside America's Households", *American Demographics,* March 1989, pp. 22–3; *National Income and Expenditure Survey* (London: Central Statistical Office, 1990).
9. Wroe Alderson, *Dynamic Marketing Behavior* (Homewood, Ill.: Irwin, 1965), pp. 195–7.

Chapter 3

1. R. Frank and Y. Wind, *Market Segmentation* (Englewood Cliffs, N.J.: Prentice-Hall, 1972).
2. Yoram Wind, "Issues and advances in segmentation research", *Journal of Marketing Research,* August 1978, pp. 317–7.
3. Donald K. Clifford, Jr and Richard E. Cavanagh, *The Winning Performance: How America's High-Growth Companies Succeed* (New York: Bantam Books, 1985), p. 53.
4. Joseph G. Albonetti and Luis V. Dominguez, "Major influences on consumer goods marketers' decision to target US Hispanics", *Journal of Advertising Research,* February–March 1989, pp. 9–11.
5. John L. Lastovicka and Erich A. Joachimsthaler, "Improving the detection of personality-behavior relationships in consumer research", *Journal of Consumer Research,* March 1988, pp. 583–7.
6. Joseph T. Plummer, "The concept and application of life style segmentaton", *Journal of Marketing,* January 1974, p. 33.
7. James F. Engel, Roger D. Blackwell and Paul W. Miniard, *Consumer Behavior* (Orlando, Fla.: Dryden Press, 1990), pp. 348–9.
8. Russell I. Haley, "Benefit segmentation: a decision-oriented research tool", *Journal of Marketing,* July 1968, pp. 30–5.
9. Y. Wind, "Going to market: new twist for some old tricks", *Wharton Magazine,* 4, 1980.
10. T. Harrison, *A Handbook of Advertising Techniques* (London: Kogan Page, 1987), p.7.
11. A. Ries and J. Trout, *Positioning: The Battle for Your Mind* (New York: McGraw-Hill, 1981).
12. Philip Kotler, *Marketing Management: Analysis, Planning, and Control,* 6th ed. (Englewood Cliffs, N.J., Prentice-Hall, 1988), p. 257.

Chapter 4

1. James F. Engel, Roger D. Blackwell and Paul W. Miniard, *Consumer Behavior,* 5th ed. (Hinsdale, Ill.: Dryden Press, 1986), p. 5.
2. John A. Howard and Jagdish N. Sheth, *The Theory of Buyer Behavior* (New York: Wiley, 1969), pp. 27–8.
3. G. Foxall, "Consumer behaviour", in *The Marketing Book,* M. Baker, ed. (London: Heinemann/Chartered Institute of Marketing, 1987).
4. Kevin L. Keller and Richard Staelin, "Effects of quality and quantity of information on decision effectiveness", *Journal of Consumer Research,* September 1987, pp. 200–13.
5. Gabriel Biehal and Dipankar Chakravarti, "Consumers' use of memory and external information in choice: macro and micro perspectives", *Journal of Consumer Research,* March 1986, pp. 382–405.
6. Bobby J. Calder and Brian Sternthal, "Television commercial wearout: an information processing view", *Journal of Marketing Research,* May 1980, pp. 173–86.
7. Michael J. Houston, Terry L. Childers and Susan E. Heckler, "Picture-word consistency and the elaborative processing of advertisements", *Journal of Marketing Research,* November 1987, pp. 359–69.
8. James R. Bettman and Mita Sujan, "Effects of framing on eval-

uation of comparable and noncomparable alternatives by expert and novice consumers", *Journal of Consumer Research,* September 1987, pp. 141–54.

9. Robert A. Westbrook, "Product/consumption-based affective responses and postpurchase processes", *Journal of Marketing Research,* August 1987, pp. 258–70.

10. Patricia Sellers, "The ABC's of marketing to kids", *Fortune,* 8 May 1989, p. 115.

11. Judith Waldrop, "Inside America's households", *American Demographics,* March 1989, pp. 20–7.

12. Houston, Childers and Heckler, pp. 359–69.

13. Thomas S. Robertson and Hubert Gatignon, "Competitive effects on technology diffusion", *Journal of Marketing,* July 1986, pp. 1–12.

14. Robertson and Gatignon, pp. 1–12.

15. Al Ries and Jack Trout, *Positioning the Battle for Your Mind* (New York: McGraw-Hill Book Co., 1986).

16. James R. Bettman, *An Information Processing Theory of Consumer Choice* (Reading, Mass.: Addison-Wesley, 1979), pp. 18–24.

17. Joseph W. Alba and J. Wesley Hutchinson, "Dimensions of consumer expertise", *Journal of Consumer Research,* March 1987, pp. 411–54.

18. Akshay R. Rao and Kent B. Monroe, "The moderating effect of prior knowledge on cue utilization in product evaluations", *Journal of Consumer Research,* September 1988, pp. 253–64.

19. Ibid.

20. John L. Lastovika and Erich A. Joachimsthaler, "Improving the detection of personality-behavior relationships in consumer research", *Journal of Consumer Research,* March 1988, pp. 583–7.

21. Martha T. Moore, "Spring break: brand names chase sales", *USA Today,* 17 March 1989, p. B1.

22. Henry Assael, *Consumer Behavior and Marketing Action* (Bos-ton: Kent Publishing, 1987), p. 369.

23. Leonard L. Berry, "The time-sharing consumer", *Journal of Retailing,* Winter 1979, p. 69.

24. Mona Doyle, "The metamorphosis of the consumer", *Marketing Communications,* April 1989, pp. 18–22.

Chapter 5

1. Gregory D. Utah and Monroe M. Bird, "Changes in industrial buying: implications for industrial marketers", *Industrial Marketing Management,* 9, May 1980, pp. 117–21.

2. P. Green, P. Robinson and Y. Wind, "The determinant of vendor selection. The evaluation function approach", *Journal of Purchasing,* August 1968.

3. John I. Coppett, "Auditing your customer service activities", *Industrial Marketing Management,* November 1988, pp. 277–84.

4. Thomas L. Powers, "Identify and fulfill customer service expectations", *Industrial Marketing Management,* November 1988, pp. 273–6.

5. Mary Jo Bitner, Bernard H. Booms and Mary Stanfield Tetreault, "The service encounter: diagnosing favorable and unfavorable incidents", *Journal of Marketing,* 54, January 1990, pp. 71–84.

6. Jim Shaw, Joe Giglierano and Jeff Kallis, "Marketing complex technical products: the importance of intangible attributes", *Industrial Marketing Management,* 18, 1989, pp. 45–53.

7. Frederick E. Webster, Jr. and Yoram Wind, *Organizational Buying Behavior* (Englewood Cliffs, N.J.: Prentice-Hall, 1972), pp. 78–80.

8. Nigel C. G. Campbell, John L. Graham, Alan Jolibert and Hans Gunthe Meissner, "Marketing negotiations in France, Germany, the United Kingdom and the United States", *Journal of Marketing,* 52, April 1988, pp. 49–62.

Chapter 6

1. "Research" is accredited by The Market Research Society (Great Britain). Reprinted by permission.

2. Sally Dibb and Lyndon Simkin, *The Marketing Casebook* (London: Routledge, 1993).

3. Andrea Dunham, "Information systems are the key to managing future business needs", *Marketing News,* 23 May 1986, p. 11.

4. R. Birn, *The Effective Use of Market Research* (London: Kogan Page, 1990).

5. P. M. Chisnall, *Marketing Research* (London: McGraw-Hill, 1992).

6. Johny K. Johansson and Ikujiro Nonaha, "Market research the Japanese way", *Harvard Business Review,* May–June 1987, pp. 16–22.

7. Raymond E. Taylor, "Using the Delphi method to define marketing problems", *Business,* October–December 1984, p. 17.

8. Ronald L. Vaughn, "Demographic data banks: a new management resource", *Business Horizons,* November–December 1984, pp. 38–42. See also Chapter 5.

9. Gary Levin, "IRI says data can now link ads to sales", *Advertising Age,* 26 January 1987, pp. 3, 74.

10. Based on a survey conducted by Market Facts, Inc., 28 April 1983.

11. Martha Farnsworth Riche, "Who says yes?", *American Demographics,* February 1987, p. 8; George Gallup, Jr, "Survey research: current problems and future opportunities", *Journal of Consumer Marketing,* Winter 1988, pp. 27–9.

12. Jeffrey S. Conant, Denise T. Smart and Bruce J. Walker, "Main survey facilitation techniques: an assessment and proposal regarding reporting practices" (working paper, Texas A&M University, 1990).

13. *Practices, Trends and Expectations for the Market Research Industry 1987,* Market Facts, Inc., 29 April 1987.

14. Ibid.

15. Riche, p. 8.

16. Diane K. Bowers, "Telephone legislation", *Marketing Research,* March 1989, p. 47.

17. Stephen M. Billig, "Go slow, be wary when considering switch to computer assisted interviewing system", *Marketing News,* 26 November 1982, secl. 2, p. 2.

18. Practices, *Trends and Expectations for the Market Research Industry 1987,* Market Facts, Inc., 29 April 1987.

19. Alan J. Bush and A. Parasuraman, "Mall intercept versus telephone interviewing environment", *Journal of Advertising Research,* April–May 1985, p. 42.

20. Alan J. Bush and Joseph F. Hair, Jr, "An assessment of the mall intercept as a data collecting method", *Journal of Marketing Research,* May 1985, p. 162.

21. Jeff Wiss, "Meet MAX: computerized survey taker", *Marketing News,* 22 May 1989, p. 16.

22. Yorkshire Television's *The Marketing Mix* series.

23. Hal Sokolow, "In-depth interviews increasing in importance", *Marketing News*, 13 September 1985, p. 26.
24. D. S. Tull and D. I. Hawkins, *Marketing Research* (New York: Macmillan, 1990).
25. Michael J. Olivette, "Marketing research in the electric utility industry", *Marketing News*, 2 January 1987, p. 13.
26. Hanjoon Lee, Frank Acits and Ralph L. Day, "Evaluation and use of marketing research by decision makers: a behavioral simulation", *Journal of Marketing Research,* May 1987, p. 187.
27. Lynn Colemar, "It's selling disguised as research", *Marketing News*, 4 January 1988, p. 1.
28. O. C. Ferrell and Steven J. Skinner, "Ethical behavior and bureaucratic structure in marketing research organizations", *Journal of Marketing Research*, February 1988, pp. 103–4.
29. Brandt Allen, "Make information services pay its way", *Harvard Business Review*, January–February 1987, p. 57.

Chapter 7

1. Part of this definition is adapted from James D. Scott, Martin R. Warshaw and James R. Taylor, *Introduction to Marketing Management*, 5th ed. (Homewood, Ill.: Irwin, 1985), p. 215.
2. Theodore Levitt, "Marketing intangible products and product intangibles", *Harvard Business Review*, May-June 1981, pp. 94–102.
3. Robert W. Haas, *Industrial Marketing Management*, 3rd ed. (Boston: Kent Publishing, 1986), pp. 15–25.
4. M.J. Thomas, "Product development management", in *The Marketing Book*, M. Baker, ed. (London: Heinemann/The Chartered Institute of Marketing, 1987).
5. "New product failure: a self-fulfilling prophecy?" *Marketing Communications*, April 1989, p. 27.
6. Levitt, "Marketing intangible products and product intangibles", p. 96.
7. Christopher W. L. Hart, "The power of unconditional service guarantees", Harvard Business Review, July-August 1988, pp. 54–62.

Chapter 8

1. Peter D. Bennett, ed., *Dictionary of Marketing Terms* (Chicago: American Marketing Association, 1988), p. 18.
2. James U. McNeal and Linda Zeren, "Brand name selection for consumer products", *MSU Business Topics,* Spring 1981, p. 35.
3. Peter Doyle, "Building successful brands: the strategic options", *The Journal of Consumer Marketing,* Vol. 7, No. 2 (1993), pp. 5–20.
4. Henry Assael, *Consumer Behavior and Marketing Action,* 4th ed. (Boston: PWS-Kent, 1992).
5. Ronald Alsop, "Brand loyalty is rarely blind loyalty; rise in coupons, choices blamed for '80s erosion", *Wall Street Journal,* 19 October 1989, pp. B1, B6.
6. Chip Walker, "What's in a name?" *American Demographics,* February 1991, pp. 54–7.
7. Alan Miller, "Gains share in dollars and units during 1990 third quarter", *Private Label,* January–February 1991, pp. 85–9.
8. Judann Dagnoli, "New study blasts private labels", *Advertising Age,* 19 June 1989, p. 34.
9. "No brand like an old brand", *Forbes,* 11 June 1990, p. 180.
10. Leonard L. Berry, Edwin E. Lefkowith and Terry Clark, "In

services, what's in a name?" *Harvard Business Review,* September–October 1988, pp. 2–4.
11. Dorothy Cohen, "Trademark Strategy", *Journal of Marketing,* January 1986, p. 63.
12. "Trademark Stylesheet", U.S. Trademark Association, no. 1A.
13. Ronald F. Bush, Peter H. Bloch and Scott Dawson, "Remedies for product counterfeiting", *Business Horizons,* January–February 1989, pp. 59–65; Pete Engardio, with Todd Vogel and Dinah Lee, "Companies are knocking off the knockoff outfits", *Business Week,* 26 September 1988, pp. 86–8; and Michael Harvey, "A new way to combat product counterfeiting", *Business Horizons,* July–August 1988, pp. 19–28.
14. Fred W. Morgan, "Tampered goods: legal developments and marketing guidelines", *Journal of Marketing,* April 1988, pp. 86–96.
15. Ibid.
16. James U. McNeal, *Consumer Behavior: An Integrative Approach* (Boston: Little, Brown, 1982), pp. 221–2.
17. "Not in my backyard", CNN Special Report, Cable News Network, 19 December 1988.
18. Alecia Swasy, "Ecology and buyer wants don't jibe", *Wall Street Journal,* 23 August 1989, p. B1.
19. Laura Bird, "Romancing the package", *Adweek's Marketing Week,* 21 January 1991, p. 11.
20. CGM, *Marketing Guide 14: 3D Packaging Design,* Haymarket Publishing Services Ltd, 1992.

Chapter 9

1. Roger C. Bennet and Robert G. Cooper, "The Product Life Cycle Trap", *Business Horizons,* September-October 1984, pp. 7–16.
2. Lynn W. Phillips, Dae R. Chang and Robert D. Buzzell, "Product quality, cost position and business performance: a test of some key hypotheses", *Journal of Marketing,* Spring 1983, pp. 26–43.
3. Douglas M. Lambert and Jay U. Sterling, "Identifying and eliminating weak products", *Business,* July-September 1988, pp. 3–10.
4. Peter F. Drucker, "The discipline of innovation", *Harvard Business Review,* May-June 1985, pp. 67–8.
5. Lawrence Ingrassia, "By improving scotch paper, 3M gets new product winner", *Wall Street Journal,* 31 March 1983, p. 27.
6. Jonathan B. Levine, "Keeping new ideas kicking around", *Business Week,* Innovation 1989 issue, p. 128.
7. Joseph Weber, "Going over the lab wall in search of new ideas", *Business Week,* Innovation 1989 issue, p. 132.
8. Joshua Hyatt, "Ask and you shall receive", *Inc.,* September 1989, pp. 90–101.
9. "Winging it at McDonald's", *USA Today,* 5 September 1989, p. 1B.
10. Eleanor Johnson Tracy, "Testing time for test marketing", *Fortune,* 29 October 1984, pp. 75–6.
11. Adapted from Everett M. Rogers, *Diffusion of Innovations* (New York: Macmillan, 1962), pp. 81–6.
12. Graham J. Hooley and John Saunders, *Competitive Positioning: The Key to Market Success* (Englewood Cliffs, N.J.: Prentice-Hall, 1993).
13. F. Stewart DeBruicker and Gregory L. Summe, "Make sure your customers keep coming back", *Harvard Business Review,* January-February 1985, pp. 92–8.

Chapter 10

1. Wroe Alderson, *Marketing Behavior and Executive Action* (Homewood, Ill.: Irwin, 1957), pp. 201–11.
2. Leo Aspinwall, "The marketing characteristics of goods", in *Four Marketing Theories* (Boulder: University of Colorado Press, 1961), pp. 27–32.
3. Bert Rosenbloom, *Marketing Channels: A Management View* (Hinsdale, Ill.: Dryden, 1987), p. 160.
4. Ibid., p. 161.
5. Ibid., pp. 254–5.
6. Wroe Alderson, *Dynamic Marketing Behavior* (Homewood, Ill.: Irwin, 1965), p. 239.
7. Lanny J. Ryan, Gaye C. Dawson, and Thomas Galek, "New distribution channels for microcomputer software", *Business*, October–December 1985, pp. 21–2.
8. Adel I. El-Ansary, "Perspectives on channel system performance", in *Contemporary Issues in Marketing Channels,* ed. Robert F. Lusch and Paul H. Zinszer (Norman: University of Oklahoma Press, 1979), p. 50.
9. Kenneth G. Hardy and Allan J. Magrath, "Ten ways for manufacturers to improve distribution management", *Business Horizons,* November–December 1988, p.68.
10. Ronald D. Michman and Stanley D. Sibley, *Marketing Channels and Strategies* (Columbus, Ohio: Grid Publishing, 1980), pp. 412–17.
11. John F. Gaski and John R. Nevin, "The differential effects of exercised and unexercised power sources in a marketing channel", *Journal of Marketing Research,* July 1985, p. 139.
12. Bert Rosenbloom, *Marketing Channels: A Management View* (Hinsdale, Ill.: Dryden Press, 1987), p. 98.
13. Ibid., pp. 96–7.

Chapter 11

1. Clarence Casson, "1988 wholesaler giants; making all the right moves", Building Supply Home Centers, September 1988, p. 56.
2. "Wholesaling without borders", Rebecca Rolfes, *Medical Marketing & Media,* February 1991, pp. 74–6.
3. Bert Rosenbloom, *Marketing Channels: A Management View* (Hinsdale, Ill.: Dryden Press, 1987), p. 63.
4. *US Census of Wholesale Trade,* May 1985, p. 207.
5. Rosenbloom, p. 34.
6. Ibid., p. 63.
7. Arthur Meidan and Anne Tomes, "Cash and carry customers' shopping habits and supplier choice criteria", *International Journal of Retail & Distribution Management,* or 19 May 1991, pp. 29–36.
8. Elizabeth Jane Moore "Grocery distribution in the UK: recent changes and future prospects", *International Journal of Retail & Distribution Management,* 19 July 1991, pp. 18–24.
9. "Drop-shipping grows to save depot costs", *Supermarket News,* 1 April 1985, pp. 1, 17.
10. *US Census of Wholesale Trade,* May 1985, p. 207.
11. *US Census of Wholesale Trade,* May 1985, p. 207.
12. Rosenbloom, p. 61.
13. Ibid.
14. Ibid., p. 62.
15. Thomas V. Bonoma, "Get more out of your trade shows", *Harvard Business Review,* January–February 1983, pp. 75–83.
16. Rosenbloom, p. 185.

17. "Trade shows—part 1; a major sales and marketing tool", *Small Business Report,* June 1988, pp. 34–9.
18. Rosenbloom, p. 185.
19. Richard K. Swandby and Jonathan M. Cox, "Trade show trends: exhibiting growth paces economic strengths", *Business Marketing,* May 1985, p. 50.
20. Joseph Weber, "Mom and Pop move out of wholesaling", *Business Week,* 9 January 1989, p. 91.
21. Ibid.

Chapter 12

1. H. Carter, The Study of Urban Geography (London: Edward Arnold, 1972), pp. 205–47.
2. J. A. Dawson. *Shopping Centre Development* (Harlow: Longman, 1983), Chapter 2.
3. Ibid.
4. Russell Schiller, "Out of town exodus", in *The Changing Face of British Retailing* (London: Newman Books, 1987), pp. 64–73.
5. Kenneth C. Schneider, "Telemarketing as a promotional tool—its effects and side effects", *Journal of Consumer Marketing*, Winter 1985, pp. 29–39.
6. Joel Dreyfuss, "Reach out and sell something", *Fortune,* 26 November 1984, pp. 127–8.
7. "V/T census of the industry issue—1988," *Vending Times*, 1988, p. 49. Reprinted by permission.
8. Ronald Alsop, "Food giants take to mails to push fancy product lines," *Wall Street Journal*, 28 February 1985, p. 85.
9. Keynote Publications, 1989.
10. Al Urbanski, "The franchise option", *Sales & Marketing* Management, February 1988, pp. 28–33.
11. Statistical Abstract of the US, 1989, p. 760.
12. C. H. Anderson, *Retailing* (St. Paul, Minn.: West, 1993).
13. R. L. Davies and D. S. Rogers, *Store Location and Store Assessment Research* (Chichester: Wiley, 1984).
14. R. L. Davies, *Marketing Geography* (London: Methuen 1976).
15. L. Simkin, "SLAM: store location assessment model—theory and practice", *OMEGA*, 17(1) (1989), pp. 53–8.
16. C. Glenn Walters and Blaise J. Bergiel, *Marketing Channels*, 2nd ed. (Glenview, Ill.: Scott, Foresman, 1982), p. 205.
17. J. R. Maier and L. Simkin, "Prioritising stock phasing for multiple retailers", *OMEGA*, 18(1), 1988, pp. 33–40.
18. D. Cook and R. D. Walters, *Retail Marketing* (London: Prentice-Hall, 1991).
19. George H. Lucas, Jr., and Larry G. Gresham, "How to position for retail success", *Business*, April–June 1988, pp. 3–13.
20. G. J. Davies and J. M. Brooks, *Positioning Strategy in Retailing* (London: Paul Chapman, 1989).
21. Leslie Wayne, "Rewriting the rules of retailing", The New York Times, 15 October 1989, p. F6.
22. Terence Conran, "The retail image", in The Retail Report (London: Healey & Baker, 1985).
23. Francine Schwadel, "Little touches spur Wal-Mart's rise; shoppers react to logo, decor, employee vests", *Wall Street Journal*, 22 September 1989, p. B1.
24. Stanley C. Hollander, "The wheel of retailing", *Journal of Marketing*, July 1960, p. 37.
25. W. S. Howe, "UK retailer vertical power, market competition and consumer welfare", *International Journal of Retail and Distribution Management*, 18(2), 1990, pp. 16–25.

26. K. K. Tse, "Marks & Spencer: a manufacturer without factories", *International Trends in Retailing*, 6(2), 1989, pp. 23–36.

27. R. M. Grant, "Manufacturer-retailer relations: the shifting balance of power", in Gerry Johnson, *Business Strategy and Retailing* (Chichester: Wiley, 1987), pp. 43–58.

28. Lynd Morley, "Mapping the Future", *Retail Technology*, 2(7), 1988, pp. 40–2.

29. Tony Rudd, "Trends in Physical Distribution," in The Changing Face of British Retailing (London: Newman Books, 1987), pp. 84–93.

30. C. Doherty, J. R. Maier and L. Simkin, "DPP decision support in retail merchandising", *OMEGA* 21(1), 1993, pp. 25–33.

Chapter 13

1. Carl M. Guelzo, *Introduction to Logistics Management* (Englewood Cliffs, N.J.: Prentice-Hall, 1986), p. 32

2. John T. Mentzer, Roger Gomes and Robert E. Krapfel, Jr., "Physical distribution service: a fundamental marketing concept?" *Journal of the Academy of Marketing Science*, Winter 1989, p. 59.

3. Lloyd M. Rinehart, M. Bixby Cooper and George D. Wagenheim, "Furthering the integration of marketing and logistics through customer service in the channel", *Journal of the Academy of Marketing Science*, Winter 1989, p. 67.

4. Charles A. Taff, *Management of Physical Distribution and Transportation* (Homewood, Ill.: Irwin, 1984), p. 250.

5. Judith Graham, "IKEA furnishing its US identity", *Advertising Age*, 14 September 1989, p. 79; and Jonathan Reynolds, "IKEA: a competitive company with style", *Retail & Distribution Management (UK)*, May/June 1988, pp. 32–4.

6. Rinehart, Cooper and Wagenheim, p. 67.

7. Guelzo, pp. 35–6.

8. Taff, p. 240.

9. Ibid., p. 244.

10. Guelzo, p. 102.

11. Adapted from John F. Magee, *Physical Distribution Systems* (New York: McGraw-Hill, Inc., 1967). Reprinted by permission of the author.

12. James C. Johnson and Donald F. Wood, *Contemporary Physical Distribution & Logistics*, 2nd ed. (Tulsa, Okla.: Penn Well Publishing Company, 1982), p. 356.

13. Guelzo, p. 102.

14. The EOQ formula for the optimal order quantity is $EOQ = 2DR/I$, where EOQ = optimum average order size, D = total demand, R = cost of processing an order and I = cost of maintaining one unit of inventory per year. For a more complete description of EOQ methods and terminology, see Frank S. McLaughlin and Robert C. Pickardt, *Quantitative Techniques for Management Decisions* (Boston: Houghton Mifflin, 1978), pp. 104–119.

15. "Watch for these red flags", *Traffic Management*, January 1983, p. 8.

16. David N. Burt, "Managing suppliers up to speed", *Harvard Business Review*, July-August 1989, p. 128.

17. Ibid., p. 129.

18. Peter D. Bennett, ed., *Dictionary of Marketing Terms* (Chicago: American Marketing Association, 1988), p. 204.

19. Guelzo, pp. 50–2.

20. John Gattorna, *Handbook of Physical Distribution Management* (Aldershot: Gower Publishing Co. Ltd, 1983), pp. 263–6.

21. Donald F. Wood and James C. Johnson, *Contemporary Transportation* (Tulsa, Okla.: Petroleum Publishing, 1980), p. 289.

22. Taff, p. 126.

23. Guelzo, p. 53.

24. John J. Coyle, Edward Bardi and C. John Langley, Jr., *The Management of Business Logistics* (St. Paul, Minn.: West, 1988), pp. 327–9.

25. Thomas A. Foster and Joseph V. Barks, "Here comes the best", *Distribution*, September 1984, p. 25.

26. Allen R. Wastler, "Intermodal leaders ponder riddle of winning more freight", *Traffic World*, 19 June, 1989, pp. 14–15.

Chapter 14

1. Richard W. Pollay, "On the value of reflections on the values in 'The distorted mirror' ", *Journal of Marketing*, July 1987, pp. 104–9.

2. Morris B. Holbrook, "Mirror, mirror, on the wall, what's unfair in the reflections on advertising", *Journal of Marketing*, July 1987, pp. 95–103.

3. Richard N. Farmer, "Would you want your granddaughter to marry a Taiwanese marketing man?" *Journal of Marketing*, October 1987, pp. 111–16.

4. Colin Coulson-Thomas, *Marketing Communications* (London: Heinemann, 1986).

5. P. "Rajan" Varadarajan and Anil Menon, "Cause-related marketing: a coalignment of marketing strategy and corporate philanthropy", *Journal of Marketing*, July 1988, pp. 58–74.

6. John Rossiter and Larry Percy, *Advertising and Promotion Management* (New York: McGraw-Hill, 1987).

7. In case you do not read Chinese, this says, "In the factory we make cosmetics, and in the store we sell hope." Prepared by Chih Kang Wang.

8. Terence A. Shimp and M. Wayne Delozier, *Promotion Management and Marketing Communication* (Hinsdale, Ill.: Dryden Press, 1986), pp. 25–6.

9. Carlos E. Garcia, "Hispanic market is accessible if research is designed correctly", *Marketing News*, 4 January 1988, p. 46.

10. Adapted from Everett M. Rogers, *Diffusion of Innovations* (New York: Free Press, 1962), pp. 81–6, 98–102.

11. Lawrence J. Marks and Michael A. Kamins, "Product sampling and advertising sequence, belief strength, confidence and attitudes", *Journal of Marketing Research*, August 1988, pp. 266–81.

12. Rogers, pp. 247–50.

13. Rossiter and Percy.

14. M. Flandin, E. Martin and L. Simkin, "Advertising effectiveness research: a survey of agencies, clients and conflicts", *International Journal of Advertising*, 11 March 1992, pp. 203–14.

15. This definition is adapted from John F. Luick and William L Ziegler, *Sales Promotion and Modern Merchandising* (New York: McGraw-Hill, 1968), p. 4.

16. Roger A. Kerin and William L. Cron, "Assessing trade show functions and performance: an exploratory study", *Journal of Marketing*, July 1987, pp. 87–94.

17. Marcy Magiera, "Holy Batvideo! Christmas already?" *Advertising Age*, 11 September 1989, p. 6.

18. *Advertising Statistics Yearbook* (London: The Advertising Association, 1990), p. 68.

19. Alvin A. Achenbaum and F. Kent Mitchel, "Pulling away from push marketing", *Harvard Business Review*, May-June 1987, p. 38.

Chapter 15

1. *Students' Briefs* (London: The Advertising Association, 1988).
2. *CBS This Morning*, CBS (TV), 11 April 1990.
3. Scott Hume, "Pizza Hut is frosted; new ad takes slap at McDonald's test product", *Advertising Age,* 18 September 1989, p. 4.
4. Torin Douglas, *The Complete Guide to Advertising* (London: Macmillan, 1985).
5. "Alberto bounces back", *Marketing,* 24 May 1990, p. 2
6. Laurie Freeman, "P&G to unveil refill package", *Advertising Age,* 6 November 1989, pp. 1, 69.
7. James E. Littlefield and C. A. Kirkpatrick, *Advertising Mass Communication in Marketing* (Boston: Houghton Mifflin, 1970), p. 178.
8. S. Watson Dunn and Arnold M. Barban, *Advertising: Its Role in Modern Marketing,* 6th ed. (Hinsdale, Ill.: Dryden Press, 1986), p. 493.
9. Patrick Quinn, *Low Budget Advertising* (London: Heinemann, 1988).
10. M. Flandin, E. Martin and L. Simkin, "Advertising effectiveness research: a survey of agencies, clients and conflicts", *International Journal of Advertising,* 11(3), 1992, pp. 203–214.
11. Ronald Alsop, "TV ads that are likeable get plus ratings for persuasiveness", *Wall Street Journal,* 20 February 1986, p. 21.
12. Marvin E. Goldberg and Gerald J. Gorn, "Happy and sad TV programmes: how they affect reactions to commercials", *Journal of Consumer Research,* December 1987, pp. 387–403.
13. *Marketing,* 24 May 1990, p. 5.
14. *Public Relations Practice—Its Role and Parameters* (London: The Institute of Public Relations, 1984).
15. The Advertising Association, London, 1990; *The Independent,* 12 August 1990; Robin Cobb, "The art of gentle persuasion", *Marketing,* 6 September 1990, pp. 25–6; and Bill Britt, "PR leads from front as buy-up battles rage", *Marketing,* 1 February 1990, p. 13.
16. David Wragg, *Public Relations for Sales and Marketing Management* (London: Kogan Page, 1987).
17. Frank Jefkins, *Public Relations Techniques* (London: Heinemann, 1988).
18. BBC and ITN news broadcasts, February and March 1993.
19. Marc G. Weinberger and Jean B. Romeo, "The impact of negative product news", *Business Horizons,* January-February 1989, p. 44.

Chapter 16

1. *Marketing,* 28 June 1990, p. 13.
2. Julian Cummins, *Sales Promotion* (London: Kogan Page, 1989).
3. Myron Gable and B. J. Reed, "The current status of women in professional selling", *Journal of Personal Selling & Sales Management,* May 1987, pp. 33–9.
4. William A. Weeks and Darrel D. Muehing, "Students' perceptions of personal selling", *Industrial Marketing Management,* May 1987, pp. 145–51.
5. "Getting ahead and staying ahead as the competition heats up", *Agency Sales Magazine,* June 1987, pp. 38–42.

6. Chris de Winter, *Telephone Selling* (London: Heinemann, 1988).
7. Thomas W. Leigh and Patrick F. McGraw, "Mapping the procedural knowledge of industrial sales personnel: a script-theoretic investigation", *Journal of Marketing,* January 1989, pp. 16–34.
8. Thayer C. Taylor, "Xerox: who says you can't be big and fast?" *Sales & Marketing Management,* November 1987, pp. 62–5.
9. Leigh and McGraw, pp. 16–34.
10. John Nemec, "Do you have grand finales?" *American Salesman,* June 1987, pp. 3–6.
11. William C. Moncrief, "Five types of industrial sales jobs", *Industrial Marketing Management,* 17 (1988), p. 164.
12. A. J. Magrath, "Are you overdoing 'lean and mean'?" *Sales & Marketing Management,* January 1988, pp. 46–53.
13. Tony Adams, *Successful Sales Management* (London: Heinemann, 1988).
14. Coleman, pp. 6, 21.
15. Patrick C. Fleenor, "Selling and sales management in action: assessment center selection of sales representatives," *Journal of Personal Selling & Sales Management,* May 1987, pp. 57–9.
16. René Y. Darmon, "The impact of incentive compensation on the salesperson's work habits: an economic model", *Journal of Personal Selling & Sales Management,* May 1987, pp. 21–32.
17. Aimee Stern, "Commissions catch on at department stores", *Adweek's Marketing Week,* 1 February 1988, p. 5.
18. Terese Hudson, "Holding meetings sharpens employees' sales skills", *Savings Institutions,* July 1987, pp. 109–111.
19. Dan Woog, "Taking sales high tech", *High Tech Marketing,* May 1987, pp. 17–22.
20. Sandra Hile Hart, William C. Moncrief and A. Parasuraman, "An empirical investigation of salespeople's performance, effort and selling method during a sales contest", *Journal of the Academy of Marketing Science,* Winter 1989, pp. 29–39.
21. Robert Martinott, "The traveling salesman goes high tech", *Chemical Week,* 10 June 1987, pp. 22–24.
22. John F. Luick and William L. Ziegler, *Sales Promotion and Modern Merchandising* (New York: McGraw-Hill, 1968), and Don E. Schultz and William A. Robinson, *Sales Promotion Management* (Chicago: Crain Books, 1982).
23. Thomas McCann, "Promotions will gain more clout in the '90s," *Marketing News,* 6 November 1989, pp. 4, 24.
24. Cummins, p. 14.
25. "Factfile," *Marketing,* 12 July 1990, p. 18.
26. W. E. Phillips and Bill Robinson, "Continued sales (price) promotion destroys brands: yes; no", Marketing News, 16 January 1989, pp. 4, 8.
27. Emin Babakus, Peter Tat and William Cunningham, "Coupon redemption: a motivational perspective", *Journal of Consumer Marketing,* Spring 1988, p. 40.
28. Donna Campanella, "Sales promotion: couponmania", *Marketing and Media Decisions,* June 1987, pp. 118–122.
29. Alison Fahey, "Coupon war fallout", *Advertising Age,* 4 September 1989, p. 2.
30. Campanella, pp. 118–122.
31. Ibid.
32. Joe Agnew, "P-O-P [P-O-S] displays are becoming a matter of consumer convenience", *Marketing News,* 9 October 1987, p. 14.
33. Ibid., p. 16.
34. Alison Fahey, "Study shows retailers rely on P-O-P [P-O-S]", *Advertising Age,* 27 November 1989 , p. 83.

35. "Sampling accelerates adoption of new products", *Marketing News*, 11 September 1987, p. 21.
36. Peter Tat, William A. Cunningham and Emin Babakus, "Consumer perceptions of rebates", *Journal of Advertising Research*, August-September 1988, p. 48.
37. Gerrie Anthea, "Sales promotion putting up the premium", *Marketing*, 16 April 1987.
38. Steven W. Colford, "Marriott sets largest promo", *Advertising Age*, 2 October 1989, p. 58.
39. Eileen Norris, "Everyone will grab at a chance to win", *Advertising Age*, 22 August 1983, p. M10.
40. Ed Crimmins, "A co-op myth: it is a tragedy that stores don't spend all their accruals", *Sales & Marketing Management*, 7 February 1983, pp. 72–3.
41. Gillian Upton, "Sales promotion: getting results Barbados style", *Marketing*, 16 April 1987, pp. 37–40.

Chapter 17

1. Michael J. O'Connor, "What is the logic of a price war?" Arthur Andersen & Company, *International Trends in Retailing*, Spring 1986.
2. Saeed Samier, "Pricing in marketing strategies of U.S. and foreign based Companies," *Journal of Business Research*, 1987, pp. 15–23.
3. Robert P. Ford, "Pricing operating services", *Bankers Magazine*, May–June 1987.
4. George S. Day and Liam Fahey, "Valuing market strategies", *Journal of Marketing*, July 1988, pp. 45–57.
5. David Landis, "It's cutting prices to win lost ground", *USA Today*, 4 October 1989, pp. 1B, 2B.
6. JCB company literature, 1992.
7. *What Car?* magazine, 1993.
8. J. Winkler, "Pricing", M. Baker, ed., in *The Marketing Book* (London: Heinemann, 1987).
9. Joseph P. Guiltinan, "The price-bundling of services: a normative framework", *Journal of Marketing*, April 1987, pp. 74–85.
10. Susan M. Petroshius and Kent B. Monroe, "Effect of product-line pricing characteristics on product evaluations", *Journal of Consumer Research*, March 1988, pp. 511–19.
11. Valerie A. Zeithaml, "Consumer perceptions of price, quality and value: a means-end model and synthesis of evidence", *Journal of Marketing*, July 1988, pp. 2–22.
12. Andrew T. Chalk and John A. Steiber, "Managing the airlines in the 1990's", *Journal of Business Strategy*, Winter 1987, pp. 87–91.
13. James B. Wilcox, Roy D. Howell, Paul Kuzdrall and Robert Britney, "Price quantity discounts: some implications for buyers and sellers", *Journal of Marketing*, July 1987, pp. 60–1.
14. Robert G. Eccles, "Control with fairness in transfer pricing", *Harvard Business Review*, November-December 1983, pp. 149–61.
15. Michael H. Morris, "Separate prices as a marketing tool", *Industrial Marketing Management*, 16, 1987, pp. 79–86.

Chapter 18

1. Reprinted from Peter D. Bennett, ed., *Dictionary of Marketing Terms* (American Marketing Association, 1988), p. 54. Used by permission.
2. Bennett, p. 150. Reprinted by permission.
3. Kent B. Monroe, "Effect of product line pricing characteristics on product evaluation", *Journal of Consumer Research*, March 1987, p. 518.
4. Marylin Chase, "Burroughs-Wellcome cuts price of AZT under pressure from AIDS activists", *Wall Street Journal*, 19 September 1989, p. A3.
5. National Federation of Consumer Groups, *A Handbook of Consumer Law, Which?* Books (London, 1989).
6. "Frantic cheap phone buy-up reveals a lot about Japanese marketing", *Ann Arbor News* (Ann Arbor, Mich.), 14 February 1988, p. C9.

Chapter 19

1. B. A. Weitz and R. Wensley, *Readings in Strategic Marketing* (Chicago: Dryden, 1988).
2. Derek F. Abell and John S. Hammond, *Strategic Market Planning* (Englewood Cliffs, N.J.: Prentice-Hall, 1979), p. 10.
3. P. Rajan Varadarajan, Terry Clark and William Pride, "Determining your company's destiny", working paper, Texas A&M University, 1990.
4. David A. Aaker, *Strategic Market Management*, 2nd ed. (New York: Wiley, 1988), p. 35.
5. John Saunders, "Marketing and competitive success", Michael J. Baker, ed., in *The Marketing Book* (London: Heinemann, 1987), pp. 10–28.
6. Zachary Schiller, with Russell Mitchell, Wendy Zellner, Lois Therrien, Andrea Rothman and Walecia Konrad, "The great American health pitch", *Business Week*, 9 October 1989, p. 116.
7. Derek F. Abell, "Strategic windows", *Journal of Marketing*, July 1978, p. 21.
8. Abell and Hammond, p. 213.
9. Liam Fahey, William K. King and Vodake K. Naraganan, "Environmental scanning and forecasting in strategic planning—the state of the art", *Long Range Planning*, February 1981, p. 38.
10. David M. Georgaff and Robert G. Mundick, "Managers' guide to forecasting", *Harvard Business Review*, January-February 1986, p. 120.
11. "Energy efficient house design", *House Builder Magazine*, September 1986.
12. "The 'bumpy road to clean fuels' ", *U.S. News & World Report*, 26 June 1989, pp. 10–11.
13. Ibid.
14. Philip Kotler, "Strategic planning and the marketing process", *Business*, May-June 1980, pp. 6–7.
15. Nigel Piercy, *Market-Led Strategic Change* (Oxford: Butterworth-Heinemann Ltd, 1992).
16. Joseph P. Guiltinan and Gordon W. Paul, *Marketing Management: Strategies and Programmes* (New York: McGraw-Hill, 1982), p. 31.
17. George S. Day, "Diagnosing the Product Portfolio", *Journal of Marketing*, April 1977, pp. 30–1.
18. Robert Jacobson, "Distinguishing among competing theories of the market share effect", *Journal of Marketing*, October 1988, pp. 68–80.
19. George S. Day, *Analysis for Strategic Market Decisions* (St. Paul, Minn.: West, 1986), pp. 117–118.
20. Robert D. Buzzell and Bradley T. Gale, *The PIMS Principles: Linking Strategy to Performance* (New York: Free Press, 1987).
21. Day, *Analysis for Strategic Market Decisions*, p. 10.

22. David W. Cravens, "Strategic marketing's new challenge", *Business Horizons*, March-April 1983, p. 19.

23. Yoram Wind, Vijay Majahan and Donald J. Swire, "An empirical comparison of standardised portfolio models", *Journal of Marketing*, Spring 1983, pp. 89–99.

24. Jonathan B. Levine, "This cyclone is out to rain on IBM's parade", *Business Week*, 23 October 1989, p. 114.

25. Roger A. Kerin, Vijay Majahan and P. Rajan Varadarajan, *Contemporary Perspectives on Strategic Marketing Planning* (Boston: Allyn & Bacon, 1990).

26. Ronald Grover, "When Columbia met Sony . . . a love story", *Business Week*, 9 October 1989, pp. 44–5.

27. David Woodruff, "Has Dow Chemical found the right formula?" *Business Week*, 7 August 1989, pp. 62, 64.

28. Mark Maremont, with Judith H. Dobrzynski, "Meet Asil Nadir, the billion-dollar fruit king", *Business Week*, 18 September 1989, p. 32.

29. Al Ries and Jack Trout, *Marketing Warfare* (New York: McGraw Hill, 1986); John Saunders, "Marketing and competitive success", in Michael Baker, ed., *The Marketing Book* (London: Heinemann, 1987).

Chapter 20

1. Sally Dibb and Lyndon Simkin, *The Marketing Casebook* (London: Routledge, 1993).

2. David Hurwood, Elliot S. Grossman and Earl Bailey, *Sales Forecasting* (New York: Conference Board, 1978), p. 2.

3. D. S. Tull and D. I. Hawkins, *Marketing Research* (New York: Macmillan, 1990).

4. Kenneth E. Marino, *Forecasting Sales and Planning Profits* (Chicago: Probus Publishing, 1986), p. 155.

5. Hurwood, Grossman and Bailey, p. 61.

6. G. L. Lilien and P. Kotler, *Marketing Decision-Making* (New York: Harper & Row, 1983).

7. P. Naert and P. Leeflang, *Building Implementable Marketing Models* (Leiden: Martinus Nijhoff, 1978).

8. *Accurate Business Forecasting* (Boston's Harvard Business Review Booklet, 1991).

9. Ronald D. Michman, "Linking futurists with marketing planning, forecasting, and strategy", *Journal of Consumer Marketing*, Summer 1984, pp. 17, 23.

10. Vasudevan Ramanujam and N. Venkatraman, "Planning and performance: a new look at an old question", *Business Horizons*, May-June 1987, pp. 19–25.

11. David J. Luck, O. C. Ferrell and George Lucas, *Marketing Strategy and Plans*, 3rd ed. (Englewood Cliffs, N.J.: Prentice-Hall, 1989), p. 328.

12. Malcolm McDonald, *Marketing Plans: How to Prepare Them, How to Use Them* (Oxford: Butterworth-Heinemann, 1989).

13. Yoram Wind and Thomas S. Robertson, "Marketing strategy: new directions for theory and research", *Journal of Marketing*, Spring 1983, p. 12.

14. M. E. Porter, *Competitive Strategy: Techniques for Analysing Industries and Competitors* (New York: Free Press, 1980).

15. William A. Band, "A marketing audit provides an opportunity for improvement", *Sales & Marketing Management in Canada*, March 1984, pp. 24–6.

16. Ely S. Lurin, "Audit determines the weak link in marketing chain", *Marketing News*, 12 September 1986, pp. 35–7.

17. Ibid.

Chapter 21

1. Larry Reibstein, "IBM's plan to decentralise may set a trend—but imitation has a price", *Wall Street Journal*, 19 February 1988, p. 17.

2. Rohit Despande and Frederick E. Webster, Jr., "Organisational culture and marketing: defining the research agenda", *Journal of Marketing*, January 1989, pp. 3–15.

3. Michael D. Hutt and Thomas W. Speh, "The marketing strategy centre: diagnosing the industrial marketer's interdisciplinary role", *Journal of Marketing*, Fall 1984, pp. 16–53.

4. John Bussy, "Manufacturers strive to slice time needed to develop products", *Wall Street Journal*, 23 February 1988, p. 18.

5. John C. Narver and Stanley F. Slater, "Creating a market orientated business", *The Channel of Communications*, Summer 1989, pp. 5–8.

6. Dave Ulrich, "Strategic human resources planning: why and how?" *Human Resources Planning*, 10, No. 1, 1987, pp. 25–57.

7. Steven Lysonski, "A boundary theory investigation of the product manager's role", *Journal of Marketing*, Winter 1985, pp. 26–40.

8. Richard Gibson and Robert Johnson, "Why Pillsbury's chief from the 70's is again taking firm's helm", *Wall Street Journal*, 1 March 1988, p. 25.

9. James H. Donnelly, Jr., Leonard L. Berry and Thomas O. Thompson, *Marketing Financial Services* (Homewood, Ill.: Dow Jones-Irwin, 1985), pp. 229–45.

10. Sybil F. Stershic, "Internal marketing campaign reinforces service goals", *Marketing News*, 31 July 1989, p. 11.

11. David C. Jones, "Motivation the catalyst in profit formula", *National Underwriter*, 13 July 1987, pp. 10, 13.

12. The example is adapted from Edward B. Deakin and Michael W. Maher, *Cost Accounting*, 2nd ed. (Homewood, Ill.: Irwin, 1987), pp. 838–9.

13. Jerry McAdams, "Rewarding sales and marketing performance", *Management Review*, April 1987, p. 36.

14. "Higher education in doughnuts", *Ann Arbor News*, 9 March 1988, p. B7.

15. Bernard J. Jaworski, "Toward a theory of marketing control: environmental context, control types, and consequences", *Journal of Marketing*, July 1988, pp. 23–39.

16. See Theo Haimann, William G. Scott and Patrick E. Connor, *Management*, 5th ed. (Boston: Houghton Mifflin, 1985), pp. 478–92.

17. Jeffrey A. Tannenbaum, "Video games revive—and makers hope this time the fad will last", *Wall Street Journal*, 8 March 1988, p. 35.

18. "Carbonates and concentrates", *Marketing Intelligence*, January 1990, pp. 2.10–2.17.

19. Kevin Kelly and Neil Gross, "A weakened Komatsu tries to come back swinging", *Business Week*, 22 February 1988, p. 48.

Chapter 22

1. Donald P. Robin and R. Eric Reidenbach, "Social responsibility, ethics in marketing strategy, closing the gap between concept and application", *Journal of Marketing*, January 1987, pp. 44–58.

2. Vernon R. Loucks, Jr., "A CEO looks at ethics", *Business Horizons*, March-April 1987, p. 4.

3. Clare Sambrook, "Do free flights really build brands?" *Marketing*, 15 October 1992, p. 11.

4. James R. Rest, *Moral Development Advances in Research and Theory* (New York: Praeger, 1986), p. 1.
5. *CNN Worldday*, Cable News Network (TV), 5 January 1990.
6. F. Neil Brady, *Ethical Managing: Rules and Results* (New York: Macmillan, 1990), pp. 4–6.
7. O. C. Ferrell and Larry G. Gresham,"A contingency framework for understanding ethical decision making in marketing", *Journal of Marketing*, Summer, 1985, p. 90.
8. Ibid.
9. John Fraedrich, "Philosophy type interaction in the ethical decision making process of retailers", Ph.D. dissertation, Texas A&M University, 1988.
10. William C. Frederick and James Weber, "The value of corporate managers and their critics: an empirical description and normative implications", in William C. Frederick and Lee E. Preston, eds., *Research in Corporate Social Performance and Social Responsibility* (Greenwich, Conn.: JAI Press, 1987), pp. 149–50.
11. Charles L. Tomkovick, "Time for a cease-fire with strategic marketing warfare", in Peter J. Gordon and Bert J. Kellerman, eds., *Advances in Marketing* (Southwest Marketing Association, 1990), p. 212.
12. Eric H. Beversluis, "Is there 'no such thing as business ethics'?" *Journal of Business Ethics*, No. 6, 1987, pp. 81–8.
13. O. C. Ferrell, Larry G. Gresham, and John Fraedrich, "A synthesis of ethical decision models for marketing", *Journal of Macromarketing*, Fall 1989, pp. 58–9.
14. Ferrell and Gresham, p. 92.
15. Damon Darlin, "Where trademarks are up for grabs", *Wall Street Journal*, 5 December 1989, p. B1.
16. Jacob Scheslinger, "Chrysler finds a way to settle odometer issue", *Wall Street Journal*, 10 December 1987, p. 7.
17. Scott Hume, "Squawk over KFC ads—company challenges Y&R with new strategy", *Advertising Age*, 15 January 1990, p. 16.
18. Archie B. Carroll, *Business and Society: Ethics and Stakeholder Management* (Cincinnati: South-Western Publishing, 1989), pp. 228–30.
19. Lanny J. Ryan, Gay C. Dawson and Thomas Galek, "New distribution channels for microcomputer software", *Business*, October-December 1985, pp. 21–2.
20. Linda K. Trevino and Stuart Youngblood, "Bad apples in bad barrels: a causal analysis of ethical decision making behavior", *Journal of Applied Psychology*, 1990.
21. Ibid.
22. Robin and Reidenbach, pp. 44–58.
23. Carroll, *Business and Society*, p. 45.
24. Margaret A. Stroup, Ralph L. Newbert and Jerry W. Anderson, Jr., "Doing good, doing better: two views of social responsibility", *Business Horizons*, March-April 1987, p. 23.
25. "McD ads draw protests from nutritional experts", *Nation's Restaurant News*, 22 June 1987, p. 26.
26. Gregory A. Patterson, "Lexus to recall all its LS 400 luxury models", *Wall Street Journal*, 5 December 1989, pp. B1, B11.
27. Sir Adrian Cadbury, "Ethical managers make their own rules", *Harvard Business Review*, September-October 1987, p. 33.

Chapter 23
1. Edward F. Fern and James R. Brown, "The industrial/consumer marketing dichotomy: a case of insufficient justification", *Journal of Marketing*, Spring 1984, pp. 168–177.

2. Robert W. Haas, *Industrial Marketing Management* (New York: Petrocelli Charter, 1976), pp. 37–48.
3. *Standard Industrial Classification Revision* (London: Central Statistical Office, 1979).
4. Peter Doyle and John Saunders, "Market segmentation and positioning in specialized industrial markets", *Journal of Marketing*, Spring 1985, p. 25.
5. Doyle and Saunders, p. 25.
6. Erin Anderson and Anne T. Coughlan, "International market entry and expansion via independent or integrated channels of distribution", *Journal of Marketing*, January 1987, pp. 71–82.
7. Hiram C. Barksdale, Jr., Terry E. Powell and Ernestine Hargrove, "Complaint voicing by industrial buyers", *Industrial Marketing Management*, May 1984, pp. 93–9.
8. James D. Hlavacek and Tommy J. McCuiston, "Industrial distributors: when, who, and how?" *Harvard Business Review*, March-April 1983, p. 97.
9. Gary L. Frazier, Robert E. Spekman and Charles R. O'Neal, "Just-in-time exchange relationships in industrial markets", *Journal of Marketing*, October 1988, pp. 52–67.
10. Daniel H. McQuiston, "Novelty, complexity, and importance as casual determinants of industrial buyer behavior", *Journal of Marketing*, April 1989, pp. 66–79.
11. Laboratory of Advertising Performance (LAP) report 8052.3 McGraw-Hill Research.
12. Steve Sulerno, "The close of the new salesmanship", *PSA*, April 1985, p. 63.
13. "Aircraft industry emerging from engineering dominance", *Marketing News*, 2 August 1985, p. 7.
14. Roger A. Kerin and William L. Cron, "Assessing trade show functions and performance; an exploratory study", *Journal of Marketing*, July 1987, pp. 87–94.
15. John C. Narver and Stanley F. Slater, "Creating a market-oriented business", *The Channel of Communications*, Summer 1989, pp. 5–8.
16. Robert Jacobson and David A. Aaker, "The strategic role of product quality", *Journal of Marketing*, October 1987, pp. 31–44.
17. Douglas G. Brooks, "Bidding for the sake of follow-on contracts", *Journal of Marketing*, January 1978, p. 35.

Chapter 24
1. Leonard L. Berry, "Services marketing is different", *Business Horizons*, May-June 1980, pp. 24–9.
2. David Pottruck, "Building company loyalty and retention through direct marketing", *Journal of Services Marketing*, Autumn 1987, p. 56.
3. Donald Cowell, *The Marketing of Services* (London: Heinemann, 1984).
4. Valarie A. Zeithaml, A. Parasuraman and Leonard L. Berry, "Problems and strategies in services marketing", *Journal of Marketing*, Spring 1985, pp. 33–46.
5. John E. G. Bateson, "Why we need service marketing", in O. C. Ferrell, S. W. Brown and C. W. Lamb, Jr., ed., *Conceptual and Theoretical Development in Marketing* (Chicago: American Marketing Association, 1979), pp. 131–46.
6. Valarie A. Zeithaml, "How consumer evaluation processes differ between goods and services", in James H. Donnelly and William R. George, ed., *Marketing of Services* (Chicago: American Marketing Association, 1981), pp. 186–90.
7. Leonard L. Berry, Valarie A. Zeithaml and A. Parasuraman,

"Responding to demand fluctuations: key challenge for service businesses", in Russell Belk et al., ed., *AMA Educators' Proceedings* (Chicago: American Marketing Association, 1984), pp. 231–4.

8. Brian Moores, *Are They Being Served?* (Oxford: Philip Allan, 1986).

9. Christopher H. Lovelock, "Classifying services to gain strategic marketing insights", *Journal of Marketing,* Summer 1983, p. 15.

10. Christopher H. Lovelock, *Services Marketing* (Englewood Cliffs, N.J.: Prentice-Hall, 1984), pp. 46–64.

11. G. Lynn Shostack, "Breaking free from product marketing", *Journal of Marketing,* April 1977, pp. 73–80.

12. Sak Onkvisit and John J. Shaw, "Service marketing: image, branding, and competition", *Business Horizons,* January-February 1989, p. 16.

13. Tom Peters, "More expensive, but worth it", *U.S. News & World Report,* 3 February 1986, p. 54.

14. Valarie A. Zeithaml, "Consumer perceptions of price, quality, and value: a means-end model and synthesis of evidence", *Journal of Marketing,* July 1988, pp. 2–22.

15. Leonard L. Berry, "8 keys to top service at financial institutions", *American Banker,* August 1987.

16. A. Parasuraman, Valarie A. Zeithaml and Leonard L. Berry, "SERVQUAL: a multiple item scale for measuring consumer perceptions of service quality", *Journal of Retailing,* Spring 1988, pp. 12–40.

17. Stephen W. Brown and Teresa A. Swartz, "A gap analysis of professional service quality", *Journal of Marketing,* April 1989, pp. 92–8.

18. Ibid.

19. G. Lynn Shostack, "Service positioning through structural change", *Journal of Marketing,* January 1987, pp. 34–43.

20. William R. George and Leonard L. Berry, "Guidelines for the advertising of services", *Business Horizons,* July-August 1981, pp. 52–56.

21. S. Dibb and L. Simkin, "The strength of branding and positioning in services", *International Journal of Service Industry Management,* January 1993, pp. 25–33.

22. Heskett, pp. 118–25.

23. George and Berry, pp. 55–70.

24. William R. George and J. Patrick Kelly, "The promotion and selling of services", *Business,* July-September 1983, pp. 14–20.

25. John M. Rathmell, *Marketing in the Services Sector* (Cambridge, Mass.: Winthrop, 1974), p. 100.

26. George and Kelly, pp. 14–20; George and Berry, pp. 55–70.

27. Doris C. Van Doren and Louise W. Smith, "Marketing in the restructured professional services field", *Journal of Services Marketing,* Summer 1987, pp. 69–70.

28. James B. Ayers, "Lessons from industry for healthcare", *Administrative Radiology,* July 1987, p. 53.

29. Joseph R. Guiltinan, "The price bundling of services: a normative framework", *Journal of Marketing,* April 1987, p. 74.

30. James H. Donnelly, Jr., "Marketing intermediaries in channels of distribution for services", *Journal of Marketing,* January, 1976, pp. 55–70.

31. Ibid.

32. Nigel A. L. Brooks, "Strategic issues for financial services marketing", *Journal of Services Marketing,* Summer 1987, p. 65.

33. S. Dibb and L. Simkin, "Strategy and tactics: Marketing leisure facilities", *The Services Industry Journal,* March 1993, pp. 110–124.

34. Yoram Wind, "Financial services: increasing your marketing productivity and profitability", *Journal of Services Marketing,* Fall 1987, p. 8.

35. Lovelock, *Services Marketing,* pp. 279–89.

36. Ibid.

37. Berry, Zeithaml and Parasuraman, pp. 231–4.

38. Heskett, pp. 118–26.

39. Leonard L. Berry, "Big ideas in services marketing", *Journal of Services Marketing,* Fall 1987, pp. 5–9.

40. J. Whyte, "Organisation, person and idea marketing as exchange", *Quarterly Review of Marketing,* January 1985, pp. 25–30.

41. John Garrison, "Telethons—the positive story", *Fund Raising Management,* November 1987, pp. 48–52.

42. Philip Kotler, *Marketing for Non-profit Organisations,* 2nd ed. (Englewood Cliffs, N.J.: Prentice-Hall, 1982) p. 37.

43. Ibid.

44. Meryl Davids, "Doing well by doing good", *Public Relations Journal,* July 1987, pp. 17–21.

45. Leyland F. Pitt and Russell Abratt, "Pricing in non-profit organisations—a framework and conceptual overview", *Quarterly Review of Marketing,* Spring-Summer 1987, pp. 13–15.

46. Kelly Walker, "Not-for-profit profits", *Forbes,* 10 September 1984, p. 165.

Chapter 25

1. Vern Terpstra, *International Marketing,* 4th ed. (Hinsdale, Ill.: Dryden Press, 1987), p. 4.

2. Theodore Levitt, "The globalisation of markets", *Harvard Business Review,* May-June 1983, p. 92.

3. Ibid.

4. Subhash C. Jain, "Standardisation of international marketing strategy: some research hypotheses", *Journal of Marketing,* January 1989, pp. 70–9.

5. "Global brands need local ad flavor", *Advertising Age,* 3 September 1984, p. 26.

6. Vern Terpstra, "Critical mass and international marketing strategy", *Journal of the Academy of Marketing Science,* Summer 1983, pp. 269–82.

7. C. Min Han, "Country image: halo or summary construct?", *Journal of Marketing Research,* May 1989, pp. 222–9.

8. Nigel G. G. Campbell, John L. Graham, Alain Jolibert and Hans Gunther Meissner, "Marketing negotiations in France, Germany, the United Kingdom, and the United States", *Journal of Marketing,* April 1988, pp. 49–62.

9. Brian Oliver, "UK soccer advertising in trouble", *Advertising Age,* 8 July 1985, p. 36.

10. Laurel Wentz, "Local laws keep international marketers hopping", *Advertising Age,* 11 July 1985, p. 20.

11. Lee Smith, "Japan wants to make friends", *Fortune,* 2 September 1985 p. 84.

12. John Hillkirk, "It could be trade boom or bust", *USA Today,* 12 January 1989, p. 4B.

13. Nicholas Colchester, "1992 = 1990 + 2 or thereabouts", in *The World in 1990* (London: Economist Publications, 1990), pp. 49–50; and Stephen Young, James Hamill, Colin Wheeler and J. Richard Davies, *International Market Entry and Development* (London: Harvester Wheatsheaf, 1989), pp. 280–82.

14. Sandra Vandermerwe and Marc-André L'Huillier, "Euro-con-

sumers in 1992", *Business Horizons,* January-February 1989, pp. 34–40.

15. Eric G. Friberg, "1992: moves Europeans are making", *Harvard Business Review,* May-June 1989, p. 89.

16. Leslie Helm, with Laxmi Nakarmi, Jang Jung Soo, William J. Holstein and Edith Terry, "The Koreans are coming", *Business Week,* 25 December, 1985, pp. 46–52.

17. Dori Jones Yang and Dinah Lee, with William J. Holstein and Maria Shao, "China: the great backward leap", *Business Week,* 19 June 1989, pp. 28–32.

18. Dori Jones Yang, with Dirk Bennett and Bill Javerski, "The other China is starting to soar", *Business Weekly,* 6 November 1989, pp. 60–2.

19. Louis Kraar, "Asia's rising export powers", *Fortune,* Special Pacific Rim 1989 issue, pp. 43–50.

20. "East bloc business", *USA Today,* 19 March 1990, p. 6B.

21. Richard L. Kirkland, "Russia: where Gorbanomics is leading", *Fortune,* 28 September 1987, pp. 82–4; and Misha G. Knight, "The Russian bear turns bullish on trade", *Business Marketing,* April 1987, pp. 83–4.

22. Peter Gumbel, "Soviet reformers urge bold push to liberalise faltering economy", *Wall Street Journal,* 27 October 1989, p. A9.

23. Paul Meller, "Back to the USSR", *Marketing,* 9 August 1990, pp. 22–3.

24. John Templeman, Thane Peterson, Gail E. Schares and Jonathan Kapstein, "The shape of Europe to come", *Business Week,* 27 November 1989, pp. 60–4.

25. Kevin Maney, "Eager East's welcome mat is a bit shabby", *USA Today,* 23 October 1989, pp. 1B, 2B; and Peter Gumbel, "Corporate America flocking to Moscow", *Wall Street Journal,* 24 October 1989, p. A18.

26. Albert G. Holzinger, "A new era in trade", *Nation's Business,* September 1989, p. 67.

27. Gordon Bock, "Big hug from Uncle Sam", *Time,* 19 October 1987, p. 50; Madelaine Drohan, "A critical concern", *Maclean's,* 4 January 1988, pp. 42–3; Mushtaq Luqmani and Zahir A. Quraeshi, "The US–Canada free trade pact: issues and perspectives", *Developments in Marketing Science,* Vol. XII, Academy of Marketing Science Proceedings, 1989, pp. 113–15; Edith Terry, Bill Javerski, Steven Dryden and John Pearson, "A free-trade milestone", *Business Week,* 19 October 1987, pp. 52–3; "The trade pact benefits both sides", *Business Week,* 19 October 1987, p. 154.

28. Holzinger, pp. 67–9.

29. Warren J. Keegan, *Global Marketing Management,* 4th ed. (Englewood Cliffs, N.J.: Prentice-Hall, 1989), pp. 378–82.

30. Kamran Kashani, "Beware the pitfalls of global marketing", *Harvard Business Review,* September-October 1989, pp. 93–4.

31. Allecia Swasy, "After early stumbles, P&G is making inroads overseas", *Wall Street Journal,* 6 February 1989, p. B1.

32. Douglass G. Norvell and Robert Morey, "Ethnodomination in the channels of distribution of Third world nations", *Journal of the Academy of Marketing Science,* Summer 1983, pp. 204–35.

33. Erin Anderson and Anne T. Coughlan, "International market entry and expansion via independent or integrated channels of distribution", *Journal of Marketing,* January 1987, pp.71–82.

34. John A. Quelch, "How to build a product licensing program", *Harvard Business Review,* May-June 1985, pp. 186–7.

35. Andrew Kupfer, "How to be a global manager", *Fortune,* 14 March 1988, pp. 52–8.

36. Kathryn Rudie Harrigan, "Joint ventures and competitive advantage", *Strategic Management Journal,* May 1988, pp. 141–58.

37. A. Dunlap Smith, "Europe's truckmakers face survival of the biggest", *Business Week,* 6 November 1989, p. 68.

38. S. C. Jain, "Some perspectives on international strategic alliances", in *Advances in International Marketing* (New York: JAI Press, 1987), pp. 103–20.

39. "More companies prefer liaisons to marriage", *Wall Street Journal,* 12 April 1988, p. 35.

40. Thomas Gross and John Neuman, "Strategic alliances vital in global marketing", *Marketing News,* June 1989, pp. 1–2.

41. Margaret H. Cunningham, "Marketing's new frontier: international strategic alliances", working paper, Queens University (Ontario), 1990.

42. Stephen Young, James Hamill, Colin Wheeler and J. Richard Davies, *International Market Entry and Development. Strategies and Management* (Englewood Cliffs, N.J.: Prentice-Hall, 1989).

Appendix

1. T. Jackson, "Writing the targeted résumé", *Business Week's Guide to Careers,* Spring 1983, pp. 26–7.

2. Burke Marketing Research for Robert Hall Inc. Reported in *USA Today,* 2 October 1987, p. B–1.

3. Marcia Fleschner, "Evolution of research takes the profession to new heights", *Collegiate Edition Marketing News,* March 1986, p. 1.

4. Judith George, "Market researcher", *Business Week Careers,* October 1987, p. 10.

5. "What it's like to work in marketing research depends on where you work—supplier, ad agency, manufacturer", *Collegiate Edition Marketing News,* December 1985, pp. 1, 3.

6. The Institute of Public Relations, 15 Northburgh Street, London.

7. Jan Greenberg, "Inside public relations", *Business Week Careers,* February 1988, p. 47.

8. Nicholas Basta, "Inventory and distribution", *Business Week's Guide to Careers,* Spring-Summer 1985, p. 23.

9. The Institute of Practitioners in Advertising, 44 Belgrave Square, London, and the Advertising Association, 15 Wilton Road, London.

10. Kevin Higgins, "Economic recovery puts marketers in catbird seat", *Marketing News,* 14 October 1983, pp. 1, 8.

11. Nicholas Basta, "Direct marketing", *Business Week Careers,* March 1986, p. 52.

12. "Wonderman urges: replace marketing war muskets with the authentic weapon—direct marketing", *Marketing News,* 8 July 1983, pp. 1, 12.

Glossary

A

Ability Competence and efficiency in performing tasks.

Accessory equipment Equipment used in production or office activities; does not become a part of the final physical product.

Accommodation strategy Assumes responsibility for all actions of the company.

Accumulation A process through which an inventory of homogeneous products that have similar production or demand requirements is developed.

ACORN (A Classification of Residential Neighbourhoods) A market segmentation/analysis system which allows consumers to be classified according to the type of residential area in which they live. Developed by CACI.

Actual product Is a composite of several factors: the features and capabilities offered; quality and durability; design and product styling; packaging; brand name.

Administered pricing A process in which the seller sets a price for a product, and the customer pays that specified price.

Advertising A paid form of non-personal communication about an organisation and/or its products that is transmitted to a target audience through a mass medium.

Advertising budget (Advertising appropriation) The amount of money set aside to cover all the expenses and cost of a particular campaign.

Advertising campaign Involves designing a series of advertisements and placing them in various advertising media to reach a particular target market.

Advertising platform The basic issues or selling points that an advertiser wishes to include in the advertising campaign.

Advertising Standards Authority (ASA) An independent body which handles the public's and companies' complaints relating to dishonest or misleading, shocking or unethical advertising.

Advertising target The group of people at whom advertisements are aimed.

Agent A marketing intermediary who receives a commission or fee for expediting exchanges; represents either buyers or sellers on a permanent basis.

Aided (prompted) recall test A post-test method of evaluating the effectiveness of advertising in which subjects are asked to identify advertisements they have seen recently; they are shown a list of products, brands, company names, or trade marks to jog their memory.

Allocation The breaking down of large homogeneous inventories into smaller lots.

Allowance Concession in price to achieve a desired goal; for example, industrial equipment manufacturers give trade-in allowances on used industrial equipment to enable customers to purchase new equipment.

Approach The manner in which a salesperson contacts a potential customer.

Arbitrary approach A method for determining the advertising appropriation in which a high level executive in the firm states how much can be spent on advertising for a certain time period.

Area sampling A variation of stratified sampling, with the geographic areas serving as the segments, or primary units, used in random sampling.

Artwork The illustration in an advertisement and the layout of the components of an advertisement.

Assessment centre An intense training centre at which sales candidates are put into realistic, problematic settings where they must prioritise activities, make decisions, and act on their decisions to determine whether each candidate will make a good salesperson.

Assorting Combining products into collections, or assortments, that buyers want to have available at one place.

Assortment A combination of similar or complementary products put together to provide benefits to a specific market.

Atmospherics The conscious designing of a store's space to create emotional effects that enhance the probability that consumers will buy.

Attitude The knowledge and positive or negative feelings about an object.

Attitude scale A measurement instrument that usually consists of a series of adjectives, phrases, or sentences about an object; subjects are asked to indicate the intensity of their feelings towards the object by reacting to the statements in a certain way. It can be used to measure consumer attitudes.

Augmented product Support issues such as sales assistance, delivery, payment terms, installation, warranty and after sales back up.

Automatic vending Non-store, non-personal retailing; includes coin operated, self-service machines.

Average cost Total costs divided by the quantity produced.

Average fixed cost The fixed cost per unit produced; it is calculated by dividing the fixed costs by the number of units produced.

Average revenue   Total revenue divided by the quantity produced.

Average total cost   The sum of the average fixed cost and the average variable cost.

Average variable cost   The variable cost per unit produced; it is calculated by dividing the variable cost by the number of units produced.

B

Balance of retailing   The balance of negotiating and buying power between retailers and their suppliers.

Barcode   Universal product code—series of thick and thin black lines identifying inventory and pricing, read by a computer scanner.

Barter   The trading of products.

Base point pricing   A geographic pricing policy that includes the price at the factory, plus transport charges from the base point nearest the buyer.

Base variables   In market segmentation these are variables used to form the basis for identifying homogeneous groups of consumers in a market: *demographic, geographic, psychographic* and *behaviouralistic* variables in consumer markets; *geographic location, type of organisation, customer characteristics, product usage* in organisational markets.

Benefit segmentation   The division of a market according to the various benefits that customers want from the product.

Bid pricing   A determination of prices through sealed bids or open bids.

Bonded storage   A storage service provided by many public warehouses, whereby the goods are not released until customs duties, taxes, or other fees are paid.

Brand   A name, term, symbol, design, or combination of these that identifies a seller's products and differentiates them from competitors' products.

Brand attitude   The buyer's overall evaluation of the brand with respect to its perceived ability to meet a relevant motivation. This evaluation generally takes account of competing brands' ability to meet the need. The third communication effect.

Brand awareness   The buyer's ability to identify (recognise or recall) the brand within the category in sufficient detail to make a purchase. The second communication effect.

Brand extension branding   A type of branding in which a firm uses one of its existing brand names as part of a brand for an improved or new product that is usually in the same product category as the existing brand.

Brand management   *See* Product management; Brand manager.

Brand manager   A person who holds a staff position in a multi-product company and is responsible for a single brand.

Brand mark   The element of a brand, such as a symbol or design, that cannot be spoken.

Brand name   The part of a brand that can be spoken—including letters, words, and numbers.

Brand purchase intention   The buyer's "self-instruction" to purchase the brand: a conscious decision to buy. The fourth communication effect.

Break down approach   A general approach for measuring company sales potential based on a general economic forecast—or other aggregate data—and the market sales potential derived from it; company sales potential is based on the general economic forecast and the estimated market sales potential.

Break even point   The point at which the costs of producing a product equal the revenue made from selling the product.

Broker   A functional middleman who performs fewer functions than other intermediaries; the primary function is to bring buyers and sellers together for a fee.

Build up approach   A general approach to measuring company sales potential in which the analyst initially estimates how much the average purchaser of a product will buy in a specified time period and then multiplies that amount by the number of potential buyers; estimates are generally calculated by individual geographic areas.

Business analysis   An analysis providing a tentative sketch of a product's compatibility in the market-place, including its probable profitability.

Business services   Include executive recruitment; fleet car management; consulting; business, advertising and marketing research services.

Business-to-business marketing   Business marketing or industrial marketing involves marketing activities between organisations in business-to-business markets, and not with end user consumers.

Buy back allowance   A certain sum of money given to a purchaser for each unit bought after an initial deal is over.

Buyer behaviour, consumer   The decision processes and acts of individuals involved in buying and using products or services.

Buyer behaviour, organisational   The purchase behaviours of producers, resellers, government units and institutions.

Buyer behaviour influences, consumer   Person specific, psychological, social.

Buyer behaviour influences, organisational   Business environment, company aims/policies/resources, personal relationships, characteristics of personnel.

Buyer behaviour process, consumer   Problem recognition; information search; evaluation of alternatives; purchase; post-purchase evaluation.

Buyer behaviour process, organisational   Problem

recognition; product specification; product/supplier search; evaluation of options; selection of product/supplier; evaluation of product/supplier performance.

Buying allowance   A temporary price reduction to resellers for purchasing specified quantities of a product.

Buying behaviour   The decision processes and acts of people involved in buying and using products.

Buyer centre   The group of people within an organisation who are involved in making organisational purchase decisions; these people take part in the purchase decision process as users, influencers, buyers, deciders, technologists, and gatekeepers.

Buying power   Resources such as money, goods, and services that can be traded in an exchange situation.

Buying power index   A weighted index consisting of population, effective buying income, and retail sales data. The higher the index number, the greater the buying power. Common usage in the USA.

C

"Campaign"   The weekly trade magazine published in London by Haymarket Publishing; news and features primarily from the advertising industry, with updates on the rest of the marketing communications industry.

Campaign   Organised course of action, planned carefully to achieve predetermined goals. Can relate to sales drives or any part of the promotional mix, but typically is applied to advertising.

Capabilities   Firm's distinctive competencies to tackle something well and efficiently.

Captioned photograph   A photograph with a brief description that explains the picture's content.

Cash and carry warehouses   Retail extensive ranges of groceries, tobacco, alcohol, beverages and confectionery to newsagents, small supermarkets, convenience stores and the catering trade.

Cash and carry wholesaler   A limited service wholesaler that sells to customers who will pay cash and furnish transport or pay extra to have products delivered.

Cash cows   In the BCG growth-share matrix have dominant market shares and generate significant cash flow, but are in positions set to decline.

Cash discount   A price reduction to the buyer for prompt payment or cash payment.

Catalogue retailing   A type of mail order retailing in which selling may be handled by telephone or in-store visits and products are delivered by post or picked up by the customers.

Catalogue showrooms   A form of warehouse showroom in which consumers shop from a mailed catalogue and buy at a warehouse where all products are stored out of buyers' reach. Products are provided in the manufacturer's packaging.

Category need   The buyer's perception of requiring a product or service to remove or satisfy a perceived discrepancy between current motivational state and the desired motivational state. The first communication effect.

Causal forecasting   This set of techniques includes *barometric, surveys of buyer intentions, regression analysis*, and various *econometric models*. These tools examine changes in sales due to fluctuations in one or more market variables.

Causal study   Research planned to prove or disprove that x causes y or that x does not cause y.

Central Business District (CBD)   The traditional city centre or downtown hub containing most retail, financial, legal and office functions in the city, plus many transport foci and public transport stations.

Centralised organisation   An organisation in which the top level managers delegate very little authority to lower levels of the organisation.

Channel   A marketing channel is a channel of distribution, a group of interrelated intermediaries which direct products to consumers.

Channel capacity   The limit on the volume of information that a communication channel can handle effectively.

Channel conflict   Friction between marketing channel members, often resulting from role deviance or malfunction; absence of an expected mode of conduct that contributes to the channel as a system.

Channel cooperation   A helping relationship among channel members that enhances the welfare and survival of all necessary channel members.

Channel leadership   The guidance that a channel member with one or more sources of power gives to other channel members to help achieve channel objectives.

Channel of distribution   *See* Marketing channel.

Channel power   The ability of one channel member to influence another channel member's goal achievement.

Client public   The direct consumers of the product of a non-business organisation; for example, the client public of a university is its student body.

Closing   The element in the selling process in which the salesperson asks the prospect to buy the product.

Code of ethics   Formalised statement of what a company expects of its employees with regard to ethical behaviour.

Coding process   The process by which a meaning is placed into a series of signs that represent ideas; also called encoding.

Cognitive dissonance   Dissatisfaction that may occur shortly after the purchase of a product, when the buyer questions whether he or she should have purchased the product at all or would have been better off purchasing another brand that was evaluated very favourably.

Combination compensation plan   A plan by which salespeople are paid a fixed salary and a commission based on sales volume.

Commercialisation   A phase of new product development in which plans for full scale manufacturing and marketing must be refined and settled and budgets for the product must be prepared.

Commission merchant An agent often used in agricultural marketing who usually exercises physical control over products, negotiates sales, and is given broad powers regarding prices and terms of sale.

Communication A sharing of meaning through the transmission of information.

Communications effects *See Brand attitude; Brand awareness; Brand purchase intention; Category need; Purchase facilitation.*

Company sales forecast The amount of a product that a firm actually expects to sell during a specific period at a specified level of company marketing activities.

Comparative advertising Advertising that compares two or more identified brands in the same general product class; the comparison is made in terms of one or more specific product characteristics.

Competition Generally viewed by a business as those firms that market products similar to, or substitutable for, its products in the same target market.

Competition matching approach A method of ascertaining the advertising appropriation in which an advertiser tries to match a major competitor's appropriations in terms of absolute budget or in terms of using the same percentage of sales for advertising.

Competition orientated pricing A pricing method in which an organisation considers costs and revenue secondary to competitors' prices.

Competitive advertising Advertising that points out a brand's uses, features, and advantages that benefit consumers but may not be available in competing brands.

Competitive edge *See* Differential advantage.

Competitive positions *Warfare strategy* believes an organisation must know its position in a market relative to its competitors. A *market leader* has market share leadership in a market and must grow its market by finding new applications for its products or services, by market development, or by market penetration, while defending its position against rival challengers. A *challenger* is aggressively attacking the market and the market leader to gain market share. A *market follower* has low market share and few resources to contend for market leadership. A *nicher* specialises in terms of market/product/customers by finding a small, safe, non-competitive niche.

Competitive scanning Monitoring of competitors' marketing strategies and programmes.

Competitive structure The model used to describe the number of firms that control the supply of a product and how it affects the strength of competition; factors include number of competitors, ease of entry into the market, the nature of the product, and knowledge of the market.

Competitors These are generally viewed by an organisation as those rival organisations which market similar or substitutable products or services to the same *target market.*

Complexity Is determined by the number of steps required to perform a service.

Component part A finished item ready for assembly or a product that needs little processing before assembly and that becomes a part of the physical product.

Comprehensive spending patterns The percentages of family income allotted to annual expenditures for general classes of goods and services.

Concentration strategy A market segmentation strategy in which an organisation directs its marketing efforts towards a single market segment through one marketing mix.

Conflict of interest Results from marketers' taking advantage of situations for their own selfish interests rather than for the long run interest of the business.

Consumable supplies Items that facilitate an organisation's production and operations, but do not become part of the finished product.

Consumer buying behaviour The buying behaviour of ultimate consumers—people who purchase products for personal or household use and not for business purposes.

Consumer buying decision process The five stage decision process consumers use in making purchases.

Consumer contest A sales promotion device for established products based on the analytical or creative skill of contestants.

Consumer focus group The marketing research discussion group of actual or potential buyers of a product or service.

Consumer jury A panel used to pre-test advertisements; it consists of a number of persons who are actual or potential buyers of the product to be advertised.

Consumer market Purchasers and/or individuals in their households who intend to consume or benefit from the purchased products and who do not buy products for the main purpose of making a profit.

Consumer movement A social movement through which people attempt to defend and exercise their rights as buyers.

Consumer movement forces The major forces in the consumer movement are consumer organisations, consumer laws, consumer education, and independent consumer advocates. The three major areas stressed are product safety, disclosure of information, and protection of the environment.

Consumer panels In marketing research, consumer panels consist of volunteers—usually paid—who either offer jury style instantaneous opinions or who keep records of their general household, personal, leisure, and occasionally business purchases. The information is collected by marketing research agencies which sell on the findings to marketers.

Consumer product Product purchased for ultimate satisfaction of personal and family needs.

Consumer protection legislation Laws enacted to protect consumers' safety, to enhance the amount of information available, and to warn of deceptive marketing techniques.

Consumer sales promotion techniques A sales promotion method that encourages or stimulates customers to patronise a specific retail store and/or to purchase a particular product.

Consumers' Association Is funded by the subscriptions of over one million members and works to further consumer interests.

Consumer services Include house cleaning, home maintenance, preparation of tax returns, etc.

Consumer spending patterns Information indicating the relative proportions of annual family expenditures or the actual amount of money that is spent on certain types of goods or services.

Consumer sweepstakes A sales promotion device for established products in which entrants submit their names for inclusion in a drawing for prizes.

Containerisation The practice of consolidating many items into one container that is sealed at the point of origin and opened at the destination.

Convenience products Relatively inexpensive, frequently purchased items for which buyers want to exert only minimal effort.

Convenience stores Neighborhood stores, selling groceries, beverages and newspapers, open long hours and often family run.

Co-operative advertising An arrangement in which a manufacturer agrees to pay a certain amount of a retailer's media costs for advertising the manufacturer's products.

Copy The verbal portion of advertisements; includes headlines, subheadlines, body copy, and signature.

Copy writing Written material for direct mail and advertising must be in tune with target audience requirements.

Core product The perceived or real core benefit to be gained from the product acquired.

Corporate strategy The strategy that determines the means for utilising resources in the areas of production, finance, research and development, personnel, and marketing to reach the organisation's goals.

Correlation methods Methods used to develop sales forecasts as the forecasters attempt to find a relationship between past sales and one or more variables, such as population, per capita income, or gross domestic product.

Cost comparison indicator Allows an advertiser to compare the costs of several vehicles within a specific medium relative to the number of persons reached by each vehicle.

Cost orientated pricing A pricing policy in which a firm determines price by adding a monetary amount or percentage to the cost of a product.

Cost plus pricing A form of cost orientated pricing in which first the seller's costs are determined and then a specified monetary amount or percentage of the cost is added to the seller's cost to set the price.

Costs: Fixed *See* Fixed cost.

Costs: Marginal *See* Marginal cost.

Costs: Variable *See* Variable cost.

Count and recount A sales promotion method based on the payment of a specific amount of money for each product unit moved from a reseller's warehouse in a given period of time.

Coupon A new product sales promotion technique used to stimulate trial of a new or improved product, to increase sales volume quickly, to attract repeat purchasers, or to introduce new package sizes or features.

Credence qualities Qualities of services that cannot be assessed even after purchase and consumption; for example, few consumers are knowledgeable enough to assess the quality of an appendix operation, even after it has been performed.

Crisis management Involves the identification of key targets (publics) for which to provide material or publicity, the need for a well rehearsed contingency plan; the organisation's skills and ability to respond; the provision of access for journalists.

Culture Everything in our surroundings that is made by human beings, consisting of tangible items as well as intangible concepts and values.

Cumulative discount Quantity discount that is aggregated over a stated period of time.

Customary pricing A type of psychological pricing in which certain goods are priced primarily on the basis of tradition.

Customer forecasting survey The technique of asking customers what types and quantities of products they intend to buy during a specific period so as to predict the sales level for that period.

Customer orientation An approach to marketing in which a marketer tries to provide a marketing mix that satisfies the needs of buyers in the target market.

Cycle analysis A method of predicting sales by analysing sales figures for a period of three to five years to ascertain whether sales fluctuate in a consistent, periodic manner.

D

Dealer listing An advertisement that promotes a product and identifies the names of participating retailers that sell the product.

Dealer loader A gift, often part of a display, that is given to a retailer for the purchase of a specified quantity of merchandise.

Decentralised organisation An organisation in which decision-making authority is delegated as far down the chain of command as possible.

Decline stage The stage in a product's life cycle in which sales fall rapidly and profits decrease.

Decoding process The stage in the communication process in which signs are converted into concepts and ideas.

Defence strategy Tries to minimise or avoid additional obligations linked to a problem or problems.

Defensive advertising Advertising used to offset or lessen the effects of a competitor's promotional programme.

Defensive warfare Is really for a market leader, which must await market developments or competitors' thrusts, and proactively parry competitor's action.

Delphi Survey seeks managers' views and forecasts; collates these centrally, then provides the managers with an opportunity to revise their forecasts.

Demand curve A line showing the relationship between price and quantity demanded.

Demand orientated pricing A pricing policy based on the level of demand for the product—resulting in a higher price when demand for the product is strong and a lower price when demand is weak.

Demand schedule The relationship, usually inverse, between price and quantity demanded; classically, a line sloping downward to the right, showing that as price falls, quantity demanded will increase.

Demographic factors Personal characteristics such as age, sex, race, nationality, income, family, life-cycle stage, and occupation; also called socio-economic factors.

Demonstration A sales promotion method manufacturers use temporarily to encourage trial use and purchase of the product or to show how the product works.

Department for Trade and Industry (DTI) The UK's central government department controlling all aspects of trade and industry.

Department store A type of retail store having a wide product mix; organised into separate departments to facilitate marketing efforts and international management.

Dependent variable A variable contingent on, or restricted to, one or a set of values assumed by the independent variable.

Depression A stage of the business cycle during which unemployment is extremely high, wages are very low, total disposable income is at a minimum, and consumers lack confidence in the economy.

Depth (of product mix) The average number of different products offered to buyers in a firm's product line.

Depth interview Personal interview within an open, informal atmosphere; this interview may take several hours. It is used to study motives.

Derived demand A characteristic of industrial demand that arises because industrial demand derives from the consumer demand.

Descriptive study A type of study undertaken when marketers see that knowledge of the characteristics of certain phenomena is needed to solve a problem; may require statistical analysis and predictive tools.

Descriptors Variables used to describe individuals, groups, or organisations that have been grouped into segments.

Differential advantage If a marketing mix is developed which is exactly in line with the targeted consumers' needs and expectations, which is a superior marketing mix to those offered by direct competitors, then there is a real or perceived *differential advantage*: something a product or an organisation has, desired by consumers and not matched by competitors.

Direct cost approach An approach to determining marketing costs in which cost analysis includes direct costs and traceable common costs but does not include non-traceable common costs.

Direct costs Costs directly attributable to the performance of marketing functions.

Direct distribution channels Distribution channels in which products are sold directly from producer to ultimate users.

Direct mail Printed material mailed direct to customers' addresses to entice prospective customers or donors.

Direct mail package More than just an envelope: a mix of mailing envelopes, covering letter, circular, response device and return device.

Direct marketing The use of non-personal media to introduce products by mail or telephone.

Director General of Fair Trading Reporting to the Secretary of State for Trade and Industry, the Director General of Fair Trading can investigate any business practice which restricts, distorts or prevents competition and hinders fair trading.

Direct ownership A long run commitment to marketing in a foreign nation in which a subsidiary or division is owned by a foreign country through purchase.

Discount sheds Are cheaply constructed one storey retail stores orientated towards discounted merchandise and car borne shoppers.

Discretionary income Disposable income that is available for spending and saving after an individual has purchased the basic necessities of food, clothing, and shelter.

Disposable income After tax income.

Distribution The activities that make products available to customers when and where they want to purchase them.

Distribution centre A large, centralised warehouse that receives goods from factories and suppliers, re-groups the goods into orders, and ships the orders to customers quickly, with the focus on active movement of goods rather than passive storage.

Distribution (place) variable The marketing mix variable in which marketing management attempts to make products available in the quantities desired, with adequate service, to a target market and to keep the total inventory, transport, communication, storage, and materials handling costs as low as possible.

Diversified growth A type of growth that occurs in three forms, depending on the technology of the new products and the nature of the new markets the firm enters; the three forms are horizontal, concentric, and conglomerate.

Dogs In the RCG growth-share market have low market shares and very poor prospects. They need to be killed off.

Drop shipper A limited service wholesaler that takes title to products and negotiates sales but never physically handles products.

Dual distribution A channel practice whereby a producer distributes the same product through two or more different channels.

Dumping The sale of products in foreign markets at lower prices than those charged in the domestic market (when all costs are not allocated or when surplus products are sold).

E

Early adopters Individuals who choose new products carefully and are viewed by persons in the early majority, late majority, and laggard categories as being "the people to check with."

Early majority Individuals who adopt a new product just prior to the average person; they are deliberate and cautious in trying new products.

Economic forces Forces that determine the strength of a firm's competitive atmosphere and affect the impact of marketing activities because they determine the size and strength of demand for products.

Economic institutions An environmental force in international markets made up of producers, wholesalers, retailers, buyers, and other organisations that produce, distribute, and purchase products.

Economic order quantity (EOQ) The order size that minimises the total cost of ordering and carrying inventory.

Edge of town In retail terms, recent expansion of superstores and discount warehouses away from the traditional city centre to the edge of conurbations close to ring roads and residential suburbs.

Effective buying income Similar to disposable income; it includes salaries, wages, dividends, interest, profits, and rents, less taxes.

Electronic Funds Transfer at Point of Sale (EFTPOS) The use of scanning equipment for both product sale data capture and cash transfer from consumer to retailer (typically via the debit or credit card).

Electronic Point of Sale (EPOS) Data capture, typically with scanning equipment reading product barcodes in retail stores.

Encoding *See* Coding process.

Environmental analysis Is the process of assessing and interpreting the information gathered through environmental scanning.

Environmental monitoring The process of seeking information about events and relationships in a company's environment to assist marketers in identifying opportunities and in planning.

Environmental scanning The collecting of information about the forces in the marketing environment.

Equalised workload method A method of determining sales force size in which the number of customers multiplied by the number of sales calls per year required to serve these customers effectively is divided by the average number of calls each salesperson makes annually.

Ethical formalism Develops specific rule for behaviour by determining if an action is "safe" to repeat, as a general rule.

Ethical issue Is an identifiable problem, situation or opportunity requiring an individual or organisation to choose from among several actions which must be evaluated as being right or wrong.

Ethical pricing A form of professional pricing in which the demand for the product is inelastic and the seller is a professional who has a responsibility not to overcharge the client.

European Community (EC) Twelve member countries in Europe promoting common agricultural, trade, economic, and legislative policies.

Exchange Participation by two or more individuals, groups, or organisations, with each party possessing something of value that the other party desires. Each must be willing to give up its "something of value" to get "something of value" held by the other, and all parties must be willing to communicate with each other.

Exclusive dealing A situation in which a manufacturer forbids an intermediary to carry products of competing manufacturers.

Exclusive distribution A type of market coverage in which only one outlet is used in a geographic area.

Executive judgement A sales forecasting method based on the intuition of one or more executives.

Exhibition hall *See* Trade market.

Experience curve pricing A pricing approach in which a company fixes a low price that high cost competitors cannot match and thus expands its market share; this approach is possible when a firm gains cumulative production experience and is able to reduce its manufacturing costs to a predictable rate through improved methods, materials, skills, and machinery.

Experience qualities Qualities of services that can be assessed only after purchase and consumption (taste, satisfaction, courtesy, and the like).

Experimentation Research in which the factors that are related to or may affect the variables under investigation are maintained as constants so that the effects of the experimental variables may be measured.

Expert forecasting survey Preparation of the sales forecast by experts, such as economists, management consultants, advertising executives, academics, or other persons outside the firm.

Exploratory studies   A type of research conducted when more information is needed about a problem and the tentative hypothesis needs to be made more specific; it permits marketers to conduct mini-studies with a very restricted database.

Extended marketing mix for services   In addition to the "standard" 4Ps of product, place, price and promotion, there are 3Ps: process, people and physical evidence.

Extensive decision-making   The considerable time and effort a buyer spends seeking alternative products, searching for information about them, and then evaluating them to determine which one will be most satisfying.

External search   The process of seeking information from sources other than one's memory.

F

Facilitating agency   An organisation that performs activities helpful in performing channel functions but does not buy, sell, or transfer title to the product; it can be a transport company, an insurance company, an advertising agency, a marketing research agency, or a financial institution.

Family branding   Three choices for an organisation naming and branding its products or services: *individual brand names* for each separate product; *blanket family name* across the portfolio; *company name combined with individual brand name* for each product or service.

Family packaging   A policy in an organisation that all packages are to be similar or are to include one major element of the design.

Feature article   A form of publicity that is up to three thousand words long and is usually prepared for a specific publication.

Federal Trade Commission   A US governmental group established to prevent the free enterprise system from being stifled or fettered by monopoly or anticompetitive practices; it provides direct protection to consumers from unfair or deceptive trade practices.

Feedback   The receiver's response to a decoded message.

Field public warehouse   A warehouse established by a public warehouse at the owner's inventory location; the warehouser becomes the custodian of the products and issues a receipt that can be used as collateral for a loan.

Financial Services Act 1986   Supervised by the Director General of Fair Trading, legislation in the UK for the protection of investors.

Fixed cost   The cost that does not vary with changes in the number of units produced or sold.

Flashes   Headers printed on a direct mail package in order to gain the recipient's attention.

F.O.B. (free-on-board) destination   Part of a price quotation, used to indicate who must pay shipping charges. F.O.B. destination price means that the producer absorbs the costs of shipping the merchandise to the customer.

F.O.B. (free-on-board) factory   Part of a price quotation; used to indicate who must pay shipping charges. F.O.B. factory price indicates the price of the merchandise at the factory, before it is loaded onto the carrier vehicle; the buyer must pay for shipping.

Focus group   Between six and eight people, usually single sex, who—for a small fee or product sample—take part in, typically, discussions for two hours or three hours. These discussions commence in a general manner examining a particular market or product field before narrowing to focus on a specific brand or product.

Food broker   An intermediary that sells food and other grocery products to retailer owned and merchant wholesalers, grocery chains, industrial buyers, and food processors. Both buyers and sellers use food brokers to cope with fluctuating market conditions.

Forecasting   Predicting future events on the basis of historical data, opinions, trends, known future variables. Principally there are three categories of forecasting models in marketing: *see* Causal forecasting, Judgemental forecasting, Time series forecasts.

Franchising   An arrangement in which a supplier (franchisor) grants a dealer (franchisee) the right to sell products in exchange for some type of consideration.

Free merchandise   A sales promotion method aimed at retailers whereby free merchandise is offered to resellers that purchase a stated quantity of product.

Free samples   A new product sales promotion technique that marketers use to stimulate trial of a product, to increase sales volume in early stages of the product's lifecycle, or to obtain desirable distribution.

Freight absorption pricing   Pricing for a particular customer or geographical area whereby the seller absorbs all or part of the actual freight costs.

Freight forwarders   Businesses that consolidate shipments from several organisations into efficient lot sizes, which increases transit time and sometimes lowers shipping costs.

Full cost approach   An approach to determining marketing costs in which cost analysis includes direct costs, traceable common costs, and non-traceable common costs.

Full service wholesaler   A marketing intermediary that provides most services that can be performed by wholesalers.

Functional discount   *See* Trade discount.

Functional middleman   A marketing intermediary that does not take title to products but usually receives a fee for expediting exchanges.

Functional modification   A change that affects a product's versatility, effectiveness, convenience, or safety, usually requiring the redesigning of one or more parts of the product.

Functional wholesaler A marketing intermediary that expedites exchanges among producers and resellers and is compensated by fees or commission.

G

General Electric's Strategic Business Planning Grid A variation of the market attractiveness-business position model.

General merchandise wholesaler Full service merchant wholesaler that carriers a very wide product mix.

General public The indirect consumers of the product of a non-business organisation; for instance, the general public of a university includes alumni, trustees, parents of students, and other groups.

Generic brand A brand that indicates only the product category (such as *aluminum foil*), not the company name and other identifying terms.

Generic strategies Porter's strategies to help firms maintain leadership: cost leadership, differentiation or focus.

Geographic pricing A form of pricing that involves reductions for transport costs or other costs associated with the physical distance between the buyer and the seller.

Globalisation The development of marketing strategies as if the entire world (or regions of it) were a single entity; products are marketed the same way everywhere.

Good A tangible item.

Government markets Markets made up of national and local government, spending millions of pounds annually for goods and services to support their internal operations and to provide such products as defence, energy, and education.

Green marketing Refers to the specific development, pricing, promotion and distribution of products that do not harm the environment.

Green movement Society's concern about pollution, waste disposal, manufacturing processes and the so called "greenhouse effect" has led to the green movement.

Gross Domestic Product (GDP) Total output of goods and services by the national economy in a full year.

Gross National Product (GNP) An overall measure of a nation's economic standing in terms of the value of all products produced by that nation for a given period of time.

Growth stage The product life-cycle stage in which sales rise rapidly; profits reach a peak and then start to decline.

Guarantee Document that specifies what the producer will do if the product malfunctions.

H

Heterogeneity A condition resulting from the fact that people typically perform services; there may be variation from one service provider to another or variation in the service provided by a single individual from day to day and from customer to customer.

Heterogeneous market A market made up of individuals with diverse product needs for products in a specific product class.

Horizontal channel integration The combining of institutions at the same level of operation under one management.

Hypermarkets Take the benefits of superstores further using their greater size (9,000 m^2 or 100,000 ft^2).

Hypothesis A guess or assumption about a certain problem or set of circumstances; reasonable supposition that may be right or wrong.

I

Idea A concept, image, or issue.

Idea generation The search by businesses and other organisations for product ideas that help them achieve their objectives.

Illustrations Photographs, drawings, graphs, charts, and tables, used to encourage an audience to read or watch an advertisement.

Implicit bargaining A method of employee motivation that recognises the various needs of different employees and is based on the theory that there is no one best way to motivate individuals.

Impulse buying An unplanned buying behaviour that involves a powerful, persistent urge to buy something immediately.

Income The amount of money received through wages, rents, investments, pensions, and benefit payments for a given period.

Incremental productivity method A plan by which a marketer should continue to increase the sales force as long as the additional sales increases are greater than the additional selling costs that arise from employing more salespeople.

Independent Broadcasting Authority (IBA) Responsible for control and monitoring of non-BBC broadcasting companies in the UK Replaced by the Independent Television Commission.

Independent Television (ITV) The regional television stations in the UK which compete with the national networks.

Independent Television Commission *See* Independent Broadcasting Authority.

Independent variable A variable free from the influence of, or not dependent on, other variables.

In-depth interviews Marketing research tool in which the subject is encouraged to talk freely about the topic in question.

Individual branding A branding policy in which each product is named differently.

Industrial buying behaviour *See* Organisational buying behaviour.

Industrial distributor An independent business organisation that takes title to industrial products and carries inventories.

Industrial market A market consisting of individuals, groups, or organisations that purchase specific kinds of products for resale, for direct use in producing other products, or for use in day to day operations; also called organisational market.

Industrial marketing A set of activities directed towards facilitating and expediting exchanges involving industrial markets and industrial products.

Industrial product A product purchased to be used directly or indirectly to produce other products or to be used in the operations of an organisation.

Industrial service An intangible product that an organisation uses in its operations, such as a financial product or a legal service.

Inelastic demand A type of demand in which a price increase or decrease will not significantly affect the quantity demanded.

Inflation A condition in which price levels increase faster than incomes, causing a decline in buying power.

Information inputs The sensations we receive through our sense organs.

In-home retailing A type of non-store retailing that involves personal selling in consumers' homes.

Innovators The first consumers to adopt a new product; they enjoy trying new products and tend to be venturesome, rash, and daring.

Input-output data A type of information, sometimes used in conjunction with the SIC system, that is based on the assumption that the output or sales of one industry are the input or purchases of other industries.

Inseparability A condition in which the consumer frequently is directly involved in the production process because services normally are produced at the same time they are consumed.

Institutional advertising A form of advertising promoting organisational images, ideas, and political issues.

Institutional market A market that consists of organisations seeking to achieve goals other than such normal business goals as profit, market share, or return on investment.

Intangibility A characteristic of services: because services are performances, they cannot be seen, touched, tasted, or smelled, nor can they be possessed.

Integrated growth The type of growth that a firm can have within its industry; three possible growth directions include forward, backward, and horizontal.

Intense growth The type of growth that can occur when current products and current markets have the potential for increasing sales.

Intensive distribution A form of market coverage in which all available outlets are used for distributing a product.

Intermediaries In marketing channels, these are agents or brokers, wholesalers or retailers for consumer goods, and agents or distributors for industrial goods. They *sort out, accumulate, allocate* goods.

Intermodal transport Combining and coordinating two or more modes of transport.

Internal marketing Refers to the managerial actions required to make all employees understand and help implement the chosen marketing strategy.

Internal search An aspect of an information search where buyers first search their memory for information about products that might solve their problem.

International marketing Marketing activities which are performed across national boundaries.

Introduction stage The stage in a product's life-cycle beginning at a product's first appearance in the marketplace, when sales are zero and profits are negative.

Intuition In many situations managers have neither time nor resources to access marketing intelligence or commission marketing research to address a problem; instead they make decisions based on their experience and understanding of their market.

J

Job enrichment A method of employee motivation that gives employees a sense of autonomy and control over their work, with employees being encouraged to set their own goals.

Joint demand A characteristic of industrial demand that occurs when two or more items are used in combination to produce a product.

Joint venture A partnership between a domestic firm and foreign firms and/or governments.

Judgemental forecasting Subjective opinions of managers, aggregated and averaged: *sales force composite* seeks the views and predictions from the field force; *expert consensus* includes the opinions of industry experts; *Delphi* attains forecasts from the field force, centrally collates and revises them before returning the updated forecasts to the field force for further modification and opinion.

Junk mail Unwanted direct mail consigned straight to the dust bin.

K

Kinesic communication Commonly known as body language, this type of interpersonal communication occurs in face to face selling situations when the salesperson and customers move their heads, eyes, arms, hands, legs, and torsos.

Knowledge Familiarity with a product and expertise in applying the product.

L

Labelling An important dimension of packaging for promotional, informational, and legal reasons; regulated by numerous national and EC laws.

Laggards The last consumers to adopt a new product; they are orientated towards the past and suspicious of new products.

Late majority People who are quite sceptical of new products; they eventually adopt new products because of economic necessity or social pressure.

Layout The physical arrangement of the illustration, headline, subheadline, body copy, and signature of an advertisement.

Learning A change in an individual's behaviour that arises from prior behaviour in similar situations.

Legal forces Forces that arise from the legislation and interpretation of laws; these laws, enacted by government units, restrain and control marketing decisions and activities.

Level of involvement The intensity of interest that one has for a certain product in a particular buying decision.

Licensing Is an alternative to direct involvement: the licensee (holder) pays commissions or royalties on sales.

Licensing (international) An arrangement in international marketing in which the licensee pays commissions or royalties on sales or supplies used in manufacturing.

Limited decision-making Consumer decision-making used for products that are purchased occasionally. Also used when a buyer needs to acquire information about an unfamiliar brand in a familiar product category.

Limited line wholesaler Full service merchant wholesaler that carries only a few product lines.

Limited service wholesaler A marketing intermediary that provides only some marketing services and specialises in a few functions.

Line family branding A branding policy in which an organisation uses family branding only for products within a line, not for all its products.

Location For retailers, a key factor. Location is the general locality. Site is the specific terrain on which the store stands.

Long range plan A plan that covers more than five years.

M

Mailing lists Of addresses for direct mail campaigns.

Mail order retailing A type of non-personal, non-store retailing that uses direct mail advertising and catalogues and is typified by selling by description. The buyer usually does not see the actual product until it is delivered.

Mail order wholesaler A firm that sells through direct mail by sending catalogues to retail, industrial, and institutional customers.

Mail surveys Questionnaires sent to respondents, who are encouraged to complete and return them.

Major equipment A category of industrial products that includes large tools and machines used for production purposes.

Manufacturer brand A brand initiated by a producer; makes it possible for a producer to be identified with its product at the point of purchase.

Manufacturers' agent An independent businessperson who sells complementary products of several producers in assigned territories and is compensated through commission.

Marginal cost (MC) The cost associated with producing one more unit of a product.

Marginal revenue (MR) The change in total revenue that occurs after an additional unit of a product is sold.

Market An aggregate of people who, as individuals or as organisations, have needs for products in a product class and who have the ability, willingness, and authority to purchase such products.

Market attractiveness/business position model A two dimensional matrix designed to serve as a diagnostic tool to highlight SBUs that have an opportunity to grow or that should be divested.

Market challengers Are non-market leaders which aggressively attack the market and the market leader in order to capture market share and to dominate the market.

Market coverage The intensity of market coverage presents three options: *intensive* with many distribution outlets; *selective* with fewer outlets but with larger catchments; *exclusive* with deliberately restricted and limited distribution.

Market density The number of potential customers within a unit of land area, such as a square mile.

Market followers Are low share competitors without resources or courage to attack the leader and the challengers for market share: "me too" companies.

Marketing Individual and organisational activities that facilitate and expedite satisfying exchange relationships in a dynamic environment through the creation, distribution, promotion, and pricing of goods, services, and ideas.

Marketing The weekly trade magazine published in London by Haymarket Publishing; news and features from the world of practising marketers.

Marketing assets Properties or features which can be used to advantage in the market place: *customer* based, such as image and reputation, brand name; *distribution* based such as coverage; *internal* assets, including skills and experience, economies of scale, technology.

Marketing audit A systematic examination of the objectives, strategies, organisation, and performance of a firm's marketing unit.

Marketing audit report A written summary produced after the marketing audit has been conducted; it includes recommendations that will increase marketing productivity and develops a recommendation as to the business's general direction.

Marketing channel A group of interrelated intermediaries who direct products to customers; also called channel of distribution.

Marketing communications The communication of information which facilitates or expedites the exchange process.

Marketing concept A managerial philosophy that an organisation should try to satisfy customers' needs through a coordinated set of activities that at the same time allows the organisation to achieve its goals.

Marketing control process A process that consists of establishing performance standards, evaluating actual performance by comparing it with established standards, and reducing the differences between desired and actual performance.

Marketing cost analysis A method for helping to control marketing strategies whereby various costs are broken down and classified to determine which costs are associated with specific marketing activities.

Marketing databank A file of data collected through both the marketing information system and marketing research projects.

Marketing environment The environment that surrounds both the buyer and the marketing mix; it consists of political, legal, regulatory, societal, consumer movement, economic, and technological forces. Environmental variables affect a marketer's ability to facilitate and expedite exchanges.

Marketing ethics Moral evaluation of decisions based on accepted principles of behaviour that result in an action being judged right or wrong.

Marketing experimentation A set of rules and procedures under which the task of data gathering is organised to expedite analysis and interpretation.

Marketing function account Classification of costs that indicates which function was performed through the expenditure of funds.

Marketing information system (MIS) A system that establishes a framework for the day to day managing and structuring of information gathered regularly from sources both inside and outside an organisation.

Marketing intelligence All the data gathered as a basis for marketing decisions.

Marketing intermediary A member of a marketing channel, usually a merchant or an agent, acting to direct products to buyers.

Marketing management A process of planning, organising, implementing, and controlling marketing activities to facilitate and expedite exchanges effectively and efficiently.

Marketing manager A person responsible for the mar-

keting activities that are necessary to serve a particular group or class of customers.

Marketing mix The tools available to the marketing manager, often referred to as "the 4 Ps": *product, place (distribution), promotion,* and *pricing.* For the marketing of services, the 4 Ps are extended to "the 7 Ps", with the addition of *people, process,* and *physical environment (ambience).* Increasingly, marketers of consumer goods and industrial products are including aspects of the extended *marketing mix* in their work.

Marketing objective A statement of what is to be accomplished through marketing activities.

Marketing orientated organisation An organisation that attempts to determine what target market members want and then tries to produce it.

Marketing plan The written document or blueprint for implementing and controlling an organisation's marketing activities related to a particular marketing strategy.

Marketing planning A systematic process that involves assessing marketing opportunities and resources, determining market objectives, and developing a plan for implementation and control.

Marketing programme A set of marketing strategies that are implemented and used at the same time.

Marketing research The part of marketing intelligence that involves specific inquiries into problems and marketing activities to discover new information so as to guide marketing decisions.

Marketing research process Define and locate the problem (task); develop hypotheses; collect data; analyse and interpret findings; report research findings and conclusions.

Marketing strategy A plan for selecting and analysing a target market and creating and maintaining a marketing mix.

Marketing Week The weekly trade magazine published in London by Centaur Communications; news and features from the marketing and agency world.

Market leader Is the company with largest market share. There can be only one market leader.

Market nichers Are companies which specialise by focusing on a narrow range of products or a select band of customers.

Market opportunity An opportunity that arises when the right combination of circumstances occurs at the right time to allow an organisation to take action towards generating sales from a target market.

Market planning cycle The five step cycle that involves developing or revising marketing objectives relative to performance, assessing marketing opportunities and resources, formulating marketing strategy, developing the plan for implementation and control, and implementing the marketing plan.

Market potential Is the total amount of a product that customers will purchase within a specified time period at a specific level of industry wide marketing activity.

Market requirement   Related to customers' needs or desired benefits, the market requirement is satisfied by components of the marketing mix that provide benefits to buyers.

Market sales potential   The amount of a product that specific customer groups would purchase within a specified period at a specific level of industry wide marketing activity.

Market segment   A group of individuals, groups, or organisations sharing one or more similar characteristics that make them have relatively similar product needs.

Market segmentation   The process of dividing a total market into groups of people with relatively similar product needs, for the purpose of designing a marketing mix (or mixes) that more precisely matches the needs of individuals in a selected segment (or segments).

Market segmentation process   *Segmentation; targeting; positioning.* How does the market break down? Which segment should be targeted? How should the product be offered to the targeted market; how should it be positioned relative to competitors' products?

Market share   A firm's sales in relation to total industry sales, expressed as a decimal or percentage.

Market test   A stage of new product development that involves making a product available to buyers in one or more test areas and measuring purchases and consumer responses to promotion, price, and distribution efforts.

Mark-up   A percentage of the cost or price of a product added to the cost.

Mark-up pricing   A pricing method in which the price is derived by adding a predetermined percentage of the cost to the cost of the product.

Materials handling   Physical handling of products.

Maturity stage   A stage in the product life cycle in which the sales curve peaks and starts to decline as profits continue to decline.

Mechanical observation devices   Cameras, recorders, counting machines, and equipment to record movement, behaviour, or physiological changes in individuals.

Media plan   A plan that sets forth the exact media vehicles to be used for advertisements and the dates and times that the advertisements are to appear.

Medium/Media   Choice of *medium of transmission* for a promotional campaign: print, TV/radio, cinema, posters, personal selling, etc.

Medium of transmission   That which carries the coded message from the source to the receiver or audience; examples include ink on paper and vibrations of air waves produced by vocal cords.

Medium range plans   Plans that usually encompass two to five years.

Megacarrier   A freight transport company that provides many methods of shipment, such as rail, truck, and air service.

Merchandise allowance   A sales promotion method aimed at retailers; it consists of a manufacturer's agreement to pay resellers certain amounts of money for providing special promotional efforts, such as setting up and maintaining a display.

Merchant   A marketing intermediary who takes title to merchandise and resells it for a profit.

Merchant wholesaler   A marketing intermediary who takes title to products, assumes risk, and is generally involved in buying and reselling products.

Misleading prices   Pricing policies which confuse or dupe consumers.

Missionary salesperson   A support salesperson, usually employed by a manufacturer, who assists the producer's customers in selling to their own customers.

Moderator   The market researcher who controls, runs, and prompts a focus group discussion.

Modified rebuy purchase   A type of industrial purchase in which a new task purchase is changed the second or third time, or the requirements associated with a straight rebuy purchase are modified.

Money off offer   A sales promotion device for established products whereby buyers receive a certain amount off the regular price shown on the label or package.

Money refund   A new product sales promotion technique in which the producer mails a consumer a specific amount of money when proof of purchase is established.

Monopolies and Mergers Commission   In the UK where at least a quarter of a particular good or service is supplied by a single person or a group of connected companies, restricting and distorting competition, the Department for Trade and Industry and the Director General of Fair Trading seek an investigation by the Monopolies and Mergers Commission.

Monopolistic competition   A market structure in which a firm has many potential competitors; to compete, the firm tries to develop a differential marketing strategy to establish its own market share.

Monopoly   A market structure existing when a firm produces a product that has no close substitutes and/or when a single seller may erect barriers to potential competitors.

Moral philosophies   Are principles or rules that individuals use to determine the right way to behave.

Motive   An internal energising force that directs a person's behaviour towards his or her goals.

MRO items   An alternative term for supplies: supplies can be divided into maintenance, repair, and operating (or overhaul) items.

Multi-branding   Each product or service in an organisation's portfolio is given its own unique name and brand identity.

Multinational enterprise   A firm that has operations or subsidiaries in several countries.

Multisegment strategy   A market segmentation strategy in which an organisation directs its marketing efforts at two or more segments by developing a marketing mix for each selected segment.

Multivariable segmentation   Market division achieved by using more than one characteristic to divide the total market; this approach provides more information about the individuals in each segment than does single variable segmentation.

N

Natural account   Classification of costs based on what the money is actually spent on; typically a part of a regular accounting system.

Negotiated pricing   A determination of price through bargaining even when there are stated list prices and discount structures.

Negotiation   Mutual discussion or communication of the terms and methods of an exchange.

New product   Any product that a given firm has not marketed previously.

New product development   A process consisting of six phases: idea generation, screening, business analysis, product development, test marketing, and commercialisation.

New task purchase   A type of industrial purchase in which an organisation is making an initial purchase of an item to be used to perform a new job or to solve a new problem.

Noise   A condition in the communication process existing when the decoded message is different from what was coded.

Non-business marketing   Marketing activities conducted by individuals and organisations to achieve some goal other than ordinary business goals such as profit, market share, or return on investment.

Non-cumulative discount   A once only price reduction based on the number of units purchased, the size of the order, or the product combination purchased.

Non-price competition   A policy in which a seller elects not to focus on price and instead emphasises distinctive product features, services, product quality, promotion, packaging, or other factors to distinguish its product from competing brands.

Non-profit organisation marketing   The application of marketing concepts and techniques to such non-profit groups as hospitals and colleges.

Non-store retailing   A type of retailing where consumers purchase products without visiting a store.

Non-traceable common costs   Costs that cannot be assigned to any specific function according to any logical criteria and thus are assignable only on an arbitrary basis.

O

Objective and task approach   An approach to determining the advertising budget: marketers first determine the objectives that a campaign is to achieve, and then ascertain the tasks required to accomplish those objectives; the costs of all tasks are added to ascertain the total budget.

Observation method   A research method in which researchers record the overt behaviour of subjects, noting physical conditions and events. Direct contact with subjects is avoided; instead, their actions are examined and noted systematically.

Odd-even pricing   A type of psychological pricing that assumes that more of a product will be sold at £99.99 than at £100.00, indicating that an odd price is more appealing than an even price to customers.

Offensive warfare   The challengers must aggressively seek market share gains from each other and from the market leaders, by identifying competitors' weaknesses.

Office of Fair Trading   Exists in the UK to oversee government policy for monopolies and mergers.

Oligopoly   A competitive structure existing when a few sellers control the supply of a large proportion of a product; each seller must consider the actions of other sellers to make changes in marketing activities.

Omnibus survey   Continuous survey used to examine a number of topics together. Client companies "buy in" to the survey having a limited number of questions included in the survey on their behalf. Marketing research agencies sell on the findings to a wide audience.

Open bids   Prices submitted by several, but not all, sellers; the amounts of these bids are not made public.

Opportunity cost   The value of the benefit that is given up by selecting one alternative rather than another.

Order getter   A type of salesperson who increases the firm's sales by selling to new customers and by increasing sales to present customers.

Order processing   The receipt and transmission of sales order information in the physical distribution process.

Order taker   A type of salesperson who primarily seeks repeat sales.

Organisational buying behaviour   The purchase behaviour of producers, government units, institutions, and resellers; also called industrial buying behaviour.

Organisational (industrial) market   Individuals or groups who purchase a specific kind of product for one of three purposes: resale, direct use in producing other products, or use in general daily operations; also called industrial market.

Overall family branding   A policy of branding all of a firm's products with the same name or at least a part of the name.

Own label/brand (private label)   Many large retail groups have in stock, in addition to manufacturers' brands, their own retail brand. This can simply be the name of the retailer or a name especially created for a retailer's use to allow competition with the manufacturers' brands. The brand name is owned and controlled by the retailer.

P

Patronage motives   Motives that influence where a person purchases products on a regular basis.

Penetration price   A lower price designed to penetrate

the market and thus quickly produce a larger unit sales volume.

Per cent of sales approach A method for establishing the advertising budget whereby marketers simply multiply a firm's past sales, forecasted sales, or a combination of the two by a standard percentage based on both what the firm traditionally has spent on advertising and what the industry averages.

Perception The process by which an individual selects, organises, and interprets information inputs to create a meaningful picture of the world.

Perceptual mapping A variety of mathematical approaches designed to place or describe consumers' perceptions of brands or products on one or a series of "spatial maps." A means of visually depicting consumers' perceptions.

Perfect competition Ideal competitive structure that would entail a large number of sellers, none of which could significantly influence price or supply.

Performance standard An expected level of performance against which actual performance can be compared.

Perishability A condition where, because of simultaneous production and consumption, unused capacity to produce services in one time period cannot be stockpiled or inventoried for future time periods.

Personal factors Factors influencing the consumer buying decision process that are unique to particular individuals.

Personal interview survey A face-to-face interview that allows more in-depth interviewing, probing, follow-up questions, or psychological tests.

Personality An internal structure in which experience and behaviour are related in an orderly way.

Personal selling A process of informing customers and persuading them to purchase products through personal communication in an exchange situation.

Persuasion The activity of convincing or prevailing upon an individual or organisation to bring about an exchange.

Physical distribution An integrated set of activities that deal with managing the movement of products within firms and through marketing channels.

Pioneer advertising A type of advertising that informs persons about what a product is, what it does, how it can be used, and where it can be purchased.

Point-of-sale (POS) materials A sales promotion method that uses such items as outside signs, window displays, and display racks to attract attention, to inform customers, and to encourage retailers to carry particular products.

Political and legal institutions Public agencies, laws, courts, legislatures, and government bureaux.

Political forces Forces that strongly influence the economic and political stability of a country, not only through decisions that affect domestic matters but through their authority to negotiate trade agreements and to determine foreign policy.

Population All elements, units, or individuals that are of interest to researchers for a specific study.

Porter's Competitive Strategies The competitive arena is affected by outside forces: *bargaining power of suppliers; bargaining power of buyers; threat of substitute products or services; threat of new entrants.*

Porter's Generic Strategies Three generic strategies resulting in success for organisations competing for position in any particular market: *cost leadership; differentiation; focus.*

Positioning *See* Product positioning.

Post-campaign test or post-test An evaluation of advertising effectiveness after the campaign.

Premiums Items that are offered free or at a minimum cost as a bonus for purchasing.

Press conference A meeting used to announce major news events.

Press (news) release A form of publicity that is usually a single page of typewritten copy containing fewer than three hundred words. A news release.

Prestige pricing Setting prices at a high level to facilitate a prestige or quality image.

Pre-test Evaluation of an advertisement before it is actually used.

Price The value placed on what is exchanged.

Price competition A policy whereby a marketer emphasises price as an issue and matches or beats the prices of competitors also emphasising low prices.

Price differentiation A demand orientated pricing method whereby a firm uses more than one price in the marketing of a specific product; differentiation of prices can be based on several dimensions, such as type of customers, type of distribution used, or the time of the purchase.

Price discrimination A policy of charging some buyers lower prices than other buyers, which gives those paying less a competitive advantage.

Price elasticity of demand A measure of the sensitivity of demand to changes in price.

Price leaders Products sold at less than cost to increase sales of regular merchandise.

Price lining A form of psychological pricing in which an organisation sets a limited number of prices for selected lines of products.

Price off sales A discount off the regular price shown on the label.

Price skimming A pricing policy whereby an organisation charges the highest possible price that buyers who most desire the product will pay.

Price variable A critical marketing mix variable in which marketing management is concerned with establishing a value for what is exchanged.

Pricing method A mechanical procedure for setting prices on a regular basis.

Pricing objectives Overall goals that describe the role of price in an organisation's long range plans.

Pricing policy   A guiding philosophy or course of action designed to influence and determine pricing decisions.

Primary data   Information observed and recorded or collected directly from subjects.

Primary data collection   In marketing research this is the act of collecting bespoke information for specific research requirements. There are two types: observation (mechanical or personal) and surveys (mail/postal, telephone or personal).

Private brand   *See* Private distributor brand.

Private distributor brand   A brand that is initiated and owned by a reseller; also called private brand and own label. *See* Own label.

Private warehouse   A storage facility operated by an organisation for the purpose of distributing its own products.

Proactive strategy   Assumes responsibility for the company's actions and responds to accusations, without outside pressure to do so.

Problem children   Or "question marks" in the BCG growth-share matrix are not obviously "dogs," but equally are not obviously going to be successful products.

Problem definition   The first step in the research process toward finding a solution or launching a research study; the researcher thinks about the best ways to discover the nature and boundaries of a problem or opportunity.

Process materials   Materials used directly in the production of other products; unlike component parts, they are not readily identifiable.

Procompetitive legislation   Laws enacted to preserve competition.

Producer market   A market consisting of individuals and business organisations that purchase products for the purpose of making a profit by using them to produce other products or by using them in their operations.

Product   Everything (both favourable and unfavourable) that one receives in an exchange; it is a complexity of tangible and intangible attributes, including functional, social, and psychological utilities or benefits. A product may be a good, a service, or an idea.

Product adoption process   The five stage process of buyer acceptance of a product: awareness, interest, evaluation, trial, and adoption.

Product advertising   Advertising that promotes goods and services.

Product assortment   A collection of a variety of different products.

Product (brand) management   A form of marketing management where the marketing function is orientated around individual products/brands or product portfolios. *Product management* is proactive, taking responsibility for both marketing strategy and the implementation of marketing mixes; it is not marketing as a service or ancillary resource.

Product deletion   The elimination of some products that no longer satisfy target market customers or contribute to achievement of an organisation's overall goals.

Product development   A stage in creating new products that moves the product from concept to test phase and also involves the development of the other elements of the marketing mix (promotion, distribution and price).

Product differentiation   The use of promotional efforts to differentiate a company's products from its competitors' products, with the hope of establishing the superiority and preferability of its products relative to competing brands.

Production orientated organisation   A firm that concentrates on either improving production efficiency or producing high quality, technically improved products; it has little regard for customers' desires.

Production orientation   The viewpoint that increasing the efficiency of production is the primary means of increasing an organisation's profits.

Product item   A specific version of a product that can be designated as a unique offering among an organisation's products.

Product life-cycle   The course of product development, consisting of several stages: introduction, growth, maturity, and decline. As a product moves through these stages, the strategies relating to competition, pricing, promotion, distribution, and market information must be evaluated and possibly changed.

Product line   A group of closely related products that are considered a unit because of marketing, technical, or end use considerations.

Product manager   Is responsible for a product, a product line or several distinct products that make up an interrelated group within a multiproduct organisation.

Product mix   The composite of products that an organisation makes available to consumers.

Product mix depth   *See* Depth (of product mix).

Product mix width   *See* Width (of product mix).

Product modification   The changing of one or more of a product's characteristics.

Product portfolio   The portfolio approach to marketing attempts to manage the product mix so as to balance short term gains with longer term profitability. There are various analytical tools available to assist in this management process: *The Boston Consultancy Group* (BCG) *Growth-Share Matrix* and the *Directional Policy Matrix* (DPM) are the most popular for analysing the relative attraction and positions of an organisation's various products or brands.

Product portfolio analysis   A strategic planning approach based on the philosophy that a product's market growth rate and its relative market share are important considerations in determining its marketing strategy.

Product portfolio approach   An approach to managing the product mix that attempts to create specific marketing strategies to achieve a balanced mix of products that will produce maximum long run profits.

Product positioning   The decisions and activities that are directed towards trying to create and maintain the firm's intended product concept in customers' minds. The creation of a product's perceived image.

Products, Consumer   Goods consumed by the general public; consumers as individuals: *convenience goods, shopping goods, specialty goods, unsought goods.*

Products, Industrial   Supplies used in the manufacture of other products: *raw materials, component parts, capital items, accessory equipment, consumable supplies, ancillary services.*

Products, Services   Service products tend to be intangible, requiring the participation of the consumer in their production and consumption: *tourism/catering, travel, health, leisure/entertainment, education, financial, consultancy, retailing, government/administration, non-profit/voluntary/charitable.*

Product specific spending patterns   The monetary amounts families spend for specific products within a general product class.

Product variable   That aspect of the marketing mix dealing with researching consumers' product wants and planning the product to achieve the desired product characteristics.

Professional pricing   Pricing used by persons who have great skill or experience in a particular field or activity, indicating that a price should not relate directly to the time and involvement in a specific case; rather, a standard fee is charged regardless of the problems involved in performing the job.

Professional services   Complex and frequently regulated services that usually require the provider to be highly skilled; for example, accounting or legal services.

Profit Impact on Marketing Strategy (PIMS)   A Strategic Planning Institute (SPI) research programme which provides reports on the products of SPI member firms; these reports assist the member firms in analysing marketing performance and formulating marketing strategies.

Projective technique   A test in which subjects are asked to perform specific tasks for particular purposes while in fact they are being evaluated for other purposes; assumes that subjects will unconsciously "project" their motives as they perform the tasks.

Promotion   The communication with individuals, groups, or organisations to directly or indirectly facilitate exchanges by influencing audience members to accept an organisation's products.

Promotional mix   The core elements of promotional activity: traditionally *advertising, sales promotion, personal selling* and *public relations/publicity,* with the more recent additions of *sponsorship* and *direct mail.*

Promotion variable   A major marketing mix component

used to facilitate exchanges by informing an individual or one or more groups of people about an organisation and its products.

Prospecting   Developing a list of potential customers for personal selling purposes.

Prosperity   A stage of the business cycle characterised by a combination of low unemployment and relatively high aggregate income, which causes buying power to be high (assuming a low inflation rate).

Proxemic communication   A subtle form of interpersonal communication used in face-to-face interactions when either party varies the physical distance that separates them.

Psychological factors   Factors that operate within individuals to partially determine their general behaviour and thus influence their behaviour as buyers.

Psychological pricing   A pricing method designed to encourage purchases that are based on emotional reactions rather than rational responses.

Publicity   Non-personal communication in news story form, regarding an organisation and/or its products, that is transmited through a mass medium at no charge.

Public relations   A broad set of communication activities used to create and maintain favourable relations between the organisation and its publics, such as customers, employees, stockholders, government officials, and society in general.

Publics   The target audiences for public relations: customers, employees, shareholders, trade bodies, suppliers, government officials, society in general.

Public warehouses   Business organisations that provide rented storage facilities and related physical distribution facilities.

Pull policy   Promotion of a product directly to consumers with the intention of developing strong consumer demand.

Purchase facilitation   The final communication effect. The product or brand has to be suitably accessible for the buyer to make the purchase: the elements of the marketing mix must facilitate the purchase.

Purchasing power   A buyer's income, credit, and wealth available for purchasing products.

Push money   An incentive programme designed to push a line of goods by providing salespeople with additional compensation.

Push policy   The promotion of a product only to the next institution down the marketing channel.

Q

Quali-depth interviews   A relatively new marketing research approach: 20–25 minute interviews conducted in halls or meeting rooms close to, for example, a high street.

Qualitative research   Deals with information too difficult or expensive to quantify; value judgements typically involving group discussions or personal interviews.

Quality modification A change that relates to a product's dependability and durability and is generally executed by alterations in the materials or production process used.

Quality of life The enjoyment of daily living, enhanced by leisure time, clean air and water, an unlittered earth, conservation of wildlife and natural resources, and security from radiation and poisonous substances.

Quantitative research Research findings which can be analysed and expressed numerically; often large sample surveys from mailed questionnaires or telephone interviewing, or analysis of sales data and market forecasts.

Quantity discounts Deductions from list price that reflect the economies of purchasing in large quantities.

Quota sampling Non-probability sampling in which the final choice of respondents is left to the interviewers.

R

Rack jobbers Middlemen (also called service merchandisers) similar to truck wholesalers but providing the extra service of cleaning and filling a display rack.

Random factor analysis A method of predicting sales whereby an attempt is made to attribute erratic sales variations to random, non-recurrent events, such as a regional power failure or a natural disaster.

Random sampling A type of sampling in which all the units in a population have an equal chance of appearing in the sample; probability sampling.

Ratchet effect The impact of using sales promotion (short term sales brought forward) and advertising (longer term sales build up) together.

Raw materials Basic materials that become part of a physical product; obtained from mines, farms, forests, oceans, and recycled solid wastes.

Reaction strategy Allows a condition or potential problem to go unresolved until the public learns about it.

Real estate brokers Brokers who, for a fee or commission, bring buyers and sellers together to exchange real estate.

Receiver The individual, group, or organisation that decodes a coded message.

Recession A stage in the business cycle during which unemployment rises and total buying power declines, stifling both consumers' and businesspeople's propensity to spend.

Reciprocity A practice unique to industrial sales in which two organisations agree to buy from each other.

Recognition test A post-test method of evaluating the effectivenesss of advertising; individual respondents are shown the actual advertisement and asked whether they recognise it.

Recovery A stage of the business cycle during which the economy moves from recession towards prosperity.

Recruiting A process by which the sales manager develops a list of applicants for sales positions.

Reference group A group with which an individual identifies so much that he or she takes on many of the values, attitudes, or behaviours of group members.

Regional issues Versions of a magazine that differ across geographic regions so that a publisher can vary the advertisements and editorial content.

Regulatory forces Forces arising from regulatory units at all levels of government; these units create and enforce numerous regulations that affect marketing decisions.

Reinforcement advertising An advertisement attempting to assure current users that they have made the right choice and telling them how to get the most satisfaction from the product.

Reliability A condition existing when a sample is representative of the population; it also exists when repeated use of an instrument produces almost identical results.

Reminder advertising Advertising used to remind consumers that an established brand is still around and that it has certain uses, characteristics, and benefits.

Reorder point The inventory level that signals that more inventory should be ordered.

Reseller market A market consisting of intermediaries, such as wholesalers and retailers, that buy finished goods and resell them for the purpose of making a profit.

Restrictive Trade Practices Act, 1976 The Restrictive Practices Court in the UK, following recommendations from the Director General of Fair Trading, examines trading agreements which limit freedom of choice in terms of trade and price setting which may be against the public interest.

Retailer An intermediary that purchases products for the purpose of reselling them to ultimate consumers.

Retailer coupon A sales promotion method used by retailers when price is a primary motivation for consumers' purchasing behaviour; usually takes the form of a "money off" coupon that is distributed through advertisements and is redeemable only at a specific store.

Retailing Activities required for exchanges in which ultimate consumers are the buyers.

Retail park In the 1970s most superstores were freestanding, isolated stores. Throughout Europe, as planning regulations were relaxed, developers found sites either formerly used by heavy industry or adjacent to suburbs on the edge of towns to accommodate several neighbouring superstores. Recently full scale covered shopping malls have appeared on such retail parks, along with the superstores.

Retail positioning Involves identifying an unserved niche or segment and serving it through a strategy that distinguishes the retailer from others in the minds of people in that segment.

Retail technology Systems such as EPOS and EFTPOS which increase retailers' efficiency and productivity.

Role A set of actions and activities that a person in a particular position is supposed to perform, based on the expectations of both the individual and the persons around the individual.

Routine response behaviour The type of decision-making used by a consumer when buying frequently purchased, low cost items that require very little search and decision effort.

S

Safety stock The inventory needed to prevent running out of stock.

Sales analysis A process for controlling marketing strategies whereby sales figures are used to evaluate performance.

Sales branches Similar to merchant wholesalers in their operations; may offer credit, delivery, give promotional assistance, and furnish other services.

Sales contest A sales promotion method used to motivate distributors, retailers, and sales personnel through the recognition of outstanding achievements.

Sales force forecasting survey Estimation by members of a firm's sales force of the anticipated sales in their territories for a specified period.

Sales forecast The amount of a product that a company expects to sell during a specific period at a specified level of marketing activities.

Sales office Provides service normally associated with agents; owned and controlled by the producer.

Sales orientated organisation An organisation acting on its belief that personal selling and advertising are the primary tools used to generate profits and that most products—regardless of consumers' needs—can be sold if the right quantity and quality of personal selling and advertising are used.

Sales orientation A focus on increasing an organisation's sales as the major way to increase profits.

Sales potential The maximum percentage of market potential that an individual firm within an industry can expect to obtain for a specific product.

Sales promotion An activity and/or material that acts as a direct inducement to resellers, salespeople, or consumers; it offers added value or incentive to buy or sell the product.

Salience Level of importance of buying choice criteria.

Sample A limited number of units that are believed to be representative of the total population under study for marketing research purposes.

Sampling Selecting representative units from a total population.

Scientific decision-making An approach that involves systematically seeking facts and then applying decision-making methods other than trial and error or generalisation from experience.

Scrambled merchandising The addition of unrelated products and product lines to an existing product mix, particularly fast moving items that can be sold in large volume.

Screening ideas A stage in the product development process in which the ideas that do not match organisational objectives are rejected and those with the greatest potential are selected for further development.

Sealed bids Prices submitted to a buyer, to be opened and made public at a specified time.

Search qualities Tangible attributes of services that can be viewed prior to purchase.

Seasonal analysis A method of predicting sales whereby an analyst studies daily, weekly, or monthly sales figures to evaluate the degree to which seasonal factors, such as climate and holiday activities, influence a firm's sales.

Seasonal discounts A price reduction that sellers give to buyers who purchase goods or services out of season; these discounts allow the seller to maintain steadier production during the year.

Secondary data In marketing research this is "second hand" information previously collected or published for another purpose, but readily available to consult. There are two types: internal sources (information within an organisation) and external sources (in libraries, publications, etc.).

Segmentation variable A dimension or characteristic of individuals, groups, or organisations that is used to divide a total market into segments. *See* Base variables.

Selective distortion The changing or twisting of currently received information that occurs when a person receives information inconsistent with his or her feelings or beliefs.

Selective distribution A form of market coverage in which only some available outlets in an area are chosen to distribute a product.

Selective exposure Selection of some inputs to be exposed to our awareness while many others are ignored because of the inability to be conscious of all inputs at one time.

Selective retention The phenomenon of remembering information inputs that support personal feelings and beliefs and forgetting inputs that do not.

Self-concept One's own perception of oneself.

Selling A process of persuasion leading to a continuing trading arrangement, initiated and perpetuated at either a personal or impersonal level but commonly confined to oral representation supported by visual aids. The focus is off loading goods, services or ideas; is one way with no customer feedback into the marketing mix.

Selling agents Intermediaries who market all of a specified product line or the entire output of a manufacturer; they have control over the manufacturer's marketing effort and may be used in place of a marketing department.

Service   An intangible product that results from applying human and mechanical efforts to people or objects.

Service heterogeneity   *See* Heterogeneity.

Service inseparability   *See* Inseparability.

Service intangibility   *See* Intangibility.

Service perishability   *See* Perishability.

Service provider   Is generally the person in the service organisation who interfaces with the customer and provides the actual product or service.

Services marketing mix   This is extended from "the 4 Ps" to "the 7 Ps": *product, price, place (distribution), promotion;* plus, *people, physical evidence (ambience), process.*

Shopping mall intercept   Typified by the market researcher on a street corner or in a shopping centre, with a clipboard and 3 or 4 minutes of questions.

Shopping product   An item for which buyers are willing to put forth considerable effort in planning and making the purchase.

Shop within a shop   Concessions operated in most department stores operated by retail companies independent of the host department store company.

Short range plans   Plans that cover a period of one year or less.

Single variable segmentation   The simplest form of segmentation, achieved by using only one characteristic to divide—or segment—the market.

Situational analysis   Takes the four elements of the *SWOT* analysis and combines them into just two sets of issues: factors external to the organisation and those within the organisation.

Situational factors   The set of circumstances or conditions that exist when a consumer is making a purchase decision.

Social class   An open aggregate of people with similar social ranking.

Social factors   The forces that other people exert on one's buying behaviour.

Social institutions   An environmental force in international markets, including the family, education, religion, health, and recreational systems.

Social marketing   Marketing that involves the development of programmes designed to influence the acceptability of social ideas or causes.

Social responsibility   An approach to marketing decisions that takes into account how these decisions may affect society as a whole and various groups and individuals within society.

Societal/green forces   Forces that pressure marketers to provide high living standards and enjoyable lifestyles through socially responsible decisions and activities; the structure and dynamics of individuals and groups and the issues of concern to them.

Socio-economic factors   *See* Demographic factors.

Sorting activities   The way channel members divide roles and separate tasks, including the roles of sorting out, accumulating, allocating, and assorting products.

Sorting out   The first step in developing an assortment; involves breaking down conglomerates of heterogeneous supplies into relatively homogeneous groups.

Source   A person, group, or organisation that has a meaning that it intends and attempts to share with a receiver or an audience.

Special event pricing   Advertised sales or price cutting to increase revenue or lower costs.

Specialty line wholesaler   A merchant wholesaler that carries a very limited variety of products designed to meet customers' specialised requirements.

Specialty product   An item that possesses one or more unique characteristics that motivates a significant group of buyers to obtain it.

Specialty shops   A type of store that carries a narrow product mix with deep product lines.

Sponsorship   The financing or partial funding of an event, personality, activity, programme or product in order to gain consumer awareness and media coverage from the association; most commonly in sports, the arts and entertainment.

Standard Industrial Classification (SIC) System   A system developed by the government for classifying industrial organisations, based on what the firm primarily produces; also classifies selected economic characteristics of commercial, financial, and service organisations; uses code numbers to classify firms in different industries.

Stars   In the BCG growth-share matrix are highly successful products, but are a drain on resources in order to achieve such good sales.

Statistical interpretation   An analysis that focuses on what is typical or what deviates from the average; indicates how widely respondents vary and how they are distributed in relation to the variable being measured.

Stockout   A condition that exists when a firm runs out of a product.

Storyboard   A blueprint used by technical personnel to produce a television commercial; combines the copy with the visual material to show the sequence of major scenes in the commercial.

Straight commission compensation plan   A plan according to which a salesperson's compensation is determined solely by the amount of his or her sales for a given time period.

Straight rebuy purchase   A type of industrial purchase in which a buyer purchases the same products routinely under approximately the same terms of sale.

Straight salary compensation plan   A plan according to which salespeople are paid a specified amount per time period.

Strategic alliance   Is a partnership created to seek competitive advantage on a worldwide basis; companies pool their assets and strengths.

Strategic business unit (SBU)   A division, product line, or other profit centre within a parent company that sells a distinct set of products and/or services to an identifiable group of customers and competes against a well defined set of competitors.

Strategic marketing planning A process through which an organisation can develop marketing strategies that, when properly implemented and controlled, will contribute to achieving the organisation's overall goals.

Strategic market plan A comprehensive plan that takes into account not only marketing but all other functional areas of a business unit that must be coordinated, such as production, finance, and personnel, as well as concern about the environment.

Strategy The key decision or plan of action required to reach an objective or set of objectives.

Stratified sampling A type of sampling in which units in a population are divided into groups according to a common characteristic or attribute; then a probability sample is conducted within each group.

Style modification Modification directed at changing the sensory appeal of a product by altering its taste, texture, sound, smell, or visual characteristics.

Sub-culture A division of a culture based on geographic regions or human characteristics, such as age or ethnic background.

Suburban centre Many cities and towns have large shopping centres in their suburbs, not just the one CBD retail centre. Typically near or on major road intersections.

Superficial discounting A deceptive mark-down sometimes called "was-is pricing" (the firm never intended to sell at the higher price); fictitious comparative pricing.

Supermarket A large, self-service store that carries broad and complete lines of food products, and perhaps some non-food products.

Superstore A giant store that carries all food and non-food products found in supermarkets, as well as most products purchased on a routine basis; sales are much greater than at discount stores or supermarkets.

Supplies *See* Consumable supplies.

Support personnel Members of the sales staff who facilitate the selling function but usually are not involved solely in making sales.

Survey methods Interviews conducted by mail, telephone, or in person to obtain factual information from or about those being interviewed, or to find out their opinions and values.

SWOT analysis Central to marketing planning, the SWOT is an analysis of an organisation's Strengths, Weaknesses, Opportunities and Threats, product group by product group. The strengths/weaknesses are internal considerations, while the opportunities/threats relate to the market and the marketing environment.

Symbolic pricing A type of psychological pricing in which prices are set at an artificially high level to provide prestige or a quality image.

Syndicated data services External sources of information that a marketer uses to study a marketing problem. Examples are provided by AGB, Selling Areas Marketing, Inc. (SAMI), and A. C. Neilson Company. They collect general information that is sold to subscribing clients.

T

Tactile communication Interpersonal communication through touching.

Target audience Group of people or a market segment at which a specific promotional campaign is aimed.

Targeting Part of the market segmentation process, *targeting* is the act of identifying which market segments (or sectors) on which to concentrate resources and marketing activity: *mass marketing, single segment,* or *multi-segments.*

Target market A group of people for whom a firm creates and maintains a marketing mix.

Target public A group of people who have an interest in or a concern about an organisation, a product, or a social cause.

Technical salesperson A support salesperson who directs efforts towards the organisation's current customers by providing technical assistance in system design, product application, product characteristics, or installation.

Technological forces Forces that influence marketing decisions and activities because they affect people's lifestyles and standards of living, influence their desire for products and their reaction to marketing mixes, and have a direct impact on maintaining a marketing mix by influencing all its variables.

Technology The knowledge of how to accomplish tasks and goals.

Technology assessment A procedure by means of which managers try to foresee the effects of new products and processes on the firm's operation, on other business organisations, and on society in general.

Telemarketing A form of personal selling where highly trained account executives do everything over the telephone that face to face salespeople do.

Telephone retailing A type of non-store retailing based on a cold canvass of the telephone directory or a screening of prospective clients before calling.

Telephone surveys The soliciting of respondents' answers to a questionnaire over the telephone, with the answers being written down by the interviewer.

Telesales *See* Telemarketing.

Test marketing A limited introduction of a product in areas chosen to represent the intended market to determine probable buyers' reactions to various parts of a marketing mix.

Third party endorsement In public relations, apparently independent recommendation by a person or organisation separate from the brand owner (the manufacturer or supplier) gives the product credibility, particularly if the recommendation is from an influential body or well known personality.

Time series analysis   A technique in which the forecaster, using the firm's historical sales data, tries to discover patterns in the firm's sales volume over time.

Time series forecasts   A set of observations, such as monthly or annual sales returns, examined and extrapolated to produce predictions for future figures. The main approaches are: *naive, moving averages, exponential smoothing, statistical trend analysis,* and *box jenkins.*

Total costs   The sum of fixed costs and variable costs.

Total market (or undifferentiated) approach   An approach in which an organisation designs a single marketing mix and directs it at an entire market for a specific product category; also called undifferentiated approach.

Total revenue   The price times quantity.

Traceable common costs   Costs that can be allocated indirectly, using one or several criteria, to the functions that they support.

Trade (or functional) discount   A reduction off the list price a producer gives to a middleman for performing certain functions.

Trade mark   A legal designation indicating that the owner has exclusive use of a brand or part of a brand and that others are prohibited by law from using it.

Trade market   A relatively permanent facility that firms can rent to exhibit products year round.

Trade name   The legal name of an organisation, rather than the name of a specific product.

Trade salesperson   A type of salesperson not strictly classified as support personnel because he or she performs the order taking function as well.

Trade sales promotion method   A category of sales promotion techniques that stimulate wholesalers and retailers to carry a producer's products and to market these products aggressively.

Trade show   A show whose purpose is to let manufacturers or wholesalers exhibit products to potential buyers; therefore assists in the selling and buying functions; commonly held annually at a specified location.

Trading company   A company that provides a link between buyers and sellers in different countries; it takes title to products and provides all the activities necessary to move the product from the domestic country to a market in a foreign country.

Trading stamps   A sales promotion method used by retailers to attract consumers to specific stores and to increase sales of specific items by giving extra stamps to purchasers of those items.

Transfer pricing   The type of pricing used when one unit in a company sells a product to another unit; the price is determined by one of the following methods: actual full cost, standard full cost, cost plus investment, or market based cost.

Transit time   The total time that a carrier has possession of the goods.

Transport   Moving a product from where it is made to where it is purchased and used, and thus adding time and place utility to the product.

Transport modes   Railways, motor vehicles, waterways, pipelines, and airways used to move goods from one location to another.

Treaty of Rome   Prohibits agreements or concertive practices which may affect trade between member states.

Trend analysis   An analysis that focuses on aggregate sales data, such as company's annual sales figures, over a period of many years to determine whether annual sales are generally rising, falling, or staying about the same.

Tying contract   An agreement in which a supplier agrees to sell certain products to a dealer if the dealer consents to buy other products the supplier sells.

U

Unaided (spontaneous) recall test   A post-test method of evaluating the effectiveness of advertising; subjects are asked to identify advertisements that they have seen or heard recently but are not shown any clues to stimulate their memories.

Undifferentiated approach   An approach in which an organisation designs a single marketing mix and directs it at an entire market for a specific product category; same as total market approach.

Uniform geographic pricing   A type of pricing, sometimes called "postage stamp price," that results in fixed average transport; used to avoid the problems involved in charging different prices to each customer.

Unit loading   Grouping one or more boxes on a pallet or skid.

Universal product code (UPC)   *See* Barcode.

Unsought products   Products purchased because of a sudden need that must be solved (e.g. emergency automobile repairs) or when aggressive selling is used to obtain a sale that otherwise would not take place (e.g. encyclopaedias).

Utilitarianism   Maximises the greatest good for the greatest number of people.

V

Validity   A condition that exists when an instrument does measure what it is supposed to measure.

Variability   Reflects the amount of diversity allowed in each stop of service provision.

Variable cost   A cost that varies directly with changes in the number of units produced or sold.

Variety stores   Slightly smaller and more specialised than department stores.

Vending   *See* Automatic vending.

Venture team   An organisational unit established to create entirely new products that may be aimed at new markets.

Vertical channel integration The combining of two or more stages of a marketing channel under one management.

Vertical marketing system (VMS) A marketing channel in which channel activities are co-ordinated or managed by a single channel member to achieve efficient, low cost distribution aimed at satisfying target market customers.

W

Warehouse showroom A type of retail store with high volume and low overhead; lower costs are effected by shifting some marketing functions to consumers, who must transport, finance, and perhaps even store merchandise.

Warehousing Designing and operating facilities for storing and moving goods.

Warfare strategies The analysis of competition linked to military warfare strategies. These include *principles of defensive warfare; principles of offensive warfare; strategies for market leaders, challengers, followers, nichers.*

Wealth The accumulation of past income, natural resources, and financial resources.

Wheel of retailing A hypothesis that holds that new types of retailers usually enter the market as low status, low margin, low price operators but eventually evolve into high cost, high price merchants.

Wholesaler An intermediary that buys from a producer or another intermediary and sells to another reseller; performs such marketing activities as transport, storage, and information gathering necessary to expedite exchanges.

Wholesaling All marketing transactions in which purchases are intended for resale or are used in making other products.

Width (of product mix) The number of product lines a company offers.

Willingness to spend A disposition towards expected satisfaction from a product; influenced by the ability to buy, as well as numerous psychological and social forces.

Z

Zone prices Regional prices that vary for major geographic zones, as the transport costs differ.

Name Index

Brown, Stephen W., 695n
Brown and Tawse, 357
Bryant, David, 673n
Brylcreem, 239
BSB, 411(table)
BSB Dorland, 397
BSN-Gervais Danone, 403(table)
BSN Groupe, 14
BT, 425(table), 516
Buchan, David, 281n
Bud Dry beer, 311
Bud Light beer, 311
Budweiser beer, 311
Buell, Barbara, 661n
BUPA, 672–673
Burberry, 316
Burger King, 67(illus.), 224, 316, 333
Burke, Kevin, 661n
Burlingham, Bo, 628n
Burnett, Leo, 679
Burnetts, 411(table)
Burroughs-Wellcome, 513
Burt, David N., 371n
Burton, 327, 342(table)
Burton Group, 316, 327, 336, 666
Burtons, 66–67
Bush, Alan J., 190n
Bush, Ronald F., 237n
Bussy, John, 611n
Buzzell, Robert D., 555n

Caballe, Monserrat, 433
Cable & Co., 66, 327
Cable News Network (CNN), 227, 725
Cabriolet cars, 483
CACI, 80(illus.), 164(illus.), 336, 683
Cadbury, 74, 179, 514, 514(illus.), 564
Cadbury, Adrian, 637n
Cadbury Caramel, 425(table)
Cadbury Schweppes, 41
Cadbury's Dairy Milk chocolate, 201
Cadillac cars, 219
Café Racer motorcycles, 261
Calais, Port of, 482(illus.)
Calder, Bobby J., 128n
California Raisins toys, 397
Callahan, Joseph M., 724n
Camay soap, 220
Campaign, 167
Campanella, Donna, 474n
Campanelli, Melissa, 611n
Campbell, Nigel G.C., 154n, 726n
Campbell Soup Co., 74, 226
Canary, 316
C&A, 217, 321, 403(table)

Canion, Rod, 660
Cannon theatres, 693
Canon, 516, 595, 709
Carat cars, 483
Cardwines, 299
Carlsberg Bryggerierne, 403(table)
Caroline, Princess of Monaco, 488
Carrefour, 267, 284, 324, 324(table), 325, 356
Carriage III watches, 610
Carroll, Archie B., 637n
Carter, H., 348n
Carter, M., 377n
Cartier watches, 196
Case, 95, 269
Casey Jones, 316
Casino, 324(table)
Casio, 103
Casson, Clarence, 314n
Cast, 355(illus.)
Caterpillar Tractor Co., 95, 138, 140, 242, 515, 602, 656, 715–716
Cathay Pacific Airways, 720
Cavanagh, Richard E., 71, 96n
Cavusgil, S. Tamer, 701(table), 702(table)
CBS, 620
CCN, 188
CCN Mosaic profiling system, 188
CDP, 411(table)
Cecchini, Paolo, 281n
Cellnet, 204, 379
Center for Auto Safety, 60
Cerus, 600(table)
Chakravarti, Dipankar, 128n
Chakravarty, S.N., 265n
Chalk, Andrew T., 497n
Chamber of Commerce, 687
Champion Sport, 327
Chanel, 20, 197, 221, 497, 600(table)
Chanel No. 5 perfume, 20, 496
Channel Tunnel, 18, 19, 363, 560
Chase, Marylin, 525n
Cheer detergent, 715
Cheers (television programme), 608
Chef's Larder, 314
Chelsea beverage, 625
Cherry Coca-Cola soft drink, 91
Chiat/Day/Mojo, 396–397
Chicago Lithuanian festival, 312
Chicago Tribune, 660
Childers, Terry L., 128n
Children in Need, 685
Children's Supermarket, 523–524
Children's World, 265, 524

Chisnall, Peter M., 119(table), 190n
Chitose Airport, 720
Christian Dior, 488, 600(table)
Chrysler Corporation, 588, 619, 703, 719(table)
CIGNA, 552
Circle K, 328
Citicorp, 715
Citroën, 249, 281, 403(table), 720
Citroën Hispania, 403(table)
Citroën Xantia cars, 259
Clairol Nice'n' Easy, 425(table)
Claris Works software, 210
Clark, Terry, 237n, 555n
Clarke, Kenneth, 58
Classica washing machine, 457
Cleese, John, 603(table)
Clemons, Eric, 293n
Clendinen, Dudley, 212n
Clifford, Donald K., Jr., 71, 96n
Clinique, 413, 462, 600(table)
Clio award, 397
Clothkits, 347
Club Med, 72(table)
Club World, 437
Clutterbuck, David, 96n
CND, 685
Cobb, Robin, 438n
Coca-Cola classic soft drink, 91
Coca-Cola Company, 4, 41, 212, 214, 215, 225, 228, 239, 251, 252, 253, 280, 333, 391, 529, 531, 544, 545(illus.), 546, 552, 594, 596, 600, 700, 712, 713, 720
Coca-Cola Cup, 432
Coca-Cola European Community Group, 531, 532(illus.)
Coca-Cola soft drink, 3, 91, 425(table)
Coco Pops cereal, 73, 221, 425(table)
Cohen, Dorothy, 237n
Cohen, Nick, 523n
Coin, 324(table)
Colchester, Nicholas, 726n
Cole, Robert J., 524n
Coleman, Lynn G., 190n, 447n
Coley Porter Bell, 239, 684
Colford, Steven W., 474n
Colgate-Palmolive, 222, 248, 460, 460(illus.), 715
Collins, Phil, 687
ColourWorks, 583
Colt Car Company, 466, 703
Columbia Pictures, 547, 601
Comet, 58, 326, 327, 342(table), 411(table)

Hanson Trust, 405
Happy Eater restaurants, 522
Happy Shopper, 217, 314
Hardy, Kenneth G., 291n
Hargrove, Ernestine, 661n
Harley-Davidson Motor Co., 225, 260–261
Harrigan, Kathryn Rudie, 726n
Harris, C., 121n
Harris, Jim, 660
Harrison, T., 89, 96n
Harrods, 316, 497
Hart, Christopher W.L., 212n
Hart, Sandra Hile, 474n
Hartley, Robert F., 337(illus.), 340(illus.)
Harvester restaurants, 694
Harvey, Michael, 237n
Harvey-Jones, John, 591
Harvey Nichols, 327
Hasbro, 239
Haslam, Colin, 281n
Havers, Nigel, 603(table)
Hawkins, D.I., 190n, 583n
Hawkins, Steve L., 212n
Hayes, Thomas C., 661n
Haynes, Walter, 259
Head & Shoulders shampoo, 220
Heathrow airport, 316
Heckler, Susan E., 128n
Hedgehog baseball jackets, 214
Heineken, 41, 116, 193, 291, 312, 388, 432
Heineken Export Strength beer, 193
Heinz Baked Beans, 222, 425(table)
Heinz Salad Cream, 222
Heinz Spaghetti, 222
Heinz Tomato Soup, 222
Helena Rubinstein, 600(table)
Helm, Leslie, 474n, 726n
Hemp, Paul, 312n
Henkel, 403(table)
Henkel France, 403(table)
Henry Howell Chaldecott Lury, 613
Hercules, 719(table)
Heritage hotels, 26
Hermes, 76(illus.)
Hertz, 333, 464, 489
Heskett, J.L., 365(table)
Hewlett-Packard, 103, 246, 472, 586, 629, 656
Higgins, Kevin, 567(table)
Hill, Michelle, 477n
Hillkirk, John, 726n
Hilton Grey, 411(table)

Hilton hotels, 522, 668
Hitachi, 95, 139
H.J. Heinz, 20, 62, 63, 72(table), 164, 216, 222, 223(illus.), 226, 227, 232, 313
H.K. McCann, 425(table)
Hlavacek, James D., 661n
Hobbs, Roger, 62
Hogan, Paul, 603(table)
Hoggan, Karen, 128n, 720n
Hoki, 324(table)
Holbrook, Morris B., 399n
Holiday Inn, 26–27, 333, 522, 547
Holland & Barrett, 333
Hollander, Stanley C., 348n
Holstein, William J., 726n
Holzinger, Albert G., 726n
Homan, Richard, 582n
Homebase, 286, 327
Home Furnishing Mart, 308
Honda, 260, 386, 533, 588, 709, 719(table)
Honeywell, 719(table)
Honeywell Information Systems, 453
Hoover, 430, 432–433, 457, 615
Hope, Bob, 312
Hornes, 327
Horton, Cleveland, 60n
Hoskyns Group plc, 658–660
Hotpoint appliances, 347, 457
Hotpoint dishwashers, 107
Houghton Mifflin Company, 169
House of Fraser, 320, 321, 497
Houston, Michael J., 128n
Hoverspeed, 18
Howard, John A., 128n
Howe, W.S., 348n
Howell, Roy D., 497n
H. Samuel, 327
Hudson, Teresa, 474n
Huggins, Francis, 457
Hula Hoops, 235
Hume, Scott, 212n, 438n, 637n
Hunt for Red October, The (film), 608
Hurwood, David, 583n
Hutchinson, J. Wesley, 128n
Hutt, Michael D., 154n, 611n
Huxtable, Bernice, 628n
Hydrotechnica, 438
Hyundai, 709

Iacocca, Lee, 619
IBM AS/400 mainframe computer, 660
IBM PC, 219
IBM PS2, 219

ICA, 403(table)
Ice Cream Mars, 165, 204, 377
ICI, 591, 721
ICI fibre, 199(illus.), 199–200
ICL, 719(table)
Ifa Española, 324(table)
Iglo-Industrias Gelados, 403(table)
IKEA, 9, 94, 126–127, 275, 284, 325, 326, 338, 353, 666
IMS International, 159(table)
Independent Grocers' Alliance (IGA), 276
Independent on Sunday, The, 497
Indiana Jones (film), 608
Indiana Jones and the Last Crusade (film), 609
Industrias Lever Portuguesa, 403(table)
InfoMart, 308
Infoplan, 438
Information Resources, Inc., 169
Infratest Burke, 159(table)
Ingram, Thomas N., 447n
Initiative, 425(table)
Insight Database Systems, 660
Insight Software, 660
Interbrew Belgium, 403(table)
InterCity, 534
Intermeaché, 324(table)
International Anti-Counterfeiting Coalition, 221
International Business Machines (IBM), 69–70, 209–210, 331, 472, 535, 547, 552, 586, 591, 592(illus.), 595, 620, 629, 660, 661
International Convention Centre (Birmingham), 669, 670(illus.)
International Red Cross, 389
Intersport, 284
Intersun, 505
Invergordon, 245
Investors' Chronicle, 167
IRI, 159(table), 188
IRI Infoscan, 188
Irish Industrial Development Authority (IDA), 552–553
Iron Man Triathlon, 312
Isoceles, 323(table)
Istel, 659
Ivey, Mark, 661n
Ivie, Robert, 365(table)

Jackson, Darryl, 350
Jackson, Michael, 376, 725
Jacob, Rahul, 628n

Porsche, Ferdinand, 724
Porsche, Ferry, 724, 725*n*
Porsche 911 Carrera Cabrie cars, 495
Porter, Michael E., 572, 573(*illus.*), 574, 583*n*
Porterhouse restaurants, 694
Postbank, 403(*table*)
Postcard, 375
Posthouse hotels, 26
Post-It note pads, 245, 246
Postopankki, 403(*table*)
Pot Noodles, 120
Pot Rice, 120
Pottruck, David, 695*n*
Powell, Terry E., 661*n*
Powers, Thomas L., 154*n*
Power-Supermarkets, 324(*table*)
PPA, 188
PPG Industries, 130
Pratt & Whitney, 552
Presil Micro, 425(*table*)
Presse Publishing, 255
Pressley, Milton M., 174(*table*)
Prestige Group UK PLC, 115(*illus.*)
Pretty Polly, 111–112, 112(*illus.*)
Pricerite, 345
Pride, William, 555*n*
Pride & Joy, 95, 327
Principles for Men, 327
Procter & Gamble, 39, 73, 74, 100, 170, 202, 203(*illus.*), 206, 212, 216, 220, 222, 231, 249, 278, 283, 286, 287, 376, 403(*table*), 406, 409, 411(*table*), 413, 557, 589, 590, 619, 620, 710, 715
Promedès, 324(*table*)
Pronto Print, 220
Pronuptia, 333
Pro Performance, 327
Prudential Insurance, 433
Prudential Series, 432
Pryca, 324(*table*)
PSA-Citroën, 403(*table*)
PSA-Peugeot, 403(*table*)
PTT Telecom, 403(*table*)
Publicis, 411(*table*), 425(*table*)
Purina Cat Chow, 397

Quadra-Pak, 370
Quaker Oats Company, 170, 171, 331, 536
Qualcast, 388
Queen, 375
Queens Moat Houses hotels, 26, 522
Queensway, 326

Quelch, John A., 726*n*
Quelle, 324(*table*)
Questor Corporation, 718
Quicks, 281
Quinn, Patrick, 438*n*
Quintessence, 711
Quraeshi, Zahir A., 726*n*

Rabobank, 289
Radius, 327
Ragu pasta sauce, 410
Raiders of the Lost Ark (film), 608
Rainforest Action Network and Cultural Survival, 635
Raleigh, 572
Ralston Purina Co., 397
Ramanujam, Vasudevan, 583*n*
Rao, Ashkay R., 128*n*
Rathmell, John M., 695*n*
Ratners, 327, 342(*table*)
RCA, 709
Reagan, Ronald, 477
Real McCoys, 235
Red Cross, 687
Redmond, S., 127*n*
Reebok International, 17, 111, 401
Reebok Pump shoes, 401
Reed, B.J., 474*n*
Reed, Lou, 376
Rees-Jones, Elizabeth, 255
Reger, Janet, 66
Reibstein, Larry, 611*n*
Reichhold Chemicals, 199
Reidenbach, R. Eric, 637*n*
Reilly, Rick, 537*n*
"Relax" (recording), 375
Reliant Robin cars, 618–619
Remix Album, The (recording), 634
Renault, 281, 403(*table*), 425(*table*), 718, 719(*table*)
Renault Espace cars, 259
Renault Portuguesa, 403(*table*)
Renault R21 cars, 259
Renault Safrane cars, 259
Rentokil, 682
Research International, 159(*table*)
Rest, James R., 637*n*
Revlon perfume, 496
Rewe, Zentral, 324(*table*)
Reynolds, J., 127*n*
Reynolds, Jonathan, 371*n*
Richard Shops, 327
Riche, Martha Farnsworth, 190*n*
Ricoh Mirai camera, 10
Riddle, Ken, 583*n*

Riemer, Blanca, 488*n*
Ries, Al, 128*n*, 555*n*
Right Guard deodorant, 206, 219
Rijksvoorlichtingsdienst, 403(*table*)
Rikli, Steve, 661*n*
Rinascente, 324(*table*)
Rinehart, Lloyd M., 371*n*
Ritchie, John Knowles, 230(*illus.*)
Ritz crackers, 231
River Island, 82
RJR Nabisco, 14, 158
Robertson, Thomas S., 128*n*, 583*n*
Robin, Donald P., 637*n*
Robinson, P., 154*n*
Robinson, William A., 474*n*
Roca, 217, 301
Rock Against Drugs (RAD), 376
Roddick, Anita, 628
Roel, Raymond, 212*n*
Rogers, D.S., 348*n*
Rogers, Everett H., 385(*illus.*)
Rogers, Everett M., 399*n*
Roland Cartier, 327
Rolex watches, 216, 221, 574
Rolfes, Rebecca, 314*n*
Rolls-Royce, 216, 499, 719(*table*)
Romeo, Jean B., 438*n*
Ronald Homes, 433
Ronald McDonald Children's Charities (RMCC), 636–637
Ronald McDonald Houses, 378, 636–637
Rosenbloom, Bert, 291*n*, 314*n*
Rossiter, John, 399*n*, 459(*illus.*)
Rothman, Andrea, 555*n*
Rover, 37, 183, 205, 242, 281, 425(*table*), 567, 719(*table*)
Rover 800 cars, 200
Row, Michael, 293*n*
Roxy theatre, 693
Royal Copenhagen, 278, 279(*illus.*)
Royal National Lifeboat Institution (RNLI), 683
Royal Shakespeare Company, 433
Royal Society for the Protection of Birds, 39(*illus.*)
Roysters, 235
Roysters Steam Nuts, 235–236
RSPCA, 682
Rudd, Roland, 534*n*
Rudd, Tony, 348*n*
Rudolph, Barbara, 488*n*
Ruffles, 235
Ruibal, Sal, 398*n*
Russell, John A., 725*n*

Subject Index

Brand loyalty, 216, 217(*illus.*)
Brand manager, 240
Brand mark, 216
Brand names, 215(*table*), 215–216
  choosing, 220–222
Brand purchase intention, 385
Break down approach, 559
Break even analysis, 508–509,
  509(*illus.*)
Break even point, 508–509, 509(*illus.*)
Bribery, 621–622, 622(*table*)
Brokers, 302, 305
Budget
  advertising, 410–411
  in marketing plan, 574
Build up approach, 559, 561,
  561(*table*)#
Business(es), *see* Organisation(s)
Business analysis, 247
Business position, 542, 542(*illus.*)
Business-to-business distributors,
  650–652
Business-to-business marketing,
  640–658
  marketing mixes for, 645–657
  target markets for, 642–645
Business-to-business marketing mix,
  645–657
  distribution in, 649–652, 650(*illus.*)
  price in, 656–657
  products in, 646, 646(*illus.*),
  648–649
  promotion in, 652–655, 653(*illus.*),
  654(*table*)
Business-to-business target markets,
  642–645
  estimating purchase potential of,
  644–645
  identifying potential customers and,
  642–644, 643(*table*), 644(*table*)
  locating customers and, 644,
  645(*illus.*)
Buy-back allowances, 464
Buyers
  benefits of branding for, 216
  consumers, *see* Consumer(s);
  Consumer buying decision
  process
  organisational, *see* Organisational
  buying; Organisational buying
  decision process
  perceptions of, pricing and, 487–489
  See also Buying behaviour
Buying, impulse, 100
Buying allowance, 465

Buying behaviour
  channel selection and, 280
  See also Consumer buying behaviour; Consumer buying decision
  process; Organisational buying
  decision process
Buying centre, 143–145
Buying power, 45–46, 46–50(*table*),
  48–51

Canada
  Free Trade Agreement and, 712
  growth of GDP in, 706(*table*)
Capabilities, 538–539
Captioned photograph, 428
Carrying costs, 358
Cash and carry warehouses, 328
Cash and carry wholesalers, 300–302
Cash cows, 540
Cash discounts, 491
Cash flow, as pricing objective, 484
Catalogue retailing, 332(*illus.*),
  332–333
Catalogue showrooms, 328
Category consistent packaging, 231
Category need, 385
Causal studies, 165, 165(*table*)
Cause related marketing, 376
Central business district (CBD), 319,
  319(*illus.*)
Centralised organisation, 586
Central Statistical Office, 35
Channel capacity, communication and,
  380–381
Channel conflict, 282–283
Channel co-operation, 282
Channel integration, 274–276
  horizontal, 276
  vertical, 275–276, 276(*illus.*),
  277(*illus.*)
Channel leadership, 283–284,
  284(*illus.*), 286–287
Channels of distribution, *see*
  Marketing channels
China, 709
CIS (Commonwealth of Independent
  States), 710
Citizens' Advice Bureaux, 34
Clayton Act (U.S.), 34
Client publics, 685, 687
Closing, in personal selling, 444
Codes of ethics, 623–624,
  624–625(*table*)
Coding process, in communication,
  379

Cognitive dissonance, 104
Colours, packaging and, 226–227
Combination compensation plan, 451,
  452(*table*)
Commercialisation, 250–252
  managing products after, 253–257
Commission, 478
Commission merchants, 304–305
Common Market, *see* European
  Community
Commonwealth of Independent States
  (CIS), 710
Communication
  defined, 378
  kinesic, 387
  within marketing unit, 593
  promotion and, 378–381, 379(*illus.*),
  381(*illus.*)
  proxemic, 387
  in services marketing, 677
  tactile, 387
Community relations, social responsibility issues and, 629, 629(*table*)
Comparative advertising, 406
Compensation, of sales force, 451–453,
  452(*table*), 592
Competition, 45–54
  advertising and, 406, 410
  assessment of, 52–54
  consumer demand and spending
  behaviour and, 45–51
  monitoring, 54
  monopolistic, 52, 53(*table*)
  non-price, 481–483, 482(*illus.*)
  perfect, 52, 53(*table*)
  positioning and, 252–253, 253(*illus.*)
  price, 479(*illus.*), 480–481
  pricing and, 489
  procompetitive legislation and,
  32–34
  warfare and, 548–549
Competition matching approach, 410
Competition oriented pricing, 519
Competitive advantage, 656
Competitive advertising, 406
Competitive edge, in services, 680
Competitive positions, 548
Competitive structure, 52
Competitive tools, 52–53
Competitor(s), prices of, 510
Competitor analysis, market segmentation and, 69
Competitor scanning, 549
Completeness, of product assortment,
  336–337

freight absorption, 492
geographic, 491–492
for industrial and organisational
      markets, 490–493
mark up, 516–517
method for, 515–519
negotiated, 657
objectives of, 483–484, 486, 500–501
odd-even, 512
pioneer, 510–512
policy for, 510–515
prestige, 512–513
professional, 513
promotional, 513–514
psychological, 512–513
special event, 514, 514(*illus.*)
transfer, 492
Primary data, 165, 166(*illus.*),
      167(*illus.*), 168–181
Primary demand, 405–406
Private warehouses, 356, 357
Proactive strategy, 632
Problem children, 540
Problem definition, in marketing
      research, 163, 164(*illus.*)
Problem recognition, in consumer
      buying decision process, 100–101,
      102(*illus.*)
Process, in marketing mix, 678–679
Process materials, 199(*illus.*), 199–200
Procompetitive legislation, 32–34
   European Community and, 33–34
   monopolies and mergers and,
      32–33
Producer(s), wholesalers' services for,
      294–295
Producer markets, 131, 133(*illus.*)
Product(s), 7, 192–208
   accumulation of, 273
   actual, 200–201
   assorting, 274
   assortment of, 272, 336–337,
      337(*illus.*)
   augmented, 200–201
   channel selection and, 280
   consumer, 194–197, 267–268,
      268(*illus.*)
   convenience, 195
   core, 200–201, 201(*illus.*)
   defined, 194
   ethical issues and, 619
   evoked set of, 103
   increasing uses of, 406
   industrial, 194–195, 197–200,
      268–269, 269(*illus.*)

international marketing and,
      712–713, 715
   in marketing mix, 5(*table*), 19–20,
      646, 646(*illus.*), 648–649,
      672–675, 674(*illus.*), 675(*illus.*),
      676(*table*), 687, 712–713, 715
   new, *see* New product development
   non-business marketing and, 687
   organising by, 590
   physical characteristics of, 205–206
   positioning, *see* Positioning
   promoting, 404–405
   promotional mix and, 392–393
   quality of, *see* Quality
   shopping, 195–196, 196(*illus.*)
   sorting out, 272–273
   specialty, 196–197
   supportive services related to,
      206–207
   unsought, 197
   use of, as segmentation variable, 84
Product adoption, 251
   adopter categories and, 384–385,
      385(*illus.*)
   promotion and, 381–386, 382(*illus.*),
      384(*illus.*)
Product advertising, 405
Product deletion, 242, 244(*illus.*),
      244–245
Product development, 247, 249
   See also New product development
Product development strategy, 547
Production era, 12
Product item, 201
Product life-cycles, 202–205,
      204(*illus.*)
   decline stage of, 205, 256–257
   growth stage of, 204, 254, 255
   introduction stage of, 203–204
   marketing strategy during, 254–257
   maturity stage of, 204–205, 254, 256
Product line, 201–202, 202(*illus.*)
   full line forcing and, 285
Product management, 238–258
   after commercialisation, 253–257
   organising for, 240–241
   positioning and, 252–253, 253(*illus.*)
   product mix and, 241–252
Product manager, 240
Product/market background, in mar-
      keting plan, 569
Product mix, 202, 203(*illus.*), 241–252
   deleting products and, 242,
      244(*illus.*), 244–245
   depth and width of, 202, 203(*illus.*)

developing new products and,
      245–252, 246(*illus.*)
   modifying existing products and,
      241–242
Product modification, 241–242
Product portfolio analysis, 539–541,
      540(*illus.*), 541(*illus.*), 545
Product portfolio approach, 241
Product positioning, 252–253,
      253(*illus.*)
   See also Positioning
Product-related behavioural character-
      istics, as segmentation variable,
      81–82, 83
Product-specific spending patterns, 51
Professional pricing, 513
Profit
   demand and cost and, 505–509
   as pricing objective, 483
Profit Impact on Marketing Strategy
      (PIMS), 543(*illus.*), 543–545,
      544(*table*)
Projective techniques, 113, 114(*illus.*)
Project (venture) team, 240–241
Promotion, 374–395
   aims of promotion communication
      and, 385–396
   communication process and,
      378–381, 379(*illus.*), 381(*illus.*)
   cost and availability of methods for,
      393
   ethical issues and, 619–622
   international marketing and,
      712–713, 714(*illus.*), 715
   in marketing mix, 5(*table*), 20,
      652–655, 653(*illus.*), 654(*table*),
      675–677, 687–688, 712–713,
      714(*illus.*), 715
   non-business marketing and,
      687–688
   packaging and, 226
   product adoption process and,
      381–386, 382(*illus.*),
      384(*illus.*)
   resources, objectives and policies
      for, 391
   role of, 376–378, 378(*illus.*)
   of services, 675–677
   See also Advertising; Promotional
      mix; Sales promotion
Promotional mix, 386–394, 387(*illus.*)
   ingredients of, 386–390
   push policy versus pull policy for,
      393–394, 394(*illus.*)
   selecting ingredients for, 391–393

Spurious loyalty, 216
Standard(s), for performance, 594–595
Standard Industrial Classification
    (SIC) system, 642–644,
    643(*table*), 644(*table*)
Stars, 540
Statistical interpretation, 181
Status, of product assortment, 336
Status quo, as pricing objective, 484
Stock out(s), 358
Stock out costs, 358
Stores
    atmospherics of, 338–339
    image of, 339
    types of, 320–330
    wheel of retailing and, 340(*illus.*),
        340–341
Straight commission compensation
    plan, 451, 452(*table*)
Straight re-buy purchases, 141
Straight salary compensation plan, 451,
    452(*table*)
Strategic alliances, international mar-
    keting and, 718–719, 719(*table*),
    720
Strategic Business Planning Grid, 542,
    542(*illus.*)
Strategic business unit (SBU), 531
Strategic market planning
    market segmentation and, 70
    plan and, 531
    significance of approaches to,
        545–546
    tools for, 539–546
Strategic window, 536
Strategy
    accommodation, 631(*illus.*),
        631–632
    concentration, 86–87
    corporate, 539
    cost leadership, 572, 573(*illus.*)
    defence, 630–631
    differentiation, 572, 573(*illus.*), 574
    focus, 573(*illus.*), 574
    generic, 572, 573(*illus.*), 574
    market development, 546
    multisegment, 87(*illus.*), 87–88,
        88(*illus.*)
    physical distribution and, 366–367
    proactive, 632
    product development, 547
    reaction, 630
    retailing and, 335–343
    for social responsibility, 630–632,
        631(*illus.*)

targeting, *see* Targeting strategies
    See also Marketing strategies
Stratified sampling, 172
Style modifications, 242
Subcultures, in consumer buying
    decision process, 122
Suburban centres, 318–319
"Sugging," 184
Supermarkets, 322–324, 323(*table*),
    324(*table*), 325
Superstores, 322–324, 323(*table*),
    324(*table*), 326
Suppliers, prohibition of refusal to deal
    by, 285
Supplies, consumable, 200
Support personnel, 446
Surveys, 173–179, 174–177(*table*)
    sales forecasting and, 562–563
Survival, as pricing objective, 483
Sweden
    advertising in, 403(*table*), 416(*table*)
    growth of GDP in, 706(*table*)
Sweepstakes, 464
Switzerland
    advertising in, 403(*table*)
    growth of GDP in, 706(*table*)
SWOT analysis, in marketing plan, 569,
    571
Syndicated data services, 167

Tactile communication, 387
Taiwan, 709–710
Tangibility concept, 664, 664(*illus.*)
Target, advertising, 408
Targeting strategies, 70–71, 86–88
    concentration, 86–87
    multisegment, 87(*illus.*), 87–88,
        88(*illus.*)
Target markets
    for business-to-business marketing,
        see Business-to-business target
        markets
    evaluation of price and ability to buy
        and, 501
    for non-business marketing, 685,
        686(*illus.*), 687
    promotional mix and, 391–392
    selection of, 17, 64–66
Target public, 685
Taxes, 478
Technical salespeople, 446
Technology, 40, 42–44
    adoption and use of, 43–44
    impact of, 42–43, 43(*illus.*)

international marketing and, 708
    retailing and, 341, 342(*table*)
Technology assessment, 43
Telemarketing, 331
    in business-to-business marketing,
        653
Telephone surveys, 174(*table*),
    175–178
Test marketing, 249–250, 250(*table*)
Thailand, 710
Third party endorsement, 429
Time series analysis, 563–564
Time utility, 318
Toll, 478
Total cost, 506
Total-market approach, 64, 65(*illus.*),
    66, 66(*illus.*)
Traceable common costs, 603
Trade associations, as data source,
    168(*table*)
Trade (functional) discounts, 490
Trade journals, as data source,
    168(*table*)
Trade mark, 216
Trade markets, 308
Trade name, 216
Trade salespeople, 446
Trade sales promotion methods, 459,
    464–466
Trade shows, 307–308
    in business-to-business marketing,
        655–656
Trading companies, international
    marketing and, 719
Trading stamps, 462–463
Training, of salespeople, 450–451
Transactions, organisational, 136,
    137(*illus.*)
Transfer pricing, 492
Transportation, 361–366, 362(*table*)
    coordinating, 365–366
    pricing and, 491–492
    transport modes and, 361–365,
        362(*table*)
Transport companies, 307, 308(*illus.*)
Transport modes, 361–365, 362(*table*)
    criteria for selecting, 364–365,
        365(*table*)
Treaty of Rome, 33
Trend analysis, 563
Tying contracts, 285

Unaided (spontaneous) recall test,
    424–425, 425(*table*)

Undifferentiated (mass) market approach, 64, 65(*illus.*), 66, 66(*illus.*)
Unethical behaviour, controlling, 624
Uniform geographic pricing, 491
United Kingdom
  advertising in, 415, 416(*table*)
  in European Community, 708
  growth of GDP in, 706(*table*)
  monopolies and mergers in, 32–33
  regulation in, 35–37
UK Consumer Protection Act (1987), 34, 285, 515, 627
UK Consumer Protection departments, 34
UK Department of Employment, 35
UK Department of the Environment (DoE), 35
UK Department of Trade and Industry (DTI), 35–36, 38, 700
UK Department of Transport, 36
UK Fair Trading Act (1973), 34, 284, 627
UK Financial Services Act (1986), 33, 34
UK Food Act (1984), 34, 627
UK Medicines Act (1968), 34
UK Misrepresentations Act (1967), 34
UK Monopolies and Mergers Commission, 32, 284
UK National Consumer Council, 34
UK Prices Act (1974), 34, 284
UK Restrictive Trade Practices Act (1976), 33
UK Sale of Goods Act (1979), 34
UK Supply of Goods and Services Act (1982), 34
UK Trade Descriptions Act (1968), 34, 284, 627

UK Trading Standards departments, 34
UK Unfair Contract Terms Act (1977), 34
UK Weights and Measures Act (1985), 34, 627
United States
  Free Trade Agreement and, 712
  growth of GDP in, 706(*table*)
  procompetitive legislation in, 34
US Federal Trade Commission Act, 34
US Robinson-Patman Act, 34
US Sherman Antitrust Act, 34
Unit loading, 354
Universal product code (UPC), 232
Unsought products, 197
UPC (universal product code), 232
Utilitarianism, 616
Utility, retailing and, 318

Validity, 169
Variability, of services, 674–675
Variable(s), independent and dependent, 169, 169(*illus.*)
Variable costs, 506
Variety stores, 321–322
Vending, automatic, 331
Venture (project) team, 240–241
Vertical channel integration, 275–276, 276(*illus.*), 277(*illus.*)
Vertical marketing system (VMS), 275–276, 276(*illus.*), 277(*illus.*)

Warehouses, 356–358
  cash and carry, 328
  public, 306
Warehousing, 354–358
  functions of, 355–356
Warfare, 548–549

Waterways, as transport mode, 362(*table*), 363
Wealth, 48–50
West Germany
  growth of GDP in, 706(*table*)
  retailers in, 324(*table*)
  See also Germany
Wheel of retailing, 340(*illus.*), 340–341
Wholesalers
  activities of, 294–296, 295(*table*)
  agents and brokers, 302–305, 303(*illus.*), 304(*table*)
  cash and carry, 300–302
  consolidation of power of, 309
  defined, 294
  drop shippers, 302
  general merchandise, 297
  limited line, 298
  mail order, 302
  manufacturers' sales branches and offices and, 305–306
  merchant, 296–302, 297(*illus.*)
  new types of, 309
  rack jobbers, 299–300
  specialty line, 298(*illus.*), 298–300
Wholesaling, 292–310
  changing patterns in, 308–309
  facilitating agencies and, 306–308
  nature and importance of, 294
  See also Wholesalers
Width, of product mix, 202, 203(*illus.*)
Willingness to spend, 51
Word of mouth communication, in services marketing, 677

Zone prices, 491–492